D1191223

Annual Review of
INFORMATION SCIENCE AND TECHNOLOGY

Annual Review of
INFORMATION SCIENCE AND TECHNOLOGY

Volume 41 • 2007

Blaise Cronin, Editor

Published on behalf of the
American Society for Information Science and Technology
by Information Today, Inc.

Information Today, Inc.
Medford, New Jersey

ISBN: 1-57387-276-8
ISSN: 0066-4200
CODEN: ARISBC
LC No. 66-25096

Published and distributed by
Information Today, Inc.
143 Old Marlton Pike
Medford, NJ 08055-8750

On behalf of

The American Society for Information Science and Technology
1320 Fenwick Lane, Suite 510
Silver Spring, MD 20910-3602, U.S.A.

Contents

SECTION I
Historical Perspectives

SECTION II
Availability, Access, and Use

Introduction

Blaise Cronin

What is the most cited work in *ARIST*'s history? I confess I had no idea until two of our doctoral students, Peter Hook and Weimao Ke, decided to crunch the numbers: roughly 60,000 references from 400 chapters covering 40 years. Vannevar Bush's 1945 *Atlantic Monthly* piece, "As We May Think," came first, albeit with a fairly modest 22 citations, just pipping Dervin and Nilan's 1986 *ARIST* review at the post. Should Peter and Weimao rerun their study a year hence, Bush will almost certainly have consolidated his lead. Not only do we have a chapter by Ronald Houston and Glynn Harmon devoted exclusively to the many interpretations and enduring influence of his seminal paper over the course of the last six decades, but several other chapters—notably those by Colin Burke and William Jones—also make generous mention of the Bush/Memex legacy. Within the literature of information science—and not just between the covers of *ARIST*—Bush's article is indubitably a citation classic. But his footprint extends more widely: A recent editorial in the *Communications of the ACM* (Crawford, 2006, p. 5) introducing a special section on Personal Information Management, co-edited by the aforementioned Mr. Jones as it happens, acknowledged "Bush's inspirational vision."

This year's volume opens with three historically inclined chapters, a good way of reminding ourselves that information science is a field with a solid pedigree and, for those who take the trouble to familiarize themselves with the canonical literature, a clear sense of its own intellectual roots and identity, virtues that really should not be sacrificed to capricious latitudinarianism. Here, if I may be permitted an aside, it is hard not to think of the so-called I-schools movement and its discursive contortions

(Cronin, 2005). As an antidote to the occasionally overblown rhetoric of the new that swirls around us, I recommend Bernd Frohmann's (2004) aptly titled *Deflating Information*, one of the most cogently argued books to have come out of our field in recent years. But back to matters historical: Burke, although a professional historian, does not here attempt to provide *the* history, or even *an* history, of information science—the original title of his chapter, "The Emergence of the History of Information Science as a Field of Study, 1994–2004: An Overview of the Literature and Comments and Cautions," clearly delineates his ambitions—but the appetite is whetted. Just as it is with Stephen Bensman's chapter on the impact factor (IF), a citation-based indicator that is loved and reviled in near equal measure by journal editors and authors alike. Bensman, who also, incidentally, trained as an historian, provides an historico-biographical account of the IF, viewed through the prism of Eugene Garfield's picaresque life. This is certainly not a conventional *ARIST* chapter, but it is a novel, exegetical approach, one which, inter alia, allows us to reacquaint ourselves with the "the Sage"—J. D. Bernal (see Brown, 2006)—a polymath, whose formative thinking on scientific information and scholarly communication probably deserves wider recognition. A more technical chapter by Bensman dealing with the validity and utility of the impact factor is planned for the next volume of *ARIST*.

The remaining 12 chapters of this year's volume are forward-looking and, taken together, demonstrate rather convincingly that information science has neither lost its early vitality nor resorted, in its maturity, to excessive navel gazing. Some of the topics I have selected for coverage (e.g., digital libraries, Arabic information retrieval [IR], and universal access by, respectively, David Bearman, Ibrahim Abu El-Khair, and Harmeet Sawhney and Krishna Jayakar) may be par for the *ARIST* course, but they are none the less valuable for that: The national security implications of research in Arabic IR, for instance, hardly need stating, and the pace of developments in digital libraries—a procrustean label, to be sure—is such that regular updates are required, an observation that could be applied equally well to policy and empirical research addressing access issues such as the digital divide.

Other chapters, in particular those by Christina Courtright, Jeppe Nicolaisen, Soo Young Rieh and David Danielson, and Diane Sonnenwald, approach familiar topics from an original, or revised, angle: context in the case of information seeking; signaling in the case of citation behavior; credibility in the case of information systems use; factors and stages in the case of scientific collaboration. In each instance, the authors enrich our theoretical understanding of complex information practices and phenomena, adding incrementally to the field's knowledge base. One could quite easily add to this list the chapters by Birger Hjørland ("Semantics and Knowledge Organization") and Catherine Legg ("Ontologies on the Semantic Web"), both of which deal with axial concerns of information science, namely, meaning and representation.

Thanks to the development of the Web, the practical significance of these abstract issues has become much more widely appreciated of late by scholars of all stripes and, indeed, by sections of the general public. One of the Grand Challenges facing computer scientists, information scientists, and artificial intelligence researchers is to create the Semantic Web, which will provide metadata on the semantics, not just the syntax, of Web resources. Thus, if you want to know something about Turkey, you won't be fobbed off with information on the feathered variety.

One of the fastest-growing and potentially most important fields of contemporary research in academia—one that straddles many academic disciplines and fields, from biology and physics to sociology, epidemiology, and information science—is network science (e.g., Barabási, 2003), profiled here by Katy Börner (electrical engineering), Soma Sanyal (physics), and Alessandro Vespignani (physics). Together they review a diversity of approaches to analyzing the self-organizing properties of biological, transport, social, and other networks. There is much that will be new to *ARIST* readers in this chapter, both conceptually and methodologically, but also not a little that will be familiar: Bibliometrics and co-citation mapping are, after all, established techniques for revealing socio-cognitive networks and have been staples of the information science research literature for many years.

Volume 41 concludes with a chapter by Greg Downey, a geographer with a strong interest in the history of science and technology and author of the engaging *Telegraph Messenger Boys* (Downey, 2002). He makes the case that current thinking in human geography, especially notions of process, context, and relationality, should be of interest to the information science research community. Downey introduces us to "the geographical turn"—shades of the "cognitive turn" in information retrieval research (Ingwersen & Järvelin, 2005)—in the social sciences and humanities and reacquaints *ARIST* readers with concepts such as the space of flows and the social shaping of space. Downey is not the first, nor will he be the last, geographer to appear between the covers of *ARIST*; there are assuredly potential intellectual synergies between (classical) information science and (postmodern) human geography (e.g., Raper, Dykes, Wood, Mountain, Krause, & Rhind, 2002; Turner & Davenport, 2005). But, of course, the same could be said of information science and several other disciplines, a fact that is beginning to be recognized by scholars both within and outside our particular intellectual community, I am pleased to note.

References

Barabási, A.-L. (2003). *Linked: How everything is connected to everything else and what it means for business, science, and everyday life*. New York: Plume.

Brown, A. (2006). *J. D. Bernal: The sage of science*. Oxford, UK: Oxford University Press.

Crawford, D. (2006). Editorial pointers. *Communications of the ACM, 49*(1), 5.

Cronin, B. (2005). An I-dentity crisis? The information schools movement. *International Journal of Information Management, 25,* 363–365.

Downey, G. (2002). *Telegraph messenger boys: Labor, technology, and geography, 1850–1950.* New York: Routledge.

Frohmann, B. (2004). *Deflating information: From science studies to documentation.* Toronto: Toronto University Press.

Ingwersen, P., & Järvelin, K. (2005). *The turn: Integration of information seeking and retrieval in context.* Dordrecht, NL: Springer.

Raper, J., Dykes, J., Wood, J., Mountain, D., Krause, A., & Rhind, D. (2002). A framework for evaluating geographical information. *Journal of Information Science, 28,* 39–50.

Turner, P., & Davenport, E. (Eds.). (2005). *Spaces, spatiality and technology.* Dordrecht, NL: Springer.

Acknowledgments

Many individuals are involved in the production of *ARIST*. I readily acknowledge the contributions of our Advisory Board members and outside reviewers. Their names are listed in the pages that follow. Thomas Dousa and Dorothy Pike were enormously helpful with copyediting and bibliographic checking. Amy Novick produced the thorough index. As always, Debora Shaw did what a first-rate associate editor is supposed to do.

ARIST Advisory Board

Judit Bar-Ilan
Bar-Ilan University of Jerusalem, Israel

Micheline Beaulieu
University of Sheffield, UK

Nicholas J. Belkin
Rutgers University, New Brunswick, USA

David C. Blair
University of Michigan, Ann Arbor, USA

Christine L. Borgman
University of California at Los Angeles, USA

Terrence A. Brooks
University of Washington, Seattle, USA

Elisabeth Davenport
Napier University, Edinburgh, UK

Susan Dumais
Microsoft Research, Redmond, USA

Abby Goodrum
Ryerson University, Toronto, Canada

Glynn Harmon
University of Texas at Austin, USA

Leah A. Lievrouw
University of California at Los Angeles, USA

Katherine W. McCain
Drexel University, Philadelphia, USA

Charles Oppenheim
Loughborough University, UK

Chapter Reviewers

Ahmed Abdelali
Marcia Bates
Nicholas Belkin
Gerald Benoît
Alistair Black
Christine Borgman
Terrence Brooks
Michael Buckland
Ian Cornelius
Elisabeth Davenport
Charles Davis
Ron Day
Susan Dumais
Sanda Erdelez
Noriko Hara
Glynn Harmon
Roberta Lamb
Leah Lievrouw

Ziming Liu
Katherine McCain
Jens-Erik Mai
Lokman Meho
Javed Mostafa
David Muddiman
Tom Nisonger
Jim Nyce
Charles Oppenheim
Uta Priss
Boyd Rayward
Alice Robbin
Howard Rosenbaum
Candy Schwartz
Ben Shneiderman
Linda Smith
Sanna Talja
Mike Thelwall

Contributors

Ibrahim Abu El-Khair is an Assistant Professor in the Department of Library and Information Science, Faculty of Arts, El-Minia University, Egypt. He received a B.A. in library and information science from the Department of Documentation and Librarianship, Faculty of Arts, Cairo University. He was awarded a government scholarship to study in the United States, which enabled him to earn a master's degree in Library and Information Science from the University of Wisconsin, Milwaukee. He received his Ph.D. in information science from the School of Information Sciences at the University of Pittsburgh. His major research areas are Arabic information retrieval and text processing, data mining, and digital libraries.

David Bearman is President of Archives & Museum Informatics. He consults on issues relating to electronic records and archives, integrating multi-format cultural information and museum information systems and is Founding Editor of the quarterly journal *Archives and Museum Informatics*. He has served as Deputy Director of the Smithsonian Institution Office of Information Resource Management and as Director of the National Information Systems Task Force of the Society of American Archivists (1980–1982). He also served as Director of Strategy and Research for the Art Museum Image Consortium. Bearman is the author of over 125 books and articles on museum and archives information management issues.

Stephen J. Bensman is a technical services librarian at Louisiana State University Libraries in Baton Rouge. His main duties have been in cataloging and classification, collection development, and statistical analyses for purposes of collection development and management. He holds a master's degree in library science and a doctorate in history, both from the University of Wisconsin in Madison, where he worked as the foreign law librarian. He has published articles on Soviet legal bibliography and bibliometrics, as well as the socioeconomic structure of the scholarly and scientific journal system.

Katy Börner is an Associate Professor of Information Science in the School of Library and Information Science, Adjunct Associate Professor in the School of Informatics, a member of the Cognitive Science core faculty, Research Affiliate of the Biocomplexity Institute, Fellow of the Center for Research on Learning and Technology, and Member of the Advanced Visualization Laboratory at Indiana University, Bloomington, where she directs the Information Visualization Laboratory and is the Founding Director of the Cyberinfrastructure for Network Science Center. Her research focuses on the development of data analysis and visualization techniques that inform access, understanding, and management of scholarly data and the design of cyberinfrastructures (CI) for large-scale scientific collaboration and computation such as the Information Visualization CI and the recently funded Network Workbench CI.

Colin Burke is a historian who has published on many subjects during his career. Among them are histories of American voting, residential segregation, 19th-century higher education and its students, nonprofit organizations, the development of code-breaking technologies, and various information technology projects and policies. Among the awards and positions in his background are a Social Science Research Council Fellow, a Scholar-in-Residence at the NSA, a Research Fellow at Yale University, and a Eugene Garfield Fellow. Dr. Burke is currently working on a biography of an American Cold War agent and on a general history of information science.

Christina Courtright is a doctoral candidate at the School of Library and Information Science at Indiana University, Bloomington, with research interests that include social aspects of information behavior and computerization, information policy, and international information issues. Her dissertation research explores the nature of context for information needs, seeking, and use; the fieldwork focuses on Spanish-speaking immigrants in southern Indiana.

David R. Danielson is a doctoral candidate in Communication Theory and Research at Stanford University, specializing in human–computer interaction. He is on the editorial board of the *Encyclopedia of Human–Computer Interaction* (Idea Group, 2005) and leads the Web Credibility project in the Persuasive Technology Lab at Stanford. His research and professional activities focus on information seeking behavior, trust and credibility, consumer behavior, usability metrics and processes, and usability engineering.

Greg Downey is an Assistant Professor in both the School of Journalism and Mass Communication and the School of Library and Information Studies at the University of Wisconsin-Madison. He is the author of *Telegraph Messenger Boys: Labor, Technology, and Geography, 1850–1950* (Routledge, 2002) and is currently working on a history and geography of the intertwined technologies and labors of court reporting and video captioning, tentatively titled *From Court Reporters to Closed Captioners: The Hidden Technology and Labor of Subtitling and Stenography in Translating Speech into Text* (The Johns Hopkins University Press, forthcoming).

Glynn Harmon is a Professor in the School of Information, University of Texas at Austin. His research centers on the dynamics of scientific discovery, philosophy of information science, information impact, unconscious cognition, and health informatics. He has served twice as Interim Dean of the School of Information. Previously, he served as a U.S. Navy pilot for eight years. His degrees include B.A. and M.A. degrees (Public Administration) from the University of California at Berkeley, an M.S. and Ph.D. (Information Science) from Case Western Reserve University, and an M.B.A. from Southwest Texas State University.

Birger Hjørland holds an M.A. in Psychology and a Ph.D. in Library and Information Science. He is a Professor of Library and Information Science (Knowledge Organization) at the Royal School of Library and Information Science (RSLIS) in Copenhagen. He worked formerly as an information researcher on a Nordic research project (1971–1973), taught reference work and documentation at RSLIS (1972–1978), and served as a research librarian at the Royal Library in Copenhagen (1978–1990). He also taught information science at the Department of Applied Linguistics, University of Copenhagen (1983–1986); was Head of the Department of Humanities and Social Sciences Information Studies at RSLIS (1990–2000); taught history and philosophy of psychology at the University of Copenhagen (1994–1997); and served as Professor of Knowledge Organization at the University College of Borås, Sweden (2000–2001). Dr. Hjørland is the author of *Information Seeking and Subject Representation: An Activity-Theoretical Approach to Information Science* (1997) as well as numerous journal articles.

Ronald D. Houston, D.A. (Psychology), B.B.A. (International Business), B.S. (Geology), M.L.I.S. (Archival Enterprise), is a doctoral candidate in information science at the School of Information at the University of Texas at Austin. His research and writing efforts center on the societal implications of information behavior, particularly on manifestations of compelled non-use of information. He has published in the *Journal of Information Ethics*.

Krishna P. Jayakar is an Associate Professor in the College of Communications at the Pennsylvania State University and teaches telecommunications management and media economics. Dr. Jayakar completed his bachelor's degree in mechanical engineering from the Institute of Technology-BHU, Banaras, India, and holds an M.A. and Ph.D. in Mass Communications from Indiana University, Bloomington. His research interests include telecommunications policy, intellectual property rights, and film industry economics. Dr. Jayakar's research has been published in several journals, including *Telecommunications Policy, Journal of Media Economics,* and *The Information Society.*

William Jones is a Research Associate Professor in the Information School at the University of Washington, where he manages the Keeping Found Things Found project in collaboration with Harry Bruce (http://kftf.ischool.washington.edu/index.asp; see also http://pim.ischool. washington.edu). He received his Ph.D. from Carnegie-Mellon University for research on human memory. Dr. Jones has published basic research in cognitive psychology and more applied research in personal information management, information retrieval, and human–computer interaction. He has worked as a program manager at Microsoft, where he was involved in the production of information management features for both Microsoft Office and MSN Search.

Catherine Legg holds a B.A. in Philosophy from the University of Melbourne and an M.A. in Philosophy from Monash University. After completing her Ph.D., which was a deep investigation of the philosophical categories of the noted American polymath and pragmatist Charles Peirce, at the Australian National University, she worked for two years at Cycorp (Austin, Texas) as an ontological engineer. She is now a Lecturer in Philosophy at the University of Waikato (on the North Island of New Zealand), where she continues to pursue research interests in ontology within the contexts of both classical philosophy and information science.

Jeppe Nicolaisen is an Assistant Professor at the Royal School of Library and Information Science in Copenhagen, Denmark. He obtained his Ph.D. in 2004 for his dissertation entitled *Social Behavior and Scientific Practice: Missing Pieces of the Citation Puzzle.* The thesis was designated "Highly commended" in the First Annual Emerald/EFMD Outstanding Doctoral Research Awards in 2005. His 2002 article on the J-shaped distribution of citedness, published in the *Journal of Documentation,* won him the VALFRID Award in 2004. In 2006, he consulted for the Danish National Library Authority.

Soo Young Rieh is an Assistant Professor at the School of Information, University of Michigan. She has conducted research on information quality and cognitive authority, information seeking and retrieval, and Web searching behavior. Her current research activities include a study on the credibility judgments of college students and a project entitled Making Institutional Repositories a Collaborative Learning Environment (MIRACLE), which is funded by the IMLS. She earned her Ph.D. in Communication, Information, and Library Studies from Rutgers University, received the Eugene Garfield-ALISE Dissertation Award in 2002, and the John Wiley Best *JASIST* Paper Award in 2005.

Soma Sanyal received her Ph.D. in Physics from the Institute of Physics, Bhubaneswar, India. She is currently a postdoctoral research associate at the School of Library and Information Science, Indiana University, Bloomington. Previously she worked on phase transitions and other aspects of statistical physics. Her current research investigates the structure and co-evolution of scholarly networks, such as citation and co-authorship networks. She uses a combination of empirical methods from statistical physics and computer simulations to model the merging and splitting of existing scientific topics, the emergence of new topics, and also the diffusion of scientific concepts via scholarly networks.

Harmeet Sawhney is an Associate Professor in the Department of Telecommunications, Indiana University, Bloomington. His academic background includes a B.S. in Electrical Engineering from the Birla Institute of Technology, Ranchi, India; an M.B.A. in Marketing from XLRI, Jamshedpur, India; an M.A. in Communication from the State University of New York at Buffalo; and a Ph.D. in Communication from the University of Texas at Austin. His research interests focus on areas related to telecommunications infrastructure planning and policy. He currently serves as the Editor-in-Chief of *The Information Society*.

Diane H. Sonnenwald is a Professor at the Swedish School of Library and Information Science at Göteborg University and University College of Borås and the Director of the Center for Collaborative Innovation. She is also an adjunct professor at the University of North Carolina (Chapel Hill) and previously worked at Bell Communications Research. Dr. Sonnenwald conducts research on social aspects of collaboration and use of collaboration technology in a variety of contexts. Her research has been funded by the National Institutes of Health, National Science Foundation, European Science Foundation, Stiftelsen FöreningsSparbanken Sjuhärad, and the National Library of Medicine.

Alessandro Vespignani is a Professor of Informatics and Cognitive Science and Adjunct Professor of Physics at Indiana University, Bloomington. He is also affiliated with the Biocomplexity Institute at Indiana University and is a member of the French National Scientific Research Council. Previously he worked on non-equilibrium phenomena, critical phase transitions, growth processes, and complex systems. Recently, Vespignani's research activity has focused on the interdisciplinary application of statistical physics and numerical simulation methods to the analysis of spreading phenomena and the study of biological, social, and technological networks. He is a co-author of the book *Evolution and Structure of the Internet*, published by Cambridge University Press.

About the Editor

Blaise Cronin is the Rudy Professor of Information Science at Indiana University, Bloomington, where he has been Dean of the School of Library and Information Science for 15 years. From 1985 to 1991 he held the Chair of Information Science and was Head of the Department of Information Science at the University of Strathclyde Business School in Glasgow. He has also held visiting professorships at the Manchester Metropolitan University and Napier University, Edinburgh. Professor Cronin is the author of numerous research articles, monographs, technical reports, conference papers, and other publications. Much of his research focuses on collaboration in science, scholarly communication, citation analysis, the academic reward system, and cybermetrics—the intersection of information science and social studies of science. He has also published extensively on topics such as information warfare, information and knowledge management, competitive analysis, and strategic intelligence. Professor Cronin sits on a number of editorial boards, including *Journal of the American Society for Information Science and Technology*, *Scientometrics*, *Cybermetrics*, and *International Journal of Information Management*.

Professor Cronin has extensive international experience, having taught, conducted research, or consulted in more than 30 countries. Clients have included the World Bank, NATO, Asian Development Bank, UNESCO, U.S. Department of Justice, Brazilian Ministry of Science and Technology, European Commission, British Council, Her Majesty's Treasury, Hewlett-Packard Ltd., British Library, Commonwealth Agricultural Bureaux, Chemical Abstracts Service, and Association for Information Management. He has been a keynote or invited speaker at scores of conferences, nationally and internationally. Professor Cronin was a founding director of Crossaig, an electronic publishing start-up in Scotland, which was acquired in 1992 by ISI (Institute for Scientific Information) in Philadelphia. He was educated at Trinity College Dublin (M.A.) and the Queen's University of Belfast (Ph.D., D.S.Sc.). In 1997, he was awarded the degree Doctor of Letters (D.Litt., *honoris causa*) by Queen Margaret University College, Edinburgh, for his scholarly contributions to information science.

About the Associate Editor

Debora Shaw is a Professor at Indiana University, Bloomington and also Associate Dean of the School of Library and Information Science. Her research focuses on information organization and information seeking and use. Her work has been published in the *Journal of the American Society for Information Science and Technology*, the *Journal of Documentation*, *Online Review*, and *First Monday*, among others. She serves on the editorial board of the *Journal of Educational Resources in Computing*.

Dr. Shaw served as President of the American Society for Information Science & Technology (1997), and has also served on the Society's Board of Directors. She has been affiliated with *ARIST* as both a chapter author and as indexer over the past 18 years. Dr. Shaw received bachelor's and master's degrees from the University of Michigan and her Ph.D. from Indiana University. She was on the faculty at the University of Illinois before joining Indiana University.

Historical Perspectives

CHAPTER 1

History of Information Science

Colin Burke
University of Maryland, Baltimore County

Introduction: The Emergence of the History of Information Science as a Field of Study

After a decade of stimulating interest, establishing an infrastructure, and encouraging the creation of a body of literature, a group of information science professionals, in tandem with library history organizations around the world, has achieved the first stages of academic recognition for a field of study, the history of information science. That field encompasses more than the history of theory, methods, and techniques. It includes institutions, people, politics, and economics. Although information science is an international activity, the existing literature and this chapter attend mainly to its development in the United States and Western Europe. The number of historical works published in the last decade, 1994–2004, is now in the hundreds and the list continues to grow. There are too many to cite and the attached bibliography contains only a sampling of the literature.

Several events signaled that the mid-1990s was a landmark period for the historical study of the diverse set of activities and institutions in the United States and Europe that have been at the core of what has been variously named documentation, information retrieval, informatics, and information science. Major events in the early and mid-1990s were the appearance of special historical issues of the *Journal of Documentation, Information Processing & Management*, the *Journal of the American Society for Information Science (JASIS)*, the *Documentaliste*, and then the publication of a volume of historical articles by the American Society for Information Science, *Historical Studies in Information Science* (Hahn & Buckland, 1998; Rauzier, 1993; Rayward, 1996; Vickery, 1994).

Those publications were the result of much encouragement of historical research in the 1980s. By the early 1990s, there was enough scholarship and public interest to lead editors of major professional information journals to think that special historical issues were possibilities. They began soliciting papers and quickly received many more than the expected number of submissions. The papers were somewhat different from those in historical and commemorative compilations of earlier decades. There

3

were many more that were interpretive and depended on original and primary research. For example, in 1996 *Information Processing & Management* (Rayward, 1996) published half a dozen articles embodying this new type of work. Importantly, the articles targeted a general audience and avoided the use of specialized language. These interpretive pieces also helped to place the present in perspective. Included in the collection were explorations of how early twentieth-century concepts of information handling anticipated many recent ideas: They showed that the "Web" generation was not the first to conceive of creatively organizing and reorganizing separate chunks of information through "links" rather than through rigid forms, such as books or documents.

Information historians were not alone in focusing on their history. Librarians were also attending to information science history as well as to their traditional interest in the evolution of the library. Information historians contributed to the library organizations' mid-1990s reinvigorated interest in topics connected to the history of information processing. One of the United States' library history meetings led to the publication of a collection of relevant papers (Davis, 1996). Librarians' bibliographies of historical works also began to include works on information science (Passet, 1994).

Meanwhile, information scientists were encouraging additional research and publication. The two special issues of *JASIS* published in 1997 were of broad scope, tapped more approaches to history than usual, and reflected the international character of the growing interest in the history of information (Buckland & Hahn, 1997a, 1997b). Their articles explored topics ranging from Hebrew citation indexing to the development of libraries and scientific information systems in France and the Soviet Union. The value of the *JASIS* and *Information Processing & Management* issues was recognized by combining them to create a book devoted to presenting the best of the current historical scholarship, *Historical Studies in Information Science* (Hahn & Buckland, 1998).

Interest continued to grow, even among scholars from other disciplines. That led to the first Conference on the History and Heritage of Science Information Systems, held in Pittsburgh during October 1998. Of especial importance to this meeting was support provided by the American Society for Information Science (ASIS), which also aided in the production of another pivotal volume: Containing almost two dozen new papers given by historians of science, as well as those generated by scholars and practitioners focusing upon information science, the *Proceedings of the 1998 Conference on the History and Heritage of Scientific Information Systems* (Bowden, Hahn, & Williams, 1999) provided public access to the text of most of the meeting's presentations. This publication demonstrated that information history was beginning to move into the mainstream of historical study. Concurrently, chemists looked at their own information system history, a long and important one predating World War II (Williams & Bowden, 1999). *JASIS* then joined in with a double commemorative issue that included several historical articles (Bates, 1999b, 1999c).

These publications of the late 1990s and the 1998 meeting were not parochial: They included papers and people from around the modern world and gave recognition to previous efforts in information history. Importantly, some of the participants attempted to place their information science histories in larger historical/explanatory contexts, such as the modernization of the Western World, the rise of "post-industrial society," and the early twentieth-century struggle between socialism and capitalism.

The 1998 Pittsburgh meeting was significant for other reasons. In addition to the presentation of some explanatory studies, the meeting indicated that scholars other than practitioners of information science were likely to become involved in recording and interpreting its history; that information histories could be more than reflections on methods and could be made attractive to the general public; and that institutions other than professional ones, such as ASIS, would be willing to support scholarly research in the field. The Chemical Heritage Foundation and the National Science Foundation, for example, were major contributors to the late 1990s projects and an important fellowship in information history was established by Eugene Garfield.

Although the early twenty-first century stock market debacle, government retrenchment, and the economic recession made financial support difficult to obtain, historical work has continued. There is a growing list of institutions and people attending to information science history. In addition to the efforts of those groups associated with the American Society for Information Science and Technology (ASIST), the Special Libraries Association is devoting resources to a centennial history. The Charles Babbage Institute in the United States has been shifting its attention from computer hardware and its creators to the history of software, databases, and information retrieval. Researchers in France, Spain, Germany, and other countries have been generating their own histories (Behrends, 1995; Fayet-Scribe, 2000; Fernandez & Moreno, 1997; Hapke, 1999; Marloth, 1996). Finnish information scientists have continued their tradition of exploring the roots and nature of information science (Makinen, 2004). By the mid-1990s, Asian scholars had begun another round of historical initiatives, producing important bibliographies, anthologies, and very impressive books and articles of historical import (Muranushi, 1994) whose results American researchers quickly incorporated into their own work (Satoh, 1999).

In England, in addition to the 1994 *Journal of Documentation* effort, the Library History Group (recently renamed the Library and Information History Group) has been expanding its historical reach into information history in general. Furthermore, Leeds Metropolitan University has secured funding for broadly defined information history initiatives. In addition, British information science leaders have been making their own individual contributions, such as the important works by Brian Vickery (1994, 2000, 2004).

But scholars and institutions within the United States seem the most active in supporting meetings and publications. A volume containing the many papers presented at a conference at the Chemical Heritage Foundation in Philadelphia held in conjunction with the ASIST 2002 conference was quickly published (Rayward & Bowden, 2004). The books from the 2002 and 1998 conferences are a resource for the general public and for the presently small but significant number of scholars, such as Alistair Black, Mark Bowles, Ron Day, Thomas Haigh, and Shawne Miksa who may well be the first generation of academics to center their careers on the history of information science and related topics.

A special 2004 issue of *Library Trends* (Rayward, 2004) that focused upon library and information science pioneers, the historical articles published in recent volumes of the *Annual Review of Information Science and Technology* (*ARIST*) (Black, 2006; Buckland & Liu, 1996; Warner, 2005), a University of Illinois symposium on the role of information in the rise of the modern world ("modernity"), and the recent appearance of a work on the history of the relationship of intelligence work and information science, edited by Robert V. Williams and Ben-Ami Lipetz (2005, published after completion of this chapter), indicate that the historical initiative in the United States will continue. No less important, the recent *IEEE Annals of the History of Computing* issues on history of library automation (Graham & Rayward, 2002a, 2002b) and the publication by MIT Press of the long-awaited and valuable history of the early online industry by Bourne and Hahn (2003) show that more than "library-oriented" publishers will support information history.

More to Be Done

In spite of all the work accomplished thus far, there is not enough accumulated scholarship to allow the writing of a comprehensive narrative history of information science. Many essential questions remain unanswered and much of the existing technical historical literature awaits translation into common language and concepts. Moreover, there are some roadblocks to progress. University information science and history departments have yet to reshape promotion and tenure orientations so as to encourage information history research. In addition, most of those scholars writing information histories have come out of information science rather than computer science, communications engineering, or special libraries backgrounds: This skew in the representation of academic disciplines may have fostered a somewhat unbalanced view as to origins, the nature of the field, and the sources of innovations (Aspray, 1985). But, it may soon be acceptable practice to include at least the outline of the history of information science in the curricula of professional degree programs. In time, a scholar may be able to compose an inclusive narrative, like those for computer history, that will make the history of information science attractive to students and, perhaps, the general public (Ceruzzi, 1998).

This chapter reviews new literature from the last decade and points to the many questions still to be answered in the hope of stimulating researchers to fill the historical gaps and correct any imbalances so that the history of information science may come to be considered as a mature and independent academic subject.

Information History Before the 1990s

There was, of course, interest in information science history and related subjects prior to the 1990s. More than a decade before the current group of academic and practitioner information history advocates began their work, historical articles on information theory, automated information retrieval, and information policy appeared in journals such as *Libraries and Culture*, *Library Trends*, *The Annals of the History of Computing*, and *JASIS* (Redmond, 1985; Williams, Whitmire, & Bradley, 1997). The *Encyclopedia of Library and Information Sciences* also served as a source for historical information. Even though it did not usually publish explicitly historical articles, from its inception its editors encouraged contributors to provide the historical background of their subjects. Furthermore, *ARIST*'s state-of-the-art pieces frequently included some historical material.

In the United States, an initial wave of interest in information science history and the state of the profession during the 1970s and early 1980s led to a few special collections and some issues of professional journals (Chartrand, Henderson, & Resnick, 1988; Heilprin, 1988; Library and information science: Historical perspectives, 1985). Library historians went further, and in 1986 published an issue of *Library Trends* devoted to library and information history (Davis & Dain, 1986). Historians of the library began writing on the evolution of classification and indexing systems and the impact of new technologies on them (Davis & Tucker, 1989). Added to this literature were the beginnings of a continuing string of commemorative in-house histories of the U.S. government's various library and information centers (Miles, 1982; Thompson, 2004; Vaden, 1992).

Most of the contributions of the era were by practitioners, were addressed to specialists, and dealt with topics of immediate interest, such as establishing the ideal nature of information science. Two seminal articles were published in *ARIST* and *JASIS* (Herner, 1984; Shera & Cleveland, 1977). Among the early major efforts was Anthony Debons's (1974) contribution, *Information Science: Search for Identity*, which pursued a theme that information historians continue to explore.

Several works of the early period, written by recognized leaders in information science such as Jack Meadows (1987), received much attention. Also important, but less well known, were several histories of subfields and organizations, such as Brenner and Saracevic's (1985) *Indexing and Searching in Perspective* and the National Federation of Abstracting and Indexing Services' (NFAIS) *Abstracting and Indexing Services in Perspective* (Granick & Cornog, 1983). The Association of Computing Machinery

(ACM) published a conference proceedings volume, *History of Medical Informatics* (Blum & Duncan, 1990). That publication was followed by a series of works on medical information systems (e.g., Collen, 1995).

Like their North American counterparts, European and Asian professional journals published historical works before the mid-1990s—typically written by information professionals who relied upon their own experiences, memories, and personally held documents (Williams, Whitmire, & Bradley, 1998).

Establishing a Context

Works serving to help place information science in context also appeared. Importantly, a few classic books and articles on the history of the United States government's information policies were published in the 1970s and 1980s. Their authors typically were persons involved in policy creation and implementation. Burton W. Adkinson's (1978) *Two Centuries of Federal Information* remains a central work. Harold Wooster's (1987) "Historical Note: Shining Palaces, Shifting Sands: National Information Systems," written a decade later, is also outstanding.

From the 1970s, concerns over America's role in what was named the "post-industrial age" led to efforts that continue to influence historians, including how they classify someone as an information professional (Bell, 1973). Among several studies attempting to define precisely the size and boundaries of the emerging "information economy" was Porat's (1977) multi-volume work for the U.S. Commerce Department. This topic has continued to fascinate economists (Martin, 1998; Schement, 1990).

The United States' worries over its declining competitive position in the reshaped world economy of the 1970s and threats to its lead in scientific research created another round of intense and focused interest on the dissemination of government-sponsored scientific and technical information (STINFO). Adding to their older concerns over information for Cold War science, journals such as *Government Information Quarterly, Government Publications Review,* and the *Journal of Government Information* published many significant historical pieces concentrating on information policy and its relation to economic competition. Furthermore, work began on what became a valuable series of monographs and bibliographies on STINFO and government information programs in general (Dahlin, 1990; Pinelli, Henderson, Bishop, & Doty, 1992).

Important Contributions from the Social Sciences: Helpful but Potentially Confusing

Whereas information professionals of the 1970s were producing the first historical studies and economists were trying to judge the size of the information economy, academics working within social science frameworks, such as Fritz Machlup and Una Mansfield (1983) and, later, James

R. Beniger (1986) and Joanne Yates (1989), drew grand outlines of the history of the developing "information" economy and culture of twentieth-century America. They defined the information field much more broadly than previous historical researchers. Most historical works on information science had been rather uncomplicated descriptions of the development of the methods and techniques of book and document cataloging, indexing, and retrieval. Other works had monitored the careers of established information organizations and leaders. In contrast, the books by Yates and Beniger provided sweeping, high-level views and explanations. However, they did limit their target somewhat, for they attended to the role of all types of information and its tools—but only within the economic and business realms, paying little attention to information needs in the sciences or the humanities.

Machlup's contribution was of special importance because it was interdisciplinary and looked at information in a wider range of subject areas. It included efforts by various types of economists and, importantly, studies by information specialists already engaged in historical research on information science topics, such as Boyd Rayward (1983). Machlup was familiar with the latest trends in European historiography and his work served as a bridge between American and foreign scholarship and between practitioners and social scientists. For unknown reasons, Machlup's initiative did not lead to ongoing support for such all-encompassing interdisciplinary research on information science itself. This has left important gaps in the accumulated historical literature.

The broad works of the Beniger-Machlup genre remained influential, however—but with a few negative consequences. By defining information history as the history of nearly all types of communications and record keeping, they offered the temptation to investigators to avoid the difficulties involved in precisely identifying information science professionals and their contributions. Another result of the use of an all-inclusive definition of "information" has been to situate the origins of information systems and information science in a distant past (Brown, 1989; Headrick, 2000; Stockwell, 2001). Also, the approaches taken by the broad works' authors have added to the difficulties historians face as they attempt to write the story of information science professionals since World War II (Chandler & Cortada, 2000; Cortada, 1998). For example, while focusing on the massive shift away from manual labor in the twentieth century the United States statistical agencies have not usefully identified and tracked what we commonly refer to as "information scientists." United States government reports do not provide the data needed to determine the number of those who were trained as or considered themselves as professionals. The Bureau of Labor Statistics has a category for "information scientists" but does not report their numbers separately from those of computer scientists.

Other types of work in the post-Machlup era were more limited in scope but also somewhat off-target with regard to the needs of information science historians. Additional business histories, which focused on the role of information in management, only partially filled the gaps (Lamoreaux, Raff, & Temin, 1997; Levenstein, 1998; Temin, 1987).

However, during the 1980s a useful detailed literature on subjects interconnected with information science history was accumulating. The emphasis was on technology, but there were intellectual and general policy histories. By the mid-1980s, the history of computers, especially their hardware, was maturing and popular enough to support specialized college classes and textbooks. The texts showed that, because of the revolution in microelectronics, the power/price ratio of computing was ushering in a new information era (Williams, 1985). Some computer historians, such as William Aspray (1985), brought new insights to the history of the intellectual aspects of the mathematical and scientific conceptualization of information. Among many others, the economist Peter Temin (1987) explored the critical AT&T deregulation decision that has shaped so many of the United States' communications policies, technologies, prices—and, therefore, the work of information scientists.

The New Information History Literature Begins to Emerge

The technological histories, the expanded visions of the role of information in society and the economy, and a growing body of practitioner-generated literature provided a foundation and motivations for the historical initiatives of the 1990s. The flow of reminiscences by practitioners continued; however, in the late 1980s, a new breed of information history began to appear. Much of it continued to be written by authors working as information specialists or associated with practitioners' organizations; however, they introduced a new approach. Their ambitions were great but temperate. The leading works of the genre had broader visions, were marked by more original research, and were more successful at meeting scholarly standards for explanation than had been typical. Furthermore, the authors avoided using an imperialistic definition of information.

The first of these publications emerged without much fanfare. Two extensive American institutional histories appeared in 1989 and 1990: Lilley and Trice's (1989) *A History of Information Science, 1945–1985* and the more integrated and scholarly *From Documentation to Information Science* by Irene Farkas-Conn (1990), which sensitively described the rather strange birth of America's predecessor to information science, "documentation." Farkas-Conn's history of Watson Davis and his elite research librarian and scientist allies in the 1930s–1950s, who first concentrated on speeding the dissemination of academic scientific literature through microfilm technology, gave historical continuity to information as both a science and a profession. Her book's inclusion of insights into the history of the American Documentation Institute (ADI), the predecessor of the American Society for Information Science, enhanced the work's positive reception and amplified the rise of interest in the record of America's information professionals.

Importantly, recognition of the value of historical research was soon institutionalized. Beginning in the early 1990s, a new round of historical panels at various association meetings was held and, by mid-decade, ASIST gave formal acknowledgment to the field. By that time, ASIST had assisted in the creation of a database for information pioneers' biographies (www.libsci.sc.edu/bob/ISP/ISP.htm) and *ARIST* soon published its first historical chapter in more than a decade (Buckland & Liu, 1996). ASIST's encouragement also aided the effort to compile the first comprehensive bibliographies on the history of information, a project that continues to this day (Williams, 2005; Williams et al., 1998). In addition, the Chemical Heritage Foundation began plans to conduct what has become an invaluable series of oral history interviews with information pioneers.

At the same time, European information professionals and academics were creating their own new approaches to information history. They sponsored and published the results of the historically oriented 1991 conference on information science in Tampere, Finland. Vakkarri and Cronin's (1992) seminal collection, *Conceptions of Library and Information Science: Historical, Empirical and Theoretical Perspectives*, remains a major source. It contained more than just assertions of the ideal nature of information science. Rayward's and Saracevic's papers in the volume and their contacts with America's history advocates were catalysts for future work on the origins and character of information science in the Western world. In addition, France's *Documentaliste* put out a historically oriented issue in 1993 and, a year later, England's Aslib published a fifty-year commemorative issue of the *Journal of Documentation* (Vickery, 1994).

In the United States, there were other significant developments. Pamela Spence Richards's (1981, 1994) earlier writings on how nations obtained foreign scientific information during World War II and the Cold War were evolving into an interpretive monograph. Roy MacLeod (1999) began his research on information in World War I and Michael Buckland (1992) started publishing well-researched articles that challenged the idea that modern information retrieval techniques and such concepts as hypertext were solely the result of pragmatic developments within the United States. Furthermore, Boyd Rayward's (1975, 1994) intellectual histories of Paul Otlet achieved recognition just as an intense interest was developing concerning the origins of the Internet and hypertext.

The Role of Some Other "Outsiders"

That interest in the World Wide Web had already led a few nonpractitioners to write on the origins of the Internet and related information concepts and techniques. The 1991 volume edited by Nyce and Kahn, which examined Vannevar Bush's prescient intellectual contributions and his proposed information devices, reflected the common belief that Bush's mid-1940s vision of the advanced retrieval machine, the Memex, was unique and causally related to the most advanced system and methodological ideas of the 1980s (Nyce & Kahn, 1989, 1991).

The Bush mystique, including appraisals of his role in organizing American science during World War II, had already launched two non-practitioners on long-term research that touched on the history of information. The reporter, G. Pascal Zachary, and the historian of science, Larry Owens (1996), explored Bush's personality in addition to much of his engineering work and policy making. Zachary (1997) eventually published a full-length biography of Bush.

Another historian, who had been researching the supersecret code-breaking machines of World War II, found that the story of the proto-computers used against the German and Japanese codes and ciphers was intimately tied to Bush's efforts to build what became famous as the first automated information retrieval machine, the electronic/microfilm Rapid Selector. In turn, the Selector's rather disappointing history, before and after World War II, was entwined with the establishment of military-sponsored document retrieval centers and their new methods and machines for processing scientific reports and intelligence and military data (Burke, 1994).

William Aspray began a study of the first information science programs in American universities that led to his superb 1999 article in the *IEEE Annals of the History of Computing*, in which he situated the formation and early history of the University of Pittsburgh's information science program within the contexts of the university's drive to become a recognized research/entrepreneurial institution and the visions and ambitions of the department's founding generation (Aspray, 1999).

Bush's biography, the Selector's career, Aspray's curricular study, and the history of the fabled INTREX project at the Massachusetts Institute of Technology (MIT)—an effort that promised to build a fully automated library in the 1960s (Burke, 1996)—pointed to one of the many topics being explored in the more recent historical literature: the sometimes competitive relations between those trained as engineers or entrepreneurs and those from information/library backgrounds as the age of information automation unfolded. The INTREX history also highlighted the difficulties faced by even well-funded sponsoring institutions, such as the Ford Foundation and the Council on Library Resources, as they attempted to modernize the leading American universities' general libraries. When they attempted to create equality of access to the extremely expensive information technology then available only at the largest government and military centers, they faced many disappointments (Marcum, 2002).

What the New Histories of the Later 1990s Tell Us: The Diverse Nature of the Contributions and Areas of Concentration

The summaries of the historical literature from the last decade presented here are based upon a search of relevant bibliographic databases and the classification and frequency analysis of the articles and books by subjects and historical approaches.

The new historical publications that followed the initial works by non-practitioners were not confined to a few topics nor to a few approaches. There are as yet no schools of what professional historians call "interpretation" that have succeeded in dominating the field and no demands have surfaced that publication be restricted to those with historical credentials. Moreover, publication has not been confined to those whose interests and political orientations fit narrow editorial agendas. Fortunately, there are few indications that authors will be required, as in some historical fields, to orient their attention to such ideologically laced items as, for example, race-gender-class conflicts, in each of their publications.

Much of the work has been straightforward and is being done by "insiders," that is, information professionals or academics in information science departments. An increasing number of publications reflect a methodological consciousness and, in some cases, the authors make use of currently popular theories or interpretive frameworks from the fields of literary criticism, mainstream history, the sociology of knowledge, and the philosophy of science.

The "Building Block" Type of Contributions of the Last Decade

In terms of frequency, however, the latest historical works have been rather uncomplicated short biographies, autobiographical reminiscences, and participant descriptions of methods, projects, and devices. Almost all have appeared in publications sponsored by information science and library organizations. A growing and impressive body of interviews supplements the articles (Bjorner & Ardito, 2003; see also the Chemical Heritage Foundation's Oral History Collection [www.chemheritage.org/exhibits/ex-nav2.html]). Both the publications and interviews will serve as valuable building blocks for broader integrative histories. But a note of caution should be sounded. As mentioned, the biographies and interviews tend to focus on those persons previously identified as major contributors from within post-World War II information science, not from computer science or other related fields. Future historians will need to compensate for that and to sort through differing views of information science history resulting from participant authors' varied career experiences.

The building-block articles and interviews have concentrated on the people and advances during what some quite aptly term a "golden age" of information science in the United States, the 1950s–1970s. Those thirty-odd years constitute the period when the Cold War's technological needs, the growth of highly funded applied science projects, and the rise of giant universities with applied research contracts led to a search for novel approaches to indexing, new retrieval technologies, formal information management tools, and innovative online bibliographic systems. The government supplied unprecedented amounts of money for information systems and research and helped define what promised to be a distinct and homogeneous profession and discipline (Hayes, 1999; Saracevic, 1992, 1999).

The majority of the building-block historical works of the 1990s and similar, earlier contributions are in agreement about the core of the "golden age." Although most of the literature has been about trends in the United States, the patterns found in its Cold War information age seem, to this author, to fit those in Western Europe (East, 1998).

The building-block histories find some continuity with the past: Both the older 1930s documentalists and the emerging information scientists focused on scientists' and academics' needs (Walker, 1997). But the 1950s witnessed a shift. The early generation of documentalists had been committed to serving typical pre-World War II sponsors: elite universities, older types of faculties who worked independently, and established non-profit science organizations. After the outbreak of World War II, a new generation appeared, the first to be called "information scientists." Their different professional backgrounds made them central to the creation of an information science linked to new varieties of patrons. Engineers, physicists, chemists, and even psychologists began playing critical and prominent roles in building new systems and in creating the methodological core of information science's "golden age."

The Cold War and the growth of government regulation over industry in the United States provided resources and power for those reworking scientific, intelligence, and military information systems. These first information scientists looked to the needs of the entrepreneurial university, defense and mission-oriented government agencies and their contractors, and a few expanding businesses with special information needs, such as those in the chemical industry. The primary mission of the new information specialists was to improve what are called "secondary" bibliographic services (Cragin, 2004; Kaser & Kaser, 2001; Kualnes, 1999). Added to that work on indexing and efficient document (and fact) retrieval were, at some of the new centers, more esoteric efforts. Some projects attempted to develop automatic language translation, automatic indexing, and new tools for the identification of photographs and their contents. Military and intelligence needs led to an even more expansive definition of the "science" (Debons & Horne, 1997; Gimbel, 1990).

The work also included some new challenges. Many government centers had to ensure that secret information was kept secret. Security needs went beyond the older corporate desire to protect business information. Intelligence and other agencies needed innovative systems to handle a torrent of data and to protect it from outsiders. Embedded in the challenges were frustrating issues of balancing mandates for the free flow of scientific information with privacy laws and the secrecy demands of national security (Kenzo, 2003; Seidel, 1999).

Technology was also new. The period was marked by the appearance of a cohort of practitioners who were among the first to have access to the then exorbitantly expensive yet limited computer technology. That technology made previously impractical approaches to indexing and retrieval seem possible.

Much of the work took place within the vastly expanded government agencies, which produced a challenging form of publication, the "technical report." Unlike books and academic articles, these reports and other irregular documents had a short life span, were used by only a few readers, and had to be made available almost instantly. Importantly, older classification systems did not meet the needs of the "technical report" literature. That led to searches for quick and ideally inexpensive ways to index and retrieve materials, including patents and even pictures. New methods and new terms appeared: uniterms, inverted files, keyword in context (KWIC), and keyword out of context (KWOK) (Austin, 1998; Gull, 1987; Kilgour, 1997; Ohlman, 1999; Stewart, 1993).

Most information professionals working on the new types of publications and documents paid little attention to traditional types of all-inclusive classification systems because they were focusing on providing information to specialists as quickly as possible. The terms used by contemporary subject specialists appeared to be satisfactory for many indexing tasks and there seemed no need for systems based on comprehensive and intellectually pleasing classification schemes. The goal of creating tools useful to non-specialists was, at best, of secondary importance.

There was a faith that new technologies for retrieval, ranging from massive microfilm devices to the electronic computer, would overcome, by brute technological force, any logical weaknesses of the new, simpler approaches to classification and indexing (Burke, 1994). But there were exceptions. In Europe, several documentalists sought integrated classification structures that could manage the new documents without ignoring nonspecialists' desires (Justice, 2004; McIlwaine, 1997).

Meanwhile, some of the United States' information practitioners focused on filling the scientific information gaps left by the weaknesses of the established nonprofit professional bibliographic and publishing services. Those older providers and their patrons could not afford to modernize and had continued with traditional types of bibliographies and professional journals. They and the established academic infrastructure were unable to meet the needs for speedy indexing and publication. Their systems were overwhelmed by the flood of publications caused by the expansion of higher education and the growing pressures on all types of university faculty for research and publication as "publish or perish" became a national standard. Even the rich medical profession and its suppliers in the chemical industry felt besieged and hoped for an information retrieval and dissemination revolution to meet the extraordinary intellectual demands of their sciences. Resource-starved public school educators scrambled for ways to bring research findings to the classroom teacher. They all soon called on the government for support and protection (Altman, 1993; Horn & Clements, 1989; Kaser & Kaser, 2001; Neufeld, Cornog, & Sperr, 1983; Powell, 2000).

While a few information scientists concentrated on refurbishing the older but expanding nonprofit sector, a smaller number of information pioneers created for-profit companies and extended their reach into law, various technical literatures, patent searching, and even the newsroom (Bjorner & Ardito, 2003; Brown, 2002a, 2002b, 2003a, 2003b; Hahn, 1996; Pemberton, 1983; Power, 1990). One innovative scientific entrepreneur, Eugene Garfield, developed a company whose products became essential to academia. His citation indexing soon played a role in promotion and tenure considerations, library materials purchasing, and departmental certification (Cronin & Atkins, 2000; Wouters, 1999).

All of the "golden age" information science sectors shared in an outpouring of direct and indirect support from the American government. Federal monies for the Cold War and, later, the Great Society social reform initiatives were important to most all those efforts (Altman, 1993; Brandhorst, 1993; National Science Foundation, Office of Science Information Service, 1960).

There was more to the "golden age," for it seemed that a profession was being created. The Cold War decades, which matured into a relatively stable set of technologies, tasks, markets, and sponsors, saw what many interpreted as the emergence of a clear, uncontested, and permanent professional identity for information science. There appeared to be a fairly well-marked employment territory, there were signs that a science with its own theory might develop, and there were reasons to expect that high-status university information science departments would become full, independent, and self-determining members of the university community (Kline, 2004; Varlejs, 1999).

There may also have been hopes that the new information research and, perhaps, theories would lead to the discovery of fundamental laws of information, ones beyond the earlier statistical regularities in word use and publication rates created in the pre-war years by such innovators as Zipf and Bradford. Reflecting that vision and the appearance of full-time information science programs and educators, the United States' older documentation organization changed its name: ADI became ASIS (later ASIST). Distinguishing itself from librarians' organizations, and continuing its relationship with the scientific research community, ASIS focused its major journal on research rather than professional news or practitioners' comments.

There was more than a name change. With much government support through institutions such as the National Science Foundation, mathematically/statistically oriented research into information retrieval methods (and results) seemed to be fulfilling the scientific promise of the field. Novel tools, such as statistical techniques to examine the nature of scientific and scholarly communications, promised even more for the new information science. The continued development of methods and perspectives, such as bibliometrics (a forerunner of data mining), suggested that information science could provide important insights into all the sciences (Bensman, 2004; Hertzel, 1987; Olaisen, Munch-Peterson, & Wilson, 1995;

Oluić-Vuković, 1997; Shapiro, 1992). By the early 1980s, the hopes for academic status seemed bright as publications in the field became more abstract and formalized (Lipetz, 1999). Information research had already been conducted in the most prestigious universities and by respected scholars such as Gerald Salton, whose work was lauded by academics outside the field (Harman, 1997; Lesk, 1996).

The academic progress went beyond research. A promising job market led to information science programs for professional training being established throughout the country. Another new generation of information scientists was rising—the first to have been formally trained in the practice, if not science, of information.

The building-block literature yields more than an outline of the "golden age." It provides insight into the human side of the rising profession. Many of the articles present details on the lives of the members of the founding generation, a group with various and fascinating backgrounds. Not all of those who contributed to the rise of information science have been included, however. Most of the biographies are about those persons who identified themselves as information science professionals concerned with retrieval and worked in government agencies or what became large nonprofit information organizations such as Chemical Abstracts Service or the Ohio College Library Center (now the Online Computer Library Center [OCLC]). A few of the biographical works inform us about the lives of those who ventured into the nascent for-profit scientific information sector and some tell of the experiences of those working within larger corporate information centers. Not explicit, but identifiable in even these works, is the theme of how people without formal library or information backgrounds were reshaping methods, professional organizations, and college-based training and research during the era (Chemical Abstract Service, 1997; Wouters, 1999).

Works other than biographical ones have appeared in the building-block literature and will be important for a future general history. There have been studies on early technological advances, such as Susan Cady's (1999) article on the birth and early life of the microfilm industry. A young scholar, Shawne Miksa (2002), has contributed an insightful dissertation that summarizes much that is known about early technology and information processing. An "outsider's" book on the Cold War's Itek Corporation provided tantalizing hints about the development of advanced techniques for information retrieval and processing for the U-2 and early satellite photography programs (Lewis, 2002). As mentioned earlier, chemists have looked at their own information system history, a long and important one that predates World War II (Meyer & Funkhouser, 1998).

The contributions of two building-block researchers stand out. Among many other activities (such as his Pioneers of Information Project), Robert V. Williams is collecting and encouraging the preservation of documentary records on precomputer information machines (and allied methods of the 1930s–1950s) and is rescuing and translating into common language descriptions of the information methods used during the earliest stages of computer hardware development. He is also tracking the relationship of work in Cold War codebreaking and intelligence centers to information science.

Although she reportedly does not claim to be an historian, Marcia Bates has given us a major contribution. Her 1999 article presented a list and brief description, arranged by topic, of the major articles that had appeared in *JASIS* and its predecessor since 1950 (Bates, 1999a). It thus outlined the development of the research agenda of the new field, which continues to focus on information retrieval methods. Although not an interpretive or evaluative history, Bates's article is a foundation piece for the sorely needed integrated history of American information concepts and methods. That future history should incorporate earlier studies and should compare contributions to *JASIS* by authors who were trained as information scientists with those by authors who had not received such training in order to evaluate the impact of formal training in the field. It is to be hoped that a new round of similar surveys of the contents of *ARIST*, *Special Libraries*, and the proceedings of organizations such as ASIST will appear (Järvelin & Vakkari, 1992; Lipetz, 1999).

Beyond the Building Blocks—The Interpretive Literature

Fewer in number than the building blocks, but not of less importance, are the thematic, analytic, and interpretive articles and books that have been published in the last decade. They touch on several topics and place building-block items in larger contexts. Some of the topics appear to have been selected because they are of current interest to practitioners and academics. Although picking topics because of their relevance for currently important and possibly ideologically or emotionally charged issues holds the dangers of what are called "presentism" and "ahistoricism" (the shaping of the view of the past to conform to contemporary contexts or ideologies), researching the history of contemporary issues is quite acceptable and does not necessarily lead to biased conclusions (Fischer, 1970). Thus, although current concerns over the future of academic programs and the role of the information scientist in the age of the World Wide Web, as well as a general postmodern cultural malaise, seem to have driven many recent historical projects, the new thematic histories have yielded much of value.

Especially significant among the prominent themes in the analytic works are the theses that the "golden age" of information science did not lead to a permanently stable profession; that the founding era was not as harmonious as the building block and previous histories pictured; and that the decades of the Cold War and Great Society social reform programs were not marked by a deep and lasting consensus about the nature of information science. Furthermore, the new interpretive historical literature gives strong indications that many early professional and scientific dreams have not been completely fulfilled. Certainly, the hopes that an information science theory would bridge the intellectual and institutional divides between library, computer, cognitive, and information sciences remain unrealized.

These conclusions seem justified, but we await verification. Hardly any publications have explored the post-"golden age" years in depth. Even the recent informative article by Griffiths and King (2002) and the important book by Bourne and Hahn (2003), which bring together much material about the tools and trends of the 1950s–1970s, say little about the science of information or the information business after the mid-1970s. Moreover, a critical and analytic review of the intellectual and professional foundations laid during the Cold War is just beginning (Day, 2005).

We do have some indications of the conditions the science and profession faced in the post-"golden age" years, however. The 1980s brought social, economic, and technological changes that altered both the profession and, perhaps, the science. Certainly, job and employment conditions changed: Information science moved into what has been called the era of "post-professionalism" (Cronin & Davenport, 1988; M. Day, 2002).

The transformations since the 1970s appear profound, but have not been subjected to detailed examination (Hayes, 1999). There has as yet been little investigation of the impact of new types of for-profit employers and their demands on the profession and its allied educational programs. We know that America's social context also played a role in post-professionalism, placing all professions under ideological pressures. But we await the details on what happened to information science as political turmoil and economic change led to less respect and self-determination for many professionals. Did information scientists experience changes similar to those in the medical professions, where old hierarchies were displaced by new ones staffed with accountants? We also need answers concerning the impact of user-friendly software as it de-skilled information retrieval (and even indexing) as the newly competitive American economy demanded cost cutting and the outsourcing of work to low-wage areas. We need investigations of what happened in response to the call for new skills, ones that were taught in computer and business information management programs and on the shop floor—as well as in information and library programs (M. Day, 2002).

We also await investigations of the influence of the increasing size of information firms on professional status and culture. What happened as professionals became employees within complex, profit-driven businesses? Deep histories of the growth of the once small nonprofit bibliographic companies into massive, worldwide corporations might reveal a major change in professional culture as significant as the spread of multinational for-profit information companies dealing with other than scientific and academic information (Powell, 2000; Schultz & Georgy, 1994; Smith, 1998).

Although gaps remain in the history of the pre-1980s profession and a rigorous effort on the post-Cold War period has not been launched, the existing thematic literature does provide some insights into the record of the last three decades—as well as into the history of the formative era of information professionalism. A brief review of the writings, organized around the major categories in the thematic historical literature, also helps, as the authors probably intended, to place present concerns in perspective.

The Search for Intellectual and Institutional Roots

As might be expected of any historical initiative, much attention has been paid to the origins of information science. Some two dozen related articles and books have appeared since the mid-1990s. They agree that the field began with an emphasis on the processing of report-like documents and scientific information. Furthermore, there is agreement that such a focus continued for decades. However, although no competing, distinct schools of interpretation have yet formed, there are noticeable differences within the thematic literature as to the timing and nature of the discipline's beginnings. Tied to those differences, in many instances, are beliefs as to what information science should be in the future.

What is currently known about information science history helps explain the varied stories of origins. The mix of people from different disciplines, institutions, and orientations within information science, both today and at its birth, has much to do with the present historical ambivalence. The interpretive variations are also due to the application of different historical methods and assumptions. Some authors rely upon the history of ideas while others take a behavioral approach. Furthermore, there are semantic difficulties. A researcher is faced with a swirl of unstable definitions of basic terms such as information and information science (Capurro & Hjørland, 2002; Hjørland, 2000; Schrader, 1984). A solution to the disagreements over origins is possible, but it will take much logical and empirical work. Fundamental to a resolution is the need to overcome any temptation to allow desires concerning an ideal information science to determine the interpretation of its origins.

Among the many versions of origins are several emphasizing the European and humanistic roots of the field and its institutions. These histories trace information science back to at least the beginnings of the twentieth century—not the 1950s. Michael Buckland and Boyd Rayward have spotlighted early idealistic contributions of Europeans such as Paul Otlet, whose vision of a total library was anchored as much in the ideals of the humanities as in the needs of the expanding realms of science and engineering. For those historians pointing to Europe, broad intellectual hopes, not practical demands, gave birth to information science and, later, the profession (Rayward, 1994). H. G. Wells's dream of a universal library, a World Brain, and pre-World War II academically linked efforts at advancing general classification methods are also a part of the humanistic histories (Muddiman, 1998). In addition, Buckland (1992, 1995) has demonstrated that path-breaking technologies, such as automated microfilm catalogs and various information retrieval methods, were born as much in Europe as in the United States.

Such works also make claims of institutional continuities and assert a huge domain for information science. Like Farkas-Conn (1990), they trace the birth of America's major new information science organization, the American Society for Information Science (now American Society for Information Science and Technology) from Otlet through America's science advocate, Watson Davis, whose work had ties to America's intellectual and university elites, their academic expectations, and their social/political connections (Varlejs, 1999).

The Buckland/Rayward variety of historical claims can easily be interpreted as entailing a set of unspoken assertions about obligations and professional futures: Information science was and should continue to be wedded to the extraordinary heritage of the liberal arts; it should demand advanced and interdisciplinary training; it should have theoretically oriented programs; it should study all types of communication, including art and music; and its practitioners should be represented by an organization with expansive intellectual and cultural visions (Buckland, 1991, 1997; McCrank, 1995, 2001).

Other historians point to slightly different and much later beginnings, although they too emphasize intellectual roots and university connections rather than techniques or technologies. Recently, the theoretical orientation of the first university-level library graduate program in the United States, at the University of Chicago, has been treated as maturing by the 1950s into "social epistemology." That theory, developed by Jesse Shera and his colleagues (such as Margaret Egan) was an early version of the sociology of knowledge, which treats information as the result of individuals' and society's complex backgrounds and needs, not just as an intellectual item. The advocates of social epistemology view it as a precursor of theoretically driven user studies. They also make a greater claim, interpreting Shera's work as the first academically viable, high-level theory for the entire field of information science because it stood at the same prestige level as the most advanced sociology of the era (Furner, 2004; Smiraglia, 2002; Wright, 1985; Zandonade, 2004). Social epistemology foresaw an information science and its curriculum that were to be intellectual and analytic, not technical and vocational.

There are other versions of intellectual and institutional origins that look to methods and techniques rather than theories. In contrast to the more humanistic and social science-linked views, the perspective of some commentators rests upon the implicit claim that the core of modern information science emerged from the application of advanced mathematical and statistical tools and the use of computers during the Cold War era, especially through the work of the American academic Gerald Salton (Dubin, 2004; Harman, 1997).

The social/professional connections of those associated with all of these claims explain in part ASIST members' advantages in seeking support from the larger, post-World War II funding agencies. Information scientists in prestigious university departments, whether liberal arts or scientific, had much more success obtaining governmental grants and subsidies for information research than did librarians, special librarians, or non-academic information scientists (Harter & Hooten, 1992). The organization founded to upgrade research in American academia, the National Science Foundation, and many military agencies tended to sponsor information projects and programs run by those who were members of elite universities and their established academic "scientific" departments and professional organizations (National Science Foundation, Office of Science Information Service, 1960).

There are other claims about beginnings. Some European and North American university information science programs have traced their origins to semiotics and various other communications theories. Many of those theories arose from language studies and even from computer-related artificial intelligence research being conducted by newcomers to information studies in the post-World War II period. Other historical investigators place emphasis on roots in more traditionally library-related work. They trace information science to explorations of alternative classification philosophies in England and the statistical analysis of publications and word frequencies during the 1930s. In the eyes of some, those efforts are what led to the formation of the United Kingdom's now defunct Institute of Information Scientists (IIS) in 1958 (Hjørland, 2000; Olaisen et al., 1995).

To others, the methodological foundations were laid much earlier and by different types of people. Robert V. Williams has shown how many of the tasks and methods that differentiated regular librarians from information professionals came from the early twentieth-century work of floor-trained American "special librarians" who were employed in business and corporate libraries. Their methodological contributions were the result of responding to immediate and practical users' needs through the application of technologies created for purposes other than document processing. They built the United States' Special Libraries Association (SLA) into a large-scale organization before the emergence of the American documentalists and before anyone dreamed of the electronic computer (Williams, 1997; Williams & Zachert, 1983). Claims of origins in special libraries are not confined to the United States. Jack Meadows saw England's more inclusive version of special librarians as laying out the fundamentals of information theory, as well as contributing techniques—and doing so in the period immediately following World War I (Hjørland, 2000; Meadows, 1987). Other explorations of England's special library organization's 1930s (Aslib) history are proving informative. But Europeans who have a more theoretical and academic orientation see the work of the Classification Research Group (CRG), which was building a new and intellectually warranted library classification system, as the true originator of the "science" (Justice, 2004; La Barre, 2004; Mohanrajan, 1992; Ranganathan, 2001; Satija, 1992).

In contrast, Alistair Black (1998, 2004) of England, taking a very wide view, has bundled office information management techniques with those of practicing librarians. This has led him to a picture of a field evolving out of what he sees as the "information revolution" of the nineteenth century. For him, the first information professionals emerged without the guidance (or perhaps need) of theory, advanced academic training, or sophisticated technologies.

Others, especially in the United States, continue to locate origins and obligations in the engineering and applied computer science realms. Vannevar Bush's 1940s papers on the MEMEX, the statistical/engineering theory of information developed by Claude Shannon, and cybernetics have been treated as the intellectual foundations of the field. These claims come with only a few salutes to the need for other theories or philosophies, such as linguistics, to guide information research or curriculum building (Chomsky, 2002; Garfinkel & Abelson, 1999; Hayes, 1999; Kline, 2004).

Some of the more frequent claims about the origins and nature of the field are in greater accord with the building block's "golden age" interpretation. These versions center on practical needs, related funding, and markets in the post-World War II period. According to Tefko Saracevic (1992, 1999), the profession originally was, and continues to be, oriented around problems rather than theories or techniques. On this view, information science was born of the World War II- and Cold War-era demands by applied scientists for fast access to new types of documents and has lived around practical issues since then (Jackson, 1992). Donald Windsor (1999) goes further: He also emphasizes the practical orientation of the profession but locates its beginnings in the needs of particular industries as corporate growth and government regulations forced a search for new methods, which were devised primarily by subject specialists who trained themselves to be information professionals. Only later, Windsor claims, would academics displace the founding types at the head of information professionals' organizations. Despite the emergence of the academic "scientists," historians like Windsor and Saracevic see a constancy in information science history: It was, and is, a pragmatic and ever-shifting "science" dependent on an always changing set of tools, technologies, and perspectives—all taken from other disciplines.

Can a future historian reconcile these differing claims? Can a credible estimate be made of the degree of influence of the various asserted beginnings? The answer is yes, reasonable answers can be found. For example, in terms of intellectual roots, solutions are possible if distinctions are made between parallel and free-floating intellectual contributions and the behavior of historical actors. An historian, perhaps using bibliometric and content-analysis tools, can show how ideas did or did not migrate from person to person and how those people used (or did not use) such ideas in their work and in institution building (Smith, 1991). Empirical studies of curricula also can determine influences over time and space. A survey of the educational backgrounds and institutional associations of information innovators would also be of help (Lipetz, 1999).

There may also be progress on the questions concerning the ideas of those seen as the founders of information science. Some analyses of the nature and consequences of the premises behind the documentalists' and the "golden age's" faith in the possibility of a science of information are beginning to appear (Day, 2001). So far, the techniques used by such authors have been those of current brands of literary criticism and rhetorical analysis. This work has yet to reach the depth and maturity of the analytical literature on the ideas of the major contributors to the established sciences (e.g., Herbert, 2005).

The Search for an Identity and Status for Information Science

Additional topics, entwined with the questions of institutional origins and intellectual heritage, have received much attention in the interpretive historical writings of the last decade although they have often been treated as only a secondary part of a history. The identity of information science is one such topic. Since at least the 1960s, there have been efforts to distinguish information science from other disciplines and to establish the uniqueness and the academic status of the profession.

Among the new historical explorations, more than a dozen major works (in addition to those on origins) have tried to use history to ascertain or establish information science's boundaries (Hjørland, 2000; Warner, 2004). A dozen more have appeared dealing with the related issue of the history of information theory. As with the works on origins, there are many different assertions about the identity of information science and what it can claim as its own territories in academia and the job market (Schrader, 1984).

There are areas of agreement, however. The new histories point to a long-term struggle to achieve recognition and to secure a domain. The tensions generated during the struggles are reflected in the histories of the first American university-level information science programs. Research has shown that early programs found it difficult to differentiate themselves from library and computer science/artificial intelligence efforts or to sustain a harmonious interdisciplinary full-time faculty (Buckland, 1999; Sweeney, 2003).

Historical studies of two of the earliest well-known university programs highlight the frictions resulting from the attempt to blend librarians, information retrieval specialists, and systems/operations analysts into cohesive departments. A history of Western Reserve University's famous initiative, creating the Center for Documentation and Communication Research, revealed a librarian versus subject specialist/entrepreneurial split. An investigation of the University of Pittsburgh's ambitious department showed that even those faculty who came from non-library backgrounds, such as chemical information, engineering, or psychology, had difficulties agreeing on the nature of the "science" (Aspray, 1999; Bowles, 1999).

An information scientist active during the founding "golden age" has recently taken an extreme historical view of the history of information science education (Saracevic, 1999). He claims that departments and curricula began with, and continue to have, two fundamentally different orientations. One followed a service idea set by Jesse Shera who took a librarian/human-centered view, the other by the hard science approach of Gerald Salton of Harvard and Cornell universities. Of course, these two approaches were, and are, difficult to reconcile and make the establishment of a single identity for information science elusive.

Other evidence suggests that more than a few departments and individuals faced difficulties. A collective biography of the post-World War II generation will likely reinforce the conclusions that the demands and enticements of Cold War science, especially in applied and mission-oriented programs (such as missile and space efforts), as well as intelligence programs, shifted indexing, cataloging, and retrieval into the hands of subject specialists and engineers whose focus was the immediate solution of problems for a specialized audience. They could welcome deviations from established library procedures but few of them, it seems, were able to find ways to live comfortably in the social/professional worlds of either theoretical information science or library-oriented programs as they responded to new technological opportunities (Cragin, 2004; Crowley, 1999). A study of the INTREX project at MIT showed that attempts at blending computer scientists, librarians, subject specialists, and self-described information scientists into a long-term program faced considerable hurdles (Burke, 1996).

Another complication contributed to the difficulties of forming a unified and distinct identity: Differences over the roles of sponsored research/academic entrepreneurship versus teaching made departmental definition and harmony elusive (Aspray, 1999; Bowles, 1999). In parallel with this and Saracevic's two-world thesis, some of the historical literature, although not focused specifically on the definition and boundary issues, suggests that there has been an underlying tension between those who see the information profession as part of the nonprofit service sector and those who view it as a resource for the for-profit database world.

A significant empirical bibliometric study of the information science literature from the 1970s to the mid-1990s revealed yet another division: The information research world was itself partitioned into two separate realms (White & McCain, 1998). Those engaged in quantitative work on questions such as the best document retrieval techniques and the relevance to users of the results of information searches rarely cited those whose work was more philosophical or humanistic in orientation. The two clusters of intellectual and professional researchers seem to have persisted into the twenty-first century. A similar investigation of the interaction among professionals engaged in research on users' needs and those working on system design also revealed divisions (Buckland, 1999; Ellis, Allen, & Wilson, 1999).

Time and social and economic forces have played roles in shaping professional identities. One important remembrance of the innovative program at the University of California at Berkeley showed that information science and library science were diversely defined over time as well as space (Bates, 2004). During the 1960s, Berkeley's library and information science program placed emphasis on training in operations research, statistical analysis, and social science theory. The program was then relying upon the current ideas, and even used textbooks, of what was called the "behavioral" social sciences. The devotion to that particular social science orientation soon changed as "behavioralism" declined in popularity, as did the social sciences themselves, perhaps because of the ideological ferment of the years of the Vietnam war (Bates, 2004; Rau, 2000). Market forces also played a part in determining programs. At Drexel University in Philadelphia, early commitments to theory and research gave way to practical courses designed to serve the needs of the area's large scientific information industry (Flood, 2000). In spite of the continuities of research patterns discernable in Bates's (1999a) list of significant articles in *JASIS*, Berkeley's and Drexel's experiences reinforce the conclusion that information science has always found it difficult to carve out a domain distinct from other fields and to establish a stable identity.

In addition, a recent long-term history of the information science program at the University of Pittsburgh brings into question how much theory and independent professionalism contributed to determining information science research and education (Bleier, 2001). Academic self-determination of content and programs was limited. Reliance on outside funding targeted for problem solutions, typically from government agencies, seems to have driven faculty selection as well as course and program content. In traditional higher-educational contexts, departments without a significant degree of independence are unlikely to be seen as a true part of the academy—although they may generate a great deal of money for the institution.

Unfortunately, there is not yet a comprehensive, empirical, historical survey of information science curricula or faculty, either in the United States or abroad. Studies of university catalogs and textbooks will yield needed evidence on identity and status, including important information on the credentials and disciplinary backgrounds required to become a faculty member in an information science department (Lipetz, 1999). There are hints that such research will show long-term and continued significant variations, at least among American programs. Some have been, and are, technologically oriented and are hard to differentiate from computer science programs. Others emphasize cognitive psychology. And some, like those at Illinois and Berkeley, have had, during parts of their histories, ties to library training, the liberal arts, and broad, near-humanistic theory (Aspray, 1999).

Although there are suggestions about the nature of the history of curricula and faculty, there is a void concerning students and alumni. That void could be eliminated. Many types of data are available to researchers for developing a history of students' backgrounds and careers. College and alumni records, society membership data, and even employment advertisements can serve as an empirical base (Cronin, Stiffler, & Day, 1993).

What were admissions standards? What were the social and economic backgrounds of students? What jobs did they take after completing their education? How did information science students compare with those trained as librarians, special librarians, computer scientists, or even those who were shop trained? Answering these questions will help determine the identity and domain of the science.

Professional Status and Organizations

Professions are seen as established and worthy of deference when they have a significant degree of control over the discovery and application of methods, exercise power with respect to employment, and play a significant role in monitoring professional behavior. Control of employment is important, for it tends to ensure relatively high economic returns to the professionals. Established professions also shape academic programs and are able to manipulate legislation of concern (Haber, 1991; Lynn, 1965; MacDonald, 1995).

High-status professions such as law and medicine have gained the right, to an important extent, to be self-regulating. They have maintained much of that power through their professional organizations, which engage in effective political lobbying and legal work. In the United States, the power of the legal and medical professions is accounted for by their historical evolution from guild-like beginnings and also by their connection to long formal training in difficult and intellectually demanding methods. Although the medical profession in the United States has recently experienced a status decline and American lawyers have lost full control over the numbers entering the profession, both retain much of their formal legal status and popular respect.

In some instances professional domains have been defended through linkage to theory that predicts and explains research and practice (see Abbott, 1988, Chapter 8). Theory seems to justify any special powers that have been granted to a profession and its institutions. A profession of a type different from medicine and law, physics, serves as perhaps the best model for those seeking academic recognition through theory. Physicists hold claim to theories that yield fundamental explanations. The status of the field within the intellectual community came about because of these grand theories, as well as its startling practical accomplishments in the twentieth century (Kevles, 1978).

It seems that historians of information science have yet to explore that field's identity puzzle by looking directly at the nature and power of professional organizations. A few of the accumulating historical works do give us hints at professional status, arguing that the major information science organizations seem to have played a role in setting some technical standards (Kokabi, 1996; McCallum, 2002; Spicher, 1996). But historians have yet to show the influence of organizations such as ASIST or those representing other practitioners (information brokers or indexers and abstractors) in such activities as accrediting academic programs, setting certification standards, establishing and enforcing standards of professional conduct, controlling job markets, and forming and enforcing codes of ethics (Rubin, 2000). Traditional librarians' organizations, such as the American Library Association (ALA), appear to have developed more professional power than information scientists over job entry. None of the information organizations in the United States seems ever to have been involved in enforcing professional standards through any form of sanctions (Kister, 2002).

Professional Status and Theory

One cornerstone of professional status is in the first stages of investigation by information historians: theory. Much of this work on the history of information theory has been tied to the questions of origins and the range of conclusions about the nature and status of theory echoes the divisions over beginnings. The history of theory is also linked to the surprising amount of recent attention to the history of classification and to the appearance of an approach brought from the field of literary criticism, poststructuralism, which has been recommended as a theoretical foundation for both information science and information history (Herold, 2004).

Although much attention has been devoted to classification, only a few of the many theories mentioned as important in the history of information science have been explored by information historians. Apart from Jesse Shera and his social epistemology, only a few varieties of comprehensive theory and higher-level methodological mandates have received extensive historical treatment. Many aspects of this topic require translation into language understandable to non-specialists.

There have been examinations of what many saw as being the theoretical guides for information research in engineering and computer science programs. Scholars have looked into the career of Claude Shannon's statistical theory as well as the many versions of the post-World War II systems/cybernetics theories (Cole, 1993; Kline, 2004; Verdu, 1998). Approaches guiding other types of information programs are also being investigated. Dubin (2004) has explored Gerald Salton's theories and Rau (2000) has looked at the career of operations analysis in academic, military, and industrial information departments. Scholars such as Day (2005) and Smiraglia (2002) are beginning to use and, to a degree, delve into the nature and impact of theories brought from the humanities since the 1970s. Mizzaro (1997) has surveyed the evolution of theories and methods for measuring the relevance of materials produced through automated document searching. Tague-Sutcliffe (1994) provided a monumental work on quantitative methods. However, we still lack historical insights into the nature and role of linguistics, semiotics, graphics, and communication theory (Tufte, 2001).

The recent efforts devoted to the history of theories are only the first steps toward an understanding of which theories, if any, have been employed to define and guide professionals. Importantly, no histories have yet shown more than the most general relationship between the use of a particular higher-level theory, the methods researchers employed, and the resultant findings. Nor has it been demonstrated that theory has played a significant part in providing status for the profession, even within academic circles. Furthermore, it may be found that a major role of theory has been to enhance the post-facto justification of work, just as there are hints that formal scientific publications have not, in many instances, been directly related to work by established scientists or even to communicating information to other scientists. Rather, theory and formal publication may have been of more value in determining academic status and in guiding students during initial stages of professional training (Frohmann, 1999).

The Unexplored

There are many unexplored questions linked to the issues of origins, identity, and status that are relevant to the history of information science in both the pre- and post-1970s eras. Significantly, the persistence of these questions suggests that there are many historical parallels between the two periods. One is the apparent disconnect between American documentalists' methods of the 1940s–1950s and any previous methods—and the apparent discontinuity between the birth of Web search engines and established information science in the 1980s–1990s. Another task for historians is a comparison of the critical role of federal priorities during the Cold War to the impact of the privatization and increased commercialization of information services since the 1980s in shaping information programs. In both instances, non-professionals seem to have been in charge. Allied with both of these points is the question of the disproportionate influence of engineers and applied scientists in the design and management of early online systems and a similar profile for the Internet—although information science had matured by the time of the Web (Berners-Lee & Fischetti, 1999; Bourne & Hahn, 2003). As has been discussed, there is a parallel between the struggle in the 1950s–1970s to create a profession that could determine itself and the turmoil created by shifts and declines in academic funding in conjunction with what appears to be an increasing importance of the for-profit sector in reshaping curricula and professional attitudes (Crowley, 1999; Ørom, 2000).

Technology, Methods, and the Business Aspect

Some other topics have received rather more attention in the thematic literature. Historians of the computer have produced another round of informative general histories (Campbell-Kelley & Aspray, 1996; Ceruzzi, 1998). There are some works on the history of software, including insights into systems for library automation (Campbell-Kelly, 2003; Cortada, 2002; Grad & Johnson, 2002; Haigh, 2004). The vast changes in communications technology, such as the development of high-capacity fiber optics and high-speed routers, are at least being addressed (Verdu, 1998). Many historical explorations of the intellectual and policy origins of the Internet have appeared, but it is perhaps too early to expect balanced works on the development of more recent Web software and search engines (Abbate, 1999; Berners-Lee & Fischetti, 1999; Hafner, 1996; Reid, 1997).

It is also too early to expect insightful historical analyses of the Web's impact on the delivery of scientific and scholarly information, the heart of American information science in the "golden years." Historians of the new era of scientific communication will certainly have to explore four related themes: the increasing cost of scientific publications despite the technological revolutions in communications and printing, the reluctance of academia to alter its reward systems so that electronic publications by faculty might receive credit in promotion and tenure decisions, the ways in which the Web has altered the training and definition of information scientists, and the degree to which the Web has contributed to the development of an alternative informal communications system for scientists and academics (Case, 2002; Schiffrin, 2000). The broader question of whether the Web will create one worldwide culture or foster the recognition of many different cultures will take decades to answer.

Other, perhaps more fundamental topics await historical work. One is at the core of the professional identity issue. Although historians such as Robert V. Williams have been diligently gathering information on early methods, there is as yet no general historical survey of the intellectual tools of information science. Notably lacking are studies directed to nonspecialists about the creation and applications of methods after the "golden age." We await a history of the intellectual tools, their creators, their relationship to technological innovations, and their significance. And, no matter the intellectual origin, a basic question about methods has to be answered: Were there enough methodological contributions to defend the claim that there was, and is, a distinct and valuable information "science?"

Surprisingly, there has been almost no new historical work on the economics of information despite increasing interest in the problem of building an abstract general theory of information economics (Stiglitz 2000; Warner, 2005). (See also Braman's [2006] chapter, which has recently been called to the author's attention.) We lack the most fundamental knowledge about the history of the information and "knowledge" businesses and about the role of information science in shaping the cost of information. For example, in spite of the long-term contributions of Robert Hayes (1999), the pricing of products, salaries, and profit margins remain historical unknowns. We do know that the information domains treated as extensions of information science, such as online textual/bibliographic information services, became big businesses by at least the 1980s. Yet, we have only snippets about their financial struggles and about the information businesses as employers (Meyer, 1997).

Bourne and Hahn (2003) have provided some insight into the financial aspects of the online industry during its early years and there is a fascinating series of articles by one of the early leaders of the for-profit provider, Lexis-Nexis (Brown, 2002a, 2002b, 2003a, 2003b). The troubled history of early online newspaper experiments received some attention in the 1980s (Pemberton, 1983). But, although researchers (e.g., Williams, 2001) have conducted surveys of the database industry, no historian has pulled together the evidence to yield an overview of the growth of the industry and to explain the apparent trend toward consolidation. Certainly, there is not enough information to begin judging the comparative contributions of advances in communications/computing technology versus those of information science's tools to the cost of information delivery. Of course, the commercialization of the Internet/Web and reactions by practitioners need an historian's touch.

Other neglected fields are the history of government information policy and its relation to the specific nature and growth of the information industry. As noted, scholars have monitored American government policies, but no historian has directly linked policy history to the course of the industry and information practice. The legal battles that helped set the framework for the profession also await examination (Eisenberg, 1995). We have glimpses of the importance of the United States' telecommunications deregulation and the importance of the Web (Hundt, 2000; Stone, 1999); there have been mentions of Freedom of Information Act policies and the careers of online services (Bourne & Hahn, 2003); and, there have also been hints of the influence of some information organizations in the debates over intellectual property. We know of episodes such as the formation of NFAIS to block government domination of scientific information and have caught some glimpses into the counterpressure by others in the information profession to increase government's role. Nevertheless, a full-press historical effort is needed on economic policy and legal history (Ryan, 1998).

On the other hand, historians have begun to look at the interaction of political philosophies (or ideologies) and the nature of information science and its institutions. We know, for example, that Vannevar Bush's political conservatism fueled his determination to keep scientific information in the hands of the older academic/nonprofit institutions (Burke, 1994; Zachary, 1997). Muddiman (2004) and others have charted the influence of socialistic dreams on British information societies in the pre- and post-World War II period and Kister (2002) has shown the role of ideology in Eric Moon's determination to swing the ALA toward the service of the poor in the Great Society years. Moreover, the role of communist ideology in creating a different STINFO world in the Soviet bloc has been made clear (Mikhailov, Chernyi, & Gilairevskii, 1984; Richards, 1999; Volodin, 2000).

Classification

One topic related to professional contributions and identity has received much attention in thematic and interpretive histories. The history of classification has been the subject of at least two dozen historical works during the last decade. Both universal classification systems, such as the Dewey Decimal Classification (DDC) and the Universal Decimal Classification (UDC), and less ambitious ones covering a single specialty have been used as a basis for claims of professional status by librarians and, sometimes, information scientists. But status concerns do not seem to be the motives for the recent, vigorous historical interest.

Other, rather incompatible reasons account for the attention. Some historians of science, using traditional approaches, have returned to the subject (Frangsmyr, 2001). But most of the literature has been created by practicing librarians and information scientists who have maintained a faith in professional classification work or, more recently and significantly, by those who have become adversaries of what they see as intellectual and cultural imposition through classification (Hjørland & Albrechtsen, 1999; Osborn, 1991).

Historians and practitioners who are appreciative of classification were the first to make contributions. They focused upon the history of the librarians/documentalists who began exploring alternatives to the great established classification schemes and theories. Although many of the founding generation of "golden age" information scientists, at least in the United States, thought they could avoid dealing with any all-encompassing ordering of knowledge, others from more traditional backgrounds, especially in Europe, had not abandoned faith in wide-ranging classification systems. They sought to devise better and more modern schemes and theories. Their 1930s work continued, even in North America, and several members of related groups have contributed historical articles and books on such major contributors to modern classification theory as Ernest Richardson and Henry Bliss (e.g., Miksa, 1998). The work of pre-World War II English librarians/documentalists and the group they founded to devise intellectually elegant classification schemes have been the subject of several articles (see, e.g., Justice, 2004). An intellectual godfather of their Classification Research Group, Shiyali Y. Ranganathan, has a book-length biography (Ranganathan, 2001; cf. Sharma, 1992).

In contrast to the classifiers' approaches to their history are the works of two groups with less benign views of classification. The first group's findings came from applying what is termed a "sociology of knowledge" perspective. An early insightful work by Paul Starr (1987) on the United States census perhaps served as an inspiration to Susan Leigh Star and Geoffrey Bowker (1998), whose books and articles on classification became prominent in the 1990s. They (Bowker & Star, 1999) have presented balanced, well researched, and clearly written histories of particular classification schemes (such as those for the international classification of diseases and for nursing practice), showing how practical, social, and cultural factors shaped the classifications and giving examples of how non-scientific pressures and needs helped determine whether popular (but transient) terms rather than those from established medical/scientific lexicons were adopted. Bowker and Star do not conclude, however, that classifications are without any objective basis. They hold that classifications are inescapable, and, importantly, there can, and will be, real world feedback on the worth of various schema. Some will have a better fit with reality and will be of more utility to more people than others. Professionalism and expertise are not, in their view, unjustified impositions by elites.

The second group's approach is less positive. Its historical interpretation of classification is marked by degrees of doubt about the worth of classification schemes (Frohmann, 2004a, 2004b; Smiraglia, 2002; Wersig, 1993). The members of this group share a pronounced skepticism about the possibility of objectivity, possibly because they rely upon criteria and methods associated with recently adopted versions of literary criticism and rhetorical analysis rather than those associated with traditional approaches to the history of ideas or the sociology of knowledge. Some of these critics call themselves postmodernists: their stance—postmodernism—and its acceptance in historical work will be addressed in the next section.

As a consequence of applying "post-isms," the resulting histories are critical of classification in general. Unfortunately, these interpretive frameworks sometimes produce evaluations rather than descriptions, with the histories telling more about an envisioned radicalized cultural future than about the history of classification systems (Radford, 1998). An example of the application of the premises of such schools of analysis is an article by a critic of the well-known DDC that bears the revealing title, "The Ubiquitous Hierarchy: An Army to Overcome the Threat of a Mob" (Olson, 2004). Dewey's system is treated as a "privileged" ordering of nature. Instead of viewing his system as a practical and user-friendly schema for the people of its, and our, time (McIlwaine, 1997), the author treats Dewey's work as an attempt at cultural domination. Viewed from the postmodern perspective, Dewey and his like revealed their intellectual limits by attempting to order all knowledge in a single system and in a hierarchical fashion. The result, it is claimed, was an embodiment of the biases of the post-1600 "modern" Western Civilization. Dewey's critic has not been alone in applying a dislike of the Enlightenment's and similar ways of organizing information in the West, for postmodernists generally tend to interpret all classification schemes as indicators of unjustified social control exercised over others by power holders (McCullagh, 2004).

There have been less extreme historical applications of postmodernist views that have also been recommended as a new theoretical basis for contemporary information science. Their advocates emphasize the need for pluralism in the process of categorization, not the complete abandonment of systems. Some see postmodernism as a mandate to have classifications determined by users rather than being created by professionals. Others, believing that there are many "truths" (or none at all) and that all elites have narrow vision, call for the inclusion, at minimum, of popular terms and concepts in any classification or indexing system (Jasanoff, 2004; Joachim, 2003; Star & Bowker, 1998).

Ironically, as is the case with the more extreme postmodern critics, the moderates' visions of social/cultural diversity in knowledge organization seem plausible only because of the rise of those most modern of technologies, the computer and the Web. For many advocates, the Internet, search engines, and full-text systems seem to have ended the need for traditional classification hierarchies and indexing schemes. Few of the postmodernists appear to have noticed that the Internet has had to turn to hierarchical classification systems and information professionals' modernist methods to avoid overwhelming users.

There has been another blind spot resulting from the application of "post" approaches to the history of classification. Although postmodernism is premised on the idea that there is no natural order and thus all is historical, some extreme versions of the anti-classification interpretations suffer from a lack of attention to history and historical contexts. They seem unaware, for example, of the long history of research on, and development of, user-oriented systems and their philosophical/methodological commitments to post-isms may have prevented them from appreciating work that dates from at least the 1940s, when the first document retrieval systems were being designed (Griffiths & King, 2002; Saracevic, 1997; Siatri, 1999). As a result, they attribute an unwarranted degree of cultural insensitivity to the librarians and information professionals of the modern era. As already mentioned, postmodernists have also failed to place previous indexing and classification efforts within changing technological contexts.

A Problematic Time to Join the Historical Mainstream

Of all information history topics, the history of classification has received the most attention from postmodernists and their intellectual cousins. There are indications that their approaches will be more frequently applied to other topics in information history. The reason is that, as information science historians have sought their own recognized academic niche, they have imported currently fashionable perspectives from mainstream history, which, in turn, has recently favored historical philosophies developed in the fields of literary criticism and rhetorical analysis: postmodernism, poststructuralism, and deconstructionism. These approaches have often been filtered through political ideologies. In the United States, many applications of these "methods" have more than a hint of the New Left beliefs, politics, and values of the 1960s and 1970s (Berkhofer, 1995, 1998). More than the possibility of political influence makes an uncritical reliance on post-isms questionable and an over-reliance on them may well have negative consequences for the future of the history of information science. Indeed, information history runs the risk of being misdirected by transient and often conflicting mandates just as it is emerging as a separate field of study.

Information history scholars are turning to mainstream historians when the American historical profession itself is at a critical juncture (Novick, 1988; Ross, 1995). Since World War II, the profession has traveled through a long series of methodological/historiographic fashions, to which graduate students and untenured professors have had to defer if not adhere. Each of these theoretically oriented approaches has made contributions, but they have been accompanied by a temptation to force historical findings that confirm, rather than test, a theory's substantive conclusions about the historical experience.

The vast majority of practicing historians in America have used a commonsense framework for writing both descriptive and explanatory works. A few have borrowed low-level explanatory theories from the social sciences (Benson, 1972). However, a long list of grand theories and interpretive schemata, one succeeding, if not displacing, another, has received attention and favor. Within the last 50 years the profession has traveled through interpretive schools using frameworks as diverse as those of liberal progress, Marxist determinism, socialist reformism, Freudian psychology, behavioral/social science mid-level theories, quantitative methods, anthropological theories, variants of France's Annales school of social history, New Left culturalism, political correctness, and feminist and queer theory (Appleby, 1998; Lynd, 2001).

Postmodernism, poststructuralism, and deconstructionism are the latest major and prominent overarching orientations. Although they seem to have reached their high points since their introductions in the 1970s, they continue to attract adherents, sometimes very fervent ones. Postmodernism and its intellectual allies hold special types of temptations and dangers because they include premises concerning objectivity that undermine the fundamental credibility of the historical enterprise. Because of this and other internal weaknesses of postmodernism and deconstructionism, their use presents enticements to assert explanations and evaluations before what is to be explained or judged is established through empirically grounded and comprehensive research. There are also temptations to treat historical investigation as exclusively an exercise in the new type of literary analysis of textual dialogues or "discourses" and to ignore behaviors, actions, and historical contexts. Furthermore, attempts to place information science history in broader historical contexts by using current cutting-edge conceptual schemes associated with the post-isms, such as viewing information history as a critical part of the long-term imposition of social control through modernization or as part of the imminent implosion of capitalism (R. Day, 2002), may deflect needed research and lead to interpretive dead ends.

Most worrisome is the possibility of information science historians abandoning a belief in objectivity and, thus, the need to create testable histories as they adopt currently fashionable methods. Many of the prominent spokeswomen and spokesmen for post-isms in the American historical profession question whether there can be any true histories. Some have gone beyond declaring the great universal histories, such as Marx's deterministic saga, to have been culture-bound and thus biased. They now tag such works as merely subjective stories (Iggers, 1997). Some historians have purchased, under the name of postmodernism, a more extreme version of epistemic relativism: In their view, there is no way to use evidence to differentiate between contending histories. But it should be noted that many proclaimed relativists write histories that lay claim to be telling the "truth" about the past (Foucault, 1997; Jenkins, 1997; Lyotard, 1984).

Why have the post-isms achieved recognition? Some intellectual dissection and historical background are needed to understand the attraction and acceptance of relativist and "post" ideas by American historians. Unfortunately, these relativistic theories are classic examples of intellectual moving targets. There are many versions of the theories and methods, and a critic encounters ambiguities at every step. In addition, the field is experiencing its own version of revisionism as a new generation of philosopher/historians replaces the 1960s founders. Some of the younger contributors are even asserting versions of the once rejected deterministic history (R. Day, 2002). There is another problem: All the "post" theorists tend to use special and ill-defined vocabularies. However, an acceptable general outline of the theories is possible. It must include a brief history of the use of theory by historians.

The historical profession in America emerged in the late nineteenth century when the idea of human progress was accompanied by a hope that the social and humanistic sciences could produce the type of sweeping and useful theories based on fixed and universal laws that marked the rise of the physical and biological sciences. Europeans took the lead in creating such objective, large-scale histories. Some pictured a progressive world inexorably emerging, with liberalism and reason (and perhaps capitalism) being the driving forces. But the most influential historical theory, at least since the Russian Revolution, was even more committed to forces above individual or even group action as determining the course of world history. Marxism looked to economics and material forces (structures) as the universal determinates, not the power of reason, mind, or individual will. For Marxists, out of the conflict of uncontrollable opposing forces, the dialectic, the old oppressive hierarchical order would disappear to be replaced eventually by an unstructured egalitarian paradise (Novick, 1988).

Although Marxism was developed and polished in European academic circles, it gained some adherents within American academia. Using a modified, less law-like version, Frederick Jackson Turner in the late nineteenth century and then Charles Beard in the early twentieth century introduced grand, socialistic interpretations of American history. They did not see a world marked by an automatic march of progress and feared that industrialization would lead to revolution unless government policies were altered. Unlike Marxists, they had faith in gradual reform and human action. Their work, however, inspired others in America to adopt purer versions of Marxist economic determinism, leading them to focus their research on exposing economic and social injustices. Some of these historians looked to the Soviet Union and its revolution as the model for achieving true "progress." Both the socialist and communist historians believed that they were writing truth-testable history. Like Turner and Beard, the writings of the more radical left-wing historians penetrated some of American academia's highest circles (Benson, 1960; Zinn, 1999, 2001).

The early left-wing critics of the theory of liberal, Enlightenment-driven history were joined by those who forcefully claimed that all such progressive history was insensitive to cultures other than those of the Western World's "imperialistic" middle class. As a result of those criticisms and of world events, by the 1960s, progressive history was out of fashion. Then reactions to the discovery of Stalin's excesses, the failure of the working classes in Europe and America to behave as the intellectual elites had expected, and the later collapse of the Soviet Union fueled a rejection of traditional Marxism and its determinism. With progressivism and Marxism declared "dead," there was an explanatory void.

Some influential historians went further than rejecting the great deterministic histories. Using a stereotyped picture of historical practice as their basis of evaluation, they not only declared themselves against all forms of deterministic historical theory but also showed their disbelief in the objectivity of any historical research by substituting the words "narrative" or "story" for history. Another important shift occurred. Leading theoretically oriented historians focused on cultural issues, turning away from economics. Reflecting the political issues of the time, race, gender, and sexuality became favored topics and, to some, the driving forces in history.

Many in America in the turbulent 1960s and 1970s looked to France for intellectual and methodological aid. The intellectual/social history approach of Fernand Braudel and the Annales school, which did hold to a belief in testable histories, attracted many historians in the United States who wished to continue to write grand histories covering long periods of time (Braudel, 1981; Stoianovich, 1976). Others, especially students and faculty in activist English departments (usually on the ideological left), turned to French literary critics/philosophers and their methods. Michel Foucault provided a devastating critique of Western thought and culture, declaring the Enlightenment a foe that had led to false beliefs in objectivity and the dangerous belief in the existence of a natural order. For him, reason was only one way—but a privileged one—of knowing. Reason, he emphasized, had allowed elites to impose "surveillance" and "social control," which limited the potential for the full realization of cultural and human diversity and self-determination (also called "agency"). Foucault's generalizations implied something that turned an important aspect of the progressive interpretation of history on its head: The growth of information resources was more for the benefit of the dominating elites than for the liberation of the common man. Although his critique of the intellectual and social history of the West implicitly claimed to be "truthful," because an historian could determine the nature of "discourses" through his "archeology of knowledge," Foucault denied the possibility of truth in history (Radford, 2003). To many observers, agreeing with Foucault meant agreeing that the most an historian could do was to tear down old intellectual constructs and the false structures of what had been claimed as being natural systems, whether intellectual or social. There was no way to do positive history—there was no historical truth. And, explanations could certainly not rest on universal laws but had to be local and complex (Foucault, 1988, 1997).

Jacques Derrida (1997, 1998) went further toward relativism, a focus on culture, and a reliance on the writings of influential intellectuals as evidence about the past (Borradori, 2003; Royle, 2000). He saw historical research as an exercise in literary analysis, a perspective that contrasted sharply with the beliefs of those in the Annales school who treasured historical research as an exercise in the exploration of economic, demographic, and other behavioral data. Derrida devised his deconstructionism to deal with "texts" because he believed language (writing) was all. And, although it did not match reality, it shaped it. It was the duty of researchers to show how society (perhaps even the material world) was "constructed" through language and a new version of the Hegelian-Marxist dialectic, "discourse." It was the duty of the critic or historian to deconstruct the discourses of the West, showing how they were built on false oppositions, such as man-woman, that supported socioculturally constructed hierarchies. Like Foucault, Derrida did not spell out a method that would allow the replication of studies—he did not believe in testable history, although he implicitly laid claims to asserting truths. Importantly, he did not reconcile his claim that an observer would never know what a document meant by analyzing its text with his claim that, through knowledge of historical contexts, the "real" meaning of a text could be determined. He never showed how a "context" could be truthfully established.

As the "post" ideas moved into history departments in the United States, nuances were added. Over time, the ideas became more than guides to research in the form of questions to be asked of evidence. They now hold the possibility of becoming dicta—mandates that certain conclusions must always be reached. The list of such embedded demands is long, including that "agency" always be found, that particular types of social diversity be saluted, that analysis of texts and discourse trump other historical evidence, and that hierarchies of any sort, in any realm, be shown as unnatural social constructions. The many variations of deconstructionism also carry a host of assumptions about historical processes, human psychology, social structures, and even common historical practice. Those assumptions are rarely questioned or tested, perhaps because of the nature of deconstructionist and postmodernist historical approaches. Reliance on vague and shifting definitions of key terms and the use of truisms as the basis for explanation do not lead to testable histories.

Although post-isms deny the possibility of objective history, many postmodern historians feel warranted in imposing sweeping concepts on evidence and structuring their work around deterministic forces such as the desire for social control. Certainly, the history of information science should not be subjected to that. There are too many gaps in the grounded history of information science to justify concentration on any sweeping and speculative interpretations and evaluations of the field. Furthermore, an uncritical reliance on questionable high-level interpretations can make causal explanations non-informative. For example, there is a danger of explaining the growth of the information profession by reference to the rise of an "age of information"—a bit of circular logic.

Important and inherently interesting questions have to be answered before an interpretive history of the field can be written. The nature of the information profession and its role in providing, one hopes, the most information to the widest possible audience at the least cost cannot be adequately described, let alone judged, without such empirical foundations. Significantly, the "post" and deconstructionist views have limiting agendas as to topics, methods, and types of evidence. Such limited research agendas have always discouraged fresh and wide-ranging explorations by historians. The adoption of epistemic relativism can also lead to overly hasty research (Berkhofer, 1995). The emerging history of information science should continue to build a literature of empirically grounded building-block and mid-level interpretive works that explore and utilize all types of evidence about all related topics.

References

Abbate, J. (1999). *Inventing the Internet*. Cambridge, MA: MIT Press.

Abbott, A. (1988). *The system of professions: An essay on the division of professional labor*. Chicago: University of Chicago Press.

Adkinson, B. W. (1978). *Two centuries of federal information*. Stroudsburg, PA: Dowden, Hutchinson & Ross.

Altman, E. (1993). National Science Foundation's support of information research. In A. Kent (Ed.), *Encyclopedia of library and information science* (Vol. 52, Suppl. 15, pp. 273–291). New York: Dekker.

Appleby, J. (1998). The power of history. *American Historical Review*, *103*, 1–14.

Aspray, W. F. (1985). The scientific conceptualization of information: A survey. *IEEE Annals of the History of Computing*, *7*(2), 117 140.

Aspray, W. F. (1999). Command and control, documentation, and library science: The origins of information science at the University of Pittsburgh. *IEEE Annals of the History of Computing*, *21*(4), 4–20.

Austin, D. (1998). Derek Austin: Developing PRECIS, Preserved Context Index System. *Cataloging & Classification Quarterly*, *25*(2–3), 23–66.

Bates, M. J. (1999a). A tour of information science through the pages of *JASIS*. *Journal of the American Society for Information Science*, *50*, 1043–1062.

Bates, M. J. (Ed.). (1999b). Special topic issue: The 50th anniversary of the *Journal of the American Society for Information Science*: Part 1: The journal, its society, and the future of print. *Journal of the American Society for Information Science*, *50*(11), 906–1041.

Bates, M. J. (Ed.). (1999c). Special topic issue: The 50th anniversary of the *Journal of the American Society for Information Science*: Part 2: Paradigms, models, and methods of information science. *Journal of the American Society for Information Science*, *50*(12), 1042–1162.

Bates, M. J. (2004). Information science at the University of California at Berkeley in the 1960s: A memoir of student days. *Library Trends, 52,* 683–701.

Behrends, E. (1995). *Technisch-wissenschaftliche Dokumentation in Deutschland von 1900 bis 1945: Unter besonderer Berücksichtigung des Verhältnisses von Bibliothek und Dokumentation* [Technical and scientific documentation in Germany from 1900 to 1945: With special reference to the relationship between library and documentation] (Buchwissenschaftliche Beiträge aus dem Deutschen Bucharchiv München, 51). Wiesbaden, Germany: Harrassowitz.

Bell, D. (1973). *The coming of post-industrial society: A venture in social forecasting.* New York: Basic Books.

Beniger, J. R. (1986). *The control revolution: Technological and economic origins of the information society.* Cambridge, MA: Harvard University Press.

Bensman, S. (2004). Urquhart and probability: The transition from librarianship to library and information science. *Journal of the American Society for Information Science and Technology, 56,* 189–214.

Benson, L. (1960). *Turner and Beard: American historical writing reconsidered.* Glencoe, IL: Free Press.

Benson, L. (1972). *Toward the scientific study of history: Selected essays of Lee Benson.* Philadelphia: Lippincott.

Berkhofer, R. E., Jr. (1995). *Beyond the great story: History as text and discourse.* Cambridge, MA: Belknap Press.

Berkhofer, R. E., Jr. (1998). Self-reflections on Beyond the Great Story: The ambivalent author as ironic interlocutor. *American Quarterly, 50,* 365–375.

Berners-Lee, T., & Fischetti, M. (1999). *Weaving the Web: The original design and ultimate destiny of the World Wide Web by its inventor.* San Francisco: Harper San Francisco.

Bjorner, S., & Ardito, S. (2003). Online before the Internet: Early pioneers tell their stories: parts 3 and 4: Carlos Cuadra and Roger Summit. *Searcher, 11*(9), 20–34.

Black, A. (1998). Information and modernity: The history of information and the eclipse of library history. *Library History, 14,* 39–45.

Black, A. (2004). Technical libraries in British industrial and commercial enterprises before 1950. In W. B. Rayward & M. E. Bowden (Eds.), *The history and heritage of scientific and technological information systems: Proceedings of the 2002 conference* (pp. 267–280). Medford, NJ: Information Today.

Black, A. (2006). Information history. *Annual Review of Information Science and Technology, 40,* 441–473.

Bleier, C. (2001). *Tradition in transition: A history of the School of Information Sciences, University of Pittsburgh.* Lanham, MD: Scarecrow Press.

Blum, B. I., & Duncan, K. (Eds.). (1990). *A history of medical informatics.* New York: ACM Press.

Borradori, G. (2003). *Philosophy in a time of terror: Dialogues with Jürgen Habermas and Jacques Derrida.* Chicago: University of Chicago Press.

Bourne, C. P., & Hahn, T. B. (2003). *A history of online information services, 1963–1976.* Cambridge, MA: MIT Press.

Bowden, M. E., Hahn, T. B., & Williams, R. V. (Eds.). (1999). *Proceedings of the 1998 Conference on the History and Heritage of Science Information Systems.* Medford, NJ: Information

Today for the American Society for Information Science and the Chemical Heritage Foundation.

Bowker, G. C., & Star, S. L. (1999). *Sorting things out: Classification and its consequences.* Cambridge, MA: MIT Press.

Bowles, M. D. (1999). The information wars: Two cultures and the conflict in information retrieval, 1945–1999. In M. E. Bowden, T. B. Hahn, & R. V. Williams (Eds.), *Proceedings of the 1998 Conference on the History and Heritage of Science Information Systems* (pp. 156–166). Medford, NJ: Information Today for the American Society for Information Science and the Chemical Heritage Foundation.

Braman, S. (2006). The micro- and macroeconomics of information. *Annual Review of Information Science and Technology, 40,* 3–52.

Brandhorst, T. (1993). The Educational Resources Information Center (ERIC). In A. Kent (Ed.), *Encyclopedia of library and information science* (Vol. 51, Suppl. 14, pp. 208–225). New York: Dekker.

Braudel, F. (1981). *The structures of everyday life: The limits of the possible* (S. Reynolds, Trans.). New York: Harper & Row.

Brenner, E. H., & Saracevic, T. (1985). *Indexing and searching in perspective.* Philadelphia: National Federation of Abstracting and Indexing Services.

Brown, P. (2002a). How a digital idea became a multi-billion dollar business. *Logos, 13*(3), 128–133.

Brown, P. (2002b). How a digital idea became a multi-billion dollar business: Part II. *Logos, 13*(4), 212–219.

Brown, P. (2003a). How a digital idea became a multi-billion dollar business: Part III. *Logos, 14*(1), 31–36.

Brown, P. (2003b). How a digital idea became a multi-billion dollar business: Part IV. *Logos, 14*(2), 79–84.

Brown, R. D. (1989). *Knowledge is power: The diffusion of information in early America, 1700–1865.* New York: Oxford University Press.

Buckland, M. K. (1991). Information retrieval of more than text. *Journal of the American Society for Information Science, 42,* 586–588.

Buckland, M. K. (1992). Emanuel Goldberg, electronic documentation retrieval, and Vannevar Bush's Memex. *Journal of the American Society for Information Science, 43,* 284–294.

Buckland, M. K. (1995). The centenary of "Madame Documentation": Suzanne Briet 1894–1989. *Journal of the American Society for Information Science, 46,* 235–237.

Buckland, M. K. (1997). What is a "document"? *Journal of the American Society for Information Science, 48,* 804–809.

Buckland, M. K. (1999). The landscape of information science: The American Society for Information Science at 62. *Journal of the American Society for Information Science, 50,* 1030–1031.

Buckland, M. K., & Hahn, T. B. (Eds.). (1997a). Special topic issue: History of documentation and information science. *Journal of the American Society for Information Science, 48*(4).

Buckland, M. K., & Hahn, T. B. (Eds.). (1997b). Special topic issue: History of documentation and information science. *Journal of the American Society for Information Science, 48*(9).

Buckland, M. K., & Liu, Z. (1996). The history of information science. *Annual Review of Information Science and Technology, 30,* 383–416.

Burke, C. (1994). *Information and secrecy: Vannevar Bush, Ultra, and the other Memex.* Metuchen, NJ: Scarecrow Press.

Burke, C. (1996). A rough road to the information highway. Project Intrex: A view from the CLR archives. *Information Processing & Management, 32,* 19–32.

Cady, S. A. (1999). Microfilm technology and information systems. In M. E. Bowden, T. B. Hahn, & R. V. Williams (Eds.), *Proceedings of the 1998 Conference on the History and Heritage of Science Information Systems* (pp. 177–186). Medford, NJ: Information Today for the American Society for Information Science and the Chemical Heritage Foundation.

Campbell-Kelly, M. (2003). *From airline reservations to Sonic the Hedgehog: A history of the software industry.* Cambridge, MA: MIT Press.

Campbell-Kelly, M., & Aspray, W. (1996). *Computer: A history of the information machine.* New York: Basic Books.

Capurro, R., & Hjørland, B. (2002). The concept of information. *Annual Review of Information Science and Technology, 37,* 343–411.

Case, M. (2002). Igniting change in scholarly communication: SPARC, its past, present, and future. *Advances in Librarianship, 26,* 1–27.

Ceruzzi, P. E. (1998). *A history of modern computing.* Cambridge, MA: MIT Press.

Chandler, A. D., & Cortada, J. W. (Eds.). (2000). *A nation transformed by information: How information has shaped the United States from colonial times to the present.* New York: Oxford University Press.

Chartrand, R. L., Henderson, M. M., & Resnik, L. (Eds.). (1988). ASIS 50th anniversary issue. *Bulletin of the American Society for Information Science, 14*(5).

Chemical Abstract Service. (1997). *CAS anniversary, 1907–1997: Celebrating 90th [year].* Columbus, OH: Chemical Abstracts Service.

Chomsky, N. (2002). *Syntactic structures.* New York: Mouton de Gruyter.

Cole, C. (1993). Shannon revisited: Information in terms of uncertainty. *Journal of the American Society for Information Science, 44,* 204–211.

Collen, M. F. (1995). *A history of medical informatics in the United States, 1950 to 1990.* Indianapolis, IN: American Medical Informatics Association.

Cortada, J. W. (Ed.). (1998). *The rise of the knowledge worker.* Boston: Butterworth-Heinemann.

Cortada, J. W. (2002). Researching the history of software from the 1960s. *IEEE Annals of the History of Computing, 41*(1), 72–79.

Cragin, M. (2004). Foster Mohrdardt: Connecting the traditional world of libraries and the emerging world of information science. *Library Trends, 52,* 833–852.

Cronin, B., & Atkins, H. B. (Eds.). (2000). *The web of knowledge: A Festschrift in honor of Eugene Garfield.* Medford, NJ: Information Today.

Cronin, B., & Davenport, E. (1988). *Post-professionalism: Transforming the information heartland.* London: Taylor Graham.

Cronin, B., Stiffler, M., & Day, D. (1993). The emergent market for information professionals: Educational opportunities and implications. *Library Trends, 42,* 257–276.

Crowley, B. (1999). The control and direction of professional education. *Journal of the American Society for Information Science, 50,* 1127–1135.

Dahlin, T. C. (1990). *Books and documents on government information policy: A selected bibliography.* Monticello, IL: Vance Bibliographies.

Davis, D. G. (Ed.). (1996). *Libraries and philanthropy: Proceedings of Library History Seminar IX, March 30-April 1, University of Alabama, Tuscaloosa.* Austin: Graduate School of Library and Information Science, University of Texas at Austin.

Davis, D. G., & Dain, P. (Eds.). (1986). History of library and information science. *Library Trends, 34*(3), 357–531.

Davis, D. G., & Tucker, J. M. (1989). *American library history: A comprehensive guide to the literature.* Santa Barbara, CA: ABC-CLIO.

Day, M. (2002). Discourse fashions in library administration and information management: A critical history and bibliometric analysis. *Advances in Librarianship, 26,* 231–285.

Day, R. (2001). *The modern invention of information: Discourse, power, and history.* Carbondale: Southern Illinois University Press.

Day, R. (2002). Social capital, value, and measure: Antonio Negri's challenge to capitalism. *Journal of the American Society for Information Science and Technology, 53,* 1074–1082.

Day, R. (2005). Poststructuralism and information studies. *Annual Review of Information Science and Technology, 39,* 575–610.

Debons, A. (Ed.). (1974). *Information science: Search for identity.* New York: Dekker.

Debons, A., & Horne, E. E. (1997). NATO Advanced Study Institutes of Information Science and foundations of information science. *Journal of the American Society for Information Science, 48*(9), 794–803.

Derrida, J. (1997). *Deconstruction in a nutshell: A conversation with Jacques Derrida.* New York: Fordham University Press.

Derrida, J. (1998). *The Derrida reader: Writing performances.* Lincoln: University of Nebraska Press.

Dubin, D. (2004). The most influential paper Gerard Salton never wrote. *Library Trends, 52,* 748–764.

East, H. (1998). Towards the schism: Information officers at the Royal Society Scientific Information Conference, 1948. *Journal of Information Science, 24,* 271–275.

Eisenberg, K. (1995). *Privatizing government information: The effects of policy on Landsat satellite data.* Metuchen, NJ: Scarecrow Press.

Ellis, D., Allen, D., & Wilson, T. (1999). Information science and information systems: Conjoint subjects disjoint disciplines. *Journal of the American Society for Information Science, 50,* 1095–1107.

Farkas-Conn, I. (1990). *From documentation to information science: The beginnings and early development of the American Documentation Institute-American Society for Information Science.* New York: Greenwood Press.

Fayet-Scribe, S. (2000). *Histoire de la documentation en France: Culture, science et technologie de l'information, 1895-1937.* Paris: CNRS Editions.

Fernandez, F. S., & Moreno, A. G. (1997). History of information science in Spain: A selected bibliography. *Journal of the American Society for Information Science, 48,* 369–372.

Fischer, D. H. (1970). *Historians' fallacies: Toward a logic of historical thought.* New York: Harper & Row.

Flood, B. (2000). Drexel's information science M.S. degree program, 1963–1971: An insider's recollections. *Journal of the American Society for Information Science, 51,* 1137–1148.

Foucault, M. (1988). *Madness and civilization: A history of insanity in the Age of Reason* (R. Howard, Trans.). New York: Vintage Books.

Foucault, M. (1997). *The essential works of Michel Foucault, 1954–1984*. New York: New Press.

Frangsmyr, T. (Ed). (2001). *The structure of knowledge: Classification of science and learning since the Renaissance*. Berkeley, CA: Office for the History of Science and Technology.

Frohmann, B. (1994). Discourse analysis as a research method in library and information science. *Library & Information Science Research, 16,* 119–138.

Frohmann, B. (1999). The role of the scientific paper in science information systems. In M. E. Bowden, T. B. Hahn, & R. V. Williams (Eds.), *Proceedings of the 1998 Conference on the History and Heritage of Science Information Systems* (pp. 63–73). Medford, NJ: Information Today for the American Society for Information Science and the Chemical Heritage Foundation.

Frohmann, B. (2004a). *Deflating information: From science studies to documentation*. Toronto: University of Toronto Press.

Frohmann, B. (2004b). Discourse analysis as a research method in library and information science. *Library & Information Science Research, 16,* 119–138.

Furner, J. (2004). "A Brilliant Mind": Margaret Egan and social epistemology. *Library Trends, 52,* 792–818.

Garfinkel, S. L., & Abelson, H. (1999*). Architects of the information society: Thirty-five years of the Laboratory for Computer Science at MIT*. Cambridge, MA: MIT Press.

Gimbel, J. (1990). *Science, technology and reparations: Exploitation and plunder in postwar Germany*. Stanford, CA: Stanford University Press.

Grad, B., & Johnson, L. (Eds.). (2002). [Special issue on the history of the software industry]. *IEEE Annals of the History of Computing, 24*(1).

Graham, R., & Rayward, W. B. (Eds.). (2002a). [Special issue on computer applications in libraries, part 1]. *IEEE Annals of the History of Computing, 24*(2).

Graham, R., & Rayward, W. B. (Eds.). (2002b). [Special issue on computer applications in libraries, part 2]. *IEEE Annals of the History of Computing, 24*(3).

Granick, L., & Cornog, M. (1983). The history of NFAIS, 1972–1982. In M. L. Neufeld, M. Cornog, & I. L. Sperr (Eds.), *Abstracting and indexing services in perspective: Miles Conrad Memorial Lectures, 1969–1983* (pp. 21–26). Arlington, VA: Information Resources Press.

Griffiths, J., & King, D. (2002). U.S. information retrieval system evaluation and evolution (1945–1975). *IEEE Annals of the History of Computing, 24*(3), 35–55.

Gull, C. D. (1987). Information science and technology: From coordinate indexing to the global brain. *Journal of the American Society for Information Science, 38,* 338–374.

Haber, S. (1991). *The quest for authority and honor in the American professions, 1750–1900*. Chicago: University of Chicago Press.

Hafner, K. (1996). *Where wizards stay up late: The origins of the Internet*. New York: Simon and Schuster.

Hahn, T. B. (1996). Pioneers of the online age. *Information Processing & Management, 32,* 33–48.

Hahn, T. B., & Buckland, M. K. (Eds.). (1998). *Historical studies in information science*. Medford, NJ: Information Today.

Haigh, T. (2004). "A veritable bucket of facts": Origins of data base management systems, 1960–1980. In W. B. Rayward & M. E. Bowden (Eds.), *The History and Heritage of Scientific and Technological Information Systems: Proceedings of the 2002 Conference* (pp. 75–88). Medford, NJ: Information Today.

Hapke, T. (1999). History of scholarly information and communication: A review of selected German literature. *Journal of the American Society for Information Science, 50*, 229–232.

Harman, D. (Ed.). (1997). [Series of articles/reminiscences about Gerald Salton by former students, including a bibliography of his publications]. *SIGIR Forum: A Publication of the Special Interest Group on Information Retrieval, 31*(1), 2–22.

Harter, S. P., & Hooten, P. A. (1992). Information science and scientists: *JASIS*, 1972–1990. *Journal of the American Society for Information Science, 43*, 583–593.

Hayes, R. M. (1999). History review: The development of information science in the United States. In M. E. Bowden, T. B. Hahn, & R. V. Williams (Eds.). *Proceedings of the 1998 Conference on the History and Heritage of Science Information Systems* (pp. 223–236). Medford, NJ: Information Today for the American Society for Information Science and the Chemical Heritage Foundation.

Headrick, D. (2000). *When information came of age: Technologies of knowledge in the age of reason and revolution, 1700–1850.* New York: Oxford University Press.

Heilprin, L. B. (1988). *Annual Review of Information Science and Technology (ARIST)*: Early historical perspective. *Journal of the American Society for Information Science, 39,* 273–280.

Herbert, S. (2005). *Charles Darwin, geologist.* Ithaca, NY: Cornell University Press.

Herner, S. (1984). A brief history of information science. *Journal of the American Society for Information Science, 35,* 157–163.

Herold, K. (Ed). (2004). The philosophy of information [Special issue]. *Library Trends, 52*(3).

Hertzel, D. (1987). Bibliometrics, history of the development of the ideas. In A. Kent (Ed.), *Encyclopedia of Library and Information Science* (Vol. 42, Supp. 7, pp. 144–219). New York: Dekker.

Hjørland, B. (2000). Documents, memory institutions and information science. *Journal of Documentation, 56,* 27–41.

Hjørland, B., & Albrechtsen, H. (1999). An analysis of some trends in classification research. *Knowledge Organization, 26,* 131–139.

Horn, S. K., & Clements, S. K. (1989). ERIC: The past, present and future federal role in education dissemination. *Government Information Quarterly, 6,* 183–197.

Hundt, R. (2000). *You say you want a revolution: A story of information age politics.* New Haven, CT: Yale University Press.

Iggers, G. (1997). *Historiography in the twentieth century: From scientific objectivity to the postmodern challenge.* Hanover, NH: Wesleyan University Press.

Jackson, E. B. (1992). Operational information science (documentation) activities at Wright Field, Ohio, before 1950, with emphasis on foreign-language technical reports. *Proceedings of the ASIS Annual Meeting,* 288–290.

Järvelin, K., & Vakkari, P. (1992). The evolution of library and information science, 1965–1985: A content analysis of journal articles. In P. Vakkari & B. Cronin (Eds.), *Conceptions of library and information science: Historical, empirical and theoretical perspectives* (pp. 109–125). London: Taylor Graham.

Jasanoff, S. (2004). *States of knowledge: The co-production of science and social order.* New York: Routledge.

Jenkins, K. (1997). *The postmodern history reader.* New York: Routledge.

Joachim, M. (Ed.). (2003). *Historical aspects of cataloging and classification.* New York: Haworth Press.

Justice, A. (2004). Information science as a facet of the history of British science: The origins of the Classification Research Group. In W. B. Rayward & M. E. Bowden (Eds.), *The History and Heritage of Scientific and Technological Information Systems: Proceedings of the 2002 Conference* (pp. 267–280). Medford, NJ: Information Today.

Kaser, R. T., & Kaser, V. C. (2001). *BIOSIS: Championing the cause: The first 75 years*. Philadelphia: National Federation of Abstracting and Information Services.

Kenzo, G. (2003). *Federal security controls over scientific and technical information: History and current controversy*. New York: Novinka Books.

Kevles, D. J. (1978). *The physicists: The history of a scientific community in modern America*. New York: Knopf.

Kilgour, F. G. (1997). Origins of coordinate searching. *Journal of the American Society for Information Science, 48*, 340–348.

Kister, K. (2002). *Eric Moon: The life and library times*. Jefferson, NC: MacFarland.

Kline, R. (2004). What is information theory a theory of? Boundary work among information theorists and information scientists in the United States and Britain during the Cold War. In W. B. Rayward & M. E. Bowden (Eds.), *Conference on the History and Heritage of Scientific and Technological Information Systems* (pp. 15–28). Medford, NJ: Information Today for the American Society of Information Science and Technology and the Chemical Heritage Foundation.

Kokabi, M. (1996). The internationalization of MARC. Part I: The emergence and divergence of MARC. *OCLC Systems and Services, 12*(1), 21–31.

Kualnes, F. H. (1999). The history of managing technical information at DuPont. In M. E. Bowden, T. B. Hahn, & R. V. Williams (Eds.), *Proceedings of the 1998 Conference on the History and Heritage of Science Information Systems* (pp. 107–114). Medford, NJ: Information Today for the American Society for Information Science and the Chemical Heritage Foundation.

La Barre, K. (2004). Weaving webs of significance: The Classification Research Study Group in the United States and Canada. In W. B. Rayward & M. E. Bowden (Eds.), *The History and Heritage of Scientific and Technological Information Systems: Proceedings of the 2002 Conference* (pp. 249–257). Medford, N.J.: Information Today.

Lamoreaux, N. R., Raff, D. M. G., & Temin, P. (1997). New economic approaches to the study of business history. *Business and Economic History, 26*(1), 57–79.

Lesk, M. E. (1996). Gerald Salton, Mar. 8, 1927 to Aug. 28, 1995: In memoriam. *Journal of the American Society for Information Science, 47*, 110–111.

Levenstein, M. (1998). *Accounting for growth: Information systems and the creation of the large corporation*. Stanford, CA: Stanford University Press.

Lewis, J. E. (2002). *Spy capitalism: ITEK and the CIA*. New Haven, CT: Yale University Press.

Library and information science: Historical perspectives [Special issue containing papers from a Library History Round Table session at the 1984 ALA conference] (1985). *Journal of Library History, Philosophy & Comparative Librarianship, 20*(2), 120–178.

Lilley, D. B., & Trice, R. W. (1989). *A history of information science, 1945–1985*. San Diego, CA: Academic Press.

Lipetz, B. A. (1999). Aspects of *JASIS* authorship through five decades. *Journal of the American Society for Information Science, 50*, 994–1003.

Lynd, S. (2001). Reflections on radical history. *Radical History Review, 79*, 104–107.

Lynn, K. S. (1965). *The professions in America*. Boston: Houghton Mifflin.

Lyotard, J.-F. (1984). *The postmodern condition: A report on knowledge*. Minneapolis: University of Minnesota Press.

MacDonald, K. M. (1995). *The sociology of the professions*. Thousand Oaks, CA: Sage.

Machlup, F., & Mansfield, U. (Eds.). (1983). *The study of information: Interdisciplinary messages*. New York: Wiley.

MacLeod, R. (1999). Secrets among friends: The Research Information Service and the "special relationship" in Allied scientific information and intelligence, 1916–1918. *Minerva, 37*, 201–233.

Makinen, I. (2004). Finnish information services for technology during the first half of the twentieth century. In W. B. Rayward & M. E. Bowden (Eds.), *The History and Heritage of Scientific and Technological Information Systems: Proceedings of the 2002 Conference* (pp. 300–309). Medford, NJ: Information Today.

Marcum, D. B. (2002). Automating the library: The Council on Library Resources. *IEEE Annals of the History of Computing, 24*(3), 2–13.

Marloth, H. (1996). *Zeittafel zur internationalen Entwicklung des Informationswesens nach 1945* [Chronology of the international development of information science since 1945]. Retrieved December 12, 2005, from http://fs-infowiss.phil.uni-sb.de/BuFaTa/thesen.marloth.html#Zeit

Martin, S. B. (1998). Information technology, employment, and the information sector: Trends in information employment, 1970–1995. *Journal of the American Society for Information Science, 49*, 1053–1069.

McCallum, S. H. (2002). MARC: Keystone for library automation. *IEEE Annals of the History of Computing, 24*(2), 34–39.

McCrank, L. J. (1995). History, archives, and information science. *Annual Review of Information Science and Technology, 30*, 281–382.

McCrank, L. J. (2001). *Historical information science: An emerging unidiscipline*. Medford, NJ: Information Today.

McCullagh, C. (2004). *The logic of history: Putting postmodernism in perspective*. London: Routledge.

McIlwaine, B. H. (1997). The Universal Decimal Classification: Some factors concerning its origins, development, and influence. *Journal of the American Society for Information Science, 48*, 331–339.

Meadows, A. J. (Ed.). (1987). *The origins of information science*. London: Taylor Graham, Institute of Information Scientists.

Meyer, E., & Funkhouser, N. F. (Eds.). (1998). Papers invited to celebrate the 50th anniversary of the Division of Chemical Information. *Journal of Chemical Information and Computer Science, 38*(6).

Meyer, R. W. (1997). Monopoly power and electronic journals. *Library Quarterly, 67*, 325–349.

Mikhailov, A. I., Chernyi, A. I., & Gilairevskii, R. S. (1984). The ideas of Lenin on the problems, methods, and forms of the scientific information activity. In R. H. Burger (Trans.), *Scientific communications and informatics* (pp. 247–260). Arlington, VA: Information Resources Press.

Miksa, F. L. (1998). *The DDC, the universe of knowledge, & the post-modern library*. Albany, NY: OCLC Forest Press.

Miksa, S. (2002). *Pigeonholes and punchcards: Identifying the division between library classification research and information retrieval research, 1952–1970.* Unpublished doctoral dissertation, Florida State University, Tallahassee.

Miles, W. D. (1982). *A history of the National Library of Medicine: The nation's treasury of medical knowledge.* Bethesda, MD: U.S. National Library of Medicine.

Mizzaro, S. (1997). Relevance: The whole history. *Journal of the American Society for Information Science, 48,* 810–832.

Mohanrajan, P. A. (1992). *Library science: Dr. S. R. Ranganathan's contribution, 1924–1944: An analysis.* Madras, India: Mohanavalli Publications.

Muddiman, D. (1998). The universal library as modern utopia: The information society of H. G. Wells. *Library History, 14,* 85–101.

Muddiman, D. (2004). Red information science: J. D. Bernal and the nationalization of scientific information in Britain from 1930 to 1949. In W. B. Rayward & M. E. Bowden (Eds.), *The History and Heritage of Scientific and Technological Information Systems: Proceedings of the 2002 Conference* (pp. 258–266). Medford, NJ: Information Today.

Muranushi, T. (1994). The framework and methodology for the history of information. *Library & Information Science, 32,* 43–64.

National Science Foundation, Office of Science Information Service. (1960). *A review of science information activities: Fiscal years 1951–1959.* Washington, DC: The Foundation.

Neufeld, M. L., Cornog, M., & Sperr, I. L. (1983). *Abstracting and indexing services in perspective: Miles Conrad Memorial Lectures, 1969–1983.* Arlington, VA: Information Resources Press.

Novick, P. (1988). *That noble dream: The "objectivity question" and the American historical profession.* Cambridge, UK: Cambridge University Press.

Nyce, J. M., & Kahn, P. (1989). Innovation, pragmaticism, and technological continuity: Vannevar Bush's Memex. *Journal of the American Society for Information Science, 40,* 214–220.

Nyce, J. M., & Kahn, P. (Eds.). (1991). *From Memex to hypertext: Vannevar Bush and the mind's machine.* San Diego, CA: Academic Press.

Ohlman, H. (1999). Mechanical indexing goes public [Pioneers' reminiscences]. In M. E. Bowden, T. B. Hahn, & R. V. Williams (Eds.), *Proceedings of the 1998 Conference on the History and Heritage of Science Information Systems* (p. 276). Medford, NJ: Information Today, Inc. for the American Society for Information Science and the Chemical Heritage Foundation.

Olaisen, J., Munch-Peterson, E., & Wilson, P. (Eds.). (1995). *Information science: From the development of the discipline to social interaction.* Oslo, Norway: Scandinavian University Press.

Olson, H. A. (2004). The ubiquitous hierarchy: An army to overcome the threat of a mob. *Library Trends, 52,* 604–617.

Oluić-Vuković, V. (1997). Bradford's distribution: From the classical bibliometric "law" to the more general stochastic models. *Journal of the American Society for Information Science, 48,* 833–842.

Ørom, A. (2000). Information science, historical changes and social aspects: A Nordic outlook. *Journal of Documentation, 56,* 12–26.

Osborn, A. D. (1991). From Cutter and Dewey to Mortimer Taube and beyond: A complete century of change in cataloguing and classification. *Cataloging & Classification Quarterly, 12*(3–4), 35–50.

Owens, L. (1996). Vannevar Bush: An engineer builds a book. *Science as Culture, 34,* 373–399.

Passet, J. E. (1994). The literature of American library history, 1991–1992. *Libraries & Culture, 29,* 415–439.

Pemberton, J. (1983). A backward and forward look at the New York Times Information Bank: A tale of ironies compounded ... and an analysis of the Mead deal. *Online, 7*(4), 7–17.

Pinelli, T. E., Henderson, M., Bishop, A. P., & Doty, P. (1992). *Chronology of selected literature, reports, policy instruments, and significant events affecting federal scientific and technical information (STI) in the United States, 1945–1990* (Report No. 11; NASA TM-101662). Washington, DC: National Aeronautics and Space Administration, NASA/DoD Aerospace Knowledge Diffusion Research Project.

Porat, M. (1977). *The information economy: Definition and measurement.* Washington, DC: U.S. Department of Commerce, Office of Telecommunications.

Powell, E. C. (2000). A history of Chemical Abstracts Service, 1907–1998. *Science & Technology Libraries, 18*(4), 93–110.

Power, E. B. (1990). *Edition of one: The autobiography of Eugene B. Power, founder of University Microfilms.* Ann Arbor, MI: University Microfilms International.

Radford, G. P. (1998). Flaubert, Foucault, and the Bibliotheque [*sic*] fantastique: Toward a postmodern epistemology for library science. *Library Trends, 46,* 616–634.

Radford, G. (2003). Trapped in our own discursive formations: Towards an archaeology of library and information science. *Library Quarterly, 73,* 1–18.

Ranganathan, Y. (2001). *S. R. Ranganathan, pragmatic philosopher of information science: A personal biography.* Mumbai, India: Bharatiya Vidya Bhavan.

Rau, E. (2000). The adoption of operations research in the United States during World War II. In A. C. Hughes & T. P. Hughes (Eds.), *Systems, experts and computers: The systems approach on management and engineering, World War II and after* (pp. 57–92). Cambridge, MA: MIT Press.

Rauzier, J.-M. (Ed.). (1993). Special historical issue. *Documentaliste, 30*(4–5).

Rayward, W. B. (1975). *The universe of information: The work of Paul Otlet for documentation and international organisation* (FID 520). Moscow: VINITI.

Rayward, W. B. (1983). Librarianship and information research: Together or apart. In F. Machlup & U. Mansfield (Eds.), *The study of information: Interdisciplinary messages* (pp. 343–364). New York: Wiley.

Rayward, W. B. (1994). Visions of Xanadu: Paul Otlet (1868–1944) and hypertext. *Journal of the American Society for Information Science, 45,* 235–250.

Rayward, W. B. (Ed.). (1996). History of information science [Special issue]. *Information Processing & Management, 32,* 1–88.

Rayward, W. B. (Ed.). (2004). Pioneers in library and information science [Special issue]. *Library Trends, 52*(4).

Rayward, W. B., & Bowden, M. E. (2004). *Conference on the History and Heritage of Scientific and Technological Information Systems.* Medford, NJ: Information Today for the American Society of Information Science and Technology and the Chemical Heritage Foundation.

Redmond, A. D. (1985). American Society for Information Science: History. In A. Kent (Ed.). *Encyclopedia of library and information science* (Vol. 38, Suppl. 3, pp. 11–31). New York: Dekker.

Reid, R. (1997). *Architects of the web: 1,000 days that built the future of business*. New York: Wiley.

Richards, P. S. (1981). Gathering enemy scientific information in wartime: The OSS and the periodical reproduction program. *Journal of Library History, 16*, 253–264.

Richards, P. S. (1994). *Scientific information in wartime: The Allied-German rivalry, 1939–1945*. Stamford, CT: Greenwood Press.

Richards, P. S. (1999). The Soviet overseas information empire and the implications of its disintegration. In M. E. Bowden, T. B. Hahn, & R. V. Williams (Eds.), *Proceedings of the 1998 Conference on the History and Heritage of Science Information Systems* (pp. 201–214). Medford, NJ: Information Today for the American Society for Information Science and the Chemical Heritage Foundation.

Ross, D. (1995). Grand narrative in American historical writing: From romance to uncertainty. *American Historical Review, 100*, 651–677.

Royle, N. (Ed.). (2000). *Deconstructions: A user's guide*. New York: Palgrave.

Rubin, R. (2000). *Foundations of library and information science*. New York: Neal-Schuman.

Ryan, M. P. (1998). *Knowledge diplomacy: Global competition & the politics of intellectual property*. Washington, DC: Brookings Institution Press.

Saracevic, T. (1992). Information science: Origin, evolution and relations. In P. Vakkari & B. Cronin (Eds.). *Conceptions of library and information science: Historical, empirical and theoretical perspectives* (pp. 5–27). London: Taylor Graham.

Saracevic, T. (1997). Users lost: Reflections on the past, future, and limits of information science. *SIGIR Forum, 31*(2), 16–27.

Saracevic, T. (1999). Information science. *Journal of the American Society for Information Science, 50*, 1051–1062.

Satija, M. P. (1992). *S. R. Ranganathan and the method of science*. New Delhi, India: Aditya Prakashan.

Satoh, T. (1999). Restoration of Japanese academic libraries and development of library and information science: The contributions of Shigenori Baba. In M. E. Bowden, T. B. Hahn, & R. V. Williams (Eds.), *Proceedings of the 1998 Conference on the History and Heritage of Science Information Systems* (pp. 215–220). Medford, NJ: Information Today for the American Society for Information Science and the Chemical Heritage Foundation.

Schement, J. R. (1990). Porat, Bell, and the information society reconsidered: The growth of information work in the early twentieth century. *Information Processing & Management, 26*, 449–465.

Schiffrin, A. (2000). *The business of books: How international conglomerates took over publishing and changed the way we read*. London: Verso.

Schrader, A. M. (1984). In search of a name: Information science and its conceptual antecedents. *Library and Information Science, 6*, 227–271.

Schultz, H., & Georgy, U. (1994). *From CA to CAS online* (2nd ed.). Berlin: Springer-Verlag.

Seidel, R. W. (1999). Secret scientific communities: Classification and scientific communication in the DOE and DOD. In M. E. Bowden, T. B. Hahn, & R. V. Williams (Eds.), *Proceedings of the 1998 Conference on the History and Heritage of Science Information Systems* (pp. 46–60). Medford, NJ: Information Today for the American Society for Information Science and the Chemical Heritage Foundation.

Shapiro, F. R. (1992). Origins of bibliometrics, citation indexing, and citation analysis: The neglected legal literature. *Journal of the American Society for Information Science, 43,* 337–339.

Sharma, R. N. (Ed.). (1992). *S. R. Ranganathan and the West.* New Delhi, India: Sterling Publishers.

Shera, J. H., & Cleveland, D. (1977). The history and foundation of information science. *Annual Review of Information Science and Technology, 12,* 249–275.

Siatri, R. (1999). The evolution of user studies. *Libri, 49,* 132–141.

Smiraglia, R. (2002). The progress of theory in knowledge organization. *Library Trends, 50,* 330–349.

Smith, K. W. (Ed.). (1998). *OCLC, 1967–1997: Thirty years of furthering access to the world's information.* New York: Haworth Press.

Smith, L. C. (1991). Memex as an image of potentiality revisited. In J. M. Nyce & P. Kahn (Eds.), *From Memex to hypertext: Vannevar Bush and the mind's machine* (pp. 281–286). San Diego, CA: Academic Press.

Spicher, K. M. (1996). The development of the MARC format. *Cataloging and Classification Quarterly, 21*(3–4), 75–90.

Star, S. L., & Bowker, G. (Eds.). (1998). How classification works [Special issue]. *Library Trends, 42*(2).

Starr, P. (1987). *The politics of numbers.* New York: Russell-Sage.

Stewart, R. K. (1993). The office of technical services. *Knowledge: Creation, Diffusion, Utilization, 15,* 44–77.

Stiglitz, J. E. (2000). The contributions of the economics of information to twentieth century economics. *Quarterly Journal of Economics, 115,* 1441–1478.

Stockwell, F. (2001). *The history of information storage and retrieval.* Jefferson, NC: McFarland.

Stoianovich, T. (1976). *French historical method: The Annales paradigm.* Ithaca, NY: Cornell University Press.

Stone, A. (1999). *How America got on-line.* Armonk, NY: M. E. Sharpe.

Sweeney, L. (2003). *That's AI? A history and critique of the field* (Technical Report, CMU-CS-03-106). Pittsburgh, PA: Carnegie Mellon University, School of Computer Science.

Tague-Sutcliffe, J. (1994). Quantitative methods in documentation. In B. C. Vickery (Ed.), *Fifty years of information progress: A Journal of Documentation review* (pp. 147–188). London: Aslib.

Temin, P. (1987). *The fall of the Bell System: A study in prices and politics.* New York: Cambridge University Press.

Thompson, T. (2004). *The fifty-year role of the United States Air Force in advancing information technology: A history of the Rome, New York, Ground Electronics Laboratory* (Studies in American history, Vol. 10). Lewiston, NY: Edwin Mellen Press.

Tufte, E. R. (2001). *The visual display of quantitative information.* Cheshire, CT: Graphics Press.

Vaden, W. M. (1992). *The Oak Ridge Technical Information Center: A trailblazer in federal documentation.* Oak Ridge, TN: U.S. Department of Energy, Office of Scientific and Technical Information.

Vakkari, P., & Cronin, B. (Eds.). (1992). *Conceptions of library and information science: Historical, empirical and theoretical perspectives*. London: Taylor Graham.

Varlejs, J. (1999). The continuing professional education role of ASIS: Fifty years of learning together, reaching out, seeking identity. *Journal of the American Society for Information Science, 50*, 1032–1036.

Verdu, S. (1998). Fifty years of Shannon theory. *IEEE Transactions on Information Theory, 44*, 2057–2078.

Vickery, B. C. (Ed.). (1994). *Fifty years of information progress: A Journal of Documentation review*. London: Aslib.

Vickery, B. C. (2000). *Scientific communication in history*. Lanham, MD: Scarecrow Press.

Vickery, B. C. (2004). *A long search for information* (Occasional Papers 213). Champaign: Graduate School of Library and Information Science, University of Illinois at Urbana-Champaign.

Volodin, B. F. (2000). History of librarianship, library history, or information history: A view from Russia. *Library Quarterly, 70*, 446–467.

Walker, T. D. (1997). *Journal of Documentary Reproduction*, 1938–1942: Domain as reflected in characteristics of authorship and citation. *Journal of the American Society for Information Science, 48*, 361–368.

Warner, J. (2004). *Humanizing information technology*. Lanham, MD: Scarecrow Press.

Warner, J. (2005). Labor in information systems. *Annual Review of Information Science and Technology, 39*, 551–575.

Wersig, G. (1993). Information science: The study of postmodern knowledge usage. *Information Processing & Management, 29*, 229–239.

White, H. D., & McCain, K. W. (1998). Visualizing a discipline: An author co-citation analysis of information science, 1972–1995. *Journal of the American Society for Information Science, 49*, 327–355.

Williams, M. E. (2001). Highlights of the online database industry and the Internet: 2001. *National Online 2001: Proceedings*, 1–4.

Williams, M. R. (1985). *A history of computing technology*. Englewood Cliffs, NJ: Prentice-Hall.

Williams, R. V. (1997). The documentation and special libraries movements in the United States, 1910–1960. *Journal of the American Society for Information Science, 48*, 775–781.

Williams, R. V. (2005). *Bibliography of the history of information science, 1900–2004* (5th ed.). Retrieved December 12, 2005, from www.libsci.sc.edu/bob/istchron/Isbiblio5.pdf

Williams, R. V., & Bowden, M. E. (1999). *Chronology of chemical information science*. Philadelphia: Chemical Heritage Foundation. Retrieved December 12, 2005, from www.chemheritage.org/explore/timeline/CHCHRON.HTM

Williams, R. V., Whitmire, L., & Bradley, C. (1997). Bibliography of the history of information science in North America, 1900–1995. *Journal of the American Society for Information Science, 48*, 373–379.

Williams, R.V., Whitmire, L., & Bradley, C. (1998). Bibliography of the history of information science in North America, 1900–1997. In T. B. Hahn & M. Buckland (Eds.), *Historical studies in information science* (pp. 296–314). Medford, NJ: Information Today.

Williams, R. V., & Zachert, M. J. K. (1983). Knowledge put to work: SLA at 75. *Special Libraries, 74*, 370–382.

Windsor, D. (1999). Industrial roots of information science. *Journal of the American Society for Information Science, 50,* 1064–1065.

Wooster, H. (1987). Historical note: Shining palaces, shifting sands: National information systems. *Journal of the American Society for Information Science, 38,* 321–335.

Wouters, P. (1999). The creation of the *Science Citation Index.* In M. E. Bowden, T. B. Hahn, & R. V. Williams (Eds.), *Proceedings of the 1998 Conference on the History and Heritage of Science Information Systems* (pp. 127–136). Medford, NJ: Information Today for the American Society for Information Science and the Chemical Heritage Foundation.

Wright, H. C. (1985). Shera as a bridge between librarianship and information science. *Journal of Library History, 20,* 137–156.

Yates, J. (1989). *Control through communication: The rise of system in American management.* Baltimore: Johns Hopkins Press.

Zachary, G. P. (1997). *Endless frontier: Vannevar Bush, engineer of the American century.* New York: Free Press.

Zandonade, T. (2004). Social epistemology from Jesse Shera to Steve Fuller. *Library Trends, 52,* 810–832.

Zinn, H. (1999). *A people's history of the United States: 1492-present.* New York: HarperCollins.

Zinn, H. (2001). *Howard Zinn on history.* New York: Seven Stories Press.

CHAPTER 2

Vannevar Bush and Memex

Ronald D. Houston and Glynn Harmon
University of Texas at Austin

Introduction

This review examines the history, historiography, influences, and apparent misunderstandings surrounding Vannevar Bush's memex concept and discusses the manner in which the literatures of information science and other areas have cited the memex and its central idea of knowledge management (KM) by associative trails. The review also challenges the central memex premise that the mind works exclusively through associative thinking by reviewing some competing psychological movements and theories that emerged before and after Bush framed the memex concept.

Vannevar Bush (1890–1974), who directed the U.S .Office of Scientific Research and Development during World War II, led the huge wartime research effort (Kochen, 1967, p. 23). He thus acquired a broad perception of the dynamics of accelerated research and the frustrations of digging out critically needed recorded information. Bush expressed dissatisfaction with the ineffective and awkward ways in which libraries and other research organizations managed information and, on the eve of World War II, he proposed a radically different form of information technology, which he called the "memex." According to Bush, the memex would provide information storage and access based on personal relevance judgments and corresponding associative trails of reasoning and retrieval. Together with the world encyclopedia concept of H. G. Wells (1938), the memex has for several decades inspired countless scholars working in a host of various disciplines. This review assesses the legacy and impact of the memex and its central concept of associative trails from specious invocation, to source of inspiration, and finally to Web development and application.

The memex concept and its underlying assumption that the mind works only or essentially through associative reasoning have had a broad, enduring impact throughout information science and technology. Although the present review is the first *Annual Review of Information Science and Technology* (*ARIST*) chapter to be devoted solely to considering the memex, a perusal of volumes 1 through 39 (1966–2005) reveals that it has been cited in a wide variety of information science areas:

records management, documentation, artificial intelligence, information storage and retrieval, interactive computing, electronic publishing, scholarly publishing, multimedia, optical media, information portals, office automation, psychometrics, hypertext and hypermedia, virtual reality, the history of information science, distributed information management, librarianship, digital library design, communication via the Web, collaboratories, visualization of knowledge domains, cognition through associative reasoning and latent semantic analysis, and archival enterprise. Earlier *ARIST* chapters tended to center on the application of memex concepts to emerging problems of online retrieval. During the 1980s, the deployment of personal computers and the subsequent development of hypertext and the Web revived discussion about memex-related concepts and extended them to other areas of information science. Although Bush's notion of the memex was criticized somewhat unfairly for vagueness that "could have won the admiration of the Oracle at Delphi" (Rorvig, 1988, p. 158) or because "few of his suggestions were original" (Fairthorne, 1958, p. 135), the memex has been, and continues to be, cited by authors in various information science publications as well as by those working in other fields, such as literary theory, marketing, and education.

Following Davenport and Prusak (2000), this review focuses on the two KM behaviors of *personal* KM and *shared* KM. Although some commentators have dismissed memex KM as a reinvention of existing approaches to indexing, this review highlights novel features of the memex concept, such as its high degree of scalability, its high cross-indexing potential through links, and its extension from personal KM through memory augmentation to shared KM, which constituted a departure from earlier KM approaches. The distinction between personal and shared KM appears to be particularly applicable to the memex, inasmuch as Bush proposed the development of a personal knowledge base that would have the capability of linking a pre-existing document or set of documents both to personally generated documents and to selected documents published by others.

The literature cited in this review constitutes a representative sample of the literature discovered through searches for "Bush" and "memex" in the *ARIST* annual indexes and in print and online databases. Works acknowledged include those that cited the memex for substantive conceptual reasons and, for illustrative purposes, a few that cited the memex to lend authority to their arguments or to comply with perceived social conventions. Our sources included Academic Search Premier, the Association for Computing Machinery Digital Library, Book History Online, Computer Science Index, the ERIC database, Emerald Insight, the *Encyclopedia Americana Yearbooks* published from1945 to 2005, the second edition of the *Encyclopedia of Library and Information Science*, Eugene Garfield's *Essays of an Information Scientist* (volumes 1–15), Expanded Academic ASAP, Internet and Personal Computing Abstracts, *Library and Information Science Abstracts*, Library

Literature & Information Science Full Text, *Readers' Guide*, and *Readers' Guide Retrospective*. In this review, we have followed Bush's practice of not capitalizing the term "memex" except in those cases where we quote titles of, and passages from, works that used the capitalized form.

Bush on the Memex

Bush took the memex concept quite seriously. He formulated recognizable parts of it in 1932–1933 in an attempt to improve information retrieval (IR), noting that library research required individuals "to paw over cards, thumb pages, and delve by the hour" (Bush, 1991b, p. 74). This work was spurred on by Bush's dissatisfaction with the library practices of the day, which he described in the following terms:

> Our ineptitude in getting at the record is largely caused by the artificiality of systems of indexing. When data of any sort are placed in storage, they are filed alphabetically or numerically, and information is found (when it is) by tracing it down from subclass to subclass. It can be in only one place, unless duplicates are used; one has to have rules as to which path will locate it, and the rules are cumbersome. Having found one item, moreover, one has to emerge from the system and re-enter on a new path. (Bush, 1991a, p. 101)

Although some librarians reacted negatively to these criticisms, others registered their agreement: "Dr. Bush's article is chiefly of interest today for its account of the inadequacies of conventional systems of library classification and the resulting tendency to neglect existing information in research work" (Joyce & Needham, 1958, p. 192; cf. Sloan, 1998, p. 122). Given that Bush directed the frantic scientific effort for the U.S. during World War II, when a large number of projects had to be completed under tight deadlines, his frustrations, particularly those related to obtaining current information, were well justified.

In 1939, Bush wrote an unpublished article "Mechanization and the Record," in which he formulated his concept of a filing and retrieval system, designed largely for experienced researchers and trained librarians, into a "memex" for anyone, which, as he conceived it, would operate in ways resembling human associative thought processes (Bush, 1939; cited in Waldrop, 2001, pp. 27–28). Following World War II, he published his classic article "As We May Think" (AWMT) in the July 1945 *Atlantic Monthly* (Bush, 1945a), followed by an illustrated condensation in *Life* (Bush, 1945b), an anonymous summary in *Time* (A machine that thinks, 1945), and a reprint of the full article in his 1946 book, *Endless Horizons* (Bush, 1946). In 1959, he described an improved "memex II" (Kahn & Nyce, 1991; citing Bush, 1991c, p. 168). In 1967 and 1970, Bush printed a revision in "Memex Revisited" (Bush, 1967b, pp. 75–101) and a summary in his autobiographical *Pieces of the Action* (Bush, 1970, pp. 190–192). The period between 1964 and 1974, the year of Bush's death, saw further reprintings of AWMT, presumably with Bush's consent (Bush, 1967a, pp. 23–35; Pylyshyn, 1970, pp. 47–59; Sharp, 1964, pp. 19–41).

Some scholars (e.g., Nyce & Kahn, 1991) have offered comprehensive and reasonably laudatory reviews of the entire 38-year history of the memex, but hasty words by Bush may have led others into confusion, as evidenced by Oppenheim's review of commentaries by Zachary (1997) and Burke (1994). In a review of Zachary's *Endless Frontier*, Oppenheim (1999, p. 373) stated, "In particular, Zachary fails to pick up with what contempt Bush himself viewed the piece [AWMT], which, according to Burke, he wished he had never written." Oppenheim (1994, p. 95) had previously said in the course of his review of Burke's *Information and Secrecy* that "Burke has shown that Bush considered the article [AWMT] as a 'fantasy' and did not take it seriously himself." However, Burke actually wrote something different: "Although later generations have viewed Memex as Bush's greatest contribution to information science, he [Bush] had a different view" (Burke, 1994, p. 329). This statement was apparently based on Bush's 1947 letter to the head of the Massachusetts Institute of Technology (MIT) library system, entitled "Selector Speech to Librarians," in which he wrote:

> I am now weary and the thought of trying to present this subject to a group of librarians appals [*sic*] me. It was all right to stir them up with the article on Memex, for they could not possibly tell whether I was being serious or not and besides it was an arm's length affair anyway. (Bush, 1947; quoted in Burke, 1994, p. 329)

Given Bush's (1991a, p. 101) critical but constructive stance toward librarians' "artificiality of systems of indexing" and in the absence of any other derogation of the memex and AWMT by Bush, this quotation probably reflects an attempt to avoid a speaking engagement rather than "contempt" for AWMT. Indeed, some members of the library profession might have viewed interventions by the "outsider" Bush with a hostile spirit of territorial protectionism or responded in a reactionary fashion to the technological innovations proposed in AWMT. Thus, Bush's attitudes toward his memex have been the subject of various interpretations, some of which have become distorted.

Bush's memex was centered on the individual researcher and anchored in a concept that he thought to be the dominant mode of individual mental functioning—thinking by *association* from one concept to another and, via associative mental trails, to knowledge represented in recorded documents. The doctrine of associative thinking, however, had been significantly challenged prior to, during, and especially after the 1940s by other theories of cognition. Nevertheless, associationism became embedded in the memex legacy and, for better or worse, continues to have an impact in spite of the relevance to information science and technology of several competing psychological theories. Accordingly, the next section briefly reviews the psychological doctrine of associationism and explores the development of competing approaches to the study of the mind and cognition before and after Bush's publication of AWMT.

Challenges to Bush's Associative Thinking Premise

Although Bush did acknowledge the need to go beyond formal logical relations and apply creativity and intuitive judgment in research, he subscribed to associationism, a leading theory of cognition at the time. Thus, he stated in AWMT that

> The human mind ... operates by association. With one item in its grasp, it snaps instantly to the next that is suggested by the association of thought, in accordance with some intricate web of trails carried by the cells of the brain. (Bush, 1967a, p. 32)

Associationism had a strong following among American psychologists, who were preoccupied at that time with the entrenched dogmas of behaviorism. Focusing on stimulus-response links—which were compatible with the associationist doctrine—in order to study relationships between stimuli and behavioral responses, the behaviorist approach to cognition was characterized by rigid empiricism, reductionism, and operationalism in order to produce "scientific" psychological findings. Behaviorists tended to dismiss methods such as introspection for the study of thought processes and to dismiss constructs such as "the mind." Herbert Simon, referring to the first half of the twentieth century, stated: "You couldn't use a word like mind in a psychological journal or you would get your mouth washed out with soap" (quoted in Santrock, 2000, p. 255).

By contrast, gestaltist psychology maintained that associationist theories were far too limited and that thinking is best characterized by the visualization of holistic patterns and concepts, the development of problem-solving structures, language learning, and the interplay of organisms with their environments. The German term *Gestalt* refers to "configurations" or "wholes" of entities (including thought patterns) that differ from the simple sum of their parts. In their compilation entitled *Thinking: From Association to Gestalt*, Mandler and Mandler (1964) have provided multiple perspectives on the battles between the followers of associationism and Gestalt scholars, which took place mainly during the first half of the twentieth century. It is important to note, however, that gestaltism was not well known in the U.S. until after World War II. Given his heavy wartime responsibilities, Bush probably had not followed these developments in psychology. His strong associationist stance thus appears to have been a product of his time and environment.

During the 1950s, fresh psychological theories were beginning to compete with behaviorism and associationism. Vinacke (1952) noted that the Gestalt school was just beginning to have broad influence and that structuralism, which depended on introspection, was re-emerging. Marx and Hillix (1963) reviewed the key systems and theories of psychology that had emerged by the early 1960s: structuralism, functionalism, associationism, behaviorism, gestaltism, and psychoanalysis. Eighteen years later, Hampden-Turner (1981) published *Maps of the Mind*, which illustrated 60 perspectives that could be applied to study of the mind. Gardner (1985) noted that the cognitive revolution arose in the early 1950s to address epistemological questions about the nature of knowledge and its development and deployment, producing a coalition of epistemological philosophers, cognitive and Gestalt psychologists, artificial intelligence specialists, linguists, anthropologists, and neuroscientists. But these various perspectives likely were neither available nor apparent to Bush in 1945, when he published AWMT. Associationism was then the choice of the day.

But as newer and theoretically more appealing explanations of cognition have arisen to compete with associationism, we should ask whether the mimicking of associationism by Bush's followers and authors who invoke his name has been entirely justified. On one hand, associationism has proved to be enormously successful in explaining many thought processes and in providing a basis for hyperlinking and Web technologies; as a consequence, the current task is often seen to consist in building on that associationist infrastructure. On the other hand, some observers have argued that new technologies and approaches are needed to compensate for the shortcomings of Web associationism. For example, Vakkari (2003) has made the Gestalt-like case that the development of task-based information searching is needed and Cole, Leide, Large, Beheshti, and Brooks (2005) have questioned associationism, suggesting that information needs can be addressed by working with users' cognitive maps or structures and their transformation—an approach that is even more reminiscent of gestaltism. As new theories emerge and the debate continues, associationism might be considered to provide an explanation of cognitive phenomena that is necessary but not, of itself, sufficient.

Interpretations of the Memex Legacy

Many remember Bush's notion of the memex for its suggestions of technological innovations: ideas of input devices (i.e., the "Cyclops" miniature camera and the Vocoder voice recorder), storage (on reels of indexed 35 mm microfilm), processing (by means of a "logical calculator"), and a workstation incorporating these components (the memex).

Others remember it for its suggestions of personal KM in the form of associative "trails" involving user-created links between associated ideas stored in the user's machine, and shared KM in the form of those trails and other knowledge resources transferable from one researcher to another. Over the years, Bush himself came to downplay the *technological* aspects of his memex machine (Nyce & Kahn, 1991, p. 113) in favor of stressing its *associative* KM functions.

The memex's legacy also rests in part on the subsequent conflation of its *analog* ideas with their *digital* realizations some decades later. For example, Turoff (1977, p. 401) suggested that AWMT had predicted the FORTRAN programming language. Other commentators noted the impossibility of a literal, physical memex, due to the comparatively primitive state of technology when Bush published his article. Oettinger (2000, p. 11) mentioned a yet more fundamental problem with the memex—the "excessively high recall, excessively low precision" that characterizes (digital) online bibliographic database or Web searching even today. Bolter (2000, p. 35) has extrapolated Bush's analog-based vision further than most: "Computer technology was already far enough advanced for Bush to see the possibility of hypertext and to proclaim nothing less than 'a new relationship between thinking man and the sum of knowledge.' "

Did Bush really foresee what we know as hypertext via digital computers? In 1937–1938, he wrote several memoranda about the feasibility of an electronic computer. Radford (1938) summarized these and implied that Bush had suggested "perforated tapes, optically coded films or plates, and magnetically recorded steel strips" for data input (Randell, 1982a, p. 66; citing Radford, 1938; Radford, 1939). As new technology appeared, Bush (1991c, p. 168) postulated data storage on the magnetized edges of steel drums and, ultimately, in phase-change organic crystals. However, although Bush *did* know the state of development of digital computers (Randell, 1982c, p. 409; citing Bush, 1936) and had tried to build a digital computer in 1937–1938 (Randell, 1982a, pp. 66–67; citing Radford, 1938, 1939), he abandoned digital computers in 1940 (Randell, 1982a, pp. 66–67), disavowed any part in their development (Bush, 1970, p. 185), and ignored the development of the ENIAC, the first digital computer (Stern, 1978, p. 46; Kurzweil, 1990, p. 198). It was only in 1967 that Bush (1967b, pp. 75–101) finally published an endorsement of digital technology.

Three factors may have influenced Bush's reported 25-year dismissal of the benefits of digital technology. First, his own digital computer was rejected (Randell, 1982a, 1982b, 1982c). Second, Skagestad (1996, p. 224) has accused Bush of "actively opposing the ENIAC," citing and exaggerating Kurzweil's (1990, p. 198) statement that Bush "apparently did not respond [to Norbert Weiner's letter proposing a digital computer]." However, Bush may have been too preoccupied with other matters or simply may have chosen not to respond. Third, according to Buckland (1992), Nyce and Kahn (1989, 1991), Burke (1991, 1992, 1994), and Zachary (1997), Bush may have tried to preserve a niche for human-imitative analog technology in an increasingly digital world. This interpretation finds support in passages from Bush's (1967b, pp. 75–101; reprinted in Nyce & Kahn, pp. 197, 211) writings such as the following:

> I proposed a machine for personal use [the memex] rather than the enormous computers which serve whole companies. … We will not expect our personal machine of the future, our memex, to do the job of the great computers. But we can expect it to do clever things for us in the handling of the mass of data we insert into it.

Indeed, Waldrop (2001, p. 31; cf. Lee, 1992, p. 22, quoting Robert Faro) has expressed in emphatic terms Bush's preference for analog technology in the face of a digital future:

> Doggedly, and without success, the Best Apparatus Man in America [Wiener's term for Bush] kept on trying to come up with a workable analog design for his Memex until his death, in 1974. And until the end, his colleagues used to hear him grumbling about the "damn digital computer."

However, to define the memex solely by its technology is to divert attention from Bush's (1965, p. 174) primary theme—the creation of a machine to assist, and even to mimic, the imaginative and associative nature of the human mind:

> As always he [the next generation developer] will build his own concepts, and his own loyalties. He will follow science where it leads, but will not attempt to follow where it cannot lead. And, with a pause, he will admit a faith.

Indeed, Bush's (1967b) entire book, *Science Is Not Enough*, pursued the theme that science has a place in the world up to, but not entering, the world of imagination and faith. Bush's belief in limits on the human mind may well have resulted from respect for the faith of his Universalist minister father (Zachary, 1997, p. 20).

In summary, the memex is remembered largely as a technological vision that proposed a combination of personal and shared KM through associative links, as a precursor to hypertext, and as a projected means to augment limited human memory. The following sections take advantage of hindsight and draw on the scholarship of Smith, Meyrowitz, Nyce and Kahn, Buckland, Burke, and Zachary to trace the evolution of references to the memex primarily through its KM functionality.

Some Early Reactions to the Memex

Shortly after the publication of AWMT in 1945, *Time* accompanied a photograph of Bush with the caption "Prof Bush: Just turn the crank" (A machine that thinks, 1945), referring ambiguously to Bush as a crank, to the mechanical nature of the memex, or to both. Others echoed this ambiguous attitude toward Bush's proposal. In 1957, the self-described "information science logician" Bar-Hillel (1957, p. 110) said that Bush's ideas "certainly show a great deal of vision, but are also unfortunately rather vague and indefinite." A year later, Fairthorne (1958, pp. 135–136) took a somewhat skeptical view of the memex, pointing out its limitations:

> Bush's paper was timely, even though few of his sugges-
> tions were original. ... Though Dr. Bush had stated early on
> that we could benefit from machines only if we changed our
> linguistic and clerical habits, by the time he arrived at the
> Rapid Selector proposal he himself had forgotten his earlier
> stipulation. ... The Memex conception ... would have been
> useful only to an individual who could apply his own criteria
> of relevance to cumulatively stored micro-copy of world liter-
> ature, and who, having read and digested all of this already,
> had marked it appropriately for retrieval.

Later, however, Bush (1991c) did revise the memex concept to suggest that microfilm rolls be published with their documents precoded for association and retrieval. And in the same 1958 article, Fairthorne noted a positive contribution by Bush: "he had an immediate and lasting effect in stimulating others" (Buckland, 1992, p. 292; quoting Fairthorne, 1958).

Criticism continued. Foskett (1964, p. 103) paid a back-handed compliment to Bush with the observation that "no doubt we [librarians] are all equipped with suitable quotations from Milton, from Carlyle, from Ruskin, or perhaps from Vannevar Bush." In a skeptical and adversarial 1966 article, "As We May *Have* Thought" (emphasis added), Wilson (1966, p. 117) described the memex as a technology beset with "mechanical problems impeding its development" and echoed Fairthorne's identification of its human problems as "cultural, philosophical, and psychological." Apparently unaware of the memex's pre-war provenance, Wilson (p. 118) inferred questionable motives on Bush's part: "Dr. Bush's article rings with victorious post-war optimism compounded with an exuberant confidence that technology could remake the peace-time world, and that it had the obligation to do so." Citing an American Psychological Association (APA) (1963, pp. 6–9) study, Wilson (1966, p. 119) also denied Bush's fundamental premise that a flood of information was stifling scientific advance, claiming that "31 oral or written papers, reports, or presentations are made for each research project at several stages." Therefore, Wilson (p. 119) argued, a scientist could chance across one of those thirty-one manifestations or telephone a fellow scientist: in his view, Bush was "hawking for butterflies." On this point, however, Wilson apparently erred. A close reading of pages 6 through 9 of the APA study indicates that its scope was limited to the field of *psychology* (not science in general), that approximately *16* (not 31) oral and written presentations accompanied each *published article* (not project), reaching *at most* .01 percent to 7 percent of APA psychologists, and that the existing publication lag of up to *five years* was equivalent to "sending stale bread to China via air express" (American Psychological Association, 1963, p. 9).

Taking up a theme similar to Wilson's and Fairthorne's identification of human problems, less specific but no less serious concerns about humans placing trust in a machine appeared in print from 1965 to 1983: These have been chronicled by Smith (1991) in an article on "Memex as an Image of Potentiality Revisited." Recently, Cambor (1999, p. 56) has provided a succinct summary of humanist concerns:

> The danger with reducing everything to information, of course, is that one is inevitably left with an impoverished sense of the human. (What are we to make of the fact that in 1983, Time magazine named the computer Man of the Year?) Bush and Wiener both worried about this. Bush emphasized in his later writings those powers he believed to be uniquely human—emotional judgment, spirituality, art.

Interestingly, Bush (1967a, p. 32) conceived his memex as "an enlarged intimate supplement" to memory (i.e., a memory extender) that would augment human intellectual prowess, not diminish it. In his view, the memex was designed to enhance human cognition—a fact that should have mitigated humanist objections, but did not.

In short, from 1945 through the 1960s, the memex concept stirred public imagination but also brought forth critical reactions from the scholarly community about its technological, social, and psychological shortcomings. Some humanists saw the memex as a dehumanizing threat, whereas others tended to distort or misinterpret the memex vision and its possible impact.

Positive Reactions to the Memex: The 1960s and 1970s

Following the initially mixed reactions, the tide began to turn positive. In *State of the Library Art*, Hawkins (1960, p. 145) wrote of Bush's de facto advocacy of personal KM, which he referred to as "basic principles of organization of knowledge":

> Shaw [Hawkins' editor] credited Dr. E. Goldberg with the first practical application of electronics to the selection of

data on film and Dr. Vannevar Bush with the basic principles of organization of knowledge and the basic electronic system used in the Rapid Selector.

All other discussions of Bush and the memex in *State of the Library Art* focused on microphotographic technology (Hawkins, 1960, p. 21; Stewart & Hickey, 1960, pp. 64–65, 89, 150, 156, 168, 169) but did not mention the far more important "basic principles."

In the same year, Brownson (1960, p. 631) described the personal KM function of the memex, referring to it as "associative retrieval." Ten years later, the second edition of Hayes and Becker's (1970, p. 25) seminal book on IR referred to the memex positively but without explanation, describing it as "the earliest and perhaps the most important, single description of the potential uses of computers for information processing." Curiously, Hayes and Becker omitted this statement in prior and subsequent versions of the work (Becker & Hayes, 1963; Hayes & Becker, 1974). Other commentators made note of the personal KM function of the memex (Overhage & Harman, 1967, p. 86; Sharp, 1964, p. 19); yet others merely cited the memex's existence or confused it with Bush's Rapid Microfilm Selector (Sharp, 1965, p. 115). Nevertheless, favorable evaluations continued to appear. Toward the end of the 1970s, De Gennaro (1979, p. 2406) wrote that the memex, as described in AWMT,

> could store and have instant access to the equivalent of a million volumes. The article had an immediate and lasting impact, and it has been cited as a seminal piece ever since. Rider and Bush dramatized the library and information problem in the postwar period and set the stage for the technical developments that followed.

Already in the 1940s, Fremont Rider (1944) had studied the publishing industry, concluding that the volume of publications with which a research library had to deal was doubling every sixteen years. To address this and other KM concerns, De Gennaro (1979) recommended the combination of microforms, interlibrary sharing, and online computer and communications technology as a solution. Yet, as De Gennaro's (1985, p. 39) microform solution began to appear antiquated, he seemed to demonstrate *less* enthusiasm for Bush's ideas:

> Despite the fact that Bush postulated a mechanical device with an improved form of microfilm as the storage medium, it has become an article of faith in the folklore of information science that he was visualizing something like the computer-based Scholar's Workstation. In one sense, Bush was as wrong about the Memex as he was about the intercontinental ballistics [*sic*] missile which he flatly declared to be an impossibility.

De Gennaro's statement, however, exaggerated Bush's position on the intercontinental ballistic missile (ICBM). In 1945, Bush actually said:

> In my opinion such a thing is impossible and will be impossible for many years. ... I say technically I don't think anybody in the world knows how to do such a thing [build an accurate ICBM] and I feel confident it will not be done for a long period of time to come. (McDougal, 1985, p. 98; cf. Hall, 1963, p. 411)

Four years later, Bush (1949, pp. 84–85) stated that the ICBM would be possible but at "astronomical" cost (McDougal, 1985, p. 98) and, in 1957, he told the U.S. Senate that he had underestimated the pace of ICBM development (p. 153). De Gennaro thus brought up a point that had already faded into obscurity 28 years prior to his statement. However, he also offered a perceptive comment: "The point is that our field thrives on visions. Some of those visions turn out to be pipe dreams; others, like the Memex, eventually become realities—one way or another" (De Gennaro, 1985, p. 39).

The Memex Inspires: 1962 Onward

The early positive reactions to the memex did indeed inspire visions. By 1962, Theodor H. Nelson and Douglas C. Engelbart had begun to react to AWMT and to influence the work of other individuals, such as J. C. R. Licklider and Tim Berners-Lee (see Figure 2.1).

Citing the memex as an inspiration, Nelson (1965, p. 84) began the project that was to become Xanadu in 1960 (McCracken, 1999, p. 138; Project Xanadu, 2001). Nelson also coined the term "hypertext" in either 1960 (Nelson, 1987, p. 0/2), 1963 (Project Xanadu, 2001), or 1965 (Nelson, 1965, p. 96), coming to define it as "non-sequential writing with reader-controlled links" in his *Literary Machines* (Nelson, 1987, p. 0/2). Nelson has been cited numerous times across many disciplines; these citations, among other things, reflect the continued influence of the memex idea and its associative underpinnings.

Engelbart read AWMT in 1945 and cited it in an article published 16 years later (Engelbart, 1961, p. 124). In a letter to Bush that he wrote in 1962, he stated somewhat ambiguously that AWMT "probably influenced me quite basically. ... I wouldn't be surprised at all if the reading of this article sixteen and a half years ago hadn't had a real influence upon the course of my thoughts and actions" (Engelbart, 1991, pp. 235–236). To this, Waldrop (2001, p. 216) has added the following observation:

> Engelbart later explained that the guidance must have been subliminal, because he did not consciously remember the memex until after he had envisioned the digital computer

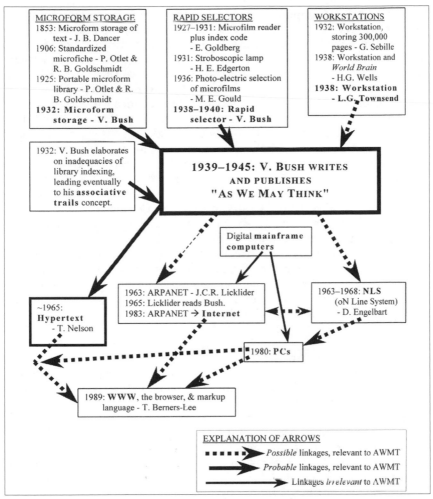

Figure 2.1 **The first author's approximately chronological visualization of the degrees of developmental influence related to AWMT and the Web, based on statements by Nelson, Engelbart, Licklider, Berners-Lee, and leading Bush historians.**

with its cathode ray tube display. … Although he hadn't consciously based his own ideas on Bush's, says Engelbart … he still believed that even unconscious debts should be acknowledged.

Licklider essentially planned ARPANET, which evolved into the Internet (Waldrop, 2001, p. 201), but he did not read AWMT until 1965 (Kahn & Nyce, 1991, pp. 136–137). Thus, Licklider's (1960) famous manifesto "Man-Computer Symbiosis" does not refer to Bush or the memex, whereas his 1965 book entitled *Libraries of the Future* refers to the memex only in its prefatory materials: "I had often heard about Memex and its 'trails of references.' ... But I had not read the article. Now that I have read it, I should like to dedicate this book, however unworthy it may be, to Dr. Bush" (Licklider, 1965, pp. xii–xiii).

In response to the question "Have your first ideas in regard to the Web been influenced by any specific work or published paper like Vanevar [*sic*] Bush's 'As we my [*sic*] think', a publication of Doug Engelbart or Ted Nelson?" Berners-Lee (circa 2000) published a statement on his Web site that acknowledged the *influence* of hypertext on Web development, the *parallel work* of Engelbart, the *necessity* of the Internet for his development of the Web, and the *greatness* of AWMT, but did not avow a "direct line" to any of them (cf. Berners-Lee & Fischetti, 1999, p. 5). In other words, Bush appears to have served as something of a godparent to the godparents of Berners-Lee, the father of the Web.

The memex concept, then, along with its provision for associative linkages, did inspire some key figures who pioneered the development of the Internet, hyperlinking, the Web, and digital libraries. Significantly, very few of these pioneers seriously questioned its heavy reliance on associationist models of mind and reasoning.

Apparent Misinterpretation: 1965 Onward

Disregard for, or de-emphasis of, the memex concept (i.e., defining memex as simply an IR tool) became so frequent that Nelson (1972, p. 248) republished excerpts from AWMT in his article "As We *Will* Think" (emphasis added), stating that the memex "runs counter to virtually all work being pursued under the name of information retrieval today." He lamented the fact that the memex and personal KM concepts had not been incorporated into the system-oriented brand of IR that dominated thinking at the time.

In addition to being obscured by insufficient emphasis of its conceptual aspects, the idea of the memex was subjected to various forms of misinterpretation. For example, Vagianos (1976, p. 155) stated that the memex could revolutionize libraries through the librarian's giving, rather than lending, "a new unit of information" on microform: He thus appeared to focus on the microform storage function of memex rather than KM by association.

In 1981, Smith used citation context to analyze the impact of AWMT and updated her analysis 10 years later (Smith, 1981, 1991). Examining the historical context, hardware, and IR and KM functionality presented in AWMT, she concluded that "the article has been used as a symbol for a number of different concepts. Although most citing authors affirm various viewpoints presented by Bush, there have been critics" (Smith, 1991, p. 278). Smith (1991, p. 272) cited Bar-Hillel (1957) as a critic of memex-based KM by association who had held that the idea of approximating the association of ideas in the human mind by a co-occurrence chain of indexes to be traced by machine held very little promise.

Recently Buckland (2003, p. 680) has cited both his own and Smith's analyses in summing up nicely the state of misinterpretation of AWMT.

> the iconic status of Vannevar Bush and his essay "As We May Think" is doubly interesting as a case study: first as a cult [phenomenon] in its own right, examined by Smith (1981,1991); and secondly in showing how a lack of historical awareness results in an uncritical, mythic tradition, and the erasure of history (Buckland, 1992).

Buckland's phrase "erasure of history" refers here to his exposure and critique of the tendency in some sectors of information science literature to identify the birth of the discipline with the 1945 publishing of AWMT, thus ignoring such earlier landmarks as the 1920s innovations of Emanuel Goldberg, the 1930s prognostications of Paul Otlet and Walter Schurmeyer, Bush's earlier writings about the memex (1932–1939), and electronic document retrieval technology (Buckland, 1992, p. 284; cf. Buckland, 2002).

The Memex in *ARIST*, 1966–2005

Throughout four decades of *ARIST*, authors from many areas of information science have cited the memex. Already in the inaugural volume, Taylor's (1966, p. 16) statement that "Bush's far-sighted predictions are only beginning to be realizable now" offered a plausible temporal explanation for the frequency of references to the memex: technology had begun to catch up with AWMT. Seventeen years later, Kochen (1983, p. 299) offered a different explanation when he said that memex and World Brain made information science "visibly relevant and central to society." But how extensively had memex and associationism diffused through the various areas of information science and technology? A search of *ARIST* indexes revealed that 24 chapters from 19 volumes mentioned Bush or the memex. These chapters covered several areas of information science, which are enumerated here in approximate chronological order of first mention:

- **Records management** used the memex file organization by association (van Dam & Michener, 1967, p. 197). Four decades later, metadata, still linkable through association, aided records management (Gilliland-Swetland, 2005, p. 230).

- Memex "opened the way for a new era in **documentation**" following World War II, replacing the American Documentation Institute's focus on microforms with the broader issues that AWMT had suggested (Shera & Cleveland, 1977, pp. 254–255).

- **Artificial intelligence** drew on Bush's belief that a machine could augment human mental powers. This augmentation dealt primarily with **information storage and retrieval** as it applied to artificial intelligence (Smith, 1980, 1987).

- Commentators on **interactive computing** credited the memex with providing inspiration for this field and even with being its ultimate point of origin (Hjerppe, 1986, p. 143; citing Rheingold, 1985, p. 176). However, Rheingold's assertion that AWMT influenced computer pioneers such as Engelbart, Licklider, and Berners-Lee contradicts the statements of these pioneers (see, respectively, Waldrop, 2001, p. 216; Kahn & Nyce, 1991, pp. 136–137; Berners-Lee & Fischetti, 1999, p. 5) that no direct, conscious link connected AWMT to their work (cf. Figure 2.1). Hjerppe (1986) also cited the interactive nature of the memex as the foundation of **electronic publishing**, a theme echoed by Peek and Pomerantz (1998, p. 323), who also noted the influence of memex on **scholarly publishing**, as did Fox and Urs (2002, p. 504).

- **Multimedia** systems have used the memex as a benchmark (e.g., Lunin, 1987), because of its integration of text, graphics, and sound recordings. Buckland and Liu (1995, p. 391) cited AWMT as one of the inspirations for multimedia systems.

- In discussing the concepts of **optical media** and of inter-item association, Fox described the memex as "a desktop portal to the world's store of recorded knowledge that would build on and give expression to the manifold associations among information items," thus identifying it as a precursor to the concept of **information portals**, so important in Web design today (Fox, 1988, p. 100; cf. Börner, Chen, & Boyack, 2003, p. 187).

- "The dream [of **office automation**] began with Bush and his Memex ..." (Martin, 1988, p. 217).

- Rorvig (1988) mentioned Bush in a survey of the development of **psychometrics**.

- In their review of **hypertext and hypermedia** (i.e., the combination of hypertext and multimedia), Cronin and Davenport (1993, p. 19) cited "The role of hypertext in training and orientation—[as] one of the memex applications envisaged by Bush." Speaking more broadly, Blustein and Staveley (2001, p. 299) stated that "Vannevar Bush is often cited as the visionary who described semi-automated hypertext" (cf. Börner et al., 2003, p. 187).

- Newby (1993, p. 214) measured **virtual reality** against the memex, stating that "information access in this virtual world would be as easy as, say, Memex."

- As regards the **history of information science**, Buckland and Liu (1995) detailed the influence of AWMT on hypermedia and multimedia (p. 391) and placed Bush accurately in context with other pioneers such as Paul Otlet (p. 392) and Emanuel Goldberg (p. 393).

- Pottenger, Callahan, and Padgett (2001, p. 104) noted that "it is Bush's 'memex' which still drives much conceptual work in **distributed information management** ... much of what is being done now ... is an attempt to fulfill Bush's seminal vision of 50 years ago."

- Pottenger et al. (2001, p. 83) also noted the relevance of Bush's notion of researchers as "trailblazers" for **librarianship** in the electronic age, with the suggestion that it implied a new role for librarians as "knowledge navigators," "explorers," and "trackers" who "carve paths" through knowledge network environments. Fox and Urs (2002, p. 541) echoed this emphasis on trails in their article on **digital library design**.

- As Tim Berners-Lee continued to develop **communication via the Web,** he encountered AWMT and the writings of Ted Nelson. Herring (2002, p. 126) may have been referring to Berners-Lee's acknowledgment of these parallel ideas when she wrote that the memex influenced Berners-Lee's *goal* (rather than his accomplishments).

- According to Finholt (2002, p. 78), Bush anticipated **collaboratories** as he explored ways for scientists to keep up with the "explosion of scientific knowledge."

- With regard to **human cognition**, Börner et al. (2003, p. 187) attributed "thinking-by-association" in the **visualization of knowledge domains** (more specifically, the visualization of the domain structure of the scientific disciplines) to memex. Dumais (2004, p. 208) discussed **cognition through associative reasoning** and **latent semantic analysis** in terms of a memex that "would be an extension of the personal memory belonging to an individual, and would work in a fashion analogous to the human brain, that is, by association." Pottenger et al. (2001, p. 82) viewed such an extension of personal memory as "a hint of cyborgian melding of reader and machine."

- AWMT's connections with **archival enterprise** were adumbrated in Gilliland-Swetland's (2005, p. 230) description of archivists' and records managers' reactions to the memex.

As documented in the pages of *ARIST*, then, authors writing about some 25 information science topical areas have acknowledged the memex. In some cases this was simply paying homage to Bush's notion of the memex, largely as a matter of scholarly ritualism. In others, memex-related contributions were presented as landmarks that catalyzed or gave impetus to the areas. Overall, reference to the memex in the pages of *ARIST* might be characterized as widespread and continual, with citations being both ritualistic and substantive in character. Interestingly, KM by association appears in 14 of the 25 memex-related areas, supporting the view that associationist assumptions, which continue to exert an influence on information science, have played a significant role in generating references to memex.

The Hand of Mammon: 1985 Onward

Alongside episodes of ignorance, omission, and misinterpretation, one can also discern, from 1985 on, the *commercialization* of the memex name, which has frequently been accompanied by misuse of the concept or wholesale distortion of it. As some companies and other organizations assumed the memex name, they tended to relate their projects loosely to the KM concepts inherent in the memex. For example, Memex Information Engines, Ltd., marketed a database of cataloging records that appeared to bear minimal relationship to Bush's original idea (Neate, 1985). In 1986, vendors and reviewers began to compare CD-ROMs with the memex (De Gennaro, 1985; Hegarty, 1988; Mason, 1986; Rogers, 1986), thus envisioning an integration of the IR functions of CD storage and access with memex KM capabilities. Indeed, Nyce and Kahn (1991, p. ix) noted that AWMT was "discovered" at the first CD-ROM conference in 1986, hosted by Microsoft.

However, some commercial usage of the memex name revealed a true awareness of AWMT. In 1988, Rice (1988b, p. 141) stated that microcomputer database management systems that interface to online catalogs "will create the potential for an end user remote-access workstation that will be more like Vannevar Bush's Memex than anything to date." He also noted that "online searching and the use of CD-ROM databases and database-management systems on microcomputers fit the memex image well" (Rice, 1988a, p. 14). In spite of the commercial interest and activity, Brunelle and McClelland (1987, p. 42) wrote in "As We May Think, *Revisited*" (emphasis added) that "perhaps one reason that available technologies have not been developed to the point where they could represent a prototype memex is that the economic motivation is not present." In 1990, the MemRI (Memex Research Institute) of California State University at Chico proposed MARC standards for the cataloging of electronic information as an "intermediate step on the road to a true 'memex'" (Brownrigg & Butler, 1990, p. 22). Given Bush's own critical stance vis-à-vis the awkward and time-consuming demands of the library-based knowledge retrieval of his day, one wonders what he would have thought of these library cataloging references to the memex by Memex Information Engines, Rice, and the MemRI (Bush, 1970, p. 191; Sloan, 1998, pp. 122–123; citing Bush, 1945a).

Commercial usage of the memex name moved even further away from the memex-based concept of KM by association. Cawkell (1989) compared MediaMaker, a multimedia editor, to the memex, but offered no obvious attribution to Bush. In reporting on the Memex database system created by Content Legal Systems, Williamson (1989) did not note any connection to Bush. Kinney (1992) proposed a personal information management technology called Memex-TV, which combined IR and entertainment but bore little resemblance to Bush's memex. Wildstrom (1998, p. 19) promoted the reliability of e-books, terming memex the first e-book and Bush "the first casualty in a long line of failed electronic Gutenbergs" (cf. Hughes, 2003; Wang, 2003). In 1988, Memex Press, Inc., announced a database of American colleges and universities (Jacsó, 1998). The U.K.-based Memex Technology, Ltd., provides security organizations with IR products, called "intelligence software" (Gardner, 2002). Memex Electronics, Inc., manufactures micro-machines with no obvious tie to Bush, whereas Memex Optical Media Solutions, based in Switzerland, develops phase-change DVD technology. All these uses of the term "memex" illustrate the breadth of the concept's diffusion into contemporary culture and the appeal of the name to information technology developers and promoters.

Displaying some knowledge of Bush's memex vision, Tehrani (2000) echoed the title of AWMT in that of his article "Publisher's Outlook: As We May *Communicate*" (emphasis added). He used a description of the associative personal KM function of the memex and Bush's predictions in *Science, the Endless Frontier* to introduce Internet server technology developed by Lucent. Thomas (2000, pp. 169–170) compared ALPS (A Language for Process Specification) to the memex, noting that they shared the capability to specify a hypertext trail external to the documents being linked. Displaying a thorough understanding of the shared

KM potential of the memex, Chakrabarti, Srivastava, Subramanyam, and Tiwari (2000) named their Web browser assistant "Memex" and designed in it many of the features now called "computer assisted [or supported] collaborative work" (CSCW) (Kerven, 1993; Mills, 2003). In 2003, Microsoft promoted its MyLifeBits as at least a partial fulfillment of the memex, in that it would permit the scientist (or anyone else) to record and retrieve memories and life experiences (Pescovitz, 2003, p. 34; reporting on Gemmell, Bell, Lueder, Drucker, & Wong, 2002): In similar fashion, Bush had envisioned that the Cyclops camera and Vocoder could be used to store experiences on the memex. In the same year, Cohn (2003, p. 10) traced the ancestry of the tablet PC to Bush's ideas, noting that "the concept of a tablet PC goes back at least as far as 1945, with plans for a machine called the Memex."

Vannevar Bush Reanimated

Neither Bush nor the memex appeared in the *Library Literature* index from 1964 to 1989, in spite of numerous commercial uses of "Memex" in periodicals directed toward librarians. During this period, the memex fared better in the pages of *ARIST*, as has been noted. In 1989, Bush began to receive wider and more thoughtful notice. Two books about information science began with brief histories that included nods to Bush (Gabriel, 1989, pp. 2, 41; Lilley & Trice, 1989, pp. 4, 6, 11, 16). Moreover, Nyce and Kahn (1989) published an analysis of the memex, tracing Bush's inspirations and aspirations and the subsequent history of memex-inspired technology and KM. Nyce and Kahn's article was written prior to the emergence of the World Wide Web, but they presented an extensive analysis of the KM technology then available. Concurrently, Meyrowitz (1991) evaluated the development of hypertext technology with respect to the memex.

Nyce and Kahn (1991, p. ix) expanded their 1989 work "to determine what was known about Bush's Memex," gathering together many of Bush's writings on the memex and interspersing them with scholarly commentary to contextualize its creation, development, and legacy. One article in the book deserves special mention because of its emphasis on the heart of the memex concept—the associative KM function. In that piece, Oren (1991) examined the memex concept of associative trails as it changed over the years and discussed its treatment in memex-related literature. For example, in 1945 Bush envisioned the memex as slower than the human mind but generating associative trails that "do not fade" (Bush, 1991a, pp. 103–104; Oren, 1991, p. 319; citing Bush, 1945a). However, by 1967, the memex would operate "at lightning speed" and weight trails by their recentness and frequency of use: In other words, less-used trails would fade, whereas those receiving greater use would be retained and refined (Oren, 1991, p. 320; citing Bush, 1967b, p. 22; 1970). In his essay, Oren noted that memex mimicked the associative trails of the human mind, even to the point of "forgetting" associations:

This second-generation "adaptive memex" would not follow trails that were relatively faint or old (p. 320). The endpoints of trails, however, would remain undimmed and unaltered, unlike human memories. Oren likened this functionality to agent software, in which intelligent software makes decisions about information based on the user's previous interactions. The modern computer and World Wide Web make use of this agent function, lending a glow of prescience to the memex legacy. Nevertheless, Oren did ask whether associationism could serve as an adequate or exclusive model of mental functioning.

Shortly after the appearance of Nyce and Kahn's volume, Buckland (1992, 2002) published historical studies of the events that led, and did not lead, to the memex concept. Furthermore, Burke (1992) expanded an earlier essay (Burke, 1991) into a thorough history of Bush's success in founding the National Science Foundation (NSF) despite failures in other areas, such as the work on the Rapid Selector. In 1994, Burke published yet another authoritative work on trans-memex technology, which dealt with the code-breaking functions of another Bush contraption, the Comparator. The Rapid Selector and the Comparator, which never advanced beyond the prototype stage, represented an approach very close to Bush's conceptualization of the memex; Buckland's and Burke's studies demonstrated just how ethereal the memex notion was. The fact that the memex design was never implemented in physical form does not gainsay the inspiration Bush provided to Engelbart and Nelson.

Patterson and Yaffe presented literature supporting Bush's view of human thought processes as "omni-directional association" (1994, p. 270; quoting Tsai, 1988, p. 4) and as nodes with associative connections (Patterson & Yaffe, 1994, p. 270; citing Bobrow & Norman, 1975). Skagestad (1996, pp. 228, 239), in an article about patterns of human and machine "cognition," suggested that Bush had vindicated philosophers Charles Sanders Peirce (1887) and Alan M. Turing (1965) in viewing the computing machine not as a mind-*imitating* machine, but as a mind-*complementing* machine. In this context, Skagestad referred explicitly to memory: "The Memex, finally, was intended to replicate, not indeed the human mind, but one very important function of the human mind, namely memory, as is signified by its name [memory extender]" (Skagestad, 1996, p. 231; citing Nyce & Kahn, 1991, pp. 61–64). Similarly, Zachary's lucid biography of Bush provided insight into his preoccupation with creating a machine capable of performing KM in a manner that would mimic and augment the organic human mind through association (Zachary, 1997, pp. 400–401). However, neither Skagestad, nor Zachary, nor other reviewers delved much into the psychological literature covering alternative models of cognition, memory, and reasoning, or other closely related psychological topics.

Mentions of memex in 1994 and 1995 frequently implied (somewhat incorrectly) that AWMT inspired computer technology. For example, Levy (1994, p. 47) stated that "[Engelbart] was the first to implement windows in computer screens, transforming a single video monitor to the multiscreened hydra envisioned by Bush with his memex machine," whereas Hafner (1995, p. 76), in her *Newsweek* article "Have Your Agent Call My Agent," implied a connection between the memex and contemporary computer agents—programs enabling a computer to act as an agent for a person.

In sum, various authors and editors (Smith, Meyrowitz, Nyce and Kahn, Buckland, Burke, Zachary, and others) returned Bush to the public eye in the late 1980s and 1990s. Their probing analyses set the stage for a more accurate examination of subsequent references to the memex.

Memex Influence on Shared KM and the World Wide Web, 1993

Some scholars (e.g., Fairthorne, 1958, pp. 135–136) criticized the KM features of the memex as representing merely another form of conventional personal KM. However, a key strength of the memex concept (whether it was original or not) lay in its expansion of indexing through links (what librarians might have called cross-indexing) and the sharing of links among users. Memex links could scale to handle vast quantities of information far more easily than cross-indexed indexes. Further, memex users could transfer these chains from one machine to another, facilitating shared KM. Contemporaneous librarians and scholars would have had some difficulty in instantiating these ideas with the tools of their day. However, the personal KM that Fairthorne knew has since metamorphosed into shared KM of the World Wide Web, as developed by Berners-Lee (see Figure 2.1).

The memex idea of true shared KM began to receive attention in 1993, as evidenced by Kerven's citation of the memex in his dissertation on CSCW via hypermedia:

> The origins of the hypermedia can be traced back to 1945 with the conception of the memex system, a mechanized scientific literature browsing system. ... With the advent of computers, and later, high-power workstations, the concepts behind memex became realizable. (Kerven, 1993, abstract; cf. Mills, 2003)

Furthermore, Rivera and Singh (1994, p. 91) drew parallels between the hypermedia technology of the memex and Mosaic, the first popular Web browser, whereas Oettinger pursued a more pragmatic theme in his keynote address to the 2000 annual meeting of the American Society for Information Science and Technology, as reported by Rogers and Oder (2000, p. 20):

> The Harvard info guru [Oettinger] called Vannevar Bush's famous "Memex" vision "the holy grail of the artificial

intelligentsia" and charged that it had become a meaningless "bait and switch" vision. He went on to assert that "we have made great progress on information technology as applied to information transfer, but we are losing ground on the problem of extracting knowledge from data."

The Influence of Memex on Literary Theory

To provide some examples of how and when the memex concept has diffused through different areas, this and the following sections consider its influence on literary theory, marketing, library science, and education. References to memex in these fields demonstrate the spreading impact of the memex concept, often involving a rather uncritical acceptance of associationism.

Manifestations of what we know today as hypertext literature appear to have a longer history than is generally supposed; indeed, they are already discernable in medieval Byzantine manuscripts. For example, the eleventh-century Theodore Psalter contains an elaborate system of connections between marginal illustrations and the Psalm text, as well as special marks that link the disconnected texts that comprise various liturgical rites (Nikolova-Houston, 2004). As a result, the Theodore Psalter may be read linearly or in reader-controlled segments.

In more recent times, Ted Nelson (drawing on AWMT) contributed heavily to hypertext literary theory (Jonassen, 1986; Patterson & Yaffe, 1994, p. 270; Tsai, 1988, pp. 3–4) and has published *Literary Machines*, itself a hypertextual book that defines and promotes the use of non-linear text (Nelson, 1987). However, it was only in the 1990s that the literature of literary theory began to cite the memex directly. Donatelli and Winthrop-Young (1995) included "Memex Revisited" (Bush, 1967b, pp. 75–101) and *From Memex to Hypertext* (Nyce & Kahn, 1991) in a bibliography of the history and theory of mediality (i.e., relatedness to media) of literature. Landow (1992, pp. 17–18) expressed eloquently the memex influence on critical and cultural theory:

> Perhaps most interesting to one considering the relation of Bush's ideas to contemporary critical and cultural theory is that this engineer began by rejecting some of the fundamental assumptions of the information technology that had increasingly dominated—and some would say largely created—Western thought since Gutenberg. Moreover, Bush wished to replace the essentially linear fixed methods that had produced the triumphs of capitalism and industrialism with what are essentially poetic machines—machines that work according to analogy and association, machines that capture the anarchic brilliance of human imagination. Bush,

we perceive, assumed that science and poetry work in essentially the same way.

Hypertextual literature (i.e., text with a variable sequence of passages rather than a strictly linear progression) comprises one facet of contemporary critical and cultural theory. For example, Crawford (1996) has presented the parallels in the associative thought processes used in the memex and in the poetry of William Carlos Williams. This parallel becomes less *outré* in light of an attested meeting between Williams and Bush, each of whom impressed the other favorably (p. 665). Travis (1996, pp. 116–117) traced the origin of hypertextual fiction to AWMT and suggested that the genre would not survive unless it changed to adopt more of the multimedia aspect of the memex, a change that would appeal to the portion of the population enamored of television, cinema, and video games. Johnson (1997, p. 119; quoting Bush, 1945a) discussed the memex's impact on literature, contrasting it with traditional librarianship:

> The Memex would not see the world as a librarian does, as an endless series of items to be filed away on the proper shelf. It would see the world the way a *poet* does: a world teeming with associations, minglings, continuities. And the trails would keep that radiant universe bound together.

Hypertext fiction has its supporters. In a book entitled *Writing Space*, Bolter (2000, pp. 42–43) explored the differences between hypertext and conventional fiction, citing Bush, Nelson, and several philosophers of literary theory:

> Nelson argued that hypertext was natural or true to our tradition of literacy, as when he claimed to have discovered the fact that "literature" is a system of interconnected writing. By this logic, ironically, hypertext becomes a transparent form that actually captures and reveals the structure of the underlying written record. The supporters of print ... will challenge the hypertextual definition of interactivity: letting the reader choose links only gives the illusion of control, which is really withheld from the reader. If authors prescribe links, they deny the reader the choice of making her own associations, so that a printed novel or essay actually gives the reader greater freedom to interact with the ideas presented. This debate turns on the question: which form is better at constituting the real, the authentic, or the natural?

Interestingly, an author's prescribing hypertext links to "deny the reader the choice," as postulated by these advocates of print fiction, confounds Nelson's (1987, p. 0/2) definition of hypertext as "non-sequential writing with reader-controlled links." Compounding the issue is the fact that Bush actually presented two different concepts under the guise of "trails." In one, he postulated *fixed* trails of associated ideas, "blazed" by researchers or professional "trailblazers" and published with microfilms or transferred from one researcher to another (Bush, 1945a, p. 108). Bush's second concept, coming later in his career, involved *variable* trails of ideas linked by association, in parallel to idea linkages in the human mind (cf. Savage-Knepshield & Belkin, 1999). Literary theory will require firmer definitions of its terms before resolving this issue, but the associative concept articulated in AWMT and Nelson's notion of hypertextuality will continue to figure prominently in the debate.

Some Recent Influence of AWMT on Marketing Thought

Various for-profit and nonprofit organizations and their representatives had used, and even exploited, the memex name since at least 1985, as has already been noted. With the commercial adoption of Internet and Web technologies in the 1990s, marketing theorists began anew to cite the memex. For example, Hoffman and Novak (1996, p. 53) presented marketing applications of hypertext theory, citing "Bush, Nelson, and others with regard to hypertext/hypermedia marketing." In an article subtitled "As We May *Buy*" (emphasis added), Dorman (1997, p. 84) praised Bush's prescience while noting that marketplace logic and imperatives "significantly alter not only the blueprints of visionaries [such as Bush], but even the short-range plans of vendors as they constantly strive to extend the capabilities of our information processing systems for their own economic advantage." In both of these cases, the authors seem to imply that the memex may have *inspired* some part of hypertext-assisted marketing, but the links between the memex per se and the theory and practice of marketing seem to be indirect.

Memex in the Library

Although many *pre*-Web librarians recognized the potentially broad role that memex could play in changing overall library practice and KM, some did not. Virtually all of the pre-Web library literature that mentions the memex does so in the context of information storage and retrieval rather than in the broader context of KM: For example, Harter and Kister (1981, p. 1600) mentioned the memex in the course of describing online encyclopedias. Upham (1991, p. 72) remarked on the prevalence of memex-like IR in the practice of serials librarianship and noted the potential applicability of memex to overall KM functionality:

> I am reminded of the classic article "As We May Think" written by Vannevar Bush at the end of the second world war wherein he hypothesizes the MEMEX. I was, in fact, surprised that none of the authors mentioned it, although several

sounded as though it was in their thoughts. ... I believe we will have machines that will allow us to access and extract data from information sources throughout our country and ultimately from around the world, and that we can use this data to create files capable of fulfilling our own particular needs that can be set up in a format with which we are comfortable.

Post-Web librarians, however, came to embrace both the personal and the shared KM functionalities of memex as an inspiration for contemporary hypertext practice. Sloan (1998, pp. 122–123) emphasized the "profession of trailblazers" in AWMT to describe the future of librarianship in an environment of increasingly privatized information access. Wills (1999) elaborated on the incorporation of hypertext into library practice and Wright (2000, p. 591) noted the accuracy of Bush's vision of the widespread use of associative trails as expressed in AWMT. McFadden (2001, p. 1) invoked the name of memex in proposing that instruction in library science education should present a "seamless environment of tutorial or classroom learning managed and presented by electronic media and computing machines." In tandem with the birth and development of the Web, the flood of memex-related writings from 1989 and subsequent years accelerated recognition of the utility of memex ideas among librarians and influenced virtual or digital library development.

Influence of Memex on Education

The literature of education also saw its share of memex citations. However, these usually referred to the multimediality of memex, rather than KM by association. The emphasis on multimedia applications calls to mind the references to memex in the previous decade's information science literature (e.g., Lunin, 1987). Generally, the focus was interactive, multimedia-based electronic teaching. For example, Davis (1998) wrote an article entitled "As We May *Teach*" (emphasis added)—an obvious reference to AWMT—in which, drawing upon Bush's memex-related concepts, he proposed that the computer might serve as a hypertext learning and teaching tool. Barab, Young, and Wang (1999, p. 283) used the "fully active engagement conceptualized by Vannevar Bush in describing the historical precursor of hypertext, the 'Memex,'" as a benchmark for interactive learning exercises. Butler (2000, p. 630) called for geoscience education to "perfect the memex," by which he meant the development of teaching modules, available online without password protection and designed with "instructors providing the content and graphic designers, programmers, and cognitive experts adding their skills to produce the final product." Thus, the memex has influenced the development of educational theory and practice, albeit generally in an indirect fashion.

The foregoing sections on literary theory, marketing, library science, and education illustrate minimally how the memex concept diffused, how it was or could be applied, and how it tended to be accompanied by a somewhat routine acceptance of associationism.

Summary and Conclusions

First, we can safely say that the legacies of Bush and his memex endure and remain positive despite their 60-year journey over rocky roads. Although controversies may continue about whether Bush's concepts or technologies were original, or about his true place in history, his AWMT article retains its inspirational magic. Responses to Bush's concepts have been mixed over the years. Initial reactions to the memex were negative, but this state of affairs began to change by about 1960. Positive responses developed into invocation and inspiration in the 1960s, particularly as reflected in the pages of *ARIST*. And there was misinterpretation, as Nelson noted in 1972. In the 1980s various businesses, including software vendors, adopted the memex name, occasionally without knowing the origins and implications of the original concept. Between 1989 and 1994, the memex reemerged in the scholarly literature of information science. Bolstered by the advent of the Web, this reemergence prompted a new wave of interest as theorists in such fields as computer science, literature, marketing, post-Web librarianship, and education discovered and developed associative ("trails") thinking and applications in their respective fields. However, few writers in these fields questioned the psychological soundness of the associationist models underlying the memex concept or considered alternative models of human thinking and reasoning.

Second, although some textbooks since 1995 have tended to credit AWMT as a key root or origin of information science, personal computers, the Internet, the Web, and hypertext, that position distorts the historical record. The roots of information science reach much further back than 1945 and are more diverse than the memex, documentation, or IR; information science has roots in the behavioral and communication sciences as well (Harmon, 1971).

Third, future research on Bush's memex concept might well address other aspects of the overall context within which he formulated it. Some commentators find it easy to fault Bush for being vague or unoriginal in his writing, overlooking the fact that he shouldered the responsibility of managing several thousand scientists who worked on several hundred projects during World War II. The memex was not altogether original, but neither were many other breakthrough concepts, such as calculus, universal gravitation, or numerous Nobel laureate discoveries (Harmon, 1973): For example, the 1903 Wright Flier essentially was an amalgam of pre-existing air frame, bicycle, control, and engine technologies (Goodard, 2003). Breakthroughs often consist of new syntheses or *Gestalten* that are more than the sum of their parts: The memex qualifies as such a breakthrough.

Fourth, the memex concept provided an exemplary and relatively early integration of the personal and shared approaches to KM. Bush's successful emphasis on augmenting individual memory through the deployment of systems external to the mind highlights an enduring challenge. Indeed, Saracevic (1999, p. 1062) has posed the question:

> Are we evolving into two information sciences—plural? One that is computer science-based [e.g., SIGIR, TREC] focusing on IR, digital libraries, search engines and the like, and the other that is information science-based [e.g., ASIST], more attuned to interaction, users, and use, with little direct connection with development of systems, but still completely dependent on systems, thus, changing them relentlessly. ... The greatest payoff for information science will come if and when it successfully integrates systems and user research and applications.

Although Bush's mind-system synthesis proposal was not wholly original, it was sufficiently novel, appealing, and elegant to acquire a quasi-paradigmatic status over the years. Had the memex integrative vision been realized, would we have the apparent "two information sciences" gap that Saracevic laments?

Fifth, in line with the integration of personal and shared KM concepts, the memex legacy suggests the need for a more global approach to both KM orientations. In regard to personal KM, there is a need to bridge the disparate literatures of areas that can contribute to the study of information behavior, such as cognitive science, artificial intelligence, management and decision sciences, and particularly the literatures and schools of psychology (neo-behaviorism, gestaltism, consciousness, structuralism, functionalism, associationism, etc.) and the subfields of psychology (personality theory, motivation, cognitive, individual differences, consciousness, emotions, learning, development, etc.). A more global approach to personal KM might have averted our preoccupation with associationism, among other things. As regards shared KM, a more global approach might build on recent studies of information behavior, such as those oriented to occupation, role, or demographics (Case, 2006; MacIntosh-Murray & Choo, 2006). Such an approach might bring into system design the many research methods that have been developed and successfully utilized in the sciences, humanities, and social sciences. *The Sage Encyclopedia of Social Science Research Methods* (Lewis-Beck & Liao, 2004), for example, summarizes dozens of research approaches and explains hundreds of methodologies. The topics of research, search, and inquiry (not to mention search engines) are close topical neighbors in the KM arena. In short, there appears to be a need to adopt a more global approach to the study of personal information behavior to avoid, for example, instances of chronic insularity such as the long preoccupation with associationism. More global approaches to shared KM and information behavior are needed as well. More importantly, the broad personal and shared realms appear to require closer integration if we are to bridge Saracevic's "two information sciences." Recent memex-inspired thinking on personal information management appears to be bridging the systems-user divide (Teevan, Jones, & Bederson, 2006) through such applications as personal image monitoring and storage (Czerwinski, Gage, Gemmell, Marshall, Pérez-Quiñones, Skeels, et al., 2006), autobiographical databases (Gemmell, Bell, & Lueder, 2006), and reducing the cognitive effort involved in organizing personal information (Cutrell, Dumais, & Teevan, 2006). Nevertheless, it is important to reestablish the bridge between current information behavior studies and (at least) the concepts presented in introductory psychology courses and other key areas.

Sixth, as argued earlier, authors who cite Bush, AWMT, or the memex need to do so less ritualistically, more critically, and for substantive reasons. Lessons from the memex are perhaps better incorporated into studies as one of many fundamental idea sets, rather than as the *alpha* and *omega*. We should move beyond the memex and its heavy reliance on associationism as the sole explanation of the way the mind works. We need, for example, to heed critics such as Bar-Hillel (1957), who warned that approximating human brain associations and matching them with co-occurrence indexes via a machine held little promise because matches would essentially produce similarity and equivalence relations rather than links to different, more novel items. Similarly, Verhoeff, Goffman, and Belzer (1961) demonstrated mathematically the inherent, basic inefficiency of using Boolean functions for information retrieval and the prospect of sub-optimal retrieval because of relevance/recall tradeoffs. These early criticisms are all the more remarkable when one considers that associative links depend on Boolean operators for connectivity and that hybridization of associative linking with Boolean functions might thus be doubly ineffective. We need to build upon both the legacies of pioneers, such as Bush, Wells, and others, and the dialectics initiated by their critics.

Epilogue

For years, the world recognized Vannevar Bush primarily for his administration of scientific research during World War II (particularly the atomic bomb program), for his 1930s Differential Analyzer analog computer, and for his role in the founding of the U.S. NSF Foundation. Since 1980, the NSF has given the "Vannevar Bush Award" to numerous scientists (National Science Board, 2005). Yet, not until the 1990s did the world come to appreciate the magnitude of Bush's vision of KM by associative trails. Wang (1999, p. 15) has said: "Bush had great ideas, and he made great errors. Pointing out these errors does not undermine his accomplishments; rather, it reminds us that error is an unavoidable part of imagination and invention." Bush believed that individuals should be judged not by their words, family, position, beliefs, or efforts, but by their accomplishments (Zachary, 1997, pp. 8, 408). Bush had many accomplishments and the products of his creative vision, among which the memex looms large, have garnered favorable judgment. Over six decades after its initial formulation, the legacy of Bush's memex endures, in spite of shortcomings and critics, and continues to be written.

Acknowledgments

The authors wish to thank Don Turnbull for initiating the discussion that led to this paper and the *ARIST* editors and reviewers who helped so much to modify and focus the review.

References

American Psychological Association. (1963). *Reports of the American Psychological Association's project on scientific information exchange in psychology.* Washington, DC: The Association.

Barab, S. A., Young, M. F., & Wang, J. (1999). The effects of navigational and generative activities in hypertext learning on problem solving and comprehension. *International Journal of Instructional Media, 26,* 283–309.

Bar-Hillel, Y. (1957). A logician's reaction to recent theorizing on information search systems. *American Documentation, 8,* 103–113.

Becker, J., & Hayes, R. M. (1963). *Information storage and retrieval: Tools, elements, theories.* New York: Becker & Hayes.

Berners-Lee, T. (circa 2000). *Frequently asked questions.* Retrieved July 22, 2005, from www.w3.org/People/Berners-Lee/FAQ.html#Influences

Berners-Lee, T., & Fischetti, M. (1999). *Weaving the Web: The original design and ultimate destiny of the World Wide Web by its inventor.* New York: Harper Collins.

Blustein, J., & Staveley, M. S. (2001). Methods of generating and evaluating hypertext. *Annual Review of Information Science and Technology, 35,* 299–335.

Bobrow, D. G., & Norman, D. A. (1975). Memory schemata. In D. G. Bobrow & A. Collins (Eds.), *Representation and understanding: Studies in cognitive science* (pp. 131–149). New York: Academic Press.

Bolter, J. D. (2000). *Writing space: Computers, hypertext, and the remediation of print* (2nd ed.). Mahwah, NJ: Erlbaum.

Börner, K., Chen, C., & Boyack, K. W. (2003). Visualizing knowledge domains. *Annual Review of Information Science and Technology, 37,* 179–255.

Brownrigg, E., & Butler, B. (1990). An electronic library communications format: A definition and development proposal for MARC III. *Library Hi Tech, 8*(3), 21–26.

Brownson, H. L. (1960). Research on handling scientific information. In H. S. Sharp (Ed.), *Readings in information retrieval* (pp. 630–659). New York: Scarecrow.

Brunelle, B., & McClelland, B. (1987). As we may think, revisited. *National Online Meeting Proceedings,* 41–46.

Buckland, M. K. (1992). Emanuel Goldberg, electronic document retrieval, and Vannevar Bush's memex. *Journal of the American Society for Information Science, 43*, 284–294.

Buckland, M. K. (2002, November). *Histories, heritages, and the past: The case of Emanuel Goldberg.* Paper presented at the History and Heritage of Scientific and Technical Information Systems Conference, Philadelphia, PA.

Buckland, M. K. (2003). Five grand challenges for library research. *Library Trends, 51*, 675–686.

Buckland, M. K., & Liu, Z. M. (1995). History of information science. *Annual Review of Information Science and Technology, 30*, 385–416.

Burke, C. (1991). A practical view of memex: The career of the Rapid Selector. In J. M. Nyce & P. Kahn (Eds.), *From memex to hypertext: Vannevar Bush and the mind's machine* (pp. 145–164). Boston: Academic Press.

Burke, C. (1992). The other memex: The tangled career of Vannevar Bush's information machine, the Rapid Selector. *Journal of the American Society for Information Science, 43*, 648–657.

Burke, C. (1994). *Information and secrecy: Vannevar Bush, Ultra, and the other memex.* Metuchen, NJ: Scarecrow Press.

Bush, V. (1936). Instrumental analysis. *Bulletin of the American Mathematical Society, 42*, 649–669.

Bush, V. (1939). *Mechanization and the record.* Unpublished manuscript, Washington, DC.

Bush, V. (1945a, July). As we may think. *Atlantic Monthly, 176*(1), 101–108.

Bush, V. (1945b, November). As we may think: A top US scientist foresees a possible future world in which man-made machines will start to think. *Life, 19*, 112–114, 116, 118, 121, 123–124.

Bush, V. (1946). *Endless horizons.* Washington, DC: Public Affairs Press.

Bush, V. (1947). *Selector speech to librarians.* Library of Congress, Papers of Vannevar Bush, Burchard File, Washington, DC.

Bush, V. (1949). *Modern arms and free men: A discussion of the role of science in preserving democracy.* New York; Simon and Schuster.

Bush, V. (1965, May). Science pauses. *Fortune, 71*, 116–119, 167–168, 172, 174.

Bush, V. (1967a). As we may think. In M. Kochen (Ed.), *The growth of knowledge: Readings on organization and retrieval of information* (pp. 23–35). New York: Wiley. (Originally published in 1945)

Bush, V. (1967b). *Science is not enough.* New York: Morrow.

Bush, V. (1970). *Pieces of the action.* New York: Morrow.

Bush, V. (1991a). As we may think. In J. M. Nyce & P. Kahn (Eds.), *From memex to hypertext: Vannevar Bush and the mind's machine* (pp. 85–110). Boston: Academic Press. (Originally published in 1945)

Bush, V. (1991b). The inscrutable 'thirties: Reflections upon a preposterous decade. In J. M. Nyce & P. Kahn (Eds.), *From memex to hypertext: Vannevar Bush and the mind's machine* (pp. 67–79). Boston: Academic Press. (Originally published in 1946)

Bush, V. (1991c). Memex II. In J. M. Nyce & P. Kahn (Eds.), *From memex to hypertext: Vannevar Bush and the mind's machine* (pp. 165–184). Boston: Academic Press. (Originally published in 1959)

Butler, J. C. (2000). An academic challenge for the year 2000: Perfect the memex. *Computers & Geosciences, 26,* 627–633.

Cambor, K. (1999). Remember this. *American Scholar, 68*(4), 51–58.

Case, D. O. (2006). Information behavior. *Annual Review of Information Science and Technology, 40,* 293–327.

Cawkell, T. (1989). From memex to mediamaker. *Electronic Library, 7,* 278–286.

Chakrabarti, S., Srivastava, S., Subramanyam, M., & Tiwari, M. (2000). Using memex to archive and mine community Web browsing experience. *Computer Networks, 33,* 669–684.

Cohn, M. (2003). Tablet PCs fill the slate. *Internet World, 9*(1), 10.

Cole, C., Leide, J. E., Large, A., Beheshti, J., & Brooks, M. (2005). Putting it together online: Information need identification for the domain novice user. *Journal of the American Society for Information Science and Technology, 56,* 684–694.

Crawford, T. H. (1996). *Paterson,* Memex, and Hypertext. *American Literary History, 8,* 665–682.

Cronin, B., & Davenport, E. (1993). Social intelligence. *Annual Review of Information Science and Technology, 28,* 3–44.

Cutrell, E., Dumais, S. T., & Teevan, J. (2006). Searching to eliminate personal information management. *Communications of the ACM, 49*(1), 58–64.

Czerwinski, M., Gage, D. W., Gemmell, J., Marshall, C. C., Pérez-Quiñones, M. A., Skeels, M. M., et al. (2006). Digital memories in an era of ubiquitous computing and abundant storage. *Communications of the ACM, 49*(1), 44–50.

Davenport, T. H., & Prusak, L. (2000). *Working knowledge: How organizations manage what they know.* Retrieved April 7, 2004, from www.lib.utexas.edu:2048/login?url=http://www.netlibrary.com/urlapi.asp?action=summary&v=1&bookid=7259

Davis, T. (1998). As we may teach. *Education + Training, 40,* 347–352.

De Gennaro, R. (1979). Research libraries enter the information age. *Library Journal, 104,* 2405–2410.

De Gennaro, R. (1985). Integrated online library systems: Perspectives, perceptions, & practicalities. *Library Journal, 110*(2), 37–40.

Donatelli, J., & Winthrop-Young, G. (1995). Literature and media change: A selective multidisciplinary bibliography. *Mosaic, 28*(4), 165–186.

Dorman, D. (1997). Exhibits reveal San Francisco's high-tech "underground": As we may buy. *American Libraries, 28*(7), 84.

Dumais, S. T. (2004). Latent semantic analysis. *Annual Review of Information Science and Technology, 38,* 189–230.

Engelbart, D. C. (1961). Special considerations of the individual as a user, generator, and retriever of information. *American Documentation, 12,* 121–125.

Engelbart, D. C. (1991). Letter to Vannevar Bush and program on human effectiveness. In J. M. Nyce & P. Kahn (Eds.), *From memex to hypertext: Vannevar Bush and the mind's machine* (pp. 235–236). Boston: Academic Press. (Originally written in 1962)

Fairthorne, R. A. (1958). Automatic retrieval of recorded information. In R. A. Fairthorne (Ed.), *Towards information retrieval* (pp. 135–138). London: Butterworths.

Finholt, T. A. (2002). Collaboratories. *Annual Review of Information Science and Technology, 36,* 73–107.

Foskett, D. J. (1964). *Science, humanism, and libraries*. London: C. Lockwood.

Fox, E. A. (1988). Optical disks and CD-ROM: Publishing and access. *Annual Review of Information Science and Technology, 23*, 85–124.

Fox, E. A., & Urs, S. R. (2002). Digital libraries. *Annual Review of Information Science and Technology, 36*, 503–589.

Gabriel, M. R. (1989). *A guide to the literature of electronic publishing: CD-ROM, desktop publishing, and electronic mail, books, and journals* (Foundations in Library and Information Science, Vol. 24). Greenwich, CT: JAI Press.

Gardner, D. (2002, June 16). Memex know-how adding inches to long arm of the law. *Scottish Media Newspapers Limited, The Sunday Herald*, p. 4.

Gardner, H. (1985). *The mind's new science: A history of the cognitive revolution*. New York: Basic Books.

Gemmell, J., Bell, G., & Lueder, R., (2006). MyLifeBits: A personal database for everything. *Communications of the ACM, 49*(1), 88–95.

Gemmell, J., Bell, G., Lueder, R., Drucker, S., & Wong, C. (2002). MyLifeBits: Fulfilling the memex vision. *ACM International Conference on Multimedia*, 235–238.

Gilliland-Swetland, A. (2005). Electronic records management. *Annual Review of Information Science and Technology, 39*, 219–253.

Goodard, S. B. (2003). *Race to the sky: The Wright brothers versus the United States government*. Jefferson, NC: McFarland.

Hafner, K. (1995, February 27). Have your agent call my agent. *Newsweek*, 76.

Hall, R. C. (1963). Early U.S. satellite proposals. *Technology and Culture, 4*, 411.

Hampden-Turner, C. (1981). *Maps of the mind*. New York: Collier.

Harmon, E. G. (1971). On the evolution of information science. *Journal of the American Society for Information Science, 22*, 235–241.

Harmon, E. G. (1973). *Human memory and knowledge: A systems approach* (Contributions in Librarianship and Information Science, No. 6). Westport, CT: Greenwood Press.

Harter, S. P., & Kister, K. F. (1981). Online encyclopedias: The potential. *Library Journal, 106*(15), 1600–1602.

Hawkins, R. R. (1960). *Production of micro-forms* (The State of the Library Art, v. 5, pt. 1). New Brunswick, NJ: Graduate School of Library Service, Rutgers University.

Hayes, R. M., & Becker, J. (1970). *Handbook of data processing for libraries*. New York: Becker & Hayes.

Hayes, R. M., & Becker, J. (1974). *Handbook of data processing for libraries* (2nd ed.). Los Angeles: Melville.

Hegarty, K. (1988). Build your own CD public access catalog. *Library Journal, 113*(12), 40–43.

Herring, S. C. (2002). Computer-mediated communication on the Internet. *Annual Review of Information Science and Technology, 36*, 109–168.

Hjerppe, R. (1986). Electronic publishing: Writing machines and machine writing. *Annual Review of Information Science and Technology, 21*, 123–166.

Hoffman, D. L., & Novak, T. P. (1996). Marketing in hypermedia computer-mediated environments: Conceptual foundations. *Journal of Marketing, 60*(3), 50–68.

Hughes, C. A. (2003). E-books. In M. A. Drake (Ed.), *Encyclopedia of library and information science* (2nd ed., Vol. 2, pp. 993–998). New York: Dekker.

Jacsó, P. (1998). Critical comparisons of American colleges and universities: Demotables, demographics, and world databases. *Database, 21*(5), 80–81.

Johnson, S. (1997). *Interface culture: How new technology transforms the way we create and communicate.* San Francisco: Harper Edge.

Jonassen, D. H. (1986). Hypertext principles for text and courseware design. *Educational Psychologist, 21*, 269–292.

Joyce, T., & Needham, R. M. (1958). The thesaurus approach to information retrieval. *American Documentation, 9*, 192–197.

Kahn, P., & Nyce, J. M. (1991). The idea of a machine: The later memex essays. In J. M. Nyce & P. Kahn (Eds.), *From memex to hypertext: Vannevar Bush and the mind's machine* (pp. 113–144). Boston: Academic Press.

Kerven, D. S. (1993). *An abstract architecture for distributed, object-oriented hypermedia systems.* Unpublished doctoral dissertation, University of Southwestern Louisiana.

Kinney, T. (1992). Memex meets Madonna: Multimedia at the intersection of information and entertainment. *Electronic Library, 10*, 133–138.

Kochen, M. (1967). The encyclopedia system idea. In M. Kochen (Ed.), *The growth of knowledge: Readings on organization and retrieval of information* (pp. 9–10). New York: Wiley.

Kochen, M. (1983). Information and society. *Annual Review of Information Science and Technology, 18*, 277–304.

Kurzweil, R. (1990). *The age of intelligent machines.* Cambridge, MA: MIT Press.

Landow, G. P. (1992). *Hypertext: The convergence of contemporary critical theory and technology.* Baltimore: Johns Hopkins University Press.

Lee, J. A. N. (Ed.). (1992). Time-sharing and interactive computing at MIT: Part II—Project MAC [Special issue]. *IEEE Annals of the History of Computing, 14*(2).

Levy, S. (1994). *Insanely great: The life and times of Macintosh, the computer that changed everything.* New York: Viking.

Lewis-Beck, B. A., & Liao, T. F. (2004). *The Sage encyclopedia of social science research methods* (3 Vols.). Thousand Oaks, CA: Sage.

Licklider, J. C. R. (1960). Man-computer symbiosis. *IRE Transactions on Human Factors in Electronics HFE-1, 1*(1), 4–10.

Licklider, J. C. R. (1965). *Libraries of the future.* Cambridge, MA: MIT Press.

Lilley, D. B., & Trice, R. W. (1989). *A history of information science, 1945–1985.* San Diego, CA: Academic Press.

Lunin, L. F. (1987). Electronic image information. *Annual Review of Information Science and Technology, 22*, 179–224.

A machine that thinks. (1945, July 23). *Time, 46*, 93–94.

MacIntosh-Murray, A., & Choo, C. W. (2006). Information failures in health care. *Annual Review of Information Science and Technology, 40*, 357–391.

Mandler, J. M., & Mandler, G. (1964). *Thinking: From association to Gestalt.* New York: Wiley.

Martin, T. H. (1988). Office automation. *Annual Review of Information Science and Technology, 23*, 217–235.

Marx, M. H., & Hillix, W. A. (1963). *Systems and theories in psychology.* New York: McGraw-Hill.

Mason, R. M. (1986). Woodstock in Seattle? CD-ROM & CD-I. *Library Journal, 111*(9), 50–51.

McCracken, H. (1999). How the Web was spun. *PC World, 17*(12), 138–139.

McDougal, W. A. (1985). *The heavens and the earth: A political history of the space age.* New York: Basic Books.

McFadden, T. G. (2001). Introduction. *Library Trends, 50,* 1–7.

Meyrowitz, N. (1991). Hypertext: Does it reduce cholesterol, too? In J. M. Nyce & P. Kahn (Eds.), *From memex to hypertext: Vannevar Bush and the mind's machine* (pp. 287–318). Boston: Academic Press.

Mills, K. L. (2003). Computer-supported cooperative work. In M. A. Drake (Ed.), *Encyclopedia of library and information science* (2nd ed., Vol. 1, pp. 678–684). New York: Dekker.

National Science Board. (2005, October 14). *Vannevar Bush Award.* Retrieved December 13, 2005, from www.nsf.gov/nsb/awards/bush/bush.htm

Neate, G. (1985). *Memex: Evaluation of a search engine.* Oxford, UK: Bodleian Library.

Nelson, T. H. (1965). A file structure for the complex, the changing and the indeterminate. *Proceedings of the ACM 20th National Conference,* 84–100.

Nelson, T. H. (1972). As we will think. *Online 72 Conference Proceedings, 1,* 439–454.

Nelson, T. H. (1987). *Literary machines: The report on, and of, Project Xanadu concerning word processing, electronic publishing, hypertext, thinkertoys, tomorrow's intellectual revolution, and certain other topics including knowledge, education and freedom.* Swarthmore, PA: Theodor H. Nelson.

Newby, G. B. (1993). Virtual reality. *Annual Review of Information Science and Technology, 28,* 187–229.

Nikolova-Houston, T. (2004). *Byzantine hypertexts.* Retrieved November 7, 2005, from http://translate.google.com/translate?hl=de&sl=en&u=www.ischool.utexas.edu/ ~slavman/hypertexts

Nyce, J. M., & Kahn, P. (1989). Innovation, pragmaticism, and technological continuity: Vannevar Bush's memex. *Journal of the American Society for Information Science, 40,* 214–221.

Nyce, J. M., & Kahn, P. (Eds.). (1991). *From memex to hypertext: Vannevar Bush and the mind's machine.* Boston: Academic Press.

Oettinger, A. G. (2000). Knowledge innovations: The endless adventure. *Bulletin of the American Society for Information Science, 27*(2), 10–15.

Oppenheim, C. (1994). [Review of Colin Burke, *Information and secrecy: Vannevar Bush, Ultra, and the other memex*]. *International Journal of Information and Library Research, 6,* 94–96.

Oppenheim, C. (1999). [Review of G. P. Zachary, *Endless frontier*]. *Education for Information, 17,* 372–373.

Oren, T. (1991). Memex: Getting back on the trail. In J. M. Nyce & P. Kahn (Eds.), *From memex to hypertext: Vannevar Bush and the mind's machine* (pp. 319–338). Boston: Academic Press.

Overhage, C. F. J., & Harman, R. J. (1967). The on-line intellectual community and the information transfer system at MIT in 1975. In M. Kochen (Ed.), *The growth of knowledge: Readings on organization and retrieval of information* (pp. 77–95). New York: Wiley.

Patterson, D. A., & Yaffe, J. (1994). Hypermedia computer-based education in social work education. *Journal of Social Work Education, 30,* 267–277.

Peek, R. P., & Pomerantz, J. P. (1998). Electronic scholarly journal publishing. *Annual Review of Information Science and Technology, 33,* 321–356.

Peirce, C. S. (1887). Logical machines. *American Journal of Psychology, 1,* 165–170.

Pescovitz, D. (2003). Digital memories to last a lifetime. *Business 2.0, 4*(8), 34.

Pottenger, W. M., Callahan, M. R., & Padgett, M. A. (2001). Distributed information management. *Annual Review of Information Science and Technology, 35,* 79–113.

Project Xanadu. (2001, October 5). *Project Xanadu history.* Retrieved October 16, 2004, from http://xanadu.com/xuhistory.html

Pylyshyn, Z. W. (1970). *Perspectives on the computer revolution.* Englewood Cliffs, NJ: Prentice-Hall.

Radford, W. H. (1938). *Notes on arithmetical machine memoranda.* Unpublished manuscript, Cambridge, MA.

Radford, W. H. (1939). *Report on an investigation of the practicality of developing a rapid computing machine.* Unpublished manuscript, Cambridge, MA.

Randell, B. (1982a). The case of the missing memoranda. *IEEE Annals of the History of Computing, 4,* 66–67.

Randell, B. (1982b). From analytical engine to electronic digital computer: The contributions of Ludgate, Torres, and Bush. *IEEE Annals of the History of Computing, 4,* 327–341.

Randell, B. (1982c). *Origins of digital computers: Selected papers.* Berlin: Springer-Verlag.

Rheingold, H. (1985). *Tools for thought: The people and ideas behind the next computer revolution.* New York: Simon & Schuster.

Rice, J. G. (1988a). The dream of the memex. *American Libraries, 19*(1), 14–17.

Rice, J. G. (1988b). Serendipity and holism: The beauty of OPACs. *Library Journal, 113*(3), 138–141.

Rider, F. (1944). *The scholar and the future of the research library: A problem and its solution.* New York: Hadham Press.

Rivera, J. C., & Singh, S. K. (1994). MOSAIC: An educator's best friend. *T. H. E. Journal, 22*(3), 91–94.

Rogers, M. (1986, April 21). A library on a disc. *Newsweek,* 73.

Rogers, M., & Oder, N. (2000). Over 800 attend ASIS(&T) revival. *Library Journal, 125*(20), 20–22.

Rorvig, M. E. (1988). Psychometric measurement and information retrieval. *Annual Review of Information Science and Technology, 23,* 157–189.

Santrock, J. W. (2000). *Psychology.* New York: McGraw-Hill.

Saracevic, T. (1999). Information science. *Journal of the American Society for Information Science, 50,* 1051–1063.

Savage-Knepshield, P. A., & Belkin, N. J. (1999). Interaction in information retrieval: Trends over time. *Journal of the American Society for Information Science, 50,* 1067–1082.

Sharp, H. S. (1964). Preface to "As we may think." In H. S. Sharp (Ed.), *Readings in information retrieval* (p. 19). New York: Scarecrow.

Sharp, J. R. (1965). *Some fundamentals of information retrieval*. New York: House & Maxwell.

Shera, J. H., & Cleveland, D. B. (1977). History and foundations of information science. *Annual Review of Information Science and Technology, 12*, 249–275.

Skagestad, P. (1996). The mind's machines: The Turing machine, the memex, and the personal computer. *Semiotica, 111*, 217–243.

Sloan, B. (1998). Service perspectives for the digital library remote reference services. *Library Trends, 47*, 117–143.

Smith, L. C. (1980). Artificial intelligence applications in information systems. *Annual Review of Information Science and Technology, 15*, 67–105.

Smith, L. C. (1981). The influence of Bush's "memex" as an image of potentiality in information retrieval research and development. In R. N. Oddy, S. E. Robertson, C. J. van Rijsbergen, & P. W. Williams (Eds.), *Information Retrieval Research: Proceedings of the Symposium in Research and Development in Information Retrieval; 1980 June; Cambridge, England*. London: Butterworths.

Smith, L. C. (1987). Artificial intelligence and information retrieval. *Annual Review of Information Science and Technology, 22*, 41–77.

Smith, L. C. (1991). Memex as an image of potentiality revisited. In J. M. Nyce & P. Kahn (Eds.), *From memex to hypertext: Vannevar Bush and the mind's machine* (pp. 261–286). Boston: Academic Press.

Stern, N. F. (1978). *From ENIAC to UNIVAC: A case study in the history of technology*. Bedford, MA: Digital Press.

Stewart, J., & Hickey, D. (1960). *Reading devices for micro-images* (The State of the Library Art, v. 5, pt. 2). New Brunswick, NJ: Rutgers University Press.

Taylor, R. S. (1966). Professional aspects of information science and technology. *Annual Review of Information Science and Technology, 1*, 15–40.

Teevan, J., Jones, W., & Bederson, B. B. (2006). Personal information management. *Communications of the ACM, 49*(1), 40–43.

Tehrani, R. (2000). Publisher's outlook: As we may communicate. *Communications Solutions, 5*(1), 6, 8.

Thomas, B. (2000). ALPS (a language for process specification): A definition language for hypertext trails. *Information Services and Use, 20*, 169–187.

Travis, M. A. (1996). Cybernetic esthetics, hypertext and the future of literature. *Mosaic, 29*, 115–129.

Tsai, C. J. (1988). Hypertext: Technology, applications, and research issues. *Journal of Educational Technology Systems, 17*, 3–14.

Turing, A. M. (1965). On computable numbers, with an application to the Entscheidungsproblem. In M. Davis (Ed.), *The undecidable* (pp. 116–154). Hewlett, NY: Raven Press. (Originally published in 1936)

Turoff, M. (1977). An online intellectual community or "MEMEX" revisited. *Technological Forecasting and Social Change, 10*, 401–412.

Upham, L. N. (1991). The future of serials librarianship revisited. *Serials Review, 17*(2), 71–75.

Vagianos, L. (1976). Today is tomorrow. *Library Journal, 101*(1), 147–156.

Vakkari, P. (2003). Task-based information searching. *Annual Review of Information Science and Technology, 37*, 413–464.

van Dam, A., & Michener, J. C. (1967). Hardware developments and product announcements. *Annual Review of Information Science and Technology, 2,* 187–222.

Verhoeff, J., Goffman, W., & Belzer, J. (1961). Information efficiency of the use of Boolean functions for information retrieval. *Communications of the ACM, 4*(12), 557–559.

Vinacke, W. E. (1952). *The psychology of thinking.* New York: McGraw-Hill.

Waldrop, M. M. (2001). *The dream machine: J. C. R. Licklider and the revolution that made computing personal.* New York: Viking.

Wang, C. (2003). Electronic publishing: Significant landmarks. In M. A. Drake (Ed.), *Encyclopedia of library and information science* (2nd ed., Vol. 2, pp. 1011–1015). New York: Dekker.

Wang, J. (1999). V. Bush as computer visionary: Was role key or only memex? Reply. *Physics Today, 52*(5), 15.

Wells, H. G. (1938). *World brain.* Garden City, NY: Doubleday, Doran.

Wildstrom, S. H. (1998, November 2). A new chapter for e-books. *Business Week,* 19.

Williamson, R. (1989). Putting information into context. *Advanced Information Report, 10*(9), 4–6.

Wills, D. (1999). The nature of hypertext: Background and implications for librarians. *Journal of Academic Librarianship, 25,* 134–139.

Wilson, J. H. (1966). As we may have thought. *Proceedings of the American Documentation Institute 1966 Annual Meeting,* 117–122.

Wright, H. S. (2000). Technology: In music libraries. *Notes, 56,* 591–597.

Zachary, G. P. (1997). *Endless frontier: Vannevar Bush, engineer of the American century.* New York: Free Press.

CHAPTER 3

Garfield and the Impact Factor

Stephen J. Bensman
Louisiana State University

Introduction

This is the first of two chapters on Eugene Garfield and the impact factor, the second part of which will be published in next year's volume of the *Annual Review of Information Science and Technology*. Garfield is the founder of the Institute for Scientific Information (ISI), now Thomson Scientific, which launched the *Science Citation Index* (*SCI*), the *Social Sciences Citation Index* (*SSCI*), and the *Arts & Humanities Citation Index* (*A&HCI*). The impact factor is a citation measure that Garfield created during the process of developing these indexes. Simply defined, the impact factor is the ratio of the total number of citations in the journals covered by ISI during a processing year to the issues a given journal published during the two years preceding the processing year divided by the number of citable source items published in this journal during those two preceding years.

This chapter is historical, comprising an intellectual biography of Garfield. It discusses in detail the political, social, and intellectual influences affecting Garfield in his creation of the impact factor. The focus is on Garfield himself, the small group of intellectuals comprising his mentors and colleagues—Garfield's "invisible college" in Price's (1963, pp. 85–91) terminology—and his company, ISI. The thought processes and analyses surrounding the creation of the impact factor are described and placed in the theoretical structure that Garfield developed. Finally, the way the impact factor was utilized in determining the journal coverage of ISI's indexes is analyzed.

This chapter is not a comprehensive treatment of citation indexing, citation measures, or the use of the latter for the evaluation of journals, academic personnel, and academic programs. The emphasis is upon Garfield's own writings about these matters and upon those of persons who either greatly influenced his intellectual development or to whom he felt compelled to respond.[1] Other writings are discussed only insofar as they highlight or validate the principles on which Garfield based his ideas.

The Life and Career of Eugene Garfield

Eugene Garfield created an essential component of the empirical bases for modern information science through the application of citation indexing to the sciences, social sciences, arts, and humanities. He was born in the Bronx borough of New York City on September 16, 1925, to Henry and Edith (née Wolf) Garfinkle, who were themselves the children of immigrants. Garfield's parents separated while his mother was pregnant. As a result, his upbringing was heavily influenced by his uncles, whom Garfield has described in the following manner:

> Three of my uncles were radicals, involved in labor organizing and socialist-communist politics. There were two sides to the family. Two uncles were capitalists and they were always opposed to that. So there was a lot of turmoil going on. They cultivated my interest in science, classical music—in fact almost everything. Atheism was part of it. I was discouraged from going to any kind of religious school, so I did not go. Most Jewish kids of that age would have been Bar Mitzvahed, but I was not. (Garfield, 1987a, p. 2)

Garfield (1999a) reports being affected by political discussions with his uncles. However, it should be noted that Garfield's surrogate father was one of the capitalist uncles, who was a successful ladies' garment manufacturer and helped support his mother. Garfield's biological father was a successful newspaper-magazine distributor, whose firm's name was the Garfield News Company. Over the father's objections, the uncle had Garfield adopt the name of this company. It seems that the capitalist family influences predominated over the Marxist ones, but this family turmoil made Garfield an ideologically complex character. On the one hand, he was attracted to radical ideas; yet, on the other, he was a consummate businessman capable of implementing these radical ideas through the formation of a private corporation when governmental and societal organizations were too conservative and hidebound to do so.

Garfield came to information science by way of chemistry. Upon his graduation from high school in 1942, he enrolled at the University of Colorado to study chemical engineering. This choice may have been influenced by one of his uncles having a chemistry set. Because of a combination of personal problems and the patriotic fervor of World War II, Garfield lasted at Colorado only one semester. Not yet old enough for military service, he worked as a shipyard welder until he was drafted into the Army. After the war, Garfield obtained a B.S. in chemistry in 1949 from Columbia University in his native New York City and worked for a while as a laboratory assistant at Columbia for Professor Louis W. Hammett. In 1951 Garfield attended the Diamond Jubilee Conference of the American Chemical Society, where he discovered its Division of Chemical Literature and the possibility of a career in scientific information.

The turning point in Garfield's life occurred in 1951, when he was hired as a staff member of the Welch Medical Library Indexing Project. This project was headed by Sanford V. Larkey, director of the William H. Welch Medical Library at Johns Hopkins University in Baltimore. It had begun in 1948 and was sponsored by the Army Medical Library, which eventually became the National Library of Medicine. The Welch Project's mission was to investigate the size of biomedical literature, the extent of this literature's coverage by existing indexes, the structure of medical subject headings, and the application of machine methods to medical indexing. In his accounts of the project, Garfield (1985b; 1987a, pp. 10–13; 1997b, pp. 1–26; 1999c, pp. 240–244; 2000, pp. 1–2; 2002, p. 22) has stated that he was hired for his chemical expertise and that much of his time was spent in subject authority work involving the definition and classification of subject headings. His special task was to standardize chemical nomenclature. A sign of his strong interest in this area is that at the same time he voluntarily worked for *Chemical Abstracts*, summarizing articles on pharmacology in Spanish journals. Also taking an interest in machine indexing, Garfield worked out the "programs" needed to wire the punched-card machines that were used to prepare and tabulate subject-heading lists, and played a key role in the First Symposium on Machine Methods in Scientific Documentation that was organized by the Welch Project. While working on this project, Garfield manifested that combination of scientific interest and entrepreneurship which typified his career. To keep himself better informed on what was happening worldwide in documentation, he started in 1952 the first contents-page service he ever published: entitled *Contents in Advance*, it covered library science as well as documentation journals.

Garfield's participation in the Welch Medical Library Indexing Project set the course of his life, for through it he came to know most of the pioneers in information science. After leaving the project, Garfield strengthened his academic credentials in information science. In 1954 he obtained an M.S. in library science from Columbia University. Garfield (1997b, p. 32) has described the library degree as making him "official or Kosher" for librarians. He further reinforced his academic credentials in 1961, earning a doctorate in structural linguistics from the University of Pennsylvania with a dissertation entitled "An Algorithm for Translating Chemical Names to Molecular Formulas." During this period, Garfield continued his pattern of combining scientific interest with entrepreneurialism. He accepted a position as a consultant with the pharmaceutical firm Smith Kline and French in Philadelphia, a move that led him to make that city his permanent base of operations. At the same time, he launched a firm called Eugene Garfield Associates, whose name he changed in 1960 to the Institute for Scientific Information (ISI). Garfield (1999c, p. 249; personal communication, Oct. 5, 2005) reports that he was inspired in this choice of corporate name by the U.S.S.R.'s All-Union Institute of Scientific and Technical Information, citing two reasons for this selection: to cause the company to be perceived as a nonprofit organization and to highlight his small company's ability to achieve what the huge Soviet organization was attempting to do. This firm published two contents-page services on the model of *Contents in Advance*. These services marked the start of the *Current Contents* publications that were for a long time ISI's financial mainstay. One covered management literature and was secured by a contract with AT&T's Bell Laboratories. The other was dedicated to chemical, medical, pharmaceutical, and life sciences publications.

Garfield had conceptualized the citation indexing of science before he established ISI. While still at the Welch Project, he mentally assembled the various elements of this method of covering scientific journal literature. As Garfield (1998a, p. 68) reports, in early 1954 he wrote a term paper proposing the creation of citation indexes at the Columbia University School of Library Service. With the help of Johns Hopkins biologist Bentley Glass, Garfield (1955) revised this paper and was able to publish it in the prestigious journal *Science* in 1955. The article attracted the attention of Joshua Lederberg (2000), a Stanford University geneticist who received the 1958 Nobel Prize for medicine. Lederberg wrote to Garfield about the latter's idea, starting a vigorous correspondence that opened the way for Garfield to implement his idea of applying citation indexing to science. Under Lederberg's guidance, Garfield obtained in 1961 a National Institutes of Health (NIH) grant to produce a citation index for genetics. The NIH grant had to be converted into a National Science Foundation (NSF) contract because ISI was a private company. ISI approached the construction of the genetics citation index by first preparing a multidisciplinary science index. Garfield proposed that the NIH and NSF publish this multidisciplinary science citation index. When these bodies rejected the proposal, he decided to launch the index himself at considerable financial risk to his own company. The rejection fortified Garfield's (1975, p. 5) belief that private enterprise was "the best and most economical way to serve the scientific community."

ISI began regular publication of the *Science Citation Index* in 1964. It introduced the *Social Sciences Citation Index* in 1973 and the *Arts & Humanities Citation Index* in 1978. By showing how many times a given work has been referenced by other works, these indexes made practical the widespread use of citations in evaluating the importance—or "impact"—of works, scientists, and scholars, as well as research institutions. They also created an opening for new methods in exploring the history, sociology, and relational structure of science and scholarship. ISI added to the analytical capabilities of the *SCI* in 1975 by making a regular component of this index a volume entitled *Journal Citation Reports* (*JCR*) and made the same addition to the *SSCI* in 1977. These *JCR*s contained numerical data on the journals covered by ISI's citation indexes during a given year, such as total number of citations to these journals, the number of source items in these journals, the rapidity with which an average journal item was cited, how many times a given journal cited itself and other journals, as well as how many times other journals cited a given journal. However, the centerpiece of the *JCR*s came to be a measure called the "impact factor." In its original form, it was the ratio of the total number of citations during a processing year to the issues a given journal published during the two years preceding the processing year divided by the total—not just "citable"—number of source items published in this journal during those two preceding years. The impact factor can be, and has often been, considered an arithmetic mean. Thus, in the first *SCI JCR* (Garfield, 1976b, p. 6), the impact factor was defined as "a measure of the frequency with which the 'average cited article' in a journal has been cited in a particular year." In spite of its seeming simplicity, the impact factor is an exceedingly complex measure. It has become widely used for purposes that go far beyond the original intention of the measure and for which it is structurally flawed. Such utilization of the impact factor has occurred primarily in Europe in regard to the evaluation of scientists and scientific programs, raising such a storm of controversy that Garfield (1999a, p. 26) commented:

> I do find it hard to keep up with the large literature involving journal impact factors. I am especially frustrated that I can't respond to the portion containing misstatements or misuses. There is much controversy about the validity of impact factors, which are used for many purposes. ... *SCI* and *Journal Citation Reports* (*JCR*) data have become institutionalized. People often criticize the impact factor because it is so pervasive.

Garfield's (2005) level of frustration on this matter is revealed by the title of his talk at the International Congress on Peer Review and Biomedical Publication: "The Agony and the Ecstasy—the History and Meaning of the Journal Impact Factor." He even considered as an alternative title "Citation Sanity and Insanity—the Obsession and Paranoia of Citations and Impact Factors." However, a major reason for this situation is that Garfield himself made the impact factor seemingly his main measure of scientific value, doing so for reasons peculiar to his own intellectual development. Moreover, many of the problems in the validation of the impact factor arise from actions he took and processes he discovered.

The Theoretical Framework of the Science Citation Index

Early British Intellectual Influences

The theoretical framework within which Garfield developed his ideas was constructed in Britain during a scientific revolution that laid the bases for modern information science. This revolution was a consequence of World War I, which demonstrated the need for a modern scientific information system. The persons driving the information science revolution in Britain can be categorized as either reformists or revolutionaries. The reformists wanted, or were willing, to retain the journal as the basis of the scientific information system, whereas the revolutionaries wanted to make the scientific paper the basis of this system.

The Reformist Program

S. C. Bradford, head of the Science Museum Library (SML) in London, was the main theorist of the reformist camp. He was also a leading figure in information science—or "documentation," as it was known in this period—at the national and international level, being the director of the British Society for International Bibliography. Bradford approached the problem of scientific literature from the perspective of its adequate coverage by indexing and abstracting services. To analyze this coverage, he conducted research at the SML, the results of which showed that, although the 300 abstracting and indexing journals in existence at the time noticed 750,000 articles each year, only 250,000 articles were covered due to duplication of effort (Bradford, 1934). Suspecting that the reason for this oversight lay in the way articles on a given scientific subject were distributed among journals, Bradford investigated this distribution in two subject areas: applied geophysics and lubrication. The distributions in both areas were found to be remarkably similar, leading to the formulation of the Law of Scattering that is associated with Bradford's name. According to this law, the articles on a given scientific topic concentrate in a small nucleus of journals and then scatter across other journals in zones that must increase exponentially in number of titles to contain the same number of articles on the topic as contained in the journals of the nucleus. For example, in 1928–1931 the articles on applied geophysics were distributed across journals in the following manner: a small nucleus of nine journals (2.8 percent) contained 429 articles (32.2 percent), a second zone of 59 journals (18.1 percent) encompassed 499 articles (37.5 percent), and a third zone of 258 journals (79.1 percent) comprised 404 articles (30.3 percent). Bradford pointed out two practical consequences of the Law of Scattering. First, to gain complete coverage of articles on a subject, an indexing service would have to scrutinize for long periods thousands of journals, the vast bulk of which would haphazardly provide only occasional references. Second, no special library could gather all the literature on its subject without becoming a general science library. Bradford noted that in practice only one-third of the content of special libraries was definitely related to their subject scope, with the other two-thirds comprising literature on borderline and less related subjects. He pointed out that this situation led to much duplication in special library holdings.

World War II was a quintessentially technological war that severely stressed the British scientific information system, particularly affecting special libraries. The war exacerbated the problem of handling a scientific literature growing exponentially in both size and complexity. As a result, the Royal Society Empire Scientific Conference of 1946 dedicated a session to scientific information services at which Bradford (1948a) delivered a paper that summarized both the development of the international documentation movement and his lifetime's work. The paper contained a detailed explanation of the Law of Scattering and the practical dilemmas arising from it. Shortly after the conference, Bradford (1948b) gave further prominence to his ideas by publishing his classic book *Documentation*. Together, the conference paper and the book set forth Bradford's recommendations on how to handle the dilemmas resulting from his law. In respect to indexing and abstracting services, Bradford (1948b, pp. 28–29) urged the adoption of the Universal Decimal Classification (UDC), which he believed would improve bibliographical cooperation by enabling the collaboration of many persons in the task of indexing by subject the world's literature. At the conference, Bradford (1948a, p. 745) suggested using the UDC to classify journals according to the subjects treated by existing abstracting agencies; the agencies would then forward any article outside their scope but published in their allotted periodicals to the agency interested in that subject. Aware of objections, he emphasized, *"No interference is involved with the internal work of any abstracting agency"* (italics in original). As for the problems afflicting special libraries, Bradford (1948b, pp. 64–84) in his book made a detailed case for developing one of the great libraries of the U.K. into a comprehensive national central library of science and technology, on which the special libraries could rely for articles in journals dedicated to subjects peripheral to their own area of interest. One of Bradford's life ambitions had been to convert the SML into just such a library: He made it into Britain's main backup library in science, pioneering the concept of document delivery.

The Revolutionary Program

The primary theorist of the revolutionary wing of British information science was J. D. Bernal. One of Britain's most eminent scientists, Bernal pioneered x-ray crystallography and was one of the founders of molecular biology. In 1937 he was elected a fellow of the Royal Society and was appointed to the Chair of Physics at Birbeck College of the University of London, where he spent most of his career. Bernal had been born in Ireland in 1901. His father was a descendant of Spanish Sephardic Jews who had converted to Catholicism; his mother, the daughter of an American Presbyterian clergyman. As an undergraduate at Cambridge University, Bernal became a Marxist and joined the Communist Party of Great Britain in 1923.

Bernal's conversion to Marxism led him to become a pioneer in the study of the relationship of science to society. His biographer Hodgkin (1980, p. 64) states that his interest in this facet of science was powerfully strengthened and sharply focused in 1931 at the Second International Congress of the History of Science and Technology, where a Soviet delegation of theoreticians, historians, and scientists led by Bukharin (1931) set forth before Western intellectuals for the first time the view of science then predominant in the U.S.S.R. The Russian contribution to this conference had a profound impact in Britain—especially upon Bernal (1931, p. 43), who summed up this impact in a report entitled "Science and Society":

> The old conception of the history of science, the bare enumeration of discoveries and inventions, the telling of lives and deeds of great men, and the drawing up of the genealogical tree of present knowledge, is now seen as a partial though necessary basis for the study of the interaction of science with economics and politics, with religion, art and industry, throughout the whole course of history, not least in the present.

Hodgkin (1980, p. 64) considers this article as a point of departure for Bernal's subsequent writings on the history of science and science policy.

Bernal's (1940) most important contribution to the study of the relationship of science to society was his book entitled *The Social Function of Science*, first published in 1939. In a Festschrift celebrating the 25th anniversary of its publication, Goldsmith and Mackay (1964, p. 11) point out that *The Social Function of Science* presented the views not only of Bernal himself but also of a large school of scientists and others, who formed a kind of "invisible college," most of whose members were influenced by Marxism to a greater or lesser degree. Outlandish as it may seem in the light of the mass famines of collectivization, forced labor camps, and political purges of Stalin's rule, Bernal (1940, p. xiii) pointed to the Soviet Union as a model of "the possibility of combining freedom and efficiency in scientific organization." As any good Marxist, Bernal (pp. 10–11) considered science to be a part of industrial production and its importance, a result of its contribution to profits. However, although Bernal (pp. 408–416) thought capitalism essential to the early development of science, he now regarded the continuance of this economic system as incompatible with the full development of science in the service of humanity. For Bernal, science implied a unified, coordinated, and conscious control of the whole of social life. He thought that the function of science was to serve as the main engine of social change. According to Bernal, the relevance of Marxism to science was that it showed science to be an important part of economic and social development. Bernal defined science as communism because in science men had learned consciously to subordinate themselves to a common purpose. The doctrine expounded in the book came to be called "Bernalism," which was defined by one of its opponents, Oxford biologist John Baker (1939, p. 174), in the following manner:

Bernalism is the doctrine of those who profess that the only proper objects of scientific research are to feed people and protect them from the elements, that research workers should be organised in gangs and told what to discover, and that the pursuit of knowledge for its own sake has the same value as the solution of crossword puzzles.

Bernal's role in the effort to nationalize the British scientific information system has been well documented by Muddiman (2003, 2004). Bernal was a leading member of the Association of Scientific Workers (AScW), a trade union of Communist, socialist, and liberal scientists. *The Social Function of Science* contains the most detailed exposition of his ideas on the proper scientific communication system. Bernal (1940, pp. 292–293) summarized the main problem affecting this system and his proposed solution in the following terms:

The present mode of scientific publication is predominantly through the 33,000 odd scientific journals. It is ... incredibly cumbersome and wasteful, and is in danger of breaking down on account of expense. What can we put in its place? The prime function of scientific publications is to convey information about acquired knowledge, but it is clear that whereas certain information is needed by certain workers in full detail, the great bulk of it is only needed by any given worker in outline, if at all. An adequate system of communication would consist in principle of a limited distribution of detailed accounts, a wider distribution of summaries or abstracts, and the frequent production of reports or monographs covering the sum of recent advances in any given field. Behind this must be a body of readily accessible archives in which reference can be made to the work of the past.

He likened the problem of scientific communication to the problem of distribution and storage that was being solved every day by large businesses and mail order houses.

Bernal's proposed reform entailed the abolition of all existing scientific journals and their replacement by a service that would record, file, coordinate, and distribute scientific information. He regarded the publication of scientific journals as an inefficient method plagued by overlap and lack of coordination for distributing large amounts of scientific information. Bernal stated that a scientific publication was read to an extent of only 10 percent, when taken by an individual, but demanded simultaneously by a dozen persons, when taken by a library. The obvious solution was to make the separate paper, rather than the journal, the unit of communication between scientists. The science service that Bernal envisioned would ensure that all relevant information would be available to each research worker in amplitude proportional to the degree of its relevance and without any effort on the part of the worker. He suggested as a model Watson Davis's (1940) proposal for a science service for the U.S., which Bernal published as an appendix in his book. Davis was an interesting character who, in 1925 as managing editor of Science Service, covered the Scopes Monkey Trial in Tennessee and in 1937 founded the American Documentation Institute, which ultimately became the American Society for Information Science and Technology. Davis's proposal was typical of the era of the Great Depression and New Deal. He called for a central organization, called the Scientific Information Institute (SII), which would take over the publication functions of many existing societies and journals. All scientific bibliographical and abstracting services as well as many of the journals then under financial stress were to be brought under the SII, which, he envisaged, would be a monopoly in the same sense as the post office was a monopoly, that is, one operated for the public benefit without profit. Davis listed three factors he considered essential to his project: (1) centralization of scientific publication and bibliography with resulting economy of operation and improvement of service, (2) substitution of photographic duplication for printing-from-type duplication, and (3) the utilization of a comprehensive scheme of numerical indexing and automatic finding and sorting devices for filing and selecting bibliography.

In *The Social Function of Science*, Bernal essentially endorsed the type of scientific communication system Davis had proposed, notably its organizational and technological aspects. In addition, he emphasized two aspects of such a system that would prove to be of great import. First, Bernal (1940, pp. 297–298) stressed the importance of review literature in scientific communication. In doing so, he recommended following Lord Stamp's suggestion that the responsible body in each scientific discipline periodically review its field and report for each period what it deemed to be the chief discoveries and improvements in its subject. Bernal also desired that qualified authors be persuaded to write up their scientific fields at suitable intervals in monographs and textbooks. He suggested as a model for such works the monumental series of German *Handbücher*, which had conscientiously followed the details of scientific advances in every field. Second, Bernal (pp. 298–301) tried to forestall objections based on the dangers arising from the centralization of science. To counter these, he stated that he did not propose putting editorial functions of publication in the hands of a permanent administrative staff. Instead, this administrative staff was to act merely as a link between the writers of papers and the persons who, under the existing system, were editors of scientific journals. Exemplifying this with the same analogy that Davis had used, Bernal (p. 300) wrote, "The publication service would come to be more and more a kind of convenient post office between scientific workers." He responded to potential opposition to his reforms from the scientific societies in the following manner:

A more serious difficulty would have to be met in the opposition of the existing scientific societies that undertake the bulk of scientific publication. Although in most cases this publication is a serious financial burden to the societies, it gives them in many cases their main *raison d'être*, and the abolition of scientific journals might also be resented for purely sentimental reasons. (p. 30)

In this assessment Bernal was correct, for his proposals were to be almost universally rejected by the scientific societies.

Toward the end of World War II, the British political left took up the cause of a planned scientific state and within the Association of Scientific Workers interest arose in Bernal's proposals for the centralized publication and dissemination of scientific information. The result was what Muddiman (2003, pp. 393–398; 2004, pp. 261–264) has described as a campaign to nationalize scientific information. Bernal obtained the opportunity to advance his ideas by delivering a paper at the 1946 Royal Society Empire Scientific Conference at the same session where Bradford presented his paper. There, Bernal (1948a, p. 698) outlined a set of reforms, whose main purpose was to provide scientific workers with "the maximum of information relevant to their work and the minimum of irrelevant information." The way to do this, he stated, was to organize better the production and distribution of the basic unit of scientific publication—the individual scientific paper. Envisioning reforms at the international level, Bernal proposed that the scientific societies and other publishing bodies in each country jointly establish central agencies, which would use modern methods of reproduction and distribution to disseminate papers and abstracts. In an effort to win the support of the scientific societies, he stipulated that individual papers would be submitted in each country to the appropriate scientific society, which would accept and edit them; the central agency would then print and distribute the papers to members of the society in its country and to corresponding distribution agencies in other countries. Bernal noted that extra copies of papers could be made available to libraries and that the individuality of journals could be retained, as scientists and libraries would have the option of binding papers published by a given society into volumes in accordance with contemporary practice. He suggested that the cost of such a service be borne by general budgets of the participating countries or through subscriptions to UNESCO.

Victory of the Reformist Program

The scientific information session of the 1946 Royal Society Empire Conference recommended that the Royal Society hold another conference specifically dedicated to improving the management of scientific literature. This recommendation was implemented in 1948 with the convening of the Royal Society Scientific Information Conference. By this time the positions of the reformist and revolutionary camps had become fairly clearly defined. As set forth by Bradford (1948a), the main elements of the reformist program were: (1) maintenance of the scientific journal as the basis of scientific communication, (2) maintenance of publication of scientific journals in the hands of scientific societies and other publishing bodies, (3) cooperation among the existing indexing and abstracting services to ensure complete bibliographic coverage of scientific literature, and (4) provision of scientific information through the existing library system improved by the creation of a central document delivery library. In contrast, the revolutionary program advocated by Bernal (1940, 1948a) can be summarized by the following points: (1) replacement of the journal by the individual paper as the basis of scientific communication, (2) centralization of publishing as well as indexing and abstracting functions in a single administrative agency, and (3) transfer of the main distribution function from libraries to the central administrative agency.

Bernal (1948c) had intended to present to the Royal Society Scientific Information Conference a paper outlining a plan for the central distribution of scientific papers. This paper, which was submitted and circulated to the delegates prior to the opening of the conference, was essentially a more detailed elaboration of the proposals and considerations set forth by Bernal and Davis in *The Social Function of Science*. Bernal (1948c) introduced the scheme by describing its aim as the more effective distribution to scientific workers of those papers in which they were most interested. In an attempt to win the support of the scientific societies for the plan, he declared:

> This is to be effected not by radical reorganization of the methods of presentation of scientific papers, but the existing machinery of the scientific societies is to be supplemented by a distributing body functioning as the agency of the societies and in no way interfering with their editorial functions. (p. 253)

Bernal then proposed establishing a small number of central organizations called the National Distributing Authorities (NDA). These NDA were to combine the functions of publishing, abstracting, and distributing scientific papers, so that the whole of scientific publication and distribution would operate together as one unit. Bernal envisioned the establishment of such a system on the national, Commonwealth, and world levels.

In spite of Bernal's attempt to tone down the radicalism of his plan, it provoked a storm of criticism in the British press and infuriated the scientific societies. East (1998, pp. 295–296) has described the campaign in the British press, which was so virulent that it caused Sir Robert Robinson (1948, p. 16), President of the Royal Society, to comment wryly in his opening address that "the writers of certain notices in the newspapers have allowed themselves to dwell, with evident relish, on the prospect of a clash of ideologies and the probable conflict between the planners and those who don't want to be planned." The reactions of the scientific societies and others to Bernal's plan, which were printed in the conference proceedings, were overwhelmingly hostile. Thus, a memorandum signed by sixteen representatives of scientific societies ranging from the Anatomical Society to the Zoological Society of London as well as two journal editors (Memorandum on Section I, 1948, p. 518) deemed Bernal's plan "unacceptable" and declared that "the present system of production of journals by societies ... is not only adequate but essential in principle." Under these conditions Bernal withdrew his plan from consideration of the conference.

Muddiman (2003, p. 396; 2004, p. 263) has interpreted Bernal's withdrawal of his paper in a political sense as marking the defeat of the leftist campaign to nationalize the British scientific information system. However, close examination of the reasons Bernal stated for withdrawing the paper suggests that there may have been very good technical reasons underlying his decision to do so. Bernal's (1948c, p. 258) statement referred to another paper he had submitted for the conference, in which he presented the results of a survey of scientists at leading research institutions in the U.K. on their use of scientific literature (1948b). This survey yielded findings of great import for the further development of the scientific information system. First, it revealed that libraries were the primary source of the scientific journals whose articles scientists either browsed (54 percent) or carefully read (56 percent). In comparison to libraries, personally owned journals and article reprints played relatively small roles. Second, the survey found that scientists were extremely multidisciplinary in their reading habits. Of the journals respondents read, 43 percent were in their own fields, 29 percent classed in related fields, and 28 percent were general journals. Bernal (p. 595) was surprised by this phenomenon. He also (pp. 596–597) noted that the distribution of articles on a given subject across journals conformed to Bradford's Law of Scattering, which stipulated that, although most articles on a topic were in a small number of journals, recourse had to be made to a large number of journals to find all the relevant literature. A third important finding of the survey (p. 599) was that an overwhelming proportion of scientists (76 percent) read reviews and that reviews must form a very important and increasing part of background reading. This finding conformed to the importance Bernal had assigned such literature in *The Social Function of Science*. The first two findings caused Bernal (1948c, p. 258) to make the following explanation in his withdrawal statement:

> It seemed much more profitable to concentrate on improved library systems and on the possibility of copies of papers through libraries rather than from the original publishing body. The scatter of references in journals also

revealed in the survey, though it could be greatly reduced by good grouping, could never from the very nature of science be altogether eliminated. As a consequence an ideal system would be one which would (a) ensure a wide and rapid spread through all libraries of papers from the few great common journals; (b) use special libraries to distribute copies on request of papers in the middle rank of special journals whose numbers at present only run into hundreds; [and] (c) provide a service from central libraries in conjunction with abstracting agencies and special research institutions of papers from the many thousand small, local, or highly specialized journals.

Muddiman (2003, p. 396; 2004, p. 263) has dismissed this explanation as "a fig leaf" to cover political defeat, but Bernal (1965, p. 456) reiterated these conclusions some 17 years later when he divided physics journals into three categories: the most cited and the most read papers, which should be in every physics laboratory library; the less often cited ones, which could be in the library of the university or large-scale research institute; and, finally, the group containing by far the largest number of journals but not the largest number of papers, which would be sufficiently accessible if they were found in some national science library. It thus seems that, through scientific analysis, Bernal had come to endorse Bradford's reformist position.

In general, the 1948 Royal Society Scientific Information Conference can be considered a victory for Bradford's reformist concepts. Bernal's proposal for the centralized distribution of scientific papers was blocked from consideration and the conference made several recommendations that dovetailed with Bradford's position (Recommendations, 1948). In particular, the conference (p. 199) concluded that more active cooperation among the abstracting agencies would be of benefit to science and made several proposals in that regard. Together with this, it (p. 203) came out in favor of the wider application of the Universal Decimal Classification. The conference (pp. 201–202) also urged further development of information services and special libraries, including increased funding for central scientific libraries such as the Science Museum Library to expand their collections and greater cooperation among libraries to reduce unnecessary duplication and extend access to the world's scientific literature. However, Bernal did win a victory in that the conference (p. 201) recognized the importance of reviews and urged senior scientists to regard the provision of reviews as an important ancillary to the pursuit of new knowledge. In 1956, D. J. Urquhart, who had attended the conference as a representative of the government department charged with promoting scientific research, obtained authorization from his agency to establish the National Lending Library for Science and Technology—the central document delivery library that Bradford had envisaged—which ultimately evolved into today's British Library Document Supply Centre.

Conceptualization of the Science Citation Index

Bernal's Influence on Garfield

Garfield (1982b) was introduced to British developments in information science through Bernal's writings. Upon his graduation from high school, an uncle gave him Bernal's *The Social Function of Science*. He took the book with him to the University of Colorado, where he discussed it intensely with a group of friends, including a Marxist woman who became his wife (Garfield, personal communication, December 5, 2005). The chapter on scientific communication made a great impression on Garfield (1982b, p. 13), who considered it as anticipating the modern revolution in science communication. According to Garfield, Bernal foresaw the need for a reference work that would give scientists access to a large body of past and present scientific literature. Garfield regarded the Scientific Information Institute, which Watson Davis had advocated in the appendix of Bernal's book, as a predecessor to his own company, the Institute for Scientific Information. While working on the Welch Project at Johns Hopkins, Garfield (p. 5) was further heavily influenced by Bernal in the latter's role at the 1946 Royal Society Empire Scientific Conference and the 1948 Royal Society Scientific Information Conference. These conference proceedings became a bible for Garfield as a fledgling investigator. Garfield always considered Bernal something of a "hero figure" (p. 6). In 1962 he sent samples of the *Science Citation Index*, then under development, to Bernal, who agreed in 1964 to serve on its editorial advisory board. Garfield (1976b, p. vii) acknowledged his intellectual debt to Bernal in the dedication to the first *Science Citation Index Journal Citation Reports* (*SCI JCR*): "Dedicated to the memory of the late *John Desmond Bernal* whose insight into the societal origins and impact of science inspired an interest that became a career." As will be discussed, the creation of the *Science Citation Index* itself was partially an attempt to solve the problem posed by Bradford's Law of Scattering for Bernal's plan for the central distribution of scientific papers. Ironically, Garfield himself was to make his greatest theoretical breakthrough by further developing Bradford's law, a breakthrough that was to reveal the complications of employing citation measures such as the impact factor for evaluative purposes.

Leake and Review Articles

The initial impetus for Garfield's conceptualization of the *Science Citation Index* came from Chauncey D. Leake, whom he met in 1951 while working on the Welch Project. Leake, who was the chairman of the project's advisory committee, was a polymath, being both an accomplished scientist and a poet: Over the course of his career, he served terms as president of the American Association for the Advancement of Science, the American Association for the History of Medicine, the History of Science Society, and the American Pharmacology Society. He had an enormous influence on Garfield (1976b, p. vii), who placed his name immediately after Bernal's and right before Lederberg's in the dedication of the first *SCI JCR*. Leake admonished Garfield (1970a, 1974b, 1978) to study review articles and try to understand why they were so important in science. He regularly called Garfield's attention to the failure of conventional abstracting and indexing services to take advantage of the real bibliographic significance of the references in review papers. This advice probably fell on willing ears because, as has been noted, Bernal had also believed in the importance of review papers and had validated this belief in the paper he had presented to the 1948 Royal Society Scientific Information Conference, which, in turn, had officially endorsed this view and urged senior scientists to write such papers. As a result of his study, Garfield came to recognize that the sentences in review articles are implicit indexing statements and that the process of producing a scientific index could be automated by making these sentences the grist for such an index. This idea eventually led to creation of the *SCI*. Garfield continued to hold review articles in high esteem because he remained convinced that it is impossible for artificially intelligent machines to produce the indexing statements that authors contribute when writing critical reviews.

Adair and Legal Citators

Although Leake had pointed Garfield toward the review article as a possible pathway to the automation of indexing scientific literature, the latter still lacked a method for connecting the review article to an index. This was provided by William C. Adair, who had retired as executive vice-president of the Frank Shepard Company. In 1873, this company had begun publishing a system of legal citation indexes called *Shepard's Citations*. U.S. common law is based upon the principle of *stare decisis*, which dictates that all courts must follow precedents laid down by higher courts and each court also follows its own precedents. This makes it essential that lawyers know how a particular case, statute, or other document has been cited by subsequent legal documents. *Shepard's Citations* provided such information. Its legal indexes became popularly known as "citators," and the term "Shepardize" became the common terminology for tracing how a given legal document had been cited in the legal literature. Garfield came into contact with Adair through the First Symposium on Machine Methods in Scientific Documentation sponsored by the Welch Project. As Garfield (1987a, p. 13) has reported, the vice-president of Johns Hopkins University, Lowell J. Reed, delivered the symposium's opening address, in which he stated, "Man is going to be drowned in a flood of paper." This statement was given national coverage by the press, resulting in a flood of letters from all over the country asking for information about the symposium. One letter came to Garfield from Adair, who explained the principle of citators. Garfield (pp. 13–14) has related the moment of discovery thus:

> I didn't know what *Shepard's* was so I went down to the Enoch Pratt Free Library and went into the reference room. I found *Shepard's Citations* and I literally screamed, "Eureka." I had been trying to devise a system around review articles which Chauncey Leake had been pushing me to do. He kept saying, "Review articles are extremely important to scientists. Study them carefully. Find out why they are so successful." I had done a primitive kind of linguistic analysis of reviews. Essentially if you parse a review article, each sentence becomes an indexing statement. ... I was taking the review article and analyzing each sentence and tagging it with the article it had cited. When I saw the *Shepard's Citations* I found the methodology that I needed for linking all these things, for indexing all these cited references that were cited in the review.

Garfield had become the youngest associate editor of *American Documentation*, the journal of the American Documentation Institute founded by Watson Davis. He was so excited by his discovery that he invited Adair (1955) to write an article for *American Documentation* on the possibility of using citators for scientific literature.

First Major Theoretical Paper and the Impact Factor

Garfield put together these elements in an article entitled "Citation Indexes for Science," which appeared in the journal *Science* in 1955. In this article, which Garfield (1987a, p. 16) himself has characterized as "my most important paper," he listed the advantages of a citation index over conventional alphabetical and subject indexes, using *Shepard's Citations* as a tested and successful model. The first advantage, he said, was that its different construction allowed it to bring together material that would never be collated by means of the usual methods of subject indexing. Garfield described a citation index as "an association-of-ideas" index that allowed readers as much leeway as they needed (Garfield, 1955, p. 108). In his opinion, conventional indexes were inadequate because scientists were often concerned with a particular idea rather than a complete concept. The basic problem was to build subject indexes that could anticipate the infinite number of possible approaches that scientists might require in order to bridge the gap between the subject approach of those who created the documents and the subject approach of those who were seeking the information. Garfield stated that the utility of a citation index had to be considered from the viewpoint of the transmission of ideas. He pointed out that scientists could not rely on conventional indexes alone to establish the history of an idea but also had to do much eclectic reading because it was impossible for any one person (the indexer) to anticipate all the thought processes of a user.

Garfield (1955, p. 110) described the advantage of a citation index from this perspective:

> By using authors' references in compiling the citation index, we are in reality utilizing an army of indexers, for every time an author makes a reference he is in effect indexing that work from his point of view. This is especially true of review articles where each statement, with the following reference, resembles an index entry, superimposed upon which is the function of critical appraisal and interpretation.

This perspective, together with the technical discussion in the article about how to code entries for machine processing, shows that Garfield viewed the citation index as a vehicle for using automation to capture more fully the multiplicity of thought processes operative in the scientific information system.

Flexibility in collating materials from different subject areas underlay another advantage that Garfield (1955, p. 109) saw in citation indexes. In his 1955 *Science* article, he alluded briefly to this advantage, stating that the listing of articles that had cited a given article could "provide each scientist with an individual clipping service." This was only the tip of a very deep iceberg, whose full dimensions Garfield (1956, p. 11) revealed one year later:

> An intriguing application of the Citation Index is its potential use in disseminating scientific information as well as for retrieval. Bernal proposed some time ago that a centralized reprint clearing house be established. Each scientist would then regularly receive papers in designated areas of interest. The proposal is excellent in its simplicity. Its execution is not so simple. How would one spell out his interests? By decimal class numbers of index headings or specific compounds? In time any conventional system of classification would break down even if the individual did decide on class numbers or headings. However, a reprint distribution plan based on the principle of the Citation Index could overcome this difficulty. The flow of reprints to each scientist would be reasonable and geared to his individual specialized needs. His changing frame of reference would not periodically disrupt the entire classification scheme.

Thus, Garfield saw in citation indexes a way to circumvent the rock on which Bernal's proposal to nationalize Britain's scientific information system had foundered: Bradford's Law of Scattering. It should be noted that it also offered a way to upgrade the contents-page services on which Garfield was building his business. Garfield (1982b, p. 5) has written that this passage was his first public acknowledgment of Bernal's impact on his career. Shortly after this public acknowledgment, Garfield (1999a, p. 28) first met Bernal in person in Washington, DC at the 1958 International Conference on Scientific Information, which was the successor to the 1948 Royal Society Scientific Information Conference. Both men presented papers there, Garfield's (1959, p. 461) being on the construction of a unified index of science, by which he meant "a single interdisciplinary index to *all* documents, primarily periodical literature in *all* fields of science."

Garfield's (1955) *Science* paper is notable also because it was the first time that he used the term "impact factor," mentioning this term in two places, which are quoted here:

> In effect, the system would provide a complete listing, for the publications covered, of all the original articles that had referred to the article in question. This would clearly be particularly useful in historical research, when one is trying to evaluate the significance of a particular work and its impact on the literature and thinking of the period. Such an "impact factor" may be much more indicative than an absolute count of the number of a scientist's publications. (p. 108)

> Thus, in the case of a highly significant article, the citation index has a quantitative value, for it may help the historian to measure the influence of the article—that is, its "impact factor." (p. 111)

Garfield is clearly speaking here of measuring the "impact factor" of a given scientific paper in terms of the total number of citations to it. He was to change this meaning when he created a measure he called the "impact factor" to determine which journals should be covered by the *SCI*. This term came to be defined as the average number of citations to the papers of a given journal. Nevertheless, the importance Garfield assigned to this measure was determined by his prior intellectual development, which was conditioned by two major determinants in his thinking. First, Garfield considered the paper, not the journal, as the chief vehicle of scientific information. Therefore, he would be inclined to consider important a measure designed to evaluate the significance not of a given journal but of the articles of a given journal. Second, he developed his idea of the citation index on the basis of the review article, which he regarded as the epitome of scientific writing. Therefore, he would favor a measure that ranked the review article higher than the research article. This view of scientific value was at considerable variance with the opinion of many—if not most—scientists. Given that the impact factor was used to rank journals in the *Journal Citation Reports*, there was always inherent in this measure a certain ambiguity as to what actually was being ranked—the journal or the article—and, if the article, then what type of article.

Citation Measures, Bibliometric Laws, and the Journal Citation Reports

Early Statistical Analyses

Definition of the Basic Method of Calculating the Impact Factor

From the very beginning, Garfield combined the development of the *Science Citation Index* with statistical analyses of the citation data being collected for this index. These analyses afforded him great insight into the social structure of science and how it related to the scientific journal system. As part of this process, he created citation measures and formulated bibliometric laws, which he used to improve the journal coverage of the *SCI*. The culmination of this process was the launching of the *Journal Citation Reports* in the mid-1970s as integral parts of the *Science Citation Index* and the *Social Sciences Citation Index*. These *JCR*s were compilations of journal citation measures, of which the two most important qualitative measures were total citations and impact factor.

The first report of such research was written by Garfield and Sher (1963) while the *SCI* was still in its embryonic stage as the Citation Index Project, which, under the sponsorship of the National Institutes of Health and the National Science Foundation, was focused on genetics. This paper is notable as the first one in which the term "impact factor" was defined in the form that the Institute for Scientific Information was to employ it and the reasoning behind this form was stated. Garfield and Sher (p. 199) reported that their concern was not so much the "vital statistics" of scientific publishing; rather, they were "more interested in certain 'impact' factors such as how often a particular paper, author, or journal is cited compared to corresponding average values in a given Citation Index file" (p. 199). They then proceeded to demonstrate that the larger the number of citations taken into account, the more positively and highly skewed became the distribution of the citations to the papers within the data set. Thus, Garfield and Sher calculated that, whereas 95 percent of the papers were cited merely one to three times, certain papers were highly cited, with the range running from the vast bulk of the articles cited only once to an article by Oliver H. Lowry cited 305 times. They also reported that the first year preceding the citing source was the most heavily cited and that half the references were to the eight-year period preceding the source. Garfield and Sher (p. 200) then introduced what they termed "journal impact factor":

> One of the most interesting correlations is the "journal impact factor." In the usual citation count methods ... the importance of a journal is determined by the absolute number of citations to it. The J AM CHEM SOC ranks first on such a list. However, this count is largely a reflection of the fact that more articles are published in this journal than

most. This approach is not much more sophisticated than ranking the importance of a journal by the quantity of articles published. The first step in obtaining a more meaningful measure of importance is to divide the number of times a journal is cited by the number of articles that journal has published. This linear relationship is valid at least as long as self-citations are not eliminated ... nor multiple citations omitted. ... When this calculation is performed, the J AM CHEM SOC no longer ranks first. In our own citation counts, the PROC NAT ACAD SCI, NATURE, SCIENCE and other journals move towards the top—including some journals which publish many articles and others which do not.

Here, the concept of "impact factor" has undergone an interesting and important evolution from its initial form in Garfield's 1955 *Science* paper. First, the "impact factor" is no longer the total number of citations to a given scientific paper but the mean number of citations per paper in a given journal to be used for explicitly comparative purposes. Second, Garfield explicitly rejects size as a component of "importance." However, the focus is still on the paper instead of the journal, as is evident in a statement by Garfield and Sher (pp. 200–201) that clearly reflects Bernal's influence:

Librarians and information scientists can organize collections of frequently used papers. It seems utterly foolish to be sending out bound volumes of journals which are being borrowed for a small group of frequently cited articles. The citation data now available makes such a determination possible without intimate knowledge of the subject matter. Thus, we can say with reasonable certainty that any biochemistry librarian would be well advised to have Lowry's article on protein analysis readily available, since it is the most frequently cited paper in the field.

Garfield and Sher then issued a caveat that such information should be used with caution for personnel selection and evaluation such as that done by the Nobel committees, even though many people were interested in this application of citation indexing. They concluded with a declaration that the basic purpose of their project was not "to take a statistical inventory of scientific publication" but "to develop an information system which is economical and which contributes significantly to the process of information discovery—that is, the correlation of scientific observations not obvious to the searcher" (p. 201) through the new insights provided by citation indexes that are not possible through descriptor-oriented systems.

Initial Application of Citations to Evaluating Scientific Research

Immediately after this paper's appearance, Garfield (1963) published another one on the use of citation indexes in sociological and historical research. Here again he stressed the dangers of using citations to evaluate scientists and scientific research, declaring that his purpose in this paper was "to record my forewarning concerning the possible promiscuous and careless use of quantitative citation data for sociological evaluations, including personnel and fellowship selection" (pp. 289–290). In particular, Garfield wanted to disassociate himself from the idea that one could measure the importance of a paper by citation counting, declaring, "*Impact* is not the same as *importance* or *significance*" (p. 290, italics in original). He wrote that citation indexes could be used to facilitate personnel and fellowship evaluation because they synthesize a consensus of scientific opinion needed in a careful appraisal of research. But, he argued, it would be preposterous to conclude blindly that the most cited author deserves a Nobel prize because on this basis Lysenko might have been judged the greatest scientist of the last decade. The reference to Lysenko, the Stalinist scientist who destroyed genetics in the U.S.S.R., possesses a certain amount of irony, because Garfield's mentor Bernal was held in disrepute for openly and steadfastly supporting the Soviet scientist.

Two years later Sher and Garfield (1966) took up the sensitive issue of using citations to evaluate scientists and their work. In this paper, presented at a conference on research program effectiveness sponsored by the U.S. Office of Naval Research, they touted ISI's products as being able to "provide, for administrators, interesting capabilities that can be used in studying, evaluating, and improving the effectiveness of research programs" (p. 137). Cautioning that ISI was on record as being against the promiscuous use of quantitative citation data for research evaluation, Sher and Garfield then declared that "this by no means implies that such evaluations are not possible" (p. 138). The method they selected for demonstrating the validity of the impact factor involved an extreme case—the comparison of the citation rates of Nobelists to the citation rates of average scientists. To do this, Sher and Garfield tallied the citations in the 1961 *SCI* to the persons awarded Nobel Prizes in physics, chemistry, and medicine in 1962 and 1963. They then constructed the "impact factor" of the Nobelists by calculating the number of citations per prize winner, finding that as a group there were thirty times as many citations per average Nobelist as there were per average cited author in the 1961 *SCI* database. Having done this, Sher and Garfield then stated that administrators could use the "individual journal impact factors" (p. 140), which they had just created, to evaluate the effectiveness of specific publications.

The ISI Citation Analysis of Scientific Journals of 1971

Garfield conducted ISI's most important research project on citation analysis as a means to evaluate the significance of scientific journals in 1971. The aims and progress of this research were reported in his essays entitled "Current Comments," which appeared as a regular feature of the weekly *Current Contents*. Garfield (1972a) summarized the results of this project in an article published in *Science* in 1972. The gist of this article was succinctly stated in the following sentence beneath the article's title: "Journals can be ranked by frequency and impact of citations for science policy studies" (p. 471). Garfield began his description of the citation data for the project by stating that the *SCI* had international and multidisciplinary coverage that included the world's most important scientific and technical journals in most disciplines. Data for the study were collected by extracting from ISI's database all the references published during the last quarter of 1969 in the 2,200 journals then covered by the *SCI*. To ensure that this three-month sample was representative of the year as a whole, it was compared to a random sample of every twenty-seventh reference from the approximately four million references collected over all of 1969. The two samples were sufficiently similar to validate the three-month sample, from which three listings were produced. The first listing showed the total citations received by each title and the distribution of these citations over the journal's backfile by year. The second displayed how many times each title was cited by the other titles and the distribution of these citations over the titles' backfile by year. The third was a listing of how many times each journal referenced the other journals and the distribution of these references over the journals' backfile by year. The purpose of these listings, which were to become incorporated into the *JCR*s, was "to map the network of journal information transfer" (p. 472).

Total Citations and Garfield's Law of Concentration

Garfield (1972a) split his discussion of the ISI project into two basic parts: the ranking of journals by total citations and the ranking of journals by impact factor. Concerning the first, the major finding was that, in terms of absolute counts, scientific journal frequency distributions are highly and positively skewed. Pointing out that the majority of all references cited relatively few journals, Garfield (p. 474) described the findings on total citations:

> [The plot of the distribution of citations among cited journals] shows that only 25 journals (little more than 1 percent of *SCI* coverage) are cited in 24 percent of all references; that only 152 journals ... are cited in 50 percent of all references; that only 767 journals are cited in 75 percent of all references; and that only 2000 or so journals are cited in 85 percent of all references. In addition, the data ... show that only

540 journals are cited 1000 or more times a year, and that only 968 journals are cited even 400 times a year.

He also demonstrated that this same pattern held for the distributions of journals by number of articles and number of references to other journals. According to his figures, of the 2,200 journals covered by the *SCI* in 1969, about 500 published approximately 70 percent of all the articles, while a small group of 250 journals provided almost half of the 3.85 million references processed for the *SCI* in 1969. These figures caused Garfield to conclude that "many journals now being published seem to play only a marginal role, if any, in the effective transfer of scientific information" (p. 475).

In analyzing the *SCI* data structure in his *Science* summary article, Garfield (1972a, p. 475) observed, "The predominance of cores of journals is ubiquitous." This observation marked his greatest theoretical breakthrough and provided a solution to the problem that Bradford's Law of Scattering posed for abstracting and indexing services. Garfield (1971) discussed this problem in a "Current Comments" essay written while the ISI project was in progress. Here he noted that Bradford's law dictated that "no matter what the specialty, a relatively small core of journals will account for as much as 90 percent of the significant literature, while attempts to gather 100 percent of it will add journals to the core at an exponential rate" (p. 5). He then stated that "[a]ny abstracting or indexing service that ignores Bradford's law in attempting to realize the myth of complete coverage does so at its great financial peril" and echoed Bradford himself in noting that "no special library can gather the complete literature of its subject *without becoming a general scientific library*" (p. 5). Garfield (p. 5) declared that Bradford's law explains why a multidisciplinary index like the *SCI* is generally more effective than any discipline-oriented index, no matter the specialty:

> At ISI, we are completing a study which has resulted in a generalization of Bradford's law which, in a sense, "unifies" the demonstration of its validity in studies of individual fields. Allow me the eponymic shorthand of calling this unified theory or generalization "Garfield's law of concentration." The name is intended to suggest that, in opposition to scattering, a basic concentration of journals is the common core or nucleus of all fields.

He described his law as postulating for science as a whole what Bradford's law had postulated for a single discipline, declaring that his law held true no matter whether journals were considered as a source of citing articles or as a collection of cited articles. In his *Science* article Garfield (1972a, p. 476) stated his law thus:

The data reported here demonstrate the predominance of a small group of journals in the citation network. Indeed, the evidence seems so conclusive that I can with confidence generalize Bradford's bibliographical law concerning the concentration and dispersion of the literature of individual disciplines and specialties. Going beyond Bradford's studies, I can say that a combination of the literature of individual disciplines and specialties produces a multidisciplinary core for all of science comprising no more than 1,000 journals. The essential multidisciplinary core could, indeed, be made up of as few as 500 journals.

In his monograph on citation indexing, Garfield (1979a, pp. 21–23, 160) used as a physical analogy for Bradford's law a comet, whose nucleus represents the core journals of a literature and whose tail of debris and gas molecules widening in proportion to the distance from the nucleus depicts the additional journals that sometimes publish material relevant to the subject. According to Garfield, his Law of Concentration postulates that the tail of the literature of one discipline largely consists of the cores of the literatures of other disciplines. He had theoretically solved the problem posed by Bradford's Law of Scattering, but the processes described by his Law of Concentration ensure that any citation analysis seeking to validate the impact factor as a measure of scientific value will be plagued by exogenous subject citations, which render accurate estimates of parameters almost impossible and cause extreme outliers that distort the results.

The Meaning, Methodology, and Consequences of Impact Factor

Garfield's (1972a, pp. 476–477, 478–479; 1972c) discussion of the impact factor in his "Current Comments" essay on this measure and his *Science* article on the 1971 ISI project was more tentative than his discussion of total citations. Indeed, no major conclusions were presented with respect to the impact factor. This was because at the time of this project, Garfield had not fully worked out how to calculate the impact factor, even though he had conceptualized the measure some eight years earlier. Therefore, the discussion of impact factor in both the essay and the article was focused on various ways to construct the impact factor and the reasoning underlying them. These writings provide evidence that Garfield was still keeping a close eye on work in Britain as a source of ideas. For example, in his essay, Garfield (1972c, p. 5) cited a letter in *Nature* written by Sandison (1971), who had been working on the problem of journal obsolescence. Sandison (p. 368) emphasized that in studies of citations or library use the following rule had to be observed:

To be useful as parameters of the relative value to scientists of groups of volumes, the data must be presented as the number of references per available item, and not as the numbers from groups of differing size. The need to correct "obsolescence rates" for the fact that there is much less of the older literature to cite or read is becoming generally recognized.

Garfield (1972c, p. 5) termed Sandison's rule a "recent rediscovery of the impact factor."

However, Garfield (1972a, p. 476) seemed to be particularly influenced by Martyn and Gilchrist (1968), whose work on evaluating British scientific journals he cited in his *Science* article. For their work, Martyn and Gilchrist utilized data from the 1965 *SCI*, which they obtained from ISI. In structuring their data, their first decision was to restrict the sample to the citations made by the journals covered by the 1965 *SCI* to issues of the British journals under evaluation that were published in 1963 and 1964. Their reasoning for this echoed Sandison's logic:

> We decided that our most practical course would be to confine our study to citations made during 1965 to journals published in the two preceding years. It was already known that 26.1 percent of all the 1965 citations were to the literature of 1964 and 1963, so in terms of number of citations this would give us an adequate sample. There is no reason to suppose that, so far as the more important journals are concerned, the ranking we obtained would have been materially altered had our sample covered a greater time span, and by confining ourselves to the two years prior to 1965, we avoided the problem of correcting for cited journal age. (Martyn & Gilchrist, 1968, p. 2)

Then, citing Garfield and Sher's (1963) article on the impact factor, Martyn and Gilchrist (1968) stated that they required, for the journals cited, some measure of their relative sizes in terms of the number of citable items. In this way, adjustments could be made to the number of times each title was cited in order to allow for the increased probability of citations of journals with the greater number of citable items. For this purpose, they deemed it sufficient to count the number of citable items contained in each journal in 1964. Of great import for the future was the fact that they found it difficult to define just what a "citable item" was and had to proceed on an ad hoc basis. To capture various aspects of importance, Martyn and Gilchrist ranked British scientific journals in three different ways: (1) by total number of citations, (2) by ratio of 1964 items cited to 1964 items published, and (3) by number of citations per cited item. There is evidence that Garfield carefully considered Martyn and Gilchrist's work, for he explored their options and incorporated, with important modifications, much of what they did in his construction of the impact factor.

Garfield (1972c) first discussed the findings of the 1971 ISI project on the impact factor in one of his "Current Comments" essays. There, he introduced the impact factor by pointing out the need of librarians for objective criteria in the selection of journals. He also noted that citation frequency is biased in favor of large journals and that ISI had developed the concept of a journal's impact some 10 years earlier. According to Garfield, impact could be measured in a number of ways, of which two had been used by Martyn and Gilchrist. First, one could use the ratio of citations to the number of articles actually cited one or more times, disregarding those that were not cited. Garfield described this as "the *putative* impact factor" (p. 5). Second, a very different ratio could be constructed by calculating the fraction of articles cited. Garfield also observed that one could try to discount the "inbreeding" effect of journal self-citations and that one could compare "*journal utilization* factors" indicating number of different citing journals involved (p. 5, italics in original). The method of calculating the impact factor Garfield chose during the 1971 project became ISI's standard method. This method, some of whose main features had been pioneered and justified by Martyn and Gilchrist, computed the ratio between citations to particular years of a journal and the number of articles published in those years. Garfield noted that this method differs from that used to calculate the putative impact factor, which discounts the negative influence of articles that are never cited, and that such discounting can have a significant effect for certain journals, depending on the definition of an article or citable item. Garfield considered the ratio of citations to sources as providing an overall measure of impact, but he cautioned that the ratio can be skewed by a few super-cited classics unless limited by chronological criteria, observing that a single article cited 500 times has the same effect as 100 articles cited five times. Garfield established these chronological criteria in the same way as Martyn and Gilchrist had, by dividing the number of citations of the source year of the ISI project—1969—to the issues of a given journal published during the two years preceding the source year— 1967 and 1968—by the total number of articles published in these issues in 1967 and 1968. Like Martyn and Gilchrist, he justified the two-year limitation by pointing out that about 25 percent of all citations were made to the two-year period prior to the source year chosen. However, years later, he would elaborate further that this figure of 25 percent of all citations to the two years preceding the source year held true basically for the two fields—molecular biology and biochemistry—that were of greatest interest to the users of *Current Contents* and the *SCI* (Garfield, 2003, p. 366). Garfield (1972c, p. 6) declared that, by establishing this two-year limitation, ISI had chosen "a current impact factor" that discounts the effects of most super-cited classics.

At the end of the "Current Comments" essay, Garfield (1972c) published two lists: (1) the 50 most-cited journals ranked in descending order by total citations and (2) the fifty journals highest in impact factor ranked in descending order. His analysis of these lists made two important points. First, the list of 50 journals highest in impact factor was quite different from the list of the 50 most-cited journals: Indeed, only 11 titles appeared on both lists. Second, almost half of the high-impact journals could be categorized as review journals, none of which appeared among the top 50 most-cited list. For example, the title highest in total citations was the *Journal of the American Chemical Society*—the society's main research journal—whereas the title highest in impact factor was *Accounts of Chemical Research*—a review journal of the society. This was to be a consistent feature of all such citation rankings and, given Garfield's intellectual development, the impact factor's capturing of the importance of review articles and journals was bound to influence his evaluation of what was to be considered the most valid citation measure.

Garfield (1972a, pp. 476–477, 478–479, nn. 27–28) developed these considerations concerning the impact factor more fully in his *Science* article on the 1971 ISI project. He began by emphasizing the relationship of citation frequency to journal size, writing that he had very rarely found among the 1,000 most frequently cited journals one that is not also among the 1,000 journals that are most productive in terms of articles published. Garfield (p. 476) carefully distinguished scientific significance from size, declaring that "[i]n view of the relation between size and citation frequency, it would seem desirable to discount the effect of size when using citation data to assess a journal's importance." He then outlined the method by which the effect of size had been discounted for the ISI project:

> We have attempted to do this by calculating a relative impact factor—that is, by dividing the number of times a journal has been cited by the number of articles it has published during some specific period of time. The journal impact factor will thus reflect an average citation rate per published article. (p. 476)

Garfield went on to spell out the details of the calculation of "relative impact factor":

> With the *SCI* data base, it is easy to determine how frequently a journal has been cited within a given period of time, but it is much more difficult to agree on a total-items-published base to which such citation counts can properly be related because the items may have been published at any point in the journal's history. In selecting an items-published base for each journal, I have been guided by the chronological distribution of cited items in each annual edition of the *SCI*. An analysis of this distribution has shown that the typical cited article is most heavily cited during the 2 years after its year of publication. ... Therefore, since my sample consists of references made in 1969, I have taken as the items-published

base for each journal the number of items it published during
1967 and 1968. To calculate an impact factor for each journal,
I divided the number of times 1967 and 1968 articles were
cited in 1969 by the number of articles published in 1967 and
1968. (p. 476)

He also pointed out that Martyn and Gilchrist had used a similar
method in ranking British journals in their analysis of 1965 *SCI* data.

In presenting the method he chose for calculating journal impact factors, Garfield (1972a, p. 476) wrote that "the development of impact factors that fairly relate the size of a journal during the cited years to its
current citation rate is a formidable challenge to statistical analysis." He
then analyzed the difficulties of calculating this measure in two lengthy
footnotes to the article. In the first footnote, Garfield (p. 478, n. 27)
stated that the impact factor discussed in the paper—which he defined
as the "average citation rate per published item"—gives some idea of the
frequency with which the "average" paper in a particular journal is
cited. He then stated that the impact factor is both adversely affected by
papers in the journal that are not cited at all and favorably affected by
papers with unusual citation frequency. According to Garfield, the influence of uncited and very frequently cited papers can be discounted either
by considering the total number of citations in relationship to cited items
only (rather than in relation to all published items) or by considering
only the number of cited items (rather than total citations) in relation to
all published items. It is not without interest that these two ranking
methods were used by Martyn and Gilchrist. Although Garfield
acknowledged the potential usefulness of these methods for assessing
the impact of journals, he noted their impracticality, stating that their
derivation would require enormous amounts of computer time.

Garfield's second footnote dealt specifically with the problem of defining what should be in the denominator of the impact factor equation.
This problem was to play such a significant role in the subsequent history of the impact factor that it is worth directly quoting Garfield's
(1972a, pp. 478–479, n. 28) own words on the matter:

> The problem of selecting an items-published base is fur-
> ther complicated by the variety in the kinds of items pub-
> lished in scientific journals. Many journals publish only
> full-length reports of original research. Many others publish,
> in addition, editorials, technical communications, letters,
> notes, general correspondence, scientific news surveys and
> notes, book reviews, and so on; all of these are potentially
> citable items. I have not attempted in this article to limit the
> definition of items-published to lead articles, original com-
> munications, or the like. Even assuming it were possible to
> construct an acceptable classification that would accommo-
> date all of the different kinds of published material, it would

have been impossible for me, within the resources available for this article, to have examined individually each of the approximately 600,000 items that I use for the items-published base.

In Garfield's view, it was reasonable to assume that, had such a differentiation among kinds of material been made part of the analysis, the lead articles of such journals as *Science, Nature, Lancet*, and the *Journal of the American Medical Association* would have had higher impact factors than those calculated for these journals.

Garfield's Constant and Its Implications

In addition to the aforementioned statistical problems with the impact factor, Garfield (1972a) encountered another difficulty that he did not fully discuss in his *Science* article on the 1971 ISI project. Although he referred, somewhat obliquely, to this problem, he did not explicitly analyze its possible consequences. In the article, Garfield (pp. 474–475) observed that, as a result of the highly skewed distribution of citations over journals, the impact of most papers was relatively slight: The average paper is cited only 1.7 times per year, he noted, citing statistics that showed that from 1964 to 1970 the number of *SCI* citations per cited item per year was consistently around 1.7 (p. 478, n. 19). Later, Garfield (1976a) was to call this ratio "Garfield's constant" and puzzle about its significance. In later years, Garfield (1998b, p. 72) observed that, given the growth of scientific literature, the constant was remarkably stable over time, rising from 1.33 to 2.25 over the course of the 50-year period 1945–1995. Garfield's constant suggests that, as estimates of the average citation rates for most articles, impact factors will be extremely low. This was demonstrated by the impact factor statistics Garfield (1972a, p. 477) presented in his *Science* paper on the 1971 ISI project. He ranked the 152 journals with the highest impact factor, and, even over this select group, the impact factor dropped from 29.285 to 1.948—already close to Garfield's constant. What is most interesting but unstated in the *Science* article is how this ranking differed from the ranking of the 50 journals with the highest impact factors that Garfield (1972c, p. 8) presented in his *Current Contents* essay on the same project. There, the impact factor was calculated to only two decimal places, whereas, in the *Science* article, it was calculated to three—a practice that ISI continues to this day. Many years later, Garfield (2000, p. 10) publicly stated the reason for the calculation to three decimal places:

> I keep telling journal people that they should never mention JIF [journal impact factor] beyond the first decimal place. I mean, to quote a JIF like "12.345" is ridiculous. Its JIF is "12.3"; why do you need these two extra digits? It gives

a false idea of precision. Now you say that ISI does report these numbers. We only do this to give an easy way to separate journals; otherwise we would have many journals with 12.3, and these journals would have to be listed in an alphabetical order. In order to solve this problem, ISI reports the numbers as exactly as they come out. That practice probably should be abandoned.

In a recent conference paper, Garfield (2005, p. 5) has declared, "I myself deplore the quotation of impact factors to three decimal places." In spite of the passion of these comments, Garfield actually understated the problem: Because of the skewed distribution of citations over journals, their impact factors necessarily concentrate at, or beneath, his constant, which, over the course of 50 years, rose merely from 1.33 to 2.25. Given Garfield's own assessment of the imprecision of the measure, this means that there is considerable randomness in impact factor rankings, particularly at the lower end of the range, where the measure cannot meaningfully distinguish one journal from another.

The Creation of the Journal Citation Reports

The Sociological Approach to Journals and Its Intellectual Origins

The 1971 ISI project laid the foundations for the creation of the *Journal Citation Reports*. In fact, the 1969 *SCI* data used in this project were published in-house in 1973 as a preliminary version of the *JCR* in the form of three bound volumes of computer printouts. The first official *Journal Citation Reports* (Garfield, 1976b), published as volume 9 of the 1975 *SCI*, consisted of a bibliometric analysis of references processed for the 1974 *SCI*. It marked an important evolution in Garfield's conceptualization of scientific journals, for, in his introduction to the volume, Garfield adopted a sociological approach toward the analysis of scientific journals. This can be attributed in part to the influence of Bernal, whose Marxism had led him to pioneer the consideration of science in relationship to other aspects of society. Garfield's (p. vii) dedication in the first *JCR* specifically thanks Bernal for the latter's "insight into the societal origins and impact of science." However, Bernal's influence in this respect was reinforced by that of two other men, whose names also appear in Garfield's dedication of the volume: Robert K. Merton and Derek J. de Solla Price, whose names Garfield added to those of Leake and Lederberg in the secondary dedication beneath the main dedication to Bernal. All four men in the secondary dedication are described as ones "whose acumen, criticism, and encouragement as scientists and friends envigored and guided the early research that led to the publication of the *Science Citation Index* and to its use not only for information retrieval but also for the social study of science" (p. vii). Indeed, in 1962, Garfield had sent samples of the *SCI* then under development to Merton and Price as well as to Bernal.

Merton is generally considered the founder of the sociology of science. He began to develop his ideas on the relationship of science to society in the 1930s contemporaneously with Bernal, whose work did not overly impress him. In his review of Bernal's *The Social Function of Science*, Merton (1941, p. 623) described the proposals outlined in the book as "avowedly an attempt at social engineering" and "the most complete and apparently well-grounded program that has appeared since the days of the founders of the Royal Society in the seventeenth century." However, he went on to offer the following assessment:

> The book contributes a great body of substantive materials in a field which has long needed cultivation. It would be ungracious to suggest that the physicist-author has failed to interpret these materials sociologically or has done so in an excessively simplified fashion—*ce n'est pas son métier*. This task may rather be conceived as a challenge to the sociologist of science who has all too often divorced theoretical specula-tion from empirical investigation. (p. 623)

Merton himself took up the challenge issued in this assessment. His student Jonathan R. Cole (2000, p. 283) credits him with demonstrating in his own work that "the social study of science, beyond the Marxian treatment of it, could yield important results."

Garfield developed an extraordinarily close relationship with Merton, with whom he shared both ethnic and institutional links. Merton was born Meyer R. Schkolnick in 1910 in South Philadelphia to Jewish immi-grant parents from East Europe. For most of his career, he taught at Garfield's alma mater, Columbia University. In the mid-1960s Merton's interest in science as an exemplar of sociological theory caused him to establish a Columbia research program in the sociology of science, to which he recruited as its first students Jonathan Cole, Stephen Cole, and Harriet Zuckerman. By his own admission, Merton (1983) was slow to recognize the importance of the *Science Citation Index* for the sociol-ogy of science. This was probably because Merton was a qualitative, rather than a quantitative, sociologist. Indeed, Garfield (1977d, p. 6) has remarked, "I have always had the kind of reaction to much of Merton's writing that I associate with a great novelist, not a great scientist." Merton himself did no quantitative citation analyses, but his students were among the pioneers in the use of ISI data for the sociology of sci-ence. Employing citation and content analysis, Garfield (1980a) proved not only that Merton's influence extended far beyond his home discipline of sociology, being widely cited throughout the social and natural sci-ences, but also that he was cited much more for his unique sociological concepts than for his empirical findings. Garfield classified Merton's concepts in the sociology of science into five categories: priority disputes, the Matthew effect, the information structure of science, multiple dis-coveries, and norms of science.

Of Merton's concepts, the one most important for information science is the Matthew effect. Merton (1968) introduced it in a *Science* article on the psychosocial processes affecting the allocation of awards to scientists for their contributions. According to Merton, the scientific reward system is governed by the Matthew effect—a name he derived from the Gospel according to Matthew (13:12, 25:29), which states (in the King James translation he preferred): "For unto every one that hath shall be given, and he shall have abundance; but from him that hath not shall be taken away even that which he hath." Merton (1968, p. 58) argued that the Matthew effect caused a complex pattern of misallocation of credit for scientific work:

> The Matthew effect consists in the accruing of greater increments of recognition for particular scientific contributions to scientists of considerable repute and the withholding of such recognition from scientists who have not yet made their mark.

Merton traced the consequences of the Matthew effect on the scientific communication system, using the highly stratified institutional structure of U.S. academic science to point out that the Matthew effect embodies the principle of cumulative advantage operative in many systems of social stratification and produces the same result: The rich get richer at a rate that makes the poor become relatively poorer. Garfield (1977d, p. 7) has observed, "I would have an opportunity to confirm the Mertonian 'law' called 'the Matthew effect,' by which scientific recognition is bestowed upon one who already has it." That he did so is certified by Merton (1988, pp. 611–612) himself, who, in a follow-up article on the Matthew effect, cited the inequality below as evidence:

> The distributions are even more skewed in the use of scientists' work by their peers, as that use is crudely indexed by the number of citations to it. Much the same distribution has been found in various data sets: typical is Garfield's finding that, for an aggregate of some nineteen million articles published in the physical and biological sciences between 1961 and 1980, 0.3 percent were cited more than one hundred times; another 2.7 percent between twenty-five and one hundred times; and, at the other extreme, some 58 percent of those that were cited at all were cited only once in that twenty-year period. This inequality, you will recognize, is steeper than Pareto-like distributions of income.

From this it can be seen that Merton's Matthew effect bears a strong resemblance to the Marxist doctrine of the concentration of the means of the production in the hands of the capitalist elite and the impoverishment of the masses.

Whereas Merton was the putative father of the sociology of science, Price played a major role in the development of the history of science. The two men differed in the nature of their contributions to their respective disciplines: Merton's were qualitative and conceptual, whereas Price made the greatest impact with his quantitative work. Garfield was related to Price both ethnically and intellectually. Price was born in 1922 in London to parents descended from early 19th-century Jewish immigrant families. Like Bernal, Price came from Sephardic stock, although not through the father but through the mother; around 1950 he adopted his mother's maiden name—de Solla—as his middle name to indicate his Sephardic roots. Price was educated in British state schools, received his first doctorate in experimental physics from the University of London, and obtained his second doctorate in the history of science from Cambridge University. He thus stemmed from the British intellectual tradition that had so influenced Garfield. Like Garfield, Price (1964) was an admirer of Bernal, contributing an article to the Festschrift celebrating the 25th anniversary of the publication of *The Social Function of Science*. It is thus fitting that Price was the first recipient of the John Desmond Bernal Award established by the Society for Social Studies of Science in collaboration with ISI.

As Price (1980) has recorded, he first met Garfield shortly after becoming a professor of the history of science at Yale University in 1959, where he spent the bulk of his academic career. He was serving on the NSF Science Information Council when Garfield applied for support to publish the *SCI*. Although the council rejected the proposal, Price (p. v) writes that he was "inoculated with Citation Fever." During this early period, Price (1963) published his most influential book, *Little Science, Big Science*, which originated as a series of lectures delivered in 1962 at the Brookhaven National Laboratory. The approach of this book was "to deal statistically ... with general problems of the shape and size of science and the ground rules governing growth and behavior of science-in-the-large" (p. viii). Price was particularly concerned with the exponential nature of science in both its growth and distributional patterns. In respect to the first, he analyzed the logistic character of scientific growth, comparing it to similar growth patterns in biology and human society. Concerning the second, he discussed the skewed distributions in the productivity of scientists posited by Lotka's Law and in scientific journal use discovered by D. J. Urquhart in his pioneer study of loans made by London's Science Museum Library in preparation for the establishment of the National Lending Library for Science and Technology. Price (p. 75) described these distributions as "the same Pareto curve as in the distributions of incomes or sizes of cities." *Little Science, Big Science* became an ISI Citation Classic. In commenting upon its evolution, Price (1983, July 18, p. 18) made the following interesting observations about his interests and the intellectual influences upon him:

Although most of my time was then given to straight history of science, mainly in ancient astronomy and scientific instrumentation, the exponential growth business needled me a lot, and I began to pursue other quantitative researches about science, stimulated much by Robert Merton's writings in the sociology of science, by Eugene Garfield's new book on citation indexing, and by rereading Desmond Bernal's books which had prepared my mind for the initial sensitivity that led me to this field in the first place.

In a bold attempt at a theoretical coup, Price (1976, 1978) attempted to unify all the empirical laws describing the skewed distributions governing science such as Bradford's and Lotka's laws together with the Pareto distribution by deriving a stochastic model he named the Cumulative Advantage Distribution (CAD) after the pioneering work of Merton and the Coles on the social stratification of science. He described Merton's Matthew effect as double-edged in that success increases the probability of success and failure decreases the probability of success. Price regarded Merton's Matthew effect as the stochastic model for the negative binomial distribution, which had been developed on the basis of industrial accidents and smallpox contagion. In contrast, he stated, his CAD was single-edged in that success increases the probability of further success but failure is a non-event that has no effect on subsequent probabilities. In Price's view, the CAD modeled the appropriate probabilistic theory for all the empirical results of citation frequency analysis.

The combined effect of the work of Bernal, Merton, Price, and Garfield was to open the way for analysis of the scientific journal system in terms of social stratification and its mechanisms—a field of study which Karl Marx can justifiably be said to have played a major role in pioneering. This is evident in Garfield's (1976b, p. ix) focus on the social aspects of scientific journals in the preface and introduction to the first *SCI JCR*:

> As, during the years, I and many others used the *SCI* for its planned and advertised purpose of information retrieval, I came to see that I had been advised not only to consider the meaning and usefulness of references and citations, but advised especially to consider their meaning *in a particular type of journal*. The data bank amassed over the years to produce the *SCI* gave me a unique and unprecedented opportunity to look at references and citations not just as tools for information retrieval, but to look at them also as characteristics of the journals they linked. Using the *SCI* data bank, I began to study journals as socio-scientific phenomena as well as communications media.

This conceptualization of scientific journals as sociological entities marked a distinct evolution in Garfield's thinking away from Bernal's idea of scientific journals as inefficient bundles of articles that needed to be broken down into more convenient packages for delivery to individual scientists. Garfield expressed the hope that the *JCR* would prove uniquely useful in exploring the relatively new field of the sociology of science.

Garfield (1976b) opened his introduction to the new *JCR* by elaborating upon the sociological aspects of scientific journals. He pointed out that a citation index is based upon the principle that there is some meaningful relationship between one paper and another that cites it and, thus, between the work of the two authors or two groups of authors who published the papers. Garfield (p. 1) then observed that an author's or a paper's frequency of citation has been found to correlate well with professional standing and argued that the same principle could be applied to the evaluation of journals: "The more frequently a journal's articles are cited, the more the world's scientific community implies that it finds the journal to be a carrier of useful information." He described the *JCR* as extending the use of citation analysis to examine the relationships among journals rather than among articles and their authors. With this conceptualization, Garfield made journals an integral part of the social stratification system of science.

Having thus defined the basic purpose of the *JCR*, Garfield (1976b) issued a number of caveats against its indiscriminate use in the evaluation of journals. He noted that citation frequency was biased both in favor of journals publishing original research findings and the indispensable summary of research findings provided by reviews, and against those published for other purposes, such as conveying scientific news. Echoing Merton's concerns about the misallocation of scientific credit, Garfield stated that citation frequency is sometimes a function of variables other than scientific merit. Among such variables, he listed first an author's reputation, followed by others such as the controversial character of subject matter, journal circulation and price, indexing coverage, society memberships, and library holdings. Garfield (p. 3) warned against the technical difficulties involved in utilizing the *JCR*:

> We have, thus, in compiling the *JCR* refrained from combining journal counts on the basis of "lineage," even when it is clearly definable. Except where a title change has been so minor ... that it neither affects the title's position in a catalog listing nor requires additional or different entries, the *JCR* does not combine counts for related journals (replacements, supersedents, continuations, descendants, etc.). Nor does it combine counts for "sections" of "the same journal." [The] *JCR* leaves it to the user to decide whether or not his purpose recommends that counts be combined in such cases.

Thus, utilization of the *JCR* requires intimate knowledge of the intricacies of serials cataloging—knowledge often absent in researchers and others who have drawn upon *JCR* data for their various purposes. Under the heading "Caution!," Garfield emphasized the need to be aware of the different citation patterns of different disciplines in comparing journals. Toward the end of the introduction, Garfield (p. 5) emphatically declared that "the *JCR* cannot be used alone in evaluating a journal's performance."

JCR Structure and Citation Measures:
Final Formulation of the Impact Factor

The structure of the first *JCR* consisted of three packages. The first of these was the Journal Ranking Package, which began with an alphabetical list of journals cited in 1974 and then ranked these journals in descending order by the following measures: total citations in 1974, impact factor in 1974, immediacy index in 1974, source items published in 1974, and 1974 citations of their 1972 and 1973 articles. The Journal Ranking Package was followed by a Citing Journal Package, which listed citing journals alphabetically with subentry listings of the journals they cited in 1974, and a Cited Journal Package, which listed cited journals alphabetically with subentry listings of the journals that cited them in 1974. With certain important modifications, this structure was to remain essentially the same through the successive print and microform editions of the *JCR*s until electronic versions with new capabilities appeared in the mid-1990s on both CD-ROM and the World Wide Web. Prior to the appearance of the electronic versions, the rankings published in the *JCR*s were rigid and could be manipulated only with great difficulty.

In order to understand fully the citation frequency rankings of the *JCR*, it is necessary to have a clear grasp of the definitions of three key *JCR* terms. These (Garfield, 1976b) are quoted below. The first two definitions involve calculations; the *JCR* data for the *Journal of the American Chemical Society* as well as the method of calculation are placed beneath them to aid in their understanding.

> Immediacy Index. A measure of how quickly the "average cited article" in a particular journal is cited. A journal's immediacy index considers citations made during the year in which the cited items were published. Thus, the 1979 immediacy index of journal *X* would be calculated by dividing the number of all journals' 1979 citations of items it published in 1979 by the *total number* of source items it published in 1979. It should be obvious that an article published early in the year has a better chance of being cited than one published later in the year. As a result, journals published weekly and monthly will theoretically have an advantage, as regards

immediacy, over journals published quarterly and semi-annually. (p. 6)

CITATIONS IN 1974 TO 1974 SOURCE ITEMS	SOURCE ITEMS IN 1974	IMMEDIACY INDEX
J AM CHEM SOC		
1835	1432	1.281

[CALCULATION: 1835/1432 = 1.281]

Impact Factor. A measure of the frequency with which the "average cited article" in a journal has been cited in a particular year. The *JCR* impact factor is basically a ratio between citations and citable items published. Thus, the 1979 impact factor of journal X would be calculated by dividing the number of all the *SCI* source journals' 1979 citations of articles journal X published in 1977 and 1978 by the *total number* of source items it published in 1977 and 1978. There are other ways of calculating journal impact. ...

The impact factor is useful in evaluating the significance of absolute citation frequencies. It tends to discount the advantage of large journals over small ones, of frequently issued journals over less frequently issued ones (weeklies vs. quarterlies or annuals), of older journals over newer journals. In each such case the first is likely to produce or have produced a larger citable corpus than the second. All things being equal, the larger that corpus, the more often a journal will be cited. The impact factor allows some qualification of quantitative data. The qualification is algorithmic and objective, but nonetheless useful in journal evaluation. (pp. 6–7)

CITATIONS IN 1974 TO 1973 1972 72+73	SOURCE ITEMS IN 1973 1972 72+73	IMPACT FACTOR
J AM CHEM SOC		
7855 9233 17088	1776 2123 3899	4.383

[CALCULATION: 17088/3899 = 4.383]

Source Item. Called also source document or source article, a source item is an item published in one of the source journals processed for the *Science Citation Index* (*SCI*). Source items may be original substantive articles, editorials, letters, technical notes, correction notes, meeting reports, reviews, and so

forth. From the references provided by a source item, citations are extracted to prepare the *Citation Index* of the *SCI*.

Some types of source items (e.g., news items, non-scientific
and non-technical correspondence) do not by their very nature
invite citation in the references of scientific reports. Such
source items are excluded from source-item counts in [the]
compilation of the *JCR*. In the *JCR* only original articles,
technical notes, and review articles are counted as source
items, except in the case of [certain] journals, whose meeting
abstracts are admitted as source items in impact-factor and
immediacy-index calculation. (pp. 7–8)

From these definitions it can be seen that the *JCR* ranked journals
by citation frequency in two different ways: the total citation frequency of journals and the citation frequency of the "average cited
article" (p. 6). Each of these was, in turn, done in two versions. The
total citation rankings were determined by calculations using both
the total citations to all the issues of a given journal and the total citations only to the issues published in the two years preceding the processing year. The latter method—that of Martyn and Gilchrist
(1968)—yielded the numerator of the impact factor. With respect to
rankings by the "average cited article," the impact factor was calculated by dividing the citations of the processing year to the issues of
the journals published in the two years preceding the processing year
by the number of "source items" published during these two preceding
years, whereas the immediacy index was calculated by adding the
citations of the processing year to the issues of the processing year
and dividing by the "source items" of the processing year (Garfield,
1976b, p. 7). This raises two contentious issues. First, both cases
involved a dichotomy between the numerator and the denominator.
The numerator was comprised of citations from all types of items published but the denominator included only the number of source items
defined as "citable." This technically converted both the impact factor
and the immediacy index from average citations per source item into
ratios of citations to "citable" source item. Second, as a measure of the
rapidity with which items are cited after publication, the immediacy
index affected the impact factor due to the latter's two-year limitation. But scientific disciplines differ in this respect—a fact that
severely complicates cross-disciplinary comparisons by means of the
impact factor.

Garfield (1976d) introduced the new *JCR* to the broader scientific
community in an article published in *Nature*, in which he analyzed its
data and compared the findings to those of the 1971 ISI project using
1969 *SCI* data. This analysis was instrumental in clarifying the structure of the impact factor. Garfield stated that the new *JCR* had two measures of journal significance—total citations and impact—and discussed
their characteristics. In his treatment of total citations, he presented

data in a table, which he divided into two sections (pp. 610–611). The first section arrayed the 206 journals ranking highest in 1974 total citations to all journal issues; the second included an additional 78 journals that ranked high in total citations to their 1972 and 1973 issues only—actually a ranking of journals by the numerator of the impact factor. The total citation rankings given in the *Nature* article exhibited significant deviations from those of the *JCR* because the table in *Nature* combined the counts for sections and retitled continuations. Analyzing these two total citation rankings, Garfield found that the section based upon citation counts to the 1972 and 1973 issues only had a large proportion of titles (63 percent) that had begun publication in the 1960s and 1970s. He declared that this second section was a necessary supplement to the first, based on counts to all issues, because "the journals have high current citation but lack historical mass to push them up into the top of a list ranked by total citations" (p. 609). Thus, this analysis revealed the effect of equalizing journals in terms of time. Comparing the journals that ranked highest in total citations to all issues in 1974 to the same category of journals in 1969, Garfield found what he considered a remarkable stability: Of the 206 journals most cited in 1969, 169 remained among the top 206 in 1974. Some 15 years later, Garfield (1991) confirmed this stability when he published two lists of journals: The 50 journals found to be most highly cited in his seminal study of 1969. *SCI* citations and the 50 titles most highly cited in the 1989 *SCI JCR*. Of the 50 titles on the 1969 list, 32 were also on the list in 1989.

Garfield (1976d, p. 613) also discussed the impact factor in his *Nature* article, using a table that ranked journals with impact factors greater than 2. He demonstrated the significance of these journals by pointing out that, out of 2,443 journals, only 150 had an impact factor above 3 and that the mean impact factor for all journals was 1.015. In presenting the impact factor data, Garfield (p. 613) issued the following warning about the denominator of the impact factor calculation:

> In using the data presented here, one should be aware that we revised our definition of "source items" used to calculate impacts. In 1969 we included as source items much material (editorials, non-scientific and non-technical correspondence, news notes, and so on) that does not by its very nature invite citation in scientific and technical reports. This policy worked to the disadvantage of some major journals. Our redefinition accounts in part for the changed impact in 1974 of journals like *Nature, Science, Lancet, Journal of the American Medical Association*, and *British Medical Journal*.

Garfield thus let it be known that ISI had begun to do what Martyn and Gilchrist (1968) found very difficult and Garfield (1972a, p. 479, n. 28) himself doubted the very possibility of doing—defining what a "citable item" is and constructing "an acceptable classification that would accommodate all of the different kinds of published material." Like the total citations table, the impact factor table in the *Nature* article ranked 284 journals and was divided into two sections (Garfield, 1976d, pp. 612–613). The first section listed 206 high-impact journals with the exclusion of review journals, whereas the second section ranked 78 high-impact review journals. Garfield found that the review journals had generally a higher impact factor, stating that this clearly showed the importance of review journals and confirmed previous ISI studies. He then made the following announcement concerning review journals: "Their extraordinary impact, along with a surge in the number of review-type articles and publications, led to ISI's decision to publish *Index to Scientific Reviews*" (p. 613).

Having analyzed the nature of total citations and impact factor as measures of journal significance, Garfield (1976d) went on to demonstrate the need for set definition in citation analysis. He did this with a table divided into three sections that listed the journals ranking highest in total citations and impact factor for three disciplines: astronomy/astrophysics, botany, and mathematics (p. 614). Garfield stated that the differences in average impact and citation between the three illustrative groups indicated that comparisons between journals in different subject areas might be invidious. He then summed up the causation of different citation patterns among disciplines and their effect on the impact factor:

> Variation from field to field is determined by the interplay of several factors. Perhaps the most important is the average number of references per paper in the field. In general, mathematicians cite less than half as many papers as do biochemists. Engineers on the other hand cite books as heavily as journals, as do social scientists. Furthermore, calculation of impact based on 1972 and 1973 publications is bound to affect the impact of journals in a field like mathematics, where citation of older literature is far more common than in others. Thus, the impact of mathematics journals would be higher if calculated on the basis of 1970 and 1971 publications. (p. 609)

In this way, Garfield pointed out the problem of selecting a fair time basis for calculating impact factor.

Modifications of the *JCRs* Affecting the Impact Factor

Over the next few years the *JCRs* underwent modifications that affected both the calculation of the impact factor and its evaluation. For the 1977 edition, with the introduction of *Social Sciences Citation Index JCR*, the database from which the *JCRs* were derived was expanded to include references processed for the *SCI* and the *SSCI*. The subject scope of the *JCR* database was further expanded for the 1979 edition by the inclusion of the references being processed for the newly established *Arts & Humanities Citation Index*. This added to the subject complexity of the *JCR*s, as Garfield (1980b, p. 8A) noted in the 1979 *SCI JCR*:

> The use of the combined data bases eliminates the often shadowy boundaries between the sciences and social sciences. Some journals are covered by *SCI* and *SSCI*; others are covered only by *SCI*, but may also be cited extensively by journals in the *SSCI* and *A&HCI* data base. To present a more accurate picture of these journals' citation rates and to include a complete list of the journals which cite them most often, citation data from *SSCI*-only and *A&HCI* journals are incorporated in the *SCI JCR*.

An equivalent announcement was put in the 1979 *SSCI JCR*. Given the interdisciplinary citation processes described by Garfield's Law of Concentration, the combination of the databases meant that the *JCR* citation measures were capturing the significance of journals not only within their specific fields but also for all branches of human knowledge. However, with the 1978 editions of both the *SCI* and *SSCI JCR*s, ISI began to compensate for the increased subject complexity of the *JCR* data by including a section listing the source journals within narrowly defined subject categories. Together with these subject changes, ISI introduced new measures and sections that aided in the clarification of citation patterns and their effect on the impact factor.

With the 1977 edition of the *SCI* and the newly created *SSCI JCR*s, ISI added a section called "Source Data Listing" that classified source items into non-review and review articles, giving the total number of items and references for each. These totals were used to calculate references-to-source-items ratios for each type and the two types combined. However, even this simple classification of source items into "non-review articles" and "review articles" proved difficult. Garfield (1982a, p. 5) later described the word "review" as "one of the more ambiguous terms in scholarship." Defining a review article in science as "an annotated summary or critical digest of the literature of a given topic," he declared that "even in science the line of demarcation is hazy." Garfield (1987b) discussed various methods of classifying review journals and articles, citing research that classified review journals into eight different types and showed that review articles could run the gamut from little more than bibliographies to highly subjective evaluations of material within a field in many bibliographic forms.

The 1978 *JCR* editions provided vastly improved measurement of the chronological patterns of citations with the introduction of a part entitled "Journal Half-Life Package," which was divided into two sections. The first cumulated the percentage of citations to each cited journal over a ten-year period. These cumulated percentages formed the basis for calculating for each cited journal a measure called "half-life," which Garfield (1979c, p. 10A) defined as "the number of journal publication years from the current year back whose articles have accounted for 50 percent of the total citations received in a given year." The second section of the "Journal Half-Life Package" ranked journals in ascending order by this measure.

The Enshrinement of the Impact Factor as ISI's Chief Measure of Journal Significance

The 1979 editions of the *JCR*s introduced a new feature that enshrined the impact factor as ISI's chief measure of journal significance. This new feature integrated many of the modifications already mentioned; Garfield (1980b, p. 1A) described it in these words:

> A refinement in the 1979 *JCR* enables researchers to access journal ranking information according to journals' subject fields. I've often stressed the importance of limiting comparisons between journals to those in the same field. The journal literature varies in importance as a means of disseminating information in different fields, and citation practices vary from field to field. Thus, a comparison of the citation data of a micro-biology journal and a journal of highway engineering would be meaningless. The researcher can avoid such "apples and oranges" comparisons by turning to Section 8 of the *JCR's Journal Ranking Package*. This new section shows journals grouped by subject category, then ranked by impact factor. Journal half-life is also provided.

No reasons were stated for the inclusion of journal half-life, but it does provide a means of comparing between journals and subject fields, whether or not the citations to journals were concentrated within the two-year limit on which the calculation of the impact factor was based. Until the appearance of the electronic versions of the *JCR*s in the mid-1990s, these impact factor rankings were the only easily and immediately accessible citation rankings of journals within narrowly defined subject fields. This must be considered the underlying reason the impact factor assumed such overwhelming importance in scientific evaluations.

The question now arises as to why Garfield accorded such prominence to the impact factor as a measure of journal significance. There are manifold reasons—some of them traceable to Bernal. First, it is possible to hypothesize that, as a youth, Garfield was indoctrinated into leftist political thinking, which tends to regard equality almost as a moral imperative. The impact factor levels the playing field, putting the measurement of all journals—big and small, old and new—on the same basis: Thus, the ostensible fairness of the impact factor may have played a role in its widespread adoption as the standard measure of journal significance. Second, quite apart from politics, Garfield was heavily influenced by Bernal's idea that the article, not the journal as a whole, is the prime vehicle of scientific communication. The impact factor is definitely an attempt to measure the significance of a journal not globally but by the importance of its individual articles. For this reason, Garfield (1972b, pp. 5–6) considered the impact factor to be helpful to scientists in selecting a journal in which to publish, observing that "[p]ublishing in a high-prestige journal which has a large circulation may have less impact on the scientific community than publication in a journal with smaller circulation but high impact." Third, for various reasons—some of which will become clearer later—Garfield was focused on measuring current, not historical, significance. As has been discussed, one of the reasons Garfield developed the impact factor was to discount the effect of older papers that had become citation classics. From the perspective of current significance, such citation classics can be highly distortional. For example, Garfield (1996) pointed out that Lowry's classic 1951 protein determination paper, which fascinated Garfield over his entire career, alone accounted for about 7,000 (3 percent) of the 265,000 citations in 1994 to the *Journal of Biological Chemistry*, which was the journal most highly ranked in total citations that year. Fourth, when journals are measured by impact factor, review journals are the most highly ranked ones. Review articles had always held a special meaning for Garfield. It has already been shown that Bernal stressed the importance of review literature in *The Social Function of Science*, which so influenced Garfield in his youth, and had uncovered the importance of review materials for scientists in the research he presented to the 1948 Royal Society Scientific Information Conference. Moreover, under Leake's guidance, Garfield had developed the entire concept of the *Science Citation Index* as a result of his analysis of review articles. Throughout his career, Garfield (1974a, 1974b, 1977c, 1982a, 1987b, 1987c) maintained his high esteem for scientific reviews, even suggesting that there be a counterpart for science of the law reviews published by American law schools and that reviewing be established as a scientific profession. In describing his attitude toward review literature, Garfield (1987b, p. 5) wrote:

> The "culture" of reviewing the literature is so fundamental to my own professional life that I too may forget that in comparison with research discoveries one reads about in the press, and for which Nobel Prizes are awarded, reviewing may seem to the uninitiated to be a relatively humdrum topic.
>
> But it is precisely this mistaken notion that I want to dispel. It is not an accident that so many of our greatest scientists have used, created, and contributed to the review literature. Like an important opinion rendered by the chief

justice of the Supreme Court, reviews can have great value and influence.

Review literature was the subject of a number of analyses by researchers at ISI, which joined with Annual Reviews Inc. in 1979 to sponsor the National Academy of Sciences Award for Excellence in Scientific Reviewing. However, Garfield (1987b) presented evidence that his opinion on the importance of review literature was at variance with that of many scientists, reporting that many authors of ISI Citation Classics believed that review articles should not be automatically granted this award and that some felt that their review articles should not be judged on the same criteria as their articles reporting original research. And, finally—a reason never stated by Garfield but obvious to anybody with a knowledge of serials cataloging who has ever worked with *JCR* data—the impact factor's restriction of the field of observation to the two most recent years minimizes the technical problems and subjective judgments occasioned by the bibliographic instability of journals, which have a tendency to change titles, continue or supersede each other, and divide into parts that subsequently do or do not recombine.

Utilization of Citation Measures in Determining ISI Journal Coverage

Development of Selection Criteria

Garfield (1972d, 1979b, 1985a) has reported that, in its early days, ISI had no objective criteria or formal policies for selecting journals to cover. Journal selection was by necessity highly subjective for most disciplines and so Garfield compiled a basic list in the same manner as any experienced scientific publisher or librarian. Although there were classic studies of scientific serials and library surveys, ISI did not need them to know that publications such as *Science, Nature, New England Journal of Medicine, Proceedings of the National Academy of Sciences-US*, were among the most important scientific journals. Garfield (1985a, p. 6) has stated that there was no question that journals of this caliber should be covered because these intuitive choices were backed up by all sorts of objective criteria. He has also pointed out that this same basic group of hard-core journals continued to maintain high quality year after year and had an uncanny way of surviving and growing. Journal selection did not become a major problem until economics permitted ISI to extend its coverage beyond this overwhelmingly important core.

With the growth of *SCI* journal coverage during the 1960s from about 600 to over 2,000 titles, ISI developed the capability of experimenting with citation measures of journal significance. One of the first of these experiments was with the impact factor. In his report Garfield (1970b) cited Martyn and Gilchrist's (1968) evaluation of British scientific journals as a study that quantified the impact measure that Garfield and

Sher (1963) had initially proposed. Defining the impact factor as "the mean number of citations to a journal's articles by papers subsequently published," he stated that, "though perhaps a somewhat crude measure, [it] does reveal some interesting characteristics of scientists, as well as of journals" (Garfield, 1970b, p. 5). Garfield (p. 5) urged caution in using measures such as the impact factor for comparative purposes, specifically warning about "the 'immediacy factor'—the 'bunching,' or more frequent citation, of recent papers relative to earlier ones." For this early experiment, ISI constructed a prototype of impact factor by selecting the 1965 *SCI* references to articles published in 1963, sorting the references by cited journal, and then ranking the journals by "impact factor." Garfield found the results revealing. The average impact factor was only 1.9, but the relatively new *Journal of Molecular Biology*, which began publication in 1961, had an impact factor of 7, whereas "long established 'significant' journals like the *Journal of Biological Chemistry*" (p. 5) had an impact factor of about 3. This caused Garfield (p. 5) to observe:

> It is generally recognized that molecular biology is a highly focussed [*sic*], "hot" field; so, the question arises whether the rapidity of developments in such a field tends to distort the impact factor. Rapid citation of one paper by others in a fast-moving field presents a picture of impact different from that of journals publishing articles that are cited in later years not only frequently but in a wide range of journals.

He then declared that "whether a journal is cited because it is in a rapidly developing field, or because it publishes articles of long-term impact, the journal is significant" (p. 6). At the end of the report, Garfield (p. 6) observed that most journals containing a large number of source items also prove to be significant, thus making the connection between size and significance, and concluded with the following recommendation:

> Hopefully, some of the less significant journals would take steps to improve their quality or to merge with other small journals to form larger ones, which ... tend to acquire a special significance, due possibly to greater exposure.

The 1971 project analyzing 1969 *SCI* data was pivotal in ISI's development of criteria for selecting which journals to cover with its indexes, and Garfield (1972d, 1973a, 1973b, 1973c) devoted a number of "Current Comments" essays to this aspect of the project. The fact that, in these essays, he initially referred to the *Journal Citation Reports* as the *Journal Citation Index* serves as a sign that they were being written as the discoveries were made. In the earliest of these essays Garfield (1972d, p. 5) made a very interesting distinction between the roles of total citations—or "absolute citation frequency" in his terminology—and the impact factor in selecting journals for coverage. With respect to the former, Garfield (p. 5) observed that "absolute citation frequency is not sufficient for the task of journal selection except perhaps to establish 'core' journal collections." He then noted the difficulty of new and small journals to make it into the top ranks of the most-cited journals, especially given that "an almost immutable 'constant' citation rate will obtain and that the average article in *SCI* is cited about 1.67 times a year" (p. 5). Garfield then went on to state that, because absolute citation frequency does not tell the entire story, ISI had developed the impact factor to discount the advantage that large, established journals have in absolute citation counts. Here we see in embryonic form the relationship of total citations and impact factor to Garfield's Law of Concentration. Total citations identify the core journals of each discipline that form the small multidisciplinary core dominating science as a whole, whereas the impact factor is a measure enabling one to select in a more rational fashion which journals should be selected for coverage from the long tails of the Bradfordian citation comets.

Garfield (1973a) joyously hailed the publication of his 1972 *Science* article on the 1971 ISI project with a "Current Comments" essay in which he summarized some of the project's key findings. Of greatest interest in this essay are his conclusions on the relationship of size to significance and his justification of the impact factor. As regards the former, Garfield (p. 5) wrote:

> The [*Science*] paper deals primarily with the use of our *Journal Citation Index* data bank to determine the frequency with which scientific and technical journals are cited in the journal literature. It shows that a "large" journal that publishes many articles is, as a rule, more frequently cited than a journal that publishes fewer articles. In addition, however, through development of "impact factors," it shows that articles in about half of these most-cited journals are cited less frequently than articles in smaller, less-cited journals.

Concerning the latter, Garfield stated that the project provided justification for ISI's coverage of review journals, despite the extreme expense required to process their many references, because it found that they ranked high in impact factor even though they were not often among the most-cited titles. He also emphasized that objective criteria alone do not solve the journal selection problem. In a follow-up essay, Garfield (1973b) declared that, although citation studies enable the identification of the obviously important journals, ISI also had to take into account other factors in evaluating the less-important titles. He pointed out that, because biochemists composed a major segment of ISI readership, a new journal in biochemistry or molecular biology would have higher priority than a journal in horticulture or a journal of a local medical society.

At the beginning of his most comprehensive essay on the implications of the 1971 project for ISI journal coverage, Garfield (1973c) announced that the company was using citation analysis to evaluate journals but then immediately reiterated his caution that neither men nor journals can be judged on the basis of citation analysis alone. He stated that citation analysis adds objectivity to the evaluation process and listed three different ways of using citation data to evaluate journals: (1) the frequency with which the journal is cited, (2) the frequency with which the average article in the journal is cited, in other words, the impact factor, and (3) the frequency with which a given journal publishes articles that become citation superstars. Garfield concentrated his attention in this essay on the second and third methods. To illustrate the third method, he used Lowry's paper on protein determination as an example of a citation superstar, noting that in 1969 only about 150 journals were cited as frequently as this single paper. Garfield then reported that he had recently examined a list of the 1,000 papers most frequently cited during the past decade. He had found that only about 200 journals had accounted for these 1,000 articles, of which half had been published in only fifteen journals. In Garfield's view, although a citation blockbuster like Lowry's paper was atypical of most scientific papers, it was not so atypical of other papers published in the *Journal of Biological Chemistry*. Summing up his main point on this matter, Garfield (p. 6) wrote that "it is remarkable that of the 1000 or more most heavily cited articles in the literature, not one appeared in an 'obscure' journal." This concentration of high-quality articles in a few high-prestige and high-visibility journals was also found by Merton's student, Stephen Cole (2000), who regarded it as a sign of the effectiveness of the scientific journal system in concentrating attention on key research and therefore making this journal system capable of playing a role in scientific evaluation. However, Cole did note that, due to the inherent difficulty of predicting quality, most of the articles even in the most prestigious journals were also of minor significance, thus hampering the journal system as a tool for scientific evaluation.

Garfield (1976c) stated that one of the most surprising discoveries of the 1971 ISI project was the relatively low impact of articles published in most journals, including journals that seem almost universally accepted as preeminent. As proof of this, he observed that there were only about 150 journals with impact factors greater than 2 and fewer than 500 journals with impact factors above 1. He then went on to translate the statement in his 1972 *Science* article that developing a fair way of calculating impact factors was "a formidable challenge to statistical analysis" (Garfield, 1972a, p. 476) in the following manner: "In less stilted prose, it offers ample opportunity for statistical carping" (Garfield, 1973c, p. 5). He also cautioned that in dealing with journals of small size and low impact—in other words, with the vast majority of journals—considerations other than citation counts had to be taken into account in justifying coverage.

In this and in two subsequent essays dedicated to coverage by *Current Contents*, Garfield (1973c, 1979b, 1985a) discussed these other considerations in detail. The most controversial ones were those he categorized under the heading "Geopolitical Representation," which consisted of two elements: language and geographical representation. Concerning language, he stated that, given two equivalent journals, ISI would choose the one that published articles in English on the grounds that most of its readership could handle English, but few could deal with Slavic or Asian languages. Failing this, preference would be given those journals that contained informative abstracts and summaries in English as it would be absurd for scientists to expect colleagues abroad to be able to read all of the exotic languages in which original data could be reported. Garfield (1976c, 1977a, 1977b) was fairly adamant on this point and he caused a scandal in France by publishing there an article on the provinciality of French science, in which he used citation analysis to prove that French science was declining in influence because of the refusal of French scientists to recognize that French was no longer a significant international language. Garfield declared English to be the true international language of science, recommending that French scientists publish in English and that French-language journals also be published in an English edition or at least have contents pages and summaries in English. This *"nouveau défi américain"* appears to have had an effect, for in a follow-up study Garfield (1988) found that French researchers were publishing much more in English and citing English (international) literature more extensively. Garfield (2002) offered much the same advice to the Germans.

In outlining ISI criteria for selecting which foreign journals to cover, Garfield described language as being closely interconnected with geographic representation. Thus, given a choice of two journals in the same subject area, ISI would choose the one with international representation. Garfield held that the fundamental issue for scientists in small countries like Finland was that research of international significance should be submitted to international journals. He reported that his own research showed that, of the 23 most-cited articles by Third World authors, none had been published in Third World journals, 13 had been published in U.S. journals, seven in the U.K., two in the Netherlands, and one in Germany (Garfield, 1983, p. 120). This research also revealed that most of the citations to these articles came from scientists in developed countries. In a paper on the implications of the quantitative analysis of scientific literature for science policymaking in Latin America and the Caribbean, Garfield (1995, p. 88) gave the following characterization of *SCI* journal coverage:

> Currently, ISI indexes about 3,300 journals for the *SCI*, all
> peer-reviewed and internationally influential. This selective

coverage is not merely a matter of economics; it reflects a virtual law of nature with regard to the use of the journal literature. Just a handful of journals in any field account for the lion's share of the really important, frequently read, and frequently cited journals.

Thus, what the ISI database represents is the set of journals that constitute the internationally influential literature. It does not represent the science of any given country or region as a whole, but it does represent the portion of research that is published within and cited within the internationally elite literature. Beyond that, it generally represents the best science performed in any nation.

Garfield (1997a) returned to the question of the internationality of ISI journal coverage in an article examining whether the *SCI* discriminated against Third World journals. This article is most interesting not only for Garfield's explanation of what he meant by *SCI*'s selective journal coverage being reflective of "a virtual law of nature" (Garfield, 1995, p. 88), but also for his description of the role of impact factor in ISI's determination of which journal to cover. With respect to the first point, Garfield identified the "virtual law of nature" with Bradford's Law of Scattering and his own Law of Concentration, pointing out that such laws are operative in other areas of human endeavor. He then commented on the alleged bias in the ISI databases:

> All such discussions are essentially concerned with the tail of a long hyperbolic curve. Once the core journals are selected, the remainder of one's effort is spent selecting from thousands of relatively small and low-impact journals published, both in the advanced as well as in the developing countries. (Garfield, 1997a, p. 640)

Garfield declared that ISI had developed the journal impact factor as just one method of supplementing the subjective appraisal of small journals by objective, unobtrusive means, and noted that citation impact was just one of many criteria used to select such journals. Of these criteria, he first mentioned that English had become the *lingua franca* of science, declaring: "Any journal which claims international significance will at minimum include English titles and abstracts" (p. 641). Garfield also pointed out that ISI coverage of articles by Third World scientists had substantially increased because they were increasingly publishing in the international journals. Returning to the relationship of size to significance, he stated that many Third World countries were suffering by publishing marginal journals and urged them to combine the best material into larger regional journals to achieve a critical mass, thereby following the precedent of the numerous European journals that had made many national journals essentially obsolete. In a later interview,

Garfield (1999b, p. 69) characterized ISI bias in journal selection, if any, not as an "American" but as an "English-language" bias.

Quantitative versus Qualitative Criteria

Garfield's (1990) most cogent description of ISI journal selection policies is a "Current Comments" essay adapted from a talk he gave in Taipei at the Symposium on Science Journal Evaluation sponsored by the National Science Council of Taiwan Science and Technology Information Center. The policies and considerations he set forth in this essay are still being largely followed by ISI today (Testa, 2004), long after his retirement as head of the company.

Garfield (1990) stated that ISI took into account three types of information, ranging from the quantitative to the qualitative, when evaluating journals for coverage: citation data, journal standards, and expert judgment. He gave the following overview of these three sources for evaluative criteria:

> Citation data are a source of quantitative indicators that can be used to evaluate existing journals with established track records. ... But selection of new journals often relies on other, more qualitative considerations. Journal standards are an example. A journal's ability to meet its declared schedule and frequency is perhaps the most basic expectation. Standards can also include editorial requirements for abstracts titles, and references set by professional associations of publishers and editors. Peer review of submissions, editorial board membership, and the reputation of the publisher or sponsoring society are other indicators of journal quality.
>
> Finally, journal selection also relies on the subjective judgment of experts in a particular field—subscribers, editors and publishers, and ISI's many editorial advisory board members and staff specialists. (pp. 5–6)

Need for Subject Set Definition

Garfield (1990) began his discussion of the utilization of citation measures in ISI journal selection policies with his oft-reiterated warning on the need for a set definition before performing any citation analysis, stating in this respect:

> It should always be stressed that citation data must be carefully interpreted—and their limitations clearly understood—when they are used for evaluating anything. ... For example, the number of authors and journals varies greatly

between and within disciplines, as do their citation levels and rates. Smaller fields like botany or mathematics do not generate as many articles or citations as, say, biotechnology or genetics. Also, in certain fields it may take 10 or more years for an article to attract a meaningful number of citations, while in other research areas citations can typically peak after only a few years. (p. 7)

Total Citations, the Law of Concentration, and the Multidisciplinary Core

Following this mandatory warning, Garfield (1990) introduced the citation measures ISI used in determining journal coverage. He presented a table listing, in descending rank order, the 25 journals with the most total citations in the 1988 *SCI*. His comments on these journals were instructive because they dealt with the characteristics of the extreme upper stratum of those journals that, according to his Law of Concentration, form the relatively small, multidisciplinary core dominating all science:

> The list of the 25 most-cited journals in the 1988 *SCI* (Table 1) probably agrees closely with most readers' mental list of the most important scientific journals. Hardly anyone would dispute the inclusion of the *Journal of Biological Chemistry, Nature*, the *Proceedings of the National Academy of Sciences of the USA*, the *Journal of the American Chemical Society, Science*, or any others. The same basic group of journals tends to be most cited year after year. A few may gradually decline or be replaced by successful newcomers like *Cell* as editors and audiences change. But most successful journals survive and prosper for decades. Not surprisingly, the list is dominated by larger journals and the big life-sciences specialties. Fourteen also ranked among the top 25 by number of articles published. (pp. 7–8)

What is to be particularly noted here is that, according to Garfield, these most highly cited journals conform to scientists' conceptions of what an important scientific journal is, that they are among the largest in terms of number of articles published, and that they maintain their dominance over time, giving the journal social stratification system a high degree of stability. It can be hypothesized that scientists deem them important because they are old, largely bibliographically stable, and historically significant in terms of the number of citation classics they have published over the years.

Impact Factor, the Bradfordian Citation Comet Tail, and Review versus Research Journals

After discussing the characteristics of the journals comprising the upper stratum of the multidisciplinary core of journals posited by his Law of Concentration as dominating all science, Garfield (1990) turned to the impact factor—the citation measure used by ISI to select journals from among those journals that the law theorized as forming the long tails of the Bradfordian citation comets of each discipline. He began by stating that the main purpose of the impact factor—or "the average number of citations per article"—was to compensate for the "putative size advantage" of the journals comprising the multidisciplinary core (p. 8). Garfield's approach to the use of the impact factor in journal selection was twofold and he presented two tables to demonstrate his method: One listed the 25 journals ranking highest in impact factor in the 1988 *SCI* and the other enumerated the 25 journals publishing at least 100 articles that ranked highest in impact factor in the 1988 *SCI*. Garfield gave the following analysis of these tables:

> In Table 2 impact is calculated as follows: the number of articles published by a journal in 1986 and 1987 is divided into the number of citations they received in 1988. For example, the *Annual Review of Biochemistry* published 67 articles in 1986 and 1987. They received a total of 3,237 citations from ISI-covered journals in 1988. Thus, its impact factor is 48.3.
>
> The list is obviously dominated by review journals, which tend to publish fewer contributions than original research journals, but these are cited much more frequently. Table 3 presents another impact ranking, showing only journals that published at least 100 articles, which effectively excludes most review journals.
>
> Eighteen life-sciences journals are listed, compared to two each for chemistry and physics. Again, although impact compensates somewhat for the size of a journal or literature, it tends to favor research areas that more heavily cite recent research published in the last two years. As we found several years ago, the average number of references cited per article is perhaps the most significant contributing factor. This may or may not be a reflection of the field size. (p. 8)

Garfield's approach was interesting from two perspectives. First, both in the passage just quoted and in the tables, the impact factor was calculated only to the first decimal place. However, Garfield was dealing only with the extreme high end of a skewed distribution, where ties in rank from such a calculation would not be as overwhelmingly common as at the lower end of the distribution, reducing the impact factor's ability to discriminate. Second, Garfield used the unadulterated impact factor to identify his all-important review journals, but, for the evaluation of research journals, he reintroduced the element of size (which his research had found to be causal in journal significance) by restricting the set to those journals publishing 100 or more articles. The results supported Garfield's theory that high-impact research articles tend to concentrate in the multidisciplinary core dominating all science: Of the 25 journals that he identified as being highest in total citations, 12 were also on his list of the 25 journals highest in impact factor but publishing 100 or more articles per year.

Garfield (1990) also dealt with three other aspects of impact factor: calculating the impact factor of journals not covered by ISI, rankings by five-year impact factor, and item-by-item impact. These topics will not be covered in this chapter, as they are exceedingly complex, are crucial elements in the validation of impact factor, and play an important role in the use of impact factor for evaluative purposes; they therefore require the introduction of an entire set of new considerations for their explanation. However, it is worth noting that, in discussing the first of these topics, Garfield observed à propos of the complaints of Third World editors about their journals having a higher impact factor than journals covered by ISI:

> This reflects another common misconception—that impact factors are the sole or single most important criterion for coverage. In fact, journal impact is only one of several quantitative and qualitative factors described in this essay that we take into account. (p. 9)

Garfield has largely himself to blame for this misconception, for he has continually stressed the need for subject set definition in citation analysis, then ranked journals within defined subject groups only by impact factor in the *JCR*s, and calculated impact factor to three decimal places to assist the ranking process, thereby giving a false impression of the measure's precision.

Qualitative Criteria

At the end of the essay, Garfield (1990) discussed the other considerations ISI took into account in the selection of journals. First among these was the "internationality" of a journal, defined by the nationality of items it publishes and the nationality of the articles that cite it (p. 10). This consideration was followed by others such as the ability of the journal to meet publication schedules, whether it followed international editorial conventions, whether its articles were written in English or at least had informative English summaries, whether its manuscripts were subject to peer review, the track record of its editorial board and contributors, the reputation of its publisher, and the judgment of ISI and outside experts.

Summary and Conclusions

This chapter represents an attempt to analyze the impact factor from the perspective of Garfield's own intellectual development. Garfield was found to be a complex and sometimes contradictory thinker, with many of his contradictions stemming from the complexity of the phenomena he was examining. His intellectual roots were traced back to the scientific revolution in Britain that laid the foundations for modern information science and established the theoretical framework within which his ideas developed. This revolution had both a reformist and a revolutionary wing. The ideas of the reformist wing were set forth by S. C. Bradford, who sought to improve the existing methods of scientific communication through the established system of journals and libraries. He justified capping this system with a central document delivery library by his Law of Scattering. Bradford's Law stemmed from the unity of science and described the skewed distribution of articles on a given topic over journals that made it impossible for any special library to have complete journal holdings on the subject of interest to it. The revolutionary wing was led by J. D. Bernal, who regarded articles as the prime vehicle of scientific communication and journals as inefficient bundles of articles. Being a Communist, Bernal sought to overthrow the established journal system and nationalize scientific communication by means of a central distribution system that would group articles into convenient packages meeting the needs of individual scientists. However, Bernal himself was forced to recognize the inapplicability of his system due to Bradford's Law, which made it virtually impossible to define such convenient packages. Bernal emphasized the importance of scientific review literature in his theoretical writings and validated this importance in his empirical research.

Due to family influences, Garfield was introduced to the British literature through the work of Bernal. As a result, he had a tendency to emphasize the importance of the article over the journal. Moreover, Bernal's stress on the importance of scientific review literature was reinforced in Garfield's thought by Chauncey D. Leake, who urged him to study the importance and function of the review article. Garfield combined the structure of the review article with that of the legal citator, to which he was introduced by William C. Adair, to create the *Science Citation Index*. As a result of these influences, Garfield came to esteem review articles as the epitome of scientific writing, whose function was to serve as arbiters in scientific controversies and direct the course of scientific research. As a further sign of Bernal's influence, one of the primary motivations in Garfield's creation of the *Science Citation Index* was to solve the problem posed by Bradford's Law of Scattering for defining convenient packages of articles of interest to individual scientists.

However, Garfield's attempt to solve the problem that stymied Bernal ultimately resulted only in confirming Bernal's conclusion. By describing the inherently interdisciplinary nature of science with his Law of Concentration, Garfield may have solved the problem posed by Bradford's Law for the comprehensive indexing of scientific journals, but he also demonstrated that Bernal's problem is perhaps impossible to solve.

Garfield's intellectual development was also heavily influenced by Bernal in another important respect. As a Marxist, Bernal pioneered the study of the societal aspects of science. His influence on Garfield in this respect was reinforced by the latter's association with the founder of the sociology of science, Robert K. Merton, and the historian of science, Derek J. de Solla Price. Together, these three men formed an invisible college. Partly as a result of these influences, Garfield came to change his concept of scientific journals from Bernal's inefficient bundles of articles to sociological entities, whose scientific and social significance could be measured by citation frequency. One of the most important contributions of Merton and Price to Garfield's thinking was to help shape his understanding of the skewed distributions underlying scientific phenomena. Merton supplied a causal theory of such distributions with his Matthew effect, describing a cumulative advantage or success-breeds-success process. For his part, Price clarified the form of these distributions with his analyses of the exponential character of science and the similarity of scientific distributions to ones in biology and society. It was with this changed concept of scientific journals that Garfield launched a series of statistical analyses of the citation structure of the scientific journal system that led to his formulation of the Law of Concentration and the creation of the *Journal Citation Reports*.

Garfield's Law of Concentration was a reformulation of Bradford's Law of Scattering, according to which articles on a given subject concentrate primarily in a small core of journals and then spread over zones of other journals that have to increase exponentially in numbers of titles to contain the same number of articles on the topic as the journals in the core. Garfield found the same pattern in the distribution of citations over the journals of a given scientific discipline and he likened the pattern to a comet, with the nucleus symbolizing the core of journals receiving the bulk of the citations and the tail symbolizing zones of the lesser journals that have to increase exponentially in numbers to receive the same number of citations as the journals in the core. Garfield's main innovation was to raise Bradford's Law from the level of individual disciplines to that of science as a whole and show that the tail journals of one discipline consist largely of core journals of other disciplines, resulting in a small multidisciplinary core of journals dominating all of science. Garfield's analyses of the journals of this multidisciplinary core found them to be large in terms of numbers of articles published and old in the sense that they maintain their dominance over decades: They are the journals in which the most significant articles in terms of citation counts concentrate. Garfield found that these core journals are also those journals that scientists, librarians, scientific publishers, and he himself have tended intuitively to identify as the most significant journals of science.

Garfield's understanding and use of the impact factor must be viewed from the standpoint of his evaluation of the importance of review articles and his Law of Concentration. Garfield found that the journals of the dominant multidisciplinary core are easily identified by total citations. Once this is done, he claimed, the main problem is to select journals from the long tail of the citation comet: This was the function of the impact factor. This measure counteracted the age and size advantage of the journals of the multidisciplinary core by restricting the observation period to the two most recent years and calculating the ratio of citations to citable items to estimate the average citation rate per article. Doing this provides a different perspective on journal significance in two respects. First, it brings review journals to the top, allowing an easy way to identify these all-important journals. Second, it allows one to estimate a journal's current, as against its historical, significance by evaluating only its most recent materials. Garfield was well aware of the impact factor's propensity to rank review journals at the top and therefore used the impact factor in two different ways. To identify review journals, he used the impact factor in its unadulterated form, but, to evaluate research journals, he reintroduced size by limiting the set under evaluation to those journals publishing 100 or more articles. The result of the latter move was a tendency to bring to the top the journals of the multidisciplinary core, because these are the journals in which the high-impact research articles tend to concentrate. Garfield was well aware of another aspect of the impact factor—the extremely low citation frequency of the vast bulk of scientific articles. This finding was expressed by his invention of "Garfield's constant"—the ratio of citations to cited items—which rose from only 1.33 to merely 2.25 over the 50-year period 1945–1995. Given the skewed distributions of journals by citations, this meant that journal impact factors had concentrated for the most part in an extremely short range of around 2 or below. As a result, the impact factor could not be used by itself to discriminate among journals at the lower range, where most journals were. Therefore, Garfield always urged that the impact factor should always be used in conjunction with other, subjective considerations.

This brings us to what seems to be a logical contradiction between the structure of Garfield's thought as it pertains to the impact factor and the structure of the *JCR*s. Garfield always mandated that citation analysis could be performed only within carefully defined subject sets. Yet in the print and microform editions of the *JCR*s, where the rankings were immutable, the only ranking of journals within defined subject sets was by impact factor. Given the identification by total citations of the titles in the multidisciplinary journal core posited by the Law of Concentration as dominating all science, it would seem to have been more logical to rank journals within defined subject sets by this measure instead of by impact factor. Moreover, the impact factor rankings were given a false sense of precision by the calculation of the impact factor to three decimal places instead of the one decimal place Garfield himself regarded as more realistic. This was done to avoid the overwhelming number of ties in ranks at the lower range that would inevitably have resulted if the impact factor would have been calculated to only one decimal place. The consequence was to enshrine the impact factor as ISI's main measure of journal significance for the outside world, spawning what can only be termed the impact factor industry. One can only speculate on the reasons for this: (1) the impact factor is an egalitarian measure and Garfield was indoctrinated into leftist political thinking as a youth, (2) the impact factor is a measure of article significance and Garfield regarded the article instead of the journal as the main vehicle of scientific communication, (3) the impact factor ranks review journals at the top and Garfield regarded the review article as the epitome of scientific writing, (4) the impact factor minimizes the problems resulting from the bibliographic instability of journals by limiting the time period to only two years, and (5) the impact factor is a measure of current, in contrast to historical, significance. This last consideration may have been of crucial importance for Garfield, because, to ensure that ISI journal coverage was current with the constant shifts in scientific importance, he needed a measure that helped him detect new rising stars and changes in journal significance.

Endnote

1. A comprehensive collection of Garfield's writings—scientific, (auto)biographical, and occasional—is available on his home page (www.garfield.library.upenn.edu).

References

Adair, W. C. (1955). Citation indexes for scientific literature? *American Documentation*, 6(1), 31–32.

Baker, J. (1939). Counterblast to Bernalism. *The New Statesman and Nation*, 18(440), New Series, 174–175.

Bernal, J. D. (1931). Science and society. *Spectator*, 147(5376), 43–44.

Bernal, J. D. (1940). *The social function of science* (2nd corrected ed.). London: Routledge.

Bernal, J. D. (1948a). The form and distribution of scientific papers. In *The Royal Society Empire Scientific Conference, June-July 1946: Report* (Vol. 1, pp. 698–699). London: The Society.

Bernal, J. D. (1948b). Preliminary analysis of pilot questionnaire on the use of scientific literature. In *The Royal Society Scientific Information Conference, 21 June-2 July 1948: Report and papers submitted* (pp. 589–637). London: The Society.

Bernal, J. D. (1948c). Provisional scheme for central distribution of scientific publications. In *The Royal Society Scientific Information Conference, 21 June-2 July 1948: Report and papers submitted* (pp. 253–258). London: The Society.

Bernal, J. D. (1965). Science Citation Index. *Science Progress, 53*, 455–459.

Bradford, S. C. (1934, January 26). Sources of information on specific subjects. *Engineering, 137*, 85–86.

Bradford, S. C. (1948a). Complete documentation. In *The Royal Society Empire Scientific Conference, June-July 1946: Report* (Vol. 1, pp. 729–748). London: The Society.

Bradford, S. C. (1948b). *Documentation*. London: Crosby Lockwood.

Bukharin, N. I. (1931). Theory and practice from the standpoint of dialectical materialism. In *Science at the cross roads: Papers presented to the International Congress of the History of Science and Technology held in London from June 29th to July 3rd, 1931, by the delegates of the U.S.S.R.* London: Kniga.

Cole, J. R. (2000). A short history of the use of citations as a measure of the impact of scientific and scholarly work. In B. Cronin & H. B. Atkins (Eds.), *The web of knowledge: A Festschrift in honor of Eugene Garfield* (pp. 281–300). Medford, NJ: Information Today.

Cole, S. (2000). The role of journals in the growth of scientific knowledge. In B. Cronin & H. B. Atkins (Eds.), *The web of knowledge: A Festschrift in honor of Eugene Garfield* (pp. 109–142). Medford, NJ: Information Today.

Davis, W. (1940). Project for scientific publication and bibliography. In J. D. Bernal, *The social function of science* (2nd corrected ed., pp. 449–457). London: Routledge.

East, H. (1998). Professor Bernal's "insidious and cavalier proposals": The Royal Society Scientific Information Conference, 1948. *Journal of Documentation, 54*, 293–302.

Garfield, E. (1955). Citation indexes for science: A new dimension through association of ideas. *Science, 122*, 108–111.

Garfield, E. (1956). Citation indexes—new paths to scientific knowledge. *Chemical Bulletin, 43*(4), 11.

Garfield, E. (1959). A unified index to science. *Proceedings of the International Conference on Scientific Information, Washington, D.C., November 16–21, 1958* (Vol. 1, pp. 461–469). Washington, D.C.: National Academy of Science, National Research Council.

Garfield, E. (1963). Citation indexes in sociological and historical research. *American Documentation, 14*, 289–291.

Garfield, E. (1970a, April 22). Calling attention to Chauncey D. Leake—Renaissance scholar extraordinaire. *Current Contents, No. 16*, 5–6.

Garfield, E. (1970b, May 6). What is a significant journal? *Current Contents, No. 18*, 5–6.

Garfield, E. (1971, Aug. 4). The mystery of transposed journal lists—wherein Bradford's Law of Scattering is generalized according to Garfield's Law of Concentration. *Current Contents, No. 17*, 5–6.

Garfield, E. (1972a). Citation analysis as a tool in journal evaluation. *Science, 178*, 471–479.

Garfield, E. (1972b, February 16). Citation statistics may help scientists choose journals in which to publish. *Current Contents, No. 6*, 5–6.

Garfield, E. (1972c, February 23). Citations-to divided by items-published gives journal impact factor; ISI lists the top fifty high-impact journals of science. *Current Contents, No. 7*, 5–8.

Garfield, E. (1972d, April 5). Is citation frequency a valid criterion for selecting journals? *Current Contents, No. 13*, 5–6.

Garfield, E. (1973a, February 7). Citation frequency and citation impact; and the role they play in journal selection for *Current Contents* and other ISI services. *Current Contents, No. 6,* 5–6.

Garfield, E. (1973b, August 22). The economics and Realpolitik of exponential information growth; or, Journal selection ain't easy! *Current Contents, No. 34,* 5–6.

Garfield, E. (1973c, September 26). Which journals attract the most frequently cited articles? Here's a list of the top fifteen. *Current Contents, No. 39,* 5–6.

Garfield, E. (1974a, November 13). So why don't we have *science* reviews? *Current Contents, No. 46,* 5–6.

Garfield, E. (1974b, October 30). So you wanted more review articles—ISI's new *Index to Scientific Reviews (ISR)* will help you find them. *Current Contents, No. 44,* 5–6.

Garfield, E. (1975, January 6). The who and why of ISI. *Current Contents, No. 1,* 5–6.

Garfield, E. (1976a, February 9). Is the ratio between number of citations and publications cited a true constant? *Current Contents, No. 6,* 5–7.

Garfield, E. (Ed.). (1976b). *Journal citation reports: A bibliometric analysis of references processed for the 1974 Science Citation Index.* (Science Citation Index 1975 Annual, v. 5). Philadelphia: Institute for Scientific Information.

Garfield, E. (1976c). La science française est-elle trop provinciale? [Is French science too provincial?] *La Recherche, 7,* 757–760.

Garfield, E. (1976d). Significant journals of science. *Nature, 264,* 609–615.

Garfield, E. (1977a, April 11). Le nouveau défi américain, I. *Current Contents, No. 15,* 5–10.

Garfield, E. (1977b, April 18). Le nouveau défi américain, II. *Current Contents, No. 16,* 5–12.

Garfield, E. (1977c, April 4). Proposal for a new profession: Scientific reviewer. *Current Contents, No. 14,* 5–8.

Garfield, E. (1977d, July 11). Robert K. Merton: Among the giants. *Current Contents, No. 28,* 5–8.

Garfield, E. (1978, February 13). To remember Chauncey D. Leake. *Current Contents, No. 7,* 5–15.

Garfield, E. (1979a). *Citation indexing: Its theory and application in science, technology, and humanities.* Philadelphia: ISI Press.

Garfield, E. (1979b, November 5). How do we select journals for *Current Contents*? *Current Contents, No. 45,* 5–8.

Garfield, E. (Ed.). (1979c). *SCI journal citation reports: A bibliometric analysis of science journals in the ISI data base.* (Science Citation Index 1978 Annual, v. 13). Philadelphia: Institute for Scientific Information.

Garfield, E. (1980a). Citation measures of the influence of Robert K. Merton. In T. F. Gieryn (Ed.), *Science and social structure: A Festschrift for Robert K. Merton* (Transactions of the New York Academy of Sciences, series 2, vol. 39, pp. 61–74). New York: New York Academy of Sciences.

Garfield, E. (Ed.). (1980b). *SCI journal citation reports: A bibliometric analysis of science journals in the ISI data base.* (Science Citation Index 1979 Annual, v. 14). Philadelphia: Institute for Scientific Information.

Garfield, E. (1982a, September 27). ISI's "new" *Index to Scientific Reviews (ISR)*: Applying research front specialty searching to the retrieval of the review literature. *Current Contents, No. 39,* 5–12.

Garfield, E. (1982b, May 10). J. D. Bernal—The sage of Cambridge: 4S award memorializes his contributions to the social studies of science. *Current Contents, No. 19*, 5–17.

Garfield, E. (1983). Mapping science in the Third World. *Science and Public Policy, 10*, 112–127.

Garfield, E. (1985a, March 18). Journal selection for *Current Contents*: Editorial merit vs. political pressure. *Current Contents, No. 11*, 3–11.

Garfield, E. (1985b, August 26). Origins of *Current Contents*, ISI, and computer-aided information retrieval. How it all began at the Welch Medical Library Indexing Project. *Current Contents, No. 34*, 3–9.

Garfield, E. (1987a). *Oral history: Transcript of an interview conducted by A. Thackray and J. Sturchio at the Institute for Scientific Information, Philadelphia, PA, on 16 November 1987*. Philadelphia: Beckman Center for the History of Chemistry. Retrieved January 20, 2006, from www.garfield.library.upenn.edu/oralhistory/interview.html

Garfield, E. (1987b, May 4). Reviewing review literature: Part 1, Definitions and uses of reviews. *Current Contents, No. 18*, 5–8.

Garfield, E. (1987c, May 11). Reviewing the review literature: Part 2, The place of reviews in the scientific literature. *Current Contents, No. 19*, 5–10.

Garfield, E. (1988, June 6). French research: Citation analysis indicates trends are more than just a slip of the tongue. *Current Contents, No. 23*, 3–11.

Garfield, E. (1990, May 28). How ISI selects journals for coverage: Quantitative and qualitative considerations. *Current Contents, No. 22*, 5–13.

Garfield, E. (1991, September 2). In truth, the 'flood' of scientific literature is only a myth. *The Scientist, 5*(17), 11.

Garfield, E. (1995). Quantitative analysis of the scientific literature and its implications for science policymaking in Latin America and the Caribbean. *Bulletin of the Pan American Health Organization, 29*(1), 87–95.

Garfield, E. (1996, September 2). The significant scientific literature appears in a small core of journals. *The Scientist, 10*(17), 14–16.

Garfield, E. (1997a). A statistically valid definition of bias is needed to determine whether the *Science Citation Index* discriminates against Third World journals. *Current Science, 73*, 639–641.

Garfield, E. (1997b). *Transcript of an interview conducted by R. V. Williams at Philadelphia, Pennsylvania, on 29 July 1997 (with subsequent corrections and additions)*. Philadelphia: Chemical Heritage Foundation. Retrieved January 20, 2006, from http://garfield.library.upenn.edu/papers/oralhistorybywilliams.pdf

Garfield, E. (1998a). From citation indexes to informetrics: Is the tail now wagging the dog? *Libri, 48*, 67–80.

Garfield, E. (1998b). Random thoughts on citationology: Its theory and practice. *Scientometrics, 43*, 69–76.

Garfield, E. (1999a, October). Deeds and dreams of Eugene Garfield: Interview by Istvan Hargittai. *Chemical Intelligencer, 5*(4), pp. 26–31.

Garfield, E. (1999b). An interview with Eugene Garfield: Conducted by Beatrice L. Caraway. *Serials Review, 25*(3), 67–80.

Garfield, E. (1999c). On the shoulders of giants. In M. E. Bowden, T .B. Hahn, & R. V. Williams (Eds.), *Proceedings of the 1998 Conference on the History and Heritage of Science Information Systems* (pp. 237–251). Medford, NJ: Published for the American

Society for Information Science and the Chemical Heritage Foundation by Information Today.

Garfield, E. (2000). In-depth interview: Interview with Eugene Garfield, Ph.D., by Chungji Kim. *Medical Writing, 8*(1). Retrieved July 20, 2005, from www.garfield.library. upenn.edu/papers/medicalwritingv8(1)1999.html

Garfield, E. (2002, June). Citation consciousness: The origins of citation indexing in science: Interview with Eugene Garfield, Chairman Emeritus of ISI, Philadelphia, U.S.A. *Password, Nr.* 6, 22–25.

Garfield, E. (2003). The meaning of impact factor. *Revista Internacional de Psicología Clínica y de la Salud, 3,* 363–369.

Garfield, E. (2005). The agony and the ecstasy—the history and meaning of the journal impact factor. Presented at the International Conference on Peer Review and Biomedical Publication. Retrieved November 18, 2005 from http://garfield.library. upenn.edu/papers/jifchicago2005.pdf

Garfield, E., & Sher, I. H. (1963). New factors in the evaluation of scientific literature through citation indexing. *American Documentation, 14*(3), 195–201.

Goldsmith, M., & Mackay, A. (1964). Introduction. In M. Goldsmith & A. Mackay (Eds.), *The science of science: Society in the technological age* (pp. 9–17). London: Souvenir Press.

Hodgkin, D. M. C. (1980). John Desmond Bernal, 10 May 1901–15 September 1971. *Biographical Memoirs of Fellows of the Royal Society, 26,* 17–84.

Lederberg, J. (2000). How the *Science Citation Index* got started. In B. Cronin & H. B. Atkins (Eds.), *The web of knowledge: A Festschrift in honor of Eugene Garfield* (pp. 25–64). Medford, NJ: Information Today.

Martyn, J., & Gilchrist, A. (1968). *An evaluation of British scientific journals* (Aslib Occasional Publication, no. 1). London: Aslib.

Memorandum on Section I dealing with the central distribution of scientific publications. (1948). In *The Royal Society Scientific Information Conference, 21 June-2 July 1948: Report and papers submitted* (pp. 516–519). London: The Society.

Merton, R. K. (1941). [Review of *The social function of science,* by J. D. Bernal]. *American Journal of Sociology, 46,* 622–623.

Merton, R. K. (1968). The Matthew effect in science. *Science, 159,* 56–63.

Merton, R. K. (1983). Foreword. In E. Garfield, *Essays of an Information Scientist: Vol. 5, 1981–1982* (pp. xv–xix). Philadelphia: ISI Press.

Merton, R. K. (1988). The Matthew effect in science, II: Cumulative advantage and the symbolism of intellectual property. *Isis, 79,* 606–623.

Muddiman, D. (2003). Red information science: The information career of J. D. Bernal. *Journal of Documentation, 59,* 387–409.

Muddiman, D. (2004). Red information science: J. D. Bernal and the nationalization of scientific information in Britain from 1930 to 1949. In W. B. Rayward & M. E. Bowden (Eds.), *The History and Heritage of Scientific and Technological Information Systems: Proceedings of the 2002 conference* (pp. 258–266). Medford, NJ: Information Today.

Price, D. J. D. (1963). *Little science, big science.* New York: Columbia University Press.

Price, D. J. D. (1964). The science of science. In M. Goldsmith & A. Mackay (Eds.), *The science of science: Society in the technological age* (pp. 195–208). London: Souvenir Press.

Price, D. J. D. (1976). A general theory of bibliometric and other cumulative advantage processes. *Journal of the American Society for Information Science, 27,* 292–306.

Price, D. J. D. (1978). Cumulative advantage urn games explained: A reply to Kantor. *Journal of the American Society for Information Science, 29*, 204–206.

Price, D. J. D. (1980). Foreword. In E. Garfield, *Essays of an information scientist: Vol. 3, 1977–1978* (pp. v–ix). Philadelphia: ISI Press.

Price, D. J. D. (1983, July 18). The week's citation classic: Price D. J. D. *Little science, big science* (New York: Columbia University Press, 1963). *Current Contents, No. 29*, 18.

Recommendations. (1948). In *The Royal Society Scientific Information Conference, 21 June–2 July 1948: Report and papers submitted* (pp. 195–208). London: The Society.

Robinson, R. (1948). [Opening address]. In *The Royal Society Scientific Information Conference, 21 June-2 July 1948: Report and papers submitted* (pp. 15–17). London: The Society.

Sandison, A. (1971). Library optimum. *Nature, 234*, 368–369.

Sher, I. H., & Garfield, E. (1966). New tools for improving and evaluating the effectiveness of research. In M. C. Yovits, D. M. Gilford, R. H. Wilcox, E. Staveley, & H. D. Lerner (Eds.), *Research program effectiveness: Proceedings of the conference sponsored by the Office of Naval Research, Washington, D.C., July 27–29, 1965* (pp. 135–146). New York: Gordon and Breach.

Testa, J. (2004). *The ISI database: The journal selection process*. Retrieved September 27, 2005, from http://scientific.thomson.com/knowtrend/essays/selectionofmaterial/journal selection

Availability, Access, and Use

CHAPTER 4

Universal Access

Harmeet Sawhney
Indiana University

Krishna P. Jayakar
Pennsylvania State University

Introduction

All review essays brim with information. Whenever we attempted to devise a coherent framework to organize this information, we found that we had left out sizeable portions of the universal access literature. On the other hand, our efforts to cover the literature exhaustively generated an organizational structure at such a high level of generality that it lost its analytical edge. The root of these problems lies in the peculiar nature of the literature on universal access. It is sprawling and diffused across many different domains. Everybody seems to have something to say about universal access but there is little common understanding of the core concepts and issues. Furthermore, the loosely defined concept has been applied to a wide range of domains, ranging from primary education to the rights of people with disabilities. In effect, we found ourselves dealing with an intellectual terrain that would not fit into typological boxes.

The breadth and diversity of the literature are mirrored in the conceptual ambiguity surrounding universal service itself. At various times in its history, universal service has been interpreted to mean an interconnected telecommunications network; universal geographical coverage; subsidized access to telecommunications services and information and communication technologies (ICTs); access for communities with specialized needs, such as the disabled; and so on. In the various literatures that we reviewed, this conceptual ambiguity continues to be in evidence—universal service is shorthand for a variety of socioeconomic objectives underlying telecommunications policy open to selective interpretation based on the ideological proclivities and policy goals of the interest group professing the viewpoint.

A critical review essay therefore has to begin by clarifying the universal service concept itself. We do so by examining the egalitarian impulse at the heart of universalism—the idea that some services need to be accessible to all citizens in a democracy. This egalitarian impulse

159

was concretized into the universal service concept through our historical experiences with four precedent-setting systems—universal postal service, universal education, universal telephone service, and broadcasting. On the basis of this review, we uncover a set of core principles about what universal service represents or should represent.

After examining how scholars have conceptualized the universal service principle, we turn to a critical review of a number of policy discourses in which universal service currently plays a role. It has been observed that when new socio-technical systems emerge, repeated calls are soon made to extend the universal service concept to new technologies and services (Dordick, 1991; Gillan, 1986; Hadden, 1991a, 1991b; Information Infrastructure Task Force, 1993; National Telecommunications and Information Administration, 1988, 1991; O'Connor, 1991; Pacific Bell, 1988; Parker, Hudson, Dillman, & Roscoe, 1989; U.S. Office of Technology Assessment, 1990; Williams, 1991; Williams & Hadden, 1991). We review the universal access literatures in three domains—minorities, people with disabilities, and rural broadband—to understand how the universal service concept came to be applied to these domains and the specific ways universal service ideals influenced these policy discourses. We conclude by identifying certain broad generalizations about the processes that extend universal service to new socio-technical systems.

Our discussions in this chapter are essentially limited to policy discourses in the United States. This is not to minimize the contributions of other jurisdictions, in Europe and elsewhere, to the universal service debate. For example, the "public service" tradition in British broadcasting and telecommunications influenced developments in many other countries, including the U.S. The public service concept showed clear evidence of the universalist impulse, interpreted to mean the obligation of state-funded, monopolistic communication systems to provide fair and equitable service to all individuals, communities, and social groups. However, discussion of the public service model would entail addressing alternative political, social, and economic traditions that would considerably expand the scope of this review essay. Moreover, the public service tradition itself is giving way to systems more closely patterned on those in the United States, as broadcasting and telecommunications are deregulated, privatized, and made competitive. We have therefore made a deliberate choice to restrict coverage of our review to the U.S. situation, fully aware that this curtailment of scope limits, to a certain extent, the picture of universal access issues that this contribution presents.

Precedents

The concept of universal service as we recognize it today seems to embody some of our most deeply held beliefs about justice and fairness, equal opportunity, individual empowerment, and, ultimately, the fundamental equality of all human beings. In fact, "equalitarianism" has deep roots in human nature (Lipson, 1993; Scanlon, 2000). In Western thought, the origins of "equalitarian" thinking are shrouded in antiquity—in the philosophy of the Stoics, Roman law (the *jus gentium,* or law of the peoples), and the Christian gospel (Lipson, 1993). Scanlon (2000) identifies some of the most common reasons that inequality feels intolerable to us. First, inequality denies basic rights to people: For example, extreme poverty can deprive individuals of the means of sustaining life. Second, even if inequality does not consign some people to extreme poverty, it may lead otherwise just institutions to treat some people differently—for example, by denying some people the right to obtain legal redress. Third, inequality may limit individual potential by leading some people to feel inferior—the shame and humiliation of being unable to afford something that everyone else has. Finally, inequality may lead to unfair differences in "starting places" in life—the basis of the ethical argument presented in John Rawls's (1971) influential *Theory of Justice* as well. Although not all of these arguments for equality have an identical hold on our conscience—the deprivation of extreme poverty seems much more unconscionable than the shame of being unable to afford something—they collectively make a strong case for equality.

In spite of such august antecedents, the idea of human equality has also faced tremendous challenges. Influential thinkers, including Plato, Hegel, Carlyle, and Nietzsche have argued that some individuals, classes, or races, through superior natural endowments, temperament, or training, are better suited to the task of governance and should therefore be accorded positions of power and influence: Philosopher kings, hereditary nobles, and master races are all instances of such assertions of privilege and inequality (Lipson, 1993). However, privilege and heredity today stand discredited as organizing principles of social and political life. The last few centuries have seen the gradual, although slow and heavily contested, establishment of the fundamental social and political equality of all human beings. Universal service is an example of a policy arena where the triumph of the equalitarian ideal is especially evident.

To examine how abstract sociocultural ideals can influence the making of policy, we observe the historical development of a set of precedent-setting "proto-systems" in which the principles of universal service as we know it today evolved. There is perhaps an element of judgment in our identification of precedent-setting proto-systems, but the consideration set is so small that any divergence in opinion is likely to be limited to the addition or subtraction of a single system. We identify as precedent-setting proto-systems universal postal service, universal education, universal telephone service, and broadcasting. The postal service, the first universal system, is especially important because it set the stage for subsequent debates about universal provision of other technologies and services. Universal education, on the other hand, in spite of much celebration of the ideal it represents, was in reality the product of a long and contested incremental process. Universal telephone service and broadcasting, which are more recent systems, provide the more immediate conceptual foils for newer systems. The former has been the source of much of the vocabulary in the universal access discourse and the latter of the "public interest, convenience, and necessity" standard. In the following discussion on the development of each of these precedent-setting systems, we examine the values and ideas that shaped their development in the United States. In each instance we demonstrate how universal access principles developed through heavily contested and incremental processes.

Universal Postal Service

The U.S. Constitution gave the Congress the right "to establish the Post Offices and Post Roads" (Article 1, Section 8), but preoccupation with other pressing matters prevented the Congress from legislating on postal issues. The 1790 and 1791 Acts extended the rules and practices developed during the colonial and revolutionary eras on a temporary basis (Kielbowicz, 1989). The Post Office Act of 1792 set the stage for the future development of the postal system. In fact, the debates that took place then and the compromises that resulted set the contours of all the subsequent debates about universal provision of other technologies and services.

From the very beginning, the development of newspapers was intertwined with that of the postal system. Newspapers constituted a great bulk of postal traffic—70 percent in 1794, rising to 90 percent in 1832 (McChesney, 2004). Yet they contributed less than 10 percent of the total revenue (Kielbowicz, 1989). Their postage was heavily subsidized with revenues from regular mail; according to one estimate, in 1765, a letter carried postage about 46 times that of a newspaper (Kielbowicz, 1989).

In spite of objections from some quarters,[1] there was wide consensus that newspapers should continue to receive postal subsidies. The question was whether only certain newspapers should be allowed into the mail. Because it was problematic for a democratic government to decide which newspapers should be allowed, Congress decided to allow all newspapers; in essence, an open access policy was adopted. The real issue of contention was whether a flat rate should be used or the rates should be graduated by distance. Representatives from the big cities and those who wanted to maximize the flow of information tended to favor a flat rate. On the other hand, the advocates of distance-sensitive rates sought to protect small town and rural papers; they were concerned that, with a flat rate, metropolitan newspapers would overwhelm those in the hinterland (John, 1995; Kielbowicz, 1989). The final legislation was based on a compromise; it created two zones for determining postage for newspaper delivery. The rate for delivery within 100 miles was set at 1 cent and, for greater distances, 1.5 cents. Interestingly, from our standpoint, some even argued that this modest delivery fee would allow only the "rich and *better sort*" to participate in the body politic as the poor would be unable to afford newspapers (Kielbowicz, 1989, p. 37).

More fundamentally, the 1792 Act represented a shift in mindset. Since the fifteenth century, when the Hapsburg emperor granted a postal monopoly to the Taxis family, European monarchs had been using the post as a source of revenue (Noam, 1992). William Blackstone, author of the influential *Commentaries on the Law of England*, characterized the postal service as a "most eligible method ... of raising money" (quoted in John, 1995, p. 26). For the first time in modern history, the 1792 Act sought to plow earnings back into the expansion of the postal system. This project inadvertently received a major boost with the transfer of the power to designate postal routes from the executive branch to the Congress.[2] Members of Congress started asking for the expansion of the system into their districts and the pre-1792 Act's logic that each route should be self-supporting no longer held sway: By 1840, the flow of subsidies from New England and the mid-Atlantic states to the South Atlantic, the Northwest, and the Southwest was well established (John, 1995). Although local politicians in the North and East often grumbled about the need to subsidize routes in the interior, they were not able to stop the growth of cross-subsidies. The higher prices that resulted from cross-subsidies motivated the rise of private carriers who could undercut the post office rates. In spite of repeated calls to ban private carriers, Congress, unlike the European governments, refused to ban them outright. But in the North and the East, areas generating surpluses that made subsidies possible, the Post Office, with congressional support, cracked down on private carriers, mainly via court orders.

The history of the postal system witnessed the growth of many policy innovations that were later to become part of universal service: cross-subsidies, geographic rate averaging, open access, and the metropolis versus hinterland conflict. These developments resulted from a potent combination of politics and idealism. The idealism was very real at the time of the birth of the new republic. For example, the routine publication of congressional proceedings to create a well-informed citizenry was unheard of in earlier times. In the same vein, many proponents of the postal expansion saw it as something essential for a democratic polity. Ironically, some of the proponents had a paternalistic attitude in the sense that they sought to educate the masses. Others, however, saw an informed citizenry as an essential check on the government. Finally, there were those, including George Washington, who saw the flow of information as essential for binding the nation together.

Universal Education

Today, the United States has a well-established system of education across the country. Although there are notable variations in the 14,000 school districts in the fifty states, the overall pattern is fairly consistent. It would seem that this system was a product of a grand design. But nothing could be further from the truth.

One could say that the idea of universal education has been in existence at least since the American Revolution. George Washington, in his first message to Congress, stressed the importance of education. Many plans for a system of education were put forward, including those by Thomas Jefferson, Benjamin Rush, and Noah Webster.[3] The American Philosophical Society even organized a contest for plans for an educational system (Cremin, 1980; Madsen, 1974). In short, there was no dearth of ideas.[4]

But no concerted effort was launched to make universal education a reality. There was a failure to "translate sentiments into appropriations" (Ditzion, 1947, p. 10). This failure of will was especially evident in Indiana, the first state to mention provision of education on a universal basis specifically in its constitution. In 1816 the state constitution directed its lawmakers to establish an educational system that would be "free and open to all." At the same time, it asked the lawmakers to delay the undertaking "until circumstances will permit" (Meyer, 1965, p. 387). This qualifying clause provided a convenient loophole for less determined spirits and the idealistic enterprise was put off for many years.

However, as had been the case before the Revolution, educational institutions continued to evolve incrementally. A great variety of institutional types sprouted up across the country. For ordinary citizens, there were dame schools, parochial schools, old field schools, and district schools, which prepared children to become tradesmen or clerks.[5] In the cities, there were venture schools and private schools that imparted practical skills such as accounting and bookkeeping. Finally, there were the preparatory schools and Latin grammar schools, which prepared future scholars, doctors, clergymen, and lawyers for college (Sawhney & Jayakar, 1999). These schools were supported by "nearly every money-raising scheme known to man" including lotteries, fines for public drunkenness, rate bills (tuition), license fees, and the sale of war booty (Madsen, 1974, p. 88).

The concerted effort toward a system of education finally began in the 1830s. As Katz (1968) has pointed out, education reform in the mid-19th century was not motivated solely by "a potpourri of democracy, rationalism, and humanitarianism" (cited in Button & Provenzo, 1989, p. 94). Although idealism certainly motivated some individuals to support public education, others had more practical motives. Industrialists, for example, wanted trained manpower for their expanding factories. Others saw the schools as a way of coping with the widespread social dislocations of the time, brought on by increasing immigration and industrialization. A tax-supported public school would be the "principal digestive organ of the body politic" that would Americanize the newcomers (Strong, 1963, p. 89). The propertied elites were apprehensive of the consequences of universal suffrage, which had become a reality during the Jacksonian era. Afraid of "mob rule," they thought that "education could play an important role in reconciling freedom and order," in other words, teach the masses to conform to the existing system and not destabilize it (Kaestle, 1983, p. 5). The conver-gence of these forces allowed people like Horace Mann, the idealistic champion of education who served as Secretary of the Massachusetts Board of Education, to build a coalition of religious, business, and other groups in support of universal education.

With greater public interest, the government's role, too, began to change. Earlier, the government had basically provided support for edu-cation via grants of land, special tax provisions, and other such assis-tance. Now, the government got into the business of building a true *system* of education (Madsen, 1974, p. 86). We start seeing this system thinking in the very first annual report Mann wrote as the Secretary of the Massachusetts Board of Education in 1838, in which he highlighted the disparities in school quality and funding that resulted from different districts making uncoordinated choices: "One party pays an adequate price, but has a poor school; the other has a good school, but at more than four-fold cost. Were their funds and their interest combined, the poorer school might be as good as the best; and the dearest almost as low as the cheapest" (Mann, 1891, p. 410). In today's parlance, Mann was talking about what is referred to as rate averaging and bypass in telecommunications and postal arenas.

This move toward systemization was resisted by those who felt that the state should not intrude in a domain that has traditionally been under the control of parents, church, and local authorities (Madsen, 1974). The different religious and ethnic groups, keen on preserving their cultures, were wary of the homogenizing impact of an organized system of education, which was seen as a nationalistic goal of universal education even at the time of independence.[6] The principle of the state's authority over education, which is even today an issue for many Americans, had to become a settled question in law for a system of uni-versal education to develop (Power, 1991).

The system of universal education was not created by a single leg-islative act or executive fiat. It developed instead through incremental innovations in particular locales and their diffusion to other school dis-tricts and states (Sawhney & Jayakar, 1999). Yet, although there is con-siderable variation in institutional arrangements from one jurisdiction to another, there is a certain coherence at the level of ideas that can be characterized as "public provision by small fiscally independent dis-tricts, public funding, secular control, gender neutrality, open access and a forgiving system, and an academic curriculum" (Goldin & Katz, 2003, p. 1). Thus we see that a few core ideas took different shapes in various locales, creating diversity of form while maintaining a coherence of prin-ciples—a hallmark of the American experience.

Universal Telephone Service[7]

The Bell Telephone Company introduced the telephone in the U.S. in the 1870s. As a monopoly provider, it had exclusive rights over the early telephone patents. When the Bell patents expired in 1894, a number of competing telephone companies (the independents) entered the market. Bell refused to interconnect with the new entrants, with the result that the entire subscriber universe in the U.S. was fragmented into several unconnected networks (Brock, 1981; Friedlander, 1995; U.S. Department of Commerce, 1975). Vail's (1907, cited in Mueller, 1997, p. 96) call for "one system, one policy, universal service" was a reaction to this chaotic situation and aimed at integrating the fragmented subscriber universe. His vision did not include making telephone service accessible to all consumers, as evidenced by his disinterest in serving rural areas (Fischer, 1992; Friedlander, 1995; Gabel, 1969).

In order to secure full access to the subscriber universe, the Bell System wanted government permission to acquire competing telephone companies in contravention of anti-trust laws. Not only that, the Bell System wanted the federal government to take an activist approach—a conscious, publicly mediated policy decision to "unify the service" "that is, to eliminate the user fragmentation created by dual service" (Mueller, 1997, p. 9). The government's response to Bell's acquisition campaign oscillated between opposition and acceptance. Initially noncommittal, the government soon became opposed to acquisitions and required Bell to make the Kingsbury Commitment of 1913 whereby it agreed to stop acquiring directly competing independent telephone companies (Barnett & Carroll, 1993). Significant market share thus remained with the independents until 1921, when the Willis-Graham Act again permitted the Bell System to acquire nonaffiliated companies. By 1926, less than 1 percent of subscribers belonged to systems not interconnecting with the Bell System and the U.S. telephone system was converted into a de facto monopoly (U.S. Department of Commerce, 1975).

Although there was no explicit commitment to universal service in the 1934 Communications Act, the accounting system put in place by the policy initiatives and court judgments of that era indirectly helped universal service. Even in the 1920s, there had been growing debate about how to allocate the costs of the local exchange. State regulators who had an interest in keeping local rate increases in check argued for the station-to-station method, which allocated parts of the local exchange costs to long distance service because the local loop was used for completing any telephone call. On the other hand the Bell System, later joined by the Federal Communications Commission (FCC), supported the board-to-board system that would raise all local loop costs from subscriptions.[8] U.S. Supreme Court decisions in 1930 and 1933 supported the station-to-station principle. Nevertheless, the conflict persisted until the National Association of Regulatory Utility Commissioners (NARUC) and the FCC jointly produced the Separations Manual in 1947 (Mueller, 1997). Beginning in 1965, regulators began to use the separations process to increase the cross-subsidies from long-distance to local service gradually, aided no doubt by the substantial cost savings then being realized through the introduction of new technologies in interstate transmission. Thus the elaborate system of cross-subsidies and rate averaging that is now recognized as "classical" universal service began to emerge. But it sprang forth neither from deliberate regulatory design nor at a specific time. Instead, it evolved over a substantial period through a heavily contested political-legal-regulatory process in which the Bell System, state-level regulators, the FCC, advocacy groups, and the courts all played prominent roles.

As Oettinger pointed out, the vision for universal service was reified after the objective was accomplished (cited in National Governors' Association, 1988). The need to justify a monopoly provided the initial impetus for universal service, and the possibility of internal cross-subsidies within an integrated system provided the means. But the Bell System became acutely mindful of the universal service mission only when competition and antitrust lawsuits threatened to unravel its monopoly. Now, universal service became a useful defense for the preservation of the status quo. Aided by Bell sympathizers and even some consumer advocates worried about the implications of competition for affordable access, universal service acquired a long historic pedigree stretching right back to Vail's original 1907 declaration, which vastly exaggerated its historical precedence.

Broadcasting

When the Congress started working on the legislation for broadcasting in the mid-1920s, it faced a fundamental choice. It could choose a system of a few high-powered stations that covered the country in large stretches or a large number of lower-powered stations that covered the country in small patches. The high-powered stations would be able to generate both the resources and the economies of scale necessary to produce high-quality programming. But they would not provide an outlet for local voices, especially in rural areas and small towns. Conversely, lower-powered stations would allow for diversity of viewpoints but would not have as many resources. The Congress left licensing decisions to the Federal Radio Commission (FRC), but it did direct the Commission to allocate licenses and frequencies "among the several States and communities as to give a fair, efficient, and equitable distribution of radio service to each ..." (quoted in Kielbowicz, 2002, p. 12). The Congress also divided the country into five zones and stipulated that one commissioner should be selected from each.

Unhappy with the FRC's decisions favoring large companies with high-powered stations, Congress passed the Davis amendment in 1928, which compelled the Commission to reallocate licenses equitably among the five zones and resulted in more licenses for the West and South. However, Congress repealed the zone system in 1936 because it found that sparsely populated areas could not sustain the number of stations assigned to them. But even the new legislation continued to call for a "fair, efficient, and equitable distribution of radio service" among communities, albeit "insofar as there is demand" (quoted in Kielbowicz, 2002, p. 12). This doctrine came to be known as localism (Kielbowicz, 2002).

The other big question the FRC faced was with regard to the ownership of the broadcast spectrum. The 1927 Radio Act and the 1934 Communications Act deemed that the broadcast spectrum was a resource in the public domain that broadcasters could use but not own. However, there were no guidelines or precedents for establishing how the spectrum should be allocated to the users. One of the tasks of the new FRC (and, later, the FCC) was to define the standards of conduct for a broadcast licensee. The Commission developed the notion of trusteeship, which regards the spectrum as a public resource that is entrusted to the licensee to be used for the public good. Taken together, the two concepts formed the "localism and trusteeship" framework (Messere, 2004, p. 1204).[9] Basically, the framework states that the licensee shall act as a trustee of a public resource, the spectrum, and be obligated to serve all programming interests in the local audience and to provide coverage of all local public issues.[10]

The localism and trusteeship framework in turn was based on language in the 1927 Radio Act that mandated the FRC to allocate the spectrum on the basis of which "prospective broadcaster best served the 'public interest, convenience, or necessity' " (McChesney, 1993, p. 18). The FRC (quoted in Krasnow & Goodman, 1998, p. 610) explained this public trust model as follows:

> The conscience and judgment of a station's management are necessarily personal ... [but] the station itself must be operated as if owned by the public. ... It is as if people of a community should own a station and turn it over to the best man in sight with this injunction: "Manage this station in our interest. ..." The standing of every station is determined by that conception.

The phrase "public interest, convenience, and necessity," which has its origins in transportation and public utility law, itself provides an insight into the processes by which policy concepts move from one domain to another. According to Krasnow and Goodman (1998), the framers of the 1927 Radio Act were at an impasse about how to describe the obligations of the licensees under the Act in a manner that would make these obligations sufficiently concrete to stand for something definite in the public mind while giving them enough flexibility to encompass all possible uses to which the technology might be put in the future. A young lawyer on loan from the Interstate Commerce Commission suggested to Senator Clarence Dill that "public interest, convenience, and necessity"[11] might be the standard, and the concept stuck (Krasnow & Goodman, 1998) in spite of the fact that broadcasting is very different from transportation systems and public utilities.[12] The vagueness and malleability of the concept allowed for this transfer from older systems to the new one and also gave the regulators considerable latitude in developing regulations for the evolving technology.

Localism, trusteeship, and the "public interest, convenience, and necessity" standard created a fairly articulate framework for regulating broadcasting. But its effectiveness is debatable, for the emergence of broadcast networks led to the concentration of programming power, and the ideal of localism was never fully realized.

Each precedent-setting system discussed in this section is different in terms of the technological artifacts and human resources it deploys and the type of service it provides. Yet, they are kindred systems as their development was animated not only by the quests for profit and market share but also by a set of similar ideas and values—our notions of democracy and equity. Furthermore, they all required the creation of systems for the provision of service and the redistribution of large amounts of monies in service of these ideas. Any situation that calls for some people to pay more so that others can pay less generates its own peculiar politics even when the exercise is motivated by widely embraced ideals. It is the reconciliation of the ideals, which cannot be avoided in a proud democracy, and the realities of taxes and subsidies, influence and power, and other such prosaic considerations that determine the architecture of these systems.

By comparing our experiences with the precedent-setting systems, some of the common elements of the universal service discourse in these diverse domains emerge. First, there seems to be a consensus in favor of greater information flow and "informatization" of all aspects of public and private life. Second, there is a belief that universal service cannot be provided without an organized systemic framework. The prevailing notion in every case seems to be that the normal processes of diffusion need to be aided and channeled toward universal coverage. Third, there is a concern that the organized systemic frameworks should not let the metropolis dominate the hinterland. Fourth, there is a consciousness that government actions invariably favor one faction, group, or service provider over another, creating a constant jockeying for position. This makes universal access not just a policy exercise but a political process as well. Finally, in consonance with the "equalitarian" origins of universal service, there is a tendency to promote uniformity in access across regions and social strata. We critically examine these unquestioned assumptions of the universal access discourse in the final section.

Diverse Literatures

With the historical background to universal service laid out in the previous section, we now turn to contemporary debates on universal service. In this section, we review the universal access literature in the following domains: minorities, people with disabilities, e-government, the E-Rate program, rural broadband, and community networks. In these reviews, our main objective is to observe how ideas about universal access have informed and influenced the discourses in these domains. Of course, we have not covered every domain of policy making where universal service is an issue or even all aspects of universal service within the domains for which we do provide coverage. For example, our review of the disabilities literature touches only on issues related to the elderly. Similarly, we cover issues related to education to a considerable extent in our review of the literature on the E-Rate program, but this federal initiative is only one of several that promote access to educational technology. The same would apply in the case of rural broadband with respect to the overall rural telecommunications literature. Also, as mentioned in the introduction, our review is by and large limited to the U.S. except for cases where developments in other countries have set important precedents. These limitations notwithstanding, we have covered a vast territory that, in our judgment, more or less tells the complete story of universal access. In the following sections we move through the reviews in the order listed.

Minority Access

One of the enduring problems in the universal service and digital divide debates has been minority access to telecommunications and ICTs. Although many studies have found evidence of this gap in contemporary data (National Telecommunications and Information Administration, 1995, 2000; Riordan, 2002; Walsh, Gazala, & Ham, 2001), others have suggested that, over long periods of time, the gap has persisted with regard to the use of some technologies—such as telephones, computers, and, now, the Internet—while narrowing and disappearing in others, such as radio and television (Schement & Forbes, 2000). However, in spite of the persistent and significant gap in some technologies, the issue of minority access did not attract much attention historically because it was considered a part of the overall universal service problem. The breakup of AT&T and increasing concern about the survivability of universal service in the new competitive environment drew attention to the problem of access—in particular, minority access. This section discusses the empirical evidence relating to the ethnic digital divide, some of the theories advanced to explain the data, and some of the proposed policy solutions.

Although agencies such as the FCC and the Census Bureau have collected data on household telephone access, a study of subscribership that includes race as a factor is harder to find. The earliest studies of this nature date to the mid-1980s, around the time of the AT&T divestiture (Gilbert, 1987; Perl, 1983). An early study of classroom computer use found that schools receiving Chapter I assistance (i.e., those serving districts with higher incidence of poverty, which are also more likely to have higher percentages of minority students) had fewer computers in the classroom (McPhail, 1985). These schools were also more likely to use "drill-and-practice" software, while higher-income schools emphasized programming skills. Later surveys have confirmed these findings for telecommunications and computers at home (Lenhart, Horrigan, Rainie, Allen, Boyce, Madden, et al., 2003; National Telecommunications Information Administration, 1995, 2000) and in the classroom (National Center for Educational Statistics, 2002; U.S. Department of Education, 2000).

In general, scholars have relied on factors other than race to explain the difference in penetration between majority and minority communities. According to these studies, much of the difference in access is due to differences in household income, education, and professional status rather than race (Garbacz & Thompson, 1997, 2003; Taylor, 1994). Other studies have included the impact of race as a factor in determining telecommunications demand (Lenhart et al., 2003; Riordan, 2002; Schement, 1995; Schement & Forbes, 2000; Walsh et al., 2001). In these studies, race and ethnicity have emerged as factors explaining both the decision to subscribe to a telecommunications service as well as the level of usage to a high enough degree to lead some to label the Internet the "world white Web" (Bolt & Crawford, 2000, pp. 95–120). However, not all minority communities are confronted with a digital divide—Asian-American and some Hispanic-American communities lead even the majority in access to computers and the Internet: As Walsh et al. (2001, p. 279) have put it, "a digital divide exists, but not all minorities show up on the wrong side of it."

The evidence that an ethnic digital divide exists is substantial, especially with regard to African-Americans, but explanations for the phenomenon are less forthcoming. As Riordan (2002, p. 427) asks,

> Are black households less likely to have a telephone because of different tastes, or because blacks tend to have lower income and telephone service is a normal good, or because blacks are discriminated against in the provision of telephone service? Or do blacks tend to live in states with less aggressive policies for promoting universal telephone service?[13]

Although African-American and Hispanic-American households are, in the aggregate, less well educated and have lower income than their white counterparts, studies have shown that, for whatever reason, the gap persists even after controlling for income and education. As described by the National Telecommunications and Information Administration (1999), the access gap between majority and minority communities tends to disappear at the highest household income levels (greater than $75,000), but lower income black households have significantly less telecommunications and Internet access than their white counterparts.

Mack (2001, p. 8) has identified prevalent distrust of science and technology as a factor that prevents minorities, especially African-Americans, from subscribing to ICTs:

> Throughout history, whites have used science, research and technology to continue their subjugation of blacks. Blacks, in turn have learned to fear and mistrust scientific and technological developments, believing that such advancements are easily manipulated to suit the purposes of the dominant society.

As evidence, she cites the 19th-century "scientific" studies of cranial measurements used to "prove" Black inferiority, the infamous Tuskegee experiments, the use of dubious measures of intelligence to track black children into remedial classes, and so forth. In another study, researchers found that African-American university students tended to believe that "the Internet and WWW were tools used by the U.S. government to track and monitor individuals" (Ervin & Gilmore, 1999, p. 404). This mistrust of government and technology kept them from going online even when access to computers, the Internet, and the World Wide Web was not an issue.

Another factor identified in the literature is "redlining," the systemic denial of service in inner city neighborhoods by telecommunications companies (Kahl, 1997). The service providers argue that no redlining is practiced, but should it occur in rare instances, it is a purely business decision due to insufficient demand in these locations. Pockets of urban poverty themselves are a consequence of the housing policies followed during the segregation era, which excluded minorities from owning homes in the "white" areas of that time. Other studies have found little evidence of redlining based on income or on Black or Hispanic concentration, but some confirmation of the practice in Native American and Asian communities (Prieger, 2001). Other factors identified as significant negative impacts on access were inner city or rural location; in contrast, market size, education, and Spanish language use increased probability of access.

Poor consumption choices, bad credit, and unscrupulous marketing practices by telecommunications firms have also been identified as factors decreasing access. In one ethnographic study, poor minority households in Camden, New Jersey, were found to have subscribed to premium cable and telephone company services that they did not need and could not afford (Mueller & Schement, 1996). As a consequence, several households lost their service owing to nonpayment of bills.

Another commonly cited factor, especially for Internet access, is the difficulty of mastering the technology (Kuttan & Peters, 2003). In a Pew Foundation study, 46 percent of nonusers said this was either a major or a minor reason why they were not online (Lenhart et al., 2003). For Hispanics especially, but all minorities in general, the lack of language- and culture-specific content might also be an issue (Kuttan & Peters, 2003). Bolt and Crawford (2000, p. 100) agree that "when minority youths go to a software store or log on to the Internet, they do not see reflections of themselves" but argue that not too much should be made of this "content theory" (p. 102): African-Americans have not let that stop them from participating in many other aspects of society and online content tailored to ethnic and linguistic minorities is, in fact, increasing. African-Americans were also found to be apprehensive about privacy to a much greater extent than Caucasian-Americans or Hispanic-Americans (Ervin & Gilmore, 1999).

Given these multiple reasons, no theme emerges in the literature as the single most important factor leading to the ethnic digital divide. The consensus seems to be that minority access to telecommunications and ICTs is a vexing and significant problem that is not amenable to easy solutions. Although a number of federal and state programs exist to address the digital divide (e.g., Lifeline and Linkup, the E-Rate, and the High Cost Areas program), none is exclusively directed at minority communities. Nevertheless, minorities end up being the major beneficiaries because of the household income and poverty provisions built into these programs. For example, grants to schools from the E-Rate program are indexed to the percentage of area children eligible for the School Lunch Program, which directs E-Rate funds to the poorer school districts in which many minority children attend school.

In addition to these general digital divide initiatives, scholars have also advocated schemes that fund community-level ICT programs. Citing one public/private partnership program called "network neighborhoods," which is funded by the Housing and Urban Development (HUD) agency, Mack (2001, p. 71) observed that such initiatives allow participants to "enhance their computer literacy, launch new careers, make the transition from welfare to work, have expanded access to necessary health services, and participate in inter-generational learning activities." Because the absence of culturally and linguistically appropriate content is considered to be one of the major reasons minorities do not venture online, Mack also recommended content creation as a significant step to bridging the digital divide.

However, scholars are not agreed that policy action is required at all—some argue that gaps in access are a natural part of technology diffusion and sometimes disappear without any form of governmental action. For example, several surveys have shown that the gap in Internet access that existed between men and women has practically disappeared: In fact, some studies have revealed that women now constitute a small majority in the Internet population commensurate with their numbers in the overall U.S. population (see especially Norris, 2001, Chapter 4, Social Inequalities). Schement and Forbes (2000) point to the case of radio and television, where no policy promoting household ownership was ever implemented in spite of the obvious advantages of citizen access to news and information. They argue that although the status quo may be unsupportable, so would any generalized policy prescription that does not recognize the complex interplay of factors that leads to the digital divide. Another observer takes the more radical position that policy action is not required just because a gap exists: For example, the fact that the poor eat fewer steaks or drive cheaper cars does not imply that the government should intervene to restore the balance. Instead, as Compaine (2001, p. 116) has put it, "If there is an issue, it is: What priorities should a society have in making decisions on what are necessities, what are frills, and what falls in a debatable middle ground?"

However, the consensus does not favor a "hands-off" approach. Policymakers and researchers agree that a persistent gap in ICT access is neither fair nor socially desirable and that something needs to be done—yet, the ethnic digital divide is a problem that permits no easy solutions.

People with Disabilities

The notion of universal service existed for quite some time, but only recently has access for people with disabilities become an issue. There were perhaps two main reasons for this lag. First, the movement for the rights of the disabled came into its own only recently. Second, the increasing role of ICTs in everyday life raised the importance of the issue of access within the disabled community. We discuss these two factors before delving into the literature on universal access for people with disabilities.

In the 19th century people with disabilities, including some with only physical disabilities, were often seen as "feebleminded" (Pfeiffer, 1993, p. 724). Such thinking was one of the factors that prompted a number of states (at one time, as many as 26) to administer sterilization laws, which were upheld by the U.S. Supreme Court. It was against this backdrop that the modern-day disabilities movement, along with other civil rights movements, arose during the social turmoil of 1960s (Pfeiffer, 1993). Early efforts focused on issues related to discrimination and affirmative action, housing, public transportation, education, and other essential services. As critical everyday functions such as banking moved onto electronic platforms, ICTs started gaining the attention of the disability community. By this time the thinking within the disability community had gone beyond the limited discourses that, according to some observers, the rest of society had been imposing on them. Goggin and Newell (2000, p. 127) identify these "discourses" as medical (passive recipient of expert care), lay (objects of pity), charity, and management (a demanding constituency that needs to be managed).[14] Although Goggin and Newell consider these to be stereotypes, because not all institutions and individuals behave the same way, their caricatured sketch does drive home the point that the dominant discourses locate the problem in the shortcomings of the disabled.

In opposition to the "able-ist" perspective, disability advocates have put forward a discourse based on rights. This approach broadens the focus beyond disabled individuals and expands it to the social systems within which they have to operate. For example, British theorists "propose a distinction between an individual's impairments (the bodily dimension) and disability which is socially produced (as in the barriers society unfairly creates for the person with impairment, for instance)" (Goggin & Newell, 2004, p. 412). Accordingly, attention is directed toward eliminating the barriers that exacerbate, even if they do not create, problems for people with disabilities. The rights discourse calls for an awareness of and sensitivity to the needs of the disabled at the time of system design instead of developing adaptive devices after the system has been created. In other words, the needs of those with disabilities should not be an afterthought (Stephanidis & Salvendy, 1998; Vanderheiden, 1990).

Disability advocates argue that this initial system design approach is not only an inherently good idea but also a practical one because the rapid pace of technological change is increasingly making the retroactive approach untenable (Stephanidis & Emiliani, 1999). Even better would be to proactively develop generic solutions as early as possible in the design process, creating products and services that are usable by the widest possible range of persons, including those with disabilities. This approach, which would minimize the need for a posteriori adaptations, is "grounded on the notions of universal access and design" (p. 24).

Universal design is based on the idea that designing for the "typical" or "average" user, which is what "conventional" design does, results in products that do not meet the needs of the largest possible population of users because many groups, especially the disadvantaged, are left out. In contrast, designs intended to serve the needs of a disadvantaged population can have benefits for the general population as well (Stephanidis & Emiliani, 1999). For example, curb cuts designed to accommodate wheelchairs help parents with strollers, delivery workers, bicyclists, and travelers with roll-on bags (Shneiderman, 2000). In the ICT realm, pay phones designed for comfortable use by wheelchair and scooter users also help parents with strollers. In addition to helping people with dexterity and mobility problems, telephones with big buttons and hands-free operability are useful for the elderly. Teletypewriter (TTY) services not only enable hearing- and speech-impaired subscribers to communicate with each other but also the rest of the community with them (Goggin & Newell, 2000).

Critics of universal design question its practicality and cost justification. They argue that a design seeking to satisfy everyone may end up satisfying no one (Stephanidis & Emiliani, 1999; Shneiderman, 2000). They also warn of the "innovation restriction scenario" wherein focus on accommodating the low end in terms of technology and skill inhibits innovation at the high end (Shneiderman, 2000, p. 88). Proponents of universal design counter that the approach does not preclude multiple designs for different groups when necessary (Stephanidis & Emiliani, 1999; Stephanidis & Salvendy, 1998). With regard to costs, sufficient data are not available to settle the question one way or another. Moreover, disability advocates point out that the disabled and the elderly make up a sizeable and growing portion of the market that would be unwise for business to ignore. However, we need to keep in mind that the long-term costs of making systems accessible via a posteriori adaptations is very high and likely to continue to increase in the future (Stephanidis & Emiliani, 1999).

In terms of telecommunications regulation, until recently universal service was seldom interpreted to include the needs of people with disabilities (Bowe, 1993). The carriers tended to see their universal service obligations limited to providing physical connectivity to the entire population. Whether or not the service was actually usable by people with special needs, such as those with disabilities, was generally not seen as the carriers' responsibility. A landmark case in Australia (*Scott, DPI v. Telstra*) heard before the Human Rights and Equal Opportunity Commission identified the key issues very clearly (Goggin & Newell, 2000, 2004; Ransom, 1994). Prior to this case, there was no legal requirement for telecommunications carriers to provide access for the disabled: The 1991 Telecommunications Act mandated universal service but excluded accessibility, while the 1992 Disability Discrimination Act explicitly left telecommunications outside its purview. The main telecommunications provider in Australia, Telstra, was thus able to claim that its service obligations were limited to the provision of technical equipment and that the accessibility of the equipment to all people was not its responsibility. The Commission sided with the plaintiff and ruled that if the standard equipment failed to make the service usable by any subscriber group, Telstra should provide alternative equipment (Bourk, 2000). Subsequently, the 1997 Telecommunications Act obligated carriers to provide a functional equivalent of voice telephone service to subscribers who need it (Goggin & Newell, 2004).

In the U.S., it was the 1990 Americans with Disabilities Act (ADA) that explicitly dealt with the telecommunications needs of people with disabilities. Title IV of the ADA guarantees to users of TTY service "full and equal access" to the public telephone network. The TTY service allows people with disabilities to send text messages to relay operators who then read them out to non-TTY users and correspondingly relay back the spoken message as text. Thus the ADA addressed the needs of hearing-impaired and speech-impaired users. It, however, still left out many people who had problems due to cerebral palsy, visual impairment, learning disabilities, and other disorders. Deborah Kaplan, director of technology policy of the World Institute on Disability (WID), organized an effort to extend similar benefits to other disabled groups (Bowe, 1993). She based her strategy on the Television Decoder Circuitry Act, which represented a new way of thinking. Instead of requiring the hearing impaired to buy special devices, the Act mandated manufacturers to produce products that were accessible. Because manufacturers were required to install special chips in all televisions, the resulting economies of scale brought down the additional cost to as little as $5 per set. Kaplan sought to do the same for the public telephone service by requiring services such as speech synthesis and speech recognition to be part the overall fabric of the network. These capabilities would allow visually impaired users to listen to information, the hearing-impaired to print out voice messages, and quadriplegics to dial numbers by speaking them aloud (Bowe, 1993). The Consumer Federation of America challenged this approach, which was akin to universal design, by asking why ordinary Americans should bear the cost of providing services that benefited people with disabilities. Kaplan countered by arguing that costs, when spread out across the entire subscriber base, would be only a dollar or two. Furthermore, the benefits would not be restricted to people with disabilities. The elderly, the rural population, and others would also benefit (Bowe, 1993).

The 1996 Telecom Act does not incorporate disability issues in its universal service section (Section 254), but deals with them in a separate section (Section 255). In developing the rules implementing Section 255, the FCC adopted the "readily achievable" concept from the ADA, obligating carriers to make changes for people with disabilities when they are "easily accomplishable and able to be carried out without much difficulty or expense" (quoted in Kanayama, 2003, p. 189). Although the industry groups applauded the FCC's decision to devise its own analytical factors (feasibility, expense, and practicality) for determining what is "readily achievable," advocates of people with disabilities expressed dismay. They argued that some of the enhanced services used by people with disabilities such as voice mail and electronic mail—labeled as information services in the 1996 Act and therefore not covered by Section 254—should be covered by universal service. They also recommended that the FCC should base the selection of new services for universal service at least partially on the extent to which these services were commonly used by the disabled (Kanayama, 2003). Largely due to these efforts, the final implementation rules applied to landline telephones as well as to cell phones, pagers, call waiting, operator services, and many other products and services.

The recommendation that the FCC identify the features "commonly used by people with disabilities" is noteworthy (Kanayama, p. 190). One of the criteria that policymakers have often used for inclusion of new services in an expanded universal service package is that its value be demonstrated through wide acceptance by ordinary consumers (Sawhney, 2000, 2003). For example, the second criterion laid out in the Telecommunications Act of 1996 asks the FCC to consider a new service for the universal service package when it has "through the operation of market choices by customers, been subscribed to by a substantial majority of customers" (Section 254 (c)(1)). Here the disability advocates were arguing that the "consumption norms" (Preston & Flynn, 2000, pp.

93–95) within a disadvantaged group, instead of within the entire population, be used as the criterion for including a service in the universal service package.

Another front in the battle for universal accessibility is the definition of Web sites and Web-based telecommunications services as "products," "promotional vehicles," "services," or "sites of accommodation." Definitions are important because classifying an ICT one way or another brings different laws into operation and places different obligations on service providers. Again, an Australian case (*Maguire v. Sidney Organizing Committee for the Olympic Games*) heard before the Human Rights and Equal Opportunities Commission identifies the issues clearly (Shneiderman, 2000). Maguire, a blind person, complained to the Human Rights and Equal Opportunities Commission (hereafter the Commission) that a number of features on the Web site maintained by the Sydney Organizing Committee for the Olympic Games (hereafter the Games Committee) were inaccessible via refreshable Braille display and screen reading technologies used by visually impaired Internet users. The issue before the Commission was whether or not this difference constituted discrimination under the 1992 Commonwealth Disability Discrimination Act, which prohibits discrimination in service provision. The Games Committee countered that its Web site was not a service but a promotional vehicle, and therefore not covered by the Act. When the Commission refused to accept this argument, the Games Committee pleaded that the cost involved constituted "unjustifiable hardship," which was grounds for exemption under the Act (Russell, 2003, p. 241). The Commission also rejected this argument and required changes to be made well before the Games were to commence (Russell, 2003).

Although the decision in the *Maguire* case was significant, it did not have as wide an impact as one might have expected. In the United Kingdom, the issue still remains unresolved whether the Internet constitutes a service falling within the remit of the U.K. Disability Discrimination Act 1992 or a product not subject to it (Russell, 2003). In the United States, the ADA (p. 242) states that people with disabilities cannot be discriminated against in accessing "places of accommodation," examples of which include hotels and grocery stores. The matter in contention now is whether Web sites constitute "places of accommodation." In a case brought about by Access Now, an advocacy group, against Claire's Stores, the court observed that it was highly uncertain whether Web sites fell within the remit of the ADA. The court dismissed a case Access Now filed against Southwest Airlines, concluding that Web sites were not "places of accommodation" because the ADA is concerned with access to physical, not virtual, spaces. The court felt that if a similar law were needed for cyberspace, Congress should pass the necessary legislation (Russell, 2003).

In a case that did not involve Web accessibility (*Carparts Distribution Center v. Automotive Wholesaler's Association of New England*), the court determined that the term "public accommodation" was ambiguous and could denote intangible "accommodations" such as a health benefit plan. The court said that "it would be irrational to conclude that persons who enter an office to purchase services are protected by the ADA, but persons who purchase the same services over the telephone or by mail are not. Congress could not have intended such an absurd result" (quoted in Russell, 2003, p. 243). In another case (*Vincent Martin et al. v. Metropolitan Atlanta Rapid Transit Authority* [MARTA]) where the complaint was that the transport authority's Web site was not accessible and its alternate means of access via Braille schedules was not easy to use, the court determined that MARTA was "violating the ADA mandate of making adequate communications capacity available, through accessible formats and technology, to enable users to obtain information and schedule service" (quoted in Russell, 2003, p. 243).

These variations in interpretation stem to some degree from differences in the laws that apply to each situation. The MARTA case was brought under Title II of the ADA, which prohibits "public entities" from denying service to people with disabilities. Furthermore, this section specifically mentions transportation services. On the other hand, Section 504 of the Rehabilitation Act prohibits discrimination by government agencies. Although the legal position is not entirely clear, it seems that under Title II and Section 504 government agencies are required to make their Web sites accessible, but private companies under Title III do not have to do so because they are not a "place of public accommodation" (Russell, 2003, p. 243).

One common thread running through the disability literature is the constant refrain that we need to extend universal access beyond simple availability of a connection to accessibility. Otherwise, as disability advocates warn, we will end up with a "two-tier" society of "haves" and "have-nots" (Stephanidis & Emiliani, 1999; Stephanidis, Salvendy, Akoumianakis, Arnold, Bevan, Dardailler, et al. 1999) or, as Kanayama (2003, p. 193) says, of those who "can" and those who "cannot." Although this broad theme resonates with those in other universal access literatures, the disability literature is notably different. Unlike other literatures that evoke and extend long-established universal access principles, the disability literature introduces new concepts into the discourses. For instance, the notion of a universal design comes from civil engineering, architecture, and interior design.

Unfortunately, the disability literature has a very strong advocacy flavor. Although writers challenge the fundamental assumptions of the institutions they seek to change, they rarely pause to reflect critically on their own. Their moral self-assuredness prevents the development of a more balanced, scholarly perspective. For instance, Stephanidis et al. (1999, p. 109) argue that universal access principles should not be limited to computers and their interfaces but should be extended to "information itself and how it is created, collected, represented, stored, transferred from one place to another, and used." Chung, Austin, and Mowbray (2000) go further and argue that the concept of accessibility should be stretched beyond Internet software to other barriers such as jargon and complicated site structure. There is little thought expended on whether such extensions are feasible and, if feasible, whether they are cost effective. Interestingly, not a single paper we reviewed situated disability initiatives within the overall universal service package. How do disability programs relate to other programs, say, for the urban poor, and how should funds be distributed among them? Without this broader framework, disability research rarely rises above the level of advocacy.

E-Government

Described variously as "e-government," "electronic government," and "digital government," the movement toward greater utilization of ICTs to deliver government services to citizens, businesses, and other government agencies is accelerating. Although e-government became a buzzword only with the tremendous growth of the Internet in the late 1990s, the utilization of ICTs in government is by no means new. As Ho (2002) points out, computers and networks have been used to improve efficiency and internal communication in government agencies for a long time. The "focus of e-government in this [early] era was primarily internal and managerial" (p. 435). As private businesses began to deploy e-commerce services in the 1990s and consumers grew accustomed to the conveniences of 24/7 service, the same expectations came to be set for government (Edmiston, 2002). In 1993 the National Performance Review included a report authored by Vice President Gore (1993) declaring the aim of "reinventing government" through the use of ICTs and identifying key action items and initiatives to make e-government a reality. The Bush administration's E-Government Act of 2002 created a special Office of Electronic Government to coordinate e-government initiatives at the federal level (E-Government Act, Public Law 107–347, 2002). The 2003 E-Government Strategy statement further developed the Bush administration's approach to electronic government. Internationally as well, e-government initiatives have attracted much attention from organizations such as the World Economic Forum (Brown, 2002), Organisation of Economic Co-operation and Development (OECD) (2003), and the European Union (Chadwick & May, 2003).

Proponents of e-government claim that it represents a fundamental transformation in the way government and its relationship to citizens are organized. Traditionally, each governmental department specialized in the provision of a few specific services. There was little communication with agencies providing other services or between different levels of government—federal, state, or local (Fountain, 2001; Ho, 2002). The use of ICTs, initially intended only to improve internal processes and procedures, gradually began to transform the nature of government itself. As Ho (2002, p. 436) points out, government departments began to experiment with "client-based" models more in tune with user expectations and "one-stop service centers," where multiple services would be available at the same place. The emerging model of user friendliness, flexibility, direct communication, and fast feedback presents several points of contrast with the old model of command and control, rule-based decision making, procedural efficiency, and hierarchy.

Scholars have described four stages of implementation of e-government (Layne & Lee, 2001). In the first, "cataloging" stage, an online presence for a government department is created and users are able to access some limited fact-finding and searching functions, for example, for forms or e-mail addresses (pp. 126–128). In the second stage, it becomes possible for users to make transactions using ICTs. This stage requires modifications to databases and retraining of workers to move from service delivery to supervision of electronic systems. In the third stage—"vertical integration"—departments providing similar services are connected across different levels of government, for example vehicle registration and health and human services (pp. 129–132). When existing services are moved online, new functionalities may also be created, for example a common Web site to obtain business licenses from both state and local governments. The fourth stage envisages "horizontal integration," which is achieved when agencies doing different things connect their systems and databases to provide "one-stop shopping" for a variety of government services (pp. 132–134). Other scholars have divided the process of e-government into different stages but follow the same logic: For example, Chadwick and May (2003) distinguish between managerial, consultative, and participatory stages, whereas West (2004) speaks of billboard, partial service delivery, portal, and interactive democracy stages.

In spite of the rhetoric surrounding e-government, progress in its implementation was relatively slow. In the year 2000, a survey of municipal governments in the United States showed that the vast majority had one-way communication/information dissemination (i.e., the cataloging stage), with only some reporting limited two-way communication (i.e., query and response) capabilities. Relatively few permitted transactions to be executed online and still fewer had vertical and horizontal integration across levels of government and functions (Moon, 2002). Since then, a number of government departments have unveiled significantly more advanced Web-based services, several of which have attracted praise (Freed, 2005; Stowers, 2004). One example is the U.S. Federal Government's FirstGov.gov, which promises to make 186 million Web pages of federal and state government information accessible to users within three clicks (U.S. Office of the President, 2003). The U.S. Internal Revenue Service (IRS), too, has significantly increased its electronic tax filing and document delivery services in recent years. The annual American Customer Satisfaction Survey conducted by the University of Michigan has given high rankings in its e-government category to agencies such as the National Library of Medicine (for *MedlinePlus*) and the Social Security Administration (for its *Medicare*

Prescription Drug Costs information site and the *Internet Social Security Benefits Application)* (Freed, 2005).

Questions about universal service and the digital divide have been prominent in discourse about e-government. Although some scholars see e-government as an opportunity, notably the ability to extend services cost-effectively to underserved areas such as rural areas and inner cities (Edmiston, 2002), others are more concerned about citizens' lack of access to computers and the Internet. Although computer and Internet penetration in the home and workplace have been steadily rising, reports such as the National Telecommunications and Information Administration's (2000) *Falling through the Net*, the Benton Foundation's (2002) *Bringing a Nation Online*, and others (e.g., National Center for Educational Statistics, 2002; Organisation for Economic Co-operation and Development, 2003) show that significant gaps still exist in terms of race, income, and place of residence. Migrating and creating services online can result in denial of service to the most needy if significant sections of the disadvantaged populations do not have access to the Internet.

A recent study found that an "e-government divide" based on race, income, and education exists even among those with Internet access: "Visitors to government Websites are more likely to be white, to have higher incomes, and to be more educated than other Internet users" (Thomas & Streib, 2003, p. 95). The study also found that, contrary to expectations, the young were more likely to visit government Web sites, a finding that the authors explain by citing the intense curiosity of youth about "this new face of government" (p. 95). The researchers did not find urban-rural differences in the frequency of accessing government Web sites among those with Internet access—perhaps because only the more motivated rural user subscribes to Internet service, given the higher prices and greater difficulty of obtaining access in rural areas.

The digital divide may be compounded if greater expenditures on creating an online presence force some government agencies to scale back on traditional face-to-face services. An OECD (Organisation for Economic Co-operation and Development, 2003) report entitled *The E-Government Imperative* points out that disadvantaged groups such as the disabled and the indigent—who often have greater need for government services like welfare, unemployment, and disability—are also specifically the groups that have difficulty accessing and using government Web sites. The report argues that a widespread move toward e-government thus presents a double threat to these groups—not only do they lack access to the enhanced services available online, but the physical facilities they had previously relied on are sometimes scaled back as governments divert funds to online services.

Given these potential pitfalls, one observer has questioned whether the government should emulate the private sector's movement toward e-commerce, arguing that businesses have the luxury of choosing their customers, whereas government is obligated to serve all Americans irrespective of whether they have a home computer or Internet access (Klima, 2003). The consequence of government services moving exclusively online would be more severe than in the case of private businesses. It was partially in response to this criticism that the 2002 E-Government Act specifically included a provision (Section 213) to enhance the effectiveness of community technology centers, public libraries, and other institutions that provide Internet access to the public and to promote public awareness of the government services accessible over the Internet from these sites (E-Government Act, Public Law 107–347, 2002). The OECD (Organisation for Economic Co-operation and Development, 2003), too, states that it is important for governments to persist with efforts to bridge the digital divide, on the grounds of e-government alone.

West (2003) has identified six other areas of concern to e-government in relation to universal service. First, online services may present significant problems of access for the disabled. Although there have been a number of efforts recently to improve accessibility by producing standards and incorporating universal design principles into government Web sites, significant issues of compliance remain unresolved at the city and municipal levels. In a cross-reference to the disability discourse, some scholars of e-government have sought to identify government Web sites as sites of accommodation where federal laws applicable to accessibility should prevail. Second, West's studies show that the content of government Web sites is presented at a reading level (11th grade) significantly higher than the competency of the average American (8th grade). Again, federal and state government Web sites do better than municipal Web sites in this regard. Third, only a minority of government Web sites provided access to bilingual content in English and a foreign language. Fourth, government Web sites were found to have limited interactivity. Although most sites provided e-mail addresses of government officials, West (p. 9) argues that this puts "government in a reactive mode," capable only of responding to citizen complaints after they have occurred. Instead, he recommends that government Web sites incorporate proactive feedback mechanisms such as online surveys and satisfaction forms, which few currently do. Fifth, West found that there was considerable variation in accessibility standards across different agencies and the result was not always sympathetic to the targeted clientele. For example, Health and Human Services Web sites used predominantly by the poor presented a majority of their content at a twelfth-grade reading level. Finally, West condemns the decision of a few government departments to charge user fees for government services or to move some types of content into premium sections requiring a subscription or registration. This is a worrisome trend because it could lead to "a two-tier society based on those who can afford information and those who cannot" (West, 2003, p. 10).

Although West's analysis raises important points about universal service in the context of e-government, his criticism also appears to be somewhat one-sided. In some cases he expects government departments to accomplish tasks for which they have no budgetary resources. In others, departments that are chartered as quasi-governmental agencies have always been allowed to charge for services; thus, charging for e-government services does not create new grounds for complaints of discrimination. Further, e-government is at a rudimentary stage of development and the evolution of online services is far from complete. Criticism, in some cases at least, may be premature.

Both Moon (2002) and Ho (2002) have discussed a geographical dimension of the digital divide related to e-government, namely the ability and willingness of municipal governments to deploy online services. Moon showed that larger cities are more likely to innovate with e-government and found that the type of administration also matters: Cities with a politically elected chief executive (i.e., a mayor) have tended to be slower with e-government deployment than cities with professional managers answerable to elected councils. Ho confirmed the results for city size and, in addition, found that affluent cities and those with smaller minority populations have tended to be quicker to deploy e-government. The underlying reason for this trend is that, although minority populations tend to be higher in large cities, the average per capita income is also lower in minority households. This results in a comparatively smaller tax base for cities with larger minority populations. The net effect is that, at every level of city size, cities with higher proportions of low-income and minority households tend to be slower to enact e-government initiatives. Ho's research also showed that cities with large minority populations have tended to take an administrative, rather than an informational or user-centered, approach to e-government deployment. The administrative approach, motivated by resource constraints, tends to favor e-government initiatives that improve cost-efficiency (process management, document flow control, etc.) rather than focusing on user needs or satisfaction. "Racial differences not only influence private usage of computers and the Internet, they may also affect the progressiveness of city governments in Web development" (Ho, 2002, p. 439).

In summary, there is tremendous variation in the provision of e-government services at the federal, state, and local levels: Some government agencies serve as exemplars in providing such services and some are clearly laggards and models of anything but good service. There are also contrasting theoretical claims about the impact of e-government on public administration and governance. Although some scholars hail it as a paradigm shift, others are much more cautious. Concerns about universal access to e-government services constitute one of several reasons why those in the latter camp advocate a more measured approach. Indeed, advocates of universal service have pointed to e-government as a reason to devote more policy attention and financial resources to bridging the digital divide. The discourse on e-government thus brings together and, in some cases, amplifies many of the concerns researchers and policy makers have voiced about universal service, the digital divide, disability, and socioeconomic justice.

Community Networks

Community networks are different from virtual communities in that they seek to strengthen ties within a local community rather than creating a virtual one in cyberspace (Carroll & Rosson, 2003; Chapman & Rhodes, 1997; Morino, 1994; Pettigrew, Durrance, & Vakkari, 1999; Schuler, 1994; Tonn, Zambrano, & Moore, 2001). As Virnoche (1998, p. 205) notes, "unlike virtual communities which can attract dispersed people with shared interests or characteristics, community networks serve geographic communities often encompassing diverse interests of stratified groups." Although they are limited to a particular community in physical space, the scope of their intended activities tends to be quite expansive. For example, the Seattle Community Network seeks to generate community cohesion, develop informed citizens, provide access to education and training, and create strong democracy (Schuler, 1994). Universal access is an important goal of community networks but their overall scope is much broader. Here we focus on only that portion of the community network literature centered on universal access issues.

Early community network projects were directed toward providing cheap access, often by establishing a nonprofit Internet Service Provider (ISP). As the technology evolved, they had to grapple with new issues. For example, in the years preceding the Web browser, there was considerable debate within community network groups on how much they should invest in interactivity. Many advocated the use of text-only interfaces. As one activist phrased it, "BCN (Boulder Community Network) is an information source. People can get interactivity somewhere else" (Virnoche, 1998, p. 209). Others argued that this approach would create another level of disparity whereby the upper classes would have two-way capabilities and the lower classes would remain passive recipients within a one-way broadcast framework (Virnoche, 1998). The development of the Web browser made this debate moot. More generally, with the plummeting costs of Internet access, community networks found that they could not compete with commercial providers (Chapman & Rhodes, 1997). Even though facilitating physical access remained a challenge, the community networks started thinking more about education, outreach, and other such activities.

The broadcast model versus two-way communication debate continues with regard to content-related issues. According to Chapman and Rhodes (1997, p. 51), much of the content on the Internet a decade ago was irrelevant to the poor and hardly any of it was produced locally in their neighborhoods: "Despite the rhetoric about shedding labels of gender, race, and social class upon entering cyberspace, the Internet reflects the culture of its principal inhabitants—upper middle-class white males." In principle, everybody agrees that local content is critical but the creation of meaningful local content is very difficult in practice, with the result that, even today, some commentators rue the lack of genuine local content online. As Pigg and Crank (2004, p. 69) point out, the hope that ICTs are still in an upward trajectory of development and that suitable "local-based" applications will eventually develop has been belied in the past decade: They opine that "waiting [longer] means taking the significant risk that the global influences so pervasive in cyberspace will never provide the opportunity for 'local' networks and content to gain a significant foothold." Although commercial providers do offer some local information, such as restaurant and shopping guides, the general sentiment is that commercial providers cannot serve the community in ways that community networks can (Beamish, 1999; Carroll & Rosson, 2003; Schuler, 1994; Virnoche, 1998; Weston, 1997).

On matters related to physical access and local content, the public library and its services are a subject of much discussion. Public libraries in African-American communities have received special attention (Bishop, Tidline, Shoemaker, & Salela, 1999; Pinkett 2003). Jue, Koontz, Magpantay, Lance, and Seidl (1999) used geographic information systems (GIS) technology to identify libraries that serve the poor. With regard to local information, Pettigrew, Durrance, and Vakkari (1999) point out that, for more than thirty years, public libraries have provided information and referral services. They note that local information was typically collected in files within the library. The Internet has changed the nature of this service because library Web sites can now link to other local sites. Chapman and Rhodes (1997) point out that although community networks almost always use libraries as access points, they are perhaps not optimal for furthering access. Libraries may be physically proximate to the poor, but they are also psychologically distant. Chapman and Rhodes recommend access locations frequented by the poor on a daily basis—laundromats, eating places, alternative schools, youth centers, sports facilities, shopping centers, and even bars.

Beyond physical access and content, there is considerable fascination with the possibility of increasing social capital with a community network. Oldenberg's notion of a "third place" other than home and workplace where people meet and talk has found considerable favor (Cohill, 2002; Schuler, 1994; Tonn et al., 2001). Correspondingly, the question whether community networks actually increase social capital has received attention (O'Neil, 2002; Tonn et al., 2001). Researchers have also sought to understand how to generate and sustain social engagement (Millen & Patterson, 2002; Tonn et al., 2001). However, Borgida, Sullivan, Oxendine, Jackson, Riedel, and Gangl (2002) point out that the preoccupation with whether community networks increase social capital is somewhat misplaced. Researchers also need to study how the existing social capital affects the deployment of community networks. They illustrate their point with a comparative study of network development in a Minnesota town that has historically had a communitarian culture with that of a more market-oriented one.

According to Chapman and Rhodes (1997), the concept of a local community tends to be stronger in poor neighborhoods than in rich ones. The people in poor neighborhoods tend to spend more time locally because they are less mobile and also because the physical boundaries of their neighborhood are often their greatest defining feature. Within this context, community networks are better placed to strengthen local connections than to create new ones to faraway places.

> The organizers of the Austin Free-Net are seeking to lay a virtual environment over real geographic places, to supplement existing connections between people, institutions, and programs with electronic ones. We are producing a web of network links and communication patterns that resemble those one finds in the community already. (Chapman & Rhodes, 1997, p. 51)

In a similar vein, Morino (1994, online) has observed that "community networking in the social sense is not a new concept, but using electronic communications to extend and amplify it certainly is." On the other hand, Contractor and Bishop (2000) argued that community networks should go beyond "substitution" (moving existing practices to ICT platforms) and "enlargement" (intensifying existing practices) to "reconfiguration" (changing social practices). In effect, they argued against the "extend and amplify" model, holding that, without reconfiguration, the existing digital divide would only deepen because the rich would benefit from the advances at a greater rate.

Contractor and Bishop (2000) employed the asset-mapping concept from the community renewal literature to develop a reconfiguration strategy. According to this "inside out" development perspective, community renewal can be catalyzed by making the community members aware of the assets—individual, associational, and institutional—that already exist within the community (Kretzmann & McKnight, 1993). Contractor and Bishop (2000) explored how community networks can reduce the high coordination costs of asset mapping and reported on the use of a new "community ware" tool they had developed to facilitate asset mapping. Pinkett (2003) has pointed out that there is an extensive literature on community building that predates our relatively recent fascination with ICTs. Yet, one rarely sees community network researchers draw on this literature. Contractor and Bishop's (2000) paper, in spite of some weaknesses, is a rare exception.

Most writings on community networks have a celebratory tinge. Any criticisms discuss inadequacies in how the ideals have been implemented and are directed toward correcting problems. For example, Tonn et al. (2001) evaluated 40 community networks and concluded that the networks did not seem to be increasing social capital, but that they could do so if appropriate actions were taken. Rarely does anybody challenge the very concept of a community network. Virnoche (1998, p. 216) noted that "there is an underlying assumption within community networking—and more generally within the electronic democracy movement—that the infusion of Internet technologies in peripheral populations is inherently positive. To do anything but share the technology would be discriminatory." She stressed the need to think through the potential negative impact of information technology, especially on an already vulnerable population. Beamish (1999), too, challenged the notion that technology will automatically make life better for the poor. What benefits do we expect access to provide and how do we know that these supposed benefits are indeed being delivered? She stressed the need for clarity of objectives and evaluation of results. She also argued that perhaps the biggest problem with community networks is the tendency to consider access to technology an end in itself rather than the means to an end.

Virnoche (1998) and Beamish (1999) offered these critical reflections in passing, but Stoecker (2005) has recently subjected community network research and the emerging field of community informatics to sustained scrutiny. If the goal is to develop strong communities, he questions the need for a field that knows a priori the solution to the social problems of the day—the computer.[15] Stoecker characterizes community informatics as a "distraction." He argues that we should think not in terms of community informatics projects but rather in terms of community development projects that incorporate informatics. In other words, community informatics should at best be seen as a "support field" and ICTs as only one development option among others that include housing, family services, and small business incubators. He also has questioned the vested interests involved. On one hand, he sees many academics making careers out of community networks:

> Yes, we all like to complain (me included) about the sacrifices we make, since our skills could easily get double the salary in the corporate market. But we still have pretty privileged lifestyles, jetting around the globe to meet with other experts in this emerging field, and writing journal articles and books for each other. (Stoecker, 2005, pp. 19–20)

On the other hand, he sees community networks integrating marginalized groups into the capitalist order. For instance, community technology centers are focused on "job training—integrating people into the lower rungs of the capitalist economy rather than helping them to question it" (Stoecker, 2005, p. 19). Similarly, community portals become sites for commerce whereby "the entire community, rather than just its individuals, become integrated into the capitalist economy" (Stoecker, 2005, p. 19).[16] Stoecker has brought almost every aspect of community network research under his critical lens and so forces us to rethink the fundamentals. He believes that the potential of community networks can only be realized if we are clearheaded and channel our energies in the right direction.

The community networks literature highlights a major weakness of our thinking on matters related to universal access—the belief that universal access is inherently good. But here we also see the beginnings of a profound critique that has implications not just for community network research but universal access research in general.

E-Rate

The proposal to include Internet connectivity for schools and libraries in the universal service program originated from a bill entitled the "National Communication Competition and Information Infrastructure Act" (HR 3636), which was introduced in November, 1993, by Representatives Markey of Massachusetts and Fields of Texas (Dickard, 2002).[17] Although the bulk of the bill dealt with cable services provided by telephone companies, one section included a broad commitment to universal service (National Communication Competition and Information Infrastructure Act, 1993, Section 102). Beyond this, there was no specific provision for telecommunications funding for schools and libraries in the bill's original version. The first reference to universal service support for schools and libraries appeared in Section 229 of the final version of the bill, which ordered the FCC to "promote the provision of advanced telecommunications services by wire, wireless, cable, and satellite technologies to (1) educational institutions; (2) health care institutions; and (3) public libraries" (National Communication Competition and Information Infrastructure Act, 1993). However, the Markey-Fields bill, as it was called, failed to become law when the 103rd Congress ended without the Senate taking up the bill (Dickard, 2002).

Meanwhile, the idea of federal support for Internet access in schools and libraries was percolating elsewhere as well. In September 1993, President Clinton constituted the National Information Infrastructure Advisory Council (NIIAC) to advise the Secretary of Commerce about the development of the National Information Infrastructure (NII) (Carvin, 2000). In 1995, the Council developed the KickStart project to help local communities launch neighborhood networking initiatives centered on schools, libraries, and community centers. The Council stated that a short-term goal should be to "deploy Information Superhighway access and service capabilities to all community-based institutions that serve the public such as schools and libraries by the year 2000" (NIIAC, quoted in Carvin, 2000, p. 7).

Legislative proposals such as the Markey-Fields bill and public-private initiatives such as KickStart served to mobilize support for federal funding of Internet access in schools and libraries. Simultaneously, organizations such as the Consortium for School Networking (CoSN) and the International Society for Technology in Education (ISTE) worked at both the grassroots and national levels to raise support for such initiatives

(Carvin, 2000). Thus, when deliberations began in Congress in 1995 for the first major rewriting of the Communications Act of 1934, school technology funding received bipartisan support. Senators Snowe, Rockefeller, Kerrey, and Exon sponsored a motion (the Snowe-Rockefeller amendment) to include a provision called the "E-Rate" in the new law. With strong White House backing, the amendment found a place in the final Telecommunications Act passed in 1996.

The final contours of the E-Rate program took shape in the Federal-State Joint Board on Universal Service, to which the Congress referred the universal service provisions of the Telecommunications Act for implementation. Funding for the E-Rate program proved especially controversial, with conflicting proposals put forward by the telecommunications industry, school groups, and community organizations. Industry groups favored block grants through local or regional authorities and offered to contribute vouchers. School and library groups favored discounts, preferably on a sliding scale indexed to the level of poverty prevailing in the community. The administration weighed in on the side of the educators, with the result that the final Joint Board recommendations to the FCC included E-Rate discounts based on economic disadvantage (Carvin, 2000).

The E-Rate program is available to all community libraries as well as public schools, and to nonprofit private and parochial schools with less than $50 million in endowments. These schools receive discounts for telecommunications access ranging from 20 to 90 percent of total eligible spending. The percentage of discounts is indexed to the poverty level prevailing among a school's students—specifically, the percentage of students enrolled in the School Lunch Program. The schools can use the funds for a variety of purposes related to telecommunications and Internet access. In order to prevent abuse or diversion of funds to ineligible uses, an elaborate list of covered and non-covered expenditure categories has been developed over time.[18] In general, telecommunications services and Internet access services are eligible for support from the E-Rate fund. In addition, internal wiring (such as cabling) and file servers for multiple users are also eligible (Universal Service Administrative Company, 2003b). End-user equipment, software (unless it is file server or e-mail software), and content are not eligible for support. Further, schools must acquire service from eligible telecommunications providers that have been approved by state and federal regulators to offer telecommunications services in that area. Any commercial vendor can install internal wiring and connections.

Currently, a nonprofit organization called the Universal Service Administration Company (USAC) implements the E-Rate program. Incorporated in 1997 on an FCC initiative, the USAC has four divisions—High Cost, Low Income, Rural Health Care, and Schools and Libraries—active in each of the areas in which Congress had mandated universal service support (Universal Service Administrative Company, 2003a). The Schools and Libraries Division (SLD) is responsible for the

E-Rate program: In addition to other duties, it generates projections of funding demand for the E-Rate program, determines discount levels, administers the review process, and disburses funds.

The source of funding for the E-Rate program, as well as for all other universal service initiatives administered by the USAC, is the federal Universal Service Fund (USF). The 1996 Telecommunications Act mandated that all telecommunications service providers must contribute in an equitable and nondiscriminatory manner to a fund that will support universal service programs for low-income customers, high-cost areas, schools and libraries, and rural health-care providers. In 2002, the USAC collected $5.27 billion from telecommunications providers and distributed over $5.3 billion through its various universal service programs (Universal Service Administrative Company, 2003a). The E-Rate program alone is authorized to distribute a maximum of $2.25 billion per year to schools and libraries—actual disbursements in the last five years have varied between $1.41 billion and $1.68 billion annually.

The process that culminated in the creation of the E-Rate program gained strength from a number of trends a long time in the making. Schofield and Davidson (2002, p. 2) identify three of these as "government policy, business interests, and community enthusiasm." The government was probably the last of the three to take an interest in advanced telecommunications access in schools. Business interests had played an important role as far back as the mid-1980s in producing well-publicized reports, such as *A Nation At Risk* and the *SCANS Report*, that advocated a major role for technology in solving the ills of the educational system (Schofield & Davidson, 2002). These initiatives were not entirely altruistic: Major computer manufacturers and telecommunications providers saw in these efforts a business opportunity as well. Community enthusiasm was also clearly evident in events such as NetDays held in the mid-1990s, in which parents, educators, community volunteers, and technology companies came together to connect schools to the Internet and install computers in classrooms. Over a quarter of a million citizen volunteers participated in the first NetDay in 1996 (Schofield & Davidson, 2002).

The creation of the E-Rate program to fund telecommunications and Internet access in schools and libraries was the result of these converging governmental, business, and community interests. However, a program using mandatory contributions from a specific industry (i.e., telecommunications) to support education was unprecedented and signified a key compromise between historically opposed ideas in public policy. In a sense, the E-Rate program bridged these contradictions and provided a politically viable action plan to policymakers. Three key trade-offs of this compromise can be identified: between the building of "social capital" or individual skills as the objective of education, between community autonomy and national coordination, and between consumer benefit and industry deregulation. We address these contradictions further in the discussion section.

Rural Broadband

With every significant technological advance come calls for policy interventions to bring about urban-rural parity. At the turn of the last century, the big issue was Rural Free Delivery—delivery of mail to each rural homestead so that rural residents, unlike city dwellers, would not have to make trips to the post office to pick up their mail (Fuller, 1964; Roper, 1917). Calls to extend telephone service to rural areas soon followed. Interestingly, the first major push for rural telephony was a grassroots phenomenon, with farmers setting up their own systems (often using barbed wire as transmission lines) when the Bell System ignored their repeated pleas for rural service. This initial and significant burst of network growth was extended further via loans provided by the Rural Electrification Administration and internal cross-subsidies from urban to rural services (Brock, 1981; Fischer, 1987; Mueller, 1993).[19] With the arrival of digital technologies, especially the Integrated Services Digital Network (ISDN),[20] alarms were again sounded about rural areas being left behind (Gabe & Abel, 2002). While documenting the disparities in the deployment pattern of the new technology, Gabe and Abel (2002, p. 1246) observed that "the patterns of ISDN investment and digital divide uncovered in the study may apply to other forms of telecommunications infrastructure available today and in the future." Soon enough, there were studies recording inequities in access to the Internet (Downes & Greenstein, 1999; Greenstein, 1998; Grubesic, 2003; Malecki, 2002, 2003; Nicholas, 2003; Strover, 2001). Today, the discussion has moved on to broadband, where we have a virtual replay of old concerns with regard to yet another new technology.[21]

In fact, authors writing on rural broadband[22] have characterized it as the "newest dimension" (Prieger, 2003, p. 346) or a "different dimension" (Skerratt & Warren, 2003, p. 485) and declared that "the 'have' and 'have not' dichotomy extends to access to broadband" (Bertot, 2003, p. 185). In keeping with the earlier pattern, there have been empirical studies showing an urban-rural gap in the patterns of broadband deployment (Gillet & Lehr, 1999; Grubesic & Murray, 2002; National Telecommunications and Information Administration, 2000; Strover, Oden, & Inagaki, 2001). These studies have been accompanied by others that examine different factors such as demand (Hollifield & Donnermeyer, 2003), costs (Glass, Chang, & Petukhova, 2003), competition (Grubesic & Murray, 2004), technological development (Glass, Talluto, & Babb, 2003), and the effectiveness of current policies that have an impact on broadband deployment (Gabel & Kwan, 2000; Grubesic, 2003; Strover, 2003). Other studies have proposed strategies for broadband deployment that include varied solutions for different locales (Parker, 2000), community networks (Matear, 2002; Rowe, 2003; Skerratt & Warren, 2003), and demand aggregation (Hollifield & Donnermeyer, 2003; Leatherman, 2000; Parker, 2000).

Then there are authors who make a case for policy interventions to further broadband deployment, a technology seen as having widespread benefits across different sectors—health care, education, e-government, entertainment, and commerce (Kalhagen & Olsen, 2002; Leatherman, 2000; Parker, 2000). Others focus on implications for a specific sector such as rural small businesses (Allen, Johnson, Leistritz, Olsen, & Sell, 1998; Locke, 2004).[23] The case for rural broadband is made around the following four points. First, in comparing broadband to railroads and highways, authors express the fear that communities unconnected to broadband networks will face the same fate as those that were bypassed by railroads and highways in an earlier era (Parker, 2000; Worstell, 2002). Sometimes comparisons are also made to early rural telephony: For example, Parker (2000, p. 281) has characterized upgrading to broadband as being as "fundamental as the transition from telegraph to telephone service at the turn of the previous century."[24] Second, authors have called for investments in rural broadband, evoking the principle of urban-rural parity (BJK Associates, 2001; Crandall & Jackson, 2003; Hollifield & Donnermeyer, 2003). For example, Hollifield and Donnermeyer (2003, p. 136) have argued that

> to remain competitive in the global information economy, rural-based businesses and individuals must acquire emerging technologies such as broadband connectivity with their urban competitors. Similarly, rural-based schools, non-governmental organizations (NGOs) and government institutions also need access in order to provide services to their constituents comparable to those available to urban-based citizens.

Third, authors have justified investment in rural broadband by pointing out the system-wide benefits or network externalities. For example, Crandall and Jackson (2003) have argued that rural broadband would enhance telemedicine, which in turn would reduce the time and cost of medical service delivery for the whole healthcare system. This argument is different from the equality of access argument. Here, Crandall and Jackson make the claim that rural broadband will offer benefits to the larger system by reducing the costs of delivering services in addition to improving the lives of rural residents. Finally, some authors make a case for including broadband in the universal service package by drawing an analogy with earlier technologies—a position that essentially sums up the previous three arguments (Matear, 2002; Solomon & Walker, 1995). For example, Matear (2002, p. 461) has suggested that

> just as universal access to traditional communications media, such as the post office and the telephone, is considered an essential service, so also should access to high-speed Internet, particularly in areas that currently lack the infrastructure to make this possible.

Rarely does a researcher seek to evaluate the actual impact of broadband availability on a rural population (LaRose, 2003). It is generally assumed, with the exception of few skeptics (Prieger, 2003; Xavier, 2003), that rural broadband is inherently good. This bias is deeply rooted in the rural telecommunications literature. Writing in 1990 before broadband entered the popular vocabulary, Samarajiva and Shields (1990, p. 234) noted that this bias perhaps arises from the fact that "those who engage in the academic and policy discourse are already committed to telecommunication through sunk costs of education, job choice, etc." They questioned whether investments in rural telecommunications are justified when there are pressing needs for resources for education, housing, and other basic necessities of life. More fundamentally, they challenged the long-distance bias of rural telecommunications projects in which connectivity to the nearest metropolis is privileged over that to the neighboring rural communities. Although we do not see a comparable critique in the rural broadband literature, Prieger (2003) and Xavier (2003) have made some important points. Prieger (2003, p. 346) has criticized studies that document the digital divide because they "commingle non-adoption of broadband access by households and non-implementation of the technology by carriers." He examined the deployment patterns of broadband carriers and found that what matters on the supply side is the demographic divide rather than urban-rural divide.[25] Xavier (2003) argued against the inclusion of broadband in the universal service package because there is little evidence that it is an essential service right now, although he remains open to the possibility that it might become so in the future. He stated that the aim of his paper was to "exert a moderating influence on (the, at times, exaggerated) calls for government support/subsidies to broadband deployment" (p. 8).

A Trans-Generation Model

One of our objectives in undertaking this review was to understand the process by which the concept of universal service is extended to new socio-technical domains. We call this process "trans-generation," a word of our own coinage that implies the transference of a concept to new policy discourses and its regeneration within these new contexts. The analysis of seven discursive domains in the previous section provided numerous examples of instances in which scholars had used precedent, analogy, appeals to values, economic rationalizations, and so forth to make a case for universal access in new policy domains. Scholars have made explicit comparisons to precedent-setting systems—for example, by comparing rural broadband to the railroads and highways. Authors have also used appeals to egalitarian ideals in calling for parity between different communities (in the case of minority access or access for the disabled), between rural and urban areas (as in the case of community networks and rural broadband), and between rich and poor school districts (in the case of the E-Rate). Economic arguments, too, have been used—for example, lower costs of health care through telemedicine as a justification for investment in rural broadband or cost savings in teacher training in the case of school telecommunications access. Here the possibility of realizing system-wide benefits or network externalities is held to mitigate the financial pain egalitarianism demands. Finally, some authors make a case for including a service in the universal service package by employing communitarian metaphors: For example, the very characterization of local networks as "community" networks elicits comparison with existing notions of community and creates a pressing case for inclusiveness, service orientation, and universal accessibility.

In the transference of the universal service concept to new policy domains, a divergence appears to occur between the actual historical precedent and how it is subsequently reconstructed, thus leaving an interpretative veil between later observers and the actual precedent. Our review of different policy discourses suggests that the "precedent veil" demonstrates a certain anatomization. Historically, regulatory concepts developed in interrelated clusters in the course of development of the precedent-setting systems. However, when new technologies are introduced, individual concepts are picked as if they were freestanding. Often the original meaning of these concepts is forgotten and the interrelations between them overlooked. The historical precedent becomes a repertoire of free-floating concepts dislodged from their historical context. For example, the "public interest, convenience, and necessity" standard current in broadcast policy owes its conceptualization to public utility law, where it originally covered the obligations of tramcar and railway line operators (Caldwell, 1930). As radio regulations were being framed in the 1920s, policymakers picked up the phrase on the grounds that everyone would recognize it as standing for something concrete yet sufficiently flexible to cover all possible future applications of radio technology.

We have also observed a process that may be labeled "reduction to historical shorthand" in the transference of the universal service concept to new issue domains. The complexities of the development of the precedent-setting proto-systems are reduced to an "imagined history." Although not necessarily false, this imagined history reconstructs the sequence of events to confer coherence and purposiveness to a process that is, in reality, chaotic and conditional. The precedent-setting systems are seen as products of a grand design and inspired action, whereas the incremental and contested nature of their development is overlooked. For example, Mueller (1993) has shown that when Vail called for "one policy, one system, and universal service" in 1907, he meant universal interconnection among different telephone networks and not service to everyone, as has been long accepted by the telecommunications policy community.

Furthermore, we have noted several instances in which the meaning of technological precedents that originated in one domain of discourse took on new aspects when applied to another. We label this process "stretching" and define it as the tendency of subsequent commentaries to broaden the scope of concepts, regulatory constructs, or policy terms beyond their original applicability. In all these instances, stretching was used to create a case for the extension of universal service to new sociotechnical domains. A few examples should help to clarify the process: Perhaps the best example of this process from the discourse domains that we surveyed can be found in the disabilities literature.

In the disability discourse, advocates in Australia were successful in arguing that Telstra's universal service obligations did not end with simply providing connectivity. They held that any technical equipment was merely a means of enabling subscribers to communicate with one another. If the standard equipment was unable to do so for a particular subscriber group, the telephone company was obligated to provide alternate means. This stretching of the notion of universal access from hardware provision to usability first convinced the Human Rights and Equal Opportunity Commission and, then, the legislature to redefine the universal service obligations of the telephone company.

Perhaps the most blatant examples of stretching were the arguments for making Web sites accessible to people with disabilities. Quite clearly the lawmakers were thinking of only physical spaces when they wrote the ADA, as all the places mentioned in the statute are physical. Yet, disability advocates have been able to make a strong argument, although not always a successful one, that Web sites should also be considered to be "places of accommodation" and hence within the purview of the ADA. There is no doubt that as more and more transactions and services move online, the case for accessible Web sites will become ever more pressing. The big question is how far should the accessibility requirements for Web sites go? In 1996, the Department of Justice's Civil Rights Division issued an opinion (which does not have the force of law) that the ADA applies to Web sites. A separate law requires that federal sites created after August 7, 2000, should be accessible to people with disabilities. In 2000, the National Federation of the Blind and the Attorney General of Connecticut persuaded four tax preparation services to agree to make their Web sites accessible (Heim, 2000; Sager, 2000). As Sager (2000, p. 62) has noted, "although the law was not written with cyberspace in mind, it looks like ADA may be ready to make the jump online."

Critique and Discussion

Having completed the reviews of the literature on precedent-setting systems and the new domains of discourse where universal service is playing an important role, we can now turn to a critique of the field. Our main concern is to identify and analyze assumptions about universal service that are sometimes unstated and often unexamined, but nevertheless exert an influence on the direction of the discourse. Our analysis of these underlying assumptions also identifies certain tentative directions for future research in the field.

Value of Informatization

The first of these unstated assumptions is that *information flow and exchange are socially and economically beneficial and that greater "informatization" is an indicator of progress*. The idea that information flow is something inherently good has a long and impressive pedigree. It harks back to the Enlightenment ideal of the worth of all knowledge, which has resurfaced repeatedly as the nation has engaged with the various proto-systems. George Washington saw postal networks as a way of binding the nation together. Madison thought it was essential to check the power of the government. Others thought it would facilitate commerce. Furthermore, the nexus between democracy and information has been taken as a given. Each successive effort to universalize a new service has been driven by the desire to increase information flows in the country, something that was expected to strengthen democracy and increase general welfare.

As new socio-technical systems emerge, we see policymakers repeatedly adopting this principle without a second thought. It is only when a writer like Schivelbusch (1978, p. 40) questions the notion that "communication, exchange, motion brings humanity, enlightenment, progress and that isolation and disconnection are evidence of barbarism and merely obstacles to be overcome" that we pause to think otherwise. In the literatures reviewed, we found only a few scholars arguing against information flow and exchange—and even they took care to qualify their criticism. For example, Cuban (2001) criticized the euphoria surrounding the introduction of computers into the classroom and found that computer and Internet use has only minimal impact on educational quality. However, his complaint was directed not against computers per se, but against the unplanned, thoughtless introduction of technology into the classroom, the misplaced sense of complacency that educational technology seems to engender, and the diversion of resources from more pressing needs. Similarly, Compaine (2001) argued against universal service programs in telecommunications, but his objection, too, was directed at those who apparently argue that every disparity in telecommunications access needs an organized government response and the concomitant expenditure of public resources and not against information flow and exchange itself. It is only in the rural broadband literature that we have found a stronger critical voice questioning the universal service project. Here scholars have questioned whether the expected impact of deploying rural broadband has actually materialized (LaRose, 2003), whether an observed digital divide is the result of conscious non-adoption by some rural households rather than deliberate denial of service by telecommunications carriers (Prieger, 2003), or if rural broadband is an "essential service" at present meriting its inclusion in the universal service package (Xavier, 2003).

As a research community, universal service scholars have been too quick to subscribe to the inherent value of information flows and use. Although there are undoubtedly benefits to greater information access and use, the apparent reluctance of many universal service scholars to examine this idea critically and articulate contrary viewpoints is a weakness of the current policy discourse. For example, Samarajiva and Shields (1990) pointed out the long-distance bias of rural telecommunications projects wherein connectivity to the nearest metropolis is privileged over that to the neighboring rural communities. They observed that in an asymmetrical relationship, the weaker communities could be harmed by this connectivity: Local businesses might be unable to compete with their now more accessible counterparts in the metropolis, and the local community might lose autonomy as its economy becomes integrated with the metropolitan economy. Samarajiva and Shields thereby took issue with the vast majority of researchers who consciously or unconsciously make the assumption that telecommunications networks are an inherent force for good. In their opinion, telecommunications enthusiasts make the erroneous assumption that two-way communication is power-neutral. The notion of communication as dialogue is often incompatible with entrenched power structures.

Samarajiva and Shields's stand is widely accepted at the global level, where it is sometimes feared that information flows can lead to electronic imperialism. However, within a nation, integration—the goal that universal service seeks to achieve—is accepted without question as something inherently good. Our aim here is not to deny the value of information flows but only to advocate a more critical perspective in discussions of universal access.

Systemic Framework

A second unexamined assumption in the universal service debates is that *universal access cannot be provided without an organized, systemic framework*. According to this viewpoint, universal access is most feasible when it is incorporated within the overall design of a system and when purposive programs are put in place for its achievement. Even services that start in a bottom-up manner (e.g., education) need to be systemized at some point to facilitate universal access. A systemic framework allows for the transfer of resources from one user group to subsidize another. Historically, these cross-subsidies have been critical for the development of the universal postal service (subsidies from regular mail to newspapers and from the North and East to South and West), universal education (subsidies via property taxes from the rich to the poor), and universal telephone service (subsidies from businesses to residential users and urban to rural users). Although broadcasting did not require an explicit system of cross-subsidy, the cost of programming was recovered via advertising charges largely from urban sponsors.

Among the literatures reviewed, the need for an organized systemic framework is most explicitly an issue in the case of E-Rate and rural broadband, which depend on subsidy flows from one part of the system to another. In fact, without these subsidy flows, neither would be possible.

Although the need for an organized systemic framework was not explicitly discussed in the case of minorities and people with disabilities, its existence is an implicit assumption because cross-subsidies, rather than direct government grants, have been the traditional way of funding initiatives in these areas. In the case of people with disabilities, Kaplan (cited in Bowe, 1993) provided a new twist when she argued that speech synthesis and speech recognition technologies should be incorporated in the very design of the network and the costs should be spread across the entire subscriber base. It is important to note that the economies of scale Kaplan (cited in Bowe, 1993) advocated would generate different kinds of subsidies from those traditionally used in the telephone industry. In the traditional system, the price at which some subscribers could access telecommunications services was raised (even though the cost of producing those services did not go up) so that the resulting profit margins could subsidize other subscribers who could not afford service. In Kaplan's model, the cost of producing telecommunications services goes up because technical enhancements are made mandatory for all equipment—although economies of scale would tend to mitigate this effect to some extent. In both cases, the prices that some subscribers pay will go up, but in different ways. In each case, however, a systemic response is clearly required.

These repeated calls for systemic solutions to problems of access may indicate a distrust of, and impatience with, the normal processes of diffusion in which subscribers individually adopt new technologies, based upon costs and benefits (Lentz, 2000). This, in turn, leads to providing services to customers through universal service programs that they may not need or be able to use appropriately: For example, schools are only now learning how to make effective use of computers and Internet access made available through E-Rate subsidies. This distrust also extends to service providers, based on the suspicion that they may deliberately, or through lack of understanding of consumer needs, withhold access to consumers. This is not to deny that cases of redlining do occur, but universal service scholars seem at times to be too eager to identify each and every gap in access as a market failure requiring the creation of systemic solutions. Few scholars have argued that some gaps will disappear over time while others might persist (Schement & Forbes, 2000) or that some gaps may be due to genuine differences in consumer needs (see Lentz, 2000, for a review of articles taking these positions). More research, informed by the extensive literature on diffusion studies, is required on which gaps actually constitute a digital divide and how long they need to persist before a systemic solution becomes necessary.

Uniformity of Access

Closely tied to the call for systemic solutions is a third assumption of the universal service discourse: *There should be uniformity in access across regions and social strata.* This requirement sustains itself on both philosophical and practical grounds. Philosophically, uniformity in access resonates with our notion of information egalitarianism and equity. Practically, uniformity of access provides a convenient and politically defensible benchmark. Disparities in the quality of service between the rich and the poor and urban and rural areas have been a concern with many of the precedent-setting technologies discussed in this chapter: In the case of postal rates, for example, there was genuine concern about their impact on rural newspapers. In the case of telephones, the FCC and the industry put in place an elaborate system of cross-subsidies and geographic rate averaging to ensure that rural and urban consumers would pay the same rates for telephone access.

In the new domains of discourse, this principle is most clearly evident in the E-Rate and rural broadband literatures, areas where mitigating the rural disadvantage is of primary concern. Geography is also an important issue in the minorities and e-government literatures because of concerns about redlining and the need for parity between the poorer parts of urban areas, usually inner cities in the U.S., and the rest of the system. Concerns about equity across social strata permeate all the literatures. We often hear warnings about a "two-tier" society, "second-class citizens," and "haves and have-nots." In the case of people with disabilities, Kanayama (2003, p. 193) has even provided a new twist to the familiar theme—gaps between those who "can" and those who "cannot."

Although eminently well-intentioned and with definite practical advantages, this insistence on uniform access also has its downside, especially in a multiple services environment. In the old, precedent-setting systems that provided a few services, it was possible to define a narrow set of services that would be supported by universal service subsidies. For example, universal telephone service centered on dial-tone access to local service, disparagingly referred to as Plain Old Telephone Service (POTS). Telephone networks today provide multiple services, analogously labeled as Pretty Advanced New Stuff (PANS). To include all of these options in the universal service package would be financially impossible, but which services should be included? Also, whatever the package, it is evident that not all consumers would find all the included services equally useful nor would all the services they might want be covered by universal service. Therefore, there are likely to be both waste and unmet demands when universal service policies support only a uniform bundle of services.

Identifying and implementing a uniform service package in a multiple services environment also presents challenges. The FCC has evolved complicated procedures of periodic reviews and trigger mechanisms to identify which services should be supported by universal service programs without abandoning the fundamental notion that the universal service package should be uniformly available. Proposals permitting regional variations in universal service packages (Hart, 1998) or allowing consumers to choose the services they want from a common menu (Schement & Forbes, 1999) have been put forward but have found little favor thus far. Universal service scholars need to explore further the possibility that universal access need not be uniform access across geographical regions and social strata.

Placelessness

In sharp contrast to scholars concerned about geographical gaps in access to telecommunications and information technology, another perspective claims that *universal service programs need no longer be concerned with geography because place has been made irrelevant in the new information and communication technology environment.* Some observers see the promise of the Internet as the "gateway to placelessness" (Knoke, 1996, p. 18), where physical location does not matter and a user can access content from anywhere on the globe. On this view, the whole world converges into a global village, generating optimism about global access to knowledge resulting from the digitization and distribution of information. By implication, universal access programs need not be concerned about physical location or geography in the coming age of informational plenty.

Yet, research in some of the new domains seems to indicate that an individual's place of residence matters in determining access. First, we should consider the possibility that some communities may not have Internet access of the highest quality or at the most affordable prices available. Second, local service providers may differ vastly in their ability to deploy services. As Ho's (2002) work has shown, cities with lower revenue bases and higher concentrations of minority populations tend to lag behind other cities of similar size when deploying e-government services. Many cities never advance beyond the first stage of "cataloging" (Layne & Lee, 2001) because of revenue constraints. Thus, neither an excessive focus on geographical differences in access nor a denial of the relevance of geography is likely to help the universal service discourse— the truth, as in so many cases, lies somewhere in between.

Local versus Metropolitan

The fifth assumption in the universal service discourse is the expectation that *the organized, systemic framework for universal service should not let the metropolis dominate the hinterland.* By its very nature, a universalized information and communication system is an integrative force and, yet, universal service scholars and policymakers have been, and continue to be, concerned that the metropolis should not dominate the hinterland. There is a peculiar paradox here that has repeatedly stymied policymakers. Historically, Americans have been distrustful of national government and strong defenders of local autonomy. This faith in community can be traced from "Thomas Jefferson's national visions of a continental republic of small landholders, through the late 19th century populist agitation's [*sic*] that challenged the nationalization of regional and local economic resources, to the more recent notion of locally-controlled information networks" (Shuler, 1999, pp. 362–363). Localism as a policy goal has been a strong influence on broadcast policy making. The emphasis on local control is especially strong in education, too, with local communities fiercely defending the right to raise local resources through taxation and to set local curricula.

There has also been a tendency toward national coordination and harmonization, especially in matters with interstate ramifications such as transportation, broadcasting, and telecommunications. This tendency has been evident in education as well. By the early decades of the 20th century, states had acquired considerable public and judicial sanction to set reasonable educational standards for local school districts. This trend was taken one step further in the second half of the 20th century, with the extension of federal authority over school testing, teacher accreditation, and educational equity (Ravitch, 1995). The tension between local autonomy and national coordination was also manifest in the flat rate versus distance-based rates in the postal system: Advocates of distance-sensitive rates sought to protect small town and rural papers against metropolitan newspapers, which they felt would overwhelm those in the hinterland under a flat rate. Similarly in broadcasting history, some scholars argued that all stations should be allowed to use only low-power transmitters so that stations in small and large markets would be able to co-exist.

Domination by metropolitan areas was an issue only in some of the later literatures reviewed. It was particularly evident in the E-Rate literature, where there was concern that local communities did not have the autonomy to deploy funds as they saw fit. Instead, the purposes for which funds could be used and the services that could be purchased were specifically enumerated and controlled (Dickard, 2002). The aim of the E-Rate program was not to promote the Jeffersonian local autonomy to which Shuler (1999) referred. Rather, the aim was to harmonize or standardize telecommunications access across classrooms and school districts and to equalize opportunity: "Building technology capacity in underserved communities diminishes the competitive disadvantage faced by certain areas, especially inner cities and rural areas" (Carvin, 2000, p. 4). As former Department of Commerce Assistant Secretary Larry Irving has argued, Internet access has become the new civil right (quoted in Carvin, 2000, p. 5)—implying thereby that it should be available universally and in qualitatively undifferentiated fashion to all citizens.

At the same time, the E-Rate program was able to mollify supporters of local autonomy by providing important incentives. By funding "vital community centers" (Shuler, 1999, p. 364) such as schools and libraries, the E-Rate program creates local community resources. This is especially true of economically disadvantaged communities where E-Rate funds often have multiplier effects on development. As one study prepared for the U.S. Department of Education pointed out, the experience of participating in the E-Rate program proved to be useful for these communities "as they look for other ways to promote e-learning opportunities for their students and thereby better develop the long-run economic strength of their communities" (Chaplin, 2001, p. 15). As the debate on the E-Rate program showed, legislators found it easy and politically advantageous to show their support for local communities: "Lawmakers did see public access in schools and libraries as a stepping stone to developing a modern communication infrastructure in communities" (Carvin, 2000, p. 5). Thus, the rhetoric on the E-Rate program managed to bridge the seemingly unbridgeable gap between local autonomy and national standardization. The benefit to local communities made the program appealing to legislators even as the strict program guidelines promoted national harmonization at the expense of local autonomy.

Universal service scholars need to engage more clearly with the fact that a universalized information and communication system by its very nature is an integrative force. One way to reconcile the centralizing tendencies of universal service policy with the exigencies of local autonomy may be to move away from prescriptive policy solutions toward the evolution of common standards and their promotion through coordinating agencies. Such standards are reminiscent of teacher training and curriculum standards in education. We have noted references to standards in many of the discursive domains. For example, in the disability arena, the Center for Information Technology Accommodation (CITA), which was created by Congress in 1998, encourages all government agencies to implement Web site accessibility standards (U.S. General Services Administration, n.d.). Private parties have also proposed Web accessibility standards such as the Priority One guidelines of the World Wide Web Consortium (W3C) (West, 2003). Similarly, in the field of e-government, hierarchies of achievement such as the four-stage model proposed by Layne and Lee (2001) may be regarded as examples of performance standards for government agencies. Such a standards-building approach may even be more compatible with a globalizing world environment in which the powers of national policymakers are eroding vis-à-vis both transnational groupings and subnational entities.

Neutrality

A final assumption evident in the universal service debates is the expectation that *universal service can and should be achieved while maintaining neutrality and balance between different policy choices and interest groups*. This is a paradoxical expectation because universal service, with its basis in egalitarianism and universalism, is a utopian ideal that does not permit any exceptions or exclusions—yet, some policymakers and scholars expect that such an outcome can be achieved while preserving balance and moderation in every other respect. The expectation is that government should ensure a level playing field even as it pursues a project with distinct redistributive outcomes. We saw this principle in postal history when Congress decided to allow all newspapers into the mail instead of favoring a few. It has also become a recurring issue in the regulation of the telephone industry, wherein the Congress and the FCC sought to ensure that their interventions via subsidies or regulatory actions should not give an unfair advantage to any particular firm—"competitive neutrality" was made one of the objectives of telecommunications policy in the Telecommunications Act (1996). However, technological convergence, intensifying competition, and the proliferation of services and litigation have enormously complicated the task of ensuring policy neutrality. The regulators now need to implement light-touch regulation that favors neither one competitor over another nor one technology platform over another. This has resulted in increasingly complicated financing mechanisms for universal service programs that are still regularly contested in the courts—for example, funding for the E-Rate program from the Universal Service Fund.

But the presence of multiple stakeholders in the universal service debates and the multifaceted impacts of its programs on society may also provide an opportunity for policymakers. In heavily contested policy terrains with multiple objectives and many stakeholders, it often becomes possible to put together winning coalitions whose members have enough overlap in interests to permit agreement on a plan of action. Such coalitions are less likely to emerge when the number of stakeholders is fewer and the policy choices less ambiguous. This sort of coalition building has precedents in the history of the American educational system that, since the beginning, has had the twin goals of building social capital and imparting skills. If social capital refers to virtues such as civic responsibility, mutual trust, and democratic participation, individual skills include the elementary "three Rs" and higher-level workplace skills. Although not mutually exclusive, these two objectives have battled for supremacy. In colonial New England, the driver of educational initiatives was communitarian concern with the religious instruction of the young and the republican ideal of the equality of all citizens (Kotin & Aikman, 1980). Meanwhile, Virginia and other southern states put in place a system of trade education based on apprenticeship that emphasized skills. In the 19th century, with rapid industrialization and increasing demands for trained labor, the "Virginia model" of skill-based education seemed to prevail. In the late 19th and early 20th centuries, the schools' potential to build social capital through assimilation came to the fore when industrialization, rural-to-urban migration, and massive immigration caused many to fear class conflict and discord. The success of educational reformers such as Horace Mann can be attributed in part to the fact that they tapped into these multiple aspirations—the assimilationists' goal of welding diverse ethnic and linguistic groups into a common American identity, as well as the industrialists' demand for skilled labor.

Similarly, universal service programs appear to offer something to all sides. On one hand, they build skills and empower individuals. On the other, they build shared knowledge, social interaction, and common cultural referents by creating community resources such as Internet access at schools and libraries, local computing centers, and community networks. The fact that its advocates claim that universal service can attain both skills and socialization has not kept its critics from saying that the balance has been shifted one way or the other: For example, Cuban (2001, pp. 191–192) states with reference to the E-Rate program that "contemporary reformers have forgotten the democratic mission at the heart of public schooling, ignored the critical importance of social capital in strengthening civic behaviors, and proven too narrowly committed to technocratic solutions of school problems." On the other hand, some note that school Internet access does nothing for basic skill development: "Opponents say that schools that cannot teach their students to read and write should not be plugging them into the Internet instead" (DeMuth & Furchtgott-Roth, 1998, p. x). Universal service programs obviously do not satisfy all stakeholders, but the fact that they exist shows that enough stakeholders have found something to agree so that the programs could be implemented.

Policymakers have been able to use the same principle to balance the conflicting demands of consumer benefit and industry deregulation. Theoretically, industries in which the conditions necessary for perfect competition are unlikely to obtain because of natural monopoly, imperfect information, scarce resources, and so on, have all been subject to regulation. In each situation, the ultimate justification for regulation has been the supposed disadvantages to consumers or potential competitors resulting from the unencumbered operations of industry. Industry deregulation therefore raises real or imagined fears that consumers will be negatively affected. With or without a rational basis, consumer benefits and industry deregulation are seen by some observers as antithetical to each other. Thus, for deregulatory initiatives to be politically acceptable, consumer concerns would need to be addressed effectively. The preamble to the 1996 Telecommunications Act specifically addressed this concern by stating that the objective of the Act is "to promote competition and reduce regulation in order to secure lower prices and higher quality services for American telecommunications consumers and encourage the rapid deployment of new telecommunications technologies." Thus, although deregulation was the principal objective of the Act, it was not the sole or ultimate objective, which was to secure certain consumer benefits in terms of lower prices, higher quality, and universal access to advanced services. However, legislators could not leave these consumer benefits to be delivered indirectly and incrementally by the market without appearing to be negligent in safeguarding the interests of their constituencies. Specific language had to be worked into the Act to guarantee these consumer benefits by mandating them. The lawmakers' need to make deregulation palatable to the electorate explains the seeming contradiction that a piece of legislation intended to deregulate the industry created a huge new fiscal liability for the industry (the Universal Service Fund), the proceeds of which would be used to fund a program that radically expanded the notion of traditional universal service (Hausman,

1998). An explanation for this apparent contradiction comes from George Stigler's (1971) widely cited paper entitled "The Theory of Economic Regulation." Stigler made the case that regulation is a product produced by government and regulatory agencies and consumed by industry. Government produces regulation by putting together coalitions of support among the public to secure passage for rule-making initiatives through the legislative/regulatory process. Industry is the "consumer" of regulation and "pays" for regulation through campaign contributions and other forms of political support to the government. Although the government might be keen to oblige one of its constituents (industry), it can produce only the regulation behind which it can put together a viable and effective coalition. (This is a key difference from Stigler's capture theory, which says that government decision making is captured by industry interests with the result that government can be made to produce any outcome at the bidding of industry.) The "supply of regulation" (p. 3) is therefore limited to the outcomes for which the government can put together winning coalitions.

When viewed from the perspective of Stigler's theory of economic regulation, universal service programs cease to be an aberration within a deregulatory initiative and can be seen as a vital component of deregulation that ensures overall political viability. Thus, by including the provisions for universal service programs in Section 254 of the Telecommunications Act, legislators succeeded in winning approval for a "regulatory product" (namely deregulation) for which there was much demand from industry. Industry willingly accepted the new financial obligation because it secured for them a relaxation of line-of-business restrictions and other deregulatory benefits. In this sense as well, the E-Rate program functioned as a bridge between the seemingly irreconcilable concepts of consumer benefits and industry deregulation.

This discussion shows that the expectation of policy neutrality in the universal service discourse is not only impractical but also counterproductive because it encourages the pursuit of exceedingly convoluted policy solutions. The ideal of "competitive neutrality" enshrined in the 1996 Telecommunications Act cannot be reconciled with the redistributive goals of universal service policy. Universal service scholars and policymakers need to recognize that universal service policymaking is an exercise not in preserving competitive neutrality but in achieving coalitions of interest through the distribution of costs and benefits. The enormous literature on coalition building and interest group politics in political science has been insufficiently utilized in universal service policy studies: As the preceding paragraphs have made clear, there is ample scope to do so.

Summary

Originally aimed at ensuring access to postal and telephone services, education, and broadcasting, universal service policies continue to influence diverse new domains of discourse including rural broadband,

Internet access in schools, and community networks. The apparent ability of the universal service concept to regenerate itself in new domains of discourse is testimony to the strength of its underlying egalitarian and universalist principles. We are repeatedly drawn to the concept because it taps deeply into our sense of equality and fairness. However, we have also seen that there are specific discursive practices that have been used by universal service scholars to argue for the application of universal access to new socio-technical systems as they emerge. These discursive practices, which include invocations of precedent, the drawing of analogies, appeals to values, economic rationalizations, anatomization, and stretching, give the demand for universal access urgency in the various debates.

Our review of the precedent-setting systems and new discursive domains also identified certain unexamined assumptions and expectations about the nature of universal service: the unquestioned value attached to informatization, the call for systemic solutions, the expectation that services will be provided uniformly, the conflict between the local and the metropolitan, and the ideal of policy neutrality. Critically evaluating these assumptions allowed us to assess the current status of the field and point out some directions for future research.

Endnotes

1. For example, Leonard Bacon, a Congregational minister, questioned the right of the government to shower resources on newspapers and give them a decided advantage over proponents of non-secular points of view, such as Methodist circuit riders (John, 1995, p. 40).

2. In 1801 the postal system was moved from the Treasury Department to the State Department (John, 1995).

3. At a time of considerable euphoria about the potential of education, Samuel Miller warned against the tendency to "assign 'intellectual and moral omnipotence' to education. Never before was there an age, he noted, when knowledge of various kinds had been so popular and widely diffused: The public mind had been awakened, the masks of ignorance and corruption had been lifted, and the love of freedom had been advanced. But in the wake of these improvements had come superficiality, infidelity, materialism, and worst of all, hubris. God would show little mercy, he warned, to a society that ignored human limitation" (Cremin, 1980, p. 5–6).

4. The U.S. Constitution makes no mention of education. However, education was debated at the Constitutional Convention. For instance, Madison and others proposed that the Congress should be empowered to establish a national university in Washington, DC. This proposal was voted down because it was felt that cluttering the constitution with specific proposals like this might generate controversy and make ratification difficult—the framers wanted to stay at

the level of general principles. Also, with jurisdiction over the District of Columbia, Congress could create a national university at any time, if it so desired, without any additional constitutional authorization. Later, when the Bill of Rights was passed, the Tenth Amendment pronounced that all powers not delegated "to the United States by the Constitution, nor prohibited by it to the States, are reserved to the States respectively, or to the people." Even the Tenth Amendment makes no specific reference to education, but it is generally seen as leaving education to the states because no mention was made to it in the Constitution (Madsen, 1974).

However, the federal government was not entirely removed from education. When the Continental Congress passed the Northwest Ordinance in 1787, it declared that "religion, morality, and knowledge, being necessary to good government and the happiness of mankind, schools and the means of education shall forever be encouraged" (quoted in Madsen, 1974, p. 86). It also reserved land in every township in the new territories for supporting a public school. On a more general level, the American Revolution "lent new urgency to the discussion of educational affairs, there being widespread agreement that in republics the nurturance of morality and intellect in the citizenry at large is a matter of the highest public responsibility" (Cremin, 1980, p. 11).

5. As the name indicates, *dame schools* were run by women in their homes where very young children were taught their letters. Old field schools, parochial schools, and district schools were all elementary schools under different forms of management. Old field schools, run on the basis of a contract between teacher and parents, got their name from being located on waste or exhausted land belonging to the town. Parochial schools, which were run by the church, derived their name from their association with parishes; district schools formed parts of school districts under the control of elected boards (Good, 1956).

6. In 1786, Benjamin Rush had written: "Our schools of learning, by producing one general and uniform system of education, will render the mass of the people more homogeneous and thereby fit them more easily for uniform and peaceable government" (Rush, 1965, p. 10).

7. The materials in this section have been extracted from Jayakar and Sawhney (2004).

8. As Mueller (1997) points out, long distance services were much more lightly regulated than local service in the 1920s and 1930s. When a firm uses common facilities to produce goods or services for both regulated and unregulated markets, it has an economic incentive to allocate as much of the common costs to the regulated market as possible (in order to substantiate demands for higher rates).

9. "The tastes, needs, and desires of all substantial groups among the listening public should be met, in some fair proportion, by a well-rounded program, in which entertainment, consisting of music both classical and lighter grades, religion, education, and instruction, important public events, discussion of public questions, weather, market reports, and news, and matters of interest to all members of the family find a place" (*Great Lakes Broadcasting Company et al. v. FRC* [37 F. 2nd 993 (D.C. Cir.)], quoted in Messere (2004, p. 1204).

10. Messere (2004) argues that there was a political reason for the FRC/FCC making localism a policy objective. The FCC's authority under the original terms of the Communications Act did not extend to the national radio networks. The network-affiliate relationship was also arguably outside the FCC's purview. However, by asserting an interest over the relationship of local stations to their communities, the FCC could have a say in the network-affiliate relationship. "Policy evaluation based on serving the interests of the city of license provided the FCC with sufficient leverage over the whole of the broadcast industry through station regulation" (p. 1205). Thus the localism and trusteeship framework was not a neutral decision-making protocol, but part of an active policy vocabulary that could be used by key participants to extend their authority or secure their objectives.

11. More detail is provided in an article by Louis Caldwell, Chairman of the Committee on Communications of the American Bar Association and the General Counsel to the FRC (Caldwell, 1930). The first law with the phrase was enacted in 1892 in New York, requiring railroads to obtain a certificate of "convenience and necessity" (p. 300). In 1895, another New York statute extended the requirement to street railways. Soon other states made the standard mandatory for all public utilities (the article does not say if this list included telephones as well). The Transportation Act of 1920, which amended the Interstate Commerce Act, required railroads participating in interstate commerce to obtain a certificate of public interest or convenience before extending old lines, constructing new lines, or acquiring a railroad. The "public interest" phrase originated in a series of Supreme Court decisions: *Munn v. Illinois* (1876), *Budd v. New York* (1892), and *Brass v. North Dakota* (1894).

12. The "public interest, convenience, and necessity" standard was used for transportation systems and public utilities on the rationale that they had exclusive right to serve a given area and used public rights of ways. Neither was an issue in the case of radio. The basis for using the standard for broadcasting was different—the broadcasters were given access to a scarce, publicly owned medium and there was need to ensure diversity of viewpoints (Krasnow & Goodman, 1998; McChesney, 1993).

13. "Normal goods" are those with a positive income elasticity of demand, i.e., goods for which people tend to increase consumption when their incomes rise and vice versa.

14. Goggin and Newell (2000) characterize the medical paradigm as one that looks at disability as a medical problem where the doctor, the expert, knows what is best for the patient, the passive recipient of medical care. They view the lay and charity paradigms as convergent on the grounds that lay people perceive the disabled as objects of pity and charities work to ameliorate the suffering of the disabled. On the other hand, corporations seek to "manage" the disability communities just as they manage labor, environmentalists, and other demanding constituencies. They talk in terms of "special needs" and "special programs" that are essentially patchwork solutions.

15. His critique of technology orientation goes deeper. According to Stoecker (2005, p. 17), "information is often confused with technology, in the sense that once you have the technology it is assumed you will get the information." This confusion becomes especially evident when organizations spend enormous amounts of effort assessing the technology needs of a community but do not even bother to understand the information needs. He therefore feels that community informatics has the best chance of flowering in library and information science environments, where information has traditionally been privileged over technology.

16. See Sawhney (2003) for a discussion on how systems in general benefit from universal access.

17. The text and legislative history of the bill can be accessed in the U.S. Library of Congress's THOMAS Legislative Information System (http://thomas.loc.gov).

18. For a full list of eligible and ineligible services, see the *Eligible Services List* maintained by the Universal Service Administrative Company (2002): www.sl.universalservice.org/reference/eligible.asp

19. In 1907, more than 18,000 rural telephone companies and cooperatives serviced about 1.5 million rural telephones, which comprised about a quarter of all telephones in the U.S. By 1920, as a result of the networks built by the independents and those their competitive pressure induced Bell to build, 39 percent of farms had telephone service as compared to 35 percent of all U.S. households. However, after the 1913 Kingsbury commitment, the independents started fading as a competitive force (Fischer, 1987).

20. According to the International Telegraph and Telephone Consultative Committee, an Integrated Services Digital Network (ISDN) is defined as a network "that provides end-to-end digital connectivity to support a wide range of services, including voice and nonvoice services" (quoted in Gabe & Abel, 2002, p. 1246). What generated considerable

enthusiasm for ISDN was that it transmits voice, data, and video over the same line. Depending on the specific technology deployed, the transmission rates of ISDNs range from 128 kilobits per second to over 150 megabits per second (Gabe & Abel, 2002).

21. See Sandvig and Sawhney (2004) for an analysis of why ICT research tends to follow the same pattern with each new technology.

22. "The term 'broadband' itself has multiple meanings. Some suggest that 'broadband' is a multitier concept and its definition should evolve as user expectations change" (Rowe, 2003, p. 86). Venkatachalam and McDowell (2002) document the varying definitions offered by different participants at a 2001 NTIA proceeding.

23. Allen et al. (1998) talk about advanced telecommunications services in general and not broadband per se.

24. Parker (2000, p. 282) hastens to add that "The main difference between the railroad and Interstate highway networks on the one hand and the telephone and broadband digital information super-highway on the other is that the costs of the information technologies are so low that our society can easily afford to make the digital information highway available to all rural communities."

25. Bertot (2003, p. 187), although not skeptical of rural broadband investments, argues that "in a telecommunications/networked environment, one needs to reconsider this location-based definition and consider the concept of 'rurality'—that being 'rural' has more to do with access to and availability of advanced, reliable, and high speed telecommunications services than geography."

References

Allen, J. C., Johnson, B., Leistritz, F. L., Olsen, D., & Sell, R. (1998). Telecommunications and rural business. *Economic Development Review, 15*(4), 53–59.

Barnett, W. P., & Carroll, G. R. (1993). How institutional constraints affected the organization of early U.S. telephony. *Journal of Law, Economics and Organization, 9*, 98–126.

Beamish, A. (1999). Approaches to community computing: Bringing technology to low-income groups. In D. Schön, B. Sanyal, & W. J. Mitchell (Eds.), *High technology and low-income communities: Prospects for the positive use of advanced information technology* (pp. 349–368). Cambridge, MA: MIT Press.

Benton Foundation. (2002). *Bringing a nation online: The importance of federal leadership.* Washington, DC: Civil Rights Education Fund.

Bertot, J. C. (2003). The multiple dimensions of the digital divide: More than the technology "haves" and "have nots." *Government Information Quarterly, 20*, 185–191.

Bishop, A. P., Tidline, T., Shoemaker, S., & Salela, P. (1999). Public libraries and networked information services in low-income communities. *Library & Information Science Research, 21*, 361–390.

BJK Associates. (2001). *Broadband Internet access for rural small businesses.* Retrieved December 16, 2005, from www.nfib.com/object/2753109.html

Bolt, D., & Crawford, R. (2000). *Digital divide: Computers and our children's future*. New York: TV Books.

Borgida, E., Sullivan, J. L., Oxendine, A., Jackson, M. S., Riedel, E., & Gangl, A. (2002). Civic culture meets the digital divide: The role of community electronic networks. *Journal of Social Issues, 58*, 125–141.

Bourk, M. J. (2000). *Universal service? Telecommunications policy in Australia and people with disabilities*. Retrieved February 23, 2005, from www.tomw.net.au/uso/index.html

Bowe, F. G. (1993). Access to the information age: Fundamental decisions in telecommunications policy. *Policy Studies Journal, 21*, 765–774.

Brock, G. (1981). *The telecommunications industry: The dynamics of market structure*. Cambridge, MA: Harvard University Press.

Brown, C. L. (2002, January). *G-8 collaborative initiatives and the digital divide: Readiness for e-government*. Paper presented at the 35th Annual Hawaii International Conference on System Sciences, Hawaii.

Button, H. W., & Provenzo, E. F. (1989). *History of education in America*. Englewood Cliffs, NJ: Prentice Hall.

Caldwell, L. G. (1930). The standard of public interest, convenience or necessity as used in the Radio Act of 1927. *Air Law Review, 1*, 295–330.

Carroll, J. M., & Rosson, M. B. (2003). A trajectory for community networks. *The Information Society, 19*, 381–393.

Carvin, A. (Ed.). (2000). *The E-Rate in America: A tale of four cities*. Washington, DC: Benton Foundation.

Chadwick, A., & May, C. (2003). Interaction between states and citizens in the age of the Internet: "E-government" in the United States, Britain, and the European Union. *Governance: An International Journal of Policy, Administration and Institutions, 16*, 271–300.

Chaplin, D. D. (2001, January 18). *Empowerment zones and e-rate application rates*. Retrieved March 7, 2005, from www.urban.org/UploadedPDF/empowerment_zones_FR.pdf

Chapman, G., & Rhodes, L. (1997). Nurturing neighborhood nets. *Technology Review, 100*(7), 48–54. Retrieved November 26, 2005, from http://cache.technologyreview.com/articles/97/10/chapman1097.asp?p=1

Chung, P., Austin, D., & Mowbray, A. (2000). A defense of plain HTML for law: AustLII's approach to standards. *The Journal of Information, Law and Technology, 1*. Retrieved October 15, 2005, from http://elj.warwick.ac.uk/jilt/00-1/chung.html

Cohill, M. (2002). *Why broadband? A community perspective*. Retrieved December 16, 2005, from www.knowledgedemocracy.org

Compaine, B. M. (2001). Information gaps: Myth or reality. In B. M. Compaine (Ed.), *The digital divide: Facing a crisis or creating a myth?* (pp. 105–118). Cambridge, MA: MIT Press.

Contractor, N., & Bishop, A. (2000). Reconfiguring community networks: The case of PrairieKNOW. In T. Ishida (Ed.), *Digital cities: Technologies, experiences, and future perspectives* (pp. 151–164). Berlin: Springer-Verlag.

Crandall, R. W., & Jackson, C. L. (2003). The $500 billion opportunity: The potential economic benefit of widespread diffusion of broadband Internet access. Washington, DC: Criterion Economics. Retrieved June 11, 2006, from www.criterioneconomics.com/docs/Crandall_Jackson_500_Billion_Opportunity_July_2001.pdf

Cremin, L. A. (1980). *American education: The national experience, 1783–1876*. New York: Harper & Row.

Cuban, L. (2001). *Oversold and underused: Computers in the classroom*. Cambridge, MA: Harvard University Press.

DeMuth, C., & Furchtgott-Roth, H. (1998). Foreword. In J. Hausman (Ed.), *Taxation by telecommunications regulation: The economics of the E-Rate* (pp. vii–xi). Washington, DC: AEI Press.

Dickard, N. (Ed.). (2002). *Great expectations: Leveraging America's investment in educational technology*. Washington, DC: Benton Foundation.

Ditzion, S. H. (1947). *Arsenals of American culture: A social history of the American public library movement in New England and the Middle States from 1850 to 1900*. Chicago: American Library Association.

Dordick, H. S. (1991). Toward a universal definition of universal service. In *Annual review, 1991: Universal telephone service: Ready for the 21st century?* (pp. 109–139). Nashville, TN: Institute for Information Studies.

Downes, T. A., & Greenstein, S. (1999). Do commercial ISPs provide universal access? In S. E. Gillett & I. Vogelsang (Eds.), *Competition, regulation, and convergence: Current trends in telecommunications policy research* (pp. 195–212). Mahwah, NJ: Erlbaum.

E-Government Act, Public Law 107–347, 116 STAT. 2899. (2002).

Edmiston, K. D. (2002). State and local e-government: Prospects and challenges. *American Review of Public Administration, 33*, 20–45.

Ervin, K. S., & Gilmore, G. (1999). Traveling the superinformation highway: African Americans' perceptions and use of cyberspace technology. *Journal of Black Studies, 29*, 398–407.

Fischer, C. S. (1987). The Revolution in rural telephony: 1900–1920. *Journal of Social History, 21*, 5–26.

Fischer, C. S. (1992). *America calling: A social history of the telephone to 1940*. Berkeley: University of California Press.

Fountain, J. E. (2001). The virtual state: Transforming American government? *National Civic Review, 90*, 241–251.

Freed, L. (2005). *E-government satisfaction index*. Retrieved November 6, 2005, from www.govexec.com/pdfs/ACSIfreedanalysis.pdf

Friedlander, A. (1995). *Natural monopoly and universal service: Telephones and telegraphs in the U.S. communications infrastructure, 1837–1940*. Reston, VA: Corporation for National Research Initiatives.

Fuller, W. E. (1964). *RFD, the changing face of rural America*. Bloomington: Indiana University Press.

Gabe, T. M., & Abel, J. R. (2002). Deployment of advanced telecommunications infrastructure in rural America: Measuring the digital divide. *American Journal of Agriculture Economics, 84*, 1246–1252.

Gabel, D., & Kwan, F. (2000, September). *Accessibility of broadband telecommunications services by various segments of the American population*. Paper presented at the 29th Research Conference on Communication, Information and Internet Policy (TPRC), Alexandria, VA.

Gabel, R. (1969). The early competitive era in telephone communication, 1893–1920. *Law and Contemporary Problems, 34*, 340–359.

Garbacz, C., & Thompson, H. G., Jr. (1997). Assessing the impact of FCC lifeline and linkup programs on telephone penetration. *Journal of Regulatory Economics, 11,* 67–78.

Garbacz, C., & Thompson, H. G., Jr. (2003). Estimating telephone demand with decennial state census data from 1970–1990: Update with 2000 data. *Journal of Regulatory Economics, 24,* 373–378.

Gilbert, P. (1987). *Universal service on hold: A national survey of telephone service among low income households.* Washington, DC: U.S. Public Interest Research Group.

Gillan, J. (1986). Universal telephone service and competition: The rural scene. *Public Utilities Fortnightly, 117,* 22–26.

Gillett, S. E., & Lehr, W. (1999, September). *Availability of broadband Internet access: Empirical evidence.* Paper presented at the 27th Annual Telecommunications Policy Research Conference, Alexandria, VA.

Glass, V., Chang, J., & Petukhova, M. (2003). Testing the validity of NECA's middle mile cost simulation model using survey data. *Government Information Quarterly, 20,* 107–119.

Glass, V., Talluto, S., & Babb, C. (2003). Technological breakthroughs lower the cost of broadband service to isolated customers. *Government Information Quarterly, 20,* 121–133.

Goggin, G., & Newell, C. (2000). An end to disabling policies? Toward enlightened universal service. *The Information Society, 16,* 127–133.

Goggin, G., & Newell, C. (2004). Disabled e-nation: Telecommunications, disability, and national policy. *Prometheus, 22,* 411–422.

Goldin, C., & Katz, L. F. (2003). *The "virtues" of the past: Education in the first hundred years of the new republic* (Working Paper No. 9958). Cambridge, MA: National Bureau of Economic Research. Retrieved October 15, 2005, from www.nber.org/papers/w9958

Good, H. G. (1956). *A history of American education.* New York: Macmillan.

Gore, A. (1993). *Reengineering through information technology: Accompanying report of the national performance review.* Retrieved May 18, 2005, from http://govinfo.library.unt.edu/npr/library/reports/it.html

Greenstein, S. M. (1998). *Universal service in the digital age: The commercialization and geography of U.S. Internet access* (Working Paper 6453). Cambridge, MA: National Bureau of Economic Research.

Grubesic, T. H. (2003). Inequities in the broadband revolution. *Annals of Regional Science, 37,* 263–289.

Grubesic, T. H., & Murray, A. T. (2002). Constructing the divide: Spatial disparities in broadband access. *Papers in Regional Science, 81,* 197–221.

Grubesic, T. H., & Murray, A. T. (2004). Waiting for broadband: Local competition and the spatial distribution of advanced telecommunication services in the United States. *Growth and Change, 35,* 139–165.

Hadden, S. (1991a). *Regulating content as universal service* (Working Paper, Policy Research Project: "Universal Service for the Twenty-First Century"). Austin: The University of Texas at Austin, Lyndon B. Johnson School of Public Affairs.

Hadden, S. (1991b). Technologies of universal service. In *Annual review, 1991: Universal telephone service: Ready for the 21st Century?* (pp. 53–92). Nashville, TN: Institute for Information Studies.

Hart, T. (1998). A dynamic universal service for a heterogeneous European Union. *Telecommunications Policy, 22,* 839–852.

Hausman, J. (1998). *Taxation by telecommunications regulation: The economics of the E-Rate.* Washington, DC: AEI Press.

Heim, J. (2000). Locking out the disabled. *PC World, 18*(9):181–185.

Ho, A. T.-K. (2002). Reinventing local governments and the e-government initiative. *Public Administration Review, 62,* 434–444.

Hollifield, C. A., & Donnermeyer, J. (2003). Creating demand: Influencing information technology diffusion in rural areas. *Government Information Quarterly, 20,* 135–150.

Information Infrastructure Task Force. (1993). *The National Information Infrastructure: Agenda for action.* Washington, DC: National Telecommunications and Information Administration.

Jayakar, K., & Sawhney, H. (2004). Universal service: Beyond established practice to policy space. *Telecommunications Policy, 28,* 339–357.

John, R. R. (1995). *Spreading the news: The American postal system from Franklin to Morse.* Cambridge, MA: Harvard University Press.

Jue, D. K., Koontz, C. M., Magpantay, J. A., Lance, K. C., & Seidl, A. M. (1999). Using public libraries to provide technology access for individuals in poverty: A nationwide analysis of library market areas using a geographic information system. *Library & Information Science Research, 21,* 299–325.

Kaestle, C. F. (1983). *Pillars of the republic: Common schools and American society, 1780–1860.* New York: Hill & Wang.

Kahl, C. M. (1997, Winter). Electronic redlining: Racism on the information superhighway? *Katherine Sharp Review, 4,* 1–8.

Kalhagen, K. O., & Olsen, B. T. (2002). Provision of broadband services in non-competitive areas of Western European Countries. *Telektronikk,* no. 2–3, 71–86. Retrieved February 15, 2006, from www.telenor.com/telektronikk/volumes/pdf/2_3.2002/Page_071-086.pdf

Kanayama, T. (2003). Leaving it up to the industry: People with disabilities and the Telecommunications Act of 1996. *The Information Society, 19,* 185–194.

Katz, M. B. (1968). *The irony of early school reform.* Cambridge, MA: Harvard University Press.

Kielbowicz, R. B. (1989). *News in the mail: The press, the post office, and public information, 1700–1860s.* New York: Greenwood Press.

Kielbowicz, R. B. (2002). *Universal postal service: A policy history, 1790–1970: A report prepared for the Postal Rate Commission.* Retrieved July 14, 2005, from www.prc.gov/tsp/116/paper.pdf

Klima, J. (2003). The E-Government Act: Promoting e-quality or exaggerating the digital divide? *Duke Law and Technology Review, 9.* Retrieved December 16, 2005, from www.law.duke.edu/journals/dltr/articles/2003dltr0009.html

Knoke, W. (1996). *Bold new world: The essential road map to the twenty-first century.* New York: Kodansha America.

Kotin, L., & Aikman, W. F. (1980). *Legal foundations of compulsory school attendance.* Port Washington, NY: Kennikat Press.

Krasnow, E. G., & Goodman, J. N. (1998). The "public interest" standard: The search for the holy grail. *Federal Communications Law Journal, 50,* 606–636.

Kretzmann, J. P., & McKnight, J. L. (1993). *Building communities from the inside out: A path toward finding and mobilizing a community's assets*. Chicago, IL: ACTA Publications.

Kuttan, A., & Peters, L. (2003). *From digital divide to digital opportunity*. Lanham, MD: Scarecrow Press.

LaRose, R. (2003). *Closing the rural broadband gap: A call for program evaluation* (Working Paper 002–2003). East Lansing, MI: Quello Center for Telecommunications Management and Law, Michigan State University.

Layne, K., & Lee, J. (2001). Developing fully functional e-government: A four stage model. *Government Information Quarterly, 18*, 122–136.

Leatherman, J. C. (2000). *Internet-based commerce: Implications for rural communities* (Reviews of Economic Development Literature and Practice, No. 5). Washington, DC: U.S. Economic Development Administration.

Lenhart, A., Horrigan, J., Rainie, L., Allen, K., Boyce, A., Madden, M., et al. (2003). *The ever-shifting Internet population: A new look at Internet access and the digital divide*. Washington, DC: Pew Internet & American Life Project.

Lentz, R. G. (2000). The e-volution of the digital divide in the US: A mayhem of competing metrics. *Info, 2*, 335–377.

Lipson, L. (1993). *Great issues of politics: An introduction to political science*. Englewood Cliffs, NJ: Prentice Hall.

Locke, S. (2004). ICT adoption and SME Growth in New Zealand. *Journal of the American Academy of Business, 4*, 93–102.

Mack, R. L. (2001). *The digital divide: Standing at the intersection of race and technology*. Durham, NC: Carolina Academic Press.

Madsen, D. (1974). *Early national education: 1776–1830*. New York: Wiley.

Malecki, E. J. (2002). The economic geography of the Internet's infrastructure. *Economic Geography, 78*, 399–424.

Malecki, E. J. (2003). Digital development in rural areas: Potentials and pitfalls. *Journal of Rural Studies, 19*, 201–214.

Mann, H. (1891). The first annual report of the Secretary of the Board of Education. In G. E. Mann (Ed.), *Life and works of Horace Mann* (Vol. 2, pp. 383–431). Boston: Lee and Shepard.

Matear, M. (2002). Canada must make broadband infrastructure a priority. *Canadian Journal of Communication, 27*, 461–467.

McChesney, R. W. (1993). *Telecommunications, mass media and democracy: The battle for the control of U.S. Broadcasting, 1928–1935*. New York: Oxford University Press.

McChesney, R. W. (2004). *The problem of the media: U.S. communication politics in the twenty-first century*. New York: Monthly Review Press.

McPhail, I. P. (1985). Computer inequities in school uses of microcomputers: Policy implications. *Journal of Negro Education, 54*, 3–13.

Messere, F. (2004). Regulation. In C. H. Sterling (Ed.), *The Museum of Broadcast Communications encyclopedia of radio* (Vol. 3, pp. 1201–1207). New York: Fitzroy Dearborn.

Meyer, A. E. (1965). *An educational history of the Western world*. New York: McGraw-Hill.

Millen, D. R., & Patterson, J. F. (2002). All ways aware: Stimulating social interaction in a community network. *Proceedings of the 2002 ACM Conference on Computer Supported Cooperative Work*, 307–313.

Moon, M. J. (2002). The evolution of e-government among municipalities: Rhetoric or reality? *Public Administration Review, 62*, 424–433.

Morino, M. (1994, May). *Assessment and evolution of community networking.* Paper presented at the "Ties That Bind" Conference on Building Community Networks, Cupertino, CA. Retrieved February 15, 2005, from http://morino.org/under_sp_asse.asp

Mueller, M. (1993). Universal service in telephone history: A reconstruction. *Telecommunications Policy, 17*, 352–369.

Mueller, M. (1997). *Universal service: Competition, interconnection, and monopoly in the making of the American telephone system.* Cambridge, MA: MIT Press.

Mueller, M., & Schement, J. R. (1996). Universal service from the bottom up: A study of telephone penetration in Camden, New Jersey. *The Information Society, 12*, 273–292.

National Center for Educational Statistics. (2002). *Internet access in U.S. public schools and classrooms, 1994–2001* (No. NCES 2002–018). Washington, DC: The Center.

National Communication Competition and Information Infrastructure Act, 103rd Congress, House of Representatives, 2nd Sess. (1993).

National Governors' Association. (1988). *A hearing of the Subcommittee on Telecommunications: Universal service, summary transcript.* Washington, DC: The Association.

National Telecommunications and Information Administration. (1988). *Telecom 2000: Charting the course for a new century* (NTIA Special Publication 88–21). Washington, DC: U.S. Government Printing Office.

National Telecommunications and Information Administration. (1991). *The NTIA infrastructure report: Telecommunications in the age of information* (NTIA Special Publication 91–26). Washington, DC: U.S. Government Printing Office.

National Telecommunications and Information Administration. (1995). *Falling through the Net: A survey of the "have nots" in rural and urban America.* Washington, DC: The Administration.

National Telecommunications and Information Administration. (1999). *Falling through the Net: Defining the digital divide.* Washington, DC: The Administration.

National Telecommunications and Information Administration. (2000). *Falling through the Net: Toward digital inclusion.* Washington, DC: U.S. Department of Commerce.

Nicholas, K. (2003). Geo-policy barriers and rural Internet access: The regulatory role in constructing the digital divide. *The Information Society, 19*, 287–295.

Noam, E. (1992). *Telecommunications in Europe.* New York: Oxford University Press.

Norris, P. (2001). *Digital divide: Civic engagement, information poverty, and the Internet worldwide.* New York: Cambridge University Press.

O'Connor, B. (1991). Universal service and NREN. In *Annual review, 1991: Universal telephone service: Ready for the 21st Century?* (pp. 93–140). Nashville, TN: Institute for Information Studies.

O'Neil, D. (2002). Assessing community informatics: A review of methodological approaches for evaluating community networks and community technology centers. *Internet Research: Electronic Networking Applications and Policy, 12*, 76–102.

Organisation for Economic Co-operation and Development. (2003). *The e-government imperative*. Paris: The Organisation.

Pacific Bell. (1988). *Pacific Bell's response to the Intelligent Network Task Force Report*. San Francisco: The Author.

Parker, E. B. (2000). Closing the digital divide in rural America. *Telecommunications Policy*, *24*, 281–290.

Parker, E. B., Hudson, H. E., Dillman, D. A., & Roscoe, A. D. (1989). *Rural America in the information age: Telecommunications policy for rural development*. Lanham, MD: University Press of America.

Perl, L. J. (1983). *Residential demand for telephone service*. White Plains, NY: National Economic Research Associates.

Pettigrew, K. E., Durrance, J. C., & Vakkari, P. (1999). Approaches to studying public library-networked community information initiatives: A review of the literature and overview of a current study. *Library & Information Science Research*, *21*, 327–360.

Pfeiffer, D. (1993). Overview of the disability movement: History, legislative record, and political implications. *Policy Studies Journal*, *21*, 724–734.

Pigg, K. E., & Crank, L. D. (2004). Building community social capital: The potential and promise of information and communication technologies. *Journal of Community Informatics*, *1*, 58–73.

Pinkett, R. (2003). Community technology and community building: Early results from the Creating Community Connections Project. *The Information Society*, *19*, 365–379.

Power, E. J. (1991). *A legacy of learning: A history of Western education*. Albany, NY: State University of New York Press.

Preston, P., & Flynn, R. (2000). Rethinking universal service: Citizenship, consumption norms, and the telephone. *The Information Society*, *16*, 91–98.

Prieger, J. E. (2001). *The supply side of the digital divide: Is there redlining in the broadband Internet access market?* (Working Paper 01–16). Washington, DC: AEI-Brookings Joint Center for Regulatory Studies.

Prieger, J. E. (2003). The supply side of the digital divide: Is there equal availability in the broadband Internet access market? *Economic Inquiry*, *41*, 346–363.

Ransom, P. (1994). Public policy/legislative trends: Telecommunications access for people with disabilities. *Technology and Disability*, *3*, 165–172.

Ravitch, D. (1995). *National standards in American education: A citizen's guide*. Washington, DC: Brookings Institution Press.

Rawls, J. (1971). *A theory of justice*. Cambridge, MA: Belknap Press.

Riordan, M. H. (2002). Universal residential telephone service. In M. E. Cave, S. K. Majumdar, & I. Vogelsang (Eds.), *Handbook of telecommunications economics* (Vol. 1, pp. 423–473). Boston: Elsevier.

Roper, D. C. (1917). *The United States Post Office*. New York: Funk & Wagnalls.

Rowe, R. (2003). Rural technology deployment and access: Successes upon which to build. *Government Information Quarterly*, *20*, 85–93.

Rush, B. (1965). Thoughts upon the mode of education proper in a republic. In F. Rudolph (Ed.), *Essays on education in the early republic* (pp. 9–23). Cambridge, MA: Harvard University Press.

Russell, C. (2003). Access to technology for the disabled: The forgotten legacy of innovation? *Information & Communication Technology Law*, *12*, 237–246.

Sager, R. H. (2000). Don't disable the Web. *American Spectator, 33*(9), 62–64.

Samarajiva, R., & Shields, P. (1990). Value issues in telecommunications resource allocation in the Third World. In S. Lundstedt (Ed.), *Telecommunications, values, and the public interest* (pp. 227–253). Norwood, NJ: Ablex.

Sandvig, C., & Sawhney, H. (2004, August). *Approaching yet another new communication technology.* Framing paper prepared for the Wireless Communication Workshop: Inspirations from Unusual Sources, Ann Arbor, MI.

Sawhney, H. (2000). Universal service: Separating the grain of truth from the proverbial chaff. *The Information Society, 16,* 161–164.

Sawhney, H. (2003). Universal service expansion: Two perspectives. *The Information Society, 19,* 327–332.

Sawhney, H., & Jayakar, K. (1999). Universal service: Migration of metaphors. In B. A. Cherry, S. S. Wildman, & A. S. Hammond, IV (Eds.), *Making universal service policy: Enhancing the process through multidisciplinary evaluation* (pp. 15–37). Mahwah, NJ: Erlbaum.

Scanlon, T. M. (2000). The diversity of objections to inequality. In M. Clayton & A. Williams (Eds.), *The ideal of equality* (pp. 41–59). New York: St. Martin's Press.

Schement, J. R. (1995). Beyond universal service: Characteristics of Americans without telephones, 1980–1993. *Telecommunications Policy, 19,* 447–485.

Schement, J. R., & Forbes, S. C. (1999, September). *Offering a menu of options: An informed choice model of universal service.* Paper presented at the Telecommunications Policy Research Conference, Washington, DC.

Schement, J. R., & Forbes, S. C. (2000). Identifying temporary and permanent gaps in universal service. *The Information Society, 16,* 117–126.

Schivelbusch, W. (1978, spring). Railroad space and railroad time. *New German Critique, 14,* 31–40.

Schofield, J. W., & Davidson, A. L. (2002). *Bringing the Internet to school: Lessons from an urban district.* San Francisco, CA: Jossey-Bass.

Schuler, D. (1994). Community networks: Building a new participatory medium. *Communications of the ACM, 37*(1), 39–51.

Shneiderman, B. (2000). Universal usability: Pushing human-computer interaction research to empower every citizen. *Communications of the ACM, 43*(5), 85–91.

Shuler, J. A. (1999). A critique of universal service, E-Rate, and the chimera of the public's interest. *Government Information Quarterly, 16,* 359–369.

Skerratt, S., & Warren, M. (2003). Broadband in the countryside: The new digital divide. *Proceedings of the European Federation for Information Technology in Agriculture (EFITA 2003) Conference, Debrecen, Hungary,* 484–491. Retrieved February 15, 2006, from www.date.hu/efita2003/centre/pdf/0802.pdf

Solomon, J., & Walker, D. (1995). Separating infrastructure and service provision: The broadband imperative. *Telecommunications Policy, 19,* 83–89.

Stephanidis, C., & Emiliani, P. L. (1999). "Connecting" to the information society: A European perspective. *Technology and Disability, 10,* 21–44.

Stephanidis, C., & Salvendy, G. (1998). Toward an information society for all: An international research and development agenda. *International Journal of Human-Computer Interaction, 10,* 107–134.

Stephanidis, C., Salvendy, G., Akoumianakis, D., Arnold, A., Bevan, N., Dardailler, D., et al. (1999). Toward an information society for all: HCI challenges and R&D recommendations. *International Journal of Human Computer Interaction, 11*, 1–28.

Stigler, G. J. (1971). The theory of economic regulation. *Bell Journal of Economics and Management Science, 2*(1), 3–21.

Stoecker, R. (2005). Is community informatics good for communities? Questions confronting an emerging field. *Journal of Community Informatics, 1*(3), 13–26.

Stowers, G. N. L. (2004, March). *Measuring the performance of e-government* (E-Government Series). Washington, DC: IBM Center for the Business of Government. Retrieved February 16, 2006, from www.businessofgovernment.org/pdfs/8493_Stowers_ Report.pdf

Strong, J. (1963). *Our country*. Cambridge, MA: Harvard University Press.

Strover, S. (2001). Rural Internet connectivity. *Telecommunications Policy, 25*, 331–347.

Strover, S. (2003). The prospects for broadband deployment in rural America. *Government Information Quarterly, 20*, 95–106.

Strover, S., Oden, M., & Inagaki, N. (2001, October). *Telecommunications and rural economies: Findings from the Appalachian region*. Paper presented at the 29th Research Conference on Communication, Information and Internet Policy, Alexandria, VA.

Taylor, L. D. (1994). *Telecommunications demand: Theory and practice*. Boston: Kluwer.

Telecommunications Act of 1996. (1996). Pub. Law No. 104–104, 110 Stat. 56.

Thomas, J. C., & Streib, G. (2003). The new face of government: Citizen-initiated contacts in the era of e-government. *Journal of Public Administration Research and Theory, 13*, 83–102.

Tonn, B. E., Zambrano, P., & Moore, S. (2001). Community networks or networked communities. *Social Science Computer Review, 19*, 201–212.

Universal Service Administrative Company. (2002). *Eligible services list of the schools and libraries support mechanism*. Washington, DC: The Company.

Universal Service Administrative Company. (2003a). *Annual report 2002*. Washington, DC: The Company.

Universal Service Administrative Company. (2003b, May 3). *Eligible services framework*. Retrieved July 20, 2003, from www.sl.universalservice.org/reference/eligserv_ framework.asp

U.S. Department of Commerce (1975). *Historical statistics of the United States: Colonial times to 1970*. Washington, DC: The Department.

U.S. Department of Education. (2000). *The condition of education, 1999*. Washington, DC: The Department.

U.S. General Services Administration. (n.d.). *Section 508*. Retrieved May 19, 2005, from www.section508.gov/index.cfm

U.S. Office of Technology Assessment. (1990). *Critical connections: Communications for the future (OTA-CIT-407)*. Washington, DC: U.S. Government Printing Office.

U.S. Office of the President. (2003). *E-government strategy: Implementing the President's management agenda for e-government*. Washington, DC: The Office.

Vanderheiden, G. C. (1990). Thirty-something million: Should they be exceptions? *Human Factors, 32*, 383–396.

Venkatachalam, S., & McDowell, S. (2002). What is broadband? Where is "rural"? *Government Information Quarterly, 20*, 151–166.

Virnoche, M. F. (1998). The seamless Web and communications equity: The shaping of a community network. *Science, Technology, & Human Values, 23,* 199–220.

Walsh, E. O., Gazala, M. E., & Ham, C. (2001). The truth about the digital divide. In B. M. Compaine (Ed.), *The digital divide: Facing a crisis or creating a myth?* (pp. 279–284). Cambridge, MA: MIT Press.

West, D. M. (2003, October 22). *Achieving e-government for all: Highlights from a national survey.* Retrieved March 28, 2005, from www.benton.org/publibrary/egov/access2003.doc

West, D. M. (2004). E-government and the tranformation of service delivery and citizen attitudes. *Public Administration Review, 64,* 15–27.

Weston, J. (1997). Old freedoms and new technologies: The evolution of community networking. *The Information Society, 13,* 195–201.

Williams, F. (1991). *The new telecommunications: Infrastructure for the information age.* New York: The Free Press.

Williams, F., & Hadden, S. (1991). *On the prospects for redefining universal service: From connectivity to content* (Working Paper, Policy Research Project: "Universal Service for the Twenty-First Century"). Austin: University of Texas at Austin, Lyndon B. Johnson School of Public Affairs.

Worstell, Robert C. (2002, May 29). *Spanning the digital divide for rural counties: Jobs and a level playing field in this information age. A preliminary report on broadband infrastructure and its impact on economic development for rural counties.* Retrieved April 30, 2005, from www.deltanetwork.org/broadband/finals/spanning02.pdf

Xavier, P. (2003). Should Broadband be part of universal service obligations? *Info, 5,* 8–25.

CHAPTER 5

Digital Libraries

David Bearman
Archives & Museum Informatics

The Domain and Its Origins

This is the third time that digital libraries have been the primary focus of a chapter in the *Annual Review of Information Science and Technology (ARIST)* and, not surprisingly, it reflects a third perspective. Five years ago, Fox and Urs (2002) reported on the literature of the digital library largely as an engineering construct and a research domain. A few years earlier, Bishop and Star (1996) had examined the digital library as an emerging phenomenon within a broader review of social informatics.

Today the digital library is a reasonably mature information service application and so we can ask who uses digital libraries and how successful such applications are in serving user needs. Because services are at the core, I do not review digital collections in isolation; for the same reason, I include libraries which service some physical items in addition to digital content—"hybrid libraries." Of course, digital libraries have boundaries—not all services applied to digital objects are "library" services. The Digital Library Federation (DLF) Working Group on a Service Framework for Digital Libraries (Dempsey & Lavoie, 2005) usefully distinguishes the digital library domain from such domains as e-learning, e-research, e-archives and e-records management, e-publishing, enterprise systems within campus environments, personal users, and search engines and other open Web services. This review of English-language publications from the past four years does not systematically examine developments in any of these domains; it does, however, occasionally reflect on their intersections with digital libraries.

The term "digital libraries" emerged from the National Information Infrastructure initiative and U.S. national political discourse in 1991 and 1992, before achieving common currency among librarians in the wake of a special issue of the *Journal of the American Society for Information Science* (Fox & Lunin, 1993). Both the political and computer science foundations for discussions concerning the digital library lay in high-speed computer networks and the technical issues associated with linking and delivering collections of multimedia content. Although the vision of a singular "Digital Library" is what captured the popular and political imagination, and was promoted especially by Vice President Al Gore in the 1992 election campaign, through the 1990s the United States government supported "digital libraries" in the plural. Large multidisciplinary teams were funded to answer technical questions about computing requirements and almost incidentally built intensively curated collections, almost exclusively for academic use. The one exception was the Library of Congress's largely privately funded American Memory project (http://memory.loc.gov/ammem) and National Digital Library Program (http://memory.loc.gov/ammem/dli2/html/lcndlp.html), which created the largest digital library of all (over 8 million objects) for public use and enabled public access over the Web.

In the pre-WWW context of 1991–1993, the period of popular discovery of the Internet and the rise and fall of gopher (which first permitted public access to remote digital resources), the focus of digital libraries on solving the technical problems faced by those building collections of multimedia content was understandable, but the orientation to discrete collections has since shifted the focus of digital library applications. More than a decade later, we are finding the core assumptions of the early 1990s—that digital library content would consist of fixed objects, that digital libraries would contain only digital works, and that individuals working alone should be the target users of digital libraries—particularly limiting as some prescient observers predicted (Levy & Marshall, 1995). The plurality of digital libraries is an ongoing technical challenge and major source of user frustration.

The Literature

Digital libraries are now crucial tools for nearly all professional communities, but the development of digital library applications is not the central focus of any single discipline. One consequence of this interdisciplinarity is that new research contributions to the digital library literature are almost always first presented at topical conferences, especially at the Joint Conferences on Digital Libraries (www.jcdl.org/index.shtml), co-sponsored by the Association for Computing Machinery (ACM) and IEEE Computer Society (IEEE-CS) division since 2001, and the European Conference on Digital Libraries, the proceedings of which are published in *Lecture Notes in Computer Science*. The International Conference of Asian Digital Libraries and the more recent International Conference on Digital Libraries, the papers of which have been published in special issues of journals since 2001, are of more regional interest but attract well over one hundred papers annually. In addition, major library association conferences include papers devoted to aspects of the digital library, especially online services, digital content acquisition and preservation, and management. Furthermore, the pre-existing conferences of information scientists, publishers, abstracting and indexing services, and online database providers all report on digital library topics from their particular perspectives.

Digital libraries are now a sufficiently mature subject to be taught in graduate school courses and, over the past four years, have been the topic of a number of monographs. Some of these are conference proceedings (Börner & Chen, 2002; Brophy, Fisher, & Clarke, 2002; Fox & Logan, 2005; Heery & Lyon, 2004; Koch & Sølvberg, 2003; Koskiala & Savolainen, 2004; Lankes, Janes, Smith, & Finneran, 2004; Lankes, McClure, Gross, & Pomerantz, 2003; Marcum, 2001; Sembok, Zaman, & Chen, 2003) but others are edited books with chapters by various authors (Bishop, Van House, & Buttenfield, 2003; Hodges, Sandler, Bonn, & Wilkin, 2003) or textbooks and treatises (Chowdhury & Chowdhury, 2003; Deegan & Tanner, 2002; Gorman, 2002; Hanson & Levin, 2002; Lesk, 2005; Levy, 2001; Lipow, 2003; Pace, 2003; Pantry & Griffiths, 2002; Rosedale, 2002; Tennant, 2004). Articles and book chapters are referenced separately throughout this review. Introductory texts presenting broad overviews that have been widely reviewed receive less attention, with preference given to more specific publications by their authors.

The core journals include *College & Research Libraries, Communications of the ACM, Electronic Library, Information Processing & Management, Information Technology and Libraries,* the *Journal of the American Society for Information Science and Technology, Library Trends,* and *Online Information Review.* Despite its irregular publication life, the *International Journal on Digital Libraries* has served as a venue for important articles from time to time.

The e-journals *ARIADNE* (www.ariadne.ac.uk), *D-Lib* (www.dlib.org), *First Monday* (www.firstmonday.org), and *Information Research* (http://informationr.net/ir), as well as the p- and e-journals *Program: Electronic Library & Information Systems* (www.aslib.co.uk/program), and *portal: Libraries and the Academy* (http://muse.jhu.edu/journals/ portal_libraries_and_the_academy) publish a steady stream of announcements, project reports, and reviews that serve the digital library community. These sources also include some important articles, especially overviews.

A number of organizations frequently publish reports and play other supporting roles for digital libraries far beyond what is represented in the published record. In the U.S., these include the Council on Library and Information Resources (www.clir.org), the National Science Foundation (NSF) (www.nsf.gov), and the National Academy of Sciences (www.nas.edu), as well as the Digital Library Federation (www.diglib.org)—which hosts twice-annual forums, the presentations of which are a record of the shifting foci of the field—and the World Wide Web Consortium (www.w3.org). The Joint Information Steering Committee (JISC) in the U.K. (www.jisc.ac.uk) supports and publishes on digital libraries. In Europe, the DELOS Network of Excellence on Digital Libraries (www.delos.info) has operated during the EU Fifth and Sixth Frameworks Programmes (since 2000), with the aim of coordinating research, standardization, evaluation, training, and international cooperation (including joint projects with the NSF).

Some Influential Recent Reports

During the past four years, a number of major reports have summarized the situation of digital libraries and articulated challenges facing the domain. These reflect the divergence of views between those who see the digital library as an institutional configuration, an engineering problem, a political challenge, and a service.

Writing for the Council on Library and Information Resources, Lougee (2002) suggested that digital libraries could allow the library profession to take on new roles in the creation and dissemination of content and in partnering with others acting as publishers. These new library roles were seen as being consonant with open paradigms and with teaching and research functions in the broader academic enterprise. Lougee described the evolution of some traditional roles, such as virtual reference services and information literacy training, to support her case. It is clear that academic librarians have accepted these new opportunities enthusiastically, seeing in them a way to reassert their importance within academia.

A report from the NSF Workshop on Research Directions for Digital Libraries held in June 2003 (Larsen & Wactlar, 2003) challenged digital libraries to become transparent and to support a ubiquitous knowledge environment in an effective manner. Their technocentric vision of infrastructures and interoperable toolsets acknowledged that "the idea of curated, network-accessible repositories—the original notion of 'digital libraries'—was (and remains) a fundamental need of scholarly inquiry" and asserted that building such digital libraries would lead to "an information ether" (p. 1). Although they talked of integrating information space into everyday life, their focus was solely on the higher education community. The workshop ultimately proposed how to transform "the conduct of disciplinary research itself," but in doing so revealed the gap between "disciplinary research" and a ubiquitous knowledge environment (p. 1). The recommendations of the workshop focused on search paradigms, metadata control orientations, and standards enforcement models.

The report of the NSF Blue-Ribbon Panel on CyberInfrastructure (Atkins, Droegemeier, Feldman, Garcia-Molina, Klein, Messerschmitt, et al., 2003) had a political objective: It called for a major investment in a national collaboratory, or grid, to fuel a revolution in scientific and scholarly activity built on a foundation of collaborative working environments, rich digital libraries, and intensive computational utilities. In order to influence the federal budget process, the report examined digital libraries in the sciences and found that they have had considerable impact as a testbed for interdisciplinary research into issues underlying cyberinfrastructure development. In this respect, it contrasted dramatically with the draft report of the American Council of Learned Societies

(ACLS) Commission on Cyberinfrastructure for the Humanities and Social Sciences (www.acls.org/cyberinfrastructure/acls-ci-public.pdf) which, although it essentially equated cyberinfrastucture for the humanities and social sciences with universally available digitized content, barely acknowledged digital libraries.

If a major report on cyberinfrastructure can overlook digital libraries, how are we to measure their impact? One way is through user studies. In her report on "Use and Users of Electronic Library Resources," Tenopir (2003) reviewed over 200 user studies of digital libraries reported between 1995 and 2003. These studies examined almost exclusively how faculty and students used academic libraries. With few exceptions, they did not measure the impact of those uses on academia and revealed virtually nothing about public or nonacademic users or uses. The literature of digital libraries does not address the impact of changing social practices as the Pew Internet and American Life Project has done over the past five years. In 2004, the Pew study found that search engines had radically changed the way people in the United States live and work, essentially by putting a digital library—the public Web—at their fingertips. Nearly one third of those who use search engines cannot imagine what they would do without them (Fallows, 2005): This is certainly a measure that libraries of any kind, digital or physical, would love to achieve.

Taken as a group, these major reports suggest that digital libraries are still firmly tethered to their academic roots and have had substantial impacts on scientific communications. However, they have not yet been acknowledged to have fundamentally changed the nature of scholarship in the humanities and social sciences and have been nowhere nearly as revolutionary as the Web in changing information-seeking behavior at large.

Ecology

The Digital Library, a singular, uniform, ubiquitous, and comprehensive digital information resource, has been a feature of prevailing political rhetoric in the U.S. and the U.K. for a decade, but the professional discourse, with few exceptions (Keller, 2004), has been largely about *digital libraries*. Because digital libraries are many and various, users experience them differently depending on whose "door" they walk through.

Discipline- and Subject-Based Digital Libraries

The predominant organization of digital libraries today is by their intellectual content or disciplinary focus. The users we know and the languages they speak are specific to disciplines (Lee, Na, & Khoo, 2003). Typically, funding is directed by agencies whose mandates are limited to a group of disciplines in science, medicine, or the humanities. We may be able to demonstrate that use is less related to the discipline served than it is to the availability of suitable resources, but the fact remains that resources are available for building digital libraries relating to specific disciplines (Törmä & Vakkari, 2004).

It is not surprising, therefore, that most detailed descriptions of digital libraries have been published in disciplinary journals with the intention of introducing them to their clientele rather than critically analyzing them from the perspective of information professionals. Nevertheless, the examination of features and tools developed to serve the needs of specialized communities could, in principle, cross-fertilize developments in other fields.

Digital libraries that are built around disciplinary subject matter can present barriers to access by nonspecialists, even when the content might be of interest to many disciplines and different types of users; for example, reports in journals in mathematics focus on the disciplinary use and benefits of a mathematics digital library (Adams, 2003; Lozier, 2003; Miller & Youssef, 2003). A digital library of classical protestant texts (Prest, 2003) contains content that could be of general interest, but the modes of access provided and the services supported are not designed to attract the general public or nonspecialists from other disciplines. Experience has shown that, when nonspecialist users are attracted to a digital library, as has occasionally been the case for digital medical libraries used by both general practitioners and the public, they have needs different from those of professionals, and serving these disparate needs presents challenges (D'Alessandro, Kreiter, & Peterson, 2004). For example, when a digital library of herbals is structured as a service designed to support scientific research, this limits its utility for chefs (Agosti, Benfante, & Orio, 2003).

Genre- and Format-Based Digital Libraries

Implementing digital libraries for particular media provides some technical advantages to support functions, interfaces, and archiving. Researchers, and the public at large, have prior experience with repositories dedicated to specific genres or formats and generally find national-level collecting institutions of this sort convenient. Countries may follow this path because national laws on copyright deposit provide for different agencies to receive texts, sounds, and motion images, as has been the case in France. Australia, for example, has created a national digital music library (Ayres, Burrows, & Holmes, 2004) and a national digital image library (Campbell, 2002). The nature of content management for academic digital libraries could change significantly if digital recorded culture were comprehensively available through national libraries worldwide and the content were open (subject to appropriate licenses) for access by digital library search engines.

Institutional Repositories

Disciplinary and format- or genre-based digital libraries may serve individual researchers well, but they could also undermine the library mission within the university. University librarians are struggling to identify a future role that the library can play within the larger institution (Atkins, 2003). One recent development in digital libraries has been to make "institutional repositories" an intrinsic part of an architectural strategy. Proponents (e.g., Lynch, 2003c) argue that if the management of radically distributed resources takes place in part by encouraging the development of institutional repositories, the identity of the institutional library and the university's commitment to its responsibility for curating digital resources are enhanced. This strategy, like that of distributed archiving, of which it forms a critical element, has a natural synergy with, and indeed might be necessitated by, new publishing paradigms in which individuals are enabled to "publish" without the gatekeepers or publishers who were the traditional collators of library content. Early experience suggested that the users of digital libraries were not very interested in contributing to institutional repositories (Smith, Rodgers, Walker, & Tansley, 2004). More thorough research comparing developments in many countries and examining the rapidly evolving nature of institutional repositories, however, gives those advocating the importance of this ecological niche cause for optimism (Lynch & Lippincott, 2005; van Westrienen & Lynch, 2005).

At the heart of the institutional argument is the economics of digital libraries. Resource sharing between institutions, new economics of publishing, and business models for digital library services all combine to drive thinking into institutionally oriented planning processes (Greenstein, Lawrence, Miller, & Dunlap, 2003). Real digital libraries, it is argued, must be grounded in institutions and in sustainable business models, not in grants and research efforts (Lynch, 2003a).

Mission- and Audience-Directed Digital Libraries

In contrast to the repository orientation, the digital library itself is increasingly viewed as a service (Bonn, Hodges, Sandler, & Wilkin, 2003) and, to some, invisibility is the ultimate goal (Borgman, 2003b). If digital libraries are to evolve this way, they will have to be constructed to support specific types of activity or missions and will not be readily identified with institutions or collections. Systems built around work processes are focused on serving those needs and are evaluated in terms of their success by those engaged in the tasks they are designed to support (Meyyappan, Foo, & Chowdhury, 2004). Increasingly we are learning how work methods and technical capabilities are discipline-specific (Adams & Blandford, 2002).

Digital libraries supporting distance education instruction are an instance of mission-directed libraries (Ho, 2004; Zia, 2004), as is CITIDEL (Fox, 2004), the NSF-funded consortial portal to educational resources related to computing and information technology. Other educational digital libraries, such as the National Science Digital Library, are broad programs under which a wide range of research is taking place, most of which is not directly related to the development of methods for delivery of educational content (Arms, Hillmann, Lagoze, Krafft, Marisa, Saylor, et al., 2002; Prey & Zia, 2002; Zia, 2004).

One of the few well-studied cases of building digital libraries for user communities without a disciplinary orientation is that of digital libraries for children (Druin, 2005; Druin, Revelle, Bederson, Hourcade, Farber, Lee, et al., 2003; Hourcade, Bederson, Druin, Rose, Farber, & Takayama, 2003; Hutchinson, Rose, Bederson, Weeks, & Druin, 2005). Having a targeted audience enables these digital libraries to design more satisfactory intellectual access methods and tools to exploit target resources. Audience orientation emphasizes services over collections.

Content

Primary Objects

Most content available in digital libraries has been born digital. Although the first decade of digital library research projects in the U.S. and Europe digitized some content in order to have material with which to test engineering solutions, digitization per se has not been considered scientifically interesting and, until very recently, it has not been conducted on a massive or comprehensive scale. Studies showing that older data have value even for the hard sciences (Liu, 2003) and that the digitization of "cultural heritage" is crucial to its future study (Sutton, 2004) were not sufficient to expand the pace of conversion from analog to digital. But institutional and national pride seem to be. Since December 2004, when Google announced plans to digitize and index the full text of more than 10 million volumes from five university libraries, there has been considerable reaction worldwide. Whether they welcomed or rejected it, the announcement led national libraries to examine the scope and speed of their current digitization plans. Before the end of 2005, major libraries, such as the British Library, the Bibliothèque Nationale de France, the Library and Archives of Canada, and the University of California Digital Library, had announced exponential increases in their text digitization programs. Together with the Open Content Alliance (www.opencontentalliance.org), which could well create the first comprehensive, public-domain digital library, these developments have engendered a realistic expectation that nearly everything ever printed might be available in digital form within a decade or so. Mechanisms such as the recently approved "info" Uniform Resource Identifier (URI) scheme will ensure that legacy content metadata is intellectually integrated into digital libraries (http://info-uri.info).

Primary digital objects in many formats will soon populate digital libraries much larger than the curated collections that have been built to date; researchers are therefore developing methods to handle massive quantities of content without human descriptions. Brute force approaches to these large collections (Cacheda, Plachouras, & Ounis, 2005) compete with methods to tease structure and genre out of scanned images of texts or full-text documents, to increase precision in retrieval, to improve understanding of context, and to exploit linkages between elements of the structure of documents (Muehlberger, 2002; Rauber & Merkl, 2003). Distributed architectures and access using content-based image retrieval (CBIR) (Tang, Avula, & Acton, 2004) are still attracting substantial research for massive image collections but these high-tech solutions seem oddly less successful than allowing user annotation in collaborative workspaces (Pisciotta, Dooris, Frost, & Halm, 2005). Music, too, can be retrieved automatically with waveforms (Clausen, Kurth, Maller, & Ribbrock, 2004), but evidence suggests that organizations which take into account work processes might better support regular users (Notess, Riley, & Hemmasi, 2004). Similarly, it seems that for huge volumes of texts, images, sound files, and video (Kim, Kim, & Hwang, 2003), or even video alone, better data models coupled with architectures to exploit them are needed (Lee, 2003; Salembier & Smith, 2001; Wang, Xing, & Zhou, 2003). It seems that huge quantities of data will require more than fast processors and clever engineering algorithms to become useful to general audiences.

The objects in digital libraries have two somewhat paradoxical properties: They are not fixed, and the metadata that describe and control them are often treated as objects in their own right. Treating metadata as a first class object, like any other resource (Karadkar, Francisco-Revilla, Furuta, Shipman, Arora, Dash, et al., 2004), creates new social and scholarly publishing opportunities and structures. Treating the annotations as first class objects, for example, enables them to be organized and annotated recursively, in the same way as any other object in the library (Agosti & Ferro, 2003; Frommholz, Brocks, Thiel, Neuhold, Iannone, Semeraro, et al., 2003; Liu, Lim, & Goh, 2002). Because metadata can then be cited, it is possible for some members of a digital library community to emerge as expert metadata authors—the kind of role once reserved for librarians or scholarly editors—just as some individuals can be respected reviewers in the Amazon.com community or have trusted profiles on e-Bay. These benefits were documented in an image library study, where metadata from a number of different professionally sanctioned schemas were augmented with user- and user group-contributed annotations (Attig, Copeland, & Pelikan, 2004). Research into how social tagging might be harnessed to generate folksonomies that contribute to retrieval by augmenting controlled vocabularies is a potential mechanism for offering broader access to museum objects than is typically provided by professional indexing (Bearman, Trant, Chun, Jenkins, Smith, Cherry, et al., 2005).

Adding shifting layers of personalized and group-annotated content on a foundation of digital library objects, which are themselves constantly changing, supports Levy's continuing assertion that digital library objects will not succeed if they treat their holdings as fixed content (Levy, 2001, 2003; Levy & Marshall, 1995). At the same time, it is a strong reminder that the primary object of interest is different for each user and that what constitutes data and metadata is simply a matter of perspective.

Value-Added Metadata and Indexing

If metadata is the answer, what is the question? Unrealistic expectations have been associated with metadata, in spite of decades of pre-digital library experience that revealed the limitations of cataloging, indexing, summarizing, and other modes of surrogation. The digital library literature includes many superficial exhortations to adhere to metadata standards (Bekaert, Van de Ville, Rogge, Strauven, De Kooning, & Van de Walle, 2002) along with very sophisticated models of how metadata namespaces can inform service models through schema mapping and semantic enhancement (Huang, Ke, & Yang, 2005). All too often both treat subject classification as objective and imagine that users share an understanding of indexing terminology that will improve retrieval. When we see how complex some systems need to be to take metadata from multiple sources and do with it what end-users probably assume it already does—that is, collocate like items—the challenge of universal digital libraries seems insurmountable (Candela, Castelli, & Pagano, 2004). Hope persists that metadata will overcome heterogeneity even when empirical findings are negative (Weiss-Lijn, McDonnell, & James, 2002). But lacking demonstrable successes on a significant scale, we are often left to celebrate the consensus building of the metadata standardization process (Weibel, 2005) or the intellectual rigor of the end product (Salembier & Smith, 2001).

Hughes and Kamat (2005) have suggested that all we need may be better interfaces to the metadata; other researchers have held that we should accept that there is a specific metadata schema for each particular user (Ismail, Yin, Theng, Goh, & Lim, 2003). One strategy for managing a multiplicity of formats, each carrying its metadata according to its own standard, is to build repositories for any type of content with arbitrary XML metadata descriptors that could serve as a uniform structure in which digital libraries are stored (Amato, Gennaro, Rabitti, & Savino, 2004). In the abstract, this approach seems to have special virtues in archival environments where the objects entering the repository are of arbitrary formats, although it conflicts with all encapsulating approaches, such as the Open Archives Information System (OAIS) reference model, which are currently the preferred strategies for archiving.

As digital libraries grow and their data become more heterogeneous and designed to serve a more diverse community of users, there is a definite trend toward obtaining ever more metadata from more sources to support distinct uses. The title pages of books may contain all we need for descriptive cataloging, but they do not carry the equivalent of the MPEG-7 (Moving Pictures Experts Group) header on which systems of multimedia digital library storage and retrieval are constructed (Lee, Kang, Myaeng, Hyun, Yoo, Ko, et al., 2003). Complex metadata and content packages describe and control anything from standard product labeled drugs to curricula, instructional Web sites, demonstrations and quizzes, and course blogs (Gold, 2003). So much has been written about these complex data-plus-metadata objects in the field of learning objects, for example, that they recently required a review of their own (Hanisch & Strasser, 2003). We can expect metadata to become increasingly important in applications that support richer services as users and content become more diverse. In the past few years we have seen growing adherence to the Metadata Encoding and Transmission Standard (METS); it is to be hoped that additional robust models and standards will enable greater interoperability among metadata schemes in the digital libraries of the near future.

One category of metadata that does not yet seem to have a literature of its own, although applications are increasingly being built to use it, is metadata about the use of digital library objects in the digital library environment. This kind of metadata, the basis for recommender systems and social tagging applications, is central to exploiting non-verbal indexes that depend on relations established in another dimension to indicate similarity. Like co-citation analysis and concept mapping, which are related methods for retrieval, exploiting this kind of metadata will support new methods of access. Interest in how these data are represented for possible sharing between repositories is bound to grow.

Technology

Architecture

One central technical problem of the digital library is providing effective access to heterogeneous, distributed, digital content. If content remains distributed at the point of its creation, we must have tools to search and retrieve content automatically in all its possible technical formats and present it seamlessly to the end user. Recognizing the complexity of distributed libraries and the need to communicate promising solutions, the Library of Congress recently launched the Distributed Open Digital Library (DODL) program (Marcum, 2004).

The first decade of digital library evolution was dominated by federated databases and distributed searching as the architectural solution to the challenges of access. With the dramatic success of search engines and the rapid adoption of the Open Archives Initiative-Protocol for Metadata Harvesting (OAI-PMH), architectures that build centralized metadatabases by federating metacontent have come to be preferred in the past several years. Architects of some universal digital libraries, such as the Open Content Alliance, are even beginning to revisit the realm of central databases with full content and metadata served from one system.

Today digital library assets are widely distributed. Case studies demonstrate (Mischo, 2001) that they include publisher-controlled data sources, the Web, secondary and tertiary information resources, local information, personal digital libraries, and institutional repositories; they are likely to include at least some paper-based content, a feature typically attributed only to "hybrid" libraries. Content from all these sources is required to serve users. In theory, all these distributed databases could employ the same standards and use their descriptive vocabularies in the same way (Bekaert et al., 2002; Lee, 2004), thus effectively acting as a single system. Because of their common "Web server" platforms, one could argue that Web sites work this way and that the digital library is another "portal" (Campbell, 2003); however, the Web certainly does not employ any descriptive content standards, and the dynamic—indeed chaotic—state of its content challenges the notion of libraries as storehouses for persistent and authoritative resources.

No matter how a search is performed, a search mechanism must resolve how to recognize and negotiate for the content it needs (Ding & Sølvberg, 2004). Most digital library developers feel that distributed content will work only if we can reliably find and persistently use the content, and can depend on favored solutions that have a built-in level of social agreement as their architectural strategy. Currently, digital libraries acquire content through deposit, obtain access to it under subscription, or acquire it through harvesting (it or its metadata) from distributed resources. Since 2001, OAI-PMH is increasingly being used. Federated search services still primarily employ the older Z39.50 search protocol to search on demand, although efforts are underway to create better metasearch protocols (www.niso.org/committees/MS_initiative. html). Some researchers advocate industry-standard protocols as crucial to long-term distributed library success (Apps, 2004; Congia, Gaylord, Merchant, & Suleman, 2004). In spite of their tremendous success within the digital library community, the OAI-PMH and Z39.50 protocols are only used in this niche market.

In interoperability research reports, we are too often presented with either metadata harvesting options (Ravindranathan, Shen, Goncalves, Fan, Fox, & Flannigan, 2004) or federated searching approaches (Campbell, 2002; Ding & Sølvberg, 2004; Eason, Harker, Apps, & MacIntyre, 2004) independently of each other. But we know that interoperability has to function on several levels (Arms et al., 2002). So it is welcome that investigations of ways to combine harvesting and federated searching have begun to appear (Congia et al., 2004). An alternative approach uses complex rules to mediate between the different repositories in a federated library, effectively making them distributed resources under the control of one system (Lee, 2003); however, it is likely to be difficult to attain this level of cooperation between systems in the real world. Promising evaluative work is being conducted comparing various approaches to federating content. If put into practice, these findings could improve any federated library service (Simeoni, 2004), including the application design challenges OAI-PMH presents for ongoing harvesting and post-processing of data (Anan, Tang, Maly, Nelson, Zubair, & Yang, 2003).

The federated library has been made significantly more complex by "sociable" and personalized computing. Just when ways to bring together content or views of content emerge, groups of users with common interests want tools to fence off areas of their own in which to collaborate, annotate with their own meanings, and re-use, or even republish, content (Candela & Straccia, 2004). The logical conclusion of such a project is personal libraries, with personal software agents in charge of acquiring the content, making the federated vision a radically distributed one in which the clients for services are an audience of one (Cho, 2004).

Knowledge Architecture

Among researchers, there is disagreement about what knowledge architecture will best make heterogeneous resources useful to diverse users. Some argue that collaboration toolsets are the way to create more useful digital libraries for each user community (Bieber, Engelbart, Furuta, Hiltz, Noll, Preece, et al., 2002; Renda & Straccia, 2002), although the added value from collaboration is effectively closed. Others suggest that ontologies will prove to be the method of overcoming even linguistic boundaries (Brisaboa, Parama, Penabad, Places, & Rodriguez, 2002), thus effectively opening up content to anyone. Ontology-oriented researchers assert that agents can overcome differences among schemas of distributed datasets (Yang, Rana, & Walker, et al., 2002), but socially oriented researchers argue that, as digital libraries succeed, users will necessarily become more remote, unknown, and unpredictable. In the latter group's view, more effort will need to be expended to understand users' needs and tasks, so that data and services can be modeled to meet heterogeneous needs (Borgman, 2003a; Borgman, Smart, Millwood, Finley, Champeny, Gilliland, et al., 2005). Actual users will benefit if they can build deeper communities of use around their datasets.

These strategies require different approaches. Building tools for a digital library to deploy an ontology service layer (X. L. Zhang, 2004) is quite different from modeling user tasks for a music metadata model (Notess et al., 2004). Social strategies involve developing and refining tools to display connections made by users and are essentially pragmatic and incremental. Creating ontologies to bridge meaning across disparate groups is a fundamental problem, even without introducing machine understanding. We each belong to a number of communities that have their own worldviews and languages and the concepts in those domains may have distinctive meaning that, for the time being, only humans can distinguish (Star, Bowker, & Neumann, 2003). We can construct systems that allow multiple schemes of knowledge to co-exist (Krowne & Fox, 2003), but this still begs the question of where a user obtains the understanding to move among them.

Application Systems

Several major groups of digital library researchers have created model digital library applications with tools that enable content holders to implement basic digital library environments with only modest technical support.

Fox and his numerous collaborators have promoted applications built on their 5S model of the digital library space, which employs formal methods to direct the design of digital libraries, purportedly even by nontechnical staff who are willing to express requirement variables formally (Fox, Goncalves, & Shen, 2005; Goncalves, Fox, Watson, & Kipp, 2004; Kelapure, Goncalves, & Fox, 2003; Zhu, Goncalves, Shen, Casse, & Fox, 2003). These applications are said to demonstrate the benefits of the 5S formal descriptions of digital library architectures (structures), content definitions (streams), clients (societies), service models (scenarios), and perspectives (spaces). If not yet exactly full-scale digital libraries in a box, these are, at least, boxes of useful components (Fox, 2003; Fox, Suleman, & Luo, 2002; Hussein, Fox, Kelapure, Krowne, & Luo, 2003).

Witten and his colleagues are working on generalized digital library "generators" that can create a variety of different libraries based on values of parameter settings (Bainbridge, Don, Buchanan, Witten, Jones, Jones, et al., 2004; Witten, Jones, Bainbridge, Cantlon, & Cunningham, 2004). They have been particularly active in Third World settings where significant success has been reported with some implementations of the Greenstone software. Their solutions are pragmatic and the approach is, overall, less theoretical than the 5S model.

Probably the most influential tool for digital library implementation over the past four years has been the Fedora open source library for a digital repository (www.fedora.info). Fedora does not claim to create full-blown digital libraries for nontechnical authors; various Fedora implementations have been reported throughout the literature, validating its claim to be a robust, generalizable platform (Dong, Xing, Zhou, Zhang, & Jiang, 2004; Pyrounakis, Saidis, Nikolaidou, & Lourdi, 2004).

The continuation and widespread implementation of projects to open and modularize digital library source code could prove a tremendous boost to the field. This would enable the construction of digital libraries in settings otherwise unable to support them, creating common structures for interoperability and advancing a profile of what functions ought to be supported.

Digital Libraries within General Computing Environments

Digital libraries are implemented within standard database and network service environments. As a consequence, every year a considerable quantity of research is reported on solutions to general computing problems as they apply to digital library applications, such as pre-fetching content to speed up display for end-users (Hollmann, Ardö, & Stenström, 2003), fault tolerance and security in Web-based digital libraries (Di Giacomo, Martinez, & Scott, 2004), and data security (Yague, Mana, Lopez, Pimentel, & Troya, 2002).

Authorization systems, which are of interest in general computing and central to digital library implementations, have been the focus of a great deal of work over the past decade (Adam, Atluri, Bertino, & Ferrari, 2002). Recently, JISC decided to abandon its ATHENS authentication service in favor of Shibboleth (http://shibboleth.internet2.edu), making it and the NSF Middleware Initiative the most widely deployed toolsets (Morgan, Cantor, Carmody, Hoehn, & Klingenstein, 2004). Because they have increasingly adopted the same authentication infrastructure, digital libraries could potentially solve a major problem of the Internet—identity control and management. More widely accepted solutions to authentication serve the interests both of groups such as the Attention Trust (www.attentiontrust.org), which are lobbying for individuals to have greater control over their digital identities, and of those in the augmented social network community, who are emphasizing the positive benefits of being "recognized" and having one's preferences and interests respected wherever one goes in virtual space.

Interfaces

Some interface issues, even though they feature in other domains as well, have particular resonance within digital libraries. We know that complexity often contributes to confusion and that the multiple layers of systems, data, and services in digital libraries are certainly capable of causing trouble for end-users unless design principles are followed rigorously (Bates, 2002). Usefully, some are beginning to trace digital library interface design principles back to human cognitive processes and extract possible guidelines for digital library interfaces from fundamental research in cognition (Rapp, Taylor, & Crane, 2003). Such work will be increasingly important if we try to scale libraries beyond the small communities for which they are now optimized.

Heterogeneous content, of course, includes content in many languages but multilingual systems are still the exception rather than the norm and strategies for multilingual digital libraries are just being developed (Lu, Wang, & Chien, 2003). A variety of programs and tools for multilingual digital libraries development is available through the Cross-Language Evaluation Forum (CLEF) at DELOS (Peters, 2005). As the Greenstone digital library project demonstrated, systems that operate effectively in several languages, or whose content is in multiple languages, require metadata management, interfaces, and end-use tools in several languages (Bainbridge, Edgar, McPherson, & Witten, 2003). But this seems a bare toehold in the face of proposals to create distributed libraries for, and for preservation of, the world's 6,500 languages (Lu, Liu, Fotouhi, Dong, Reynolds, Aristar, et al., 2004) and presumably for their literatures and users. Researchers have demonstrated some success in querying federated databases in several languages (Brisaboa et al., 2002), but years of multilingual thesaurus development have demonstrated that it is hard for such systems to scale successfully.

Digital libraries are being implemented as utilities for the general public; it is thus necessary to consider the range of abilities and disabilities of the public and how these affect use. Few digital library studies report specifically on these issues (Craven, 2003), but entire digital library research teams have been assembled, for example, at the University of Toronto (www.utoronto.ca/atrc/research.html), to design the array of interface tools required for universal accessibility.

Of course, digital libraries do not pose unique interface challenges (Hunter, Falkovych, & Little, 2004). Even when articles on interface design directly reference digital libraries, they are not the only application: For example, advice on page icons for digital library catalogs applies equally to other interfaces displaying page icons (Janssen, 2004). But as the use studies cited later in this review emphasize, we need to understand better the interaction between usability factors and the success of digital libraries. It is time to go beyond usability factors in digital libraries (Jeng, 2005) and ask users what usability really means to them (Koohang & Ondracek, 2005).

Tools for visualization of search set results are in demand (Kampanya, Shen, Kim, North, & Fox, 2004). Buzydlowski, White, and Lin (2002) have presented a simple co-occurrence analysis to collocate items retrieved from the *Arts & Humanities Index*. A more complex visualization simultaneously mapping in geographic and conceptual space was reported for geographic data using GEOVibe (Cai, 2002) and ranked information retrieval (Larsen & Wactlar, 2003). Perhaps more promising than global visualizations are simple associations that combine semantic links with usage patterns and other data to suggest possible extensions to a search. As with the Amazon.com "long tail" (Anderson, 2004, p. 170), such systems have the capacity to stir up connections that might otherwise have remained submerged (White, Lin, Buzydlowski, & Chen, 2004). If users can play a role in structuring the relations maps, these associations may have personal retrieval advantages even though this would limit their generalized applicability (Buchanan, Blandford, Thimbleby, & Jones, 2004).

Functions

Search

To date, the core function in digital libraries has been searching. Do digital library users want Web-like searching as some studies suggest (Wolfram & Xie, 2002)? Will a combination of keywords and browsing together with a few post-retrieval knowledge-based functions (Feng, Hoppenbrouwers, & Jeusfeld, 2005) serve their requirements? Or will all the tricks of information retrieval as practiced before the Web, from sophisticated Boolean query formulation to proximity searching, be necessary to improve searching in digital libraries (Buzydlowski et al., 2002; Rasmussen, 2004)? One approach to answering these questions is to study real users in a variety of settings, but of course, we are not sure whether findings from one digital library and its clientele will be applicable elsewhere. In the coming years, it may be possible to build on ethnographic studies of users of digital music libraries (Cunningham, 2002) together with studies of the users of geographic information services (Guan, Zhou, Chen, Chen, An, Bian, et al., 2003) in order to move analysis to the next level.

Although we can alter the search environment to provide traditional Boolean capabilities and study how users employ them, we must ultimately ask how actual users experience retrieval (Blomgren, Vallo, & Byström, 2004). In addition, we need to know more about potential (that is, non-) users. The broad public, often a target of digital library applications, is rarely the subject of detailed retrieval studies: A useful exception is found in an evaluation of MEDLINEPlus (Lacroix, 2001). Such studies suggest when to add different content, different indexing, and/or different tools, reminding us that search problems can originate in content, system, service, or users.

The favored approach to improving retrieval in distributed digital libraries is to create better metadata and search it more intelligently. Metadata models are appearing in almost every discipline to categorize the descriptive content so as to yield effective retrieval results (Crosier, Goodchild, Hill, & Smith, 2003). Field-specific digital libraries, such as those serving the geographical community with specialized metalanguages, have solved many of these problems. To learn from them we need to determine how much the success reflects the nature of geographical data, some of which can be formally represented. Work on place names demonstrates that this is not always an explanation (Weaver, Delcambre, Shapiro, Brewster, Gutema, & Tolle, 2003), and other research points to the underlying social cohesion of the institutional actors, rather than to the technology, as the source of success (Guan et al., 2003). Metadata need not be descriptive of the content. Contextual metadata, describing groups that share work processes and workflow process models, are more useful than content descriptors in some instances (Klas, Fuhr, & Schaefer, 2004). Search problems can be "solved" by restricting the community for which the solution is designed and defining success in terms of supporting the perspectives of the control language.

When a broader universe of users is targeted, other approaches may prove more useful. In one study, the collections targeted for searching were subjected to probabilistic analysis in an effort to reduce semantic uncertainty in the result set (Larson, 2003). We can take comfort in the thought that software might automatically recognize meaning in context (Ciravegna, Chapman, Dingli, & Wilks, 2004), but the reality is that this is the same complex problem that faces the Semantic Web (Kim, Choo, & Chen, 2003). Intelligent agents, armed with ontologies, could do some of the work (Medina, Sanchez, Chavez, & Benitez, 2004), but of course they will succeed only to the extent that ontology bridges intellectual perspectives in content description.

Some researchers suggest that in heterogeneous collections, controlled vocabularies and shared ontologies are unachievable; accordingly, they recommend brute force, full-text indexing (Arms & Arms, 2004). Research also suggests ways to use peer-to-peer networks to compute relevance in large text libraries (Lu & Callan, 2005). Others, who think the problem is more a lack of quality control (Kelly, 2004), would prefer to improve efficiency in searching. Attempts to improve searching for names, reflecting both controlled and uncontrolled approaches, help clarify whether the issue is simply lack of standards enforcement (Feitelson, 2004; Hong, On, & Lee, 2004; Wu, Na, & Khoo, 2004).

Fortunately, many of the problems attributed to searching, whether on the Web or in digital libraries, can be solved by allowing humans to use their intelligence. Browsing and annotation overcome many of the limitations of initial machine retrieval (Kornbluh, Fegan, & Rehberger, 2004). But because people are involved, these approaches will not necessarily scale well. In the Kepler environment, for example, users can both exploit and make—by browsing, annotating, and authoring—OAI metadata (Maly, Nelson, Zubair, Amrou, Kothamasa, Wang, et al., 2004). By deploying group authoring and document utilization functions, multiple individuals can be engaged, allowing more content to be handled. This may seem to be a good digital library environment for those on the inside, but it begs the question of extensibility. A more general metadata enhancer, citation analysis, is employed in some digital library contexts (He, Hui, & Fong, 2003); of course, its applicability is limited to certain classes of content. In a restricted domain (e.g., experimental context), we can put several such strategies together to create a retrieval negotiator that interacts with users in the retrieval process: It is far from clear that this would be extensible to large-scale applications (Mustapha, 2003).

As has been the case for 20 years, some researchers argue for the use of intelligent agents, but the claims are often more impressive than the results (Andersen, Andersen, Degemmis, Licchelli, Lops, & Zambetta, 2003; Detlor & Arsenault, 2002). There is a prima facie argument that personalization features should take the place of reference librarians because the use of human intermediaries does not scale well

(Chowdhury, 2002b), but the alternatives that have been studied do not scale well either. One study proposed combining intelligent harvesting agents, annotating retrieved sets, and "teaching" learning systems about additional strategies and further annotation after interacting with users (Ciravegna et al., 2004). The potential of Wikis (online, collaboratively built and edited information sources) is attracting significant research attention (Frumkin, 2005). We have seen that knowing more about what makes intermediation work could help (Southwick, 2003), but our inability to predict, for example, the huge success of social bookmarking suggests we are still far from understanding why some knowledge building is satisfying.

When it comes to searching, our objective may be wrong. Framed by years of retrieval in physical libraries, the digital library is still retrieving an "item," typically a journal article, in response to a user query rather than returning the information that the user needs (Kortelainen, 2004). If so, it may be harder than first thought to make the transition to intelligent search agents (Weiss-Lijn et al., 2002). Tools that allow users and contributors to mark up objects in digital libraries at arbitrary levels of granularity and embed meanings in them are advocated by, for example, Kumar, Bia, Holmes, Schreibman, Siemens, and Walsh (2004). This content is intended to reside in digital libraries composed primarily of larger chunks of metadata. Those who have struggled with Standard Generalized Mark-up Language (SGML) marked-up content and structure-aware queries know that relying on user-generated mark-up is not a panacea (York, Wulfman, & Crane, 2003).

Retrieval is still a goal, but digital libraries will need to take the user far beyond current practice (Lagoze, Krafft, Payette, & Jesuroga, 2005; Lynch, 2003a). For the user, success in "searching" is evaluated not by how well the single step of submitting terms and obtaining a set of results works but by how well the end-to-end process, including browsing the results and reviewing items retrieved, satisfies the information need (McKay & Cunningham, 2003). Suggestions that such contextual refinement can be automated are not completely convincing (Neuhold, Niederee, Stewart, Frommholz, & Mehta, 2004); nonetheless, research continues into automatic linking of various kinds of content in order to reduce manual metadata entry and augment user experiences (Melucci, 2004; Péter, 2004).

Most users would like the digital library to call their attention to content that might be important to the task at hand. How can a system best do so? Recommender systems exploit the notion that language and terms applied to objects in a digital library are socially constructed and that, as such, the contexts of assignment are always part of understanding their meanings (Tuominen, Talja, & Savolainen, 2003). Hwang, Hsiung, and Yang (2003) have incorporated a simple recommender system—people who asked for x, also asked for y—into a university thesis and dissertation system. Embedding such functions in digital library services has proved equally popular (Krottmaier, 2002). Systems may also improve experiences for users by ranking search results, a practice that lies somewhere between retrieval functions and recommender systems. Claims are made for automatic ranking based on various characteristics and techniques (Manolopoulos & Sidiropoulos, 2005; Mutschke, 2003), but no recent studies have examined user satisfaction with different methods of ranking.

Using, Personalizing, Sharing

Users of digital libraries want to exploit the content they retrieve in subsequent applications; personalization and collaboration systems have been explored as means to enable such uses as well as to customize interactions. At their simplest, user profiles filter the system or shape the service so that one's view, or interface, is personalized when one logs into the digital library (Zeng, Zheng, Xing, & Zhou, 2002). This kind of collection personalization can be assisted by server-side tools that profile the content of the library, maintain personal filters, and customize retrieval mechanisms (Jayawardana, Hewagamage, & Hirakawa, 2001). Ways for users to change their perspectives, and hence their interface and knowledge representations, in mid-stream take personalization further (French, Chapin, & Martin, 2004); such flexibility also introduces problems for systems designed to "know" what interface a user needs (Semeraro, Ferilli, Fanizzi, & Abbattista, 2001). Personalization features linked to artificial intelligence are said to enhance user profile-driven filtering services (Gentili, Micarelli, & Sciarrone, 2003).

Digital library services can also alert users to content or events taking place in collaboration spaces. The standard model of user profiles has been tied to narrowcasting designed to generate proactive streams of content, in one case with personalization supported by the metadata headers in MPEG-7 (Wang, Balke, Kießling, & Huhn, 2004). Doubtless many users subscribe to RSS (Rich Site Summary/Really Simple Syndication) feeds and MyLibrary (http://dewey.library.nd.edu/my library) supports them. However, no reports of their use by digital libraries were found in the literature in spite of the fact that KnowLib carries a regular meta-feed of digital-library-related RSS feeds (http://dbkit02.it.lth.se/rss/showDigLib.phtml#62).

Personalization can also be applied to functions that enable users to interact with content, such as annotating, modifying, formatting, and integrating. Tools that support "active reading"—highlighting, underlining, marking, filing, making glossaries, and summaries, for example— are all elements of personalizing if they persist for future interactions by that user. Tools to enable users to manipulate data in Extensible Markup Language (XML) (Chang, 2005); to cluster retrieved groups and, through typed annotations, prepare them for subsequent uses (Constantopoulos, Doerr, Theodoridou, & Tzobanakis, 2004); and to classify and share them (Frommholz et al., 2003) are being developed as integral features of digital libraries. All these functions together serve as an environment in which digital library materials, once retrieved, can be reused effectively (Goh, Fu, & Foo, 2002). Personal annotations have been tied back to metadata (Agosti & Ferro, 2003; Agosti, Ferro, Frommholz, & Thiel, 2004) so that users have personalized workspaces that can build communities, receive recommendations based on what others do, and construct shared knowledge structures (Candela & Straccia, 2004).

Because environments in which users actually work must bring together content in various formats, the toolsets developed for post-retrieval analysis, use, personalization, and collaboration are necessarily integrated. Image annotation and linking within environments also heavy in textual content have been a focus of several longer-term undertakings that are now reporting success (Attig et al., 2004; Pisciotta et al., 2005; Thiel, Brocks, Dirsch-Weigand, Everts, Frommholz, & Stein, 2005).

In the future, perhaps the most important class of personalization tools will be those that enable users to rediscover resources they have used previously. Bookmarks were the first such application, and the success of social tagging has raised the functional requirement. Use of the resources can lead to personal or group views being made available for later use; it can also feed content and annotations directly back into the digital libraries (Liu et al., 2002). Recent work has both modeled the varieties of these interactions between users and digital libraries and implemented numerous scenarios (Neuhold, Niederee, & Stewart, 2003). A set of studies at Microsoft on how readers have historically shared information through "clippings" has articulated requirements for digital libraries to promote the sharing of "encountered" information (Marshall & Bly, 2004, p. 218). As social software registers increasing success on the public Web, such functions will doubtless grow in importance in the digital library domain.

All personalization raises issues of privacy and control over identity. Digital libraries are likely to be affected by the interests of users in managing their digital identities so that they are portable and persistent (as proposed by the AttentionTrust.org) as well as in limiting identity-bearing information to avoid loss of control over records of their interactions.

Services

Traditional Library Services

Processes that have traditionally been internal to the library—acquisition, cataloging, and circulation—are all undergoing change in the digital library environment. In addition, many new services are imaginable in digital libraries. Kelapure et al. (2003) explored a scenario-building exercise based on abstract models of such services, but it is not clear how they will fit into institutional roles.

Acquisition

Most librarians would argue that the digital library requires selection of content by librarians and obtains its value from that selection (Wallace, 2004). Such models of selection can be implemented in purpose-built digital libraries by putting URLs in library catalogs (Burke, Germain, & Van Ullen, 2003) or by implementing versions of "others also use" recommender systems (which first proved their popularity on the Web) in front of legacy library OPACs (Geyer-Schulz, Neumann, & Thede, 2003). In any of these implementations, traditional questions about content acquisition still play a role and will continue to do so as long as the digital library is institutionally based (Miller, 2002), even though the toolsets employed in collection development may be quite different (Mitchell, 2005).

Research is pointing the way to some machine-assisted acquisition or content development mechanisms (Nicholson, 2003). But the roles of collection development staff (Dorner, 2004) are related to organizational policy and participation in a variety of different types of consortia. Collaborative agreements, for example, may have greater impact on acquisition processes than the simple fact of acquiring digital assets. Studies of how library consortia are serving to aggregate content and services in more cost-effective ways (Pandian, Jambhekar, & Karisiddappa, 2002) will be crucial to the reconfiguration of core library processes.

Cataloging

Some digital library contents are, of course, digitized books and online journals for which there is traditional cataloging, but digital libraries are also collecting some very different sorts of objects (Okerson, 2003). Cataloging online resources by engaging content creators in creating metadata was the initial impetus for the Dublin Core Initiative (http://dublincore.org). We have discovered, however, that content creators and non-librarians, even when provided with a highly simplified metadata model, do not catalog. Since then, social bookmarking has attracted widespread popular attention. Flickr.com has become popular with photographers, deli.cio.us is acting as a recommender system for Web pages, and LibraryThing (www.librarything.com) is a cross between a home book-cataloging site and a dating service. These have been reported in the digital libraries literature (Hammond, Hannay, Lund, & Scott, 2005), but experimentation by digital libraries into the benefits of social tagging is just beginning (Bearman et al., 2005; Lund, Hammond, Flack, & Hannay, 2005). It has yet to be seen if, or how, vocabularies generated as folksonomies contribute to improved retrieval.

A potentially important contribution to digital library cataloging will be the deployment of smart scanners, with learning capability, to segment print images and mark up digitized pages of print as part of large-scale retrospective scanning efforts now planned in many countries. For example, METS records in the ALTO (Analyzed Layout and Text Object) scheme can be generated from image processing software yielding full text marked up not only with descriptive cataloging but also with structured tables of contents, indexes, and citations.

Reference

The benefits of collaborative online library reference services is an area of considerable debate (Berube, 2004; Borbinha, Kunse, Spinazze, Miutschke, Lieder, Mabe, et al., 2005; Chowdhury, 2002b; Jane & McMillan, 2003; Lankes et al., 2004; Lankes et al., 2003). The OCLC/Library of Congress collaboration, which has capitalized on efforts by hundreds of libraries, is the most analyzed of these services (Gottesman, Kresh, & Takagi, 2004; Penka, 2003). Like smaller collaboratives, the benefits it provides are not technology-driven per se but rather are delivered by time shifting, interest sharing, or on the basis of some other labor-related efficiency (Jin, Huang, Lin, & Guo, 2005). For the user, the benefits may be more social or psychological than purely instrumental. Theng (2002) argues that reference is a therapeutic system that helps users understand their needs and explores how digital services might fulfill them.

Circulation

The superficially contradictory notion of circulation in digital libraries, an intersection of past practice, current legal constraints, and future functions, is illustrated by electronic reserves (Jacoby & Laskowski, 2004), a practice that reveals students' use of digital libraries for shifting both time and place. Virtually all aspects of the service—from copyright issues through technical practices—are covered in one or another chapter of Rosedale's (2002) text. As with any digital library problem involving copyright, it is useful to compare local practices and policies with what happens outside the U.S. (Trosow, 2005).

New Library Roles

Not only are digital libraries transforming traditional library practices, but they also have the potential to generate new roles for academic libraries.

Hosting Scholarly and Scientific Collaboration

Supporting "knowledge communities" is a major objective of digital library developers, but not all tools used to build communities on the Web are being adapted to digital libraries. The historical aversion to talking in the library may be responsible for the collective failure to introduce chat rooms. Libraries, including public libraries, could support private portals and host community blogs, yet few such public content creation functions have been undertaken in the digital library domain.

Perhaps more will be reported soon; the widespread popularity of instant messaging among students evidently carries over into successful digital library services when tried (Desai, 2003).

Digital libraries are beginning to exploit social computing methods in order to enable users to collaborate. For example, after retrieving digital objects, users can work together or separately in digital libraries interfaced to the National Library of Singapore's systems (Goh et al., 2002). The Collaboratory for Annotation, Indexing and Retrieval of Digitized Historical Archive Material (COLLATE) system, serving historical archives in Europe, supports the accumulation of interactions with documents to build a collective trace that can feed into uses others make of the documents. Thus a discussion forum, for example, attaches the topics to the documents it discusses, adding metadata and a context for future retrieval (Frommholz et al., 2003). Such systems are also building real (i.e., non-virtual) communities of people by supporting the needs of day-to-day life (Bieber et al., 2002).

Typically, the role of annotation has been to personalize database content (Neuhold et al., 2003), but in many implementations it also serves to support collaborative work (Agosti et al., 2004); indeed, mechanisms have been constructed to permit entire personal annotation systems to be made visible to groups (Candela & Straccia, 2004). Efforts to bootstrap annotation through text mining and other semantic analysis processes can complement social methods (Ciravegna et al., 2004). The richness of annotation has created a need to model annotation types and create faceted annotation systems (Constantopoulos et al., 2004). Annotation can, of course, be in any genre. Audio, video, and graphics can be combined to annotate each other or texts. In the case of image annotations, users are building text information on top of objects that originally had no associated textual content (Attig et al., 2004; Chang, 2005; Pisciotta et al., 2005); combinations of methods including feature extraction and collaborative annotation have been shown to work together successfully (Thiel et al., 2005).

Archiving

Before the digital age, librarians engaged in preservation activity to prevent decay of their special collections even though they did not conceive of their libraries as archives. Now, however, because the viability of digital libraries depends on their content's preservability, uncertainty surrounding whether we can maintain digital content over time is leading libraries to adopt some archival functions.

Recent years have witnessed limited progress but no breakthrough in digital preservation. The OAIS Reference Model has been more broadly accepted (Frommholz et al., 2003). The processes of encapsulation and capture at the time of creation still have technical advocates (Gladney, 2004), including this author, although some archivists hope to delay control until a later date. In general, strategies to have smarter objects and dumber repositories seem to be emerging (Nelson, 2001; Nelson & Maly,

2001). This type of strategy permits format migration, either on an ongoing basis or on the fly (Lots of Copies Keep Stuff Safe [LOCKSS]), which has generally favored in recent NSF/DELOS (Ross & Hedstrom, 2005) and National Academy of Sciences Computer Science and Telecommunications Board (NAS CTSB) (Sproull & Eisenberg, 2005) reports as the most likely means of ensuring reliable and usable content over time. Because formats will carry metadata about their technical and content characteristics, some researchers contend that this metadata will address aspects of archival access and use (Bekaert, De Kooning, & Van de Walle, 2005; Bekaert et al., 2002). Substantially more archival process metadata will need to be carried as well; however, the history of metadata migrating successfully with format migrations is not encouraging. The only confident actors are engineers charged with storing the data, who believe that developments in data grids have nearly solved their problems (Moore, Rajasekar, & Wan, 2005). Unfortunately, most others have concluded that archival preservation of digital artifacts is not primarily a technical problem but, rather, is one of those difficult issues that individuals, institutions, society, and law must solve (Kenney & McGovern, 2003). Even if one assumes that the technologies will continue to work into the future, managing the policies and collaborations that could ensure preservation is itself a major challenge (Hiiragi, Sakaguchi, Sugimoto, & Tabata, 2004).

Important foundational work is being done in the National Digital Information Infrastructure Preservation Program at the Library of Congress (Fleischaeur & Arms, 2005). Recent reports of the Archive Ingest and Handling Test (AIHT) illustrate the difficulty still associated with the post hoc ingestion of even a relatively small group of digital records into long-term preservation repositories; however, they also validate the general strategy of the AIHT approach, if archival control is not implemented until some point after the creation of the record rather than built into the record creation and transmission process (Abrams, Chapman, Flecker, Kreigsman, Marinus, McGath, et al., 2005; Anderson, Frost, Hoebelheinrich, & Johnson, 2005; DiLauro, Patton, Reynolds, & Choudhury, 2005; Nelson, Bollen, Manepalli, & Haq, 2005; Shirky, 2005). The draft report of the Research Libraries Group (RLG) and National Archives and Records Administration (NARA) Task Force on Digital Repository Certification (RLG & National Archives and Records Administration, 2005), which was out for comment at the end of 2005, is expected to make a substantial contribution to defining the parameters of the social issues involved in digital archiving and permit libraries that are willing and able to commit to this role to do so with sound standards in place.

Social Impacts

Users

Anyone can be a user of a digital library; users can be any age, have varying degrees of prior knowledge, and speak any language. However, most digital libraries are constructed with certain users and their needs in mind (Koskiala & Savolainen, 2004). For the most part, digital library users are adults with academic or professional interests in information, who are connected to high-speed networks and able to employ many post-processing systems to analyze what they find in the digital library for use in educational settings (Bieber et al., 2002). We need to know more about whether these users return month after month, year after year, and, if so, how their use of the resource changes (Cherry & Duff, 2002; Koohang & Ondracek, 2005).

One particular challenge is that when we conduct user evaluations, we study those who actually use a service but miss those who might use a service but do not (Monopoli, Nicholas, Georgiou, & Korfiati, 2002). We need to find ways to learn more about non-users in order to make digital libraries effective for all. In some cases, potential users may be easy to identify—for instance, in an academic health sciences library (Bracke, 2004) or a private law firm (Reach, Whelan, & Flood, 2003); however, in most cases the client base is not as clearly delimited.

Perhaps understanding more about why users come to digital libraries can help us understand the roles the digital library plays in their worlds (Assadi, Beauvisage, Lupovici, & Cloarec, 2003). A dozen position papers by attendees at a recent JCDL workshop studying "digital library users in the wild" explored many of the underlying questions (Khoo & Ribes, 2005) but left more unanswered. Paradoxically, as digital library use becomes integrated into day-to-day activity in a supportive way, it becomes more invisible, and users are increasingly unaware of the paths they took to and through it.

Ethnographic studies of academic and research library users in Slovakia (Steinerová, 2003), mixed method research on higher education digital services provision in the U.K. (Banwell & Coulson, 2004; Banwell, Ray, Coulson, Urquhart, Lonsdale, Armstrong, et al., 2004), comparative content analysis of written evaluation of physical reference service and virtual reference services in Canada (Nilson, 2004), and qualitative methods applied to situated use assessments in Illinois (Bishop, Neumann, Star, Merkel, Ignacio, & Sandusky, 2000) are among the approaches reported by researchers seeking to understand why users did, or did not, use digital libraries and what they felt about their experiences. Additionally, a range of in-depth usability studies have been conducted in non-laboratory but quasi-experimental use contexts focusing on specific features of digital libraries, such as a "my e-journal" personalizer and aggregator in Denmark (Hyldegaard & Seiden, 2004), the use of music library tools (Notess, 2004), and broad studies of technical strategies such as whether integrated interaction is actually preferable to common interaction (Park, 2000). These studies are valuable to systems designers, especially interface developers within the context of a particular digital library.

Evidence that the user responds more to social than technical factors has been present in general computing for a long time and so it is not surprising to find the theme appearing in studies of the users of digital medical libraries (Gosling, Westbrook, & Coiera, 2003). Users encounter boundaries that designers did not envision and perceive as boundaries some of the features that have been built into systems intentionally for security, to guide the user, or even to enhance effectiveness (Marshall, 2003). It has been suggested that users are dissatisfied because the digital library does not enable them to express themselves creatively rather than because it failed to find what they were seeking (Lee, Theng, & Goh, 2003).

User expectations are changing. Until now, it was assumed that the user operated as a "library patron" with respect to the library. Putting the digital library into the classroom (Jose, Braddick, Martin, Robertson, Walker, & MacPherson, 2002) or integrating it into other work processes changes assumptions about what the user is doing and how the digital library functions. Calls for greater focus on both users and staff in digital library research are welcome, but, as case studies show, comparability of results and, therefore, conclusions is complicated (Marchionini, Plaisant, & Komlodi, 2003). Interactions between technical, social, and personal variables are complex and constitute one of the more promising and dynamic areas developing in digital library research (Thong, Hong, & Tam, 2002).

Digital libraries influence user needs and methods of communication. The full range of issues associated with changing patterns of scholarly communications and bibliometrics was the subject of a recent *ARIST* chapter (Borgman & Furner, 2002) and will not be revisited here. It is useful, however, to note that some digital libraries, such as preprint libraries (Huwe, 2002), data repositories (Borgman et al., 2005; Brase, 2004), and primary source archives (Bruder, Finger, Heuer, & Ignatova, 2003) are not simply used by scholars in their communications but were explicitly designed to promote the transformation of scholarly communication. Evidence suggests that they are working. An influential report found that the online availability of an article in full text increases citations (Lawrence, 2001); however, recent refinements of that study have suggested that, at least in some fields, the reason for the increases in citation may be that the articles are available earlier and that articles deemed more important are selected for online presentation (Kurtz, Eichhorn, Accomazzi, Grant, Demleitner, Hennekin, et al., 2005).

Uses

Methodologically, research to discover which features of digital libraries contribute to success often involves using Web server logs (Tarr,

2001). Web server log analysis can be likened to archeology—what the users leave behind is being examined for implied meanings (Nicholson, 2005). A self-referential use of Web server log analysis occurs in the i-DLR site at the University of Missouri, which is the subject of research into how it can improve, including how the site uses Web log analysis in conjunction with a full range of other research methods (Kassim & Kochtanek, 2003). Analysis of Web logs can reveal user communities, for whom services or interfaces can then be tailored (Papatheodorou, Kapidakis, Sfakakis, & Vassiliou, 2003). Sophisticated data mining strategies are needed to obtain useful information from voluminous logs (Zhang, Gong, & Kawamura, 2004).

Sometimes what we want to know about online use is relatively straightforward. For example, Australian researchers asked whether clinicians' use of a database created for them was related to their care of patients (Westbrook, Gosling, & Coiera, 2004). Following backlinks to identify the sources that referred users to a digital library (and even what they were seeking at those sites) can provide insight into what user needs are being served by the digital library (Thelwall, 2004). Query term analysis and content analysis of comments and full-text questions presumably addressed to a reference librarian can help a digital library service identify not only the topics in which its users are interested but also the kinds of ancillary data that they expect to find in conjunction with their searches. For instance, the National Library of Medicine's MedlinePlus service found that it needed to acquire links into clinical trials and pharmacopoeia databases in order to deliver what health consumers assumed they would find in one-stop shopping (Lacroix, 2001).

Beyond the metrics of use, there are more qualitative evaluations that go to the heart of assessing the kinds of applications and services that are being created, the social expectations that they engender, and their sustainability (Borgman, 2002). Van House (2003, p. 271) applied actor-network theory to understanding the impacts in situated contexts, arguing persuasively that "designing effective digital libraries ... requires understanding knowledge work and the way that it is not only supported but potentially changed by digital libraries." Evaluations of use, often employing participatory-action research methods, explore whether digital libraries enable social outcomes that are desirable (Bishop, Mehra, Bazzell, & Smith, 2003). Most radically, we could even ask whether use of a digital library actually increases knowledge. It is not clear what evidence exists that physical libraries increase users' knowledge, but the ambivalent findings of one study of digital libraries provide food for thought (Madle, Kostkova, Mani-Saada, & Weinberg, 2003). If people with real-world motivations use digital libraries to acquire knowledge upon which they need to act and, after doing so, they have less understanding of the facts than before they began, is there a fundamental problem with digital libraries, with the specific library design with which they interacted, or with the idea that more information contributes to better decision making?

Organizational Impacts

Digital libraries have an impact on the organizations in which they are built—they require staff and cost money—and generally they change roles and practices within the organization. They are designed to support education, research, and scholarly communication. And they are presumed to have a beneficial impact on society at large. Digital libraries are themselves social institutions and not mere technical constructs. They exist in the real world and are enabled by staff. Users encounter them in their work. As such, they exist within an institutional landscape that itself requires study (Agre, 2003).

In spite of the enthusiastic rhetoric, resistance to organizational change is strong. For example, professionals who embrace change in some respects also remain seriously beholden to tradition, as is evident when the Semantic Web can be seen as another opportunity to advocate authority control (Franklin, 2003) and static views or human-maintained Web pages are still the norm (Tyler & McNeil, 2003). Although there is broadly based agreement that new service paradigms embodying a wide variety of specific approaches are necessary and valuable contributions of digital libraries, many institutional costs and barriers remain (Moyo, 2004). Dempsey (2003) has argued convincingly that disaggregated library services need to be incorporated into environments where potential users actually work, rather than hidden within library portal environments.

The digital library requires new expertise. Its builders see such institutional issues as rights management, open access policies, standards adherence, and persistence as crucial to digital library success and requiring new skills and perspectives to administer effectively (McCray & Gallagher, 2001). The change has been sufficiently dramatic to call into question the educational foundations of the profession (Marcum, 2003). The extensive literature on education for the digital library has been usefully reviewed elsewhere (Saracevic & Dalbello, 2001).

Institutional Implications

Much of the digital library literature assumes that the boundaries between archives, libraries, and museums are artificial, created because each institution stored different kinds of objects, and that the eradication of content boundaries is basically a good thing as it enables unified access to collections of "information" (Barton, 2005). This perspective overlooks the very different missions and functions of these traditional institutions. Although some superficial integration has been achieved for users, the homogenization of the Web presences of "memory institution"—all with searchable catalogs, archival roles, and exhibitions—seems to this writer to have undermined rather than enriched the quality of professional discourse in information retrieval, archival practice, and interpretation.

Cultural heritage informatics has had a salutary effect on thinking about knowledge representation issues in digital libraries (Beghtol, 2001), and cultural heritage concepts inform complex ontologies and artificial intelligence-supported searching (Abbattista, Bordoni, & Semeraro, 2003). Nevertheless, focus needs to move from the possibility of integrating abstract representation to emphasizing the concerns that cultural repositories share—such as authenticity, preservation, privacy, and appreciation for indigenous knowledge. Unfortunately, redefining archives, libraries, and museums as "memory institutions" does not seem to have helped professionals in these organizations to understand their common foundational concerns (Bradley, 2005; Chen, 2002).

Public Policy

Digital libraries raise broad public policy issues. Do they exacerbate the digital divide (Byrne, 2003; Chowdhury, 2002a)? Are they a necessary feature of national planning? If so, what place do digital libraries play in strategies for development (Vaidya & Shrestha, 2002; Witten, 2002, 2004; Witten, Loots, Trujillo, & Bainbridge, 2002)?

The National Aeronautics and Space Administration (NASA) has adopted a set of metrics to assess its distributed digital library service. These metrics point to significant economic benefits for a disciplinary community in the construction and use of such a tool (Kurtz, Eichhorn, Accomazzi, Grant, Demleitner, Murray, et al., 2005). Their impressive findings—that digital libraries increased productivity equivalent to thousands of extra workers in the field—have implications for information-intensive areas of practice, such as medical care, that should influence governments to greatly extend the scope of digital libraries' services in these areas in the coming decade.

Funding and Future Digital Library Research

Digital library funding in the U.S., which began in 1993, ran its course over the next decade. It is generally agreed that this period of direct funding by the U.S. government has ended (Lynch, 2005), but continuing direct funding is available in the U.K., Europe, and some Asian nations. Results of the productive first round of NSF funding were reported in 2002 (Fox & Urs, 2002), as were the early results from DL-2 funding, whereas final reports of the DL-2 round (www.dli2.nsf.gov/intl. html) did not become available until 2002–2004. A view of the concrete impact of these funds on digital library development is contained in the short "biographies" of digital libraries in Greenstein and Thorin (2002).

Many "research agendas" were published as these funded programs came to a close (Larsen & Wactlar, 2003). The DELOS/NSF meetings of 2002–2003 produced a lengthy set of publications in early 2005 that assessed the payoff expected for research in a variety of topical areas

(Borbinha et al., 2005; Ioannidis, 2005; Ross & Hedstrom, 2005; Smeaton & Callan, 2005). The tenth anniversary issue of *D-Lib Magazine* mixed Whig history with futurology and navel gazing (Arms, 2005; Mischo, 2005; Paepcke, Garcia-Molina, & Wesley, 2005; Weibel, 2005). As always, the images of a future of well-orchestrated and interrelated research and development sat uncomfortably beside a past characterized by opportunistic advances (Ioannidis, 2005). Nevertheless, taken as a whole, these papers outlined broad areas of consensus on future research requirements. Here, as elsewhere, participants generally agreed that digital library technology problems will recede as service challenges come to the fore, and that inherently long-term issues such as preservation, sustainability, and social impacts will require more attention (Bollen, Manepalli, Manepalli, Nandigam, & Nelson, 2005; Borgman, 2003a; Lynch, 2003b, 2005; X. X. Zhang, 2004).

The Future

So what can we expect? Digital library content will increasingly encompass all kinds of information. The proportion of past information in digital form will grow exponentially over the coming decade until nearly everything in print is available online. As a consequence, we will be forced to attend to Buckland's (2003) observation that all our digital libraries have been designed backwards, from the data we have to the users we serve, rather than from actual user needs to data. New ways will have to be found to become more responsive to a universal clientele.

I think we will be forced to do so in part because digital libraries share a technological and social space with the public Web and their success will necessarily be measured against it. Fortunately, the Web provides a readily available testbed, where users are voting with their clicks for the services and information they want. The digital library community may need to launch a collaborative "Web observatory" from which to monitor and exploit user inventions of the future, so that innovations such as BitTorrent and podcasting, which were validated within weeks by millions of users, can in the future be leveraged rapidly in digital libraries. The astonishing success of search engines on the public Web (Fallows, 2005) has challenged leading proponents of digital libraries to think anew about what digital libraries can be beyond a mechanism for search and access (Lagoze et al., 2005). The next big challenge that the Web will pose to digital libraries is reflected in the Web 2.0 services model which, if widely adopted, would render obsolete digital libraries that are equated with single digital collections and bundled toolsets (Miller, 2005).

Finally, the needs of society for confidence in a stable and shared knowledge base will grow as the malleability of content and the fragility of digital documents become more evident. We need to heed Levy's (2003, p. 38) call for study of the sociotechnical basis of emerging library services to ensure that they are providing "communicative stability." That many users find the dynamic content and changing functions and services of the Web an emotionally consistent social space, while perceiving the digital library setting as discontinuous, suggests that, for digital libraries to succeed, they will need to become more tightly woven into the fabric of everyday life.

References

Abbattista, F., Bordoni, L., & Semeraro, G. (2003). Artificial intelligence for cultural heritage and digital libraries. *Applied Artificial Intelligence, 17*, 681–686.

Abrams, S., Chapman, S., Flecker, D., Kreigsman, S., Marinus, J., McGath, G., et al. (2005). Harvard's perspective on the Archive Ingest and Handling Test. *D-Lib Magazine, 11*(12). Retrieved January 14, 2006, from www.dlib.org/dlib/december05/abrams/12abrams. html

Adam, N. R., Atluri, V., Bertino, E., & Ferrari, E. (2002). A content-based authorization model for digital libraries. *IEEE Transactions on Knowledge and Data Engineering, 14*, 296–315.

Adams, A., & Blandford, A. (2002). Digital libraries in academia: Challenges and changes. *Proceedings of the 5th International Conference on Asian Digital Libraries*, 392–403.

Adams, A. A. (2003). Digitisation, representation, and formalisation: Digital libraries of mathematics. *Proceedings of the 2nd International Conference on Mathematical Knowledge Management*, 1–16.

Agosti, M., Benfante, L., & Orio, N. (2003). IPSA: A digital archive of herbals to support scientific research. *Proceedings of the 6th International Conference on Asian Digital Libraries*, 253–264.

Agosti, M., & Ferro, N. (2003). Annotations: Enriching a digital library. *Proceedings of the 7th European Conference on Digital Libraries*, 88–100.

Agosti, M., Ferro, N., Frommholz, I., & Thiel, U. (2004). Annotations in digital libraries and collaboratories: Facets, models and usage. *Proceedings of the 8th European Conference on Digital Libraries*, 244–255.

Agre, P. E. (2003). Information and institutional change: The case of digital libraries. In A. P. Bishop, N. A. Van House, & B. P. Buttenfield (Eds.), *Digital library use: Social practice in design and evaluation* (pp. 219–240). Cambridge, MA: MIT Press.

Amato, G., Gennaro, C., Rabitti, F., & Savino, P. (2004). Milos: A multimedia content management system for digital library applications. *Proceedings of the 8th European Conference on Digital Libraries*, 14–25.

Anan, H., Tang, J. F., Maly, K., Nelson, M., Zubair, M., & Yang, Z. (2003). Challenges in building federation services over harvested metadata. *Proceedings of the 6th International Conference on Asian Digital Libraries*, 602–614.

Andersen, V., Andersen, H. H. K., Degemmis, M., Licchelli, O., Lops, P., & Zambetta, F. (2003). A methodological approach for designing and evaluating intelligent applications for digital collections. *Applied Artificial Intelligence, 17*, 745–771.

Anderson, C. (2004). The long tail. *Wired, 12*(10), 170–177.

Anderson, R., Frost, H., Hoebelheinrich, N., & Johnson, K. (2005). The AIHT at Stanford University: Automated preservation assessment of heterogeneous digital collections. *D-Lib Magazine, 11*(12). Retrieved February 2, 2006, from www.dlib.org/dlib/december 05/johnson/12johnson.html

Apps, A. (2004). zetoc SOAP: A Web services interface for a digital library resource. *Proceedings of the 8th European Conference on Digital Libraries,* 198–208.

Arms, W. Y. (2005). A viewpoint analysis of the digital library. *D-Lib Magazine, 11*(7/8). Retrieved February 2, 2006, from www.dlib.org/dlib/july05/arms/07arms.html

Arms, W. Y., & Arms, C. R. (2004). Mixed content and mixed metadata: Information discovery in a messy world. In D. Hillmann & E. Westbrooks (Eds.), *Metadata in practice* (pp. 223–237). Chicago: American Library Association.

Arms, W. Y., Hillmann, D., Lagoze, C., Krafft, D., Marisa, R., Saylor, J., et al. (2002). A spectrum of interoperability: The site for science prototype for the NSDL. *D-Lib Magazine, 8*(1). Retrieved February 2, 2006, From www.dlib.org/dlib/january02/arms/01arms.html

Assadi, H., Beauvisage, T., Lupovici, C., & Cloarec, T. (2003). Users and uses of online digital libraries in France. *Proceedings of the 7th European Conference on Research and Advanced Technology for Digital Libraries,* 1–12.

Atkins, D. E. (2003). Keeping academic libraries at the center of the university. In P. Hodges, M. Sandler, M. Bonn, & J. P. Wilkin (Eds.), *Digital libraries: A vision for the 21st century. A Festschrift in honor of Wendy Lougee on the occasion of her departure from the University of Michigan* (pp. 58–73). Ann Arbor: University of Michigan.

Atkins, D. E., Droegemeier, K. K., Feldman, S. I., Garcia-Molina, H., Klein, M. L., Messerschmitt, D. G., et al. (2003). *Revolutionizing science and engineering through cyberinfrastructure: Report of the National Science Foundation Blue-Ribbon Advisory Panel on Cyberinfrastructure.* Washington, DC: National Science Foundation.

Attig, J., Copeland, A., & Pelikan, M. (2004). Context and meaning: The challenges of metadata for a digital image library within the university. *College & Research Libraries, 65*(3), 251–261.

Ayres, M.-L., Burrows, T., & Holmes, R. (2004). Sound footings: Building a national digital library of Australian music. *Proceedings of the 8th European Conference on Digital Libraries,* 281–291.

Bainbridge, D., Don, K. J., Buchanan, G. R., Witten, I. H., Jones, S., Jones, M., et al. (2004). Dynamic digital library construction and configuration. *Proceedings of the 8th European Conference on Digital Libraries,* 1–13.

Bainbridge, D., Edgar, K. D., McPherson, J. R., & Witten, I. H. (2003). Managing change in a digital library system with many interface languages. *Proceedings of the 7th European Conference on Research and Advanced Technology for Digital Libraries,* 350–361.

Banwell, L., & Coulson, G. (2004). Users and user study methodology: The JUBILEE Project. *Information Research, 9*(2). Retrieved February 2, 2006, from http://informationr.net/ir/9-2/paper167.html

Banwell, L., Ray, K., Coulson, G., Urquhart, C., Lonsdale, R., Armstrong, C., et al. (2004). The JISC user behaviour monitoring and evaluation framework. *Journal of Documentation, 60*(3), 302–320.

Barton, J. (2005). Digital libraries, virtual museums: Same difference? *Library Review, 54*(3), 149–154.

Bates, M. J. (2002). The cascade of interactions in the digital library interface. *Information Processing & Management, 38*(3), 381–400.

Bearman, D., Trant, J., Chun, S., Jenkins, M., Smith, K., Cherry, R., et al. (2005). Social terminology enhancement through vernacular engagement: Exploring collaborative annotation to encourage interaction with museum collections. *D-Lib Magazine, 11*(9).

Retrieved February 2, 2006, from www.dlib.org/dlib/september05/bearman/09bearman. html

Beghtol, C. (2001). Knowledge representation and organization in the Iter Project: A Web-based digital library for scholars of the Middle Ages and Renaissance. *Knowledge Organization, 28*(4), 170–179.

Bekaert, J., De Kooning, E., & Van de Walle, R. (2005). Packaging models for the storage and distribution of complex digital objects in archival information systems: A review of MPEG-21 DID principles. *Multimedia Systems, 10*(4), 286–301.

Bekaert, J., Van de Ville, D., Rogge, B., Strauven, I., De Kooning, E., & Van de Walle, R. (2002). Metadata-based access to multimedia architectural and historical archive collections: A review. *Aslib Proceedings, 54*(6), 362–371.

Berube, L. (2004). Collaborative digital reference: An Ask a Librarian (UK) overview. *Program, 38*(1), 29–41.

Bieber, M., Engelbart, D., Furuta, R., Hiltz, S. R., Noll, J., Preece, J., et al. (2002). Toward virtual community knowledge evolution. *Journal of Management Information Systems, 18*(4), 11–35.

Bishop, A. P., Mehra, B., Bazzell, I., & Smith, C. (2003). Participatory action research and digital libraries: Reframing the question. In A. P. Bishop, N. A. Van House, & B. P. Buttenfield (Eds.), *Digital library use: Social practice in design and evaluation* (pp. 161–189). Cambridge, MA: MIT Press.

Bishop, A. P., Neumann, L. J., Star, S. L., Merkel, C., Ignacio, E., & Sandusky, R. J. (2000). Digital libraries: Situating use in changing information infrastructure. *Journal of the American Society for Information Science, 51,* 394–413.

Bishop, A. P., & Star, S. L. (1996). Social informatics of digital library use and infrastructure. *Annual Review of Information Science and Technology, 31,* 301–401.

Bishop, A. P., Van House, N. A., Buttenfield, B. P. (Eds.). (2003). *Digital library use: Social practice in design and evaluation.* Cambridge MA: MIT Press.

Blomgren, L., Vallo, H., & Byström, K. (2004). Evaluation of an information system in an information seeking process. *Proceedings of the 8th European Conference on Digital Libraries,* 57–68.

Bollen, J., Manepalli, G., Manepalli, S., Nandigam, G., & Nelson, M. L. (2005). Trend analysis of the digital library community. *D-Lib Magazine, 11*(1). Retrieved February 2, 2006, from www.dlib.org/dlib/january05/bollen/01bollen.html

Bonn, M., Hodges, P., Sandler, M., & Wilkin, J. P. (2003). Building the digital library at the University of Michigan. In P. Hodges, M. Sandler, M. Bonn, & J. P. Wilkin (Eds.), *Digital libraries: A vision for the 21st century. A Festschrift in honor of Wendy Lougee on the occasion of her departure from the University of Michigan* (pp. 22–41). Ann Arbor: University of Michigan.

Borbinha, J., Kunse, J., Spinazze, A., Miutschke, P., Lieder, H.-J., Mabe, M., et al. (2005). Reference models for digital libraries: Actors and roles. *International Journal on Digital Libraries, 5,* 325–330.

Borgman, C. L. (2002). Challenges in building digital libraries for the 21st century. *Proceedings of the 5th International Conference on Asian Digital Libraries,* 1–13.

Borgman, C. L. (2003a). Designing digital libraries for usability. In A. P. Bishop, N. A. Van House, & B. P. Buttenfield (Eds.), *Digital library use: Social practice in design and evaluation* (pp. 85–118). Cambridge, MA: MIT Press.

Borgman, C. L. (2003b). The invisible library: Paradox of the global information infrastructure. *Library Trends, 51*, 652–674.

Borgman, C. L., & Furner, J. (2002). Scholarly communication and bibliometrics. *Annual Review of Information Science and Technology, 36*, 3–72.

Borgman, C. L., Smart, L. J., Millwood, K. A., Finley, J. R., Champeny, L., Gilliland, A. J., et al. (2005). Comparing faculty information seeking in teaching and research: Implications for the design of digital libraries. *Journal of the American Society for Information Science and Technology, 56*, 636–657.

Börner, K., & Chen, C. M. (2002). Visual interfaces to digital libraries: Motivation, utilization, and socio-technical challenges. In K. Börner & C. Chen (Eds.), *Visual interfaces to digital libraries* (Lecture Notes in Computer Science, 2539; pp. 1–9). Berlin: Springer.

Bracke, P. J. (2004). Web usage mining at an academic health sciences library: An exploratory study. *Journal of the Medical Library Association, 92*, 421–428.

Bradley, R. (2005). Digital authenticity and integrity: Digital cultural heritage documents as research resources. *portal: Libraries and the Academy, 5*, 165–175.

Brase, J. (2004). Using digital library techniques: Registration of scientific primary data. *Proceedings of the 8th European Conference on Digital Libraries*, 488–494.

Brisaboa, N. R., Parama, J. R., Penabad, M. R., Places, A. S., & Rodriguez, F. J. (2002). Solving language problems in a multilingual digital library federation. *Proceedings of the 1st EurAsian Conference on Information and Communication Technology*, 503–510.

Brophy, P., Fisher, S., & Clarke, Z. (2002). *Libraries without walls 4: The delivery of services to distant users*. London: Facet.

Bruder, I., Finger, A., Heuer, A., & Ignatova, T. (2003). Towards a digital document archive for historical handwritten music scores. *Proceedings of the 6th International Conference on Asian Digital Libraries*, 411–414.

Buchanan, G., Blandford, A., Thimbleby, H., & Jones, M. (2004). Supporting information structuring in a digital library. *Proceedings of the 8th European Conference on Digital Libraries*, 464–475.

Buckland, M. K. (2003). Five grand challenges for library research. *Library Trends, 51*, 675–686.

Burke, G., Germain, C. A., & Van Ullen, M. K. (2003). URLs in the OPAC: Integrating or disintegrating research libraries' catalogs. *Journal of Academic Librarianship, 29*, 290–297.

Buzydlowski, J. W., White, H. D., & Lin, X. (2002). Term co-occurrence analysis as an interface for digital libraries. In K. Börner & C. Chen (Eds.), *Visual interfaces to digital libraries* (Lecture Notes in Computer Science, 2539; pp. 133–144). Berlin: Springer.

Byrne, A. (2003). Digital libraries: Barriers or gateways to scholarly information? *Electronic Library, 21*, 414–421.

Cacheda, F., Plachouras, V., & Ounis, I. (2005). A case study of distributed information retrieval architectures to index one terabyte of text. *Information Processing & Management, 41*, 1141–1161.

Cai, G. R. (2002). GeoVIBE: A visual interface for geographic digital libraries. In K. Börner & C. Chen (Eds.), *Visual interfaces to digital libraries* (Lecture Notes in Computer Science, 2539; pp. 171–187). Berlin: Springer.

Campbell, D. (2002). Federating access to digital objects: PictureAustralia. *Program, 36*, 182–187.

Campbell, J. D. (2003). Access in a networked world: Scholars portal in context. *Library Trends, 52*, 247–255.

Candela, L., Castelli, D., & Pagano, P. (2004). Enhancing the OpenDLib Search Service. *Proceedings of the 8th European Conference on Digital Libraries*, 353–365.

Candela, L., & Straccia, U. (2004). The personalized, collaborative digital library environment CYCLADES and its collections management. In J. Callan, F. Crestani, & M. Sanderson (Eds.), *Distributed multimedia information retrieval* (Lecture Notes in Computer Science, 2924; pp. 156–172). Berlin: Springer.

Chang, N. C. (2005). Data manipulation in an XML-based digital image library. *Program, 39*, 62–72.

Chen, H. C. (2002). From digital library to digital government: A case study in crime data mapping and mining. *Proceedings of the 5th International Conference on Asian Digital Libraries*, 36–52.

Cherry, J. M., & Duff, W. M. (2002). Studying digital library users over time: A follow-up survey of Early Canadiana Online. *Information Research, 7*(2). Retrieved February 2, 2006, from http://informationr.net/ir/7-2/paper123.html

Cho, Y. I. (2004). Development of a personalized digital library system based on the new mobile multi agent platform. *Proceedings of the 7th International Conference on Artificial Intelligence and Soft Computing*, 829–834.

Chowdhury, G. G. (2002a). Digital divide: How can digital libraries bridge the gap? *Proceedings of the 5th International Conference on Asian Digital Libraries*, 379–391.

Chowdhury, G. G. (2002b). Digital libraries and reference services: Present and future. *Journal of Documentation, 58*, 258–283.

Chowdhury, G. G., & Chowdhury, S. (2003). *Introduction to digital libraries*. London: Facet.

Ciravegna, F., Chapman, S., Dingli, A., & Wilks, Y. (2004). Learning to harvest information for the Semantic Web. *Proceedings of the 1st European Semantic Web Symposium*, 312–326.

Clausen, M., Kurth, F., Maller, M., & Ribbrock, A. (2004). Content-based retrieval in digital music libraries. *Proceedings of the 8th European Conference on Digital Libraries*, 292–303.

Congia, S., Gaylord, M., Merchant, B., & Suleman, H. (2004). Applying SOAP to OAI-PMH. *Proceedings of the 8th European Conference on Digital Libraries*, 411–420.

Constantopoulos, P., Doerr, M., Theodoridou, M., & Tzobanakis, M. (2004). On information organization in annotation systems. In G. Grieser & Y. Tanaka (Eds.), *Intuitive human interfaces for organizing and accessing intellectual assets* (Lecture Notes in Artificial Intelligence, 3359; pp. 189–200). Berlin: Springer.

Craven, J. (2003). Access to electronic resources by visually impaired people. *Information Research, 8*(4). Retrieved February 2, 2006, from http://informationr.net/ir/8-4/paper156.html

Crosier, S. J., Goodchild, M. F., Hill, L. L., & Smith, T. R. (2003). Developing an infrastructure for sharing environmental models. *Environment and Planning B: Planning & Design, 30*, 487–501.

Cunningham, S. J. (2002). What people do when they look for music: Implications for design of a music digital library. *Proceedings of the 5th International Conference on Asian Digital Libraries*, 177–178.

D'Alessandro, D. M., Kreiter, C. D., & Peterson, M. W. (2004). An evaluation of information-seeking behaviors of general pediatricians. *Pediatrics, 113*, 64–69.

Deegan, M., & Tanner, S. (2002). *Digital futures: Strategies for the information age*. London: Library Association Publishing.

Dempsey, L. (2003). The recombinant library: Portals and people. *Journal of Library Administration, 39*(4), 103–136.

Dempsey, L., & Lavoie, B. (2005). *DLF service framework for digital libraries*. Washington, DC: Digital Library Federation. Retrieved May 17, 2005, from www.diglib.org/architectures/serviceframe/dlfserviceframe1.htm

Desai, C. M. (2003). Instant messaging reference: How does it compare? *Electronic Library, 21*(1), 21–30.

Detlor, B., & Arsenault, C. (2002). Web information seeking and retrieval in digital library contexts: Towards an intelligent agent solution. *Online Information Review, 26*, 404–412.

Di Giacomo, M., Martinez, M., & Scott, J. (2004). A large-scale digital library system to integrate heterogeneous data of distributed databases. *Proceedings of the 10th International EuroPar Conference*, 391–397.

DiLauro, T., Patton, M., Reynolds, D., & Choudhury, G. S. (2005). The archive ingest and handling test: The Johns Hopkins University report. *D-Lib Magazine, 11*(12). Retrieved February 2, 2006, from www.dlib.org/dlib/december05/choudhury/12choudhury.html.

Ding, H., & Sølvberg, I. (2004). Exploiting extended service-oriented architecture for federated digital libraries. *Proceedings of the 7th International Conference on Asian Digital Libraries*, 184–194.

Dong, L., Xing, C. X., Zhou, L. Z., Zhang, B., & Jiang, A. R. (2004). Cataloging and preservation toolkit of a Chinese mathematics ancient books digital library. *Proceedings of the 7th International Conference on Asian Digital Libraries*, 174–183.

Dorner, D. G. (2004). The impact of digital information resources on the roles of collection managers in research libraries. *Library Collections, Acquisitions, and Technical Services, 28*, 249–274.

Druin, A. (2005). What children can teach us: Developing digital libraries for children with children. *Library Quarterly, 75*, 20–41.

Druin, A., Revelle, G., Bederson, B. B., Hourcade, J. P., Farber, A., Lee, J., et al. (2003). A collaborative digital library for children. *Journal of Computer Assisted Learning, 19*, 239–248.

Eason, K., Harker, S., Apps, A., & MacIntyre, R. (2004). Towards an integrated digital library: Exploration of user responses to a "Joined-Up"™ service. *Proceedings of the 8th European Conference on Digital Libraries*, 452–463.

Fallows, D. (2005). *Search engine users*. Washington, DC: Pew Foundation.

Feitelson, D. G. (2004). On identifying name equivalences in digital libraries. *Information Research, 9*(4). Retrieved February 2, 2006, from http://informationr.net/ir/9-4/paper192.html

Feng, L., Hoppenbrouwers, J., & Jeusfeld, M. A. (2005). Beyond information searching and browsing: Acquiring knowledge from digital libraries. *Information Processing & Management, 41*, 97–120.

Fleischaeur, C., & Arms, C. (2005). *Sustainability of digital formats: Planning for Library of Congress collections*. Washington, DC: Library of Congress. Retrieved January 21, 2006, from www.digitalpreservation.gov/formats/index.shtml

Fox, E. A. (2003). Case studies in the US National Science Digital Library: DL-in-a-box, CITIDEL, and OCKHAM. *Proceedings of the 6th International Conference on Asian Digital Libraries*, 17–25.

Fox, E. A. (2004). Digital libraries for education: Case studies. *Proceedings of the 7th International Conference on Asian Digital Libraries*, 51–60.

Fox, E. A., Goncalves, M. A., & Shen, R. (2005). The role of digital libraries in moving toward knowledge environments. In M. Hemmje, C. Niederee, & T. Risse (Eds.), *From integrated publication and information systems to virtual information and knowledge environments* (Lecture Notes in Computer Science, 3379; pp. 96–106). Berlin: Springer.

Fox, E. A., & Logan, E. (2005). An Asian digital libraries perspective. *Information Processing & Management, 41*, 1–4.

Fox, E. A., & Lunin, L. F. (1993). Perspectives on digital libraries: Introduction and overview. *Journal of the American Society for Information Science, 44*, 441–445.

Fox, E. A., Suleman, H., & Luo, M. (2002). Building digital libraries made easy: Toward open digital libraries. *Proceedings of the 5th International Conference on Asian Digital Libraries*, 14–24.

Fox, E. A., & Urs, S. R. (2002). Digital libraries. *Annual Review of Information Science and Technology, 36*, 503–589.

Franklin, R. A. (2003). Re-inventing subject access for the Semantic Web. *Online Information Review, 27*, 94–101.

French, J. C., Chapin, A. C., & Martin, W. N. (2004). Multiple viewpoints as an approach to digital library interfaces. *Journal of the American Society for Information Science and Technology, 55*, 911–922.

Frommholz, I., Brocks, H., Thiel, U., Neuhold, E., Iannone, L., Semeraro, G., et al. (2003). Document-centered collaboration for scholars in the humanities: The COLLATE system. *Proceedings of the 7th European Conference on Research and Advanced Technology for Digital Libraries*, 434–445.

Frumkin, J. (2005). The Wiki and the digital library. *OCLC Systems and Services, 21*(1), 18–22.

Gentili, G., Micarelli, A., & Sciarrone, F. (2003). Infoweb: An adaptive information filtering system for the cultural heritage domain. *Applied Artificial Intelligence, 17*, 715–744.

Geyer-Schulz, A., Neumann, A., & Thede, A. (2003). Others also use: A robust recommender system for scientific libraries. *Proceedings of the 7th European Conference on Research and Advanced Technology for Digital Libraries*, 113–125.

Gladney, H. M. (2004). Trustworthy 100-year digital objects: Evidence after every witness is dead. *ACM Transactions on Information Systems, 22*, 406–436.

Goh, D., Fu, L., & Foo, S. (2002). A work environment for a digital library of historical resources. *Proceedings of the 5th International Conference on Asian Digital Libraries*, 260–261.

Gold, A. K. (2003). Multilateral digital library partnerships for sharing and preserving instructional content and context. *portal: Libraries and the Academy, 3*, 269–291.

Goncalves, M. A., Fox, E. A., Watson, L. T., & Kipp, N. A. (2004). Streams, structures, spaces, scenarios, societies (5S): A formal model for digital libraries. *ACM Transactions on Information Systems, 22*, 270–312.

Gorman, G. E. (2002). *The digital factor in library and information services*. London: Facet.

Gosling, A. S., Westbrook, J. I., & Coiera, E. W. (2003). Variation in the use of online clinical evidence: A qualitative analysis. *International Journal of Medical Informatics, 69,* 1–16.

Gottesman, L., Kresh, D., & Takagi, K. (2004). QuestionPoint: Collaboration between the Library of Congress and the Online Computer Library Center (OCLC): An update. *Journal of Information Processing & Management, 47,* 535–540.

Greenstein, D., Lawrence, G. S., Miller, J., & Dunlap, M. (2003). New models of library service: Deep resource sharing and collaboration at the University of California. In P. Hodges, M. Sandler, M. Bonn, & J. P. Wilkin (Eds.), *Digital libraries: A vision for the 21st century. A Festschrift in honor of Wendy Lougee on the occasion of her departure from the University of Michigan* (pp. 74–93). Ann Arbor: University of Michigan.

Greenstein, D., & Thorin, S. E. (2002). *The digital library: A biography.* Washington, DC: Digital Library Federation.

Guan, J. H., Zhou, S. G., Chen, J. P., Chen, X. L., An, Y., Bian, F. L., et al. (2003). MAG2DL: A framework for information retrieval and integration of distributed geographic digital libraries. *Proceedings of the 6th International Conference on Asian Digital Libraries,* 351–364.

Hammond, T., Hannay, T., Lund, B., & Scott, J. (2005). Social bookmarking tools (I): A general review. *D-Lib Magazine, 11*(4). Retrieved February 2, 2006, from www.dlib.org/dlib/april05/hammond/04hammond.html

Hanisch, F., & Strasser, W. (2003). Adaptability and interoperability in the field of highly interactive Web-based courseware. *Computers & Graphics, 27,* 647–655.

Hanson, A., & Levin, B. L. (2002). *Building a virtual library.* Hershey, PA: Information Science Publishing.

He, Y., Hui, S. C., & Fong, A. C. M. (2003). Citation-based retrieval for scholarly publications. *IEEE Intelligent Systems, 18*(2), 58–65.

Heery, R., & Lyon, L. (Eds.). (2004). *Proceedings of the 8th European Conference on Digital Libraries* (Lecture Notes in Computer Science, 3232). Berlin: Springer.

Hiiragi, W., Sakaguchi, T., Sugimoto, S., & Tabata, K. (2004). A policy-based system for institutional Web archiving. *Proceedings of the 7th International Conference on Asian Digital Libraries,* 144–154.

Ho, C. H. (2004). Managing the e-library in a global environment: Experiences at Monash University, Australia. *Program, 38,* 168–175.

Hodges, P., Sandler, M., Bonn, M., & Wilkin, J. P. (Eds.). (2003). *Digital libraries: A vision for the 21st century. A Festschrift in honor of Wendy Lougee on the occasion of her departure from the University of Michigan.* Ann Arbor: University of Michigan.

Hollmann, J., Ardö, A., & Stenström, P. (2003). An evaluation of document prefetching in a distributed digital library. *Proceedings of the 7th European Conference on Research and Advanced Technology for Digital Libraries,* 276–287.

Hong, Y., On, B.-W., & Lee, D. (2004). System support for name authority control problem in digital libraries: OpenDBLP approach. *Proceedings of the 8th European Conference on Digital Libraries,* 134–144.

Hourcade, J. P., Bederson, B. B., Druin, A., Rose, A., Farber, A., & Takayama, Y. (2003). The International Children's Digital Library: Viewing digital books online. *Interacting With Computers, 15,* 151–167.

Huang, S. H., Ke, H. R., & Yang, W. P. (2005). Enhancing semantic digital library query using a content and service inference model (CSIM). *Information Processing & Management, 41*, 891–908.

Hughes, B., & Kamat, A. (2005). A metadata search engine for digital language archives. *D-Lib Magazine, 11*(2). Retrieved February 2, 2006, from www.dlib.org/dlib/february05/hughes/02hughes.html

Hunter, J., Falkovych, K., & Little, S. (2004). Next generation search interfaces: Interactive data exploration and hypothesis formulation. *Proceedings of the 8th European Conference on Digital Libraries*, 86–98.

Hussein, S., Fox, E. A., Kelapure, R., Krowne, A., & Luo, M. (2003). Building digital libraries from simple building blocks. *Online Information Review, 27*, 301–310.

Hutchinson, H. B., Rose, A., Bederson, B. B., Weeks, A. C., & Druin, A. (2005). The International Children's Digital Library: A case study in designing for a multilingual, multicultural, multigenerational audience. *Information Technology and Libraries, 24*, 4–12.

Huwe, T. K. (2002). Social sciences e-prints come of age: The California Digital Library's working paper repository. *Online, 26*(5), 38–42.

Hwang, S. Y., Hsiung, W. C., & Yang, W. S. (2003). A prototype WWW literature recommendation system for digital libraries. *Online Information Review, 27*, 169–182.

Hyldegaard, J., & Seiden, P. (2004). My e-journal: Exploring the usefulness of personalized access to scholarly articles and services. *Information Research, 9*(3). Retrieved February 2, 2006, from http://informationr.net/ir/9-3/paper181.html

Ioannidis, Y. (2005). Digital libraries at a crossroads. *International Journal on Digital Libraries, 5*, 255–265.

Ismail, D. M. M., Yin, M., Theng, Y. L., Goh, D. H. L., & Lim, E. P. (2003). Towards a role-based metadata scheme for educational digital libraries: A case study in Singapore. *Proceedings of the 7th European Conference on Research and Advanced Technology for Digital Libraries*, 41–51.

Jacoby, J., & Laskowski, M. S. (2004). Measurement and analysis of electronic reserve usage: Toward a new path in online library service assessment. *portal: Libraries and the Academy, 4*, 219–232.

Jane, C., & McMillan, D. (2003). Online in real-time? Deciding whether to offer a real-time virtual reference service. *Electronic Library, 21*, 240–246.

Janssen, W. C. (2004). Document icons and page thumbnails: Issues in construction of document thumbnails for page-image digital libraries. *Proceedings of the 8th European Conference on Digital Libraries*, 111–121.

Jayawardana, C., Hewagamage, K. P., & Hirakawa, M. (2001). A personalized information environment for digital libraries. *Information Technology and Libraries, 20*, 185–196.

Jeng, J. (2005). What is usability in the context of the digital library and how can it be measured? *Information Technology and Libraries, 24*, 47–56.

Jin, Y., Huang, M., Lin, H., & Guo, J. (2005). Towards collaboration: The development of collaborative virtual reference service in China. *Journal of Academic Librarianship, 31*, 287–291.

Jose, J. M., Braddick, H., Martin, I., Robertson, B., Walker, C., & MacPherson, G. (2002). Virtual Tutor: A system for deploying digital libraries in classrooms. *Proceedings of the 5th International Conference on Asian Digital Libraries*, 275–286.

Kampanya, N., Shen, R., Kim, S., North, C., & Fox, E. A. (2004). Citiviz: A visual user interface to the CITIDEL System. *Proceedings of the 8th European Conference on Digital Libraries*, 122–133.

Karadkar, U. P., Francisco-Revilla, L., Furuta, R., Shipman, F. M., Arora, A., Dash, S., et al. (2004). Metadocuments supporting digital library information discovery. *International Journal on Digital Libraries*, *4*, 25–30.

Kassim, A. R. C., & Kochtanek, T. R. (2003). Designing, implementing, and evaluating an educational digital library resource. *Online Information Review*, *27*, 160–168.

Kelapure, R., Goncalves, M. A., & Fox, E. A. (2003). Scenario-based generation of digital library services. *Proceedings of the 7th European Conference on Research and Advanced Technology for Digital Libraries*, 263–275.

Keller, M. A. (2004). Gold at the end of the digital library rainbow: Forecasting the consequences of truly effective digital libraries. *Proceedings of the 7th International Conference on Asian Digital Libraries*, 84–94.

Kelly, B. (2004). Interoperable digital library programmes? We must have QA! *Proceedings of the 8th European Conference on Digital Libraries*, 80–85.

Kenney, A. R., & McGovern, N. Y. (2003). The five organizational stages of digital preservation. In P. Hodges, M. Sandler, M. Bonn, & J. P. Wilkin (Eds.), *Digital libraries: A vision for the 21st century. A Festschrift in honor of Wendy Lougee on the occasion of her departure from the University of Michigan* (pp. 122–152). Ann Arbor: University of Michigan.

Khoo, M., & Ribes, D. (2005). JCDL Workshop report: Studying digital library users in the wild. *D-Lib Magazine*, *11*(7/8). Retrieved February 2, 2006, from www.dlib.org/dlib/july05/khoo/07khoo.html

Kim, H., Choo, C. Y., & Chen, S. S. (2003). An integrated digital library server with OAI and self-organizing capabilities. *Proceedings of the 7th European Conference on Research and Advanced Technology for Digital Libraries*, 164–175.

Kim, I., Kim, B., & Hwang, T. (2003). Multimedia data transmission using multicast delivery in digital library. *Proceedings of the 6th International Conference on Asian Digital Libraries*, 206–217.

Klas, C.-P., Fuhr, N., & Schaefer, A. (2004). Evaluating strategic support for information access in the DAFFODIL system. *Proceedings of the 8th European Conference on Digital Libraries*, 476–487.

Koch, T., & Sølvberg, I. T. (Eds.). (2003). *Research and Advanced Technology for Digital Libraries: Proceedings of the 7th European Conference on Research and Advanced Technology for Digital Libraries* (Lecture Notes in Computer Science, 2769). Berlin: Springer.

Koohang, A., & Ondracek, J. (2005). Users' views about the usability of digital libraries. *British Journal of Educational Technology*, *36*, 407–423.

Kornbluh, M., Fegan, M., & Rehberger, D. (2004). Media matrix: Creating secondary repositories. *Proceedings of the 8th European Conference on Digital Libraries*, 329–340.

Kortelainen, T. (2004). An analysis of the use of electronic journals and commercial journal article collections through the FinELib portal. *Information Research*, *9*(2). Retrieved February 2, 2006, from http://informationr.net/ir/9-2/paper168.html

Koskiala, S., & Savolainen, R. (Eds.). (2004). Selected papers from the Conference, 'Toward User-Centered Approach to Digital Libraries,' Espoo, Finland, September 8–9, 2003, [special issue]. *Information Research*, *9*(2). Retrieved March 6, 2006, from http://informationr.net/ir/9-2/infres92.html

Krottmaier, H. (2002). Automatic references: Active support for scientists in digital libraries. *Proceedings of the 5th International Conference on Asian Digital Libraries*, 254–255.

Krowne, A., & Fox, E. A. (2003). An architecture for multischeming in digital libraries. *Proceedings of the 6th International Conference on Asian Digital Libraries*, 563–577.

Kumar, A., Bia, A., Holmes, M., Schreibman, S., Siemens, R., & Walsh, J. (2004). Bridging the gap between a simple set of structured documents and a functional digital library. *Proceedings of the 8th European Conference on Digital Libraries*, 432–441.

Kurtz, M. J., Eichhorn, G., Accomazzi, A., Grant, C., Demleitner, M., Hennekin, E., et al. (2005). The effect of use and access on citations. *Information Processing & Management*, *41*, 1395–1402.

Kurtz, M. J., Eichhorn, G., Accomazzi, A., Grant, C., Demleitner, M., Murray, S. S., et al. (2005). Worldwide use and impact of the NASA Astrophysics Data System digital library. *Journal of the American Society for Information Science and Technology*, *56*, 36–45.

Lacroix, E. M. (2001). How consumers are gathering information from MEDLINEplus. *Science Communication*, *22*, 283–291.

Lagoze, C., Krafft, D. B., Payette, S., & Jesuroga, S. (2005). What is a digital library anymore, anyway? *D-Lib Magazine*, *11*(11). Retrieved February 2, 2006, from www.dlib.org/dlib/november05/lagoze/11lagoze.html

Lankes, R. D., Janes, J., Smith, L. C., & Finneran, C. M. (2004). *The virtual reference experience: Integrating theory into practice*. New York: Neal-Schuman.

Lankes, R. D., McClure, C. R., Gross, M., & Pomerantz, J. (2003). *Implementing digital reference services: Setting standards and making it real*. London: Facet.

Larsen, R. L., & Wactlar, H. D. (2003). *Knowledge lost in information: Report of the NSF Workshop on Research Directions for Digital Libraries*. Pittsburgh, PA: School of Information Sciences, University of Pittsburgh. Retrieved January 21, 2006, from www.sis.pitt.edu/~dlwkshop/report.pdf

Larson, R. R. (2003). Distributed IR for digital libraries. *Proceedings of the 7th European Conference on Research and Advanced Technology for Digital Libraries*, 487–498.

Lawrence, S. (2001). Online or invisible? *Nature*, *411*, 521.

Lee, C. H., Na, J. C., & Khoo, C. (2003). Ontology learning for medical digital libraries. *Proceedings of the 6th International Conference on Asian Digital Libraries*, 302–305.

Lee, E. (2004). Building interoperability for United Kingdom historic environment information resources. *Proceedings of the 8th European Conference on Digital Libraries*, 179–185.

Lee, M. (2003). A knowledge network approach for building distributed digital libraries. *Proceedings of the 6th International Conference on Asian Digital Libraries*, 373–383.

Lee, M. H., Kang, J. H., Myaeng, S. H., Hyun, S. J., Yoo, J. M., Ko, E. J., et al. (2003). A multimedia digital library system based on MPEG-7 and XQuery. *Proceedings of the 6th International Conference on Asian Digital Libraries*, 193–205.

Lee, S. S., Theng, Y. L., & Goh, D. H. L. (2003). Creativity in digital libraries and information retrieval environments. *Proceedings of the 6th International Conference on Asian Digital Libraries*, 398–410.

Lesk, M. (2005). *Understanding digital libraries* (2nd ed.). Boston: Elsevier.

Levy, D. M. (2001). *Scrolling forward: Making sense of documents in the digital age*. New York: Arcade.

Levy, D. M. (2003). Documents and libraries: Sociotechnical perspective. In A. P. Bishop, N. A. Van House, & B. P. Buttenfield (Eds.), *Digital library use: Social practice in design and evaluation* (pp. 25–42). Cambridge, MA: MIT Press.

Levy, D. M., & Marshall, C. C. (1995). Going digital: A look at the assumptions underlying digital libraries. *Communications of the ACM, 38*(4), 77–84.

Lipow, A. G. (2003). *The virtual librarian's handbook.* New York: Neal-Schuman.

Liu, Z. H., Lim, E. P., & Goh, D. H. L. (2002). Resource annotation framework in a georeferenced and geospatial digital library. *Proceedings of the 5th International Conference on Asian Digital Libraries,* 287–298.

Liu, Z. M. (2003). Trends in transforming scholarly communication and their implications. *Information Processing & Management, 39,* 889–898.

Lougee, W. P. (2002). *Diffuse libraries: Emergent roles for the research library in the digital age.* Washington, DC: Council on Library and Information Resources.

Lozier, D. W. (2003). NIST digital library of mathematical functions. *Annals of Mathematics and Artificial Intelligence, 38,* 105–119.

Lu, J., & Callan, J. (2005). Federated search of text-based digital libraries in hierarchical peer-to-peer networks. *Proceedings of the 27th European Conference on Information Retrieval,* 52–66.

Lu, S., Liu, D., Fotouhi, F., Dong, M., Reynolds, R., Aristar, A., et al. (2004). Language engineering for the Semantic Web: A digital library for endangered languages. *Information Research, 9*(3). Retrieved February 2, 2006, from http://informationr.net/ir/9-3/paper176.html

Lu, W. H., Wang, J. H., & Chien, L. F. (2003). Towards Web mining of query translations for cross-language information retrieval in digital libraries. *Proceedings of the 6th International Conference on Asian Digital Libraries,* 86–99.

Lund, B., Hammond, T., Flack, M., & Hannay, T. (2005). Social bookmarking tools (II): A case study: Connotea. *D-Lib Magazine, 11*(4). Retrieved February 2, 2006, from www.dlib.org/dlib/april05/lund/04lund.html

Lynch, C. (2003a). Colliding with the real world: Heresies and unexplored questions about audience, economics, and control of digital libraries. In A. P. Bishop, N. A. Van House, & D. P. Buttenfield (Eds.), *Digital library use: Social practice in design and evaluation* (pp. 191–216). Cambridge, MA: MIT Press.

Lynch, C. (2003b). Digital library opportunities. *Journal of Academic Librarianship, 29,* 286–289.

Lynch, C. (2003c). Institutional repositories: Essential infrastructure for scholarship in the digital age. *portal: Libraries and the Academy, 3,* 327–336.

Lynch, C. (2005). Where do we go from here? The next decade for digital libraries. *D-Lib Magazine, 11*(7/8). Retrieved February 2, 2006, from www.dlib.org/dlib/july05/lynch/07lynch.html

Lynch, C., & Lippincott, J. (2005). Institutional repository deployment in the United States as of early 2005. *D-Lib Magazine, 11*(9). Retrieved February 2, 2006, from www.dlib.org/dlib/september05/lynch/09lynch.html

Madle, G., Kostkova, P., Mani-Saada, J., & Weinberg, J. R. (2003). Evaluating the changes in knowledge and attitudes of digital library users. *Proceedings of the 7th European Conference on Research and Advanced Technology for Digital Libraries,* 29–40.

Maly, K., Nelson, M., Zubair, M., Amrou, A., Kothamasa, S., Wang, L., et al. (2004). Enhancing Kepler usability and performance. *Proceedings of the 8th European Conference on Digital Libraries*, 317–328.

Manolopoulos, Y., & Sidiropoulos, A. (2005). A new perspective to automatically rank scientific conferences using digital libraries. *Information Processing & Management, 41*, 289–312.

Marchionini, G., Plaisant, C., & Komlodi, A. (2003). The people in digital libraries: Multifaceted approaches to assessing needs and impact. In A. P. Bishop, N. A. Van House, & B. P. Buttenfield (Eds.), *Digital library use: Social practice in design and evaluation* (pp. 119–160). Cambridge, MA: MIT Press.

Marcum, D. B. (Ed.). (2001). *Development of digital libraries: An American perspective* (Contributions in Librarianship and Information Science, 95). Westport, CT: Greenwood Press.

Marcum, D. B. (2003). Research questions for the digital era library. *Library Trends, 51*, 636–651.

Marcum, D. B. (2004). The DODL, the NDIIPP, and the copyright conundrum. *portal: Libraries and the Academy, 4*, 321–330.

Marshall, C. C. (2003). Finding the boundaries of the library without walls. In A. P. Bishop, N. A. Van House, & B. P. Buttenfield (Eds.), *Digital library use: Social practice in design and evaluation* (pp. 43–63). Cambridge, MA: MIT Press.

Marshall, C. C., & Bly, S. (2004). Sharing encountered information: Digital libraries get a social life. *Proceedings of the 4th ACM/IEEECS Joint Conference on Digital Libraries*, 218–227.

McCray, A. T., & Gallagher, M. E. (2001). Principles for digital library development. *Communications of the ACM, 44*(5), 48–54.

McKay, D., & Cunningham, S. J. (2003). Browsing a digital library: A new approach for the New Zealand Digital Library. *Proceedings of the 6th International Conference on Asian Digital Libraries*, 329–339.

Medina, M. A., Sanchez, A., Chavez, A., & Benitez, A. (2004). Designing ontological agents: An alternative to improve information retrieval in federated digital libraries. *Proceedings of the Second International Atlantic Web Intelligence Conference*, 155–163.

Melucci, M. (2004). Making digital libraries effective: Automatic generation of links for similarity search across hyper-textbooks. *Journal of the American Society for Information Science and Technology, 55*, 414–430.

Meyyappan, N., Foo, S., & Chowdhury, G. G. (2004). Design and evaluation of a task-based digital library for the academic community. *Journal of Documentation, 60*, 449–475.

Miller, B. R., & Youssef, A. (2003). Technical aspects of the Digital Library of Mathematical Functions. *Annals of Mathematics and Artificial Intelligence, 38*, 121–136.

Miller, P. (2005). Web 2.0: Building the new library. *Ariadne,* no. 45. Retrieved January 22, 2006, from www.ariadne.ac.uk/issue45/miller/

Miller, R. G. (2002). Shaping digital library content. *Journal of Academic Librarianship, 28*, 97–103.

Mischo, W. H. (2001). The digital engineering library: Current technologies and challenges. *Science & Technology Libraries, 19*, 129–145.

Mischo, W. H. (2005). Digital libraries: Challenges and influential work. *D-Lib Magazine, 11*(7/8). Retrieved February 2, 2006, from www.dlib.org/dlib/july05/mischo/07mischo.html

Mitchell, S. (2005). Collaboration enabling Internet resource collection-building software and technologies. *Library Trends, 53*, 604–619.

Monopoli, M., Nicholas, D., Georgiou, P., & Korfiati, M. (2002). A user-oriented evaluation of digital libraries: Case study the "electronic journals" service of the library and information service of the University of Patras, Greece. *Aslib Proceedings, 54*, 103–117.

Moore, R. W., Rajasekar, A., & Wan, M. (2005). Data grids, digital libraries, and persistent archives: An integrated approach to sharing, publishing, and archiving data. *Proceedings of the IEEE, 93*, 578–588.

Morgan, R. L. B., Cantor, S., Carmody, S., Hoehn, W., & Klingenstein, K. (2004). Federated security: The Shibboleth approach: The open-source Shibboleth System extends Web-based applications and identity management for secure access to resources among multiple organizations. *Educase Quarterly, 27*(4). Retrieved February 2, 2006, from www.educause.edu/apps/eq/eqm04/eqm0442.asp

Moyo, L. M. (2004). Electronic libraries and the emergence of new service paradigms. *Electronic Library, 22*, 220–230.

Muehlberger, G. (2002). Automated digitisation of printed material for everyone: The METADATA ENGINE Project. *RLG DigiNews, 6*(3), 1–12.

Mustapha, S. M. F. D. (2003). Towards building sociable library system [*sic*] through negotiation engine. *Proceedings of the 6th International Conference on Asian Digital Libraries*, 322–328.

Mutschke, P. (2003). Mining networks and central entities in digital libraries: A graph theoretic approach applied to co-author networks. In F. Pfenning, M. R. Berthold, H.-J. Lenz, E. Bradley, R. Kruse, & C. Borgelt (Eds.), *Advances in intelligent data analysis V* (Lecture Notes in Computer Science, 2810; pp. 155–166). Berlin: Springer.

Nelson, M. L. (2001). A new digital library technology for preserving NASA research. *Journal of Government Information, 28*, 369–394.

Nelson, M. L., Bollen, J., Manepalli, G., & Haq, R. (2005). Archive ingest and handling test: The Old Dominion University approach. *D-Lib Magazine, 11*(12). Retrieved February 2, 2006, from www.dlib.org/dlib/december05/nelson/12nelson.html

Nelson, M. L., & Maly, K. (2001). Buckets: Smart objects for digital libraries. *Communications of the ACM, 44*(5), 60–62.

Neuhold, E., Niederee, C., & Stewart, A. (2003). Personalization in digital libraries: An extended view. *Proceedings of the 6th International Conference on Asian Digital Libraries*, 1–16.

Neuhold, E., Niederee, C., Stewart, A., Frommholz, I., & Mehta, B. (2004). The role of context for information mediation in digital libraries. *Proceedings of the 7th International Conference on Asian Digital Libraries*, 133–143.

Nicholson, S. (2003). Bibliomining for automated collection development in a digital library setting: Using data mining to discover Web-based scholarly research works. *Journal of the American Society for Information Science and Technology, 54*, 1081–1090.

Nicholson, S. (2005). A framework for Internet archaeology: Discovering use patterns in digital library and Web-based information resources. *First Monday, 10*(2). Retrieved February 2, 2006, from www.firstmonday.org/issues/issue10_2/nicholson/index.html

Nilson, K. (2004). The Library Visit Study: User experiences at the virtual reference desk. *Information Research, 9*(2). Retrieved February 2, 2006, from http://informationr.net/ir/9-2/paper171.html

Notess, M. (2004). Three looks at users: A comparison of methods for studying digital library use. *Information Research, 9*(3). Retrieved February 2, 2006, from http://informationr. net/ir/9-3/paper177.html

Notess, M., Riley, J., & Hemmasi, H. (2004). From abstract to virtual entities: Implementation of work-based searching in a multimedia digital library. *Proceedings of the 8th European Conference on Digital Libraries, 157–167.*

Okerson, A. (2003). Asteroids, Moore's Law, and the Star Alliance. *Journal of Academic Librarianship, 29,* 280–285.

Pace, A. K. (2003). *The ultimate digital library: Where the new information players meet.* Chicago: American Library Association.

Paepcke, A., Garcia-Molina, H., & Wesley, R. (2005). Dewey meets Turing: Librarians, computer scientists, and the Digital Libraries Initiative. *D-Lib Magazine, 11*(7/8). Retrieved February 2, 2006, from www.dlib.org/dlib/july05/paepcke/07paepcke.html

Pandian, M. P., Jambhekar, A., & Karisiddappa, C. R. (2002). IIM digital library system: Consortia-based approach. *Electronic Library, 20,* 211–214.

Pantry, S., & Griffiths, P. (2002). *Creating a successful e-information service.* London: Facet.

Papatheodorou, C., Kapidakis, S., Sfakakis, M., & Vassiliou, A. (2003). Mining user communities in digital libraries. *Information Technology and Libraries, 22,* 152–157.

Park, S. (2000). Usability, user preferences, effectiveness, and user behaviors when searching individual and integrated full-text databases: Implications for digital libraries. *Journal of the American Society for Information Science, 51,* 456–468.

Penka, J. T. (2003). The technological challenges of digital reference: An overview. *D-Lib Magazine, 9*(2). Retrieved February 2, 2006, from www.dlib.org/dlib/february03/penka/02penka.html

Péter, J. (2004). Link-enabled cited references. *Online Information Review, 28,* 306–311.

Peters, C. (2005). Comparative evaluation of cross-language information retrieval systems. M. Hemmje, C. Niederee, & T. Risse (Eds.), *From integrated publication and information systems to virtual information and knowledge environments* (Lecture Notes in Computer Science, 3379; pp. 152–161). Berlin: Springer.

Pisciotta, H. A., Dooris, M. J., Frost, J., & Halm, M. (2005). Penn State's visual image user study. *portal: Libraries and the Academy, 5,* 33–58.

Prest, L. A. (2003). Digital library of classic protestant texts. *Library Journal, 128*(2), 126–127.

Prey, J. C., & Zia, L. L. (2002). Progress on educational digital libraries: Current developments in the National Science Foundation's (NSF) National Science, Technology, Engineering, and Mathematics Education Digital Library (NSDL) Program. *Proceedings of the 5th International Conference on Asian Digital Libraries, 53–66.*

Pyrounakis, G., Saidis, K., Nikolaidou, M., & Lourdi, I. (2004). Designing an integrated digital library framework to support multiple heterogeneous collections. *Proceedings of the 8th European Conference on Digital Libraries, 26–37.*

Rapp, D. N., Taylor, H. A., & Crane, G. R. (2003). The impact of digital libraries on cognitive processes: Psychological issues of hypermedia. *Computers in Human Behavior, 19,* 609–628.

Rasmussen, E. (2004). Information retrieval challenges for digital libraries. *Proceedings of the 7th International Conference on Asian Digital Libraries, 95–103.*

Rauber, A., & Merkl, D. (2003). Text mining in the SOMLib Digital Library System: The representation of topics and genres. *Applied Intelligence, 18*, 271–293.

Ravindranathan, U., Shen, R., Goncalves, M. A., Fan, W., Fox, E. A., & Flanagan, J. W. (2004). Prototyping digital libraries handling heterogeneous data sources: The ETANA-DL case study. *Proceedings of the 8th European Conference on Digital Libraries*, 186–197.

Reach, C. S., Whelan, D., & Flood, M. (2003). Feasibility and viability of the digital library in a private law firm. *Law Library Journal, 95*, 369–381.

Renda, M. E., & Straccia, U. (2002). A personalized collaborative digital library environment. *Proceedings of the 5th International Conference on Asian Digital Libraries*, 262–274.

RLG & National Archives and Records Administration. (2005). *An audit checklist for the certification of trusted digital repositories. Draft for public comment.* Mountain View, CA: RLG. Retrieved January 21, 2006, from www.rlg.org/en/pdfs/rlgnara-repositories checklist.pdf

Rosedale, J. E. (2002). *Managing electronic reserves.* Chicago: American Library Association.

Ross, S., & Hedstrom, M. (2005). Preservation research and sustainable digital libraries. *International Journal on Digital Libraries, 5*, 317–324.

Salembier, P., & Smith, J. R. (2001). MPEG-7 multimedia description schemes. *IEEE Transactions on Circuits and Systems for Video Technology, 11*, 748–759.

Saracevic, T., & Dalbello, M. (2001). A survey of digital library education. *Proceedings of the Annual Meeting of the American Society for Information Science and Technology*, 209–223.

Sembok, T. M. T., Zaman, H. B., & Chen, H. (Eds.). (2003). *Digital libraries: Technology and management of indigenous knowledge for global access. Proceedings of the 6th International Conference on Asian Digital Libraries* (Lecture Notes in Computer Science, 2911). Berlin: Springer.

Semeraro, G., Ferilli, S., Fanizzi, N., & Abbattista, F. (2001). Learning interaction models in a digital library service. *Proceedings of the 8th International Conference on User Modeling*, 44–53.

Shirky, C. (2005). AIHT: Conceptual issues from practical tests. *D-Lib Magazine, 11*(12). Retrieved March 6, 2006, from www.dlib.org/dlib/december05/shirky/12shirky.html

Simeoni, F. (2004). Servicing the federation: The case for metadata harvesting. *Proceedings of the 8th European Conference on Digital Libraries*, 389–399.

Smeaton, A. F., & Callan, J. (2005). Personalisation and recommender systems for digital libraries. *International Journal on Digital Libraries, 5*, 299–308.

Smith, M., Rodgers, R., Walker, J., & Tansley, R. (2004). DSpace: A year in the life of an open source digital repository system. *Proceedings of the 8th European Conference on Digital Libraries*, 38–44.

Southwick, S. B. (2003). Digital intermediation: An exploration of user and intermediary perspectives. *Proceedings of the Annual Meeting of the American Society for Information Science and Technology*, 40–51.

Sproull, R. F., & Eisenberg, J. (2005). *Building an electronic records archive at the National Archives and Records Administration: Recommendations for a long-term strategy.* Washington, DC: National Academies Press.

Star, S. L., Bowker, G. C., & Neumann, L. J. (2003). Transparency beyond the individual level of scale: Convergence between information artifacts and communities of practice. In A. P. Bishop, N. A. Van House, & B. P. Buttenfield (Eds.), *Digital library use: Social practice in design and evaluation* (pp. 241–269). Cambridge, MA: MIT Press.

Steinerová, J. (2003). In search for patterns of user interaction for digital libraries. *Proceedings of the 7th European Conference on Research and Advanced Technology for Digital Libraries*, 13–23.

Sutton, S. (2004). Navigating the point of no return: Organizational implications of digitization in special collections. *portal: Libraries and the Academy, 4, 233*–243.

Tang, J. S., Avula, S. R., & Acton, S. T. (2004). DIRECT: A decentralized image retrieval system for the National STEM Digital Library. *Information Technology and Libraries, 23*, 9–15.

Tarr, B. L. (2001). Looking for numbers with meaning: Using server logs to generate Web site usage statistics at the University of Illinois Chemistry Library. *Science & Technology Libraries, 21*, 139–152.

Tennant, R. (2004). *Managing the digital library*. New York: Reed Press.

Tenopir, C. (2003). *Use and users of electronic library resources: An overview and analysis of recent research studies*. Washington, DC: Council on Library and Information Resources.

Thelwall, M. (2004). Methods for reporting on the targets of links from national systems of university Web sites. *Information Processing & Management, 40*, 125–144.

Theng, Y. L. (2002). Information therapy in digital libraries. *Proceedings of the 5th International Conference on Asian Digital Libraries*, 452–464.

Thiel, U., Brocks, H., Dirsch-Weigand, A., Everts, A., Frommholz, I., & Stein, A. (2005). Queries in context: Access to digitized historic documents in a collaboratory for the humanities. In M. Hemmje, C. Niederee, & T. Risse (Eds.), *From integrated publication and information systems to virtual information and knowledge environments* (Lecture Notes in Computer Science, 3379; pp. 117–127). Berlin: Springer.

Thong, J. Y. L., Hong, W. Y., & Tam, K. Y. (2002). Understanding user acceptance of digital libraries: What are the roles of interface characteristics, organizational context, and individual differences? *International Journal of Human–Computer Studies, 57*, 215–242.

Törmä, S., & Vakkari, P. (2004). Discipline, availability of electronic resources and the use of Finnish National Electronic Library: FinELib. *Information Research, 10*(1). Retrieved February 2, 2006, from http://informationr.net/ir/10-1/paper204.html

Trosow, S. E. (2005). The changing landscape of academic libraries and copyright policy: Interlibrary loans, electronic reserves and distance education. In M. A. Geist (Ed.), *In the public interest: The future of Canadian copyright law* (pp. 375–407). Toronto: Irwin Law.

Tuominen, K., Talja, S., & Savolainen, R. (2003). Multiperspective digital libraries: The implications of constructionism for the development of digital libraries. *Journal of the American Society for Information Science and Technology, 54*, 561–569.

Tyler, D. C., & McNeil, B. (2003). Librarians and link rot: A comparative analysis with some methodological considerations. *portal: Libraries and the Academy, 3*, 615–632.

Vaidya, B., & Shrestha, J. N. (2002). Rural digital library: Connecting rural communities in Nepal. *Proceedings of the 5th International Conference on Asian Digital Libraries*, 354–365.

Van House, N. A. (2003). Digital libraries and collaborative knowledge. In A. P. Bishop, N. A. Van House, & B. P. Buttenfield (Eds.), *Digital library use: Social practice in design and evaluation* (pp. 271–295). Cambridge, MA: MIT Press.

van Westrienen, G., & Lynch, C. (2005). Academic institutional repositories: Deployment status in 13 nations as of mid 2005. *D-Lib Magazine, 11*(9). Retrieved February 2, 2006, from www.dlib.org/dlib/september05/westrienen/09westrienen.html

Wallace, K. (2004). Digital libraries, digital containers, "library patrons," and visions for the future. *Electronic Library, 22*, 401–407.

Wang, Q., Balke, W.-T., Kießling, W., & Huhn, A. (2004). P-News: Deeply personalized news dissemination for MPEG-7 based digital libraries. *Proceedings of the 8th European Conference on Digital Libraries*, 256–268.

Wang, Y., Xing, C. X., & Zhou, L. Z. (2003). THVDM: A data model for video management in digital library. *Proceedings of the 6th International Conference on Asian Digital Libraries*, 178–192.

Weaver, M., Delcambre, L., Shapiro, L., Brewster, J., Gutema, A., & Tolle, T. (2003). A digital GeoLibrary: Integrating keywords and place names. *Proceedings of the 7th European Conference on Research and Advanced Technology for Digital Libraries*, 422–433.

Weibel, S. L. (2005). Border crossings: Reflections on a decade of metadata consensus building. *D-Lib Magazine, 11*(7/8). Retrieved February 2, 2006, from www.dlib.org/dlib/july05/weibel/07weibel.html

Weiss-Lijn, M., McDonnell, J. T., & James, L. (2002). An empirical evaluation of the interactive visualization of metadata to support document use. In K. Börner & C. Chen (Eds.), *Visual interfaces to digital libraries* (Lecture Notes in Computer Science, 2539; pp. 50–64). Berlin: Springer.

Westbrook, J. I., Gosling, A. S., & Coiera, E. (2004). Do clinicians use online evidence to support patient care? A study of 55,000 clinicians. *Journal of the American Medical Informatics Association, 11*, 113–120.

White, H. D., Lin, X., Buzydlowski, J. W., & Chen, C. M. (2004). User-controlled mapping of significant literatures. *Proceedings of the National Academy of Sciences of the United States of America, 101*, 5297–5302.

Witten, I. H. (2002). Examples of practical digital libraries: Collections built internationally using Greenstone. *Proceedings of the 5th International Conference on Asian Digital Libraries*, 67–74.

Witten, I. H. (2004). Digital libraries: Developing countries, universal access, and information for all. *Proceedings of the 7th International Conference on Asian Digital Libraries*, 35–44.

Witten, I. H., Jones, M., Bainbridge, D., Cantlon, P., & Cunningham, S. J. (2004). Digital libraries for creative communities. *Digital Creativity, 15*, 110–125.

Witten, I. H., Loots, M., Trujillo, M. F., & Bainbridge, D. (2002). The promise of digital libraries in developing countries. *Electronic Library, 20*, 7–13.

Wolfram, D., & Xie, H. I. (2002). Traditional IR for Web users: A context for general audience digital libraries. *Information Processing & Management, 38*, 627–648.

Wu, P. H.-J., Na, J.-C., & Khoo, C. S. G. (2004). NLP versus IR approaches to fuzzy name searching in digital libraries. *Proceedings of the 8th European Conference on Digital Libraries*, 145–156.

Yague, M. I., Mana, A., Lopez, J., Pimentel, E., & Troya, J. M. (2002). Secure content distribution for digital libraries. *Proceedings of the 5th International Conference on Asian Digital Libraries*, 483–494.

Yang, Y. Y., Rana, O. F., Walker, D. W., Georgousopoulos, C., Aloisio, G., & Williams, R. (2002). Agent based data management in digital libraries. *Parallel Computing, 28,* 773–792.

York, C., Wulfman, C., & Crane, G. (2003). Structure-aware query for digital libraries: Use cases and challenges for the humanities. *Proceedings of the 7th European Conference on Research and Advanced Technology for Digital Libraries*, 188–193.

Zeng, C., Zheng, X. H., Xing, C. X., & Zhou, L. Z. (2002). Personalized services for digital library. *Proceedings of the 5th International Conference on Asian Digital Libraries*, 252–253.

Zhang, X. L. (2004). Ontological service layer for digital libraries: A requirement and architectural analysis. *Proceedings of the 7th International Conference on Asian Digital Libraries*, 115–123.

Zhang, X. L., Gong, W. J., & Kawamura, Y. (2004). Customer behavior pattern discovering with Web mining. *Proceedings of the 6th Asia Pacific Web Conference*, 844–853.

Zhang, X. X. (2004). Knowledge service and digital library: A roadmap for the future. *Proceedings of the 7th International Conference on Asian Digital Libraries*, 104–114.

Zhu, Q. W., Goncalves, M. A., Shen, R., Casse, L., & Fox, E. A. (2003). Visual semantic modeling of digital libraries. *Proceedings of the 7th European Conference on Research and Advanced Technology for Digital Libraries*, 325–337.

Zia, L. L. (2004). Digital libraries for education: A progress report on the National Science Foundation's (NSF) National Science, Technology, Engineering, and Mathematics Education Digital Library (NSDL) Program. *Proceedings of the 7th International Conference on Asian Digital Libraries*, 45–50.

CHAPTER 6

Context in Information Behavior Research

Christina Courtright
Indiana University

Introduction

Studies of information needs, seeking, and use (INSU) make up approximately eight percent of research literature in library and information science (LIS) (Julien & Duggan, 2000). Over the past 20 years or so, this subfield of LIS has acknowledged a shift in focus from the study of people interacting directly with information systems to the study of the people themselves and how they seek and use information independently of specific sources and systems (Pettigrew, Fidel, & Bruce, 2001). The "user-centered paradigm" not only emphasizes the understanding of information practices from the human standpoint but also views these practices as a process that takes place within specified situations and contexts (Vakkari, Savolainen, & Dervin, 1997; Wilson & Allen, 1999).

However, conceptualizing context for the study of information needs, seeking, and use remains problematic for INSU researchers. What elements constitute a context? How are contexts understood by their participants? How and why do they change? How should information needs, seeking, and use be studied from a user-centered standpoint and in context? Although there is general agreement that context constitutes a frame of reference for information behavior (Vakkari et al., 1997), there is little agreement within the INSU literature as to how such a frame is established by or for the actor group[1] in question or how it operates with regard to information practices. In spite of a growing emphasis on the problem of context, most INSU literature fails to address it theoretically (Dervin, 1997; Johnson, 2003; Lueg, 2002).

The purpose of this review is to contribute to research on information seeking in context by examining and comparing existing models of context in this field and analyzing how context has been conceptualized in current INSU empirical research. This chapter expands and further develops previous *ARIST* reviews of INSU literature: in particular, chapters by Allen (1969), Dervin and Nilan (1986), Hewins (1990), Pettigrew et al. (2001), Solomon (2002), and Lievrouw and Farb (2003), as well as recent INSU reviews by Julien and Duggan (2000), Case (2002), and McKechnie, Baker, Greenwood, and Julien (2002).

The research selected for this review includes many of the papers published in the proceedings of five recent biennial conferences on "Information Seeking in Context,"[2] as well as other published refereed literature in library and information science that foregrounds context as an aspect of INSU research. Due to the recent growth in context-centered studies, the emphasis in this chapter is on literature published over the past 10 years; nevertheless, earlier context-centered models will be brought in for discussion as appropriate. Furthermore, in keeping with the user-centered stance that information seekers should be viewed holistically (Dervin & Nilan, 1986), this review has excluded research in which context is limited to an electronic surround (i.e., a Web site or screen interface) as well as research limited to information retrieval (i.e., the study of persons already engaged with an information system) (cf. Savolainen, 1998).

Following a brief discussion of common terms used in INSU research and in discussions of context, part two of the chapter addresses many of the larger questions involved in a conceptualization of context. This section reviews, classifies, and compares models that seek to explain context and its influence on information behavior, connecting them to empirical studies that illustrate these models and typologies. Finally, the review discusses methodological implications for research on information seeking in context.

Terminology of Information Needs, Seeking, and Use

The term "information seeking" is often used as shorthand for myriad activities. Bates (2002, p. 3) argues that information seeking must be considered "with respect to all the information that comes to a human being during a lifetime, not just in those moments when a person actively seeks information." In this view, although most information seeking research tends to stress its purposive and problem-based nature (Wilson, 1997, 1999), information seeking in the broadest sense can be active or passive, directed or undirected. Most importantly, information seeking is seen as a process, iterative and variable over time and context (e.g., Kuhlthau, 1991, 1993; Taylor, 1968).

In addition to the purposive activities typically involved in information seeking (cf. models in Ellis, 1989; Krikelas, 1983; Kuhlthau, 1988a; Wilson, 1997, 1999), Bates (1989) highlights the value and nature of both undirected and semi-directed browsing as part of a typical ensemble of information seeking activities in which the seeker does not proceed systematically through a series of rational steps but rather pursues leads as they emerge. Choo (2001) adds scanning as a semi-directed form of browsing in which the seeker is alert to informational cues but is not necessarily focused on the resolution of a specific problem. The tendency to come across, or encounter, useful information without consciously searching for it is also considered an information activity and may vary according to the seeker's knowledge, problems, state of mind, availability of a rich information environment, and other factors (Erdelez, 1996, 1997; McKenzie, 2003b; Williamson, 1998). Thus, although the role of information needs is strongly emphasized in the INSU literature (Wilson, 2000), information seeking may or may not include the identification or discovery of a need. If a need is identified, it might not always originate in the seeker but rather may be imposed on the seeker by a third party (Gross, 1999, 2001). Furthermore, in spite of the salience of research on the interactions between users and information systems, information seeking may never progress to "information searching" (Wilson, 2000), also called information retrieval. Finally, information that is sought or encountered may or may not ultimately be used (Audunson, 1999; Frohmann, 2004; Hjørland, 2000; Lievrouw, 2001; Taylor, 1991).

Wilson (2000) and others have often referred to the set of activities described above as "information behavior," which might in turn be considered a convenient shorthand for the cumbersome "information needs, seeking, and use" that underlies the INSU acronym. Yet Kari and Savolainen (2003) reject this term as too closely bound with psychological behaviorism, in which external observation of human behavior is used to draw inferences about an actor's state of mind or intentions, a pitfall Dervin and Nilan (1986) warn against in their definition of user-centered research. McKenzie (2003b) further argues that the use of the term "information behavior" removes the referenced phenomenon from the realm of the socioculturally shaped practices that, she claims, encompass all information-related activities. Instead, she proposes the term "information practices" as a more accurate way to designate the broad range of activities described in the preceding paragraph.

This review does not intend to dwell on the challenge of adequately naming the admittedly broad and diverse set of information-related activities studied in the corpus of literature on information needs, seeking, and use but will employ terms such as "information behavior," "information practices," and "information activities" interchangeably for the time being, as the review will eventually offer some epistemological and ontological observations that may contribute to future research and assist in future labeling. At the same time, the differing views on how INSU activities are to be labeled, as reflected in the preceding paragraph, do raise the question of how to define the factors that may influence these activities. Those factors that fall outside the realm of the fundamentally cognitive or psychological tend to be included, to varying degrees in both theoretical and empirical research, in the term "context" or its equivalents.

Equivalents of "Context"

Context, the problematic that inspires this chapter, is most generally considered by INSU researchers to constitute a "frame of reference" (Vakkari et al., 1997, p. 8) for information practices. Several other terms that appear to play a similar role to that of context have emerged in INSU research and studies that foreground these terms have been included in this chapter. Among these terms are "setting" (e.g., Byström, 1997; Davies & McKenzie, 2004; McKenzie, 2004; Pettigrew, 2000), "environment" (e.g., Janes & Silverstein, 2003; Lamb, King, & Kling, 2003; Rieh, 2004; Taylor, 1991), "information world" or "life-world" (e.g., Chatman, 1996; Kari & Savolainen, 2003; Lievrouw, 2001; Talja, 1997), and "information ground" (e.g., Fisher, Naumer, Durrance, Stromski, & Christiansen, 2005; Fisher, Durrance, & Hinton, 2004; Pettigrew, 1999). These alternate terms for context will be clarified through their usage as the review develops.

The term "situation" has at times been used interchangeably with context (e.g., Allen, 1997), but researchers tend to define it in contrast with context. Cool (2001, p. 8) explains: "contexts are frameworks of meaning, and situations are the dynamic environments within which interpretive processes unfold, become ratified, change, and solidify." For example, she adds, "when people interact with information resources, an interaction situation is constructed, albeit within some context" (p. 9). Sonnenwald (1999, p. 180) generally agrees: "A context is somehow larger than a situation and may consist of a variety of situations; different contexts may have different possible types of situations." For McCreadie and Rice (1999, p. 58), context is "the larger picture in which the potential user operates; the larger picture in which the information system is developed and operates, and potential information exists" and situation is "the particular set of circumstances from which a need for information arises." Thus, for the purposes of this chapter, context will include those elements that have a more lasting and predictable influence on information practices than situation; situation will be seen as a potential part of context.

INSU and the Challenge of Context

In the broad outlines of the user-centered paradigm of INSU research, marked primarily by a shift from the system-centered to the person-centered perspective, researchers are exhorted to cease attempting to determine information behavior on the basis of demographic, geographic, structural, or other similarly immutable criteria and instead to approach the problem from a fundamentally cognitive and eventually also affective perspective (Dervin & Nilan, 1986; Kuhlthau, 1988a). In order to avoid the appearance of a system-centered bias, the weaknesses of which are amply discussed by Dervin and Nilan (1986), factors external to the information actor are awarded less importance and, when addressed, tend to be stressed only insofar as they are constructed by the individual (Dervin, 1997). In effect, this tends to background the concept of context.

It remains apparent, however, that the concept of context still has a role to play in analyzing information behavior even from a user-centered perspective (Malmsjö, 1997). Now that the user-centered paradigm has achieved relatively broad acceptance among INSU researchers (Julien & Duggan, 2000), the research challenge becomes moving beyond merely cognitive and affective influences without losing sight of the actor at the center of information activity (Thomas & Nyce, 2001). The advent of the biennial "Information Seeking in Context" conferences has stimulated the growth of user-centered studies and theoretical discussions that address this challenge. Yet, with some notable exceptions that will be discussed, context as a concept appears in the research literature as largely amorphous and elusive. This section contributes by identifying and discussing the crucial issues for understanding and defining context, principally: (1) the boundaries of a context and the elements that constitute it; (2) the ontological status of context, in other words, to what extent context depends upon actors' constructions and to what extent contextual elements are external to the actor; (3) the stability of context; and (4) how context is related to information practices.

Bounding Context

From the standpoints of both the information actor and the researcher, it may be easier to identify context for information practices within a bounded organization than to define a context for everyday life activities (Fidel & Pejtersen, 2004).[3] Indeed, Savolainen (1998) notes that job-related INSU studies appear to be more focused than general studies. Johnson (2003, p. 750) explains that this is due to the greater clarity and stability of "information fields" within organizations:

> Individuals [in organizations] are embedded in a physical world that involves recurring contacts with an interpersonal network of managers and co-workers. They are also regularly exposed to the same mediated communication channels ... interpersonal communication network and information terminals. ... This physical context in organizations serves to stabilize an individual's information field and in large part determines the nature of information individuals are exposed to on a regular basis.

Thus, organizations seem to provide natural boundaries that delineate the activities taking place within them, activities that are largely purposive in nature (Aldrich, 1999). Researchers may widen or narrow the boundaries of study when examining organizational context, depending upon the plausibility of the explanations for organizational behavior obtained through selective bounding (Avgerou & Madon, 2002; Scott, 1998).

For example, the landmark model of context known as the information use environment, or IUE (Taylor, 1991), was developed to account for the information uses of professional groups such as physicians and engineers functioning in predictable workplace settings. Taylor defines the IUE as "the set of those elements that (a) affect the flow and use of information messages into, within, and out of any definable entity; and (b) determine the criteria by which the value of information messages will be judged" (p. 280). Taylor groups these elements into four categories: user demographics, primarily education and profession; how actors conceptualize the problems that would spark information practices; the constraints and opportunities that characterize actors' settings, including organizational and infrastructural attributes; and what types of problem resolutions are sought or would be acceptable. Adding Giddens's (1984) structuration theory to Taylor's framework, Rosenbaum (1993, 1996) specifies that above all, organizational rules and resources shape information practices in these environments and members' activities reinforce these rules and resources. Similar findings have been noted in several subsequent empirical studies (e.g., Allen & Wilson, 2003; Chang & Lee, 2001; Solomon, 1997b, 1999).

The "information ecologies" model developed by Nardi and O'Day (1999) is also delineated by an organizational setting, applicable not only to workplaces but also sites such as the home. Instead of Taylor's demographic criterion as a bounding element, this model stresses the diverse array of human activity that takes place within a closed setting. The home environment has been explored in related empirical studies (Davenport, Higgins, & Somerville, 1997, 2000; Green & Davenport, 1999; Rieh, 2004), with an emphasis on social interaction and the goals of information activities. For Davenport et al., the home is seen as a discrete micro-organization; Rieh, however, argues that the home is not a discrete context but instead contains contextual elements that interact with broader spheres of information activity outside the home.

Based on Scott's (1987) model of open organizational systems, Lamb et al. (2003) broaden the researcher's lens to examine the ways that extra-organizational factors such as regulations, industry-wide infrastructures, and client expectations also influence within-organization information practices. Empirical studies that highlight the shaping influence of extra-organizational factors have addressed professional populations such as police (Allen & Shoard, 2005), journalists (Attfield & Dowell, 2003), researchers (Barry, 1997; Hirsh & Dinkelacker, 2004), managers (Choo, 2001; Owens, Wilson, & Abell, 1997; Tibar, 2000), and judiciary employees (Doty & Erdelez, 2002). In a comparative study, Barnes, Spink, and Yeatts (1997) find that high-performing work teams acknowledge extra-organizational context more than do low-performing work teams. Thus, traditionally defined organizational boundaries are used by some to delineate context, but others find these must be transcended in order to understand information practices.

In other organizational models of context, the INSU research lens is narrowed to emphasize work roles. Although Leckie and Pettigrew (1997, p. 101) recommend that researchers examine "the broader working context in which professional practice is conducted," the principal contextual influences on information practices they analyze are actors' roles at work and, stemming from those roles, the tasks with which they are charged. In this model, tasks give rise to information needs and the strategies deployed to meet those needs vary according to "factors such as the corporate culture, individual habits, availability of information systems and sources, commitment to professional development etc." (p. 101). This emphasis on role is supported by Audunson (1999) in his appeal to ground INSU research in institutional theory. He argues that roles contain sets of identifiable norms that govern likely information practices and that variability in information-seeking norms across similar roles can be attributed to the "strength of rules and the cohesion and degree of social control from a centre" (p. 78). Similarly, the Cognitive Work Analysis framework by Fidel and Pejtersen (2004) foregrounds roles, tasks, and the norms that govern them; norms function as both constraints and enablers for information actions.

In a narrower view, Byström's empirical research (Byström, 1997, 2000; Byström & Järvelin, 1995) concludes that actor-perceived task complexity is the principal determinant of information sources and the number of sources consulted. Other empirical studies that bound context most closely to task involve professionals (Algon, 1997; Kuhlthau, 1996, 1997) and students (Hultgren & Limberg, 2003; Limberg, 1997, 1999).

Outside an organizational setting, contexts may be more difficult to bound (see Johnson, 2003). However, several conceptual models of context for non-organizational settings, largely grounded in sociological theories, reveal boundaries that resemble those of organizations. For example, Fisher (née Pettigrew) (Fisher et al., 2005; Fisher, Durrance, et al., 2004; Fisher, Marcoux, Miller, Sánchez, & Cunningham, 2004; Pettigrew, 1999) has developed a contextual model called an "information ground," an "environment temporarily created when people come together for a singular purpose but from whose behavior emerges a social atmosphere that fosters the spontaneous and serendipitous sharing of information" (Pettigrew, 1999, p. 811). Examples of information grounds identified through research include library classes, health clinics, places of worship, workplaces, and hair salons. An information ground is thus not only a physical setting but also is overlaid with certain social configurations, including specified actors and norms. Research on information grounds emphasizes the quality and quantity of information obtained there through social interaction (Fisher et al., 2005), with particular attention given to the informational benefits of weak social ties (Granovetter, 1973, 1983).

Another model of context involving non-professional groups is known as "small-world theory" (Chatman, 2000, p. 3) or "life in the round" (Chatman, 1999, p. 207). Chatman (1987, 1991, 1992, 1996) developed her model through the study of information practices among vulnerable populations such as low-income workers, elderly women in assisted living environments, and prisoners. The groups she studied were usually geographically bounded, although others have extended her analysis to clearly bounded groups whose members interrelate through distance connections as well (Burnett, Besant, & Chatman, 2001). The small-world concept, grounded in sociological theories (Chatman, 1996, 2000), posits that these groups live in a "small world" governed by a worldview[4] and will tend to behave within its norms and expectations until or unless something critical needs to be pursued outside of it (Chatman, 2000). Characteristics of small-world information practices are deeply social in nature: shared perceptions of insiders and outsiders, social norms that force private behaviors into public scrutiny, commonly held assumptions, and a reluctance to cross boundaries to seek information. Small worlds tend to constrain more than enable information practices: "People will not search for information if there is no need to do so. If members of a social world choose to ignore information, it is because their world is working without it" (Chatman, 2000, p. 10). Thus, as in the organizational context models previously reviewed, members of the same social world appear to carry out roles and are governed by norms in their information practices. Many characteristics of this model are reflected, for example, in empirical studies of immigrant communities (Jeong, 2004; Sligo & Jameson, 2000).

A similar type of bounding operates in Savolainen's (1995) model for everyday-life information seeking in which the sociological concept of "habitus" (Bourdieu, 1990; Bourdieu & Wacquant, 1992), the manner in which one's "way of life" is organized, is used as a proxy for context. Habitus "renders a general direction to choices made in everyday life by indicating which choices are natural or desirable in relation to one's social class or cultural group" (Savolainen, 1995, p. 262). Thus, way of life is seen as a general "order of things" that is "determined on both objective and subjective grounds" (p. 262). At the same time, "way of life" is complemented by the psychological concept of "mastery of life," defined along cognitive-affective and optimistic-pessimistic dimensions (p. 265).

In these three models of everyday-life information practices, contextual boundaries are set by the researcher and explanations for these practices are sought within those boundaries. Likewise, some researchers bound context through the concept of nested layers with the actor at the center. Examples of nested contexts are found in models of everyday-life information seeking derived from empirical study, such as Williamson (1998). In this case the information actor is ringed by intimate personal networks, then wider personal networks, the mass media, institutional sources, and finally an outer ring of context that is characterized by "personal characteristics, socio-economic circumstances, values, lifestyles and physical environments" (p. 35). Other models of nested contexts appear in the work of Kari and Savolainen (2003) Sonnenwald (1999), and in an early version of Wilson's (1981) model of person-in-context.

In contrast, Lievrouw's (2001) conceptual model views the boundaries of context as evolving dynamically through the practices of information actors. With Taylor's information use environment as a point of departure, she posits a model of context, or information environment, applicable to everyday-life information practices. She argues, however, that information environments are not necessarily limited to professions or similar traits, nor to documentary information sources and purposive information seeking. In Lievrouw's model, the information environment is conceptualized from the standpoint of the information actor or group of actors. Context takes shape, on one hand, through institutional practices of generating information, organizing it and governing its distribution and on the other hand, through social practices in which individuals share and seek information; the two parts of the environment evolve over time, interact, and shape each other. Bates (2002) also notes that actors in fact arrange their social and physical environments so that they can provide needed information.

Thus, as Nardi and O'Day (1999) report, this type of information environment is configured through human activity but is particularly suited to analysis of settings outside of a particular organizational configuration. The Lievrouw model posits that an information actor could conceivably inhabit several discrete or overlapping information environments depending upon activities and imperatives (Lievrouw & Farb, 2003). The concept of multiple and overlapping contexts is echoed in other INSU models (Johnson, 2003; Lamb & Kling, 2003; Solomon, 1999; Sonnenwald, 1999; Sonnenwald & Lievrouw, 1997) as well as in sociological theory (Friedland & Alford, 1991; Pescosolido & Rubin, 2000; Sewell, 1992; Weber, 2001) and renders more complex the research challenge of identifying contextual boundaries. At the same time, the model's dynamic, multilayered approach appears well suited to addressing the complexity of everyday-life information practices.

Contextual Factors that Shape Information Practices

Both empirical studies and theoretical models that examine the relationships among contextual elements and information activities often foreground one or two chief shaping factors that account for variability in such activities. Similarities can be found in how these factors are invoked in both organizational and everyday-life settings (see Table 6.1). For example, the concept of rules and resources, which encompasses both organizational norms and the affordances of the local setting, is explained at length by Rosenbaum (1993, 1996) and appears in a number of other studies involving workplace settings. In everyday-life information practices, rules and resources may take the form of local institutional ensembles, such as libraries, schools, and/or public agencies, whose contextual influences vary according to the perceived accessibility and trustworthiness of institutions as information suppliers and their perceived relevance to a given information need. Organizational culture is invoked explicitly as a contextual shaping factor in workplace settings. In everyday life, cultural influences are more diverse and diffuse although the concept is often mentioned as a contextual shaping factor with reference to a particular population group.

Table 6.1 Studies of rules, resources, and culture

Factors	Workplace settings	Everyday life settings
Rules and resources	Attfield & Dowell, 2003 Audunson, 1999 Chang & Lee, 2001 Eskola, 2005 Johnson, 2003 Rosenbaum, 1993, 1996 Seldén, 2001 Solomon, 1997b Taylor, 1991	Davenport et al., 1997 Green & Davenport, 1999 Harris & Dewdney, 1994 Hjørland, 2000 Johnson, 2003 Lievrouw, 2001 Lievrouw & Farb, 2003 Williamson, 1998 Williamson, Schauder, & Bow, 2000
Culture	Allen & Shoard, 2005 Allen & Wilson, 2003 Bruce et al., 2003 Fabritius, 1999 Leckie & Pettigrew, 1997 Loughridge, 1997 Mackenzie, 2003 Mutch, 2000 Owens et al., 1997 Seldén, 2001 Sundin, 2002 Widén-Wulff, 2003	Fisher, Marcoux et al., 2004 Lievrouw, 2001 Meyer, 2003 Pivec, 1998 Savolainen, 1995 Sligo & Jameson, 2000

Many empirical studies find that actors rely on interpersonal information sources in the form of both close and diffuse social networks and frequently prefer these over formal sources; however, the interpersonal or social factor is often viewed instrumentally rather than as part of context (e.g., Keane, 1999; Sprague, 1994; Wilkins & Leckie, 1997; Zach, 2005). Other researchers problematize social networks as an aspect of context that shapes information practices variably, both in workplace and everyday-life settings (see Table 6.2). This second approach often finds that social networks are not equally accessible and beneficial to all actors and that the information that circulates within social networks is not always reliable, useful, or used. Actors may draw variably upon their social networks depending on the nature of the information activity. The concept of social capital (Bourdieu, 1986) is also defined as a contextual influence, according to which access to resources, including informational resources, is shaped by the quality of an actor's social relationships. Even when social networks are not drawn upon actively for information practices, actors are often mindful of social norms and social authority in choosing sources and evaluating their credibility. Finally, some researchers note that the information environments they examine are inherently collaborative and thus the focus of these studies is on the variability of information exchange in a necessarily interpersonal context.

Table 6.2 Social factors in context

Factors	Workplace settings	Everyday life settings
Social networks or social capital	Foster, 2004 Given, 2002 Haythornthwaite & Wellman, 1998 Huotari & Chatman, 2001 Mackenzie, 2005 Seldén, 2001 Widén-Wulff, 2003	Chatman, 2000 Courtright, 2005 Hersberger, 2001 C. A. Johnson, 2004 Lievrouw, 2001 Meyer, 2003 Pettigrew, 1999 Sligo & Jameson, 2000
Social norms or social authority	Olsson, 1999 Solomon, 1997b Sundin, 2002	Chatman, 1999 Fisher, Marcoux et al., 2004 McKenzie, 2003a Savolainen, 1999 Sligo & Jameson, 2000
Collaborative requirement in workplace	Prekop, 2002 Solomon, 1997b Sonnenwald & Lievrouw, 1997 Sonnenwald & Pierce, 2000 Talja, 2002	

Tasks are seen as primary contextual shaping influences in numerous studies involving workplace settings, particularly in terms of levels of complexity and uncertainty that explain variability in types of information activities (see Table 6.3). Similarly, "situation" and "problem" figure prominently as contextual shaping elements in research that focuses on non-workplace life. The way in which "task" is operationalized in work-centered models is not unlike the concept of situation or problem as used in other INSU literature (Julien & Michels, 2004). The purposive nature of organizations is the most likely explanation for the use of the term "task" over "situation" but in both tasks and situations

Table 6.3 Tasks, problems, and situations

Factors	Workplace settings	Everyday life settings
Task or problem situation	Algon, 1997 D. Allen & Wilson, 2003 Byström & Järvelin, 1995 Byström, 1997 Chang & Lee, 2001 Fidel & Pejtersen, 2004 Gorman, 1999 Hertzum, 2000 Järvelin & Ingwersen, 2004 Kuhlthau, 1996, 1997 Leckie & Pettigrew, 1997 Pharo, 2004 Solomon, 1997b Zach, 2005	Dervin, 1997 Harris & Dewdney, 1994 Hersberger, 2001 Ikoja-Odongo & Ocholla, 2003 J. D. Johnson, 2003 Julien & Michels, 2004 Pettigrew, 1999 Rieh, 2004 Sonnenwald, 1999

the actor is confronted with a challenge that has a particular configuration and must draw upon internal and external resources to resolve it.

Many studies attribute significant variability in information practices to differences in professional domains or work roles (see Table 6.4). Others focus on the nature of human activity and interaction as the primary shaping factor (Davies & McKenzie, 2004; Keane, 1999; Malmsjö, 1997; Nardi & O'Day, 1999; Solomon, 1997a; Thivant, 2003). The two approaches are related, but the latter foregrounds actors' autonomy whereas the former stresses the prevalence of norms or rules.

Table 6.4   Contextual shaping by work domain versus human activity

Work domain or role	Human activity
Audunson, 1999	E. Davies & McKenzie, 2004
Barry, 1997	Nardi & O'Day, 1999
Bruce et al., 2003	Keane, 1999
Fidel & Pejtersen, 2004	Solomon, 1997b
Kari & Savolainen, 2003	Thivant, 2003
Leckie & Pettigrew, 1997	
Olsson, 1999	
Sonnenwald & Lievrouw, 1997	
Talja, 2003	
Talja, Savolainen, & Maula, 2004	
Taylor, 1991	
Tibar, 2000	
Törmä & Vakkari, 2004	

The Special Role of IT

Although much of INSU research portrays information technologies (IT) instrumentally as a choice actors make, some researchers posit IT as a shaping part of context (Järvelin & Ingwersen, 2004). In the latter view, a wide range of technologies is intimately and inextricably involved in everyday information practices and, to a certain extent, mediates and shapes not only the type, volume, and presentation of available information but also actors' expectations of the kinds of information that they can, should, or will seek (Allen & Shoard, 2005; Johnson, Donohue, Atkin, & Johnson, 1995; Leckie, Pettigrew, & Sylvain, 1996; Marchionini, 1995). Marchionini argues that the habit of IT use and the affordances of the technologies themselves shape individual actors' expectations as they come to rely on the speed, convenience, storage capabilities, and hypertext links that connect one resource to another. For example, the information practices of both users and producers of national statistics evolved with IT development over time (Marchionini, 2002). A longitudinal study of IT use by academics finds changes in information practices among individuals (information seeking) as well as within the professional domain (scholarly communication and collaboration) as users are increasingly offered electronic searching and communication tools (Barry, 1997). At the same time, the increasing availability of IT may contribute to actors' perceptions of information complexity and overload (Allen & Wilson, 2003). Outside the workplace, society-wide changes in IT use affect information practices at the individual or household level (Rieh, 2004) and technology practices within the household likewise reshape its internal social dynamics (Green & Davenport, 1999). Similarly, social groups form and evolve around information practices in non-work public spaces such as libraries and cybercafés (Pivec, 1998; Sandvig, 2003).

Not only does IT influence information practices, but social informatics research shows in turn that IT adoption itself varies depending upon other contextual elements such as organizational and institutional rules and resources, power differentials, resource dependencies, actor expectations and goals, and influences external to a given bounded context (Kling, McKim, & King, 2003; Lamb et al., 2003; Orlikowski & Gash, 1994). Although the design and implementation of information technologies are intended to prescribe the ways in which they are used, such contextual factors interact to engender alternate uses that may reshape not only the technologies but also the information practices themselves. For Lievrouw (2001, p. 16), IT forms an integral part of information contexts while also rendering them more complex, as technologies become either "bridges or barriers within and between the institutional and personal/relational aspects." In other words, IT plays a dual role in context, as it is both a shaper of information practices and the object of shaping by other contextual factors and by users themselves.

Although most empirical INSU studies do not combine multiple shaping factors or analyze interaction effects among two or more shaping variables (Törmä & Vakkari, 2004), many theoretical models, based on empirical study, do in fact combine a rich ensemble of shaping elements from among the factors listed throughout this section (Bates, 2002; Chang & Lee, 2001; Fidel & Pejtersen, 2004; Järvelin & Ingwersen, 2004; Kari & Savolainen, 2003; Lamb et al., 2003; Leckie & Pettigrew, 1997; Lievrouw, 2001; Reneker, Jacobson, & Spink, 2001; Rosenbaum, 1993; Sonnenwald, 1999; Taylor, 1991; Williamson, 1998; Wilson, 1997). However, how contextual shaping factors influence information activities depends in great measure on how the researcher understands the status of context in relation to the information actor, which will be discussed in the next section.

The Ontological Status of Context

Efforts to address the status of context theoretically have been many, both in terms of modeling and the creation of typologies. To illustrate the latter, both Dervin (1997) and Johnson (2003) employ a three-tiered categorization of context as used in INSU research. Dervin argues that for many, "context has the potential of being virtually anything that is not defined as the phenomenon of interest … a kind of container in which the phenomenon resides." A second group grapples with the dilemma of choosing which of "an inexhaustible list of factors" will be included in context. For a third set, context is "the carrier of meaning ... an inextricable surround without which any possible understanding of human behavior becomes impossible" (Dervin, 1997, pp. 14–15). Johnson classifies context models in LIS in a similar fashion. Beyond these three typologies, there has also been recent discussion in the literature of context as social, relational, and dynamic. This section will thus address the evolution of the status of context throughout recent INSU research.

Context as "Container"

The ontological implication of the first and second general categories above, which will together be called the "context-as-container" model,[5] is that elements of context exist objectively around an actor and could therefore be enumerated by a researcher who has observed or queried the actor's life. In this model, context is used as a "setting" whose influences on information activities are assumed. These settings are often described in detail as part of the introduction to the research paper but the research findings are not discussed in relation to context; instead, context serves as a backdrop to the findings and its relationship to the actor is implied rather than stated or problematized. Thus the information behavior is essentially described in terms of its principal features yet these features are not analyzed with relation to context.

Examples of empirical studies in which information contexts function as backdrops or settings can be found in workplaces, primarily those of professional or managerial-level employees (Byström, 1997; Fulton, 2000; Gorman, 1999; Lomax, Lowe, Logan, & Detlefse, 1999; Loughridge, 1997; Wilkins & Leckie, 1997), public libraries (Coles, 1999; Gross, 2001), school library media centers (Cooper, 2002; Enochsson, 2001; Gross, 2001), academic libraries and archives (Duff & Johnson, 2002), educational centers (Brown, 2002; Erdelez, 1997; Heinstrom, 2005), and geographically bounded communities (Rolinson, 1998; Spink, Bray, Jaeckel, & Sidberry, 1999). It is noteworthy that in several studies, "everyday life" is given as the context but without a description or analysis of what constitutes actors' everyday lives (Ellen, 2003; Hektor, 2003; Palsdottir, 2003).

This view of context, sometimes labeled "positivist" (Dourish, 2004) or "objectivist" (Talja, Keso, & Pietilainen, 1999), presents contexts as a set of stable, delineated entities that can be conceptualized independently of the activities of their participants. In practice,

> context in INS studies usually refers to any factors or variables that are seen to affect individuals' information-seeking behavior: socio-economic conditions, work roles, tasks, problem situations, communities and organizations with their structures and cultures, etc. ... Context refers to objective reality. (Talja et al., 1999, pp. 752–753)

Thus, if context is merely a container or backdrop for information practices, then research cannot explain variability among actors in the same or similar settings. Actors will either carry out the actions most likely to respond to one or more nominally verifiable elements of their context, or will act independently of context. The first alternative seems to conflict with the cognitive shift in user-centered research, which privileges the meanings that the actor confers upon the world in enacting information practices. The second alternative fails to shed light on how context helps explain variability in information practices. In order for the concept of context to play a significant role in INSU studies, contextual elements must be explicitly linked to particular information practices and comparisons among actors and contexts must be used to explain variability and thereby build more robust theories of information seeking in context.

Context as Constructed Meaning: The Person in Context

In contrast to the "context-as-container" approach is a stance that examines context from the point of view of the information actor; that is to say, information activities are reported in relation to contextual variables and influences, largely as perceived and constructed by the information actor. Several person-in-context models are cited in the literature. Principal among these is Wilson (1981), whose model presents context as a set of concentric layers, beginning with a person's physiological, affective, and cognitive needs and progressing through his or her various roles (work and leisure) and environments (socio-cultural, politico-economic, and physical). Information needs and information-seeking actions take place in relation to these factors, which should be studied qualitatively in order to understand the weight of different factors at different moments. Wilson later expands this model to analyze variability among information-seeking actions that ensue once the context has been adequately examined (Wilson, 1997). Information actions are triggered or inhibited by factors such as stress and coping and may involve a series of intervening variables arising from personal, interpersonal, environmental, situational, and source-related factors. Information practices take place in relation to a person's perceptions of risks and rewards as well as past experiences and perceptions of self-efficacy. The model incorporates a feedback loop to account for learning over time. Niedźwiedzka (2003) argues that what Wilson refers to as "intervening variables" are more properly conceptualized as part of context itself and that activating mechanisms are not purely individual in nature but may also arise from the needs of others, as in the "imposed query" model (Gross, 1999, 2001).

Sonnenwald's (1999) model of "information horizons" also places the individual at the center of a nested set of factors including social networks, situations, and contexts. Each of these factors shapes, constrains, and enables information activities variably; together they constitute an overall information world for the actor, who reflects on available resources and constraints while attempting to resolve a need or requirement. Information activities may recursively influence these contextual factors and thereby enhance the actor's information horizon, gradually constructing for the actor a "densely-populated solution space" (p. 187).

Marchionini (1995) has developed a person-in-context model that awards a stronger role to IT-enabled change, known as the "personal information infrastructure" (PII). The PII, which is framed as a context for individual information behavior, is made up of mental models, general cognitive skills, metacognitive resources, material resources, and attitudes toward information seeking and knowledge acquisition. The particular affordances of interactive information technologies and the long-term effects of their use are discussed in order to explain the prominent role of IT in this model. The model is dynamic in that the individual adapts to and applies experience as it is acquired while shaping and being shaped by outside resources as they are available or added or subtracted. In this model, information seeking occurs at the intersection of the seeker, task, system, subject domain, setting, and search outcomes, of which the last initiates a feedback loop that infuses the model with its dynamism.

Other person-in-context models are found in Williamson's (1997, 1998) presentation of the actor's information world, conceptualized as concentric circles of influence as perceived by the individual; actor-centered information seeking by Järvelin and Ingwersen (2004), which places the actor at the center, interacting with socio-cultural context on one hand, and with information objects and information systems on the other; and nested levels of context or "life-world" in Kari and Savolainen (2003, p. 159), in which the life-world is the "perceived reality in which his activities take place." For Dervin and Clark (1993), constraining and enabling structures outside the individual exist only insofar as they are constructed by actors and thus can be determined by the researcher only through the actor's perceptions.

In general, following Audunson's (1999) critique, person-in-context models largely represent individuals' linear trajectories through time and space, with external and internal factors stepping in to influence the individuals as they proceed. An underlying assumption of this type of study is that an understanding of the information needs and activities of the group or organization can be built on an accumulation of studies of individuals (e.g., Reneker et al., 2001). However, notes Frohmann (2004), the individual-constructivist stance makes generalizations implausible; instead, there lies a danger of solipsism, which has not been convincingly addressed within the traditional user-centered paradigm (*pace* Dervin, 2000; Savolainen, 1993). In addition, person-in-context models do not adequately account for the complexity, variability, and mutual interactions of contextual factors previously mentioned, such as social networks, information technologies, and organizational practices.

Socially Constructed Context: The Social Actor

Critics of the person-in-context stance argue that actors are social beings who construct information through social interaction and not only inside their heads (Audunson, 1999; Bates, 2002; Frohmann, 2004; Lievrouw, 2001; Talja, 1997; Talja et al., 1999; Tuominen, 1997; Tuominen & Savolainen, 1997). In what they term a "social-epistemological view" (Talja, Tuominen, & Savolainen, 2005, p. 88), the individual can be conceptualized as a social actor (Lamb & Kling, 2003) and knowledge as inherently social (Talja, 1997). Although, as has been mentioned, many scholars have emphasized the importance of social interaction in information practices (Julien, 1999), the concept of social actors goes beyond specific instances of social interaction. Olsson (1999, p. 140) notes that, although person-in-context models "consider the role of social forces on information behaviour, they treat them as factors which affect the individual information user (which remains the unit of analysis)." An alternate view is that information activities take place within an explicit or implicit social community whose knowledge, characteristics, expectations, and norms are internalized, to varying degrees, within the individual (Alexandersson & Limberg, 2003; Chatman, 1996, 1999, 2000; Davenport et al., 1997; Given, 2002; McKenzie, 2003b; Rosenbaum, 1993; Savolainen, 1995; Solomon, 1997b; Sundin, 2002).

Some argue, moreover, that because actors' language reveals their social constructions of reality, the best way to understand context for INSU research is to analyze the discourse of information actors, rather than simply to observe their behaviors and record their views (Given, 2002; McKenzie, 2002, 2003b, 2004; Olsson, 1999; Sundin, 2002; Talja, 1997; Talja et al., 2005; Tuominen & Savolainen, 1997).

Relational Context: Embeddedness

Related to the concept of "social actor" is the embeddedness of actors in context that includes institutional and technological factors as well (Bates, 2002; Lamb & Kling, 2003; Talja et al., 2005) and the embeddedness of information activities in actors' broader contexts (Frohmann, 2004; Vakkari, 1997). Rieh (2004, p. 751) argues that context cannot be separated from its participants, "rather, it should be understood as contextual entities interplaying with other social, cultural, situational, and individual factors that variously constrain and motivate information seeking." But this embeddedness does not imply stasis; instead, according to Dourish (2004, p. 6), "context isn't something that describes a setting; it's something that people do." Dourish (2001) posits context as relational, as produced by the interactions among people and between people and nonhuman elements. Several other models of INSU context, particularly those that see context as an ensemble of complexly interacting and dynamic factors, support this relational view (Dixon & Banwell, 1999; Introna, 1999; Lievrouw, 2001; Nardi & O'Day, 1999; Rosenbaum, 1993, 1996).

Talja et al. (1999) extend the relational standpoint to the researcher, arguing that context is also created by the latter at the intersection between actors' constructions of context-as-meaning and the researchers' examination of the actors' lives; "context is the site where a phenomenon is constituted as an object to us [the researchers]" (p. 754); context when viewed interpretively is constituted "at the crossroads between researchers and data" (p. 755). Thus, the researcher also contributes to the creation of context during research (Burawoy, 2003).

Changing Context

A relational view of context, particularly when based on human activity, implies a concept of change. Research studies that conceptualize context as a backdrop or container tend to imply contextual stability. However, other studies and models find that context is a dynamic construct and that information actors are not only shaped by context but also shape it in turn. For example, Rosenbaum's (1993, 1996) enhancement of the Information Use Environment (Taylor, 1991) adds a dynamic dimension to Taylor's context, in that context not only shapes action but is also shaped by it. The concept of "information ecologies" (Nardi & O'Day, 1999) posits an even more dynamic concept of organizational INSU context, one that foregrounds human activity more than structures or resources. Its human and non-human components are tightly interwoven, highly interdependent, and constantly evolving. The relationships among these components and information practices are explored through empirical examples although the main focus is on the use and adaptation of technologies rather than on information seeking as such. Several context-centered theoretical models and empirical studies also stipulate change as a basic characteristic and conceptualize change as a form of mutual shaping between actors and their contexts (Barry, 1997; Chang & Lee, 2001; Courtright, 2005; Foster, 2004, 2005; Hirsh & Dinkelacker, 2004; Järvelin & Ingwersen, 2004; Johnson, 2003; Kari & Savolainen, 2003; Lamb et al., 2003; Lamb & Kling, 2003; Lievrouw, 2001; Solomon, 1997b; Sonnenwald, 1999).

Conclusions and Future Directions

This brief examination of the general corpus of research on information needs, seeking, and use in context reveals a number of general tendencies. In the first place, the paradigm shift from a system-centered to user-centered stance on the part of the researcher has led to a growing body of research that takes as its point of departure the information actor. Yet the user-centered paradigm faces the challenge of how to conceptualize the shaping influences of context without regressing to a system-centered view, in which information actions are seen as predictable according to set environmental variables. The biennial Information Seeking in Context conferences have sought to address that challenge by centering on the problem of context in studies of information practices. These and related efforts have generated a wide range of contextual models, both explicit and implied, without yet arriving at a theoretical paradigm that might represent the next step forward from the classic "user-centered" stance. Much of the INSU research continues to equate context with a describable physical setting and to identify one or more contextual variables that are seen as causally or tangentially linked to actors' information practices. However, several of the models and theoretical trends discussed in this review embrace the complexity of context and the actor, in that they posit actors as embedded in complex, multiple, overlapping, and dynamic contexts, elements of which include sociality, culture, institutional rules and resources, technological change, and power relations, and that are in turn shaped by information actors (e.g., Järvelin & Ingwersen, 2004; Lamb et al., 2003; Lamb & Kling, 2003; Lievrouw, 2001; Nardi & O'Day, 1999; Talja, 1997; Talja et al., 1999).

These research trends have implications for methodology that should be addressed, particularly because of the prevalence of user-centered INSU research that introduces context as a simple setting in which information activities take place, then concludes at the end that more needs to be known about the role of context in explaining the information activities that are documented in the study (e.g., Gross, Dresang, & Holt, 2004). Perhaps researchers set out to study a given population and draw conclusions about its information practices but find that the study produces descriptions without explanations. Studies that fail to examine adequately both actors and context, or actors-in-context, may also lack an adequate theory of context. At the same time, the mix of methods implicated in the study of information practices within the complex, dynamic view of context favored in this review may also exceed the practical reach of many researchers. Nevertheless, it is worth addressing some of these methodological implications.

If context is conceptualized as dynamic and relational, then studies of information actors can foreground context without losing sight of the actor at the center of research interest. Explanations for actors' information strategies and tactics, and for source and system choices and rejections, can be explored and tested through iterative study using multiple methods, as many have advocated (Barry, 1995; Fabritius, 1999; Fisher, Durrance, et al., 2004; Savolainen, 1998; Seldén, 2001). Indeed, the use of multiple methods in INSU research seems to have increased over time (McKechnie et al., 2002). A focus on actors' actual activities and material practices, rather than specifically their information needs and uses, affords a richer view of actors-in-context as well (Frohmann, 2004), as documents and other artifacts would be studied along with organizational and/or social relations, rules, and resources (e.g., Davies & McKenzie, 2004; Ikoja-Odongo & Ocholla, 2003; Keane, 1999; Nardi & O'Day, 1999).

Among the multiple methods required to study actors-in-context, ethnographic observation and interviewing are both key to uncovering the complexity involved (Bates, 1999; Forsythe, 1998; Thomas & Nyce, 2001). The interpretive stance in research methodology recognizes that researchers contribute to actors' versions of their information worlds rather than simply documenting these transparently (Denzin, 2001; Holstein & Gubrium, 1995; Talja et al., 1999). As Thomas and Nyce (2001, pp. 112–113) note:

> Although qualitative methods have been defined as revealing the user's point of view, reliance on self report techniques limits the researchers to meanings of which the observed is aware. Masked or left unexplored are the theoretical underpinnings and the assumptions of the researcher as well as the sorts of tacit knowledge and taken for granted understandings that also constitute the context of the observed. ... Not only does ethnography provide researchers incisive ways to explore the subjective experience of information seekers, it also permits the consideration of linkages between users and information institutions, such as libraries, and the social and cultural contexts that define what "user" and "institution" mean.

Weber (2001, p. 475) argues for "multi-integrative ethnography" in order to embrace the complexity and overlapping worlds that constitute actors-in-context. For Weber, context is a combination of "setting, interactions, and things": "the universe of reference and socialization in which interactions take on meaning for their participants"; it is "not reduced to the space of physical co-presence of several individuals [but] may lie at the intersection of several settings" (p. 485) and includes "things and places" (p. 486). In this view, consistent with the user-centered approach, the researcher would begin with the actor and try through observation and questioning to map out his/her context but also follow the links across multiple social settings in order to paint a complex portrait of actor-in-context. Researchers' independent investigations of contextual factors may test their initial assumptions about contextual boundaries and may stimulate new questions to ask information actors. In addition, such inquiry may be useful in investigating variations encountered (e.g., use or non-use of particular resources or tactics).

Comparisons among nominally similar groups of actors in different settings, or of varied groups in the same nominal setting, can contribute to explanations of variability (Durkheim, 1901/1982). In INSU research, few scholars have adopted or even called for this approach (Savolainen, 1998). Notable examples of comparative studies that provide useful explanatory insights into contextual shaping factors are mostly found in workplace settings (Barnes et al., 1997; Bruce, Dumais, Fidel, Grudin, Pejtersen, & Poltrock, 2003; Lamb et al., 2003; Leckie et al., 1996; Mutch, 2000; Talja, Savolainen, & Maula, 2004; Taylor, 1991). Lievrouw and Farb (2003) advocate broadening the range of target groups addressed so that everyday-life information seeking in context is better understood. But without a theoretical concept of actors-in-context, the mere amplification of the range of study populations will simply lead to a research corpus that describes all manner of "user groups" without arriving at plausible explanations for differences among them, other than the usual system-centered variables such as education, demographics, and the like.

Durkheim (1901/1982, p. 155) argues that the purpose of comparative research is

> not to compare isolated variations, but series of variations, systematically constituted, whose terms are correlated with each other in as continuous a gradation as possible and which moreover cover an adequate range … [also] the evolution which the variations represent must be sufficiently prolonged in length for the trend to be unquestionably apparent.

Thus, following the example of research mentioned above that views context as dynamic, it is of the utmost importance to conduct longitudinal studies of actors-in-context (Savolainen, 1998), as it remains relatively scarce (Johnson, 2003). Those INSU studies that examine change over time tend to document primarily the evolution of actors only (e.g., Banwell, Gannon-Leary, & Jackson, 2002; Cothey, 2002; Klobas & Clyde, 2000; Kuhlthau, 1988b, 1999; Nicholas, Huntington, & Williams, 2003; Vakkari & Pennanen, 2001; Vakkari & Serola, 2002; Wang, 1997; Wang & Soergel, 1999; Wilson, Ford, Ellis, Foster, & Spink, 2002; Wyatt, Henwood, Hart, & Smith, 2005). The few INSU studies that foreground context and change have taken place within organizational settings (Barry, 1997; Chang & Lee, 2001; Davies, 1998; Marchionini, 2002; Solomon, 1997b), although Fisher et al. (2005) are planning to examine change over time in information grounds.

In sum, by combining multiple methods in an iterative design, particularly alternating ethnographic observation and study of artifacts with questioning of information actors, a relational and dynamic view of actors-in-context might emerge. Longitudinal and comparative research can add depth and breadth to this approach and, one might hope, begin to systematize the study of actors-in-context toward the construction of a richer corpus of theoretical and empirical research in this field.

Acknowledgments

The author wishes to thank the editors of *ARIST* for their encouragement and forbearance, Professor Alice Robbin for her assistance in shaping the theoretical concepts involved in this review, and the three anonymous reviewers for their careful reading of the draft text and detailed, helpful comments.

Endnotes

1. The term "actor" will generally be preferred to "user" to stress the active nature of information seeking and the need to separate information behavior analytically from the use of any specific resource or system (cf. Fidel & Pejtersen, 2004; Hjørland, 2000; Järvelin & Ingwersen, 2004; Kari & Savolainen, 2003; Lamb & Kling, 2003; Thivant, 2003).

2. Published in two edited volumes (Vakkari et al., 1997; Wilson & Allen, 1999) and in the journals *The New Review of Information Behaviour Research* (vols. 1–4) and *Information Research* (vol. 10).

3. The term "everyday life information seeking," or ELIS, was coined by Savolainen (1995), although the large-scale study of non-work information practices dates back to at least 1973 (Warner, Murray, & Palmour, 1973).

4. Chatman (1999) defines worldview as "a collective set of beliefs held by members who live within a small world. It is a mental picture or a cognitive map that interprets the world" (p. 213); it is also a frame of reference that "accepts certain ways in which to speak, behave, and accept or reject information" (p. 211).

5. What distinguishes the two is chiefly the selectivity in the choice of which contextual elements to include in the analysis.

References

Aldrich, H. E. (1999). *Organizations evolving*. London: Sage.

Alexandersson, M., & Limberg, L. (2003). Constructing meaning through information artefacts. *New Review of Information Behaviour Research*, 4, 17–30.

Algon, J. (1997). Classification of tasks, steps, and information-related behaviors of individuals on project teams. *Proceedings of an International Conference on Research in Information Needs, Seeking and Use in Different Contexts*, 205–221.

Allen, B. (1997). Information needs: A person-in-situation approach. *Proceedings of an International Conference on Research in Information Needs, Seeking and Use in Different Contexts*, 111–122.

Allen, D., & Wilson, T. D. (2003). Information overload: Context and causes. *New Review of Information Behaviour Research*, 4, 31–44.

Allen, D. K., & Shoard, M. (2005). Spreading the load: Mobile information and communications technologies and their effect on information overload. *Information Research*, 10(2). Retrieved January 24, 2005, from http://informationr.net/ir/10-2/paper227.html

Allen, T. J. (1969). Information needs and uses. *Annual Review of Information Science and Technology*, 4, 3–29.

Attfield, S., & Dowell, J. (2003). Information seeking and use by newspaper journalists. *Journal of Documentation*, 59, 187–204.

Audunson, R. (1999). Can institutional theory contribute to our understanding of information seeking behaviour? *Proceedings of the Second International Conference on Research in Information Needs, Seeking and Use in Different Contexts*, 67–81.

Avgerou, C., & Madon, S. (2002). *Framing IS studies* (Working Paper Series No. 112). London: Department of Information Systems, London School of Economics.

Banwell, L., Gannon-Leary, P., & Jackson, M. S. (2002). *JUBILEE JISC user behaviour in information seeking: Longitudinal evaluation of EIS. Third Annual Report.* Retrieved January 23, 2004, from http://online.northumbria.ac.uk/faculties/art/information_studies/imri/rarea/rm/rmres/JUB%20Cycle%203%20Draft%20Report%205%20adada.pdf

Barnes, D. M., Spink, A., & Yeatts, D. E. (1997). Effective information systems for high-performing self-managed teams. *Proceedings of an International Conference on Research in Information Needs, Seeking and Use in Different Contexts*, 163–178.

Barry, C. (1995). Critical issues in evaluating the impact of IT on information activity in academic research: Developing a qualitative research solution. *Library & Information Science Research*, *17*, 107–134.

Barry, C. (1997). Information-seeking in an advanced IT culture: A case study. *Proceedings of an International Conference on Research in Information Needs, Seeking and Use in Different Contexts*, 236–256.

Bates, M. J. (1989). The design of browsing and berrypicking techniques for the online search interface. *Online Review*, *13*, 407–425.

Bates, M. J. (1999). Review of *Information Seeking in Context*, edited by Pertti Vakkari. *Library Quarterly*, *69*, 378.

Bates, M. J. (2002). Toward an integrated model of information seeking and searching. *New Review of Information Behaviour Research*, *3*, 1–16.

Bourdieu, P. (1986). The forms of capital. In J. Richardson (Ed.), *Handbook of theory and research for the sociology of education* (pp. 241–258). New York: Greenwood Press.

Bourdieu, P. (1990). *The logic of practice.* Cambridge, UK: Polity Press.

Bourdieu, P., & Wacquant, L. J. D. (1992). *An invitation to reflexive sociology.* Chicago: University of Chicago Press.

Brown, C. D. (2002). Straddling the humanities and social sciences: The research process of music scholars. *Library & Information Science Research*, *24*, 73–94.

Bruce, H., Dumais, S., Fidel, R., Grudin, J., Pejtersen A. M., & Poltrock, S. (2003). A comparison of the collaborative information retrieval behaviour of two design teams. *New Review of Information Behaviour Research*, *4*, 139–153.

Burawoy, M. (2003). Revisits: An outline of a theory of reflexive ethnography. *American Sociological Review*, *68*, 645–679.

Burnett, G., Besant, M., & Chatman, E. A. (2001). Small worlds: Normative behavior in virtual communities and feminist bookselling. *Journal of the American Society for Information Science and Technology*, *52*, 536–547.

Byström, K. (1997). Municipal administrators at work: Information needs and seeking (INandS) in relation to task complexity: A case study amongst municipal officials. *Proceedings of an International Conference on Research in Information Needs, Seeking and Use in Different Contexts*, 125–146.

Byström, K. (2000). The effects of task complexity on the relationship between information types acquired and information sources used. *New Review of Information Behaviour Research*, *1*, 85–101.

Byström, K., & Järvelin, K. (1995). Task complexity affects information seeking and use. *Information Processing & Management*, *31*, 191–213.

Case, D. O. (2002). *Looking for information: A survey of research on information seeking, needs, and behavior.* San Diego, CA: Academic Press.

Chang, S.-J. L., & Lee, Y.-y. (2001). Conceptualizing context and its relationship to the information behaviour in dissertation research process. *New Review of Information Behaviour Research, 2,* 29–46.

Chatman, E. A. (1987). The information world of low-skilled workers. *Library & Information Science Research, 9,* 265–283.

Chatman, E. A. (1991). Life in a small world: Applicability of gratification theory to information-seeking behavior. *Journal of the American Society for Information Science, 42,* 438–449.

Chatman, E. A. (1992). *The information world of retired women.* Westport, CT: Greenwood Press.

Chatman, E. A. (1996). The impoverished life-world of outsiders. *Journal of the American Society for Information Science, 47,* 193–206.

Chatman, E. A. (1999). A theory of life in the round. *Journal of the American Society for Information Science, 50,* 207–217.

Chatman, E. A. (2000). Framing social life in theory and research. *New Review of Information Behaviour Research, 1,* 3–17.

Choo, C. W. (2001). Environmental scanning as information seeking and organizational learning. *Information Research, 7*(1). Retrieved May 21, 2002, from http://InformationR.net/ir/7-1/paper112.html

Coles, C. (1999). Information seeking behaviour of public library users: Use and non-use of electronic media. *Proceedings of the Second International Conference on Research in Information Needs, Seeking and Use in Different Contexts,* 321–329.

Cool, C. (2001). The concept of situation in information science. *Annual Review of Information Science and Technology, 35,* 5–42.

Cooper, L. Z. (2002). A case study of information-seeking behaviour in 7-year-old children in a semistructured situation. *Journal of the American Society for Information Science and Technology, 53,* 904–922.

Cothey, V. (2002). A longitudinal study of World Wide Web users' information-searching behavior. *Journal of the American Society for Information Science and Technology, 53,* 67–78.

Courtright, C. (2005). Health information-seeking among Latino newcomers: An exploratory study. *Information Research, 10*(2). Retrieved January 24, 2005, from http://informationr.net/ir/10-2/paper224.html

Davenport, E., Higgins, M., & Somerville, I. (1997). The appropriation of home information systems in Scottish households. *Proceedings of an International Conference on Research in Information Needs, Seeking and Use in Different Contexts,* 386–411.

Davenport, E., Higgins, M., & Somerville, I. (2000). Narratives of new media in Scottish households: The evolution of a framework of inquiry. *Journal of the American Society for Information Science, 51,* 900–912.

Davies, E., & McKenzie, P. J. (2004). Preparing for opening night: Temporal boundary objects in textually-mediated professional practice. *Information Research, 10*(1). Retrieved November 4, 2004, from http://informationr.net/ir/10-1/paper211.html

Davies, M. (1998). Impact of information technology developments on the information handling techniques of research scientists: Implications of selected results. *The New Review of Information Networking, 4,* 53–70.

Denzin, N. K. (2001). *Interpretive interactionism* (2nd ed.). Thousand Oaks, CA: Sage.

Dervin, B. (1997). Given a context by any other name: Methodological tools for taming the unruly beast. *Proceedings of an International Conference on Research in Information Needs, Seeking and Use in Different Contexts*, 13–38.

Dervin, B. (2000). Chaos, order, and sense-making: A proposed theory for information design. In R. Jacobson (Ed.), *Information design* (pp. 35–57). Cambridge, MA: MIT Press.

Dervin, B., & Clark, K. D. (1993). Communication and democracy: A mandate for procedural invention. In S. Splichal & J. Wasko (Eds.), *Communication and democracy* (pp. 103–140). Norwood, NJ: Ablex.

Dervin, B., & Nilan, M. (1986). Information needs and uses. *Annual Review of Information Science and Technology*, *21*, 3–33.

Dixon, P., & Banwell, L. (1999). School governors and effective decision making. *Proceedings of the Second International Conference on Research in Information Needs, Seeking and Use in Different Contexts*, 384–392.

Doty, P., & Erdelez, S. (2002). Information micro-practices in Texas rural courts: Methods and issues for e-government. *Government Information Quarterly*, *19*, 369–387.

Dourish, P. (2001). Seeking a foundation for context-aware computing. *Human-Computer Interaction*, *16*, 229–241.

Dourish, P. (2004). What we talk about when we talk about context. *Personal and Ubiquitous Computing*, *8*, 19–30.

Duff, W. M., & Johnson, C. A. (2002). Accidentally found on purpose: Information-seeking behavior of historians in archives. *Library Quarterly*, *72*, 472–496.

Durkheim, E. (1901/1982). *The rules of sociological method* (W. D. Halls, Trans.). New York: Free Press.

Ellen, D. (2003). Telecentres and the provision of community based access to electronic information in everyday life in the UK. *Information Research*, *8*(2). Retrieved May 21, 2003, from http://informationr.net/ir/8-2/paper146.html

Ellis, D. (1989). A behavioural model for information retrieval system design. *Journal of Information Science*, *15*, 237–247.

Enochsson, A. (2001). Children choosing Web pages. *New Review of Information Behaviour Research*, *2*, 151–165.

Erdelez, S. (1996). Information encountering on the Internet. *Proceedings of the 17th National Online Meeting*, 101–107.

Erdelez, S. (1997). Information encountering: A conceptual framework for accidental information discovery. *Proceedings of an International Conference on Research in Information Needs, Seeking and Use in Different Contexts*, 412–421.

Eskola, E.-L. (2005). Information literacy of medical students studying in the problem-based and traditional curriculum. *Information Research*, *10*(2). Retrieved January 24, 2005, from http://informationr.net/ir/10-2/paper221.html

Fabritius, H. (1999). Triangulation as a multiperspective strategy in a qualitative study of information seeking behaviour of journalists. *Proceedings of the Second International Conference on Research in Information Needs, Seeking and Use in Different Contexts*, 406–419.

Fidel, R., & Pejtersen, A. M. (2004). From information behaviour research to the design of information systems: The Cognitive Work Analysis framework. *Information Research*, 10(1). Retrieved November 4, 2004, from http://informationr.net/ir/10-1/paper210.html

Fisher, K., Naumer, C., Durrance, J., Stromski, L., & Christiansen, T. (2005). Something old, something new: Preliminary findings from an exploratory study about people's information habits and information grounds. *Information Research*, 10(2). Retrieved January 24, 2005, from http://informationr.net/ir/10-2/paper223.html

Fisher, K. E., Durrance, J. C., & Hinton, M. B. (2004). Information grounds and the use of need-based services by immigrants in Queens, New York: A context-based, outcome evaluation approach. *Journal of the American Society for Information Science and Technology*, 55, 754–766.

Fisher, K. E., Marcoux, E., Miller, L. S., Sánchez, A., & Cunningham, E. R. (2004). Information behaviour of migrant Hispanic farm workers and their families in the Pacific Northwest. *Information Research*, 10(1). Retrieved November 4, 2004, from http://informationr.net/ir/10-1/paper199.html

Forsythe, D. E. (1998). Using ethnography to investigate life scientists' information needs. *Bulletin of the Medical Library Association*, 86, 402–409.

Foster, A. (2004). A nonlinear model of information-seeking behavior. *Journal of the American Society for Information Science and Technology*, 55, 228–237.

Foster, A. (2005). A non-linear model of information seeking behaviour. *Information Research*, 10(2). Retrieved January 24, 2005, from http://informationr.net/ir/10-2/paper222.html

Friedland, R., & Alford, R. R. (1991). Bringing society back in: Symbols, practices, and institutional contradictions. In W. W. Powell & P. J. DiMaggio (Eds.), *The new institutionalism in organizational analysis* (pp. 232–263). Chicago: University of Chicago Press.

Frohmann, B. (2004). *Deflating information: From science studies to documentation.* Toronto: University of Toronto Press.

Fulton, C. (2000). The case of the missing information resources: Information seeking and coping behaviour in teleworking arrangements. *New Review of Information Behaviour Research*, 1, 117–134.

Giddens, A. (1984). *The constitution of society: Outline of the theory of structuration.* Berkeley, CA: University of California Press.

Given, L. M. (2002). Discursive constructions in the university context: Social positioning theory and mature undergraduates' information behaviours. *New Review of Information Behaviour Research*, 3, 127–141.

Gorman, P. (1999). Information seeking of primary care physicians: Conceptual models and empirical studies. *Proceedings of the Second International Conference on Research in Information Needs, Seeking and Use in Different Contexts*, 226–240.

Granovetter, M. S. (1973). The strength of weak ties. *American Journal of Sociology*, 78, 1360–1380.

Granovetter, M. S. (1983). The strength of weak ties: A network theory revisited. *Sociological Theory*, 1, 210–233.

Green, A.-M., & Davenport, E. (1999). Putting new media in its place: The Edinburgh experience. *Proceedings of the Second International Conference on Research in Information Needs, Seeking and Use in Different Contexts*, 330–342.

Gross, M. (1999). Imposed queries in the school library media center: A descriptive study. *Library & Information Science Research*, 21, 501–521.

Gross, M. (2001). Imposed information seeking in public libraries and school library media centers: A common behaviour? *Information Research, 6*(2). Retrieved May 3, 2001, from http://InformationR.net/ir/6-2/paper100.html

Gross, M., Dresang, E. T., & Holt, L. E. (2004). Children's in-library use of computers in an urban public library. *Library & Information Science Research, 26*, 311–337.

Harris, R. M., & Dewdney, P. (1994). *Barriers to information: How formal help systems fail battered women*. Westport, CT: Greenwood Press.

Haythornthwaite, C., & Wellman, B. (1998). Work, friendship, and media use for information exchange in a networked organization. *Journal of the American Society for Information Science, 49*, 1101–1114.

Heinstrom, J. (2005). Fast surfing, broad scanning and deep diving: The influence of personality and study approach on students' information-seeking behavior. *Journal of Documentation, 61*, 228–247.

Hektor, A. (2003). Information activities on the Internet in everyday life. *New Review of Information Behaviour Research, 4*, 127–138.

Hersberger, J. (2001). Everyday information needs and information sources of homeless parents. *New Review of Information Behaviour Research, 2*, 119–134.

Hertzum, M. (2000). People as carriers of experience and sources of commitment: Information seeking in a software design project. *New Review of Information Behaviour Research, 1*, 135–149.

Hewins, E. T. (1990). Information need and use studies. *Annual Review of Information Science and Technology, 25*, 43–96.

Hirsh, S., & Dinkelacker, J. (2004). Seeking information in order to produce information: An empirical study at Hewlett Packard Labs. *Journal of the American Society for Information Science and Technology, 55*, 807–817.

Hjørland, B. (2000). Information seeking behaviour: What should a general theory look like? *New Review of Information Behaviour Research, 1*, 19–33.

Holstein, J. A., & Gubrium, J. F. (1995). *The active interview*. Thousand Oaks, CA: Sage.

Hultgren, F., & Limberg, L. (2003). A study of research on children's information behaviour in a school context. *New Review of Information Behaviour Research, 4*(1), 1–15.

Huotari, M.-L., & Chatman, E. A. (2001). Using everyday life information seeking to explain organizational behavior. *Library & Information Science Research, 23*, 351–366.

Ikoja-Odongo, R., & Ocholla, D. N. (2003). Information needs and information-seeking behavior of artisan fisher folk of Uganda. *Library & Information Science Research, 25*, 89–105.

Introna, L. D. (1999). Context, power, bodies and information: Exploring the 'entangled' contexts of information. *Proceedings of the Second International Conference on Research in Information Needs, Seeking and Use in Different Contexts*, 1–9.

Janes, J., & Silverstein, J. (2003). Question negotiation and the technological environment. *D-Lib Magazine, 9*(2). Retrieved March 1, 2003, from www.dlib.org/dlib/february03/janes/02janes.html

Järvelin, K., & Ingwersen, P. (2004). Information seeking research needs extension towards tasks and technology. *Information Research, 10*(1). Retrieved November 4, 2004, from http://informationr.net/ir/10-1/paper212.html

Jeong, W. (2004). Unbreakable ethnic bonds: Information-seeking behavior of Korean graduate students in the United States. *Library & Information Science Research, 26,* 384–400.

Johnson, C. A. (2004). Choosing people: The role of social capital in information seeking behaviour. *Information Research, 10*(1). Retrieved November 4, 2004, from http://informationr.net/ir/10-1/paper201.html

Johnson, J. D. (2003). On contexts of information seeking. *Information Processing & Management, 39,* 735–760.

Johnson, J. D., Donohue, W. A., Atkin, C. K., & Johnson, S. (1995). A comprehensive model of information seeking: Tests focusing on a technical organization. *Science Communication, 16,* 274–303.

Julien, H. (1999). Where to from here? Results of an empirical study and user-centred implications for system design. *Proceedings of the Second International Conference on Research in Information Needs, Seeking and Use in Different Contexts,* 586–596.

Julien, H., & Duggan, L. J. (2000). A longitudinal analysis of the information needs and uses literature. *Library & Information Science Research, 22,* 291–309.

Julien, H., & Michels, D. (2004). Intra-individual information behaviour in daily life. *Information Processing & Management, 40,* 547–562.

Kari, J., & Savolainen, R. (2003). Towards a contextual model of information seeking on the Web. *New Review of Information Behaviour Research, 4*(1), 155–175.

Keane, D. (1999). The information behaviour of senior executives. *Proceedings of the Second International Conference on Research in Information Needs, Seeking and Use in Different Contexts,* 430–450.

Kling, R., McKim, G., & King, A. (2003). A bit more to IT: Scholarly communication forums as socio-technical interaction networks. *Journal of the American Society for Information Science and Technology, 54,* 47–67.

Klobas, J. E., & Clyde, L. A. (2000). Adults learning to use the Internet: A longitudinal study of attitudes and other factors associated with intended Internet use. *Library & Information Science Research, 22,* 5–34.

Krikelas, J. (1983). Information-seeking behavior: Patterns and concepts. *Drexel Library Quarterly, 19*(2), 5–20.

Kuhlthau, C. C. (1988a). Developing a model of the library search process: Cognitive and affective aspects. *RQ, 28,* 232–242.

Kuhlthau, C. C. (1988b). Longitudinal case studies of the information search process of users in libraries. *Library & Information Science Research, 10,* 257–304.

Kuhlthau, C. C. (1991). Inside the search process: Information seeking from the user's perspective. *Journal of the American Society for Information Science, 42,* 361–371.

Kuhlthau, C. C. (1993). *Seeking meaning: A process approach to library and information services.* Norwood, NJ: Ablex.

Kuhlthau, C. C. (1996). The concept of a zone of intervention for identifying the role of intermediaries in the information search process. *Proceedings of the 59th Annual Meeting of the American Society for Information Science,* 91–94. Retrieved May 5, 2000, from www.asis.org/annual-96/ElectronicProceedings/kuhlthau.html

Kuhlthau, C. C. (1997). The influence of uncertainty on the information seeking behavior of a securities analyst. *Proceedings of an International Conference on Research in Information Needs, Seeking and Use in Different Contexts,* 268–274.

Kuhlthau, C. C. (1999). The role of experience in the information search process of an early career information worker: Perceptions of uncertainty, complexity, construction, and sources. *Journal of the American Society for Information Science, 50*, 399–412.

Lamb, R., King, J. L., & Kling, R. (2003). Informational environments: Organizational contexts of online information use. *Journal of the American Society for Information Science and Technology, 54*, 97–114.

Lamb, R., & Kling, R. (2003). Reconceptualizing users as social actors in information systems research. *MIS Quarterly, 27*, 197–235.

Leckie, G. J., & Pettigrew, K. E. (1997). A general model of the information seeking of professionals: Role theory through the back door? *Proceedings of an International Conference on Research in Information Needs, Seeking and Use in Different Contexts*, 99–110.

Leckie, G. J., Pettigrew, K. E., & Sylvain, C. (1996). Modeling the information seeking of professionals: A general model derived from research on engineers, health care professionals, and lawyers. *Library Quarterly, 66*, 161–193.

Lievrouw, L. A. (2001). New media and the 'pluralization of life-worlds.' *New Media & Society, 3*, 7–28.

Lievrouw, L. A., & Farb, S. (2003). Information and equity. *Annual Review of Information Science and Technology, 37*, 499–540.

Limberg, L. (1997). Information use for learning purposes. *Proceedings of an International Conference on Research in Information Needs, Seeking and Use in Different Contexts*, 275–289.

Limberg, L. (1999). Experiencing information seeking and learning: A study of the interaction between two phenomena. *Information Research, 5*(1). Retrieved May 20, 2005, from http://informationr.net/ir/5-1/paper68.html

Lomax, E. C., Lowe, H. J., Logan, T. F., & Detlefse, E. G. (1999). An investigation of the information seeking behaviour of medical oncologists in metropolitan Pittsburgh using a multi-method approach. *Proceedings of the Second International Conference on Research in Information Needs, Seeking and Use in Different Contexts*, 241–256.

Loughridge, B. (1997). Investigating the management information needs of heads of academic departments in universities in the United Kingdom: A critical success factors approach. *Proceedings of an International Conference on Research in Information Needs, Seeking and Use in Different Contexts*, 147–162.

Lueg, C. (2002). On problem solving and information seeking. *New Review of Information Behaviour Research, 3*, 99–112.

Mackenzie, M. L. (2003). An exploratory study investigating the information behaviour of line managers within a business environment. *New Review of Information Behaviour Research, 4*(1), 63-78.

Mackenzie, M. L. (2005). Managers look to the social network to seek information. *Information Research, 10*(2). Retrieved January 24, 2005, from http://informationr.net/ir/10-2/paper216.html

Malmsjö, A. (1997). Information seeking behaviour and development of information systems: A contextual view. *Proceedings of an International Conference on Research in Information Needs, Seeking and Use in Different Contexts*, 222–235.

Marchionini, G. (1995). *Information seeking in electronic environments*. Cambridge, UK: Cambridge University Press.

Marchionini, G. (2002). Co-evolution of user and organizational interfaces: A longitudinal case study of WWW dissemination of national statistics. *Journal of the American Society for Information Science and Technology, 53*, 1192–1209.

McCreadie, M., & Rice, R. E. (1999). Trends in analyzing access to information. Part I: Cross-disciplinary conceptualizations of access. *Information Processing & Management, 35*, 45–76.

McKechnie, L. E. F., Baker, L., Greenwood, M., & Julien, H. (2002). Research method trends in human information literature. *New Review of Information Behaviour Research, 3*, 113–126.

McKenzie, P. J. (2002). Connecting with information sources: How accounts of information seeking take discursive action. *New Review of Information Behaviour Research, 3*, 161–174.

McKenzie, P. J. (2003a). Justifying cognitive authority decisions: Discursive strategies of information seekers. *Library Quarterly, 73*, 261–288.

McKenzie, P. J. (2003b). A model of information practices in accounts of everyday-life information seeking. *Journal of Documentation, 59*, 19–40.

McKenzie, P. J. (2004). Positioning theory and the negotiation of information needs in a clinical midwifery setting. *Journal of the American Society for Information Science and Technology, 55*, 684–694.

Meyer, H. W. J. (2003). Information use in rural development. *New Review of Information Behaviour Research, 4*, 109–125.

Mutch, A. (2000). Managers, information and teams: A tale of two companies. *New Review of Information Behaviour Research, 1*, 151–166.

Nardi, B. A., & O'Day, V. L. (1999). *Information ecologies: Using technology with heart.* Cambridge, MA: MIT Press.

Nicholas, D., Huntington, P., & Williams, P. (2003). Three years of digital consumer health information: A longitudinal study of the touch screen health kiosk. *Information Processing & Management, 39*, 479–502.

Niedźwiedzka, B. (2003). A proposed general model of information behaviour. *Information Research, 9*(1). Retrieved October 15, 2003, from http://informationr.net/ir/9-1/paper164.html

Olsson, M. (1999). Discourse: A new theoretical framework for examining information behaviour in its social context. *Proceedings of the Second International Conference on Research in Information Needs, Seeking and Use in Different Contexts*, 136–149.

Orlikowski, W. J., & Gash, D. C. (1994). Technological frames: Making sense of information technology in organizations. *ACM Transactions on Information Systems, 12*, 174–207.

Owens, I., Wilson, T. D., & Abell, A. (1997). Information and business performance: A study of information systems and services in high-performing companies. *Journal of Librarianship and Information Science, 29*, 19–28.

Palsdottir, A. (2003). Icelandic citizens' everyday life health information behaviour. *Health Informatics Journal, 9*, 225–240.

Pescosolido, B. A., & Rubin, B. A. (2000). *The Web of Group Affiliations* revisited: Social life, postmodernism, and sociology. *American Sociological Review, 65*, 52–76.

Pettigrew, K. E. (1999). Waiting for chiropody: Contextual results from an ethnographic study of the information behaviour among attendees at community clinics. *Information Processing & Management, 35*, 801–817.

Pettigrew, K. E. (2000). Lay information provision in community settings: How community health nurses disseminate human services information to the elderly. *Library Quarterly*, *70*, 47–85.

Pettigrew, K. E., Fidel, R., & Bruce, H. (2001). Conceptual frameworks in information behavior. *Annual Review of Information Science and Technology*, *35*, 43–78.

Pharo, N. (2004). A new model of information behaviour based on the search situation transition schema. *Information Research*, *10*(1). Retrieved November 4, 2004, from http://informationr.net/ir/10-1/paper203.html

Pivec, F. (1998). Surfing through the Internet: The new content of teenagers' spare time. *Aslib Proceedings*, *50*(4), 88–92.

Prekop, P. (2002). A qualitative study of collaborative information seeking. *Journal of Documentation*, *58*, 533–547.

Reneker, M., Jacobson, A., & Spink, A. (2001). Information seeking environment of a military university. *New Review of Information Behaviour Research*, *2*, 179–193.

Rieh, S. Y. (2004). On the Web at home: Information seeking and Web searching in the home environment. *Journal of the American Society for Information Science and Technology*, *55*, 743–753.

Rolinson, J. (1998). Health information for the teenage years: What do they want to know? *Information Research*, *3*(3). Retrieved September 24, 2003, from http://informationr.net/ir/3-3/paper42.html

Rosenbaum, H. (1993). Information use environments and structuration: Towards an integration of Taylor and Giddens. *Proceedings of the 56th Annual Meeting of the American Society for Information Science*, 235–245.

Rosenbaum, H. (1996). Structure and action: Towards a new concept of the information use environment. *Proceedings of the 59th Annual Meeting of the American Society for Information Science*, 152–156.

Sandvig, C. (2003). Public internet access for young children in the inner city: Evidence to inform access subsidy and content regulation. *The Information Society*, *19*, 171–183.

Savolainen, R. (1993). The sense-making theory: Reviewing the interests of a user-centered approach to information seeking and use. *Information Processing & Management*, *29*, 13–28.

Savolainen, R. (1995). Everyday life information seeking: Approaching information seeking in the context of "way of life." *Library & Information Science Research*, *17*, 259–294.

Savolainen, R. (1998). Use studies of electronic networks: A review of empirical research approaches and challenges for their development. *Journal of Documentation*, *54*, 332–351.

Savolainen, R. (1999). Seeking and using information from the Internet: The context of non-work use. *Proceedings of the Second International Conference on Research in Information Needs, Seeking and Use in Different Contexts*, 356–370.

Scott, W. R. (1987). *Organizations: Rational, natural, and open systems* (2nd ed.). Englewood Cliffs, NJ: Prentice Hall.

Scott, W. R. (1998). *Organizations: Rational, natural, and open systems* (4th ed.). Upper Saddle River, NJ: Prentice Hall.

Seldén, L. (2001). Academic information seeking: Careers and capital types. *New Review of Information Behaviour Research*, *2*, 195–215.

Sewell, W. H., Jr. (1992). A theory of structure: Duality, agency, and transformation. *American Journal of Sociology, 98*, 1–29.

Sligo, F. X., & Jameson, A. M. (2000). The knowledge-behavior gap in use of health information. *Journal of the American Society for Information Science, 51*, 858–869.

Solomon, P. (1997a). Discovering information behavior in sense making. Part II: The social. *Journal of the American Society for Information Science, 48*, 1109–1126.

Solomon, P. (1997b). Information behavior in sense making: A three-year case study of work planning. *Proceedings of an International Conference on Research in Information Needs, Seeking and Use in Different Contexts*, 290–306.

Solomon, P. (1999). Information mosaics: Patterns of action that structure. *Proceedings of the Second International Conference on Research in Information Needs, Seeking and Use in Different Contexts*, 150–175.

Solomon, P. (2002). Discovering information in context. *Annual Review of Information Science and Technology, 36*, 229–264.

Sonnenwald, D. H. (1999). Evolving perspectives of human information behaviour: Contexts, situations, social networks and information horizons. *Proceedings of the Second International Conference on Research in Information Needs, Seeking and Use in Different Contexts*, 176–190.

Sonnenwald, D. H., & Lievrouw, L. A. (1997). Collaboration during the design process: A case study of communication, information behavior, and project performance. *Proceedings of an International Conference on Research in Information Needs, Seeking and Use in Different Contexts*, 179–204.

Sonnenwald, D. H., & Pierce, L. G. (2000). Information behavior in dynamic group work contexts: Interwoven situational awareness, dense social networks and contested collaboration in command and control. *Information Processing & Management, 36*, 461–479.

Spink, A., Bray, K. E., Jaeckel, M., & Sidberry, G. (1999). Everyday life information-seeking by low-income African American households: Wynnewood Healthy Neighbourhood Project. *Proceedings of the Second International Conference on Research in Information Needs, Seeking and Use in Different Contexts*, 371–383.

Sprague, M. W. (1994). Information-seeking patterns of university administrators and non-faculty professional staff members. *Journal of Academic Librarianship, 19*, 378–383.

Sundin, O. (2002). Nurses' information seeking and use as participation in occupational communities. *New Review of Information Behaviour Research, 3*, 187–202.

Talja, S. (1997). Constituting "information" and "user" as research objects: A theory of knowledge formations as an alternative to the information man-theory. *Proceedings of an International Conference on Research in Information Needs, Seeking and Use in Different Contexts*, 67–80.

Talja, S. (2002). Information sharing in academic communities: Types and levels of collaboration in information seeking and use. *New Review of Information Behaviour Research, 3*, 143–159.

Talja, S. (2003). Reasons for the use and non-use of electronic journals and databases: A domain analytic study in four scholarly disciplines. *Journal of Documentation, 59*, 673–691.

Talja, S., Keso, H., & Pietilainen, T. (1999). The production of "context" in information seeking research: A metatheoretical view. *Information Processing & Management, 35*, 751–763.

Talja, S., Savolainen, R., & Maula, H. (2004). Field differences in the use and perceived use-fulness of scholarly mailing lists. *Information Research*, *10*(1). Retrieved November 4, 2004, from http://informationr.net/ir/10-1/paper200.html

Talja, S., Tuominen, K., & Savolainen, R. (2005). "Isms" in information science: Constructivism, collectivism and constructionism. *Journal of Documentation*, *61*, 79–101.

Taylor, R. S. (1968). Question-negotiation and information seeking in libraries. *College & Research Libraries*, *29*, 178–194.

Taylor, R. S. (1991). Information use environments. In B. Dervin & M. Voigt (Eds.), *Progress in Communication Science* (Vol. 10, pp. 217–255). Norwood, NJ: Ablex.

Thivant, E. (2003). Information seeking and use behaviour for the design of financial products. *New Review of Information Behaviour Research*, *4*, 45–61.

Thomas, N. P., & Nyce, J. M. (2001). Context as category: Opportunities for ethnographic analysis in library and information science research. *New Review of Information Behaviour Research*, *2*, 105–118.

Tibar, A. (2000). Information needs and uses in industry: The implications for information services. *New Review of Information Behaviour Research*, *1*, 185–200.

Törmä, S., & Vakkari, P. (2004). Discipline, availability of electronic resources and the use of Finnish National Electronic Library: FinELib. *Information Research*, *10*(1). Retrieved November 4, 2004, from http://informationr.net/ir/10-1/paper204.html

Tuominen, K. (1997). User-centered discourse: An analysis of the subject positions of the user and the librarian. *Library Quarterly*, *67*, 350–371.

Tuominen, K., & Savolainen, R. (1997). A social constructionist approach to the study of information use as discursive action. *Proceedings of an International Conference on Research in Information Needs, Seeking and Use in Different Contexts*, 81–96.

Vakkari, P. (1997). Information seeking in context: A challenging metatheory. *Proceedings of an International Conference on Research in Information Needs, Seeking and Use in Different Contexts*, 451–464.

Vakkari, P., & Pennanen, M. (2001). Sources, relevance and contributory information of documents in writing a research proposal: A longitudinal case study. *New Review of Information Behaviour Research*, *2*, 217–232.

Vakkari, P., Savolainen, R., & Dervin, B. (Eds.). (1997). *Proceedings of an International Conference on Research in Information Needs, Seeking and Use in Different Contexts*. London: Taylor Graham.

Vakkari, P., & Serola, S. (2002). Utility of references retrieved for preparing a research proposal: A longitudinal case study. *New Review of Information Behaviour Research*, *3*, 37–52.

Wang, P. (1997). Users' information needs at different stages of a research project: A cognitive view. *Proceedings of an International Conference on Research in Information Needs, Seeking and Use in Different Contexts*, 307–318.

Wang, P., & Soergel, D. (1999). A cognitive model of document use during a research project. Study I: Document selection. *Journal of the American Society for Information Science*, *49*, 115–133.

Warner, E. S., Murray, A. D., & Palmour, V. E. (1973). *Information needs of urban residents. Final report of the Baltimore Regional Planning Council and Westat Inc.* (ERIC: ED 088464). Washington, D.C.: U.S. Department of Health, Education and Welfare, Division of Library Programs.

Weber, F. (2001). Settings, interactions and things: A plea for multi-integrative ethnography. *Ethnography, 2*, 475–499.

Widén-Wulff, G. (2003). Information as a resource in the insurance business: The impact of structures and processes on organization information behaviour. *New Review of Information Behaviour Research, 4*(1), 79–94.

Wilkins, J. L. H., & Leckie, G. J. (1997). University professional and managerial staff: Information needs and seeking. *College & Research Libraries, 58*, 561–574.

Williamson, K. (1997). The information needs and information-seeking behaviour of older adults: An Australian study. *Proceedings of an International Conference on Research in Information Needs, Seeking and Use in Different Contexts*, 337–350.

Williamson, K. (1998). Discovered by chance: The role of incidental information acquisition in an ecological model of information use. *Library & Information Science Research, 20*, 23–40.

Williamson, K., Schauder, D., & Bow, A. (2000). Information seeking by blind and sight impaired citizens: An ecological study. *Information Research, 5*(4). Retrieved May 20, 2005, from http://informationr.net/ir/5-4/paper79.html

Wilson, T. D. (1981). On user studies and information needs. *Journal of Documentation, 37*, 3–15.

Wilson, T. D. (1997). Information behaviour: An inter-disciplinary perspective. *Proceedings of an International Conference on Research in Information Needs, Seeking and Use in Different Contexts*, 39–50.

Wilson, T. D. (1999). Models in information behaviour research. *Journal of Documentation, 55*, 249–270.

Wilson, T. D. (2000). Human information behavior. *Informing Science, 3*(2), 49–55.

Wilson, T. D., & Allen, D. K. (Eds.). (1999). *Proceedings of the Second International Conference on Research in Information Needs, Seeking and Use in Different Contexts.*

Wilson, T. D., Ford, N., Ellis, D., Foster, A., & Spink, A. (2002). Information seeking and mediated searching. Part 2: Uncertainty and its correlates. *Journal of the American Society for Information Science and Technology, 53*, 704–715.

Wyatt, S., Henwood, F., Hart, A., & Smith, J. (2005). The digital divide, health information and everyday life. *New Media & Society, 7*, 199–218.

Zach, L. (2005). When is "enough" enough? Modeling the information-seeking and stopping behavior of senior arts administrators. *Journal of the American Society for Information Science and Technology, 56*, 23–35.

CHAPTER 7

Credibility:
A Multidisciplinary Framework

Soo Young Rieh
University of Michigan

David R. Danielson
Stanford University

Introduction

This chapter reviews the theoretical and empirical literature on the concept of credibility and its areas of application relevant to information science and technology, encompassing several disciplinary approaches. An information seeker's environment—the Internet, television, newspapers, schools, libraries, bookstores, and social networks—abounds with information resources that need to be evaluated for both their usefulness and their likely level of accuracy. As people gain access to a wider variety of information resources, they face greater uncertainty regarding who and what can be believed and, indeed, who or what is responsible for the information they encounter. Moreover, they have to develop new skills and strategies for determining how to assess the credibility of an information source. Historically, the credibility of information has been maintained largely by professional knowledge workers such as editors, reviewers, publishers, news reporters, and librarians. Today, quality control mechanisms are evolving in such a way that a vast amount of information accessed through a wide variety of systems and resources is out of date, incomplete, poorly organized, or simply inaccurate (Janes & Rosenfeld, 1996).

Credibility has been examined across a number of fields ranging from communication, information science, psychology, marketing, and the management sciences to interdisciplinary efforts in human-computer interaction (HCI). Each field has examined the construct and its practical significance using fundamentally different approaches, goals, and presuppositions, all of which results in conflicting views of credibility and its effects. The notion of credibility has been discussed at least since Aristotle's examination of *ethos* and his observations of speakers' relative abilities to persuade listeners. Disciplinary approaches to investigating credibility systematically developed only in the last century, beginning within the field of communication. A landmark among these efforts was the work of Hovland and colleagues (Hovland, Jannis, & Kelley, 1953; Hovland & Weiss, 1951), who focused on the influence of various characteristics of a *source* on a recipient's message acceptance. This work was followed by decades of interest in the relative credibility of *media* involving comparisons between newspapers, radio, television, and the Internet (e.g., Meyer, 1974; Newhagen & Nass, 1989; Slater & Rouner, 1996; West, 1994). Communication researchers have tended to focus on sources and media, viewing credibility as a *perceived characteristic*. Within information science, the focus is on the evaluation of *information*, most typically instantiated in documents and statements. Here, credibility has been viewed largely as a criterion for relevance judgment (Barry, 1994; Bateman, 1999; Cool, Belkin, Frieder, & Kantor, 1993; Park, 1993; Schamber, 1991; Wang & Soergel, 1998), with researchers focusing on how information seekers assess a document's likely level of quality (Liu, 2004; Rieh, 2002; Rieh & Belkin, 1998).

This brief account highlights an often implicit focus on varying *objects of assessment* among fields and not merely variance in the relevant unit of analysis from one study to the next. A field's perspective may for a time be primarily focused on a source, medium, or type of information. Each discipline recognizes that the credibility of sources, media, and information are fundamentally and intimately linked, but differences in implicit primary interest or focus have had, we believe, profound effects on the direction of credibility research. A researcher's focus can be on speakers, as was the case for Aristotle (*people* being more or less believable) and continues in interpersonal communication and psychological research; on larger aggregations (organizations or groups), as is often the case in the management sciences; on media (e.g., television or the Internet) as in mass communication research; on information resources (texts), as is common in information science; or on messages (claims, threats, or promises) and signals (often in the form of overt behaviors which *imply* claims, threats, or promises), as is often the case in consumer research.

Further, information technology is beginning to have a significant effect on credibility research, in that it highlights the need to reexamine what constitutes a perceived *source* and the blurring lines between traditional concepts such as source, message, medium, and receiver. This shift is clearest in HCI research (e.g., Sundar & Nass, 2000, 2001), where the focus may be on devices (*computers* or *information systems* are more or less believable) and on-screen representations of real-world sources (virtual characters); on information resources that merely filter, summarize, or otherwise manipulate data but are not the actual originators (e.g., portals, news filters, and search engines); and, by extension, on messages and signals that can be manipulated or distorted—in some cases, as a result of the recipient's actions or preferences—making one simultaneously recipient and source.

Several other challenges exist in examining the concept of credibility across disciplines. Not only do different fields address different sets of questions with different goals, but they inevitably introduce related but distinct constructs into the discussion: authority, quality, trust, and persuasion. In some cases, various terms are considered to be related to credibility and, in others, they are construed as underlying dimensions of the construct.

Scope

This is the first chapter devoted to the concept of credibility to appear in the *Annual Review of Information Science and Technology (ARIST)*. Two previous *ARIST* chapters have investigated the notions of trust and belief. Marsh and Dibben (2003) examined the role and significance of trust for information system practitioners and management scientists with an interest in social informatics. They did not cover social interactionist influences such as social capital, authenticity, credibility, and authority. Fallis's (2006) *ARIST* chapter addressed the notions of truth and belief from the perspective of social epistemology. He discussed truth and beliefs with respect to the accuracy of materials that libraries provide and how librarians help people to acquire *true beliefs*.

Beyond *ARIST*, a number of previous studies have reviewed the notion of credibility within specialized domains, such as credibility assessments on the World Wide Web (Danielson, 2005), or with respect to particular academic disciplines, such as communication (Metzger, Flanagin, Eyal, Lemus, & McCann, 2003).

This chapter differs from previous studies by discussing credibility in broader and more diverse contexts that encompass a number of academic disciplines. Nevertheless, as with previous reviews, we have set certain boundaries to the discussion. Our focus is on credibility in relation to the use of information technology. We occasionally examine research that is not aimed at exploring this relationship (e.g., in the use of newspapers or in interpersonal face-to-face communication); we do so, however, primarily to illustrate the uniqueness of credibility evaluation in relation to human use of information technology. Where information technology employs increasingly human-like characteristics such as voice and virtual characters, user credibility assessments tend to mimic those of human–human interaction (Nass & Brave, 2005; Reeves & Nass, 1996). Where such social responses are not evoked through human-like characteristics, information systems introduce numerous unique pressures on credibility judgments.

The objectives of the chapter are:

- To review critically the various conceptualizations and research approaches pertaining to credibility with respect to the use of information technology across multiple disciplines

- To examine concepts related to credibility and investigate relationships among them

- To identify multiple perspectives on credibility with respect to their applications to the design of information technology and critical thinking instruction for students

- To develop a multidisciplinary framework for credibility

Organization of the Chapter

This chapter begins by discussing types of credibility and related concepts such as quality, authority, trust, and persuasion. We then discuss the underlying dimensions of credibility in general and its problems. In the following section, both empirical and theoretical studies are examined across five broad domains in which credibility is investigated in relation to human use of information technology: information seeking and retrieval, management information systems, consumer behavior, health science, and evaluation of Web resources. The focus is on the identification of critical concepts and dimensions of credibility and the factors or criteria that influence the extent of credibility assessment. Then the three application areas of critical thinking instruction, Web design, and information system design in which the concept of credibility has become increasingly significant are introduced. Finally, a multidisciplinary framework for credibility and an agenda for future research are proposed.

Credibility and Related Concepts

In this section, we situate credibility in relation to other concepts. To do so, we first briefly discuss various types of credibility. Second, we examine concepts that, although frequently discussed together with credibility and sometimes confused with it, are not equivalent. Third, we address the construct's underlying dimensions, in particular how situation-dependent variables can lead to widespread disagreement regarding which terms (e.g., expertness, trustworthiness) ought to be considered as the core dimensions.

Types of Credibility

Credibility is frequently attached to objects of assessment, as in *source credibility*, *media credibility*, and *message credibility*, reflecting the fact that assessments of these objects differ (Kiousis, 2001). At the same time, however, credibility assessments of sources and messages are fundamentally interlinked and influence one another (Slater & Rouner, 1996)—that is, credible sources are seen as likely to produce credible messages and credible messages are seen as likely to have originated from credible sources (Fragale & Heath, 2004). The extent to which source and media credibility assessments are interlinked, however, is less clear, perhaps in part because these have historically been investigated by different subdisciplines of communication. It is unclear, for example, if credible media are seen as more likely to introduce credible sources or if credible sources are seen as more likely to communicate via credible media.

For several decades, probably the best-known and most-employed media credibility comparison item was that used by Roper Research Associates for the Television Information Office: "If you got conflicting or different reports of the same news story from radio, television, magazines, and newspaper, which of the four versions would you be most inclined to believe?" (Roper, 1985). This question was aimed at discovering perceptions of the *relative credibility* of different news media. More recently, comparisons between the Web and traditional media have posed similar questions.

The problem with this approach is that such comparisons do little to illuminate either the specific *variables* that make one medium more credible than another (see Nass & Mason, 1990, for a general critique) or the processes used in evaluating different types of media and, more importantly, what characteristics of a medium influence credibility assessments (Burbules, 2001).

That credibility assessments themselves may be based upon distinct types of evaluations has been a focus of, among others, Fogg and his colleagues (Fogg, 2003a; Tseng & Fogg, 1999), who proposed four types of credibility in assessing information systems: presumed, reputed, surface, and experienced. *Presumed* credibility describes how much the perceiver believes someone or something because of general assumptions in the perceiver's mind. For example, people may assume that their friends tell the truth but view salespeople as lacking in credibility. *Reputed* credibility describes how much the perceiver believes someone or something because of what third parties have reported. For instance, if people see assessments made by *Consumer Reports* or receive recommendations from friends, they may tend to rely on them as unbiased views. *Surface* credibility refers to believability based on simple inspection, such as looking at the cover of a book or relying on the type of language people use as an indicator of credibility. *Experienced* credibility refers to believability based on first-hand experience; as people interact over time, their expertise and trustworthiness can be assessed.

For the past decade, the new term *Web credibility* has been increasingly used in a variety of disciplines. Burbules (2001) argued that Web credibility needs to be discussed independently of other types of credibility on the grounds that conventional methods for assessing credibility may not be feasible on the Web because of its speed, complex features and link structure, and lack of referencing and organizational conventions. Danielson (2005) has pointed to four general characteristics that complicate Web users' credibility assessment strategies: (1) the relative lack of filtering and gatekeeping mechanisms; (2) the form of the medium, including interaction techniques and interface attributes either inherent to the Web and other hypertext systems or emerging from common design practices; (3) a preponderance of source ambiguity and relative lack of source attributions; and (4) the novelty of the Web as a medium in conjunction with a lack of evaluation standards.

Related Concepts

Credibility and Quality

Taylor's (1986) conceptual model of information quality suggests that people make judgments in choosing particular information objects by assigning value to some but not others. To make choices about information, the kinds of questions to be asked include: Is this information error-free? Does this information cover a particular subject or discipline? Is this information recent? Does this information show consistency of quality performance over time? Can this information be judged as sound (Taylor, 1986)? Among these, one critical question to be asked is: "Can I trust this information?" or "Can I take this information seriously?" (as Wilson [1983] might have suggested). The evaluation of these questions often forces an information seeker to step back and evaluate who or what is perceived to be responsible for the information. That is precisely the question of credibility, one of the chief aspects of quality.

Taylor (1986) identified six categories of user criteria for making choices: ease of use, noise reduction, *quality*, adaptability, time saving, and cost saving. He defined quality as "a user criterion which has to do with excellence or in some cases truthfulness in labeling" and identified five values included in quality: accuracy, comprehensiveness, currency, reliability, and validity (p. 62). Although Taylor did not explicitly use the term "credibility," the notion is embedded in his derivation of quality from reliability and validity. These aspects of information quality can be used when people need to make decisions about information; however, such decisions can be difficult because a text may be of high or low quality in many different ways. For instance, a text can be comprehensive but not accurate, have validity but not be current, and so on. Therefore, information seekers sometimes must make choices about which values matter most to them. This is where credibility plays an important role. Out of a set of objects that appear to hold various information values, people tend to choose the items that appear to be most credible. That is, credibility provides one more layer of information evaluation to select items from a pool of documents that are initially judged as being of high quality.

Credibility and Authority

Wilson's (1983) theory of cognitive authority is closely related to the concept of credibility. Both feature trustworthiness and competence as their main components. Wilson argues that what people know of the world, beyond the narrow range of their own lives, is only what others have told them. People do not, however, count all hearsay as equally reliable. Only those who are deemed to "know what they are talking about" are recognized as cognitive authorities. Wilson claims that people do not attribute cognitive authority exclusively to individuals. Cognitive authority is also found in books, instruments, organizations, and institutions. Wilson points out that an authority's influence on us is thought proper because "he is thought credible, worthy of belief" (p. 15). Further, he distinguishes between the average person's competence and the expert's special competence. For instance, people often assume that their friends, neighbors, and colleagues are generally trustworthy and of ordinary competence and so consider them to be credible sources. They may, of course, fail to influence one's thoughts if they are perceived to lack expertise in a particular domain.

However, people also recognize that some sources have more than ordinary competence in particular spheres; these become the cognitive authorities within those spheres. Wilson (1983, p. 16) states that "our cognitive authorities are clearly among those we think credible sources, but we might recognize someone as credible in an area even though he did not in fact have any influence on our thoughts." People believed to be credible constitute the potential pool of cognitive authorities upon which to draw. Cognitive authorities are valued not just for their stocks of knowledge (answers to closed questions) but also for their opinions (answers to open questions) as well as for their advice on the proper attitude or stance on questions and their proposed answers. Cognitive authorities are the subset of people or information perceived to be credible. They not only possess competence and trustworthiness but also influence thoughts deeply, as people would consciously recognize as being proper.

Credibility and Trust

It can be difficult to discuss credibility without referring to trust or trusting behaviors and vice versa. Historically, trust has been a core construct in many conceptualizations of credibility (Hovland et al., 1953). Marsh and Dibben (2003) provide a good overview of the theoretical meanings of trust. They argue that trustworthy interfaces become enabling technologies because they lead the user to want to interact with them, thus increasing productivity. This notion of trust has become critical for e-commerce research because consumer trust affects online behavior. The notion of trust in information itself is also critical when one considers content, source, intent, and meaning.

Tseng and Fogg (1999) point out that, although credibility and trust have sometimes been used interchangeably, they should not be considered synonymous. Trust is different from credibility because "trust indicates a positive belief about the perceived reliability of, dependability of, and confidence in a person, object, or process" (p. 41). They suggest that, in the field of HCI, trust refers to dependability and credibility is roughly synonymous with believability. Tseng and Fogg further distinguish between the general concept of trust and "trust in information" (p. 41). Trust is often used with respect to, for example, reliance on a computer system designed to keep track of financial transactions but other uses of the term, including "trust the information," "accept the advice," and "believe the output," are more properly understood as references to credibility (p. 41). Trust frequently refers to a set of beliefs, dispositions, and behaviors associated with the acceptance of risk and vulnerability. Credibility refers to a perceived quality of a source, which may or may not result in associated trusting behaviors.

Credibility and Persuasion

Finally, we need to distinguish between credibility and its most recognizable outcome, persuasion, as operationalized by message acceptance. Aristotle's discussion of ethos is widely considered to be among the first attempts at conceptualizing what is now more commonly referred to as source credibility; indeed, a short phrase used to refer to the construct—"persuasion through character"—captures a number of underlying assumptions that have long been influential in credibility research. The most obvious of these is that credibility is intimately tied to persuasion, but it was not until the twentieth century that researchers began to test this assumption rigorously (see Pornpitakpan, 2004, for a review) and to identify conditions under which source credibility exerts no effect on persuasion or, paradoxically, decreases the effect. Thus, although source credibility is a critical determinant of message acceptance (Petty & Cacioppo, 1981), the two constructs are not equivalent.

Underlying Dimensions

Researchers, particularly in interpersonal and mass communication, have long understood credibility to be a multidimensional construct (McCroskey & Young, 1981) but have not always agreed on its underlying dimensions. Numerous labels have been suggested and have come to be influential in subsequent research, including trustworthiness, expertise, dynamism, competence, and goodwill. In order to understand the source of this disagreement, we need to understand the limitations of the prevailing approaches used to tease apart the construct's dimensions. Such approaches include two basic activities: the *creation* of candidate terms relevant to credibility and the *validation* of these candidate items, resulting in a reduced set indicative of the construct's primary dimensions. In the creation stage, researchers attempt to generate a list of terms that, at face value, are relevant to credibility. For example, Singletary (1976) and VandenBergh, Soley, and Reid (1981) asked participants in their studies to imagine a specific high-credibility source (in Singletary's case, a news person; in VandenBergh et al.'s, an advertiser) and to list as many terms as possible that, in the participant's view, gave credibility to that source. Other researchers either sampled the existing literature to create a list of candidate terms based upon their review or relied upon intuition. In the validation stage, these candidate terms are summarized and reduced, most often using factor analysis. This basic two-stage approach may in some ways seem reasonable for teasing apart the dimensions of credibility, but it has led to widespread disagreements for many reasons.

Creation methods. The first and most obvious difficulty is in choosing the right approach for generating candidate terms. One's validation stage is only as good as one's creation stage; that is, if creation methods fail to generate a sufficiently broad range of terms or if the set of terms is itself biased in some way, the results of the validation stage will be similarly biased. These methods have, out of necessity, been largely qualitative and sometimes creative endeavors. A number of relevance studies, for example, collected user-based criteria simply by asking users what made them think that the information was useful without developing a predefined set of relevance criteria—an approach similar to that of Singletary (1976) and VandenBergh et al. (1981). The user criteria were derived from content analysis of oral or written reports (Barry, 1994; Cool et al., 1993; Park, 1993; Schamber, 1991; Wang & Soergel, 1998).

Validation methods. One approach for reducing the number of candidate terms has been the use of factor analytic methods. This carries inherent limitations, particularly with respect to the subjectivity of interpreting results (Infante, Parker, Clarke, Wilson, & Nathu, 1983; Meyer, 1988). Indeed, even the labeling of factors is subjective and, consequently, it is often unclear whether dimensions identified by different researchers as representing similar but distinct sets of terms are in fact the same, "expertness" and "competence" being a case in point. Other methodological issues, such as participant response, may be set using semantically different scales and so can influence which dimensions emerge in a given study.

Dimensions versus predictors. Even relatively rigorous creation and validation stages face a fundamental problem: It is often unclear whether the factors identified are mere predictors of source credibility or representative of an underlying dimension of the construct (Newhagen & Nass, 1989). The "face validity" of proposed dimensions is largely subjective; it is debatable, for example, whether one ought to consider dimensions referring to extroversion of a communication source as a mere correlate of source credibility or a distinct dimension (McCroskey & Young, 1981).

Unit of analysis. Finally, it is important to recognize that the *target* of a researcher's interest—be it public speakers, newspapers, or Web sites—likely has a critical impact on the dimensions the researcher uncovers. Newhagen and Nass (1989) have shown that information seekers use different criteria to evaluate newspapers and television and that this can lead to differences in both assessments of those media and in what one concludes to be the important dimensions of credibility.

Thus, the various sets of dimensions reported by different studies simply reflect differing criteria for evaluating vastly different media. It is not surprising, then, that "dynamism" (encompassing such variables as animation and showmanship) was long considered a distinct dimension of credibility when the focus was on platform speakers. That changed as the credibility dimensions of print news began to interest mass communication researchers. Different media variables influence user goals and attention and these, in turn, influence the strategies users employ in making credibility assessments (Austin & Dong, 1994; Danielson, 2005; Mulder, 1980).

The fundamental fact that the underlying criteria used in evaluating credibility can be largely situation-dependent plays an important role in our analysis of multidisciplinary approaches.

Multidimensional Approaches to Credibility

Information Seeking and Retrieval

In information science, assessments of information and sources have often been discussed within the context of relevance judgments. It is often believed that users make decisions to accept or reject information based on whether they judge it to be relevant to their information problem. Relevance has been considered the primary criterion in selecting information (Mizzaro, 1997; Saracevic, 1996); indeed, the term "credibility" did not appear in the literature on information seeking and retrieval until the 1990s (Fritch & Cromwell, 2001; Janes & Rosenfeld, 1996; Wathen & Burkell, 2002; Watson, 1998). It is no coincidence that this topic has steadily gained prominence with the growth of the Web.

Credibility as a Relevance Criterion

In general, information science researchers have considered the assessment of credibility to be a part of relevance judgments. In the 1990s, several empirical studies (Barry, 1994; Cool et al., 1993; Park, 1993; Schamber, 1991; Tang & Solomon, 1998; Wang & Soergel, 1998; Wang & White, 1999) were conducted to identify user-defined relevance criteria. These studies revealed that people use much more diverse criteria than mere topicality for their relevance judgments. Interestingly, user-defined relevance criteria show common characteristics and factors across studies conducted in meteorology, health, and scholarly information (Barry & Schamber, 1998; Wang, 1997). Maglaughlin and Sonnenwald (2002) compared the findings of eleven previous studies on relevance criteria, counting the number of times each criterion was identified. The relevance criteria that consistently and frequently appeared included subject matter/topic, authority, completeness/depth, currency/recency, accuracy/quality, affectiveness, belief, credibility, clarity, and document type.

It should be noted here that information science researchers often use the broader term *quality* to denote the concept of credibility. For instance, Barry (1994) found that academic users employed criteria pertaining to evaluation of a document's source (i.e., source quality and source reputation/visibility). Wang and Soergel's (1998, p. 120) work revealed the criterion of "expected quality," which is defined as an estimation of the goodness of a document in terms of journal quality and author quality. Schamber (1991) examined user assessments of weather information and identified reliability as a criterion. She understood information to be reliable if "the source could be trusted, believed, or relied upon based on reputation or consistency" (p. 129). The results of relevance criteria research indicate that although the labels applied to categories differ from one research study to another, credibility is a notion underlying various relevance criteria such as expected quality, source quality, authority, and reliability. In both work settings (e.g., Barry and Wang & Soergel) and everyday life (e.g., Schamber), users express concerns about the credibility of the information and its source.

Bateman (1998, 1999) explored information credibility in the context of information seeking. From a survey of more than 200 graduate students, she identified the 11 most important criteria and ran a factor analysis to develop a three-dimensional model of relevance: information quality, information credibility, and information completeness. Together, these three factors explained 48 percent of the respondents' concepts of relevance. The results of Bateman's studies indicate that quality and credibility were very important to her user group. Users wanted information that was not only accurate, credible, well written, focused, understandable, and consistent but also easy to obtain, current, and on their topic.

Credibility Judgments of Information Seekers

Olaisen's (1990) research may have been the first empirical study that explicitly addressed the authority and credibility of electronic information. Based on questionnaires and interviews conducted with employees of Finnish banking companies, Olaisen (p. 113) found that the "knowledgeable person" was the most important source for both daily administrative decisions and strategic long-term decisions; these sources ranked high in credibility, influence, reliability, and relevance. Electronic information was emerging as an important source, scoring highly in relevance, perceived value, accessibility, actual value, flexibility, and browsing possibilities, but low in credibility, form, and user friendliness.

Rieh examined the problems of information quality and authority in Web searching by identifying the factors influencing people's judgments of information (Rieh, 2000, 2002; Rieh & Belkin, 1998, 2000). Using Wilson's (1983) theory of cognitive authority and Taylor's (1986) value-added model, she found that source characteristics were the primary criteria people used when making judgments on information quality. Her subjects mentioned source credibility on two different levels: institutional and individual. The Web users in Rieh's studies paid considerable attention to institutional authority, giving greater credence to academic and governmental institutions. They also took into account the affiliation of the author/creator, assigning higher levels of authority to professional experts such as professors, doctors, and librarians. Rieh's research indicates that the range of evidence people employ in ascribing source authority is much broader in the Web context than in the print realm. Moreover, people depend upon such judgments of source authority and credibility more heavily on the Web than in the print environment.

McKenzie (2003) also used Wilson's theory of cognitive authority to understand the basis upon which an individual decides whether or not a particular information source is authoritative. Her research examined "discursive action" by analyzing information seekers' descriptions of the authority of information sources in the context of pregnancy (p. 261). Based on her interviews with nineteen pregnant women, McKenzie found that this subpopulation did not blindly accept "authoritative knowledge" (p. 263). Rather, they used several forms of personal positioning to validate or contest the authority of an information source; they relied on themselves "as cognitive authorities, using their own reasoning, bodies, and experience as evidence against which to test the authority of another source" (pp. 281–282).

Scholars are generally concerned with the quality and authority of Web information based on source characteristics and domain knowledge (e.g., Rieh, 2002; Rieh & Belkin, 1998), but students may have different ways of evaluating information credibility on the Web. As Leckie (1996) has pointed out, a model of "expert researchers" that requires in-depth knowledge of the discipline, awareness of important scholars, and participation in a scholarly communication system, cannot be applied to undergraduate students who possess none of these characteristics. A few empirical studies have explicitly investigated how students address the credibility of information when they are seeking information on the Web.

Liu (2004, p. 1031) operationalized credibility assessment as "a cognitive process by which information is filtered and selected." His analysis revealed that resonance with one's beliefs, novelty of information, trustworthiness, and good quality have a positive impact on credibility perception. Liu identified two other types of source credibility—verifiable credibility and cost-effect credibility—that, in addition to the four types of credibility proposed by Tseng and Fogg (1999), play a significant role in shaping student perceptions. He noted that because students may not be well equipped for making credibility assessments (e.g., they may lack familiarity with authors' affiliations), they tend to look for verifiable sources that confirm their credibility appraisals. In terms of cost-effectiveness, Web-based information that is not free, in that it requires purchase or subscription, tends to be viewed as credible. Liu and Huang (2005) found that undergraduate students relied predominantly on an author's name/reputation/affiliation as well as Web site reputation for their credibility evaluation. In contrast, graduate students focused more on information accuracy/quality.

Based on her interviews with 15 first-year undergraduates, Whitmire (2004) examined the relationship between students' epistemological beliefs and reflective judgments on the one hand and how they searched for information in digital environments on the other. She argued that people's ideas about how to view and construct knowledge come into play when they encounter information in digital environments: They make judgments about the information on the basis of these epistemological beliefs. Whitmire introduced the reflective judgment model to examine how epistemological beliefs affect thinking and reasoning processes. Based on their Measures of Epistemological Reflection (MERs) scores, the 15 undergraduates were divided into two groups: absolute believers and transitional believers. Absolute believers selected information sources consistent with their own views and rejected those that were not consonant with their points of view. When they encountered conflicting information sources, they asked authority figures such as faculty for help in determining source authority rather than figuring things out on their own. Transitional believers used various criteria to evaluate Web sources, such as examining the URL of a Web site, assessing its author's institutional affiliation, and looking at the publisher of a print source. These students often felt that including conflicting information in their papers strengthened their academic assignments.

Agosto (2002a, 2002b) investigated how young people make decisions while using the Web. She conducted group interviews with 22 ninth- and tenth-grade female students and found that adolescents' evaluation criteria of information sources on the Web differ from those of adults. For instance, her study participants had strong positive responses to both the color and the design of graphics and multimedia. Perceived quality of information content proved to be a primary evaluation criterion, but these users tended simply to equate information quality with information quantity. Credibility and authority were not discussed extensively. Agosto's findings are consistent with those of Fidel, Davies, Douglass, Holder, Hopkins, Kushner, et al. (1999), who also did not find credibility to be a major concern of high school students when they evaluated information encountered on the Web.

In summary, discussions of credibility within the field of information seeking and retrieval have come to prominence only during the past few years. Most studies in this area have sought to understand people's perceptions and judgments of credibility in the Web context. The Web provides a unique information-seeking environment because of its relative lack of quality control mechanisms. Scholars still tend to make use of conventional indicators of credibility (such as an institution's name and an individual's affiliation) within the context of the Web; young adults, who have not yet acquired the knowledge and skills necessary for assessing credibility, give evidence of quite different perceptions about Web information. This problem will be discussed further in the section on Teaching Critical Thinking.

Management Information Systems

In a wide range of organizational settings, managers and other decision makers rely upon general judgment and advice, specific recommendations and solutions, and factual claims presented by information systems. Research in this area has examined (1) when and to what degree users of expert systems, decision support systems, and other information systems may over-rely or under-rely on advice provided by these systems; (2) whether credibility assessments of, and responses to, information system advice might differ from those produced by non-computer sources such as people; and (3) the effects of providing various types of explanations for a system's conclusions or recommendations.

Expertise and Information Systems

There is little evidence that users are generally in awe of computers' decision-making or advisory abilities; nonetheless, they may have high expectations, as the very name of one class of systems—"expert" systems—suggests. As Winograd and Flores (1986, p. 132) point out, "When we talk of a human 'expert' we connote someone whose depth of understanding serves not only to solve specific well-formulated problems, but also to put them into a larger context." Words such as "intelligence," "knowledge," and "understanding" also carry connotations above and beyond expert systems' capabilities and thus may obscure their inherent limitations (Will, 1991; Winograd & Flores, 1986). Unlike human experts, expert systems are often "brittle" in the sense of being unable either to cope with small deviations from their programmed expertise or to apply broader contextual knowledge and common sense to novel situations.

Nevertheless, expert systems are generally viewed as credible advisers in a wide range of domains and circumstances, even though such systems use static information and rules applied to dynamic problems (Murphy & Yetmar, 1996). Dijkstra (1999) has pointed out that, when users are unable to verify information from such systems, they may rely on peripheral cues, such as the degree to which the interaction with the system is enjoyable, in deciding whether to accept the system's output. This is similar to social interactions, where source credibility is often relied upon in place of a more rigorous examination of claims and arguments (Petty & Cacioppo, 1986).

Several researchers (e.g., Flake, 1991; Lerch, Prietula, & Kulik, 1997; Wærn & Ramberg, 1996) have sought to compare responses to advice derived from expert systems and other information systems to that given by humans. These researchers have found that users perceive human and computer advisers differently but do not always perceive or respond differently to advice from these two sources. Wærn and Ramberg (1996) found no differences between the perception of advice given by computers and by people but did discover evidence that humans and computers may be perceived as more or less trustworthy depending upon the task. Similarly, Dijkstra, Liebrand, and Timminga (1998) found that users perceive expert systems as more objective than humans. Lerch et al. (1997) found that users place greater confidence in human advice than in advice provided by an expert system. However, when particular expert systems were said to perform more reliably than human advisers, participants did agree more with the former in spite of having less confidence in expert systems as a whole. The researchers pointed out that users respond to predictability and dependability separately in making concurrence decisions. Dependability assessments reflect source attributions, whereas predictability assessments are based upon known or perceived behavioral consistency, not source attributions. The researchers also found that users perceive human and expert system advisers differently, attributing effort only to humans and invoking experience as an explanation for expertise only in the case of humans.

The perceived objectivity of expert systems reported by Dijkstra et al. (1998) is consistent with research indicating that users seek out, and respond differently to, human- and computer-based feedback. Kluger and Adler (1993) found people to be more likely to seek feedback from a computer when the goal was to obtain objective information about their performance. Earley (1988) reported that computer-based feedback was considered more credible than the same feedback from human superiors. In spite of these reported differences, Jiang, Klein, and Vedder (2000) found compliance patterns in human–system interactions that were consistent with human–human persuasion contexts. Users are more likely to comply if confidence in the source is high, self-confidence in the decision domain is low, and the discrepancy between the user's initial choice and the system's suggested choice is low. Finally, use of expert systems has the potential to imbue people with increased credibility in subsequent human–human interactions. Murphy and Yetmar (1996) found that managers in public accounting firms agreed more frequently with a subordinate's evaluations if told that the subordinate had used an expert system to reach the decision.

Reliance

Users of information systems often accept a recommended course of action from a system without critical examination or without considering the possibility of system errors. Such errors can result from commission, in which a rule contributing to a system's output is factually incorrect, or omission, in which a rule is missing altogether or is incorrectly constrained (Will, 1991). The limited ability of users of information systems to recognize and account for such inaccuracies is not uncommon, even for human experts in the system domain who are evaluating weak arguments (Dijkstra, 1995; Kottemann, Davis, & Remus, 1994). Expert system usage can reduce the motivation to think critically about the information upon which a decision is based, with users committing to it based solely on the credibility of the decision support system itself (Landsbergen, Coursey, Loveless, & Shangraw, 1997).

Will (1991) had a group of reservoir petroleum engineers interact with an expert system that suggested erroneous models for solving well pressure buildup problems and noted that both novices and experts relied on the incorrect models. Compared to a group of users who had arrived at incorrect conclusions using *conventional* methods (rather than an expert system), the novice group using an erroneous expert system showed greater confidence in its decisions. Will argued that this provides evidence for over-reliance on the expert system by novices.

Even in the case of critical decisions, users faced with a difficult task requiring the integration of large amounts of information may rely on decision-support systems without attempting to verify their information. Biros, Fields, and Gunsch (2003) found that operators in a military command and control scenario tended not to make use of available external safeguards for verification.

Additionally, Swinney (1999) has found that organizational norms and biases may make some types of system recommendations more acceptable than others, again leading to over-reliance. Conversely, because information systems are often used within organizational settings, factors such as word-of-mouth effects among co-workers or fear of the system's impact on job security can lead to under-reliance or general suspicion. If trust in automation is low, operators may consequently view such systems as less credible and thus reject accurate information (Muir, 1987). Moreover, overconfidence in one's own abilities can lead to under-reliance on a reliable system (Swinney, 1999).

Luthans and Koester (1976) and Koester and Luthans (1979) found evidence that experience may influence one's tendency to accept and comply with suggestions from computers. They found that highly experienced users may be overly skeptical and that inexperienced users tend to over-rely on suggestions from computers, as compared to a control condition with mimeographed lists of the same suggestions. This finding is consistent with an early belief among researchers that users are likely to be "in awe" of computers, viewing them as credible in a wide range of domains (Pancer, George, & Gebotys, 1992); however, subsequent experimental research has shown little evidence for this belief (e.g., Andrews & Gutkin, 1991; Wærn & Ramberg, 1996).

Findings of both over-reliance and under-reliance on information system advice demonstrate that developing an accurate understanding of a system's accuracy over time can be difficult. Even when evidence is considered or system behavior is observed, users may place too much weight on recent outcomes, leading to either over-reliance or under-reliance (Jiang, Muhanna, & Pick, 1996). However, users may be better equipped to detect errors if they are warned about potential data quality concerns prior to interaction with the system (Biros, George, & Zmud, 2002). As Muir (1987) has pointed out, users supported in appropriately calibrating their acceptance of information system advice will be best able to understand the circumstances under which a system's output can be reliable. Muir argues that in order to interact most effectively with such systems, users need an accurate perception of the system's level of trustworthiness (e.g., a lack of unnecessary skepticism or awe) and an understanding of the most effective criteria upon which to base this judgment.

Explanations

Expert and decision support systems are often equipped with explanation facilities that can expose the underlying processes behind system conclusions and recommendations. These explanation facilities may be invoked by the user, remain constantly present, or be presented to the user based on an analysis of user interactions with the system (Gregor & Benbasat, 1999). Explanations provided by these facilities can vary in both referent and form. Trace or line-of-reasoning explanations provide a logic behind the decision; justification or support explanations point to extensive reference material in support of a full or partial decision. Control (or "strategic") explanations indicate the problem-solving strategy used in arriving at the conclusion. Finally, terminological explanations provide definition information (Gregor & Benbasat, 1999; Ye & Johnson, 1995). Ye and Johnson (1995) found that auditors were more likely to accept expert system advice when the system's reasoning process was made clear via use of explanations, with justification explanations being the most effective. The researchers noted that different domains of human work have varying standards for what constitutes an acceptable argument.

Each explanation type may also be presented to system users in various ways. Researchers typically distinguish between natural language and production rule presentations; in some cases, the contrast has been characterized more generally by *mechanistic* dialogues versus *humanistic* ones. *Procedural* presentations of facts demonstrate IF-THEN rules, whereas *declarative* presentations simply list the involved facts without demonstrating the necessary procedural rules for arriving at a solution (Lamberti & Wallace, 1990).

Dijkstra et al. (1998) found the perceived objectivity of expert systems to be pronounced when such systems presented arguments using a production rule format. Exposing or increasing the transparency of decision-making processes does not always influence attitudes toward decisions, however, such as in the case of exposing the algorithm behind the process (Brown & Jones, 1998). Lerch et al. (1997) found that although providing explanations increased user agreement when expert system advice was given, it failed to boost user confidence in the system.

It is important to note that user desire for explanations can be driven by discrepancies between expert system advice and initial user choice or attitude. If the discrepancy is very low, the benefit of seeking an explanation may be outweighed by the cost; if the discrepancy is too high, users may see little chance of being persuaded. If users typically choose not to seek system explanations, human–system trust may not develop. Such explanations may be critical not simply for short-term compliance (as is the focus of most studies) but also for appropriately calibrating user reliance on system advice and for increasing domain knowledge, thus reducing the "black box phenomenon" (Landsbergen et al., 1997) in user interactions with complex expert systems.

Consumer Behavior

Consumers have an incentive to look for reliable cues to a product's level of quality prior to purchase as well as to avoid high costs associated with information seeking. The entities with the greatest amount of accurate information about available products are the firms themselves but they are inherently biased. Because firms and consumers have asymmetric information about the quality of available products, consumers still must incur costs in evaluating claims and assessing the credibility of firms, advertisers, and other marketing sources (Spence, 1974; Stigler, 1961). Information technology can help to reduce these asymmetries, but it also creates new pressures on credibility evaluation, often compelling consumers to integrate and assess product-relevant messages and interpret firms' overt behaviors in new ways. In this section we review the concepts of claims, verification, and signaling and their relevance to credibility assessment and discuss how the use of information technology can distort, impede, or enhance credibility assessments by consumers.

Claims

One straightforward way in which firms attempt to inform consumers of product quality is through claims made in advertisements and other marketing materials. Consumer researchers have attempted to distinguish between relative levels of objectivity and subjectivity in these claims. *Factual* claims describe objectively verifiable product features such as performance dimensions; *evaluative* claims appeal to subjective and emotional responses to intangible aspects of the product such as prestige of ownership (Holbrook, 1978). Darley and Smith (1993) have separated the two critical dimensions of objectivity (factual/impressionistic and tangible/intangible), pointing out that maximally objective claims will both be factual and refer to tangible attributes but maximally subjective claims will be impressionistic and refer to intangible attributes. Factual claims regarding intangible attributes are argued to be impossible, as is consistent with most conceptualizations of these dimensions (e.g., Ford, Smith, & Swazy, 1990).

The use of exaggerated claims ("puffery"), however, has its limits. Claims may be extreme in either a consumer-independent or consumer-dependent sense. Source credibility is a critical factor moderating the (dis)incentive for firms to overstate product quality. When source credibility is low, moderate claim extremity achieves greatest attitude change and, thus, such firms have no incentive to be deceptive beyond this point (Goldberg & Hartwick, 1990); indeed, it may be most beneficial to understate quality until source credibility is enhanced (Kopalle & Assunção, 2000). When source credibility is high, claim extremity is generally positively related to attitude change (Goldberg & Hartwick, 1990). Even for high-credibility sources, however, claims not relevant to a primary message or central argument within an advertisement can hinder the effectiveness of the message and render it less credible (Mackenzie, 1986; Meyvis & Janiszewski, 2002).

Verification

Probably the most critical aspect of product claims with respect to credibility has to do with whether and at what cost consumers can verify such claims. Nelson (1970, 1974) initially explored the fundamental differences between claims referring to *search qualities* of a product, which can be determined prior to purchase (such as the color of a dress), and *experience qualities*, which cannot be determined until after purchase (such as the taste of canned tuna fish).

The verification of both search and experience quality claims can vary in cost. A home buyer may verify both relatively objective (such as the home's dimensions and amenities) and subjective (such as the home's coziness or the beauty of its surroundings) claims prior to its purchase and still incur the costs of arranging a viewing of the home as well as travel and inspection time. Consequently, subjective claims are again inherently less credible; sellers may exaggerate such claims just enough to entice potential buyers to incur the above costs but not to the degree that discovered exaggeration overwhelms search costs (Nelson, 1974).

Experience quality claims, too, differ in typical verification costs. The price of a good is often an immediate roadblock to verification; an inexpensive good may be tried and discarded if it fails to meet a consumer's needs. Even when price does not significantly hinder "trialability" (Rogers, 1995, p. 243), some product attributes, such as the durability of a running shoe, can be assessed only after a considerable amount of usage (Davis, Kay, & Star, 1991). Darby and Karni (1973) have further distinguished experience qualities that are costly to evaluate from credence; this distinction makes verification costs impossible, for all practical purposes. Consumers may, for example, lack the skills necessary for verification (such as in the case of assessing automobile repair claims). Even in the case of search qualities, complex product attributes may require considerable skill and experience to verify prior to purchase (Shapiro & Spence, 2002). By and large, consumers place a strong belief in their own experiences (Smith, 1993). Wright and Lynch (1995) found direct usage to play a larger role than advertisements in determining belief strength for experience quality claims.

Signaling

Firms often communicate with consumers about the quality of their products and their own characteristics (e.g., reputation and production efficiency) in less explicit ways than through advertising claims, such as by offering warranties and money-back guarantees or simply by the expensive act of advertising itself (Kihlstrom & Riordan, 1984; Nelson, 1974). Credible signals are often expensive to produce, precisely because the expense of the signal can indicate production efficiency and, therefore, product reliability and quality. For a signal to be credible, however, it must also reliably indicate which firms "have the goods" and which do not. If low-quality firms have both the ability and incentive to mimic or fake the signal, then a pooling equilibrium occurs and consumers will be unable to determine which firms are of high quality, thereby reducing the usefulness of the signal. When high-quality firms have an incentive to produce a particular signal and low-quality firms have an incentive to refrain from doing so, a separating equilibrium occurs (Kirmani & Rao, 2000). Warranties, for example, signal quality only under circumstances in which they will be invoked by consumers with sufficient frequency to produce costs for low-quality firms outweighing the benefits (to those same firms) of a noisy market; consequently, they must be observably enforceable (Kirmani & Rao, 2000).

Firms may incur the cost of a signal prior to production and display (such as in the case of advertisements) or they may attempt to signal quality with the understanding that deceptive signals would lead them to incur future costs (such as in the case of warranties and money-back guarantees). For instance, sale signs can credibly signal below-market prices only when a retailer does not overuse them; if too many products are claimed to be on sale or if retailers attempt to introduce noise by placing sale signs on higher-priced items, consumers will become skeptical of the signal and cease to rely on it (Anderson & Simester, 1998, 2001). Notice, however, that credibility decisions based on the use (or overuse) of sale signs are enhanced by consumers' global view of brick-and-mortar stores as well as the impracticality of retailers dynamically and rapidly altering which products display these signals. Thus, a key aspect of in-store browsing and shopping is that consumers gain a view of the "lay of the land" for a set of products associated with a single retailer. Electronic contexts typically hide or distort this "shelved" view of the world, and often aggregate or filter sets of products from various sources.

Online Consumer Behavior

Products presented and described through information technology lack the abundance of sensory data normally available to in-store consumers. Consequently, product qualities normally verifiable prior to in-store purchase become experience qualities for online consumers: This tends to erode the credibility of the Internet as a medium (Graefe, 2003).

In few arenas is the link between credibility and subsequent trusting behaviors as immediate as in e-commerce; thus, there is likely to be a strong incentive for firms to leverage digital product experience to increase believability of experience quality claims along with a strong incentive for online consumers to verify such claims.

There are a few primary mechanisms through which these needs are partially addressed. First, online product information can be both abundant and available for processing at the consumer's pace. Such abundant information, however, can come with significant search costs, particularly for novice Internet users who must possess numerous information-gathering skills (Burbules, 2001). Because the amount of successful information gathering is heavily dependent upon user skills and motivation, the extent of reliance on source credibility and brand reputation can differ among consumers (Ward & Lee, 2000). It is well established that the elaboration of claims and importance of source credibility can differ for print, radio, and television ads (Brown, Homer, & Inman, 1998; Smith & Buchholz, 1991), as different media place varying demands on consumer attention and allow for varying amounts of reflection, claim and counterargument rehearsal, and cognitive elaboration.

Second, information technology produces massive electronic "word-of-mouth" networks that consumers might access in order to indirectly assess experience quality claims prior to purchase. Recommender systems assist and augment this process by providing appropriate recipients with recommendations from previous consumers (Resnick & Varian, 1997). Bickart and Schindler (2001) have demonstrated that users gathering product information from online forums tend to have greater product interest than those gathering information from marketing materials available from a corporate Web site. Both recommender systems and online forums carry the advantages of written text over typical spoken word-of-mouth because users may access others' stories and experiences at their own pace and depth (Bickart & Schindler, 2001).

Third, although experience qualities may sometimes drift to search qualities, Klein (1998, 2003) has demonstrated that information systems allow the reverse to occur as well. For example, a consumer might digitally observe how drapes or a vase could be situated in the home—and thus what is normally an experience quality (the attractiveness of the drapes *in context*) becomes an attribute one can examine prior to purchase. More commonly, consumer use of information technology reduces search quality verification costs. Where a consumer would once have been required to travel to a retail store in order to observe many prepurchase product features (particularly the less tangible of these), digital experiences allow for more of these features to be assessed remotely. Daugherty, Li, and Biocca (2001) found that increased levels of telepresence influenced attitude toward the brand. Presence was investigated by varying user control over the environment and the mediated sense of the environment through sensory channels (see Steuer [1992] for an overview of the construct). Klein (2003) similarly found that telepresence increases the strength of beliefs and attitudes for digital product experiences.

Biswas and Biswas (2004) have found that the online shopping context places a premium on credible product quality signals in comparison to in-store contexts. They point out that, compared with in-store contexts, consumers in electronic spaces accept inherently greater risk and thus have a strong incentive to look for the expensive signals of product quality. This increased risk is a fundamental pressure on credibility evaluations in electronic spaces. When consumers face uncertainty, they tend to rely more heavily on brand reputation (Erdem & Swait, 2004) as a general signal of product quality and without incurring search costs (Adaval, 2003; Anand & Shachar, 2004).

Consumers may frequently rely on the perceived cost of an advertisement as a signal of product quality (Kihlstrom & Riordan, 1984) but the kinds of knowledge used to make such judgments for traditional print and television advertisements (e.g., "popular programs charge more for ad time") will not always apply in electronic contexts. Moreover, it may be unclear to consumers precisely what makes it costly to produce and display an online advertisement. One cue consumers do appear to use is the quality and credibility of the Web site in which the advertisement appears, which can increase the credibility of the advertisement (Choi & Rifon, 2002). With the newer online medium, however, consumers are likely to face a number of situations in which costly signals (indeed, even those that would normally create a separating equilibrium) will go unnoticed due to the inability to recognize that the signal reliably indicates quality. In these cases, high-quality firms may need to invest resources in demonstrating as well as reminding consumers of the costliness of the signal (Kirmani & Rao, 2000).

On the other hand, in-store consumers have already incurred travel costs; comparative information is more useful when gathered prior to incurring search costs, for example when reading a comparative advertisement at home. In a store, consumers are more receptive to information confirming the fact of a "good deal" and are thereby likely to accept information promoting a preexisting intention to buy (Grewal, Marmorstein, & Sharma, 1996), consistent with cognitive dissonance theory (Festinger, 1957). The accessibility of online information allows such comparisons to be made prior to incurring travel costs and consequently may contribute to greater skepticism toward in-store claims, promoting comparative shopping.

Persuasiveness

A key aspect of consumer credibility assessments of product claims and signals is that buyers and sellers (or advertisers) interact in a context in which persuasion goals are highly salient. Consumers develop knowledge about the sorts of tactics that agents of persuasion typically use as well as beliefs about the fairness or manipulativeness of such tactics. This knowledge and set of beliefs in turn shape how they respond to persuasive tactics (Friestad & Wright, 1994). Further, these tactics may begin to take on a meaning for consumers. That is, they may come to believe that certain tactics reliably indicate something about the communicator (e.g., "If a candidate starts mudslinging, he must know he's probably going to lose the election"). Moreover, when persuasion goals are salient and consumers have gained experience in such contexts, consumers can more easily step beyond proximate sources and think about the goals and biases of the organizations that serve as puppet masters behind the exchange (Friestad & Wright, 1994). This is in contrast to the vast majority of media experiences in which the motivation to think beyond the proximate source does not exist (Reeves & Nass, 1996; Sundar & Nass, 2000).

Consequently, high source credibility in consumer behavior contexts can in some cases exert little or no effect, or even, potentially, decrease persuasion. When consumers reflect upon their own purchase behaviors to help them develop attitudes toward products and brands, for example, the use of highly credible sources in the brand's marketing mix can be a liability because consumers may attribute such behaviors to the advertising tactics rather than attributing it to their own internal motivations (Dholakia & Sternthal, 1977).

Consumer researchers have further noted an inherent trade-off in many cases between increased source credibility and persuasiveness. Including negative claims about a product may indicate lack of bias and increase credibility, for example, but at the cost of consumer intent to purchase the product (Settle & Golden, 1974). It is noteworthy here that high source credibility can in some cases undermine behavioral persistence (Dholakia & Sternthal, 1977). Appeals to source credibility involve the peripheral rather than the central route to persuasion, resulting in attitudes both more predictive of behavior and more resistant to change (Petty & Cacioppo, 1986). Thus, there is potentially a trade-off that firms face in relying too heavily upon peripheral cues in their marketing mix when consumer motivation might in some cases warrant a central route approach with its associated persuasive advantages.

Perhaps the most critical area for research at the intersection of credibility, consumer behavior, and information technology involves how the inherent risk imposed by electronic information spaces influences responses to peripheral cues such as source credibility and potentially unreliable signals of product quality. Such uncertain circumstances create two competing incentives for information seekers: to look for, and rely upon, signals that reduce the inherently high cost of uncertainty while being simultaneously skeptical of such signals due to a lack of clear pressures that would normally ensure their reliability.

Health Science

In the previous sections, we discussed three major strands of theory and research concerning credibility assessment by users of information systems. In each circumstance—evaluating the results of information seeking and retrieval, interacting with systems designed to enhance decision making, and assessing claims and signals regarding products and services—the *importance* of the information being gathered and used has been a critical determinant of how users assess credibility, as predicted by the elaboration likelihood model (Petty & Cacioppo, 1986). For professionals and information seekers alike, the potentially negative effects of inaccurate health information have undoubtedly contributed to the special attention being paid to credibility assessment within the health domain.

Information Systems and Health Professionals

As health professionals' use of information systems increases, so does the need to promote the skills necessary for gathering accurate information efficiently. There is a growing need for producing graduates capable of using information technology to improve patient care (Casebeer, Bennett, Kristofco, Carillo, & Centor, 2002). Casebeer et al. (2002) collected survey data from a sample of 2,200 U.S. physicians and found that online information is used most frequently for addressing novel patient-specific problems. Practitioners are aware of credibility concerns and recognize the need for caution in relying on information systems in patient care (Parekh, Nazarian, & Lim, 2004); however, physicians' information seeking, when compared to that of medical information experts, did not produce the highest quality health information (Groot, ter Riet, Khan, & Misso, 2001). Physicians need to learn new evaluative skills because assessing the credibility of decision support systems and Internet resources is a fundamentally different activity from assessing the credibility of professors, colleagues, and textbooks.

Using online databases frequently may require health professionals to examine unfamiliar sources critically. Nevertheless, problems of credibility assessment remain even when the network of systems used is constrained, either to a set of trusted partners or within a single organization. Systems developed to advise in patient care or assist in diagnosis involve risks resulting from both system design and organizational constraints. Edwards, Kang, Preston, and Compton (1995) claim, for example, that indicating the accuracy of an expert system or its level of agreement with human experts can be misleading because expert system errors in health care decisions may have more disastrous consequences than human errors.

The ability of information systems to assist health professionals accurately is not always built-in and static but rather depends crucially upon organizational commitments and ease of use. The difficulty of entering patient records, case histories, cautionary notes, and other practitioner data into a database can negatively affect the timeliness, accuracy, and effectiveness of the system. Gardner and Lundsgaarde (1994) surveyed physicians and nurses regarding a centralized database intended to integrate information throughout one hospital and found a common concern among nurses about the completeness of database records and the inability to enter complete medical data.

As in managerial decision-making contexts, there has been a concern about the possibility of over-reliance on expert system conclusions. The system investigated by Gardner and Lundsgaarde (1994)—the Health Evaluation through Logical Processing (HELP) system—consisted of an inference engine that could warn of drug contraindications. Over-reliance on this system, based on the presumption that HELP will always indicate contraindications successfully, when conjoined with incomplete medical records, might well prove disastrous.

Further evidence suggests that, within the health sciences, computer output is not perceived to be more credible than human communications. Honaker, Hector, and Harrell (1986) asked a group of clinicians and graduate students in psychology to evaluate personality reports labeled as being generated either by computer or by a human practitioner. They found no evidence that either group perceived reports generated by computers to be more credible than those by people. The clinicians in the sample perceived the computer-generated reports to be less comprehensive.

Online Health Information

According to the Pew Internet & American Life Project (Fox, 2005), 79 percent of Internet users have searched online for information on at least one major heath topic. Internet health information is used particularly frequently by younger people (Gray, Klein, Noyce, Sesselberg, & Cantrill, 2005; Licciardone, Smith-Barbaro, & Coleridge, 2001) and women (Baker, Wagner, Singer, & Bundorf, 2003; Escoffery, Miner, Adame, Butler, McCormick, & Mendell, 2005). There are at least two significant issues regarding the credibility of online health information from the consumer's point of view: One has to do with the quality of online health information and the other with the consumer's ability to understand the information.

There seems to be a consensus that the quality of online health information varies. Members of the general public are not simply consumers of health information but sometimes (unqualified) producers as well (Hardey, 2001). These difficulties result in widely varying strategies among consumers for evaluating online health information. For example, Peterson, Aslani, and Williams (2003) found that consumers differed greatly as to which sources they considered most credible when searching for online information about various medicines. Eastin (2001) found that college students are very concerned about the credibility of health information, paying attention to both source expertise and content knowledge.

There has been much discussion as to what constitutes quality and credibility with respect to health information. Accuracy seems to be widely used as a primary facet of information quality (e.g., Berland, Elliott, Morales, Algazy, Kravitz, Broder, et al., 2001; Fallis & Frické,

2002; Haddow, 2003). When Eysenbach, Powell, Kuss, and Sa (2002) conducted a systematic analysis of 170 health information articles, they found that the quality criteria used to evaluate Web sites were much more diverse: technical quality, design, readability, accuracy, completeness/comprehensiveness/coverage/scope. Most technical criteria identified were "transparency criteria" from the print world: references, disclosure of authorship, author's credentials, and date of creation (p. 2694).

The Internet may be perceived as a major source of low-quality information but Eysenbach et al. (2002) pointed out that inaccurate information was not a problem specific to the Web; they cited findings from other studies in which 76 percent of the information about oral hygiene from television, 53 percent from magazines, and 12 percent from newspapers was in fact inaccurate. They also reported that the inaccuracy rates of information about healthy eating in printed sources were high: 55 percent in free advertising newspapers, 30 percent in general interest magazines, 17 percent in health magazines, and 14 percent in newspapers. This indicates that the problem of credibility assessment of health information is not limited to the Internet; it is also present in other media.

When comparing the credibility of the Web with other kinds of information sources, Marton (2003) found that women perceived health care practitioners to be the most reliable source. Books were rated second-highest, followed by pamphlets and fact sheets. The lowest-rated information sources were Web-based bulletin boards and chat rooms. Web sites received slightly higher ratings than libraries.

It is important to note that people's credibility perceptions and actual judgments and behaviors are not always consistent. Eysenbach and Köhler (2002) compared the criteria identified in focus groups and in-depth interviews to the actual search behavior observed in information retrieval experiments. The kinds of criteria participants mentioned that they would use for assessing the credibility of health information on the Internet were diverse: authority of source, layout and appearance, readability, picture of the site owner, credentials and qualifications, content updating, and quality-seal and third-party endorsements. Contrary to the statements made in focus groups and interviews, none of the participants actively searched for information as to who stood behind the sites or how the information had been compiled. Most participants started their searches using general search engines, although only 20 percent were able to report the source name. Another 23 percent could recall the kinds of organizations (government agency, commercial organization, university, etc.). The results of Eysenbach and Köhler's research indicate that health consumers assess information in a manner different from that implicitly assumed in many studies about information quality and credibility on the Web.

Another important issue is consumers' lack of skills in evaluating the accuracy of online health information and their reliance on indirect cues (Eysenbach & Köhler, 2002; Freeman & Spyridakis, 2004). Using the term "context deficit," Eysenbach and Diepgen (1998, p. 1498) listed a number of ways in which health information users can be misled by information on the Web. One example is the difficulty of recognizing whether a document is directed at professionals or for patients. Patients who read materials intended for health professionals may misinterpret information and thus develop false expectations about treatment options. Again, health consumers may not realize that health information valid in a specific health care context may prove invalid in another.

The criticality of health information increases the importance of examining the information providers, owning organizations, and partnering organizations (Luo & Najdawi, 2004) as well as any related commercial interests (Morahan-Martin, 2004). Such interests are not always disclosed, however, and may be difficult for people to grasp when evaluating online health sites. Eysenbach and Diepgen (1998) propose two kinds of metadata to be assigned to online health information: metadata to help consumers assess reliability and descriptive metadata to provide context.

Online health information consumers simultaneously face difficulty in evaluating information and risk in making decisions based on this information. Possibly as a consequence, online information seeking in the health domain is often accompanied by related offline information seeking. Consumers of online health information may, for example, be influenced by offline interactions in a doctor's office in which specific Web sites might be recommended or advertised (Quintana, Feightner, Wathen, Sangster, & Marshall, 2001).

Gray et al. (2005) discovered that adolescents compared health information found online with information from offline personal sources; conversely, they used the Internet as a verification tool. This contrasts with the rarity of verification behaviors for other information topics; Metzger, Flanagin, and Zwarun (2003), for example, found that college students tended not to verify information found online. This interplay between online and offline information seeking for health information is potentially beneficial, particularly when patients discuss what they find on the Web with health professionals who are able to verify advice as well as dispel myths and clarify misconceptions resulting from inaccurate Internet resources (Benotsch, Kalichman, & Weinhardt, 2004).

Consumers may compare health information gathered online with that from other sources; in such searches, the Internet offers the advantages of privacy and anonymity. For example, on the Internet, people can gather information on topics that they may well feel uncomfortable discussing.

Evaluation of Web Resources

A substantial body of literature has addressed the issue of credibility on the Web, but it is often unclear what the objects of assessment have been. There appear to be three distinct levels of credibility assessment on the Web: evaluation of the Web, evaluation of Web sites, and evaluation of Web information. First, credibility assessment can be measured at the media level by comparing the credibility of the Web with other communication means such as television or newspapers. Credibility can be also measured by assessing individual Web sites as sources or by assessing information available on the Web.

Evaluation of the Web

Credibility assessment of the Web at the media level is frequently examined by directly inquiring of study participants if they perceive that the Web as a whole provides credible information resources. Several large-scale surveys of Internet use have included questions about Web credibility. The Oxford Internet Institute surveyed 2,190 households in Britain in 2005 and found that nearly half (48 percent) believe that most Web information is reliable and only 10 percent believed that just a small portion of the information was reliable (Dutton, Gennaro, & Hargrave, 2005). The Annenberg School Center for the Digital Future (2004) reported that 55.2 percent of its 2003 survey respondents considered the Internet to be a very important or an extremely important source of information, a figure that had fallen from 67.9 percent in 2000. The Center for the Digital Future longitudinal studies also indicated a slight decline in the number of users who believed that most or all of the information on the Internet was reliable and accurate (50.1 percent in 2003; 53 percent in 2002; 58 percent in 2001; 55 percent in 2000). The Pew Internet report on search engine users indicated that 68 percent of those surveyed said that search engines were a fair and unbiased source of information and only 19 percent said that they did not have that level of trust in search engines (Fallows, 2005). Interestingly, the 68 percent who considered search engines to be fair and unbiased were less knowledgeable, engaged, and experienced in searching than the 19 percent who were more skeptical.

A number of studies have compared people's perceptions of the credibility of information on the Web with their perceptions of the same when sourced from other media. Research on the credibility of traditional versus Internet information resources has failed to produce consistent findings (Flanagin & Metzger, 2000). Johnson and Kaye (1998) surveyed politically interested Web users and reported that online newspapers and political issue-oriented Web sites were rated as more believable than their traditional counterparts. By way of contrast, Mashek, McGill, and Powell (1997) found that users rated traditional media as less biased than their Internet equivalents when searching for political information. Johnson and Kaye (2002) conducted an online survey on the 2000 presidential campaign and found that online newspapers and news magazines were considered to be highly credible sources.

Sundar (1999) investigated the credibility criteria college students used by asking them to read and rate both print and online news stories. Factor analysis of the students' ratings revealed three measures that affected their perceptions of credibility: bias, fairness, and objectivity. A related factor was quality, which was found to be composed of the following measures: accuracy, believability, clarity, coherency, comprehensiveness, conciseness, and whether the stories were well written. Sundar argued that the results revealed a similarity between the factor structures underlying readers' perceptions of the credibility of print news and those underlying readers' perceptions of the credibility of online news.

A potential explanation for these inconsistencies may be found in the experience and confidence levels of Internet users. Flanagin and Metzger (2000) suggested that, as people become more experienced with the Internet, they become increasingly knowledgeable about sites to be trusted and sites to be ignored. Further, more experienced Internet users are more likely to verify Internet information and to judge it credible. This finding is consistent with the Annenberg School Center for the Digital Future's finding that, in 2003, 83.5 percent of very experienced users believed that most or all of the information on news pages posted by established media was reliable and accurate; only 49.1 percent of new users gave the same response. Graham and Metaxas (2003), however, found that college students' confidence in their ability to search the Internet did not significantly affect their performance. The relationship between level of confidence and critical thinking to search performance certainly warrants further investigation.

These studies compared news in print media and on the Web; Mehta (2000), on the other hand, examined differences between the Web and traditional printed sources within the context of scholarly research. She investigated authors' citation behavior, noting whether authors cited Web information sources in their published work and what types of Web sources they cited. Some 47 percent of authors' citations came from the .com domain, followed by 22 percent from the .edu domain, and 14 percent from the .org domain. This result seems to contradict the findings of Treise, Walsh-Childers, Weigold, and Friedman (2003) that sites in the .gov domain were perceived to be more credible than those in the .com domain within the context of scientific research. Apparently, as Flanagin and Metzger (2000) have pointed out, people's perceptions about the credibility of different media vary depending on the type of information being sought and on the context in which the information will be used (e.g., news, reference, entertainment, or commercial).

Evaluation of Web Sites

The issue of credibility has been investigated most thoroughly at this level of analysis. Here, the individual Web site has been viewed as the source; credibility in this context is often referred to as Web site credibility. Flanagin and Metzger (2003) conceptualized users' perceptions of credibility along three dimensions: (1) message credibility (i.e., the perceived credibility of the information residing on a Web site); (2) sponsor credibility (i.e., the perceived credibility of the individual whose site is represented); and (3) site credibility (i.e., the perceived credibility of the Web site as a whole).

Abels, White, and Hahn (1997) collected data from faculty members by asking them to engage in "brainwriting" during a focus group conducted in an electronic environment. The six clusters that reportedly influenced the use of Web sites were appearance, content, linkage, special features, structure, and use. These authors noted that "when a user states that information must be useful, they are referring not only to topic coverage but also to the source or producer of the information" (Abels, White, & Hahn, 1998, p. 42).

Fogg and other members of the Stanford Web Credibility Research project have conducted a number of studies on Web site credibility issues (Fogg, Marshall, Kameda, Solomon, Rangnekar, Boyd, et al., 2001; Fogg, Marshall, Laraki, Osipovich, Varma, Fang, et al., 2001; Fogg, Marshall, Osipovich, Varma, Laraki, Fang, et al., 2000; Fogg, Soohoo, Danielson, Marable, Stanford, & Tauber, 2003; Fogg & Tseng, 1999). By conducting an online survey, Fogg and his colleagues examined which elements boost and which hurt perceptions of Web credibility. In their first study, conducted in 1999, Fogg, Marshall, Laraki, et al. (2001) collected data from more than 1,400 participants based on seven composite scales of characteristics of Web sites. The results showed that five types of elements increased credibility perceptions (real-world feel, ease of use, expertise, trustworthiness, and tailoring), but two types of elements decreased credibility perceptions (commercial implications and amateurism). In another study, Fogg et al. (2003) asked more than 2,600 participants to compare and comment on two Web sites within a particular content category (e.g., e-commerce sites, news sites, nonprofit organizational sites, travel sites, Web search sites). They selected 10 sites within each of 10 content categories and analyzed participants' comments to ascertain which Web site features were noticed when people evaluated credibility. Their research identified a number of features including design look, information design/structure, information focus, company motive, usefulness of information, accuracy of information, name recognition and reputation, advertising, bias of information, and tone of writing. Of the top 10 issues about which participants were concerned, five dealt with information, three with design issues, and two with source characteristics. These results were compared with the credibility assessments of 15 experts in the health and finance fields (Stanford, Tauber, Fogg, & Marable, 2002). Overall, domain experts were considerably less concerned about visual appeal than were consumers; they also expressed more concern about the quality of a site's information. Stanford et al.'s study found that health experts assigned more credibility to health sites that provided information from reputable sources and relied on author credentials. Finance experts assigned more credibility to finance sites that provided unbiased educational information rather than steering consumers toward their own products and services.

Based on four years of quantitative research on Web credibility, Fogg (2003b) developed the prominence-interpretation theory, which posits two aspects of credibility assessment: the likelihood of an element related to the source or message being noticed when people evaluate credibility (prominence) and the value or meaning assigned to the element based on the user's judgment of how the element affects the likelihood of being good or bad (interpretation). Fogg identified five factors affecting prominence: user involvement, information topic, task, experience level, and other individual differences. Three factors affecting interpretation were identified: user assumptions, user skill and knowledge, and contextual factors such as the environment in which the assessment is made. Fogg explained how people repeated their evaluative processes, focusing on different Web site elements until they were satisfied with their credibility assessments or until other constraints, such as lack of time or skill, stopped them.

Young adults might have ways of assessing credibility on the Web that differ from what adult Web users do. Clark and Slotta (2000) explored the topic of how inclusion of static images with written text on the Web influenced high school students' interpretations of source authority. Although students could reliably judge the higher authority sources as being more knowledgeable and trustworthy than lower authority ones, no significant difference was revealed in students' final preference for either type of information source. Furthermore, boys tended to rate a piece of evidence as more important when it included an image, but girls believed information presented as text-only to be more important.

Wathen and Burkell (2002) have conceptualized the evaluation process of Web sites on three levels: surface credibility, message credibility, and content evaluation. In surface credibility assessments, users focus on presentational and organizational characteristics of a Web site. In message credibility assessments, users thoroughly review indicators of source and message credibility and decide whether the information provided is likely to be believable. In content assessments, users integrate source evaluations with self-knowledge of their own expertise, domain knowledge, and information need, deciding if and how to act on the information. If failure occurs at either the surface or message credibility assessment stages, the user is likely to exit the site.

Tombros, Ruthven, and Jose (2005) investigated the criteria used by Web searchers in assessing Web pages. They separated these criteria into six categories: text, structure, quality, non-textual items, physical properties, and counted mentions of page features. Each category contained several kinds of document features. For instance, the "quality" category included scope/depth, authority/source, recency, general quality, content novelty, and error on page. The component features of "text" were content, titles/headings, query terms, and numbers. The authors reported the ranking of the 10 most important features users took into account when judging a Web page to be useful and the ten they took into account when judging a Web page not to be useful. Most features mentioned for one type of judgment were mentioned for the other type as well, but authority/source was listed as an important indicator only of usefulness.

Hong (2006) examined the influence of both message and structural features on perceptions of Web site credibility as measured by five dimensions of credibility: expertise, goodwill, trustworthiness, depth, and fairness. Message features refer to the characteristics of a message that lend perceived credibility to the overall message of the source. The interactive nature of Web sites is such that the relative contribution of structural features to overall site credibility should be assessed separately. Regression analyses indicated that message features were more important than structural features in determining perceived site credibility. The presence of quotations/testimonials, statistics, authorship, source reference, information currency, and information selection criteria in Web sites was positively associated with site credibility. In contrast, structural features such as the presence of third-party endorsements, privacy policy, site authorship, site contact information, and site navigation tools did not influence perceptions of Web site credibility.

Evaluation of Web Information

This level explores the concept of credibility on the basis of individual objects of information found on the Web. For instance, when people come upon a new fact or obtain information from the Web, can they trust what they have found? The assumption is that the credibility of information can vary on the Web and even within the same site. There are two approaches to this issue, the first being to provide guidelines on the criteria that could influence users' perceptions of the quality of information they obtain. This is discussed in the next section on Teaching Critical Thinking. The second approach is to understand users' assessments based on their own statements. This method is similar to that of relevance criteria studies except that the focus is on assessments of credibility rather than on judgments of relevance.

Rieh (2000, 2002) examined the factors influencing judgments of information quality and cognitive authority by collecting users' verbal reports through think-aloud sessions and interviews. The content analysis of the criteria mentioned by Web users resulted in six major categories with 14 subcategories as follows:

1. Characteristics of information objects (type of information object, title, content, organization/structure, presentation, graphics, functionality)

2. Characteristics of sources (URL domain type, type of source, source reputation, single versus collective source, author/creator credentials)

3. Knowledge (domain knowledge, system knowledge)

4. Situation

5. Ranking in search output

6. General assumptions

Rieh's (2000, 2002) results showed that when people made choices about which Web page to visit first (predictive judgment), they relied on their previous knowledge. For instance, the study subjects went directly to sites recommended to them by other people or to sites they already knew. When people evaluated Web sites during use, prior knowledge became a less important factor as they paid more attention to the characteristics of information objects, especially content, graphics, organization/structure, and type of information object. Interestingly, the characteristics of sources—source reputation, type of source, and author/creator credentials—were consistently important for users making both predictive and evaluative judgments. Huerta's (2003) findings confirm Rieh's research by determining that out of five manipulated variables (quality of content, modality of exposure, simulation, message attractiveness, and reputation of the Web site owner), quality of content and owner reputation were statistically significant.

Addressing the issue of credibility by distinguishing among the three levels of evaluation—of the Web, of sites, and of information—clarifies some of the conflicting results and arguments. Overall, the Web itself seems to have gained a certain level of credibility as an information source over the years, comparing favorably in terms of credibility with traditional media such as television, newspapers, and magazines (Annenberg School Center for the Digital Future, 2004). In many studies, credibility has been operationalized in terms of reliability and accuracy. As these studies dealt with two aspects of credibility in one question (is the information reliable and accurate?), it remains unclear what respondents actually meant when they answered the question. They might have thought that the information on CNN.com is more accurate than that broadcast by CNN television simply because the Web tends to be updated more frequently.

Applications of the Concept of Credibility

Applying the concept of credibility to information systems can be done in three ways. Perhaps the most widely discussed application area is how to teach people to evaluate information so that they obtain it from credible sources: Two approaches are the checklist model and the critical thinking model. Second, the evaluation criteria that people are advised to use can also be employed as guidelines by Web designers who want to boost a site's credibility. The third area concerns designing information retrieval systems in which various aspects of credibility judgments can be integrated with topical relevance to improve search performance. Evaluating information credibility and designing credible systems and Web sites are two sides of the same coin. Together, they help people secure good, useful, reliable, and trustworthy information to help them with the task at hand.

Teaching Critical Thinking

Much of the literature on the instruction of information evaluation aims to teach students by addressing issues such as how to make a quality assessment when potentially relevant materials have been located (Cooke, 1999). The criteria proposed tend to be drawn from librarians' experience of selecting materials for their collections. The items suggested in the various checklists can be summarized as follows (Alexander & Tate, 1999; Cooke, 1999; Dragulanescu, 2002; Kapoun, 1998; Kjartansdóttir & Widenius, 1995; Pratt, Flannery, & Perkins, 1996; Tate & Alexander, 1996):

- Objectivity issues: Is there a statement of the aims, objectives, and intended coverage? Is the information presented with a minimum of bias? To what extent is the information attempting to sway the opinion of the audience?

- Source reputation issues: What are the reputation and experience of the author or institution responsible for the information? Is the information written by a subject expert or produced by an institution with recognized knowledge and expertise in the field?

- URL domain issues: Is the document from a government site (.gov), educational institution (.edu), commercial site (.com), or nonprofit group (.org)?

- Currency and maintenance issues: Does the site indicate the date information was posted? Is the information up-to-date? Is the site generally well maintained?

- Information accuracy issues: Is the information factually accurate? Are there any typographic, spelling, or grammatical errors? Is it an advocacy site, championing the viewpoint of a particular organization? Is the information based on research or other evidence? Are there any references to published sources of information?

- Presentation of information issues: Is the information clearly presented and arranged? Is there a site map? Is there a search facility? Is the information categorized and has it been appropriately organized? Are the individual pages aesthetically pleasing? Is the text easy to read? Is it well written?

- Accessibility issues: Is the source reliably accessible? Can the source be accessed quickly? Is any additional software or hardware required? Are there any access restrictions, such as registration, passwords, proof of eligibility, or membership in an organization?

This checklist model has some limitations because evaluation of information is, for the most part, subjective, relative, and situational rather than objective, absolute, and universally recognizable (Rieh, 2000, 2002). Individual users have different expectations, make different predictions, and, more importantly, possess different levels of knowledge. Therefore, credibility is not always determined by the characteristics of information objects and sources, although these characteristics do serve as the bases for such judgments. Given the subjective nature of credibility judgments, bibliographic instruction needs to focus on helping students make informed judgments about others' knowledge claims (Wilson, 1991).

Meola (2004) offers a contextual approach to Web site evaluation as an alternative to the checklist model. The contextual approach uses three techniques: promoting the library's subscription-based electronic resources, comparative thinking and analysis, and corroboration (i.e., having students verify information against one or more different sources). Arnold and Jayne (1998) have also emphasized that the Web needs to be presented not as a tool, but as another information resource in the context of the information-seeking process. Students need to learn how to locate, evaluate, and use information effectively on the Web. This is an issue of information literacy (Buschman & Warner, 2005).

Information literacy and critical thinking are closely linked. McGuigan (2001) has pointed out that critical thinking and information literacy share the same goals: engaging students to be proactive learners who can use critical thinking skills in locating and using information. The Association of College and Research Libraries (2000) included in its definition of an information-literate individual the ability to evaluate information and its sources critically. Critical thinking is often considered as "the intellectually disciplined process of actively and skillfully conceptualizing, applying, analyzing, synthesizing, and/or evaluating information gathered ... as a guide to belief and action" (Scriven & Paul, 2004, online). Case (2003) has proposed a range of tools that students need for critical thinking, such as background knowledge, critical thinking vocabulary, thinking strategies, and habits of mind that include open-mindedness, tolerance for ambiguity, an inquiring or critical attitude, and an intellectual work ethic.

Authors of library instruction and critical thinking literature point out the limitations of the simplistic approach of using a checklist with evaluation criteria. Critical thinking studies tend to be case studies of library instruction programs and thus are not value-neutral (Buschman & Warner, 2005; D'Angelo, 2001; Morrison & Stein, 1999; Swanson, 2004). More importantly, what seems to be missing in the current literature is the interventionist role that information professionals and librarians can play in facilitating people's judgments about the credibility of information.

Designing Web Sites

Teaching people how to evaluate information is not the only way with which information professionals can address the problem of information credibility (Fallis, 2004). Another is to help users make credibility judgments by highlighting evidence of credibility in information systems and Web sites. Although there is a substantial body of literature on teaching people how to evaluate information, there is very little research on how to design systems and Web sites to include more explicit evidence of information accuracy. Fallis (2004) insists that it is important to make information more verifiable because that would give people easier access to evidence. He suggests specific ways of making information more verifiable by offering both direct and indirect evidence. One approach is to organize information in ways that enable people to locate with ease additional evidence relevant to the topic in question. Further, information professionals can maintain metadata about the context in which information was created and disseminated.

The work of Fogg and colleagues has demonstrated various design elements that tend to influence user credibility assessments. Based on three years of research on Web credibility, Fogg (2002) developed the "Stanford Guidelines for Web Credibility" for Web designers. Its 10 guidelines are as follows:

- Design your site so it looks professional (or is appropriate for your purpose). Pay attention to layout, typography, images, consistency issues, and the like.

- Make it easy to verify the accuracy of the information on your site. You can build Web site credibility by providing third-party support (citations, references, source materials).

- Show that there's a real organization behind your site. The easiest way to do this is by listing a physical address. A photo of the offices and listing a membership with the local chamber of commerce can be helpful.

- Highlight the expertise in your organization as well as in the content and services you provide. Be sure to give the credentials of contributors and service providers. Don't link to outside sites that are not credible.

- Show that real people who are honest and trustworthy stand behind your site. In addition, find a way to convey their trustworthiness through images or text.

- Make it easy to contact you. Provide your phone number, physical address, and e-mail address.

- Make your site easy to use and useful. Web sites lose credibility whenever they make it difficult for users to accomplish the task at hand.

- Update your site's content frequently (at least show it's been reviewed recently).

- If possible, avoid having ads on your site. If you must have ads, clearly distinguish the sponsored content from your own.

- Avoid errors of all types, no matter how small they appear.

Sillence, Briggs, Fishwick, and Harris's (2005) guidelines developed specifically for health Web sites share some similarities with the Stanford Guidelines. Sillence et al. proposed three guidelines based on their empirical study of trust and selection of health Web sites: (1) make the purpose of the site clear; (2) allow a personalized, tailored experience; and (3) include markers of social identity. In addition to these specific guidelines, several studies have emphasized the implications of user evaluation criteria for the design of Web pages in terms of both content and also visual appearance and interface characteristics (e.g., Ivory & Hearst, 2002; Kim & Moon, 1998; Tombros et al., 2005).

Designing Information Retrieval Systems

In the field of information retrieval, the concept of credibility has been discussed as a part of the topic of relevance judgment rather than in its own right. With few exceptions, the notion of credibility has not been applied directly to the design of information retrieval systems. Even those studies that incorporate the credibility concept have not considered the aspect of human credibility assessment. Most assume that credibility can be represented simply as attributes of Web pages or documents. This assumption is limited, for credibility assessment is inherently a matter of human judgments and document attributes provide only the cues for such judgments. In spite of these limitations, it is still important to review a few significant studies here because the credibility concept has potential to be used as a way to filter information from a huge set of relevant pages. There seem to be two primary approaches.

The first explores the analysis of link structures. Kleinberg (1999) suggested a way to filter a small set of the most authoritative or definitive pages from a large number of relevant ones. According to Kleinberg, hyperlink structures among Web pages encode a considerable amount of latent human judgment and this type of judgment is precisely what is needed to formulate a notion of credibility. He claimed that a good hub is a page that points to many good authorities and a good authority, a page pointed to by many good hubs. PageRank, as implemented in Google, also makes use of the Web link structure to calculate a quality ranking for each Web page (Brin & Page, 1998). Amento, Terveen, and Hill (2000) computed five metrics: in- and out-degrees (Kleinberg, 1999), authority and hub scores (Kleinberg, 1999), and PageRank score (Brin & Page, 1998). They revealed that simply counting the number of pages on a site gave as good an estimate of quality as any of the link-based computations. Liu, Wang, Zhang and Ma (2005) also reported differences in non-content feature distribution between ordinary and key resources pages in terms of in-degree, URL length, in-site out-link anchor text rate, in-site out-link number, and document length.

The second approach explores the attributes of the document. Price and Hersh (1999) addressed the idea of using automatic filtering techniques to identify pages likely to be of high quality. Their prototype system examined Web pages and assigned a score to indicate the likelihood that each page would meet quality criteria such as relevance, credibility, absence of bias, quality of content, currency, and value of links. The indicator for credibility was computed via several subroutines that inspected the URL, looked for authorship of the information, determined whether the site displayed the HONcode logo, and searched for particular words or phrases such as "miracle cure." Zhu and Gauch (2000) selected quality metrics in terms of currency, availability, information-to-noise ratio, authority, popularity, and cohesiveness; they found that the authority metric was not related to search effectiveness.

Recently, Bai, Ng, Sun, Kantor, and Strzalkowski (2004) identified nine document properties and analyzed the reliability of document quality judgments. They also explored the correlation of judgments of the document properties. The document qualities examined were accuracy, source reliability, objectivity, depth, author/producer credibility, readability, verbosity/conciseness, grammatical correctness, and one-sidedness/multi-views. Factor analysis indicated that three factors of "general goodness" of documents were responsible for about 48 percent of the total variance. Document qualities of depth, objectivity, and author credibility, which were categorized as quality separators, evinced consistent patterns between two quite different kinds of collections.

A Multidisciplinary Framework

This chapter has reviewed various perspectives and empirical studies that investigate the concept of credibility across multiple disciplines and within several applied contexts. Our synthesis is organized around five topics: (1) the construct of credibility as a chief element of information quality, composed of situation-dependent dimensions and criteria for evaluation; (2) orientation toward the targets of credibility assessment; (3) credibility assessment processes, which comprise prediction, evaluation, calibration, and verification; (4) situational aspects of credibility assessment with respect to domain, user goals, motivation, environmental constraints, and organizational and social contexts; and (5) the evaluator's background, encompassing a general stance toward new sources and information, evaluative skills, and domain knowledge.

Construct of Credibility

Researchers in information science have traditionally situated credibility in relation to relevance judgments. In particular, credibility assessments are often taken to be a subset of relevance judgments. Relevance is often defined as users' perceptions of the potential usefulness of information; relevance judgments, as users' decisions to accept or reject specific information items (Schamber & Bateman, 1996). When users make such evaluations, they rely on various criteria that eventually lead them to select information. Information quality, credibility, and cognitive authority are those criteria that have appeared consistently across relevance studies (Wang, 1997).

Credibility is a principal component of information quality. People are likely to believe that information is useful and accurate if it is perceived to originate from credible sources. However, not all information perceived to be of high quality is perceived to be credible. A number of other criteria, such as consistency and recency, can lead information seekers to accept information in spite of the absence of any evidence about its credibility. That is, the absence of evidence regarding credibility does not in itself necessarily hinder the assessment of information quality. Consequently, the pool of information perceived to be credible is a subset of the pool of information perceived to be of high quality. In turn, cognitive authorities within a domain are a subset of all credible sources (Rieh, 2005). That is, the set of credible sources constitutes the potential pool from which information seekers can draw cognitive authorities (Wilson, 1983).

Finally, we reiterate the importance of the object of assessment in credibility research. Information seekers' criteria for credibility assessment are largely a function of the type of source being evaluated. Consequently, the underlying dimensions of credibility a researcher is likely to uncover can also vary as a function of the type of source, whether it is a public speaker, an organization, a Web site, or an information system. These differences are often reflective of situation-dependent evaluative criteria. Because information technology introduces a new set of candidates for source orientation, we expect the evaluative criteria of users to be in flux when interacting with computers.

Orientation toward Targets of Credibility Assessment

It is almost universally presupposed in the research literature on credibility that a specific object (e.g., a newspaper, Web site, person) has been chosen as the target of credibility assessment. What we lack is an understanding of how this initial orientation toward a particular target occurs and, ultimately, who or what is perceived to be a source when various layers imposed by information technology tend to obscure the originator of content. In every discipline applying credibility to the use of technology, users are prone to respond to information systems themselves as if they were the source of the information they were programmed to deliver; this is a direct consequence of users' social responses to technology (Reeves & Nass, 1996).

Thus, the line between traditional notions of source and medium has become blurred. Information seekers can be doubtful of a medium, without reference to more specific sources, in much the same way they are doubtful of more traditionally recognized sources such as organizations and individuals (Rieh & Belkin, 1998). Just as importantly, information technology presents users with numerous new objects that might be perceived as sources—from physical devices to applications and virtual characters to layer upon layer of information filters. In many cases, the messenger, by virtue of its proximity to the information seeker, *is* the perceived source.

Credibility Assessment Processes

A key distinction in the literature of credibility assessment processes is between two kinds of judgments: predictive judgments made prior to accessing the object of assessment and evaluative judgments made when confronting the object of assessment. The distinction originates from Hogarth's (1987) judgment and decision-making theory and has been most explicitly applied to credibility assessment in information seeking and retrieval, where it is clear that a wide range of surrogates (such as hyperlinked text, document titles, abstracts, and the like) serve as initial indicators of credibility before the evaluator has accessed a full document. Predictive judgments, which are often subtle, become increasingly critical in massive information ecologies available through information technology; each discipline, for example, notes at least category membership as a powerful assessment cue. This is likely to be a critical shift, as work by Rieh (2000, 2002) indicates that the kinds of criteria people use for predictive and evaluative judgments differ.

Each discipline additionally includes some notion of historical or behavioral observation by evaluators and subsequent *calibration* of beliefs about a source's credibility based upon the observations made. This aspect of assessment has been particularly prominent in user interaction with autonomous decision-support and other automated systems (Muir, 1987).

Finally, credibility assessment varies in the extent to which verification procedures are likely or even possible. Web sites provide links to supporting material; expert and decision-support systems provide detailed reasoning behind a particular recommendation. Avoiding the "black box" phenomenon in interactions with complex information systems helps users understand how the system gathers information or arrives at conclusions. Information completeness helps combat this problem. Information is complete to the extent that the possibility for verification exists. However, where verification is impractical because of time constraints and other situational demands, the mere *presence* of verification material can be the key factor influencing credibility judgments.

Situational Aspects of Credibility Assessment

Across disciplines, researchers recognize the importance of the *context* of credibility assessment—both the relatively idiosyncratic situational variables that can influence judgment and the broader social and organizational background within which assessments are made. The goals and motivations of the information seeker and constraints created by the evaluative environment can significantly influence credibility assessments.

In some instances, one's goal not only influences the selection of sources but can cause one to *select a particular environment in which credibility assessments will be made*. A manager who is concerned with discussions being too heavily influenced by participants' status levels might opt for a virtual meeting in which participants contribute ideas anonymously. Individuals also differ in motivation and other associated feelings of urgency; a high need for information increases one's willingness to accept whatever information is currently available. Consumers who have already incurred the costs of traveling to a store accept comparative product quality claims readily; the online shopper, however, with no costs invested in a particular vendor remains more reasonably skeptical. As discussed in the sections on online health and general Web information seeking, the importance and impact of the information sought can strongly influence strategies for credibility assessment.

Deliberate selection of sources, media, and evaluative environments, in turn, strongly influences the criteria one will use in assessing credibility. The demands created by the medium have been of special interest to communication scholars, as different modalities (e.g., text, audio, video) place varying constraints on attention and memory. For consumer researchers, at issue are the relative abilities of consumers to recognize contextual variables that may help indicate whether a product claim or signal is reliable.

A source sits within social and organizational contexts that enhance or inhibit the accuracy of what it reports. The context can be more or less transitory and an information seeker may be only vaguely aware of how a perceived source leverages (or depends upon) a network of resources. With respect to information systems, the management and health sciences have been acutely aware of the importance of this situational aspect of credibility. Managers are as sensitive to the timeliness of information and recommendation as any evaluator, one primary reason they have traditionally depended upon observation of the external environment and highly rich media in decision making (Daft & Lengel, 1984). Health professionals, too, as we saw in our discussion of the HELP system, must rely on timely patient information, often maintained by multiple individuals over time and across an organization.

Thus, information systems in such contexts inevitably possess a *distributed* intelligence. Decision makers are not simply relying on the perceived source; they are relying on an organizational commitment and ability to place the system in the best position possible to report facts and make recommendations. Similarly, information is evaluated against a background of social and organizational norms regarding, for example, the types of facts, reasoning, and argumentation that are considered acceptable within a domain.

Evaluator Background

The fact that individuals differ in general credulity as a trait is at least implicit in every discipline's approach to credibility research, even if the relative attention paid to this individual difference varies. Similarly, all disciplines recognize a set of individual differences with respect to goals, expertise, and the like that strongly influence credibility judgments. Communication and consumer researchers in particular have also investigated such differences as temporary states, noting for example that individuals assess credibility within contexts where the general level of credulity expressed by groups and communities is, or can be, fluid. Information seekers respond to newspapers and politicians, for example, in contexts where the general climate may favor one but not the other, neither, or both. More broadly, the context in which credibility assessments are made may favor or disfavor the trustworthiness of the "generalized other" (Putnam, 2000). Putnam (2000) gives the example of individuals living in large cities compared with those living in small towns. The relative stances that persons from these contrasting backgrounds tend to take toward new sources and new claims differ substantially; this may simply reflect the reality of the evaluator's context. Similarly, the competitive climate in which product claims and signals are made can enhance or reduce their believability and persuasiveness. Here, the skills of an information seeker in gaining a broad view of that competitive climate are critical, as we saw in examples of in-store assessments of various signals implying product quality as well as of comparative shopping.

Common to all credibility assessment research is the recognition that assessments are made in relation to an evaluator's existing knowledge and beliefs and that this background often drives information-seeking strategies. A second critical aspect of credibility assessment with information technology is the frequent need for users to develop novel evaluative skills. Examining a set of production rules explaining a recommendation by a decision-support system or examining the URL of a Web site as an indicator of credibility, for example, are not innate skills. New information technologies inevitably require users to develop new skills in deciding whom and what to believe. Finally, credibility judgments are not made simply against a background of factual knowledge and skills. They involve an assessment of, and attempt to understand, the source's goals and motivations, as exemplified in the persuasion knowledge model (Friestad & Wright, 1994).

Agendas for Future Research

Reviewing past research on credibility in various disciplines and the development of a multidisciplinary framework leads naturally to the identification of several avenues of future research. Researchers encounter challenges in understanding the concept of credibility outside of their own disciplinary arenas. Media, information retrieval systems, medical information systems, and management information systems have traditionally been studied in different academic disciplines, the distances between which have decreased dramatically in the current information environment. The following areas are suggested for future research: multidisciplinary approaches, broader contexts of information credibility, changing Web environments, subjective assessment processes, and tracking changes in credibility perceptions.

Multidisciplinary Approaches

Most studies about credibility in mass communication are carried out with respect to a particular type of information within a limited domain. Studies have been primarily concerned with news, personal Web sites, and political issue sites (e.g., Johnson & Kaye, 1998, 2002; Mashek et al., 1997; Sundar, 1999). Researchers in information science have tended to focus on scholarly information in work settings with either scholars (e.g., Rieh, 2002; Rieh & Belkin, 1998) or students (e.g., Liu, 2004; Liu & Huang, 2005; Whitmire, 2004). However, as the literature reviewed in this chapter demonstrates, people make credibility assessments both at work and in everyday life when they engage in seeking information pertaining, for example, to health, products, or hobbies. This is an important aspect of credibility research because people carry over both their perceptions and the judgment processes that they have acquired from one domain to another. Given the reality that people use the Web to conduct quotidian tasks and pursue the everyday pleasures of life (Fallows, 2004), it is extremely important for credibility researchers to employ multidisciplinary approaches.

Broader Contexts of Information Credibility

Researchers in a variety of disciplines have investigated the issue of credibility for quite some time and the Web has cast new light on the topic. It should be emphasized, however, that the Web is not an isolated medium for the playing out of information and communication behaviors. People continue to rely on a variety of information systems and resources in interacting with information and often use multiple media to resolve their problems. As a result, relative credibility across different information systems will remain a significant and interesting item on the research agenda.

In addition to investigating credibility assessment in terms of outcomes by asking people which media they trust most, it is important to understand how such assessments are influenced by the information system used: In other words, people make judgments of credibility not only after they gain information from a certain system but also in selecting the systems they use. Future studies should take account of credibility assessments over the entire process of human information and communication behavior, including the range of information systems to which people turn.

Changing Web Environments

The Web is viewed increasingly as a means of creating communities and fostering collaboration rather than simply a means of publishing and delivering documents and services (Liu, Harper, & Watt, 2005). A significant innovation is the emergence of open source production, which involves the free and open creation, alteration, and distribution of information from vast numbers of contributors (Anthony, Smith, & Williamson, 2005). Open source production gives one a sense of community membership. For instance, Wikipedia is a free, online, open-content encyclopedia in which content results from a community of editors rather than a single individual or small set of experts. The quality of Wikipedia content is much debated. Lih (2004) insists that an open-editing policy helps to control quality because the contributions have been evaluated and revised by the thousands of visitors to the site. From the perspective of credibility assessment, Wikipedia certainly offers a significant research opportunity as it provides a new form of collaborative quality control. In addition to issues of quality control, source orientation becomes critical, as the question of who is ultimately responsible for content becomes less clear to information seekers.

Content-based recommender systems represent one more attempt to combat information overload; as with any system that filters information selectively, they are subject to credibility assessments (O'Donovan & Smyth, 2005). One interesting area for future research is the extent to which people would be likely to believe recommendations generated by these systems, especially those leveraged from the preferences of communities of similar users.

Subjective Assessment Processes

Many studies show that credibility does not reside in the information object or source itself. Rather, it is users who recognize dimensions of credibility based on the characteristics of information objects and sources and then make credibility judgments. In other words, although objects and sources provide clues that can be used to make information more believable, individuals will eventually make different assessments of information because of their experiences and knowledge. In addition to knowledge and experience, other factors associated with individual differences should be considered explicitly in future research. For instance, levels of motivation to engage in information seeking may influence the ways people assess information credibility. Attitude might be an important factor to investigate in lieu of demographic characteristics. These variables might be related to the level of mental effort that people are willing to invest in the information evaluation process.

Tracking Changes in Credibility Perceptions

According to Metzger, Flanagin, and Zwarun (2003), credibility perceptions may change over time. As seen in Johnson and Kaye's (2000, 2002) research, the credibility of online political information changed from the 1996 to the 2000 election season. As the Web has changed in terms of both audience and content, people's perceptions of the Web have altered as well. We make two suggestions for future research. One is to conduct larger-scale studies in which credibility assessments can be examined across diverse user groups. The findings of such research can be compared to previous research to determine whether there has been an overall shift in people's perceptions of credibility. The second is to conduct longitudinal studies in which researchers can observe whether users' credibility assessment processes change over time.

Conclusion

This chapter has reviewed various perspectives and empirical studies that investigate the concept of credibility across multiple disciplines and within several applied contexts. Although research on this topic has the potential to offer a useful conceptual framework with which to understand better the nature of human judgments about information, information science researchers have traditionally limited their discussions of credibility to its role as a criterion in relevance judgments. This review has illustrated the importance of understanding credibility as a focus of research in its own right. Credibility has in fact received renewed attention in various research communities partly because there are increasing concerns about the credibility of information on the Web. However, understanding the concept of credibility only in the context of information evaluation on the Web would limit the potential usefulness of the credibility concept because assessment of credibility is a ubiquitous activity of human judgment, given that people constantly have to make decisions about the value and usefulness of information in a variety of work and everyday life contexts.

Acknowledgments

We would like to thank Beth St. Jean for providing substantial assistance in the compiling of our bibliography. Special thanks are extended to Cliff Nass, Derek Hansen, and three anonymous reviewers for their insightful suggestions on earlier versions of this chapter.

References

Abels, E. G., White, M. D., & Hahn, K. (1997). Identifying user-based criteria for Web pages. *Internet Research, 7,* 252–262.

Abels, E. G., White, M. D., & Hahn, K. (1998). A user-based design process for Web sites. *Internet Research, 8,* 39–48.

Adaval, R. (2003). How good gets better and bad gets worse: Understanding the impact of affect on evaluations of known brands. *Journal of Consumer Research, 30,* 352–367.

Agosto, D. E. (2002a). A model of young people's decision-making in using the Web. *Library & Information Science Research, 24,* 311–341.

Agosto, D. E. (2002b). Bounded rationality and satisficing in young people's Web-based decision making. *Journal of the American Society for Information Science and Technology, 53,* 16–27.

Alexander, J. E., & Tate, M. A. (1999). *Web wisdom: How to evaluate and create information quality on the Web.* Mahwah, NJ: Erlbaum.

Amento, B., Terveen, L., & Hill, W. (2000). Does "authority" mean quality? Predicting expert quality ratings of Web documents. *Proceedings of the 23rd Annual International ACM SIGIR Conference on Research and Development in Information Retrieval,* 296–303.

Anand, B. N., & Shachar, R. (2004). Brands as beacons: A new source of loyalty to multi-product firms. *Journal of Marketing Research, 41,* 135–150.

Anderson, E. T., & Simester, D. I. (1998). The role of sale signs. *Marketing Science, 17,* 139–155.

Anderson, E. T., & Simester, D. I. (2001). Are sale signs effective when more products have them? *Marketing Science, 20,* 121–142.

Andrews, L. W., & Gutkin, T. B. (1991). The effects of human versus computer authorship on consumers' perceptions of psychological reports. *Computers in Human Behavior, 7,* 311–317.

Annenberg School Center for the Digital Future. (2004). *The digital future report: Surveying the digital future: Year four.* Los Angeles: University of Southern California.

Anthony, D., Smith, S. W., & Williamson, T. (2005). *Explaining quality in Internet collective goods: Zealots and good Samaritans in the case of Wikipedia.* Retrieved February 2, 2006, from www2.scedu.unibo.it/ roversi/Blog/anthony.pdf

Arnold, J. M., & Jayne, E. A. (1998). Dangling by a slender thread: The lessons and implications of teaching the World Wide Web to freshmen. *Journal of Academic Librarianship, 24,* 43–52.

Association of College and Research Libraries. (2000). *Information literacy competency standards for higher education.* Chicago: American Library Association. Retrieved February 2, 2006, from www.ala.org/ala/acrl/acrlstandards/standards.pdf

Austin, E. W., & Dong, Q. (1994). Source v. content effects on judgments of news believability. *Journalism Quarterly, 71,* 973–983.

Bai, B., Ng, K. B., Sun, Y., Kantor, P., & Strzalkowski, T. (2004). The institutional dimension of document quality judgments. *Proceedings of the 67th Annual Meeting of the American Society for Information Science and Technology*, 110–118.

Baker, L., Wagner, T. H., Singer, S., & Bundorf, M. K. (2003). Use of the Internet and e-mail for health care information. *Journal of the American Medical Association, 289*, 2400–2406.

Barry, C. L. (1994). User-defined relevance criteria: An exploratory study. *Journal of the American Society for Information Science, 45*, 149–159.

Barry, C. L., & Schamber, L. (1998). Users' criteria for relevance evaluation: A cross-situational comparison. *Information Processing & Management, 34*, 219–236.

Bateman, J. (1998). *Modeling changes in end-user relevance criteria: An information seeking study.* Unpublished doctoral dissertation, University of North Texas.

Bateman, J. (1999). Modeling the importance of end-user relevance criteria. *Proceedings of the 62nd Annual Meeting of the American Society for Information Science*, 396–406.

Benotsch, E. G., Kalichman, S., & Weinhardt, L. S. (2004). HIV-AIDS patients' evaluation of health information on the Internet: The digital divide and vulnerability to fraudulent claims. *Journal of Consulting and Clinical Psychology, 72*, 1004–1011.

Berland, G. K., Elliott, M. N., Morales, L. S., Algazy, J. I., Kravitz, R. L., Broder, M. S., et al. (2001). Health information on the Internet: Accessibility, quality, and readability in English and Spanish. *Journal of the American Medical Association, 285*, 2612–2621.

Bickart, B., & Schindler, R. M. (2001). Internet forums as influential sources of consumer information. *Journal of Interactive Marketing, 15*, 31–40.

Biros, D. P., Fields, G., & Gunsch, G. (2003). The effect of external safeguards on human–information system trust in an information warfare environment. *Proceedings of the 36th Hawaii International Conference on System Sciences.* Retrieved March 22, 2006, from http://csdl2.computer.org/comp/proceedings/hicss/2003/1874/02/187420062b.pdf

Biros, D. P., George, J. F., & Zmud, R. W. (2002). Inducing sensitivity to deception in order to improve decision making performance: A field study. *MIS Quarterly, 26*, 119–144.

Biswas, D., & Biswas, A. (2004). The diagnostic role of signals in the context of perceived risks in online shopping: So signals matter more on the Web? *Journal of Interactive Marketing, 18*, 30–45.

Brin, S., & Page, L. (1998). The anatomy of a large-scale hypertextual Web search engine. *Proceedings of the 7th International World Wide Web Conference.* Retrieved February 2, 2006, from www7.scu.edu.au/programme/fullpapers/1921/com1921.htm

Brown, D., & Jones, D. R. (1998). Factors that influence reliance on decision aids: A model and an experiment. *Journal of Information Systems, 12*, 75–94.

Brown, S. P., Homer, P. M., & Inman, J. J. (1998). A meta-analysis of relationships between ad-evoked feelings and advertising responses. *Journal of Marketing Research, 35*, 114–126.

Burbules, N. C. (2001). Paradoxes of the Web: The ethical dimensions of credibility. *Library Trends, 49*, 441–453.

Buschman, J., & Warner, D. A. (2005). Researching and shaping information literacy initiatives in relation to the Web: Some framework problems and needs. *Journal of Academic Librarianship, 31*, 12–18.

Case, R. (2003). Making critical thinking an integral part of electronic research. *School Libraries in Canada, 22*(4), 13–16.

Casebeer, L., Bennett, N., Kristofco, R., Carillo, A., & Centor, R. (2002). Physician Internet medical information seeking and on-line continuing education use patterns. *Journal of Continuing Education in the Health Professions, 22*, 33–42.

Choi, S. M., & Rifon, N. J. (2002). Antecedents and consequences of Web advertising credibility: A study of consumer response to banner ads. *Journal of Interactive Advertising, 3*(1). Retrieved February 2, 2006, from www.jiad.org/vol3/no1/choi/index.htm

Clark, D. B., & Slotta, J. D. (2000). Evaluating media-enhancement and source authority on the Internet: The Knowledge Integration Environment. *International Journal of Science Education, 22*, 859–871.

Cooke, A. (1999). *Authoritative guide to evaluating information on the Internet.* New York: Neal-Schuman.

Cool, C., Belkin, N. J., Frieder, O., & Kantor, P. (1993). Characteristics of texts affecting relevance judgments. *Proceedings of the 14th National Online Meeting*, 77–84.

Daft, R. L., & Lengel, R. H. (1984). Information richness: A new approach to managerial behavior and organization design. *Research in Organizational Behavior, 6*, 191–233.

D'Angelo, B. J. (2001). Using source analysis to promote critical thinking. *Research Strategies, 18*, 303–309.

Danielson, D. R. (2005). Web credibility. In C. Ghaoui (Ed.), *Encyclopedia of human–computer interaction* (pp. 713–721). Hershey, PA: Idea Group.

Darby, M. R., & Karni, E. (1973). Free competition and the optimal amount of fraud. *Journal of Law and Economics, 16*, 67–88.

Darley, W. K., & Smith, R. E. (1993). Advertising claim objectivity: Antecedents and effects. *Journal of Marketing, 57*, 100–113.

Daugherty, T., Li, H., & Biocca, F. (2001). Consumer learning and 3-D ecommerce: The effects of sequential exposure of a virtual experience relative to indirect and direct product experience on product knowledge, brand attitude and purchase intention. In F. Biocca, H. Li, P. David, S. Edwards, & T. Daugherty (Eds.), *Proceedings of the Experiential E-commerce Conference* [CD-ROM]. East Lansing: M.I.N.D. Lab, Michigan State University.

Davis, E., Kay, J., & Star, J. (1991). Is advertising rational? *Business Strategy Review, 2*, 1–23.

Dholakia, R. R., & Sternthal, B. (1977). Highly credible sources: Persuasive facilitators or persuasive liabilities. *Journal of Consumer Research, 3*, 223–232.

Dijkstra, J. J. (1995). The influence of an expert system on the user's view: How to fool a lawyer. *New Review of Applied Expert Systems, 1*, 123–138.

Dijkstra, J. J. (1999). User agreement with incorrect expert system advice. *Behaviour & Information Technology, 18*, 399–411.

Dijkstra, J. J., Liebrand, W. B., & Timminga, E. (1998). Persuasiveness of expert systems. *Behaviour & Information Technology, 17*, 155–163.

Dragulanescu, N. (2002). Website quality evaluations: Criteria and tools. *International Information & Library Review, 34*, 247–254.

Dutton, W. H., Gennaro, C., & Hargrave, A. M. (2005). *The Internet in Britain: The Oxford Internet survey.* Oxford, UK: Oxford Internet Institute, University of Oxford.

Earley, P. C. (1988). Computer-generated performance feedback in the magazine-subscription industry. *Organizational Behavior and Human Decision Processes, 41*, 50–64.

Eastin, M. S. (2001). Credibility assessments of online health information: The effects of source expertise and knowledge of content. *Journal of Computer-Mediated Communication*, *6*(4). Retrieved February 2, 2006, from www.ascusc.org/jcmc/vol6/issue4/eastin.html

Edwards, G., Kang, B. H., Preston, P., & Compton, P. (1995). Prudent expert systems with credentials: Managing the expertise of decision support systems. *International Journal of Bio-Medical Computing*, *40*, 125–132.

Erdem, T., & Swait, J. (2004). Brand credibility, brand consideration, and choice. *Journal of Consumer Research*, *31*, 191–198.

Escoffery, C., Miner, K. R., Adame, D. D., Butler, S., McCormick, L., & Mendell, E. (2005). Internet use for health information among college students. *Journal of American College Health*, *53*(4), 183–188.

Eysenbach, G., & Diepgen, T. L. (1998). Towards quality management of medical information on the Internet: Evaluation, labelling, and filtering of information. *British Medical Journal*, *317*, 1496–1502.

Eysenbach, G., & Köhler, C. (2002). How do consumers search for and appraise health information on the World Wide Web? Qualitative study using focus groups, usability tests, and in-depth interviews. *British Medical Journal*, *324*, 573–577.

Eysenbach, G., Powell, J., Kuss, O., & Sa, E.-R. (2002). Empirical studies assessing the quality of health information for consumers on the World Wide Web: A systematic review. *Journal of the American Medical Association*, *287*, 2691–2700.

Fallis, D. (2004). On verifying the accuracy of information: Philosophical perspectives. *Library Trends*, *52*, 463–487.

Fallis, D. (2006). Social epistemology and information science. *Annual Review of Information Science and Technology*, *40*, 475–519.

Fallis, D., & Frické, M. (2002). Verifiable health information on the Internet. *Journal of Education for Library and Information Science*, *43*, 262–269.

Fallows, D. (2004). *The Internet and Daily Life*. Washington, DC: Pew Internet & American Life Project. Retrieved February 2, 2006, from www.pewinternet.org/pdfs/PIP_Internet_and_Daily_Life.pdf

Fallows, D. (2005). *Search engine users: Internet searchers are confident, satisfied and trusting—but they are also unaware and naive*. Washington, DC: Pew Internet & American Life Project. Retrieved February 2, 2006, from www.pewinternet.org/pdfs/PIP_Searchengine_users.pdf

Festinger, L. (1957). *A theory of cognitive dissonance*. Stanford, CA: Stanford University Press.

Fidel, R., Davies, R. K., Douglass, M. H., Holder, J. K., Hopkins, C. J., Kushner, E. J., et al. (1999). A visit to the information mall: Web searching behavior of high school students. *Journal of the American Society for Information Science*, *50*, 24–37.

Flake, W. L. (1991). Influence of gender, dogmatism, and risk-taking propensity upon attitudes toward information from computers. *Computers in Human Behavior*, *7*, 227–235.

Flanagin, A. J., & Metzger, M. J. (2000). Perceptions of Internet information credibility. *Journalism and Mass Communication Quarterly*, *77*, 515–540.

Flanagin, A. J., & Metzger, M. J. (2003). The perceived credibility of personal Web page information as influenced by the sex of the source. *Computers in Human Behavior*, *19*, 683–701.

Fogg, B. J. (2002). *Stanford guidelines for Web credibility*. Stanford Persuasive Technology Lab, Stanford University. Retrieved February 2, 2006, from www.webcredibility.org/guidelines

Fogg, B. J. (2003a). *Persuasive technology: Using computers to change what we think and do*. San Francisco: Morgan Kaufmann.

Fogg, B. J. (2003b). Prominence-interpretation theory: Explaining how people assess credibility online. *CHI '03 Extended Abstracts on Human Factors in Computing Systems*, 722–723.

Fogg, B. J., Marshall, J., Kameda, T., Solomon, J., Rangnekar, A., Boyd, J., et al. (2001). Web credibility research: A method for online experiments and early study results. *CHI '01 Extended Abstracts on Human Factors in Computing Systems*, 295–296.

Fogg, B. J., Marshall, J., Laraki, O., Osipovich, A., Varma, C., Fang, N., Paul, J., et al. (2001). What makes Web sites credible? A report on a large quantitative study. *Proceedings of the SIGCHI Conference on Human Factors in Computing Systems*, 61–68.

Fogg, B. J., Marshall, J., Osipovich, A., Varma, C., Laraki, O., Fang, N., et al. (2000). Elements that affect Web credibility: Early results from a self-report study. *CHI '00 Extended Abstracts on Human Factors in Computing Systems*, 287–288.

Fogg, B. J., Soohoo, C., Danielson, D. R., Marable, L., Stanford, J., & Tauber, E. R. (2003). How do users evaluate the credibility of Web sites? A study with over 2,500 participants. *Proceedings of the 2003 Conference on Designing for User Experiences (DUX'03)*. Retrieved April 1, 2006, from http://portal.acm.org/citation.cfm?id=997097&coll=ACM&dl=ACM&CFID=36236037&CFTOKEN=18606069

Fogg, B. J., & Tseng, H. (1999). The elements of computer credibility. *Proceedings of the SIGCHI conference on Human Factors in Computing Systems*, 80–87.

Ford, G. T., Smith, D. B., & Swazy, J. L. (1990). Consumer skepticism of advertising claims: Testing hypotheses from economics of information. *Journal of Consumer Research*, *16*, 433–441.

Fox, S. (2005). *Health information online*. Washington, DC: Pew Internet & American Life Project. Retrieved February 2, 2006, from www.pewinternet.org/pdfs/PIP_Healthtopics_May05.pdf

Fragale, A. R., & Heath, C. (2004). Evolving information credentials: The (mis)attribution of believable facts to credible sources. *Personality and Social Psychology Bulletin*, *30*, 225–236.

Freeman, K. S., & Spyridakis, J. H. (2004). An examination of factors that affect the credibility of online health information. *Technical Communication*, *51*, 239–263.

Friestad, M., & Wright, P. (1994). The persuasion knowledge model: How people cope with persuasion attempts. *Journal of Consumer Research*, *21*, 1–31.

Fritch, J. W., & Cromwell, R. L. (2001). Evaluating Internet resources: Identity, affiliation, and cognitive authority in a networked world. *Journal of the American Society for Information Science and Technology*, *52*, 499–507.

Gardner, R. M., & Lundsgaarde, H. P. (1994). Evaluation of user acceptance of a clinical expert system. *Journal of the American Medical Informatics Association*, *1*, 428–438.

Goldberg, M. E., & Hartwick, J. (1990). The effects of advertiser reputation and extremity of advertising claim on advertising effectiveness. *Journal of Consumer Research*, *17*, 172–179.

Graefe, G. (2003). Incredible information on the Internet: Biased information provision and lack of credibility as a cause of insufficient information quality. *Proceedings of the 8th International Conference on Information Quality*, 133–146.

Graham, L., & Metaxas, P. T. (2003). "Of course it's true: I saw it on the Internet!" Critical thinking in the Internet era. *Communications of the ACM, 46*(5), 71–75.

Gray, N. J., Klein, J. D., Noyce, P. R., Sesselberg, T. S., & Cantrill, J. A. (2005). Health information-seeking behavior in adolescence: The place of the Internet. *Social Science & Medicine, 60*, 1467–1478.

Gregor, S., & Benbasat, I. (1999). Explanations from intelligent systems: Theoretical foundations and implications for practice. *MIS Quarterly, 23*, 497–530.

Grewal, D., Marmorstein, H., & Sharma, A. (1996). Communicating price information through semantic cues: The moderating effects of situation and discount size. *Journal of Consumer Research, 23*, 148–155.

Groot, D., ter Riet, G., Khan, K. S., & Misso, K. (2001). Comparison of search strategies and quality of medical information of the Internet: A study relating to ankle sprain. *International Journal of the Care of the Injured, 32*, 473–476.

Haddow, G. (2003). Focusing on health information: How to assess information quality on the Internet. *Australian Library Journal, 52*, 169–177.

Hardey, M. (2001). "E-health": The Internet and the transformation of patients into consumers and producers of health knowledge. *Information, Communication, and Society, 4*, 388–405.

Hogarth, R. M. (1987). *Judgment and choice: The psychology of decision* (2nd ed.). New York: Wiley.

Holbrook, M. B. (1978). Beyond attitude structure. *Journal of Marketing Research, 15*, 546–556.

Honaker, L. M., Hector, V. S., & Harrell, T. H. (1986). Perceived validity of computer- versus clinician-generated MMPI reports. *Computers in Human Behavior, 2*, 77–83.

Hong, T. (2006). The influence of structural and message features on Web site credibility. *Journal of the American Society for Information Science and Technology, 57*, 114–127.

Hovland, C. I., Janis, I. L., & Kelley, H. H. (1953). *Communication and persuasion*. New Haven, CT: Yale University Press.

Hovland, C. I., & Weiss, W. (1951). The influence of source credibility on communication effectiveness. *Public Opinion Quarterly, 15*, 635–650.

Huerta, E. (2003). *The credibility of online information*. Unpublished doctoral dissertation, Claremont Graduate University, CA.

Infante, D. A., Parker, K. R., Clarke, C. H., Wilson, L., & Nathu, I. A. (1983). A comparison of factor and functional approaches to source credibility. *Communication Quarterly, 31*, 43–48.

Ivory, M. Y., & Hearst, M. A. (2002). Statistical profiles of highly-rated Web sites. *Proceedings of the SIGCHI Conference on Human Factors in Computing Systems*, 367–374.

Janes, J. W., & Rosenfeld, L. B. (1996). Networked information retrieval and organization: Issues and questions. *Journal of the American Society for Information Science, 47*, 711–715.

Jiang, J. J., Klein, G., & Vedder, R. G. (2000). Persuasive expert systems: The influence of confidence and discrepancy. *Computers in Human Behavior, 16*, 99–109.

Jiang, J. J., Muhanna, W. A., & Pick, R. A. (1996). The impact of model performance on users' confidence in decision models: An experimental examination. *Computers in Human Behavior, 12*, 193–207.

Johnson, T. J., & Kaye, B. K. (1998). Cruising is believing? Comparing Internet and traditional sources on media credibility measures. *Journalism and Mass Communication Quarterly, 75*, 325–340.

Johnson, T. J., & Kaye, B. K. (2000). Using is believing: The influence of reliance on the credibility of online political information among politically interested Internet users. *Journalism and Mass Communication Quarterly, 77*, 865–879.

Johnson, T. J., & Kaye, B. K. (2002). Webelievability: A path model examining how convenience and reliance predict online credibility. *Journalism and Mass Communication Quarterly, 79*, 619–642.

Kapoun, J. (1998). Teaching undergrads Web evaluation: A guide for library instruction. *College & Research Library News, 59*, 522–523.

Kihlstrom, R. E., & Riordan, M. H. (1984). Advertising as a signal. *Journal of Political Economy, 92*, 427–450.

Kim, J., & Moon, J. (1998). Designing towards emotional usability in customer interfaces: Trustworthiness of cyber-banking system interfaces. *Interacting with Computers, 10*, 1–29.

Kiousis, S. (2001). Public trust or mistrust? Perceptions of media credibility in the information age. *Mass Communication & Society, 4*, 381–403.

Kirmani, A., & Rao, A. R. (2000). No pain, no gain: A critical review of the literature on signaling unobservable product quality. *Journal of Marketing, 64*, 66–79.

Kjartansdóttir, A., & Widenius, M. (1995). The quality of business information on the Internet: Evaluation criteria applicable to Internet resources. *Swedish Library Research, 3–4*, 43–50.

Klein, L. R. (1998). Evaluating the potential of interactive media through a new lens: Search versus experience goods. *Journal of Business Research, 41*, 195–203.

Klein, L. R. (2003). Creating virtual product experiences: The role of telepresence. *Journal of Interactive Marketing, 17*, 41–55.

Kleinberg, J. M. (1999). Authoritative sources in a hyperlinked environment. *Journal of the Association for Computing Machinery, 46*, 604–632.

Kluger, A. N., & Adler, S. (1993). Person- versus computer-mediated feedback. *Computers in Human Behavior, 9*, 1–16.

Koester, R., & Luthans, F. (1979). The impact of the computer on the choice activity of decision makers: A replication with actual users of computerized MIS. *Academy of Management Journal, 22*, 416–422.

Kopalle, P. K., & Assunção, J. L. (2000). When (not) to indulge in 'puffery': The role of consumer expectations and brand goodwill in determining advertised and actual product quality. *Managerial and Decision Economics, 21*, 223–241.

Kottemann, J. E., Davis, F. D., & Remus, W. E. (1994). Computer-assisted decision making: Performance, beliefs, and the illusion of control. *Organizational Behavior and Human Decision Processes, 57*, 26–37.

Lamberti, D. M., & Wallace, W. A. (1990). Intelligent interface design: An empirical assessment of knowledge presentation in expert systems. *MIS Quarterly, 14*, 279–311.

Landsbergen, D., Coursey, D. H., Loveless, S., & Shangraw, R. F. (1997). Decision quality, confidence, and commitment with expert systems: An experimental study. *Journal of Public Administration Research and Theory, 7,* 131–157.

Leckie, G. J. (1996). Desperately seeking citations: Uncovering faculty assumptions about the undergraduate research process. *Journal of Academic Librarianship, 22,* 201–208.

Lerch, F. J., Prietula, M. J., & Kulik, C. T. (1997). The Turing effect: The nature of trust in expert systems advice. In P. Feltovich, K. Ford, & R. Hoffman (Eds.), *Expertise in context: Human and machine* (pp. 417–448). Menlo Park, CA: AAAI Press.

Licciardone, J. C., Smith-Barbaro, P., & Coleridge, S. T. (2001). Use of the Internet as a resource for consumer health information: Results of the second osteopathic survey of health care in America (OSTEOSURV-II). *Journal of Medical Internet Research, 3,* e31.

Lih, A. (2004, April). *Wikipedia as participatory journalism: Reliable sources? Metrics for evaluating collaborative media as a news resource.* Paper presented at the 5th International Symposium on Online Journalism, Austin, TX. Retrieved February 2, 2006, from http://jmsc.hku.hk/faculty/alih/publications/utaustin-2004-wikipedia-rc2.pdf

Liu, B., Harper, D. J., & Watt, S. (2005). Information sharing through rational links and viewpoint retrieval. *Proceedings of the 28th Annual International ACM SIGIR Conference on Research and Development in Information Retrieval,* 639–640.

Liu, Y., Wang, C., Zhang, M., & Ma, S. (2005). Web data cleansing for information retrieval using key resource page selection. *Proceedings of the 14th International World Wide Web Conference,* 1136–1137.

Liu, Z. (2004). Perceptions of credibility of scholarly information on the Web. *Information Processing & Management, 40,* 1027–1038.

Liu, Z., & Huang, X. (2005). Evaluating the credibility of scholarly information on the Web: A cross cultural study. *International Information & Library Review, 37,* 99–106.

Luo, W., & Najdawi, M. (2004). Trust-building measures: A review of consumer health portals. *Communications of the ACM, 47*(1), 109–113.

Luthans, F., & Koester, R. (1976). The impact of computer generated information on the choice activity of decision-makers. *Academy of Management Journal, 19,* 328–332.

Mackenzie, S. B. (1986). The role of attention in mediating the effect of advertising on attribute importance. *Journal of Consumer Research, 13,* 174–195.

Maglaughlin, K. L., & Sonnenwald, D. H. (2002). User perspectives on relevance criteria: A comparison among relevant, partially relevant, and not-relevant judgments. *Journal of the American Society for Information Science and Technology, 53,* 327–342.

Marchionini, G. (1995). *Information seeking in electronic environments.* Cambridge, UK: Cambridge University Press.

Marsh, S., & Dibben, M. R. (2003). The role of trust in information science and technology. *Annual Review of Information Science and Technology, 37,* 465–498.

Marton, C. (2003). Quality of health information on the Web: User perceptions of relevance and reliability. *The New Review of Information Behaviour Research, 4,* 195–206.

Mashek, J. W., McGill, L. T., & Powell, A. C. (1997). *Lethargy '96: How the media covered a listless campaign.* Arlington, VA: The Freedom Forum.

McCroskey, J. C., & Young, T. J. (1981). Ethos and credibility: The construct and its measurement after three decades. *The Central States Speech Journal, 32,* 24–34.

McGuigan, G. S. (2001). Databases vs. the Web: A discussion of teaching the use of electronic resources in the library instruction setting. *Internet Reference Services Quarterly, 6*(1), 39–47.

McKenzie, P. J. (2003). Justifying cognitive authority decisions: Discursive strategies of information seekers. *Library Quarterly, 73*, 261–288.

Mehta, U. (2000). On the World Wide Web: Where are you going, where have you been? *Internet Reference Services Quarterly, 5*(1), 51–66.

Meola, M. (2004). Chucking the checklist: A contextual approach to teaching undergraduates Web-site evaluation. *portal: Libraries and the Academy, 4*, 331–344.

Metzger, M. J., Flanagin, A. J., Eyal, K., Lemus, D. R., & McCann, R. M. (2003). Credibility for the 21st century: Integrating perspectives on source, message, and media credibility in the contemporary media environment. In P. J. Kalbfleisch (Ed.), *Communication yearbook* (Vol. 27, pp. 293–335). Mahwah, NJ: Erlbaum.

Metzger, M. J., Flanagin, A. J., & Zwarun, L. (2003). College student Web use, perceptions of information credibility, and verification behavior. *Computers & Education, 41*, 271–290.

Meyer, P. (1988). Defining and measuring credibility of newspapers: Developing an index. *Journalism Quarterly, 65*, 567–574.

Meyer, T. J. (1974). Media credibility: The state of the research. *Public Telecommunications Reviews, 19*(4), 48–52.

Meyvis, T., & Janiszewski, C. (2002). Consumers' beliefs about product benefits: The effect of obviously irrelevant product information. *Journal of Consumer Research, 28*, 618–635.

Mizzaro, S. (1997). Relevance: The whole history. *Journal of the American Society for Information Science, 48*, 810–832.

Morahan-Martin, J. M. (2004). How Internet users find, evaluate, and use online health information: A cross-cultural review. *CyberPsychology & Behavior, 7*, 497–510.

Morrison, J. L., & Stein, L. L. (1999). Assuring integrity of information utility in cyber-learning formats. *Reference Services Review, 27*, 317–326.

Muir, B. M. (1987). Trust between humans and machines, and the design of decision aids. *International Journal of Man-Machine Studies, 27*, 527–539.

Mulder, R. (1980). Media credibility: A use-gratifications approach. *Journalism Quarterly, 57*, 474–477.

Murphy, D. S., & Yetmar, S. A. (1996). Auditor evidence evaluation: Expert systems as credible sources. *Behaviour & Information Technology, 15*, 14–23.

Nass, C., & Brave, S. (2005). *Wired for speech: How voice activates and advances the human–computer relationship.* Cambridge, MA: MIT Press.

Nass, C., & Mason, L. (1990). On the study of technology and task: A variable-based approach. In J. Fulk & C. Steinfeld (Eds.), *Organizations and communication technology* (pp. 46–67). Newbury Park, CA: Sage.

Nelson, P. (1970). Information and consumer behavior. *Journal of Political Economy, 78*, 311–329.

Nelson, P. (1974). Advertising as information. *Journal of Political Economy, 82*, 729–754.

Newhagen, J., & Nass, C. (1989). Differential criteria for evaluating credibility of newspapers and TV news. *Journalism Quarterly, 66*, 277–284.

O'Donovan, J., & Smyth, B. (2005). Trust in recommender systems. *Proceedings of the 10th International Conference on Intelligent User Interfaces*, 167–174.

Olaisen, J. (1990). Information quality factors and the cognitive authority of electronic information. In I. Wormell (Ed.), *Information quality: Definitions and dimensions* (pp. 91–121). London: Taylor Graham.

Pancer, S. M., George, M., & Gebotys, R. J. (1992). Understanding and predicting attitudes toward computers. *Computers in Human Behavior, 8*, 211–222.

Parekh, S. G., Nazarian, D. G., & Lim, C. K. (2004). Adoption of information technology by resident physicians. *Clinical Orthopaedics & Related Research, 421*, 107–111.

Park, T. K. (1993). The nature of relevance in information retrieval: An empirical study. *Library Quarterly, 63*, 318–351.

Peterson, G., Aslani, P., & Williams, K. A. (2003). How do consumers search for and appraise information on medicines on the Internet? A qualitative study using focus groups. *Journal of Medical Internet Research, 5*(4). Retrieved February 2, 2006, from www.jmir.org/2003/4/e33

Petty, R. E., & Cacioppo, J. T. (1981). *Attitudes and persuasion: Classic and contemporary approaches*. Dubuque, IA: W. C. Brown.

Petty, R. E., & Cacioppo, J. T. (1986). The elaboration likelihood model of persuasion. *Advances in Experimental Social Psychology, 19*, 123–205.

Pornpitakpan, C. (2004). The persuasiveness of source credibility: A critical review of five decades' evidence. *Journal of Applied Social Psychology, 34*, 243–281.

Pratt, G. F., Flannery, P., & Perkins, C. L. D. (1996). Guidelines for Internet resource selection. *College & Research Library News, 57*, 134–135.

Price, S. L., & Hersh, W. R. (1999). Filtering Web pages for quality indicators: An empirical approach to finding high quality consumer health information on the World Wide Web. *Proceedings of the 1999 Annual Symposium of the American Medical Informatics Association*, 911–915.

Putnam, R. D. (2000). *Bowling alone: The collapse and revival of American community*. New York: Simon & Schuster.

Quintana, Y., Feightner, J. W., Wathen, C. N., Sangster, L. M., & Marshall, J. N. (2001). Preventive health information on the Internet· Qualitative study of consumers' perspectives. *Canadian Family Physician, 47*, 1759–1765.

Reeves, B., & Nass, C. (1996). *The media equation: How people treat computers, television, and new media like real people and places*. New York: Cambridge University Press.

Resnick, P., & Varian, H. R. (1997). Recommender systems. *Communications of the ACM, 40*(3), 56–58.

Rieh, S. Y. (2000). *Information quality and cognitive authority in the World Wide Web*. Unpublished doctoral dissertation, Rutgers, The State University of New Jersey.

Rieh, S. Y. (2002). Judgment of information quality and cognitive authority in the Web. *Journal of the American Society for Information Science and Technology, 53*, 145–161.

Rieh, S. Y. (2005). Cognitive authority. In K. E. Fisher, S. Erdelez, & E. F. McKechnie (Eds.), *Theories of information behavior: A researcher's guide* (pp. 83–87). Medford, NJ: Information Today.

Rieh, S. Y., & Belkin, N. J. (1998). Understanding judgment of information quality and cognitive authority in the WWW. *Proceedings of the 61st Annual Meeting of the American Society for Information Science*, 279–289.

Rieh, S. Y., & Belkin, N. J. (2000). Interaction on the Web: Scholars' judgment of information quality and cognitive authority. *Proceedings of the 63rd Annual Meeting of the American Society for Information Science*, 25–38.

Rogers, E. M. (1995). *Diffusion of innovations* (4th ed.). New York: The Free Press.

Roper, B. (1985). *Public attitudes toward television and other media in a time of change*. New York: Television Information Office.

Saracevic, T. (1996). Relevance reconsidered. *Information science: Integration in perspectives: Proceedings of the Second Conference on Conceptions of Library and Information Science, Copenhagen, Denmark*, 201–218.

Schamber, L. (1991). Users' criteria for evaluation in a multimedia environment. *Proceedings of the 54th Annual Meeting of the American Society for Information Science*, 126–133.

Schamber, L., & Bateman, J. (1996). User criteria in relevance evaluation: Toward development of a measurement scale. *Proceedings of the 59th Annual Meeting of the American Society for Information Science*, 218–225.

Scriven, M., & Paul, R. (2004). *Defining critical thinking*. Retrieved February 2, 2006, from www.criticalthinking.org/aboutCT/definingCT.shtml

Settle, R. B., & Golden, L. L. (1974). Attribution theory and advertiser credibility. *Journal of Marketing Research*, *11*, 181–185.

Shapiro, S., & Spence, M. T. (2002). Factors affecting encoding, retrieval, and alignment of sensory attributes in a memory-based brand choice task. *Journal of Consumer Research*, *28*, 603–617.

Sillence, E., Briggs, P., Fishwick, L., & Harris, P. (2005). Guidelines for developing trust in health Websites. *Special interest tracks and posters of the 14th International World Wide Web Conference*, 1026–1027.

Singletary, M. W. (1976). Components of credibility of a favorable news source. *Journalism Quarterly*, *53*, 316–319.

Slater, M. D., & Rouner, D. (1996). How message evaluation and source attributes may influence credibility assessment and belief change. *Journalism and Mass Communication Quarterly*, *73*, 974–991.

Smith, A. G. (1997). Testing the surf: Criteria for evaluating Internet information resources. *The Public-Access Computer Systems Review*, *8*(3). Retrieved February 2, 2006, from http://info.lib.uh.edu/pr/v8/n3/smit8n3.html

Smith, R. E. (1993). Integrating information from advertising and trial: Processes and effects on consumer response to product information. *Journal of Marketing Research*, *30*, 204–219.

Smith, R. E., & Buchholz, L. M. (1991). Multiple resource theory and consumer processing of broadcast advertisements: An involvement perspective. *Journal of Advertising*, *20*, 1–7.

Spence, A. M. (1974). *Market signaling: Information transfer in hiring and related processes*. Cambridge, MA: Harvard University Press.

Stanford, J., Tauber, E. R., Fogg, B. J., & Marable, L. (2002). *Experts vs. online consumers: A comparative credibility study of health and finance Web sites* (Consumer WebWatch Research Report). Retrieved February 2, 2006, from www.consumerwebwatch.org/dynamic/web-credibility-reports-experts-vs-online-abstract.cfm

Steuer, J. (1992). Defining virtual reality: Dimensions determining telepresence. *Journal of Communication*, *42*, 73–93.

Stigler, G. (1961). The economics of information. *Journal of Political Economy, 69*, 213–225.

Sundar, S. S. (1999). Exploring receivers' criteria for perception of print and online news. *Journalism and Mass Communication Quarterly, 76*, 373–386.

Sundar, S. S., & Nass, C. (2000). Source orientation in human–computer interaction: Programmer, networker, or independent social actor? *Communication Research, 27*, 683–703.

Sundar, S. S., & Nass, C. (2001). Conceptualizing sources in online news. *Journal of Communication, 51*, 52–72.

Swanson, T. A. (2004). A radical step: Implementing a critical information literacy model. *portal: Libraries and the Academy, 4*, 259–273.

Swinney, L. (1999). Consideration of the social context of auditors' reliance on expert system output during evaluation of loan loss reserves. *International Journal of Intelligent Systems in Accounting, Finance, & Management, 8*, 199–213.

Tang, R., & Solomon, P. (1998). Toward an understanding of the dynamics of relevance judgment: An analysis of one person's search behavior. *Information Processing & Management, 34*, 237–256.

Tate, M., & Alexander, J. (1996). Teaching critical evaluation skills for World Wide Web resources. *Computers in Libraries, 16*(10), 49–55.

Taylor, R. S. (1986). *Value-added processes in information systems*. Norwood, NJ: Ablex.

Tombros, A., Ruthven, I., & Jose, J. M. (2005). How users assess Web pages for information seeking. *Journal of American Society for Information Science and Technology, 56*, 327–344.

Treise, D., Walsh-Childers, K., Weigold, M. F., & Friedman, M. (2003). Cultivating the science Internet audience: Impact of brand and domain on source credibility for science information. *Science Communication, 24*, 309–332.

Tseng, S., & Fogg, B. J. (1999). Credibility and computing technology. *Communications of the ACM, 42*(5), 39–44.

VandenBergh, B. G., Soley, L. C., & Reid, L. N. (1981). Factor study of dimensions of advertiser credibility. *Journalism Quarterly, 58*, 629–632.

Wærn, Y., & Ramberg, R. (1996). People's perception of human and computer advice. *Computers in Human Behavior, 12*, 17–27.

Wang, P. (1997). The design of document retrieval systems for academic users: Implications of studies on users' relevance criteria. *Proceedings of the 60th Annual Meeting of the American Society for Information Science*, 162–173.

Wang, P., & Soergel, D. (1998). A cognitive model of document use during a research project. Study I. Document selection. *Journal of the American Society for Information Science, 49*, 115–133.

Wang, P., & White, M. D. (1999). A cognitive model of document use during a research project. Study II. Decisions at the reading and citing stages. *Journal of the American Society for Information Science, 50*, 98–114.

Ward, M. R., & Lee, M. J. (2000). Internet shopping, consumer search, and product branding. *Journal of Products and Brand Management, 9*, 6–20.

Wathen, C. N., & Burkell, J. (2002). Believe it or not: Factors influencing credibility on the Web. *Journal of the American Society for Information Science and Technology, 53*, 134–144.

Watson, J. S. (1998). "If you don't have it, you can't find it." A close look at students' perceptions of using technology. *Journal of the American Society for Information Science, 49*, 1024–1036.

West, M. D. (1994). Validating a scale for the measurement of credibility: A covariance structure modeling approach. *Journalism Quarterly, 71*, 159–168.

Whitmire, E. (2004). The relationship between undergraduates' epistemological beliefs, reflective judgment, and their information-seeking behavior. *Information Processing & Management, 40*, 97–111.

Will, R. P. (1991). True and false dependence on technology: Evaluation with an expert system. *Computers in Human Behavior, 7*, 171–183.

Wilson, P. (1983). *Second-hand knowledge: An inquiry into cognitive authority*. Westport, CT: Greenwood Press.

Wilson, P. (1991). Bibliographic instruction and cognitive authority. *Library Trends, 39*, 259–270.

Winograd, T., & Flores, F. (1986). *Understanding computers and cognition: A new foundation for design*. Boston: Addison-Wesley.

Wright, A. A., & Lynch, J. (1995). Communication effects of advertising versus direct experience when both search and experience attributes are present. *Journal of Consumer Research, 21*, 708–718.

Ye, L. R., & Johnson, P. E. (1995). The impact of explanation facilities on user acceptance of expert systems advice. *MIS Quarterly, 19*, 157–172.

Zhu, X., & Gauch, S. (2000). Incorporating quality metrics in centralized/distributed information retrieval on the World Wide Web. *Proceedings of the 23rd Annual International ACM SIGIR Conference on Research and Development in Information Retrieval*, 288–295.

Organization and Retrieval of Information

CHAPTER 8

Semantics and Knowledge Organization

Birger Hjørland
Royal School of Library and Information Science, Copenhagen

Introduction: The Importance of Semantics for Information Science

The aim of this chapter is to demonstrate that semantic issues underlie all research questions within Library and Information Science (LIS, or, as hereafter, IS)[1] and, in particular, the subfield known as Knowledge Organization (KO). Further, it seeks to show that semantics is a field influenced by conflicting views and discusses why it is important to argue for the most fruitful one of these. Moreover, the chapter demonstrates that IS has not yet addressed semantic problems in systematic fashion and examines why the field is very fragmented and without a proper theoretical basis. The focus here is on broad interdisciplinary issues and the long-term perspective.

The theoretical problems involving semantics and concepts are very complicated. Therefore, this chapter starts by considering tools developed in KO for information retrieval (IR) as basically semantic tools. In this way, it establishes a specific IS focus on the relation between KO and semantics.

It is well known that thesauri consist of a selection of concepts supplemented with information about their semantic relations (such as generic relations or "associative relations"). Some words in thesauri are "preferred terms" (descriptors), whereas others are "lead-in terms." The descriptors represent concepts. The difference between "a word" and "a concept" is that different words may have the same meaning and similar words may have different meanings, whereas one concept expresses one meaning.

For example, according to WordNet 2.1 (2005), the word "letter" has five senses, of which two are: (1) "a written message addressed to a person or organization" and (2) "a letter of the alphabet, alphabetic character." In a thesaurus, these meanings are distinguished by, for example, parenthetical qualifiers, as in the *Thesaurus of ERIC Descriptors* (1987, p. 136):

> Letters (Alphabet)
> Letters (Correspondence)

The thesaurus manages synonymy relations by means of "Use/Used for" relations and homonymy relations by means of parenthetical qualifiers. Furthermore, by means of semantic relations between descriptors (concepts) such as narrower term (NT), broader term (BT), and related term (RT), the thesaurus establishes the structure of a subject field:

> Most thesauri establish a controlled vocabulary, a standardized terminology, in which each concept is represented by one term, a descriptor, that is used in indexing and can thus be used with confidence in searching; in such a system the thesaurus must support the indexer in identifying all descriptors that should be assigned to a document in light of the questions that are likely to be asked. A good thesaurus provides, through its hierarchy augmented by associative relationships between concepts, a semantic road map for searchers and indexers and anybody else interested in an orderly grasp of a subject field. (Soergel, 1995, p. 369)

It should now be clear that a thesaurus is basically a semantic tool because the "road map" it provides is semantic: The relations between concepts that a thesaurus indicates are semantic relations.

What is the case with thesauri is more or less the case with all kinds of what Hodge (2000, online) has presented as knowledge organizing systems (KOS) in the following taxonomy:

> Term Lists
> > Authority Files
> > Glossaries
> > Dictionaries
> > Gazetteers
>
> Classifications and Categories
> > Subject Headings
> > Classification Schemes
> > Taxonomies
> > Categorization Schemes
>
> Relationship Lists
> > Thesauri
> > Semantic Networks
> > Ontologies

All these types of KOS represent selections of concepts more or less enriched with information about their semantic relations. Semantic networks, for example, are instances of KOS utilizing more varied kinds of semantic relations than thesauri do, whereas authority files are examples of KOS displaying limited information about semantic relations. Because such systems are basically about concepts and semantic relations, knowledge about concepts and semantics is important for research into, and the use of, any of those systems. In other words, researchers in KO should ground their work in a fruitful theory of semantics. This kind of basic research has, however, been largely absent from IS.

Having argued that the various types of items which Hodge has identified as KOS may all be considered semantic tools, we will now take a closer look at the term "knowledge organizing systems."

Hodge (2000) omits certain kinds of KOS—for example, bibliometric maps such as those provided by White and McCain (1998). In these maps, citation patterns may be generated by authors and/or by terms (e.g., from descriptors). Such maps thus display certain kinds of semantic relations on the basis of citing behavior (and the relation between terms on such a map suggests a certain kind of *semantic distance*). It is thus important to include bibliometrics within the concept of KOS for both theoretical and practical reasons.

There are other kinds of KOS that Hodge (2000) does not consider. It could be argued that encyclopedias, libraries, bibliographical databases, and many other concepts used within IS should be considered as KOS. Furthermore, concepts outside IS, such as the system of scientific disciplines or the social division of labor in society, also constitute very fundamental kinds of KOS. Indeed, KOS in a narrow, IS-oriented sense are those systems related specifically to organizing bibliographical records (in databases), whereas KOS in a wide, general sense are related to the organization of literatures, traditions, disciplines, and people in different cultures.

Although all the KOS listed by Hodge, as well as others, such as bibliometric maps, may be considered semantic tools, not all kinds of KOS can be identified as such. The system of scientific disciplines, for example, is not a semantic tool. The term "semantic tool" should be reserved for systems that provide selections of concepts more or less enriched with information about semantic relations; KOS should be used as a broader term including, but not limited to, semantic tools.

The field of KO within IS is thus concerned with the construction, use, and evaluation of semantic tools for IR. This insight brings semantics to the forefront of IS. This view is shared by Khoo and Na (2006, p. 207), who declare that "natural language processing and semantic relations, in particular, point the way forward for information retrieval in the 21st century."

Because concepts provide the meaning behind words and semantics is the study of meaning, the study of concepts, meaning, and semantics should form one interdisciplinary subject field. However, the relevant literature is very scattered and difficult to synthesize, for it covers, among other fields, philosophy, linguistics, psychology and cognitive science, sociology, computer science, and information science. In addition to the disciplinary scattering of research in semantics, the field is based on different epistemological assumptions whose roots extend back hundreds of years into the history of philosophy. Moreover, the field seems theoretically muddled.

Semantics, by the way, is not concerned solely with word meaning. Pictures as well as other signs are also the objects of semantics. The way semantics is viewed and discussed in this chapter may seem, in the eyes of many people, more like semiotics (the study of signs in general) than semantics as commonly understood. The relation between semantics and semiotics is itself a controversial issue. The focus on semantics rather than semiotics in this chapter is motivated by the fact that thesaural relations (like KOS in general) are semantic relations.

The Status of Semantic Research in Information Science

Van Rijsbergen (1986, p. 194) has pointed out that the concept of meaning has been overlooked in IS and discussed why the whole area is in crisis. The fundamental basis of all the previous work—including his own—is wrong, he claims, because it has been based on the assumption that a formal notion of meaning is not required to solve IR problems. This statement by a leading researcher should encourage closer cooperation between IS and other fields conducting research in semantics. Few researchers have, however, risen to the challenge and not much consideration has been given to the nature of semantics and its implications for IS.

Some of those addressing semantic issues in KO and IS are Bean and Green (2001); Beghtol (1986); Blair (1990, 2003); Bonnevie (2001); Brooks (1995, 1998); Budd (2004); Dahlberg (1978, 1995); Daily (1979); Doerr (2001); Foskett (1977); Frohmann (1983); Green, Bean, and Myaeng (2002); Hammwöhner and Kuhlen (1994); Hedlund, Pirkola, and Kalervo (2001); Hjørland (1997, 1998); Khoo and Na (2006); Qin (1999, 2000); Read (1973); Song and Galardi (2001); Stokolova (1976, 1977a, 1977b); and Vickery and Vickery (1987).

These contributions are very different and difficult to present in any coherent way because they are not related to each other or systematically related to broader views. Some of them try to base their view on an explicit philosophy (e.g., "Activity Theory" [Hjørland, 1997] or Wittgenstein's philosophy [Blair, 1990, 2003; Frohmann, 1983]); others, for example, Vickery and Vickery (1987), base their view on cognitive psychology, but many simply present their own commonsense views without attempting to ground them in general theories (e.g., Foskett, 1977). A book such as that by Green, Bean, and Myaeng (2002) should be praised for its attempt to present an interdisciplinary perspective. Both this book and reviews such as Khoo and Na's (2006) fail, however, to consider much previous research within IS (such as many of the references listed here) and thus lack a historical perspective on the relation between semantics and IS. They also fail to provide a discussion of basic issues in semantics or to argue systematically for a specific theoretical view. This state of the art leaves us without a clear line of progress. Without proper theoretical frames of reference, empirical research becomes fragmented and almost impossible to perceive as a whole.

Much research is also based on technicalities and does not show much concern for basic semantic issues. This is the case with bibliometric research about semantic relationships among highly cited articles (e.g., Song & Galardi, 2001), with the technique known as "latent semantic indexing" or "latent semantic analysis" (Ding, 2005; Dumais, 2004) and, of course, with a new concept considered by many the most important frontier in KO, "the semantic Web" (Antoniou & van Harmelen, 2004; Berners-Lee, Hendler, & Lassila, 2001; Fensel, Hendler, Lieberman, & Wahlster, 2003). Some authors (e.g., Budd, 2004) have introduced important philosophical and semantic views into IS, but have not fully explored their implications for KO. There is a danger that the philosophical insights remain too isolated and vague.

The question concerning the relationship between semantics and KO may be turned upside down and we may ask from which theoretical perspectives KO has been approached. Which views of semantics have been implied by those approaches? KO has a long tradition within IS: Among the classics in the field is Bliss (1929). In order to discuss the relations between semantics and KO we should ask: What approaches have been used in the field of KO in the course of its history? How do they relate to semantic theory? Broughton, Hansson, Hjørland, and López-Huertas (2005) have suggested that the following traditions are the most important ones in KO:

1. The traditional approach to KOS expressed by classification systems used in libraries and databases, including the Dewey Decimal System (DDC), the Library of Congress Classification (LCC), and the Universal Decimal Classification (UDC)

2. The facet-analytical approach founded by Ranganathan

3. The IR tradition

4. User oriented/cognitive views

5. Bibliometric approaches

6. The domain-analytic approach

7. Other approaches, including semiotic, "critical-hermeneutical," discourse-analytic, and genre-based ones, as well as those that place emphasis on document representations, document typology and description, markup languages, document architectures, and so forth

Given that KOS essentially are semantic tools, should different approaches to KO reflect different approaches to semantics? This question can be answered only briefly here. The traditional approach to classification introduced the principle of literary warrant and thus located semantic relations in the scientific and scholarly literature. This was (and is) often done on positivist premises: The scientific literature is seen as representing facts about knowledge and structures in knowledge, and subject specialists are deemed capable of making true and objective representations of it in KO (thus tending to neglect conflicting evidence and theories). The facet-analytic approach tends to base KO on a priori semantic relations. These are derived from the application of (logical) principles rather than from the study of evidence in literatures (although this latter approach, too, is visible to some degree within the facet-analytic tradition). The IR tradition sees semantic relations as statistical relations between signs and documents. It is atomistic in the sense that it does not consider how traditions, theories, and discourse communities have formed the very statistical patterns it observes. User-oriented and cognitive approaches tend to replace literary warrant with empirical user studies and thus to base semantic relations on users rather than on the scientific literature. The bibliometric approach considers documents to be semantically related if they cite each other, are co-cited, or are bibliographically coupled. Again, the semantic relations are based on some kind of literary warrant, but in a way quite different from that of the traditional approach. The domain-analytic approach is rather traditional in its identification of semantic relations based on literary warrant. However, it is not positivist, for it regards semantic relations as determined by theories and epistemologies, which more or less influence all fields of knowledge. Many recent approaches to KO, including semiotic and hermeneutic approaches may be considered to be related to the domain-analytic approach.

What this suggests is that different approaches to KO imply different views on semantics. This point, however, has not been previously considered in the literature.

Semantics and the Philosophy of Science

The different theories and epistemologies that are in competition with one another may be more or less fruitful (or harmful) for information science. It is important to realize this and to take the risk of defending a particular theory. If this is not done, other views will never be sufficiently falsified, confirmed, or clarified. In the process of defending a particular view, one learns what other views it is necessary to reject. As pragmatist philosophers have long suggested, in order to make our thoughts clear, we have to ask what practical consequences follow from taking one or another view (or meaning) as true. If our theory (or meaning) does not have any practical implications, then it is of no consequence.

Peregrin (2004) has suggested that there are two dominant paradigms in semantics: One elaborated by logical positivists such as Rudolph Carnap (and the young Wittgenstein) and another developed by pragmatist philosophers such as John Dewey, which also draws on the insights of the late Wittgenstein. Positivist semantics suggests that expressions "stand for" entities and their meanings are the entities stood for by them. Pragmatist semantics suggests that expressions are tools for interaction and their meanings are their functions within the interaction, giving them the capacity to support it in their distinctive ways.[2] Hjørland and Nissen Pedersen (2005) have used this dichotomy to set the foundations of a theory of classification for IR. Their arguments may be summarized as follows:

1. Classification is the ordering of objects (or processes or ideas) into classes on the basis of some properties. (The same is the case when terms are defined: It is determined what objects fall under the term.)

2. The properties of objects are not just "given" but are available to us only on the basis of some descriptions and pre-understandings of those objects.

3. Description (or every other kind of representation) of objects is both a reflection of the thing described and of the subject creating the description. Descriptions are more or less purposeful and theory-laden. Pharmacologists, for example, in their description of chemicals, emphasize their medical effects, whereas "pure" chemists emphasize other aspects of the chemicals such as their structural properties.

4. The selection of the properties of the objects to be classified must reflect the purpose of the classification. There is no "neutral" or "objective" way to select properties for classification because any choice facilitates some kinds of use while limiting others.

5. The (false) belief that there exist objective criteria for classification may be termed "empiricism" or "positivism," whereas the belief that classifications always reflect a purpose may be termed "pragmatism."

6. Different domains (e.g., chemistry and pharmacology) may need different descriptions and classifications of objects to serve their specific purposes in the social division of labor in society. The criteria for classification are thus generally domain-specific. Different domains develop specific languages (languages for specific purposes, or LSPs) that are useful for describing, differentiating, and classifying objects in their respective domain.

7. In every domain, there exist different theories, approaches, interests, or "paradigms," which also tend to describe and classify objects according to their respective views and goals.

8. Any given classification or definition will *always* be a reflection of a certain view or approach to the objects being classified. Ørom (2003), for example, has shown how different library classifications reflect different views of the arts. Ereshefsky (2000) has argued that Linnaean classification is based on criteria that are

pre-Darwinian and thus problematic. Sometimes, however, a given classification seems to be immune to criticism. This may be the case with the periodic table of elements in chemistry and physics. Such immunity is caused by a strong consensus in the underlying theory.

9. A given literature to be classified is always—to some extent—a merging of different domains and approaches/theories/views. Such different views may be explicit or implicit. If they are implicit, they can be uncovered by theoretical and philosophical analysis.

10. Classifications and semantic systems that do not consider the different goals and interests reflected in the literature of a given domain are "positivist." The criteria for classification should be based on an understanding of the specific goals, values, and interests at play. They are not to be established a priori, but by "literary warrant"—i.e., by examining the literature. This cannot be done in either a "neutral" or an "objective" way, but can be accomplished by considering the different arguments.

In her reply, Sparck Jones (2005, p. 601) has acknowledged this pragmatic point of view. Her final suggestion is, however:

One of the most important techniques developed in retrieval research and very prominent in recent work, namely relevance feedback, raises a more fundamental question. This is whether classification in the conventional, explicit sense, is really needed for retrieval in many, or most, cases, or whether classification in the general (i.e., default) retrieval context has a quite other interpretation. Relevance feedback simply exploits term distribution information along with relevance judgements on viewed documents in order to modify queries. In doing this it is forming and using an implicit term classification for a particular user situation. As classification the process is indirect and minimal. It indeed depends on what properties are chosen as the basic data features, e.g., simple terms and, through weighting, on the values they can take; but beyond that it assumes very little from the point of view of classification. It is possible to argue that for at least the core retrieval requirement, giving a user more of what they like, it is fine. Yet it is certainly not a big deal as classification per se: in fact most of the mileage comes from weighting. And how large that mileage can be is what retrieval research in the many experiments done in the last decade have demonstrated, and web engines have taken on board.

I agree that meanings and classification criteria are implicit in the literature to be retrieved, as outlined here. Sparck Jones asks "whether classification in the conventional, explicit sense, is really needed for retrieval." My answer to this question is that no retrieval mechanism (and also any definition of "relevance") is ever neutral; it always considers some interests at the expense of others. To distinguish between such views is to make a kind of classification. To believe in a technical solution employing "relevance feedback" is to fall into the positivist trap. The vision of automated feedback and value-free systems is seductive but based on problematic philosophical assumptions.

This *ARIST* chapter espouses the pragmatist understanding of concepts, meaning, and semantics. This perspective may be able to address fundamental problems in KO and IR from a new and promising angle. The theoretical standpoint is that expressed by the American philosopher Hilary Putnam. He gives a résumé of his criticism in a paper bearing the apt title "The meaning of 'meaning'":

> Traditional semantic theory leaves out only two contributions to the determination of extension—the contribution of society and the contribution of the real world! (Putnam, 1975, p. 164)

Putnam is also known as a philosopher in the pragmatist tradition. We may thus list three characteristics of his (and our) philosophical point of departure:

- A focus on the relation between meaning and the real world (realism)

- A focus on the functional/pragmatic nature of meaning (pragmatism)

- A focus on the development of meaning in a social context (historicism and meaning collectivism/holism)

We can say with Putnam that these principles have been very much ignored in semantic theory. We can also assert that they have also been ignored to a large extent in fields such as IS, despite the fact that, as shown here, these fields are heavily dependent on semantics.

Semantics and Subject Knowledge

Advanced semantic tools demand proper subject knowledge for their design and administration, as well as for their use and evaluation. This follows from the realist philosophical position formulated previously: Knowledge of semantic relations between terms requires world knowledge about the relations between the objects that the terms refer to. You cannot determine the semantic relations between the words

"Copenhagen" and "Denmark" unless you know that Copenhagen is a part of Denmark.

This has been well known in the world of research libraries and bibliographical databases as well as in education for librarianship. The Medline database, for example, demands that a "prospective indexer must have no less than a bachelor's degree in a biomedical science, and should also have a reading knowledge of one or more modern foreign languages. An increasing number of recent recruits hold advanced degrees in biomedical sciences" (National Library of Medicine, 2005, online).

Concerning the construction of ontologies for gene technology, Bada, Stevens, Goble, Gil, Ashburner, Blake, et al. (2004, p. 237) write:

> One of the factors that account for GO's [Gene Ontology's] success is that it originated from within the biological community rather than being created and subsequently imposed by external knowledge engineers. Terms were created by those who had expertise in the domain, thus avoiding the huge effort that would have been required for a computer scientist to learn and organize large amounts of biological functional information. This also led to general acceptance of the terminology and its organization within the community. This is not to say that there have been no disagreements among biologists over the conceptualization, and there is of course a protocol for arriving at a consensus when there is such a disagreement. However, a model of a domain is more likely to conform to the shared view of a community if the modellers are within or at least consult to a large degree with members of that community.

These quotations do not constitute a new view. Earlier, Richardson and Bliss had considered the implications of the need of subject knowledge for education in librarianship and IS:

> Again from the standpoint of the higher education of librarians, the teaching of systems of classification ... would be perhaps better conducted by including courses in the systematic encyclopedia and methodology of all the sciences, that is to say, outlines which try to summarize the most recent results in the relation to one another in which they are now studied together. (Richardson, quoted in Bliss, 1935, p. 2)

Furthermore, at the close of her linguistic investigation into semantic relations, Murphy (2003, p. 242) draws the following conclusion:

> Plainly, the topic of lexical semantic paradigms has not been exhausted, and the metalinguistic approach discussed in this book gives rise to a number of new directions for lexicological

research. It fits with (and exploits) a general trend in linguistic research to appreciate the particular relations that language engages in: the relation between language and context, language and conceptualization, language and linguistic behavior. While [Leonard] Bloomfield (1985/[1936]) argued that linguists should ignore meaning because it is not properly "linguistic," to hold such a position in the current disciplinary context is untenable, since many if not most (if not all) linguistic phenomena cross boundaries between the linguistic, the conceptual, and the communicative. In the case of lexical relations, this means that those who study it are not just linguists, but metalinguists.

The domain-analytic view in information science is an attempt to provide subject knowledge within the boundaries of IS in a way that still makes it possible for professionals to have a clear identity as information scientists (cf. Hjørland, 2002a). Teaching librarians and information specialists the content of a paper such as that of Ørom (2003) would provide a better basis for all kinds of information work related to the arts. In addition, it would provide certain possibilities for generalization to other domains. In this way, information specialists would provide domain-specific knowledge while operating within a framework that allows IS to have a specific identity.

Domain knowledge is a problem not only for IS but also for linguistics and many metasciences (such as cognitive science and the sociology of science). Much cognitive and linguistic theory regarding concepts, meaning, and semantics is strongly constrained by attempts to avoid "world knowledge." The importance of subject knowledge has theoretical implications for how concepts should be defined and semantic relations determined (whether by human or by machine). It has implications for answering the question: What kind of information is needed in order to determine the semantic relations between two terms A and B? This question is considered in the next section.

Semantics and Its "Warrant"

Theories of semantics should be formulated in ways that provide methodological implications for determining meanings and relations in semantic tools such as thesauri and semantic networks. Often such implications are not clear; this renders the theories vague and unhelpful. Murphy (2003, p. 111), for example, has observed:

> From the WordNet literature available, it is often difficult to determine the bases on which design decisions in WordNet are made. For example, Miller (1998) notes that Chaffin, Herrmann, and Winston (1988) identified eight types of meronymy and Iris, Litowitz, and Evens (1988) distinguished

four types, but he does not indicate how it was determined that WordNet should distinguish only three types.

Similarly it is often unclear on what bases specific decisions are made in classification systems such as DDC or in thesauri such as the *Thesaurus of Psychological Index Terms* (Kinkade, 1974; Walker, 1997). Frohmann (1983) has discussed the semantic bases and theoretical principles of some classification systems. His is one of the few papers in IS to recognize that problems in classification should be seen as problems related to semantic theories. He observes that concepts such as "dog," "cat," "whale," "pike," and "owl" may be grouped or classified in different ways:

> For example, one principle of division divides the set according to nocturnal and diurnal characteristics. In this case, "cat" and "owl" belong to the first category, and the other terms to the second. Another principle of division separates mammals from non-mammals. In that case, "dog," "cat," and "whale" belong to the first category, whereas "pike" and "owl" belong to the second. Other divisions may be recognized (e.g., "land creatures," "water creatures," and "flying creatures"). (Frohmann, 1983, pp. 15–16)

Frohmann presents two semantic theories. The first holds that the categories to which a concept belongs are given a priori as part of the "meaning" of the term for that concept. According to the second, the categories to which a concept belongs must be found in the specific literature or discourse of which the associated term is a part. Consequently, the semantic relations are not given a priori, but are formulated a posteriori. This distinction has implications for classification theory. Frohmann demonstrates that Austin's PRECIS system (as an example) is based on a priori semantics and therefore open to an argument from Wittgenstein's later philosophy of language. According to Frohmann, KO systems cannot be both machine-compatible and adequate, as Austin claimed (although he does not rule out other ways to construe systems that are both machine-compatible and adequate).

Thus, a basic problem in KO is whether semantic relations are a priori or a posteriori: whether they can be known before examining the literature or only after such an examination has been carried out. What kind of literary warrant (or other kind of warrant) is needed in order to identify semantic relations and classify concepts?

This question is also related to one about the possibility of universal solutions to KO because a posteriori relations are unlikely to be universal. According to Frohmann (1983), the Classification Research Group (CRG) in England realized that semantic relations are a posteriori relations and have to be determined by examining specific disciplinary literatures individually. However, neither Frohmann himself nor the literature from the CRG and the Bliss Bibliographical Classification goes into details about precisely *how* concepts should be defined and their relations identified. Although it is correct that the CRG (and the Bliss Classification System, 2nd ed.) work on the basis of examining specific literatures, it is not clear—at least to this author—to what extent semantic relations are taken from the literature to be classified or are imposed on that literature. My opinion is that those systems are based on a priori principles to a greater degree than Frohmann suggests. There is a tendency within the facet-analytic tradition to work with universal categories like time and space and to classify the literature in relation to such pre-established categories. I believe this will be clearer when we analyze different theories of concepts and semantics.

Let us look at some theoretical possibilities about the nature of concepts and semantic relations. These might be:

- Query/situation specific or idiosyncratic

- Universal, Platonic entities/relations

- "Deep semantics" common to all languages (or inherent in cognitive structures)

- Specific to specific empirical languages (e.g., Swedish)

- Domain- or discourse-specific

- Other (e.g., determined by a company or a workgroup, "user-oriented")

Before discussing these possibilities separately, let us adumbrate some general considerations about the nature of semantic relations. Semantic relations are often displayed in standard lexica—for example, in the *Longman Synonym Dictionary* (1986), WordNet, and similar semantic tools. However, it is well known that, for example, synonyms are seldom synonyms in all contexts. It thus becomes important not to think of semantic relations as simply "given," but to ask: When are two concepts A and B to be considered synonyms (or homonyms or otherwise semantically related)? When is a semantic relation? We should again ask the pragmatist question: What difference does it make whether, in a given situation, we choose to consider A and B as semantically related in a specific way? This may look strange, given that many semantic relations seem intuitively "given" or authoritatively established in standard dictionaries.[3]

This relativity of meaning is also evident from Ogden and Richards's (1923) famous triangle of meaning (Figure 8.1).[4]

The triangle implies that the referent of an expression—that is, a word or another sign or symbol—is relative to different language users. As Peirce (1931–1958, Vol. 2, p. 228) put it:

A sign, or *representamen*, is something which stands to somebody for something in some respect or capacity. It addresses somebody, that is, creates in the mind of that person an equivalent sign, or perhaps a more developed sign. That sign which it creates I call the *interpretant* of the first sign. The sign stands for something, its *object* [or referent]. It stands for that object, not in all respects, but in reference to a sort of idea, which I have sometimes called the *ground* of the representamen.

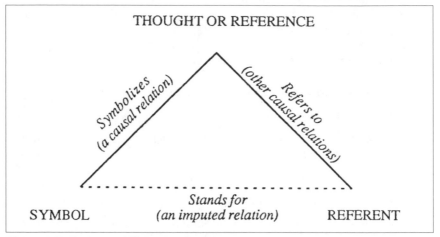

Figure 8.1   Ogden and Richards's (1923) semiotic triangle.

Concerning Query/Situation-Specific or Idiosyncratic Semantics

"*I* use a word," Humpty Dumpty said,
in rather a scornful tone,
"it means just what I choose it to mean—
neither more nor less."

"The question is," said Alice,
"whether you *can* make words mean
so many different things."

"The question is," said Humpty Dumpty
"which is to be master—that's all."
(Carroll, 1899)

It is important to keep in mind that concept determination and semantic relations are to be used in, for example, query expansion (automatic or manual) as well as in query precision and query formulation. In a way, it is the specific "information need" that determines which relations are fruitful and which are not in a given search session. A semantic relation that increases recall and precision in a given search is relevant in that situation. Creative information searchers do just that: They provide search strategies that retrieve a fruitful set of documents by combining terms in unusual ways. Different terms may be combined using the Boolean operator OR in a given search. By implication, they are regarded as equivalent terms (or synonyms) in the situation, even though they are not normally considered synonyms. For example, antonyms and contrary terms are different from synonyms. Yet, in IR, it is often useful to conduct searches using antonyms because certain phenomena may be discussed in relation to their opposites. The implication is that, in a given search, it might be useful to regard antonyms as synonyms.

This pragmatist point of departure is important to keep in mind in developing a theory of concepts and semantics. Semantic relations relate to a given task or situation and not all users of a given set of semantic relations will share the same view of which terms are equivalent. On the other hand, it is clear that if we base a semantic theory on an individualistic/idiosyncratic view of concepts and semantics, it is not possible to design systems for more than one user or situation—an absurd conclusion. We need more stable principles on which to determine semantic relations. We need a semantic theory about the meaning of words as forms of *typified practices*. Knowledge about semantics in typified practices may then be used by information searchers in order to include or exclude certain documents.

Concerning Universal, Platonic Entities/Relations

Mathematicians are, probably more than other professionals, Platonists. They believe that the mathematical concepts such as π (pi) have always existed and had only to be discovered. π is semantically related to the "radius" and the "perimeter" of a "circle" (because it is defined as the relation between those concepts). This semantic relation is universal and *given* (although the symbols chosen are conventional). According to Platonism, the meaningfulness of a general term is constituted by its connection with an abstract entity, the (possibly) infinite extension of which is determined independently of our classificatory practices (cf. Haukioja, 2005).

The question for us is: Is it also a priori in the sense Frohmann (1983) meant? It may be sufficient to say that the semantics of, for example, mathematical concepts are not simply intuited by the individual indexer. They have to be determined by considering the mathematical literature (or by people educated in that literature). Even if the basic method of knowing in mathematics involves a kind of rational intuition, this does not imply that semantic relations in mathematics should be considered to be given a priori in KO.

Concerning "Deep Semantics" Common to All Languages or Inherent in Cognitive Structures (A Priori Relations)

Much research on semantics is based on the assumption that concepts are somehow "hardwired" to our mind or brain, for example, in our so-called "mental lexicon." This is perhaps most clearly seen in research on color concepts.

Berlin and Kay's (1969) book *Basic Color Terms: Their Universality and Evolution* has had a major impact on how we view color terms. The authors argued for the universality and evolutionary development of eleven Basic Color Terms. Some salient characteristics of this universalist position have been summarized by one of its main critics, Barbara Saunders (1998, online):

> The relation between Munsell, the workings of the visual system, and the colour naming behaviour of people, is so tight it can be taken to be a causative law. Diversity of colour-naming behavior is defined as a system-regulated stability evinced by Evolution. The full lexicalisation of the human colour space is designated Evolutionary Stage Seven, as in American English; languages below this level are the fossil record.

Berlin and Kay's (1969) view of color concepts contrasts with a cultural-relative view, according to which our color concepts (and semantics in general) are determined primarily not by our visual system but by our need to act in relation to the colored environment:

> Sociohistorical psychology emphasizes the fact that sensory information is selected, interpreted, and organized by a social consciousness. Perception is thus not reducible to, or explainable by, sensory mechanisms, per se. Sapir, Whorf, Vygotsky, and Luria do not deny the existence of sensory processes—they maintain that sensory processes are subordinated to and subsumed within 'higher' social psychological functions. (Ratner, 1989, p. 361)[5]

We may thus conclude that the universality of color terms is controversial. The dominant view is cognitivist and maintains the universality of concepts, but a well-argued minority maintains a relativist view of color concepts, a position related to the pragmatist standpoint.

A certain version of "deep semantics" is the theory of semantic primitives according to which every word can be broken up into primitive kernels of meaning, *semantemes* (also called *semantic features* or *semantic components*). Semantemes are terms that are used to explain other terms or concepts but cannot themselves be explained by other terms. The process of breaking words down into semantemes is known as *componential analysis* and has been most often used to analyze kinship terms across languages. The components are often given in considerable detail. For instance, kinship terms like those shown in Table 8.1 might have three components: sex, generation, and lineage. Sex would be male or female; generation would be a number, with 0 = reference point's generation, -1 = previous generation, +1 = next generation; and lineage would be either direct, colineal (as in siblings), or ablineal (as in uncles and aunts).

Cruse (2001, p. 8758) has characterized the theory of semantic primitives as an "influential approach, much criticized but constantly reborn." He also writes (p. 8759)

> In the earliest versions of componential analysis, the components were the meanings of words, and the aim of the analysis was to extract a basic vocabulary, in terms of which all non-basic meanings could be expressed. Generally speaking, the features recognized by earlier scholars had no pretensions to universality, and indeed were often avowedly language-specific. Later scholars aimed at uncovering universals of human cognition, a finite "alphabet of thought." Accessible introductions to componential analysis can be found in Nida (1975) and Wierzbicka (1996).

According to Sparck Jones (1992, p. 1609), this theory was influential in early thesaurus construction: "A thesaurus was seen as providing a set of domain-independent *semantic primitives*."

Theories about "innate ideas" (including concepts and semantic relations) have roots far back in the history of philosophy and are particularly connected to the rationalist philosophers (e.g., Descartes and

Table 8.1   Kinship terms

Word	Semantemes
Father	male + parent
Mother	female + parent
Son	male + offspring
Daughter	female + offspring
Brother	male + sibling
Sister	female + sibling

Leibniz). The theory of semantic primitives is also related to "logical atomism" (Oliver, 1998), versions of which were put forward by Wittgenstein (1922) in his *Tractatus Logico-Philosophicus* and by Bertrand Russell (1924), both of whom were affiliated with logical positivism. (As is well known, Wittgenstein later changed his position and developed a more holistic and pragmatic view of language.) In linguistics, Chomsky has been the main representative of this rationalist strain of philosophy. Such a rationalist theory of semantics is similar to views put forward in IS, for example, in thesauri and in the facet-analytic tradition established by Ranganathan as well as in "formal concept analysis" (cf. Priss, 2006).

Although this rationalist theory dominates the literature (and is associated with the cognitive view), I do not find it fruitful for KO. First, the arguments that have been raised against it by the researchers mentioned here seem plausible. Second, semantic relations in KO are mostly a product of scientific ontological models; for example, the relations between chemical elements are not hardwired in our brains but are discovered by chemical researchers. Consequently, the creators of KOS have to identify the semantic relations in the subject literature rather than through psychological studies.

Concerning Semantics Specific to Given Empirical Languages

A paper by Hedlund et al. (2001) bears the title "Aspects of Swedish Morphology and Semantics from the Perspective of Mono- and Cross-Language Information Retrieval." The wording of this title implies that the Swedish language has a semantics of its own. In other words, semantic relations are structural relations attributed to different empirical languages. This view is also evident in the literature of structural linguistics. As demonstrated in Table 8.2, the English word "tree" does not have the same meaning as the Danish word "træ." Natural languages are structures in which the words classify the world differently.

Furthermore, many techniques in computational linguistics and natural language processing (NLP) are based on structures that are specific to a given language. For example, the commercial program Connexor (2003–2004, online) is described as giving

> a semantic interpretation of the syntactic structure, which means that many language-specific patterns are normalized. For example, the Machinese representation of the sentence "A book was given to John" shows the notional roles object and indirect object that correspond to the similar roles in "Somebody gave John a book."

The focus on differences between different natural languages has been useful for IS. Research such as that by Hedlund et al. (2001) has provided knowledge that is very fruitful for IR. On the other hand, some

Table 8.2   Cultural relativity in word meanings

English	*German	*Danish	*French	Italian	Spanish
Tree	Baum	Træ	arbre	albero	Árbol
Wood	Holz		bois	legno	Leña
		skov			Madera
Woods	Wald			bosco	Bosque
Forest			forêt	foresta	Selva

Originally presented by the Danish structural linguist Louis Hjelmslev (1943). Extended by information from Buckley (2001).

KOS (for example, the UDC) are applied across multiple languages and developed field by field. Semantic structures may be established in different domains and may diffuse into general languages. Our conceptions of uranium and radium as radioactive materials are based on scientific discoveries made within physics and transferred from there into general language. In other words, semantic structures in IS cannot be established simply by the study of natural languages: this also requires domain-specific knowledge.

Concerning Domain- or Discourse-Specific Semantics

As I noted earlier, pragmatism holds that descriptions and conceptions of objects are made from certain perspectives and involve certain pre-understandings and interests. This principle also figures prominently in other epistemological schemes, such as those of hermeneutics and Thomas Kuhn's theory of scientific paradigms. Although objects have objective properties, representation of those properties in languages and concepts is always more or less "subjective" or "biased" by individuals, social groups, or different cultures. Different human interests stress different properties of objects. Pharmacology and chemistry, for example, emphasize different properties of the same chemical elements: A chemical database emphasizes structural descriptions; a pharmacological database emphasizes medical effects.

The implication is that semantic relations reflect human interests. For example, pharmacology as a domain or discourse community emphasizes, those semantic relations that are related to medical and side effects. This does not imply that all semantic relations are domain-specific. Pharmacology as a domain is heavily dependent on chemical research and the two domains share many concepts and semantic relations. Still, parts of their descriptions contain descriptions and semantic relations that reflect the specific goals of their respective domains.

How are the basic semantic structures determined within a domain? Keil (1989, p. 159) has outlined some important developments in theories about concepts and semantics:

The history of all natural sciences documents the discovery that certain entities that share immediate properties nonetheless belong to different kinds. Biology offers a great many examples, such as the discoveries that dolphins and whales are not fish but mammals, that the bat is not a kind of bird, that the glass "snake" is in fact a kind of lizard with only vestigial limbs beneath its skin. In the plant kingdom it has been found, for example, that some "vegetables" are really fruits and that some "leaves" are not really leaves. From the realm of minerals and elements have come the discoveries, among others, that mercury is a metal and that water is a compound.

In almost all these cases the discoveries follow a similar course. Certain entities are initially classified as members of a kind because they share many salient properties with other bona fide members of that kind and because their membership is in accordance with current theories. This classification may be accepted for centuries until some new insight leads to a realization that the entities share other, more fundamentally important properties with a different kind not with their apparent kind.

Sometimes it is discovered that although the fundamental properties of the entities are not those of their apparent kind, they do not seem to be those of any other familiar kind either. In such cases a new theoretical structure must develop that provides a meaningful system of classification.

There are many profound questions about when a discovery will have a major impact on a scheme of classification, but certainly a major factor is whether that discovery is made in the context of a coherent causal theory in which the discovered properties are not only meaningful but central.

This quotation shows that concepts and semantic structures depend on our worldviews and theories, including those shaped by scientific discoveries. It is also supportive of scientific realism, according to which science uncovers deeper and deeper layers of reality and in the process changes our theories, concepts, classification schemes, and semantics. Such a view is very different from the prevailing view that concepts are inherent in the mind or in specific languages.

In the literature of any domain, different theories and epistemologies come into play (cf. the lemma "domains" in Hjørland & Nicolaisen, 2005, online). In some cases (e.g., in psychology), different "schools" or "paradigms" co-exist, each with its own journal(s) (cf. Hjørland, 2002b). In most cases, however, such different epistemologies or paradigms are not self-conscious and do not have formally established information sources and communication structures. In the case of medicine, the movement known as *evidence-based medicine* may be considered a paradigm; but there are no self-conscious alternative paradigms in medicine, a fact that challenges our view.[6] In such cases, the existence of different paradigms has to be demonstrated by analyzing different methodologies and assumptions made in the field; studies of different paradigms (e.g., by using bibliometric methods) are much more difficult to perform. A working hypothesis is that different theories, background assumptions, and paradigms are at play in *any* field of knowledge (although, of course, the degree of consensus varies from field to field and variant views may be almost absent in some fields).

The meanings of particular words or symbols are primarily influenced by the dominant view or paradigm within a given domain or discourse. Any attempt to change the dominant view implies a need to reconsider established meanings. This is often not clear to the users of those words and symbols, who may use terms and symbols with meanings that work against what they are trying to do. When the need to redefine symbols has become clear to users, they may choose to use a different term or to continue to use a term with a somewhat different meaning. In this way, meanings are linked to different views, interests, and goals; accordingly, terms can generally be considered polysemous.[7] Attempts to standardize terminology may unwittingly suppress certain views. This problem is, for example, important to consider in relation to The Unified Medical Language System (UMLS) project. Campbell, Oliver, Spackman, and Shortliffe (1998, pp. 426–427) have discussed how the ULMS has integrated the concept "Aspirin" from two different thesaural sources:

> It is obvious that the intension associated with a term in a source terminology is represented at least in part by its location in a hierarchy and by decisions made regarding synonyms and non-synonyms. Aspirin in the CRISP Thesaurus is a chemical; it is also a centrally acting drug that has antirheumatic, anti-inflammatory, analgesic, and antipyretic properties. Similarly, the UMLS equivalent of aspirin in SNOMED, acetylsalicylic acid, is a chemical. It is also a drug with several of the same properties that it has in the CRISP Thesaurus: It is a centrally acting agent, an analgesic, and an antipyretic. On the other hand, in SNOMED, acetylsalicylic acid is not synonymous with two other UMLS equivalents of aspirin, Easprin and Zorprin, because the first is a generic drug and the other two are proprietary drugs. Thus, in SNOMED, the intension of aspirin is clearly not the same as the intension of Easprin, yet aspirin and Easprin are linked to the same CUI. It may even be argued that there are subtle differences in the intension of aspirin in CRISP and SNOMED, yet these differences are obscured or lost when one moves from the source terminology to the CUI.

How a term like "aspirin" should be defined and which semantic relations should be assigned in a given KOS is thus not an objective fact but a question related to the purpose of that KOS. As Campbell et al. (1998, p. 430) write:

> In our previous discussion of how the UMLS represents "Aspirin," ... we noted that most clinicians would probably not consider these three concepts [aspirin, Aspergum, and Ecotrin] interchangeable in the prescriptions they write. However, we also assert that from some possible perspectives, such as when we are concerned primarily with medication allergies, having these concepts all linked to the same extension makes perfect sense.

In this way, semantic decisions (such as whether aspirin, Aspergum, and Ecotrin should be considered synonymous terms) have to be decided by considering the consequences, such as whether these substances can be substituted for each other for the purpose that the KOS is designed to accomplish.

The implication of different paradigms for KO and semantics is that any bibliography of a certain size must confront conflicting ways of defining concepts and determining semantic relations. Literary warrant does not mean identifying only one text from which semantic relations may be inferred. The task is to negotiate between different claims put forward in different texts and to select the one that has the highest degree of cognitive authority or is considered best in relation to the goal of the KOS. Information scientists engaged in developing a given KOS have to negotiate among different views more or less visible in the literature to be indexed. In practice, this is often not done. The DDC, for example, claims to be based on the principle of literary warrant (Mitchell, 2001, p. 217); however, as Miksa (1994, p. 149) has noted, its practice has typically involved

> arranging as many categories as possible in orders that reflected some kind of consensus among experts but thereafter simply doing something "practical" with the remainder. This appears to have been an approach characteristic of the DDC and the UDC as they developed over the years.

Systems such as the DDC are conservative because it is not economical to conduct deep literary investigations; to change the system; and, in particular, to reclassify books. Systems of this kind have to weigh the advantages of being updated in terms of literary warrant against the benefits of being a standard that is changed only rarely and reluctantly. There is a trade-off between being an optimal tool for the information seeker and a practical tool for the library manager. For the theory of IS, it is nonetheless important to describe the principles of designing optimal search tools. Such principles have to deal with the conflicting criteria of literary warrant. For example, should *social psychology* be classified with psychology or with sociology? Bibliometric arguments might claim that as psychologists are dominant in social psychology, it should be classified with psychology. However, theoretical arguments might assert that the explanation of social psychological phenomena needs to be founded in sociological theory and so it should be classified with sociology. Historical and bibliometric studies have shown that there are actually two social psychologies—*psychological social psychology* (mainly experimental) and *sociological social psychology*. Each of these types of social psychology has its own courses, textbooks, journals, and so on, and so a third possibility would be to distinguish between psychological and sociological social psychology. The point is that the kind of information presented here is necessary for any informed decision about classification practice. Exactly the same kind of information would be helpful for the information seeker (in order to discriminate between the two kinds of social psychology or in order to find related information). If a semantic tool is to be optimized as a retrieval tool, such information about conflicting views of semantic relations should be available. This implies that classification research would make such alternatives visible in the literature and that the construction of systems would be based on such knowledge, with explicit references to, and interpretation of, literary warrant. The more that is invested in designing classification systems, the greater the benefits to the user. Arbitrary, easy, standardized, or "practical" solutions from an administrative point of view do not provide the information seeker with insights into the structures of knowledge.

The existence of different paradigms thus implies that any existing KOS can be examined in relation to both dominant and alternative views. As Ørom (2003) has demonstrated, different KOS such as the UDC and the DDC are more or less biased toward different paradigms within, for example, art studies. Although some systems (e.g., the *Art and Architecture Thesaurus* [Petersen, 1994]) are easier to adapt to new tendencies, there are no neutral platforms or criteria on which to base classifications and semantic tools. Any semantic tool may be more or less in harmony, or in conflict, with the views represented in the literature. Which view should the designer choose? The majority view? It is not possible to prescribe any single "correct" view or method for selecting a particular one. If it were, then it would be possible to prescribe how to do science, something that most philosophers of science find impossible. All we can conclude is that a precondition for designing quality KOS is that the designer knows the different views and is able to provide a reasonably informed and negotiated solution. In addition, the designer of a given KOS should analyze, from a pragmatic point of view, what goals the KOS seeks to fulfill.

Information scientists should ask the pragmatic question: Given the different interests and paradigms in the field, what kinds of interest should this specific system support? What difference does it make whether some kinds of semantic relations are used at the expense of others? Perhaps the most important task of the information professional is to make the different interests and paradigms visible so that the user can make an informed choice.

Other Kinds of Warrant

In KO, as well as in IS in general, user-oriented and cognitive theories have flourished for some time. What kinds of "user warrant" exist with regard to semantic relations? Beghtol (1986) has discussed the following:

- Literary warrant and terminological warrant

- Scientific/philosophical warrant

- Educational warrant

- Cultural warrant

She does not, however, discuss user warrant. Indeed, it is difficult to imagine that the establishing of relations between terms A and B should be determined by investigating non-specialist users' perspectives (e.g., that the classification of whales as mammals should be determined by users rather than by experts). In the case of popular music (Abrahamsen, 2003), the experts on genre are generally not the musicologists because so few of them have specialized in this field. It is closer to the users' own expertise; however, journalists are presumably among those defining and naming new genres (and thus determining meaning and semantics). Other kinds of warrant may exist. Albrechtsen and Mark Pejtersen (2003) have argued for the existence of a sort of *work domain* warrant. This view may represent a tendency to prefer oral sources to written sources in IS. Yet, oral and written sources need the same kind of interpretation and argumentation. Information scientists may feel safer if they rely on "experts" rather than documents, but relevant documents are written by experts and are equally valid sources, if not more so.

Semantic Relations

Semantic relations are the relations between concepts, meanings, or senses. The concept [school] should be distinguished from the word "school." [School] is a kind of [educational institution]. This is an example of a hyponymous, or hierarchical, relationship between two concepts or meanings, which is one among many kinds of semantic relations.

The concept [school] may, for example, be expressed by the terms or expressions "school," "schoolhouse," and "place for teaching." The relation between "school" and "schoolhouse" is one of synonymy between two words, but the relation between "school" and "place for teaching" is a relation between a word and an expression. The relations between words are termed lexical relations.[8] "School" also means [a group of people who share a common outlook in relation to something] (as in "a school of thought"). This is a homonym relation: Two senses share the same word or expression—"school." Synonyms and homonyms are not relations between concepts but are about concepts expressed with identical or with different signs.

Relations between concepts, senses, or meanings should not be confused with relations between the terms, words, expressions, or signs that are used to express the concepts. It is, however, common to mix both of these kinds of relations under the heading "semantic relations" (e.g., Cruse, 1986; Lyons, 1977; Malmkjær, 1995; Murphy, 2003). For this reason, synonyms, homonyms, and so forth, are considered under the label "semantic relations" in this chapter.

How many kinds of semantic relations exist? Is the number of semantic relations finite or infinite? What determines this number? Rosario and Hearst (2001) have observed that there are contradictory views in theoretical linguistics regarding the semantic properties of noun compounds (NCs). Some researchers hold that there exists a small set of semantic relationships that NCs may imply. Others maintain that the semantics of NCs cannot be exhausted by any finite listing of relationships. Green (2001, pp. 5–6) has argued that the inventory of semantic relationships includes both a closed set of relationships (including mainly hierarchical and equivalence relationships) and an open set of relationships. For example, every time a new verb is coined, the potential for the introduction of a new conceptual relationship arises.

Is it possible to draw up an exhaustive list of semantic relations? The answer is probably that any relation between objects (or processes or anything else) may be expressed in language because languages do not contain a limited number of semantic relations. "Love" is a relation between specific people, for example, Tom and Clare. [Tom] and [Clare] are thus individual concepts conjoined through the semantic relation "love."[9] (Note that the words "Tom" and "Clare" need not refer to the [Tom] and [Clare] in question, but may also refer to other individual concepts that do not share the same semantic relations.) The limit to the number of semantic relations seems to be relations that nobody has found interesting enough to conceptualize. If this argument is correct, then the number of semantic relations is infinite.

Different domains probably develop new kinds of semantic relations continuously. Rosario and Hearst (2001, pp. 83–84) identified 38 semantic relations within medicine.[10]

> In this work we aim for a representation that is intermediate in generality between standard case roles (such as Agent, Patient, Topic, Instrument), and the specificity required for information extraction. We have created a set of relations that are sufficiently general to cover a significant number of noun compounds, but that can be domain specific enough to be useful in analysis. We want to support relationships between

entities that are shown to be important in cognitive linguistics, in particular we intend to support the kinds of inferences that arise from Talmy's force dynamics (Talmy, 1985). It has been shown that relations of this kind can be combined in order to determine the "directionality" of a sentence (e.g., whether or not a politician is in favor of, or opposed to, a proposal) (Hearst, 1990). In the medical domain this translates to, for example, mapping a sentence into a representation showing that a chemical removes an entity that is blocking the passage of a fluid through a channel.

The problem remains of determining what the appropriate kinds of relations are. In theoretical linguistics, there are contradictory views regarding the semantic properties of noun compounds (NCs). Levi (1978) argues that there exists a small set of semantic relationships that NCs may imply. Downing (1977) argues that the semantics of NCs cannot be exhausted by any finite listing of relationships. Between these two extremes lies Warren's (1978) taxonomy of six major semantic relations organized into a hierarchical structure.

We have identified the 38 relations shown in Table 1 [omitted here]. We tried to produce relations that correspond to the linguistic theories such as those of Levi and Warren, but in many cases these are inappropriate. Levi's classes are too general for our purposes; for example, she collapses the "location" and "time" relationships into one single class "In" and therefore field mouse and autumnal rain belong to the same class. Warren's classification schema is much more detailed, and there is some overlap between the top levels of Warren's hierarchy and our set of relations.

Rosario and Hearst (2001) thus seem to support the view that the number of semantic relations is infinite. In this regard, it is worth noting that semantic relations resemble commonly used grammatical categories. Now, categories and grammatical relations represent abstractions. Thus, our earlier example of a semantic relation, "love," may be seen as a special case of "being affected" (one of Aristotle's categories). Although the number of semantic relations appears to be unlimited, only a limited number of generalized relations tend to be used in practice.

In IR, the basic function of semantic relations is to contribute to the increase of recall and precision. For example, the inclusion of synonyms and broader terms in a query may contribute to increased recall, whereas the differentiation of homonyms and the specification of terms may increase precision. In this way, the wide use of the standard semantic relations employed in thesauri may be explained functionally. There are, however, recommendations that the number of relations should be expanded:

> The participants [in a NISO 1999 workshop on standards for electronic thesauri] recommended that a much richer, hierarchically organized, set of relationships be developed. ... There is reason to expect that provision for semantic relations in controlled vocabularies will become much more extensive in a future standard. (Milstead, 2001, p. 65)

How should we explain this demand for a much richer set of relationships than that ordinarily used in, for example, thesauri? The answer may imply a criticism of the traditional recall/precision way of understanding IR. What information searchers need are maps that inform them about the world (and the literature about that world) in which they live and act. They need such maps in order to formulate questions in the first instance. In order to formulate queries and to interact with information sources, advanced semantic tools are often very useful. This is probably especially so in the humanities, where concepts are more clearly associated with worldviews. The notion of conceptual history (*Begriffsgeschichte*) as developed in Germany provides a good illustration of this point. Historians and other humanistic researchers have realized that in order to use sources from a given period, one must know what the terms meant at the time. Therefore, they have developed impressive historical dictionaries that provide detailed information about conceptual developments within different domains, just as they have developed methodological principles on how to work with historical information sources (cf. Hampsher-Monk, Tilmans, & van Vree, 1998).

An example of a semantic tool developed in this tradition is *Reallexikon der deutschen Literaturwissenschaft* (Weimar, 1997–2003), which provides the following information for each term:

- The term (e.g., "bibliography")

- A definition (e.g., definition of "bibliography")

- A history (i.e., etymology) of the word (e.g., the etymology of the word "bibliography")

- A history of the concept (e.g., the history of the meanings of "bibliography")

- A history of the field (e.g., the history of bibliographies themselves)

- A history of research about the field (e.g., the history of research on bibliographies, i.e., library science)

I mention this example because it illustrates the existence of important work that may inspire IS to adopt a broader approach to semantic relations. To date, few researchers have investigated whether different domains need different kinds of semantic tools displaying different kinds of semantic relations: A notable exception is Roberts (1985), who has argued for the importance of specific kinds of relations in the social sciences.

The "Intellectual" Versus the Social Organization of Knowledge

Are there semantic relations between citing papers and their cited papers? Some authors have explicitly used this terminology (e.g., Harter, Nisonger, & Weng, 1993; Qin, 1999; Song & Galardi, 2001). Others have used bibliometric methods in order to establish semantic relations in thesauri and information retrieval (e.g., Kessler, 1965; Pao, 1993; Rees-Potter, 1989, 1991; Salton, 1971; Schneider, 2004), thus implying such a relation.

Harter et al. (1993) examined semantic relations between citing and cited papers by applying two methods: a macro analysis, based on a comparison of the Library of Congress class numbers assigned citing and cited documents, and a microanalysis, based on a comparison of descriptors assigned to citing and cited documents by three indexing and abstracting services, *ERIC*, *LISA*, and *Library Literature*. Both analyses suggested that the subject similarity among pairs of cited and citing documents is typically very small (at least in this domain). In interpreting the results of this study, one should remember that subject determination typically is a process with great uncertainty and variance. If two documents, A and B, have a citing relation (directly or indirectly by co-citations or bibliographic coupling), they might be understood as semantically related whether or not they are assigned the same descriptors or classification codes by somebody (or whether or not they contain the same words, for that matter: one might, for example, be in English, the other in Danish). I hold that the citing relation is in itself a kind of semantic relation. In support of this claim, I distinguish between "ontological" and social semantic relations and argue that citing relations belong to the latter.

The kinds of relations typically used in semantic tools are "real" relations such as geographical relations (e.g., Denmark is part of Europe), biological relations (e.g., cats are mammals), and chemical relations (such as the relations implied by the periodic table). Such relations are "ontological." Researchers produce ontological models that are used to organize knowledge.

A "social relation" is a different kind of relation. For example, disciplinary relations are social. The classification of sociology as a social science means that sociologists belong to the community of social scientists. A discipline is a social concept defined as people with similar education or other social ties, such as sharing the same organizations and journals. Disciplines typically have strong internal citation relations in comparison to their relations to other disciplines. A citation network is thus a kind of social relationship.

In some cases, ontological models of reality correspond very well with social organizations such as disciplines or citation networks. In other cases, the connections may be weak (many disciplines or "schools" may, for example, have overlapping ontological structures). Social constructivists tend to claim that ontological models and discoveries are just constructed: In other words, the social organization of knowledge is somehow primary to the intellectual organization. Scientific realists, on the other hand, tend to see ontological structures as primary and social structures as based on preexisting structures discovered by science.

Ontological models and theories developed by researchers as well as social organizations provide meaning to terms and semantic relations between terms. One may discuss which kind of meanings or relations are the most truthful or fruitful ones. However, information scientists provide semantic tools that are based on both kinds of relations. Bibliometric tools and tools based on ontological relations are available and in many cases supplement each other in IR. One should study the ways in which they supplement each other. In other words, semantic relations as provided by citing relations are legitimate in their own right. There is no need to verify them as Harter et al. (1993) and Schneider (2004) attempt to do. A traditional thesaurus and a bibliometric map may, in different ways, inform a person seeking information. Their relative value may depend on domain-specific issues such as how terminology is used and whether citation patterns reflect relevant specializations. A citation relation between two papers, A and B, is in itself a semantic relation, regardless of whether it corresponds with how A and B are otherwise determined to be related.

Conclusion

The pragmatist view of semantics suggests that words and expressions are tools for interaction and their meanings are their functions within the interaction, constituting their capacities to serve it in their distinctive ways. When information professionals classify documents or informational objects, the relevant meanings and properties are available only on the basis of some descriptions. This important consideration, which van Rijsbergen (1979) has emphasized, stands in opposition to the prevailing implicit assumption that all relevant properties of the objects are obvious to information specialists and that the latter follow certain given principles providing an optimal classification that is objective, neutral, and universal—hence, technically efficient. Hunter's (2002, p. 25) textbook on classification demonstrates how machine bolts may be classified according to their material, thread size, head shape, and finish. Admittedly, this example is probably not typical of documentary classification (it is classification made too simple). The same thing is often described differently for different purposes. Differing human interests emphasize different properties of objects. A typical database, on which IR experiments are performed, is best conceptualized as a merging of different descriptions serving different purposes.

Traditional approaches to KO have a tighter affiliation with positivism than with the pragmatist view of semantics. The solutions provided have not been based on the view that a typical database, on which IR experiments are performed, should be conceived of as a merging of different descriptions serving different purposes and based on different epistemologies. The implication is that traditional views have provided solutions that are, at best, statistical averages and thus sub-optimal. The prospect of KO based on a pragmatist understanding of semantics holds open the promise of fine-tuning KOS in different domains and genres.

Endnotes

1. LIS and IS are regarded as synonyms in this chapter. Other researchers do not regard them as synonyms. This example of semantic relations is an illustration of the problems that KO faces. Those who claim that the two terms are not synonyms should be able to say whether a given paper belongs to IS or to LIS.

2. In the sociology of science, the debate is between "meaning finitism" and "meaning determinism," a related theoretical discussion (cf. Barnes, 2002; Bloor, 1997, pp. 1–3, 9–11; Haukioja, 2005; Klaes, 2002; Larsson, 2003; and Weber, 2005). Harris (2005) provides an important critique of the semantic assumptions generally made in science.

3. Some texts define semantic relations as stable and different from "syntactic relations" (Foskett, 1977, p. 72) or from pragmatic relations (Dahllöf, 1999, p. 44). Such positions are not in accordance with the theoretical view put forward in this chapter and would make the question "Under what conditions can a semantic relation be said to exist?" meaningless.

4. Sowa (2000, online) writes about Ogden & Richards's (1923) triangle of meaning: "The triangle in Figure [8.]1 has a long history. Aristotle distinguished objects, the words that refer to them, and the corresponding experiences in the *psychê*. Frege and Peirce adopted that three-way distinction from Aristotle and used it as the semantic foundation for their systems of logic. Frege's terms for the three vertices of the triangle were *Zeichen* (sign) for the symbol, *Sinn* (sense) for the concept, and *Bedeutung* (reference) for the object."

5. Regarding relativism in color concepts see in addition to Ratner (1989) also Goodwin (2000), Lucy (1997), Roberson, Davies, and Davidoff (2000), and Saunders (1998).

6. Perhaps "narrative based medicine" (Greenhalgh & Hurwitz, 1998) should be considered a competing paradigm.

7. This is clearly seen in the German tradition of *Begriffsgeschichte*, which is discussed in the section on semantic relations.

8. "Lexical Semantics is about the meaning of words. Although obviously a central concern of linguistics, the semantic behaviour of words has been unduly neglected in the current literature, which has tended to emphasize sentential semantics and its relation to formal systems of logic" (Cruse, 1986, book cover).

9. Such relations could be drawn, for example, in semantic networks. See figure 7 in McCann (1997).

10. Rosario and Hearst (2004) described the problems involved in distinguishing seven relation types between the entities "treatment" and "disease" in biomedical texts.

References

Abrahamsen, K. T. (2003). Indexing of musical genres: An epistemological perspective. *Knowledge Organization, 30*, 144–169.

Albrechtsen, H., & Mark Pejtersen, A. (2003). Cognitive work analysis and work centered design of classification schemes. *Knowledge Organization, 30*, 213–227.

Antoniou, G., & van Harmelen, F. (2004). *A semantic Web primer*. Cambridge, MA: MIT Press.

Bada, M., Stevens, R., Goble, C., Gil, Y., Ashburner, M., Blake, J. A., et al. (2004). A short study on the success of the gene ontology. *Journal of Web Semantics, 1*, 235–240. Retrieved December 15, 2005, from www.websemanticsjournal.org/ps/pub/2004-9

Barnes, B. (2002). Thomas Kuhn and the problem of social order in science. In T. Nickles (Ed.), *Thomas Kuhn* (pp. 122–141). Cambridge, UK: Cambridge University Press.

Bean, C. A., & Green, R. (Eds.). (2001). *Relationships in the organization of knowledge*. Dordrecht, NL: Kluwer.

Beghtol, C. (1986). Semantic validity: Concepts of warrant in bibliographic classification systems. *Library Resources & Technical Services, 30*, 109–125.

Berlin, B., & Kay, P. (1969). *Basic color terms: Their universality and evolution*. Berkeley: University of California Press.

Berners-Lee, T., Hendler, J., & Lassila, O. (2001). The semantic Web. *Scientific American, 284*(5), 34–43.

Blair, D. C. (1990). *Language and representation in information retrieval*. Amsterdam: Elsevier.

Blair, D. C. (2003). Information retrieval and the philosophy of language. *Annual Review of Information Science and Technology, 37*, 3–50.

Bliss, H. E. (1929). *The organization of knowledge and the system of the sciences*. New York: Henry Holt.

Bliss, H. E. (1935). *A system of bibliographical classification*. New York: H. W. Wilson.

Bloomfield, L. (1936/1985). Language or ideas? In J. J. Katz (Ed.), *The philosophy of linguistics* (pp. 19–25). Oxford, UK: Oxford University Press.

Bloor, D. (1997). *Wittgenstein: Rules and institutions*. London: Routledge.

Bonnevie, E. (2001). Dretske's semantic information theory and meta-theories in library and information science. *Journal of Documentation, 57*, 519–534.

Brooks, T. A. (1995). Topical subject expertise and the semantic distance model of relevance assessment. *Journal of Documentation, 51*, 370–387.

Brooks, T. A. (1998). The semantic distance model of relevance assessment. *Proceedings of the Annual Meeting of the American Society for Information Science*, 33–44.

Broughton, V., Hansson, J., Hjørland, B., & López-Huertas, M. J. (2005). Knowledge organisation: Report of working group 7. In L. Kajberg & L. Lørring (Eds.), *European Curriculum Reflections on Education in Library and Information Science*. Copenhagen: Royal School of Library and Information Science. Retrieved December 15, 2005, from www.db.dk/LIS-EU/workshop.asp

Buckley, G. (2001). *Semantics*. Retrieved July 31, 2005, from www.ling.upenn.edu/courses/Spring_2001/ling001/semantics.html

Budd, J. M. (2004). Relevance: Language, semantics, philosophy. *Library Trends, 52*, 447–462.

Campbell, K. E., Oliver, D. E., Spackman, K. A., & Shortliffe, E. H. (1998). Representing thoughts, words, and things in the UMLS. *Journal of the American Medical Informatics Association, 5*, 421–431. Retrieved December 15, 2005, from www.pubmedcentral.nih.gov/articlerender.fcgi?artid=61323

Carroll, L. (1899). *Through the looking glass*. New York: M. F. Mansfield & A. Wessels.

Chaffin, R., Herrmann, D. J., & Winston, M. (1988). A taxonomy of part-whole relations. *Cognition and Language, 3*, 1–32.

Connexor. (2003–2004). *Machinese semantics*. Retrieved December 15, 2005, from www.connexor.com/software/semantics

Cruse, D. A. (1986). *Lexical semantics*. Cambridge, UK: Cambridge University Press.

Cruse, D. A. (2001). Lexical semantics. In N. J. Smelser & P. B. Baltes (Eds.), *International Encyclopedia of the Social and Behavioral Sciences* (Vol. 13, pp. 8758–8764). Amsterdam: Elsevier.

Dahlberg, I. (1978). A referent-oriented, analytical concept theory for INTERCONCEPT. *International Classification, 5*, 142–151.

Dahlberg, I. (1995). Conceptual structures and systematization. *IFID Journal, 20*(3), 9–24.

Dahllöf, M. (1999). *Språklig betydelse: En introduktion till semantik och pragmatik* [Linguistic meaning: An introduction to semantics and pragmatics]. Lund: Studentlitteratur.

Daily, J. E. (1979). Semantics. In A. Kent, H. Lancour, & J. E. Daily (Eds.), *Encyclopedia of Library and Information Science* (Vol. 27, pp. 209–215). New York: Dekker.

Ding, C. H. Q. (2005). A probabilistic model for latent semantic indexing. *Journal of the American Society for Information Science and Technology, 56*, 597–608.

Doerr, M. (2001). Semantic problems of thesaurus mapping. *Journal of Digital Information, 1*(8). Retrieved December 15, 2005, from http://jodi.ecs.soton.ac.uk/Articles/v01/i08/Doerr

Downing, P. (1977). On the creation and use of English compound nouns. *Language, 53*, 810–842.

Dumais, S. T. (2004). Latent semantic analysis. *Annual Review of Information Science and Technology, 38*, 189–230.

Ereshefsky, M. (2000). *The poverty of the Linnaean hierarchy: A philosophical study of biological taxonomy*. Cambridge, UK: Cambridge University Press.

Fensel, D., Hendler, J. A., Lieberman, H., & Wahlster, W. (Eds.). (2003). *Spinning the semantic Web: Bringing the World Wide Web to its full potential.* Cambridge, MA: MIT Press.

Foskett, A. C. (1977). Assigned Indexing I: Semantics. In *The subject approach to information* (pp. 67–85). London: Clive Bingley.

Frohmann, B. P. (1983). An investigation of the semantic bases of some theoretical principles of classification proposed by Austin and the CRG. *Cataloging & Classification Quarterly, 4,* 11–27.

Goodwin, C. (2000). Practices of color classification. *Mind, Culture and Activity, 7,* 19–36.

Green, R. (2001). Relationships in the organization of knowledge: An overview. In C. A. Bean & R. Green (Eds.), *Relationships in the organization of knowledge* (pp. 3–18). Dordrecht, NL: Kluwer.

Green, R., Bean, C. A., & Myaeng, S. H. (Eds.). (2002). *The semantics of relationships: An interdisciplinary perspective.* Dordrecht, NL: Kluwer Academic Publishers.

Greenhalgh, T., & Hurwitz, B. (1998). *Narrative based medicine: Dialogue and discourse in clinical practice.* London: BMJ Publishing Group.

Hammwöhner, R., & Kuhlen, R. (1994). Semantic control of open hypertext systems by typed objects. *Journal of Information Science, 20,* 175–184.

Hampsher-Monk, I., Tilmans, K., & van Vree, F. (Eds.). (1998). *History of concepts: Comparative perspectives.* Amsterdam: Amsterdam University Press.

Harris, R. (2005). *The semantics of science.* London: Continuum International Publishing Group.

Harter, S. P., Nisonger, T. E., & Weng, A. W. (1993). Semantic relations between cited and citing articles in library and information science journals. *Journal of the American Society for Information Science, 44,* 543–552.

Haukioja, J. (2005). A middle position between meaning finitism and meaning Platonism. *International Journal of Philosophical Studies, 13,* 35–51.

Hearst, M. A. (1990). A hybrid approach to restricted text interpretation. In P. S. Jacobs, (Ed.), *Text-based intelligent systems: Current research in text analysis, information extraction and retrieval* (pp. 38–43). Schenectady, NY: GE Research & Development Center.

Hedlund, T., Pirkola, A., & Kalervo, J. (2001). Aspects of Swedish morphology and semantics from the perspective of mono- and cross-language information retrieval. *Information Processing & Management, 37,* 147–161.

Hjelmslev, L. (1943). *Omkring sprogteoriens grundlæggelse.* Copenhagen: B. Lunos bogtrykkeri a/s.

Hjørland, B. (1997). *Information seeking and subject representation: An activity-theoretical approach to information science.* Westport, CT: Greenwood.

Hjørland, B. (1998). Information retrieval, text composition, and semantics. *Knowledge Organization, 25,* 16–31. Retrieved December 15, 2005, from www.db.dk/bh/publikationer/ Filer/ir_semant_2.pdf

Hjørland, B. (2002a). Domain analysis in information science: Eleven approaches—traditional as well as innovative. *Journal of Documentation, 58,* 422–462. Retrieved December 15, 2005, from www.db.dk/bh/publikationer/Filer/JDOC_2002_Eleven_ approaches.pdf

Hjørland, B. (2002b). Epistemology and the socio-cognitive perspective in information science. *Journal of the American Society for Information Science and Technology, 53,* 257–270.

Hjørland, B., & Nicolaisen, J. (2005). *The epistemological lifeboat.* Copenhagen: Royal School of Library and Information Science. Retrieved December 15, 2005, from www.db.dk/jni/lifeboat/home.htm

Hjørland, B., & Nissen Pedersen, K. (2005). A substantive theory of classification for information retrieval. *Journal of Documentation, 61,* 582–597. Retrieved December 15, 2005, from www.db.dk/bh/Core%20Concepts%20in%20LIS/Hjorland%20&%20Nissen.pdf

Hodge, G. (2000). *Systems of knowledge organization for digital libraries: Beyond traditional authority files* (CLIR Report 91). Washington, DC: Council on Library and Information Resources. Retrieved December 15, 2005, from www.clir.org/pubs/reports/pub91/pub91.pdf

Hunter, E. J. (2002). *Classification made simple* (2nd ed.). Aldershot, UK: Ashgate.

Iris, M. A., Litowitz, B., & Evens, M. (1988). Problems of the part-whole relation. In M. W. Evens (Ed.), *Relational models of the lexicon* (pp. 261–288). Cambridge, UK: Cambridge University Press.

Keil, F. C. (1989). *Concepts, kinds, and cognitive development.* Cambridge, MA: MIT Press.

Kessler, M. M. (1965). Comparison of the results of bibliographic coupling and analytic subject indexing. *American Documentation, 16,* 223–233.

Khoo, C., & Na, J.-C. (2006). Semantic relations in information science. *Annual Review of Information Science and Technology, 40,* 157–228.

Kinkade, R. G. (Ed.). (1974). *Thesaurus of psychological index terms.* Washington, DC: American Psychological Association.

Klaes, M. (2002). Some remarks on the place of psychological and social elements in a theory of custom. *American Journal of Economics and Sociology, 61,* 519–530. Retrieved December 15, 2005, from www.findarticles.com/p/articles/mi_m0254/is_2_61/ai_86469072#continue

Larsson, J. (2003). *Finitism and symmetry: An inquiry into the basic notions of the strong programme.* Unpublished doctoral dissertation, Göteborg University, Sweden.

Levi, J. (1978). *The syntax and semantics of complex nominals.* New York: Academic Press.

Longman synonym dictionary. (1986). Essex, UK: Longman.

Lucy, J. (1997). The linguistics of "color." In C. L. Hardin & L. Maffi (Eds.), *Color categories in thought and language* (pp. 320–346). Cambridge, UK: Cambridge University Press.

Lyons, J. (1977). *Semantics.* Cambridge, UK: Cambridge University Press.

McCann, J. M. (1997). *Generation of marketing insights: Semantic networks.* Retrieved December 15, 2005, from http://web.archive.org/web/19990127092407/http://www.duke.edu/~mccann/mwb/15semnet.htm

Malmkjær, K. (1995). Semantics. In K. Malmkjær (Ed.), *The linguistics encyclopedia* (pp. 389–398). London: Routledge.

Miksa, F. (1994). Classification. In W. A. Wiegand & D. G. Davis (Eds.), *Encyclopedia of library history* (pp. 144–153). New York: Garland Publishing.

Miller, G. A. (1998). Nouns in WordNet. In C. Felbaum (Ed.), *WordNet: An electronic lexical database* (pp. 23–46). Cambridge, MA: MIT Press.

Milstead, J. L. (2001). Standards for relationships between subject indexing terms. In C. A. Bean & R. Green (Eds.), *Relationships in the organization of knowledge* (pp. 53–66). Dordrecht, NL: Kluwer.

Mitchell, J. S. (2001). Relationships in the Dewey Decimal Classification System. In C. A. Bean & R. Green (Eds.), *Relationships in the organization of knowledge* (pp. 211–226). Dordrecht, NL: Kluwer.

Murphy, M. L. (2003). *Semantic relations and the lexicon: Antonymy, synonymy, and other paradigms*. Cambridge, UK: Cambridge University Press.

National Library of Medicine. (2005). *Frequently asked questions: Who are the indexers, and what are their qualifications?* Retrieved December 15, 2005, from www.nlm.nih.gov/bsd/indexfaq.html#qualifications

Nida, E. A. (1975). *Componential analysis of meaning: An introduction to semantic structures*. The Hague, NL: Mouton.

Ogden, C. K., & Richards, I. A. (1923). *The meaning of meaning: A study of the influence of language upon thought and of the science of symbolism*. London: Routledge & Kegan Paul.

Oliver, A. (1998). Logical atomism. In E. Craig (Ed.), *Routledge encyclopedia of philosophy* (Vol. 5, pp. 772–775). London: Routledge.

Ørom, A. (2003). Knowledge organization in the domain of art studies: History, transition and conceptual changes. *Knowledge Organization, 30*, 128–143.

Pao, M. L. (1993). Term and citation retrieval: A field study. *Information Processing & Management, 29*, 95–112.

Peirce, C. S. (1931–1958). *Collected papers of C. S. Peirce* (C. Hartshorne, P. Weiss, & A. Burks, Eds.). Cambridge, MA: Harvard University Press.

Peregrin, J. (2004). Pragmatism und Semantik [Pragmatism and semantics]. In A. Fuhrmann & E. J. Olsson (Eds.), *Pragmatisch denken* [Thinking pragmatically] (pp. 89–108). Frankfurt am Main, Germany: Ontos. English manuscript version retrieved December 15, 2005, from http://jarda.peregrin.cz/mybibl/PDFTxt/482.pdf

Petersen, T. (Ed.). (1994). *Art and architecture thesaurus* (2nd ed.). New York: Oxford University Press.

Priss, U. (2006). Formal concept analysis in information science. *Annual Review of Information Science and Technology, 40*, 521–543.

Putnam, H. (1975). The meaning of "meaning." In K. Gunderson (Ed.), *Language, mind, and knowledge* (pp. 131–193). Minneapolis: University of Minnesota Press.

Qin, J. (1999). Discovering semantic patterns in bibliographically coupled documents. *Library Trends, 48*, 109–132.

Qin, J. (2000). Semantic similarities between a keyword database and a controlled vocabulary database: An investigation in the antibiotic resistance literature. *Journal of the American Society for Information Science, 51*, 166–180.

Ratner, C. (1989). A sociohistorical critique of naturalistic theories of color perception. *Journal of Mind and Behavior, 10*, 361–372. Retrieved December 15, 2005, from http://web.archive.org/web/20031029152929/http://www.humboldt1.com/~cr2/colors.htm

Read, C. S. (1973). General semantics. In A. Kent, H. Lancour, & J. E. Daily (Eds.), *Encyclopedia of library and information science* (Vol. 9, pp. 211–221). New York: Dekker.

Rees-Potter, L. K. (1989). Dynamic thesaural systems: A bibliometric study of terminological and conceptual change in sociology and economics with application to the design of dynamic thesaural systems. *Information Processing & Management, 25,* 677–691.

Rees-Potter, L. K. (1991). Dynamic thesauri: The cognitive function. *Proceedings of the 1st International ISKO Conference, Darmstadt, Part 2,* 145–150.

Roberts, N. (1985). Concepts, structures and retrieval in the social sciences up to c. 1970. *Social Science Information Studies, 5,* 55–67.

Roberson, D., Davies, I., & Davidoff, J. (2000). Color categories are not universal: Replications and new evidence from a stone-age culture. *Journal of Experimental Psychology: General, 129,* 369–398.

Rosario, B., & Hearst, M. (2001). Classifying the semantic relations in noun compounds via a domain-specific lexical hierarchy. *Proceedings of the 2001 Conference on Empirical Methods in Natural Language Processing (EMNLP 2001),* 82–90. Retrieved December 15, 2005, from http://biotext.berkeley.edu/papers/emnlp01.pdf

Rosario, B., & Hearst, M. (2004). Classifying semantic relations in bioscience texts. *42nd Annual Meeting of the Association for Computational Linguistics (ACL 2004),* 430–437. Retrieved December 15, 2005, from http://biotext.berkeley.edu/papers/acl04-relations.pdf

Russell, B. (1924). Logical atomism. In R. C. Marsh (Ed.), *Logic and knowledge* (pp. 323–343). London: Allen & Unwin.

Salton, G. (1971). Automatic indexing using bibliographic citations. *Journal of Documentation, 27,* 98–110.

Saunders, B. (1998, August). *Revisiting Basic Color Terms.* Paper presented at conference on "Anthropology and Psychology: The Legacy of the Torres Strait Expedition," St. John's College, Cambridge. Retrieved January 31, 2006, from http://human-nature.com/science-as-culture/saunders.html

Schneider, J. (2004). *Verification of bibliometric methods' applicability for thesaurus construction.* Unpublished doctoral dissertation, Royal School of Library and Information Science, Aalborg, Denmark. Retrieved December 15, 2005, from http://biblis.db.dk/uhtbin/hyperion.exe/db.jessch04

Soergel, D. (1995). The Art and Architecture Thesaurus (AAT): A critical appraisal. *Visual Resources, 10,* 369–400. Retrieved December 15, 2005, from www.dsoergel.com/cv/B47_short.pdf (short version); www.dsoergel.com/cv/B47_long.pdf (long version)

Song, M., & Galardi, P. (2001). Semantic relationships between highly cited articles and citing articles in information retrieval. *Proceedings of the Annual Meeting of the American Society for Information Science,* 171–181.

Sowa, J. F. (2000). Ontology, metadata, and semiotics. In B. Ganter & G. W. Mineau (Eds.), *Conceptual structures: Logical, linguistic, and computational issues* (pp. 55–81). Berlin: Springer-Verlag. Retrieved December 15, 2005, from http://users.bestweb.net/~sowa/peirce/ontometa.htm

Sparck Jones, K. (1992). Thesaurus. In S. C. Shapiro (Ed.), *Encyclopedia of artificial intelligence* (Vol. 2, pp. 1605–1613). New York: Wiley.

Sparck Jones, K. (2005). Revisiting classification for retrieval. *Journal of Documentation, 61,* 598–601. Retrieved December 15, 2005, from www.db.dk/bh/Core%20Concepts%20in%20LIS/Sparck%20Jones_reply%20to%20Hjorland%20&%20Nissen.pdf

Stokolova, N. A. (1976). Syntactic tools and semantic power of information languages (Pt. II of "Elements of a semantic theory of information retrieval"). *International Classification*, *3*, 75–81.

Stokolova, N. A. (1977a). Elements of a semantic theory of information retrieval—I. The concepts of relevance and information language. *Information Processing & Management*, *13*, 227–234.

Stokolova, N. A. (1977b). Paradigmatic relations (Pt. III of "Elements of a semantic theory of information retrieval"). *International Classification*, *4*, 11–19.

Talmy, L. (1985). Force dynamics in language and thought. In W. F. Eikfont, P. D. Kroeber, & K. L. Peterson (Eds.), *Papers from the Parasession on Causatives and Agentivity* (pp. 293–337). Chicago: Chicago Linguistic Society.

Thesaurus of ERIC Descriptors (11th ed.) (1987). Phoenix, AZ: Oryx Press.

van Rijsbergen, C. J. (1979). *Information retrieval* (2nd ed.). London: Butterworths. Retrieved December 15, 2005, from www.dcs.gla.ac.uk/Keith/Chapter.3/Ch.3.html

van Rijsbergen, C. J. (1986). A new theoretical framework for information retrieval. *Proceedings of the Annual International ACM SIGIR Conference on Research and Development in Information Retrieval*, 194–200.

Vickery, B. C., & Vickery, A. (1987). Semantics and retrieval. In *Information science in theory and practice* (pp. 133–179). London: Bowker-Saur.

Walker, A. (Ed.). (1997). *Thesaurus of psychological index terms* (8th ed.). Washington, DC: American Psychological Association.

Warren, B. (1978). *Semantic patterns of noun-noun compounds* (Gothenburg Studies in English, 41). Gothenburg, Sweden: Acta Universitatis Gothoburgensis.

Weber, M. (2005, October). *How strong is the case for social relativism in science?* Lecture held at the Minnesota Center for Philosophy of Science. Retrieved December 15, 2005, from http://philosophy.duke.edu/pdf/weber_duke.pdf

Weimar, K. (Ed.). (1997–2003). *Reallexikon der deutschen Literaturwissenschaft, Band 1–3*. (3. neubearb. Aufl.). Berlin: Walter de Gruyter.

Wellisch, H. H. (2000). *Glossary of terminology in abstracting, classification, indexing, and thesaurus construction* (2nd ed.). Medford, NJ: Information Today.

White, H. D., & McCain, K. W. (1998). Visualizing a discipline: An author co-citation analysis of information science, 1972–1995. *Journal of the American Society for Information Science*, *49*, 327–355.

Wierzbicka, A. (1996). *Semantics: Primes and universals*. Oxford, UK: Oxford University Press.

Wittgenstein, L. (1922). *Tractatus logico-philosophicus*. London: Routledge & Kegan Paul. Hypertext of the Ogden bilingual edition retrieved July 31, 2005, from www.kfs.org/~jonathan/witt/tlph.html

WordNet 2.1. A lexical database for the English language. (2005). Princeton, NJ: Princeton University Cognitive Science Laboratory. Retrieved December 15, 2005, from http://wordnet.princeton.edu

Appendix

Some important kinds of semantic relations that have been presented in the literature:

1. Active relation: A semantic relation between two concepts, one of which expresses the performance of an operation or process affecting the other. The inverse of the passive relation.

2. Antonymy: A semantic relation in which A is the opposite of B (e.g., cold is the opposite of hot).

3. Associative relation: A semantic relation defined psychologically as the mental association of concepts (i.e., A is mentally associated with B by somebody). Often, associative relations are simply unspecified relations. In thesauri, antonyms are not usually specified but may be listed along with terms representing other kinds of relations under "associative relations."

4. Causal relation: A semantic relation in which A is the cause of B (e.g., a lack of vitamin C causes scurvy).

5. Homonymy: A semantic relation in which two concepts, A and B, are expressed by the same symbol (e.g., both a financial institution and the edge of a river are expressed by the word "bank"; i.e., the word has two senses).

6. Hyponymous relations (hyponym-hyperonym): Relations in which A is a kind of B; A is subordinate to B; A is narrower than B; B is broader than A. Also known as generic relation, genus-species relation, or hierarchical subordinate relation.

7. Is-a relation: A semantic relation between a general concept and individual instances of that concept; that is, A is an example, or instance, of B (e.g., Copenhagen is an instance of the general concept "capital").

8. Locative relation: A relation in which a concept indicates a location of a thing designated by another concept: that is, A is located in B (e.g., minorities in Denmark).

9. Paradigmatic relation: As defined by Wellisch (2000, p. 50), "a semantic relation between two concepts, that is considered to be either fixed by nature, self-evident, or established by convention. Examples: mother/child; fat/obesity; a state/its capital city."

10. Partitive (i.e., part-whole) relation (meronymy): a relationship between the whole and its parts; that is, A is part of B. A meronym is the name of a constituent part of, the substance of, or a member of something. Meronymy is the opposite of holonymy (i.e., B has A as part of itself).

11. Passive relation: A semantic relation between two concepts, one of which is affected by, or subjected to, an operation or process expressed by the other. The inverse of the active relation.

12. Polysemy: A mode of semantic relation in which a word has several subsenses that are related with one another (i.e., concepts A1, A2, and A3 are all expressed by the word "A"). Such a word is termed "polysemous" or "polysemantic."

13. Possessive relation: a semantic relation between a possessor and what is possessed (i.e., A belongs to B; B possesses A).

14. Related term: A term that is semantically related to another term. In thesauri, related terms are often coded RT and used for kinds of semantic relations other than synonymy (USE, UF), homonymy (separated by parenthetical qualifier), and generic relations and/or partitive relations (BT, NT). Related terms may, for example, express antagonistic relations, active/passive relations, causal relations, locative relations, or paradigmatic relations.

15. Synonymy: A semantic relation in which A denotes the same as B; A is equivalent with B.

16. Temporal relation: A semantic relation in which a concept indicates a time or period of an event designated by another concept (e.g., Second World War, 1939–1945).

17. Troponymy: According to WordNet 2.1 (2005), "the semantic relation of being a manner of [doing] something."

CHAPTER 9

Ontologies on the Semantic Web

Catherine Legg
University of Waikato

Introduction

As an informational technology, the World Wide Web has enjoyed spectacular success. In just ten years it has transformed the way information is produced, stored, and shared in arenas as diverse as shopping, family photo albums, and high-level academic research. The "Semantic Web" is touted by its developers as equally revolutionary, although it has not yet achieved anything like the Web's exponential uptake. It seeks to transcend a current limitation of the Web—that it largely requires indexing to be accomplished merely on specific character strings. Thus, a person searching for information about "turkey" (the bird) receives from current search engines many irrelevant pages about "Turkey" (the country) and nothing about the Spanish "pavo" even if he or she is a Spanish-speaker able to understand such pages. The Semantic Web vision is to develop technology to facilitate retrieval of information via *meanings*, not just *spellings*.

For this to be possible, most commentators believe, Semantic Web applications will have to draw on some kind of shared, structured, machine-readable *conceptual scheme*. Thus, there has been a convergence between the Semantic Web research community and an older tradition with roots in classical Artificial Intelligence (AI) research (sometimes referred to as "knowledge representation") whose goal is to develop a *formal ontology*. A formal ontology is a machine-readable *theory* of the most fundamental concepts or "categories" required in order to understand information pertaining to any knowledge domain.

A review of the attempts that have been made to realize this goal provides an opportunity to reflect in interestingly concrete ways on various research questions such as the following:

- How explicit a machine-understandable theory of meaning is it possible or practical to construct?

- How universal a machine-understandable theory of meaning is it possible or practical to construct?

- How much (and what kind of) inference support is required to realize a machine-understandable theory of meaning?

- What is it for a theory of meaning to be machine-understandable anyway?

The World Wide Web

The World Wide Web's key idea arguably derives from Vannevar Bush's 1940s vision of a "Memex"—a fluidly organized workspace upon which a user or group of users could develop a customized "library" of text and pictorial resources, embellishing it with an ever-expanding network of annotated connections (Bush, 1945). However, it was only in 1989 that Tim Berners-Lee (then employed at the Organisation Européenne pour la Recherche Nucléaire [CERN]) spearheaded the development that became the current Web, whose startling success may be traced to the following design factors: hypertext markup language (HTML), universal resource identifiers (URIs), and hyperlinks.

Hypertext Markup Language

HTML provided formatting protocols for presenting information predictably across an enormous variety of application programs. This for the first time effectively bypassed the idiosyncracies of particular applications, enabling anyone with a simple "browser" to read any document marked up with HTML. These protocols were possessed of such "nearly embarrassing simplicity" (McCool, Fikes, & Guha, 2003, online) that they were quickly adopted by universal agreement. A particularly attractive feature of HTML was that formatting markup was cleanly separated from the Web resource itself in angle-bracketed "metatags." Although the term "metadata" became current at this time, the concept it represents—information about information—was of course by no means new, library catalog cards being a perfect example of pre-Web metadata.

Universal Resource Identifiers

HTML took advantage of the Internet's emerging system of unique names for every computer connected to the network to assign each Web resource a unique "location," the interpretation of which was, once again, governed by a simple and clear protocol. This rendered Web resources accessible from anywhere in the world in such a "low-tech" manner that, within just a few years, anyone with a personal computer could download and view any item on the Web and anyone able to borrow or buy space on a server was able to add to the Web resources that would then become instantly available to all Web users (for better or worse).

However, URIs embrace not only Uniform Resource Locators (URLs) but also "Unique Resource Names" (URNs). Whereas URLs *locate* an information resource—that is, they tell the client program where on the Web it is hosted—URNs are intended to serve purely as a *name* for a resource, which signals its uniqueness. Thus, a resource, copies of which exist at different places in the Web, might have two URLs and one URN. Conversely, two documents on the same Web page might have one URL and two URNs, reflecting different perspectives on the documents. Of course, unique naming systems for informational resources have been realized before (for example, the International Standard Book Number [IBSN], International Standard Serial Number [ISSN], the North American Industry Classification System [NAICS], and the United Nations Standard Products and Services Code [UNSPSC]). Unsurprisingly, Semantic Web designers sought to incorporate these older naming systems (Rozenfeld, 2001).

The generality (and hoped-for power) of the URN is such that it is not confined to Web pages but may be used to name any real-world object one wishes to identify uniquely (buildings, people, organizations, musical recordings). It is hoped that, with the Semantic Web, the ambitious generality of this concept will come into its own (Berners-Lee, Hendler, & Lassila, 2001). In short, the push to develop URNs is a vast, unprecedented exercise in *canonicalizing names* (Guha & McCool, 2003). At the same time, however, the baptism of objects with URNs is designed to be as decentralized as anything on the Web—anyone may perform such naming exercises and record them in "namespaces." This tension between canonicalization and decentralization is one of the Semantic Web's greatest challenges.

Hyperlinks

The World Wide Web also provides unique functionality for linking any Web resource to any other(s) at arbitrary points. Once again, the protocol enabling this is exceedingly simple and its consequences have been very "informationally democratic," enabling users to link their resources to any other(s) no matter how official the resource so co-opted. (Thus, for example, a university department of mathematics Web site could be linked to by a page advocating the rounding down of *pi* to 4 decimal places.) However, there is no guarantee that this new resource will be read by anyone.

The World Wide Web Consortium (W3C) (www.w3c.org) was founded in 1994 by Tim Berners-Lee and others to ensure that fundamental technologies on the rapidly evolving Web would be mutually compatible ("Web interoperability"). The consortium currently has over 350 member organizations, from academia, government, and private industry. Developers of new Web technologies submit them to W3C peer evaluation. If accepted, the reports are published as new Web standards. This is the process currently being pursued with the development of the Semantic Web.

The Semantic Web

The Semantic Web is the most ambitious project that the W3C has scaffolded so far. It was part of Berners-Lee's vision for the World Wide Web from the beginning (Berners-Lee et al., 2001, Berners-Lee, 2003) and the spectacular success of the first stage of his vision would seem to provide at least some prima facie argument for trying to realize its remainder.

Semantic Web Goals

The project's most fundamental goal may be simply (if somewhat enigmatically) stated as follows: to provide metadata not just concerning the *syntax* of a Web resource (i.e., its formatting, its character strings) but also its *semantics*, in order to, as Berners-Lee has put it, replace a "web of links" with a "web of meaning" (Heflin, Hendler, & Luke 2003, p. 29). As has been noted numerous times (e.g., McCool et al., 2003; McGuinness, 2003; Patel-Schneider & Fensel, 2002), there has traditionally been a significant difference between the way information is presented for *human* consumption (for instance, as printed media, pictures, and films) and the way it is presented for *machine* consumption (for instance, as relational databases). The Web has largely followed human rather than machine formats, resulting in what is essentially a large, hyperlinked book. The Semantic Web aims to bridge this gap between human and machine readability. Given the enormous and ever-increasing number of Web pages (as of August 2005, the Google search engine claims to have indexed over 8 billion), this has the potential to open unimaginable quantities of information to any applications able to traffic in machine-readable data and, thereby, to any human able to make use of such applications.

Planned applications of the Semantic Web range across a considerable spectrum of complexity and ambition. At the relatively straightforward end sits the task of disambiguating searches—for instance distinguishing "Turkey" the country from "turkey" the bird in the example cited earlier (Fensel, Angele, Decker, Erdmann, Schnurr, Studer, et al., 2000). The spectrum then moves through increasingly sophisticated information retrieval tasks such as finding "semantic joins" in databases (Halevy, Ives, Mork, & Tatarinov, 2003), indexing text and semantic markup together in order to improve retrieval performance across the Web (Guha & McCool, 2003; Shah, Finin, Joshi, Cost, & Mayfield, 2002), or even turning the entire Web into one enormous distributed database (Fensel et al., 2000; Guha & McCool, 2003; Maedche, Motik, & Stojanovic, 2003). The most ambitious goals for the Semantic Web involve the performance of autonomous informational integrations over an arbitrary range of sources by software agents (Cost, Finin, Joshi, Peng, Nicholas, Soboroff et al., 2002; Goble & de Roure, 2002; Hendler, 2001).

Not surprisingly, the vision of the Semantic Web's founders is located at the ambitious end of this spectrum. Berners-Lee et al. (2001) have envisaged an automated medical informatics-literate personal assistant that will book a sick mother's medical appointment while rescheduling her daughter's other commitments so that she can accompany her mother and also working out insurance provider issues. Semantic Web supporters see as a further goal the Web services view—to "provide access not only to documents that collect useful information, but also to services that describe or even provide useful behavior" (Klein & Bernstein, 2004, p. 30; McIlraith, Son, & Zeng, 2001). This dimension of the Semantic Web is, however, beyond the scope of this chapter.

It is worth emphasizing that the Semantic Web is expected not to replace but to *extend* the current Web. This aspect of the vision has been expressed by Berners-Lee (2000, online) in a famous "layer-cake diagram" (Figure 9.1).

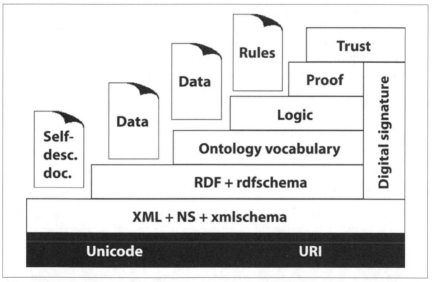

Figure 9.1   Berners-Lee's layer-cake diagram of the Semantic Web.

This diagram (Figure 9.1) represents a series of ever richer stages of informational interoperability. The first layer represents the pre-semantic Web. It provides universal character recognition and the URI system of referencing, which supports hyperlinking. At the second layer, applications exchange metatags but understand them purely qua character strings. At the third and fourth layers, with the introduction of Resource Description Framework (RDF) and ontology vocabularies, meaning is added to the tags, such that applications may be said to begin to understand the terms they are exchanging in metadata. The fifth and sixth layers add the ability to perform inferencing over shared knowledge. The final layer provides mechanisms for the verification and authentication of knowledge (which will obviously be very important, although space does not permit discussion of it in this chapter).

In a related discussion, Decker, van Harmelen, Broekstra, Erdmann, Fensel, Horrocks, et al. (2000) have defined three levels of requirement that must be satisfied for knowledge to be shared on the Web in machine-understandable form. The first is *universal expressive power*, which consists in being able to express information from any knowledge domain. The second is *syntactic interoperability,* which means that any application can "read" any data by at least parsing them and individuating their words or symbols (p. 67). The third is *semantic interoperability*, the requirement that data be (machine-) "understandable"; the authors do not, however, offer a concrete or operational explanation of this very general definition (p. 67).

On the other hand, Euzenat (2001) has divided the interoperability problem into five separate layers. Layer 1 consists in both *encoding* interoperability, that is, "being able to segment the representation in characters," and *lexical* interoperability, that is, "being able to segment the representation into words (or symbols)" (p. 20). Layer 2 pertains to *syntactic* interoperability, which is described as "being able to structure the representation in structured sentences (or formulas or assertions)" (p. 20). Layers 3, 4, and 5 are *semantic* in character, that is, "being able to construct the propositional meaning of the representation" (p. 20). Layer 6 is *pragmatic*, that is, "being able to construct the pragmatic meaning of the representation (or its meaning in context)" (p. 20). These last three categories draw on a traditional division in philosophical and linguistic analyses of meaning whereby syntax treats a language's grammatical or formal-logical structure; semantics, the reference of its words to objects in the external world; and pragmatics, the ways in which the meaning of particular uses of language is influenced by their particular contexts of use (Cruse, 2006; Sowa, 2000).

Discussions of Berners-Lee's layer-cake vision tend to agree that (1) syntax and semantics are separable, perhaps with further "pragmatic" issues concerning how language is used in context, and (2) some kind of inferencing capacity is vital to genuine representation of meaning on the Web. Beyond that, however, certain criticisms of the framework emerge. For instance, Patel-Schneider and Fensel (2002, pp. 20–21) have observed that exactly how and where "semantics start" has not been worked out and is by no means obvious technically. They have also suggested that analyzing inferencing as a separate layer might be a mistake on the grounds that inference is so tightly intertwined with meaning that it should be possible in the third and fourth layers. Moreover, they contend, "trust" does not belong on the layer cake because it is not a layer of *meaning* but a further issue that should be dealt with by separate applications.

Challenges

As has been noted, the Semantic Web has not yet enjoyed the rapid, seemingly inexorable uptake of the original Web. Four challenges have yet to be met.

The first major challenge is *inferential tractability*. The Semantic Web is not intended merely as a silo for storing and retrieving isolated data. Its realization also requires inferencing to assimilate the data and draw out their logical consequences. It is an understatement to claim that information on the Web is highly distributed. In the best-case scenario, one would like the capacity to answer queries by gathering information from an arbitrary number of unrelated sites and reasoning over the information retrieved by intelligently choosing whatever heuristics are most appropriate on a case-by-case basis. However, any potential implementation of such functionality faces enormous issues of scalability. An important concept here is that of a problem's being *decidable*, that is, formally capable of being evaluated as answerable within a finite time period (Rozenberg & Salomaa, 1994). If a Semantic Web application cannot finish processing a problem because it is not decidable, then that application will be of little use; obviously, Semantic Web applications will need some means of anticipating and bypassing such problems. Moreover, if an application is even merely very, very slow due to the vast quantities of data it is considering, it will also be of little use (Guha & McCool, 2003). An issue with enormous influence on inferential tractability is the logical expressivity of the languages used to represent and to query ontologies. This is discussed in the section on "The Logical Expressivity of Ontology Languages."

Many knowledge representation tools in classical AI made the so-called closed world assumption, which posits that the system knows all that there is to know in a given domain. Such an assumption, although often questionable in practice, makes inferencing considerably more powerful, because an application can assume that if it cannot prove a statement to be true, the statement is false. (A practical example would be allowing a human resources information system to infer that because it does not know that a particular person is employed by a company, he is not so employed.) It is impossible to make such an assumption concerning the Web (Heflin et al., 2003).

The second challenge concerns *logical consistency*. The vision of machine reasoning on the Semantic Web consists primarily in deductive (as opposed to inductive or abductive) inference. (For a defense of this claim, as well as a definition of these three different inferencing forms, see Sowa [2001, 2004].) This may be attributed at least in part to the fact that many projects have their roots in classical AI. However, it is a notorious fact that any proposition can be deduced from a logical contradiction; and, of course, on an information space of the unprecedented size and democratic character of the Web, one will find logically contradictory statements. These will include statements true at different times and circumstances (for instance, "New Orleans escaped major hurricane damage," which could be stated truly on August 30, 2005, and "New Orleans did not escape major hurricane damage," which could be stated truly on August 31, 2005), deliberate misinformation, and apparent contradictions arising from differing interpretations of the same term (for instance, the statements "John Brown was born in 1945" and "John Brown was born in 1967" when the proper name "John Brown" refers to two different men).

A related issue is the *rapid changeability* of information on the Web. Even the *rate* of change of this information is unpredictable—both across pages (some change extremely quickly; others are entirely static) and across time (some sites, after long static periods, change suddenly without warning) (Heflin et al., 2003). Thus, a further dimension of the problem of obtaining information reliably from the Semantic Web, as noted by Guha and McCool (2003), is *predictability*: If a Semantic Web application delivers one answer to a question today and a different answer to the same question tomorrow because the dataset it is encountering is subtly different, this is a problem (unless the world has changed consonantly with the changed answers, in which case this outcome is desirable). This should give one pause, particularly with respect to blithe predictions by developers that the Semantic Web will not constitute a particular application so much as a ubiquitous infrastructure, like electricity (Berners-Lee et al., 2001), because this remit must perforce include so-called mission-critical applications. At least one necessary piece of the solution to this changeability problem would seem to be some kind of ontology versioning (Heflin & Pan, 2004; Noy & Klein, 2004; Noy & Musen, 2004).

The final major challenges facing the Semantic Web are not technical so much as *political*. First of all, who will mark up Web pages with the required semantic metadata? A response might be: Who marked up the World Wide Web with HTML tags? However, this is a different, much more complex task. HTML is learnable in an hour or two, but, as will be seen, to understand Semantic Web languages requires logical, and in many cases also considerable philosophical, *nous*. The obvious solution might seem to be to automate such markup and, indeed, several research programs have vigorously pursued this goal. Some examples include SHOE (which will be discussed in the section on "Ontologies with [Largely] DL Expressivity"), "MnM" (Vargas-Vera, Motta, Domingue, Lanzoni, Stutt, & Ciravegna, 2002), OntoAnnotate (Staab, Maedche, & Handschuh, 2001), and SemTag (Dill, Eiron, Gibson, Gruhl, Guha, Jhingran, et al., 2003) (see also Roesner, Kunze, & Kroetzsch, 2005; Witbrock, Panton, Reed, Schneider, Aldag, Reimers, et al., 2004). However, such automated markup might seem to require scaffolding by a working Semantic Web, creating an infinite regress problem.

Moreover, the ambitious directive to generalize URIs from mere address locators for downloading files to canonical names for real-world things is fraught with political implications. In stark contrast to the Web, where one genius of the system was that no preexisting relationship was necessary between producers and consumers of information, canonical-ized names make necessary "a very deep relationship," namely that producers and consumers of data must agree on the references of all URIs (McCool et al., 2003, online). How is such agreement to be achieved?

It is widely appreciated that until the Web includes a significant quantity of semantic metadata, developers have little incentive to produce applications for the Semantic Web; but if few Semantic Web applications exist, there is little incentive for Web authors to mark up pages semantically. Ironically this same fact is taken by some as reason to be pessimistic about the future of the Semantic Web, while others take it as reason for optimism, on the grounds that bootstrapping will quickly accelerate development (Berners-Lee, 2001). Bray (2001) holds the Yahoo!'s hand-coded subject directories (done at considerable expense to the company) return very few hits as a consequence of the human mediation. Nonetheless, people like to use these directories, Bray contends, suggesting that the same will be true of information on the Semantic Web. Other commentators, such as Shirky (2003, online), warn of the "this will work because it would be good if it did" fallacy.

Semantic Web Technologies

The Semantic Web's core technology is, as noted, a generalization of markup tags beyond indicating a Web resource's intended *formatting,* to indicating its intended *meaning.* This has occurred primarily through the development of a series of new markup languages.

Extensible Markup Language

Extensible Markup Language (XML) (Bray, Paoli, Sperberg-McQueen, Maler, & Yergeau, 2000) was originally designed as a replacement for Standard Generalized Markup Language (SGML), which was used to share documents within government and the aerospace industry (Bailey, Bry, Furche, & Schaffert, 2005). XML was not developed specifically for the Semantic Web but has been embraced by its developers. It was initially conceived as a simple way to send documents across the Web (Swartz, 2002). In contrast to HTML's decreed list of formatting tags, XML allows Web authors to define their own tags and, thus, their own document formats, subject to a syntax specified in the XML Recommendation. Originally, these tag definitions were registered in a separate document called a Document Type Definition (DTD). However, this system has now been superseded by XML Schema. When a document conforms to XML syntax, it is said to be "well-formed"; when, in addition, it conforms to a set of tag definitions, it is also said to be "valid." Teasing apart these criteria might seem to enable the separation of a document's syntax from its semantics, at least in principle (Sowa, 2000).

As an illustration, one might define the following tags:

```
<album> </album>
<artist> </artist>
<genre> </genre>
```

One may then—without using any kind of database software infrastructure, in other words, in a flat file—construct a short document describing a three-item music collection containing the following fields:

```
<album> I
        <artist> The Magnetic Fields </artist>
        <genre> Alternative </genre>
</album>
<album> Midnight Love
        <artist> Marvin Gaye </artist>
        <genre> R&B </genre>
</album>
<album> Hounds Of Love
        <artist> Kate Bush </artist>
        <genre> Rock </genre>
</album>
```

Such a document is said to have three main elements (<album>), each of which possesses two child elements (<artist>, <genre>). XML also allows attributes for tags to be defined, as in the following example:

```
<album genre='Rock'> Hounds Of Love
        <artist> Kate Bush </artist>
</album>
```

However, it is generally preferred to define new child elements rather than using attributes in this way. At any rate, each XML document essentially consists of a document tree, with a distinguished root element, containing elements, character data, and attributes (Bailey et al., 2005).

In these examples, data such as the character strings "Kate Bush" and "Marvin Gaye" are obviously receiving *some* kind of "meaning-tagging." A human reader will probably infer that the <artist> tag applied to "Kate Bush" means that it names the artist who recorded the album listed immediately afterward. But what meaning do these tags have for a machine? As stated so far, absolutely nothing. So they need to be linked to some kind of definition. This function is served by XML namespaces. I can define a namespace (which I shall call "mc") by inserting a tag in my document as follows:

<h:html xmlns:mc=HYPERLINK "http://www.musiccollections.com/myCDs" http://www.musiccollections.com/myCDs"/>

I can then prefix all tags in my document with the name of my namespace as follows:

<mc:album> I

<mc:artist> The Magnetic Fields </mc:artist>

<mc:genre> Alternative </mc:genre>

</mc:album>

[...]

Although the term "namespace" might suggest some further document that includes definitions for the terms in tags, in practice a namespace is often just a URI, which need not point to any further location. Thus, namespaces are essentially just a way of indexing different tags (uniquely) via prefixes.

Of course, any number of XML namespaces can exist. Anyone can define one. So, how do these namespaces relate to each other, semantically speaking? Should it be stipulated that two tags from different namespaces have the same meaning if and only if they consist of the same character string? This would, of course, be a bad idea. The <artist> tag in my namespace "means" (i.e., is intended to apply only to) musicians, whereas an <artist> tag in another namespace might "mean" (i.e., be intended to apply only to) painters. Conversely, another person might document a music collection using the tag <musician> with the same meaning with which I have used my <artist> tag. Thus, to exactly the same degree that namespace prefixing allows for clear distinctions among tags that use the same character string, it drastically reduces tag shareability. Every namespace's tags are now quite distinct. How may translation between them be effected?

In spite of XML's new freedom to define tags at will, it still arguably provides syntactic interoperability at best (Swartz, 2002). We have seen that Decker et al. (2000) distinguish the interoperability requirements of universal expressive power, syntactic interoperability, and semantic interoperability. They argue that XML satisfies the first and the second, but not the third, requirement; moreover, they hold that the advantage of using it consists only in "the reusability of the parsing software components" (p. 68). In their estimation, it is "useful for data interchange between parties that both know what the data is, but not for situations where new communications partners are frequently added" (Decker et al., 2000, p. 68; see also Heflin et al., 2003).

This should not be too surprising because, as already noted, XML was not designed to share meaning so much as document format, and the latter is, in fact, a concept of enormous generality that embraces any kind of structure within data (including for instance, a document containing just four elements). In other words, XML allows for no principled distinction between "content-specific" and "presentation-specific" tags (Heflin et al., 2003, p. 30).

XML Schemas

Attempts to remedy XML's lack of semantic bite have been made by building a series of "schemas" that can be added to it. The most widely used is simply and somewhat confusingly entitled "XML Schema" because it was the first to achieve Recommendation status by the W3C, in May 2001 (Fallside, 2001); a second edition was released in October 2004 (Fallside & Walmsley, 2004). It was largely developed by Microsoft. An XML Schema instance is called an XML Schema Definition (XSD). Each application of XML Schema to a given XML document produces a further file that lists its vocabulary (i.e., element and attribute names), its content model (i.e., relationships and data structure), and its data types. This file is called the Post-Schema Validation Infoset (PSVI), and enables interoperability with many object-oriented programming tools. The following very simple XML document:

```
<h:html xmlns:mc=http://www.musiccollections.com/myCDs>
    <<mc:album> I
        <mc:artist> The Magnetic Fields </mc:artist>
        <mc:genre> Alternative </mc:genre>
    </mc:album>
```

may be described using the following XML Schema document:

```
<xs:schema xmlns:xs="http://www.w3.org/2001/XMLSchema">
    <xs:element name="album" type="xs:string"/>
        <xs:complexType>
            <xs:sequence>
                <xs:element name="artist"
                type="xs:string"/>
                <xs:element name="genre"
                type="xs:string"/>
            </xs:sequence>
        </xs:complexType>
    </xs:element>
</xs:schema>
```

As may be evident, it is, unfortunately, often easier for a human reader to understand an XML document than its schema. Further XML schema languages include the Japanese RELAX (Regular Language description for XML, www.xml.gr.jp/relax), TREX (Tree Regular Expressions for XML, http://thaiopensource.com/trex), and a later merging of these two called RELAX NG (Clark & Makoto, 2001). These languages are popular because they are considerably simpler to use than XML Schema itself; nevertheless, they are not easy to learn.

It can be seen that XML schemas categorize XML data in *some* sense. However, this is little more than the garden-variety data typing performed by relational databases (for example, "sequence" or "ComplexType"). What does such typing tell us about the *meaning* of data? Such reflections raise the interesting research question of how, in general, one distinguishes between the structure and the meaning of information in a principled way (not to mention in a machine-understandable way). In spite of the prima facie clarity of Berners-Lee's layer-cake model, this has turned out to be a thorny issue in practice (see, for instance, Patel-Schneider & Fensel, 2002, discussed in greater detail in the section "DAML+OIL/OWL"). Research into such questions is rendered even thornier by the philosophical possibility some (albeit surprisingly few) commentators have raised—namely, that the structure of information might form part of its meaning. For instance, Sowa (2004, p. 13) has suggested that it will be necessary to find a way to represent the "structure or geometry" of data in order specifically to reproduce analogical reasoning, which he argues forms a considerable part of human inference and, thus, meaning (see also Sowa & Majumdar, 2003). Thus, Semantic Web developers have sought to develop ways of representing meaning in a purer and more explicit fashion than is possible in XML; this brings us to the topic of RDF.

Resource Description Framework

Work on Resource Description Framework (RDF) was initiated by R. V. Guha while at Apple Computer, and its first version attained W3C Recommendation status in 1999. A new version (Beckett, 2004) was published as a set of related specifications in 2004.

Strictly speaking, RDF is not a language but a data model for describing a machine-readable semantics for "Web resources" (in the very general sense of "resource" identified in the earlier discussion of URIs). Mathematically speaking, this model consists of a directed graph of nodes connected by labeled arcs. (For a textbook introduction to these concepts, see Bollobas [2002].) In a key advance on XML, RDF introduces propositional structure into its data. Each RDF "proposition" has three parts. These are referred to either as "subject," "predicate," and "object" (e.g., Beckett, 2004; Swartz, 2002) or as "object," "attribute," and "value" (e.g., Decker et al., 2000). The subjects/objects and the objects/values should be understood to lie on the nodes of RDF's directed graphs and the predicates/attributes on the arcs. Semantically speaking, in each proposition the subject/object should be understood as the "thing" the proposition is about, the predicate/attribute as a property that is ascribed to the subject/object, and the object/value as a value (or some other qualifier) assigned to that trait as it pertains specifically to that subject/object. As an example, take the proposition:

Kate Winslet's age is 27.

Here the subject/object is Kate Winslet, the predicate/attribute is age, and the object/value is 27. Thus, one might argue that each RDF proposition is equivalent to one cell in a database table; the fervent hope exists one day to "slurp" the world's databases onto the Semantic Web in RDF format (Hendler, Berners-Lee, & Miller, 2002).

When RDF graphs are made available on the Semantic Web, their nodes will consist of URIs describing Web resources; so-called "literals" (scalar data such as strings or numbers); or blank (unlabelled) nodes, which may be used to group or "aggregate" properties (Bailey et al., 2005). Thus, representing the proposition about Kate Winslet will consist in representing a ternary relationship among entities such as that illustrated in Figure 9.2.

An RDF statement can itself become the subject/object or object/value of a triple, a process known as "reification." This is, of course, necessary if there is to be any reasoning about trust or levels of confidence in the propositions on the Semantic Web (Berners-Lee's sixth semantic layer). Reification does, however, introduce considerable awkwardness into RDF implementation: When an RDF graph is traversed (i.e., read by an application) via statements regarding a given property, reified statements are traversed in a way different from that used for unreified ones (Garshol, 2005).

Because RDF is a data model rather than a language, it needs to be implemented ("serialized") in a language. It is often serialized in XML, as it is in the W3C's official specification (Beckett, 2004). However, this implementation is notoriously unwieldy with regard to syntax (de Bruijn, 2003). Somewhat less complex serializations include N3 and its even simpler subset N-Triples (Berners-Lee, 2001, 2005). Another language, developed at the University of Bristol is TURTLE (Terse RDF

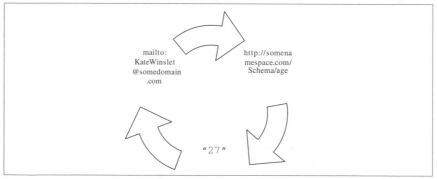

Figure 9.2 Relationships among entities representing the proposition about Kate Winslet's age.

Triple Language), which slightly extends N-Triples (Beckett, 2003); many other serializations have been proposed. In terms of the Semantic Web's goal of seamless semantic interoperability, applications that use RDF should perform serialization in independent fashion. However, this is not yet the case in practice (Bailey et al., 2005).

Bray (2001) has argued that RDF's three-part propositional structure renders it very scalable because arbitrary numbers of triples can be "stacked" in any order. By way of contrast, in XML, the order in which elements appear in a document is significant: This vastly complicates data interchange. The data structures definable in XML are also considerably more complex and syntactically unwieldy, for they can consist of arbitrary mixes of trees, graphs, and character strings. Haarslev and Moeller (2003) have also pointed out that RDF's triple-oriented style of data modeling offers means for providing graph-structured data over multiple documents; on the other hand, XML can only express graphs within a given document.

A standard RDF query language does yet exist; each language is typically tied to a particular implementation. A useful and thorough overview and comparison of query languages for XML, RDF, and Topic Maps (discussed in the section on "Ontologies with [Largely] DL Expressivity") is provided by Bailey et al. (2005), who work through a suite of test questions using each language in turn.

In spite of RDF's advantages over XML, it would be premature to conclude that RDF makes possible a "Semantic Web." In the sample proposition about Kate Winslet, a propositional structure exists with two of the three components assigned a URI. However, we have seen that URIs are just simple indices. To what are they indexed? RDF does not determine this. The problems of polysemy for metadata terms composed of identical character strings and hidden synonymy for terms composed of different character strings, which were noted with respect to XML, have not yet been resolved. Moreover, Heflin et al. (2003, p. 32) have observed that RDF provides "a very small set of semantic primitives" and, for this reason, it is logically quite inexpressive. Indeed, it does not even support an inheritance hierarchy. (This concept is explained in the section on "History of Ontology.") It has also been noted that RDF has relatively weak mechanisms for managing "schema evolution" (i.e., ontology versioning).

Something more is needed in order to determine meaning fully. Ontologies have been designated the semantic "silver bullet" (de Bruijn, 2003, p. ii). Therefore, in order to implement the Semantic Web's "ontology layer," developers have set themselves the task of building a number of further languages. These include RDF Schema and DAML-OIL/OWL, which are discussed later. First, however, an introduction to, and discussion of, ontologies in general is presented.

Introduction to Formal Ontology

History of Ontology

Ontology (which is generally, but not universally, treated as synonymous with "metaphysics") originated in a branch of philosophy as old as Aristotle, which he called "first philosophy." Etymologically, it derives from the Greek words ὄντος: (participle of εἰναι: "to be," i.e., "being") and λόγος: ("word/speech"). Ontologists seek to build a theory, at the most general level, of all the different types of things that exist (including the relationships among the different types of things that exist). As Smith and Welty (2001, p. iii) have put it, "philosophical ontology is the science of what is, of the kinds and structures of objects, properties, events, processes and relations in every area of reality" (see also Smith, 2003b). The terms coined or adapted by ontologists to refer to these most basic "kinds and structures" are called *categories* (terminology which has carried over into ontology in information science). "Material Object," "Person," "Time-point," and "Number" are just some of the basic categories proposed by traditional ontologists.

Aristotle's work "Categories" arguably represents humanity's first attempt to determine a systematic formal ontology. It is worth noting that this work was intertwined very much with Aristotle's logic—thus, understanding the inferential rules by which knowledge falling under certain categories might be transformed into further, categorized knowledge was for Aristotle inseparable from understanding the categories themselves. Interestingly, although later philosophers sought to pursue ontology and formal logic as separate disciplines, formal ontology in information technology applications has been forced to reunite them. Aristotle mapped out the first systematic logical distinction between the subject and predicate of a proposition—a significant advance in Western thought. Building on this, he defined his most basic categories ("Substance," "Quantity," "Quality," "Relation," "Place," "Time," "Posture," "State," "Action," and "Passion") as groupings of predicates according to what kinds of entities they properly pertain. To apply a predicate from one category to entities from another (e.g., "The number 8 is red.") produces a nonsensical so-called category error, something that will, of course, need to be discerned on the Semantic Web.

Famously, it was Aristotle who first formally defined the genus/species/differentia framework for categorizing groups of objects (whereby a species is defined by giving its genus—the kind under which the species falls—and its differentia—what distinguishes that species from others within that genus) (Smith, 2004). Thus were the sciences of classification born: For the first time, knowledge could be organized *taxonomically*—that is, into a hierarchy where knowledge "inherits" (is inferable downward, through an arbitrary number of genus–species relationships—a meaning that the term "inheritance" retains today in knowledge engineering). This feature alone greatly increased the organization and power of knowledge systems. Eventually, although not until the 19th century, this logical framework was developed and mathematized into modern set theory, which, as we shall see, is the basis for much formal ontology today. Most ambitiously, Aristotle sought to organize *all* branches of knowledge taxonomically, discerning the basic principles that defined each and organizing them into an integrated system (Smith, 2004; Sowa, 2001).

Medieval philosophy was built very much on Aristotle's ontological foundation. Genus–species relationships were considerably elaborated and organized into a "tree of knowledge" (Sowa, 1999, book cover). However, in the early modern period, development in formal ontology as an intellectual discipline suffered a setback, for the Scientific Revolution's new understanding of (and consequent enthusiasm for) scientific experiment led to the spread of *empiricism*—the idea that genuine knowledge is gained only through real-world experience—and a corresponding loss of focus on formal inquiries. Very few real advances in logic occurred during this period.

Such empiricism was countered to some degree by rationalists such as Kant, who sought to demonstrate that learning from experience already presupposed a prior (possibly innate) conceptual scheme and devised his own system of categories (Kant, 1998; Sowa, 2004). The early empiricists were, on the whole, logical atomists who saw knowledge as decomposable into basic building blocks (namely individual sensory experiences); Kant, however, took a more holistic view. A physical object such as a chair can be split in half, Kant noted, but what, he asked, would constitute half a proposition? The meaning of a proposition (e.g., "Trees are green.") is not reducible to the meanings of its subject ("trees") and its predicate ("are green") but constitutes a unity provided by the mind's understanding of their combination, he suggested.

Nevertheless, the spirit of the Scientific Revolution continued to pervade many currents of philosophical thought, culminating, in the early twentieth century, in logical positivism's wholesale rejection of speculative metaphysics (Schlick, 1936). During the formative years of mainstream analytic philosophy, the enormously influential Quine, partaking of this disdain for speculative metaphysics, presented his famous logical criterion of ontological commitment according to which the only mode of being is "to be the value of a [bound] variable [in our best scientific theory]" (Quine, 1953). Thus, the work of formally defining categories fell out of favor in mainstream philosophy, with the odd notable exception (e.g., Chisholm, 1996; Lowe, 1997, 1998; Weiss, 1958).

Formal logic, however, had received a new infusion of life toward the end of the 19th century with the invention of predicate logic by Frege (1970) and Peirce (1931–1958). This was the first major advance in logic since Aristotle, generalizing away from the Aristotelian framework of unary relations and two-premise arguments to relations of arbitrary complexity and arguments of arbitrary length, and it generated tremendous excitement. Set theory was invented, with the intent of using it to found all of mathematics on logic. Frege himself dreamed that this would form the basis of a genuinely clear and objective theory of meaning that would "break the domination of the word over the human spirit by laying bare the misconceptions that through the use of language often almost unavoidably arise concerning the relations between concepts" (Frege, 1970, p. 20). Frege hoped that it would now be possible to build all knowledge into an integrated, *deductively complete*, taxonomic system (i.e., one in which everything true might be proven to be true). Alas, this dream was shattered when Russell uncovered a paradox at the heart of the new logical system that rendered it inconsistent—namely, the famous class of all classes that do not contain themselves, which must perforce both contain and not contain itself (Zalta, 2005). Nevertheless, as we shall have occasion to see, Frege's dream has had a tendency to reemerge again in knowledge engineering circles.

Peirce, the other inventor of predicate logic, pursued a rather different vision. His philosophical pragmatism led him to see any attempt to formalize the entire meaning of a body of knowledge as impossible. In his view, an irreducible dimension of the meaning of any term (such as "hard" or "magnetic") is constituted by the effects that an agent situated in the world would experience in relevant situations and the sum total of such effects can never be known in advance (or there would be no need for scientific inquiry) (Peirce, 1940). Moreover, one of Peirce's major philosophical ambitions was to critique such aprioristic overreaching, which, for him, was epitomized by Descartes's famous claim for the philosophical necessity of eliminating all doubt as a precondition for serious inquiry. He also rejected attempts to reduce all useful inference to deduction, claiming that induction—generalizing from past to future cases of a relevantly similar kind (a process that, in contrast to deduction, requires experience)—and "abduction"—the generation of possible explanations of phenomena—were equally important (Peirce, 1940). As has been mentioned, classical AI was excessively deductivist in its approach to knowledge; we will see that Semantic Web developments so far have not yet departed significantly from this stance.

An aspect of the Cartesian philosophical framework to which Peirce objected with especial vehemence was its model of *meaning*, whereby the meaning of a sign is determined by the intention of the person who uses it (for Descartes himself, this intention consisted in an idea in the user's mind so private and inaccessible as to constitute a non-physical substance). Peirce sought to replace this with a new, publicly accessible, model of meaning. Whereas Descartes's model was dualist, with meaning consisting fundamentally in a binary relationship between a user's intention (a sign in the mind) and an object in the world, Peirce's was triadic, with meaning consisting in a relationship between a sign, an object signified, and further uses of the same sign *by others* to "mean" the same object. (This crucial third term in his meaning model he called the sign's *interpretant*.) An important difference between these models is that, whereas the Cartesian makes the comforting assumption that, by virtue of our intentions, we determine and have the ultimate authority as to what we mean, Peirce's implies that the meanings of one's signs consist only in their continued use by others. Thus, the meaning a sign has for initial users might be very different from the meaning it is interpreted to have subsequently, scientific terms providing a very good example of this (Peirce, 1940; Legg, 2005). The issue of predictability versus unanticipated development in meaning is highly relevant to formal ontology's goal of defining meaning in machine-understandable form.

A final issue worth mentioning—and it is an understatement to say that it has bedeviled philosophical ontology from the beginning—is the question of the degree to which the categories devised by human ontologists should be thought of as universally applicable or objective, as opposed to artifacts of particular contexts (such as a culture, a time period, a species, or a set of perceptual capacities). To what extent should an ontologist's categories be regarded as valid for all time and shareable across all communities? Or must all ontological work be done "locally" and repeatedly? This is the question of *realism*; 2,000 years of continuing controversy have not discouraged philosophers from hotly debating it today. Snapshots of some recent skirmishes in this debate are provided by Rorty (1990), Harré and Krausz (1996), and Kirk (1999).

Formal Ontology in Information Technology

In the late 1950s, formal ontology began to be reinvented in computer science (a field itself born from the 19th-century advances in logic mentioned earlier). As databases became more sophisticated and attempts to integrate them more ambitious, it was noted (McCarthy, 1995; Smith, 2003b) that certain problems encountered by database designers were actually ontological in character. For example: What is a person? Is it an entity that exists wholly at a particular time (in which case one can conveniently assume that a person has only one address)? Or is it an entity that covers a whole "person-lifetime" (in which case databases will need somehow to deal with one "person" having multiple addresses)? Are organizations individuated by the physical locations of their buildings, in which case it is not possible to have two organizations in one location? Or are they individuated by some other means and, if so, how? (For example, what is the relationship between Microsoft Germany and Microsoft U.S.A.?) Some general standardized conceptual scheme is considered desirable, at least to prevent random, ad hoc solutions to ontological problems being "hacked" by computer programmers.

Perhaps less surprisingly, ontology became a topic of interest in the field of AI. Famously, after early inspiring successes on relatively simple problems, AI encountered difficulties that led to a humbling scaling back of goals and enthusiasm (and also funding) (Lenat, Guha, Pittman, Pratt, Guha, & Shepherd,1990). In the late 1970s and early 1980s, concentrated research effort was put into so-called "expert systems," which sought to represent knowledge of a domain in such a way that questions about it could be answered at the level of a human expert. Examples included DENDRAL for organic chemistry (Lindsay, Buchanan, Feigenbaum, & Lederberg, 1980) and MYCIN for medical diagnosis (Buchanan & Shortliffe, 1984). These systems achieved success in the narrowly defined domains for which they were designed but became brittle when applied to new problems. A major stumbling block was delivering "artificial understanding" of natural languages such as English. It was realized that much natural language understanding draws on a background framework of general knowledge about the world (even at the level of simple sentence parsing, as evident in the differing interpretations we naturally give to the sentences "Aroha and Fiona are mothers" and "Aroha and Fiona are sisters").

A few farsighted individuals began to look to philosophy for aid in constructing an artificial general knowledge framework (McCarthy, 1995; Sloman, 1995). Some of this new thinking crystallized in a series of formal ontology projects, the largest and most ambitious of which was the Cyc project, whose target was identified by Lenat as capturing "common sense": everything a six-year-old knows that allows her to understand natural language and start learning independently (Lenat, 1995; Lenat & Guha, 1990). (The Cyc ontology is discussed in the section "Ontologies with First-Order Logic Expressivity [or Higher].") These ontology projects drew on AI researchers' attempts to represent knowledge in "declarative" languages explicitly modeled on formal logic (and subject to its inferencing rules). This embrace of formal logic proceeded in stages. The earliest knowledge representation systems were semantic networks (Quillian, 1967) and "frame systems," the latter so called because they embodied a collection of named data structures (frames), each of which had a series of "slots" representing attributes of the entity represented by the frame, into which values were inserted (Minsky, 1975). It was soon realized, however, that the lack of formal semantics underpinning these systems rendered them unsatisfactory. Reasons for this included profound ambiguity: For instance, if the value "green" is inserted in the "color" slot within the "frog" frame, does this mean that frogs *must* be green or merely that frogs *can* be green? Genuine confusion existed here.

The first formal semantics specifically aimed at the field of knowledge representation was developed by Brachman (1978) and resulted in a language known as KL-ONE (Brachman & Schmolze, 1985). Around this time, the idea that it might be of benefit to restrict logical expressivity in favor of inferential tractability began to emerge; unfortunately, it was shown that reasoning even in KL-ONE was undecidable (Schmidt-Schauss, 1989). From this line of research developed a branch of formal logic known as Description Logic (DL). DL is a decidable fragment of first-order logic with a series of versions of greater and lesser expressivity. Brachman and Levesque (2004) give an overview of 20 years of development in this area. Detailed investigations into the formal features and consequences for decidability of different versions of DL include SHOQ

(D) (Horrocks & Sattler, 2001), SHIQ (Horrocks, Sattler, Tobies, 2000b), and ALL (Horrocks, Sattler, & Tobies, 2000a). Borgida (1996) provides a comparison of the expressiveness of DLs and traditional predicate calculus.

However, as the field of symbolic "knowledge representation" developed, it was found necessary to add more and more logical expressivity to representation languages in order to deal with the full range of typical human assertions, including negations (e.g., "Henry has no jazz CDs."), disjunctions (e.g., "This CD is either jazz or pop."), and assertions about assertions (e.g., "Ruth's claim that Henry has no jazz CDs is not true."). As a result, the field soon acquired languages with the expressivity of full first-order, and even higher-order, logic. Examples here include Stanford's Knowledge Interchange Format (KIF) (Genesereth & Fikes, 1992), knowledge management (Clark & Porter, 2001), jointly developed at University of Texas at Austin and Boeing, and CycL, the language of the Cyc project. The difficulty of inferencing over these languages soon became more than apparent and, as the field of AI pushed on into the 1990s and turned from the explicit symbolization of "Good Old-Fashioned AI" toward brute-force, number-crunching approaches epitomized by machine learning, these projects began to languish. However, the push to create the Semantic Web has reignited interest in them, although to what degree they can be adapted to present needs remains to be seen.

The majority of formal ontologists within information technology work with Gruber's (1993, p. 199) simple definition of an ontology as "the specification of a conceptualization." This definition takes a position on the realism question, by assuming that whatever is conceptualized as reality by a particular group is all the reality there is to represent (see also Gruber, 1995). Despite its "irrealist" approach, it does satisfy Quine's criterion of ontological commitment (and one might, of course, ask how one might represent things one does not conceptualize). Even so, Gruber's definition has critics in the formal ontology community, for instance Smith (2003b), who does, however, concede that it might be appropriate for certain domains where reality is arguably wholly human-created, such as administrative systems.

The Logical Expressivity of Ontology Languages

As noted, the scalability of applications that use ontologies is strongly influenced by the logical expressivity of ontology languages (both representation and query languages, if the latter differ from the former, as they frequently do). In Figure 9.3, McGuinness (2003) usefully taxonomizes ontologies across a spectrum of increasing expressivity.

The first and simplest category, *catalogs*, consists of finite lists of terms that are used as a controlled vocabulary, although no attempt is made to define the terms. The next category, *glossaries*, consists of lists of terms along with a meaning for each term stated in natural language.

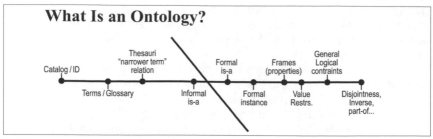

Figure 9.3 McGuinness's taxonomy of ontologies.

Thesauri add to glossaries some rudimentary semantic relationships, such as synonymy, between terms (thus, a thesaurus for the music domain might point out that "CD" and "compact disc" mean the same thing). Not infrequently, thesauri also enable informal "is-a" relationships (that is, membership of kinds or classes) to be discerned by a human user but not reasoned over in any machine-processable way.

To the right of the diagonal line, one begins to add to one's ontology properties and relations that can be reasoned over formally. The first addition is formal subclass and class membership relationships. We have now reached the complexity of frame systems. If the subclass relationship is rendered transitive, the ontology provides inheritance (sometimes also referred to as a "subsumption hierarchy"). The next logical sophistication generally added is so-called "value restrictions," whereby assertions are made about the domain and range of the ontology's relations (for instance, "Every named artist on a CD is a person"). After this, it is customary to add the standard inter-set relationships of classical set theory. These include *union* (for instance, "The category of '80s music' consists of releases from 1981, and from 1982, and from 1983, ... etc."), *intersection* (for instance, "The category of 'music recommended by dorm 10' consists of those songs that are on the iPods of every resident of dorm 10"), and *disjointness* ("No jazz CDs are heavy metal CDs"). We have now reached the complexity of some versions of DL.

One then reaches ontology languages with the expressivity of full first-order logic. First-order logic is already undecidable; however, it is possible to proceed even further, into higher-order logic, by including such features as quantifying over properties, ("All songs in Cathy's collection have something in common."), propositions about propositions ("Not all the statements Cathy has made about her CD collection are true."), modal logic ("It is possible that Miles Davis might release a hip-hop CD."), and context logic ("Whereas in the novel [X], all Kate Bush CDs were recorded by David Bowie, actually Kate Bush's CDs were recorded by Kate Bush."). The problems of inferential tractability are so compounded here that very little research has been done on such languages (in comparison to the extensive work done on DLs). Nevertheless, some ontologies have ventured this far.

Although "real-world" ontology languages do not always fit cleanly into these boxes, this framework is used here to taxonomize ontologies on the Semantic Web into three broad categories that structure the next three sections—namely, "thesaurus ontologies," ontologies with (roughly) the expressivity of DL, and ontologies with the expressivity of full first-order logic or higher. It is worth noting that the catch-all term "ontology" is somewhat misleading with respect to these three sections, as some of the developments discussed are merely ontology languages with no real knowledge represented in them (for instance, OWL); some comprise languages plus more or less extensive knowledge bases (for instance, SUMO); others (such as Cyc) constitute full knowledge representation systems (containing further tools such as inference engines, natural language interfaces, and ontology editors).

Thesaurus Ontologies

Dublin Core Metadata Element Set

The Dublin Core Metadata Initiative (DCMI) (http://dublincore.org) is a loosely affiliated group of researchers located in a variety of institutions worldwide, whose aim is to formulate interoperable metadata standards. To this end, they have dedicated themselves to developing metadata-sharing frameworks and technologies, constructing core specialized metadata vocabularies, and collecting and registering the metadata vocabularies of others. Heery and Wagner (2002, online) note that these registries trace a lineage back to "shared data dictionaries and the registration process encouraged by the ISO/IEC 11179 community."

The inaugural Dublin Core Series Workshop took place in Dublin, Ohio, in 1995. The initiative's first deliverable was the Dublin Core Metadata Element Set (DCMES), a vocabulary for describing 15 "core" information properties, such as "Description," "Creator," and "Date." The DCMES functions like a library card catalog system for Web resources. "Simple Dublin Core" uses only the canonical elements defined in the Element Set, whereas "Qualified Dublin Core" allows the addition of further data-defining qualifiers. A number of people in the DCMI are active in the W3C; indeed, Dublin Core is the application on which RDF was initially prototyped. The logical expressivity of the DCMES is particularly simple, consisting as it does merely in attribute:value pairs (with, moreover, possible attributes numbering only 15 so that it lacks the "universal expressive power" of Decker et al., [2000, p. 67]); consequentially, one might hesitate to call it an ontology at all.

WordNet

WordNet has been under development since 1985 at the Cognitive Science Laboratory of Princeton University (under the direction of the psychologist George Miller). The work has received considerable funding from government agencies interested in machine translation. WordNet is a lexicon for the English language containing approximately 150,000 words organized into more than 115,000 "synsets" (sets of synonymous words or phrases). Words typically participate in several synsets. WordNet distinguishes between nouns, verbs, adjectives, and adverbs. The meaning of the synsets is further clarified with short defining glosses. Every synset is connected to other synsets via a number of transitive relations. For nouns, the relations include synonyms, hypernyms (Y is a hypernym of X if every X is a kind of Y), "hyponyms" (Y is a hyponym of X if every Y is a kind of X), "holonyms" (Y is a holonym of X if X is a part of Y), and "meronyms" (Y is a meronym of X if Y is a part of X). The hypernym and hyponym relationships are also applied to verbs; thus, both nouns and verbs are organized into subsumption hierarchies.

The WordNet project, which is freely downloadable (http://wordnet. princeton.edu), is widely used and has spawned a number of derivative projects. Global WordNet attempts to coordinate the production and linking of wordnets for all languages (www.globalwordnet.org). The eXtended WordNet project at the University of Texas at Dallas aims to improve WordNet by semantically parsing the glosses, thus making them available for automatic knowledge processing systems (http://xwn.hlt.utdallas.edu). FrameNet, developed by Charles Filmore at the University of California at Berkeley, adds some assertions ascribing properties to entities listed in WordNet, thus bringing it closer to DL expressivity (www.icsi.berkeley.edu/framenet). SENSUS, developed at the University of Southern California's Information Sciences Institute, is an extension and reorganization of WordNet.

WordNet is very simple as regards logical expressivity, as it consists almost entirely of a lexicon of words with natural language definitions (although it does enable formal reasoning over subsumption hierarchies organized on the few relations previously mentioned). It is also simple in that it cannot, in principle, distinguish between words themselves and the concepts they express (although synsets do, in effect, create semantic clusters—thus, for example, the word "tree" participates in one synset qua biological organism and another qua mathematical structure). In spite of its simplicity, WordNet is often used as a formal ontology. Some researchers have suggested that this widespread use is precisely because of WordNet's simplicity (e.g., Sowa, 2004). Developers of other, more sophisticated ontologies have put considerable effort into mapping WordNet onto their systems (for instance, SUMO and OpenCyc, which are discussed in subsections of "Ontologies with First-Order Logic Expressivity [or Higher]").

Ontologies with (Largely) DL Expressivity

Topic Maps

Topic Maps (Pepper & Moore, 2001) derive from work in library sciences and knowledge indexing (Bailey et al., 2005) and are standardized in ISO/IEC 13250. They represent data concerning "topics" (which are named and organized into a subsumption hierarchy of topic types) by means of "associations," which are relations of arbitrary arity (i.e., numbers of places) between topics, and "occurrences," which are information resources relevant to a topic. Topic Maps can be understood, like RDF data, as directed graphs with labeled nodes and edges. However, they are more logically expressive because of the arbitrary complexity of association relations (in contrast to RDF's restriction to binary relations). Trials of large-scale Topic Maps knowledge bases have largely taken place within organizations that have voluminous in-house data, such as the U.S. Office of Naval Intelligence, the U.S. Internal Revenue Service, and the Dutch Tax and Customs Administration (Breebaart, 2004); a less centralized project, closer to the spirit of the Semantic Web, is Kulturnett 3.0 (www/kuturnett.no), a Norwegian government portal for cultural information.

Unfortunately, in spite of their similarity, RDF and Topic Maps have developed separate user communities. Initial efforts toward integrating them are described by Lacher and Decker (2001); Pepper, Vitali, Garshol, Gessa, and Presutti (2005); and Garshol (2005, p. 24), although the last notes that fully merging the two technologies does not appear "desirable or possible."

RDF Schema

RDF Schema (RDFS) (Brickley & Guha, 2003) extends RDF with some basic frame modeling primitives (de Bruijn, 2003). It allows one to declare classes and properties, populate classes with instances, and organize them into a subsumption hierarchy. It also allows adding range and domain constraints to properties and ascribing properties to individuals. All of these features render it a fragment of DL in terms of expressivity (Horrocks, Patel-Schneider, & van Harmelen, 2003).

One might ask about the relationship between RDFS and XML Schema. Does the Semantic Web really need both? If it does not, which would be preferable? Or might they be merged somehow? Unfortunately, the exact logical relationship and the extent of possible interoperability between XML Schema and RDFS are complicated and very difficult to understand. This difficulty is compounded by the polarization of their user communities along cultural lines—XML Schema is embraced by those who see themselves as "quick and dirty" real-world developers, whereas RDFS's users identify with a perceived elegance and formal correctness usually only supported by academic research funding. In 1999, the two communities met in an attempt to work out their differences; the result was a document known as the "Cambridge Communiqué" (Swick & Thompson, 1999). The participants agreed that XML Schema and RDFS should not be merged (due to their different data models), but that certain atomic data types should be shared. The communiqué also suggested that the XML Schema specification should provide an extension mechanism to (for example) allow elements from other namespaces to be included in its schema documents, possibly even including the RDF data model itself. Further details are given by Melnik (1999). Another attempt to bridge the XML-RDF gap in a common formal semantics can be found in Patel-Schneider and Siméon (2002).

RDFS is still too logically simple to express a great deal of what is said on the Web. Within its framework, it is possible to declare new classes and populate them with instances, but one cannot say anything further about these classes and instances; moreover, one cannot state axioms or inference rules concerning them (Delteil, Faron-Zucker, & Dieng, 2001). Thus, the problem with *defining* (in a machine-understandable way) the meaning of terms used in one's ontology language remains—ultimately, RDFS terms are still indexed only via namespaces whose further meaning is opaque.

DAML+OIL/OWL

DAML+OIL was initially created by merging the results of two projects: the American Defense Advanced Research Projects Agency (DARPA) Agent Markup Language (DAML) project (www.daml.org) and the largely European "Ontology Inference Layer" (OIL) project (Fensel, Horrocks, van Harmelen, McGuinness, & Patel-Schneider, 2001; Horrocks, Patel-Schneider, & van Harmelen, 2002). It is a particularly expressive DL (de Bruijn, 2003). Although it supports all XML datatypes, it does not support explicit representation of them and the making of assertions about them.

DAML+OIL has recently been reworked and renamed OWL (Web Ontology Language) (McGuinness & van Harmelen, 2004), which became a W3C Recommendation in February 2004. OWL goes beyond RDF and RDFS by providing additional vocabulary and a formal semantics. The additional vocabulary includes the ability to define classes in terms of logical relationships between other classes (such as intersection, union, complement, or enumerations of specific entities), the ability to state class cardinality (e.g., "Jones has 6 Kate Bush CDs"), equality (for both classes and individuals), and characteristics of properties (such as symmetry, transitivity, functionality, and inverse relationships between properties). A major extension over RDFS, though, is the ability to provide restrictions on how properties behave that are local to a class (e.g., defining a class "Australian Person," all of whose members have "Australia" as the value for the property "country of residence"). This, in particular, results in a much more complicated logic (Horrocks et al., 2003).

OWL has three sublanguages, each of which is an extension of the preceding one. OWL Lite, which is designed to support thesauri and other taxonomies, is limited to providing a classification hierarchy with some very simple constraints on values. OWL DL is designed for the greatest possible logical expressiveness while retaining decidability and computational completeness (all conclusions true in an OWL DL knowledge base are computable). OWL Full sacrifices computational completeness for maximal logical expressiveness. In practice, however, OWL Lite has proven to be very close to the considerably more expressive OWL DL in terms of complexity of implementation; developers have therefore tended to favor the latter. OWL Full is so expressive that it is considered too difficult to implement and, consequently, is hardly used. As a result, most tools exist for OWL DL.

The exact formal relationship between OWL and RDF (how the former "extends," in Berners-Lee's sense, the latter) is a somewhat delicate matter. OWL Full can be viewed as an extension of RDF, whereas OWL Lite and OWL DL can only be viewed as extensions of a restricted view of RDF. In other words, every OWL document is an RDF document, and every RDF document is an OWL Full document, but only some RDF documents are legal OWL Lite or OWL DL documents. Thus, considerable care has to be taken in migrating RDF documents to OWL (McGuinness & van Harmelen, 2004). An interesting perspective on current issues in OWL that arise from its original roots in DL, as well as an overview of the conflicting requirements that led to the development of three separate languages, is to be found in Horrocks et al. (2003).

A penetrating paper (Patel-Schneider & Fensel, 2002) has raised a further issue with layering OWL over RDF and RDFS—namely, that it is in fact subject to Russell's Paradox, which, as noted earlier defeated Frege's original vision of a univocal, unified, and deductively complete system of knowledge. This is because OWL is sufficiently expressive to allow users to define classes at will from sets of resources, but the syntax of RDF lacks the resources to block the creation of the class of all classes that do not contain themselves. Patel-Schneider and Fensel concede that the response to this point might be "Who cares?" on the grounds that such a situation will arise extremely rarely, if at all, "in the wild," and Semantic Web developers should stick to practical problems (see, for instance, Berners-Lee, 1998). However, they counter this, asking how practical it is to have "a complete collapse of the logical formalism" (Patel-Schneider & Fensel, 2002, p. 22). The dispute makes intriguingly vivid the divide within the Semantic Web community between application-oriented pragmatism and formal correctness.

Patel-Schneider and Fensel (2002) offer a detailed analysis of four possible solutions to this problem: (1) writing some explicit rules to limit inferences from statements in RDFS to statements in OWL (a measure that would cripple the expressiveness of the latter in bizarre and difficult-to-anticipate ways); (2) defining new syntactic constructs in OWL (which would seem to defeat the purpose of the layer-cake model according to which each layer extends the layers below it); (3) defining some new semantics for OWL that overrides certain RDFS semantics (a move that would also seem to defeat the purpose of the layer-cake model); and (4) defining a divergent syntax and semantics for OWL (which would seem the most inelegant solution of all).

In summary then, OWL, although currently the flagship ontology of the W3C group, is not problem-free; a case in point is its complex verbosity. For instance, here is Horrocks et al.'s (2003, p. 17) OWL translation of the statement "A student is a person who is enrolled in at least one class":

```
<owl:Class rdf:ID="Student">
    <owl:intersectionOf rdf:parsetype="Collection">
        <owl:Class rdfs:about="Person" />
        <owl:Restriction>
            <owl:onProperty
            rdf:resource="enrolledIn" />
            <owl:minCardinality
            rdfs:datatype="&xsd;Integer">
            </owl:minCardinality>
        </owl:Restriction>
    <owl:intersectionOf>
</owl:Class>.
```

Consider also that layering such a statement on top of RDF will entail encoding it into stackable triples which will have to be held together somehow if the statement's coherence is not to be lost (Horrocks et al., 2003).

SHOE

SHOE (Simple HTML Ontology Extensions) is an early Semantic Web ontology platform that combines characteristics of both frame systems and predicate logics (Heflin & Hendler, 2000; Heflin et al., 2003). It enables the annotation of Web pages with separate machine-readable metadata, which can be embedded directly in HTML documents or used in XML documents. The latter strategy is preferred because it exposes the metadata to a broader range of software tools (Heflin et al., 2003).

SHOE addresses the problem of the distributed nature of Web resources by providing a system for extending ontologies, using tags to specify the ID and version number of ontologies extended by a given ontology, and making use of prefixes to specify from which ontology a given term comes. It has a formal semantics. SHOE's developers claim to minimize the problem of logical contradiction on the Web by designing the language as far as possible to avoid the representation of logical contradictions. Thus, it does not permit logical negation, retractions of assertions already made, single-valued relations, or the specification of disjointness among classes. Of course, this restricts SHOE's expressive powers considerably (for instance, rendering impossible claims such as "No CDs are vinyl records").

The SHOE approach has been criticized by Fensel et al. (2000, p. 363) for its strategy of adding further data to pages rather than "mak[ing] explicit the semantics of already available data." Not only is the latter approach more elegant, but it also avoids maintenance problems caused by the presence of two sets of tags for the same data. Fensel et al. also claimed that SHOE's inferencing is too weak, barely outstripping basic database capabilities. However, it should be noted that these researchers are the developers of a rival system, Ontobroker, which, in contrast to SHOE's basic database-style inferencing, is more logic-based and infers and records additional knowledge on top of what it is given. Such proactive deduction has traditionally been known in AI circles as "forward inference." However, given the exponential growth of forwardly inferred knowledge once just a few simple inferencing rules are in place, one might ask how scalable this is for the whole Semantic Web (Fensel et al., 2000).

That SHOE might have been something of a trial Semantic Web application, now superseded, is suggested by the fact that its official Web site is no longer actively maintained and that two of its key developers (Hendler and Heflin) are now working on OWL.

Ontologies with First-Order Logic Expressivity (or Higher)

Cyc

As has been noted, the Cyc project (www.cyc.com) is the most ambitious formal ontology project yet attempted, with roots firmly planted in classical AI. It is the most ambitious in terms of size (over 600,000 categories), depth of knowledge (over two million axioms), and time devoted to it (over 700 person-years) (Sowa, 2004). Cyc began in 1984 as a project within the Microelectronics and Computer Technology Corporation (MCC), spinning off as an independent company, Cycorp, in 1994. In 2002, Cycorp released the first version (0.7.0) of OpenCyc (www.open cyc.org), an open source version of (about 40 percent of) its ontology. In February 2005, version 0.9.0 was released (about six times the size of 0.7.0). There also exists a slightly larger version for researchers, named ResearchCyc. The Cyc ontology has its own purpose-built inference engine, which is bundled with OpenCyc and ResearchCyc.

Even more ambitiously, the Cyc project was originally envisaged to move from initial hand-coding of its knowledge base by "ontological engineers" (a process that has turned out to be very expensive—a recent public trial on a high school chemistry textbook produced an estimate of $10,000 a page [Sowa, 2004]) to automated acquisition of knowledge by the system itself through reading and asking questions of untrained humans (Matuszek, Witbrock, Kahlert, Cabral, Schneider, Shah, et al., 2005). Building a natural language interface is another major plank of the project: Unlike WordNet, there is a separation, and required mapping, between terms representing concepts in the Cyc ontology and words in English or any other language.

The Cyc project has boldly addressed itself to the full-blown ontological problem of not just indexing terms but also attempting to describe their meanings in machine-understandable terms. For example, its representation of the concept of a tree (#$Tree-ThePlant, which is distinguished from #$Tree-PathSystem) comes with axiomatic assertions (e.g., "A tree is largely made of wood") and rules (e.g., "If a tree is cut down, then it will be destroyed"). This work is done in the purpose-built CycL language, which, although largely consisting of first-order predicate logic and set theory, has the expressivity of higher-order logic—allowing assertions about assertions, context logic (Cyc contains 6,000 explicitly represented contexts, known as "microtheories"), and some modal statements (although only temporal modality currently has inference support). An added complication is that the language allows assertions to be accorded not two but five different truth values: non-defeasibly true, defeasibly true, unknown, defeasibly false, and non-defeasibly false.

Because this project has gone on for so long and at such considerable expense, it has been the object of some criticism. For instance, Copeland (1997) criticized particular ontological choices that have been made with respect to the representation of substance, causation, and time. In an early but influential article, Smith (1991, pp. 252–253) argued that methodologically, Cyc's developers had "left out the middle part," accusing them of

> an assumption that you can move directly from broad intuition to detailed proposal, with essentially no need for intermediate conceptual results ... from the generality of human knowledge to the intricacies of slot inheritance; from the full flowering of intelligence to particular kinds of controlled search.

(Interestingly, critics of the Semantic Web have raised a similar complaint.) At any rate, one may fairly say that the research challenge of producing a general purpose ontology with a dedicated team of researchers and considerable cash has been much more difficult to carry through than was envisioned at the project's outset (for instance, in Lenat & Feigenbaum, 1991). This criticism is justifiable insofar as the time at which the system is to begin learning on its own continues to be pushed forward by the Cycorp itself.

What potential use does this ontology have for the Semantic Web? On one hand, Cycorp has made strenuous efforts to map other ontologies and databases into Cyc. Examples include FIPS (Federal Information Processing Standards), the Central Intelligence Agency (CIA) WorldFactbook (Reed & Lenat, 2002), and WordNet. The company also recently published a paper on automated OWL annotation of text documents (Witbrock et al., 2004); one significant challenge the authors noted is that the translation of terms in the text to terms in OWL proceeds via the CycL language, not all of which is translatable into OWL.

Unfortunately, Semantic Web developers outside the company have so far made little use of this ontology (but see Sicilia, Lytras, Rodriguez,

& Garcia-Barriocanal, 2006). Its system of categories is extremely complex, requiring philosophical training to understand (the majority of Cycorp's in-house ontologists possess philosophy Ph.D.s, and even they require six months to learn the system properly), and for a long time was poorly documented. Inferential tractability must also be a particular worry given the extreme expressivity of the CycL language. Ramachandran, Regan, and Goolsbey (2005) have recently explored to what extent this issue might be mitigated by "first-orderizing" sections of the knowledge base. Furthermore, because Cyc comprises such an integrated suite of applications (where the inference engine and other tools are custom-built and as such difficult to "unbundle"), it seems destined to remain a "located" rather than a "distributed" technology and committed to canonicalization at the expense of the decentralization fostered by notions of the Semantic Web vision. It has been the company's strongly held belief, however, (echoing Kant's rationalist skepticism that meaning might be chopped into units) that it is necessary to solve the problem of understanding basic, commonsense knowledge in an integrated, coherent manner, via one general-purpose application as a first step in building any other knowledge-based application, including the Semantic Web.

SUMO

SUMO (Suggested Upper Merged Ontology) was developed by Teknowledge Corporation (http://ontology.teknowledge.com) and first released in December 2000. Adam Pease, the current Technical Editor of the standard, has authored a number of publications presenting its key features (Niles & Pease, 2001; Pease & Niles, 2002). It can be browsed (www.ontologyportal.org), downloaded, and used freely. However, unlike the Cyc system, it does not include an inference engine.

SUMO's ontology language is (the full first-order logic expressivity) KIF and, as is the case with Cyc, the basic structure of its ontology is set-theoretic, including both axioms and rules. Its upper ontology consists of 1,000 concepts, defined using 4,000 assertions. A complete mapping from WordNet synsets to SUMO classes has been defined. There is also a Mid-Level Ontology (MILO) (Niles & Allan, 2004). An attempt has been made to sell SUMO to Semantic Web developers (Pease, Niles, & Li, 2002). Unfortunately this ontology is subject to many of the same concerns as Cyc—indeed, it is merely a smaller version of the same basic design—and has seen just as little external uptake.

SUO

SUO (Standard Upper Ontology) is a voluntary effort spearheaded by researchers concerned that, given the potential worldwide reach and importance of any real-world solution to the ontological problem, a viable, free, open source alternative to proprietary solutions should be presented. It largely consists of an Institute of Electrical and Electronics

Engineers (IEEE) working group (http://suo.ieee.org) and an e-mail list. A motion was passed in June 2003 to define an ontology registry into which members might enter ontologies that will be "related in a generalization/specialization hierarchy" (IEEE, Standard Upper Ontology Working Group, 2003, online). However, given the voluntary nature of participation in this forum, contributions have largely been confined to parties proffering their own already-worked-out ontologies as "starting documents" (for instance, OpenCyc, SUMO). Sustained independent development within the forum has not occurred: This seems to offer further confirmation that the Semantic Web's most difficult challenge may be political.

The list of ontologies discussed here is representative rather than comprehensive. Other general-purpose upper ontologies include Philippe Martin's (2003) MSO (Multi-Source Ontology), which was built by integrating a series of others onto a cleaned-up WordNet, and Barry Smith's (2003a) BFO (Basic Formal Ontology). BFO claims to distinguish itself by being based not on set theory, but on mereology (a theory of wholes and their parts as opposed to a theory of classes and their members); however, applications based on it seem still to make some use of a traditional subsumption hierarchy (Dos Santos, Dhaen, Fielding, & Ceusters, 2004).

To sum up the last three sections, then, ontologies were meant to be the "silver bullet" that delivered a machine-understandable theory of meaning; however, none of the applications examined here seems to have succeeded. They appear to fall across a spectrum whereby terms used by the simpler systems are defined at most in the form of URIs pointing to unique namespaces (Dublin Core) or in natural language glosses (WordNet). Some kind of machine-understandable definitions of the meanings of terms is needed if more robust results are to be achieved. And what is needed for that? It would appear axiomatic assertions and inferential rules concerning all the terms in one's ontology, at least when working within a deductivist inferencing paradigm. (As has already been mentioned, it is admittedly a big assumption to posit reliance on deductive inferencing, but other forms of automated reasoning have been slow to appear on the Semantic Web.) To be able to formulate axioms and rules, though, one is forced to build considerable logical expressivity into the ontology language. At this point, one encounters a raft of new problems: the complexity of one's language, the need to determine its formal semantics, and the inferential tractability, scalability, and brittleness of applications built using it. What noble attempts do exist suffer from obscurity and lack of uptake by others.

It might be argued, however, that the real problem actually lies with the attempt to build one all-embracing, general-purpose ontology and that local, distributed ontologies are the solution, a consideration that brings us to the next section.

Domain Ontologies

"Domain ontology" is the term of art for ontologies that pertain to specific, integrated areas of knowledge (such as individual sciences, for instance physics or chemistry, or real-world subject areas such as film or adventure sports). A bewildering variety of domain ontologies, in a wide range of formats, exists at present.

The knowledge domain in which ontology development is currently most advanced (in both size and sophistication) is bioinformatics. Notable examples here include the Gene Ontology (www.geneontology. org), which is downloadable in XML or OWL (Ashburner, Ball, Blake, Botstein, Butler, Cherry, et al., 2000), and SNOMED (the Systematized Nomenclature of Medicine), developed by the College of American Pathologists, which attempts the complete capture of healthcare terminology (www.snomed.org) (Spackman, Campbell, & Côté, 1997). Both of these are closer to glossaries or controlled vocabularies than to ontologies proper, however. Although they do provide subsumption hierarchies, they are very simple (containing very few roles). The fact that they have been constructed largely by domain experts ignorant of the tradition of formal knowledge representation has resulted in criticism by philosophically trained ontologists for various alleged metaphysical and logical blunders. For instance, Smith, Williams, and Schulze-Kremer (2003) have claimed that the Gene Ontology's "is-a" relationship is deeply ambiguous. As SNOMED has been under development for twenty years and contains 150,000 "records," it is particularly unruly, and Ceusters, Smith, Kumar, and Dhaen (2004) have recently alleged that it contains numerous logical errors. It should be noted that Smith himself is developing an alternative biomedical ontology based on BFO, which has been mentioned earlier. His Leipzig National Center for Biomedical Ontology (http://bioontology.org) includes a library of 50 stackable modular ontologies designed to be merged and used together.

Another ontology domain in which work is proceeding apace is geographical and spatio-temporal reasoning (a subject area currently very well funded because of its potential military applications). This is an extremely difficult domain to ontologize because spatial information is necessarily mathematical and mathematical relationships pose a significant challenge to the set-theoretic framework in which ontologies are traditionally built. (This is so because set-theoretic relations represent only a tiny subset of mathematical functions.) Nevertheless, the problem is currently being addressed by a large project at the University of Bremen (Bateman & Farrar, 2004), as well as by the nonprofit Open Geospatial Consortium (www.opengeospatial.org). The latter seems currently mainly to provide standards for Web services, but has sponsored the development of a Geographical Markup Language (GML) (http://opengis.net/gml).

Ontology Libraries and Related Resources

A number of ontology repositories or libraries exist. The original, and now relatively dated, site is the DAML Ontology Library (www.daml.org/ontologies). More recent offerings include SemWebCentral (www.semwebcentral.org) and SchemaWeb (www.schemaweb.info).

Resources to search across domain ontologies are, of course, a natural development, and are beginning to emerge. These include search engines, one notable example of which is Swoogle, a Google-like search engine for the Semantic Web developed at the University of Maryland, Baltimore County (UMBC) (http://swoogle.umbc.edu). This tool searches and indexes the world's metadata using both character string and URI references. It also seeks to provide "ontology rank," an equivalent to Google's Web page ranking service, although it is worth noting that the top-ranked ontologies as of 2004 were the W3C's own specification documents for RDF, RDFS, and DAML+OIL (Ding, Finin, Joshi, Pan, Cost, Peng, et al., 2004). Resources to explore Semantic Web ontologies also include browsers, of which an oft-cited example is Ontaria (www.w3c.org/2004/ontaria), which site is currently down for overhaul (as of December 2005).

Whether local, distributed ontologies might prove more useful than their general, all-purpose cousins for the Semantic Web it is arguably too early to tell. Even the most highly developed domains, bioinformatics and geographical and spatio-temporal reasoning, ontologies still require considerable development. Ontologies for most other domains are tiny, with numbers of categories in the tens rather than the hundreds or thousands. Burton-Jones, Storey, Sugumaran, and Ahluwalia (2005, p. 98) studied the DAML library and claimed that both the size and the quality of publicly available ontologies were currently questionable: "For the average ontology, 18 percent of its syntax is incorrect, 37 percent of its terms are uninterpretable, 22 percent of its terms are polysemous and 18 percent of its statements are irrelevant." A further question concerns how local distributed ontologies are going to interoperate, given that Semantic Web information integration operations are meant to be performable not merely within "domain islands," but across the Web as a whole. Will a further ontology be required to perform ontology integration? How will *its* terms be defined?

Conclusion

The Challenges Revisited

Throughout this chapter, a number of significant challenges have been identified with regard to the ontological dimension of the original vision of the Semantic Web. The first is the trade-off in ontology languages between logical expressivity and inferential tractability. Is there a way of resolving this tension? The various languages of DL expressivity might seem to provide a happy medium between, on the one hand, extreme expressivity and inferential intractability and, on the other, extreme inferential tractability and inexpressivity by providing the maximum expressivity obtainable while retaining decidability. But still, in contrast to the original Semantic Web vision of rendering machine-readable the entire Web's human-readable knowledge, there is an enormous amount that cannot be said in these languages (to give just one example, "Bill Evans recorded exactly one album with Miles Davis").

It is sometimes claimed that ever more powerful computer hardware will solve this problem, rendering tractable tomorrow inferential problems that are intractable today. This is not correct, however, because inferential tractability decreases exponentially with such simple matters as the number of variables in a question, for which no principled upper limit has yet been set on the Semantic Web. In a position paper written in the early days of the Semantic Web, Berners-Lee (1998, online) blithely stated that the Semantic Web will not "require every application to use expressions of arbitrary complexity" but gave no further details regarding what might constitute a principled means of determining which applications would, and would not, use such expressions; whether the Semantic Web itself might be forced to divide this labor when serving up knowledge; and, if so, how. In the same paper, Berners-Lee also attempted to dodge the inferential tractability issue by claiming that the Semantic Web need not supply "proof generation," only "proof validation" (an example of such being the way access control is provided by Web sites). Once again, however, some details would be helpful—regarding, for example, how this might work for information integration over a number of independent sources (so as to answer, for instance, Berners-Lee et al.'s [2001] question: Which medical specialist would be able to see the ailing mother at a mutually convenient time?)

The second significant challenge is the trade-off between decentralization and canonicalization in the definitions of ontological terms. (This includes both terms for general concepts, such as "CD," and terms for individuals, such as "Kate Bush," which may well require differing solutions.) The invention of URIs qua unique character strings goes only the first, easy step toward solving the problem of uniquely identifying resources. The rest of the issue concerns how humans are to agree on a particular character string/resource alignment. (In an interesting twist, it has even been suggested that resources are most effectively picked out not by such pure names, but via uniquely identifying—"discriminant"—descriptions [Guha & McCool, 2003].) In an echo of Smith's complaint back in 1991 about Cyc's insouciance regarding the hard methodological middle ground, Shirky (2003, online) has observed that the modus operandi of Semantic Web development is to "take some well-known problem. Next, misconstrue it so that the hard part is made to seem trivial and the trivial part hard. Finally, congratulate yourself for solving the trivial part." The combined effect of these challenges has generated significant skepticism in some quarters regarding the Semantic Web (for a particularly pungent critique that draws morals from library science, see Brooks, 2002).

Possible Alternatives to the Semantic Web

If the goals of the Semantic Web cannot be achieved by the current W3C development framework, might they be achieved by other means? And if not, what is the Web's future? Some recent Web developments are worth mentioning insofar as they seem to partake of the giddy momentum of the original technology. The first development is *tagging*. Tags are labels users voluntarily add to the Web. Ontologically speaking, the practice is entirely uncontrolled—no categories are prepared or agreed upon in advance. (Thus a given CD might be labeled "boring," "amazing," "Mike_likes_this," "driving_music," and "songs_about_fish.") The practice began as a means of labeling Web pages with words or phrases meaningful to oneself so that one might rediscover them quickly; it has spread to embrace a number of other, much more public uses as a variety of Web sites has emerged to serve as tag clearinghouses. Examples of such sites include del.icio.us. for the sharing of tagged bookmarks to Web sites (http://del.icio.us) and Flickr for tagged photographs (www.flickr.com). Unsurprisingly, developers have begun to develop search engines for this new slew of metadata (e.g., Technorati: www.technorati.com).

Tagging is said to produce not a *taxonomy* (in the sense of a mark-up according to a pre-given structure of categories) but the newly coined term *folksonomy* (Weinberger, 2005). In spite of the "feral" source of tags, it has been argued that, at the level of the entire Web, semantic patterns emerge among them, thus lessening the impact of individual idiosyncrasy, and that, "by forgoing formal classification, tags enable a huge amount of user-produced organizational value, at vanishingly small cost" (Shirky, 2005, online). This new development is interesting from the perspective of the Cartesian-versus-Peircean philosophical debate with respect to meaning. We saw that the Cartesian perspective holds that the meaning of a sign consists in the idea its user intends to convey by using it. In Semantic Web development terms, this model naturally generates the attempt to anticipate and define every possible aspect of a term's future meaning through explicit axioms and rules (as is epitomized, for instance, in the Cyc project). According to the Peircean perspective, on the other hand, the meaning of a sign consists merely in the way it continues to be used. Consider, for example, the popular pairing between the terms "blonde" and "joke." From the Cartesian perspective, for the Semantic Web to work, these terms will need to be defined so that the meaning of their pairing might be anticipated, an obviously Herculean task. The Peircean perspective allows that the phrase might be a new development in the meaning of both terms—somehow consisting in the new uses of the phrase themselves.

A further runaway development in the recent Web is *RSS autodiscovery*. Via software of simplicity reminiscent of early HTML, this technology "syndicates" Web sites (frequently Weblogs) by providing summaries of their content, links to the full version, and other metadata in an XML file called an RSS (Really Simple Syndication/RDF Site Summary) feed. Content is filtered for individual receivers using keywords (the choice of which once again is wholly personal and idiosyncratic). There has been some speculation among Web developers that such advances might result in a "lowercase semantic web," which will implement at least some of the original founders' goals while bypassing (or, less charitably, precisely by bypassing) the formal standards they have labored so hard to create. (For an attempt to merge the two, see Cayzer [2004].)

This review makes evident that inferencing capability is inseparable from machine-understandable meaning; it is currently difficult to envisage how coherent inferencing rules might be built on such a turbulent, ambiguous, and amateur base as tags and RSS feeds. In direct contrast to formal ontologies, such "do-it-yourself" metadata seem to demonstrate an extreme version of the decentralization at the expense of the canonicalization plank of the Semantic Web vision. Still, these criticisms might equally well be leveled at Google's deployment of its (in fact spectacularly successful) page-rank algorithm across the turbulent, ambiguous, and amateur World Wide Web. Shirky (2005) has suggested that, just as it was Google's genius to realize how to leverage vast quantities of hyperlinks to create a meaning (namely, the significance of a given Web site) that the authors of hyperlinks never intended them to have, something analogous and as-yet-unanticipated, substituting order of magnitude of data for authorial intention, will surely happen to generate the requisite metadata.

An even more subversive question worth at least some thought is: "Is the Web really the future of the Internet?" Recent discussions on the popular U.K. information technology news and gossip site *The Register* have speculated that it might not be, suggesting that the Web is "much less important, compared to other Internet services, than the giant Web search engines like to think" and making reference to a so-called "Asian way of using Internet," which focuses rather on games, Internet chat rooms, and Web radio and Television (Google can take the Web, yawn readers, 2005, online).

The Semantic Web vision is audacious and tempting. However, attempts to realize it may mean pursuing a "machine-understandable meaning at the end of the rainbow." The more one attempts to build a formal system that explicitly and antecedently states what terms used on the Web will mean, the more it appears that the meaning of the terms in the formal system itself elude one's grasp. It can easily appear that one needs an ontology behind one's ontology in order to determine *its* meaning—an issue philosophers (the original ontologists) have been struggling with for centuries. The only alternative would seem to be to explore with Peirce the surprising idea that machine-understandable data about the meaning of Web resources already exist precisely in the form of those resources themselves, if we can only find the means to leverage them.

Acknowledgments

For feedback and discussion that considerably improved this chapter, I am indebted to Ajeet Parhar, Lars Marius Garshol, Sally-Jo Cunningham, and the anonymous reviewers.

References

Ashburner, M., Ball, C. A., Blake, J. A., Botstein, D., Butler, H., Cherry, J. M., et al. (2000). Gene ontology: Tool for the unification of biology. *Nature Genetics, 25*, 25–29.

Bailey, J., Bry, F., Furche, T., & Schaffert, S. (2005). *Web and Semantic Web query languages: A survey*. Retrieved February 26, 2006, from www.pms.ifi.lmu.de/publikationen/PMS-FB/PMS-FB-2005-14.pdf

Bateman, J., & Farrar, S. (2004). Towards a generic foundation for spatial ontology. *Proceedings of the Third International Conference on Formal Ontology in Information Systems*, 237–248.

Beckett, D. (2003). *TURTLE: Terse RDF triple language*. Retrieved February 26, 2006, from http://ilrt.org/discovery/2003/11/ntriplesplus

Beckett, D. (2004). *RDF/XML syntax specification* (Revised). Retrieved February 26, 2006, from www.w3.org/TR/2004/REC-rdf-syntax-grammar-20040210

Berners-Lee, T. (1998). *What the Semantic Web can represent*. Retrieved February 26, 2006, from www.w3.org/DesignIssues/RDFnot.html

Berners-Lee, T. (2000, December). *Semantic Web*. Paper presented at XML 2000, Washington, DC. Retrieved March 22, 2006, from www.w3.org/2000/Talks/1206-xml2k-tbl/slide10-0.html

Berners-Lee, T. (2001). *Notation 3*. Retrieved February 26, 2006, from www.w3.org/DesignIssues/Notation3

Berners-Lee, T. (2003). Foreword. In D. Fensel (Ed.), *Spinning the Semantic Web: Bringing the World Wide Web to its full potential* (pp. xi–xxiii). Cambridge, MA: MIT Press.

Berners-Lee, T. (2005). *Primer: Getting into RDF and Semantic Web using N3*. Retrieved February 26, 2006, from www.w3.org/2000/10/swap/Primer.html

Berners-Lee, T., Hendler, J., & Lassila, O. (2001). The Semantic Web. *Scientific American, 284*(5), 34–43.

Bollobas, B. (2002). *Modern graph theory* (2nd ed.). Berlin: Springer.

Borgida, A. (1996). On the relative expressive power of description logics and predicate logics. *Artificial Intelligence, 82*, 353–367.

Brachman, R. (1978). *Structured inheritance networks* (Technical Report No. 3742). Cambridge, MA: Bolt Beranek & Newman.

Brachman, R., & Levesque, H. (2004). *Knowledge representation and reasoning*. Boston: Morgan Kaufmann.

Brachman, R., & Schmolze, J. (1985). An overview of the KL-ONE knowledge representation system. *Cognitive Science*, *9*, 171–216.

Bray, T. (2001). *What is RDF?* Retrieved February 26, 2006, from www.xml.com/pub/a/2001/01/24/rdf.html?page=2

Bray, T., Paoli, J., Sperberg-McQueen, C. M., Maler, E., & Yergeau, F. (2000). *Extensible Markup Language (XML) 1.0* (Third Edition). Retrieved February 26, 2006, from www.w3.org/TR/REC-xml

Breebaart, M. (2004). *Using topic maps and XML to implement a closed-loop search service for the Dutch Tax and Customs Administration website.* Retrieved February 26, 2006, from www.idealliance.org/papers/dx_xmle04/papers/04-01-03/04-01-03.html

Brickley, D., & Guha, R. V. (2003). *RDF vocabulary description language 1.0: RDF schema.* Retrieved February 26, 2006, from www.w3.org/TR/rdf-schema

Brooks, T. A. (2002). The Semantic Web, universalist ambition and some lessons from librarianship. *Information Research*, *7*(4). Retrieved March 19, 2006, from http://informationr.net/ir/7-4/paper136.html

Buchanan, B. G., & Shortliffe, E. H. (1984). *Rule-based expert systems: The MYCIN experiments of the Stanford Heuristic Programming Project.* Reading, MA: Addison-Wesley.

Burton-Jones, A., Storey, V. C., Sugumaran, V., & Ahluwalia, P. (2005). A semiotic metrics suite for assessing the quality of ontologies. *Data and Knowledge Engineering*, *55*, 84–102.

Bush, V. (1945, July). As we may think. *Atlantic Monthly*, *176*(1), 101–108.

Cayzer, S. (2004). Semantic blogging and decentralized knowledge management. *Communications of the ACM*, *47*(12), 47–52.

Ceusters, W., Smith, B., Kumar, A., & Dhaen, C. (2004). Ontology-based error detection in SNOMED-CT. *Proceedings of the 11th World Congress on Medical Informatics*, 482–486.

Chisholm, R. (1996). *A realistic theory of categories: An essay on ontology.* Cambridge, UK: Cambridge University Press.

Clark, J., & Makoto, M. (2001). *RELAX NG specification.* Retrieved December 3, 2001, from www.oasis-open.org/committees/relax-ng/spec-20011203.html

Clark, P., & Porter, B. (2001). *KM–The Knowledge Machine: Users manual and situations manual.* Retrieved February 26, 2006, from www.cs.utexas.edu/users/mfkb/RKF/km.html

Copeland, J. (1997). CYC: A case study in ontological engineering. *Electronic Journal of Philosophy*, *5*(6). Retrieved March 19, 2006, from http://ejap.louisiana.edu/EJAP/1997.spring/copeland976.2.html

Cost, R. S., Finin, T., Joshi, A., Peng, Y., Nicholas, C., Soboroff, I., et al. (2002). ITTalks: A case study in the Semantic Web and DAML+OIL. *IEEE Intelligent Systems*, *17*(1), 40–47.

Cruse, D. A. (2006). *Meaning in language: An introduction to semantics and pragmatics.* Oxford, UK: Oxford University Press.

de Bruijn, J. (2003). *Using ontologies: Enabling knowledge sharing and reuse on the Semantic Web* (DERI Technical Report, DERI-2003-10-29). Innsbruck, Austria: Digital Enterprise Research Institute. Retrieved February 26, 2006, from www.deri.org/fileadmin/documents/DERI-TR-2003-10-29.pdf

Decker, S., van Harmelen, F., Broekstra, J., Erdmann, M., Fensel, D., Horrocks, I., et al. (2000). The Semantic Web: On the respective roles of XML and RDF. *IEEE Internet Computing, 4*(5), 63–74.

Delteil, A., Faron-Zucker, C., & Dieng, R. (2001). Extension of RDFS based on the CG formalisms. *Proceedings of the 9th International Conference on Conceptual Structures*, 275–289.

Dill, S., Eiron, N., Gibson, D., Gruhl, D., Guha, R., Jhingran, A., et al. (2003). SemTag and Seeker: Bootstrapping the Semantic Web via automated semantic annotation. *Proceedings of the 12th International World Wide Web Conference*. Retrieved February 26, 2006, from wwwconf.ecs.soton.ac.uk/archive/00000508/01/p831-dill.html

Ding, L., Finin, T., Joshi, A., Pan, R., Cost, R. S., Peng, Y., et al. (2004). Swoogle: A search and metadata engine for the Semantic Web. *Proceedings of the Thirteenth ACM Conference on Information and Knowledge Management*, 652–659.

Dos Santos, M., Dhaen, C., Fielding, M., & Ceusters, W. (2004). Philosophical scrutiny for run-time support of application ontology development. *International Conference on Formal Ontology and Information Systems*, 342–352.

Euzenat, J. (2001). Towards a Principled Approach to Semantic Interoperability. *Proceedings of the International Joint Conference on Artificial Intelligence Workshop on Ontologies and Information Sharing*, 19–25. Retrieved March 28, 2006, from http://ftp.informatik.rwth-aachen.de/Publications/CEUR-WS/Vol-47

Fallside, D. (2001). *XML schema part 0: Primer*. Retrieved February 26, 2006, from www.w3.org/TR/2001/REC-xmlschema-0-20010502

Fallside, D., & Walmsley, P. (2004). *XML schema part 0: Primer* (2nd ed.). Retrieved February 26, 2006, from www.w3.org/TR/xmlschema-0

Fensel, D., Angele, J., Decker, S., Erdmann, M., Schnurr, H., Studer, R., et al. (2000). Lessons learned from applying AI to the Web. *International Journal of Cooperative Information Systems, 9*(4), 361–382.

Fensel, D., Horrocks, I., van Harmelen, F., McGuinness, D., & Patel-Schneider, P. (2001). OIL: An ontology infrastructure for the Semantic Web. *IEEE Intelligent Systems, 16*(2), 38–45.

Frege, G. (1970). Begriffsschift: A formula language, modeled upon that of arithmetic, for pure thought. In J. Van Heijenoort (Comp.), *Frege and Gödel: Two fundamental texts in mathematical logic* (pp. 1–82). Cambridge, MA: Harvard University Press. (Original work published 1879.)

Garshol, L. M. (2005). *Living with topic maps and RDF*. Retrieved February 26, 2006, from www.idealliance.org/papers/dx_xmle03/papers/02-03-06/02-03-06.pdf

Genesereth, M., & Fikes, R. (1992). *KIF: Knowledge Interchange Format version 3.0 reference manual*. Stanford, CA: Stanford University, Knowledge Systems AI Laboratory.

Goble, C., & de Roure, D. (2002). The Grid: An application of the Semantic Web. *SIGMOD Record, 31*(4), 65–70.

Google can take the Web, yawn readers. (2005, May 18). *The Register*. Retrieved February 26, 2006, from www.theregister.co.uk/2005/05/18/google_domination_letters

Gruber, T. R. (1993). A translation approach to portable ontology specifications. *Knowledge Acquisition, 5*, 199–220.

Gruber, T. R. (1995). Toward principles for the design of ontologies used for knowledge-sharing. *International Journal of Human–Computer Studies, 43*, 907–928.

Guha, R., & McCool, R. (2003). TAP: A Semantic Web platform. *Journal of Network Computing*, *42*, 557–577.

Haarslev, V., & Moeller, R. (2003). Racer: A core inference engine for the Semantic Web. *Proceedings of the 2nd International Workshop on Evaluation of Ontology-based Tools*, 27–36. Retrieved February 26, 2006, from www.racer-systems.com/technology/contributions/2003/HaMo03e.pdf

Halevy, A. Y., Ives, Z. G., Mork, P., & Tatarinov, I. (2003). Piazza: Data-management infrastructure for Semantic Web applications. *Proceedings of the 12th International World Wide Web Conference*, 556–567.

Harré, R., & Krausz, M. (1996). *Varieties of relativism*. Oxford, UK: Blackwell.

Heery, R., & Wagner, H. (2002). A metadata registry for the Semantic Web. *D-Lib Magazine*, *8*(5). Retrieved March 19, 2006, from www.dlib.org/dlib/may02/wagner/05wagner.html

Heflin, J., & Hendler, J. (2000). Dynamic ontologies on the Web. *Proceedings of the Seventeenth National Conference on Artificial Intelligence*, 443–449.

Heflin, J., Hendler, J., & Luke, S. (2003). SHOE: A blueprint for the Semantic Web. In D. Fensel, J. Hendler, H. Lieberman, & W. Wahlster (Eds.), *Spinning the Semantic Web: Bringing the World Wide Web to its full potential* (pp. 29–63). Cambridge, MA: MIT Press.

Heflin, J., & Pan, Z. (2004). A model theoretic semantics for ontology versioning. *Proceedings of the Third International Semantic Web Conference*, 62–76.

Hendler, J. (2001). Agents and the Semantic Web. *IEEE Intelligent Systems*, *16*(2), 30–37.

Hendler, J., Berners-Lee, T., & Miller, E. (2002). Integrating applications on the Semantic Web. *Journal of the Institute of Electrical Engineers of Japan*, *122*, 676–680.

Horrocks, I., Patel-Schneider, P., & van Harmelen, F. (2002). Reviewing the design of DAML+OIL: An ontology language for the Semantic Web. *Proceedings of the 18th National Conference on Artificial Intelligence*, 792–797.

Horrocks, I., Patel-Schneider, P., & van Harmelen, F. (2003). From SHIQ and RDF to OWL: The making of a Web ontology language. *Journal of Web Semantics*, *1*, 7–26.

Horrocks, I., & Sattler, U. (2001). Ontology reasoning in the SHOQ(D) description logic. *Proceedings of the International Joint Conference on Artificial Intelligence Workshop on Ontologies and Information Sharing*, 199–204.

Horrocks, I., Sattler, U., & Tobies, S. (2000a). Practical reasoning for very expressive description logics. *Logic Journal of the IGPL*, *8*(3), 239–264.

Horrocks, I., Sattler, U., & Tobies, S. (2000b). Reasoning with individuals for the description logic SHIQ. *Proceedings of the 17th International Conference on Automated Deduction*, 482–496.

IEEE. Standard Upper Ontology Working Group. (2003). *Cumulative resolutions*. Retrieved March 30, 2006, from http://suo.ieee.org/SUO/resolutions.html

Kant, I. (1998). *Critique of pure reason* (P. Guyer & A. Wood, Trans.). Cambridge, UK: Cambridge University Press.

Kirk, R. (1999). *Relativism and reality: A contemporary introduction*. London: Routledge.

Klein, M., & Bernstein, A. (2004). Towards high-precision service retrieval. *IEEE Internet Computing*, *8*, 30–36.

Lacher, M., & Decker, S. (2001). On the integration of topic maps and RDF data. *Extreme Markup Languages 2001: Proceedings*. Retrieved February 26, 2006, from www.mulberry tech.com/Extreme/Proceedings/html/2001/Lacher01/EML2001Lacher01.html

Legg, C. (2005). The meaning of meaning-fallibilism. *Axiomathes, 15*, 293–318.

Lenat, D. B. (1995). Cyc: A large-scale investment in knowledge infrastructure. *Communications of the ACM, 38*(11), 32–59.

Lenat, D. B., & Feigenbaum, E. (1991). On the thresholds of knowledge. *Artificial Intelligence, 47*, 185–250.

Lenat, D. B., & Guha, R. V. (1990). *Building large knowledge-based systems: Representation and inference in the Cyc project.* Reading, MA: Addison Wesley.

Lenat, D. B., Guha, R. V., Pittman, K., Pratt, D., & Shepherd, M. (1990). Cyc: Toward programs with common sense. *Communications of the ACM, 33*(8), 30–49.

Lindsay, R. K., Buchanan, B. G., Feigenbaum, E. A., & Lederberg, J. (1980). *Applications of artificial intelligence for organic chemistry: The DENDRAL project.* New York: McGraw-Hill.

Lowe, E. J. (1997). Ontological categories and natural kinds. *Philosophical Papers, 26*, 29–46.

Lowe, E. J. (1998). *The possibility of metaphysics: Substance, identity, and time.* Oxford, UK: Oxford University Press.

Maedche, A., Motik, B., & Stojanovic, L. (2003). Managing multiple and distributed ontologies on the Semantic Web. *VLDB Journal, 12*, 286–302.

Martin P. (2003). Correction and extension of WordNet 1.7. *Proceedings of the 11th International Conference on Conceptual Structures*, 160–173.

Matuszek, C., Witbrock, M., Kahlert, R., Cabral, J., Schneider, D., Shah, P., et al. (2005). Searching for common sense: Populating Cyc from the Web. *Proceedings of the Twentieth National Conference on Artificial Intelligence.* Retrieved February 26, 2006, from www.cyc.com/doc/white_papers/AAAI051MatuszekC.pdf

McCarthy, J. (1995). What has AI in common with philosophy? *Proceedings of the 14th International Joint Conference on AI*, 2041-2044. Retrieved March 19, 2006, from www-formal.stanford.edu/jmc/aiphil/aiphil.html

McCool, R., Fikes, R., & Guha, R. (2003). *Semantic issues in Web-scale knowledge aggregation* (KSL 03-15). Stanford, CA: Stanford University, Knowledge Systems AI Laboratory. Retrieved February 26, 2006, from www-ksl.stanford.edu/KSL_Abstracts/KSL-03-15.html

McGuinness, D. (2003). Ontologies come of age. In D. Fensel, J. Hendler, H. Lieberman, & W. Wahlster (Eds.), *Spinning the Semantic Web: Bringing the World Wide Web to its full potential* (pp. 171–194). Cambridge, MA: MIT Press.

McGuinness, D., & van Harmelen, F. (2004). *OWL Web ontology language: Overview.* Retrieved February 26, 2006, from www.w3.org/TR/owl-features

McIlraith, S., Son, T. C., & Zeng, H. (2001). Semantic Web services. *IEEE Intelligent Systems, 16*, 46–53.

Melnik, S. (1999). *Bridging the gap between RDF and XML.* Retrieved February 26, 2006, from www-db.stanford.edu/~melnik/rdf/fusion.html

Minsky, M. (1975). A framework for representing knowledge. In P. Winston (Ed.), *The Psychology of Computer Vision* (pp. 211–277). New York: McGraw-Hill.

Niles, I., & Pease, A. (2001). Towards a standard upper ontology. *Proceedings of the 2nd International Conference on Formal Ontology in Information Systems.* Retrieved March 19, 2006, from http://projects.teknowledge.com/HPKB/Publications/FOIS.pdf

Niles, I., & Allan, T. (2004). The MILO: A general-purpose, mid-level ontology. *Proceedings of the International Conference on Information and Knowledge Engineering*, 5–19.

Noy, N., & Klein, M. (2004). Ontology evolution: Not the same as schema evolution. *Knowledge and Information Systems*, *6*, 428–440.

Noy, N., & Musen, M. (2004). Ontology versioning in an ontology-management framework. *IEEE Intelligent Systems*, *19*(4), 6–13.

Patel-Schneider, P. F., & Fensel, D. (2002). Layering the Semantic Web: Problems and directions. *Proceedings of the First International Semantic Web Conference*, 16–29.

Patel-Schneider, P. F., & Siméon, J. (2002). The yin/yang Web: XML syntax and RDF semantics. *Proceedings of the 11th international conference on World Wide Web*, 443–453.

Pease, A., & Niles, I. (2002). IEEE standard upper ontology: A progress report. *Knowledge Engineering Review*, *17*, 65–70.

Pease, A., Niles, I., & Li, J. (2002). The suggested upper merged ontology: A large ontology for the Semantic Web and its applications. *Working Notes of the AAAI-2002 Workshop on Ontologies and the Semantic Web*. Retrieved March 19, 2006, from http://home.earthlink. net/~adampease/professional/Pease.ps

Peirce, C. S. (1931–1958). *Collected papers* (C. Hartshorne, P. Weiss, & A. Burks, Eds.). Cambridge, MA: Harvard University Press.

Peirce, C. S. (1940). *Philosophy of Peirce: Selected writings* (J. Buchler, Ed.). London: Routledge and Kegan Paul.

Pepper, S., & Moore, G. (2001). *XML topic maps (XTM) 1.0*. Retrieved February 26, 2006, from www.topicmaps.org/xtm/1.0

Pepper, S., Vitali, F., Garshol, L., Gessa, N., & Presutti, V. (2005, March). *A survey of RDF/topic maps interoperability proposals*. Retrieved February 26, 2006, from www.w3.org/TR/2005/WD-rdftm-survey-20050329

Quillian, M. R. (1967). Word concepts: A theory and simulation of some basic semantic capabilities. *Behavioral Science*, *12*, 410–430.

Quine, W. V. (1953). On what there is. *From a logical point of view: 9 logico-philosophical essays* (pp. 1–19). Cambridge MA: Harvard University Press.

Ramachandran, D., Reagan, P., & Goolsbey, K. (2005). First-orderized ResearchCyc: Expressivity and efficiency in a common-sense ontology. *Papers from the AAAI Workshop on Contexts and Ontologies: Theory, Practice and Applications*. Retrieved March 19, 2006, from www.cyc.com/doc/white_papers/folification.pdf

Reed, S., & Lenat, D. (2002). Mapping ontologies into Cyc. *AAAI 2002 Conference Workshop on Ontologies for the Semantic Web*. Retrieved March 19, 2006, from www.cyc.com/doc/white_papers/mapping-ontologies-into-cyc_v31.pdf

Roesner, D., Kunze, M., & Kroetzsch, S. (2005). *Transforming and enriching documents for the Semantic Web*. Retrieved February 26, 2006, from http://arxiv.org/PS_cache/ cs/pdf/0501/0501096.pdf

Rorty, R. (1990). *Objectivity, relativism, and truth: Philosophical papers, Vol. 1*. Cambridge, UK: Cambridge University Press.

Rozenberg, G., & Salomaa, A. (1994). *Cornerstones of undecidability*. New York: Prentice Hall.

Rozenfeld, S. (2001). *Using the ISSN (International Serial Standard Number) as URN (Uniform Resource Names) within an ISSN-URN namespace* (RFC 3044). Retrieved February 26, 2006, from ftp://ftp.isi.edu/in-notes/rfc3044.txt

Schlick, M. (1936). Meaning and verification. *Philosophical Review, 45,* 339–369.

Schmidt-Schauss, M. (1989). Subsumption in KL-ONE is undecidable. *Proceedings of the First International Conference on Principles of Knowledge Representation and Reasoning,* 421–431.

Shah, U., Finin, T., Joshi, A., Cost, R. S., & Mayfield, J. (2002). Information retrieval on the Semantic Web. *Proceedings of the 11th International Conference on Information and Knowledge Management,* 461–468.

Shirky, C. (2003). *The Semantic Web, syllogism, and worldview.* Retrieved February 26, 2006, from www.shirky.com/writings/semantic_syllogism.html

Shirky, C. (2005). *Ontology is over-rated: Categories, links, and tags.* Retrieved February 26, 2006, from www.shirky.com/writings/ontology_overrated.html

Sicilia, M. A., Lytras, M., Rodriguez, E., & Garcia-Barriocanal, E. (2006). Integrating descriptions of knowledge management learning activities into large ontological structures: A case study. *Data and Knowledge Engineering, 57,* 111-121.

Sloman, A. (1995). A philosophical encounter: An interactive presentation of some of the key philosophical problems in AI and AI problems in philosophy. *Proceedings of the 14th International Joint Conference on AI.* Retrieved March 19, 2006, from http://www.cs.bham.ac.uk/research/cogaff/Sloman.ijcai95.pdf

Smith, B. (2003a). *BFO/MedO: Basic formal ontology and medical ontology. Draft 0.0006.* Retrieved February 26, 2006, from http://ontology.buffalo.edu/bfo/BFO.htm

Smith, B. (2003b). Ontology. In L. Floridi (Ed.), *Blackwell guide to the philosophy of computing and information* (pp. 155–166). Oxford, UK: Blackwell.

Smith, B., & Welty, C. (2001). Ontology: Towards a new synthesis. *Proceedings of the International Conference on Formal Ontology in Information Systems,* iii–x.

Smith, B., Williams, J., & Schulze-Kremer, S. (2003). The ontology of the gene ontology. *Proceedings of AMIA Symposium,* 609–613.

Smith, B. C. (1991). The owl and the electric encyclopedia. *Artificial Intelligence, 47,* 251–288.

Smith, R. (2004). Aristotle's logic. *Stanford encyclopedia of philosophy.* Stanford, CA: Stanford University. Retrieved February 26, 2006, from http://plato.stanford.edu/entries/aristotle-logic

Sowa, J. (1999). *Knowledge representation: Logical, philosophical, and computational foundations.* Pacific Grove, CA: Brooks Cole.

Sowa, J. (2000). Ontology, metadata, and semiotics. In B. Ganter & G. W. Mineau (Eds.), *Conceptual structures: Logical, linguistic, and computational issues* (Lecture Notes in Computer Science, 1867; pp. 55–81). Berlin: Springer.

Sowa, J. (2001). *Signs, processes, and language games.* Retrieved February 26, 2006, from www.jfsowa.com/pubs/signproc.htm

Sowa, J. (2004). *The challenge of knowledge soup.* Retrieved February 26, 2006, from www.jfsowa.com/pubs/challenge.pdf

Sowa, J., & Majumdar, A. (2003). Analogical reasoning. In A. de Moor, W. Lex, & B. Ganter (Eds.), *Conceptual structures for knowledge creation and communication* (Lecture Notes in Computer Science, 2746; pp. 16–36). Berlin: Springer.

Spackman, K., Campbell, K., & Côté, R. (1997). SNOMED RT: A reference terminology for health care. *Proceedings American Medical Informatics Association, Annual Fall Symposium,* 640–644.

Staab, S., Maedche, A., & Handschuh, S. (2001). An annotation framework for the Semantic Web. *Proceedings of the First Workshop on Multimedia Annotation*. Retrieved March 19, 2006, from www.aifb.uni-karlsruhe.de/WBS/ama/publications/mma01_staabetal.pdf

Swartz, A. (2002). *The Semantic Web in breadth*. Retrieved February 26, 2006, from http://logicerror.com/semantic-Web-long

Swick, R., & Thompson, H. (1999). *The Cambridge communiqué: W3C Note 7*. Retrieved February 26, 2006, from www.w3.org/TR/1999/NOTE-schema-arch-19991007

Vargas-Vera, M., Motta, E., Domingue, J., Lanzoni, M., Stutt, A., & Ciravegna, F. (2002). Ontology-driven semi-automatic and automatic support for semantic markup. *Proceedings of the 13th International Conference on Knowledge Engineering and Management*, 379–391.

Weinberger, D. (2005). Taxonomies to tags: From trees to piles of leaves. *Release 1.0, 23*(2), 1–33.

Weiss, P. (1958). *Modes of being*. Carbondale: Southern Illinois University Press.

Witbrock, M., Panton, K., Reed, S. L., Schneider, D., Aldag, B., Reimers, M., et al. (2004). Automated OWL annotation assisted by a large knowledge base. *Workshop Notes of the 2004 Workshop on Knowledge Markup and Semantic Annotation at the 3rd International Semantic Web Conference*, 71–80.

Zalta, E. (2005). Frege's logic, theorem and foundations for arithmetic. *Stanford Encyclopedia of Philosophy*. Stanford, CA: Stanford University. Retrieved February 26, 2006, from http://plato.stanford.edu/entries/frege-logic

CHAPTER 10

Personal Information Management

William Jones
University of Washington

Introduction

Personal Information Management (PIM) refers to both the practice and the study of the activities a person performs in order to acquire or create, store, organize, maintain, retrieve, use, and distribute the information needed to complete tasks (work-related or not) and fulfill various roles and responsibilities (for example, as parent, employee, friend, or community member). PIM places special emphasis on the organization and maintenance of personal information collections (PICs) in which information items, such as paper documents, electronic documents, e-mail messages, Web references, and handwritten notes, are stored for later use and repeated reuse.

One ideal of PIM is that we always have the right information in the right place, in the right form, and of sufficient completeness and quality to meet our current needs. Tools and technologies help us spend less time with labor-intensive and error-prone information management activities (such as filing). We then have more time to make creative, intelligent use of the information at hand in order to get things done.

This ideal is far from the reality for most people. A wide range of tools and technologies is now available for the management of personal information. But this diversity has become part of the problem, leading to *information fragmentation* (Jones, 2004). A person may maintain several separate, roughly comparable but inevitably inconsistent, organizational schemes for electronic documents, paper documents, e-mail messages, and Web references. The number of organizational schemes may increase if a person has several e-mail accounts, uses separate computers for home and work, makes use of a personal digital assistant (PDA) or a smart phone, or uses any of a bewildering array of special-purpose PIM tools.

Interest in the study of PIM has increased in recent years, spurred by the growing realization that new applications and new gadgets, for all the targeted help they provide, often do so by increasing the overall complexity of PIM. Microsoft's OneNote, for example, provides many useful features for note-taking but also requires the use of a separate tabbed system for the organization of notes that does not integrate with existing

453

schemata for files, e-mail messages, or Web references. Users reasonably complain that this is one organization too many (Boardman & Sasse, 2004; Boardman, Spence, & Sasse, 2003).

Interest in building a stronger community of PIM inquiry is further driven by an awareness that much of the research relating to the study of PIM is also fragmented by application and device. Many excellent studies have focused on uses of, and possible improvements to, e-mail (for example, Bälter, 2000; Bellotti, Ducheneaut, Howard, Neuwirth, & Smith, 2002; Bellotti, Ducheneaut, Howard, & Smith, 2003; Bellotti, Ducheneaut, Howard, Smith, & Grinter, 2005; Bellotti & Smith, 2000; Ducheneaut & Bellotti, 2001; Gwizdka, 2000, 2002a, 2002b; Mackay, 1988; Whittaker, 2005; Whittaker & Sidner, 1996; Wilson, 2002). Other studies have examined the use of the Web or specific features such as bookmarks or history information (for example, Abrams, Baecker, & Chignell, 1998; Byrne, John, Wehrle, & Crow, 1999; Catledge & Pitkow, 1995; Tauscher & Greenberg, 1997a, 1997b). Yet other studies have considered the organization and retrieval of documents in paper and electronic form (for example, Carroll, 1982; Case, 1986; Malone, 1983; Whittaker & Hirschberg, 2001).

Research that focuses on people and what they want or need to be able to do with their information also comes under the PIM umbrella. The completion of a task depends critically on certain information: For example, returning a telephone call may require knowing a person's first name and telephone number. Thus, the study of how people manage various tasks in their lives is relevant to PIM (Bellotti, Dalal, Good, Flynn, Bobrow, & Ducheneaut, 2004; Bellotti et al., 2003; Bellotti et al., 2005; Czerwinski, Horvitz, & Wilhite, 2004; Gwizdka, 2002a; Matthews, Czerwinski, Robertson, & Tan, 2006; Whittaker, 2005; Williamson & Bronte-Stewart, 1996). Research into digital memories (Gemmell, Bell, Lueder, Drucker, & Wong, 2002) and the "record everything" and "compute anywhere" possibilities enabled by advances in hardware are also germane (Dempski, 1999; Lucas, 2000).

The past few years have seen a revival of interest in PIM as an area of serious inquiry that draws upon the best work from a range of disciplines including cognitive psychology, human–computer interaction, database management, artificial intelligence, information and knowledge management, information retrieval, and information science.[1]

Renewed interest in PIM is double-edged. On one side, the pace of improvements in various PIM-relevant technologies gives us reason to believe that earlier visions of PIM may actually be realized in the near future. Digital storage is cheap and plentiful. Why not keep a record of everything we have encountered? (See Czerwinski, Gage, Gemmell, Marshall, Pérez-Quiñones, Skeels, et al., 2006 for a recent review.) Digital storage can hold not only conventional kinds of information but also pictures, photographs, music—even films and full-motion video. Better search support can make it easy to pinpoint the information we need. The ubiquity of computing and the miniaturization of computing devices can make it possible to take our information with us wherever we go and stay connected to a still larger world of information. Improvements in technologies of information input and output (e.g., better voice recognition, voice synthesis, integrated displays of information) can free us from the mouse, keyboard, and monitor of a conventional computer.

However, renewed interest in PIM is also spurred by the awareness that developments in technology and tools, for all their promise, invariably create new problems and sometimes exacerbate old ones, too. Information that once existed only in paper form is now scattered in multiple versions in both paper and digital copies. Digital information is further scattered into "information islands," each supported by a separate application or device. This other side to renewed interest in PIM recognizes that new tools and applications—for all the help they provide—can further complicate the challenge of information management.

The Problems of PIM

In the real world, we do not always find the right information in time to meet our current needs. The necessary information may never be found or it may arrive too late to be useful. Information may also enter our lives too soon and then be misplaced or forgotten entirely before opportunities for its application arrive.

Information is not always in the right place: The information we need may be at home when we are at work or vice versa. It may be on the wrong computer, PDA, smart phone, or other device. Information may be "here" but locked away in an application or a different format so that the hassles of extraction outweigh the benefits of its use. We may forget to use information even when (or sometimes because) we have taken pains to keep it at hand. We may fail to make effective use of information even when it is directly in view.

These are failures of PIM. Some of these may be memorable. Many of us, for example, can remember the frustration of failing to find an item of information—for example, a paper document, a digital document, an e-mail message—that we know is "there somewhere." Over the course of an already busy day, we may spend precious minutes, sometimes hours, looking for lost information. Other failures of PIM may go unnoticed as part of background *information friction* associated with getting things done. In his highly influential article, "Man–Computer Symbiosis," Licklider (1960, p. 4) made the following observations about his own work day:

> About 85 per cent of my "thinking" time was spent getting into a position to think, to make a decision, to learn something I needed to know. ... My choices of what to attempt and what not to attempt were determined to an embarrassingly

great extent by considerations of clerical feasibility, not intellectual capability.

Many of us might reach similar conclusions concerning our own interactions with information. A seemingly simple e-mail request, for example, can often cascade into a time-consuming, error-prone chore as we seek to bring together, in coherent, consistent form, information that lies scattered, often in multiple versions, in various collections of paper documents, electronic documents, e-mail messages, Web references, and so on. Can you give a presentation at a meeting next month? That depends. ... What did you say in previous e-mail messages? When is your child's soccer match? Better check the paper flyer with scheduled games. Does the meeting conflict with an upcoming conference? Better check the conference Web site to get dates and program information. What have you already scheduled in your calendar? And so on. In their observations of people processing e-mail, Belloti et al. (2005) have noted instances in which a single e-mail message initiates a task involving several different software applications and lasting an hour or more.

The Potential of PIM

Information is a means to an end. Not always, not for everyone, but often. We manage information in order to have it when we need it—to complete a task, for example. Information is not an inherently precious resource. In truth, we usually have far too much of it. Even a document we have spent days or weeks writing is typically available in multiple locations (and, sometimes confusingly, in multiple versions). We manage information because information is the most visible, "tangible" way to manage other resources that *are* precious. Herbert Simon (1971, p. 40) elegantly expressed this point with respect to resource optimization:

> What information consumes is rather obvious: it consumes the attention of its recipients. Hence, a wealth of information creates a poverty of attention and a need to allocate that attention efficiently among the overabundance of information sources that might consume it.

This quotation still rings true even if we replace "attention" with "time," "energy," or "well-being." Certainly the nagging presence of papers representing unpaid bills, unanswered letters, or unfiled documents can distract, enervate, and demoralize. We cannot "see" our well-being, our attention, our energy, or even our time—except through informational devices such as a calendar. But we can see—and manage—our paper documents, our e-documents, our e-mail messages, and other forms of information. It is through these personal information items that we seek to manage the precious resources of our lives.

The payoffs for advances in PIM are large and varied:

- For each of us as individuals, better PIM allows us to make better use of our precious resources (time, money, energy, attention) and thus, ultimately, improves the quality of our lives.

- Within organizations, better PIM means better employee productivity and teamwork in the near term. Over time, PIM is key to the management and leveraging of employee expertise.

Advances in PIM may also translate into:

- Improvements in information literacy programs (Eisenberg, Lowe, & Spitzer, 2004). Progress in PIM is made not only with new tools and technologies but also with new teachable techniques of information management.

- Better support for our aging workforce and population in order to increase the chances that our mental lifespan matches our physical lifespan.

The payoffs for better PIM may be especially significant in domains such as intelligence analysis or medical informatics. Better PIM may help doctors and nurses to balance a large and varied caseload. Potentially of even greater impact may be PIM support for individuals undergoing long-term or sustained treatments for chronic or acute health conditions (Pratt, Unruh, Civan, & Skeels, 2006).

Objectives, Scope, and Structure for this Chapter

The remainder of this chapter covers the following:

- *Influences on PIM* reviews key historical influences on the study of PIM and also considers the considerable synergistic overlap with existing disciplines including cognitive science, information science, and human–computer interaction.

- *Analysis of PIM* introduces key concepts of PIM and its conceptual framework, which, in turn, provides the organizational structure of the subsequent review of PIM-related research.

- *Research to Understand How People Do PIM* reviews research squarely focused on PIM and also considers a sampling from a much larger collection of PIM-related research.

- *Methodologies of PIM Inquiry* discusses some of the special challenges associated with the conduct of PIM fieldwork and with the evaluation of PIM tools and techniques.

- *Approaches to PIM Integration* includes a sampling of computer-based, tool-building efforts that show special promise in addressing PIM challenges. Some discussion is also given to techniques and teachable strategies of PIM.

The chapter concludes with a return to a key problem of PIM: information fragmentation. Research relating to PIM is similarly fragmented. The progress in PIM depends upon an integrated approach involving several fields of inquiry. This progress, in turn, may promote important integrations in the practice of PIM.

Influences on PIM

Broadly defined, PIM includes the management of information going into our own memories as well as the management of external information. As such, an interest in PIM-related matters is evidenced in the study of mnemonic techniques going back to ancient times (see, for example, Yates, 1966).

Although definitions of PIM vary (see the section "Analysis of PIM"), they generally include, as a central component, the management of external forms of information. The difficulties of managing paper-based information have long been recognized and tools have been developed over time to address these challenges. Yates (1989) notes, for example, that the vertical filing cabinet that is now such a standard (if increasingly old-fashioned) feature of office, home, and workplace was first commercially available in 1893.

The modern dialogue on PIM probably began with Vannevar Bush's inspirational article "As We May Think" (Bush, 1945), in which he presented his vision of a memex device that would greatly increase a person's ability to record, retrieve, and interrelate information (see the chapter by Houston and Harmon in the present volume). Licklider (1960, 1965), Engelbart (1963), and Nelson (1982) each advanced the notion that the computer could be used to extend the human ability to process information and, even, to enhance the human intellect. The phrase "Personal Information Management" was apparently first used in the 1980s (Lansdale, 1988) in the midst of general excitement over the potential of the personal computer to augment the human ability to process information (Goldstein, 1980; Johnson, Roberts, Verplank, Smith, Irby, Beard, et al., 1989; Jones, 1986). The 1980s also saw the advent of so-called "PIM tools" that provided limited support for the management of appointments and scheduling, to-do lists, telephone numbers, and addresses.

A community dedicated to the study and improvement of human–computer interaction (HCI) also emerged in the 1980s (Card, Moran, & Newell, 1983; Norman, 1988) and much of the applied research reviewed in this chapter was initiated by practitioners in this field. However, much HCI research has remained focused on specific forms of information (e.g., e-mail messages, Web pages, digital photographs), specific devices to aid interaction, and, increasingly, group and organizational issues. The study of PIM focuses primarily on the individual but also broadens to include key interactions with information over time and across tools. PIM considers our personal use of information in all of its various forms—including paper. Although today it is difficult to imagine a practice of PIM that does not involve computers, *information* in all its forms is the primary focus.

In recent years, there has been discussion of human–information interaction (HII) by way of contrast to HCI (Fidel & Pejtersen, 2004; Gershon, 1995; Lucas, 2000; Pirolli, in press). Interest in HII is due in part to a realization that our interactions with information are more central to our lives than are our interactions with computers. This realization is reinforced by developments in ubiquitous computing. Success in computing and, perhaps paradoxically, in HCI, may mean that the computer will come to "disappear" (Streitz & Nixon, 2005) into the background of our daily lives, much as electricity currently does. With "transparent interfaces," we are left with information. Much in HII remains to be defined, but when this happens, PIM will likely be an important element.

The study of human cognition also informs, and is informed by, PIM. The common ground shared by PIM and cognitive science is considerable and largely unexplored. Of relevance are not only the classic findings of cognitive psychology (e.g., Neisser, 1967) but also more recent work on situated cognition, distributed cognition, and social cognition (e.g., Fiske & Taylor, 1991; Hutchins, 1994; Suchman, 1987). Also very relevant is the study of affordances provided by the environment and by the "everyday" (and often overlooked) objects of a person's environment (Gibson, 1977, 1979; Norman, 1988, 1990, 1993).

Synergies with the field of information science and the study of human information behavior are largely unrealized. For example, the work by Erdelez and Rioux (2000) on information encountering has clear relevance to an essential decision of PIM—whether and how to keep new information. To take another example, Dervin's (1992, 1999) work on sense-making certainly relates to a person's efforts to maintain and organize personal information collections (PICs) over time. The large subfield of information seeking, although focused on the retrieval of public information from external sources (e.g., a conventional library or the Web), certainly relates to the PIM activities of finding and refinding (see Pettigrew, Fidel, & Bruce, 2001).

The study of information and knowledge management in organizations also has relevance to the study of PIM (e.g., Garvin, 2000; Selamat & Choudrie, 2004; Taylor, 2004; Thompson, Levine, & Messick, 1999). Issues seen first at an organizational level often migrate to the PIM domain. The merits of various schemes of classification or the use of controlled vocabularies, for example, have long been topics of discussion at the organizational level (Fonseca & Martin, 2004; Rowley, 1994). But these topics may find their way into the realm of PIM as the amounts of personally held digital information continue to increase. This migration has already happened with regard to privacy, protection, and security (e.g., Karat, Brodie, & Karat, 2006).

Several other fields, including information retrieval, database management, and artificial intelligence, have potential relevance to the development of supporting tools for PIM. A proper review of PIM and its overlap with any one of the fields just mentioned would require a chapter in its own right. This review focuses on core activities of PIM, the challenges people face in the completion of these activities, and, in a much more limited way, approaches to the support of these activities.

Analysis of PIM

A deeper understanding of what PIM is begins with definitions and core concepts. This section sets out a conceptual framework that helps to connect several key concepts of PIM and compares PIM to related fields of inquiry.

Information and the Information Item

The question of what information "is" has been a topic of repeated discussion, excellent overviews of which have been provided by Cornelius (2002) and Capurro and Hjørland (2003) in recent volumes of the *Annual Review of Information Science and Technology (ARIST)*.

This chapter focuses on the capacity of information to effect change in our lives and in the lives of others. The information we receive influences our actions and our choices. For example, we decide which of several hotels to book based on the information we are able to gather concerning price, location, availability, and so on. Incoming information helps us to monitor the state of our world. Did the hotel send a confirmation? What about directions?

We also send information to effect change. We send information in the clothes we choose to wear, in the car we choose to drive, and in the way we choose to act. We send information—often more than we intend—with every sentence we speak or write. It is with respect to the information we send, that it is most clearly necessary to go beyond Shannon's (1948) original notion of information as a collaborative exchange between sender and recipient. As Machiavelli might have said, we send information to serve our own purposes. Certainly one of these purposes is to be helpful and inform others. But we also send information to persuade, convince, impress, and, sometimes, to deceive.

An *information item* is a packaging of information. Examples of information items include:

1. Paper documents

2. Electronic documents and other files

3. E-mail messages

4. Web pages

5. References (e.g., shortcuts, aliases) to any of the above

Items encapsulate information in a persistent form that can be created, stored, moved, given a name and other properties, copied, distributed, deleted, transformed, and so forth.

Our interactions with paper-based information items are supported by, among other things, the desktop, paper clips, staplers, and filing cabinets. Our interactions with digital information items depend upon the support of various computer-based tools and applications such as an e-mail application, a file manager, and a Web browser. The "size" of current information items is determined in part by these applications. There are certainly situations in which some of us might like information items to be packaged in smaller units. A writer, for example, might like to treat paragraphs or even individual sentences as information items to be reaccessed and combined in new ways (e.g., Johnson, 2005).

An information item has an associated *information form*, which is determined by the tools and applications that are used to name, move, copy, delete, or otherwise organize or assign properties to an item. The most common forms we consider in this chapter are paper documents, e-documents and other files, e-mail messages, and Web bookmarks.

Consider how much of our interaction with the world is now mediated by information items. We consult the newspaper or, increasingly, a Web page to read the headlines of the day and to find out the weather (perhaps before we even bother to look outside). We learn of meetings via e-mail messages and receive the documents for these meetings via e-mail as well.

As regards sending information items, we fill out Web-based forms; we send e-mail messages; we create and send out reports in paper and digital form; we create personal and professional Web sites. These and other information items serve, in a real sense, as proxies. We project ourselves and our desires across time and space in ways that would never have occurred to our forebears.

Another point concerning information items, in contrast to what we hear or see in the physical world, is that we can often defer processing until a later point in time: We can accumulate large numbers of information items for a "rainy day." This is quite different from the scenarios of situation awareness where acceptable delays in processing information are measured in seconds (Durso & Gronlund, 1999).

Personal Information

The term *personal information* has several senses:

1. The information people keep for their own personal use.

2. Information about a person kept by and under the control of others. Doctors and health maintenance organizations, for example, maintain health information about their patients.

3. Information experienced by a person but outside his or her control. The book a person browses (but puts back) in a traditional

library or the pages a person views on the Web are examples of this kind of personal (or personally experienced) information.

This chapter is concerned primarily with the first sense of personal information.

A Personal Space of Information

A personal space of information (PSI) includes all the information items that are, at least nominally if not exclusively, under an individual's control. A PSI contains a person's books and paper documents, e-mail messages (on various accounts), e-documents, and other files (on various computers). A PSI can contain references to Web pages as well as include applications, tools (such as a desktop search facility), and constructs (e.g., associated properties, folders, "piles" in various forms) that support the acquisition, storage, retrieval, and use of the information.

There are several other things to note about a PSI:

- Although people have some sense of control over the items in their PSIs, this is partly illusory. For example, once an e-mail message has been deleted, it will no longer appear in one's inbox; however, the message is very likely still in existence (as some figures in the public eye have learned to their chagrin).

- A PSI does not include the Web pages we have visited but does include copies we make (or that are cached on our computers) and the bookmarks we create to reference these pages.

- A person has only one PSI.

Personal Information Collections

Several researchers have discussed the importance of collections in managing personal information. Karger and Quan (2004) define a collection quite broadly, taking it to comprise a variety of objects ranging from menus, to portals, to public taxonomies. Boardman (2004, p. 15) understands a collection of personal information to be "a self-contained set of items. Typically the members of a collection share a particular technological format and are accessed through a particular application."

The characteristic features of a personal information collection (PIC) will be listed here but no attempt will be made to provide a formal definition. A PIC might best be characterized as a personally managed subset of a PSI. PICs are "islands" in our PSIs where we have made some conscious effort to control both the information that goes in and the manner in which it is organized. PICs can vary greatly with respect to the number, form, and content coherence of their items. Examples of PICs include:

- The papers in a well-ordered office and their organization, including the layout of piles on a desktop and the folders inside filing cabinets.

- The papers in a specific filing cabinet and their organizing folders (when perhaps the office as a whole is a mess).

- Project-related information items that are initially "dumped" into a folder on a notebook computer and then organized over time.

- A carefully maintained collection of bookmarks to useful reference sites on the Web.

- An EndNote database of article references.[2]

A PIC includes not only a set of information items but also their organizing representations, including spatial layout, properties, and containing folders. The items in a PIC will often take the same form—all will be e-mail messages, for example, or all files. But this is not a necessary feature of a PIC. Later on, we review research aimed at supporting an integrative organization of information items, regardless of form. Such efforts aim at building a "form-neutral" layer of support for the management of information items.

The concept of a PIC will prove useful as we review research on the ways people approach the organization of their information. Statements such as "I've got to get my ___ organized!" often refer to a PIC. The organization of "everything" in one's PSI is a daunting, perhaps impossible, task. But we can imagine organizing our Web bookmarks, our e-mail inbox, or our laptop filing system (but probably only selected areas thereof).

Definitions of PIM

PIM is easy to describe and discuss, for we all do it and we all have had first-hand experiences with its challenges. But it is much harder to define.

Lansdale (1988, p. 55) defined PIM as "the methods and procedures by which we handle, categorize and retrieve information on a day-to-day basis," whereas Bellotti et al. (2002, p. 182) understood it to be "the ordering of information through categorization, placement, or embellishment in a manner that makes it easier to retrieve when it is needed." Barreau (1995, p. 327) characterized PIM as a "system developed by or created for an individual for personal use in a work environment." Such a system includes "a person's methods and rules for acquiring the information, ... the mechanisms for organizing and storing the information, the rules and procedures for maintaining the system, the mechanisms for retrieval and procedures for producing various outputs" (p. 327). Recently, Boardman (2004, p. 13) noted that "many definitions of PIM draw from a traditional information management perspective—that information is stored so that it can be retrieved at a later date." In keeping with this observation, and guided by Barreau's definition, we might analyze PIM with respect to our interactions with a large and amorphous PSI. From the perspective of such a store, the essential operations are input, storage (including organization), and output.

In rough equivalence to the input-storage-output model of actions associated with a PSI, the framework used in this chapter to help organize its discussion of PIM-related research will provide the following grouping of essential PIM activities:[3]

- *Finding/refinding activities* move from need to information and affect the output of information from a PSI.

- *Keeping activities* move from information to need and affect the input of information into a PSI.

- *Meta-level activities* focus on the PSI itself and on the management and organization of PICs within it. Efforts to "get organized" in a physical office, for example, constitute one kind of meta-level activity.

The remainder of this review is guided by a framework that derives from a basic assumption—namely, that *PIM activities help to establish, use, and maintain a mapping between information and need*. This simple statement can be expanded and the relationship between the various PIM activities visualized by reference to the diagram in Figure 10.1. Needs, as depicted in the leftmost column, can be expressed in several ways. The need may, more or less, originate internally—that is, within a person as she recalls, for example, that she needs to make plane reservations for an upcoming trip. Or it may be derived from an external source—for example, a question from a colleague in the hallway or a manager's request. Needs are evoked by an information item such as an e-mail message or a Web-based form.

Information, as depicted in the rightmost column, is also expressed in various ways—for example, as aural comments from a friend, as a billboard seen on the way to work, or via any number of information items including documents, e-mail messages, Web pages, and hand-written notes.

To make a connection between need and information is to create a mapping. Only small portions of the mapping have observable external representations. Much of the mapping has only a hypothesized existence in the memories of an individual: Indeed, large portions thereof are potential and not realized in any form, external or internal. A sort function or a search facility, for example, has the potential to guide one from a need to desired information.

But parts of the mapping can be observed and manipulated. The folders of a filing system (whether for paper documents, electronic documents, e-mail messages, or Web references); the layout of a desktop (physical or virtual); and the choice of names, keywords, and other

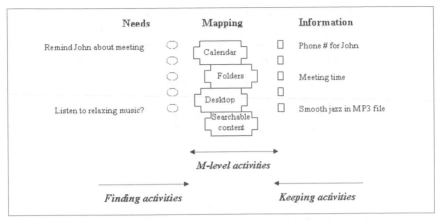

Figure 10.1   PIM activities viewed as an effort to establish, use, and maintain a
mapping between needs and information.

properties for information items all form parts of an observable fabric
helping to knit need to information.

Research to Understand How People Do PIM

Finding: From Need to Information

A person has a need and finds information in order to meet it. Needs
can be large and amorphous—the need for information to complete a
review of a research area, for example—or small and simple—the need
for a telephone number. Many needs correspond to tasks (e.g., "get
schedules and make airplane reservations"). But other needs may not fit
tasks except by the broadest definition (e.g., "see that photograph of our
vacation again").

Wilson's (2000, p. 49) definition for *information seeking* applies
equally well to *information finding*, or simply *finding* as used in this
chapter:

> the purposive seeking for information as a consequence of a
> need to satisfy some goal. In the course of seeking, the indi-
> vidual may interact with manual information systems (such
> as a newspaper or a library), or with computer-based systems
> (such as the World Wide Web).

In their efforts to meet a need, people seek. They search, sort, and
browse; they scan through a results list or the listing of a folder's contents in an effort to recognize information items that relate to a need.
These activities are all examples of finding activities. Finding includes
both acts of new finding, where there is no previous memory of the

needed information, and acts of refinding. The information found can be personal, residing in a PSI, or public, originating outside of the PSI.

There are several reasons for preferring the term "information finding," or "finding," to that of "information seeking" in relation to PIM:

- Although Wilson's definition of information seeking is inclusive, research on information research has tended to focus primarily on efforts to find information outside a PSI—from a "brick and mortar" library, for example, or from the Web (Pettigrew et al., 2001).

- "Finding" more directly expresses the goal of a finding activity: the location of items meeting a current need.

- People find, or try to find, not only information items but also physical items such as their car keys, cell phones, or television remote controls.

- The act of "finding" is complementary to that of "keeping." "Finders, keepers," as the saying goes: What we find, we can (try to) keep. With both physical items and information items, there is often a trade-off between investing more time now to keep or more time later to find. For example, time can be invested now to carefully pair the socks in a pile of freshly washed laundry—an act of keeping. Or, instead, more time can be spent later to find a matching pair of socks within the pile in order to meet the current need (e.g., nicer black socks for a business meeting).

This chapter focuses on *refinding private information*—that is, situations in which people are attempting to return to information they believe is in their PSI. But other variations of information finding are also PIM activities as discussed briefly here.

Finding and Refinding Public Information

There is an impressive body of work on information seeking and information retrieval that applies especially to finding public information (see, for example, Marchionini, 1995; Marchionini & Komlodi, 1998; Pettigrew et al., 2001; Rouse & Rouse, 1984); however, a comprehensive review of this literature is beyond the scope of this chapter.

There is a strong personal component in efforts to find new information from a public store such as the Web. For example, our efforts to find information may be directed by an outline or a to-do list that we maintain in our PSI. And information inside the PSI can be used to support a more targeted, personalized search of the Web (e.g., Teevan, Dumais, & Horvitz, 2005).

An online search to meet a need for information is often a sequence of interactions rather than a single transaction. Bates (1989) has presented a *berrypicking* model of online searching according to which needed information is gathered in bits and pieces in the course of a series of steps where the user's expression of need, as reflected in the current query, evolves. Teevan, Alvarado, Ackerman, and Karger (2004) note that users often favor a stepwise *orienteering* approach even in cases where the user knows where the information is and could presumably access it directly using a well-formed query. The stepwise orienteering approach may preserve a greater sense of control and context over the search process and may also lessen the cognitive burden associated with query articulation. The examples of berrypicking and orienteering suggest that it might be useful to preserve the search state within the PSI.

Finding (Discovery of) Personal Information

Items may enter a PSI automatically (e.g., via the inbox, automated downloads, Web cookies, the installation of new software). People may have no memory or awareness of the existence of these items. If they are ever retrieved, it is through an act of finding, not refinding. Memories of a previous encounter with an information item may also fade so that its retrieval is more properly regarded as an act of finding rather than refinding. Personal stores tend to become enormous over time: Some items may be decades old. As the use of integrative desktop search facilities increases, people may be surprised by the information they already "have."

Refinding Personal Information

The remainder of this section focuses on the refinding of information in the PSI. Clearly, the ability to refind information in a PSI is essential if people are to make effective use of their personal information. If an information item is in the PSI and people remember that the information item is there, it is often because of some earlier, explicit act of keeping. Failure to find information is frustrating in general but would appear to be especially so for information that we know "is in there somewhere."

Lansdale (1988) has described a two-step process involving an interplay between recall and recognition. Recall may constitute typing in a search string or even an exact address for the desired information. In other cases, it is less precise. A person may recall in which pile a paper document lies but not its exact location within that pile. Or one may have a rough idea when an e-mail message was sent or an electronic document last modified. In a second step, then, information items or a representation of these, as delimited by the recall step, are scanned and, if one is successful, the desired item is recognized and retrieved. The steps of recall and recognition can iterate to narrow progressively the search for the desired information—as happens, for example, when we move through a folder hierarchy to a desired file or e-mail message or when we navigate through a Web site to a desired page. The two steps of recall and recognition can be viewed as a dialogue between people and their information environments.

But a successful outcome in a finding effort depends upon completion of another step preceding recall: A person must remember to look. One may know exactly where an item is and still forget to look for it in the first place. It is also useful to consider a final "repeat?" step, although this is essentially a variation of remembering to look. Meeting an information need often means assembling or reassembling a collection of information items relating to the task at hand. The finding activity must then be repeated until the complete set of items is collected.

Failure to collect a complete set of information can sometimes mean failure for the entire finding episode. For example, a person may collect three of four items needed in order to decide whether to accept a dinner invitation next week. She consults a paper flyer, an events Web site, and her online calendar and, then, seeing no conflicts, accepts. Unfortunately, she did not think to look at a fourth item—a previously sent e-mail in which she agreed to host a meeting of her book club that same evening.

Finding events—especially when directed to previously experienced personal information—can, therefore, be viewed as a four-step process with a possibility of failure at each step:

1. Remembering to look.

2. Recalling information about the information that can help to narrow the subsequent scan.

3. Recognizing the desired item(s).

4. Repeating as needed in order to "re-collect" the set of items required to meet the current need.

Remembering (To Look)

Many opportunities to refind and reuse information are missed simply because people forget to look. This failure occurs across information forms. In a study by Whittaker and Sidner (1996), for example, participants reported that they forgot to look inside to-do folders containing actionable e-mail messages. Because of mistrust in their ability to remember to look, people elected to leave actionable e-mail messages within an already overloaded inbox. Inboxes were often further loaded with copies of outgoing e-mail messages that might otherwise have been forgotten in a "sent mail" folder.

Web information is also forgotten. In one study of Web use, for example, participants often complained that, while engaged in non-targeted activities such as "spring cleaning," they encountered bookmarks that would have been very useful for a project whose time had now passed (Jones, Dumais, & Bruce, 2002). Another study reported that, when participants were cued to return to a Web page for which they had a Web bookmark, this bookmark was used in less than 50 percent of the trials

(Bruce, Jones, & Dumais, 2004). Marshall and Bly (2005) have observed a similar failure to look for paper information (newspaper clippings). Many of us have had the experience of writing a document and then later discovering a similar document that we had previously authored.

If the old adage "out of sight, out of mind" is frequently true, then one way to aid memory is to keep items in view. Reminding is an important function, for example, of paper piles in an office (Malone, 1983). E-mail messages in an inbox provide a similar function, at least until the messages scroll out of view (Whittaker & Sidner, 1996). Barreau and Nardi (1995) have observed that users often placed a file on their computer desktop in order to be reminded of its existence and of associated tasks to be completed.

Visibility helps. But a person must still be prepared to look. Piles on a physical desktop can, over time, recede into a background that receives scant attention. Likewise, as online advertisers surely know, people can learn to ignore portions of a computer's display. Also, the ability to manage items and keep them in view—whether on a computer screen or on the surfaces of a physical office—degrades, sometimes precipitously, as the number of items increases (see, for example, Jones & Dumais, 1986).

Attempts to compensate for the limitations of visible reminders can introduce other problems. People who adopt a strategy of repeatedly checking their e-mail inboxes in order to respond to messages before these scroll out of view (and out of mind) may end up "living" in their e-mail application with little time or attention left to accomplish work requiring sustained levels of concentration. People who immediately click through to interesting Web pages, for fear of forgetting to look at these later (even if they bookmark them) may let their Web use degenerate into an incoherent sequence of page views scattered across a wide range of topics with little to show for the experience.

A computer-based device might remind people of potentially useful information in many ways (Herrmann, Brubaker, Yoder, Sheets, & Tio, 1999) including, for example, the spontaneous execution of searches that factor in words and other elements of the current context (Cutrell, Dumais, & Teevan, 2006). However, such reminding devices, like visible space, compete for a very precious and fixed resource—a person's attention—and so must walk a fine line to avoid the extremes of either being annoying or being ignored.

Why is reminding so important in the first place? Why do people forget? Part of the answer goes back to a key problem of PIM: information fragmentation. Information items are scattered in different forms across various organizational devices. Support for grouping and interrelating items is not well developed. The folder, for example, has changed little in its basic function since its introduction, as part of the desktop metaphor, over 20 years ago. Support for grouping, interrelating, and, more generally, creating external representations (e.g., of tasks or projects) that might complement our internal representations is a topic of further discussion in both the keeping and meta-level sections of this chapter.

Recall and Recognition

Recall and recognition constitute two parts of a dialogue between a person and his information world. For example, somebody types a search word (recall) and then scans through a list of results (recognition). He clicks on a folder (recall) and then scans through a listing representing the items (e.g., e-mail messages, files, Web references) within the folder. He sorts inbox e-mail messages by sender (recall) and then scans through messages from "Sally" (recognition).

Even as desktop search utilities improve, a preference persists for returning to information through what is known as location-based finding, orienteering, or browsing (Barreau & Nardi, 1995; Marchionini, 1995; O'Day & Jeffries, 1993; Teevan, 2003). Habits change slowly and desktop search support continues to improve. For example, in the author's informal survey of persons who have installed and use an integrative desktop search facility (i.e., one able to search quickly across files, e-mail messages, recently visited Web sites), people still expressed a preference for browsing their desktops, "My Documents," or through their folders. Over 90 percent of the respondents indicated that they used their search facility only as a "last resort" after other methods had failed.

And yet, desktop search is becoming increasingly integrative and ever closer to an ideal in which anything that can be remembered about an information item or the circumstances surrounding encounters with it (e.g., time of last use or nearby "landmark" events) can be used to help find this item (Cutrell et al., 2006; Lansdale, 1988, 1991; Lansdale & Edmonds, 1992). It is possible, then, that people may gradually shift to a greater reliance on search.

But the reasons underlying the preference for browsing may be more basic. In response to a cue (such as an expression of information need) people are usually, but not always, better at recognizing an item from a set of alternatives than at recalling it (Tulving & Thomson, 1973). Browsing reduces and distributes the amount that must be recalled and relies more on recognition (Lansdale, 1988). Teevan et al. (2004) discuss additional considerations favoring what they term "orienteering," such as cognitive ease (smaller steps, less burden on working memory), sense of location (and a greater sense of control), and a richer context in which to recognize and understand results. Basic research underlines the importance of context in recognition (Tulving, 1983; Tulving & Thomson, 1973).

If one assumes that people remember to look, how difficult is it to return to an information item such as an e-document, e-mail message, or Web page that has been previously seen? In a study on delayed cued recall by Bruce et al. (2004), participants were asked to return to Web pages they had last visited up to six months prior by whatever means they chose. Participants did so quickly (retrieval times were under a minute on average) and with success rates approaching 100 percent. The small number of failures and time-out delays (less than five minutes) that did occur seemed primarily due to information fragmentation. For example, one participant looked for a Web reference first in her "Favorites," then in selected e-mail folders, then in folders under "My Documents" before finally locating the Web reference inside a presentation she had saved to a network drive.

When people actually name an information item, such as a file, the research suggests that recognition accuracy is quite high (Carroll, 1982). High rates of recognition relate to a *generation effect* that has been identified in research in human cognition (Slamecka & Graf, 1978; see also Jones & Landauer, 1985). Thinking of a name for an item causes people to elaborate on connections between the name and the item. These connections persist in memory and aid in later recognition (and, to a lesser extent, recall).

We do not always name the information items in our PSIs. Abrams et al. (1998) report, for example, that when creating a Web bookmark, users rarely change the default name provided by the browser. However, 86 percent of users in their survey reported that the descriptiveness of bookmarks was a problem.

One powerful aid to the recognition of items in a results list returned by a search is to include excerpts from items in which matching search terms are highlighted (Golovchinsky, 1997a, 1997b). The highlighting of search terms is now a standard feature of many search facilities.

Repeating?

In many instances, one needs to find not a single, isolated information item but rather a set of items whose members may be scattered in different forms within different organizations. In the dinner scheduling example given earlier, four different items needed to be retrieved in order to decide whether to accept the invitation. If the likelihood of successful retrieval of each item is strictly independent of the others, then the chances of successfully retrieving all the relevant items decreases as their number increases. So even if the likelihood of success for each item is, say, 95 percent, retrieval of all four items drops to only 81 percent. In situations of *output interference,* items retrieved first may interfere with the retrieval of later items in a set—perhaps because the act of retrieval itself strengthens recollection of the items first recalled at the expense of unrecalled items (Rundus, 1971). Some of us may experience this effect when we try to think of everyone in a group of eight or nine friends. No matter whom we list first—and this can vary from time to time—the last one or two people are often the hardest to remember.

The chances of successfully retrieving all members of a set can also be much better than predicted by a strict independence of individual retrievals. Obviously, retrieval improves if all items are in the same larger unit—a folder or a pile, for example. It may also be better than predicted by strict independence if the items comprising a set have an internal organization or are interrelated so that the retrieval of one item actually facilitates the retrieval of others (e.g., Bower, Clark, Lesgold, &

Winzenz, 1969; Jones & Anderson, 1987). One quotidian instance of what we might call *output facilitation* seems to occur, for example, when remembering the characters of a well-told story or a good movie. Of potential relevance are studies of information foraging and the notion of an *information scent* (Pirolli & Card, 1999) that might guide people from one to another of the items in a fragmented set.

Summary: Finding Is a Multi-Step Process

Finding is a multi-step process with a possibility of stumbling at each step. First, people must *remember* to look. An item is retrieved through variations of searching or, more commonly for items in the PSI, browsing. Both browsing and searching involve an iterative interplay between basic actions of *recall* and *recognition*. Finally, in many situations of information need, people must *repeat* the finding activity several times in order to "re-collect" a complete set of information items.

Keeping: From Information to Need

Many events of daily life are the converse of finding events: People encounter information and try to determine what, if anything, they should do with it—that is, people must match the information to anticipated need(s). Decisions and actions relating to encountered information are collectively referred to in this chapter as *keeping* activities.

People may encounter information unexpectedly (more or less): For example, they may come across an announcement for an upcoming event in the morning newspaper or an "FYI" e-mail with a pointer to a Web site may arrive in their inbox. The ability to handle effectively information that is encountered by happenstance may be key to one's ability to discover new material and make new connections (Erdelez & Rioux, 2000).

People also keep information that they expect to receive and have actively sought but do not have time to process in real time. A search on the Web, for example, often produces much more information than can be consumed in the current session. Both the decision to keep this information for later use and the measures taken to do so constitute keeping activities.

People keep information not only to have it available at a later point in time but also to remember to look for it. A failure to remember to use information that has been kept is one kind of *prospective memory failure* (Ellis & Kvavilashvili, 2000; O'Connail & Frohlich, 1995; Sellen, Louie, Harris, & Wilkins, 1996; Terry, 1988). People may, for example, self-e-mail a Web reference in addition to, or instead of, making a bookmark so that an e-mail message with the reference appears in the inbox, where it is more likely to be noticed and used (Jones et al., 2002).

Keeping, more broadly considered, applies not only to information but also to channels of information. Subscribing to a magazine or setting the car radio to a particular station is a keeping decision. Even the cultivation of friends and colleagues can be seen as an act of keeping (and certainly friends and colleagues often represent important channels of information).

Keeping activities are triggered when people are interrupted in the course of performing a task and look for ways of preserving the current state so that work can be resumed quickly later on (Czerwinski et al., 2004). For example, people keep appointments by entering reminders into a calendar or record good ideas or "things to pick up at the grocery store" by writing down a few cryptic lines on a loose piece of paper. For some professionals, task interruptions have been observed to occur as many as four times per hour (O'Connail & Frohlich, 1995) and this is quite possibly an underestimate.

Research relating to information keeping points to several conclusions: (1) keeping is difficult and error-prone; (2) "keeping right" has become more difficult as the diversity of information forms and supporting tools has increased; and (3) some costs of "keeping wrong" have gone away, but challenges remain.

Keeping Is Difficult and Error-Prone

Keeping actions, such as bookmarking a Web site or setting a reminder flag on an e-mail, are sometimes difficult both in the mechanics of execution and because these actions interrupt the current task (e.g., browsing the Web, reading e-mail). Even more difficult is the decision that guides these actions.

The keeping decision is multifaceted. Is the information useful? If so, do special steps need to be taken to keep it for later use? How should the information be kept? Where? On what device? In what form? Jones (2004) has characterized each keeping decision as a signal detection task[4] subject to a rational analysis of alternatives (Anderson, 1990).

There is a "gray area" where determination of costs, reciprocal benefits, and outcome likelihoods is not straightforward. In the logic of signal detection, this middle area presents us with a "damned if you do, damned if you don't" choice. If we keep the information, we may never use it. If we do not keep it, we may need it later. Moreover, if we keep information in the wrong way—in the wrong folder, for example—we may pay twice: We do not find the information when we need it and, worse yet, when we later need other information in the folder, the incorrectly filed information becomes an impediment to finding it.

Filing information items—whether paper documents, e-documents, or e-mail messages—into the right folders is a cognitively difficult and error-prone activity (Bälter, 2000; Kidd, 1994; Lansdale, 1988, 1991; Malone, 1983; Whittaker & Sidner, 1996). Difficulty arises in part because the definition or purpose of a folder is often unclear from the label (e.g., "stuff") and may change in significant ways over time (Kidd, 1994; Whittaker & Hirschberg, 2001; Whittaker & Sidner, 1996). Determining a folder's definition may be at least as problematic as determining a category's definition (e.g., Rosch, 1978; Rosch, Mervis,

Gray, Johnson, & Boyes-Braem, 1976; Wittgenstein, 1953; Zadeh, 1965). Worse, people may not even recall the folders they have created and so create new folders for the same, or similar, purposes (Whittaker & Sidner, 1996).

If a person's use of folders is sometimes inconsistent, such is also the case when it comes to the handling of incoming information. One's experience of the same information item can change considerably as a function of context (Martin, 1968; Tulving & Thomson, 1973). Kwasnik (1989) identified many dimensions that might influence the placement and organization of paper-based mail and documents in an office. In addition to attributes of the document itself (e.g., title, author), keeping behavior was influenced by disposition (e.g., discard, keep, postpone), order/scheme (e.g., group, separate, arrange), time (e.g., duration, currency), value (e.g., importance, interest, and confidentiality), and cognitive state (e.g., "don't know" and "want to remember"). Overall, the classification of a document was heavily influenced by its intended use or purpose—a finding subsequently corroborated by Barreau (1995).

Jones, Bruce, and Dumais (2001, 2002) have observed that the choice of method for keeping Web information for later use was influenced by a range of considerations or functions. Marshall and Bly (2005) also noted that the reasons for keeping information vary and are not necessarily task-related or even consciously purposeful. Some participants in their study appeared to keep some information (e.g., newspaper clippings) for the pleasure of expanding their collection of like items (e.g., recipes) and a few used the term "packrat" to describe their keeping behavior (p. 117).

Sellen and Harper's (2002) work suggested that 3 percent of the paper documents in a typical office were misfiled and 8 percent were eventually lost. Perhaps the only surprise is that these percentages were not higher. Even when filing is done correctly, it is often not worth the trouble. Whittaker and Hirschberg (2001) have coined the phrase "premature filing" to describe a situation in which people go to the trouble to file information that turns out to have little or no value.

Placing (or leaving) information items in piles, as an alternative to filing, has its own problems. In Malone's (1983) study, participants indicated that they had increasing difficulty keeping track of the contents of different piles as their number grew. Experiments by Jones and Dumais (1986) suggested that the ability to track information by location alone is quite limited. Moreover, the extent to which piles were supported for different forms of information was variable, limited, and poorly understood (Mander, Salomon, & Wong, 1992). The computer desktop may serve as a place to pile items for fast access or high visibility (Barreau, 1995; Barreau & Nardi, 1995), but if it is often obscured by various open windows, the accessibility and visibility of its items are much reduced (Kaptelinin, 1996). The e-mail inbox provides pile-like functions of accessibility and visibility, but these functions are clearly reduced as the number of items in the inbox increases—especially for older messages that scroll out of view.

If filing is error-prone and costly and if the ability to manage piles is limited, it is hardly surprising that people sometimes decide to do nothing at all—even for information they believe will be useful. This is especially true for Web information. For example, Abrams et al.'s (1998) study showed that users bookmarked only a portion of the Web pages they wanted to reaccess at a future date. A study of delayed, cued recall examined how people re-found Web information they considered useful (Bruce et al., 2004; Jones et al., 2003). Participants used one of three "do nothing" methods (i.e., ones requiring no keeping activity) in over two-thirds of the trials:

1. Searching again (using a Web-based search service).

2. Typing in the first few characters of the URL for a Web site and accepting one of the suggested completions of the Web browser.

3. Navigating to the Web site from another Web site. Overall, participants were very good at getting back to "useful" Web sites even when these were accessed only once or twice per year and had not been accessed for up to six months.[5]

Keeping "Right" Is Harder When Information Is More Fragmented

An act of keeping might be likened to throwing a ball into the air toward a point where one expects it to be at some future time. Keeping information in accordance with future need has never been easy (Bruce, 2005), but the current proliferation of information forms and supporting tools and gadgets makes keeping all the more difficult. The information people need may be at home when they are at work and vice versa. It may be on the wrong computer, PDA, smart phone, or other device. Information may be "here" but locked away in an application or in the wrong format so that the difficulty associated with its extraction outweighs the benefits of its use.

The information world that Malone (1983) described was largely paper-based. Today, paper documents and books are still an important part of the average person's PSI (Sellen & Harper, 2002; Whittaker & Hirschberg, 2001). However, people must also contend with the organization of e-documents, e-mail messages, Web pages (or references to these), as well as a number of additional forms of digital information (each with their own special-purpose tool support) including phone messages, digitized photographs, music, and videos. The number of keeping considerations increases further if a person has different e-mail accounts, uses different computers for home and work, or makes use of a PDA, smart phone, or some other special-purpose PIM tool(s).

People freely convert from one form of information to another (Jones et al., 2002). They make paper printouts of e-documents, Web pages, and e-mail messages and scan paper documents for inclusion in e-documents. They send e-documents and Web references via e-mail. They save e-mail messages and Web pages into the same filing system that holds their e-documents.

People can keep information in several different ways in order to ensure that they have it later (Jones et al., 2002). Somebody may, for example, enter a client's telephone number into a calendar (as a reminder to call) and into a contact database. But doing so can increase the later challenges of updating and synchronization (e.g., when the telephone number changes). Moreover, such multiple registering of information may not cover all the contingencies when the information might be needed. Neither the calendar nor contact entry will help, for example, if the person needs to contact the client from his cell phone while stuck in traffic. We can hope that someday our information will be more integrated.

Some Costs of Keeping "Wrong" Have Gone Away, but Challenges Remain

Recent developments in technology have greatly reduced or even nullified some costs associated with mistakes made in the process of keeping. These reductions invite a consideration of two "decision-free" extremes in keeping strategy: that of keeping everything and that of keeping nothing at all (Jones, 2004). Unless one is engaged in video editing, the storage cost of a false positive—that is, of keeping digital information that is never used—is negligible. Why not keep it all? Facilities to sort, search, and filter may even help to clear away the clutter so that one can focus on the more useful information. Many people appear to be following a modified "keep everything" approach, for example, in the management of incoming e-mail by leaving it in the inbox, perhaps with occasional efforts to "spring clean" (Whittaker & Sidner, 1996).

Some costs associated with a "miss"—not keeping information that turns out to be useful—are also decreasing dramatically. With ever-increasing amounts of information available in readily searchable form on the Web (or intranet counterparts), people often rely on refinding methods that require no explicit keeping activity (Bruce et al., 2004). These "do nothing" methods include searching again or navigating from another Web site.

System support can also automate keeping in ways that combine local storage and reliance on the Web. The history and the "auto-complete" facilities in most Web browsers, for example, keep references locally to information that remains on the Web.

Approaches that automate keeping or that free individuals from the need to decide what is to be kept point to a dilemma identified by Lansdale (1988). People may not make the effort to keep information for later use either because doing so is too much trouble or because they are overly confident of their ability to retrieve the information at a later point in time (Koriat, 1993). Automated keeping can save people time and, more importantly, the distraction of leaving the current task in order to decide whether and how an item in view should be kept for future uses. But if people do not take measures to keep the information that they have encountered, they may be less likely to remember to look for it at a later date when the need arises. The *generation effect* (Slamecka & Graf, 1978) has been observed in the assignment of names for text editing commands (Jones & Landauer, 1985) and in the assignment of tags to documents (Lansdale, 1991). Research in *prospective memory*—used to perform an action in the future—also supports a prediction that steps taken when information is encountered may reduce the likelihood of memory failure later on (Ellis & Kvavilashvili, 2000; O'Connail & Frohlich, 1995; Sellen et al., 1996; Terry, 1988).

An alternative to the "keep everything," "keep nothing," and "keep automatically" strategies is the "keep smarter" approach—making better decisions concerning future uses of current information (Jones, 2004). If a person has prepared a clear plan, for example, he is often more effective at keeping relevant information (including a recognition of its relevance) even when the plan and its goal are not the current focus of attention (Seifert & Patalano, 2001). One strategy is to apply technologies of information filtering to support the automation or partial automation of keeping decisions (e.g., Foltz & Dumais, 1992). E-mail applications, for example, commonly support the creation of special rule-based folders into which incoming messages can be copied or moved automatically. Establishing the rules, however, is not an easy task (Bälter, 2000). A step further in automation are tools that attempt to induce the rules for a folder based upon an analysis of its current members. Full automation of filing is problematic for two reasons: (1) rules, whether induced by the computer or created by people, are faulty; and (2) full automation reintroduces the dilemma already discussed—that without some involvement in the keeping activity, people may forget to look again later. One way to address both problems is for the computer to present a selection of likely folder destinations from which the person selects one or more (Segal & Kephart, 1999): He or she is then involved in the final decision and always has the option of selecting "none of the above."

A second approach is to tie acts of information access and creation (e.g., sending an e-mail message, making a new document, accessing a Web page) closely to the planning and completion of associated tasks and projects. The design of the Project Planner prototype (Jones, Munat, Bruce, & Foxley, 2005), for example, follows a guiding principle that information management and task/project management are two sides of the same coin. Moreover, with the right support, an integrative organization of information can emerge as a consequence of the efforts expended to plan a project and manage its tasks. Related to the advantage of a clear plan—at a higher level—is the potential keeping benefit of having an overall scheme of classification—a personal unifying taxonomy (Jones, 2004).

Summary: Keeping Is Multifaceted

Certainly keeping, like finding, can involve several steps. It may even trigger an act of finding—as in refinding the right folder or pile in which to place an information item. But the essential challenge of keeping stems from the multifaceted nature of the decisions about information needs. Is the information useful? Do special actions need to be taken to keep it for later use? Where? When? In what form? On what device? With no crystal ball to see into the future, answering these questions is a difficult and error-prone endeavor. But the attempt helps us to remember the information item subsequently. Some caution is advised against an overreliance on well-intended attempts to automate these decisions. Complementary tool support for planning may be one way to ensure that key connections are made between encountered information and expected need. And a well-formulated plan has other benefits as well.

The Meta-Level: Mapping between Need and Information

Meta-level activities, which constitute the third set of PIM activities, operate broadly upon collections of information within the PSI and on the mapping that connects need to information for these collections. At the level of keeping and finding, "managing" often equates with "getting by" (as in the sentence, "I finally managed to find the information"). The meta-level seeks to enhance personal control of one's PSI by stressing proactivity. How can people take charge of their PIM practice? How should the information be structured? According to what schema? Following which strategies? How can tools help either to structure or to obviate structuring? How is the effectiveness of current practice measured? Issues of privacy and security are also addressed at the meta-level (Karat et al., 2006). Who has access to what information under what circumstances? How can information (e.g., medical information, airplane seating preferences, a résumé) be distributed to best effect?

This section considers two meta-level activities that are (and should be even more) related to one another: (1) maintenance and organization, and (2) making sense of information and planning its use.

Maintaining (Too) Many Organizations

Differences between people are especially apparent in their approaches to the maintenance and organization of information. Malone (1983) distinguished between "neat" and "messy" organizations of paper documents. Messy people had more piles in their offices and appeared to invest less effort than neat people in filing information. Comparable differences have been observed in the ways people approach e-mail (Bälter, 1997; Gwizdka, 2002a; Mackay, 1988; Whittaker & Sidner, 1996), e-documents (Boardman & Sasse, 2004; Bruce et al., 2004), and Web bookmarks (Abrams et al., 1998; Boardman & Sasse, 2004).

Across information forms, differences in approaches to organization correlate with differences in keeping strategy. For example, people who have a more elaborate folder organization—whether for paper documents, e-documents, e-mail messages, or bookmarks—tend to file sooner and more often. However, people are often selective in their maintenance of different organizations. Boardman and Sasse (2004), for example, classified 14 of 31 participants in their study as "pro-organizing" with respect to e-mail and e-documents but not with respect to bookmarks; only seven of the 31 participants took the trouble to organize their e-documents. (The study did not look at the organization of paper documents.)

The fragmentation of information by form poses special challenges for maintenance and organization. Folders with similar names and purposes may be created in different information organizations, especially for e-mail messages and e-documents (Boardman & Sasse, 2004). Maintaining consistency is difficult; for example, people may have a "trips" e-mail folder and a "travel" e-document folder. The fragmentation of information across forms also poses problems in the study of PIM (see the section on methods and methodologies). It is difficult and time-consuming to study and compare a participant's organizational schemes across several different forms of information and tempting to focus primarily on a single form of information such as e-mail messages or Web pages.

However, several studies have now examined how the same person manages across different forms of information (Boardman & Sasse, 2004; Jones, Phuwanartnurak, Gill, & Bruce, 2005; Ravasio, Schär, & Krueger, 2004). The following composite picture has emerged:

- People tend not to take time out of a busy day to assess their organizations or their PIM practice in general.

- People complain about the need to maintain many separate organizations of information and the fragmentation of information that results.

- Even within the same folder organization, competing organizational schemes may suffer an uneasy co-existence with each other. People may apply one scheme on one day and another on the next.

- Several participants in one study (Jones et al., 2002) reported making special efforts to consolidate organizations, for example by saving Web references and e-mail messages into a file folder organization or by sending e-documents and Web references in e-mail messages.

The prefix "meta-" is commonly used to mean "beyond" or "about."[6] But the studies referenced here also invoke the original sense of "meta-" as "after."[7] For many people, meta-level activities such as maintenance and organization occur only after the more pressing activities of keeping and finding have been done. In many cases, this means not at all. Keeping and finding are triggered by many events in a typical day.

Information is encountered and keeping decisions are made (even if the decision is to do nothing). The information needed for a variety of routine activities (e.g., calling someone, planning the day's schedule, preparing for a meeting) triggers various finding activities.

Events triggering maintenance and organization of information are fewer and less frequent. For some people, these activities may be triggered by a corporate "clean desk" policy, a system administrator's message that an inbox is too full, or possibly a New Year's resolution to get organized. Studies of PIM themselves often serve as a trigger. For example, Boardman and Sasse (2004) reported that 12 participants in their study performed ad hoc tidying during the interview itself. In Jones, Phuwanartnurak, et al.'s (2005) study, all 14 participants made comments at the outset concerning a need to move or delete material that was outdated or no longer belonged in their files. Four participants actually insisted on interrupting the interview while they moved or deleted files or old folders.

As digital storage continues to increase in capacity and decrease in cost, maintenance and organization activities are seldom prompted by "disk full" events. People are freed from the need to delete or organize their digital information, and in many ways this is a good thing. The decision to delete information can be time-consuming and difficult to make. This has been referred to as the *old magazine effect* (Jones, 2004). The potential uses or benefits of the item in focus (e.g., an old magazine) may be more salient than the ongoing cost of keeping (and never finding the time to read and use) the item. Similarly, Bergman, Beyth-Marom, and Nachmias (2003) refer to the *deletion paradox* to describe a situation where people may spend precious time on information items that are of little value to them (e.g., old, never-used information items that are candidates for deletion). With the dramatic increases in digital storage capacity in the past few years, most people are no longer forced to delete anything, ever.

Even so, people often express unease about their current maintenance activities with apologetic comments or references to themselves as "a packrat" (Marshall & Bly, 2005, p. 117). Or, as one participant in Boardman and Sasse's study (2004, p. 585) said, "stuff goes in but doesn't come back out—it just builds up."

Making Sense of Information and the Value of External Representations

Much of the experimental work reviewed so far may make us question the value of organizing information in our PSI. We have too many folder organizations to maintain and we frequently postpone or ignore issues of maintenance just as we might avoid tidying a messy closet. Keeping (filing) information in a folder structure is difficult and mistakes are common. Storage is cheap. Search continues to improve. Is it worthwhile to organize information anymore? Or can we leave our information "flat" and depend upon search (and possibly sorting) as a primary means of access?

We now review research demonstrating that people organize information not only to ensure its retrieval but for several other reasons as well. In a study conducted by Jones, Phuwanartnurak, et al. (2005, pp. 1506–1507), participants listed a number of reasons for using folders even if they had access to a perfect desktop search facility:

- "I want to be sure all the files I need are in one place."

- "Folders help me see the relationship between things."

- "Folders remind me what needs to be done."

- "Folders help me to see what I have and don't have."

- "I use empty folders for information I still need to get."

- "Putting things into folders helps me to understand the information better."

In this study, a folder hierarchy developed for a project such as "wedding" often resembled a project plan or partial problem decomposition in which subfolders stood for project-related goals and also for the tasks and subprojects associated with the achievement of these goals. A "wedding dress" subfolder, for example, organized information and tasks associated with the goal of selecting and fitting a wedding dress (including, for example, a "wedding dress trials" sub-subfolder).

Barsalou (1983, 1985, 1991) has long argued that internal categories are used to accomplish goals. His research demonstrates people's ability to group together seemingly dissimilar items according to their applicability to a specific goal. For example, weight watchers might form a category "foods to eat on a diet." Rice cakes, carrot sticks, and sugar-free soda are all members of the category, even though they differ considerably in other ways. The best member is not necessarily like other category members. Instead, the best exemplar is the item that best accomplishes the goal or the ideal. Research by Markman and Ross (2003) suggests that an internal, goal-based organization for a set of items emerges as a by-product of the use of these items to accomplish goals. A person need not think explicitly about the goal-relatedness of items in order to internalize this organization.

This is not to suggest that a direct mapping exists between goal-directed folders as an external form of information organization and goal-directed categories as an internal organization of concepts. However, it is reasonable to suppose that folders (and piles, properties/value combinations, views, and so on) can form an important part of external representations (ERs), which, in turn, can complement and combine with internal representations (IRs) to form an integrated cognitive system (Hutchins, 1994; Kirsh, 2000).

Finding the right ER helps in *sense-making* (Dervin, 1992)—in efforts to make sense of information. For example, the right diagram can allow one to make inferences more quickly (Larkin & Simon, 1987). The way in which information is represented externally can produce huge differences in one's ability to use it in short-duration, problem-solving exercises (Kotovsky, Hayes, & Simon, 1985). Different kinds of representations, such as matrices and hierarchies, are useful in solving different types of problems (Cheng, 2002; Novick, 1990; Novick, Hurley, & Francis, 1999). Russell, Stefik, Pirolli, and Card (1993) have shown that ERs are acquired and discarded according to an assessment of relative costs and benefits.

What are the long-term costs and benefits associated with the use of ERs for PIM—the ER that results from use of a particular filing scheme, for example? And, can tools change the cost/benefit equation? What comes after the folder?

Efforts in tool support can benefit from basic research into how people plan. For example, support for progressive refinement (top-down or bottom-up) must also allow for the dynamic, flexible changes people make to accommodate new information or to exploit new opportunities. This opportunistic aspect of planning has been noted in experiments ranging from ill-structured domains, such as errand planning (Hayes-Roth & Hayes-Roth, 1979), to the highly structured Tower of Hanoi problem (Davies, 2003).

Summary: Meta-Level Activities Are Important but Easily Overlooked

Meta-level activities are critical to a successful PIM practice, but they are rarely urgent. Few events in a typical day direct our attention to meta-level activities such as maintenance and organization, making (overall) sense of an information collection, managing privacy and security, or measuring and assessing the effectiveness of strategies and supporting tools. As a result, meta-level activities can easily become afterthoughts. Research into meta-level activities and their support also appears to receive less attention than, for instance, research into finding (which can draw upon support from established communities in information seeking and information retrieval). But it is at the meta-level that we may realize some of the most productive synergies between applied research in PIM and basic research in cognitive science.

Methodologies of PIM Inquiry

The development of methodologies especially suited to PIM is still in its infancy. There is need for both methodologies in *descriptive* studies aimed at better understanding how people currently practice PIM and *prescriptive* evaluations to understand better the efficacy of proposed

PIM solutions (usually involving a tool but sometimes focused on a technique or strategy).

The descriptive and the prescriptive can form a complementary and iterative relationship with one another:

1. Descriptive data from fieldwork observations, interviews, and, possibly, broader-based surveys can suggest directions for exploratory prototyping of supporting tools (and supporting techniques as well).

2. Prototypes are built and evaluated to reach more definite, prescriptive conclusions concerning support that *should* be provided. The development and evaluation of prototypes can frequently suggest specific areas of focus for the next round of fieldwork.

This is a familiar, if somewhat idealized, process for the study of human–computer interaction (HCI)—although, all too often it seems, the descriptive component is overlooked or disconnected from the rush to build new tools (Whittaker, Terveen, & Nardi, 2000).

PIM poses special challenges with respect to both descriptive study and prescriptive evaluation of proposed solutions:

1. *A person's practice of PIM is unique.* There is tremendous variation among people—even among those who have a great deal in common with each other with respect to profession, education, and computing platform—as demonstrated by many fieldwork studies (e.g., Jones et al., 2001). People develop (and continue to experiment with) their own practice of PIM, including supporting strategies, structures, tools, and habits, with little or no formal guidance. PIM practice is uniquely tailored to the individual's needs and information. This uniqueness makes it very difficult to abstract tasks or extract datasets that can be used meaningfully in a laboratory setting.

2. *PIM happens broadly across many tools, applications and information forms.* People freely convert information from one form to another to suit their needs—e-mailing a document, for example, or printing a Web page. Studies and evaluations that focus on a specific form of information and supporting applications—e-mail, for example—run the risk of optimizing for that form of information but at the expense of a person's ability to manage other forms of information.

3. *PIM happens over time.* Personal information has a life cycle—moving, for example, from a "hot" pile to a "warm" project folder and then, sometimes, into "cold" archival storage. The keeping and finding activities directed to a particular information item may be separated by days, weeks, or months. Basic PIM events of interest—such as filing, the creation of a new folder, or the protracted search for a lost item of information—occur unpredictably

and cannot be scheduled. The effectiveness of an action to file information, for example, cannot be assessed without looking at later efforts to retrieve this information. People may initially embrace a solution but, over time, tire of its use. Single-session studies and evaluations sample a point in time and can easily mislead. For example, a single-session evaluation of an automated categorization tool might show that users are quite happy with its categorization and the time savings that it appears to offer. But these users may subsequently find that they have more trouble finding information with the tool than without it (perhaps because they attend less to the information initially when categorization is automated).

One approach is to create ethnographies of PIM in which a person and his/her practice of PIM are the subject of an exploratory, longitudinal case study. Design methodologies that place an emphasis on context and situation have obvious relevance, including *contextual inquiry* (Beyer & Holtzblatt, 1998), *situated activity* (Suchman, 1983), and *situated design* (Greenbaum & Kyng, 1991). These and other methodologies have emerged from a participatory design movement that originated in Scandinavia (Schuler & Namioka, 1993). Participants in PIM studies might also be encouraged to practice participatory observation or, more simply, self-observation. People are often interested in talking about their PIM practices. Participants in longitudinal studies seem to derive therapeutic value from the opportunity to talk about their information management problems with a sympathetic observer.

But longitudinal case studies are time-consuming, and it is not easy to find a representative sample of participants able or willing to commit to a multi-session study. The results of case studies may be very enlightening but they do not, by themselves, form a proper basis for generalization. However, a longitudinal case study can be followed by a much more targeted single-session study or survey. The case study can help to identify the effects to focus on and the questions to ask in a single-session study or survey.

The effectiveness of PIM research can be improved through:

1. *Development of reference tasks* (Whittaker et al., 2000). For example, there is a need for validated keeping and finding tasks that can be administered to participants as they work with their information.

2. *Tractable units of analysis.* One potential unit of analysis is the personal project (Jones, Munat, et al., 2005). The study of PIM emphasizes helping people manage their information over time in ways that cross the many boundaries set by current tools. This is a worthy, if somewhat daunting, ambition. How much personal information should we study? For how long? In what contexts? A personal project (e.g., planning a trip, taking a course, planning a

remodel) is bounded in time and scope and still typically requires the use of a range of tools, computer-based and otherwise, and the use of many forms of information. Studying people's management of information as they work to complete a project may, therefore, provide practical ways to approach PIM other than tool-based analyses (e.g., the study of e-mail use alone or Web use alone).

It is important to note also that methodologies of PIM need to support the development and evaluation not only of tools but also of techniques and strategies.

Approaches to PIM Integration

As research has made clear, information fragmentation creates problems for keeping, finding, and meta-level activities such as maintenance and organization. The obvious antidote to fragmentation is integration (or unification). This section considers some approaches to integration.

Integration through E-Mail

The uses of e-mail now extend well beyond the sending of text messages between people separated from each other by time and distance. For example, e-mail is now used for task management, personal archiving, and contact management (Bellotti et al., 2003; Ducheneaut & Bellotti, 2001; Mackay, 1988; Whittaker & Sidner, 1996). Many of us practically "live" in e-mail in a typical work day. (On the other hand, many of us may also go "offline" in order to do concentrated work without the constant interruption of e-mail.) One approach to current problems of PIM—in particular, the fragmentation of information by application—is to accept the primacy of e-mail and build additional PIM functionality into an expanded e-mail application.

This approach is exemplified by *Taskmaster* (Bellotti et al., 2003), a prototype that deliberately builds task management features into an e-mail client application. Taskmaster introduces support for *thrasks* as a way to automatically connect task-related e-mail messages based upon an analysis of message content. The thrask is intended to be an improvement on threads. E-mail discussion within a thread can diverge widely from the original task even as other task-related e-mail messages are sent outside the context of a thread. On the other hand, a thrask can also include links (e.g., Web references) and documents that relate to the task. In this way, several forms of information are brought together.

Following an "equality of content" principle, Taskmaster also displays attachments (links and documents) at the same level as the e-mail messages associated with their delivery. Attachments are no longer buried within the e-mail messages. This makes it easier for the user to see and access all information related to a task, regardless of its form.

E-mail messages and associated content can be sorted and grouped by thrask but otherwise remain in the inbox until moved by the user. Users can also fine-tune by changing the thrask associated with an e-mail message. The design intent is that Taskmaster adds new task-related functionality without taking away the functionality already familiar to the user. Taskmaster provides several means of viewing thrask-related e-mail messages and also supports the assignment of task-relevant properties.

One potential limitation of the "integration through e-mail" approach has already been mentioned—people may want to spend *less*, not more, time in e-mail. Also, adding functionality for task management and other PIM-related activities may increase the complexity of an e-mail application that is already difficult to grasp for many users. Furthermore, users are likely to have other reasons for continuing to use files in the file system—better backup, for example, or better, finer-grained control over access rights and security.

Integration through Search

Desktop search facilities that can search across different forms of information—especially files, e-mail, and the Web pages that a person has visited—have a tremendous potential to support a more integrative access to information. Some of this potential has already been realized in facilities such as Google Desktop.[8]

Fast, integrative, cross-form searches are supported in the Spotlight features of the Macintosh Operating System X (Mac OS X) (www.apple.com/macosx/features/spotlight). Spotlight also includes support for persistent searches and the related notion that "smart folders" can be populated and constantly updated to include the results returned for an associated query. Similar features are also planned for inclusion in the next major release of Microsoft Windows (Spanbauer, 2005).

Microsoft's Stuff I've Seen (SIS) project is exploring additional integrations that build upon a basic ability to search quickly through the content and associated properties for the information items of a PSI. The user interface for SIS supports the sorting of returned results on several properties including a "useful date" (with a definition that varies slightly depending on the information form). Time intervals can be further bracketed in the *Memory Landmarks* add-on through the inclusion of representations for memory events, both public and personal. An Implicit Query (IQ) add-on to SIS is a further step in integration. As a user views an e-mail message, content and properties associated with the message are used to form a query. Matching results are shown in a side panel. The panel may sometimes list useful information items that are in the user's PSI but have been forgotten.

These and other search features make it clear that search is about more than typing a few words into a text box and waiting for a list of results. We return to a question posed earlier: Will the constellation of features enabled by fast, indexed search of content *and all associated properties* for information items in a PSI eventually eliminate the need for many PIM activities? In particular, does the need actively to keep information and to maintain and organize this information largely go away? Can people leave their information "flat" so that the need for conventional folders disappears? There are two very different reasons for believing that the answer is "no."

First, a search can return many versions of the needed information. People create multiple versions of a document, for example, in order to represent important variations, to "freeze" the document at key points in its composition, or, simply, because they need to use it on different projects and/or in different contexts. (Moreover, it's easier to copy than to reference.) People may also save external items into their PSI several times because they cannot recall whether they have done so before or, again, because they want to access this item in different "places." Or people may receive several different versions of information in e-mail. Airlines, for example, sometimes send several different e-ticket confirmations.

When multiple versions are returned, considerable time may be spent deciding which version is correct or which collection of items provides the necessary information. The problem of multiple versions intensifies when people modify or correct a document or save a new version of an item without tracking down and removing all the old versions. A chief executive officer of a major financial services company told the author that he had recently spent over an hour trying to decide which of several versions of a PowerPoint presentation was the right one to modify and use for an upcoming meeting with a customer.

The second reason to believe keeping and organizing will remain essential PIM activities is more speculative but also more fundamental: The acts of keeping an item and organizing a collection of items may be essential to our understanding of information and our memory of it later on. If filing is cognitively difficult, it is also cognitively engaging. Filing, as an act of classification, may cause people to consider aspects of an item they might otherwise fail to notice. If people do not make some initial effort to understand the information in their collection of items, they may forget to search for it subsequently. Folders, properties, and other constructs can be seen as an aid in understanding information. Even if a tool such as Implicit Query is successful at retrieving relevant information, people may fail to recognize this information or its relevance to a current need.

In a better world, we might hope to realize the advantages associated with the current use of folders and other means of ER without experiencing the disadvantages. The penalty currently associated with misfiling, for example, is too severe: We may, for all practical purposes, lose the misfiled information. If folders become more "transparent" or more like tags, we might be more inclined to reference than to copy and more inclined to tag an item in several ways in order to represent different anticipated uses. We might still be able to search or sort through items as part of a larger set.

In this regard, improving desktop search facilities may have a paradoxical effect. With search, the cost of misfiling decreases. Even if an item is misfiled, it can still be found again, using search if necessary. Moreover, regardless of folder location, search can be used to construct a useful set of results that can be quickly sorted by time and other useful properties.

Integration through Projects

It might be argued that information management and task or project management are two sides of the same coin. It certainly makes sense to try to organize information according to expected future use and people are known to do this (Kwasnik, 1989). Rooms (Henderson & Card, 1986) represents an early attempt to integrate information items and other resources (e.g., tools, applications) with respect to a user's activity. For example, one could set up a "room" for a programming project in which each window provided a view into a project-related resource. A task-based approach to integration, Taskmaster, has been discussed in the context of extensions to an e-mail application.

Another approach in tool support is the notion of a "project" as a basis for the integration of personal information. When a distinction is made between tasks and projects, it is typically with respect to length and complexity. In HCI studies of task management (Bellotti et al., 2004; Czerwinski et al., 2004), for example, a task is typically something we might put on a to-do list—e.g., "check e-mail," "send mom flowers for Mother's Day," "return Mary's phone call," or "make plane reservations." With respect to everyday planning, tasks are atomic. A task such as "make plane reservations" can certainly be decomposed into smaller actions—"get travel agent's phone number," "pick up phone," "check schedule," and so on—but there is little utility in doing so. In these studies, therefore, the focus is on management *between* tasks, including handling interruptions, switching tasks, and resuming an interrupted task.

A project, by contrast, can last from several days to several years and is made up of any number of tasks and subprojects. Again, the informal to-do measure is useful, although it makes sense to put tasks like "call the real estate broker" or "call our financial planner" on a to-do list, it makes little sense to place a containing project like "buy a new house" or "plan for our child's college education" into the same list.

In the UMEA (User-Monitoring Environment for Activities) prototype, Kaptelinin (2003) used the idea of a current project to bring together various forms of information—electronic documents, e-mail messages, Web references—and associated resources (applications, tools). One of UMEA's design goals was to minimize the user costs in setting up a project by automatically labeling items as they were accessed. Unfortunately, UMEA depended upon the user to signal a change in a current project. Because users frequently forgot to do this, items were frequently associated with the wrong project. Users could go back and edit project/item associations to correct for mislabeling but they rarely took the time and trouble to do this. Kaptelinin sketched possible ways in which the system might detect a change in project but, to the author's knowledge, nothing along these lines has been implemented that can do this with any degree of accuracy. Another limitation of UMEA is that the project is essentially just a label and has no internal structure.

Another approach in integration through projects is to label items as an incidental part of an activity that people might do in any case. When people plan projects, some of their planning finds external expression in, for example, to-do lists or outlines. The Project Planner prototype (Jones, Munat, et al., 2005), described earlier, encourages users to develop a project plan using a Project Planner module. The Planner provides a rich-text overview for any selected folder hierarchy that looks much like the outline view of Microsoft Word. A hierarchy of folders appears as a hierarchy of headings and subheadings. The view enables users to work with a folder hierarchy just as they would with an outline. As headings are added, moved, renamed, or deleted, corresponding changes are made to the folder hierarchy. The Planner is simply another view into the file folder hierarchy and is, in fact, integrated into the file manager. But, as part of more general support for shortcuts, the folders of a project plan can be used to reference project-related e-mail messages and Web pages as well as files.

Behind the scenes, the Planner is able to support its more document-like outline view by distributing Extensible Markup Language (XML) fragments as hidden files, one per file folder, that contain information concerning notes, links, and ordering for the folder. The Planner assembles fragments on demand to present a coherent project plan view including notes, excerpts, links, and an ordering of subfolders (and sub-subfolders). The architecture can handle other views as well. Efforts are currently underway, for example, to support a "mind map" view (Buzan & Buzan, 2004).

Integration through Properties

Dourish, Edwards, and their colleagues have argued that the folder hierarchy is limited, antiquated, and should be abandoned outright in favor of a property-based system of filing and retrieval such as that featured in their PRESTO/Placeless Documents prototype (Dourish, Edwards, LaMarca, Lamping, Petersen, Salisbury, et al., 2000; Dourish, Edwards, LaMarca, & Salisbury, 1999a, 1999b). Such proposals are not new. Ranganathan's (1965) colon, or faceted, classification scheme (Ranganathan, 1965) is essentially an organization of information by a set of properties in which an item's value assignment for one property can vary independently of its value assignment for another. Recipes, for example, might be organized by properties such as "preparation time," "season," and "region or style."

However, organization of information by properties depends upon an understanding of the information so organized. Meaningful, distinguishing, useful properties for special collections such as recipes may be readily apparent but this analysis is more difficult for newly acquired information. In particular, information relating to a project may be easier to organize into a hierarchy representing a plan or problem decomposition for the project.

One property of clear relevance across most items is time (as in "time of encounter" or "last accessed"). Several projects and prototypes are motivated by the integrative power of time as a means to organize information. The MEMOIRS system (Lansdale & Edmonds, 1992) organizes information items in a sequence of events (which can also include meetings, deadlines, and so on). Perhaps the best known of the time-based approaches to information integration is LifeStreams (Fertig, Freeman, & Gelernter, 1996; Freeman & Gelernter, 1996). In LifeStreams, documents and other information items and memorable events in a person's life are all placed in a single, time-ordered "stream." LifeStreams also permits users to place items into the future portion of the stream at points where a need for these items is anticipated. But it is with respect to the future that the LifeStreams timeline metaphor begins to falter. Some future events are "fixed" (to the best of our ability to fix anything in the future)—meetings, for example. It makes sense to place a presentation or report that is needed for a meeting at a point in the stream's future to coincide with the meeting. However, we often have no clear notion of when we will need an item or have an opportunity to use it. In these cases, it may make more sense to organize items according to a need (goal, task, project). Needs, in turn, are often organized into a hierarchy.

Integration through a Common Underlying Representation

The digital information items discussed in this chapter—in particular the file—are high-level. The operations we can perform at the file level are useful but limited. We can create, move, rename, and delete files. The data within a file are typically in a "native format" and readable by only a single application—the word processor, spreadsheet, or presentation software used to create the file. In this circumstance, opportunities to share, consolidate, and normalize data (e.g., to avoid problems with updating) are extremely limited. The user can initiate a transfer of data from one file to another ("owned" by another software application) via mechanisms such as "copy and paste" and "drag and drop," but this transfer is often little more than an interchange of formatted text. Information concerning the structure and semantics of the data stays behind in the source application. Moreover, the data are copied, not referenced, and this can lead to many problems with updating.

As a result, data concerning a person we know—say, Jill Johnson—may appear in many, many places within our PSI. Because of this fragmentation, even simple operations, such as correcting for a spelling mistake in Jill's name or updating her e-mail address, become nearly impossible to complete. We may update some of the copies but not all.[9] Also, we may experience the frustration of having some operations— name resolution, for example—available in one place (when sending e-mail) but not in another (when working with photographs). Underlying these issues is the problem that there is no concept or "object" for a "person named 'Jill Johnson'" in the PSI and no means by which data associated with this person can be referenced—not copied— for multiple uses (as managed through various software applications).

The situation may improve with increasing support for standards associated with the Semantic Web (Berners-Lee, 1998) including XML, RDF (Resource Description Framework), and the URI (Uniform Resource Identifier). RDF and XML, for example, can be used to include more semantics with a data interchange. URIs might be used to address data, in place, so that they do not need to be copied at all (thus avoiding problems with updating information about Jill Johnson, for example). Support for these standards may make it possible to work with data and information packaged around concepts such as "Jill Johnson" rather than with files. Data for Jill would be primarily referenced, not copied. We could readily add more information about Jill or make a comment such as "she's a true friend." And we could group information about Jill together, as needed, with other information. We could, for example, create a list of e-mail addresses and telephone numbers for "true friends" we would like to invite to a birthday celebration.

These and other possibilities are explored in the Haystack project (Adar, Karger, & Stein, 1999; Huynh, Karger, & Quan, 2002; Karger, Bakshi, Huynh, Quan, & Sinha, 2005; Quan, Huynh, & Karger, 2003). Haystack represents an effort to provide a unified data environment in which it is possible to group, annotate, and reference or link to information in units smaller and more meaningful than the file. In the Haystack data model, a typical file will be disassembled into many individual information objects represented in RDF. Objects can be stored in a database or in XML files. When an object is rendered for display in the user interface, a connection is kept to the object's underlying representation. Consequently, the user can click on anything in view and navigate to get more information about the associated object (e.g., to find Jill Johnson's birth date) and also to make additions or corrections to this information.

Haystack offers the potential to explore, group, and work with information in many ways that are not possible when it is "hidden" behind files. However, several issues must be addressed before the Haystack vision is realized in commercial systems. For example, the use of RDF, whether via XML files or a database, is slow. Beyond performance improvements, major changes in attitudes and practices will be required if application developers are eventually to abandon the control they currently have with data in native format in favor of a system where data come, instead, from an external source such as RDF.

Integration through a Digital Recording of "Everything"

If a sequence of information events is recorded—for example, those surrounding the viewing of a Web page—it should be possible to retrieve not only the Web page itself but also other items that were in close temporal proximity to it. We might hope, for example, to be able to access "the e-mail message I was looking at right before I looked at this Web page."

If enough events in our daily life were recorded, we might move significantly closer to a situation where virtually anything recalled about a desired item—the contexts of our interaction with the item as well as its content—could provide an access route back to the item. For example, we might direct the computer to "go back to the Web site that Mary showed me last week."

In his article "As We May Think," Vannevar Bush (1945) described a vision of a personal storage system, the memex, which could include snapshots of a person's world taken from a walnut-sized, head-mounted camera supplemented by a voice recorder. This vision has been realized and extended in wearable devices that can record continuous video and sound (Clarkson, 2002; Mann, 2004; Mann & Niedzviecki, 2001).

A bigger question is what to with all this data once they have been recorded. *MyLifeBits* (Gemmell et al., 2002; Gemmell, Lueder, & Bell, 2003) is an exploratory project aimed at addressing this by digitizing the life of computer pioneer Gordon Bell. The study of "record everything" approaches, also called "digital memories," is becoming a very active area of research (Czerwinski et al., 2006). For example, workshops on Continuous Archival and Retrieval of Personal Experience (CARPE) were sponsored by the Association for Computing Machinery (ACM) in both 2004 and 2005.

A continuous recording of our life's experiences has many potential uses. For example, we might use it to refresh our internal memories concerning a meeting. It might be useful in some cases to support our version of events later on. Or we might like to review our digital recording in an effort to learn from our mistakes. Sometimes, we might review just for fun. But clearly, digital memories raise serious concerns of privacy and security that can only be partially addressed by technology alone.

Integration through Organizing Techniques and Strategies

Approaches to integration are predominantly tool-based and thus are generally inspired by developments in technology. But a degree of integration can also be accomplished through techniques and strategies that make use of existing tool support. As has been noted, people sometimes focus on a single form of information and the development of organizing structures for this form. Other forms of information are "squeezed" into this organization. Everything is printed, for example; or everything is sent as an e-mail; or everything becomes a file.

Some people create a single organizing schema, which is then applied to different forms of information. This prompted Jones (2004) to speculate on the possible value of a *Personal Unifying Taxonomy (PUT)*. A person's PUT would be developed after a review, guided by a trained interviewer, of organizations for e-mail, e-documents, paper documents, Web references, and other forms of information. Top-level elements in a PUT would represent areas with enduring significance in a person's life (high-level goals, important roles). A PUT would also represent recurring themes in the folders and other constructs of various information organizations.

However, a great deal of work will be required to establish a process and lay down principles of PUT development and to determine whether a PUT can be maintained over time to realize benefits that compensate for the costs of creation and maintenance. In the development of a process and principles of PUT development, we might hope to borrow from the field of library and information science. For example, many considerations that apply to library schemes of classification and their effective, consistent, sustainable use over time may have relevance to the development of a PUT. The larger point is that, in our fascination with the potential of new tools and technology, we should not overlook that of improving PIM through changes in our techniques, strategies, and habits.

Conclusions

PIM activities are usefully grouped according to their role in our ongoing effort to establish, use and maintain a mapping between information and need.

- *Finding* activities move us from a need to information that meets that need. Finding, especially in cases where we are trying to re-access items in our PSI, is multi-step and problems can arise with each step. We have to remember to look, we have to know where to look, we have to recognize the information when we see it, and we often have to do these steps repeatedly to "re-collect" a set of items.

- *Keeping* activities move us from encountered information to expected future needs for which this information might be useful (or a determination that the information will not be needed). Reflecting the multifaceted nature of future needs, keeping activities are themselves multifaceted. We must make choices concerning location, organizing folder, form, and associated devices/applications.

- *Meta-level* activities focus on the mapping that connects information to need and on meta-level issues concerning organizing structure, strategies, and supporting tools. We maintain and organize collections of personal information; we manipulate, make sense of, and "use" information in a collection; we also seek to manage privacy and security and we measure the effectiveness of the structures, strategies, and tools we use.

One ideal of PIM is that we always have the right information in the right place and in the right form, and that it be of sufficient completeness and quality to meet our current need. Although this ideal is far from reality for most of us, the research reviewed in this chapter should provide some reason to believe that we are moving in the right direction. There is clear interest in building a stronger community of PIM research to address the pervasive problem of information fragmentation in the practice of PIM.

Progress in PIM also depends upon overcoming related fragmentation in the conduct of PIM-related research. PIM, as an emerging field of inquiry, provides a productive point of integration for research that is currently scattered across a number of disciplines including information retrieval, database management, information and knowledge management, information science, human–computer interaction, cognitive psychology, and artificial intelligence. Ultimately, improvements in our ability to manage personal information should bring improvements not only to our personal productivity but also to our overall quality of life.

Acknowledgments

I thank the three anonymous reviewers for their good comments and helpful suggestions. I would also like to thank Maria Staaf for her careful review and proofreading of previous drafts of this chapter.

Endnotes

1. Thirty researchers from these disciplines and with a special interest in PIM met to discuss the challenges of, and promising approaches to, PIM at a special workshop (see the final workshop report at http://pim.ischool.washington.edu). Participants identified the potential of PIM to promote a synergistic dialogue between practitioners from various disciplines. Another sentiment expressed in several ways was that research problems relating to PIM often "fell through the cracks" between existing research and development efforts.

2. In a personal communication, one researcher told me she uses 12 separate custom properties and "lives by" her EndNote database.

3. Certainly some events of finding and keeping involve no observable manipulation of information items and, therefore, fall outside the focus of PIM. A manager may see a recently hired employee, for example, and experience the need to retrieve his name. She may remember that the employee's name is "Ted" without reference to external information items. (But she might also find out the employee's name by referring to a paper printout that lists names of new employees.) Similarly, a salesperson with a facility for remembering telephone numbers might choose to commit the telephone number of a new client to memory. But if, instead, he writes the number on a piece of

paper, he has created an information item to be managed as part of his PSI.

4. The theory of signal detectability (TSD) (Peterson, Birdsall, & Fox, 1954; Van Meter & Middleton, 1954) has been applied elsewhere to a basic question of information retrieval: What does, and does not, get returned in response to a user query (see, for example, Swets, 1963, 1969)?

5. Given that the cue was effective in eliciting a memory for the Web site, success rates were between 90 and 100 percent (across different conditions of access frequency).

6. See, for example, the entry for "meta-" in the online encyclopedia Wikipedia (http://en.wikipedia.org/wiki/Meta-).

7. See, for example, the entry for "meta-" in the Merriam-Webster Online Dictionary (www.m-w.com/dictionary/Meta-).

8. For a more complete review of desktop search engines currently available for use, see Answers.com (www.answers.com) and then search, of course, for "desktop search."

9. But we might have good reasons not to update some copies. We may be keeping an older version of an address list. Her name and address may appear in an old paper that has already been published and is part of our archive.

References

Abrams, D., Baecker, R., & Chignell, M. (1998). Information archiving with bookmarks: Personal Web space construction and organization. *Proceedings of the SIGCHI Conference on Human Factors in Computing Systems*, 41–48.

Adar, E., Karger, D., & Stein, L. A. (1999). Haystack: Per-user information environment. *Proceedings of the 8th Conference on Information and Knowledge Management*, 413–422.

Anderson, J. R. (1990). *The adaptive character of thought*. Hillsdale, NJ: Erlbaum.

Bälter, O. (1997). Strategies for organising email messages. *Proceedings of the Twelfth Conference of the British Computer Society Human–Computer Interaction Specialist Group*, 21–38.

Bälter, O. (2000). Keystroke level analysis of email message organization. *Proceedings of the SIGCHI Conference on Human Factors in Computing Systems*, 105–112.

Barreau, D. K. (1995). Context as a factor in personal information management systems. *Journal of the American Society for Information Science, 46*, 327–339.

Barreau, D. K., & Nardi, B. (1995). Finding and reminding: File organization from the desktop. *SIGCHI Bulletin, 27*(3), 7.

Barsalou, L. W. (1983). Ad hoc categories. *Memory & Cognition, 11*, 211–227.

Barsalou, L. W. (1985). Ideals, central tendency, and frequency of instantiation as determinants of graded structure in categories. *Journal of Experimental Psychology: Learning, Memory, & Cognition, 11*, 629–654.

Barsalou, L. W. (1991). Deriving categories to achieve goals. *Psychology of Learning and Motivation, 27*, 1–64.

Bates, M. J. (1989). The design of browsing and berrypicking techniques for the online search interface. *Online Review, 13*, 407–424.

Bellotti, V., Dalal, B., Good, N., Flynn, P., Bobrow, D. G., & Ducheneaut, N. (2004). What a to-do: Studies of task management towards the design of a personal task list manager. *Proceedings of the SIGCHI Conference on Human Factors in Computing Systems*, 735–742.

Bellotti, V., Ducheneaut, N., Howard, M., Neuwirth, C., & Smith, I. (2002). Innovation in extremis: Evolving an application for the critical work of email and information management. *Proceedings of the Conference on Designing Interactive Systems: Processes, Practices, Methods, and Techniques*, 181–192.

Bellotti, V., Ducheneaut, N., Howard, M., & Smith, I. (2003). Taking email to task: The design and evaluation of a task management centered email tool. *Proceedings of the SIGCHI Conference on Human Factors in Computing Systems*, 345–352.

Bellotti, V., Ducheneaut, N., Howard, M., Smith, I., & Grinter, R. (2005). Quality vs. quantity: Email-centric task management and its relationship with overload. *Human–Computer Interaction, 20*, 89–138.

Bellotti, V., & Smith, I. (2000). Informing the design of an information management system with iterative fieldwork. *Proceedings of the Conference on Designing Interactive Systems: Processes, Practices, Methods, and Techniques*, 227–237.

Bergman, O., Beyth-Marom, R., & Nachmias, R. (2003). The user-subjective approach to personal information management systems. *Journal of the American Society for Information Science and Technology, 54*, 872–878.

Berners-Lee, T. (1998). *Semantic Web roadmap: An attempt to give a high-level plan of the architecture of the Semantic Web.* Retrieved December 15, 2005, from www.w3.org/DesignIssues/Semantic.html

Beyer, H., & Holtzblatt, K. (1998). *Contextual design: Defining customer-centered systems.* San Francisco, CA: Morgan Kaufmann.

Boardman, R. (2004). *Improving tool support for personal information management.* Unpublished doctoral dissertation, Imperial College, London.

Boardman, R., & Sasse, M. A. (2004). "Stuff goes into the computer and doesn't come out": A cross-tool study of personal information management. *Proceedings of the SIGCHI Conference on Human Factors in Computing Systems*, 583–590.

Boardman, R., Spence, R., & Sasse, M. A. (2003, June). *Too many hierarchies? The daily struggle for control of the workspace.* Paper presented at the HCI International 2003: 10th International Conference on Human–Computer Interaction, Crete, Greece.

Bower, G. H., Clark, M. C., Lesgold, A. M., & Winzenz, D. (1969). Hierarchical retrieval schemes in recall of categorized word lists. *Journal of Verbal Learning and Verbal Behavior, 8*, 323–343.

Bruce, H. (2005). Personal, anticipated information need. *Information Research, 10*(3). Retrieved March 6, 2006, from http://informationr.net/ir/10-3/paper232.html

Bruce, H., Jones, W., & Dumais, S. (2004). Information behavior that keeps found things found. *Information Research, 10*(1). Retrieved March 6, 2006, from http://informationr.net/ir/10-1/paper207.html

Bush, V. (1945, July). As we may think. *Atlantic Monthly, 176*(1), 101–108.

Buzan, T., & Buzan, B. (2004). *The mind map book: How to use radiant thinking to maximize your brain's untapped potential.* London: BBC.

Byrne, M. D., John, B. E., Wehrle, N. S., & Crow, D. C. (1999). The tangled Web we wove: A taskonomy of WWW use. *Proceedings of the SIGCHI Conference on Human Factors in Computing Systems*, 544–551.

Capurro, R., & Hjørland, B. (2003). The concept of information. *Annual Review of Information Science and Technology*, 37, 343–411.

Card, S. K., Moran, T. P., & Newell, A. (1983). *The psychology of human–computer interaction*. Hillsdale, NJ: Erlbaum.

Carroll, J. M. (1982). Creative names for personal files in an interactive computing environment. *International Journal of Man–Machine Studies*, 16, 405–438.

Case, D. O. (1986). Collection and organization of written information by social scientists and humanists: A review and exploratory study. *Journal of Information Science*, 12, 97–104.

Catledge, L. D., & Pitkow, J. E. (1995). Characterizing browsing strategies in the World-Wide Web. *Third International World Wide Web Conference*, 1065–1073.

Cheng, P. C.-H. (2002). Electrifying diagrams for learning: Principles for complex representational systems. *Cognitive Science*, 26, 685–736.

Clarkson, B. P. (2002). *Life patterns: Structure from wearable sensors*. Unpublished doctoral dissertation, Massachusetts Institute of Technology, Cambridge, MA.

Cornelius, I. (2002). Theorizing information. *Annual Review of Information Science and Technology*, 36, 393–425.

Cutrell, E., Dumais, S., & Teevan, J. (2006). Searching to eliminate personal information management. *Communications of the ACM*, 49(1), 58–64.

Czerwinski, M., Gage, D., Gemmell, J., Marshall, C. C., Pérez-Quiñones, M., Skeels, M. M., et al. (2006). Digital memories in an era of ubiquitous computing and abundant storage. *Communications of the ACM*, 49(1), 44–50.

Czerwinski, M., Horvitz, E., & Wilhite, S. (2004). A diary study of task switching and interruptions. *Proceedings of the SIGCHI Conference on Human Factors in Computing Systems*, 175–182.

Davies, S. P. (2003). Initial and concurrent planning in solutions to well-structured problems. *Quarterly Journal of Experimental Psychology*, 56A, 1147–1164.

Dempski, K. L. (1999). Augmented workspace: The world as your desktop. *Handheld and Ubiquitous Computing: First International Symposium*, 356–358.

Dervin, B. (1992). From the mind's eye of the user: The sense-making qualitative-quantitative methodology. In J. Glazier & R. Powell (Eds.), *Qualitative research in information management* (pp. 61–84). Englewood, CO: Libraries Unlimited.

Dervin, B. (1999). On studying information seeking methodologically: The implications of connecting metatheory to method. *Information Processing & Management*, 35, 727–750.

Dourish, P., Edwards, W. K., LaMarca, A., Lamping, J., Petersen, K., Salisbury, M., et al. (2000). Extending document management systems with user-specific active properties. *ACM Transactions on Information Systems*, 18, 140–170.

Dourish, P., Edwards, W. K., LaMarca, A., & Salisbury, M. (1999a). Presto: An experimental architecture for fluid interactive document spaces. *ACM Transactions on Computer-Human Interaction*, 6, 133–161.

Dourish, P., Edwards, W. K., LaMarca, A., & Salisbury, M. (1999b). Using properties for uniform interaction in the Presto Document System. *Proceedings of the 12th Annual ACM Symposium on User Interface Software and Technology*, 55–64.

Ducheneaut, N., & Bellotti, V. (2001). E-mail as habitat. *Interactions, 8*(5), 30–38.

Durso, F. T., & Gronlund, S. (1999). Situation awareness. In F. T. Durso, R. Nickerson, R. W. Schvaneveldt, S. T. Dumais, D. S. Lindsay, & M. T. H. Chi (Eds.), *The Handbook of applied cognition* (pp. 284–314). Chichester, UK: Wiley.

Eisenberg, M., Lowe, C. A., & Spitzer, K. L. (2004). *Information literacy: Essential skills for the information age* (2nd ed.). Westport, CT: Libraries Unlimited.

Ellis, J., & Kvavilashvili, L. (2000). Prospective memory in 2000: Past, present and future directions. *Applied Cognitive Psychology, 14*, 1–9.

Engelbart, D. C. (1963). A conceptual framework for the augmentation of man's intellect. In P. W. Howerton & D. C. Weeks (Eds.), *The augmentation of man's intellect by machine* (Vistas in Information Handling, vol. 1; pp. 1–29). Washington, DC: Spartan Books.

Erdelez, S., & Rioux, K. (2000). Sharing information encountered for others on the Web. *New Review of Information Behaviour Research, 1*, 219–233.

Fertig, S., Freeman, E., & Gelernter, D. (1996). Lifestreams: An alternative to the desktop metaphor. *Conference Companion on Human Factors in Computing Systems: Common Ground*, 410–411.

Fidel, R., & Pejtersen, A. M. (2004). From information behaviour research to the design of information systems: The Cognitive Work Analysis framework. *Information Research, 10*(1). Retrieved March 6, 2006, from http://informationr.net/ir/10-1/paper210.html

Fiske, S. T., & Taylor, S. E. (1991). *Social cognition* (2nd ed.). New York: McGraw-Hill.

Foltz, P. W., & Dumais, S. T. (1992). Personalized information delivery: An analysis of information filtering methods. *Communications of the ACM, 35*(12), 51–60.

Fonseca, F. T., & Martin, J. E. (2004). Toward an alternative notion of information systems ontologies: Information engineering as a hermeneutic exercise. *Journal of the American Society for Information Science and Technology, 56*, 46–57.

Freeman, E., & Gelernter, D. (1996). Lifestreams: A storage model for personal data. *ACM SIGMOD Record, 25*(1), 80–86.

Garvin, D. (2000). *Learning in action: A guide to putting the learning organization to work.* Boston: Harvard Business School Press.

Gemmell, J., Bell, G., Lueder, R., Drucker, S., & Wong, C. (2002). Mylifebits: Fulfilling the memex vision. *Proceedings of the Tenth ACM International Conference on Multimedia*, 235–238.

Gemmell, J., Lueder, R., & Bell, G. (2003). The MyLifeBits lifetime store. *Proceedings of the 2003 ACM SIGMM Workshop on Experiential Telepresence*, 80–83.

Gershon, N. (1995, December). *Human–information interaction.* Paper presented at the Fourth International World Wide Web Conference, Boston, MA.

Gibson, J. J. (1977). The theory of affordances. In R. E. Shaw & J. Bransford (Eds.), *Perceiving, acting, and knowing: Toward an ecological psychology* (pp. 67–82). Hillsdale, NJ: Erlbaum.

Gibson, J. J. (1979). *The ecological approach to visual perception.* Boston: Houghton Mifflin.

Goldstein, I. (1980, June). *Pie: A network-based personal information environment.* Paper presented at the Workshop on Research in Office Semantics, Chatham, MA.

Golovchinsky, G. (1997a). Queries? Links? Is there a difference? *Proceedings of the SIGCHI Conference on Human Factors in Computing Systems*, 407–414.

Golovchinsky, G. (1997b). What the query told the link: The integration of hypertext and information retrieval. *Proceedings of the Eighth ACM Conference on Hypertext*, 67–74.

Greenbaum, J. M., & Kyng, M. (1991). *Design at work: Cooperative design of computer systems.* Hillsdale, NJ: Erlbaum.

Gwizdka, J. (2000). Timely reminders: A case study of temporal guidance in PIM and e-mail tools usage. *Proceedings of the SIGCHI Conference on Human Factors in Computing Systems*, 163–164.

Gwizdka, J. (2002a). Reinventing the inbox: Supporting the management of pending tasks in email. *CHI '02 Extended Abstracts on Human Factors in Computing Systems*, 550–551.

Gwizdka, J. (2002b). TaskView: Design and evaluation of a task-based email interface. *Proceedings of the 2002 Conference of the Centre for Advanced Studies on Collaborative Research*, 4.

Hayes-Roth, B., & Hayes-Roth, F. (1979). A cognitive modeling of planning. *Cognitive Science, 3*, 275–310.

Henderson, A., & Card, S. (1986). Rooms: The use of multiple virtual workspaces to reduce space contention in a Windows-based graphical user interface. *ACM Transactions on Graphics, 5*, 211–243.

Herrmann, D., Brubaker, B., Yoder, C., Sheets, V., & Tio, A. (1999). Devices that remind. In F. T. Durso, R. Nickerson, R. W. Schvaneveldt, S. T. Dumais, D. S. Lindsay, & M. T. H. Chi (Eds.), *Handbook of applied cognition* (pp. 377–407). Chichester, UK: Wiley.

Hutchins, E. (1994). *Cognition in the wild.* Cambridge, MA: MIT Press.

Huynh, D., Karger, D., & Quan, D. (2002). *Haystack: A platform for creating, organizing and visualizing information using RDF.* Paper presented at the Semantic Web Workshop. Retrieved February 24, 2006, from http://semanticweb2002.aifb.uni-karlsruhe.de/proceedings/Research/huynh.pdf

Johnson, J., Roberts, T. L., Verplank, W., Smith, D. C., Irby, C. H., Beard, M., et al. (1989). The Xerox Star: A retrospective. *Computer, 22*(9), 11–26, 28–29.

Johnson, S. B. (2005, January 30). Tool for thought. *New York Times.* Retrieved March 6, 2006, from www.nytimes.com/2005/01/30/books/review/30JOHNSON.html?ex=1264741200&en=c85978ec1eacfbe9&ei=5090&partner=rssuserland

Jones, W. (1986). On the applied use of human memory models: The Memory Extender personal filing system. *International Journal of Man Machine Studies, 25*, 191–228.

Jones, W. (2004). Finders, keepers? The present and future perfect in support of personal information management. *FirstMonday, 9*(3). Retrieved February 24, 2006, from www.firstmonday.dk/issues/issue9_3/jones/index.html

Jones, W., & Anderson, J. R. (1987). Short vs. long term memory retrieval: A comparison of the effects of information load and relatedness. *Journal of Experimental Psychology: General, 116*, 137–153.

Jones, W., Bruce, H., & Dumais, S. (2001). Keeping found things found on the Web. *Proceedings of the Tenth International Conference on Information and Knowledge Management*, 119–126.

Jones, W., Bruce, H., & Dumais, S. (2003). How do people get back to information on the Web? How can they do it better? *Proceedings of the 9th IFIP TC13 International Conference on Human–Computer Interaction (INTERACT 2003)*, 793–796.

Jones, W., & Dumais, S. (1986). The spatial metaphor for user interfaces: Experimental tests of reference by location versus name. *ACM Transactions on Office Information Systems, 4*, 42–63.

Jones, W., Dumais, S., & Bruce, H. (2002). Once found, what then? A study of "keeping" behaviors in the personal use of Web information. *Proceedings of the Annual Meeting of the American Society for Information Science and Technology*, 391–402.

Jones, W., & Landauer, T. K. (1985). Context and self-selection effects in name learning. *Behaviour & Information Technology*, *4*, 3–17.

Jones, W., Munat, C. F., Bruce, H., & Foxley, A. (2005). The Universal Labeler: Plan the project and let your information follow. *Proceedings of the Annual Meeting of the American Society for Information Science and Technology* [CD-ROM]. Silver Spring, MD: American Society for Information Science and Technology.

Jones, W., Phuwanartnurak, A. J., Gill, R., & Bruce, H. (2005). Don't take my folders away! Organizing personal information to get things done. *Proceedings of the SIGCHI Conference on Human Factors in Computing Systems*, 1505–1508.

Kaptelinin, V. (1996). Creating computer-based work environments: An empirical study of Macintosh users. *Proceedings of the 1996 ACM SIGCPR/SIGMIS Conference on Computer Personnel Research*, 360–366.

Kaptelinin, V. (2003). UMEA: Translating interaction histories into project contexts. *Proceedings of the SIGCHI Conference on Human Factors in Computing Systems*, 353–360.

Karat, C. M., Brodie, C., & Karat, J. (2006). Usable privacy and security for personal information management. *Communications of the ACM*, *49*(1), 56–57.

Karger, D. R., Bakshi, K., Huynh, D., Quan, D., & Sinha, V. (2005). Haystack: A customizable general-purpose information management tool for end users of semistructured data. *Proceedings of the Second Biennial Conference on Innovative Data Systems Research*. Retrieved March 6, 2006, from www-db.cs.wisc.edu/cidr/cidr2005/papers/P02.pdf

Karger, D. R., & Quan, D. (2004). Collections: Flexible, essential tools for information management. *CHI '04 Extended Abstracts on Human Factors in Computing Systems*, 1159–1162.

Kidd, A. (1994). The marks are on the knowledge worker. *Proceedings of the SIGCHI Conference on Human Factors in Computing Systems*, 186–191.

Kirsh, D. (2000). A few thoughts on cognitive overload. *Intellectica*, *30*(1), 19–51. Retrieved March 6, 2006, from http://adrenaline.ucsd.edu/kirsch/articles/overload/cognitive_overload.pdf

Koriat, A. (1993). How do we know that we know? The accessibility model of the feeling of knowing. *Psychological Review*, *100*, 609–639.

Kotovsky, K., Hayes, J. R., & Simon, H. A. (1985). Why are some problems hard? Evidence from Tower of Hanoi. *Cognitive Psychology*, *17*, 248–294.

Kwasnik, B. H. (1989). How a personal document's intended use or purpose affects its classification in an office. *Proceedings of the 12th Annual International SIGIR Conference on Research and Development in Information Retrieval*, 207–210.

Lansdale, M. (1988). The psychology of personal information management. *Applied Ergonomics*, *19*, 55–66.

Lansdale, M. (1991). Remembering about documents: Memory for appearance, format, and location. *Ergonomics*, *34*, 1161–1178.

Lansdale, M., & Edmonds, E. (1992). Using memory for events in the design of personal filing systems. *International Journal of Man–Machine Studies*, *36*, 97–126.

Larkin, J. H., & Simon, H. A. (1987). Why a diagram is (sometimes) worth ten thousand words. *Cognitive Science, 11*, 65–99.

Licklider, J. C. R. (1960). Man–computer symbiosis. *IRE Transactions on Human Factors in Electronics, HFE-1*, 4–11.

Licklider, J. C. R. (1965). *Libraries of the future*. Cambridge, MA: MIT Press.

Lucas, P. (2000). Pervasive information access and the rise of human–information interaction. *CHI '00 Extended Abstracts on Human Factors in Computing Systems*, 202.

Mackay, W. E. (1988). More than just a communication system: Diversity in the use of electronic mail. *Proceedings of the ACM Conference on Computer-Supported Cooperative Work*, 344–353.

Malone, T. W. (1983). How do people organize their desks: Implications for the design of office information systems. *ACM Transactions on Office Information Systems, 1*, 99–112.

Mander, R., Salomon, G., & Wong, Y. Y. (1992). A "pile" metaphor for supporting casual organization of information. *Proceedings of the SIGCHI Conference on Human Factors in Computing Systems*, 627–634.

Mann, S. (2004). Continuous lifelong capture of personal experience using Eyetap. *Proceedings of the 1st ACM Workshop on Continuous Archival and Retrieval of Personal Experiences*, 1–21.

Mann, S., & Niedzviecki, H. (2001). *Cyborg: Digital destiny and human possibility in the age of the wearable computer*. Toronto: Doubleday Canada.

Marchionini, G. (1995). *Information seeking in electronic environments*. Cambridge, UK: Cambridge University Press.

Marchionini, G., & Komlodi, A. (1998). Design of interfaces for information seeking. *Annual Review of Information Science and Technology, 33*, 89–130.

Markman, A. B., & Ross, B. H. (2003). Category use and category learning. *Psychological Bulletin, 129*, 592–613.

Marshall, C. C., & Bly, S. (2005). Saving and using encountered information: Implications for electronic periodicals. *Proceedings of the SIGCHI Conference on Human Factors in Computing Systems*, 111–120.

Martin, E. (1068). Stimulus meaningfulness and paired-associate transfer: An encoding variability hypothesis. *Psychological Review, 75*, 421–441.

Matthews, T., Czerwinski, M., Robertson, G., & Tan, D. (2006). Clipping lists and change borders: Improving multitasking efficiency with peripheral information design. *Proceedings of the SIGCHI Conference on Human Factors in Computing Systems*, 989–998.

Neisser, U. (1967). *Cognitive psychology*. New York: Appleton-Century Crofts.

Nelson, T. H. (1982). *Literary machines*. Sausalito, CA: Mindful Press.

Norman, D. A. (1988). *The psychology of everyday things*. New York: Basic Books.

Norman, D. A. (1990). *The design of everyday things*. New York: Doubleday.

Norman, D. A. (1993). *Things that make us smart: Defending human attributes in the age of the machine*. Reading, MA: Addison-Wesley.

Novick, L. R. (1990). Representational transfer in problem solving. *Psychological Science, 1*, 128–132.

Novick, L. R., Hurley, S. M., & Francis, M. (1999). Evidence for abstract, schematic knowledge of three spatial diagram representations. *Memory & Cognition, 27*, 288–308.

O'Connail, B., & Frohlich, D. (1995). Timespace in the workplace: Dealing with interruptions. *SIGCHI Conference Companion on Human Factors in Computing Systems*, 262–263.

O'Day, V., & Jeffries, R. (1993). Orienteering in an information landscape: How information seekers get from here to there. *Proceedings of the SIGCHI Conference on Human Factors in Computing Systems*, 438–445.

Peterson, W. W., Birdsall, T. G., & Fox, W. C. (1954). The theory of signal detectability. *Institute of Radio Engineers Transactions, PGIT-4*, 171–212.

Pettigrew, K. E., Fidel, R., & Bruce, H. (2001). Conceptual frameworks in information behavior. *Annual Review of Information Science and Technology, 35*, 43–78.

Pirolli, P. (in press). Cognitive models of human–information interaction. In F. T. Durso, R. S. Nickerson, R. W. Schvaneveldt, S. T. Dumais, D. S. Lindsay, & M. T. H. Chi (Eds.), *Handbook of applied cognition* (2nd ed.). West Sussex, UK: Wiley.

Pirolli, P., & Card, S. (1999). Information foraging. *Psychological Review, 106*, 643–675.

Pratt, W., Unruh, K., Civan, A., & Skeels, M. (2006). Personal health information management. *Communications of the ACM, 49*(1), 51–55.

Quan, D., Huynh, D., & Karger, D. R. (2003, October). *Haystack: A platform for authoring end user Semantic Web applications*. Paper presented at the 2nd International Semantic Web Conference (ISWC 2003), Sanibel Island, FL. Retrieved March 20, 2006, from http://haystack.lcs.mit.edu/papers/iswc-haystack.pdf

Ranganathan, S. R. (1965). *The colon classification* (Rutgers Series on Systems for the Intellectual Organization of Information, Vol. 4). New Brunswick, NJ: Graduate School of Library Service, Rutgers, the State University.

Ravasio, P., Schär, S. G., & Krueger, H. (2004). In pursuit of desktop evolution: User problems and practices with modern desktop systems. *ACM Transactions on Computer–Human Interaction, 11*, 156–180.

Rosch, E. (1978). Principles of categorization. In E. Rosch & B. B. Lloyd (Eds.), *Cognition and categorization* (pp. 27–48). Hillsdale, NJ: Erlbaum.

Rosch, E., Mervis, C. B., Gray, W., Johnson, D., & Boyes-Braem, P. (1976). Basic objects in natural categories. *Cognitive Psychology, 8*, 382–439.

Rouse, W. B., & Rouse, S. H. (1984). Human information seeking and design of information systems. *Information Processing & Management, 20*, 129–138.

Rowley, J. (1994). The controlled versus natural indexing languages debate revisited. *Journal of Information Science, 20*, 108–119.

Rundus, D. (1971). An analysis of rehearsal processes in free recall. *Journal of Experimental Psychology, 89*, 63–77.

Russell, D. M., Stefik, M. J., Pirolli, P., & Card, S. K. (1993). The cost structure of sensemaking. *Proceedings of the SIGCHI Conference on Human Factors in Computing Systems*, 269–276.

Schuler, D., & Namioka, A. (Eds.). (1993). *Participatory design: Principles and practices*. Hillsdale, NJ: Erlbaum.

Segal, R. B., & Kephart, J. O. (1999). MailCat: An intelligent assistant for organizing e-mail. *Proceedings of the Third Annual Conference on Autonomous Agents*, 276–282.

Seifert, C. M., & Patalano, A. L. (2001). Opportunism in memory: Preparing for chance encounters. *Current Directions in Psychological Science, 10*, 198–201.

Selamat, M. H., & Choudrie, J. (2004). The diffusion of tacit knowledge and its implications on information systems: The role of meta-abilities. *Journal of Knowledge Management*, *8*, 128–139.

Sellen, A. J., & Harper, R. H. R. (2002). *The myth of the paperless office*. Cambridge, MA: MIT Press.

Sellen, A. J., Louie, G., Harris, J. E., & Wilkins, A. J. (1996). What brings intentions to mind? An in situ study of prospective memory. *Memory & Cognition*, *5*, 483–507.

Shannon, C. E. (1948). A mathematical theory of communication. *The Bell System Technical Journal*, *27*, 379–423, 623–656.

Simon, H. A. (1971). Designing organizations for an information-rich world. In M. Greenberger (Ed.), *Computers, communications and the public interest* (pp. 40–41). Baltimore: Johns Hopkins University Press.

Slamecka, N. J., & Graf, P. (1978). The generation effect: Delineation of a phenomenon. *Journal of Experimental Psychology*, *4*, 592–604.

Spanbauer, S. (2005, August). Longhorn preview: The newest versions of the next Windows add graphics sizzle and more search features but lack visible productivity enhancements. *PC World*, *23*(8), 20–22.

Streitz, N., & Nixon, P. (2005). The disappearing computer: Introduction. *Communications of the ACM*, *48*(3), 32–35.

Suchman, L. (1983). Office procedure as practical action: Models of work and system design. *ACM Transactions on Office Information Systems*, *1*, 320–328.

Suchman, L. (1987). *Plans and situated actions: The problem of human–machine communication*. Cambridge, UK: Cambridge University Press.

Swets, J. A. (1963). Information retrieval systems. *Science*, *141*, 245–250.

Swets, J. A. (1969). Effectiveness of information retrieval methods. *American Documentation*, *20*, 72–89.

Tauscher, L. M., & Greenberg, S. (1997a). How people revisit Web pages: Empirical findings and implications for the design of history systems. *International Journal of Human–Computer Studies*, *47*, 97–137.

Tauscher, L. M., & Greenberg, S. (1997b). Revisitation patterns in World Wide Web navigation. *Proceedings of the SIGCHI Conference on Human Factors in Computing Systems*, 399–406.

Taylor, A. G. (2004). *The organization of information* (2nd ed.). Westport, CT: Libraries Unlimited.

Teevan, J. (2003). "Where'd it go?": Re-finding information in the changing Web. *Proceedings of the MIT LCS/AI Student Oxygen Workshop*. Retrieved March 20, 2006, from http://sow.csail.mit.edu/2003/proceedings/Teevan.pdf

Teevan, J., Alvarado, C., Ackerman, M. S., & Karger, D. R. (2004). The perfect search engine is not enough: A study of orienteering behavior in directed search. *Proceedings of the SIGCHI Conference on Human Factors in Computing Systems*, 415–422.

Teevan, J., Dumais, S. T., & Horvitz, E. (2005). Personalizing search via automated analysis of interests and activities. *Proceedings of the 28th Annual International ACM SIGIR Conference on Research and Development in Information Retrieval*, 449–456.

Terry, W. S. (1988). Everyday forgetting: Data from a diary study. *Psychological Reports*, *62*, 299–303.

Thompson, L. L., Levine, J. M., & Messick, D. M. (Eds.). (1999). *Shared cognition in organizations: The management of knowledge*. Mahwah, NJ: Erlbaum.

Tulving, E. (1983). *Elements of episodic memory*. Oxford, UK: Oxford University Press.

Tulving, E., & Thomson, D. M. (1973). Encoding specificity and retrieval processes in episodic memory. *Psychological Review, 80*, 359–380.

Van Meter, D., & Middleton, D. (1954). Modern statistical approaches to reception in communication theory. *Institute of Radio Engineers Transactions, PGIT-4*, 119–145.

Whittaker, S. (2005). Collaborative task management in email. *Human–Computer Interaction, 20*, 49–88.

Whittaker, S., & Hirschberg, J. (2001). The character, value and management of personal paper archives. *ACM Transactions on Computer–Human Interaction, 8*, 150–170.

Whittaker, S., & Sidner, C. (1996). Email overload: Exploring personal information management of email. *Proceedings of the SIGCHI Conference on Human Factors in Computing Systems*, 276–283.

Whittaker, S., Terveen, L., & Nardi, B. A. (2000). Let's stop pushing the envelope and start addressing it: A reference task agenda for HCI. *Human–Computer Interaction, 15*, 75–106.

Williamson, A. G., & Bronte-Stewart, M. (1996). Moneypenny: Things to do on the desk. *Adjunct Proceedings of the 11th British Computer Society Annual Conference on Human–Computer Interaction*, 197–200.

Wilson, E. V. (2002). Email winners and losers. *Communications of the ACM, 45*(10), 121–126.

Wilson, T. (2000). Human information behavior. *Informing Science, 3*(2), 49–55.

Wittgenstein, L. (1953). *Philosophical investigations* (G. E. M. Anscombe, Trans.). New York: Macmillan.

Yates, F. A. (1966). *The art of memory*. Chicago: University of Chicago Press.

Yates, J. (1989). *Control through communication: The rise of system in American management*. Baltimore: Johns Hopkins University Press.

Zadeh, L. A. (1965). Fuzzy sets. *Information and Control, 8*, 338–353.

CHAPTER 11

Arabic Information Retrieval

Ibrahim Abu El-Khair
El-Minia University, Egypt

Introduction

Most information retrieval (IR) research to date has focused on the English language; recently, however, a considerable amount of work and effort has been devoted to developing information retrieval systems for languages other than English, including Arabic. Research on Arabic IR is still much less extensive than that on English-language IR, which has dominated the field for the past 50 years, despite the fact that Arabic is one of the five languages of the United Nations, the mother tongue of over 256 million people, and, because it is the language of the Qur'an, the second language of many Muslims and Muslim countries around the world (Brunner, 2005).

The lack of research in Arabic IR is due in part to the fact that Arabic is a unique language with a structure that differs from Latin-based languages. Research in Latin languages or even Hebrew, which belongs to the same language group as Arabic, is not directly applicable to it because of the difficulties of dealing with its different characteristics and structure. Another important reason is the lack of funding and standard evaluation sources for practitioners in the field of Arabic IR.

The quality of any IR system's response to an information need stated in a query is usually referred to as effectiveness. The effectiveness of an IR system in a language other than English and the ability of this system to perform efficiently depend on the system's capacity to conform to the specific language in use. This means that understanding the characteristics of the language in hand is of great importance. An IR system created, for instance, for the English language cannot be used for retrieval in another language before adjusting to that language. Such adjustment can be minimal, especially with languages written with the Roman alphabet. However, when dealing with a language written in a non-Roman script, such as Arabic, the adjustment can be significant.

This chapter reviews research and applications in Arabic information retrieval, a research area that has become increasingly important in the past few years. The field of Arabic computational linguistics and applications has received considerable attention—in particular, Arabic IR.

The rapidly growing interest in Arabic IR has resulted in a considerable body of work on the subject.

Scope

The literature on Arabic IR is quite diverse and has increased dramatically in the past few years. This review attempts to survey contemporary research on the subject, emphasizing comparative evaluative studies that try to compare the effectiveness of more than one technique during the retrieval process using standard evaluation measures. It focuses on text retrieval studies, or more specifically, text processing techniques that have been developed for, and applied to, Arabic-like stemming and stop-words elimination. Other issues discussed include term weighting, corpora, cross-language information retrieval (CLIR), and evaluation. The level of treatment for each subject varies. The aim of this review is to provide an overall framework for Arabic IR and present, in a selective manner, methodological research papers.

This is not meant to be a comprehensive review of term weighting schemes, which have been reviewed fully by Belkin and Croft (1987), Sparck Jones, Walker, and Robertson (2000a, 2000b), and Liu and Croft (2005). Rather, the discussion of term weighting schemes is restricted to the use of different schemes in Arabic IR. Likewise, the discussion of CLIR does not cover all aspects of this domain; Oard and Diekema (1998) have already reviewed CLIR techniques in *ARIST* and Gey, Kando, and Peters (2005) and Kishida (2005) have recently discussed state-of-the-art methods and techniques for enhancing the effectiveness of CLIR. The corpora section of the review deals exclusively with text corpora; spoken and conversational corpora are not covered. Studies reporting the efficiency of morphs, as compared to stems, in the retrieval process are addressed, but those focusing on developing morphological analyzers and different morphology techniques are excluded, for the latter subject has received a thorough review at the hands of Al Sughaiyer and Al Kharashi (2004). In the evaluation section, the review provides an introduction to IR evaluation and describes the role of the Text REtrieval Conference (TREC), which has provided the venue for some of the most important milestones in Arabic IR. Arabic optical character recognition (OCR) and lexical semantic relationship studies have been excluded; they are beyond the scope of this review.

Sources of Information

Research on Arabic language retrieval is conducted primarily by information scientists and computer scientists and is scattered across many different sources. The search for relevant papers on the topic was conducted with the aid of several online bibliographic databases including the ACM Portal (Association for Computing Machinery, http://portal. acm.org/portal.cfm), the CiteSeer database (Computer and Information

Science Papers, CiteSeer Publications ResearchIndex, http://citeseer.ist. psu.edu; note that CiteSeer incorporated links to the ACM portal and the DBLP in September 2005), and the DBLP (Digital Bibliography & Library Project: Computer Science Bibliography, http://dblp.uni-trier.de). Other databases used include LISA (Library and Information Science Abstracts), ISA (Information Science Abstracts), and search engines such as Google Scholar (http://scholar.google.com). The primary sources of information on the topic were journals such as *Information Processing & Management* and *Journal of the American Society for Information Science and Technology*. Other sources included work presented at conferences, particularly the Text REtrieval Conference's Cross-Language Information Retrieval track, which introduced Arabic into its field of investigation in 2001/2002, and the annual ACM SIGIR (Association for Computing Machinery, Special Interest Group on Information Retrieval) Conference on Research and Development in Information Retrieval.

Characteristics of the Arabic Language

According to the *Encyclopaedia Britannica* (Arabic Language, 2005, online),

> Arabic is the language of the Qur'an ... and the religious language of all Muslims. Literary Arabic ... is essentially the form of the language found in the Qur'an, with some modifications necessary for its use in modern times; it is uniform throughout the Arab world. Colloquial Arabic includes numerous spoken dialects, some of which are mutually unintelligible. The chief dialect groups are those of Saudi Arabia, Iraq, Syria, Egypt, and North Africa; with the exception of the dialect of Algeria, Arabic dialects have been strongly influenced by the literary language.

A distinguishing characteristic of the Arabic language is the right-to-left orientation of its script. Another is that vowels can be explicitly spelled out in the writing of a word or excluded (in which case they are represented by diacritic marks). The Arabic language has eight main diacritic marks (ٌ ً ٍ ِ ْ ّ ُ َ) that can change the meaning of a word drastically based on their position: for example, كَتَبَ means "he wrote" and كُتِبَ signifies "written," whereas كُتُب means "books." We may consider these diacritics to function in a manner analogous to case endings or suffixes. They are spelled out fully only in the Qur'an (to ensure a correct reading), in some school textbooks, and in many theological books. In almost all other Arabic texts, these diacritics are omitted—a practice that can lead to homonymy (Moukdad & Large, 2001).

The Arabic alphabet consists of 28 characters representing consonants and (semi)vowels:

ا, ب, ت, ث, ج, ح, خ, د, ذ, ر, ز, س, ش, ص, ض, ط, ظ, ع, غ, ف, ق, ك, ل, م, ن, هـ, و, ي

Each character may have up to four different forms in writing—isolated,
initial, middle, or final—depending on its position within a word token.
Moreover, there are three symbols (ء, ~, ى) that can be added to a character or a word, thus changing the pronunciation of the character or the
meaning of the word. In all, this makes 31 characters. The name of every
Arabic letter is pronounced as a word (e.g., ا is *alif* and ل is *lam*) so that
a single sound cannot be used to refer to an alphabetic character; therefore, acronyms or abbreviations are not used in Arabic as much as in
English (Moukdad & Large, 2001).

The Arabic language belongs to the Semitic language group, which
includes such languages as Hebrew and Aramaic, and it shares with the
other Semitic languages a distinctive morphological feature—word formation based on consonantal roots (most frequently consisting of three
consonants). Most Arabic words are morphologically derived from a
short list of generative roots, which constitute the bare verb form. These
roots can be trilateral (F'L فعل), quadrilateral (F'LL فعلل), or pentalateral
(F'LLL فعلل) (Bateson, 1967). The basic meaning of the root is furnished
by the consonants and is altered by changes in the word's vowel pattern
(i.e., changes to, or omission of, vowels) and by the addition of various
affixes. Gender, which can be masculine or feminine, is expressed in the
forms of Arabic verbs, as well as in those of nouns, pronouns, and adjectives. As regards number, Arabic distinguishes singular, dual, and plural
forms. Arabic plurals are morphologically quite complex, for they exhibit
greater irregularity in form than their English counterparts: "depending
on the root and singular form of the word, the plural might be produced
by the addition of suffixes, prefixes or infixes" or by the repatterning of
the word's vocalic structure (Moukdad & Large, 2001, p. 64).

Table 11.1 shows how a simple trilateral root, كتب (KTB), whose basic
semantic field is that of "writing," can take on many forms and different
meanings. The table indicates the word form, its transliteration, and its
translation. The transliteration uses the ALA (American Library
Association) and the Library of Congress Arabic Transliteration scheme
(Library of Congress, Cataloging Policy and Support Office, 2002).

Morphological analysis of written Arabic can be complex. For example, it is common to find a word token such as " ورأيتهم " which means
"and you (singular) saw them." This "word" is actually a sentence consisting of a conjunction (و-), a verb (-رأي-), a subject (ت —), and a direct
object (-هم). The verb alone is marked for mood, tense, number, and gender, while the object, in this case a personal pronoun, must be parsed for
person, number, gender, and case (Farghaly 2004; Moukdad & Large,
2001).

Table 11.1 Some derived forms from the root كتب

Word form	Transliteration	Translation
كَتَبَ	Kataba	He wrote
يَكْتُبُ	Yaktubu	He writes
تَكْتُبُ	Taktubu	She writes
مَكْتُوب	Maktūb	Written/Letter
كَاتِب	Kātib	Writer
كَتَبَة	Katabah	Writers
كُتّاب	Kuttāb	Writers
كَاتَبَ	Kātaba	Correspond
تَكَاتَبَ	Takātaba	Write to
مَكْتَب	Maktab	Office/Desk
مَكْتَبَة	Maktabah	Library
مُكَيْتِب	Mukaytib	Small office/Desk
كِتَاب	Kitāb	Book
كُتُب	Kutub	Books
كِتَابَة	Kitābah	Writing
كُتِبَ	Kutiba	Written
إنْكَتَبَ	Inkataba	Became written
إسْتَكْتَبَ	Istaktaba	Dictate
سَيَكْتُبُ	Sayaktubu	Will write

Early Work in Arabic IR

One of the earliest approaches to Arabic retrieval (Kasem, 1978) attempted to compare the efficiency of Arabic retrieval techniques with that of English retrieval techniques. The study used the FAMULUS bibliographic package, which was available at the University of London at the time. Kasem created his own data set, drawing a sample from Arabic journal literature in linguistics and formulating 27 queries along with their relevance judgments. He also created a transliteration system to enable the retrieval package to avoid dealing with letters written in Arabic script. The system used a simple word matching technique. The results indicated that there were no significant differences between English and Arabic retrieval using recall and precision measures. This is because the system used Kasem's transliteration scheme, which meant that it did not read actual Arabic and so did not have to deal with the problems posed by Arabic script.

The major challenge that faced Kasem and others working with Arabic IR at that time was how to represent Arabic in machines that did not support it. Nowadays, this does not constitute a problem, largely because of advances in computer technology. The issue of how and in which form to represent Arabic distracted researchers from actually addressing the main problems concerning the ambiguities present in Arabic language and script; when they did so, it was only on a theoretical basis.

Test Corpora

Corpora are the most important resource for IR research. The Arabic language has a limited number of corpora available for research and experimentation, the majority of which are built on newspaper texts. The following is a brief description of the corpora available for Arabic IR experiments.

LDC Corpus

The *LDC corpus* or the *Arabic Newswire A* corpus was created by David Graff and Kevin Walker at the University of Pennsylvania's Linguistic Data Consortium (LDC) (Linguistic Data Consortium, 2001). The corpus is composed of articles from the Agence France Presse (AFP) Arabic Newswire published between May 13, 1994 and December 20, 2000. The source material was tagged using TIPSTER-style Standard Generalized Markup Language (SGML) and was transcoded to Unicode (UTF-8). The data are stored in 2,337 compressed Arabic text data files. There are 209 megabytes of compressed data (869 Mb when uncompressed), with 383,872 documents containing 76 million tokens over approximately 666,094 unique words.

An-Nahar Newspaper Text Corpus

This corpus (European Language Resource Association, 2001, online) comprises articles published in the Lebanese newspaper An-Nahar (Al-Nahçr, or *The Daytime*) from 1995 to 2000, which are stored as Hypertext Markup Language (HTML) files. Each year contains 45,000 articles and 24 million words. Each article includes information such as title, newspaper's name, date, country, type, and page.

Al-Hayat Corpus

The *Al-Hayat corpus* (European Language Resource Association, 2002, online) was

> developed in the course of a research project at the University of Essex, in collaboration with the Open University. It contains Al-Hayat newspaper articles with value added for Language Engineering and Information Retrieval applications development purposes. The data have been distributed into seven subject-specific databases in accordance with Al-Hayat's subject tags: General, Car, Computer, News, Economics, Science, and Sport. Markup, numbers, special characters, and punctuation have been removed. The total size of the file is 268 megabytes. The dataset contains 18,639,264 distinct tokens in 42,591 articles.

Arabic Gigaword

Recently, the Arabic Newswire A, Al-Hayat, and An-Nahar corpora were aggregated into one resource entitled *Arabic Gigaword* (Maamouri & Cieri, 2002). Subsequently, a fourth source has been added, the Xinhua Arabic content from Xinhua News Agency (Linguistic Data Consortium, 2003). *Arabic Gigaword* is a comprehensive archive of newswire text data acquired from different Arabic news sources by the LDC. It consists of 319 files, totaling approximately 1.1 gigabytes in compressed form; 4,348 megabytes when uncompressed, and 391,619,000 words. All text files in this corpus have been converted to UTF-8 character encoding.[1]

U.N. Arabic English Parallel Text

The *U.N. Arabic English Parallel Text* corpus was collected, cleaned, and aligned from the United Nations Web site (www.ods.un.org/ods) by Xu, Fraser, Makhoul, Noamany, and Osman (2001) at BBN. They describe the corpus as containing 34,575 document pairs and 3,270,200 sentence pairs. Its constituent documents were published by the U.N. between January 1993 and December 1999. A special-purpose crawler extracted the documents from the U.N. Web site. The extracted documents, which were in either WordPerfect or Microsoft Word format, were converted to UTF-8-encoded plain text at BBN. They were then aligned at the sentence level with software developed at BBN. The aligned corpus was further cleaned by removing document/sentence pairs that appeared to be incorrect.

Other Corpora

Although very small in terms of their size, two other corpora are worth mentioning because they were created by individuals working with systems that had limited Arabic computational abilities. Abu-Salem (1992) and Hmeidi (1995) at the Illinois Institute of Technology (IIT) created the *SACS corpus*. It consists of 242 Arabic abstracts collected from the proceedings of the Saudi Arabia National Computer Science Conference, containing 46,968 words in all. Each abstract comprises 36 fields including title, authors, sources, and abstract. Each field starts with three characters that represent the name of the field followed by a space and the text. Hasnah (1996) created the *Al-Raya corpus*, which comprises 187 full newspaper articles selected from the Al-Raya newspaper, which is published in Qatar. This corpus contains 219,978 words in all and 30,096 different words.

Stemming

Stemming is a procedure that reduces a word to its core or root. The stem of a word represents a broader concept, enabling the system to retrieve both the word itself and a set of etymologically related terms. Stemming may or may not improve the retrieval effectiveness of IR systems depending on the language in question, its characteristics, and, naturally, the efficiency of the stemmer itself. For example, Lochbaum and Streeter (1989) found that stemming did not significantly improve retrieval performance for the English language. Harman (1991) used three different algorithms—the S algorithm, Porter algorithm, and Lovins algorithm—with three different collections and found that stemming did not significantly improve retrieval performance.

On the other hand, stemming has proved to be effective for other languages—for example, French (Savoy, 1999); Italian, Spanish, and German (Savoy, 2001); and Finnish and Dutch (Savoy, 2002). With respect to East Asian languages (specifically Chinese, Japanese, and Korean), Vines and Zobel (1999) have indicated that N-grams have proved to be very effective for retrieval. Another successful method for retrieving this type of text is using word segmentation for stemming and retrieval (Chen, 2001; Hasan & Matsumoto, 2000).

Stemming is a language-dependent technique so its effectiveness may vary from one language to another. In Arabic, it is essential for retrieval. Because Arabic is highly inflected, a good stemming algorithm can improve the retrieval performance significantly for both small (Al-Kharashi & Evens, 1994) and large collections (Larkey, Ballesteros, & Connell, 2002; Larkey & Connell, 2002).

Most studies in Arabic IR focus on comparison of stems and roots. It is important to note that there is clear distinction between roots and stems in Arabic. A root is the bare form of the verb and gives the basic lexical meaning of the word. The Arabic language has approximately 5,000 roots in modern usage (Beesley, 1996); each root can generate hundreds of words with different meanings. A stem, on the other hand, is derived from the root morpheme by adding different prefixes, infixes, and/or suffixes to construct morphological patterns. Figure 11.1 provides an example of a word and its stems with the common prefixes and suffixes.

Xu, Fraser, and Weischedel (2002) have classified Arabic stemming algorithms into two categories according to the level of analysis—stem-based and root-based algorithms; the latter is more aggressive.

Frakes (1992) has distinguished four different ways of stemming—affix removal, successor variety, table look-up, and N-grams:

- *Affix removal* is primarily a linguistic method that uses specific rules to eliminate the affixes from the words, thus isolating the stems.

- *Successor variety* or *word segmentation* uses letter sequences to divide words into stems on the basis of predetermined rules.

- *Table look-up* assumes that all word variants and stems are entries in a table.

Root	كَتَبَ	"write"
Pattern	فاعِل	FĀ'IL (noun/adjective pattern)
Prefixes	ال	"the" (definite article)
Stem	كاتِب	"writer"
Suffixes	يْن , ان	dual ending (first form: nom.; second form: acc./gen.)
Suffixes	ين , ون	plural ending
Suffixes	ة	feminine ending
Word	الكـــاتبين	"the (two) writers" (dual, acc./gen.)
	الكاتبـــان	"the (two) writers" (dual, nom.)
	الكـــاتبين	"the writers" (plural,)
	الكاتـــب	"the writer" (masculine, singular)
	الكاتبـــة	"the writer" (feminine, singular)

Figure 11.1   Arabic word = prefixes + stem (root + pattern) + suffixes.

- *N-grams* are overlapping character sequences that can vary in length from 2- to 6-grams creating word fragments used in the retrieval process.

Affix Removal

Affix removal extracts common stems of word variants by removing prefixes and suffixes in accordance with specific rules; it is perhaps the most common way of isolating stems in Arabic language processing. This approach has formed the basis for several stemmers employed in Arabic IR experiments. "Light stemming" removes a relatively small set of the most common prefixes and suffixes (Larkey et al., 2002).

One such stemmer, the Light-10 stemmer, was created over the course of several experiments using different stemming algorithms. The stemmer is built into the Lemur Toolkit (*Lemur Toolkit Overview & Documentation*, 2005) and uses the affix removal method to provide five different stemming functions:

arabic_stop : arabic_stop

arabic_norm2 : table normalization

arabic_norm2_stop : table normalization with stopping

arabic_light10 : light stemming

arabic_light10_stop : light stemming with stopping

The first function removes stopwords from the text, the second is a normalization process, and the third combines both functions. The fourth function is the light stemming function, which removes seven prefixes ال،وال،بال،كال،فال،و،لل and 10 suffixes—ي، ة، ه، ية، يه، ين، ون، ات، ان، ها . The last function combines the first and fourth functions.

The Light-10 stemmer was developed through extensive work by the University of Massachusetts group for TREC 2001/2002 and SIGIR 2 (Larkey, Allen, Connell, Bolivar, & Wade, 2003; Larkey, Ballesteros, & Connell, 2002; Larkey & Connell, 2002). They modified a stemmer created by Khoja and Garside (1999) to extract stems but not roots and added some normalizing techniques. They also compared different versions of the stemmer they created with a stemmer using vowel removal and co-occurrence analysis. The results were highly similar to those of Khoja and Garside and showed significant improvement with light stemming as against using words or roots.

Darwish (2002a) designed a light Arabic stemmer *(Al-Stem)* that removes twenty-four frequently encountered prefixes and 22 commonly occurring suffixes. This stemmer, which was subsequently modified by Leah Larkey, is available for research purposes and was used by several groups in TREC 2002. Accepting input in either CP-1256 or UTF-8 encoding, it transliterates the input string into Roman characters, removes diacritics, and normalizes the letters. Al-Sughaiyer and Al-Kharashi (2004) have observed that the main advantages of this stemmer are its simplicity and compactness, but have also noted that it may produce too many erroneous analyses. Errors tend to occur for words having start or end characters that are similar to affixes. Darwish and Oard (2003) compared three stemmers in their monolingual runs—the Light-8 stemmer, a slight modification of it, and Al-Stem. They found small differences in the performance of the stemmers, but these were not statistically significant.

Darwish (2002b) also developed a morphological analyzer for Arabic, which he described as being "shallow" because it gives only the possible roots of any given Arabic word. Therefore, it can be considered a stemmer. The *Sebawai* stemmer (www.glue.umd.edu/~kareem/hamlet/arabic/sebawai.tar.gz) consists of two modules. The "Build-Model" module uses a list of word-root pairs as inputs "(1) to derive a list of prefixes and suffixes, (2) to construct stem templates, and (3) to compute the likelihood that a prefix, suffix, or template might appear" (p. 49). The word list is constructed automatically using the Arabic morphological analyzer ALP-NET (www.xrce.xerox.com/competencies/content-analysis/arabic). The Detect Root module calculates the probabilities of stems, suffixes, and templates occurring in a particular combination. Darwish, Doermann, Jones, Oard, and Rautiainen (2002) used this stemmer to create roots and stems for their experiments. They compared retrieval by words, by roots, by stems, and by 2- to 4-character N-grams for roots and by 3- to 5-character N-grams for words. Word character trigrams and stems yielded the best results in CLIR and in the monolingual run.

Aljlayl, Beitzel, Jensen, Chowdhury, Holmes, Lee, et al. (2002) developed a root-based algorithm to detect the root of a given word and a stem-based algorithm that is not as aggressive as the root-based one; at TREC 10, the stem-based approach yielded better results. Subsequently, their team developed two new stemmers for monolingual runs (Chowdhury, Aljlayl, Jensen, & Beitzel, 2003). The first is a light stemmer designed to extract the most common prefixes and suffixes from a corpus consisting of one million words that was drawn from articles published in two major Saudi Arabian newspapers (*Al-Riyadh* and

Al-Jazirah) in the period 1999–2001. The second is a pattern-based stemmer that detects stems using common affix patterns in Arabic words. The results with the light stemmer had an average precision of 0.3419, whereas the results with the pattern-based stemmer had an average precision of 0.3473.

For TREC 10, Chen and Gey (2002) built a simple corpus-based stemmer that removed only four common suffixes and the definite article prefix (الـ) from words in the Arabic Newswire A corpus. They subsequently continued their experiments and developed two new stemmers (Chen & Gey, 2003). One of these was based on clustering Arabic words according to their English translations, with the Arabic words clustered together if their English translations were conflated to the same English stem. The other stemmer used lists of common one-, two-, and three-character prefixes and suffixes to identify which elements of words in the Arabic Newswire A corpus should be removed to obtain stems. Chen and Gey tested different combinations of these techniques, comparing them with the *Al-Stem* stemmer that Darwish and Larky had created. The affix removal stemmer performed better than the cluster-based and *Al-Stem* stemmers.

At TREC 2001, Tomlinson (2002) used the Hummingbird SearchServer retrieval system and experimented with both stopwords and stemming. The improvement in precision was greater with stopwords than with stemming. That may be because the stems were created by the same system using Unicode and did not adapt to the Arabic language. He repeated the experiment at TREC 2002 (Tomlinson, 2003), with the addition of a stoplist obtained from Yaser Al-Onizan; this led to a slight improvement in the results.

Word Segmentation/Table Look-Up

Stemming can be accomplished through the use of word segmentation, table look up, or a combination of these two techniques. The *Buckwalter Stemmer* (Buckwalter, 2002) uses both methods to create stems. It begins by segmenting each word into prefix, stem, and suffix strings using lexicon files of prefixes (299 entries), suffixes (618 entries), and stems (82,158 entries representing 38,600 lemmas). Each segment is then searched in a dictionary to verify its existence. The verified segments are then checked for compatibility of their morphological categories using tables for each pair (prefix-stem combinations [1,648 entries], stem-suffix combinations [1,285 entries], and prefix-suffix combinations [598 entries]). If all three pairs are compatible, the word is considered valid.

Although it is a very impressive work, the Buckwalter Stemmer has a few weaknesses. It gives more than one solution for stemming a word—up to 20 solutions or more—and this is impractical in some IR experiments (Abu El-Khair, 2003). Moreover, the output consists of text transliterated from Arabic to English according to a transliteration scheme created by the stemmer's author. Beesley (2003) has noted the disadvantages of using such a nonstandard scheme, the difficulty of mixing Arabic and Roman characters in the same document, and the stemmer's lack of capability to represent Arabic punctuation. Also, because the stemmer is based on word segmentation and table look-up, its effectiveness is limited by the size of the tables used. However, the Arabic language is much richer than can be easily represented in tables. Such criticisms notwithstanding, the Buckwalter Stemmer has been used extensively by the BBN group at recent TREC and SIGIR 2 meetings (Fraser, Xu, & Weischedel, 2003; Xu, Fraser, & Weischedel, 2002; Xu, Weischedel, & Fraser, 2002) and commentators have judged that the availability of this remarkable work has given a boost to Arabic IR in general (Farghaly, 2004).

N-grams

Hegazi, Ali, and Abed (1987) were the first to use N-gram methods of different sizes of n (1 to 8) to determine the characteristics of character sequences in Arabic text. They used letter frequency, rank frequency distribution, and Shannon estimates of the nth order entropy and redundancy. Hegazi, Ali, and Abed found that, compared to English, Arabic entropy is higher and that the Arabic language is more redundant because of its morphological nature. In addition, they found that the average Arabic word is longer than the average English word. They showed that as the value of n increases, redundancy increases and the entropy value decreases, resulting in a high degree of compression.

Darwish et al. (2002) used 2- to 4-character N-grams for roots and 3- to 5-character N-grams for words, with word character trigrams yielding the greatest precision. Kwok et al. (2002) tried to process the Arabic text using PIRCS, a probabilistic retrieval system for the Chinese language. They experimented with 4- and 5-character N-grams and used the Ajeeb English-to-Arabic translation Web site (http://tarjin.ajeeb.com); however, the mean precision was well below the median. Mayfield, McNamee, Costello, Piatko, and Banerjee (2002) experimented with 6-character N-grams, using a probabilistic retrieval system. McNamee, Piatko, and Mayfield (2003) subsequently investigated the use of 3-, 4-, and 5-character N-grams and combinations of those N-gram lengths. Their best results were obtained using a combination of the various lengths of N-grams and words.

Mustafa and Al-Radaideh (2004) examined the performance of 2- to 3-character N-grams in Arabic IR. They used a small corpus drawn from a number of sources representing various disciplines. The results indicated that digrams had better performance in retrieval than trigrams. Mustafa (2005) assessed the performance of two N-gram techniques using three different levels of word stemming: no stemming, light stemming, and higher-order stemming. The first technique was based on the conventional approach of generating adjacent digrams; the second adopted a hybrid approach that mixed adjacent and non-adjacent digrams. The hybrid approach outperformed the conventional one under all conditions.

The use of N-grams in Arabic IR does not appear to have produced effective retrieval results. This is because it is a statistical method and does not really address problems of ambiguity in the Arabic language. The results obtained by using the N-grams technique are poor in comparison with those obtained through the use of other stemming techniques. In addition, many errors may occur during the text preprocessing step; in most cases, this can yield conflicting and inconsistent results.

Stopword Elimination

Stopwords are very common words that carry little meaning. They serve a syntactic function but do not indicate subject matter (Lancaster, 1998). Such words affect the IR process in several ways. First, they can have an impact on retrieval effectiveness because they occur with a very high frequency and tend to diminish the effect of frequency differences among less common words, thus affecting the weighting process. The removal of stopwords also changes document length. This, too, affects the weighting process. Furthermore, they can also affect the efficiency of retrieval: Because of their frequency of occurrence and their relatively empty semantic content, their presence may result in a large amount of unproductive processing (Korfhage, 1997). Stopword removal can also increase indexing efficiency because 30 to 50 percent of the tokens in a large text collection can represent stopwords (Schauble, 1997).

Generating a list of stopwords, or stoplist, in order to eliminate them from text processing is essential to an IR system. Stoplists can be divided into two categories—domain-independent stoplists and domain-dependent stoplists. They can be created by specifying certain syntactic classes for inclusion or by using corpus statistics to identify those words occurring with greatest frequency. The latter is a more domain-dependent approach typically used for well-defined fields. They can also be created by combining certain syntactic classes with corpus statistics to obtain the benefits of both approaches.

Eliminating stopwords is considered an important step in text processing. Unfortunately, a solid theoretical basis or clear methodology for developing stoplists does not yet exist.

General Stoplists

Fox (1990) created a stoplist to be used for general texts, which he based on analysis of word usage in English. Beginning with a corpus of 1,014,000 words drawn from a broad range of literature, he drew up a list of words that occurred more than 300 times in the corpus. He then removed from the list those words that had the potential of being used as index terms and added others. He then incorporated into the list different forms of words and verbs using common suffixes and prefixes such as "-ed," "-ing," "-thing," and "-er." The final list consisted of 421 words. Because Fox's goal was the creation of a general stoplist for the English language, he did not test this list in an IR evaluation; however, it was used later in the Okapi retrieval system.

This method of stoplist generation has been used frequently and is viewed as a domain-independent approach. Its weakness lies in the absence of an objective basis for the decisions to be taken during the creation of the list. For example, the choice of cut-off point, upon which the list is built, is arbitrary. The elimination of some words and addition of others is based on personal judgment of the list's creator(s), which requires a certain expertise in the language for which the list is being prepared.

There is currently no standard Arabic stoplist for use in IR experiments. Khoja (2001) created a stoplist while developing her Arabic stemmer. This relatively short list, which totals only 168 words, forms part of the Lemur Toolkit. It has also been used by Larkey and Connell (2002) and by Larkey, Ballesteros, and Connell (2002). However, a standard general stoplist for Arabic is needed. Such a list should base itself on the structure and characteristics of the Arabic language, without any additions. In order to ensure completeness, it should incorporate all words that may be considered as stopwords; these should be drawn in a systematic way from the different syntactic classes of Arabic. The word categories (Abdul-Rauf, 1996; Al-Raghi, 1981) that should be used are: adverbs, conditional pronouns, interrogative pronouns, prepositions, pronouns, referral names/determiners, relative pronouns, transformers (verbs, letters), and verbal pronouns.

Corpus-Based Stoplists

A corpus-based stoplist is based on the statistics of the test corpus in hand. A cut-off point determining the number of words at which the list will stop should be decided based on the corpus statistics. Preliminary examination of the corpus word frequency statistics allows the researcher to decide which number is a reasonable cut-off point: Words occurring more than this number of times in the corpus are then used to create the list. Ultimately, this is an arbitrary decision.

Savoy (1999) developed a stoplist for French, using two document collections to extract that language's 200 most frequently occurring words. From this preliminary list, he removed numbers, as well as nouns and adjectives that he believed might be useful for retrieval purposes, while adding categories of words—that is, personal pronouns, possessive pronouns, prepositions, and conjunctions—that were not sufficiently "information-bearing" for use in queries (p. 945). Savoy (2001) also applied the same method to create stoplists for Italian, German, and Spanish. In the following year, he added Finnish and augmented the previously created stoplists with more words (Savoy, 2002).

Work in these languages formed the basis for Savoy's work in Arabic. At TREC 2002, Savoy and Rasolofo (2003) used the same techniques to create a stoplist for the Arabic language.[2] The stoplist was based on the LDC corpus and consisted of 347 words. This domain-dependent list encountered three problems. First, the authors used some words preceded by the letter *waw* (و), which means "and" in 17 words, including 11 duplicates. The separate form of this letter is used in the writing of many Arabic words. It also can precede all the words in the language, without any exceptions. A more efficient way to handle this ambiguity is to remove it with the help of a good stemming algorithm. Second, they removed several other single letters along with the *waw*, namely the *hamza* (ء), *'alif* (ا إ), *ba* (بـ), and *ha* (ه). Because of the way the Arabic language is written, these letters can be written as separate characters, even when they form part of a word. Removing them changes the word's meaning or leaves it meaningless. For example, the word token "كتاب" which could mean "book," "writers," or "a place for learning," has its terminal letter (بـ) written as a single separate letter; when it is removed, the remaining word fragment is meaningless. The third problem is that some of the words that Savoy and Rasolofo used were not stopwords, even though they appeared with great frequency in the corpus. Over thirty words in the list appeared in some of the queries. Perhaps the reason why their results with a longer version of the queries were more successful lies in the fact that some of the words in the short query—for example, الولايات "States," المتحدة "United," and القاهرة "Cairo"—were included in the stoplist. Finally, it should be noted that, because this is essentially a domain-dependent list, it may not be suitable for other collections.

Term Weighting Schemes

Salton and Buckley (1988) note that term weighting is a crucial component of any IR system and has the potential to improve retrieval effectiveness significantly. Indexing assigns a set of index terms to represent the content of each document in a collection. In most IR systems, every word in the text (excluding those registered in the stoplist) is used as an index term. In order to indicate the relative values of terms for describing the subject of a document, a term weight or value may be assigned to each word in the document during indexing (Korfhage, 1997; Salton & McGill, 1983).

Three term weighting schemes—TF*IDF, BM25, and LM—have proven effective in IR experiments over a wide range of systems and document collections with different properties. The success of these term weights is due to the fact that they incorporate more than one factor from the document, the query, or both to calculate the final weight for each term. Even though these statistical approaches are considered to be language-independent, their use in Arabic language retrieval still requires more research, especially in light of other factors affecting the weight, such as stemming and stopword elimination.

TF*IDF

The significance of a particular term in a given document can be determined by calculating the term frequency (TF) of that term in the document, with more frequent terms considered to be more significant. This assumption can be traced back to the observations made by Luhn (1958) when he was conducting exploratory research on creating automatic abstracts of scientific documents. Use of the TF*IDF scheme and its variations in IR experiments has led to substantial improvement in performance over simple term matching techniques. Several studies (Harman, 1986; Harman & Candela, 1990; Salton & Buckley, 1988; Sparck Jones, 2000) have found it to be relatively successful in weighting document terms over a wide range of collections with different properties, such as size and scope. In the case of Arabic language retrieval experiments, the TF*IDF weighting scheme has been successfully used in several studies (Abu-Salem, Al-Omari, & Evens, 1999; Hasnah & Evens, 2001; Aljlayl, Frieder, & Grossman, 2002; Chowdhury et al., 2003; Tomlinson, 2002, 2003).

Probabilistic Weighting

Maron and Kuhns (1960) introduced the probabilistic retrieval model almost a half-century ago. Systems using this model attempt to estimate the probability that the user will find documents relevant to his/her query. This probability is assumed to depend on the query and the document representation or description; a further assumption is that there exists a relevant subset of documents. All documents in this subset are predicted to be relevant and documents that are not in it are predicted to be non-relevant (Baeza-Yates & Ribeiro-Neto, 1999).

Probability-based indexing has proved to be relatively successful over the years, as Sparck Jones, Walker, and Robertson (2000a, 2000b) have noted in their extensive review of the model. It has been implemented in the Okapi system, a retrieval system developed at City University that has been tested heavily with various collections, specifically the large ones used at TREC. Robertson, Walker, Hancock-Beaulieu, Gatford, and Payne (1996) created what is now known as BM25 (Best Match), a probability-based weighting function that has been very successful over the years. BM25 has been used for different languages, not just English, and has out-performed a number of vector space model weights with French, Italian, German, and Spanish (Savoy, 2001), as well as Finnish and Dutch (Savoy, 2002).

The general framework of the probabilistic model, including BM25, has been used several times in Arabic retrieval experiments, with successful results (Chen & Gey, 2002, 2003; Darwish et al., 2002; Darwish

& Oard, 2003; Kwok, Grunfeld, Dinstl, & Chan, 2002; Larkey, Ballesteros, & Connell, 2002; Larkey & Connell, 2002; Mayfield et al., 2002; McNamee et al., 2003; Sanderson & Alberair, 2002; Xu, Weischedel, & Fraser, 2002). It should be noted that these studies used the weighting function on the assumption that it would be as successful with Arabic as it had been with English because it is a statistical method; however, Savoy and Rasolofo (2003) compared the Okapi model with TF*IDF function and found Okapi to be superior.

Statistical Language Modeling

Statistical language modeling is a newer weighting algorithm that has proven to be effective. Ponte and Croft (1998) were the first to apply language modeling to IR and found it superior to the traditional TF*IDF weight. Over the past few years, language modeling has emerged within a new probabilistic framework. It involves estimating a probability distribution that captures statistical regularities of natural language use.

> Applied to information retrieval, language modeling is used to estimate the likelihood that a query and a document could have been generated by the same language model, given the language model of the document either with or without a language model of the query. (Liu & Croft, 2005, p. 3)

Ogilvie and Callan (2002) compared a unigram language modeling algorithm with the Okapi retrieval function. Their language modeling approach achieved greater precision, indicating the effectiveness of this algorithm even when compared with the highly regarded Okapi approach. Fraser, Xu, and Weischedel (2003); Larkey et al. (2003); Larkey and Connell (2005); and Xu and Weischedel (2005) used this weighting function with successful results. Larkey and Connell (2005) also compared the model to the probabilistic approach available in the INQUERY retrieval system. They carried out several studies, but these did not reveal any consistent differences between the two models.

Cross-Language Information Retrieval

Cross-language information retrieval (CLIR)

> allows users to state queries in their native language and then retrieves documents in any supported language. This can simplify searching by multilingual users and, if translation resources are limited, can allow searchers to allocate those resources to the most promising documents. (Oard & Diekema, 1998)

In this section, we consider briefly some of the techniques used with CLIR and the Arabic language, such as machine translation systems, translation lexicons, and parallel corpora. For more detailed reviews of CLIR-related issues in general, see Gey, Kando, and Peters (2005); Kishida (2005); and Oard and Diekema (1998).

Machine translation (MT) *systems* are the most heavily used in CLIR experiments. For Arabic, there are several freely available MT systems, such as Ajeeb (http://tarjim.ajeeb.com), which was developed by Sakhr, and Almisbar (http://almisbar.com), formerly Al-Mutargim, which was produced by ATA Software Technology Limited.

Machine-readable bilingual dictionaries come second with Ajeeb, Ectaco (www.ectato.com/online) by Ectaco Inc., Al-Mawrid by Dar El-Ilm Lilmalayin (Chen & Gey, 2002), and Al-Mutarjim Al-Arabey (The Arabic Translator) by ATA software (Hasnah & Evens, 2001).

Parallel corpora are used as well in Arabic CLIR experiments, for example, the U.N. parallel corpus created by the BBN Group (Larkey & Connell, 2005; Xu et al., 2002; Xu & Weischedel, 2005). Mention should be made of the Buckwalter bilingual lexicon, which forms part of the stemmer. It received heavy use at TREC 2002 (Oard & Gey, 2003) and has also been used by Xu and Weischedel (2005).

The success of these different approaches in terms of retrieval performance varies in accordance with the conditions applied in different experiments. However, Darwish and Oard (2003) argue that, because there is no complete translation resource, we should always use a combination of different resources to increase the performance of CLIR. This is confirmed by research that shows improvement in retrieval results when translation resources are combined (e.g., Chen & Gey, 2002; Larkey et al., 2003).

Evaluation in Arabic IR

The primary objective IR is to provide users with the necessary documents to meet an information need. In addition to retrieving the relevant documents, an IR system should have the capacity to eliminate the non-relevant documents.

The quality of any IR system's response to an information need stated in a query is usually referred to as its effectiveness. Many studies and experiments have examined the effectiveness of different systems. Most of these studies have examined the systems in terms of recall and precision, two classical measures in IR that are used to assess the ability of the system to retrieve relevant documents (Figure 11.2). These measures are inversely related: On average, high recall is associated with low precision and vice versa. The use of specific or nonspecific terms in a query, in tandem with term weighting, can have a great effect on those measures (Korfhage, 1997; Salton & Buckley, 1988).

$$Recall = \frac{Number \ of \ relevant \ documents \ retrieved}{Number \ of \ relevant \ documents \ in \ the \ collection}$$

$$Precision = \frac{Number \ of \ relevant \ documents \ retrieved}{Total \ number \ of \ documents \ retrieved}$$

Figure 11.2 Recall and precision measures.

Recall is the proportion of relevant items retrieved, measured by the ratio of the number of relevant items retrieved to the total number of relevant items in the collection.

Precision is the proportion of retrieved items that are relevant, measured by the ratio of the number of relevant items retrieved to the total number of retrieved items.

The primary assumption underlying the use of these measures is that "the average user is interested in retrieving large amounts of relevant materials (producing a high recall performance), while at the same time rejecting a large proportion of the extraneous items (producing high precision)" (Salton, 1992, p. 442). As Salton (1992, p. 442) has noted, these two measures "have formed the basis for IR system evaluation in both operational and laboratory systems for decades" (p. 442). This is true regardless of the language involved: all comparative retrieval experiments use these measures.

TREC

TREC (http://trec.nist.gov) has been active for over 10 years, with teams from various academic, governmental, and commercial institutions around the world conducting series of experiments in many different tracks (Harman & Voorhees, 2006). So far, TREC has been successful in achieving its goals (Voorhees, 2003, p. 1):

- to encourage research in information retrieval based on large test collections;

- to increase communication among industry, academia, and government by creating an open forum for the exchange of research ideas;

- to speed the transfer of technology from research labs into commercial products by demonstrating substantial improvements in retrieval methodologies on real-world problems; and

- to increase the availability of appropriate evaluation techniques for use by industry and academia, including development of new evaluation techniques more applicable to current systems.

In 2001, TREC included, for the first time, a track for Arabic language retrieval, more specifically a CLIR track testing the use of English or French queries with regard to Arabic documents, as well as monolingual retrieval using Arabic queries. Retrieval experiments were conducted with stems, roots, and N-grams using machine translation systems, translation lexicons, parallel corpora, and transliteration (Gey & Oard, 2002). The CLIR track at TREC 2002 focused on three major issues: "(1) a greater focus on CLIR techniques ... , (2) continued investigation of Arabic-specific issues, such as stemming and stopword removal, and (3) increasing reliance on multiple sources of evidence to overcome the limitation of any single source" (Oard & Gey, 2003, p. 21).

Introducing Arabic into TREC has solved several problems regarding the standardization of tools and the generalizability of results. Prior to TREC, these problems were overlooked: Researchers worked with small data sets and had no systematic way of creating queries and relevance judgments. Results obtained using a large corpus with its queries and relevance judgments could now be applied to other research under different circumstances.

Four basic types of evaluation measures have been consistently used at TREC. All results for the ad hoc retrieval were obtained using the trec_eval package (ftp://ftp.cs.cornell.edu/pup/smart) written by Chris Buckley (Voorhees & Harman, 2002), which provides:

- summary table statistics consisting of statistics such as the number of topics used in the experiments, the number of documents retrieved across all topics, the number of relevant documents retrieved, and the total number of relevant documents that could have been retrieved.

- recall-precision average (R-P), expressed in the form of a table, graph, or both, with the average precision across the standard recall levels.

- document level averages reporting the average precision, calculated over specified document cutoff values.

- average precision histograms that illustrate the difference between the average R-P and the R-P of each individual topic.

Pooling Problems at TREC

The query set associated with the LDC corpus was created for TREC 2001 and 2002. Consisting of 75 queries, the set was developed at the LDC by native Arabic speakers, then translated into English and French.[3] The relevance judgments for these queries were obtained using assessment pools from different runs at TREC 2001 and 2002, and using the top 70 documents from each run with an average size of 910 documents for each pool. For TREC 2001, "the average number of relevant documents over the 25 [queries] was 164.9 with five topics having more than 300 relevant documents" and another five with fewer than 25 (Voorhees & Harman, 2002, pp. 7–8). For TREC 2002, "the average number of relevant documents over the 50 queries was 118.2" with eight topics having more than 300 relevant documents and 16 topics having fewer than 25 (Voorhees, 2003, p. 7).

Documents not included in the pool are not judged and their relevance is not assessed; therefore, they are assumed to be non-relevant. Because the candidate pool size is relatively small (approximately 1,000 documents), many documents will appear as non-relevant. Voorhees and Harman (2002) have observed that the difference in the relevance judgments for the Arabic corpus across queries and research groups in TREC 2001 was greater than that reported for previous TREC cross-language experiments. Thus, "for seven topics, more than half of the relevant documents were retrieved by only one group and for another six topics between 40 and 50 percent of the relevant documents were retrieved by one group" (p. 8). Voorhees and Harman recommended that, when experimenting with this type of collection, researchers "who find unjudged documents in the top-ranked list of only one of a pair of runs to be contrasted should proceed with care" (p. 8). The extent of this problem was investigated during the actual retrieval experiments.

The pooling problem has been addressed previously and some researchers believe that TREC experiments provide reliable results (Zobel, 1998). Nevertheless, this problem still needs more in-depth investigation and analysis. The effect of the pool size and the bias caused by it should be considered after the results of the experiments are obtained. There is a simple test to determine whether the pooling affects the experiments (Voorhees, personal communication, January 6, 2003):

> The number of unjudged documents retrieved should be counted, bearing in mind that the only legitimate use of a test collection is to compare different retrieval strategies. Therefore, pool size should not be a problem unless one method being compared retrieved a disproportionately large number of unjudged documents, especially at low (close to 1) ranks. If all of the runs being compared have roughly the same number of unjudged documents in the top (for instance top 100) ranks, then there is no problem. If some run does retrieve a substantially larger number of unjudged documents, then caution about any conclusions drawn from that comparison is required.

Rasmussen (2003) criticized the TREC experiments for the absence of systematic failure analysis across individual query results. Such analysis could reveal any significant differences in retrieval related to the characteristics of individual queries. The standard deviation of individual query results from the average result could identify queries that perform poorly. By analyzing the results for these queries, it should be possible to determine whether characteristics of Arabic, or any language, interact with the stemming, stopwords, term weighting, or other methods used to result in poor performance for certain query terms or types.

Conclusion and Future Research

Research on IR in English began in the 1950s, with the Cranfeld experiments and the MEDLARS project, and has made considerable progress since then (Salton, 1989). IR experiments in any language can provide great benefits for the development of the field, as seen with the TREC experiments, which started more than a decade ago.

Experimentation with Arabic language retrieval is still in its infancy. Researchers in Arabic IR can benefit greatly from the work that has been done in English, which has led to the development of many new techniques and has generated a vast specialized literature. Indeed, some of the research that has been done in English could be replicated for Arabic.

Research has shown that, in Arabic language retrieval, the use of stems and roots as the basis for searches yields superior results to the use of words for that purpose. They improve retrieval effectiveness, especially at high recall levels, by introducing a broader concept for a given term, thus increasing the number of retrieved documents. Similarly, when one compares the retrieval effectiveness of stems and roots, roots yield higher recall levels than stems. Pre-TREC experiments indicated that roots were better in retrieval than both words and stems (Abu-Salem et al., 1999; Al-Kharashi & Evens, 1994; Hasnah & Evens, 2001; Hmeidi, Kanaan, & Evens, 1997), but this was probably due to the small size of the corpora used. When one uses words to search in a small corpus, it is hard to find matches because of the complexity of Arabic morphology. Stems improve the results a little, but roots improve the results significantly: This is because words are reduced to the bare forms of their generating verbs, a move that increases the probability of matching query terms to document terms.

In larger corpora, however, a single verbal root can generate hundreds of different forms of nouns and verbs. Many studies have shown that the use of stems yields better results than the use of roots and words in retrieving documents from larger Arabic-language corpora (Aljlayl, Frieder, & Grossman, 2002; Chen & Gey, 2003; Chowdhury et al., 2003; Fraser, Xu, & Weischedel, 2003; Larkey et al., 2003; Larkey, Ballesteros & Connell, 2002; Larkey & Connell, 2002; Mayfield et al., 2002; McNamee et al., 2003; Sanderson & Alberair, 2002; Savoy & Rasolofo, 2003; Tomlinson, 2002, 2003; Xu, Weischedel, & Fraser, 2002).

More research with term weighting algorithms is required, especially as regards the application of the language modeling and probabilistic models to Arabic IR. Further investigations using these approaches could assess how effective they are in dealing with Arabic. Even though they are statistical methods, applying them to language-specific issues presented by Arabic could reveal some new interesting facts. For example, developing a weighting algorithm that uses the characteristics of the BM25 algorithm and takes into account the syntactical structure of the Arabic sentence in calculating term weight could improve upon the efficiency of this algorithm.

The need to use stemming for Arabic retrieval has been established, but no standard stemming algorithm (such as, e.g., the Porter stemmer, which is used heavily for English) has been developed. Even though the Light-10 stemmer has proven effective, further comparison and investigations for stemming algorithms in Arabic are needed. Exploring different algorithms may lead to a successful stemmer: Either the Light-10 will become a standard, stable algorithm or a better one may be found. The same principle applies for stopwords: Although they improve retrieval effectiveness and various lists have been compiled, there is no standard stoplist for use in Arabic IR experiments.

Finally, developing a new stemming algorithm that could handle broken plurals in Arabic would be very useful for retrieval. Arabic broken plurals are similar to the irregular noun plural forms in English—e.g., "man (sg.), men (pl.): رجل (sg.), رجال (pl.)": They do not follow a specific pattern. Arabic has many such forms and an efficient algorithm to reduce them to their singular form would improve retrieval results significantly.

Endnotes

1. A second edition of *Arabic Gigaword*, retaining all data from the first edition and adding content from Ummah Press, was released in January, 2006 (Linguistic Data Consortium, 2006, online).

2. The stoplists for all the languages are available at www.unine.ch/info/clef

3. The query sets are available at http://trec.nist.gov/data/topics_noneng/arabic_topics.txt (Arabic); http://trec.nist.gov/data/topics_noneng/english_topics.txt (English). The relevance judgments are available at http://trec.nist.gov/data/qrels_noneng/xlingual_t10qrels.txt

References

Abdul-Rauf, M. (1996). *Arabic for English speaking students.* Alexandria, VA: Al-Saadawi Publications.

Abu El-Khair, I. (2003). *Effectiveness of document processing techniques for Arabic information retrieval.* Unpublished doctoral dissertation, University of Pittsburgh, Pittsburgh, PA.

Abu-Salem, H. (1992). *A microcomputer based Arabic bibliographic information retrieval system with relational thesauri (Arabic-IRS).* Unpublished doctoral dissertation, Illinois Institute of Technology, Chicago.

Abu-Salem, H., Al-Omari, M., & Evens, M. (1999). Stemming methodologies over individual query words for an Arabic information retrieval system. *Journal of the American Society for Information Science, 50*, 524–529.

Aljlayl, M., Beitzel, S., Jensen, E., Chowdhury, A., Holmes, D., Lee, M., et al. (2002). IIT at TREC-10. *The Tenth Text REtrieval Conference (TREC 2001)*, pp. 265–274. Retrieved January 25, 2006, from http://trec.nist.gov/pubs/trec10/papers/IIT-TREC10.pdf

Aljlayl, M., Frieder, O., & Grossman, D. (2002). On bidirectional English-Arabic search. *Journal of the American Society for Information Science and Technology, 53*, 1139–1151.

Al-Kharashi, I., & Evens, M. (1994). Comparing words, stems, and roots as index terms in an Arabic information retrieval system. *Journal of the American Society for Information Science, 45*(8), 548–560.

Al-Raghi, A. (1981). التطبيق النحوى [*Grammatical application*]. Beirut, Lebanon: Dar al-Nahda al-Arabiyya Lelteba'ah wa al-Nashr.

Al-Sughaiyer, I. A., & Al-Kharashi, I. A. (2004). Arabic morphological analysis techniques: A comprehensive survey. *Journal of the American Society for Information Science and Technology, 55*, 189–213.

Arabic language. (2005). *Encyclopædia Britannica*. Retrieved June 20, 2005, from http://search.eb.com/eb/article-9008157

Baeza-Yates, R., & Ribeiro-Neto, B. (1999). *Modern information retrieval*. New York: ACM.

Bateson, M. C. (1967). *Arabic language handbook*. Washington, DC: Center for Applied Linguistics.

Beesley, K. R. (1996). Arabic finite-state morphological analysis and generation. *COLING 96: Proceedings of the 16th International Conference on Computational Linguistics* (vol. 1), 89–94.

Beesley, K. R. (2003). *Xerox Arabic morphological analyser surface-language (Unicode) documentation*. Retrieved June 20, 2005, from www.xrce.xerox.com/competencies/content-analysis/arabic-inxight/arabic-surf-lang-unicode-pdf

Belkin, N. J., & Croft, W. B. (1987). Retrieval techniques. *Annual Review of Information Science and Technology, 22*, 109–145.

Brunner, B. (Ed.). (2005). *Time almanac 2005 with information please*. Boston, MA: Information Please.

Buckwalter, T. (2002). *Buckwalter Arabic morphological analyzer* (Version 1.0): Philadelphia: Linguistic Data Consortium.

Chen, A. (2001). Multilingual information retrieval using English and Chinese queries. In C. Peters, M. Braschler, J. Gonzalo, & M. Kluck (Eds.), *Revised papers from the Second Workshop of the Cross-Language Evaluation Forum on Evaluation of Cross-Language Information Retrieval Systems* (Lecture Notes in Computer Science, vol. 2406, pp. 44–58). London: Springer.

Chen, A., & Gey, F. (2002). Translation term weighting and combining translation resources in cross-language retrieval. *The Tenth Text REtrieval Conference (TREC 2001)*, 529–533. Retrieved January 25, 2006, from http://trec.nist.gov/pubs/trec10/papers/berkeley_trec10.pdf

Chen, A., & Gey, F. (2003). Building an Arabic stemmer for information retrieval. *The Eleventh Text REtrieval Conference (TREC 2002)*, 299–310. Retrieved January 25, 2006, from http://trec.nist.gov/pubs/trec11/papers/ucalberkeley.chen.pdf

Chowdhury, A., Aljlayl, M., Jensen, E., & Beitzel, S. (2003). IIT at TREC-2002: Linear combinations based on document structure and varied stemming for Arabic retrieval. *The*

Eleventh Text REtrieval Conference (TREC 2002), 631–639. Retrieved January 25, 2006, from http://trec.nist.gov/pubs/trec11/papers/iit.grossman.pdf

Darwish, K. (2002a). *Al-stem: A light Arabic stemmer.* Retrieved June 20, 2005, from www.glue.umd.edu/~kareem/research

Darwish, K. (2002b, July). Building a shallow Arabic morphological analyzer in one day. *Proceedings of the ACL-02 Workshop on Computational Approaches to Semitic Languages, University of Pennsylvania, Pennsylvania, PA, USA.* Retrieved January 26, 2006, from http://acl.ldc.upenn.edu/W/W02/W02-0506.pdf

Darwish, K., Doermann, D., Jones, R., Oard, D., & Rautiainen, M. (2002). TREC-10 experiments at University of Maryland: CLIR and video. *The Tenth Text REtrieval Conference (TREC 2001)*, 549–561. Retrieved January 25, 2006, from http://trec.nist.gov/pubs/trec 10/papers/umdTREC2000.pdf

Darwish, K., & Oard, D. (2003). CLIR experiments at Maryland for TREC-2002: Evidence combination for Arabic-English retrieval. *The Eleventh Text REtrieval Conference (TREC 2002)*, 703–710. Retrieved January 25, 2006, from http://trec.nist.gov/pubs/trec 11/papers/umd.darwish.pdf

European Language Resource Association. (2001). *An-Nahar newspaper text corpus.* Retrieved June 20, 2005, from www.elda.org/catalogue/en/text/W0027.html

European Language Resource Association. (2002). *Arabic data set* [Al-Hayat newspaper text corpus]. Retrieved June 20, 2005, from www.elda.org/catalogue/en/text/W0030.html

Farghaly, A. (2004). Computer processing of Arabic script-based languages: Current state and future directions. *COLING 2004: Workshop on Computational Approaches to Arabic Script-based Languages: University of Geneva, Geneva, Switzerland*, 1. Retrieved January 25, 2006, from http://acl.ldc.upenn.edu/coling2004/W5/pdf/W5-1.pdf

Fox, C. (1990). A stop list for general text. *SIGIR Forum, 24*(1–2), 19–35.

Frakes, W. B. (1992). Stemming algorithms. In W. B. Frakes & R. Baeza-Yates (Eds.), *Information retrieval: Data structures and algorithms* (pp. 131–160). Englewood Cliffs, NJ: Prentice Hall.

Fraser, A., Xu, J., & Weischedel, R. (2003). 2002 cross-linguistic retrieval at BBN. *The Eleventh Text REtrieval Conference (TREC 2002)*, 102–106. Retrieved January 25, 2006, from http://trec.nist.gov/pubs/trec11/papers/bbn.xu.cross.pdf

Gey F., Kando N., & Peters, C. (2005). Cross-language information retrieval: The way ahead. *Information Processing & Management, 41*, 415–431.

Gey, F., & Oard, D. (2002). The TREC-2001 cross-language information retrieval track: Searching Arabic using English, French or Arabic queries. *The Tenth Text REtrieval Conference (TREC 2001)*, 16–25. Retrieved January 25, 2006, from http://trec.nist.gov/pubs/trec10/papers/clirtrack.pdf

Harman, D. (1986). An experimental study of factors important in document ranking. *Proceedings of the 9th Annual International ACM SIGIR Conference on Research and Development in Information Retrieval, Pisa, Italy*, 186–193.

Harman, D. (1991). How effective is suffixing? *Journal of the American Society for Information Science, 42*, 7–15.

Harman, D., & Candela, G. (1990). Retrieving records retrieved from a gigabyte of text on a mini-computer using statistical ranking. *Journal of the American Society for Information Science, 41*, 581–589.

Harman, D. K., & Voorhees, E. M. (2006). TREC: An overview. *Annual Review of Information Science and Technology, 40*, 113–155.

Hasan, M. M., & Matsumoto, Y. (2000). Japanese-Chinese cross-language information retrieval: An interlingual approach. *International Journal of Computational Linguistics and Chinese Language Processing, 5*(2), 59–86.

Hasnah, A. (1996). *Full text processing and retrieval: Weight ranking, text structuring, and passage retrieval for Arabic documents.* Unpublished doctoral dissertation, Illinois Institute of Technology, Chicago.

Hasnah, A., & Evens, M. (2001). Arabic/English cross language information retrieval using a bilingual dictionary. *ACL/EACL 2001 Workshop: Arabic Language Processing: Status and Prospects, Toulouse, France.* Retrieved January 26, 2005, from www.elsnet.org/arabic2001/hasnah.pdf

Hegazi, N., Ali, N., & Abed, E. (1987). Information content in textual data: Revisited for Arabic text. *Journal of the American Society for Information Science, 38,* 133–137.

Hmeidi, I. (1995). *Design and implementation of automatic word and phrase indexing for information retrieval with Arabic documents.* Unpublished doctoral dissertation, Illinois Institute of Technology, Chicago.

Hmeidi, I., Kanaan, G., & Evens, M. (1997). Design and implementation of automatic indexing for information retrieval with Arabic documents. *Journal of the American Society for Information Science, 48,* 867–881.

Kasem, H. (1978). *Arabic in specialist information systems.* Unpublished doctoral dissertation, University of London.

Khoja, S. (2001). *Khoja's Arabic stemmer* (version 1.0). London: Khoja.

Khoja, S., & Garside, R. (1999). *Stemming Arabic text.* Retrieved June 20, 2005, from www.comp.lancs.ac.uk/computing/users/khoja/stemmer.ps

Kishida K. (2005). Technical issues of cross-language information retrieval: A review. *Information Processing & Management, 41,* 433–455.

Korfhage, R. R. (1997). *Information storage and retrieval.* New York: Wiley.

Kwok, K. L., Grunfeld, L., Dinstl, N., & Chan, M. (2002). TREC2001 question-answer, Web and cross language experiments using PIRCS. *The Tenth Text REtrieval Conference (TREC 2001),* 452–456. Retrieved January 25, 2006, from http://trec.nist.gov/pubs/trec10/papers/queenst2001.pdf

Lancaster, F. W. (1998). *Indexing and abstracting in theory and practice* (2nd ed.). Champaign, IL: Graduate School of Library and Information Science, University of Illinois.

Larkey, L. S., Allan, J., Connell, M. E., Bolivar, A., & Wade, C. (2003). UMass at TREC 2002: Cross language and novelty tracks. *The Eleventh Text REtrieval Conference (TREC 2002),* 721–732. Retrieved January 25, 2006, from http://trec.nist.gov/pubs/trec11/papers/umass.wade.pdf

Larkey, L. S., Ballesteros, L., & Connell, M. E. (2002). Improving stemming for Arabic information retrieval: Light stemming and co-occurrence analysis. *SIGIR 2002: Proceedings of the 25th Annual International ACM SIGIR Conference on Research and Development in Information Retrieval, Tampere, Finland,* 275–282.

Larkey, L. S., & Connell, M. E. (2002). Arabic information retrieval at UMass in TREC-10. *The Tenth Text REtrieval Conference (TREC 2001),* 562–570. Retrieved January 25, 2006, from http://trec.nist.gov/pubs/trec10/papers/UMass_TREC10_Final.pdf

Larkey, L. S., & Connell, M. E. (2005). Structured queries, language modeling, and relevance modeling in cross-language information retrieval. *Information Processing & Management, 41,* 457–473.

Lemur Toolkit Overview & Documentation. (2005). Retrieved June 20, 2005, from www.lemurproject.org

Library of Congress. Cataloging Policy and Support Office. (2002). *ALA-LC romanization tables, Arabic language*. Retrieved June 20, 2005, from www.loc.gov/catdir/cpso/romanization/arabic.pdf

Linguistic Data Consortium. (2001). *Arabic Newswire Part 1*. Retrieved June 20, 2005, from www.ldc.upenn.edu/Catalog/LDC2001T55.html

Linguistic Data Consortium. (2003). *Arabic Gigaword*. Retrieved June 20, 2005, from www.ldc.upenn.edu/Catalog/LDC2003T12.html

Linguistic Data Consortium. (2006). *Arabic Gigaword* (2nd ed.). Retrieved January 26, 2006, from www.ldc.upenn.edu/Catalog/CatalogEntry.jsp?catalogId=LDC2006T02

Liu, X., & Croft, W. B. (2005). Statistical language modeling for information retrieval. *Annual Review of Information Science and Technology*, *39*, 3–31.

Lochbaum, K. E., &. Streeter, L. A. (1989). Comparing and combining the effectiveness of latent semantic indexing and the ordinary vector space model for information retrieval. *Information Processing & Management*, *25*, 665–676.

Luhn, H. P. (1958). The automatic creation of literature abstracts. *IBM Journal of Research and Development*, *2*, 159–165.

Maamouri, M., & Cieri, C. (2002). Resources for Arabic natural language processing at the Linguistic Data Consortium. In A. Braham (Ed.), *Proceedings of the International Symposium on the Processing of Arabic* (pp. 125–146). Manouba, Tunisia: Faculté des Lettres, Université de la Manouba.

Maron, M. E., & Kuhns, J. L. (1960). On relevance, probabilistic indexing and information retrieval. *Journal of the Association for Computing Machinery*, *7*, 216–244.

Mayfield, J., McNamee, P., Costello, C., Piatko, C., & Banerjee, A. (2002). JHU/APL at TREC 2001: Experiments in filtering and in Arabic, video, and Web retrieval. *The Tenth Text REtrieval Conference (TREC 2001)*, 332–340. Retrieved January 26, 2005, from http://trec.nist.gov/pubs/trec10/papers/jhuapl01.pdf

McNamee, P., Piatko, C., & Mayfield, J. (2003). JHU/APL at TREC 2002: Experiments in filtering and Arabic retrieval. *The Eleventh Text REtrieval Conference (TREC 2002)*, 358–363. Retrieved January 25, 2006, from http://trec.nist.gov/pubs/trec11/papers/jhuapl.mcnamee.pdf

Moukdad, H., & Large, A. (2001). Information retrieval from full-text Arabic databases: Can search engines designed for English do the job? *Libri*, *51*, 63–74.

Mustafa, S. H. (2005). Character contiguity in N-gram-based word matching: The case for Arabic text searching. *Information Processing & Management*, *41*, 819–827.

Mustafa, S. H., & Al-Radaideh, Q. A. (2004). Using N-grams for Arabic text searching. *Journal of the American Society for Information Science and Technology*, *55*, 1002–1007.

Oard, D., & Diekema, A. R. (1998). Cross-language information retrieval. *Annual Review of Information Science and Technology*, *33*, 223–256.

Oard, D., & Gey, F. (2003). The TREC 2002 Arabic/English track. *The Eleventh Text REtrieval Conference (TREC 2002)*, 17–26.

Ogilvie, P., & Callan, J. (2002). *Experiments using the Lemur Toolkit. The Tenth Text REtrieval Conference (TREC 2001)*, 332–340. Retrieved January 26, 2005, from http://trec.nist.gov/pubs/trec10/papers/cmu-dir-lemur-trec10-final.pdf

Ponte, J. M., & Croft, W. B. (1998). A language modeling approach to information retrieval. *SIGIR '98: Proceedings of the 21st Annual International ACM SIGIR Conference on Research and Development in Information Retrieval, Melbourne, Australia*, 275–281.

Rasmussen, E. (2003). Evaluation in information retrieval. In J. S. Downie (Ed.), *The MIR/MDL Evaluation Project white paper collection* (3rd ed., pp. 45–49). Champaign, IL: Graduate School of Library and Information Science.

Robertson, S. E., Walker, S., Hancock-Beaulieu, M. M., Gatford, M., & Payne, A. (1996). Okapi at TREC-4. *The Fourth Text REtrieval Conference (TREC-4)*, 73–96.

Salton, G. (1989). *Automatic text processing*. Reading, MA: Addison-Wesley.

Salton, G. (1992). The state of retrieval system evaluation. *Information Processing & Management, 28*, 441–449.

Salton, G., & Buckley, C. (1988). Term-weighting approaches in automatic text retrieval. *Information Processing & Management, 24*, 513–523.

Salton, G., & McGill, M. (1983). *Introduction to modern information retrieval*. New York: McGraw-Hill.

Sanderson, M., & Alberair, A. (2002). Keep it simple Sheffield: A KISS approach to the Arabic track. *The Tenth Text REtrieval Conference (TREC 2001)*, 642–644. Retrieved January 26, 2005, from http://trec.nist.gov/pubs/trec10/papers/sheffield_arabic.pdf

Savoy, J. (1999). A stemming and stopword list for general French corpora. *Journal of the American Society for Information Science, 50*, 944–952.

Savoy, J. (2001). Report on CLEF-2001 experiments: Effective combined query-translation approach. In C. Peters, M. Braschler, J. Gonzalo, & M. Kluck (Eds.), *Evaluation of cross-language information retrieval systems: Second Workshop of the Cross-Language Evaluation Forum, CLEF 2001, Darmstadt, Germany: Revised papers*. (Lecture Notes in Computer Science, vol. 2406, pp. 27–43). Berlin: Springer.

Savoy, J. (2002). Report on CLEF-2002 experiments: Combining multiple sources of evidence. In C. Peters, M. Braschler, J. Gonzalo, & M. Kluck (Eds.), *Advances in cross-language information retrieval: Third Workshop of the Cross-Language Evaluation Forum, CLEF, 2000, Rome, Italy: Revised papers*. (Lecture Notes in Computer Science, vol. 2785, pp. 66–90). Berlin: Springer.

Savoy, J., & Rasolofo, Y. (2003). *Report on the TREC-11 experiment: Arabic, named page and topic distillation searches. The Eleventh Text REtrieval Conference (TREC 2002)*, 765–775. Retrieved January 25, 2006, from http://trec.nist.gov/pubs/trec11/papers/uneuchatel.pdf

Schauble, P. (1997). *Multimedia information retrieval: Content-based information retrieval from large text and audio databases*. Boston, MA: Kluwer.

Sparck Jones, K. (2000). Further reflections on TREC. *Information Processing & Management, 36*, 37–85.

Sparck Jones, K., Walker, S., & Robertson, S. E. (2000a). A probabilistic model of information retrieval: Development and comparative experiments: Part I. *Information Processing & Management, 36*, 779–808.

Sparck Jones, K., Walker, S., & Robertson, S. E. (2000b). A probabilistic model of information retrieval: Development and comparative experiments: Part II. *Information Processing & Management, 36*, 809–840.

Tomlinson, S. (2002). Hummingbird SearchServer™ at TREC 2001. *The Tenth Text REtrieval Conference (TREC 2001)*, 216–227. Retrieved January 26, 2005, from http://trec.nist.gov/pubs/trec10/papers/HumTREC2001.pdf

Tomlinson, S. (2003). Experiments in named page finding and Arabic retrieval with Hummingbird SearchServer™ at TREC 2002. *The Eleventh Text REtrieval Conference (TREC 2002)*, 248–259. Retrieved January 25, 2006, from http://trec.nist.gov/pubs/trec11/papers/hummingbird.tomlinson.pdf

Vines, P., & Zobel, J. (1999). Efficient building and querying of Asian language document databases. In *Proceedings of the 4th International Workshop on Information Retrieval with Asian Languages, Taipei, Taiwan (IRAL'99)* (pp. 118–125). Taipei: Academica Sinica.

Voorhees, E. M. (2003). Overview of TREC 2002. In E. M. Voorhees & L. P. Buckland (Eds.), *The Eleventh Text REtrieval Conference (TREC 2002)*, 1–16. Retrieved January 25, 2006, from http://trec.nist.gov/pubs/trec11/papers/OVERVIEW.11.pdf

Voorhees, E. M., & Harman, D. (2002). Overview of TREC 2001. *The Tenth Text REtrieval Conference (TREC 2001)*, 1–15. Retrieved January 26, 2005, from http://trec.nist.gov/pubs/trec10/papers/overview_10.pdf

Xu, J., Fraser, A., Makhoul, J., Noamany, M., & Osman, G. (2001). *UN Arabic English parallel text version 1.0 beta* [CD-ROM]. Philadelphia: University of Pennsylvania, Linguistic Data Consortium.

Xu, J., Fraser, A., & Weischedel, R. (2002). Empirical studies in strategies for Arabic retrieval. *SIGIR 2002: Proceedings of the 25th Annual International ACM SIGIR Conference on Research and Development in Information Retrieval, Tampere, Finland*, 269–274.

Xu, J., & Weischedel, R. (2005). Empirical studies on the impact of lexical resources on CLIR performance. *Information Processing & Management, 41*, 475–487.

Xu, J., Weischedel, R., & Fraser, A. (2002). TREC 2001 cross-lingual retrieval at BBN. *The Tenth Text REtrieval Conference (TREC 2001)*, 68–77. Retrieved January 26, 2005, from http://trec.nist.gov/pubs/trec10/papers/BBNTREC2001.pdf

Zobel, J. (1998). How reliable are the results of large-scale information retrieval experiments? *Proceedings of the 21st Annual International ACM SIGIR Conference on Research and Development in Information Retrieval*, 307–314.

Space and Place

CHAPTER 12

Network Science

Katy Börner
Soma Sanyal
Alessandro Vespignani
Indiana University

Introduction

This chapter reviews the highly interdisciplinary field of network science, which is concerned with the study of networks, be they biological, technological, or scholarly in character. It contrasts, compares, and integrates techniques and algorithms developed in disciplines as diverse as mathematics, statistics, physics, social network analysis, information science, and computer science. A coherent theoretical framework, including static and dynamical modeling approaches, is provided along with discussion of non-equilibrium techniques recently introduced for modeling growing networks. The chapter also provides a practical framework by reviewing major processes involved in the study of networks such as network sampling, measurement, modeling, validation, and visualization. For each of these processes, we explain and exemplify commonly used approaches. Aiming at a gentle yet formally correct introduction of network science theory, we explain terminology and formalisms in considerable detail. Although the theories come from a mathematical, formulae-laden world, they are highly relevant for the effective design of technological networks, scholarly networks, communication networks, and so on. We conclude with a discussion of promising avenues for future research.

At any moment we are driven by and are an integral part of many interconnected, dynamically changing networks[1]: Our neurons fire, cells signal to each other, our organs work in concert. The attack of a cancer cell might have an impact on all of these networks and it could also affect our social and behavioral networks if we became conscious of the attack. Our species has evolved as part of diverse ecological, biological, social, and other networks over thousands of years. As part of a complex food web, we learned how to find prey and to avoid predators. We have created advanced socio-technical environments in the shape of cities, water and power systems, streets, and airlines. In 1969, researchers started to interlink computers leading to the largest and most widely used networked infrastructure in existence: the Internet. The Internet facilitated the emergence of the World Wide Web, a virtual network that interconnects billions of Web pages, datasets, services, and human users. Thanks to the digitization of books, papers, patents, grants, court cases, news reports, and other material, along with the explosion of Wikipedia entries, e-mails, blogs, and such, we now have a digital copy of a major part of humanity's knowledge and evolution. Yet, although the amount of knowledge produced per day is growing at an accelerating rate, our main means of accessing mankind's knowledge are search engines that retrieve matching entities and facilitate local search based on connections—for example, references or Web links. But, it is not only factual knowledge that matters. The more global the problems we need to master as a species, the more we need to identify and understand major connections, trends, and patterns in data, information, and knowledge. We need to be able to measure, model, manage, and understand the structure and function of large, networked physical and information systems.

Network science is an emerging, highly interdisciplinary research area that aims to develop theoretical and practical approaches and techniques to increase our understanding of natural and man-made networks. The study of networks has a long tradition in graph theory and discrete mathematics (Bollobas, 1998; Brandes & Erlebach, 2005), sociology (Carrington, Scott, & Wasserman, 2004; Wasserman & Faust, 1994), communication research (Monge & Contractor, 2003), bibliometrics/scientometrics (Börner, Chen, & Boyack, 2003; Cronin & Atkins, 2000), Webometrics/cybermetrics (Thelwall, 2004), biology (Barabási & Oltvai, 2004; Hodgman 2000), and more recently physics (Barabási, 2002; Buchanan, 2002; Dorogovtsev & Mendes, 2003; Pastor-Satorras & Vespignani, 2004; Watts, 1999). Consequently, there is impressive variety in the work styles, approaches, and research interests among network scientists. Some specialize in the detailed analysis of a certain type of network, for example, friendship networks. Others focus on the search for common laws that might influence the structure and dynamics of networks across domains. Some scientists apply existing network measurement, modeling, and visualization algorithms to new datasets. Others actively develop new measurements and modeling algorithms. Depending on their original field of research, scientists will emphasize theory development or the practical effects of their results and present their work accordingly. Data availability and quality differ widely from large but incomplete and uncertain datasets to high quality datasets that are too small to support meaningful statistics. Some research questions require descriptive models to capture the major features of a (typically static) dataset; others demand process models that simulate, statistically describe, or formally reproduce the statistical and dynamic characteristics of interest. This variety, coupled with a lack of communication among scientists in different domains has led to many parallel, unconnected strands of network science research and a diversity of nomenclature and approaches.

Today, the computational ability to sample and the scientific need to understand large-scale networks call for a truly interdisciplinary approach to network science. Measurement, modeling, or visualization algorithms developed in one area of research, say physics, might well increase our understanding of biological or social networks. Datasets collected in biology, social science, information science, and other fields are used by physicists to identify universal laws. For example, unexpected similarities between systems as disparate as social networks and the Internet have been discovered (Albert & Barabási, 2002; Dorogovtsev & Mendes, 2002; Newman, 2003). These findings suggest that generic organizing principles and growth mechanisms may give rise to the structures of many existing networks.

Network science is a very young field of research. Many questions have still to be answered. Often, the complex structure of networks is influenced by system-dependent local constraints on node interconnectivity. Node characteristics may vary over time and there may be many different types of nodes. The links between nodes may be directed or undirected; they may have weights and/or additional properties that change over time. Many natural systems never reach a steady state and non-equilibrium models are required to characterize their behavior. Furthermore, networks rarely exist in isolation but are embedded in "natural" environments (Strogatz, 2001, p. 273).

This chapter reviews network science by introducing a theoretical and practical framework for the scientific study of networks. Although different conceptualizations of the general network science research process are possible, we adopt the process depicted in Figure[2] 12.1. A network science study typically starts with an hypothesis or research question, for example, does the existence of the Internet have an impact on social networks or citation patterns? Next, an appropriate dataset is collected or sampled, represented, and stored in a format amenable to efficient processing. Subsequently, network measurements are applied to identify features of interest. At this point the research process may proceed on parallel tracks, analyzing and/or modeling the system. Given the complexity of networks and the results obtained, the application of visualization techniques for the communication and interpretation of results is important. Interpretation frequently results in the further refinement (for example, selection of different parameter values or algorithms) and re-running of sampling, modeling, measurement, and visualization stages. As indicated in Figure 12.1, there is a major difference between *network analysis* that aims at the generation of descriptive models that explain and describe a certain system and *network modeling* that attempts to design process models that not only reproduce the empirical data but can also be used to make predictions. The latter models provide insights into why certain network structures and/or dynamics exist. These models can also be run with different initializations or

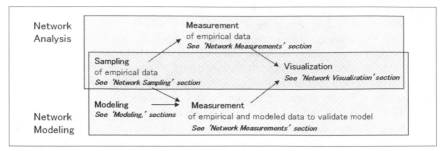

Figure 12.1   General network science research process.

parameters to make predictions for "what if" scenarios, for example: If the National Science Foundation (NSF) decided to double its budget in a given area over the next five years, what would be the impact in terms of numbers of publications, patents, and citations?

This chapter aims to provide a gentle introduction to the affordances and needs that the different network science disciplines pose. The background knowledge, pre-conceptualizations, and the ways of conducting science that the different disciplines employ vary widely. Yet, being able to translate among the different conceptualizations and terminologies and to identify similarities and differences among network science algorithms, concepts, and approaches is the basis for effective collaboration and the exchange of techniques and practices across disciplinary boundaries. Whenever possible, we will point out commonalities and differences, alternative terminology, and the relevance of alien-seeming concepts to core information science questions such as: How does one ensure that technological infrastructures (Internet, World Wide Web) are stable and secure? What network properties support/hinder efficient information access and diffusion? What are the structures of scholarly networks; how do they evolve and how can they be used for the efficient communication of scholarly knowledge?

The remainder of this review is organized as follows: First we introduce notions and notations used throughout the chapter. The next section discusses the basics of network sampling as the foundation of network analysis or modeling. This is followed by a presentation of basic measurements and some examples. Next, a discussion of the major elements of a unifying theoretical framework for network science aims to contrast, compare, and integrate major techniques and algorithms developed in diverse fields of science. The next section reviews dynamic network models. This is followed by an overview of network visualization techniques as a means of interpreting and effectively communicating the results of network sampling, measurement, and/or modeling. The concluding section discusses challenges and promising avenues for future research.

Notions and Notations

In this section we provide the basic notions and notations needed to describe networks. Not surprisingly, each field concerned with network science has its own nomenclature. The natural framework for a rigorous mathematical description of networks, however, is found in graph theory and we adopt it here. Indeed, graph theory can be traced back to the pioneering work of Euler (1736) to solve the Königsberg bridges problem. Building on the introduction of the *random graph model* by Erdös and Rényi (1959) (see also the section on modeling static networks), graph theory has reached a maturity in which a wealth of rigorous mathematical yet practically relevant results is available for the study of networks. The main sources for the subsequent formalizations are the books by Chartrand and Lesniak (1986) and Bollobas (1998). It is our intention to select those notions and notations that are easy to understand for the general *ARIST* readership and sufficient to introduce the basic measurements, models, and visualization techniques introduced in the subsequent sections.

Graphs and Subgraphs

Networks—hereafter also called graphs—have a certain structure (or topology) and can have additional quantitative information. The structure might be rooted or not and directed or undirected. Quantitative information about types, weights or other attributes for nodes and edges might exist. This section introduces different types of networks, their definition, and representation. We start with a description of graph structure.

Undirected Graphs

An *undirected graph* G is defined by a pair of sets $G = (V,E)$, where V is a non-empty countable set of elements, called *nodes* or *vertices*, and E is a set of *unordered* pairs of different nodes, called *edges* or *links*. We will refer to a node by its order i in the set V. The edge (i, j) joins the nodes i and j, which are said to be *adjacent*, *connected*, or *neighbors*. The total number of nodes in the graph equals the cardinality of the set V and is denoted as N. It is also called the *size* of the graph. The total number of edges equals the cardinality of the set E and is denoted by M. For a graph of size N, the maximum number of edges is $N(N-1)/2$. A graph in which all possible pairs of nodes are joined by edges, that is, $M = N(N-1)/2$, is called a *complete N-graph*. Undirected graphs are depicted graphically as a set of dots, representing the nodes, joined by lines between pairs of nodes that represent the corresponding edges (see Figure 12.2a-d).

Directed Graphs

A *directed graph* D, or *digraph*, is defined by a non-empty countable set of nodes V and a set of *ordered* pairs of different nodes E_D that are called directed edges. In a graphical representation, the ordered nature of the edges is usually depicted by means of an arrow, indicating the direction of an edge (see Figure 12.2e and 12.2f). Note that the presence of an edge from i to j, also referred to as $i < j$, in a directed graph does not necessarily imply the presence of the reverse edge $i > j$. This fact has important consequences for the connectedness of a directed graph, as we will discuss later in this section.

Trees

A *tree graph* is a hierarchical graph where each edge (known as a child) has exactly one parent (node from which it originates). If there is a parent node from which the whole structure arises, it is known as the *rooted tree*. It is easy to prove that the number of nodes in a tree equals the number of edges plus one, that is, $N = E+1$. The deletion of any edge will break a tree into disconnected components.

Multigraphs

The definition of both graphs and digraphs does not allow the existence of *loops* (edges connecting a node to itself) or *multiple edges* (two nodes connected by more than one edge). Graphs with either of these two elements are called *multigraphs* (Bollobas, 1998). Most networks of interest to the *ARIST* readership are not multigraphs. We therefore discuss definitions and measures that are applicable to undirected graphs and directed graphs but not necessarily to multigraphs.

Graph Representation

From a mathematical point of view, it is convenient to define a graph by means of an *adjacency matrix* $x = \{x_{ij}\}$. This is an $N \times N$ matrix defined such that $x_{ij} = 1$ if $(i,j) \in E$ and $x_{ij} = 0$ if $(i,j) \notin E$. For undirected graphs the adjacency matrix is symmetric, $x_{ij} = x_{ji}$, and therefore it conveys redundant information. For directed graphs, the adjacency matrix is not necessarily symmetric. Figure 12.2 shows the adjacency matrices and graphical depictions for four undirected (a–d) and two directed (e and f) graphs. Note that the adjacency matrix is also called a *sociomatrix* in the social network literature.

Subgraphs

A graph $G' = (V', E')$ is said to be a *subgraph* of the graph $G = (V, E)$ if all the nodes in V' belong to V and all the edges in E' belong to E, that is, $E' \subseteq E$ and $V' \subseteq V$. The graphs in Figure 12.2b, d, and f are subgraphs of the graphs shown in Figure 12.2a, c, and e, respectively. A *clique* is a complete n-subgraph of size $n < N$. For example, the graph in Figure 12.2b is a *3*-subgraph of the complete N-graph shown in Figure 12.2a.

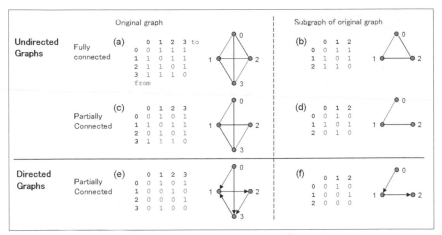

Figure 12.2 Adjacency matrix and graph presentations of different undirected and directed graphs.

The definitions so far have been qualitative descriptions of the structure of a graph. However, we can also have quantitative information about a graph, such as weights for edges.

Weighted Graphs

Many real networks display a large heterogeneity in the capacity and intensity values of edges. For example, in social systems the strength and frequency of interactions are very important in characterizing the corresponding networks (Granovetter, 1973). Similarly, the amount of traffic among Internet routers (Pastor-Satorras, & Vespignani, 2004) or the number of passengers using various airlines (Barrat, Barthelemy, Pastor-Satorras, & Vespignani, 2004; Guimera, Mossa, Turtschi, & Amaral, 2005) are crucial quantities in the study of these systems.

Where data are available, it is therefore desirable to go beyond the mere topological representation and construct a weighted graph where each edge (i,j) is associated with a weight w_{ij} representing the intensity or value of the connection. As with the adjacency matrix $x = \{x_{ij}\}$, it is possible to define a weighted adjacency matrix $W = \{w_{ij}\}$. Like the adjacency matrix, the weighted adjacency matrix can be used to represent undirected weighted graphs where $w_{ij} = w_{ji}$ and directed weighted graphs with $w_{ij} \neq w_{ji}$ (however this may not be true always). Altogether, the weighted graph representation provides a richer description because it considers the topology along with quantitative information.

Bipartite Graphs

A simple undirected graph is called *bipartite* if it has two distinctly different sets of nodes that can be decomposed into two independent sets. It is often represented as $G = (V_1 + V_2, E)$, where V_1 and V_2 are the two independent sets.

Graph Connectivity

This section introduces the standard set of nodes, edge, and graph measurements that is commonly used in graph theory. The section on network measurements reviews additional measurements commonly used by network scientists. Table 12.2 in the section on discussion and exemplification of network measurements depicts common measures.

Node Degree

In undirected graphs, the degree k of a node is termed the number of edges connected to it. In directed graphs, the degree of a node is defined by the sum of its in-degree and its out-degree, $k_i = k_{in,i} + k_{out,i}$, where the in-degree $k_{in,i}$ of the node i is defined as the number of edges pointing to i; its out-degree $k_{out,i}$ is defined as the number of edges departing from i. In terms of the adjacency matrix, we can write

$$k_{in,i} = \sum_j A_{ji}, \ k_{out,i} = \sum_j A_{ij}. \tag{1}$$

For an undirected graph, with a symmetric adjacency matrix, $k_{in,i} = k_{out,i} \equiv k_i$ holds. For example, node 1 in Figure 12.2a has a degree of three. Node 1 in Figure 12.2e has an in-degree of two and an out-degree of one.

Nearest Neighbors

The *nearest neighbors* of a node i are the nodes to which it is connected directly by an edge, so the number of nearest neighbors of the node is equal to the node degree. For example, node 1 in Figure 12.2a has nodes 0, 2, and 3 as nearest neighbors.

Path

A *path* $P_{i0,in}$ that connects the nodes i_0 and i_n in a graph $G = (V, E)$ is defined as an ordered collection of $n+1$ nodes $V_P = \{i_0, i_1, ..., i_n\}$ and n edges $E_P = \{(i_0, i_1), (i_1, i_2), ..., (i_{n-1}, i_n)\}$, such that $i_\alpha \in V$ and $(i_{\alpha-1}, i_\alpha) \in E$, for all α. The *length* of the path $P_{i0,in}$ is n. For example, the path in Figure 12.2f that interconnects nodes 0, 1, and 2 has a length of two.

Cycle

A *cycle* is a closed path $(i_0 = i_n)$ in which all nodes and all edges are distinct. For example, there is a path of length three from node 1 to node 2 to node 3 and back to node 1 in Figure 12.2e. A graph is called *connected* if there exists a path connecting any two nodes in the graph (see, for example, Figure 12.2a and 12.2b).

Reachability

A very important issue is the *reachability* of different nodes, that is, the possibility of going from one node to another following the connections given by the edges in a network. A node is said to be reachable from another node if there exists a path connecting the two nodes, even if it goes through multiple nodes in between.

Shortest Path Length

The *shortest path length* ℓ_{ij} is defined as the length of the shortest path going from nodes i to j. We will use l_s to refer to a continuous variable, which may represent any length value.

Diameter

The *diameter* d_G is defined as the *maximum shortest path length* l_s in the network. That is, the diameter is the longest of all shortest paths among all possible node pairs in a graph. It states how many edges need to be traversed to interconnect the most distant node pairs.

Size

The *size* of a network is the *average shortest path length* $\langle l_s \rangle$, defined as the average value of ℓ_{ij} over all the possible pairs of nodes in the network. Because some pairs of nodes can have the same value for the shortest path length, we can define $P_l(l_s)$ as the probability of finding two nodes being separated by the same shortest length l_s. The size of the network can then be obtained by using this probability distribution as well as the individual path lengths between different nodes.

$$\langle \ell_s \rangle = \sum_\ell \ell_s P_\ell(\ell_s) \equiv \frac{2}{N(N-1)} \sum_{i<j} \ell_{ij} \tag{2}$$

The average shortest path length is also called *characteristic path length*. In the physics literature, the average shortest path length has been also referred to as the *diameter* of a graph. By definition, $\ell_{ij} \leq l_s$ holds. If the shortest path length distribution is a well behaved and bounded function, that is, a continuous function that has defined starting and end points, then it is possible to show heuristically that in many cases the characteristic path length and the shortest path length have the same increasing behavior with increasing graph size.

Density

The *density* of a graph is defined as the ratio of the number of edges in the graph to the square of the total number of nodes. If the number of edges in a graph is close to the maximum number of edges possible between all the nodes in the graph, it is said to be a dense graph. If the graph has only a few edges, it is said to be a sparse graph.

Graph Components

A *component* C of a graph is defined as a connected subgraph. Two components $C_1 = (V_1, E_1)$ and $C_2 = (V_2, E_2)$ are disconnected if it is not always possible to construct a path $P_{i,j}$ with $i \in V_1$ and $j \in V_2$. A major issue in the study of graphs is the distribution of components, in particular the existence of a *giant component* G, defined as a component whose size scales with the number of nodes of the graph and therefore diverges in the limit $N \to \infty$. The presence of a giant component implies that a large fraction of the graph is connected, in the sense that it is possible to find a way across a certain number of edges joining any two nodes.

The structure of the components of directed graphs is somewhat more complex as the presence of a path from the node i to the node j does not necessarily guarantee the presence of a corresponding path from j to i. Therefore, the definition of a giant component becomes fuzzy. In general, the component structure of a directed graph can be decomposed into a *giant weakly connected component* (GWCC), corresponding to the giant component of the same graph in which the edges are considered as undirected, plus a set of smaller *disconnected components* (DC) (see Figure 12.3). The GWCC is itself composed of several parts because of the directed nature of its edges: The *giant strongly connected component* (GSCC), in which there is a directed path joining any pair of nodes; the *giant IN-component* (GIN), formed by the nodes from which it is possible to reach the GSCC by means of a directed path; the *giant OUT-component* (GOUT), formed by the nodes that can be reached from the GSCC by means of a directed path. Finally, there are the *tendrils* that contain nodes that cannot reach or be reached by the GSCC (among them, the *tubes* that connect the GIN and GOUT) that form the rest of the GWCC.

The component structure of directed graphs has important consequences for the accessibility of information in networks such as the World Wide Web (Broder, Kumar, Maghoul, Raghavan, Rajagopalan, Stata, et al., 2000; Chakrabarti, Dom, Gibson, Kleinberg, Kumar, Raghavan, et al., 1999).

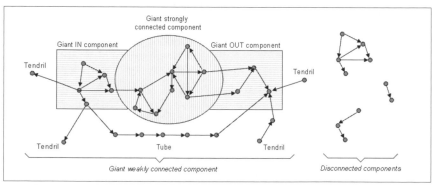

Figure 12.3   Component structure of directed networks such as the WWW. Adapted from Broder et al. (2000).

Network Sampling

Using the foregoing notions and notations, this section provides a short discussion of the issues related to the gathering of network data. Different application domains have very different affordances ranging from the size, type, and richness of network data to the scientific questions that are asked. In some domains it is relatively easy to gain access and work with a complete network dataset such as social network studies of smaller social groups—for example, all school children in a certain grade at a certain school. However, for many applications the acquisition of a complete network dataset is impossible due to time, resource, or technical constraints. In this case, network sampling techniques are employed to acquire the most reliable dataset that exhibits major properties of the entire network. Network sampling thus refers to the process of acquiring network datasets and the discussion of statistical and technical reliability. Sampling may be based on the *features of nodes and or links* or based on the *structure of the network*. For example, a dataset could be compiled by selecting "all papers that cite a set of core papers" or "all Web pages that link to the home page of a certain research group." Sampling based on node and edge features refers to the selection of a subset of nodes and/or edges that match or exceed a certain attribute value. In some domains it is reasonable to select a set of nodes with certain attributes, for example, "all Web pages of universities in California," "all papers that have been cited at least once," or "all computers that had a computer virus in the last year." Sampling based on the structure of a network is very common in Internet studies, large-scale social network analysis, semantic network studies, Webometrics, and scientometrics. Here the network's structure (not the attribute values of single nodes or edges) is exploited to acquire a meaningful subset. Link-tracing designs such as *snowball sampling* are applied to acquire information about all nodes connected to one given node. Link tracing, when performed recursively, quickly produces rather large datasets. This sampling strategy is considered the most practical way of acquiring social network data of hidden and hard-to-access human populations or of datasets of unknown size. Crawling strategies to gather Web data rely on exhaustive searches by following hyperlinks. Internet exploration consists of sending probes along computer connections and storing the physical paths of these probes. These techniques can be applied recursively or repeated from different vantage points in order to maximize the discovered portion of the network. That is, an initial dataset is acquired in a "first wave" and a subset of the features or nodes of this first wave dataset is used as a query/starting point for the "second wave" sampling.

It is clear that sampling techniques may introduce statistical biases. Therefore, a large number of *model based techniques*, such as *probabilistic sampling design* (Frank, 2004) developed in statistics, provide guidance in the selection of initial datasets. These techniques try to quantify the statistical biases that may be introduced during sampling.

Better knowledge of these biases helps us to draw inferences that have less uncertainty, which in turn increases the confidence in the tests.

In many cases, however, the discovery process is constrained by the techniques available. For example, crawling strategies on the Internet usually have intrinsic biases that cannot be avoided due to the directed nature of the exploration. These biases may lead to wrong conclusions. For example, even though it is widely known that the Internet has a power-law degree distribution, it is possible to show that sampling biases can cause a Poissonian degree distribution to appear as a power-law distribution (Clauset & Moore, 2005). So, it is difficult to determine whether the Internet is truly a power-law distribution. For this reason, each particular sampling process requires a careful study of the biases introduced and the reliability of the results obtained. The recent explosion in large-scale data gathering has spurred several studies devoted to the bias contained in the sampling of specific information networks (Clauset & Moore, 2005; Dall'Asta, Alvarez-Hamelin, Barrat, Vazquez, & Vespignani, 2005; Lakhina, Byers, Crovella, & Xie, 2002; Petermann & De Los Rios, 2004).

Finally, there are other sources of bias relating to the intrinsic experimental error of specific sampling methods. In some cases, this causes a false positive or negative on the presence of a node or edge. High throughput techniques in biological network measurements, such as in experiments for detecting protein interactions (Bader & Hogue, 2002; Deane, Salwinski, Xenarios, & Esenberg, 2002), are a case in point. For these reasons, it is important to test the results obtained against null models, which are pattern-generating models that replace the mechanisms thought to be responsible for a particular pattern with a randomization. The randomization produces a null statistical distribution for the aspect of the pattern controlled by the replaced mechanism. The observed empirical values are compared with the null distribution, which is then used to assess the importance of the replaced mechanism. So, in all these sampling cases a careful examination of the data quality and a test of the results obtained against null models are important elements for the validation of the corresponding network analyses.

Network Measurements

Basic measurements for the characterization of networks can be divided into measures for properties of nodes and edges, local measures that describe the neighborhood of a node or the occurrence of subgraphs and motifs, and global measures analyzing the interconnectivity structure and statistical properties of the entire network. Note that some node/edge measures as well as some local measures require the examination of the complete network. We next review the standard set of measures and statistical observables commonly used in network science. The section concludes with a discussion of network types and an exemplification of the different measures.

Node and Edge Properties

Nodes

A multitude of measures is available to characterize node properties (Hanneman & Riddle, 2005). The *degree* of a node (see definition in the section on graph connectivity) is a very basic indicator of a node's centrality. Obviously, it is a local measure that does not take into account the global properties of the network. The *Bonacich power index* takes into account not only the degree of a node but also the degree of the nodes connected to a node. For example, the more connections a social actor has in its neighborhood, the more central/powerful it is. *Closeness centrality* computes the distance of a node to all others. *Reach centrality* computes what portion of all other nodes can be reached from a node in one step, two steps, three steps, and so on. The *eigenvector approach* is an attempt to find the most central node in terms of the "global" or "overall" structure of the network. It uses factor analysis (Kim & Mueller, 1978) to identify "dimensions" of the distances among nodes. The dimensions are associated with a unit "eigenvector." The location of each node with respect to each dimension is called an "eigenvalue." Each unit eigenvector is associated with an eigenvalue. When the unit eigenvectors and their corresponding eigenvalues are known, one can construct a "general eigenvector" as a matrix whose columns are the unit eigenvectors. The collection of eigenvalues is then expressed as a diagonal matrix associated with the general eigenvector. It is assumed that the first dimension captures the global aspects of distances among nodes and the higher dimensions capture more specific, local sub-structures. *Betweenness centrality* is a measure that aims to describe a node's position in a network in terms of the flow it is able to control. As an example, consider two highly connected subgraphs that share one node but no other nodes or edges. Here, the shared node controls the flow of information: for example, rumors in a social network. Any path from any node in one subgraph to any node in the other subgraph leads through the shared node. The shared node has a high betweenness centrality. Mathematically, the betweenness centrality is defined as the number of shortest paths between pairs of nodes that pass through a given node (Freeman, 1977). More precisely, let $L_{h,j}$ be the total number of shortest paths from h to j and $L_{h,i,j}$ be the number of those shortest paths that pass through the node i. The betweenness b of node i is then defined as $b_1 = \sum L_{h,i,j}/L_{h,j}$, where the sum runs over all h,j pairs with $j \neq h$.

Brandes (2001) reported an efficient algorithm to compute betweenness centrality. The betweenness centrality is often used in transportation networks to provide an estimate of the traffic handled by different nodes, assuming that the frequency of use can be approximated by the number of shortest paths passing through a given node. It is important to stress that although the betweenness centrality is a local attribute of any given node, it is calculated by looking at all paths among all nodes in the network and therefore it is a measure of the node centrality with respect to the global topology of the network.

The above definitions of centrality rely solely on topological elements. When data on the edge weights w is available, the centrality of a node can be computed based on the intensity or flows associated with the node. This type of centrality is commonly called the *strength s* of a node i and is formally defined as $s_i = \sum_j w_{ij}$.

Edges

The *betweenness centrality of edges* can be calculated analogously to the node betweenness as the number of shortest paths among all possible node pairs that pass through a given edge. Edges with the maximum score are assumed to be important for the graph to stay interconnected. These high scoring edges are the "weak ties" that interconnect clusters of nodes (Granovetter, 1973, p. 1360). Removing them frequently leads to unconnected clusters of nodes. Granovetter was the first to examine the importance of weak ties; they have proved to be particularly important for decreasing the average path length among nodes in a network, for speeding up the diffusion of information, or for increasing the size of one's network for a given path length. However, networks with many weak ties are more fragile and less clustered.

Local Structure

This subsection discusses commonly used local network measures that describe the level of cohesiveness of the neighborhood of a node/edge and the occurrence of specific patterns or structures such as cliques and components.

Clustering Coefficient

The *clustering coefficient C* indicates the degree to which k neighbors of a particular node are connected to each other. It can be used to answer the question "are my friends also friends of each other?" The clustering coefficient should not be confused with measures used to identify how good a particular clustering of a dataset is, for example, in how far the similarity between clusters is minimal while similarity within a cluster is maximal. The clustering coefficient is commonly used to identify whether a network is a lattice, small-world, random, or scale-free network.

Two definitions of C are commonly used. Both use the notion of a *triangle D* that denotes a clique of size three, that is, a subgraph of three nodes that is fully connected. Basically, this means looking at cases where the node i has a link to node j and j has a link to m, then asking whether i is linked to m. If i is linked to m, we have a *triangle D*. Three nodes may also be connected without forming a triangle; for example, a single node may be connected to an unordered pair of other nodes, a *connected triple*.

The clustering coefficient is then defined as a ratio of the number of triangles to the number of connected triples in the network:

$$C = \frac{3 \times (number\ of\ triangles)}{(number\ of\ connected\ triples\ of\ nodes)}. \tag{3}$$

The factor three is used because each triangle is associated with three nodes. This can be expressed in a more quantitative way for a node i which has a degree k_i. The total number of connected triples in the graph can be obtained by summing over all possible combinations that the neighbors can have, which is given by $k_i\ (k_i\ -1)/2$. The clustering coefficient for *undirected graphs* is then defined by

$$C = \frac{3 \times \Delta}{\sum_i k_i(k_i-1)/2}. \tag{4}$$

This definition corresponds to the concept of *fraction of transitive triples* used in sociology. To obtain a statistical measure for any quantity we have to deal with a large collection of graphs (which are basically similar); these are called *ensembles* of graphs. Equation 3 then needs to be modified to consider the averages of the two quantities yielding the clustering coefficient as:

$$\langle C \rangle = \frac{6 \times \langle \Delta \rangle}{\left\langle \sum_i k_i(k_i-1) \right\rangle}. \tag{5}$$

Watts and Strogatz (1998) introduced an alternative definition of the clustering coefficient for the analysis of small-world networks (see also discussion in the section on network types). Assume there is a node i with degree k_i and let e_i denote the number of edges existing between the k_i neighbors of i. The clustering coefficient, C_i, of i, is then defined as the ratio between the actual number of edges among its neighbors e_i and the maximum possible value of edges between its neighbors which is $k_i\ (k_i\ -1)/2$, thereby giving us

$$C_i = \frac{2e_i}{k_i(k_i-1)}. \tag{6}$$

Thus, this clustering coefficient C_i measures the average probability that two neighbors of the node i are also connected. Note that this local measure of clustering has meaning only for $k_i > 1$. For $k_i \leq 1$ we define $C_i \equiv 0$ and, following work by Watts and Strogatz (1998), the clustering coefficient of a graph $\langle C_{ws} \rangle$ is defined as the average value of C_i over all the nodes in the graph

$$\langle C_{ws} \rangle = \frac{\sum_i C_i}{N}, \tag{7}$$

where N is the total number of nodes.

The two definitions give rise to different values of a clustering coefficient for a graph (see Table 12.2 in the discussion and exemplification section). Hence, the comparison of clustering coefficients among different graphs must use the very same measure. However, both measures are normalized and bounded to be between 0 and 1. The closer C is to one, the larger is the interconnectedness of the graph under consideration (see also discussion in the section on network types and Figure 12.7). Because the clustering coefficient considers the neighbors of a node and not its degree alone, it provides more information about the node. This can be illustrated by a simple example. A scientist (say i) collaborating with a large number of other scientists in only one discipline will have many collaborators who are also collaborating among themselves. However, a scientist (say j) who collaborates with other scientists in many different disciplines will have fewer collaborators collaborating among themselves. Although the important nodes (scientist i and scientist j) in both these networks may have the same degree (number of collaborators), the network of the collaborators of scientist i will have a larger clustering coefficient than the network of collaborators of scientist j.

Similar to the clustering coefficient, which analyzes the density of triangles, the study of the density of *cycles* of n connected nodes (for example, rectangles) is another useful approach to understanding the local and global cohesiveness of a network (Bianconi & Capocci, 2003; Zhou & Mondragon, 2004).

Motifs

Most networks are built up of small patterns, called *motifs*. Motifs are local patterns of interconnections that occur throughout a network with higher probability than in a completely random network. They are represented as subgraphs and contribute to the hierarchical set-up of networks (Milo, Shen-Orr, Itzkovitz, Kashtan, Chklovskii, & Alon, 2002; Shen-Orr, Milo, Mangan, & Alon, 2002; Vazquez, de Menezes, Oltvai, & Barabási, 2004). They have also been identified as relevant building blocks of network architecture and evolution (Wuchty, Oltvai, & Barabási, 2003). Diverse approaches have been taken to identify cliques and subgraphs in a graph. Bottom-up approaches include cliques, n-cliques, n-clans, k-plexes, and k-cores. The bottom-up approach tries to explore how large networks can be built up out of small and tight components. In the simplest case, the complete network is built out of cliques or fully connected subgraphs. However, not all networks can be constructed using this limited set of building blocks. In the n-clique approach, the definition is relaxed to allow nodes to be connected over a longer path length. Here, the n stands for the length of the path that interconnects nodes. In some cases, this approach tends to find long and stringy subgraphs rather than tight and discrete ones. The n-clans approach tries to overcome this problem by requiring that connections to new nodes of a subgraph can be made only via existing nodes. The k-plexes approach was introduced to relax the strong clique definition by stipulating that a node could become a member of a particular subgraph if it had connections to all but k members of the subgraph. It is similar to the k-core approach that requires that all members have to be connected to k other members of the subgraph.

Various top-down approaches, in addition to the bottom-up approaches, also help determine components, cut points, blocks, lambda sets, and bridges or factions. Components were defined in the section on graph connectivity. *Cut points* are nodes whose removal leads to a disintegration of a network into unconnected subgraphs. The resulting divisions into which cut points divide a graph are called *blocks*. Instead of the weak points one can also look for certain connections that link two different parts; these are the *lambda sets* and *bridges*. A node that is well connected to nodes in many other groups is called a *hub*.

Modules and Community Detection

In directed networks, the edge directionality introduces the possibility of different types of local structures (see component structure of directed networks in Figure 12.3). The characterization of local structures and communities is particularly relevant in the study of the Web where a large number of studies deals with the definition and measurement of directed subgraphs (Adamic & Adar, 2003; Flake, Lawrence, & Giles, 2000; Gibson, Kleinberg, & Raghavan, 1998; Kleinberg & Lawrence, 2001; Kumar, Raghavan, Rajagopalan, & Tomkins, 1999). One mathematical way to account for these local, cohesive groups is to look at the number of *bipartite cliques* present in the graph (Dill, Kumar, McCurley, Rajagopalan, Sivakumar, & Tomkins, 2002; Kumar et al., 1999). A bipartite clique $K_{n,m}$ identifies a group of n nodes, all of which have a direct edge to the same m nodes. Naively, we can think of the set as a group of "fans" with the same interests and thus their Web pages point to the same set of relevant Web pages of their "idols" (see Figure 12.4a).

Another way to detect communities is to look for subgraphs where nodes are highly interconnected among themselves and poorly connected with nodes outside the subgraph. Figure 12.4b depicts within-community links as full lines and between-community links by a dashed line. In this way, different communities can be determined with respect to varying levels of cohesiveness: for example, based on the diameter of the subgraphs representing the communities. In general, the Web graph presents a high number of bipartite cliques and interconnected subgraphs, all identified by an unusually high density of edges.

Many networks exhibit a considerable degree of modularity (Ravasz, Somera, Mongru, Oltvai, & Barabási, 2002). That is, the complete network can be partitioned into a collection of modules, each being a discrete entity of several nodes that performs an identifiable task, separable from the tasks of the other modules. Clustering techniques can be employed to determine major clusters. They comprise both nonhierarchical methods (for example, single pass methods or reallocation methods), as well as hierarchical methods (for example, single-link, complete-link, average-link, centroid-link, Ward), and linkage based methods (de Jong, Thierens, & Watson, 2004). Nonhierarchical and

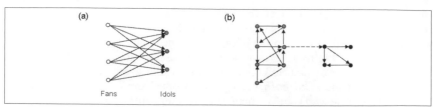

Figure 12.4 (a) A clique $K_{4,3}$ in which four pages of *fans* (white nodes) point to the same set of three pages, the *idols* (in gray). (b) A community of nodes (in gray) weakly connected to other nodes (in black) of the network. The dashed edge denotes the "weak link" with the highest betweenness centrality value. In a community, each node has a higher density of edges within the set than with the rest of the network. Adapted from Kleinberg and Lawrence (2001).

hierarchical clustering methods typically work on attribute value information. For example, the similarity of social actors might be judged based on their hobbies and ages. Nonhierarchical clustering typically starts with information on the number of clusters a dataset is expected to have and then sorts the data items into clusters to satisfy an optimality criterion.

Hierarchical clustering algorithms create a hierarchy of clusters grouping similar data items. Clustering starts with a set of singleton clusters, each containing a single data item. The number of singleton clusters equals the number of data items N. The two most similar clusters over the entire set are merged to form a new cluster that covers both. Merging of clusters continues until a single, all-inclusive cluster remains. At termination, a uniform, binary hierarchy of $N-1$ partitions results. Frequently, only a subset of all partitions is selected for further processing.

Linkage based approaches exploit the topological information of a network to identify dense subgraphs. They include measures such as betweenness centrality of nodes and edges (Girvan & Newman, 2002; Newman & Girvan, 2004) (see the section on node and edge properties), superparamagnetic clustering (Blatt, Wiseman, & Domany, 1996, 1997; Domany, 1999), and hubs and bridging edges (Jungnickel, 1994) (similar to the bridges described previously in motifs). Recently, a series of sophisticated overlapping and nonoverlapping clustering methods has been developed, aiming to uncover the modular structure of real networks (Palla, Derenyi, Farkas, & Vicsek, 2005; Reichardt & Bornholdt, 2004).

Structural Equivalence

The local network structure of a node determines not only the degree of this node but also, for example, whether my neighbors are connected, what nodes are reachable, and in how many steps. Being part of a large clique is different from being a node on a grid lattice. A short path length to hub nodes is beneficial for spreading information. In many cases, sub-networks of similar structure can be assumed to exhibit similar properties and to support similar functionality. Two nodes are said to be *structurally equivalent* if they have the same relationships with all other nodes in the network. Two nodes are said to be *automorphically equivalent* if they are embedded in local sub-networks that have the same patterns of ties, that is, "parallel" structures. Two nodes are said to be *regularly equivalent* if they have the same kind of ties with members of other sets of nodes that are also regularly equivalent. Diverse approaches are available to determine the *structural equivalence,* the *automorphic equivalence*, or the *regular equivalence* of sub-networks; they use popular measures such as the Pearson correlation coefficient, Euclidean distances, rates of exact matches, or Jaccard coefficient to determine the correlation between nodes (Chung & Lee, 2001).

Statistical Properties

A statistical analysis is beneficial when one is interested in the characteristics of the entire network rather than the characteristics of single nodes or sub-networks. This is especially relevant in the case of very large networks where local descriptions often do not suffice to answer scientific or practical questions. For example, to study the spreading of computer viruses on the Internet, the complete network has to be analyzed (see the section on modeling dynamics on networks for details on virus spreading models).

Next, we introduce the statistical distributions of the various quantities defined in the previous sections to describe the aggregate properties of the many elements that compose a network.

Node Degree Distribution

The degree distribution $P(k)$ of an undirected graph is defined as the probability that any randomly chosen node has degree k. Because each edge end contributes to the degree of a node, the average degree $\langle k \rangle$ of an undirected graph is defined as the number of all edges divided by the number of all nodes times two:

$$\langle k \rangle = \sum_k kP(k) \equiv \frac{2E}{N} \ . \tag{8}$$

A *sparse* graph has an average degree $\langle k \rangle$ that is much smaller than the size of the graph, that is, $\langle k \rangle << N$.

In the case of directed graphs, one has to consider the in-degree $P(k_{in})$ and out-degree $P(k_{out})$ distributions, defined as the probability that a randomly chosen node has in-degree k_{in} and out-degree k_{out}, respectively. Given that an edge departing from any node must arrive at another node, the average in-degree and out-degree are equal:

$$\langle k_{in} \rangle = \sum_{k_{in}} k_{in}P(k_{in}) = \langle k_{out} \rangle = \sum_{k_{out}} k_{out}P(k_{out}) \equiv \frac{<k>}{2}. \tag{9}$$

Because we are dealing with statistical probabilities, there will always be some fluctuations in the degree distribution. Highly heterogeneous networks will have large fluctuations from the average value. Homogeneous networks, for example a ring lattice, will have low fluctuations. The standard method for measuring the *heterogeneity* of a network is to study the *moments* of the degree distribution. The moment is nothing else than a property of a probability distribution. The n-th moment of the degree distribution is formally defined as

$$\langle k^n \rangle = \sum_k k^n P(k). \tag{10}$$

Note that the second moment of the degree distribution $\langle k^2 \rangle$ governs the *variance* of the distribution. It indicates how close we are to the average value of the distribution. As will be shown in the section on network types, the level of heterogeneity of the degree distribution defines different network types.

Degree Correlation Function

Some networks show degree correlations among neighboring nodes. For example, experts seem to prefer collaborations with other experts. That is, highly connected nodes are interconnected, a phenomenon also called *assortative mixing*. In biological and technological networks we find a hierarchical arrangement in which high degree nodes provide connectivity to low degree nodes, also called *disassortative mixing* (Newman, 2002). In mathematical terms, the degree correlation can be measured by the *average nearest neighbor's degree* $k_{nn,i}$ of a node i:

$$\bar{k}_{nn}(k) = \frac{1}{N_k} \sum_i k_{nn,i} \delta_{k_i,k}, \tag{11}$$

where the sum runs over all nearest neighbor nodes of node i. The average degree of the nearest neighbors $k_{nn}(k)$ for all nodes of degree k can then be defined as

$$\bar{k}_{nn}(k) = \frac{1}{N_k} \sum_i k_{nn,i} \delta_{k_i,k}, \tag{12}$$

where the sum runs over all possible nodes, N_k is the total number of nodes with degree k_i, and $\delta_{k_i,k}$ is the Kronecker delta, which has values $\delta_{i,j} = 1$ if $i = j$ and $\delta_{i,j} = 0$ if $i \neq j$. The correlations among the degree of connected nodes can then be expressed as

$$\bar{k}_{nn}(k) = \sum_{k'} k' P(k'|k), \tag{13}$$

where $P(k'|k)$ is the conditional probability that an edge of a node with degree k is pointing to a node with degree k'. If no degree correlations among neighbor nodes exist, $\bar{k}_{nn}(k)$ is independent of k; uncorrelated random networks provide an example. In the presence of correlations, the behavior of $\bar{k}_{nn}(k)$ identifies two general classes of networks (Newman,

2002): If $\bar{k}_{nn}(k)$ is a function that increases with increasing k, nodes with high degree have a larger probability to be connected with large degree nodes indicative for *assortative mixing*. On the contrary, a decreasing behavior of $\bar{k}_{nn}(k)$ defines a *disassortative mixing*, in the sense that high degree nodes have a majority of neighbors with low degree; the opposite holds for low degree nodes.

Node Betweenness Distribution

Similarly, it is possible to characterize betweenness statistically by considering the probability distribution $P_b(b)$ that a node has betweenness b. As with Equation 9, it is now possible to obtain different properties of the distribution by defining the moments of the distribution. The n-th moment of distribution $\langle b^n \rangle$ is then defined as

$$\langle b^n \rangle = \sum_b b^n P_b(b) \equiv \frac{1}{N} \sum_i b^{ni}. \tag{14}$$

As explained with respect to Equation 9, the distribution moments quantify the level of heterogeneity of the networks for the betweenness property of the nodes. As before, the significance of the observed average behavior can be quantified by using the second moment of the distribution (see also the section on network types).

Average Clustering Coefficient

The average clustering coefficient can be used to determine whether a type of network is modular or hierarchical on a global statistical level (Pastor-Satorras & Vespignani, 2004; Ravasz et al., 2002). This is determined by computing the clustering coefficient of smaller subgraphs. The subgraph selection procedure ensures they have the same average degree distribution. In mathematical terms, the average clustering coefficient $\langle C(k) \rangle$ of nodes with degree k is defined as:

$$\langle C(k) \rangle = \frac{1}{N_k} \sum_i C_i \delta_{k_i, k} \tag{15}$$

where N_k is the total number of nodes with degree k, the sum runs over all possible nodes, and $\delta_{k_i, k}$ is the Kronecker delta as defined for Equation 11. In many real networks, $\langle C(k) \rangle$ exhibits a highly non-trivial behavior with a power-law decay as a function of k, signaling a hierarchy in which most low degree nodes belong to well interconnected communities (high clustering coefficient) and hubs connect many nodes that are not directly connected (small clustering coefficient) (Pastor-Satorras & Vespignani, 2004; Ravasz et al., 2002) (see also the section on network types).

Distribution of Node Distances

There are two main statistical characterizations of the distribution of node distances. The first simply considers the probability distribution $P_\ell(\ell)$ of finding two nodes separated by a distance ℓ. A second indicator, the so-called *hop plot* $M(\ell)$, is expressed as the average number of nodes within a distance less than or equal to ℓ from any given node:

$$M(\ell) = N\sum_{\ell'=0}^{\ell} P\ell(\ell').$$ (16)

At $\ell = 0$ we find the starting node; thus $M(0) = 1$. At $\ell = 1$ we have the starting node plus its nearest neighbors; therefore $M(1) = k + 1$. If the graph is connected and l_s is the maximum shortest path length, then $M(l_s) = N$ holds. Because the average number of nodes within a certain distance is very different for a regular network, a random network, and a small-world network, the hop plot is especially useful in studying the structure of the network. Note that an increase in the number of nodes within a certain distance increases the hop plot value. Therefore, the hop plot is often referred to as a measure of the *average mass* of a graph. The hop plot can also be related to the spanning tree construction used in mathematics and statistics.

Network Types

The statistical properties identified in the previous section make possible the detailed analysis of the structural and functional properties of large networks. They form the basis for seeking large-scale regularities and asymptotic patterns that can be considered manifestations of the underlying laws governing the dynamics and evolution of complex networked systems (Albert & Barabási, 2002; Dorogovstev & Mendes, 2002; Newman, 2003; Wolf, Karev, & Koonin, 2002). For instance, many real world networks show the *small-world* property, which implies that the network has an average characteristic path length that increases very slowly with the number of nodes (logarithmically or even slower), in spite of showing a large degree of local interconnectedness that is typical of more ordered lattices. These two opposing tendencies—the intrinsic randomness with a memory of local ordering—were first reconciled by Watts and Strogatz's (1998) *small-world model*. This model starts with a regular ring lattice of N nodes in which each node is symmetrically connected to its *2m* nearest neighbors in clockwise and counterclockwise sense. Then, for every node, each edge is rewired with probability p, and preserved with probability *1-p*. The rewiring connects the edge endpoint to a randomly chosen node, avoiding self connections. The parameter p therefore tunes the level of randomness present in the graph, keeping the number of edges constant. Using this model, one can analyze the characteristic path length $\langle l \rangle$ and clustering coefficient $\langle C \rangle$ of a network as a function of the rewiring probability p (see Figure 12.5). A *regular lattice* with p close to 0 has a high characteristic path length and a high clustering coefficient. A *small-world network* with intermediate p has a low characteristic path length and a high clustering coefficient. A *random network* with p close to 1 has a low characteristic path length and a low clustering coefficient. Therefore, there is a broad region of p in which both properties—low characteristic path and high clustering—are found at the same time. In particular, it has been shown (Barrat & Weigt, 2000; Barthelemy & Amaral, 1999a, 1999b) that this region depends on the size of the network and that in the case of infinite networks any infinitesimal presence of randomness is enough to yield a small-world network.

Note that a small-world network can also be generated by adding edges instead of rewiring existing edges (Barabási, Albert, & Jeong, 1999).

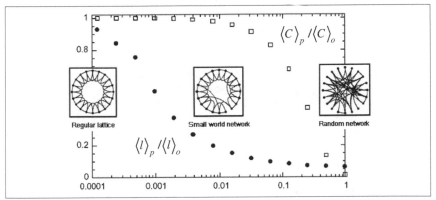

Figure 12.5 Characteristic path length and clustering coefficient as a function of the rewiring probability p for the Watts-Strogatz model. The characteristic path length and clustering coefficient are normalized by the initial shortest path length $\langle l \rangle_0$ (filled circles) and clustering coefficient $\langle C \rangle_0$ (open squares) for the original regular lattice with p = 0. Adapted from Watts and Strogatz (1998).

Another important recent finding is that many networks are characterized by the presence of "hubs," that is, nodes with a large number of links to other nodes. This implies that many networks are extremely heterogeneous, their topology being dominated by a few hubs that link to a majority of the less connected nodes (Albert & Barabási, 2002). This has led to the definition of two broad classes of networks, depending on the statistical properties of the degree distribution. The first are the so-called *homogeneous networks*, which exhibit degree distributions with an exponentially fast decaying tail such as *Poissonian distributions* (see Table 12.2). The second are *scale-free networks* with heterogeneous connectivity pattern. These networks have a heavy-tailed degree distribution; that is, the probability that a given node has degree k is in many cases well approximated by a *power-law distribution P(k) ~ k^{-g}* (see general degree distribution of a scale-free network in Table 12.2).

Interestingly, in a heavy-tail distribution, there is a finite probability of finding nodes with a degree value much larger than the average $\langle k \rangle$. This leads to errors if we assume that every node in the network has degree $\langle k \rangle$.

As has been mentioned, the heterogeneity of a network is measured by the moments of the degree distribution (Equation 10). In particular, the second moment of the degree distribution obtained by putting $n = 2$ in Equation 10 controls the standard deviation defined by $\sigma^2 = \langle k^2 \rangle - \langle k \rangle^2$. The standard deviation reveals the diversity of values in the degree distribution; it is therefore a very important quantity for networks with heavy-tailed distributions. Fluctuations in systems with a power-law exponent $2 \leq \gamma \leq 3$ are unbounded (they can be infinitely large) and depend only on the system size. The absence of any intrinsic scale for the fluctuations implies that the average value is not a characteristic scale for the system. This also holds for $\gamma \leq 2$. In other words, the average behavior of a *scale-free* system is not typical: A node selected at random will have a low degree most of the time. However, there is an appreciable probability of finding nodes with very large degree values. All intermediate values are possible and knowing the average node degree does not help to describe the degree distribution. This is clearly different from *Poissonian* distributions with fast decaying tails, in which the average k value is very close to the maximum of the distribution and represents the most probable value for the degree of a node.

Scale-free networks can be constructed by the use of generalized random graph, p^*-models, and many other techniques (Holland & Leinhardt, 1981; Molloy & Reed, 1995; Park & Newman, 2004) (see also the section on modeling static networks). Barabási and Albert (1999) developed a dynamical approach to modeling scale-free networks. This novel type of network model can simulate large networks that evolve rapidly by the continuous addition of new nodes. The *Barabási-Albert model* is based on the *preferential attachment* mechanism observed in many real world networks and also known as the *rich get richer* phenomenon, the *Matthew effect* (Merton, 1968), the *Gibrat principle* (Simon, 1955), or *cumulative advantage* (Price, 1976). It defines a simple class of growing models based on the following two rules:

> *Growth*: The network starts with a small core graph of m_0 connected nodes. The nodes could be fully connected or any other core graph density except zero could be used. The initial number of edges does not influence the properties of the network in the limit. Every time step we add a new node and connect it with m edges ($m < m_0$) to already existing nodes.
> *Preferential attachment*: The new edges are connected to an existing s-th node with a probability proportional to the degree of the node k_s.

These rules define a dynamical algorithm model that can be easily implemented in computer simulations and, starting from a connected initial core graph, generates connected graphs with fixed average degree $<k> = 2m$ and a power-law degree distribution. The interest raised by the Barabási-Albert construction resides in its capacity to generate graphs with a power-law degree distribution and small-world properties from very simple dynamical rules. Other features, however, such as the clustering coefficient or the fact that older nodes are always the most connected, do not match what we observe in real world networks.

Many extensions of the Barabási-Albert model have been proposed. They extend the original model to account for local geographical factors, rewiring among existing nodes, or age effects (Albert & Barabási, 2002). The importance of the Barabási-Albert model is at the conceptual level. It introduces a simple paradigm that suffices to exemplify the network self-organization, which spontaneously generates highly non-trivial topological properties. In addition, the model shifts the focus to micro-scopic dynamical rules as the starting point of the modeling strategy (see discussion in the sections on network modeling and modeling dynamics of networks).

Discussion and Exemplification

This section links the terminology and approaches introduced in the four previous sections in a more systematic manner. It also presents an illustrative example to point out the commonalities and differences among regular, random, small-world, and scale-free networks. Table 12.1 gives an overview of the terminology used in different scientific disciplines and their interrelations. Obviously, these disciplines have developed similar techniques in parallel; commonalities are just now being discovered. Confusion of terminology is easy and commonplace.

Table 12.1 Terminology used in various scientific disciplines

Discipline	Mathematics, Physics	Statistics, Social Network Analysis
Terminology used	Adjacency matrix	Sociomatrix
	Average shortest path length or diameter	Characteristic path length
	Clustering coefficient	Fraction of transitive triples

Table 12.2 lists properties of a random, a small-world, and a scale-free network for means of comparison. The scale-free network was generated using the Barabási-Albert model introduced in the section on network types. The model was initialized with a core of two nodes, one edge, and 40 time steps. In each time step, one node is added and connected via two edges to nodes already present in the network. There is a preference to connect to highly connected nodes. The lattice, small-world, and random networks were generated using the Watts-Strogatz model, also introduced in the section on network types. The model was initialized with 42 nodes, a node degree of four, and a rewiring probability of 0.0,

0.5, and 1.0 respectively. Note that all networks have approximately the same number of nodes and edges. All three networks are undirected, fully connected, and have neither parallel edges nor loops.

Table 12.2 Properties of regular lattice, small-world, random, and scale-free networks

Network type	Regular lattice	Small-world	Random	Scale-free / Heavy-tail
Layout				
Number of nodes	42	42	42	42
Number of edges	84	84	84	81
Diameter	11	5	5	5
Characteristic path length	5.6	2.9	2.76	2.6
Clustering coeff. (Eq.4)	1	0.31	0.21	0.26
Clustering coeff. (Eq.6)	0.5	0.16	0.13	0.22
Average degree	4	4	4	3.86
General degree distribution				
After removal of the five most highly connected nodes				

Also presented are the general degree distributions for all four network types. In the regular lattice, all nodes have a degree of four and hence the degree distribution has a *Dirac* delta function at four. For random graphs $P(k)$ is Poissonian—it is strongly peaked at $k = <k>$ and decays exponentially for large k. The network is rather homogeneous, that is, most nodes have approximately the same number of links. An example of a network with a Poisson distribution is a highway network in which nodes represent cities and links represent highways that connect cities. The degree distribution of a scale-free network decays as a power law $P(k) \sim k^{-g}$ at large k. The majority of nodes have one or two edges but a few nodes have a large number of edges and act as hubs. An example of a scale-free network is an airline network where nodes represent cities and links represent airline flights connecting them. The last column of Table 12.2 shows the network after removal of the five most highly interconnected nodes. This is relevant for the discussion of network attacks presented in the section on modeling dynamics of networks.

Network Modeling

The section on network types introduced two simple network models that generate small-world and scale-free networks. Here, we provide a general review of diverse network modeling approaches. A detailed exposition of all modeling approaches is far beyond the scope of the present review; the interested reader is encouraged to consult Wasserman and Faust (1994) and Carrington et al. (2004) for reviews of social network analysis and Kumar, Raghavan, Rajagopalan, Sivakumar, Tomkins, and Upfall (2000) and Pastor-Satorras and Vespignani (2004) for a computer science- or physics-driven approach on modeling the Internet. The attempt here is to show how the modeling paradigms, developed in different disciplines, can be unified in a common conceptual framework. It is our hope that this will encourage researchers to study approaches developed in other disciplines, help interrelate approaches, and generally promote the application and comparison of approaches across disciplinary boundaries. Selected concepts will be presented in considerable mathematical detail to give the interested reader an introduction to the strong quantitative foundations of most modeling techniques. The first sub-section starts with an introduction to models that assume that the network to be simulated is static or in equilibrium. Examples are networks of co-occurring words in a text or scholarly networks at a given point in time. The next sub-section introduces models that aim to capture the dynamic evolution of networks. These models are called dynamical models or non-equilibrium models. The third sub-section discusses modeling frameworks and model validation. Note that models of dynamic activities on networks, for example, the spreading of computer viruses on the Internet or the diffusion of knowledge in paper-citation networks, are discussed in the section on modeling dynamics of networks. An overview of the diverse modeling approaches and their applicability is provided in the discussion and model validation section (see also Table 12.4).

Modeling Static Networks

Mathematicians, statisticians, and physicists have made major contributions to models that capture the structure of networks. Interestingly, it is only now that major commonalities among the rather abstract mathematical theories developed by mathematicians and statisticians and theories describing physical systems developed by physicists are being uncovered. This section reviews known commonalities and uncovers previously unknown commonalities of graph theoretic approaches to network modeling.

Statistical graph models have been used for almost 60 years for the quantitative examination of the stochastic properties of networks; "stochastic" here refers to the involvement of a probabilistic or random process. We will also refer to various ensembles; the statistical ensemble of graphs, for example, means a group of all possible graphs having the same number of nodes, edges, and probability of connection. Statistical ensembles are a collection of similar objects that differ from one another only because of some probabilistic process that defines the collection.

Next, we review the pioneering work on random graph models, then introduce the class of exponential random graphs, and finally show that this class has interesting similarities with the statistical mechanics approach developed by physicists.

Static Random Graph Models and Topology Generators

Approaches such as the paradigmatic *Erdös-Rényi model* (1959) and the *Molloy-Reed construction* (1995) are the simplest conceivable and have been used as the basic modeling paradigm in several disciplines. They are characterized by an absolute lack of knowledge of the principles that guide the creation of edges between nodes. Lacking any information, the simplest assumption one can make is that it makes sense to connect pairs of nodes at random with a given connection probability p. The first theoretical model of random networks was proposed by Erdös and Rényi in the early 1960s. In its original formulation, the undirected graph $G_{N,E}$ is constructed from a set of N different nodes, which are joined by E edges whose ends are selected at random among the N nodes. Gilbert (1959) proposed a variation of this model. Here, the graph $G_{N,p}$ is constructed from a set of N different nodes in which each of the $N(N-1)/2$ possible edges is present with probability p (the connection probability) and absent with probability $1-p$. Both these models generate random graphs whose important properties can then be calculated. For instance, to compute the average degree, the average number of edges $\langle E \rangle$ generated in the construction of the graph is calculated and is found to be $\langle E \rangle = \frac{1}{2} N(N-1)p$.

Exponential Random Graph Family

A more general and well founded group of models, in some respects the mathematically and conceptually more sophisticated group, is represented by the *exponential random graph family* (Frank & Strauss,

1986; Holland & Leinhardt, 1981; Strauss, 1986; Strauss & Ikeda, 1990; Wasserman & Pattison, 1996). By *"exponential random graphs"* physicists often mean graphs with a *Poissonian* degree distribution; this is not the case of the exponential random graph family, which may have different degree distributions. In the statistical and social sciences literatures, these models are also referred to as *Logit models, p*-models,* and *Markov random graphs*, depending on the specific assumptions and methods used in the model construction.

This group of models treats the adjacency matrix $x = \{x_{ij}\}$ characterizing a graph of cardinality N as a random matrix whose realization occurs with probability

$$P(x) = \frac{\exp(\sum_i \theta_i z_i(x))}{K(\theta_i)}, \tag{17}$$

where θ_i is a set of model parameters and $z_i(x)$ is a set of network statistical observables, for example, the average degree of the graph $<k>$ or probability distribution of attributes.

In a co-authorship network, the set of model parameters θ_I might represent the likelihood of two authors collaborating as a result of their geographical proximity. The term $z_i(x)$ might represent the average number of collaborators in a field. After the relevant statistics and assumptions are included in the model, the parameter θ_i has to be estimated by comparison with the real data. This has spurred the development of a wide array of parameter estimation techniques such as pseudo-likelihood estimation and *Monte Carlo* maximum likelihood estimation (Frank & Strauss, 1986; Strauss, 1986; Strauss & Ikeda, 1990; Wasserman & Pattison, 1996). Monte Carlo methods are used to obtain an approximate solution to a variety of mathematical problems that deal with random processes. The function $K(\theta_i)$ ensures the correct normalization upon summing the probability distribution over all possible graphs x allowed in the *sample space*, also called *phase space* in physics and engineering. This space can be conceptually schematized as hyper-dimensional space in which each coordinate represents the possible values that each degree of freedom (in the case of a graph the variables x_{ij}) may have (see Figure 12.6).

Note that Equation 18 defines the probability for the occurrence of an edge for any pair of nodes described by the adjacency matrix x. Therefore, the individual elements x_{ij} do not explicitly occur in the equation. Instead, the matrix x as a whole is considered.

For co-authorship networks, adding a new author node increases the degrees of freedom for the existing authors as they have the possibility of collaborating with one more person. The degrees of freedom are thus related to the particular network that is being studied. For the co-authorship network, this means that if an author A collaborates with both B and C, the point representing this state would be different from the point in the phase space where A collaborates with B and not with C. The dimension of the phase space is the sum of the number of authors

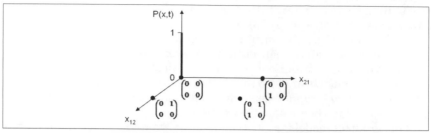

Figure 12.6 *Sample space* or *phase space* of the possible realization of a directed network with two nodes. Each x_{ij} axis represents the existence or not of the corresponding edge. Each point in the phase space thus represents a possible microscopic realization of the network, corresponding to the relative adjacency matrix. Using a third axis, it is possible to report the corresponding occurrence probability $P_{(x,t)}$ associated with each configuration. The dimensionality of the sample space increases with the number of nodes. In principle it is possible to associate each network of size N to an N^2 dimensional hyper-space. Exemplarily depicted is the phase space realization for an unconnected network.

and $P(x)$. The complete phase space consists of points representing all possible co-authorships of all authors.

Statistical Mechanics of Networks

These models assume that the probability for a system, for example a network, to be in a specific microscopic configuration x is given by the distribution $P(x)$ that maximizes the *Gibbs* entropy (Parisi, 1988)

$$S[P] = -\sum_x P(x)\ln P(x), \tag{18}$$

where the sum is over all possible stochastic realizations allowed. The Gibbs entropy $S[P]$ is a measure of the disorder encoded in the probability distribution. This is similar to the *information entropy* measure Shannon (1948) introduced to describe how much information can be processed when it is transmitted through a discrete *Markovian* process. The Shannon-Weaver model of communication (Shannon & Weaver, 1949) has led to several theoretical models in information science (Lynch, 1977). Information scientists have used these concepts in developing models for analyzing the hyperbolic distribution of letters in English text (Lynch, 1977) or the scholarly referencing process (Rettig, 1978). The general similarities and differences between the information theoretic approach and the statistical physics approach have been discussed in detail elsewhere (Jaynes, 1957). Just as the best choice for the probability distribution in information theory is the one that maximizes the information entropy (Shannon's maximum entropy assumption), in physics one expects that in the equilibrium state[3] the statistical disorder reaches its maximum. In the context of physical systems, this assumption can be more formally stated and related to the microscopic dynamics of the physical system. Again, similar to information theory, the maximization of the entropy is constrained by the statistical observables $z_i(A)$, for which one assumes there are statistical estimates:

$$\langle z_i \rangle = \sum_x P(x) z_i(x) \qquad (19)$$

and the normalization condition $\sum_x P(x) = 1$. Whenever one has to obtain the maximum of a function based on several constraints, the standard mathematical technique used is that of the *Lagrange multipliers*. Each constraint $\langle z_i \rangle$, is associated with an as-yet-undetermined constant α known as the *Lagrange* multiplier, with α_0 being the multiplier relative to the normalization condition. Note that this is similar to the model parameters in the *exponential family of random graphs* approach, which had to be determined from the actual data. The derivative of the distribution must be zero at the maximum, subject to the constraint conditions. The distribution must therefore satisfy the equation:

$$\frac{\partial}{\partial P(x)} \left[S[P + \alpha_0 \left(1 - \sum_x P(x) \right) + \sum_i \alpha_i \left(\langle z_i \rangle - \sum_x P(x) z_i(x) \right) \right] = 0 \qquad (20)$$

for all possible realizations x. This simple derivative yields the equation:

$$\ln P(x) + 1 + \alpha_0 + \sum_i \alpha_i z_i(x) = 0 \qquad (21)$$

that gives the solution

$$P(x) = \frac{\exp(-\sum_i \alpha_i z_i(x))}{Z(\alpha_i)}, \qquad (22)$$

where the normalization condition imposes

$$Z(\alpha_i) = e^{\alpha_0 + 1} = \sum_x e^{(-\sum_i \alpha_i z_i(x))}. \qquad (23)$$

Finally, the explicit values of the parameters α_i are found by imposing the self-consistent condition on the statistical observables

$$\langle z_i \rangle = \sum_x z_i(x) \frac{\exp(-\sum_i \alpha_i z_i(x))}{Z(\alpha_i)} \qquad (24)$$

for all the observables z_i used in the model construction.

Comparison

From the previous discussion it can be seen that the exponential family of distributions is equivalent to the statistical mechanics of Gibbs for networks used by physicists (Burda, Jurkiewicz, & Krzywicki, 2003; Burda & Krzywicki, 2003; Dorogovtsev, Mendes, & Samukhin, 2003; Farkas, Derenyi, Palla & Vicsek, 2004; Fronczak, Fronczak, & Holyst, 2005; Krzywicki, 2001; Park & Newman, 2004). Indeed, Equation 17 can be obtained from Equation 22 by a simple substitution of $\theta_i = -\alpha_i$ and $K(\theta_i) = Z(\theta_i)$, yielding an identical probability distribution $P(x)$. In physics, the statistical weight of each system configuration $H(x) = \sum_i \alpha_i z_i(x)$ is named *Hamiltonian* and the function Z is called the *partition function*. The Hamiltonian and the partition function are used to describe completely all properties of a system under study.

For example, in a co-authorship network with N author nodes, the partition function gives the sum over all the possible graphs in the network. The Hamiltonian describes the constraints on the co-author relations in the network. Together the partition function and the Hamiltonian of a network tell us the structure of the network (Berg & Lassig, 2002). Analogies can be pushed further; it is possible to show that different statistical constraints correspond to different statistical ensembles in the statistical mechanics definition. Moreover, it is possible to show that this formalism also describes random graphs such as that of Erdös and Rényi. For instance, the random graph family $G_{N,p}$ can be recovered by imposing as a constraint the corresponding value $<E>$ (see Park and Newman [2004] for details). The *exponential random graph* family used in statistics thus corresponds to the equilibrium ensembles of statistical mechanics developed in physics. Table 12.3 presents a comparison of the terminology used in the different disciplines.

Table 12.3 Modeling terminology in mathematics/statistics and physics

Discipline	Mathematics / Statistics	Physics (statistical mechanics)
Terminology used	All graphs in the same *exponential random graph* family	Equilibrium ensembles
	Sample space	Phase space
	Probability of occurrence of a graph in the exponential random graph family $$P(x) = \frac{\exp(\sum_i \theta_i z_i(x))}{\kappa(\theta_i)}$$	Probability of a system being in an equilibrium state based on the maximum entropy principle $$P(x) = \frac{\exp(-\sum_i \alpha_i z_i(x))}{Z(\alpha_i)}$$
	Set of statistical observables z_i that define the graph structure	Set of statistical observables z_i that constrain the physical system
	Set of model parameters θ_i that are necessary to generate the graph (obtained from data)	Set of parameters α_i corresponding to the constraints of the system known as *Lagrange* multipliers
	Normalization factor $\kappa(\theta_i)$ that equals the sum of all possible graphs in an ensemble or group	Partition function $Z(\alpha_i)$ of the system that normalizes the probability distribution in the phase space

Modeling Evolving Networks

The modeling approaches we have introduced in the previous section focus on the stationary properties of the network for which they derive the probability distribution in the phase space. However, many networks are not static but evolve over time. The creation of a social relation, the introduction of a hyperlink to a Web page, or the peering of two Internet service providers are dynamic events that shape the evolution of a network based on local interactions among individual nodes.

The *exponential random graph family* framework has been adapted to introduce network evolution by the addition (or deletion) of edges within a fixed number of nodes (Banks & Carley, 1996; Sanil, Banks, & Carley, 1995). Based on this, numerical techniques have been developed for estimating the model distribution parameters (Snijders, 2002) and subsequently implemented in the *Simulation Investigation for Empirical Network Analysis* (SIENA) package (http://stat.gamma.rug.nl/snijders/siena.html).

The dynamic evolution of networks can be generally modeled by formally introducing a time variable t that indicates the changes of the network quantities in time. In this general approach the number of nodes can vary with time and we do not need the constraint of a fixed number of nodes. However, a note of caution is in order. Because the dynamical approach is extremely dependent on the specific network dynamics, it is potentially risky and, unless we have precise experimental information on the system dynamics, it does not give quantitatively accurate predictions. Moreover, it does not provide a systematic theoretical framework, with each model focusing on specific features of the system of interest. On the other hand, the study of the dynamics is well suited to identifying general growth mechanisms out of seemingly very different dynamical rules.

Master Equation Approach

We now explain the dynamical modeling perspective, in which the probability of a particular network realization x at time t is given by the distribution $P(x,t)$. The *master equation* approach, developed in physics, can be employed to express the temporal evolution of the probability distribution. This approach assumes that a network has a particular realization in each time step and that the change in the realization over time is controlled by the microscopic dynamics of the model. The microscopic dynamics are expressed as a *rate* $r_{(x \to y)}$ that gives the transition from a particular realization x at a certain time t to a realization y at a later time $t+\partial t$. The master equation then expresses the temporal change in the distribution as a linear differential equation of the form

$$\partial_t P(x,t) = \sum_{y \neq x} [P(y,t)r_{(y \to x)} - P(x,t)r_{(x \to y)}]. \tag{25}$$

The transition rates have to satisfy the relation $\sum_Y r(x \rightarrow y) = 1$, which means that the sum of the rate of all possible configurations Y must be unitary. This condition is necessary as the transition between any two realizations is probabilistic and the total probability of any processes must be unitary. The probability distribution $P(k,t)$ is normalized and, because the sum of the rates is unitary, normalization is preserved on both sides of the equation.

As an example, we model the degree distribution of a paper node in an evolving paper citation network. Over time the paper receives more citations and its degree distribution changes. Here the term $P(x,t)$ in Equation 25 corresponds to $P(k,t)$ where k is the degree of the paper node at time t. If a new paper cites this node, the distribution $P(k,t)$ changes to $P(k+1,t)$. These are the x and y realizations described in Equation 25. Whether a paper is going to be cited might depend on many factors such as its age or the number of citations it has already accumulated. All these factors make up the microscopic dynamics used to calculate the rate $r_{(x \rightarrow y)}$. For simplicity, we assume that there is only one factor that determines the change: the degree distribution k. So, $r_{(x \rightarrow y)}$ is a function of k only and we denote this by $p(k)$. $p(k)$ can simply be k, but in real networks there are often other factors involved and hence it is usually a far more complex function of k. The other rate $r_{(x \rightarrow y)}$ will then be given by $1-p(k)$ to maintain the unitary condition. Thus all the terms in Equation 25 are defined and we can solve the equation to obtain the probability distribution $P(x,t)$ for any state of the system.

Master Equation Approach for Equilibrium Networks

Some systems eventually reach a stationary state in which the probability distribution of finding the system in any given configuration does not depend on time, that is, $P_s(x) = \lim_{t \rightarrow \infty} P(x,t)$. In equilibrium systems the stationary probability $P_s(x)$ obeys the maximum entropy principle, yielding $P_s(x) = P(x)$ where $P(x)$ is given by Equation 17 or equivalently Equation 22. In this case the solution to the master equation is obtained by simply imposing the *detailed balance condition* ensuring that the probability of leaving a state and arriving in it from another state is the same individually for every pair of states that the system can have. This reads as

$$P(y)r_{(y \rightarrow x)} = P(x)r_{(x \rightarrow y)} \ \forall y,x, \tag{26}$$

where the right-most symbol means that the relationship holds for all values of y and x (for a description of the equation elements see Equation 25). The *detailed balance condition* allows the assignment of rates according to the relation

$$\frac{r_{(y \rightarrow x)}}{r_{(x \rightarrow y)}} = \frac{P(x)}{P(y)} = \exp\left(\sum_i \theta_i [z_i(x) - z_i(y)]\right), \tag{27}$$

which defines the dynamic and ensures the convergence to the correct equilibrium probability distribution in the stationary state.

From a computational point of view these kinds of techniques are at the core of *Monte Carlo* simulations in both the statistics and the physics literature. They circumvent the explicit calculation of the partition function k (see Equation 23) that is often hard or impossible. Because Equation 27 describes ratios between transition rates, it suffices to have one of those rates as the reference time scale to obtain all the others in terms of the equilibrium distribution $P(x)$. The rates may be used to produce simulations of the evolution of the network and find the values of the parameters θ_i that better fit the real data when the analytical calculations are too complicated.

Master Equation Approach for Non-Equilibrium Networks

Unfortunately, not all systems have a stationary solution that is given by equilibrium $P(x)$. For instance, systems may achieve a stationary state without satisfying the *detailed balance condition*. Remember that the stationary distribution means that there is no change in the distribution with time whereas the detailed balance condition means that there is no change in the distribution for each pair of states.

These cases define *non-equilibrium systems* that still have a stationary state but whose dynamics do not allow a detailed balance and a maximum entropy calculation. In addition, other networks exhibit a continuously increasing number of nodes and edges. For those, the dimensionality of the phase space increases continuously, rendering equilibrium calculation infeasible.

For *non-equilibrium systems*, it is more convenient to rely on approaches dealing directly with the master equation that does not need an exact solution and for which many approximate and numerical techniques exist.

In the master equation approach, it is crucial to consider transition rates or probabilities reflecting the actual dynamics of a system. In order to model a system, the dynamical laws governing its evolution must be known. If they remain unidentified, the dynamical approach is often a difficult exercise in which rough assumptions and uncontrolled approximations must be made. Yet, it has the advantage of being more intuitive and suitable to large-scale computer simulations. An example is Krapivsky and Redner's (2005) application of the master equation approach to model paper-citation networks. In general, the master equation cannot be solved exactly and it is more practical to work with a specific projection of the probability distribution, such as the degree distribution or any other statistical observables in the network.

A continuously growing citation network in which new nodes appear and wiring processes take place (Krapivsky & Redner, 2003) can also be modeled in a way similar to that discussed near Equation 24. For the sake of simplicity we also assume that once an edge is established it will not rewire (this does hold true for a citation network, as citation links once established do not change). Further assume that we are interested in the node degree distribution (which changes over time due to increases in citations) specified by the number N_k of nodes with degree k. The master equation for such a growing scheme is given by:

$$\partial_t N_k = r_{(k-1 \to k)} N_{k-1} - r_{(k \to k+1)} N_k + \delta_{k,m}. \tag{28}$$

Here, the first term on the right corresponds to processes in which a node with k-1 links is connected to a new node, thus yielding a gain to the number N_k. The second term corresponds to nodes with degree k that acquire a new edge, thus representing a loss for N_k. The last term, the Kronecker delta (defined in Equation 11), corresponds to the entering of the new node with degree m. The eventual solution of this equation depends on the rates $r_{(k-1 \to k)}$ and $r_{(k \to k+1)}$ that specify the network dynamics.

This approach was used by Redner (2005) to model a *Physical Review* citation network. He was able to show that the growth in the average number of references per paper (the out-degree distribution) obtained from the model was consistent with the actual data. However, Krapivsky and Redner (2005) showed the growth predicted by their model was not robust for different model parameters. It will be worthwhile to test their model against other datasets.

Another possibility is to study the average degree values $k_s(t)$ of the *s-th* node at time t as proposed by Albert and Barabási (2002), Dorogovtsev and Mendes (2003), Newman (2003), and Pastor-Satorras and Vespignani (2004). For the sake of analytical simplicity the degree k and the time t are assumed to be continuous variables. Here, the properties of the system can be obtained by studying the differential equation governing the evolution of $k_s(t)$ over time. This equation can be obtained formally by assuming that the degree growth rate of the *s-th* node increases proportionally to the attachment probability $\Pi[k_s(t)]$ that an edge is attached to it. In the simplest case, edges come only from new nodes. Here the rate equation reads:

$$\frac{\partial k_s(t)}{\partial t} = m \Pi[k_s(t)], \tag{29}$$

where the proportionality factor m indicates the number of edges emanating from every new node. This equation is constrained by the boundary condition $k_s(s) = m$, meaning that at the time of their introduction, all nodes have degree m. In this formulation all the dynamic information is contained in the probability $\Pi[k_s(t)]$. The properties of each model are defined by the explicit form of the probability $\Pi[k_s(t)]$. Both formulations allow the calculation of the degree distribution, degree correlation, and clustering functions. The projection could consider other quantities such as the number of nodes $N(k \mid \ell)$ with degree k that share an edge with a node of degree ℓ and so forth; but this would result in increasing complications for the dynamical equations. Dynamics might be complicated by other dynamical processes, too, such as edge removal, rewiring, and inheritance, as well as node disappearance. For a review of dynamical models see Watts (1999), Barabási (2002), Buchanan (2002), Dorogovtsev and Mendes (2003), Pastor-Satorras and Vespignani (2004), and references therein.

As examples of this let us first consider the case of two models that contain the *preferential attachment* mechanism introduced in the section on network types: the Barabási-Albert model and the *copy model*. The Barabási-Albert model assumes that a new node is linked to an already existing node s with a probability proportional to its degree k_s. This immediately produces a probability of attraction

$$\Pi[k_s(t)] = \left[\frac{k_{in,s}(t)}{\sum_j k_j(t)}\right] \tag{30}$$

where the sum of all the degrees of all nodes in the network is the required normalization factor in the denominator. This class of models has been studied in detail as a candidate for a general mechanism to generate *power-law* degree distributions in growing networks. A second, completely different mechanism—the *copy model*—has been proposed in the context of Web simulations as a mechanism for the generation of skewed degree distributions (Kumar et al., 2000). The copy model was inspired by the observation that creators of new Web pages tend to copy hyperlinks from existing Web pages with similar content. This mechanism was translated into a growing model in which, at each time step, a new node (Web page) is added to the network and a *prototype node* is selected at random from among the already existing nodes. The outgoing edge of the new node is then distributed based on a *copy factor*, which is constant for all new nodes. A new edge is rewired with probability α to a randomly chosen node of the network. With probability $1-\alpha$ it is attached to a node already having a common edge with the prototype node. At first sight the model seems completely unrelated to the preferential attachment mechanism but a closer look reveals interesting similarities. This second process of attaching actually increases the probability of high degree nodes to receive new incoming edges.

As an example, let us focus on a generic network node and calculate its probability of receiving an edge during the addition of a new node. Given that a new node will add m new edges, a random node in the network is chosen with probability α. Thus any node has a probability α/N to receive an edge, where N is the size of the network. With probability $1-\alpha$, the node that is pointed to by one of the edges of the prototype node is selected. The probability that an existing node is linked to the new node equals the number of incoming edges of that node divided by the sum of all node degrees in the network, that is, $k_s(t)/\sum_j k_j(t)$. By combining the two terms we determine that the probability of receiving an edge is

$$\Pi[k_s(t)] = m\left[\frac{\alpha}{N(t)} + (1-\alpha)\frac{k_{in,s}(t)}{\sum_j k_j(t)}\right] . \tag{31}$$

When comparing Equations 30 and 31, we see that the second term on the right-hand side of Equation 31 is very similar to the right-hand side of Equation 30, which indicates that both have a preferential attachment component. Hence, both generate networks that exhibit *power-law* degree distributions using very different mechanisms. One strength of the dynamical approach is that systems with shared properties at the macroscopic level also often exhibit shared elements in their description at the microscopic level.

Agent Based Modeling

If a stationary solution satisfying all the constraints of the system cannot be found analytically, numerical simulations and agent-based modeling (ABM) approaches are the only viable alternatives. Numerical simulations are widely used in physics and biology as probes to study the behavior of very complicated models not amenable to analytical solutions. Stochastic simulations have been widely used in research on complex networks (Albert & Barabási, 2002; Dorogovtsev & Mendes, 2003; Newman, 2003; Pastor-Satorras & Vespignani, 2004). The availability of large-scale, dynamic network datasets (e.g., the Internet, the Web) and the need to understand, manage, and secure these networks have fueled a major increase of realistic ABM research and led to a change of the modeling perspective. The focus is on single individuals or elements of the system, including the most possible complete description of the reality. Here ABM can be applied to model local interactions in large-scale computer simulations, which ideally generate a network that shows global properties observable in real world systems. Such models have been successful in simulating the co-evolution of paper-citation and co-author networks (Börner, Maru, & Goldstone, 2003), analyzing trade and commerce networks spanning different locations (McFadzean & Tesfatsion, 1997), and other social and ecological processes (Gimblett, 2002).

Discussion

Table 12.4 provides an overview of the models that are discussed in this section and the subsequent section on modeling dynamics on networks.

The *static random graph models* and *topology generators*, as well as the *exponential random models* (introduced in the section on modeling static networks), and the very similar *statistical mechanics models* build on solid statistical foundations and have been mathematically and conceptually developed for many years. However, they are less intuitive and in many practical instances they present intractable technical problems. For example, they cannot be applied to model networks whose size is rapidly changing or to non-equilibrium networks. In these cases the dynamical approach, even if based on a large number of assumptions, is the only viable option. This is especially true if we are interested in studying very large-scale networks for which global equations cannot be specified but the local interactions—the microscopic dynamics—of nodes are known.

Table 12.4 Networking properties modeled and applicable models developed in mathematics, statistics, social networks, and physics

Section	Network properties modeled	Mathematics / Statistics / Social Network Analysis	Physics (statistical mechanics)
Modeling static networks	Structural properties	**Static random graph models and topology generators** **Exponential random graph family** (e.g., Logit models, $p*$-models, and Markov random graphs); all these graphs have a Poissonian degree distribution.	**Statistical mechanics models using Gibbs entropy maximization via Lagrange multipliers**
Modeling evolving networks	Evolution and structure (equilibrium)	**Exponential random graph family** for fixed number of nodes, edges are changed over time.	**Master Equation**
Modeling evolving networks	Evolution and structure (non-equilibrium)		**Master Equation** **Agent-Based Modeling**
Modeling dynamics on networks	Dynamical processes over network		**Master Equation** **Agent-Based Modeling**

In many ways, the recent explosion in dynamical modeling approaches is a consequence of the informatics revolution. The advent of high-throughput biological experiments, the possibility of gathering and handling massive datasets on large information structures, and the ability to track the relations and behavior of million of individuals have challenged the community to characterize and model networks of unprecedented sizes. Today, the Internet comprises more than 10^4 service providers with 10^5 routers keeping track of the behavior of 10^6 users; and its size is continuously increasing. Web crawls offer maps of the Web with more than 10^7 nodes. In addition, networks of similar size and dynamical characteristics are gathered every day for communication infrastructures such as mobile telephone and ad hoc networks, transportation networks, and digital documents. In biomedical research, we are witnessing a paradigm shift with an increasing focus on the so-called system's biology and the many large interaction networks that may be measured by taking advantage of high-throughput experiments. In almost all cases, the dynamical features of these systems cannot be neglected because we are typically dealing with networks growing exponentially as a consequence of their intrinsic dynamics. In this context, dynamical modeling offers an intuitive way to understand the evolution and non-equilibrium properties of these networks and enables the construction of basic generators that capture the rapidly evolving dynamics of such systems.

The availability of large-scale datasets and the ability to run large-scale simulations pose new conceptual questions. One asked by physicists addresses the "universality" of network properties, for example, *small-world* or *scale-free* degree distributions (see also discussion in the section on network types). In recent years, networks from diverse domains and serving very different functions have been analyzed. Many of these appear to share similar properties when the total number of nodes in the network is very large. This has raised the prospect of general and common self-organizing principles that go beyond the particulars of individual systems.

Model Validation

All models make assumptions that reflect our understanding of the world and our theoretical and/or practical interests. *Statistical modeling* based on maximum entropy considerations is most suitable for taking account of the statistical observables at hand; *dynamic modeling*, however, is well suited for large-scale and evolutionary properties. Both types of models need to be validated against empirical data: They do this in very different ways.

Statistical models such as the exponential random graph modeling or equilibrium statistical physics use empirical data to obtain the parameters (θ_i in Equation 17 and a_i in Equation 22) necessary for generating the probability distribution of a network. These distributions then provide statistical predictions that can be validated through new measurements on the dataset. Dynamical models define the local dynamics of a network—for example, what papers a new paper should cite based on information that, in general, is not related to the statistical observables of the complete network. Here the distribution of the network is assumed to emerge based on the local dynamics, and the properties of the generated network are compared with the properties of the empirical network. Hence, the network properties are not an input to the model but are instead used in the model validation process.

Generally, it is impossible to model all properties of a network in realistic detail. Suitable approximations have to be made. Depending on which questions the model wants to tackle, different properties will be given prominence. In this sense, all models are incomplete and most address only a limited set of questions. As we show in the next section, these considerations also apply to models that aim to reproduce the dynamics occurring on networks.

Modeling Dynamics on Networks

Networks provide the substrate on which the dynamical behavior of a system unfolds. At the same time, the various dynamical processes affect the evolution of a network's structure. Network structure, its evolution over time, and network usage are mutually correlated and need to be studied in concert.

To give an example, epidemiologists, computer scientists, and social scientists use very similar models to study spreading phenomena such as the diffusion of viruses, knowledge, or innovations. Detailed knowledge of the contact networks defining the interactions of the nodes at various scales, that is, path lengths over which neighboring nodes interact, is required to model these systems. Similarly, in technological networks—such as the power grid, the Internet, or transportation systems—it is crucial to understand the dynamics of information or traffic flow taking place along the nodes. The resilience of a network depends on basic dynamical processes, as the failure of one network component increases the burden on other elements, potentially overloading them and disrupting their functions as well. To model dynamics on networks, the theoretical framework presented in the section on network modeling needs to be extended so that the impact of the various network characteristics on the basic features of the dynamical processes can be investigated in a systematic way.

As has been mentioned, diffusion modeling is very similar across different applications, such as the spreading of viruses, diseases, rumors, knowledge, or fashion. For instance, epidemiological models (Pastor-Satorras & Vespignani, 2001) are based on categorizing people as "susceptible," "infected," or "removed." For rumor-spreading models (Daley, Gani, & Cannings, 1999), people may be categorized as "ignorant," "spreaders," or "stiflers." For knowledge diffusion purposes they are known as "innovators," "incubators," or "adopters." If we are interested in the spread of computer viruses, epidemiological models can be readily applied even though the virus host is now a computer instead of a living being (Bettencourt, Cintron-Arias, Kaiser, & Castillo-Chavez, 2005; Tabah, 1999).

In each of these models, transitions from one state to another are probabilistically obtained from contacts among individuals in the different categories. We explain the diffusion process using epidemiological models, as these are well studied and easy to understand. It is our hope that the interested reader will keep in mind the relation of "susceptible" and "infected" to the rumor-spreading and knowledge-diffusion analogies previously discussed.

Master Equation Approach to Dynamical Processes on Networks

The master equation approach introduced in the section on modeling evolving networks can also be applied to the study of epidemiological models and other dynamical processes. Let us consider the susceptible-infected-susceptible (SIS) model. This simple model is used to study infectious diseases leading to an endemic state with a stationary and constant value for the prevalence of infected individuals, that is, the degree to which the infection is widespread in the population. In the SIS model, each node in a network is characterized by a specific state or a vector of states s_i.

In the simplest case, each node can only exist in two discrete states, namely, susceptible ($s_i = S$) and infected ($s_i = I$). The respective *phase space* (see also Figure 12.6) for a network with two nodes is shown in Figure 12.7.

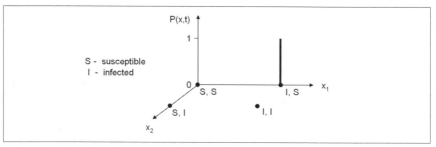

Figure 12.7 **Phase space of realizations for two nodes that can be in a susceptible or infected state. Each axis represents the existence or not of a node property such as S and I. Exemplarily shown is a configuration in which node x_1 is infected and x_2 is susceptible, that is, the probability of I, S is one and all other probabilities are 0.**

Let us examine how the SIS model can be implemented for a network with N nodes using the master equation approach. For the sake of simplicity we assign the variable 1 to the infected state and the variable 0 to the susceptible state. Let $\{\sigma^a\} = (\sigma_1 = 1, \sigma_2 = 0,...,\sigma_N = 1)$ denote a particular configuration a specifying the state of each node i and let $P(\{\sigma^a\},t)$ represent the probability that the system is in state a. In each time step, the state of any node can change. Hence in each time step, the system might be in a different configuration; for example, there might be a time step in which a majority of nodes is susceptible and other time step in which the majority of nodes is infected. Let $w_{(\{\sigma^b\} \to \{\sigma^a\})}$ denote the transition probability to go from state a to state b. The overall dynamics of the network can then be written down in the form of a *master equation*:

$$\partial_t P(\{\sigma^a\},t) = \sum_{\sigma^b \neq \sigma^a} \left[P(\{\sigma^b\},t)w_{(\{\sigma^b\} \to \{\sigma^a\})} - P(\{\sigma^a\},t)w_{(\{\sigma^{Sa}\} \to \{\sigma^b\})} \right]. \tag{32}$$

The transition probabilities $w_{(\{\sigma^a\} \to \{\sigma^b\})}$ are a function of the probability that susceptible nodes are infected by their neighbors ($0 \to 1$) and that an infected individual is cured ($1 \to 0$).

The probability that a susceptible node acquires the infection from any given neighbor in an infinitesimal time interval dt is λdt, where λ defines the virus *spreading rate* (see Figure 12.9). At the same time, infected nodes are cured and become susceptible again with probability μdt. Individuals thus run stochastically through the cycle susceptible $\rightarrow$ infected $\rightarrow$ susceptible, hence the name of the model. The SIS model does not take into account the possibility of individuals being removed due to death or acquired immunization, which would lead to the so-called susceptible-infected-removed (SIR) model. Recent epidemic modeling (Pastor-Satorras & Vespignani, 2004) that simulates the spreading of computer viruses shows that the SIR model is particularly suited to the initial stages of a computer virus attack. This is because infected computers are switched off as soon as the virus is detected and return to the network only when they have been screened by an antivirus. However, researchers have found that, in the long run, the clean-up stage reaches a steady state in which the SIS model better represents the overall endemic nature of the infection. The SIR model has also been used to model knowledge diffusion through blogspaces (Gruhl, Guha, Tomkins, & Liben-Nowell, 2004). In the blogspace, a "virus" resembles a "topic" that might be a URL, phrase, name, or any other representation of a meme that can be tracked from page to page. A blogspace is assumed to be "susceptible" to a topic and may be "infected" by it. Subsequently, the blogspace may become immune or the infection may be "removed." The authors make the assumption that all occurrences of a topic except the first are the result of communication via edges in the network, that is, the topic is not discussed offline, spread via news, or by other means. Because blogspaces can be overwritten by the authors at a later time, the SIR model was extended to the Susceptible—Infected—Removed (but temporarily)—Susceptible again (SIRS) model to include this property. Both the SIR and SIRS are extensions of the SIS model.

In the SIS model, the virus spreads by infecting its neighboring nodes. Hence, the connectivity of the nodes in the network influences the transition probability w of each node. The transition probabilities for a random network differ from those for a small-world network. Referring back to Equation 32, the global evolution of $P(\{\sigma^a\},t)$ (given by the left-hand side of the equation) depends on the transition probability w of each node (present in the terms on the right-hand side of the equation). The master equation considers the network connectivity pattern by means of the transition probabilities.

As discussed in the section on modeling evolving networks, the complete solution of the master equation is rarely achievable even for very simple dynamical processes. Again, we have the same two options to model such systems: the *continuum approach* and the *agent-based modeling* approach.

The continuum approach averages over all nodes in each category defined by the possible states of the nodes. Densities of the different node states, rather than total numbers, are used so that equations become independent of the number of nodes in the system. At time t, the density of infected nodes is represented by $I(t)$. Assuming that the total density is 1, the density of susceptible nodes is $1-I(t)$. It is also assumed that all nodes have the same degree k, that is, the same number of neighbors. We thus have a regular network. Based on these assumptions, we can write down the change in the average density of infected nodes over time for the SIS model as

$$\partial_t I = -\mu I(t) + \lambda k I(t)(1-I(t)). \tag{33}$$

In Equation 33 the first term on the right-hand side considers infected nodes spontaneously recovering with unit rate μ. The second term represents the rate at which newly infected nodes are generated in the network, that is, the density of healthy nodes acquiring the infection. It is proportional to the infection spreading rate λ, the density of susceptible nodes that might become infected $(1-I(t))$, and the number of (potentially infected) nodes in contact with a node given by the number of edges k. This last factor assumes the *homogeneous mixing hypothesis*, which asserts that the force of the infection—the per capita rate of acquisition of the disease for the susceptible nodes—is proportional to the average number of contacts with infected individuals that is approximated as $kI(t)$.

Interestingly, even such a simple approximation of the SIS model can be applied to central concepts in the modeling of spreading phenomena. Imposing the stationary condition $dI(t) / dt = 0$, we can obtain a nonzero stationary solution only if $\lambda > \mu/k$. This inequality defines the epidemic threshold λ_c below which the epidemic will die in a finite time; that is, $I = 0$ (see also Figure 12.8). Mathematically, it states that epidemics may propagate throughout the network only if the rate of contagion is sufficiently high to sustain or increase the number of infected nodes. This result may be recovered in many other models with complicated interactions. Finally, it is worth remarking that the continuum approach may be extended to consider stochastic formulations that allow the analytic inspection of the effect of noise in the dynamical process.

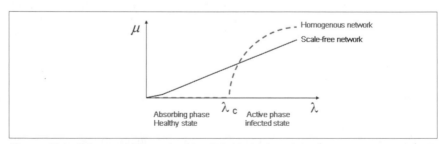

Figure 12.8 Schematic diagram of the SIS model for a homogeneous network and a scale-free network. As can be seen, there is no absorbing phase or healthy state for scale-free networks.

We must also keep in mind that the continuum approach is intrinsically a coarse-grained perspective that does not take into account individual heterogeneity or other possible fluctuations. These include certain nodes in the system being more susceptible than others to attacks: for example, a computer virus may be targeted to attack specific operating systems or specific software. Possible fluctuations may also arise due to the non-uniformity in the degree distribution of the nodes or a change in behavior after infection has occurred—for example, staying in bed when infected with a cold instead of spreading it at school.

Agent-Based Modeling Approach

In most real-world networks node attributes differ from node to node. Sub-networks within a larger network might also exhibit very different structure and behavior. For example, a computer network may be made of computers with different kinds of operating systems, which respond to a virus attack in different ways. In these cases, the continuum approach might not lead to solvable equations because of the large number of parameters to be included in the analytical description. ABMs that can simulate non-heterogeneous nodes and local sub-networks must be applied. Because ABMs can actually specify the interaction between the nodes, they can, to some extent, simulate complex and varied interactions between the individual nodes.

When modeling SIS using ABM, each individual node is again assumed to be either susceptible or infected. At each discrete time step, a model-specific update procedure is applied to each node. A node changes its state depending on the state of its neighboring nodes. Whether a node gets infected is a probabilistic process that can be simulated using *Monte Carlo* methods in which random number generators are used to simulate the random events of the dynamic process. The probabilities for changing from one state to another are the same. Because the simulations are based on random number generators we do not know exactly which nodes will become infected or healed. However, when applied over multiple time steps, this approach ideally leads to a system behavior that resembles the dynamics of a real-world system. Also, there is the added advantage that all attributes of each node can be determined in each time step and saved for further analysis.

Although extremely powerful, ABMs are often very intricate and the effect of any modeling assumption or parameter is not easy to study. ABMs in general have very few analytical tools by which they can be studied; and often no backward sensitivity analysis can be performed because of the large number of parameters and dynamical rules incorporated. This calls for a careful balance of the details included in the model and the interpretation of results obtained from computer simulations.

Ideally, the modeling approach to dynamical processes includes both methodologies at the same time: The microscopic model is formulated and the continuum equations are accordingly derived. The analytical predictions are then tested with ABM techniques in order to assess the role of noise and recover the predictions obtained.

Importance of Network Topology for Diffusion Processes

It is important to stress that the network topology, that is, the contact pattern among nodes, heavily influences the properties of dynamical processes. In the case of epidemic modeling, it is understood that there is no one-size-fits-all social network that might, even approximately, function as the prototypical substrate for epidemic modeling. Recently, major progress has been made in the understanding of how diseases spread through a wide array of networks with complex topological properties, for example, small-world and scale-free distributions. Work by May and Lloyd (2001) and Pastor-Satorras and Vespignani (2001, 2002) has shown that scale-free networks do not have any epidemic threshold below which the infection cannot initiate a major outbreak. In other words, the threshold above which the epidemics can spread is zero in the limit of an infinitely large network (see Figure 12.8). This new scenario is of practical interest in computer virus diffusion and the spreading of diseases in heterogeneous populations (Liljeros, Edling, Amaral, Stanley, & Aberg, 2001; Schneeberger, Mercer, Gregson, Ferguson, Nymukapa, Anderson, et al., 2004). It also raises questions about how to protect a network and how to develop optimal strategies for the deployment of immunization resources. Based on the notion of a critical threshold in a homogeneous network, the usual strategy is to immunize at random a certain percentage of the population to decrease the epidemic transmission rate. However, this will not work for a scale-free network, as is evident from Figure 12.8. A better strategy is to give immunization to highly connected individuals. Indeed, it is possible to show in mathematical terms that the immunization of a tiny fraction of the most connected individuals decreases the spreading of epidemics dramatically (see also the response of scale-free networks to the attack on highly connected nodes in Figure 12.9).

We have focused on epidemic modeling but it is clear that many of the approaches and insights can be readily transferred to other processes such as the spread of ideas, scholarly knowledge, and information. Heavy-tailed distributions have been observed in co-authorship networks (Newman, 2001) and paper-citation networks (Börner et al., 2003; Redner 1998). Understanding the diffusion of knowledge through co-author collaborations and paper-citation linkages can be enhanced by knowledge of how epidemics spread, leading to improved models of knowledge diffusion. Obviously, the goals are very different: We are typically interested in minimizing the spread of computer viruses and maximizing the spread of good ideas. The latter might be achieved by infecting the most connected individuals with the "idea."

Finally, we point out the analogy between diffusion processes and search processes. Although a detailed discussion of a subject that has received considerable attention in recent years is beyond the scope of

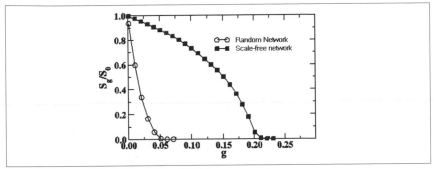

Figure 12.9 **Topological resilience to targeted attacks of the scale-free Internet Router level network and an Erdös-Rényi random graph with the same average degree. As can be seen, the scale-free network is the more fragile. Even a removal density as low as g = 0.05 suffices to fragment the whole network.**

this chapter, it is clear that the topological properties of networks affect search and retrieval results. Search strategies that take into account the structure of a network have been demonstrated to be superior over those that do not. Two important quantitative measures for information retrieval are *recall* and *precision*. Recall is defined as the number of relevant documents retrieved as a fraction of all relevant documents and precision is defined as the total number of relevant documents as a fraction of all the documents retrieved. The best results in terms of both recall and precision are achieved if global knowledge of all nodes and edges is available. In this case, the shortest path from the starting node to the target node can be computed and used to retrieve the desired information. In real-world search scenarios, such global knowledge is rarely available, but knowledge about general network properties can be exploited to improve search results. Examples are Kleinberg's (2000) work on search in small-world networks and the work on search in scale-free networks by Adamic, Lukose, Puniyani, and Huberman (2001). A comparison of topological properties and search performance in structured and unstructured peer-to-peer networks has been presented by Fletcher, Sheth, and Börner (2004).

Network Stability, Optimization, and Protection

Deep understanding of dynamical processes on networks has increased the attention given to the stability, optimization, and protection of networks. These problems are emerging as fundamental issues in, for example, homeland security and reliability assessment of critical infrastructure networks.

A first empirical analysis of the robustness of large-scale networks in the event of failures can be obtained by studying the topological response to the removal of nodes or edges. In this case, nodes are divided into two simple classes: one of functional nodes and the other of malfunctioning and, thus, removed nodes. Focusing on the effect of node removal, and assuming that all nodes are equally susceptible to failure, an instructive experiment can be performed on a connected graph of size N by looking at the effect achieved by removing a fraction g of randomly selected nodes. In order to monitor the response of the network to the damage, one can control several topological quantities related to network connectivity. A first and natural quantity to study is the size S_g of the largest component of connected nodes in the network after damage with respect to the size of the undamaged network. In particular, a ratio $S_g/N > 0$ indicates that a macroscopic fraction of nodes is still able to communicate. On the other hand, $S_g/N \cong N^{-1}$ signals that the whole network has been *compromised* by a fragmentation into very small, disconnected components. A second quantity is the diameter of the network as a function of the fraction of removed nodes (Albert, Jeong, & Barabási, 2000). A natural question to ask in this context concerns the maximum amount of damage that the network can take, that is, the *threshold* value of the fraction of nodes that can be removed before the network functionality abruptly drops to zero. Regular meshes and random graphs with an exponentially fast decaying degree distribution have a threshold value g_c denoting the number of nodes that need to be removed before a network can be considered compromised.

Scale-free and heavy-tailed networks, however, present two aspects in response to component failures: They are extremely robust when faced with the loss of a large number of randomly selected nodes but extremely fragile in response to a targeted attack (see Figure 12.11). When removing nodes at random, chances are that the largest fraction of deleted elements will have a very small degree. Hence, their deletion disconnects only a small number of adjacent edges and the overall damage of the network is limited. In order to do major damage, almost all nodes have to be randomly removed (Albert et al., 2000; Cohen, Erez, Ben-Avraham, & Havlin, 2000). In contrast, a targeted attack of high degree nodes has a very disruptive effect. Scale-free networks are more vulnerable to a targeted attack than random graph models or regular meshes.

Propagation and Adaptation

Not all dynamical processes, however, concern the change of state of the nodes in a network. In many cases, we have dynamical entities such as people, information packets, energy or matter flowing through a network. Here, the dynamic description focuses on the entities and the state of each node depends on the entities present at that node. In all cases, a straightforward generalization of continuum and ABM approaches is possible. Both models allow the study of the dynamics of information or traffic flow taking place over a network. In particular, it is possible to study the robustness of networks as a dynamical process, which takes into account the time response of elements to different damage configurations. For instance, after any router or connection fails, the Internet responds very quickly by updating the routing tables of the routers in the neighborhood of the failure point. In general, this adaptive response is able to circumscribe the damage but in some cases failures may cascade through the network, causing far more disruption than one would expect from the initial cause (Lee, 2005; Moreno, Pastor-Satorras, Vazquez, & Vespignani, 2003; Motter & Lai, 2002). This is typical of complex systems where emergent properties imply that events and information spread over a wide range of length and time scales. This also means that small variations generally have a finite probability of triggering a system-wide response, so-called *critical behavior*. This happens through chains of events that may eventually involve a macroscopic part of the system and, in some cases, lead to a global failure. It is important to realize that in a large networked system this property is inherent to the system's complexity and cannot be changed by using local reinforcements or technological updates. We can vary the proportion of small or large events but we have to live with appreciable probabilities for very large events: We must deal with the inherent complexity of the real world.

Coupling of Dynamics and Network Topology

As we have seen, the dynamical processes and the underlying topology are mutually correlated and it is very important to define appropriate quantities and measures capable of capturing their impact on the formation of complex networks. To carry out this task, we need to develop large empirical datasets that simultaneously capture the topology of the network and the time-resolved dynamics taking place on it. At the same time, a modeling paradigm that considers the dynamical processes on top of the evolving network is needed.

Many real world networks have nodes and edges of different strength and weights and are better described as weighted graphs; this has fostered the development of models that couple strength features with the dynamic evolution of a network (Barrat et al., 2004). Moreover, modeling techniques based on the topology of the network incorporating only the net effect of regulatory interactions between components can provide a starting point for understanding the downstream impact of mutations or new drugs in biological networks. This is the case of the Boolean descriptions of networks in which the state of each component is either 1 (ON) or 0 (OFF). In this sort of model, time is divided into discrete steps, and the next state for each node in the control network is determined by a Boolean function of its state and the state of the nodes that influence it. This mapping defines a discrete dynamical system that is much easier to analyze than the differential equations described in the master equation approach. The Boolean function for each node is determined from its state and the known activating and inhibiting interactions between nodes. When both activators and inhibitors act on a node, we assume that the inhibition is dominant; the node will turn off. The first step in validating a model like this is to determine whether it reproduces the normal behavior of the system. Recent evidence (Kauffman, Peterson, Samuelsson, & Troein, 2003) suggests that a Boolean model correctly integrates the topology and the nature of interactions in a gene control network and can also produce important insights into the dynamics of these networks. Although Boolean networks were initially proposed for genetic networks they have since been used to study other network types as well. They are easy to handle computationally and even dynamics can be modeled on these networks by allowing the Boolean variables to evolve continuously.

Network Visualization

Visualization techniques can be applied to communicate the results of network measurement, modeling, and validation or to compare visually the structure and dynamics of empirical and simulated networks. Techniques range from well-designed tables that support easy comparison, via standard or customized graphs, to the layout of networks and the visualization of network dynamics. This section focuses on the visualization of network structure and dynamics and the research challenges that arise as a consequence of the size and complexity of real networks and the diversity of network science applications.

We now introduce the basics of visualization design; give an overview of major matrix, tree, and graph layout algorithms; and discuss the visualization of network dynamics as well as interactivity design.

Visualization Design Basics

The design of effective visualizations that support visual exploration and decision making requires detailed knowledge about the intended user group and their information needs. This knowledge, together with knowledge about human visual perception and cognitive processing, constrain the "solution space" and guide the design of effective visualizations. Combined with existing knowledge on network sampling, measuring, and modeling, it provides a solid basis for the design of effective visualizations. Here, we provide information on how to acquire knowledge on users and their tasks, give pointers to research results on human visual perception and cognitive processing, and postulate basic network visualization design guidelines.

User and Task Analysis

Detailed knowledge of users and their tasks is needed to design visualizations that are legible and informative. If one does not understand how users conceptualize their worlds and what they need to see in what context and when, then the visualization will be little more than "eye candy."

Information on users and their tasks can be acquired via interviews, questionnaires, observation, or analysis of existing documents and manuals. Excellent introductions on how to conduct a user/task analysis can be found in interface design textbooks, for example, Hackos and Redish (1998). Issues to bear in mind include the following:

- Who are the users (profession, location, gender, age, lifestyle preferences)?

- What is their level of technical and subject expertise? The visual language used will have to match the users' understanding.

- What is the visualization context? Describe the users' physical and social environments. Note any environmental challenges, such as poor lighting or noise, and any technical challenges such as screen size, resolution, color quality, and number of displays. Determine what hardware, browser software, monitors, and screen resolutions your audience uses.

- Describe scenarios of use or those situations or circumstances in which the visualizations may be used.

- Exactly what do the users need to understand, discover, or communicate; and in what sequence?

It is important to clarify the task(s) the visualization is intended to support. Examples include the identification of trends in the data, outliers, maxima and minima, boundaries, clusters and structure, dynamics, and related information. Each of these tasks potentially demands a very different visualization design; discovering which tasks to support entails observation, exploration, model construction, simulation, verification, interpretation, and communication of results (Hanson, 1958; Popper, 1959).

Human Visual Perception and Cognitive Processing

Human visual perception and processing capabilities are nearly constant. What you learn about them today will likely be valid 50 years hence. It thus makes sense to acquire detailed knowledge on human perception and processing and to use it to constrain the quite large design solution space. Books by MacEachren (1995), Palmer (1999), and Ware (2000) are excellent resources for a detailed examination of human perception and cognition. It is beyond the scope of this chapter, however, to provide a comprehensive review of research in this area.

Basics of Network Visualization Design

Knowledge of users and their tasks, as well as of human visual perception and cognitive processing, forms the basis for the design of effective visualizations. In general, visualization design comprises decisions about (a) employed metaphors and reference systems, (b) the number and type of data layers, and (c) visual mappings. There is a strong interplay among the three elements; for example, the selection of a different metaphor might very well influence the number of data layers and the visual mappings employed. Therefore, all three elements should be dealt with in concert. Extensive knowledge of existing algorithms and visualizations (e.g., Di Battista, Eades, Tamassia, & Tollis, 1999; Freeman, 2000; Herman, Melancon, & Marshall, 2000), close collaboration with users, and thorough testing and patient (re)design of visualizations will provide the best results.

Metaphors and Reference Systems

Metaphors should be selected so that they best match the conceptualization and information needs of the intended user group(s). Diverse metaphors have been suggested for network visualization, including time lines, subway maps, galaxy visualizations of networks, and the overlay of nodes and edges on reference systems such as geospatial maps.

Reference systems refer to temporal, geospatial, semantic, and other substrates that can be used to contextualize and ease understanding of network layouts. If time is important and a 2D layout desirable, using one axis to order nodes, for example by time, is appropriate. *Historiograph* visualizations of paper-citation networks generated by Garfield's HistCite™ tool (Garfield, Sher, & Torpie, 1964; Pudovkin & Garfield, 2002) are an example of time-ordered network layouts (see Figure 12.10, left). If a highway, airline, or Internet traffic network is to be visualized, a geospatial substrate map might be best (see Figure 12.10, middle). In some cases, for example when visualizing a co-author network, a free layout of nodes that reveals the topology of the network might be preferred (see Figure 12.10, right).

Visual Layers

Visual layers ease the readability of network visualizations. In most cases, a network visualization will comprise a base map (e.g., a map of the U.S.), an information overlay (router nodes and edges representing Internet traffic), labels (names of major cities), and a legend (a title, short explanation of unique features, a description of all visual encodings). Note that the credibility of any visualization can be considerably improved if the name of the map maker and date of creation are given and information on the displayed dataset and its manipulation are provided. Many visualizations benefit from being interactive (see the section on interaction and distortion techniques). Interactivity design can be conceptualized as an additional layer that is receptive to and reflects user actions, for example by indicating the zoom level.

Visual Mappings

Given appropriate metaphors, reference systems, and visual layers, one needs to define the following: What data entities should be represented as

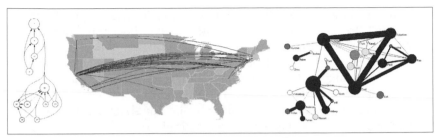

Figure 12.10 Temporal reference system used to display a citation network as an "Historiograph" (left), layout of paper citations on a geospatial map of U.S. (middle), and semantic space of co-author relations (right).

nodes? What relationships are important and should be represented as edges? What node/edge attributes are important and need to be visually encoded? Are there any sub-networks or backbone structures that need to be made visible? What subset of nodes, edges, subgraphs, and backbones needs to be labeled and how? If the network is large, one also has to decide what data can be omitted to provide users with a meaningful overview of the dataset and to enable the user to gain access to the omitted data.

In some cases the answers to these questions are straightforward. In others, considerable thought is required to come up with the right conceptualization and representation. Examples that inspired subsequent breakthroughs are Euler's (1736) rendering of the Königsberg bridges problem as a graph in which nodes represent land masses and edges represent bridges, or Moreno's (1934) first visualizations of social networks by graph structures. Moreno's *sociograms* used directed edges, color, different node shapes, and the location of nodes to show the status of a person, to depict the relationships among people in a group, or to stress structural features of a network (Moreno, 1943).

Today, a multitude of software libraries and tools makes it easy to analyze a network and to generate a network visualization. Some of the tools support dynamic changes of the mapping between data and their visual representation. Huisman and Van Duijn (2005) provide a comprehensive review and comparison of software for social network analysis.

Matrix Visualization

As discussed in the section on graphs and subgraphs, graphs are commonly represented by adjacency matrices (see Figure 12.2 for examples). The adjacency matrices can be visualized by dense pixel displays, also called structure plots, which use the space created by an ordered list of all nodes as a typically two-dimensional reference system. The existence of an edge between two nodes *(a,b)* is indicated by the shading of the area *(i,j)* where *i* is the row for *a* and *j* is the column for *b*.

Figure 12.11 a–f shows dense pixel displays for the six graphs given in Figure 12.2. Our visual system quickly identifies the symmetrical nature of the interlinkage patterns that is indicative of undirected graphs (see Figure 12.11 a–d). Only the lower or upper half of the matrix needs to be displayed. Directed graphs can be identified quickly by their non-symmetric nature (see Figure 12.11 e and f).

Dense pixel displays can be used to display the structure of very large graphs. Figure 12.11g shows a medium-sized graph in which the existence of an edge between two nodes is indicated by the shading of exactly one pixel. Networks that have more nodes than there are pixels on a monitor can be represented by averaging over a certain number of nodes and edges; for example, when displaying the interlinkage pattern of 10,000 nodes using a space of 1,000 X 1,000 pixels, each pixel represents the linkage density of 10 X 10 nodes. Edge weights can be represented by supplementing black and white pixel values with gray tones or color.

Dense areas in the matrix reveal graph structure. For example, the high density of node linkages in the diagonal of the plot in Figure 12.11g indicates that most of the nodes have links to themselves. This network property is very common, for example, in citation networks where it indicates a high level of self citation. Vertical or horizontal lines can be easily spotted, representing nodes with high in, out, or total degree. Other dense pixel areas might indicate clusters.

Obviously, the ordering of the nodes has a strong effect on the patterns that are visible. Hartigan (1972) introduced block clustering. The concept of reordering was first suggested by Bertin (1981). Chen (1999) developed and applied generalized association plots. Blockmodeling (Doreian, Batagelj, & Ferligoj, 2005) is an empirical technique that can be used to reduce a large, potentially incoherent network into a smaller comprehensible structure that can be visualized and interpreted more readily. Current research seeks to develop reordering algorithms to reduce noise and emphasize structural features (Mueller, 2004). Common choices are ordering by degree, by connected components, by core number or core levels, and according to other node properties and otherwise identified clusters.

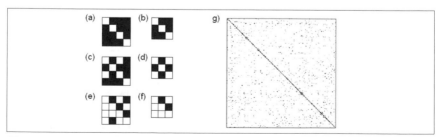

Figure 12.11 Dense pixel displays structure plots of small and larger graphs.

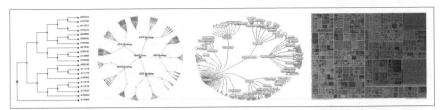

**Figure 12.12 Dendrogram (left), radial layout (middle left), hyperbolic tree layout
(middle right), and treemap layout (right).**

Tree Layout

Many networks are trees. Examples of trees include family trees, phylogenetic trees, organizational charts, classification hierarchies, and directory structures. Diverse algorithms are available to lay out trees (see Figure 12.12). The choice of algorithm depends on the dataset, users, and their tasks.

Dendrograms are a simple yet effective method for representing tree data. Most commonly, dendrograms are drawn in a *Cartesian* layout, as an upright or left-to-right tree. The branching, tree-like diagram effectively represents the hierarchical relationships among nodes. The length of edges might vary to represent edge attribute values. An illustrative use of dendrograms is the display of phylogenetic trees.

Radial tree layout (Di Battista et al., 1999; Herman et al., 2000) supports visualization and manipulation of large hierarchies. In a radial tree, the focused node is placed in the center of the display and all other nodes are rendered on appropriate circular levels around the selected node. The farther a node is from the center, the smaller it appears. This way, focus and context of very large tree structures can be displayed on a screen of limited size.

Hyperbolic tree layout is based on Poincaré's model of the (hyperbolic) non-Euclidean plane. Lamping, Rao, and Pirolli (1995) rediscovered hyperbolic spaces in 1995 for information visualization and Munzner (1998) developed the first 3D hyperbolic viewer. In a hyperbolic tree, the root is placed at the center; the children are placed at an outer ring in equal distance from their parents. The circumference jointly increases with the radius and more space becomes available for the growing number of intermediate and leaf nodes. Whereas the radial tree uses a linear layout, the hyperbolic layout uses a nonlinear (distortion) technique to accommodate focus and context for a large number of nodes.

In radial tree and hyperbolic tree layouts, node overlap is prevented by assigning an open angle for each node. All children of a node are then laid out in this open angle. Frequently the tree visualization is interactive—users can click on a node to initiate its fluent movement into the center or can grab and reposition a single node.

Treemaps, developed in the Human–Computer Interaction Lab at the University of Maryland (Shneiderman 1992, 2005), trace their ancestry back to Venn diagrams (Venn, 1894/1971). They use a space-filling technique to map a tree structure (for example, a file directory) into nested rectangles with each rectangle representing a node. A rectangular area is first allocated to hold the representation of the tree; this area is then subdivided into a set of rectangles that represents the top level of the tree. This process continues recursively on the resulting rectangles to represent each lower level of the tree, each level alternating between vertical and horizontal subdivision. Upon completion, all child rectangles are enclosed by their parent rectangle. Area size and color can be used to encode two node attribute values, for example, file size and age, respectively. Node children can be ordered by area size, providing a better understanding of their size differences. Tree maps have been successfully used to identify large files in nested directory structures or to make sense of stock option trends.

Graph Layout

Graph layout algorithms can be applied to arbitrary graphs (see Figure 12.14). They aim to sort a set of randomly placed nodes into a layout that satisfies aesthetic criteria for visual presentation such as non-overlapping, evenly distributed nodes, symmetry, uniform edge lengths, minimized edge crossings, and orthogonal drawings that minimize area, bends, slopes, and angles. The criteria may be relaxed to speed the layout process (Eades, 1984).

In some cases, it is desirable to order nodes by their attributes, for example time or size, or by their structural features, for example, their degree. An example is *Historiographs*, introduced in the section on visualization design basics and shown in Figure 12.10, left. They organize nodes (representing papers) vertically according to their publication date. Nodes are then placed horizontally in a way such that the resulting layout of nodes and edges (representing citation links) fulfills the aesthetic criteria previously discussed.

Force-directed layout (FDL) algorithms were introduced by Eades (1984). They are commonly used to display general graphs, both directed and undirected, cyclic and acyclic. Here repulsive forces F_r are applied in inverse proportion to the distance d between any two nodes i and j and attractive forces F_a in logarithmic proportion to the distance between two nodes linked by an edge:

$$F_r(i,j) = \frac{C_3}{d} \text{ and } F_a(i,j) = C_1 * \log(\frac{d}{C_2}), \tag{34}$$

where C_1, C_2 and C_3 are constant values. For all nodes, the algorithm calculates each force against all other nodes, sums them as the force of all connected nodes, and moves the node appropriately. This way, a set of randomly placed nodes is sorted into a desirable layout. However, the complexity of the algorithm increases quadratically with the number of nodes, that is, $O(N^2)$, making it unsuitable for large data sets.

Extensions of Eades's algorithm provide methods for the intelligent initial placement of nodes, cluster the data to perform an initial coarse layout followed by successively more detailed placement, and use grid-based systems for dividing the dataset. For example, Graph EMbedder (GEM) attempts to recognize and forestall non-productive rotation and oscillation in the motion of nodes in the graph as it cools (Frick, Ludwig, Mehldau, 1994). Walshaw's (2000) multilevel algorithm provides a divide-and-conquer method for laying out very large graphs by using clustering. VxOrd (Davidson, Wylie, & Boyack, 2001) uses a density grid in place of pair-wise repulsive forces to speed execution; it achieves computation times in the order of $O(N)$. It also employs barrier jumping to avoid trapping clusters in local minima. An extremely fast layout algorithm for visualizing large-scale networks in three-dimensional space was proposed by Han and Ju (2003). Today, the algorithms developed by Kamada and Kawai (1989) and Fruchterman and Reingold (1991) are most commonly employed, partly because they are available in the widely used *Pajek* visualization toolkit (de Nooy, Mrvar, & Batagelj, 2005).

Because of the major differences in the visualization of small, medium size, and large networks, they are discussed separately.

Small Networks

Small networks have up to 100 nodes: for example, social networks, food webs, or import and export among countries. Here, all nodes and edges and many of their attributes can be shown. The node (area) size is commonly used to encode a primary value such as size, importance, power, or activity level. Node color is often employed to encode secondary values such as intensity or age. Node types are often encoded by node shapes—especially if only a few node types can be defined or node types can be aggregated into a small number of main types for which an easily distinguishable shape encoding exists. Sample layouts of one small-world network using different layout algorithms are shown in Figure 12.13.

Medium-Sized Networks

Examples of medium-sized networks, with more than 100 and up to 1,000 nodes, include gene association networks, metabolic networks, and economic networks. Most nodes can be shown, but not all their attributes or labels. Typically, it is not possible to show all edges; the number of nodes, edges, and their displayed attributes need to be reduced intelligently. For example, it might be beneficial to identify major components in a network and to represent all network components of size one and two simply by displaying one and two nodes respectively and using a number next to them to indicate how many components of this size

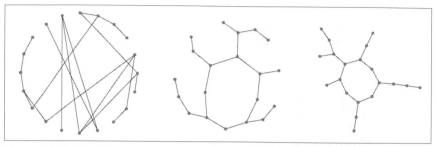

Figure 12.13 Circle layout (left), Fruchterman-Rheingold layout (middle), and Kamada-Kawai layout (right) of a small-world network.

exist. In other cases, it might suffice to determine and depict the giant connected component of the network exclusively and to provide information on the size and number of other components in a tabular format.

Major design strategies include showing only important nodes, edges, labels, and attributes; using most appropriate metaphors and reference systems to lay out nodes spatially, to supply landmarks that guide orientation and navigation, and to provide focus and context.

Large Networks

Large networks have more than 1,000 nodes. Neither all nodes nor all edges can be shown at once; sometimes there are more nodes than pixels. Examples include communication networks such as the Internet, telephone networks, and wireless networks; network applications such as the Web; e-mail interaction networks; transportation networks/road maps; relationships between objects in a database such as function/module dependency graphs; knowledge bases; and scholarly networks. Major challenges are the selection of important nodes, edges, subgraphs, and backbones and their positioning; the de-cluttering of links; labeling; as well as navigation and interaction design. A major design strategy is the tight coupling of data analysis and visualization.

For example, important nodes, edges, or subgraphs can be identified using the measurements introduced in the section on node and edge properties. It is important to show strong and weak links. *Pathfinder network scaling* (Schvaneveldt, 1990) is frequently used to identify the backbone of a network. Major network components can be identified using the algorithms introduced in the section on local structure. These components can each be presented as a "super node," the (area) size of which might correspond to the number of nodes it represents.

Hierarchy visualizations of the nested structure of a network or a visualization of major clusters and their interconnections help us to understand the global structure of a network. Cutting out sub-networks or focus and context visualizations support the examination of local network properties. The focus and context approach shows only one cluster in detail; other clusters are indicated by single nodes to provide context. Careful interactivity design aims to support overview, zoom, and filter, as well as the retrieval of details on demand (see the section on interaction and distortion techniques).

Visualization of Dynamics

Almost all networks are optimized to support diverse dynamic processes. Electricity and transportation systems are optimized to distribute tangible and intangible objects effectively. Friendship networks are often support networks; our brain cells grow in response to the input they receive. As discussed in the section on modeling dynamics on networks, studying the evolution of networks differs remarkably from studying dynamic processes on networks. Ideally, both could be studied, understood, and communicated together.

Visualizing Network Evolution

Visualizations that show the evolution of networks in terms of attribute changes or structural changes (decreases or increases in the number of nodes and edges) can be divided into two general types: algorithms that process data on network changes incrementally and algorithms that identify and aim to visualize network changes based on a complete dataset. Examples of incremental visualizations, also called organic visualizations (Fry, 2000), are Fry's Anemone (http://acg.media. mit.edu/people/fry/anemone) and Gnutellavision (Dhamija, Fisher, & Yee, 2000; Yee, Fisher, Dhamija, & Hearst, 2001) (see Figure 12.14). Note that Gnutellavision provides interactive exploration of subregions of a graph from different perspectives.

Examples of visualizations that aim to depict the change of a network over time based on a complete dataset are *Netmap* (Standish & Galloway, 2002), which visualizes Tierra's tree of life or routers and their

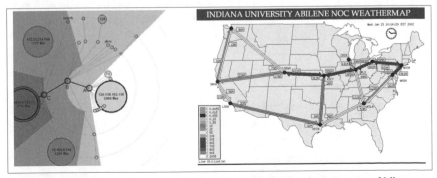

Figure 12.14 Dynamic network visualizations with fixed substrate map: Abilene network (right) and variable radial tree layout: Gnutellavision (left).

interconnections around a certain host, and Chen's (2004) *CiteSpace* system, which visualizes intellectual turning points in scholarly networks.

Visualizing Dynamics on Networks

In some application domains, the structure of a network is fixed and the flow dynamics over this fixed substrate is of interest. An example is the Abilene Weather forecast map (http://loadrunner. uits.iu.edu/weathermaps/abilene, shown in Figure 12.14). Other examples are weather forecast maps or migration maps that often use a geospatial substrate map. Here the reference system, the network, and the activity need to be depicted. Activity is often indicated by line overlays. Arrowheads can be used to indicate directedness; but many arrows going to one node leads to an increase in the size of the node. Hence line thickness, shading, color, and other forms of coding are frequently employed to indicate edge directions. High amounts of traffic quickly lead to cluttered displays. Intelligent aggregation methods that identify and visually encode major traffic flows need to be employed. Note that visualizations of network dynamics can be static or animated.

Interaction and Distortion Techniques

Many network datasets are too large to be displayed at once. Often, only the backbone or major subgraphs of a network and important landmark nodes can be displayed. Additional information associated with single nodes, links, or subgraphs might be retrievable on demand. Even if large, tiled display walls are available or high density printouts can be used, in many cases a user does not want to see a million nodes at one time. Instead, and in accordance with Shneiderman's (1996) information seeking mantra, users prefer to have an overview of the most general structure (major clusters, backbone of the network) first. Then, they may pan, zoom, and filter out sub-networks of interest. Finally, they might request details of a certain sub-network. Consequently, network visualizations should be designed with interactivity in mind. Most commonly, network visualizations support:

- Conditioning: filter, set background variables, and display foreground parameters
- Identification: highlight, color, shape code
- Parameter control: line thickness, length, color legend, time slider, and animation control
- Navigation: bird's eye view, zoom, and pan
- Information requests: Mouse over or click on a node to retrieve more details or collapse/expand a sub-network

When designing interactive visualizations one needs to keep in mind that the bandwidth from computer to human is much higher than in the other direction. Ideally, occasional user steering leads to the computer-generated display of visualization sequences that can be readily perceived via the high bandwidth channel of our visual system and cognitively understood. If possible, the user should obtain the illusion of direct control. Hence, visual feedback should be provided within 1/10 second (Shneiderman, 1987). When transitioning from one visualization to another, it is advantageous to use animation instead of jumps to support object constancy and navigation. Keeping information density almost constant at all zoom levels is important.

Curiosity is an important ingredient of scientific discovery. It can be supported by implementing a universal undo, making it impossible for a user to irrevocably get lost or to founder. In general, the user needs to be kept in "flow" (Csikszentmihalyi, 1991, p. 1). Boredom (too little information, too slowly) and anxiety (too much information, too fast) should be avoided (Bederson, 2004).

Discussion and Outlook

As we have seen, networks can be found in biological, social, economic, informational, and many other systems and processes. Although the advances that we have witnessed in the past few years have been spectacular, in terms of both impact on basic science and practical implications, they have highlighted the incompleteness of our knowledge as well. Network science is going to face a number of important challenges and questions in the next few years.

To give a concrete example, let us consider the area of scholarly information access and management that represents an important focus for the readership of this volume. Today, our main means of accessing our collective knowledge base are search engines. Companies such as Google and Microsoft claim that a few good keywords and local link traversal suffice to make use of mankind's collective knowledge. Search does work well for fact retrieval. Yet, it is instructive to see what coverage a dataset has, what major clusters exist, from which clusters search results were drawn, or how retrieved documents interrelate. Private and commercial entities have expended great effort to develop directory structures, classification hierarchies, and other means to organize knowledge. However, it appears to be difficult—if not humanly impossible—to design and update an organizational schema comprising hundreds of thousands of classes so that it captures the evolving structure of a rapidly increasing scholarly document data set of potentially millions of entries. Without organizational schemas that expeditiously and comprehensively organize scholarly data we are bound to the ground. Today, our bird's-eye views are at best one meter above the landscape of science, whereas a global view would be possible only from a 1,000-meter height. Given nearly constant human abilities, our distance above ground is decreasing as the amount of information grows. Scientists are forced into narrow specialties, scrutinizing a tiny portion of science's shoreline. They are largely ignorant of a vast hinterland containing mountain ranges of data and vast floodplains of experience. A more global view of science is required to identify major experts, to learn how knowledge evolves and interrelates, to understand what duplications or complementary approaches exist, to see what research areas are emerging. Such information is vital for funding agencies, companies, and researchers (for example, for setting research priorities) but is also beneficial to science education and appreciation. The study of science by scientific means requires the analysis of terabytes of scholarly data. It requires the measurement and modeling of large-scale, coupled networks of authors, inventors, awardees, investors, papers, grants, patents, and so on, and their many interrelations (Börner et al., 2003). These networks grow continuously and they are used to diffuse knowledge, money, and reputation. The study of feedback cycles—for example, the fact that authors who publish highly cited papers have a greater chance of having their proposals funded and, hence, securing more resources to increase their chances of publishing yet more highly cited papers—seems to be particularly important for understanding the structure and dynamics of science.

These considerations translate into a set of theoretical and practical challenges that ranges from the study of multiple overlapping and interacting networks to the design of effective visualizations that show the structure, evolution, and dynamics of very large scale (more than a million nodes) networks. We need to understand the interfacing and interaction of *networks of networks* and to start large-scale measurement projects for gathering empirical data that comprise not only the physical properties of multi-scale networks but also their usage. The theory and tool development required to address these challenges will benefit enormously from a cyberinfrastructure for network science research. This infrastructure will need to provide access to data, services, and computing resources, as well as expertise (Börner, 2006).

It is clear that different application domains will pose different challenges depending on the availability of data as well as scientific and practical demands. In addition, the different sciences will make very different contributions: Mathematicians and statisticians will advance network science theory; physicists will continue their search for universal laws; biologists will aim to uncover the secrets of life; social scientists will continue to study the social fabric in which we are embedded; computer scientists and information scientists will develop effective and scalable algorithms and infrastructures; and graph drawing experts and designers will aim to improve our ability to visually communicate network structure, evolution, and usage. Network science has true potential to integrate the knowledge acquired in diverse fields of science. Given the ubiquity of networks in our world, the results of the theoretical and practical study of networks might help solve some of the major challenges confronting society. It is our hope that this chapter succeeds in paving the way for an adoption of approaches and theories developed outside information science and computer science yet directly applicable to information science and computer science problems. We also hope that the chapter inspires new collaborations across scientific disciplines and the development of theoretical approaches with the potential for practical application.

Acknowledgments

We would like to thank Rebecca Rutherford for her assistance in the conversion of formulas and citation entries in the preparation of the manuscript. We benefited from discussions with Stanley Wasserman, Ariel Balter, Kevin W. Boyack, Joseph Cottam, Ketan K. Mane, Shashikant Penumarthy, and Elijah Wright. We thank the anonymous reviewers who provided detailed comments on a draft of the chapter. This work is supported by a National Science Foundation grant under IIS-0513650 to the first and third author and an NSF CHE-0524661 and CAREER IIS-0238261 award to the first author. The second author is supported by a James S. McDonnell Foundation grant.

Endnotes

1. By "networks" we refer to any system that allows its abstract/mathematical representation as a graph, that is, a set of nodes and edges.
2. Selected figures in this chapter are available in color at www.asis.org/Publications/ARIST/Vol41/BornerFigures.html
3. The word *equilibrium* refers to a situation in which the probability distribution describing the possible states is not biased or constrained. This happens when external forces constrain the system to be on a specific subset of the allowed states. This will be properly defined in the context of dynamical modeling; see sub-section on modeling evolving networks.

References

Adamic, L., & Adar, E. (2003). Friends and neighbors on the Web. *Social Networks, 25,* 211–230.

Adamic, L. A., Lukose, R. M., Puniyani, A. R., & Huberman, B. A. (2001). Search in power-law networks. *Physical Review E, 64,* 46135.

Albert, R., & Barabási, A.-L. (2002). Statistical mechanics of complex networks. *Reviews of Modern Physics, 74,* 47–97.

Albert, R., Jeong, H., & Barabási, A.-L. (2000). Error and attack tolerance in complex networks. *Nature, 406,* 378.

Bader, G. D., & Hogue, C. W. V. (2002). Analyzing yeast protein–protein interaction data obtained from different sources. *Nature Biotechnology, 20,* 991–997.

Banks, B. D., & Carley, K. (1996). Models for network evolution. *Journal of Mathematical Sociology, 21,* 173–196.

Barabási, A.-L. (2002). *Linked: The new science of networks.* New York: Plume.

Barabási, A.-L., & Albert, R. (1999). Emergence of scaling in random networks. *Science, 286,* 509–512.

Barabási, A.-L., Albert, R., & Jeong, H. (1999). Mean-field theory for scale-free random networks. *Physica A, 272,* 173.

Barabási, A.-L., & Oltvai, Z. N. (2004). Network biology: Understanding the cell's functional organization. *Nature Reviews Genetics,* I, 101–113.

Barrat, A., Barthelemy, M., Pastor-Satorras, R., & Vespignani, A. (2004). The architecture of complex weighted networks. *Proceedings of the National Academy of Sciences of the United States of America, 101,* 3747–3752.

Barrat, A., & Weigt, M. (2000). On the properties of small-world network models. *European Physical Journal B, 13,* 547–560.

Barthelemy, M., & Amaral, L. A. N. (1999a). Erratum: Small-world networks: Evidence for a crossover picture. *Physical Review Letters, 82,* 5180.

Barthelemy, M., & Amaral, L. A. N. (1999b). Small-world networks: Evidence for a crossover picture. *Physical Review Letters, 82,* 3180–3183.

Bederson, B. B. (2004). Interfaces for staying in the flow. *Ubiquity, 5*(27). Retrieved March 22, 2006, from www.acm.org/ubiquity/views/v5i27_bederson.html

Berg, J., & Lassig, M. (2002). Correlated random networks. *Physical Review Letters, 89,* 228701–228705.

Bertin, J. (1981). *Graphics and graphic information-processing.* Berlin: Walter de Gruyter.

Bettencourt, L. M. A., Cintron-Arias, A., Kaiser, D. I., & Castillo-Chavez, C. (2005). The power of a good idea: Quantitative modeling of the spread of ideas from epidemiological models. Retrieved March 22, 2006, from http://arxiv.org/PS_cache/physics/pdf/0502/0502067.pdf

Bianconi, G., & Capocci, A. (2003). Number of loops of size h in scale-free networks. *Physical Review Letters, 90,* 078701-1–078701-4.

Blatt, M., Wiseman, S., & Domany, E. (1996). Superparamagnetic clustering of data. *Physical Review Letters, 76,* 3251–3254.

Blatt, M., Wiseman, S., & Domany, E. (1997). Data clustering using a model granular magnet. *Neural Computing, 9,* 1805–1842.

Bollobas, B. (1998). *Modern graph theory.* New York: Springer.

Börner, K. (2006). Semantic association networks: Using Semantic Web technology to improve scholarly knowledge and expertise management. In V. G. C. Chen (Ed.), *Visualizing the Semantic Web* (pp. 183–198). Berlin: Springer.

Börner, K., Chen, C., & Boyack, K. (2003). Visualizing knowledge domains. *Annual Review of Information Science and Technology, 37,* 179–255.

Börner, K., Maru, J. T., & Goldstone, R. L. (2003). The simultaneous evolution of author and paper networks. *Proceedings of the National Academy of Sciences of the United States of America, 101*(Suppl. 1), 5266–5273.

Brandes, U. (2001). A faster algorithm for betweenness centrality. *Journal of Mathematical Sociology, 25,* 163–177.

Brandes, U., & Erlebach, T. (2005). *Network analysis: Methodological foundations.* Berlin: Springer.

Broder, A. Z., Kumar, R., Maghoul, F., Raghavan, P., Rajagopalan, S., Stata, R., et al. (2000). Graph structure in the Web. *Computer Networks, 33*, 309–320.

Buchanan, M. (2002). *Nexus: Small worlds and the groundbreaking science of networks.* New York: Norton.

Burda, Z., & Krzywicki, A. (2003). Uncorrelated random networks. *Physical Review E, 67*, 046118.

Burda, Z., Jurkiewicz, J., & Krzywicki, A. (2003). *Statistical mechanics of random graphs.* Retrieved March 22, 2006, from http://arxiv.org/PS_cache/cond-mat/pdf/0312/0312494.pdf

Carrington, P., Scott, J., & Wasserman, S. (2004). *Models and methods in social network analysis.* New York: Cambridge University Press.

Chakrabarti, S., Dom, B., Gibson, D., Kleinberg, J., Kumar, S. R., Raghavan, P., et al. (1999). Hypersearching the Web. *Scientific American, 280*(6), 44–52.

Chartrand, G., & Lesniak, L. (1986). *Graphs and digraphs.* Menlo Park, CA: Wadsworth & Brooks/Cole.

Chen, C. (2004). Searching for intellectual turning points: Progressive knowledge domain visualization. *Proceedings of the National Academy of Sciences of the United States of America, 101*(Suppl. 1), 5303–5310.

Chen, C. H. (1999, August). *Extensions of generalized association plots (GAP).* Paper presented at the Annual Meeting of the American Statistical Association, Baltimore, MD.

Chung, Y. M., & Lee, Y. J. (2001). A corpus-based approach to comparative evaluation of statistical term association measures. *Journal of the American Society for Information Science and Technology, 52*, 283–296.

Clauset, A., & Moore, C. (2005). Accuracy and scaling phenomena in Internet mapping. *Physical Review Letters, 94*, 018701.

Cohen, R., Erez, K., Ben-Avraham, D., & Havlin, S. (2000). Resilience of the Internet to random breakdowns. *Physical Review Letters, 85*, 4626–4629.

Cronin, B., & Atkins, H. B. (Eds.). (2000). *The web of knowledge: A Festschrift in honor of Eugene Garfield.* Medford, NJ: Information Today.

Csikszentmihalyi, M. (1991). *Flow: The psychology of optimal experience.* New York: HarperCollins.

Daley, D. J., Gani, J., & Cannings, C. (1999). *Epidemic modeling: An introduction.* Cambridge, UK: Cambridge University Press.

Dall'Asta, L., Alvarez-Hamelin, I., Barrat, A., Vazquez, A., & Vespignani, A. (2005). Traceroute-like exploration of unknown networks: A statistical analysis. In A. López-Ortiz & A. Hamel (Eds.), *Combinatorial and algorithmic aspects of networking* (pp. 140–153). Berlin: Springer.

Davidson, G. S., Wylie, B. N., & Boyack, K. W. (2001). Cluster stability and the use of noise in interpretation of clustering. *Proceedings of the IEEE Symposium on Information Visualization*, 23–30.

Deane, C. M., Salwinski, L., Xenarios, I., & Esenberg, D. (2002). Protein interactions: Two methods for assessment of the reliability of high throughput observations. *Molecular Cell Proteomics, 1*, 349–356.

de Jong, E. D., Thierens, D., & Watson, R. A. (2004). Hierarchical genetic algorithms. *Parallel Problem Solving from Nature: Proceedings of the 8th International Conference*, 232–241.

de Nooy, W., Mrvar, A., & Batagelj, V. (2005). *Exploratory social network analysis with Pajek*. Cambridge, UK: Cambridge University Press.

Dhamija, R., Fisher, D., & Yee, K.-P. (2000). *Gnutellavision: Real-time visualization of a peer-to-peer network*. Retrieved March 10, 2006, from http://bailando.sims.berkeley.edu/infovis/gtv

Di Battista, G., Eades, P., Tamassia, R., & Tollis, I. G. (1999). *Graph drawing: Algorithms for the visualization of graphs*. Upper Saddle River, NJ: Prentice Hall.

Dill, S., Kumar, S. R., McCurley, K. S., Rajagopalan, S., Sivakumar, D., & Tomkins, A. (2002). Self-similarity in the Web. *ACM Transactions on Internet Technology, 2*, 205–223.

Domany, E. (1999). Superparamagnetic clustering of data: The definitive solution of an ill-posed problem. *Physics A, 263*, 158–169.

Doreian, P., Batagelj, V., & Ferligoj, A. (2005). *Generalized blockmodeling*. Cambridge, UK: Cambridge University Press.

Dorogovtsev, S. N., & Mendes, J. F. F. (2002). Evolution of random networks. *Advances in Physics, 51*, 1079–1187.

Dorogovtsev, S. N., & Mendes, J. F. F. (2003). *Evolution of networks*. Oxford, UK: Oxford University Press.

Dorogovtsev, S. N., Mendes, J. F. F., & Samukhin, A. N. (2003). Principles of statistical mechanics of random networks. *Nuclear Physics B, 666*, 396.

Eades, P. (1984). A heuristic for graph drawing. *Congressus Numerantium, 42*, 149–160.

Erdös, P., & Rényi, P. (1959). On random graphs. *Publicationes Mathematicae, 6*, 290–297.

Euler, L. (1736). Solutio problematis ad geometriam situs pertinentis. *Commetarii Academiae Scientiarum Imperialis Petropolitanae, 8*, 128–140.

Farkas, I., Derenyi, I., Palla, G., & Vicsek, T. (2004). Equilibrium statistical mechanics of network structures. In E. Ben-Naim, H. Frauenfelder, & Z. Toroczkai (Eds.), *Complex networks* (Lecture Notes in Physics, 650) (pp. 163–187). Berlin: Springer.

Flake, G., Lawrence, S., & Giles, C. L. (2000). Efficient identification of Web communities. *Proceedings of the Sixth ACM SIGKDD International Conference on Knowledge Discovery and Data Mining*, 150–160.

Fletcher, G., Sheth, H., & Börner, K. (2004). Unstructured peer-to-peer networks. In G. Moro, S. Bergamaschi, & K. Aberer (Eds.), *Topological properties and search performance* (Lecture Notes in Computer Science, 3601) (pp. 14–27). Berlin: Springer.

Frank, O. (2004). Network sampling and model fitting. In P. Carrington, J. Scott, & S. Wasserman (Eds.), *Models and methods in social network analysis* (pp. 31–56). New York: Cambridge University Press.

Frank, O., & Strauss, D. (1986). Markov graphs. *Journal of the American Statistical Association, 81*, 832–842.

Freeman, L. C. (1977). A set of measuring centrality based on betweenness. *Sociometry, 40*, 35–41.

Freeman, L. C. (2000). Visualizing social networks. *Journal of Social Structure, 1*(1). Retrieved March 22, 2006, from www.cmu.edu/joss/content/articles/volume1/Freeman.html

Frick, A., Ludwig, A., & Mehldau, H. (1994). A fast adaptive layout algorithm for undirected graphs. *Proceedings of Graph Drawing '94*, 388–403.

Fronczak, P., Fronczak, A., & Holyst, J. A. (2005). *Interplay between network structure and self-organized criticality*. Retrieved March 22, 2006, from http://arxiv.org/PS_cache/cond-mat/pdf/0509/0509043.pdf

Fruchterman, T. M. J., & Reingold, E. M. (1991). Graph drawing by force-directed placement. *Software-Practice & Experience, 21*, 1129–1164.

Fry, B. (2000). *Organic information design*. Unpublished master's thesis, Massachusetts Institute of Technology.

Garfield, E., Sher, I. H., & Torpie, R. J. (1964). *The use of citation data in writing the history of science*. Philadelphia: Institute for Scientific Information.

Gibson, D., Kleinberg, J. M., & Raghavan, P. (1998). Inferring Web communities from link topology. *Proceedings of the Ninth ACM Conference on Hypertext and Hypermedia*, 225–234.

Gilbert, E. N. (1959). Random graphs. *Annals of Mathematical Statistics, 30*, 1141–1144.

Gimblett, H. R. (Ed.). (2002). *Integrating geographic information systems and agent-based modeling techniques for simulating social and ecological processes*. Oxford, UK: Oxford University Press.

Girvan, M., & Newman, M. (2002). Community structure in social and biological networks. *Proceedings of the National Academy of Sciences of the United States of America, 99*, 7821–7826.

Granovetter, M. (1973). Strength of weak ties. *American Journal of Sociology, 78*, 1360–1380.

Gruhl, D., Guha, R., Tomkins, A., & Liben-Nowell, D. (2004, May). Information diffusion through blogspace. Paper presented at the Thirteenth International World Wide Web Conference. Retrieved March 10, 2006, from www2004.org/proceedings/docs/1p491.pdf

Guimera, R., Mossa, S., Turtschi, A., & Amaral, L. A. N. (2005). Structure and efficiency of the world-wide airport network. *Proceedings of the National Academy of Sciences of the United States of America, 102*, 7794–7799.

Hackos, J. T., & Redish, J. C. (1998). *User and task analysis for interface design*. New York: Wiley.

Han, K., & Ju, B.-H. (2003). A fast layout algorithm for protein interaction networks. *Bioinformatics, 19*, 1882–1888.

Hanneman, R. A., & Riddle, M. (2005). *Introduction to social network methods: Centrality and power*. Retrieved September 19, 2005, from http://faculty.ucr.edu/~hanneman/nettext/C10_Centrality.html

Hanson, N. (1958). *Patterns of discovery*. Cambridge, UK: Cambridge University Press.

Hartigan, J. (1972). Direct clustering of a data matrix. *Journal of the American Statistical Association, 67*(337), 123–129.

Herman, I., Melancon, G., & Marshall, M. S. (2000). Graph visualization and navigation in information visualization: A survey. *IEEE Transactions on Visualization and Computer Graphics, 6*, 24–43.

Hodgman, T. C. (2000). A historical perspective on gene/protein functional assignment. *Bioinformatics, 16*, 10–15.

Holland, P. W., & Leinhardt, S. (1981). An exponential family of probability distributions for directed graphs. *Journal of the American Statistical Association, 76*(373), 33–50.

Huisman, M., & Van Duijn, M. A. J. (2005). Software for social network analysis. In P. J. Carrington, J. Scott, & S. Wasserman (Eds.), *Models and methods in social network analysis* (pp. 270–316). New York: Cambridge University Press.

Jaynes, E. T. (1957). Information theory and statistical mechanics. *Physical Review, 106,* 620–630.

Jungnickel, D. (1994). *Graphs, networks and algorithms.* Heidelberg, Germany: Springer.

Kamada, T., & Kawai, S. (1989). An algorithm for drawing general undirected graphs. *Information Processing Letters, 31,* 7–15.

Kauffman, S., Peterson, C., Samuelsson, B., & Troein, C. (2003). Random Boolean network models and the yeast transcriptional network. *Proceedings of the National Academy of Sciences of the United States of America, 100,* 14796–14799.

Kim, J.-O., & Mueller, C. (1978). *Factor analysis: Statistical methods and practical issues.* Thousand Oaks, CA: Sage.

Kleinberg, J. (2000). The small-world phenomenon: An algorithmic perspective. *Proceedings of the 32nd ACM Symposium on Theory of Computing,* 163–170.

Kleinberg, J., & Lawrence, S. (2001). The structure of the Web. *Science, 294,* 1849–1850.

Krapivsky, P. L., & Redner, S. (2003). Rate equation approach for growing networks. In R. Pastor-Satorras, M. Rubi, & A. Diaz-Guilera (Eds.), *Statistical mechanics of complex networks* (Lecture Notes in Physics 625) (pp. 3–22). Berlin: Springer.

Krapivsky, P. L., & Redner, S. (2005). Network growth by copying. *Physical Review E, 71,* 036118-1–036118-8.

Krzywicki, A. (2001). *Defining statistical ensembles of random graphs.* Retrieved March 22, 2006, from http://arxiv.org/PS_cache/cond-mat/pdf/0110/0110574.pdf

Kumar, R., Raghavan, P., Rajagopalan, S., Sivakumar, D., Tomkins, A., & Upfall, E. (2000). Stochastic models for the Web graph. *Proceedings of the 41st IEEE Symposium on Foundations of Computer Sciences,* 57–65.

Kumar, R., Raghavan, P., Rajagopalan, S., & Tomkins, A. (1999). Trawling the Web for emerging cyber-communities. *Computer Networks, 31,* 1481–1493.

Lakhina, A., Byers, J., Crovella, M., & Xie, P. (2002). *Sampling biases in IP topology measurements* (Technical Report BUCS-TR-2002-021). Boston: Boston University Computer Science Department.

Lamping, J., Rao, R., & Pirolli, P. (1995). A focus+context technique based on hyperbolic geometry for visualizing large hierarchies. *Proceedings of the SIGCHI Conference on Human Factors in Computing Systems,* 401–408.

Lee, E. J. (2005). Robustness of the avalanche dynamics in data packet transport on scale-free networks. *Physical Review E, 71,* 056108.

Liljeros, F., Edling, C. R., Amaral, L. A. N., Stanley, H. E., & Aberg, Y. (2001). The web of sexual contacts. *Nature, 411,* 907–908.

Lynch, M. F. (1977). Variety generation: A reinterpretation of Shannon's mathematical theory of communications, and its implication for information science. *Journal of the American Society for Information Science, 28,* 19–25.

MacEachren, A. M. (1995). *How maps work: Representation, visualization and design.* New York: Guildford Press.

May, R. M., & Lloyd, A. L. (2001). Infection dynamics on scale-free networks. *Physical Review E, 64,* 066112.

McFadzean, D., & Tesfatsion, L. (1997). An agent-based computational model for the evolution of trade networks. *Computing in Economics and Finance, 110*. Retrieved March 16, 2006, from http://bucky.stanford.edu/cef97/abstracts/mcfadzean.html

Merton, R. K. (1968). The Matthew effect in science: The reward and communication systems of science are considered. *Science, 159*(810), 56–63.

Milo, R., Shen-Orr, S., Itzkovitz, S., Kashtan, N., Chklovskii, D., & Alon, U. (2002). Network motifs: Simple building blocks of complex networks. *Science, 298*(5594), 824–827.

Molloy, M., & Reed, B. (1995). A critical point for random graphs with a given degree sequence. *Random Structures Algorithms, 6*, 161–174.

Monge, P. R., & Contractor, N. (2003). *Theories of communication networks*. New York: Oxford University Press.

Moreno, J. L. (1934). *Who shall survive? A new approach to the problems of human interrelations*. Washington, DC: Nervous and Mental Disease Publishing Company.

Moreno, J. L. (1943). Sociometry and the social order. *Sociometry, 6*, 299–344.

Moreno, Y., Pastor-Satorras, R.,Vazquez, A., & Vespignani, A. (2003). Critical load and congestion instabilities in scale-free networks. *Europhysics Letters, 62*, 292.

Motter, A. E., & Lai, Y. C. (2002). Cascade based attacks on complex networks. *Physical Review E, 66*, 065102.

Mueller, C. (2004). *Sparse matrix reordering algorithms for cluster identification*. Retrieved March 20, 2006, from www.osl.iu.edu/~chemuell/projects/bioinf/sparse-matrix-clustering-chris-mueller.pdf

Munzner, T. (1998). Exploring large graphs in 3D hyperbolic space. *IEEE Computer Graphics and Applications, 18*(4), 18–23.

Newman, M. (2003). The structure and function of complex networks. *SIAM Review, 45*, 167–256.

Newman, M., & Girvan, M. (2004). Finding and evaluating community structure in networks. *Physical Review E, 69*, 026113.

Newman, M. E. J. (2001). The structure of scientific network collaborations. *Proceedings of the National Academy of Sciences of the United States of America, 98*, 404–409.

Newman, M. E. J. (2002). Assortative mixing in networks. *Physical Review Letters, 89*, 208701.

Palla, G., Derenyi, I., Farkas, I., & Vicsek, T. (2005). Uncovering the overlapping community structure of complex networks in nature and society. *Nature, 435*(7043), 814–818.

Palmer, S. E. (1999). *Vision science: From photons to phenomenology*. Cambridge, MA: MIT Press.

Parisi, G. (1988). *Statistical field theory*. Redwood City, CA: Addison-Wesley.

Park, J., & Newman, M. E. J. (2004). The statistical mechanics of networks. *Physical Review E, 70*, 066117.

Pastor-Satorras, R., & Vespignani, A. (2001). Epidemic spreading in scale-free networks. *Physical Review Letters, 86*, 3200–3203.

Pastor-Satorras, R., & Vespignani, A. (2002). Epidemic dynamics and endemic states in complex networks. *Physical Review E, 63*, 036104.

Pastor-Satorras, R., & Vespignani, A. (2004). *Evolution and structure of the Internet: A statistical physics approach*. Cambridge, UK: Cambridge University Press.

Petermann, T., & De Los Rios, P. (2004). Exploration of scale-free networks. *European Physical Journal B*, *38*, 201–204.

Popper, K. (1959). *The logic of scientific discovery*. New York: Basic Books.

Price, D. J. D. (1976). A general theory of bibliometric and other cumulative advantage processes. *Journal of the American Society for Information Science*, *27*, 292–306.

Pudovkin, A. I., & Garfield, E. (2002). Algorithmic procedure for finding semantically related journals. *Journal of the American Association of Information Science and Technology*, *53*, 1113–1119.

Ravasz, E., Somera, A. L., Mongru, D. A., Oltvai, Z. N., & Barabási, A.-L. (2002). Hierarchical organization of modularity in metabolic networks. *Science*, *297*, 1551–1555.

Redner, S. (1998). How popular is your paper? An empirical study of the citation distribution. *European Physical Journal B*, *4*, 131–134.

Redner, S. (2005). Citation statistics from 110 years of *Physical Review*. *Physics Today*, *58*, 49–54.

Reichardt, J., & Bornholdt, S. (2004). Detecting fuzzy community structures in complex networks with a Potts model. *Physical Review Letters*, *93*(21), 218701.

Rettig, J. L. (1978). A theoretical model and definition of the reference process. *RQ*, *18*, 19–29.

Sanil, A., Banks, D., & Carley, K. (1995). Models for evolving fixed node networks: Model fitting and model testing. *Social Networks*, *17*, 65–81.

Schneeberger, A., Mercer, C. H., Gregson, S. A., Ferguson, N. M., Nyamukapa, A., Anderson, R. M., et al. (2004). Scale-free networks and sexually transmitted diseases: A description of observed patterns of sexual contacts in Britain and Zimbabwe. *Sexually Transmitted Diseases*, *31*, 380–387.

Schvaneveldt, R. W. (1990). *Pathfinder associative networks: Studies in knowledge organization*. Norwood, NJ: Ablex.

Shannon, C. E. (1948). A mathematical theory of communication. *Bell System Technical Journal*, *27*, 379–423, 623–656.

Shannon, C. E., & Weaver, W. (1949). *The mathematical theory of communication*. Urbana: University of Illinois Press.

Shen-Orr, S., Milo, R., Mangan, S., & Alon, U. (2002). Network motifs in the transcriptional regulation network of Escherichia coli. *Nature Genetics*, *31*, 64–68.

Shneiderman, B. (1987). *Designing the user interface: Strategies for effective human–computer interaction*. Reading, MA: Addison-Wesley.

Shneiderman, B. (1992). Tree visualization with tree-maps: A 2-D space filling approach. *ACM Transactions on Graphics*, *11*, 92–99.

Shneiderman, B. (1996). The eyes have it: A task by data type taxonomy for information visualizations. *Proceedings of the IEEE Symposium on Visual Languages*, 336–343.

Shneiderman, B. (2005). Treemaps for space-constrained visualization of hierarchies. Retrieved August 6, 2005, from www.cs.umd.edu/hcil/treemap-history/index.shtml

Simon, H. A. (1955). On a class of skew distribution functions. *Biometrika*, *42*, 425–450.

Snijders, T. (2002). Markov chain Monte Carlo estimation of exponential random graph models. *Journal of Social Structure*, *3*. Retrieved March 22, 2006, from www.cmu.edu/joss/content/articles/volume3/Snijders.pdf

Standish, R. K., & Galloway, J. (2002). *Visualising Tierra's tree of life using Netmap*. Retrieved March 10, 2006, from http://parallel.hpc.unsw.edu.au/rks/docs/netmap

Strauss, D. (1986). On a general class of models for interaction. *SIAM Review, 28*, 513–527.

Strauss, D., & Ikeda, M. (1990). Pseudolikelihood estimation for social networks. *Journal of the American Statistical Association, 85*, 204–212.

Strogatz, S. H. (2001). Exploring complex networks. *Nature, 410*, 268–276.

Tabah, A. N. (1999). Literature dynamics: Studies on growth, diffusion, and epidemics. *Annual Review of Information Science and Technology, 34*, 249–286.

Thelwall, M. (2004). *Link analysis: An information science approach*. Amsterdam: Academic Press.

Tufte, E. R. (1983). *The visual display of quantitative information*. Cheshire, CT: Graphics Press.

Vazquez, A., de Menezes, M. A., Oltvai, Z. N., & Barabási, A.-L. (2004). *Predicting the location and behavior of metabolic switches based on an optimal growth efficiency principle* (Technical Report). South Bend, IN: University of Notre Dame.

Venn, J. (1971). *Symbolic logic*. Bronx, NY: Chelsea Publishing Company. (Original work published 1894)

Walshaw, C. (2000). A multilevel algorithm for force-directed graph drawing. *Proceedings of the 8th International Symposium Graph Drawing*, 171–182.

Ware, C. (2000). *Information visualization: Perception for design*. San Francisco: Morgan Kaufmann.

Wasserman, S., & Faust, K. (1994). *Social network analysis: Methods and applications*. Cambridge, UK: Cambridge University Press.

Wasserman, S., & Pattison, P. (1996). Logit models and logistic regressions for social networks. *Psychosometrika, 61*, 401–426.

Watts, D. J. (1999). *Small world*. Princeton, NJ: Princeton University Press.

Watts, D. J., & Strogatz, S. H. (1998). Collective dynamics of small-world networks. *Nature, 393*, 440–442.

Wolf, Y. I., Karev, G., & Koonin, E. V. (2002). Scale-free networks in biology: New insights into the fundamentals of evolution? *Bioessays, 24*, 105–109.

Wuchty, S., Oltvai, Z. N., & Barabási, A.-L. (2003). Evolutionary conservation of motif constituents in the yeast protein interaction network. *Nature Genetics, 35*, 176–177.

Yee, K.-P., Fisher, D., Dhamija, R., & Hearst, M. (2001). Animated exploration of graphs with radial layout. *Proceedings of the IEEE Symposium on Information Visualization*, 43–50.

Zhou, S., & Mondragon, R. J. (2004). Accurately modeling the Internet topology. *Physical Review E, 70*, 066108-1–066108-8.

CHAPTER 13

Citation Analysis

Jeppe Nicolaisen
Royal School of Library and Information Science, Copenhagen

Introduction

This chapter presents a critical review of the theories that have formed and/or continue to form the basic assumptions underlying citation analysis. Unless stated otherwise, the term *citation* is used synonymously with the term *bibliographic reference*. *Citation analysis* is consequently taken to represent the analysis of bibliographic references, which form part of the apparatus of scholarly communication. Thus, studies of citations appearing in abstracting and indexing services, in subject bibliographies, or in lists or catalogs of the holding of libraries fall outside the scope of this chapter. The essence of this distinction was first noted by Martyn (1975, p. 290) who argued that "citation in the primary literature expressly states a connection between two documents, one which cites and the other which is cited, whereas citation in other listings does not usually imply any connection between documents other than that effected by the indexing machinery." The two main foci of the chapter are citing behavior (or "citationology" [Garfield, 1998]) and symbolic characteristics of citations (i.e., how citations reflect the characteristics of science and scholarship. These topics, the distinction between which stems from Wouters (1999b), have attracted a great deal of attention from researchers in information science and other fields.

Knowledge about citing behavior and the symbolic characteristics of citations is essential in order to determine whether it makes sense to use citation analysis in various areas of application. As Zunde (1971) noted, citation analysis has three main applications:

1. Qualitative and quantitative evaluation of scientists, publications, and scientific institutions

2. Modeling of the historical development of science and technology

3. Information search and retrieval

Moreover, the introduction of two special citation-analytical techniques has paved the way for a fourth application: Knowledge organization based on bibliographic coupling (Kessler, 1963) and co-citation analysis (Marshakova, 1973; Small, 1973).

The chapter contains three main sections. The first serves as a historical preface, reviewing briefly both the scientific tradition of citing and the recurring calls by scholars for a theory of citation. The second provides an overview of theories and studies of citing behavior. It considers, in turn, the widespread belief that citing is best understood as a psychological process, studies of citer motivations, the normative theory of citing, the social constructivist theory of citing, and contemporary theories of citing behavior based on evolutionary accounts of science and scholarship. The final section presents a critical analysis of Wouters's reflexive citation theory.

Historical Preface

This is the first *ARIST* chapter explicitly entitled *Citation Analysis*. However, previous *ARIST* chapters on bibliometrics (Borgman & Furner, 2002; Narin & Moll, 1977; White & McCain, 1989) and informetrics (Wilson, 2001) partly overlap with the topics addressed in the present chapter.

The Scientific Tradition of Citing

Scientific tradition requires that scientists, when documenting their own research, refer to earlier works that relate to the subject matter of their reported work. These bibliographic references are supposed to identify those earlier researchers whose concepts, theories, methods, equipment, and so on, inspired or were used by the author in the process of conducting and presenting his or her own research. Although this tradition is sometimes said to be as old as science itself (e.g., Price, 1963, p. 65), historians of science disagree about the origins of the reference. According to Grafton (1997), historians of science have variously placed the birth of the modern reference in the twelfth, seventeenth, eighteenth, or nineteenth century. Mustelin (1988), however, maintains that, prior to the sixteenth century, authors often duplicated the work of their predecessors without proper recognition. From the latter part of the sixteenth century, authors of scientific works strove to give their texts greater evidential weight by noting and referring to other sources. Among the earliest proponents of this practice were philologists and editors of texts, with historians and others following later. Nowadays, explicit references are believed to be essential in order to communicate "effectively" and "intelligently" about scientific and technical matters (Garfield, 1977, p. 8), and the act of citing is deemed to be "second nature" to anyone writing a scholarly or scientific paper (Kaplan, 1965, p. 179).

An important feature of citations is that each reference is an inscription (Latour & Woolgar, 1986, pp. 45–53) describing a certain text by a standardized code. Although different publication manuals give different codes and many publishers and journals use their own standards, these manuals and standards usually instruct the author to write his or her references as a combination of author name, title, journal name or publisher, year of publication, and page numbers. References themselves are thus texts pointing to other texts (Wouters, 1998). This does not entail that the cited texts are always to be found where the citing texts say they are. Garfield (1990, p. 40) reviewed a number of studies dealing with bibliographic errors and concluded, that "to err bibliographically is human." For instance, in a study of the incidence and variety of bibliographic errors in six medical journals, De Lacey, Record, and Wade (1985) found that almost a quarter of the references contained at least one mistake and 8 percent of these were judged serious enough to prevent retrieval of the article. Moed and Vriens (1989) examined discrepancies between 4,500 papers from five scientific journals and approximately 25,000 articles that cited these papers, finding that almost 10 percent of the citations in the cited reference dataset showed a discrepancy in either the title, the author name, or the page number. They concluded that one cause for the multiplication of errors seemed to be authors' copying of erroneous references from other articles. Broadus (1983) came to the same conclusion in a study of a 1975 textbook on sociobiology that included among its references an erroneous reference to a 1964 article (one word was incorrectly substituted in the title). By examining 148 subsequent papers that cited both the book and the article, Broadus could see how many authors repeated the book's mistaken reference. He found that 23 percent of the citing authors also listed the faulty title. A similar study by Simkin and Roychowdhury (2003) reported an almost 80-percent repetition of misprints.

Recurring Calls for a Theory

During the 1970s, claims such as Cawkell's (1974, p. 123) that deductions can be made from a citation network without knowledge of its subject content appeared less frequently. Instead, sociologists, information scientists, and others began to recognize the need for a theory of citing that could explain why authors cite the way they do. Among the first contributors was Mulkay (1974), who argued that there had been no clear demonstration of the way in which citations reflect the process of scientific influence. The absence of such a demonstration led him to conclude that "in fact we know very little about who cites whom in science, and why" (Mulkay, 1974, p. 111). A few years later, Swanson (1977, p. 145) called for a "convenient and rapid method for discovering the *nature* of the relevance link which the citing author has established." In 1981, three more authors raised this problem independently from different perspectives: Cozzens (1981) reviewed existing theories of citing from the perspective of sociology, Cronin (1981) called for a theory of citing from the perspective of information retrieval, and L. C. Smith (1981, p.

99) concluded that not enough was known about the citing behavior of authors and that such knowledge is essential in order to know whether it makes sense to use citation analysis for particular applications. Some years later, Zuckerman (1987) repeated the call for a theory of citing, despite her conclusion that such a call seemed redundant. In 1998, a whole issue of the journal *Scientometrics* was devoted to the discussion of, and a renewal of the call for, a theory of citing. Leydesdorff (1998) initiated this discussion with a paper entitled "Theories of Citation?" in which he argued that, although a variety of contexts for citation analysis had been proposed, a comprehensive theory had not been formulated.

Citing Behavior

As Kochen (1987, p. 54) has noted, "a paper that conforms to the norms of scholarly perfection would explicitly cite every past publication to which *it* owes an intellectual debt." This ideal has long been debated by information scientists and others, with discussion centering around two fundamental questions: (1) What makes authors cite/not cite their influences? and (2) To what extent is the ideal exemplified?

Citing as a Psychological Process

A number of commentators apparently share the belief that citing is best understood as a psychological or cognitive process and that, accordingly, theories of citing should be constructed from studies of individual citers conducted by interview techniques, thinking aloud methods, or the recording of behavioral patterns (see, for example, Case & Higgins, 2000). The focal point of this subsection is a specific theory about citing behavior proposed by Harter (1992, p. 614), who has argued that the act of citing is "a dynamic, complex, cognitive process."

Harter's (1992) starting point was a theory of the relevance of everyday speech utterances to listeners that had been proposed six years earlier by Sperber and Wilson (1986) in their book *Relevance: Communication and Cognition*. At the end of their book, Sperber and Wilson asserted that their theory was applicable not only to human speech, but to thought processes in general. Convinced that this conjecture was correct and drawing a number of its implications for information retrieval and bibliometric theory, Harter outlined his theory of citing:

> Relevant references found by a researcher in an IR search (or in another way) cause cognitive change. As the research progresses, the references (and the knowledge found in them) have their effect on the conceptual framework for the work, the choice of problems and methods, and the interpretation of the results. Finally, when the research has been completed, those references that are especially relevant, or that have led

> to especially relevant sources, will be incorporated into the
> list of references at the end of the published work that reports
> the results of the research. An author who includes particu-
> lar citations in his list of references is announcing to readers
> the historical relevance of these citations to the research; at
> some point in the research or writing process the author
> found each reference relevant. (Harter, 1992, pp. 612–613)

Although Harter's theory has received some support from White and
Wang's (1997) longitudinal study of citing behavior, the account of relevance upon which it is based has been shown to be quite problematic
(see, for example, the critical reviews of Gibbs [1987a, 1987b], Hjørland
[2000b], Mey & Talbot [1988], and Talbot [1997]), primarily because of
its disregard of sociocultural issues. Sperber and Wilson (1986) viewed
human beings as information processors with an inbuilt capacity to infer
relevance: Assuming this capacity to be of fundamental importance, they
constructed around it what they claimed to be a unified theory of cognition that could serve as a basis for studying human communication.
Harter (1992, p. 604) claimed that Sperber and Wilson had understood
human beings as being in command of a number of manifest assumptions, which are products of each individual's cognitive ability, cultural
and social group identity, educational background, and physical environment. But this is actually not true. Mey and Talbot (1988) and Talbot
(1997) have noted that considerations of cultural, social, and epistemological affiliation are absent from Sperber and Wilson's characterization
of individuals' cognitive environments. In the second edition of their
book, Sperber and Wilson (1995, p. 279) admitted that they had developed their theory without taking sociocultural issues into account and
acknowledged that "the social character and context of communication
are, of course, essential to the wider picture, to the study of which we
hope relevance theory can contribute, and from which it stands greatly
to benefit." Two years later, Sperber and Wilson (1997, p. 145) observed
that most relevance-theoretic work had largely ignored aspects of communication discussed in the sociological literature, but argued that this
is more "a reflection of a sound initial research strategy (which is likely
to change as the field develops) than some silly anti-sociological bias."
Sperber and Wilson's (1986) view that differences between human
beings derive solely from variations in physical environment and cognitive ability, makes it difficult to understand how a listener may infer a
speaker's intentions. According to their theory, a listener can infer a
speaker's intentions on the basis of knowledge of the speaker's cognitive
environment because the knowledge manifest to different individuals is
largely the same. However, as Talbot (1997, p. 447) has observed, reading *Relevance* leaves one with the impression that everyone lives in the
same kind of white, middleclass, educated world:

While this may be true, to some extent, of the linguists and cognitive scientists comprising the authors' audience, it is a serious inadequate provision of social context for a study of either communication or cognition. ... Their ad hoc choice of unrelated facts known both to themselves and their readers for the potentially endless production of negative assumptions betrays an unsystematic approach. ... In the absence of any social element, with which to locate and specify kinds of knowledge that might be mutually accessible to different individuals, this is inevitable.

Harter (1992) must, perhaps unconsciously, have seen this. Why else would he have included *cultural and social group identity* along with cognitive ability, educational background, and physical environment in his definition of what an individual's manifest assumptions are? Viewed in this light, the title of his article and his conclusion that relevance is a theoretical concept of cognitive psychology are difficult to comprehend. On the other hand, Harter simply declared the significance of sociocultural issues without developing the point further, focusing instead on the technical aspects of how a phenomenon (a stimulus) such as a retrieved citation may cause cognitive changes in a user's mental state. He did ask why an item is initially found relevant and what criteria users employ when they select bibliographic items for subsequent citation in their published works (Harter, 1992, p. 614). But his narrow focus on cognitive issues prevented him from giving an adequate answer to these questions and so diminished the cogency of his theory of citing.

Motives for Citing

Baldi (1998, p. 831) has noted that, between 1965 and 1979, trying to capture the various motives for citing became a "cottage industry" that produced a number of schemes and typologies. This subsection highlights the most significant of these.

Moravcsik and Murugesan (1975) constructed a classification scheme and used it to categorize 706 references in 30 articles in the field of theoretical high-energy physics that had been published in the journal *Physical Review* during the period 1968–1972. Their study revealed, among other things, that 41 percent of the references were nonessential (*perfunctory*) and 14 percent were negative (*negational*). Shortly after Moravcsik and Murugesan's study, Chubin and Moitra (1975) published their results of a similar study, in which they had developed their own classification scheme and categorized the references from 43 physics articles published in the period 1968–1969. The results of their content analysis revealed that 20 percent of the references were nonessential and 5 percent were negative. However, Chubin and Moitra (1975, p. 426) criticized the content-analytical method as incapable of describing authors' actual motives for citing and suggested that future studies should take a phenomenological approach focusing on "the private process by which authors choose references (i.e., when writing, do authors have an implicit set of categories which guide the kind and number of references they make?)." They also discussed how to conduct such an investigation, concluding that "direct questioning of authors about why they referenced who they did, and in what fashion, may be a beginning" (Chubin & Moitra, 1975, p. 426).

Brooks (1985) analyzed a number of theoretical models and isolated seven motives for citing posited by all of them. He then asked 26 researchers to complete a questionnaire regarding the motivations for their references in their recent articles. His survey found that persuasiveness was the most common purpose for citing and that only 2 percent of the references were negational. In a similar study, Cano (1989) asked a group of engineers to complete a questionnaire, based on Moravcsik and Murugesan's (1975) classification scheme, concerning their motives for their references in 42 articles published in three different journals. She found that 26 percent of the references were deemed nonessential by the authors, and only 2 percent were negational. Shadish, Tolliver, Gray, and Sen Gupta (1995) conducted the first major investigation of social scientists' motives for citing. Using a questionnaire that listed 28 potential purposes for citing, they surveyed researchers who had published articles in psychological journals. The results showed that psychologists rarely made use of negational references.

Unfortunately, all of these studies suffer from the same fundamental problem: They cannot clarify why a cited reference was found relevant to begin with. An individual is often partly unconscious of, or fails to recognize, his or her reasons for citing a particular source and not citing another. Thus, questioning an author about his or her motives for citing/ not citing cannot reveal the actual reasons why an author has cited as he or she has done. This dilemma is a variant of *the relevance dilemma*. According to Hjørland (2000a, 2002) and Hjørland and Sejer Christensen (2002), there are important precepts to science that are so integral to the researcher's life and culture that he or she is partially or wholly unaware of them. But the researcher's lack of awareness of their influence does not render them unimportant. In fact, the opposite is true. It is important to recognize and understand what these precepts are, and how they affect the individual. In stressing the necessity of understanding the sociocultural environment of an individual in order to comprehend his or her relevance criteria, Hjørland (2000a; 2002) and Hjørland and Sejer Christensen (2002) break with the psychological understanding of relevance.

The Normative Theory of Citing

In his article "The Norms of Citation Behaviour," which is usually held to be the first explicit account of citing as normative behavior, Kaplan (1965) argued that footnoting practices are passed on both by word of mouth from professor to student and by examination of the varying practices of different journals. Ravetz (1971, pp. 256–257) likewise held citing to be governed by an etiquette based on purely informal, perhaps tacit and unselfconscious, craft knowledge. According to Kaplan (1965), the major function of footnoting practice was the reaffirmation of the underlying norms of scientific behavior. The normative theory of citing is based on the assumption that science is a normative institution governed by internal rewards and sanctions. It holds that scientists exchange information (in the form of publications) for recognition (in the form of awards and citations). This view suggests that citations are a way to acknowledge intellectual debts and, thus, are mostly influenced by the perceived worth, as well as the cognitive, methodological, or topical content of the cited articles (Baldi, 1998).

Early sociologists of science generally believed that consensus in science was governed by a particular scientific ethos, that is, a set of rules supposed to establish trust in, and guarantee the reliability of, the knowledge claims produced by scientists. This view was given its most succinct and influential formulation by the Merton (1942/1973), who defined the ethos of science in terms of four basic norms—communism, universalism, disinterestedness, and organized skepticism. Merton (p. 269) held these norms to be binding on the man of science. Although he never claimed that the ethos of science operates explicitly at all times, his remark that "it has become manifest that in each age there is a system of science that rests upon a set of assumptions, usually implicit and seldom questioned by most of the scientific workers of the time" (Merton, 1938/1973, p. 250) reveals a profound conviction that the ethos is always decisive. Merton and the early sociologists of science knew, of course, about many instances of scientists resisting scientific discoveries and disagreeing on the merits of particular findings. But sociologists such as Merton and Barber (1961) explained these deviations from the expected consensus by arguing that cultural factors occasionally serve as institutional and intellectual obstacles to scientists otherwise behaving as faithful disciples of the norms of science.

It is not my intention to attribute a "naïve, idealized, Arcadian image of scientists" to Merton, for I agree with his biographer (Sztompka, 1986, p. 56) that such ascription would be a mistake. Merton reworked and modified his sociology of science throughout his career and made numerous adjustments and corrections to it. For example, in 1963 he acknowledged "the often painful contrast between the actual behavior of scientists and the behavior ideally prescribed for them" (Merton, 1963/1973, p. 393). However, his earlier writings on the ethos of science and the extent to which scientists adhere to certain norms were not hedged with similar reservations. On the contrary, the "younger" Merton (1942/1973, p. 276) wrote about "the virtual absence of fraud in the annals of science" and even claimed that "deviant practices ... are extremely infrequent" (Merton, 1957/1973, p. 311). Indeed, the "older" Merton sometimes seemed to forget the reservations expressed in 1963.

Discussing why he did not come up with the idea of the citation index before Garfield, Merton (1977, p. 49) wrote that "all the substantive ingredients for invention of that tool were being observed back in 1942." Merton (1977) apparently believed his 1942 theory of scientific practice to be a sound foundation for a citation index and, thus, for a theory of citing. Many have concurred with Merton and have attempted to construct a normative theory of citing based on the early sociology of science, including the work of the "younger" Merton. This theory posits that investigators cite those materials that have proved to be of value to them (i.e., communism). It also holds that scientists, when evaluating the work of others, are behaving universalistically—that is to say, their decisions about what to cite are not influenced by functionally irrelevant characteristics such as a scientific author's sex, race, religion, or rank (i.e., universalism). Furthermore, it assumes that scientists are disinterested and do not seek to gain personal advantages by flattering others or citing themselves (i.e., disinterestedness). Moreover, it holds that scientists treat their own work with the same skepticism as the work of others (i.e., organized skepticism). These assumptions have motivated many citation analyses, as illustrated by L. C. Smith's (1981, p. 87–89) list of basic assumptions underlying citation analysis in general:

1. Citation of a document implies use of that document by the citing author.

2. Citation of a document (author, journal, etc.) reflects the merit (quality, significance, impact) of that document (author, journal, etc.).

3. Citations are made to the best possible works.

4. A cited document is related in content to the citing document.

5. All citations are equal.

The second assumption in Smith's list reflects the Mertonian norm of communism and its inherent principle that scientists should give credit where credit is due whenever they have made use of the work of others. In the foreword to Garfield's (1979) book *Citation Indexing: Its Theory and Application in Science, Technology, and Humanities*, Merton (1979, p. viii) emphasized this particular responsibility of the academy by stating that

> the anomalous character of intellectual property in science becoming fully established only by being openly given away (i.e., published) links up with the correlative moral as well as cognitive requirement for scientists to acknowledge their having made use of it. Citations and references thus operate within a jointly cognitive and moral framework. In their cognitive aspect, they are designed to provide the historical lineage of knowledge and to guide readers of new work to

sources they may want to check or draw upon for themselves. In their moral aspect, they are designed to repay intellectual debts in the only form in which this can be done: through open acknowledgment of them.

Merton was convinced that authors generally cite the materials that have proved of value to them because of the social control mechanisms of science. He addressed the issue again in 1995, claiming that

> the process of socialization in the culture of science joins with such social arrangements as published and unpublished "peer review" that serve as agencies of social control which see to it, among other things, that authors generally abide by the norm of indicating their predecessors and sources. (Merton, 1995, p. 389)

Early Tests of the Normative Theory of Citing

According to the normative theory, failure to give credit where credit is due is unusual. For example, Cole and Cole (1972, p. 370) stated that "sometimes ... a crucial intellectual forebear to a paper is not cited. The omission is rarely due to direct malice on the part of the author but more often to oversight or lack of awareness. ... We can assume that omitted citations to less influential work are random in nature. ..." Garfield (1977, p. 7) took a similar view, declaring that "the vast majority of citations are accurate and the vast majority of papers do properly cite the earlier literature." However, in the very next sentence, Garfield admitted that this assertion had not been empirically substantiated: "Unfortunately, there has never been a definitive study of this assertion." The basic assumption of the normative theory of citing was not tested until the 1980s. The pioneers of this work were not adherents of the normative theory, but a group of skeptics including, among others, the biologists Michael and Barbara MacRoberts and the information scientist Terrence Brooks.

The MacRobertses published a number of articles in which they argued that citation analysis was an invalid tool for research evaluation (MacRoberts, 1997; MacRoberts & MacRoberts, 1984, 1986, 1987a, 1987b, 1988, 1989a, 1989b, 1996). In these articles, they challenged the basic assumption of the normative theory of citing—that scientists cite their influences. MacRoberts and MacRoberts (1986) tested this assumption by reading and analyzing 15 randomly selected papers in the history of genetics, a subject with which they claimed to be familiar. They found that from 0- (i.e., the paper had no references or footnotes) to 64-percent influence was captured in references and footnotes. After reconstructing the bibliographies of the papers in their sample, the MacRobertses were able to estimate that the 15 papers required some

719 references at a minimum to cover the influences manifested in them, whereas, in fact, they contained only 216—a coverage of 30 percent for the entire sample. A decade later, they claimed that this percentage typified all the fields with which they were familiar (botany, zoology, ethology, sociology, and psychology) and concluded that

> if one wants to know what influence has gone into a particular bit of research, there is only one way to proceed: head for the lab bench, stick close to the scientist as he works and interacts with colleagues, examine his lab notebooks, pay close attention to what he reads, and consider carefully his cultural milieu. (MacRoberts & MacRoberts, 1996, p. 442)

Brooks (1985, 1986) mounted another challenge to the basic assumptions of the normative theory of citing in two papers reporting on a survey of 26 researchers at the University of Iowa who indicated their motivations for giving each reference in their recently published articles by rating seven motives for citing. According to Brooks, the survey results suggested that authors cite for many reasons, with the allotment of credit being the least important motivation for citation. Of the 900 references studied, Brooks (1985, p. 228) found that about 70 percent were multiply motivated, concluding that "no longer can we naively assume that authors cite only noteworthy pieces in a positive manner. Authors are revealed to be advocates of their own points of view who utilize previous literature in a calculated attempt to self-justify. However, as White (2004b, p. 98) has pointed out, the results of Brooks's survey need to be assessed with caution, for one of the motives listed was "persuasiveness" and the respondents almost certainly understood "persuasion" to mean citing to "help build a case" not manipulative name-dropping or distortion of citees' meanings.

The Social Constructivist Theory of Citing

This section examines the phenomenon of citation from a social constructivist perspective (e.g., Baldi, 1997, p. 17; MacRoberts & MacRoberts, 1996, p. 439; Small, 1998, p. 143; White, 2004b). At the outset, it is important to note that the label *social constructivists* has historically been applied to two distinct groups of scholars. Collin (1997) admits that both groups are commonly termed social constructivists, but reserves that name for the first of these, which includes Emile Durkheim, Peter Berger, Thomas Luckmann, Don Zimmerman, Melvin Pollner, Alasdair MacIntyre, and Peter Winch. These social constructivists concentrate on how social reality is produced by the cognitive efforts of ordinary social agents. On the other hand, members of the second group, whom Collin (1997, p. 13) terms *science constructivists*, focus specifically on scientific communities and scientific research. Because the theories propounded by this latter group form the focus of this section, the term *social constructivists* is used here to refer to scientific constructivists such as Barry Barnes, David Bloor, Michel Callon, Harry Collins, Karin Knorr Cetina, Bruno Latour, and Steve Woolgar.

The social constructivists believe that scientific closure is the outcome of a negotiation process in which one party convinces the other by mere persuasion. In fact, Latour and Woolgar (1986, p. 69) have maintained that science is the art of persuasion. In their view, successful scientists are those who most skillfully manage to persuade others that they are not just being persuaded, that no mediations intercede between what is said and the truth (Latour & Woolgar, 1986, p. 70).

In the art of persuasion, no holds are barred. According to the social constructivists, the successful scientist makes use of many persuasive moves when reporting research. According to this view, when authors cite, they are marshalling earlier documents in such a way as to persuade readers of the goodness of their claims. Indeed, MacRoberts and MacRoberts (1987b, p. 294) have argued that persuasion, not a desire to give credit where credit is due, is the major motivation for citing. This position, which stands in direct opposition to the normative theory of citing, has been much influenced by Gilbert's (1977, p.116) article "Referencing as Persuasion," in which he claimed that

> Authors preparing papers will tend to cite the "important and correct" papers, may cite "erroneous" papers in order to challenge them and will avoid citing the "trivial" and "irrelevant" ones. Indeed, respected papers may be cited in order to shine in their reflected glory even if they do not seem closely related to the substantive content of the report.

Latour (1987, pp. 33–34) speculated along the same lines, arguing that in order to put up a persuasive facade, authors engage in chicanery: "First, many references may be misquoted or wrong; second, many of the articles alluded to might have no bearing whatsoever on the claim and might be there just for display." Latour (1987, p. 33) did not consider such actions to be inconsequential. On the contrary, he maintained that if readers were to find out what is actually going on—e.g., the use of citations purely for display—the result would be "disastrous" for the authors. As White (2004b) has pointed out, the issue is not the ordinary claim that scientists and scholars write to persuade and use citations as a rhetorical resource. The persuasion hypothesis, rather, is the idea that persuasion in science and scholarship relies on manipulation indistinguishable from that used in commercial advertising. For example, MacRoberts and MacRoberts (1996, p. 441) have claimed that "papers are meant to sell a product," and Law and Williams (1982, p. 543) have likened scientists' choice of references to "packaging a product for market."

White (2004b) has recently presented a careful analysis of the persuasion hypothesis, arguing that it consists of two parts. The first has to do with what citers say about cited works or, more precisely, the contexts in which they discuss them. He calls this part "persuasion by distortion," noting that "citers often misrepresent the works they allude to, twisting their meaning for their own ends" (p. 96). The second has to do with the choice of the cited works themselves, regardless of what is being said about them. White (2004b, p. 96) calls this part "persuasion by name-dropping" and notes that it is more or less independent of context: "Citers disproportionately cite works by established authorities, so as to gain credibility by association."

Empirical Tests of the Persuasion Hypothesis

Researchers have usually tested either the first or the second part of the persuasion hypothesis. One important exception is Baldi's network-analytic study of normative versus social constructivist processes in the allocation of citations. Baldi (1997, 1998) studied articles about celestial masers, an area of astrophysics research, and discovered that "authors are most likely to cite articles that are relevant to their work in terms of subject, recency of knowledge, [and] theoretical orientation, and seem to have little concern with the characteristics of authors who wrote them" (Baldi, 1998, p. 843). However, both Small (1998) and Collins (2000) have questioned the adequacy of Baldi's method.

According to the first part of the persuasion hypothesis (i.e., persuasion by distortion), citers often misrepresent the works to which they refer, twisting their meaning for their own ends. In the words of Latour (1987, p. 34): "Many of the articles alluded to might have no bearing whatsoever on the claim and might be there just for display." The first part of the persuasion hypothesis is thus the negation of the normative assumption that "a cited document is related in content to the citing document" (Smith, 1981, p. 89). The normative theory assumes that references signal direct semantic relationships between the citing and the cited works. For instance, Garfield (1979, p. 3) maintained, after discussing the semantic problems of subject indexes, that the citation is a precise, unambiguous representation of a subject. However, the assumption has been tested only a few times in studies that have yielded contradictory results (Harter, Nisonger, & Weng, 1993; Peters, Braam, & Van Raan, 1995; Song & Galardi, 2001; Trivison, 1987). Thus, it is not possible to conclude to what extent cited and citing documents are semantically related. Cronin (1994) has noted that texts may be cited at different levels of granularity or aggregation. This, he argues, may influence similarity scores and explain why the degree of subject similarity between pairs of cited and citing documents is frequently found to be small.

According to the second part of the persuasion hypothesis (i.e., persuasion by name-dropping), authors disproportionately cite works by established authorities in order to gain credibility by association. As MacRoberts and MacRoberts (1996, pp. 440–441) have put it, "an author's main objective is not to cite their influences but to present as authoritative an argument as possible." However, at least three studies have questioned the validity of this claim (Moed & Garfield, 2003; White, 2004b; Zuckerman, 1987).[1]

Zuckerman (1987, p. 334) posed the question: If persuasion really were the major motivation to cite, would citation distributions look as they do? Basing her argument on data provided by Garfield (1985), she concluded that the answer was "plainly not." Garfield (1985, p. 6) had presented a table illustrating the number of citations retrieved by items cited one or more times in the 1975–1979 cumulated *Science Citation Index* (*SCI*). The table revealed that only 6.3 percent of the 10.6 million citations went to documents cited ten or more times during the five-year period. Zuckerman (1987) pointed to the low percentage as evidence against the plausibility of the persuasion hypothesis, which would predict a much higher percentage. Zuckerman (1987, p. 334) referred to Gilbert (1977, p. 113), one of the proponents of the persuasion hypothesis, who had stated that it is the papers seen as "important and correct" that "are selected because the author hopes that the referenced papers will be regarded as authoritative by the intended audience." However, if one adopts a modest criterion of *authoritative papers* as those that have been cited at least ten times in five years (or twice annually), the persuasion hypothesis needs to be radically adjusted, for Garfield's data do not support the social constructivist suggestion that an author's main objective is not to cite his or her influences but to present as authoritative an argument as possible.

White (2004b) realized that if an author cites "a world figure" (e.g., Noam Chomsky or Thomas Kuhn), he or she might be accused of name-dropping no matter what works by these world figures are cited. Accordingly, it makes little sense to believe that cited authors' levels of prestige and authority vary much from work to work. Instead of testing the persuasion hypothesis, as Zuckerman (1987) had done, by determining the percentage of citations received by authoritative papers, White realized that one could test the hypothesis by determining the percentage of citations received by authoritative authors. White's test did not support the persuasion hypothesis, for he found that authors do not exclusively favor high-end names with authoritative reputations, but tend to cite at all levels over the entire scale of reputation. Indeed, his findings suggest, if anything, that authors tend slightly to favor low-end names. White (2004a) pointed out that if the persuasion hypothesis were correct, widespread and unwarranted citations of prestigious authors should be detectable in the writings of the social constructivists as well (e.g., Gilbert & Mulkay, 1984; Latour, 1987; Myers, 1990). "Yet," he concluded, "I find no evidence of empty name-dropping on their part; in my reading, they play the citation game straight" (White, 2004a, p. 111).

Moed and Garfield (2003, p. 192) added yet another dimension to the critique of the persuasion hypothesis in a study seeking to answer the question "how does the relative frequency at which authors in a research field cite 'authoritative' documents in the reference lists in their papers vary with the number of references such papers contain?" They reasoned that "if this proportion decreases as reference lists become shorter, it can be concluded that citing authoritative documents is less important than other types of citations, and is not a major motivation to cite" (p. 192). The authors analyzed the references cited in all source items denoted as "normal articles" that were included in the 2001 edition of the *SCI* on CD-ROM. The source papers were arranged by research fields, which were defined in terms of aggregates of journal categories. The authors focused on four such fields: molecular biology and biochemistry, physics and astronomy, applied physics and chemistry, and engineering. Their findings clearly suggest that authors in all four fields cited proportionally fewer "authoritative" documents as their bibliographies became shorter. In other words, when the authors displayed selective referencing behavior, references to "authoritative" documents dropped radically. From this, Moed and Garfield (2003, p. 195) drew the conclusion that "in this sense, persuasion is not the major motivation to cite."

The Standard Account

A number of commentators have questioned whether a theory of citing is needed at all. Indeed, one has even suggested calling a halt to *theorizing* and returning to the standpoint of logical positivism: "I think the current state of our field calls for more empirical and practical work, and all this theorising should wait till a very large body—beyond a threshold—of empirical knowledge is built" (Arunachalam, 1998, p. 142). Many citation analysts seem to accept the standard account (Nicolaisen, 2004). Although readily granting that authors frequently do not give credit where credit is due, they claim that, *on average*, authors do give due credit by properly citing their inspirations and sources. This claim, they maintain, does not invalidate citation analyses. For example, Small (1987, p. 339) has argued that "the issue is not whether we can rely on reference lists in individual cases as complete sets of influences (we cannot), but rather whether references can be used statistically, in the aggregate, as an indicator of influence." Nederhof and Van Raan (1987, p. 326) have put forth much the same argument:

> If one looks at the references contained in one individual paper, many irregularities may be found, such as missing references to important papers, or to the work of authors which have made important contributions to the body of knowledge in a field. Thus, a seriously mistaken picture of the main influences in a particular field would be obtained when only one particular paper is used for this purpose.

Commentators have frequently suggested that the biases and deficiencies of individual citers are repaired to a tolerable degree by the combined activity of the many (e.g., White, 2001, p. 102). For example, Nederhof and Van Raan (1987, p. 326) have maintained that "even if all papers would to a large extent (but not completely) cite in an arbitrary way, it would still be possible to detect valid patterns in the citations, if a sufficiently large number of papers would be sampled."

White (1990, p. 91) has thus asked: "Why not believe that there *is* a norm of citing—straightforward acknowledgement of related documents—and that the great majority of citations conform to it?" The answer is, of course, that an existence claim or even an existence proof—Kurtz, Eichhorn, Accomazzi, Grant, Demleitner, Murray, et al. (2005, p. 116) claim to have proven that the normative theory of citing is true in the main—does not explain the phenomenon in question. For that, we need some kind of theory. A theory is normally conceived as a set of formally specified and interconnected general propositions that can be used for the successful explanation and prediction of some phenomenon (Geuss, 1998). Consequently, White's belief or conviction does not qualify. Although it may help to predict citing behavior, it does not help to explain the phenomenon.

Evolutionary Accounts of Science and Scholarship

Kuhn (1962) concluded *The Structure of Scientific Revolutions* by proposing an evolutionary view of science. Ten years later, Toulmin (1972) argued that it is possible to produce a single analysis of selection processes that would be equally applicable to social, conceptual, and biological evolution. Others have subsequently taken up the challenge and sought to develop Kuhn's and Toulmin's suggestions. Prominent among these is David L. Hull, who, in his book *Science as a Process: An Evolutionary Account of the Social and Conceptual Development of Science* (Hull, 1988) and in a number of essays (Hull, 2001), has demonstrated that science and scientific behavior closely resemble selection processes normally studied in evolutionary biology.

Evolutionary theories of human behavior have also inspired research in information science. One example is Sandstrom's work on scholarly communication as a socio-ecological system (Sandstrom, 1994, 1998, 1999, 2001, 2004; see also Cronin & Hert, 1995). Sandstrom's view of scholarly communication derives its inspiration from the socio-ecological theory of optimal foraging, the basic assumption of which is that "organisms will behave as if they are optimizing some fitness-related currency or set of currencies" (Sandstrom, 1994, p. 417 [citing Kaplan & Hill, 1992]). According to optimal foraging theory, "a particular prey type will be included in the optimal diet only if its net energy return per unit handling time is greater than the average return rate (including search time) for all prey types of higher rank" (Sandstrom, 1994, p. 425 [citing E. A. Smith, 1983]). In other words, the foraging behavior of any organism is thought to be a balance between cost and benefit. If the cost of including a particular prey type within an organism's diet exceeds the benefit of doing so, the organism simply will not include it. Sandstrom (1994, p. 428) has suggested that it is probable that scholars choose among information resources according to the same basic principle: "Scholars (both as readers and writers) are likely to maximize their interaction with an array of resources offering higher returns in terms of handling and to minimize their efforts in procuring the obscure ones." The socio-ecological theory of optimal foraging has been challenged for more than two decades. A number of anthropological studies have revealed that human foragers often violate the cost-benefit principle underlying the theory. The anthropologist Eric Alden Smith, one of the leading figures of optimal foraging theory in the 1980s, now concedes that the theory fails to explain much of human foraging behavior. In fact, he acknowledged the limitations of optimal foraging theory a year before Sandstrom's first publication on the subject (Smith, 1993). Like many others, Smith now subscribes to the handicap principle, otherwise known as the theory of costly signaling (e.g., Bliege Bird, Smith, & Bird, 2001; Smith, Bliege Bird, & Bird, 2003).

Nicolaisen (2004) has recently outlined a theoretical explanation for citation behavior that draws its inspiration from models developed within the domain of evolutionary biology, especially the handicap principle developed by the Israeli biologist Amotz Zahavi.

The Handicap Principle

Nicolaisen (2004) likens references to *threat signals*. Although this may seem puzzling at first, it is not an entirely new idea. In fact, Latour (1987, p. 33) seems to have proposed the very same in his book *Science in Action*: "Attacking a paper heavy with footnotes means that the dissenter has to weaken each of the other papers, or will at least be *threatened* with having to do so" (italics added).

Although Latour and Nicolaisen apparently share the idea that references are threat signals, they do not agree on how authors may utilize them. According to Latour (1987, p. 33), an author "can turn a fact into a fiction or a fiction into a fact just by adding or subtracting references." However, to pull off this trick, the author must know and exercise the right strategies. Latour examined two such strategies: *stacking* and *modalizing*. He maintained that the presence or absence of references in a scientific text signifies whether the text is serious and strong. In order to appear serious and strong, the author should cite a number of other documents—a practice that Latour (1987, p. 33) called "stacking masses of references." Stacking can often be an effective means of transforming fiction into fact, for it requires that a potential reader read, or be acquainted with, the cited documents to be able to determine the strength and accuracy of the citing text—a difficult task to accomplish when many documents are cited. However, Latour (1987, p. 33) himself noted that stacking masses of references is not sufficient to appear serious and strong if the author is confronted with "a bold opponent." Such an opponent might just trace all of the references and probe their degree of attachment to the author's argument: "If the reader is courageous enough, the result may be disastrous for the author" (p. 33). Therefore, another move is needed to pull off the trick. The author has to *modalize* the status of the cited documents—i.e., to modify or qualify the reference to make it more in keeping with the argument of the citing text.

Apparently, Latour believed that authors are free to do whatever they need to the earlier literature to render it as helpful as possible for their own arguments. This belief is founded on an understanding of scientific communication portrayed in Figure 1.3 in Latour's (1987, p. 38) *Science in Action*. This figure shows a citing author, her article, and its (modalized) references; other elements include authors of the cited documents, as well as an unidentified man and an "isolated reader." It is unclear what, precisely, Latour means by "isolated reader." However, for the sake of argument, let us suppose he means one who is unacquainted with the literature cited in the citing article. Now, if all readers were isolated readers like the one portrayed by Latour, it seems reasonable to assume that authors would be free to do whatever they needed to the earlier literature to align it as much as possible with their own arguments. However, as Nicolaisen (2004) has pointed out, this situation is highly unlikely and Latour's assumption seems rather naïve. Most readers are not isolated in the sense given here. On the contrary, potential readers are generally well-read subject specialists possessing a broad knowledge of the literature and field covered by the text. This becomes evident if one reflects on the typical life cycle of what is currently the most common scientific or scholarly text type—the journal article. Most journal articles face two potential groups of readers: those who read them prior to publication and those who read them after publication. Potential readers prior to publication include, among others, editors and referees, who participate in the typical pre-publication peer review of academic journals. Among the potential post-publication readers are others working in the field and, perhaps most important, the authors who are cited in the article. Like the editors and referees, many of these potential post-publication readers possess expert knowledge of the field and its literature. Authors who bend the earlier literature to their own purposes and thus commit willful acts of deceit risk exposure as the cheaters they are by their potential readers. Honest authors, who cite their sources of information and inspiration properly, need not fear such exposure. The two types of authors may appeal to the same set of sources as backup for their arguments, but not at the same potential cost, which is much higher for the cheating authors than for the honest ones. Thus, the essential requirement allowing the handicap principle to work is in place.

As explained by its originator (Zahavi, 2003, p. 860), the handicap principle "suggests that if an individual is of high quality and its quality is not known, it [the individual] may benefit from investing a part of its advantage in advertising that quality, by taking on a handicap, in a way that inferior individuals would not be able to do, because for them the investment would be too high." According to this line of reasoning, costliness is essential to the evolution of honesty. Honest signals have evolved because they take forms that require considerable cost to produce, a condition that would result in ineffective communication if the sender could not bear that cost. Zahavi (1975) referred to the costly signals as handicaps and his theory thus came to be known as *the handicap principle*. Shortly after formulating his theory, Zahavi found himself debating the logic of the handicap principle with mathematicians and theoreticians (Arnold, 1983; Davis & O'Donald, 1976; Kirkpatrick, 1986; Maynard Smith, 1976), who could not prove the handicap principle with genetic models and therefore rejected it. The simple argument of the handicap principle was deemed overly intuitive and the skeptics insisted that the development of mathematical models was necessary to demonstrate the feasibility of its operation in evolution. In 1990, the Oxford biologist Alan Grafen (1990a, 1990b) successfully formulated the required model and made the handicap principle acceptable to mathematically minded evolutionary biologists. He also demonstrated that signals need be honest only on average to be evolutionary stable. Zahavi (1987, p. 319) had already put forward this idea three years earlier, recognizing that deception may be possible, but only if there is a limit to the frequency of bluffing so that receivers, on average, benefit from trusting the signals:

> I do not claim that cheating is never encountered in nature. Several types of mimicry seem to provide false information. It is interesting to note that in most cases mimicry is concerned with a third party mimicking a communication channel that has evolved due to the honest interaction of other parties. Such cheating can only exist when the toll it levies on that communication channel is kept within limits that render uncovering it too costly.

There are several well-documented examples of such a mixture of honest and deceptive signals in nature (Számadó, 2000). In all of these cases, the cheating exists because its incidence is low enough for receivers on average to benefit from the interaction.

The notion of honest signals as costly handicaps has gained considerable backing and interest in recent years (Johnstone, 1995). Moreover, the handicap principle has proved useful for unraveling an array of biological and anthropological puzzles, such as the extreme expenditures often involved in sexual advertisement, the evolutionary mystery of animal altruism, the workings of collaborative systems in the animal kingdom (Zahavi & Zahavi, 1997), human foraging (e.g., Bliege Bird, Smith, & Bird, 2001; Hawkes & Bliege Bird, 2002; Smith, Bliege Bird, & Bird, 2003), decoration of the human body (Zahavi & Zahavi, 1997), and the evolution of art (Zahavi & Zahavi, 1997). The handicap principle has also provided an explanation for threatening behavior. Zahavi and Zahavi (1997) noted that rivals rarely attack each other without initially signaling their intentions. Indeed, most of the time, they do not attack at all. Instead, the conflict is typically solved by the exchange of threats. Zahavi and Zahavi pointed out that all living creatures that communicate in any way make use of threats. Resolving a conflict simply by threatening prevents the loss of time, energy, and the risk of injury or death. It is obvious what the winner gains from threatening rather than fighting, but why should threats alone make the other party back down? What convinces one of the rivals to give up without a fight? Maynard Smith and Parker (1976) proposed that if one is going to lose anyway, it is better to lose without being defeated in a fight. But how does one know that one is going to lose? What convinces one of the rivals that defeat is inevitable, or that the possible returns from winning are not worth the risk of fighting? Zahavi (1977) answered these questions by proposing that threats are reliable indicators of each rival's chance in a fight. Threat displays communicate reliable information about one's opponent's ability and willingness to fight. Assessing such information against one's own ability and willingness provides a good idea of one's chances in a fight. If the chances are slim, then one had better give up the fight and back off. Yet, how can threat displays work in this way? Why can the party who is most likely to win a fight threaten more effectively than the other? Zahavi (1977) proposed that, in order to function in this way, the threat itself must increase the risk that the threatening party will be attacked or will be at a disadvantage if attacked. An individual who is genuinely willing to fight and has confidence in his own abilities will accept such a risk, whereas another, who lacks the requisite strength or motivation, will find the stakes too high and thus be unwilling to threaten to the same extent. In Zahavi's (1977, p. 256) words:

> The use of a threat signal which endangers the threatening individual, in correlation to the magnitude of the threat signal, deters fighters of poor quality from threatening too much. Only the high quality fighters may threaten without great harm to their potential as fighters.

Latour (1987) was surely right to argue that attacking a text full of references requires weakening the documents it cites. However, like the coiled body of an animal, the cited documents of a citing text are a sign of confidence (Nicolaisen, 2004). A stack of references is a handicap that only an honest author can afford. Like a jutting chin, it presents an inviting target for a bold opponent. Modalized references expose themselves like the vocalization of a bluffing rival. A skilled rival will detect the false note right away and know where to attack. The potential cost of such a move will often make the author reconsider his deceitful behavior. When the references are made in public, the stakes are raised even higher. Like a shouting human, references may have witnesses. Yet, only a confident author can afford to shout before the crowd. Authors who are uncertain of themselves will usually not risk the potential loss of reputation. However, in keeping with Zahavi's theory, Nicolaisen (2004) does *not* propose that all references are honest, for there are enough cases of fraud and deceit in science and scholarship to falsify such a proposal. Rather, he suggests that the handicap principle ensures that citing authors honestly credit their inspirations and sources to a tolerable degree—enough to save the scientific communication system from collapsing.

The validity of the handicap principle has not been discussed much in the information science literature: the only example, other than Nicolaisen (2004), seems to be Kock and Davison (2003). However, Zahavi's theory has received ample discussion in the literature of evolutionary biology. A fairly recent critique of the handicap principle is that of Hagstrom (2002).

Symbolic Characteristics of Citations

Van der Veer Martens (2001, online) considers "the current 'holy grail' in scientometrics" to be the development of indicator theories rather than the development of theories of citing behavior. Indicator theorists are concerned with the symbolic characteristics of the citation and its indicative abilities. They seek to understand how citations reflect and represent science—not the reasons why authors cite: Small's (1978) pioneering theory about highly cited documents being "concept symbols" is an important example. One of the most fervent advocates of this line of research is Wouters, whose notion of a reflexive citation theory has been presented in his Ph.D. thesis (Wouters, 1999b) and in two articles (Wouters, 1998, 1999a).

Wouters's Reflexive Citation Theory

Wouters (1999b, p. 211) considers the quest for a citation theory that seeks to explain the citation by relating it to the citing behavior of the scientist to be "a dead end"; therefore, we must abandon this pursuit and, instead, focus our attention on the symbolic characteristics of the citation and its indicative abilities. He sees citations as indicators constituting a "formalized representation" of science that initially neglects meaning (Wouters, 1999b, p. 209). However, in order to interpret these formalized representations, one needs to attribute meaning to the self-same indicators. According to Wouters (1999b, p. 209), "this attribution of meaning can be postponed" and should be based not on the citing behavior of the citing scientists, but on how citations reflect the characteristics of science. Wouters (1999b, p. 213) entitles this "the reflexive citation theory."

Wouters's theory rests on his interpretation of the *reference* and the *citation* as two different signs. Others have noted the technical difference between the two, but Wouters considers the difference to be fundamental:

> The reference is completely defined by the citing text it belongs to and the cited text to which it points. In semiotic terms the reference is a sign—the elementary unit of a representational system with the cited text as its referent. ... The citation is the mirror image of the reference. ... By organizing the references not according to the texts they belong to, but according to the texts they point at—they become attributes of the cited instead of the original, citing text. Semiotically, the citing text is the referent of the citation. (Wouters, 1998, pp. 232–233)

Wouters thus sees the citation as a new sign—one that is different from the reference upon which it builds. Unlike the reference, the citation is dimensionless and meaningless (Wouters, 1999b, p. 209), and acquires meaning only at the hands of the citation analyst: in other words, the (ISI) indexer's desk, not the scientist's, is the birthplace of the citation. Studies of scientists' citing behavior, therefore, facilitate the explanation of patterns of references, not patterns of citations:

> Since the citation and the reference have different referents and are actually each other's mirror image, it does not seem very wise to blur the distinction between them. This distinction has moreover the advantage that the quest for a citation theory in scientometrics and the sociology of science splits into two different, analytically independent research problems: the patterns in the citing behaviour of scientists, social scientists and scholars in the humanities on the one hand, and the theoretical foundation of citation analysis on the other. (Wouters, 1999b, p. 195)

Wouters's theory reflects the main idea of *informational semantics*, a family of theories seeking to provide a naturalistic and reductive explanation of the semantic and intentional properties of thought and language. Basically, the informational approach explains truth conditional content in terms of causal, nomic, or simply regular correlation between a representation (a signal) and a state of affairs (a situation). Signals may be reliably correlated with the situation and hence indicate that situation.

The central work of informational semantics is that of Dretske (1981). His point of departure was Shannon's (1948) theory of information, which provides a mathematical measure of the amount of information carried by a signal. Dretske (1981) supplemented Shannon's work with an account of the meaning that a signal carries. His idea was that a signal carries the meaning p if and only if the signal naturally means (that is, indicates) p, as is the case, for example, when smoke indicates fire. Thus, the main idea of informational semantics is to ignore the actual history of a signal and to focus on what the signal reliably indicates. But informational semantics faces a major problem that has been noted by a number of commentators (e.g., Devitt, 1991, 1998; Godfrey-Smith, 1989, 1992; McLaughlin & Rey, 1998): It does not allow for error. Informational semantics cannot explain how a representation can acquire a determinate content and yet be false. This problem arises precisely because informational semantics holds that representation is a kind of correlation or causation. As Godfrey-Smith (1989) has asked, how can a representation be caused by, or be correlated with, a state of affairs that does not obtain?

Devitt (1991) provides a good example of the error problem. Occasionally, he says, we see a muddy zebra but misrepresent it by thinking "horse." So, some zebras are among the things that would cause "horse" signals. What "horse" is reliably correlated with is really the presence of horses, muddy zebras, odd cows, etcetera. Thus, it should refer to horses, muddy zebras, odd cows, and so on. To solve this problem, the informational semanticist claims that the circumstances in which muddy zebras and odd cows cause "horse" are not appropriate for fixing its reference—that is, a "horse" signal represents what such signals are caused by in normal circumstances. However, as Godfrey-Smith (1989) has noted, this solution raises another problem for informational semantics, the problem of providing a naturalistic account of *normal instances*.

The error problem is logically unsolvable and, thus, any theory of representation that depends on reliable causation is doomed. The reason is simply that certain recognition of p is impossible. Misrepresentation is common—$q, r, s \ldots$ are often confused with p. For instance, in nature it is common for an organism to represent the presence of a predator when none is there. Thus, what it indicates is mostly not what it represents. According to Devitt (1991, p. 434), this situation is common in nature because it has an evolutionary payoff:

> Consider the typical bird that is the prey of hawks. A high proportion of the time that it registers the presence of a predator it is wrong; it has responded to a harmless bird, a shadow, or whatever. These false positives do not matter to its survival. What matters is that it *avoid false negatives*; what matters is that it registers the hawk when there is one. The price the bird has to pay for that is frequently registering a hawk when there isn't one. What nature has selected is a *safe* mechanism not a *certain* one.

However, informational semantics seeks not to provide safe mechanisms, but to uncover signals that are reliably correlated with specific situations and hence indicate these situations. In other words, informational semantics attempts to establish certain mechanisms, but only safe ones are logically possible.

Wouters's reflexive citation theory suffers from the same unsolvable problem as informational semantics, for it cannot handle false positives, that is, citations that do not in fact indicate the situation they are spontaneously understood to indicate. Wouters himself does not attempt to determine the correlatives of citations, but the bibliometric literature is loaded with such attempts. Perhaps most notable is the attempt to show that citations are indicators of quality. This approach posits that citations and research quality go hand in hand and thus are linearly related. Studies of the predictive validity of citation analysis have consequently sought to demonstrate the existence of a linear relationship between research quality and citation counts.[2] However, most of these studies suffer from a number of problems (Nicolaisen, 2002). Their biggest problem is that they have often focused narrowly on the opposite extremes of citation distributions. Only a few studies have dealt with entire citation distributions. These have documented low to moderate degrees of linear correlation (e.g., Gottfredson, 1978; Schubert, Zsindely, Telcs, & Braun, 1984; Virgo, 1977; Wolfgang, Figlio, & Thornberry, 1978). Moreover, Bornstein's (1991) hypothesis about a J-shaped relationship between research quality and citation counts has recently received empirical confirmation (Nicolaisen, 2002). It thus seems justified to conclude that not all citations are indicators of quality. But what, then, do they indicate? Garfield (1979) tried to answer this question in his book *Citation Indexing*. In his view, citations do not indicate elegance, importance, quality, or significance. Rather, they are indicators of utility and impact.

> A highly cited work is one that has been found useful by a relatively large number of people, or in a relatively large number of experiments. ... The citation count of a particular piece of scientific work does not necessarily say anything about its elegance or its relative importance to the advancement of science or society. ... The only responsible claim made for citation counts as an aid in evaluating individuals is that they provide a measure of the utility or impact of scientific work. They say nothing about the nature of the work, nothing about the reason for its utility or impact. (Garfield, 1979, p. 246)

What Garfield established was nothing other than a safe mechanism. A citation indicates that a cited work has been referred to, and used by, a citing work—nothing more, nothing less. He expressly avoided claiming any other correlation between citations and the world—a clever move in light of the error problem.

Conclusion

Garfield's introduction of the *SCI* in 1963 marked a very important stage in the history of information science. The unique possibility of retrieving documents according to received citations represented a significant improvement on previous term-based retrieval techniques. Moreover, as Hjørland and Kyllesbech Nielsen (2001, p. 257) have noted, citation-based retrieval has changed our understanding of the concept of subject relatedness and subject matter. However, as Small (2000, p. 451) has correctly observed, the *SCI* did not invent the citation, as Wouters seems to think, any more than the dictionary invented words. The citation is just the mirror image of the reference. Thus, if we are to understand the nature of the citation, we need to understand the nature of the reference. And if we are to understand the nature of the reference, we need a theory of citing that explains why authors cite the way they do. Ignoring the reference (i.e., ignoring the history of the citation) in order to understand the citation is logically impossible. Moed (2005, p. 216) seems to arrive at the same conclusion in his recent monograph on citation analysis: "Reference and citation theories, although analytically distinct, should be grounded in a notion of what scientists tend to express in their referencing practices."

The quest for a theory of citation that seeks to explain the citation by relating it to the citing behavior of the scientist is not a dead end. It is, on the contrary, the only way forward if we are to realize the full potential of citation analysis. A good deal of the previous research on citing behavior has provided only a few pieces for solving the citation puzzle. Studies have tended to rest on the assumption that citing is best understood as a psychological process and that theories of citing should be constructed from studies of individual citers that utilize interview techniques, thinking aloud methods, or the recording of behavioral patterns. This line of research has produced a number of classification schemes capturing various reasons for citing. But these are, as Baldi (1998, p. 832) and Cronin (1994, p. 537) have correctly observed, only of limited use.

In his recent book on academic writing and its rewards, Cronin (2005, p. 154) referred to a number of the studies dealt with here and concluded that "we are still left with a black-box explanation of citing behavior." This chapter has sought to make clear that, in order to explain such behavior, we must cease taking the individual's knowledge structures as our starting point. Rather, we should focus our attention on knowledge domains, disciplines, or other collective knowledge structures. Attempts to explain citation behavior should thus refrain from psychologizing the act of citing and instead recognize it as embedded within the sociocultural conventions of collectives.

Acknowledgments

I gratefully acknowledge the inspiration provided by the kind suggestions of, and fruitful discussions with, Blaise Cronin, Birger Hjørland, Jesper W. Schneider, Howard D. White, and Paul Wouters. I would also like to thank the three anonymous referees for their thoughtful comments.

Endnotes

1. See also the studies by Stewart (1983) and Van Dalen and Henkens (2001), which report minor impact of author reputations on citation frequencies.

2. One of the reviewers commented that s/he was not aware of anyone having claimed that there is a linear relationship between research quality and citation counts and, thus, that a straw-man argument was possibly being set up here. This is, of course, not the case. The vast majority of studies of the predictive validity of citation counts have made use of linear regression analysis as a measure of the co-variation between research quality and citation counts. A basic premise of this test is that the dependent mean of Y is assumed to be a linear function of the values of the independent variable. Thus, by employing this test, a number of analysts have implicitly assumed that there indeed exists a linear relationship between research quality and citation counts.

References

Arnold, S. J. (1983). Sexual selection: The interface of theory and empiricism. In P. Bateson (Ed.), *Mate choice* (pp. 67–108). Cambridge, UK: Cambridge University Press.

Arunachalam, S. (1998). Citation analysis: Do we need a theory? *Scientometrics, 43,* 141–142.

Baldi, S. (1997). *A network approach to the analysis of citation flows: A comparative study of two research areas in the natural and the social sciences.* Unpublished doctoral dissertation, Ohio State University.

Baldi, S. (1998). Normative versus social constructivist processes in the allocation of citations: A network-analytic model. *American Sociological Review, 63,* 829–846.

Barber, B. (1961). Resistance by scientists to scientific discovery. *Science, 134,* 596–602.

Bliege Bird, R., Smith, E. A., & Bird, D. W. (2001). The hunting handicap: Costly signaling in human foraging strategies. *Behavioral Ecology and Sociobiology, 50,* 9–19.

Borgman, C. L., & Furner, J. (2002). Scholarly communication and bibliometrics. *Annual Review of Information Science and Technology, 36,* 3–72.

Bornstein, R. F. (1991). The predictive validity of peer review: A neglected issue. *Behavioral and Brain Sciences, 14,* 138–139.

Broadus, R. N. (1983). An investigation of the validity of bibliographic citations. *Journal of the American Society for Information Science, 34,* 132–135.

Brooks, T. A. (1985). Private acts and public objects: An investigation of citer motivations. *Journal of the American Society for Information Science, 36,* 223–229.

Brooks, T. A. (1986). Evidence of complex citer motivations. *Journal of the American Society for Information Science, 37,* 34–36.

Cano, V. (1989). Citation behavior: Classification, utility, and location. *Journal of the American Society for Information Science, 40,* 284–290.

Case, D. O., & Higgins, G. M. (2000). How can we investigate citation behavior? A study of reasons for citing literature in communication. *Journal of the American Society for Information Science, 51,* 635–645.

Cawkell, A. E. (1974). Search strategy, construction and use of citation networks, with a socio-scientific example: "Amorphous semi-conductors and S. R. Ovshinsky." *Journal of the American Society for Information Science, 25,* 123–130.

Chubin, D. E., & Moitra, S. D. (1975). Content analysis of references: Adjunct or alternative to citation counting? *Social Studies of Science, 5,* 426–441.

Cole, J. R., & Cole, S. (1972). The Ortega hypothesis. *Science, 178,* 368–375.

Collin, F. (1997). *Social reality.* London: Routledge.

Collins, H. M. (2000). Surviving closure: Post-rejection adaptation and plurality in science. *American Sociological Review, 65,* 824–845.

Cozzens, S. E. (1981). Taking the measure of science: A review of citation theories. *International Society for the Sociology of Knowledge Newsletter, 7*(1–2), 16–20.

Cronin, B. (1981). The need for a theory of citation. *Journal of Documentation, 37,* 16–24.

Cronin, B. (1994). Tiered citation and measures of document similarity. *Journal of the American Society for Information Science, 45,* 537–538.

Cronin, B. (2005). *The hand of science: Academic writing and its rewards.* Lanham, MD: Scarecrow Press.

Cronin, B., & Hert, C. A. (1995). Scholarly foraging and network discovery tools. *Journal of Documentation, 51,* 388–403.

Davis, G. F. W., & O'Donald, P. (1976). Sexual selection for a handicap: A critical analysis of Zahavi's model. *Journal of Theoretical Biology, 57,* 345–354.

De Lacey, G., Record, C., & Wade, J. (1985). How accurate are quotations and references in medical journals? *British Medical Journal, 291,* 884–886.

Devitt, M. (1991). Naturalistic representation: A review article on David Papineau's *Reality and Representation. British Journal of the Philosophy of Science, 42,* 425–443.

Devitt, M. (1998). Reference. In C. Edward (Ed.), *Routledge encyclopedia of philosophy* [compact disc]. London: Routledge.

Dretske, F. (1981). *Knowledge and the flow of information.* Cambridge, MA: MIT Press.

Garfield, E. (1977, August 29). To cite or not to cite: A note of annoyance. *Current Contents, 35,* 5–8.

Garfield, E. (1979). *Citation indexing: Its theory and applications in science, technology, and humanities.* New York: Wiley.

Garfield, E. (1985, October 28). Uses and misuses of citation frequency. *Current Contents, 43,* 3–9.

Garfield, E. (1990, October 8). Journal editors awaken to the impact of citation errors: How we control them at ISI. *Current Contents, 41,* 33–41.

Garfield, E. (1998). Random thoughts on citationology: Its theory and practice. *Scientometrics, 43,* 69–76.

Geuss, R. (1998). Critical theory. In C. Edward (Ed.), *Routledge encyclopedia of philosophy* [compact disc]. London: Routledge.

Gibbs, R. W. (1987a). Mutual knowledge and the psychology of conversational inference. *Journal of Pragmatics, 11*, 561–88.

Gibbs, R. W. (1987b). The relevance of Relevance for psychological theory. *Behavioral and Brain Sciences, 10*, 718–719.

Gilbert, G. N. (1977). Referencing as persuasion. *Social Studies of Science, 7*, 113–122.

Gilbert, G. N., & Mulkay, M. (1984). *Opening Pandora's box: A sociological analysis of scientists' discourse.* Cambridge, UK: Cambridge University Press.

Godfrey-Smith, P. (1989). Misinformation. *Canadian Journal of Philosophy, 19*, 533–550.

Godfrey-Smith, P. (1992). Indication and adaptation. *Synthese, 92*, 283–312.

Gottfredson, S. D. (1978). Evaluating psychological research reports: Dimensions, reliability, and correlates of quality judgements. *American Psychologist, 33*, 920–939.

Grafen, A. (1990a). Biological signals as handicaps. *Journal of Theoretical Biology, 144*, 517–546.

Grafen, A. (1990b). Sexual selection unhandicapped by the Fisher process. *Journal of Theoretical Biology, 144*, 473–516.

Grafton, A. (1997). *The footnote: A curious history.* Cambridge, MA: Harvard University Press.

Hagstrom, C. (2002). *Critique of the handicap principle.* Retrieved June 24, 2005, from www.passionateape.com/id108.htm

Harter, S. P. (1992). Psychological relevance and information science. *Journal of the American Society for Information Science, 43*(9), 602–615.

Harter, S. P., Nisonger, T. E., & Weng, A. (1993). Semantic relationships between cited and citing articles in library and information science journals. *Journal of the American Society for Information Science, 44*, 543–552.

Hawkes, K., & Bliege Bird, R. (2002). Showing off, handicap signals, and the evolution of men's work. *Evolutionary Anthropology, 11*, 58–67.

Hjørland, B. (2000a). Relevance research: The missing perspective(s): "Non-relevance" and "epistemological relevance." *Journal of the American Society for Information Science, 51*, 209–211.

Hjørland, B. (2000b). *A problematic understanding of relevance.* Retrieved June 3, 2005, from www.amazon.com/exec/obidos/tg/detail/-/0631198784/103-4664838-4415840?v= glance

Hjørland, B. (2002). Epistemology and the socio-cognitive perspective in information science. *Journal of the American Society of Information Science and Technology, 53*, 257–270.

Hjørland, B., & Kyllesbech Nielsen, L. (2001). Subject access points in electronic retrieval. *Annual Review of Information Science and Technology, 35*, 249–298.

Hjørland, B., & Sejer Christensen, F. (2002). Work tasks and socio-cognitive relevance: A specific example. *Journal of the American Society for Information Science and Technology, 53*, 960–965.

Hull, D. L. (1988). *Science as a process: An evolutionary account of the social and conceptual development of science.* Chicago: University of Chicago Press.

Hull, D. L. (2001). *Science and selection: Essays on biological evolution and the philosophy of science.* Cambridge, UK: Cambridge University Press.

Johnstone, R. A. (1995). Sexual selection, honest advertisement and the handicap principle: Reviewing the evidence. *Biological Reviews, 70,* 1–65.

Kaplan, H., & Hill, K. (1992). The evolutionary ecology of food acquisition. In E. A. Smith & B. Winterhalder (Eds.), *Evolutionary ecology and human behavior* (pp. 167–202). New York: Aldine de Gruyter.

Kaplan, N. (1965). The norms of citation behavior: Prolegomena to the footnote. *American Documentation, 16,* 179–184.

Kessler, M. M. (1963). Bibliographic coupling between scientific papers. *American Documentation, 14,* 10–25.

Kirkpatrick, M. (1986). The handicap mechanism of sexual selection does not work. *American Naturalist, 127,* 222–240.

Kochen, M. (1987). How well do we acknowledge intellectual debts? *Journal of Documentation, 43,* 54–64.

Kock, N., & Davison, R. (2003). Dealing with plagiarism in the information systems research community: A look at factors that drive plagiarism and ways to address them. *MIS Quarterly, 27,* 511–532.

Kuhn, T. S. (1962). *The structure of scientific revolutions.* Chicago: University of Chicago Press.

Kurtz, M. J., Eichhorn, G., Accomazzi, A., Grant, C. S., Demleitner, M., Murray, S. S., et al. (2005). The bibliometric properties of article readership. *Journal of the American Society for Information Science and Technology, 56,* 111–128.

Latour, B. (1987). *Science in action: How to follow scientists and engineers through society.* Cambridge, MA: Harvard University Press.

Latour, B., & Woolgar, S. (1986). *Laboratory life: The construction of scientific facts.* Princeton, NJ: Princeton University Press.

Law, J., & Williams, R. J. (1982). Putting facts together: A study in scientific persuasion. *Social Studies of Science, 12,* 535–558.

Leydesdorff, L. (1998). Theories of citation? *Scientometrics, 43,* 5–25.

MacRoberts, M. (1997). Rejoinder. *Journal of the American Society for Information Science, 48,* 963.

MacRoberts, M. H., & MacRoberts, B. R. (1984). The negational reference: Or the art of dissembling. *Social Studies of Science, 14,* 91–94.

MacRoberts, M. H., & MacRoberts, B. R. (1986). Quantitative measures of communication in science: A study of the formal level. *Social Studies of Science, 16,* 151–172.

MacRoberts, M. H., & MacRoberts, B. R. (1987a). Another test of the normative theory of citing. *Journal of the American Society for Information Science, 38,* 305–306.

MacRoberts, M. H., & MacRoberts, B. R. (1987b). Testing the Ortega hypothesis: Facts and artefacts. *Scientometrics, 12,* 293–295.

MacRoberts, M. H., & MacRoberts, B. R. (1988). Author motivation for not citing influences: A methodological note. *Journal of the American Society for Information Science, 39,* 432–433.

MacRoberts, M. H., & MacRoberts, B. R. (1989a). Citation analysis and the science policy arena. *Trends in Biochemical Science, 14,* 8–10.

MacRoberts, M. H., & MacRoberts, B. R. (1989b). Problems of citation analysis: A critical review. *Journal of the American Society for Information Science, 40,* 342–349.

MacRoberts, M. H., & MacRoberts, B. R. (1996). Problems of citation analysis. *Scientometrics*, *36*, 435–444.

Marshakova, I. V. (1973). A system of document connection based on references. *Scientific and Technical Information Serial of VINITI*, *6*(2), 3–8.

Martyn, J. (1975). Citation analysis. *Journal of Documentation*, *31*(4), 290–297.

Maynard Smith, J. (1976). Sexual selection and the handicap principle. *Journal of Theoretical Biology*, *57*, 239–242.

Maynard Smith, J., & Parker, G. A. (1976). The logic of asymmetric contests. *Animal Behaviour*, *24*, 159–175.

McLaughlin, B. P., & Rey, G. (1998). Semantics, informational. In C. Edward (Ed.), *Routledge encyclopedia of philosophy* [compact disc]. London: Routledge.

Merton, R. K. (1973). The puritan spur to science. In R. K. Merton (Ed.), *The sociology of science: Theoretical and empirical investigations* (pp. 228–253). Chicago: University of Chicago Press. (Original work published 1938)

Merton, R. K. (1973). The normative structure of science. In R. K. Merton (Ed.), *The sociology of science: Theoretical and empirical investigations* (pp. 267–278). Chicago: University of Chicago Press. (Original work published 1942)

Merton, R. K. (1973). Priorities in scientific discovery. In R. K. Merton (Ed.), *The sociology of science: Theoretical and empirical investigations* (pp. 286–324). Chicago: University of Chicago Press. (Original work published 1957)

Merton, R. K. (1973). The ambivalence of scientists. In R. K. Merton (Ed.), *The sociology of science: Theoretical and empirical investigations* (pp. 383–412). Chicago: University of Chicago Press. (Original work published 1963)

Merton, R. K. (1977). *The sociology of science: An episodic memoir*. Carbondale: Southern Illinois University Press.

Merton, R. K. (1979). Foreword. In E. Garfield, *Citation indexing: Its theory and application in science, technology, and humanities* (pp. vii-xi). New York: Wiley.

Merton, R. K. (1995). The Thomas theorem and the Matthew effect. *Social Forces*, *74*, 379–424.

Mey, J. L., & Talbot, M. (1988). Computation and the soul. *Semiotica*, *72*, 291–339.

Moed, H. F. (2005). *Citation analysis in research evaluation*. Berlin: Springer.

Moed, H. F., & Garfield, E. (2003). Basic scientists cite proportionally fewer "authoritative" references as their bibliographies become shorter. *Proceedings of the 9th International Conference on Scientometrics and Informetrics*, 190–196.

Moed, H. F., & Vriens, M. (1989). Possible inaccuracies occurring in citation analysis. *Journal of Information Science*, *15*, 94–107.

Moravcsik, M. J., & Murugesan, P. (1975). Some results on the function and quality of citations. *Social Studies of Science*, *5*, 86–92.

Mulkay, M. J. (1974). Methodology in the sociology of science: Some reflections on the study of radio astronomy. *Social Science Information*, *13*, 107–119.

Mustelin, O. (1988). Källhänvisningar och fotnoter i svenskspråkiga Åbodissertationer under 1700-talet [References and footnotes in Swedish-language dissertations at Åbo during the eighteenth century]. In E. Kolding Nielsen et al. (Eds.), *Bøger, biblioteker, mennesker: Et nordisk Festskrift tilegnet Torben Nielsen, Universitetsbiblioteket i København* [*Books, libraries, people: A Nordic Festschrift offered to Torben Nielsen, the*

University Library in Copenhagen] (pp. 105–126). Copenhagen, DK: Det kgl. Bibliotek i samarbejde med Det danske Sprog- og Litteraturselskab.

Myers, G. (1990). *Writing biology: Texts in the social construction of knowledge.* Madison: University of Wisconsin Press.

Narin, F., & Moll, J. K. (1977). Bibliometrics. *Annual Review of Information Science and Technology, 12,* 35–58.

Nederhof, A. J., & Van Raan, A. F. J. (1987). Citation theory and the Ortega hypothesis. *Scientometrics, 12,* 325–328.

Nicolaisen, J. (2002). The J-shaped distribution of citedness. *Journal of Documentation, 58,* 383–395.

Nicolaisen, J. (2004). *Social behavior and scientific practice: Missing pieces of the citation puzzle.* Unpublished doctoral dissertation, Royal School of Library and Information Science, Copenhagen.

Peters, H. P. F., Braam, R. R., & Van Raan, A. F. J. (1995). Cognitive resemblance and citation relations in chemical engineering publications. *Journal of the American Society for Information Science, 46,* 9–21.

Price, D. J. D. (1963). *Little science, big science.* New York: Columbia University Press.

Ravetz, J. R. (1971). *Scientific knowledge and social problems.* Oxford, UK: Oxford University Press.

Sandstrom, P. E. (1994). An optimal foraging approach to information seeking and use. *Library Quarterly, 64,* 414–449.

Sandstrom, P. E. (1998). *Information foraging among anthropologists in the invisible college of human behavioral ecology: An author co-citation analysis.* Unpublished doctoral dissertation, Indiana University.

Sandstrom, P. E. (1999). Scholars as subsistence foragers. *Bulletin of the American Society for Information Science, 25*(3), 17–20.

Sandstrom, P. E. (2001). Scholarly communication as a socioecological system. *Scientometrics, 51,* 573–605.

Sandstrom, P. E. (2004). Anthropological approaches to information systems and behavior. *Bulletin of the American Society for Information Science and Technology, 30*(3), 1–8.

Schubert, A., Zsindely, S., Telcs, A., & Braun, J. (1984). Quantitative analysis of a visible tip of the peer review iceberg: Book reviews in chemistry. *Scientometrics, 6,* 433–443.

Shadish, W. R., Tolliver, D., Gray, M., & Sen Gupta, S. K. (1995). Author judgments about works they cite: Three studies from psychology journals. *Social Studies of Science, 25,* 477–498.

Shannon, C. E. (1948). A mathematical theory of communication. *Bell System Technical Journal, 27,* 379–423, 623–656.

Simkin, M., & Roychowdhury, V. P. (2003). Read before you cite! *Complex Systems, 14,* 269–274.

Small, H. (1973). Co-citation in the scientific literature: A new measurement of the relationship between two documents. *Journal of the American Society of Information Science, 24,* 265–269.

Small, H. (1978). Cited documents as concept symbols. *Social Studies of Science, 8,* 327–340.

Small, H. (1987). The significance of bibliographic references. *Scientometrics, 12,* 339–341.

Small, H. (1998). Citations and consilience in science. *Scientometrics, 43,* 143–148.

Small, H. (2000). Charting pathways through science: Exploring Garfield's vision of a unified index to science. In B. Cronin & H. B. Atkins (Eds.), *The web of knowledge: A Festschrift in honor of Eugene Garfield* (pp. 449–473). Medford, NJ: Information Today/ASIS.

Smith, E. A. (1983). Anthropological applications of optimal foraging theory: A critical review. *Current Anthropology, 24*, 625–651.

Smith, E. A. (1993). Comment on "Why hunter-gatherers work" by Kristen Hawkes. *Current Anthropology, 34*, 356.

Smith, E. A., Bliege Bird, R., & Bird, D. W. (2003). The benefits of costly signalling: Meriam turtle hunters. *Behavioral Ecology, 14*, 116–126.

Smith, L. C. (1981). Citation analysis. *Library Trends, 30*, 83–106.

Song, M., & Galardi, P. (2001). Semantic relationships between highly cited articles and citing articles in information retrieval. *Proceedings of the 64th ASIST Annual Meeting*, 171–181.

Sperber, D., & Wilson, D. (1986). *Relevance: Communication and cognition*. Cambridge, MA: Harvard University Press.

Sperber, D., & Wilson, D. (1995). *Relevance: Communication and cognition* (2nd ed.). Cambridge, MA: Harvard University Press.

Sperber, D., & Wilson, D. (1997). Remarks on relevance and the social sciences. *Multilingua, 16*, 145–151.

Stewart, J. A. (1983). Achievement and ascriptive processes in the recognition of scientific articles. *Social Forces, 62*, 166–189.

Swanson, D. R. (1977). Information retrieval as a trial-and-error process. *Library Quarterly, 47*, 128–148.

Számadó, S. (2000). Cheating as a mixed strategy in a simple model of aggressive communication. *Animal Behaviour, 59*, 221–230.

Sztompka, P. (1986). *Robert K. Merton: An intellectual profile*. London: Macmillan.

Talbot, M. M. (1997). Relevance. In V. Lamarque (Ed.), *Concise encyclopedia of the philosophy of language* (pp. 445–447). New York: Pergamon.

Toulmin, S. (1972). *Human understanding*. Princeton, NJ: Princeton University Press.

Trivison, D. (1987). Term co-occurrence in cited/citing journal articles as a measure of document similarity. *Information Processing & Management, 23*(3), 183–194.

Van Dalen, H. P., & Henkens, K. (2001). What makes a scientific article influential? The case of demographers. *Scientometrics, 50*, 455–482.

Van der Veer Martens, B. (2001). Do citation systems represent theories of truth? *Information Research, 6*(2). Retrieved June 23, 2005, from http://InformationR.net/ir/6-2/paper92.htm

Virgo, J. A. (1977). A statistical procedure for evaluating the importance of scientific papers. *Library Quarterly, 47*, 415–430.

White, H. D. (1990). Author co-citation analysis: Overview and defence. In C. L. Borgman (Ed.), *Scholarly communication and bibliometrics* (pp. 84–106). Newbury Park, CA: Sage.

White, H. D. (2001). Authors as citers over time. *Journal of the American Society for Information Science and Technology, 52*, 87–108.

White, H. D. (2004a). Citation analysis and discourse analysis revisited. *Applied Linguistics, 25*, 89–116.

White, H. D. (2004b). Reward, persuasion, and the Sokal hoax: A study in citation identities. *Scientometrics, 60*, 93–120.

White, H. D., & McCain, K. W. (1989). Bibliometrics. *Annual Review of Information Science and Technology, 24*, 119–186.

White, M. D., & Wang, P. (1997). A qualitative study of citing behavior: Contributions, criteria, and metalevel documentation concerns. *Library Quarterly, 67*, 122–154.

Wilson, C. S. (2001). Informetrics. *Annual Review of Information Science and Technology, 34*, 107–247.

Wolfgang, M. E., Figlio, R. M., & Thornberry, T. (1978). *Evaluating criminology*. New York: Elsevier.

Wouters, P. (1998). The signs of science. *Scientometrics, 41*, 225–241.

Wouters, P. (1999a). Beyond the holy grail: From citation theory to indicator theory. *Scientometrics, 44*, 561–580.

Wouters, P. (1999b). *The citation culture*. Unpublished doctoral dissertation, University of Amsterdam.

Zahavi, A. (1975). Mate selection: Selection for a handicap. *Journal of Theoretical Biology, 53*, 205–214.

Zahavi, A. (1977). Reliability in communication systems and the evolution of altruism. In B. Stonehouse & C. Perrins (Eds.), *Evolutionary ecology* (pp. 253–259). London: Macmillan.

Zahavi, A. (1987). The theory of signal selection and some of its implications. In V. P. Delfino (Ed.), *Proceedings of the International Symposium of Biological Evolution*. Bari, Italy: Adriatica Editrica, 305–327.

Zahavi, A. (2003). Indirect selection and individual selection in socio-biology: My personal views on theories of social behaviour. *Animal Behaviour, 65*, 859–863.

Zahavi, A., & Zahavi, A. (1997). *The handicap principle*. New York: Oxford University Press.

Zuckerman, H. (1987). Citation analysis and the complex problem of intellectual influence. *Scientometrics, 12*, 329–338.

Zunde, P. (1971). Structural models of complex information sources. *Information Storage and Retrieval, 7*, 1–18.

CHAPTER 14

Scientific Collaboration

Diane H. Sonnenwald
Göteborg University and University College of Borås, Sweden

Introduction

Scientific collaboration is increasing in frequency and importance. It has the potential to solve complex scientific problems and promote various political, economic, and social agendas, such as democracy, sustainable development, and cultural understanding and integration. Bibliometric studies over the past two decades have shown a continuous increase in the number of co-authored papers in every scientific discipline, as well as within and across countries and geographic areas (Cronin, 2005; Cronin, Shaw, & La Barre, 2003, 2004; Grossman, 2002; Moody, 2004; National Science Board, 2004; Wagner & Leydesdorff, 2005).[1] Subauthorship, as measured by the number of colleagues thanked in acknowledgment sections of papers, has also increased consistently (Cronin, 2005; Cronin et al., 2003, 2004). In general, co-authored publications are cited more frequently than single-authored papers (Persson, Glänzel, & Danell, 2004). Increasingly, public and private research funding agencies require interdisciplinary, international, and inter-institutional collaboration. Examples include the National Science Foundation Science & Technology Center (www.nsf.gov/od/oia/programs/stc) and Industry/University Cooperative Research Center (www.nsf.gov/eng/iucrc) programs, as well as the European Science Foundation Sixth Framework Programme (http://europa.eu.int/comm/research/fp6/index_en.cfm?p=0).

As a research topic, scientific collaboration has been discussed in diverse disciplines including information science, psychology, management science, computer science, sociology, research policy, social studies of science, and philosophy, as well as each discipline in which scientific collaboration occurs. In some instances, specialized communities that focus on specific aspects of collaboration have emerged. For example, scientometrics investigates patterns of collaboration using quantitative methods such as co-authorship statistics. This research can be found in journals such as *Scientometrics* and the *Journal of the American Society for Information Science and Technology* (*JASIST*) as well as in conference proceedings of the International Society for Scientometrics and Informetrics (ISSI) and the American Society for Information Science and Technology (ASIST). The computer-supported cooperative work (CSCW) and social informatics research communities examine how information and communications technology (ICT) affects cooperation and work in a variety of contexts, including science. This research is often published in proceedings of the ACM Conference on Computer Supported Cooperative Work, the ACM Conference on Supporting Group Work, the ACM Conference on Human Factors in Computing Systems and ASIST conferences, as well as such journals as *ACM Transactions on Computer-Human Interaction, Computer Supported Cooperative Work*, and *JASIST*. Research within the domain of social studies of science considers the development of science, technology, and medicine and investigates their social nature. Publication venues include the 4S conference and the journals *Social Studies of Science* and *Science, Technology, & Human Values*. Discussions of research policy regarding collaboration can be found in conferences such as the Triple Helix conference and in the journals *Research Policy* and *Science Public Policy*. Thus, there is not one single body of literature that focuses on collaboration but rather a strand of literature that cuts across many disciplines and forums.

The diversity of research on scientific collaboration means that a variety of terminologies, research approaches, and methods can be found in the literature. Scientific collaboration is also referred to as research collaboration, R&D collaboration, and team science. Terms that are used to categorize scientific collaboration include "university-industry collaboration"; "inter-," "multi-," "trans-" and "cross-disciplinary collaboration"; "international scientific collaboration"; "intradisciplinary" or "disciplinary collaboration"; "science-society collaboration"; "remote and inter-institutional collaboration"; "large-scale collaboration" (also known as "big science" or "teams of teams"); and "participatory" or "university-community collaboration" (Ziman, 2000). These categories are neither universally defined nor mutually exclusive. For example, the terms "inter-" and "multi-disciplinary collaboration" may be used interchangeably by some authors yet defined as different and distinct concepts by others. An international scientific collaboration may also be an interdisciplinary collaboration, and it may be difficult to ascertain how each component of the collective contributed to the scientific process. Research methods that are used to investigate scientific collaboration include bibliometrics, interviews, observations, controlled experiments, surveys, simulations, self-reflection, social network analysis, and document analysis.

The variety of both terminological designations and research methods, together with the diversity of publication forums, presents considerable challenges to understanding scientific collaboration. Those studying collaboration can find it difficult to know where to begin and when to end their literature searches. Researchers may focus on previous research conducted within their own fields and be unaware of results found in others; furthermore, they may have a difficult time interpreting the results because of the variety of research methods used. These challenges, of course, are not unique to scientific collaboration; however, they are perhaps more acute there than in other areas.

This chapter synthesizes the diverse research literature of scientific collaboration, including case studies of collaboration, with the goal of increasing our understanding of scientific collaboration. First, terminology and concepts found in the literature are described. Second, the process of scientific collaboration is illuminated by synthesizing research results pertinent to stages of the scientific collaboration process. Collaboration in both the natural and social sciences is included in these discussions; however, research on collaboration in the natural sciences is more prevalent and this is reflected in the content of the discussions.

No previous volume of the *Annual Review of Information Science and Technology (ARIST)* has included a chapter focusing exclusively on scientific collaboration; however, several chapters have dealt with different aspects of scientific collaboration. Borgman and Furner (2002), Kling and Callahan (2003), and Kling (2004) discussed scientific publishing, including bibliometrics and emerging socio-technical developments in scientific publishing. Finholt (2002) considered scientific collaboratories, that is, Internet-based collaboration. Van House (2004) reviewed social studies of science, focusing on the construction of scientific knowledge in general. Other *ARIST* chapters have discussed issues related to collaboration in general, such as virtual communities (Ellis, Oldridge, & Vasconcelos, 2004), organizational knowledge and communities of practice (Davenport & Hall, 2002), and trust and information technology (Marsh & Dibben, 2003).

Terminology and Concepts

Defining Scientific Collaboration: Human Behavior, Tasks, and Social Settings

Scientific collaboration can be defined as interaction taking place within a social context among two or more scientists that facilitates the sharing of meaning and completion of tasks with respect to a mutually shared, superordinate goal. Scientists who collaborate may also bring additional, individual goals to a collaboration (Sonnenwald, 2003a). A typical example is a junior scientist who, in addition to contributing to a given collaboration, wishes to be promoted and to receive tenure. Individual goals can influence a scientist's ongoing commitment to a collaboration and his or her perspective on many aspects of the work. Tasks within a scientific collaboration often have a high degree of uncertainty, more so than is typically found in other types of work. For example, in research it is typically not clear at the outset whether the goal can be achieved or what the best way to achieve it might be. Trial and error are integral parts of the process (Latour, 1987).

Research tasks can be shared among scientists in various ways. Some tasks are divisible and may be performed either sequentially or concurrently (Steiner, 1972; Whitley, 2000). Other tasks may be conjunctive, requiring everyone to complete the task. For example, in a social science collaboration, researchers may jointly develop data collection instruments, separately collect data with these instruments from similar populations in different geographic regions, and then analyze and interpret the results together. In a natural science collaboration, one scientist may suggest a research question and develop data samples. A second scientist may analyze the samples using specialized scientific instrumentation. Research suggests that task demands, available resources, group interaction, the degree of functional dependence among the researchers, and the degree of strategic dependence determine how tasks are allocated and shared among scientists in a collaboration (Steiner, 1972; Whitley, 2000).

Scientific collaboration occurs within the larger social context of science, which includes elements such as peer review, reward systems, invisible colleges, scientific paradigms, and national and international science policies, as well as disciplinary and university norms (Crane, 1972; Kuhn, 1970; Latour, 1987; Traweek, 1988). This context imposes constraints and enables possibilities not always found in other settings, such as, for example, the service industry. Characteristics of scientific contexts are often used in the literature to categorize, or classify, collaborations. The characteristics most frequently invoked are disciplinary, geographic, and organizational.

Classifying Scientific Collaboration

Disciplinary Focus

The terms "intra-," "inter-," "cross-," "multi-," and "trans-disciplinary collaboration" stress the importance of the role of disciplines in scientific collaboration and refer to disciplinary knowledge that is incorporated into a scientific collaboration and, in turn, produced from it. "Intra-disciplinary" or "disciplinary collaboration" denotes collaboration in which each participant derives his or her knowledge from the same discipline or field and applies this knowledge within the collaboration, which, ideally, produces new knowledge within that same discipline or field.

Interdisciplinary collaboration, on the other hand, involves the integration of knowledge from two or more disciplines (Palmer, 2001; Salter & Hearn, 1996). Typically, participants come from different disciplines and work together, integrating knowledge drawn from their respective domains to create new knowledge. The terms "multidisciplinary" and "cross-disciplinary" are sometimes used interchangeably to refer to interdisciplinary collaboration (Cummings & Kiesler, 2003; Jeffrey, 2003). However, many authors differentiate between multidisciplinary and interdisciplinary collaboration, defining multidisciplinary collaboration as research that uses knowledge from different disciplines but does not integrate or synthesize it (Bruce, Lyall, Tait, & Williams, 2004). For example, a collaboration may use methods or scientific instruments that were developed within the framework of one discipline to investigate a research question arising in another. The differences between inter- and multidisciplinary research can be difficult to distinguish in practice because integration of knowledge may be subtle and may take time to detect.

Transdisciplinary collaboration has been defined as the integration of all knowledge or the integration of all knowledge relevant to a particular problem. Recently, this definition has been extended in several ways. Klein (2004) defined it as broad interdisciplinary research that advocates both the integration of natural sciences, social sciences, and the humanities and the involvement of multiple stakeholders from all aspects of society. A related concept is that of mode 2 knowledge production, in which research questions emanate not from disciplines but from contexts of use. Mode 2 knowledge production incorporates heterogeneous skills and knowledge and involves diverse organizations and social accountability (Gibbons, Limoges, Nowotny, Schwartzman, Scott, & Trow, 1994). The involvement of communities in research is also a major theme of participatory action research.

Geographic Focus

The geographic location of scientists participating in a collaboration provides another focus for classifying scientific collaboration. Terms such as "remote collaboration," "distributed collaboration," "scientific collaboratories," and "international collaboration" are now common in the literature. "Remote" and "distributed collaboration" refer to collaborations in which participants are not collocated. Collocation may be defined in terms of the geographic propinquity of collaborating scientists (irrespective of their institutional affiliations) or in terms of their institutional affiliations (where geographic separation is assumed, e.g., Bos, Zimmerman, Cooney, Olson, Dahl, & Yerkie, in press). The latter form of collocation is also known as "inter-institutional collaboration."

The term "scientific collaboratory" originally designated "a laboratory without walls" allowing scientists to conduct research across geographic distances (National Research Council, 1993; Wulf, 1993). Initially, scientific collaboratories provided remote access to scientific instruments (Finholt, 2002). The definition and vision of scientific collaboratories have expanded over the years, as is apparent from the wording of a more recent definition, according to which a scientific collaboratory is:

> a network-based facility and organizational entity that spans distance, supports rich and recurring human interaction oriented to a common research area, fosters contact between researchers who are both known and unknown to each other, and provides access to data sources, artifacts and tools

required to accomplish research tasks. (Science of Collaboratories, 2003, online)

This definition emphasizes remote collaboration although it does not preclude the possibility that some participants may be collocated. It also incorporates the notion that collaboratories constitute socio-technical interaction networks (Kling, McKim, & King, 2003).

"International scientific collaboration" refers to collaboration that occurs when participants work in different countries. It is a special case of remote collaboration and includes collaboration among scientists in developed and developing countries, which is also known as "North-South collaboration" (Drake, Ludden, Nzongola-Ntalaja, Patel, & Shevtsova, 2000; Duque, Ynalvez, Sooryamoorthy, Mbatia, Dzorgbo, & Shrum, 2005; Olson, Teasley, Bietz, & Cogburn, 2002). International collaboration crosses international boundaries but may be located within the same cultural region—for example, the Barents region that shares a common cultural heritage and language but is located in Russia, Finland, Sweden, and Norway (Iivonen & Sonnenwald, 2000). Although cultural differences based on national affiliation or cultural heritage are mentioned in the literature, a term such as "intercultural scientific collaboration" has not emerged. Perhaps this reflects a bias toward the ideal of a universal scientific culture.

Organizational and Community Focus

Collaboration across organizational boundaries may include collaboration across geographic distances as well. However, here the focus is on factors that emerge due to differences between academia and business or between government and non-government organizations, including communities. The terms "university-industry collaboration" and "academic-industry collaboration," as well as the less frequently used "collaborative practice research" (Mathiasson, 2002), all refer to collaboration between scientists working at universities and scientists and other professionals working in industry. Science parks that house industrial research offices and labs near, or on, university campuses provide one mechanism to promote collaboration, knowledge transfer, and innovation development among industrial and university scientists.

The term "participatory action research" refers to collaborations between scientists and research participants in general; however, a focus on collaboration between scientists and communities, including non-government organizations (NGOs) and citizen groups, has emerged over time (Brydon-Miller, 1997; Fisher & Ball, 2003; Secrest, Lassiter, Armistead, Wyckoff, Johnson, Williams, et al., 2004; Wilson, 1999). Synonymous terms include "participatory research," "investigator-community collaboration," "science-society collaboration," and "community collaboration." Participatory action research values the knowledge, experiences, and norms of community members and seeks to incorporate these into research projects. Its goal is to create new knowledge that leads to effective social action that solves real-life problems. The effectiveness of social action is to be determined by participants. Science shops[2] have emerged in Europe to help communities and scientists identify and establish participatory action research projects (Leydesdorff & Ward, 2005; Pax Mediterranea, 2003).

Related concepts include the triple helix model of innovation and use-inspired research. The triple helix model of innovation examines relationships between research, industry, and government in knowledge-based economies (Etzkowitz & Leydesdorff, 2000). Use-inspired research proposes a new paradigm in which science is "directly influenced both by the quest of general understanding and by considerations of use" (Stokes, 1997, p. 79). Both concepts have influenced public and private research agencies to encourage, and sometimes require, scientific collaboration as a way to support socioeconomic development.

Stages of Scientific Collaboration

The four stages of scientific collaboration—foundation, formulation, sustainment, and conclusion—presented in this chapter provide a platform to highlight and understand the complexity of scientific collaboration. The stages are based on an approximate temporal view of the scientific process and correspond to stages suggested by others (Kraut, Galagher, & Egido, 1988; Maglaughlin, 2003). The stages frame the progressive emergence of factors that have an impact on collaboration during the scientific process. However, scientific collaboration is dynamic. Over the course of a collaboration, new research questions or topics may emerge because of external or internal forces and may require many changes in the collaboration. Similarly, new partners may join a collaboration at various points and formulation issues may then re-emerge as important. Individuals and organizations who wish to facilitate or conduct scientific collaborations should not ignore these dynamics.

In the following sections, the results of research carried out in different contexts or settings of scientific collaboration are synthesized by research stage. Although the results emerged from specific contexts, as is acknowledged in the text, some are similar across contexts and others may be applicable in additional contexts. For example, findings regarding the need to provide training opportunities for local staff can be found in research on university-minority community collaboration (Fisher & Ball, 2003), collaboration between research-intensive and historically minority universities in the U.S. (Adessa & Sonnenwald, 2003), and between universities in the developed and developing world (Oldham, 2005). Similarly, the finding that remote collaboration requires, and benefits from, explicit identification of task responsibilities in the formulation stage (Olson, Olson, & Cooney, in press) may also be useful when one is considering collocated collaboration. All findings applicable to one of the stages in the collaboration process are discussed within that stage in order to allow readers to consider the lessons learned as plausible strategies or areas of further investigation.

Foundation Stage

The foundation stage focuses on factors that provide, or have an impact on, the foundation for collaboration, in other words, factors that are required in order for collaborations to be considered and subsequently initiated, or factors that can inhibit the formation of collaborations. It can also be viewed as a "prehistory" stage, that is, one that includes knowledge, norms, policies, and relationships existing before a collaboration is formulated. Five categories of factors—scientific, political, socioeconomic, resource accessibility, and social networks and personal—emerged from a review of the literature.

Scientific Factors

The opportunity to discover new knowledge and solve complex problems in a timely manner motivates many scientists to consider collaborating. For example, when the World Health Organization (WHO) issued a global alert concerning the health threat posed by Severe Acute Respiratory Syndrome (SARS), scientists began to collaborate in order to find the cause of the disease and develop a cure. Five weeks after the global alert was announced, Dr. David Heyman, executive director of the WHO Communicable Diseases program, commented that "the pace of SARS research has been astounding. Because of an extraordinary collaboration among laboratories from countries around the world, we now know with certainty what causes SARS" (quoted in World Health Organization, 2003, online).

Increasing specialization within science, the growing complexity of scientific instruments, and the need to combine different types of knowledge and expertise to solve complex problems can also motivate and provide a foundation for collaboration (Katz & Martin, 1997). Certain types of research can no longer be conducted by a single scientist. For example, single-investigator research does not occur within high energy physics: Rather, research is conducted by large teams comprising several thousand individuals, with each team member making a specific type of contribution (Hofer, McKee, Birnholz, & Avery, in press; Traweek, 1988).[3]

Scientific collaboration can also help extend the scope of a research project and foster innovation because additional expertise is made available (Beaver, 2001; Cummings & Kiesler, 2003; Lambert, 2003). It can increase scientific reliability and the probability of success because more than one person is considering the accuracy, quality, and meaning of the results (Beaver, 2001; Thagard, 1997). It may lead to the emergence of new branches of science and to new careers at the frontiers of science (Cummings & Kiesler, 2003). Collaboration can also increase a scientist's credibility, for it is viewed as a form of acceptance, or a rite of passage, within the scientific community (Hara, Solomon, Kim, & Sonnenwald, 2003; Mervis & Normile, 1998).

There are potentially negative aspects of scientific collaboration as well, such as concerns that collaborations are sometimes used to hide unethical conduct. For example, collaborations between advanced and developing countries may occur in order to conduct unethical clinical trials, biological warfare experiments, or investigations involving natural resources that are prohibited in advanced countries (Oldham, 2005). In other instances, scientists may collaborate for purposes of intellectual espionage and scooping the results of others (Beaver, 2001).

Wray (2002) has discussed additional concerns. Collaborations can lead to a diffusion of epistemic and ethical responsibility: When many scientists collaborate, no one scientist may feel responsible for the work. Collaborations can also become powerful lobby groups, influencing research policy and funding decisions in their favor. When this occurs, the balance between single-investigator and collaborative research funding may become skewed so that single investigators do not receive funding.

Collaborations can also hinder an individual's career advancement, especially in the case of junior scientists. Tenure committees may undervalue a junior scientist's contribution to research conducted with a well-known, senior scientist. Furthermore, when junior scientists have special expertise that is in demand and accept many offers to collaborate, their research may become fragmented and they may find it difficult to develop their own research program (Burroughs Wellcome Fund & Howard Hughes Medical Institute, 2004). A recently published brochure, entitled *Making the Right Moves* (Burroughs Wellcome Fund et al., 2004), offers a checklist of items for junior scientists to consider before entering into a collaboration.

Political Factors

National and international politics are influenced by—and, in turn, influence—scientific collaboration. Informal and formal scientific collaboration can increase understanding between countries and promote world peace even when relationships between countries are strained (Collaboration in extremis, 2002; De Cerreño & Keynan, 1998). For example, during the Cold War, scientists in the U.S. and U.S.S.R. established and maintained relationships that were valuable in promoting the end of their countries' geopolitical conflict (U.S. Office of Science & Technology Policy, 2000). Another example is the International Arid Lands Consortium (http://ag.arizona.edu/OALS/IALC/Home.html). Its scientific goal is to explore problems and solutions that emerge in arid and semiarid regions; its political goal is to be a catalyst for peace (McGinley & Charnie, 2003). Partners include universities and research organizations in the U.S., Egypt, Israel, and Jordan. The consortium, with its Wayne Owens Peace Fellowship Program (http://ag.arizona.edu/OALS/IALC/PF/PF-index.html), sponsors collaborative research projects that include scientists from these countries.

Scientific collaboration can also help heal post-war wounds (Arunachalam & Doss, 2000) and redirect military research into peacetime applications (U.S. Office of Science & Technology Policy, 2000). For example, the International Science and Technology Center (www.istc.ru) supports the collaboration of former weapons researchers in Russia and the Commonwealth of Independent States with scientists throughout the world in nonmilitary projects.

Nations also use scientific collaboration to promote political unity within their borders or in their broader region (Banda, 2000). For example, during the past decade the European Science Foundation's research programs have required scientific participation from at least three countries in the European Union (E.U.) and associated states in an effort to increase understanding between countries. When political barriers are removed, scientific collaboration between the countries increases, as measured by co-authorship and joint projects (Havemann, 2001; Williams, 1998).

National and international political situations and policies may also impede scientific collaboration. For example, scientific collaborators left Rwanda in 1994 when genocide occurred and many remain reluctant to return (Cohen & Linton, 2003). In 2002, research on AIDS conducted by scientists at the U.S. Centers for Disease Control and NGOs in Myanmar (formerly Burma) was halted by the U.S. government when the Myanmar government prohibited NGOs from performing voluntary counseling and testing (Cohen & Linton, 2003). Recent changes in U.S. national security policy have also served to hinder collaboration. Some scientists cannot attend conferences and meetings in the U.S. because of visa delays, for example, or if a foreign scientist leaves the U.S., he or she may not be able to return. Additionally, restrictions can be placed on U.S. government funding contracts regarding the publication of results classified as "sensitive but not classified" (Gast, 2003, p. 10).

Establishing collaborations among nations whose official relationships are strained can be challenging, as national policies and funding mechanisms may not be in place to support such efforts. To address this problem, scientists have been encouraged to benchmark previous and ongoing achievements, identify global scientific problems that are important to satisfy a national need in each country, and specify how funds can address these problems (Collaboration in extremis, 2002; Mervis & Normile, 1998). Three-way collaborations that include one partner from a "neutral" country are encouraged, as are conferences to share ideas and develop projects, and training opportunities (Collaboration in extremis, 2002).

Collaborations established solely in response to political forces are seldom successful.[4] For example, Velho and Velho (1996) described a collaboration between U.K. and Brazilian scientists that their respective governments promoted in spite of objections from the Brazilian scientific community. Agreements regarding access to, and handling of, resources were not honored; local scientists were excluded; and co-authorship among scientists from the two countries was minimal. When such collaborations occur between developed and developing countries, perceptions of scientific and economic imperialism can emerge (Velho & Velho, 1996).

Socioeconomic Factors

Scientific collaboration has been called a "springboard for economic prosperity and sustainable development" (U.S. Office of Science & Technology Policy, 2000, online). In the near term, businesses can realize economic benefits from collaboration through research and development tax credits and access to public research funding otherwise not available to them (Autio, Hameri, & Nordberg, 1996; Lambert, 2003). The latter is achieved by collaborating with universities in government-sponsored industry-university research programs.

In the long term, collaboration can spread the financial risk of research for businesses, as well as provide access to local and scientific markets, motivate a company's workforce, and provide access to students and scientists for employment recruitment purposes (Autio et al., 1996; Grey, Lindblad, & Rudolph, 2001; Lambert, 2003). Companies can often hire scientists in developing countries at salary rates that are one-tenth of those in advanced countries but ten times the local rates (Oldham, 2005).

Countries also look to collaboration to support national and regional economic development. Many nations have research programs that require collaboration between universities and industries, including small and medium-sized enterprises. For example, the Swedish agency VINNOVA (www.vinnova.se) was established to support national and regional innovation and economic growth through collaboration between academia and industry. It requires all research proposals to include both academic and business participants.

In comparison, developing countries tend to realize a larger return on investment in science when portions of their research funds are spent to support collaboration with scientists in developed countries (Arunachalam & Doss, 2000; Oldham, 2005). Such collaborations can provide advice, key laboratory materials, equipment, student and staff training, and project funding, all of which help to increase the return on investment (Third World Academy of Sciences, 2004).

Universities can also benefit from funded collaborative research, but disagreements can occur regarding the distribution of the overheads associated with collaborative research grants (Maglaughlin & Sonnenwald, 2005). Typically, the largest share of overhead monies is allocated to the university (or department) that is the lead or primary grantee; for this reason, each university (department) involved in a collaboration wishes to be the lead. This can hinder, and even prevent, collaboration with scientists who work at universities and departments known to have inflexible policies regarding overhead allocation.

National policies that limit access to financial resources can also impede collaboration. Smith and Katz (2000) have pointed out that the university ranking system in the U.K. constrains university-industry collaboration in some instances. New universities and those with lower Research Assessment Exercise (RAE) rankings cannot apply for research funding or research student fellowships. However, these universities often have the strongest links to small and medium-sized enterprises and are thus in a position to easily form collaborations with them. Their only solution is to allow a highly ranked university be the lead on the grant application.

Resource Accessibility

Scientific collaboration is often motivated by the need to gain access to expensive instruments, unique scientific data, scarce natural and social resources, and large amounts of scientific funding (Birnholz & Bietz, 2003; Katz & Martin, 1997; Wagner, Staheli, Silberglitt, Wong, & Kadtke, 2002; Wray, 2002). For example, the William R. Wiley Environmental Molecular Sciences Laboratory (EMSL) (www. emsl.pnnl.gov) at the Pacific Northwest National Laboratory as well as National Center for Research Resources (NCRR), established by the National Institutes of Health, invite scientists to collaborate with them (Chin, Myers, & Hoyt, 2002; Kouzes, Myers, & Wulf, 1996; National Institutes of Health, 2000). The visiting scientists typically bring research questions and biological samples; the centers provide expertise on, and access to, specialized instruments that are needed to analyze the samples in order to answer research questions. Human geneticists may collaborate in order to gain access to unique reagents, clones, probes, and family resource data (Atkinson, Batchelor, & Parsons, 1998). Biologists collaborate to gain access to natural resources such as rain forests that may be located in politically sensitive areas (Oldham, 2005; Velho & Velho, 1996). The National Science Foundation, the European Science Foundation, and other funding agencies often require groups of scientists, either working within the same discipline or coming from different disciplines, to collaborate in order to help ensure that expensive instruments are used frequently. Some scientific instruments are so expensive that funding from multiple agencies and countries is needed to finance them. For example, 56 countries contribute to the construction and operating costs of the new large hadron collider (LHC) located at CERN (Centre Européen pour la Recherche Nucleaire) (http://public.web.cern.ch/Public/Welcome.html). Such large collaborations have not emerged in disciplines that do not require expensive resources of these kinds.

Collaboration is typically more successful when each participating scientist provides and receives resources—even when the scientists come from different countries and disciplines. For example, whenever Africans and non-Africans have successfully collaborated in medical research, the Africans provided access to local communities and the non-Africans supplied free treatment, lab equipment, and training (Bietz, Naidoo, & Olson, in press; Cohen, 2000). Collaboration between China and Taiwan is proceeding in spite of political differences: Taiwan provides a pool of experienced, mid-career scientists that China lacks because of the Cultural Revolution, whereas China supplies a large number of younger scientists who increase the size of Taiwan's scientific community (Normile, 2003).

Social Networks and Personal Factors

Social networks and personal factors provide a foundation for collaboration. Social networks may span disciplinary, organizational, and national boundaries. Collaboration frequently emerges from, and is perpetuated through, social networks. For example, the "small network" phenomenon has been observed to hold with respect to scientific collaborations: Two scientists are more likely to collaborate and co-author a paper if they have a co-author in common (Newman, 2001). In his study of the social networks formed by the one million scientists in the biomedical research community who publish in MEDLINE, Newman (2001) found that the typical distance between any two randomly selected scientists was approximately six links—in other words, it is possible to reach any one scientist from another by following about six co-authorship linkages. There may be more than one shortest path between scientists, and those working in the same field may be linked through scientists in other fields (Newman, 2004).

Scientists look to their social networks both for ideas regarding new research projects and in order to identify and select collaborators (Beaver, 2001; Bozeman & Boardman, 2003; Crane, 1972; Katz & Martin, 1997; Maglaughlin & Sonnenwald, 2005; Traweek, 1988). Personal factors play a role in establishing and sustaining social networks and, subsequently, collaborations. Personal compatibility, including similar approaches to science, comparable working styles, mutual respect, trust, and the ability to get along and enjoy one another's company are also used to identify and select collaborators (Creamer, 2004; Hara et al., 2003; Maglaughlin & Sonnenwald, 2005). Scientists also describe successful collaborations as fun and use dating and marriage analogies when describing successful relationships (Maglaughlin & Sonnenwald, 2005).

Cultural heritage influences social networks and personal relationships. For example, there tends to be more collaboration among scientists in countries with historical or colonial ties (Wagner & Leydesdorff, 2005). Typical collaborations in computer science within China include one or two students working with an older scientist, an arrangement that reflects both the traditional cultural pattern of an elder mentoring the young and the effects of the Cultural Revolution when no students were educated to become scientists, with the result that there is a dearth of mid-career scientists today (Liang, Guo, & Davis, 2002). Traweek (1988) has described how cultural differences between American and Japanese high energy physicists had a negative impact on their collaboration. The scientists, however, did not recognize that their problems stemmed from cultural differences. They mistakenly believed that their membership in the same research community would eliminate problems stemming from different cultural values and practices.

Gender may also play a role in social network formation and collaboration. In a survey of researchers at elite national research centers in the U.S., Bozeman and Corley (2004) found that 83 percent of the scientists who collaborated with non-tenure-track women were other women. Overall, men in their sample had an average of 14 collaborators and women, an average of 12. Yet, many women scientists do not work at elite research centers. Eisenhart and Finkel (1998) found that women scientists chose non-elite scientific places of work because these institutions offered alternatives to the impersonal and inflexible practices that characterize elite science. We know that status plays a role in science (Kuhn, 1970); however, we do not know how gender in conjunction with status affects social network formation and collaboration.

Social networks can be expanded through both informal, chance encounters and formal meetings and activities (Beaver, 2001). It is sometimes said that universities should have only one water cooler or coffee machine, so that scientists would meet and get to know each another informally. Informal meetings can lead to collaboration (e.g., Lambert, 2003). Formal meetings can also serve as seedbeds of collaboration. Research centers often host seminars and events that bring scientists together to help build social networks. For example, the London Technology Network (www. ltnetwork.org) organizes activities that bring together scientists from industry and universities in order to foster collaboration (Lambert, 2003).

Social networks have been analyzed to identify areas of strengths and weaknesses within and among research organizations and institutions, businesses, and nations in order to direct scientific development and funding policies (Owen-Smith, Riccaboni, Pammolli, & Powell, 2002; Parent, Bertrand, Côté, & Archambault, 2003). Bibliometric analyses of co-authorship, co-citation, and acknowledgment patterns, as well as sociometric surveys in which scientists identify their collaborators, are used in such analysis. Thus, social networks can influence collaboration in multiple ways.

Formulation Stage

During the formulation stage, scientists initiate and plan collaborative research projects. Collaborative research is not divorced from traditional scientific norms and practices. However, because it involves multiple scientists, some of who may have different disciplinary backgrounds, work in different institutions, and not be collocated, additional planning and sufficient time for planning are required for success. The literature suggests that research vision, goals, and tasks; leadership and organizational structure; use of ICT; and intellectual property (IP) and other legal issues need to be considered in greater detail than in single-investigator research.

Research Vision, Goals, and Tasks

A vision or complex problem can motivate scientists to collaborate (Olson et al., in press; Schiff, 2002; Sonnenwald, 2003b). Thus, as has been mentioned, scientists were spurred to collaborate in identifying the cause, and developing methods of halting the spread, of SARS in order to stop a global health threat: As Dr. Klaus Stöhr, coordinator of the SARS collaborative effort, observed, "the people in this network [collaborating on SARS] have put aside profit and prestige to work together" (quoted in World Health Organization, 2003, online). Research visions and goals often appear obvious and straightforward after they have been, or are close to being, achieved; in the early stages of formulating a collaboration, however, visions and goals can be difficult to articulate. This difficulty arises to some degree when formulating any new research question (as many doctoral students have experienced). However, in collaborative research, the visions and goals are often scientifically more complex than those tackled by a single investigator and require buy-in by the many scientists who have the expertise and other resources needed to achieve the vision. Personal motivation and excitement regarding a vision and research goals can help scientists overcome other challenges that emerge when conducting research collaboratively.

Because they are ambitious, visions and goals may require buy-in from other stakeholders as well, including participating institutions, one or more funding agencies, and citizen and community groups. Articulating clear visions and goals that multiple individuals and groups can understand and support is a skill scientists need when initiating large and complex scientific collaborations.

In addition, research tasks should be clearly defined and owned by individual scientists. This is particularly important when the collaboration occurs across distance (Maglaughlin & Sonnenwald, 2005; Olson et al., in press). When scientists are collocated, they can informally observe and discuss task progress, but this is more difficult across distances and disciplines; therefore, defining tasks and task responsibility from the outset is important.

Language and epistemological differences can hinder the formulation of visions, goals, and tasks (Jeffrey, 2003; Maglaughlin & Sonnenwald, 2005; Olson et al., in press; Palmer, 2001; Traore & Landry, 1997). Disciplines and subfields use specific terminology that varies across domains. The same term may have different meanings in different disciplines and different terms may have the same meaning. Research methods also vary across disciplines and scientists may not know what they do not know. A materials scientist may not know that it can take a biologist six months or longer to create a biological sample. A chemist may not know that it can take a sociologist six months or longer to analyze ethnographic data. Because it is common knowledge within their own disciplines, the biologist and sociologist may not realize that "outsiders" do not know these things. Disagreement and conflict may emerge when scientists have misconceptions regarding the resources, including time, required to conduct various research tasks.

When scientists collaborate with others from different types of organizations, universities, communities, and countries, additional challenges may arise from different perspectives regarding what constitutes a research goal, realistic tasks, and task completion time frames. Differing ethical practices, as well as participants' previous negative experiences and feelings of distrust, also have to be taken into account. Businesses may want research goals and tasks to be more pragmatic, directly contributing to new and existing products, services, and practices, whereas scientists may have a longer-term focus (Mathiassen, 2002). Historically black and minority colleges and universities in the U.S. typically do not have the same resources to support research as research-intensive universities. Infrastructure services, such as purchasing, accounting, and computer support; scientific equipment; time dedicated to research; as well as trained graduate students and postdoctoral fellows are often less available (Adessa & Sonnenwald, 2003). Groups that have experienced historical trauma and prejudice, such as Native American tribes and African-American communities, may distrust scientists, whereas scientists may exhibit bias and ignorance in formulating research goals and tasks involving such groups (Fisher & Ball, 2003; Secrest et al., 2004). Developing nations may not want scientists from developed countries to remove biological specimens from their jurisdictions; on the other hand, scientists in developed countries may see this as a natural or necessary activity (Velho & Velho, 1996).

To help manage such issues, scientists can include participants and stakeholders from the participating organizations and communities in this stage (Cohen, 2000; Fisher & Ball, 2003; Secrest et al., 2004). For example, when establishing a collaboration with a Native American tribal community, Fisher and Ball (2003) worked with that community for two years to plan their research project. A facilitator assisted them, helping to elucidate and negotiate the scientists' and tribal perspectives and expectations. The Tribal Council, the local controlling authority, retained the right to approve or disapprove project activities and control of the research data. A tribal research code (in addition to the university research code), a culturally specific assessment, and intervention methods were developed. Plans were made to employ and train community members as project staff. These staff members later became ombudsmen for the research within the community, helping to establish trust and cooperation. Some communities may have established research codes and practices but many do not have such measures in place; in those communities, scientists should identify the social authorities and work with them. In some instances, the social authorities may be local church groups, mothers in the community, or workers' unions. Holding focus group sessions with these constituencies can help researchers learn more about the values, expectations, and language of the community and receive feedback on materials to be used in the research (Secrest et al., 2004).

Additional best practices include sharing information about budgets (Cohen, 2000); ensuring that everyone receives benefits from the collaboration (Olson et al., in press); developing a shared statement of principles, expected benefits, and mutual obligations (Cohen, 2000); formulating a shared vocabulary (Olson et al., in press); ensuring that differences in resources are accounted for and aligned (Adessa & Sonnenwald, 2003); and establishing community and scientific advisory boards (Secrest et al., 2004; Sonnenwald, 2003b).

Leadership and Organizational Structure

Studies of successful collaboration show that leadership is important for success (Olson et al., in press; Schiff, 2002; Stokols, Harvey, Gress, Fuqua, & Phillips, 2005). Collaborations are more successful when leadership has project management experience and is respected by participants (Olson et al., in press). Some large collaborations have hired professional managers to be part of the leadership team and consultants to provide leadership and managerial training. Scientific, financial, and administrative leadership may be shared among several individuals to take advantage of individual strengths and to help ensure that no one scientist is overburdened by leadership responsibilities (Sonnenwald, 2003b).

Collaborations can be organized in different ways. Chompalov, Genuth and Shrum (2002) studied 53 interinstitutional scientific collaborations in physics and allied sciences to identify how collaborations are typically organized. Four types of organizations emerged from their analysis: bureaucratic, leaderless, nonspecialized, and participatory. According to Chompalov et al. (2002, p. 756), bureaucratic collaborations have a "hierarchy of authority, written rules and regulations, formalized responsibilities, and a specialized division of labor." They typically also have extensive external evaluations, numerous committees and boards, and officially appointed project leaders. A history of competition among participants and the large amount of money involved has led to the bureaucratic organization format (Warnow-Blewett, Genuth, & Weart, 2001).

Leaderless collaborations have administrative, but no scientific, leaders (Chompalov et al., 2002). The administrative leaders solicit input from scientists and put them in charge of specific projects. These collaborations also have formal rules and regulations for participation, as well as a board of directors in whom ultimate authority is vested. These collaborations operate well when collegial relations exist among scientists and the collaboration staff. In nonspecialized collaborations, there is hierarchical management but less formalization and differentiation of roles and responsibilities (Chompalov et al., 2002). Multiple teams perform similar tasks—for example, analyzing different data sets using identical, standard algorithms. In these collaborations, scientific leadership is needed to establish and maintain standards. Administrative tasks are shared among members.

Participatory collaborations are egalitarian in that there is no one scientific or administrative leader (Chompalov et al., 2002). There are no formal rules and regulations but rather nonbinding memos of understanding. Members publish results collectively, thus reflecting a lack of competition over IP. These collaborations are primarily found in particle physics. Several characteristics of particle physics contribute to the viability of this type of organizational structure: Particle physicists are widely dispersed across universities and require highly specialized and complex equipment that demands many types of expertise and large amounts of funding to design, develop, and operate. No single person or group can procure the necessary resources to conduct science under these conditions; a consensual, participatory approach is needed.

Chompalov, Genuth, and Shrum's work certainly contributes to our understanding of the organization of collaborations. Their study, however, focuses on natural science collaborations that occur among elite research institutions in developed countries. New research focusing on collaborations in different disciplines, institutions, and countries may yield additional insights regarding effective organizations.

Information and Communications Technology

Research continues to demonstrate that the introduction of ICT that does not complement, or is incompatible with, existing policies and practices will not increase scientific collaboration (Duque et al., 2005; Sooryamoorthy, Duque, Ynalvez, & Shrum, 2005; Star & Ruhleder, 1996). Yet ICT can facilitate scientific collaboration and give rise to new types of collaboration, especially when scientists cannot, and perhaps even should not, be collocated. For example, in developing countries, ICT can support the "migration of minds without the migration of bodies" (Oldham, 2005, online). Bos et al. (in press) have identified seven forms of remote scientific collaborations based on their use of ICT: shared instrument systems, community data systems, open community contribution systems, virtual communities of practice, virtual learning communities, distributed research centers, and community infrastructure projects. Each category is made possible or enhanced through the use of ICT.

ICT applications that are used to support collaboration include e-mail, instant messaging/chat, listservs, videoconferencing, voice over IP (VOIP), Wikis, blogs and other types of Web pages, shared applications (e.g., to support synchronous data analysis), electronic lab notebooks, shared remote access to instrumentation, shared electronic whiteboards (e.g., used during videoconferences to support information sharing and knowledge construction), project management tools, scheduling/calendar tools to arrange experiments in labs as well as meetings, manuscript submission, and review systems; and digital libraries and shared data repositories, including thesauri, metadata, and information retrieval tools. For an in-depth review of ICT used in remote scientific collaboration, see Hofer, Bos, and Olson (in press).

In order to be adopted and used within any setting, including scientific collaboration, ICT should provide benefits over current practices; be compatible with scientists' values, experiences, and needs; and be easy to try out or to use, with clearly defined results (Rogers, 1995). ICT can influence research tasks in unexpected ways and a participatory design process in which technology and work practices are codesigned may be needed. For example, Sonnenwald, Solomon, Hara, Bolliger, and Cox (2002) found that the introduction of videoconferencing and an electronic whiteboard during group meetings increased the level of formality, thus reducing the effectiveness of the meetings. Changes to the implementation and operation of the videoconferencing technology, as well as to the meeting format and content (explicitly adding and supporting informal interaction), were introduced in collaboration with technical staff and scientists. As a result, the effectiveness of the meetings increased.

Disciplines, institutions, and countries tend to adopt ICT at different rates (Duque et al., 2005; Kling & McKim, 2000; Walsh & Bayma, 1996; Walsh, Kucker, Maloney, & Gabbay, 2000). For example, physicists and mathematicians began using e-mail in 1988 and 1989 respectively, whereas biologists began using it only in 1992 (Walsh et al., 2000). Differences in adoption rates among disciplines may be attributed to the nature of research in those disciplines. For example, Birnholtz and Bietz (2003) have suggested that sharing data via ICT is easiest in disciplines where there is low task uncertainty and high mutual dependency, including consensus on the types of problems to be researched. Examples include the Genbank and Inter-university Consortium for Political and Social Research. Barriers to data sharing include competition and the large amount of work involved in making data reusable when compared to the benefits and risks of sharing (Birnholz & Bietz, 2003). E-mail is still being introduced in many developing countries and its use in collaboration appears to be primarily influenced by organizational and social factors (Duque et al., 2005).

ICT may be adopted at different rates and initially used in different ways, yet, over time, consensus and convergence of use appears to emerge. Walsh et al. (2000) found that between 50 and 65 percent of sociologists, biologists, mathematicians, and physicists surveyed (in developed countries) used e-mail as their first choice of communications media to share conference information and meeting agendas, coordinate schedules, ask/answer a quick question, solicit input for a decision, and give progress updates. On average, only 13 percent chose to use e-mail to support social interaction.

Scientific collaboration continues to inspire innovations in ICT. The needs of scientific research today continue to motivate research and development in ICT. Research programs such as the cyberinfrastructure program in the U.S. (Atkins, Droegemeier, Feldman, Garcia-Molina, Klein, Messerschmitt, et al., 2003; Berman & Brady, 2005) and e-science and e-social science programs in the U.K. (Hey & Trefethen, 2003; U.K. Research Council, 2005) are funding developments in ICT to meet the needs of remote scientific collaboration, including applications that support collaborative, synchronous access to remote scientific instruments (Sonnenwald, Maglaughlin, & Whitton, 2004); the secure and rapid transport of billions of terabytes of scientific data among scientists around the world;[5] and secure high-speed distributed computation to construct complex scientific models and 3D telepresence environments (e.g., Welch, Fuchs, Cairns, Mayer-Patel, Sonnenwald, Yang, et al., in press). Papers presented at the First International Conference on e-Social Science (www.ncess.ac.uk/events/conference/2005/papers) and Berman and Brady (2005) provide additional examples of current and future ICT support for e-social science and e-science projects. Security, data integrity, very high-speed telecommunications and computation, data privacy, effective retrieval (especially across multiple disciplines, each with its own unique terminology), and long-term archival access are several of the technical challenges facing these projects.

Reconciling the emerging cyberinfrastructure with social aspects of the scientific process may be extremely challenging (David, 2005). The design of new ICT infrastructures and applications will continue to benefit from research on the social aspects of collaboration. A new area of research is emerging, that of evaluating the potential impacts of ICT on scientific collaboration before very large sums of money are spent on technology development and deployment. This type of evaluation increases in complexity when the technology is targeted for remote scientific collaborations that include a variety of scientists from different disciplines, institutions, and countries. Current evaluation approaches include lab experiments that mirror current scientific practice (Sonnenwald, Whitton, & Maglaughlin, 2003), socio-technical interaction network analysis (Kling et al., 2003), and computer simulations (Nan, Johnston, Olson, & Bos, 2005).

Intellectual Property and Other Legal Issues

Although it is outside the scope of this chapter to review IP and legal issues in depth, it is important to recognize that IP rights and other legal issues have a bearing on collaboration. IP rights and their globalization are in flux and increasingly driven by private interests, including a merging of university-industry-government relationships linked to innovation and free trade (Etzkowitz & Leydesdorff, 2000; Sell, 2003). The Science Commons (www.sciencecommons.org) and the Creative

Commons (www.creativecommons.org) are developing alternative, flexible copyright licenses for scientific publishing, licensing, and data (Lessig, 2004; Let data speak to data, 2005).

Issues concerning IP that may emerge from a collaboration and the legal relationships among its participants should be negotiated in the formulation stage to avoid misunderstandings and conflict later on, after IP that appears to have market potential has been created or after liability issues have arisen (David & Spence, 2003; Lambert, 2003). Specific issues vary depending on the focus of the collaboration. They can include participants' claims to IP emerging from the collaboration; ownership and licensing of IP; dissemination of scientific data; and apportionment of liability with respect to violations of competition law, violations of human and animal subjects rights, and loss of reputation due to incompetent or unethical conduct (David & Spence, 2003; Reichman & Uhlir, 2003). Existing laws and formal policies regarding these issues vary across organizational and political entities, and new laws, interpretations of law, and policies are inchoate (David & Spence, 2003; Reichman & Uhlir, 2003). For example, in Sweden, university scientists are the sole owners of IP they create even when their research is supported by university and government funding.[6] By way of contrast, in the U.S., the Bayh-Dole Act passed by the federal government in 1980 has encouraged universities to claim ownership rights and commercialize results from government-funded research performed by their faculty members (Reichman & Uhlir, 2003). David and Spence (2003) and Reichman and Uhlir (2003) provide in-depth reviews of current laws and regulations.

Scientific practice is not influenced solely by legal practice. Much of science follows informal traditions and norms, which may vary among the participants in a collaboration. For example, disciplines have different informal traditions regarding how IP is shared. Experimental biologists tend to be secretive about their work and often patent their ideas, whereas mathematicians tend to be more open about their ideas (Walsh & Hong, 2003). This difference is reflected in these disciplines' formal publication policies and practices. *Science*, a leading journal for biologists and other natural scientists, does not allow preprints of articles to be distributed by authors, whereas mathematics journals allow the distribution of preprints (Walsh & Hong, 2003). Disciplines also have different perspectives regarding what constitutes IP. For example, when social scientists and computer scientists collaborate to develop novel types of software applications or new functionality for a software application, who owns the copyright on the software? The computer scientists may consider themselves sole owners because they developed the algorithms and wrote the code. However, the social scientists may want to share ownership because they view their original ideas for the software as a significant contribution.

Model agreements and contracts provided by funding agencies are emerging and the use of such models can reduce the time needed to develop a shared understanding regarding IP and other legal issues (David & Spence, 2003; Lambert, 2003). All participants, including students, should become aware of their rights and responsibilities. Without formal agreements, benefits from the scientific results may be claimed and/or liability denied by the strongest partner. For example, universities and businesses in developed countries may claim all benefits from IP when collaborating with others in developing countries irrespective of the actual source of the IP (Oldham, 2005).

Sustainment Stage

After a collaboration has been formulated and work has begun, it needs to be sustained over a period of time if it is to achieve its goals. Even with the best foundation and plans, numerous challenges can emerge during this stage. Research can be unpredictable and the hoped-for results may not be forthcoming (Atkinson et al., 1998; Latour, 1987) or the results may increase competition and secrecy among participants (Atkinson et al., 1998). Challenges can be identified and addressed through an ongoing process of evaluation in which organizational structure, tasks, communication, and learning are examined and evolve. Without such examination and evolution, a collaboration may fail (Olson & Zimmerman, in press).

Emergent Challenges

When a collaboration is not making progress toward its goals, it may be necessary to revisit its organizational structure, management practices, and goals (Shortliffe, Patel, Cimino, Barnett, & Greens, 1998). Depending on the size of the collaboration and the diversity of its participants, it may take up to a year to reach a shared working understanding, effective organizational structure, and management practices (Fisher & Ball, 2003; Shortliffe et al., 1998). Even after an effective organization has emerged, collaborations may benefit from periodic reviews of their organizational structure and practices. These reviews can be conducted by external stakeholders, including funding agencies and boards of visitors, as well as informal and formal internal review teams (Sonnenwald, 2003c).

When scientists are not collocated, it can be helpful to have one person at each location designated as a site coordinator (Sonnenwald, 2003c). The site coordinator can handle location-specific administrative issues, ranging from reserving a videoconference room for weekly meetings to distributing allocated budget funds. In this way, he or she buffers local scientists from having to deal individually with administrative issues related to the collaboration. In addition, site coordinators can share information about local problems and jointly develop solutions.

Changes in administration and university or departmental policy may also have unforeseen negative effects on a collaborative project. Understandings and agreements not documented in writing may disappear when personnel change or other pressures arise. When a department has only one scientist involved in a specific collaboration, that work may be marginalized and discounted within the department because of its miniscule local presence (Cummings & Kiesler, 2003). Because many university and departmental procedures and systems were designed for intra-departmental or intra-university collaboration, challenges with respect to interdepartmental and interuniversity accounting and reporting procedures may persist throughout this stage (Katz & Martin, 1997).

When resources are not distributed effectively in the formulation stage, scientists may be unable to buy the equipment or hire the students necessary to complete research tasks in this stage. Even when resources have been initially well planned, funding agencies may not grant all monies requested and/or some participants may discover that they need additional funds. When this occurs, there is a tendency to reduce travel among participants and to diminish, or even eliminate, funding for those scientists who are most isolated either in terms of geography or discipline (Cummings & Kiesler, 2003). Individual scientists may understand the need to reallocate funds, but university administrators may be less tolerant of such changes (Olson & Zimmerman, in press). In addition, there may be unexpected delays in obtaining equipment and materials, as well as visas for traveling to other locations because of changes in international politics. Poor infrastructure in developing countries, including unreliable electricity and phone lines, poor roads, and outsiders' lack of knowledge and understanding about these and other local conditions, can cause misunderstandings (Jones, Degu, Mengistu, Wondmikum, Sato, & Kusel, 2004).

Scientists may also discover additional, unexpected differences. For example, they may come to realize they do not have shared norms with respect to students' participation (Cummings & Kiesler, 2003) or sharing information about the research with outsiders (Walsh & Maloney, 2002). As scientists learn from each other during a collaboration, they may come to feel that they need their partners less (Atkinson et al., 1998). Ongoing challenges may also arise from illnesses, deaths, and family problems; honest disagreements regarding plans (Burroughs Wellcome Fund & Howard Hughes Medical Institute, 2004); and staff turnover (Jones et al., 2004). In addition, some individuals may behave inappropriately by not honoring some aspect of the plan, failing to complete tasks, withholding needed information from their partners, or not sharing credit appropriately.

Trust among scientists is an integral aspect of collaboration (Chin et al., 2002; Olson & Olson, 2000), and conflicting views of cooperation and competition may emerge (Atkinson et al., 1998). There are different types of trust that have different managerial implications. Cognitive trust focuses on judgments of competence and reliability, whereas affective trust focuses on interpersonal bonds among individuals. To manage situations where there is a high level of affective trust but a low level of cognitive trust, scientists may assign non-critical tasks to the person who is considered not cognitively trustworthy and establish controls to monitor task progress (Sonnenwald, 2003c). When there is a high level of cognitive trust and a low level of affective trust, controls to monitor research activities and constraints on research activities can be established (Sonnenwald, 2003c). Trust is more easily developed among scientists within the same institution or within the same research team in multi-team, multi-institutional "big science" projects than across institutions or research teams (Shrum, Chompalov, & Genuth, 2001; Zucker, Darby, Brewer, & Peng, 1995).

The size of a collaboration, geographic distances between participating scientists, task interdependency, and competitiveness can exacerbate these challenges (Walsh & Maloney, 2002). Such challenges can make a collaboration stronger and more effective if they are handled constructively (Sonnenwald & Pierce, 2000; Stokols et al., 2005) with "an appropriate balance between diversity and debate among investigators on the one hand, and intellectual integration and social support on the other" (Stokols et al., 2005, p. 212).

Learning

Learning is an integral component of scientific collaboration, especially interdisciplinary collaboration (Klein, 1994; Maglaughin & Sonnenwald, 2005; Solomon, Boud, Leontis, & Staron, 2001). In fact, collaboration is viewed as "one of the most effective forms of knowledge transfer" (Lambert, 2003, p. 38). Scientists need to learn from each other to develop a common working understanding regarding their research project and how they can integrate their specialized knowledge to create new knowledge. Both explicit and tacit knowledge are exchanged among collaborators. Scientists may recognize this in the formulation stage (learning can be a motivation to initiate a collaboration), but it is in the sustainment stage that it may be most challenging. Unfortunately, learning is not traditionally discussed or included in research proposals as a research activity (Davenport, 2005).

Learning requires time, reflexivity, disclosure, risk taking, and trust (Solomon et al., 2001). It takes time to teach and learn from others. As has been mentioned, disciplines and specialized areas of expertise have their own concepts, methods, and languages; it is important to identify and understand these differences. Collaboration with scientists in developing countries may pose additional challenges with respect to learning. Research staff may need additional training and, once trained, they may leave the project for higher paying jobs (Bietz et al., in press; Mervis & Normile, 1998; Oldham, 2005).

These challenges can be met by allocating additional time and resources to learning. Specific strategies to facilitate learning include frequent and regularly scheduled presentations by students to all the scientists working on a project (Sonnenwald et al., 2002). Typically, students are advised by one scientist, or at most two, in specialized areas of research. When students in a collaboration present the purpose of their research, their recent research activities and results, and the challenges they are facing, they help others learn about their and their advisors' specialized area. Scientists' personal Web pages can also facilitate learning by making available copies of their recent publications and pointers to other resources in their areas of expertise (Maglaughlin, 2003). Drafts of publications, including proposals, project reports, and research papers, can also be used to facilitate learning (Creamer, 2004). The drafts help identify differences among scientists' ideas and this can lead to constructive discussions and learning.

Communication

Communication is another fundamental component of collaboration in the sustainment stage. Without ongoing communication, tasks will not be coordinated, scientists will not learn from each other, research results will not be integrated, and perceptions of distrust may emerge. Projects that use more coordination and communication mechanisms have been found to be more successful (Cummings & Kiesler, 2003). It can be difficult to schedule meetings in geographically dispersed collaborations because time zones, national holidays, and organizational calendars differ. As has been discussed, the use of ICT, including e-mail, electronic calendars, audio conferences, videoconferences, and shared electronic boards, can facilitate communication across both time and distance. However, for some tasks, such as brainstorming, face-to-face meetings appear to be the most effective form of interaction (Olson & Olson, 2000).

Stokols et al. (2005) found off-site retreats useful in reducing interdisciplinary tension and increasing intellectual integration. Project meetings can be held in conjunction with national and international conferences. Some projects also have postdoctoral and graduate students learn techniques from scientists in other relevant disciplines (Cummings & Kiesler, 2003). Others seek out individuals who understand the scientific principles and practices of the various disciplines pertinent to the collaboration and who can thus help resolve discipline-based differences and language barriers among the other scientists (Maglaughlin & Sonnenwald, 2005). Still other projects use videoconferences in conjunction with electronic whiteboards to present and discuss group policy and practices (Sonnenwald et al., 2002).

It is important to revisit communication practices, including the use of ICT, periodically during a collaboration. Questionnaires, social network analysis, interviews, and focus group discussions can help identify communication practices that are working well, those that should be improved, and the ways in which they could be improved. Without effective formal and informal communication, successful collaboration is not possible.

Conclusion Stage

Ideally, in this final stage, successful results from the collaboration emerge, although it can happen that funding and other resources simply expire without the hoped-for results having been produced. However, there can be different types of successful results; moreover, the dissemination and publication of results help others to learn from the collaboration.

Definitions of Success

An important result, of course, is the creation of new scientific knowledge, including new research questions and proposals as well as new theories and models (Stokols et al., 2005). These are traditionally measured by publication and citation counts. Lee and Bozeman (2005) have reported that the total number of peer-reviewed journal publications for scientists in U.S. university research centers is significantly associated with the total number of collaborations in which the scientists take part. However, when the number of publications is divided by the number of authors, this association disappears (Lee & Bozeman, 2005). Duque et al. (2005) also found that, in the developing areas of Ghana, Kenya, and the state of Kerala (India), collaboration was not associated with an increase in scientific publication. Thus, there are open questions regarding how collaboration influences publication counts.

Another established measure of success is citation counts. Numerous bibliometric studies have illustrated that co-authored papers in all disciplines investigated tend to be published in higher-impact journals, cited more frequently, and cited for longer periods of time (Frenken, Hölzl, & de Vor, 2005; Glänzel, 2002; Goldfinch, Dale, & DeRouen, 2003; Leimu & Koricheva, 2005; Persson et al., 2004).[7] It appears that having an international co-author can increase a paper's citation rate more than having a national co-author (Frenken et al., 2005). Beaver (2004) has argued that these results occur because co-authorship increases a paper's epistemic authority. Co-authors contribute different types of knowledge and collaborative work may foster more rigorous review of papers, thus increasing the quality of the final publication. Moreover, co-authors can increase the visibility of a paper when they share information about it in conference and workshop presentations, discuss it informally with colleagues, and distribute preprints to colleagues (Katz & Martin, 1997). This increased visibility may also lead to higher citation rates.

Not all successful outcomes have the concreteness of publication and citation counts; they are nonetheless important. These include career, educational, administrative, instrumental, business, and sociopolitical developments (Cummings & Kiesler, 2003; De Cerreño & Keynan, 1998; Olson et al., in press; Sonnenwald, 2003a). Over the course of a collaboration, scientists and staff may acquire new knowledge and skills—not only new scientific knowledge but also that pertaining to research methods, use of ICT, and project management—that can lead to new career opportunities. Educational outcomes include students who successfully complete their studies, as well as those who have been influenced by the research through outreach activities or as project participants. Other educational results are the adoption of more effective teaching methods and practices that are shared among scientists across disciplines and countries or that emerge from innovative collaborative activities, such as joint supervision of students across distances.

Administrative systems and practices may also be changed as a result of a collaboration. For example, when a collaboration is interinstitutional and/or international, it may require and help establish new ways of working with respect to the administration of grants and project accounting. Such changes within an institution may make it easier for subsequent collaborations and new forms of collaboration to be established and sustained at that institution.

Innovative tools and improvements to existing ones may emerge from a collaboration. These tools may be scientific instruments as well as project management, collaboration, and other research support tools. Economic or business results may include patents, licenses, or new products and services that are used to form start-up companies or enable growth opportunities for existing companies.[8] When scientists from different cultures and countries collaborate, improved cross-cultural understanding may be another successful outcome. In sum, scientific collaborations make many different types of contributions and can be an inspiration to others (Olson et al., in press).

Dissemination of Results

Dissemination of research results is an important component of all scientific research. A traditional method of disseminating results of a collaboration is through co-writing presentations and publications. Scientists value most highly those co-authors who show consideration (e.g., exercise tact when criticizing ideas, show appreciation for others' contributions, and are willing to go beyond one's formal commitment as co-author) and who are dependable (e.g., keep commitments, keep others informed about a manuscript's status and changes, and complete writing tasks in a timely fashion) (Bozeman, Street, & Fiorito, 1999).

When a collaboration is interdisciplinary, there may be some disagreement regarding the publication forum (Maglaughlin, 2003). It may be difficult to find an appropriate journal in which to publish interdisciplinary results that do not clearly belong to one discipline or another. In some areas, new interdisciplinary journals (e.g., the *Journal of Biomedical Discovery and Collaboration*, www.j-biomed-discovery.com) are being launched to help address this problem. In addition, scientists from different disciplines may value publications differently. For example, computer scientists highly regard the publication of a paper at an ACM conference where the acceptance rates may range from 15 to 25 percent. However, conferences in fields such as business and psychology may have 75- to 100-percent acceptance rates and, thus, publication at those conferences is not as highly regarded. Furthermore, disciplines have different expectations with respect to paper content and publication speed. In the social sciences, papers can be 20 to 30 pages in length and take two years from time of submission to final publication. In chemistry, papers may be two to 10 pages in length and be published within three months of submission. Problems can emerge when scientists do not know about these differences and fail to discuss the rationale behind their suggestions regarding where and what to publish.

Reaching consensus regarding authorship inclusion and order may also be a delicate issue, and these difficulties increase as competition intensifies (Atkinson et al., 1998). Who among the students, lab technicians, and co-principal investigators should be included as an author? What constitutes a significant contribution meriting co-authorship versus inclusion in the acknowledgments section of a paper? When should authors cite their collaborators' papers? It is recommended that these issues are best discussed when there is a sense of what the research results are and before papers are written (Burroughs Wellcome Fund & Howard Hughes Medical Institute, 2004).

Disciplines have different expectations about the meaning conveyed in authorship order. For example, library and information science typically assumes that authorship order is linked to level of contribution, with descending order indicating descending contribution. On the other hand, biology assumes that the first author is the student or junior scientist who did the bench or lab work and the last author is the principal investigator who developed the initial idea and/or procured the funding necessary for the research. Tenure and promotion committees as well as colleagues may not take into account disciplinary differences with respect to publication forums and authorship order when evaluating a scientist's contributions.

There is a danger of honorary co-authorship where authors are included for political reasons, for example, to help increase the acceptance of the work (Cronin, 2001, 2005). Questions of content responsibility and erasure of style also arise (Cronin, 2001). With large numbers of authors, who is responsible for a paper's content? Whose writing style dominates or whose voice is heard? Cronin (2001, 2005) uses the term "hyperauthorship" to refer to those papers that include massive numbers of authors. For example, the high energy physics and biomedical research communities are proposing that co-authors' contributions be identified on each paper, similar to the way movie credits are handled today. Some journals, such as the *Journal of the American Medical Association (JAMA)*, have established criteria for authorship; they require one or two authors to assume responsibility for the work's integrity and all authors to identify their contributions to the work (for details, see http://jama.ama-assn.org/ifora_current.dtl). Collaborations may, of course, create their own policies regarding co-authorship. For example, the Laser Interferometer Gravitational Wave Observatory

Table 14.1   Emergence of factors during the scientific collaboration process

		Stages of Scientific Collaboration		
	Foundation	Formulation	Sustainment	Conclusion
F **a** **c** **t** **o** **r** **s**	Scientific	Research vision, goals & tasks	Emergent challenges	Definitions of success
	Political	Leadership & organizational structure	Learning	Dissemination of results
	Socio-economic	Information & communications technology	Communication	
	Resource accessibility	Intellectual property & other legal issues		
	Social networks & personal			

(LIGO) has created a publication policy that outlines the co-authorship requirements and publication review procedures that its members must follow (see www.ligo.org/T010168-02.pdf).

Conclusion

The factors that influence scientific collaboration, as reported in the literature and presented in this chapter, are summarized in Table 14.1. A factor first emerges as important during a specific stage of collaboration, yet its importance does not necessarily diminish in subsequent stages. However, as one would hope, the number of new factors emerging decreases as a collaboration progresses through its various stages.

Some of these factors can also crop up in single-investigator scientific research and, yet, in such cases, they may be less complex and easier to address. For example, IP can be easier to handle when there is only one inventor affiliated with an organization. On the other hand, other factors do not emerge at all in single-investigator research. For instance, publication issues, such as co-authorship order and selection of publication forum, are not matters that need to be negotiated in single-investigator work.

Scientists and organizations should consider the benefits and costs of collaboration before deciding to collaborate. Collaboration for its own sake does not seem warranted, given the number of critical success factors that should be taken into account before and during a collaboration. Furthermore, as the number and diversity of participants and the complexity and uncertainty of the scientific work increase, so does the complexity of the factors. The negative consequences of not addressing the factors can be considerable. There is a real need to consider the various factors reviewed here and the effort and other costs required to manage them before embarking on a collaboration. However, when a collaboration can provide new possibilities, it is well worth the effort. The possibilities offered by collaboration can be many and diverse, including the development of new ways of conducting science and the production of new knowledge for the benefit of many.

Although research on scientific collaboration has been on the rise during the past decade, many challenges remain. Important research questions to consider include the following: How do gender and cultural issues affect scientific collaboration, both in the selection of collaborators and in the process of collaboration? How can scientists from different disciplines most effectively develop a common understanding? How does trust emerge and how can it be sustained across distances, cultures, disciplines, and institutions? What methods can be used to evaluate the impact emerging ICT may have on scientific collaboration, and to influence ICT development, before large sums of money and time are spent? How should IP rights and other legal issues be managed in order to support effectively collaboration across disciplines, institutions, and countries? Given today's systems and institutions, how can we best capture and reward the many diverse outcomes of scientific collaboration?

Scientific collaboration continues to increase in importance because it can uniquely address complex, critical problems. As fresh challenges emerge and introduce new goals for science and as the contexts in which science takes place continue to evolve, new collaboration strategies will be required. The need to discover new strategies and to address the many currently unanswered questions illustrates the importance of continuing and expanding research on scientific collaboration.

Acknowledgments

My thanks to Christine Borgman, Ralph Schroeder, and the anonymous reviewers for their valuable feedback on this chapter, as well as to Ida Nolke and Alf Stenbrunn who conducted several literature searches for me.

Endnotes

1. The rate of increase and total percentage of papers co-authored differs between disciplines. Current co-authorship rates range from 99 percent in chemistry (Cronin, Shaw, & La Barre, 2004) and 71 percent in psychology (Cronin, Shaw, & La Barre, 2003) to 46 percent in mathematics (Grossman, 2002) and 4 percent in philosophy (Cronin, Shaw, & La Barre, 2003). The practice can also differ within disciplines: Moody (2004) found that approximately 50 percent of all sociology papers are now co-authored; however, this ranges from 8 percent in Marxist sociology to 53 percent in social welfare.

2. See www.scienceshops.org for more information about science shops.

3. A recent co-author list of a high energy physics paper had 1,699 names (Hofer, McKee, et al., in press).

4. The various types of success that may emerge from a collaboration are discussed in the section entitled "definitions of success."

5. For example, the ATLAS experiment, involving the Large Hadron Collider (LHC) at CERN, is expected to generate 40 million megabytes of data per second, and will need to archive and share among scientists worldwide one petabyte (one million gigabytes) of data per year when it comes online in 2007 (CERN, 2005).

6. However, businesses may ask Swedish scientists to sign over all rights to IP when they fund their research.

7. However, work by Goldfinch et al. (2003, p. 326) suggests that citation rates may differ in countries on the periphery of science: "Increasing the number of domestic institutions involved in co-authorship significantly reduces expected average citation rates."

8. These results may, of course, also emerge from single-investigator research.

References

Adessa, C., & Sonnenwald, D. H. (2003, June). Exploring collaboration among historically black universities and doctoral/research universities in the USA. *UNESCO Conference on Teaching and Learning for Intercultural Understanding. Human Rights and a Culture of Peace.* Jyväskylä, Finland.

Arunachalam, S., & Doss, J. J. (2000). Science in a small country at a time of globalization: Domestic and international collaboration in new biology research in Israel. *Journal of Information Science, 26,* 39–49.

Atkins, D. E., Droegemeier, K. K., Feldman, S. I., Garcia-Molina, H., Klein, M. L., Messerschmitt, D. G., et al. (2003). *Revolutionizing science and engineering through cyberinfrastructure: Final report of the National Science Foundation Blue-Ribbon Advisory Panel on Cyberinfrastructure.* Retrieved June 14, 2005, from www.cise.nsf.gov/evnt/reports/toc.htm

Atkinson, P., Batchelor, C., & Parsons, E. (1998). Trajectories of collaboration and competition in medical discovery. *Science, Technology, & Human Values, 23,* 259–284.

Autio, E., Hameri, A., & Nordberg, M. (1996). A framework of motivations for industry-big science collaboration: A case study. *Journal of Engineering and Technology Management, 13,* 301–314.

Banda, E. (2000). A Europe of science. *Science, 288,* 1963.

Beaver, D. D. (2001). Reflections on scientific collaboration (and its study): Past, present and future. *Scientometrics, 52,* 365–377.

Beaver, D. D. (2004). Does collaborative research have greater epistemic authority? *Scientometrics, 60,* 399–408.

Berman, F., & Brady, H. (2005). *NSF SBE-CISE Workshop on Cyberinfrastructure and the Social Sciences: Final report.* Retrieved May 19, 2005, from www.sdsc.edu/sbe/reports/SBE-CISE-FINAL.pdf

Bietz, M., Naidoo, M., & Olson, G. (in press). International AIDS research collaboratories: The HIV Pathogenesis Program. In G. M. Olson, A. Zimmerman, & N. Bos (Eds.), *Science on the Internet.* Boston: MIT Press.

Birnholtz, J. P., & Bietz, M. J. (2003). Data at work: Supporting sharing in science and engineering. *Proceedings of the 2003 International ACM SIGGROUP Conference on Supporting Groupwork*, 339–348.

Borgman, C. L., & Furner, J. (2002). Scholarly communication and bibliometrics. *Annual Review of Information Science and Technology, 36*, 3–72.

Bos, N., Zimmerman, A., Cooney, D., Olson, J. S., Dahl, E., & Yerkie, J. (in press). From shared databases to communities of practice: A taxonomy of collaboratories. In G. M. Olson, A. Zimmerman, & N. Bos (Eds.), *Science on the Internet.* Boston: MIT Press.

Bozeman, B., & Boardman, C. (2003). *Research and technology collaboration and linkages: Implications from two U.S. case studies: Report prepared for the Council of Science and Technology Advisors (CSTA) Study on Federal S&T Linkages.* Retrieved July 12, 2005, from www.csta-cest.ca/files/usa.pdf

Bozeman, B., & Corley, E. (2004). Scientists' collaboration strategies: Implications for scientific and technical human capital. *Research Policy, 33*, 599–616.

Bozeman, D. P., Street, M. D., & Fiorito, J. (1999). Positive and negative behaviors in the process of research collaboration. *Journal of Social Behavior and Personality, 14*, 159–176.

Bruce, A., Lyall, C., Tait, J., & Williams, R. (2004). Interdisciplinary integration in Europe: The case of the Fifth Framework Program. *Futures, 36*, 457–470.

Brydon-Miller, M. (1997). Participatory action research: Psychology and social change. *Journal of Social Issues, 53*, 657–666.

Burroughs Wellcome Fund & Howard Hughes Medical Institute. (2004). *Making the right moves: A practical guide to scientific management for postdocs and new faculty.* Retrieved June 14, 2005, from www.hhmi.org/grants/office/graduate/lab_book.html

CERN. (2005). *The technical challenges of ATLAS.* Retrieved July 23, 2005, from http://atlas.ch/atlas_brochures/atlas_brochures_pdf/atlas_tech_full.pdf

Chin, G., Myers, J., & Hoyt, D. (2002). Social networks in the virtual science laboratory. *Communications of the ACM, 45*(8), 87–92.

Chompalov, I., Genuth, J., & Shrum, W. (2002). The organization of scientific collaborations. *Research Policy, 31*, 749–767.

Cohen, J. (2000). Balancing the collaboration equation. *Science, 288*, 2155–2159.

Cohen, J., & Linton, M. (2003). The next frontier for HIV/AIDS. *Science, 301*, 1650–1655.

Collaboration in extremis. (2002, May 16). *Nature, 417*, 207.

Crane, D. (1972). *Invisible colleges: Diffusion of knowledge in scientific communities.* Chicago: University of Chicago Press.

Creamer, E. G. (2004). Collaborators' attitudes about differences of opinion. *The Journal of Higher Education, 75*, 556–571.

Cronin, B. (2001). Hyperauthorship: A postmodern perversion or evidence of a structural shift in scholarly communication practices? *Journal of the American Society for Information Science and Technology, 52*, 558–569.

Cronin, B. (2005). *The hand of science: Academic writing and its rewards.* Lanham, MD: Scarecrow Press.

Cronin, B., Shaw, D., & La Barre, K. (2003). A cast of thousands: Coauthorship and subauthorship collaboration in the 20th century as manifested in the scholarly journal literature of psychology and philosophy. *Journal of the American Society for Information Science and Technology, 54*, 855–871.

Cronin, B., Shaw, D., & La Barre, K. (2004). Visible, less visible, and invisible work: Patterns of collaboration in 20th century chemistry. *Journal of the American Society for Information Science and Technology, 55*, 160–168.

Cummings, J., & Kiesler, S. (2003). *KDI Initiative: Multidisciplinary scientific collaborations* (NSF Report). Arlington, VA: National Science Foundation. Retrieved November 14, 2004, from www.cise.nsf.gov/kdi/links.html

Cummings, J., & Kiesler, S. (2005). Collaborative research across disciplinary and organizational boundaries. *Social Studies of Science, 35*, 703–722.

Davenport, E. (2005, June). *Understanding interdisciplinary research design. Case study: Compliance and compromise.* Presentation at the Social Factors in Scientific Collaboration Workshop, First International Conference on e-Social Science, Manchester, UK.

Davenport, E., & Hall, H. (2002). Organizational knowledge and communities of practice. *Annual Review of Information Science and Technology, 36*, 171–227.

David, P. A. (2005, January). *Towards a cyberinfrastructure for enhanced scientific collaboration: Providing its "soft" foundations may be the hardest part.* Paper prepared for the international conference on Advancing Knowledge and the Knowledge-Economy, National Academy of Science, Washington, DC.

David, P. A., & Spence, M. (2003). *Towards institutional infrastructures for e-science: The scope of the challenge* (Oxford Internet Institute Research Reports). Oxford, UK: University of Oxford. Retrieved September 12, 2005, from www.oii.ox.ac.uk/resources/publications/RR2.pdf

De Cerreño, A. L. C., & Keynan, A. (Eds.). (1998). Scientific cooperation, state conflict: The roles of scientists in mitigating international discord. *Annals of the New York Academy of Sciences, 866.*

Drake, P., Ludden, D., Nzongola-Ntalaja, G., Patel, S., & Shevtsova, L. (2000). *International scholarly collaboration: Lessons from the past. A report of the Social Science Research Council Inter-regional Working Group on International Scholarly Collaboration* (SSRC Working Paper Series, 3). New York: Social Science Research Council. Retrieved March 9, 2006, from www.ssrc.org/programs/humancap/publications/workingpaper3.pdf

Duque, R. B., Ynalvez, M., Sooryamoorthy, R., Mbatia, P., Dzorgbo, D. S., & Shrum, W. (2005). Collaboration paradox: Scientific productivity, the Internet, and problems of research in developing areas. *Social Studies of Science, 35*, 755–785.

Eisenhart, M. A., & Finkel, E. (1998). *Women's science: Learning and succeeding from the margins.* Chicago: University of Chicago Press.

Ellis, D., Oldridge, R., & Vasconcelos, A. (2004). Community and virtual community. *Annual Review of Information Science and Technology, 38*, 145–186.

Etzkowitz, H., & Leydesdorff, L. (2000). The dynamics of innovation: From national systems and 'mode 2' to a triple helix of university-industry-government relations. *Research Policy, 29*, 109–123.

Finholt, T. (2002). Collaboratories. *Annual Review of Information Science and Technology, 36*, 73–108.

Fisher, P. A., & Ball, T. J. (2003). Tribal participatory research: Mechanisms of a collaborative model. *American Journal of Community Psychology, 32*, 207–216.

Frenken, K., Hölzl, W., & de Vor, F. (2005). The citation impact of research collaborations: The case of European biotechnology and applied microbiology (1988–2002). *Journal of Engineering and Technology Management, 22*, 9–30.

Gast, A. P. (2003). *The impact of restricting information access on science and technology.* Retrieved June 14, 2005, from www.aau.edu/research/gast.pdf

Gibbons, M., Limoges, C., Nowotny, H., Schwartzman, S., Scott, P., & Trow, M. (1994). *The new production of knowledge: The dynamics of science and research in contemporary societies.* Thousand Oaks, CA: Sage Publications.

Glänzel, W. (2002). Co-authorship patterns and trends in the sciences (1980–1998): A bibliometric study with implications for database indexing and search strategies. *Library Trends, 50*, 461–471.

Goldfinch, S., Dale, T., & DeRouen, K. (2003). Science from the periphery: Collaboration, networks and 'periphery effects' in the citation of New Zealand Crown Research Institute articles, 1995–2000. *Scientometrics, 57*, 321–337.

Grey, D., Lindblad, M., & Rudolph, J. (2001). Industry-university research centers: A multivariate analysis of member retention. *Journal of Technology Transfer, 26*, 247–254.

Grossman, J. W. (2002). The evolution of the mathematical research collaboration graph. *Congressus Numeratium, 158*, 202–212.

Hara, N., Solomon, P., Kim, S., & Sonnenwald, D. H. (2003). An emerging view of scientific collaboration: Scientists' perspectives on factors that impact collaboration. *Journal of the American Society for Information Science and Technology, 54*, 952–965.

Havemann, F. (2001). Collaboration behavior of Berlin life science researchers in the last two decades of the twentieth century as reflected in the Science Citation Index. *Scientometrics, 52*, 435–443.

Hey, T., & Trefethen, A. (2003). e-Science and its implications. *Philosophical Transactions of the Royal Society London A: Mathematical, Physical and Engineering Sciences, 361*, 1809–1825.

Hofer, E. C., Bos, N., & Olson, J. (in press). Collaborative technologies. In G. M. Olson, A. Zimmerman, & N. Bos (Eds.), *Science on the Internet.* Boston: MIT Press.

Hofer, E. C., McKee, S., Birnholz, J., & Avery, P. (in press). High energy physics: The large hadron collider collaborations. In G. M. Olson, A. Zimmerman, & N. Bos (Eds.), *Science on the Internet.* Boston: MIT Press

Iivonen, M., & Sonnenwald, D. H. (2000). The use of technology in international collaboration. *Proceedings of the Annual Meeting of the American Society for Information Science*, 78–92.

Jeffrey, P. (2003). Smoothing the waters: Observations on the process of cross-disciplinary research collaboration. *Social Studies of Science, 33*, 539–562.

Jones, J. T., Degu, G., Mengistu, G., Wondmikum, Y., Sato, H., & Kusel, J. R. (2004). Factors involved in international scientific collaborations in Ethiopia, using a research project on schistosomiasis as an example. In R. Mita & K. Satoh (Eds.), *International collaboration in community health: Proceedings of the 7th meeting of the Hirosaki International Forum of Medical Science held in Hirosaki, Japan between 28 and 29 October 2003* (International Congress Series, 1267; pp. 71–78). Amsterdam: Elsevier.

Katz, J. S., & Martin, B. R. (1997). What is research collaboration? *Research Policy, 26*, 1–18.

Klein, J. T. (1994). Finding interdisciplinary knowledge and information. In J. Klein & W. Doty (Eds.), *Interdisciplinary studies today* (pp. 7–33). San Francisco: Jossey Bass.

Klein, J. T. (2004). Prospects for transdisciplinarity. *Futures, 36*, 515–526.

Kling, R. (2004). The Internet and unrefereed scholarly publishing. *Annual Review of Information Science and Technology, 38*, 591–637.

Kling, R., & Callahan, E. (2003). Electronic journals, the Internet, and scholarly communication. *Annual Review of Information Science and Technology, 37*, 127–177.

Kling, R., & McKim, G. (2000). Not just a matter of time: Field differences and the shaping of electronic media in supporting scientific communication. *Journal of the American Society for Information Science, 51*, 1306–1320.

Kling, R., McKim, G., & King, A. (2003). A bit more to IT: Scholarly communication forums as socio-technical interaction networks. *Journal of the American Society for Information Science and Technology, 54*, 47–67.

Kouzes, R. T., Myers, J. D., & Wulf, W. A. (1996). Collaboratories: Doing science on the Internet. *IEEE Computer, 29*, 40–46.

Kraut, R. E., Galegher, J., & Egido, C. (1988). Relationships and tasks in scientific research collaboration. *Human-Computer Interaction, 3*, 31–55.

Kuhn, T. S. (1970). *The structure of scientific revolutions* (2nd ed.). Chicago: University of Chicago Press.

Lambert, R. (2003). *Lambert Review of Business-University Collaboration: Final Report.* London, UK: HM Treasury. Retrieved June 12, 2005, from www.hm-treasury.gov.uk/media/DDE/65/lambert_review_final_450.pdf

Latour, B. (1987). *Science in action.* Cambridge, MA: Harvard University Press.

Lee, S., & Bozeman, B. (2005). The impact of research collaboration on scientific productivity. *Social Studies of Science, 35*, 673–702.

Leimu, R., & Koricheva, J. (2005). Does scientific collaboration increase the impact of ecological articles? *BioScience, 55*, 438–443.

Lessig, L. (2004). *Free culture.* New York: Penguin Press.

Let data speak to data. (2005). *Nature, 438*, 521. Retrieved December 16, 2005, from www.nature.com/nature/journal/v438/n7068/full/438531a.html

Leydesdorff, L., & Ward, J. (2005). Science shops: A kaleidoscope of science-society collaborations in Europe. *Public Understanding of Science, 14*, 353–372.

Liang, L., Guo, Y., & Davis, M. (2002). Collaborative patterns and age structures in Chinese publications. *Scientometrics, 54*, 473–489.

Maglaughlin, K. L. (2003). *An exploration of interdisciplinary scientific collaboration factors.* Unpublished doctoral dissertation, University of North Carolina, Chapel Hill.

Maglaughlin, K. L., & Sonnenwald, D. H. (2005). Factors that impact interdisciplinary natural science research collaboration in academia. *Proceedings of the Conference of the International Society for Scientometrics and Informetrics*, 499–508.

Marsh, S., & Dibben, M. R. (2003). The role of trust in information science and technology. *Annual Review of Information Science and Technology, 37*, 465–498.

Mathiasson, L. (2002). Collaborative practice research. *Information Technology & People, 15*, 321–345.

McGinley, S., & Charnie, J. (2003). Peace building through scientific collaboration. *Arizona Land & People, 48*(1). Retrieved July 25, 2005, from http://ag.arizona.edu/landand people/spring2003/article7_l&p.pdf

Mervis, J., & Normile, D. (1998). North-South relations: Lopsided partnerships give way to real collaboration. *Science, 279,* 1477.

Moody, J. (2004). The structure of a social science collaboration network: Disciplinary cohesion from 1963 to 1999. *American Sociological Review, 69,* 213–238.

Nan, N., Johnston, E. W., Olson, J. S., & Bos, N. (2005). Beyond being in the lab: Using multi-agent modeling to isolate competing hypotheses. *Proceedings of the ACM Conference on Human Factors in Computing Systems,* 1693–1696.

National Institutes of Health. (2000). *NCRR Biomedical Collaboratories Workshop report.* Bethesda, MD: National Institutes of Health, National Center for Research Resources. Retrieved December 31, 2005, from www.ncrr.nih.gov/biotech/btcollabwrkshprpt10-2000.pdf

National Research Council. (1993). *National collaboratories: Applying information technology for scientific research.* Washington, DC: National Academy Press.

National Science Board. (2004). *Science and engineering indicators.* Arlington, VA: National Science Foundation. Retrieved December 16, 2005, from www.nsf.gov/sbe/srs/seind04/start.htm

Newman, M. E. J. (2001). The structure of scientific collaboration networks. *Proceedings of the National Academy of Sciences, 98,* 404–409.

Newman, M. E. J. (2004). Coauthorship networks and patterns of scientific collaboration. *Proceedings of the National Academy of Sciences, 191*(Suppl. 1), 5200–5205.

Normile, D. (2003). Taiwan-China collaboration: A bridge over troubled waters. *Science, 300,* 1074–1075.

Oldham, G. (2005). *International scientific collaboration: A quick guide.* Retrieved June 30, 2005, from www.scidev.net/dossiers/index.cfm?fuseaction=policybrief&dossier=13&policy=60

Olson, G. M., & Olson, J. S. (2000). Distance matters. *Human–Computer Interaction, 15,* 139–178.

Olson, G. M., Teasley, S., Bietz, M., & Cogburn, D. L. (2002). Collaboratories to support distributed science: The example of international HIV/AIDS research. *Proceedings of the Conference of the South African Institute of Computer Scientists and Information Technologists,* 44–51.

Olson, G. M., & Zimmerman, A. (in press). Time matters: The evolution of collaboratories. In G. M. Olson, A. Zimmerman, & N. Bos (Eds.), *Science on the Internet.* Boston: MIT Press.

Olson, J. S., Olson, G. M., & Cooney, D. (in press). Success factors: Bridging distance in collaboration. In G. M. Olson, A. Zimmerman, & N. Bos (Eds.), *Science on the Internet.* Boston: MIT Press.

Owen-Smith, J., Riccaboni, M., Pammolli, F., & Powell, W. W. (2002). A comparison of U.S. and European university-industry relations in the life sciences. *Management Science, 48,* 24–42.

Palmer, C. L. (2001). *Work at the boundaries of science: Information and the interdisciplinary research process.* Dordrecht, NL: Kluwer.

Parent, A., Bertrand, F., Côté, G., & Archambault, E. (2003). *Scientometric study on collaboration between India and Canada, 1990–2001.* Montreal, Canada: Science-Metrix.

Retrieved July 10, 2005, from www.science-metrix.com/pdf/SM_2003_009_DFAIT_Indo-Canadian_S&T_Collaboration.pdf

Pax Mediterranea. (2003). *The future collaboration between university and civic associations in Sevilla* (INTERACTS WP5 National Report). Retrieved June 14, 2005, from http://members.chello.at/wilawien/interacts/interacts_easw_spain.pdf

Persson, O., Glänzel, W., & Danell, R. (2004). Inflationary bibliometric values: The role of scientific collaboration and the need for relative indicators in evaluative studies. *Scientometrics, 60*, 421–432.

Reichman, J. H., & Uhlir, P. F. (2003). A contractually reconstructed research commons for scientific data in a highly protectionist intellectual property environment. *Law and Contemporary Problems, 66*, 315–462. Retrieved September 12, 2005, from www.law.duke.edu/journals/lcp/articles/lcp66dWinterSpring2003p315.htm

Rogers, E. (1995). *Diffusion of innovations*. New York: The Free Press.

Salter, L., & Hearn, A. (Eds.). (1996). *Outside the lines: Issues in interdisciplinary research*. Montreal, Canada: McGill-Queen's University.

Schiff, L. (2002). *Developing successful models for large-scale, collaborative biomedical research projects* (Boston Cure Project Educational Paper). Retrieved July 14, 2005, from www.bostoncure.org/downloads/collaborative-science.pdf

Science of Collaboratories. (2003). *Workshops: The social underpinnings of collaboration: Final summary*. Retrieved June 14, 2005, from www.scienceofcollaboratories.org/Workshops/WorkshopJune42001/index.php?FinalSummary

Secrest, L. A., Lassiter, B. S., Armistead, L. P., Wyckoff, S. C., Johnson, J., Williams, W. B., et al. (2004). The Parents Matter! program: Building a successful investigator-community partnership. *Journal of Child and Family Studies, 13*, 35–45.

Sell, S. K. (2003). *Private power, public law: The globalization of intellectual property rights*. Cambridge, UK: Cambridge University Press.

Shortliffe, E. H., Patel, V. L., Cimino, J. J., Barnett, G. O., & Greenes, R. A. (1998). A study of collaboration among medical informatics research laboratories. *Artificial Intelligence in Medicine, 12*, 97–123.

Shrum, W., Chompalov, I., & Genuth, J. (2001). Trust, conflict and performance in scientific collaborations. *Social Studies of Science, 31*, 681–730.

Smith, D., & Katz, J. S. (2000). *HEFCE fundamental review of research policy and funding: Collaborative approaches to research: Final report*. Retrieved July 7, 2005, from www.sussex.ac.uk/Users/sylvank/pubs/collc.pdf

Solomon, N., Boud, D., Leontios, M., & Staron, M. (2001). Researchers are learners too: Collaboration in research on workplace learning. *Journal of Workplace Learning, 13*, 274–281.

Sonnenwald, D. H. (2003a). Expectations for a scientific collaboratory: A case study. *Proceedings of the 2003 International ACM SIGGROUP Conference on Supporting Group Work*, 68–74.

Sonnenwald, D. H. (2003b). The conceptual organization: An emergent collaborative R&D organizational form. *Science Public Policy, 30*, 261–272.

Sonnenwald, D. H. (2003c). Managing cognitive and affective trust in the conceptual R&D organization. In M. Huotari & M. Iivonen (Eds.), *Trust in knowledge management and systems in organizations* (pp. 82–106). Hershey, PA: Idea Publishing.

Sonnenwald, D. H., Maglaughlin, K. L., & Whitton, M. C. (2004). Designing to support situational awareness across distances: An example from a scientific collaboratory. *Information Processing & Management, 40*, 989–1011.

Sonnenwald, D. H., & Pierce, L. (2000). Information behavior in dynamic group work contexts: Interwoven situational awareness, dense social networks, and contested collaboration in command and control. *Information Processing & Management, 36*, 461–479.

Sonnenwald, D. H., Solomon, P., Hara, N., Bolliger, R., & Cox, T. (2002). Collaboration in the large: Using video conferencing to facilitate large group interaction. In A. Gunasekaran & O. Khalil (Eds.), *Knowledge and information technology in 21st century organizations: Human and social perspectives* (pp. 136–155). Hershey, PA: Idea Publishing.

Sonnenwald, D. H., Whitton, M. C., & Maglaughlin, K. L. (2003). Evaluating a scientific collaboratory: Results of a controlled experiment. *ACM Transactions on Computer–Human Interaction, 10*(2), 150–176.

Sooryamoorthy, R., Duque, R. B., Ynalvez, M. A., & Shrum, W. (2005). *Scientific collaboration and the Kerala Model: Does the Internet make a difference?* Retrieved March 20, 2006, from http://worldsci.net/papers.htm

Star, S. L., & Ruhleder, K. (1996). Steps towards an ecology of infrastructure: Design and access for large information spaces. *Information Systems Research, 7*, 111–134.

Steiner, I. D. (1972). *Group processes and productivity.* New York: Academic Press.

Stokes, D. E. (1997). *Pasteur's quadrant: Basic science and technological innovation.* Washington, DC: Brookings Institution Press.

Stokols, D., Harvey, R., Gress, J., Fuqua, J., & Phillips, K. (2005). In vivo studies of transdisciplinary scientific collaboration. *American Journal of Preventative Medicine, 28*, 202–213.

Thagard, P. (1997). Collaborative knowledge. *Nous, 31*, 242–261.

Third World Academy of Sciences. (2004). *Building scientific capacity.* Trieste, Italy: The Academy. Retrieved June 14, 2005, from www.ictp.trieste.it/~twas/pdf/CapBuild Report.pdf

Traore, N., & Landry, R. (1997). On the determinants of scientists' collaboration. *Science Communication, 19*, 124–140.

Traweek, S. (1988). *Beamtimes and lifetimes: The world of high energy physicists.* Cambridge, MA: Harvard University Press.

U.K. Research Council. (2005). *e-Science Core Program.* Retrieved June 14, 2005, from www.research-councils.ac.uk/escience

U.S. Office of Science and Technology Policy. (2000). *Examples of international scientific collaboration and the benefits to society.* Retrieved June 14, 2005, from http://clinton4.nara.gov/WH/EOP/OSTP/html/00426_7.html

Van House, N. A. (2004). Science and technology studies and information studies. *Annual Review of Information Science and Technology, 38*, 3–86.

Velho, L., & Velho, P. (1996). Scientific collaboration of advanced/developing countries in biological sciences: The case of the Maraca Rain Forest project. *Cadernos de Ciência & Tecnologia, Brasília, 13*, 9–20.

Wagner, C., & Leydesdorff, L. (2005). Mapping the network of global science: Comparing international co-authorships from 1990 to 2000. *International Journal of Technology and Globalization, 1*, 185–208.

Wagner, C. S., Staheli, L., Silberglitt, R., Wong, A., & Kadtke, J. (2002). *Linking effectively: Learning lessons from successful collaboration in science and technology* (RAND Documented Briefing, DB-345-OSTP). Santa Monica, CA: RAND Corporation. Retrieved June 16, 2005, from www.rand.org/publications/DB/DB345/

Walsh, J. P., & Bayma, T. (1996). Computer networks and scientific work. *Social Studies of Science, 26*, 661–703.

Walsh, J. P., & Hong, W. (2003). Secrecy is increasing in step with competition. *Nature, 422*, 801–802.

Walsh, J. P., Kucker, S., Maloney, N. G., & Gabbay, S. (2000). Connecting minds: Computer-mediated communication and scientific work. *Journal of the American Society for Information Science, 51*, 1295–1305.

Walsh, J. P., & Maloney, N. G. (2002). Computer network use, collaboration structures and productivity. In P. Hinds & S. Kiesler (Eds.), *Distributed work* (pp. 433–458). Cambridge, MA: MIT Press.

Warnow-Blewett, J., Genuth, J., & Weart, S. R. (2001). *AIP study of multi-institutional collaborations: Final report.* College Park, MD: Center for the History of Physics, American Institute of Physics.

Welch, G., Fuchs, H., Cairns, B., Mayer-Patel, K., Sonnenwald, D. H., Yang, R., et al. (in press). Remote 3D medical consultation. *Journal of Mobile Multimedia.*

Whitley, R. (2000). *The intellectual and social organization of the sciences.* Oxford, UK: Oxford University Press.

Williams, N. (1998). Ireland: Peace process set to boost collaboration. *Science, 280*, 1519.

Wilson, D. (1999). *Fisheries science collaboration: The critical role of the community* (Institute for Fisheries Management and Coastal Community Development, Research Publication 45). Retrieved July 10, 2005, from www.ifm.dk/reports/45.pdf

World Health Organization. (2003). *Severe acute respiratory syndrome (SARS) – Multi-country outbreak – Update 31.* Retrieved June 14, 2005, from www.who.int/csr/don/2003_04_ 16/en/index.html

Wray, K. B. (2002). The epistemic significance of collaborative research. *Philosophy of Science, 69*, 150–168.

Wulf, W. A. (1993). The collaboratory opportunity. *Science, 261*, 854–855.

Ziman, J. (2000). *Real science: What it is and what it means.* Cambridge, UK: Cambridge University Press.

Zucker, L. G., Darby, M. R., Brewer, M. B., & Peng, Y. (1995). *Collaboration structure and information dilemmas in biotechnology: Organizational boundaries as trust production* (NBER Working Paper No. W5199). Retrieved December 6, 2005, from http://ssrn.com/abstract=225262

CHAPTER 15

Human Geography and Information Studies

Greg Downey
University of Wisconsin-Madison

Introduction: The Foundations of LIS in an Environment of Change

At the small but well-respected library and information studies (LIS) program where I work as an assistant professor, I recently confronted an interesting contradiction in my doctoral education duties. I was slated to teach a required doctoral seminar on the "foundations of library and information studies," which, as a philosophical and historical survey taught well by many senior faculty before me, should have involved relatively little work to prepare and present (always an attraction when one is on the tenure track). Yet as a young faculty member hired as much for my professional experience in "new media" as for my academic training in historical scholarship, I knew that both my peers and my students expected me to teach "foundations" from an innovative, if not radical, new angle. And the timing of my turn at this task was fraught with tension—a quick review of the LIS literature through the 1990s revealed a clear sense among both practitioners and academics that in the post-Reagan (neoliberal governance), post-Cold War (economic globalization), post-World Wide Web (internetworked communication), and, now, post-9/11 (security-conscious) world, all of the rules of the game had changed, both for librarianship as a profession and information studies as a domain of research. Where was I to look in the large and diverse literature of LIS for some way through these changes?

My first assessment was that certain strands of the "IS" side of LIS seemed to be doing the most creative work in analyzing and theorizing these changes, especially as they connected to social practice. Indeed, thanks to interdisciplinary scholars such as the late Rob Kling (see for example Kling, 1996), a whole new field of "social informatics" had grown in the short moment between the rudimentary information appliances and proprietary online networks of the 1980s and the explosion of information infrastructure and open standards of the 1990s (Sawyer & Eschenfelder, 2002). It was the "L" side of LIS, however, that seemed to be wrestling with the contradiction between foundations and change most urgently—where, in accord with the four "posts-" enumerated earlier, abstract proposals for government budget cuts, privatized technological services, equitable Internet access, and restrictions on information freedom became concrete problems. The oft-cited Benton Foundation (1997) report *Buildings, Books, and Bytes*, juxtaposing the views of library professionals with those of library publics, warned that "Americans continue to have a love affair with their libraries, but they have difficulty figuring out where libraries fit in the new digital world" (p. 184). Academics such as Molz and Dain (1999, pp. 2, 184) replied that, contrary to fears of the "disintermediation" of librarians in the relationship between information seekers and information sources, libraries would retain their place as "agencies offering to the public the means of acquiring information, knowledge, education, aesthetic experience, and entertainment." And although, as Buschman (2003, pp. 3, 7) has suggested, "we have been declaring crises in the field [of librarianship] for more than thirty years," even he recently argued that in order to secure both funding and legitimacy from states and publics, libraries need to reformulate "a meaningful, consistent, and sustainable intellectual basis" for their existence. The solution to the perils of change was, in each of these cases, a reassertion of foundations—that information remained a valuable public good and that funding the collective organization of, and access to, that information remained a legitimate public expenditure.

But simply reasserting these foundational LIS claims at this historical moment of rapid change was not a satisfying solution to my seminar dilemma. Repeated claims of the almost ahistorical importance of the "things" of LIS study—from individual information artifacts and information workers to larger-scale information/communication technologies (ICTs), such as networks, and information/communication agencies (ICAs), such as libraries—suggested that something might be missing from these foundations. Consider, for a moment, that each of the "posts" involved shifts not only in the meaning of such things, but also in the space and time relations in which they are situated: In the post-Reagan era, the locus of state funding for information agencies has shifted away from long-term policies of national governments to crisis funding by local communities; in the post-Cold War economy, the circulation of economic information through transnational corporations now penetrates every corner of the globe in real time; post-Web, the old models of physical publishing and mass broadcasting have been augmented by virtual online networking; and post-9/11, the risks to human capital and human life from crime, corruption, and terror are managed more and more through increased surveillance and control over the flows of global communication. Could part of our contradictory moment be that the foundations of LIS simply do not provide us with all the tools to conceptualize such rapid change in the spatial and temporal aspects of information production, organization, distribution, and consumption? Where might

LIS researchers and professionals find the tools to shift their focus away from "things" in abstract isolation toward "processes" and "relations" unfolding across space and time?

For me, the answer to the contradiction of teaching a foundations seminar in a time of endemic change was to introduce my students to the relevance of human geography in library and information research. After all, ICTs and ICAs are, by definition, sets of tools and systems, practices and organizations that allow informational objects (like ideas) to transcend the time and space of human activity. And human geography is, by definition, the study of the interlinked temporality and spatiality of human activity:

> Geographical knowledge records, analyzes and stores information about the spatial distribution and organization of those conditions (both naturally occurring and humanly created) that provide the material basis for the reproduction of social life. At the same time it promotes conscious awareness of how such conditions are subject to continuous transformation through human action. (Harvey, 1984, p. 1)

A newcomer to both fields might assume it would be easy to find direct connections between LIS and human geography in the literature of each discipline. However, even though the LIS literature is suffused with arguments for treating libraries as "places" and considering information in "networks," such appeals are often made without any but the most superficial connection to the human geography literature (for example, Martell, 1999). And for its part, although human geography has been quick to acknowledge the importance of ICTs and ICAs to the new landscape of globalized social action being constructed in the 21st century, it has not engaged very deeply with the long history of conceptual and theoretical work in LIS. As Brown and O'Hara (2003, p. 1566) recently argued in the geography journal *Environment and Planning A,*

> technology in geography has been a topic which has been explored ... mainly in terms of politics, social theory, and measurable changes to geographic organization. What has been much less researched is how technology impacts on the way individuals manage places and their activities in space.

This disconnect between LIS and geography is all the more surprising because, over the last few decades, certain strands within geography—especially qualitative research in human geography—have increasingly intersected with other academic areas of research. Some have termed this the "spatial turn" in the social sciences and humanities, a shift in direction bringing with it both familiar interpretive methods, such as ethnographic interviewing and theory-building, and new analytical concepts, such as "place," "space," and "scale," on par with the so-called "linguistic turn" that reinforced methods of textual analysis and introduced the concepts of "metaphor," "text," and "audience" to social science and humanities scholars decades before (Day, 2005; Pickles, 1999; Rorty, 1967; Winchester, 2000). Of course, such connections also meant that human geography was caught up in the same debate over postmodernity (as a social condition) and postmodernism (as an academic and political response to that social condition) as the rest of the humanities and the social sciences—an encounter which is still playing out today (Dear & Flusty, 2002; Harvey, 1989). Crucially important to the spatial turn, however, was that it incorporated not only ideas about space, but notions of time as well—thus allowing geographers to engage both with historians in talking about spatial change over time and with sociologists in talking about temporal changes with regard to place (Hornbeck, Earle, & Rodrigue, 1996). Yet dialogue with those who study the technologies and practices of overcoming space and time—especially ICTs—has been minimal.

In this chapter, I will introduce the discipline of human geography as a way of asking questions, conceptualizing answers, and seeing "things" such as information objects and information actors, information technologies, and information agencies both relationally and dialectically—that is, as operating in, on, and through material, social, and virtual landscapes. I argue that, especially at this historical moment, such ways of seeing can be productive for scholars in LIS—above all, those scholars who focus on human interactions with information in all its technological and social forms. Three powerful connections between LIS and human geography—the geography of the Internet (Zook, 2006), the exploration of "virtual community" (Ellis, Oldridge, & Vasconcelos, 2004), and the question of "information and equity" (Lievrouw & Farb, 2003)—have already been explored by recent *ARIST* writers; I will not duplicate their work here. Instead, in the first part of this chapter, I consider the discipline of human geography in terms of "what it produces," for, as geographer Erica Schoenberger (2001, p. 371) has pointed out, "Disciplines do not merely name a particular combination of object and method. They *generate* abstractions—such as 'economy' or 'society' or 'nature'—that become the focus of our work and they define appropriate ways of studying these entities." In other words, they produce "epistemological and ontological commitments" (p. 371). The most basic abstractions that human geography has generated, such as place, space, and scale, must be understood through particular commitments within human geography to studying *processes* rather than *things*—meaning that human geography attempts to move beyond reductionist conceptions and explanations and instead embrace messier but more productive relational, dialectical, and critical representations of change (Harvey, 1996, pp. 49–56). Given this disciplinary groundwork, in the second part of the chapter, I consider two key terrains where geographers have attempted to engage ICTs and ICAs relationally, dialectically, and critically: (1) the production of meaningful virtual geographies for social action as a result of material investment (and disinvestment) choices in wired and wireless infrastructure and (2) the reimagining of the importance of material sites of knowledge production, consumption, and labor (especially in urban areas) and the connections between these physical places and the virtual spaces swirling around them. Because this work in geography has been focused heavily on "e-commerce" topics, in the last part of the chapter I return to the question of the "place" of the library (and of LIS) in the new hybrid geography and suggest some ways that researchers in both fields might engage with each other's work. My readings and representations of both geography and LIS in this chapter are inevitably partial. I hope the intersection of these two fields that I describe will provide a useful starting point for researchers on both sides wishing to travel into new territory.

Defining the Discipline of Human Geography

On the surface, human geography and LIS already share many characteristics. Each discipline appreciates both idiographic (descriptive) and nomothetic (explanatory) forms of research; each discipline demands both the novel pursuit of basic research and the regular production of professional knowledge (often with a different set of journals for each); each discipline has its opposing wings of administrative versus critical theory (each pointing out the normative and political-economic grounding of the other); and each discipline embraces both positivist quantitative methods and interpretive qualitative methods (with only a few practitioners able to integrate the two effectively) (Kitchin & Tate, 2000). For example, within LIS, Benoît (2002, p. 452) has warned of "an uncritical emphasis on philosophies of science [i.e., logical positivism] employed in LIS [that] favor data and diminish the role of the individual's interest" and argued that LIS should also embrace "the philosophies of interpretation, as articulated in communicative, pragmatic, and hermeneutic thought." Similarly, human geographers have heard Sheppard (2001, p. 536) explain how "progressive human geography can take advantage of quantitative practices," especially when these practices are disentangled from the assumptions of neoclassical economic theory.

Another point of connection is that for both fields, over the last few decades, the social worlds they analyze have been radically transformed by both technological innovation and political-economic restructuring. Recent "postmodern" innovations in geography especially have been driven by the need to find new concepts, theories, and methods for representing and understanding a world in which "postindustrial" computer-based ICTs and ICAs have enabled new possibilities for economic expansion, geopolitical tension, and knowledge production. Within LIS, journals such as *The Information Society* have arisen to address explicitly these new realities, which are often centered around a threefold definition of globalization, such as that offered by Stolfi and Sussman (2001, pp. 51–53): (1) a neoliberal ideological shift in the course of which "the dominant discourse on collectively held values shifted from an emphasis on equity (e.g., participatory values, affirmative action, welfare) to efficiency (e.g., raising productivity, increasing competition, deregulation)"; (2) digital convergence, which "accelerated throughout the Cold War era with the generous support of government-sponsored technological R&D"; and (3) the rise of transnational corporations, "actors which were positioned to derive the greatest advantage from a global information and communications infrastructure." At least two out of these three characteristics of globalization are well-worn territory for human geography.

The two fields also share similar problems. Both human geography and LIS have been accused of "borrowing" methods and theories from other disciplines rather than growing their own, resulting in regular and public identity crises for each field. LIS scholars have heard Wiegand's (1999, p. 24) warning that LIS is "a profession trapped in its own discursive formations, where members speak mostly to each other and where connections between power and knowledge that affect issues of race, class, age, and gender, among others, are either invisible or ignored." In a similar vein, Andrew P. Carlin (2003, p. 3) recently argued that, historically, LIS has "imported" research techniques and standards of evidence from other disciplines and it might thus be time for LIS to develop its own interdisciplinary research ethics. These sentiments echo Schoenberger's (1998, p. 1) call to human geographers for "analyzing ourselves as social and historical actors and assessing the way we work and the way we use language in order to strengthen our research and improve the standing of the discipline."

Of course, comparing the units of analysis in the two fields provides the greatest contrast. LIS research focuses on the concept of information, techniques and technologies for manipulating information, and human organizations for managing it; human geography focuses on the concepts of place, space, and scale (each one wrapped up with "time" as well). The most basic way of dealing with these concepts in geography has been the rather reductionist investigation into "areal differentiation"—how, why, and when patterns of difference in natural, built, and social environments emerge across places, spaces, and scales—such as the international comparative studies of "natural resources" for which geography was known in the 19th century (the question "resources for whom?" was rarely asked). *Human* geography, however, rooted as it is in the complexities of human societies, must by definition move beyond such reductionist inquiry into more relational, dialectical, and critical investigations. Let us consider each one of these in turn.

Reductionism within geography—especially the tendency to see place, space, and scale simply as containers for human activity—reached its pinnacle during the "positivist turn" in the field starting in 1960, which assumed (incorrectly) that "human activity does not restructure space, it simply rearranges objects in space" (Smith, 1990, p. xi). In contrast to this reductionist stance, human geography must study not only the areal differentiation of human practices and human productions across the map, but also the material relationships between these different practices and productions on one hand and the normative meanings of these practices and productions on the other.

Relational concepts and theories are necessary to human geography because humans are not reductionist monads but relational creatures who communicate with each other, organize themselves into groups, and imagine meaningful identities based on both individual and group contexts. Smith (1990, p. 66) provided a useful way of thinking about relational geographies when he defined "geographical space" in particular as "the space of human activity, from architectural space at a lower scale up to the scale of the entire surface of the earth" and argued that such a conception of space must simultaneously embrace both the "absolute" space of Cartesian, geometric landscapes (where, for example, a kilometer is always a kilometer) and the "relative" space of social landscapes (where, for example, both technology and context alter the meaning of a kilometer as either a small or large distance).

Dialectical concepts and theories allow geographers to deal with the often confounding ability of humans not only to act as active agents of change over the environment, but also to be enabled and constrained in those very actions by environmental factors—including environmental factors of their own earlier creation. A common strategy in historical human geography is to trace the ways in which humans in a particular time and place are able to (and choose whether to) produce new environments, reproduce those environments, and finally destroy them. In an industrial, capitalist political economy, such a process might be called "creative destruction" (Schumpeter, 1942). The best examples of this through the 20th century have been urban built environments, which, according to Sheppard (2004, p. 474) were "shaped to meet the requirements of capital accumulation, only later to become a barrier once technological change alters those requirements." Thus, we might think of cities as the prime example of how the material aspects of place, space, and scale are "socially produced" again and again over time.

The dialectic of change in human geography does not apply only to material landscapes, however, precisely because humans are not automatons but conscious creatures who create and experience meaning as they create and experience places and spaces. For example, Schoenberger (1997, p. 6) illustrated in *The Cultural Crisis of the Firm* that, during the beginnings of globalization in the automobile and technology industries, when the spatial and temporal geographies of competition were changing rapidly, "corporate cultures and managerial identities and commitments exerted a powerful force that structured the possibilities for change in ways that proved unavailing given the actual circumstances in which firms found themselves." Thus, spatial and temporal relations and environments are not only "socially produced" through labor and technology, but also "socially constructed" through communication about shared understandings and contested claims. These meanings and claims then scale up into what we might call culture. Thus, another meaning of "geographical space" might be "shorthand for the socially constructed spaces produced on the earth's surface" (Aoyama & Sheppard, 2003, p. 1151).

Finally, human geography tends to adopt a critical stance—its advocates tend to question power relations, are suspicious of utopian claims, and do not fear to engage in rational, normative arguments—precisely because such social productions and social constructions, rarely uncontested as they come into being, have important consequences for all of society. Much as LIS research tends to embody a normative agenda, "to bring together information in all its cultural forms and the people who need or want it, thereby contributing to individual and collective knowledge, productivity, and well-being" (to quote from the mission statement of my own particular LIS program), geographers tend to strive for a world of "territorial social justice" (Harvey, 1973, p. 117)—although they may differ markedly in their claims of what that means. Either way, a critical research stance does not mean that the knowledge one produces is "biased" or "flawed." As Harvey (1984, p. 11) has argued,

> Geographers cannot remain neutral. But they can strive toward scientific rigor, integrity and honesty. The difference between the two commitments must be understood. There are many different windows from which to view the same world, but scientific integrity demands that we faithfully record and analyze what we see from any one of them.

Thus, human geography works with the same concepts of space, place, and scale as other flavors of geographic inquiry and is one of the few pursuits forced to recognize that all three are, paradoxically, both universal (as realities experienced by all human cultures regardless of technology or practice) and contingent (as "concrete abstractions" given form and meaning depending on particular human cultures and particular technological practices). Human geography theorizes that place, space, and scale are not only socially produced out of particular political economies and divisions of labor, but socially constructed out of particular cultural milieux and leaps of imagination. As a result, instead of thinking in terms of *things* set upon the landscape in a reductionist sense, human geographers tend to think about more relational and dialectical *processes* that constantly challenge current notions of place, space, and scale.

Contested Tools of Geographical Inquiry

All concepts and theories aside, one of the things most commonly thought to distinguish geography as a discipline—correctly or incorrectly—

has been the production and consumption of a specific form of knowledge-bearing artifact: the map. Many human geographers claim that they can function perfectly well without creating maps (let alone computerizing them), but fluency in the language of maps is something of a prerequisite both to participating in the debates of the field and in popularizing the knowledge accumulated by the field. And as not only an informational commodity, but increasingly a technological commodity—with the recent rise of geographic information systems (GIS) on personal computers, analytical maps and the spatial data behind them are often seen as the most direct and natural link between geography and LIS.

The question over GIS within LIS research and practice is often painted in terms of professional survival rather than academic inquiry (Smith & Gluck, 1996). Special and academic librarians increasingly need to be able to understand, if not use, GIS software in order to help patrons with reference and research questions relating to geocoded government data—especially census data (Abbott & Argentati, 1995). Public librarians, too, are increasingly fielding spatial questions from individual users (Gluck, Danley, & Lahmon, 1996; Lim, Liu, Yin, Goh, Theng, & Ng, 2005) as community action groups become more familiar with these tools, both for making claims about neighborhood development options and for recruiting new stakeholders (Craig & Ellwood, 1998). They are also discovering the potential of GIS as tools for internal tracking of patron locations and branch statistics, for formulating arguments and preparing presentations against further reductions in library budgets (Adkins & Sturges, 2004), and for reaching out to underserved and oppressed populations (Jue, Koontz, Magpantay, Lance, & Seidl, 1999). Some centers of LIS instruction, especially Florida State University, are assisting in this process by constructing Web-accessible "front end" systems to deliver spatial maps and data on U.S. libraries to those without a GIS themselves (Koontz, Jue, McClure, & Bertot, 2004). Digital library projects must increasingly deal with digital spatial data (Boxall, 2003), helping to define evolving standards of both metadata and security in concert with the federal government (Zellmer, 2004). Human-computer interface researchers have contributed to our knowledge of the various ways in which GIS users interact with spatial data presentations—even using tactile interfaces (Jeong & Gluck, 2003). And information professionals of all sorts working on digital knowledge management are increasingly attempting to "spatialize" everything from Web-page searches (Watters & Amoudi, 2003) to shelf-browsing behaviors (Xia, 2004) using GIS tools.

LIS, however, has a deeper contribution to make here. The long tradition within LIS of understanding how power is embedded in the production, distribution, and consumption of both knowledge-bearing artifacts (e.g., books) and the very methods of identifying and organizing those artifacts (catalogs, indexes, citations, and the like) can help GIS users avoid one of the most common misconceptions about maps and mapmaking: "the premise that mappers engage in an unquestionably 'scientific' or 'objective' form of knowledge creation" (Harley, 1989, p. 423). Once again drawing together the "linguistic turn" with the "spatial turn," the late geographer J. B. Harley (1989, p. 3) was one of the most vocal proponents for "deconstructing" cartographic artifacts:

> Deconstruction urges us to read between the lines of the map—'in the margins of the text'—and through its tropes to discover the silences and contradictions that challenge the apparent honesty of the image. We begin to learn that cartographic facts are only facts within a specific cultural perspective.

Harley (1989, p. 11) understood that maps, like both individual texts and channels of mass media, were, in the end, tools of strategic communication:

> All maps strive to frame their message in the context of an audience. All maps state an argument about the world and they are propositional in nature. All maps employ the common devices of rhetoric such as invocations of authority (*especially* in 'scientific maps') and appeals to a potential readership through the use of colors, decoration, typography, dedications, or written justifications of their method.

Thus, in his view, "the steps in making a map—selection, omission, simplification, classification, the creation of hierarchies, and 'symbolization'—are all inherently rhetorical" (p. 11). Just as the philosopher Langdon Winner (1986) famously argued that "artifacts can have political qualities," so did Harley hold that maps have politics: Power is exerted both *on* cartography (by governments, corporations, advertisers, and activists) and *with* cartography (through the production of state, corporate, marketing, or activist maps supporting one argument over another).

Nowhere is such an understanding of maps both as tools forged out of social relations *and* as tools used to influence social relations more crucial than in considering the maps we produce using new information technologies. For example, when digital GIS first moved from the expensive workstation to the individual desktop personal computer in the early 1990s, a crisis quickly emerged within geography. In one camp were boosters like Openshaw (1991, p. 622) who praised GIS as finally providing a common toolset to all of geography, even if that meant excluding the "soft and the so-called intensive and squelchy-soft qualitative research paradigms [that] could fade into insignificance if they cannot be adequately linked into the new data and computer age that is all around us." LIS researchers will recognize Openshaw's argument as both technologically determinist and technologically triumphalist. Unfortunately this argument ignores a stubborn reality that the "squelchy-soft" qualitative geographers would likely be quick to point out: data is not "found" waiting in rich veins to be tapped by heroic geographers at their GIS stations but is instead created—tediously produced through human labor, technological sensing, and patron funding—and therefore subject to the same questions of political-economic power as any other form of produced knowledge.

The diverse field of geography spent the next decade coming to terms with GIS, a process that would make a fascinating historical case study. One of the most useful contributions came from the human geographer Eric Sheppard (1995, p. 5) who argued that "an understanding of both the social nature and implications of GIS as a technology and the technical characteristics and possibilities of GIS are necessary for successful research to take place." Sheppard's view of GIS was, like that of many LIS social informatics researchers, a dialectical one: "Society affects the development of GIS at the same time that GIS affects the development of society" (p. 5). For example, he pointed out five main factors that influenced the trajectory of GIS development in the U.S.: (1) "the priorities of U.S. society, such as demands for military surveillance, given both its internal structure and its position within the global system"; (2) "the degree to which the private sector has dominated the development of GIS"; (3) "the types of problems that principal potential customers for GIS wish to solve and the price they are prepared to pay"; (4) "factors affecting data availability and cost"; and (5) "the weakness of geography as an intellectual discipline in the United States, which affects the degree to which geographic expertise is utilized to evaluate the development and application of GIS" (p. 8). This particular history meant that GIS privileged reductionist views of individuals, places, and regions in the landscape over relational views of the flows, processes, and connections in which they might be embedded. Sheppard (p. 11) offered a recent and relevant political-economic example to illustrate this point:

> the major theoretical split in theories of spatial economic development is arguably between those who believe that it is the attributes of places which determine their evolution (such as in modernization theory, rigid historical materialism, and neo-liberal economic policy), and those who believe that differences in situation create asymmetrical dependencies between places that lead to very different development opportunities (as in dependency theory and world systems theory).

Yet "data describing flows are much more expensive to collect and store than attribute data because they increase geometrically rather than arithmetically" (p. 11) and, furthermore, the GIS may itself be constructed to privilege one source of data over another.

Another example (of which all LIS professionals should be aware) can be found in the currently widespread practice of "geodemographic analysis"—i.e., using a GIS to combine publicly available geographic and demographic data, especially from the U.S. Census and U.S. Postal Service, with privately produced marketing profiles and purchase histories—in the service of ever more targeted marketing schemes. Goss (1995, p. 172) has pointed out that geodemographics is based on "reductionist models of consumer identity" (you are what you buy) and "the inference of unobserved behavior from residential location" (you are where you live). Thus this "science" falls prey to the "ecological fallacy": "the erroneous assumption that patterns or relationships between data observed at an aggregate level of analysis also apply to data at the level of the individual (or to any lower level of aggregation)" (p. 181). Yet, at the same time, the practice "works" in that it seems to sell not only products to consumers, but also consulting services and GIS systems to marketers. Thus, in this case, GIS is wrapped up in a dialectical (and somewhat self-fulfilling) practice of producing/constructing ideal geographies of consumers, deepening the market for capitalism as a whole by fragmenting it into precise—and presumably less risky—spatial segments: "The marketer purchases detailed psychodemographic data about consumer identity in digital form and sells these identities back to consumers in material form as consumer goods and services" (p. 191), but "the goal of marketing, of course, is to preemptively determine the meanings that consumers would make for themselves from commodities in order to sell these meanings to them in the form of commodities" (p. 193). What all this means for human geography—and for LIS—is that, although GIS may be a useful tool, it does not represent a new paradigm of knowledge production apart from human geography's traditional focus on relational, dialectical, and critical examination of spatial and temporal social change. If anything, it represents a new case to be studied.

Theories of Spatial Fixes and Uneven Geographical Development

The use of GIS for geodemographic marketing might best be understood as an example of one of the most generative concepts to come out of human geography: Harvey's (1982) idea of the "spatial fix," first articulated in his classic *The Limits to Capital*. The title was a play on words that represented both the analytical limits to Karl Marx's 19th-century analysis and critique of capitalism, *Capital*—bereft as it was of a consistent theoretical foundation in geography—and the political-economic limits to capitalism itself, prone to crisis through numerous internal contradictions but incredibly resilient in pushing the "limits" of its own influence to ward off those crises. Harvey's (2004, p. 544) aim in this book was "to take fragmentary comments about spatiality, territoriality and geography and try to weld them into a more systematic theory of the production of space, urbanization, and of uneven geographical development." In a recent retrospective assessment of Harvey's ideas,

Schoenberger (2004, p. 428) explained the spatial fix as "a way to productively soak up capital by transforming the geography of capitalism":

> Although there is no permanent solution to the crisis tendencies of capitalism, the system does generate some important ways of delaying them or diverting them into reasonably productive pathways. Harvey's great insight in *Limits* was that restructuring the geography of capital—altering its very earthly foundations—was a particularly effective way of productively absorbing these excesses. This is the spatial fix. It is a very general notion that can have different expressions historically and geographically.

Three well-known historical forms of the spatial fix include: (1) the commodification of land, where land is, over time, continually and differentially valued and revalued according to new technological opportunities for accumulation; (2) the global expansion of capitalism, both in mustering wider and wider regions for production and in selling commodities and services to wider and wider consumer markets; and (3) investment into the built environment—either in place, in the form of cities, or across space, in the form of transportation and communication infrastructure—especially when such investment is orchestrated by the state but works to benefit the competitive risks of accumulation for capital by decreasing the "friction of distance" and thus the cost of doing business (Sheppard, 2004). Other examples of spatial fixes might include reorganizing territorial systems of governance, privatizing spatial realms and assets that were previously collectively held, or even investing in those ephemeral and virtual spaces of electronic action known as "mediaspaces" or "cyberspaces." It is important, however, to realize that all of these examples of spatial fix strategies share four key elements: (1) they each involve temporal, as well as spatial, parameters; (2) they each involve opportunities for action by the state as well as by capital; (3) they each confer to the public use values (and/or "use risks") other than those values allowing for further capital accumulation; and (4) they each contain built-in contradictions, which do not solve, but merely defer or displace, the problem of crisis.

One of the most important of these contradictions comes from the fact that spatial fixes must themselves be produced out of the current spatial arrangements of a society—historical barriers that, in their own day, were often considered great leaps forward. In other words, it takes new time-and-space innovation and investment to overcome time-and-space frictions and legacies left over from previous rounds of innovation and investment. As Harvey (1989, p. 258) put it, "space can be conquered only through the production of space." For example, consider the paradox of the "last mile" in broadband ICT networks. As Graham (2001, p. 405) has observed,

> These days, telecommunications and digital media indus-
> tries endlessly proclaim the 'death of distance' and the 'ubiq-
> uity of bandwidth'. Paradoxically, however, they actually
> remain driven by the old-fashioned geographic imperatives of
> putting physical networks (optic fibers, mobile antennas and
> the like) in trenches, conduits and emplacements to drive
> market access. ... [in such a way that] fully 80 percent of the
> costs of a network are associated with this traditional,
> 'messy' business of getting it into the ground in highly con-
> gested, and contested, urban areas.

Optical fiber is laid following buried sewer conduits, disrupting vehicle travel on city streets; new cell phone towers enabling mobile telework
appear first on skyscrapers meant to congregate laborers in one place
throughout the working day; and all manner of communication systems
meant to build a cost-free virtual space nevertheless need substations
for switches, offices for managers, and fleets of vehicles for maintenance
workers placed strategically throughout costly physical space.

The inevitable result of repeated rounds of spatial fixes of all sorts,
especially in an increasingly global, capitalist political economy, is a
landscape of uneven geographic development. Rather than conceptualizing such patterns of wired and unwired, affluent and poor, well-serviced
and under-provisioned, as merely statistical—generated through random variation and contingency—human geographers theorize such patterns as structural and, often, as the logical expression of the
contradictions inherent in a society's mode of development (Smith,
1990). The twist is that certain powers within any society actually stand
to benefit from an uneven social and technological landscape—especially
if such a landscape helps to maintain monopoly power in terms of political influence, market dominance, or social importance. Thus, "uneven
development is a social inequality blazoned into the geographic landscape, and it is simultaneously the exploitation of that geographic
unevenness for certain socially determined ends" (p. 155). Reductionist
geographical research would simply identify, map, and perhaps try to
explain differences based on individual characteristics of sites and social
groupings. But a relational, dialectical, and critical human geography
sees each area of uneven development as tied to the other, being produced and reproduced over time as a result of contradictory social
processes, and often working in support of particular power relations
and normative goals.

As LIS researchers might expect, the place of ICTs and ICAs in the
production and reproduction of uneven geographies is of key interest to
human geographers—so much so that a series of concepts has emerged
in support of defining the crucial ability of information and communication technologies and agencies to help humans reorganize time and
space to new ends. Janelle (1991, pp. 49–52) has long spoken of "time-
space convergence" as a measure of "the rates at which places move

closer together or further away in travel or communication time." For example, from 1800 to 1965, the time needed to traverse the 210-mile distance between Boston and New York using various kinds of contemporary transport technology shrank from several full days by stagecoach to a mere few hours by car. Similarly, Janelle's "cost-space convergence" could be used to compare the declining cost over time of a coast-to-coast telephone call in 1920 to the price of the same call today. Harvey (1989, p. 240) theorized similarly with his notion of "time-space compression," according to which humans use the technologies of transport and communications both to broaden the space of social action and to accelerate the pace of that social action. For Harvey (1989, p. 240), time-space compression occurs precisely when material changes in infrastructure connect to mental changes in perception: "processes that so revolutionize the objective qualities of space and time that we are forced to alter, sometimes in quite radical ways, how we represent the world to ourselves" in such a way that "the world sometimes seems to collapse inwards upon us." And Giddens (1990, p. 14) contributed a related concept with his idea of "time-space distanciation," that is, "the conditions under which time and space are organized so as to connect presence and absence." Here not only technologies, but also social structures and practices come into play. For example, transnational corporations (and their transportation/communication technologies) "are able to connect the local and the global in ways which would have been unthinkable in more traditional societies and in so doing routinely affect the lives of many millions of people" (p. 20). Commodification itself is a time-space distanciation: "Money provides for the enactment of transactions between agents widely separated in time and space" (p. 24) and "writing expands the level of time-space distanciation and creates a perspective of past, present, and future in which the reflexive appropriation of knowledge can be set off from designated tradition" (p. 37). Although these three conceptualizations of time-space reorganization come from different research programs, they share the common notion that "the reorganization of space is always a reorganization of the framework through which social power is expressed" (Harvey, 1989, p. 255).

Thinking about these infrastructures of social power, then, we might identify four categories of ICTs and ICAs that have merited attention from both LIS and human geography: (1) print publishing as information technology with geographies of infrastructure (publishers, libraries, bookstores, schools), use (reading, education), and ownership/labor (private, public); (2) electronic point-to-point communication systems as information technologies with geographies of infrastructure, use, and ownership/labor (telegraph, telephone); (3) electronic mass media systems as information technologies with geographies of infrastructure, use, and ownership/labor (radio, television); and (4) the Internet as a virtual and physical geography of infrastructure and use. All four of these topics of research can be thought of as socio-technical systems or networks, a commonality that has brought them into the realm of both social informatics (Sawyer & Eschenfelder, 2002) and science and technology studies (Van House, 2004). Moreover, all four are implicated in the same kinds of relational, dialectical, and normative processes of social production and social construction because

> communications technologies are not only designed to overcome barriers posed by geographic space, thus transforming it, but at the same time always have their own distinct geographical attributes that shape the degree to which such transformation is possible [in such a way that] the new spaces they create shape, but do not substitute for, geographical space. (Aoyama & Sheppard, 2003, p. 1153)

Graham (2000, p. 115) makes three analytical points about these kinds of networks: (1) "As capital that is literally 'sunk' and embedded within and between the fabric of cities, they represent long-term accumulations of finance, technology, and organizational and geopolitical power"; (2) "infrastructure networks, and the complex socio-technical apparatus that surrounds them, are strongly involved in structuring and delineating the experiences of urban culture"; and (3) infrastructure networks "link systems and practices of production with systems and practices of consumption and social reproduction across space and time," but do so "in sustaining sociotechnical geometries of power and social or geographical biases in very real—but often complex—ways." Thinking through these networks of ICTs and ICAs with the geographical concepts of spaces and places, spatial fixes, and time-space reorganization, then, points especially to two different realms of research: understanding cyberspaces constituted out of information networks and understanding urban places caught within information networks.

Constructing Cyberspaces and Situating Urban Places

The term "cyberspace" itself is a spatial metaphor drawn out of the literary imagination—bringing together an uneasy combination of the electronic and the geographical—and like all metaphors, it has the power to both generate productive ideas and obscure important realities (Graham, 1998; Kitchin & Kneale, 2001; Mihalache, 2002). Initial formulations of cyberspace were often focused on the bodily experience of interfacing with computer networks (Benedikt, 1991) and the presence of networked information technology in cities (Graham & Marvin, 1996). Geographical theorists have continued their attempts to integrate body and city through cyberspace: Gandy's (2005) provocative ideas on "cyborg urbanization" are a recent example of this line of thought. However, social informatics researchers had been debating the concept of the place of the citizen in the "wired city"—pinning the term to cable television in the 1970s and "videotex" systems in the 1980s—long before the World Wide Web burst on the scene in the early 1990s (Dutton,

Blumler, & Kraemer, 1987). Even urban planning and architecture have explored the idea that urban built environments are converging with networked digital systems in new ways. For example, Massachusetts Institute of Technology planning and architecture professor William Mitchell (1995, p. 5) developed an evocative "city of bits" hypothesis, arguing that:

> The most crucial task before us is not one of putting in place the digital plumbing of broadband communications links and associated electronic appliances … nor even of producing electronically deliverable 'content,' but rather one of imagining and creating digitally mediated environments for the kinds of lives that we will want to lead and the sorts of communities that we will want to have.

If we define cyberspace not as some sort of "digital city" but as a virtual realm for social processes (such as production and consumption, education and play) that is enabled through increasingly convergent, digital networked information, communication, and media systems (represented most spectacularly at this moment by the World Wide Web), then we might imagine that the dialectical relationship between cyberspace and physical space could evolve in several different ways. Graham (1998, p. 167) articulated three options: (1) "substitution and transcendence," or "the idea that human territoriality, and the spaces and place-based dynamics of human life, can somehow be replaced using new technologies"; (2) "co-evolution," or the idea that "both the electronic 'spaces' and territorial spaces are necessarily produced together, as part of the ongoing restructuring of the capitalist political-economic system"; and (3) "recombination," the idea that "a fully relational view of the links between technology, time, space and social life is necessary." Rejecting simple substitution, Graham (p. 174) eschewed (1) in favor of (2) and (3), arguing that "materially constructed urban places and telecommunications networks stand in a state of *recursive interaction*, shaping *each other* in complex ways that have a history running back to the days of the origin of the telegraph and telephone."

Most theory and research on cyberspace in both LIS and geography now takes a similar point of view. But considerable room for variation remains. Many studies proceed using the language that the urban theorist Manuel Castells (1989, p. 348) originally developed in *The Informational City*, where he famously declared the new importance of networks of real places connected through the structures of cyberspaces:

> The new international economy creates a variable geometry of production and consumption, labor and capital, management and information—a geometry that denies the specific productive meaning of any place outside its position

in a network whose shape changes relentlessly in response to the messages of unseen signals and unknown codes.

Castells called this relational geometry the "space of flows" and understood it to comprise "asymmetrical networks of exchanges which do not depend on the characteristics of any specific locale for the fulfillment of their fundamental goals" (p. 348). For Castells, action in cyberspace (a pre-World Wide Web version made up of more proprietary corporate communication tools) did not substitute for action in physical space but worked to rearrange the hierarchy of power within the "space of places"—meaning that firms, cities, and regions would succeed in the new global economy not if they possessed unique characteristics in physical space but only if they could build sufficient presence in (and connections to) the new space of flows. This assessment points, then, not only to the agency of the firm, but also to the structure of the firm's competitive environment.

As a result of Castells's influential work through the 1990s, a cottage industry has developed within geography, measuring the areal differentiation in both urban accessibility to space flows and urban concentrations of firms taking advantage of the space of flows. For example, commercial "points of presence" (POPs) on the Internet are still distributed in an uneven geography in such a way that "many midsized metropolitan areas in the United States do not have a single network POP"—a condition that does not shut them out from Internet access but does call into question "the ability to access significant amounts of bandwidth from these cities" (Grubesic & O'Kelly, 2002, pp. 273–274). And if one ranks urban areas by the number of ".com" domain-name holders registered within their borders, a clearly uneven geography emerges. According to Zook (2000, p. 415), "the San Francisco Bay region has almost three times the number of domain names per firm as either the Chicago, Philadelphia, or Houston metropolitan regions"; moreover, "together, the New York, San Francisco, and Los Angeles regions have more *com* domain names than the next eleven largest metropolitan regions combined."

Such studies provide an essential baseline of empirical data for the understanding of dialectical change between urban, national, and global economies, but many geographers have begun to question this idea of networks between places as the most important, or most useful, new social arrangement to emerge from the combination of cyberspace and urban space—above all, the all-too-easy analogy that what works for competitive business practice should also work for local, state, and national governments and nongovernmental organizations. Leitner and Sheppard (2002, p. 495) critiqued

> [the] emergent trend in both public policy and academic discourse that construes networks as a preferable mode of coordination and governance for coping with the vagaries of

globalization and internationalization, facilitating a more efficient use of public resources, increasing competitiveness, generating economic growth, and resolving social problems.

Policymakers often have too easily assumed that networks are naturally self-organizing, collaborative, nonhierarchical, and flexible; however, Leitner and Sheppard (p. 514) pointed out that more often real political-economic projects organized as networks—especially networks between disparate cities, places, or regions forged in order to bring some measure of order to unpredictable globalization processes—actually "evolve under pre-existing conditions where territorial state regulation, unequal power relations, and uneven development are pervasive." Castells (2000) himself has since expanded his analysis of the networks of political-economic action enabled by his space of flows to consider how his new geography might be "grassrooted" through the efforts of social justice activists. Thus, although technology-enabled networks of social action might offer a new set of tools for attempting meaningful political-economic action, such social networks should be seen as a means to a more just society, not as an instantiation of that just society itself. Cities, among other noncorporate actors, still matter.

Web-Based Industries, Careers, and Economies

The recent work in the geography literature on the topic of the "new economy" illustrates the diversity and utility of relational, dialectical, and critical studies of cyberspaces and urban spaces—and the individuals who inhabit them. Early pronouncements about "e-business" were both reductionist and utopian in their conceptions of geography and technology. As Murphy (2003, p. 1174) has pointed out, such conceptions often involved: (1) the assumption of perfect "spaceless" consumer markets leading to a virtual landscape of deregulated competition accessible to anyone anywhere anytime across the globe; (2) the valorization of "pure-play" Internet retailers who "eschewed store networks for cavernous warehouses"; and (3) the simple glorification of "first-mover advantage,"—the assumption that in e-commerce, "the first and fleetest attains an unassailable competitive advantage."

Such assumptions fail on two counts. First, rather than being created wholly anew within cyberspace, e-commerce ventures are intimately wrapped up in physical, cultural, and legal geographies on the ground. For example, "rather than fleeing the more regulated territories of their major markets, E-commerce firms develop strategies that enable them to operate partially within such spaces" (Aoyama & Sheppard, 2003, p. 1154). Cyberspace, when grounded in physical space, cannot be perfectly deregulated nor can it be perfectly "frictionless" or instantaneous in its own workings:

> The geographical patterns of the telecommunications infrastructure and its bandwidth, the costs, and various rules and regulations governing its use, as well as many other factors, can all significantly affect the features of the electronic space and the way it is used. (Li, Whalley, & Williams, 2001, p. 702)

Second, rather than relying on an undifferentiated space of perfect competition, e-commerce ventures are born precisely to exploit uneven geographies on the ground:

> Information systems allow organizations to exploit minute differences between places in terms of, for example, local labour-market conditions, the nature of cultural facilities and of institutional structures, in a complex yet cost-effective manner. This capacity of information systems to redefine relations between people in different places, and to resolve the conflict between the fixity of capital location and the geographical flexibility of its use, has been, and will continue to be, a main source of organisational innovations. (p. 699)

For these reasons, a 2003 issue of *Environment and Planning A* devoted to e-commerce served to "challenge the claim that virtual space is coming to dominate geographic space, and the claims about the unalloyed benefits of globalization that often accompany it" (Aoyama & Sheppard, 2003, p. 1153).

Because LIS researchers, as well as geographers, study the links between technology and globalization, this topic is an obvious point of connection between the two fields. After all, a key premise in the concept of globalization is that the "new economy" enabled by "new technology" produces a "new geography." Ó Riain, Parthasarathy, & Zook (2004, p. 617) contend that, "in spatial terms, the 'new' economy is new to the extent that it has witnessed the emergence of certain regions, hitherto considered a part of the global 'periphery', as key nodes of production." Gibbs, Kraemer, and Dedrick (2003, p. 5) have drawn on the work of Giddens to suggest that researchers tend to hold three different theories of how this new geography of globalization might unfold: (1) "convergence," where globalization is "a universal process of homogenization in which countries tend toward a common way of producing and organizing economic life with resulting common social outcomes"; (2) "divergence" in globalization, where "national diversity in the pursuit of differing social and economic outcomes will prevail and prevent convergence from taking place"; and (3) "transformation," according to which globalization is to be understood as "an uneven process involving elements of both convergence and divergence, in which countries around the world are experiencing a process of profound change as they try to adapt to a more interconnected but uncertain world."

The work of both geography and LIS researchers so far demonstrates that convergence and homogenization are clearly not occurring. Aoyama (2003, p. 1205) studied the different methods of Internet access common to consumers in two different "sociospatial systems," the U.S. and Japan, and argued that "societies vary in the manner and the speed of technological adoption even when income and educational levels are similar," because cultural, institutional, and spatial differences persist and matter. Similarly, Gibbs et al.'s (2003, p. 6) systematic comparison of case studies in 10 countries dealing with the globalization of e-commerce found that "country responses to these global forces are varied and uneven due to national characteristics such as information infrastructure, business innovation/entrepreneurship and consumer preferences, and national policies that create different market and telecommunications regimes." In other words, both "national environment" and "national policy" matter. These researchers found that e-commerce globalization differed depending on whether one considered "B2B" (business to business) or "B2C" (business to consumer) e-commerce: "For B2B e-commerce, competitive forces are the greatest driver of adoption" and "countries that are more open to such forces, whether through international trade, trade liberalization, or foreign investment, tend toward higher e-commerce diffusion": This results in a convergence pattern (p. 16). However, "B2C diffusion seems to be less affected by global forces and more affected by variables specific to the national and local environment, such as consumer preferences, retail structure, and local language and cultural factors," thus leading to a divergence pattern (p. 16). Both Aoyama's and Gibbs et al.'s studies, then, support, at a minimum, a "divergence" view of the processes and outcomes of technology-driven globalization.

To think through "transformation" processes, however, requires more than the rather reductionist counting up of e-commerce indicators for "containing" nations. Qualitative case studies of particular industries, locations, or technologies are one productive approach. For example, Wilson's (2003, p. 1246) fascinating study on the "Economic Geography of Internet Gambling" highlights "the contrast between the seamless and global appearance of the World Wide Web and the place-based realities of the law." Wilson (p. 1246) describes the typical fragmented and contradictory legal, technical, and cultural geography of one online gambling venture: "VegasLand Casino" (which of course is named after the U.S. gambling center, Las Vegas, NV) "has its domain name registered in London in the United Kingdom, its technical contact at Yahoo in the United States, its financial base in Antigua, and its Website in the United Kingdom." Although this fragmentation offers financial, legal, and technical advantages, it also holds costs: "It is much harder for online sites to build brand loyalty, especially if they do not have the physical presence of a hotel or casino to anchor their identity" (p. 1249). The basic contradiction Wilson (p. 1246) identifies is that online gambling must appear to be part of one place even as it physically and/or legally locates in another place:

> Online-gambling Websites are made to appear to be part of the mainstream businesses in their markets, yet frequently are located offshore to avoid legal restrictions. For example, many Caribbean-based Internet-gambling Websites are oriented to the United States. These sites are made to appear as if they are based in the United States in several ways, such as by avoiding reference to currency exchange and by presenting transactions only in U.S. dollars, and by using toll-free telephone numbers with 800 and 866 area codes common to U.S.-based toll-free systems.

In this case, e-commerce issues cannot easily be divorced from the social and political regulation of vice and the cultural meaning of place.

Another content-specific example comes from Leyshon's (2001) work on ICT and the music industry. He conceptualized the music industry geographically as "four distinctive musical networks which possess distinctive but overlapping functions, temporalities, and geographies":

> first, a network of creativity, formed from the fusion of networks of composition and representation, wherein music is created through multiple acts of performance; second, a network of reproduction, which is a narrower definition of the original network of repetition, and which includes the manufacture of multiple copies of audio recordings; third, a network of distribution; ... and, fourth, a network of consumption, incorporating retail organizations. (p. 60)

Leyshon then argued that the MP3 technological revolution would have different but related effects through each of these four networks. This approach illustrates well how geographers create typologies and develop conceptual tools which let them deal with processes simultaneously as social, functional, ideational, and spatial (e.g., tracking the various divisions of labor in those four categories).

What about e-commerce that deals not with virtual entertainment products, but with physical products that might otherwise be hauled home in an automobile from a local "bricks-and-mortar" retail outlet? Currah (2002, p. 1411) found that instead of positing an absolute opposition between "pure play" Web retailers and traditional stores, a fruitful research strategy was to conceptualize and investigate so-called multichannel retailers who "serve consumer markets via at least two routes, including any combination of e-commerce, catalogue or mail order, interactive television, telesales, and store-based retailing." These so-called "bricks-and-clicks" e-tailers are ideally "able to draw upon an established brand name and customer franchise, thus affirming the authenticity of the Web store and alleviating the marketing traumas experienced by the pure players" by having a "combination of an electronic and physical presence" which "provides the consumer with multiple points of access to the retailer, enabling, for example, offline purchases to be researched in the Web store or online orders to be exchanged at a traditional store" (p. 1414). These retailers "can leverage existing investments in warehousing, supply-chain management systems, customer-support centres, and product-return networks to facilitate the process of e-tailing fulfilment" (p. 1414). In his study of six such firms in the Toronto area, Currah (p. 1430) concluded that "the physical places that constitute the Internet commodity chain have remained geographically integrated with those of traditional retailing": In other words, "there is little to be found in the physical places of e-tailing fulfilment in Toronto that is fundamentally unique" (p. 1433). Thus, Currah provocatively argued, "e-tailing is merely an electronically revamped model of catalogue selling" (p. 1433).

Of course, not every commodity can be purchased through a catalog. One of the most frustrating attempts at e-business has been the cybergrocery, where local delivery areas and customer perceptions of food quality are considerable obstacles to electronic rationalization. A recent study by Murphy (2003, p. 1176) did not merely evaluate strategies of "compressing" time and space, but also considered the trade-offs involved in paying attention to one side of the dialectic of space/time versus the other: "solving problems in time may compound problems in space, and vice versa." Using qualitative, ethnographic interview and observation data, Murphy (p. 1195) found that having a third party go "picking" for groceries is a vastly different time-space activity than going "shopping" for one's self:

> The design of their selling space is not well suited to picking and packing by store employees on behalf of customers. Stores are designed to encourage customers to wander throughout the store, and thus possibly be tempted by additional items: to them the store is a puzzle, and possibly an obstacle course. Pickers rely instead on information technology to guide them and provide shortcuts to the next item: for them the store is a three-dimensional Cartesian grid, with each aisle, shelf, and bay coded and tagged. Pickers compete with customers for store space and products on shelves, and as store representatives may be waylaid. (p. 1195)

Such geographical studies of new cyberspatial processes of production, distribution, and consumption usually focus on the dialectic between the space-time of the firm and the space-time of the customer in much the same way that digital library investigations in LIS might focus on the dialectic between the space-time of the library and the space-time of the patron. But there is another geography at work in these e-commerce projects that can only be seen if one takes a step back from individual actors in place to look at collective patterns across space. The question of whether globalized e-commerce would favor one city, one region, or one labor market over another has also been investigated both reductively and relationally in the past few years. Geographies of work—whether "distributed work" that takes place over space and time through ICTs mobilized by a particular firm, or "labor guilds" that form over space and time through ICTs mobilized by a particular professional group of workers at various firms—show how individuals are both empowered and constrained by ICTs as they strive to find and keep meaningful labor in particular firms, particular industries, and particular areas.

One example from this geography literature, building on the LIS-related field of "computer supported cooperative work," is Brown and O'Hara's (2003, p. 1566) ethnographic study of so-called "hot-desking" workers, in which they argued that

> mobile workers do not work in some sort of decorporalised hyperspace, as some accounts would seem to suggest. Indeed, as we will discuss, because these workers have much less physical certainty in comparison with conventional workers, place becomes a very important practical concern. When a mobile worker goes to work, he or she must decide where that work is going to be, under pressures of task and management.

Their key finding was that mobile work is relational, not reductionist: "The mobile workers were dependent on fixed aspects of the office place by proxy—they required other people to be there in order to facilitate their own decorporealisation" (p. 1585). Thus, "to ask if mobile work is virtual is simply to ask the wrong question; mobile work is different, it does not lose its corporeality, but rather that corporeality becomes something that has to be explicitly managed" (p. 1585).

Similar work in geography has drawn inspiration from workplace studies of technical labor that, once again, sit at the boundary between LIS and science and technology studies. Building on Orr's (1996) classic study of Xerox service technicians, Ueno and Kawatoko (2003, p. 1531) explored "the practice of service technicians across multiple sites in a copying-machine company" in Japan. Ueno and Kawatoko (p. 1531) considered the new question of how "service technicians move about their area in appropriate ways and times by making their workspace visible with various technologies." They argued from their findings that "space is not something given. It is not a container filled with people, artifacts, and other things. Rather, space is continually organized, described, and made visible by people who are also in space, with various technologies" (p. 1529).

One might explore the other end of the mobility spectrum at work in the same way. For example, Boyer (2004, p. 206) studied the different spatial relations of the office for early 20th century bank workers of different status (and gender) to reveal how those spatial relations were structured by technology:

> Freed from the typewriter or dictaphone, these men worked at desks designed for conversing, reading, and thinking, in offices equipped with doors and secretaries to buffer and regulate contact with others. Meanwhile, at the bottom of the organizational hierarchy, clerical workers were "tied" or tethered to spatially fixed pieces of equipment such as a typewriter or dictaphone, in workspaces that more easily lent themselves to visual and auditory surveillance.

Her conclusion was that, "while women were free to claim authority over small, discrete pieces of office machinery, comprehending the broader sociotechnical systems of which those machines were a part was still considered men's work" (p. 209).

Place becomes important in the study of the new-media workplace as well. Building on previous studies of the Bay Area's Silicon Valley and Boston's Route 128, many geographers in the late 1990s turned their attention to New York's "Silicon Alley," described by Girard and Stark (2002, p. 1929) as "a (post)industrial district ... running south of 41st Street along Broadway through the Flatiron District and SoHo into Chelsea and down to Wall Street." These authors noted that

> By 1999, new media was one of New York's fastest growing sectors, with almost 100,000 full-time equivalent employees in Manhattan alone (that is, more than the city's traditional publishing and traditional advertising industries combined) and with an estimated 8,500 new-media companies in the larger New York City area. In that same year, the New York new-media industry produced revenues of $16.8 billion and generated $1.5 billion in venture-capital funding and $3.5 billion in IPO [Initial Public Offering] funding. (p. 1929)

Such statistics could easily be compared to other nascent new-media regions. But Girard and Stark combined this understanding of geographical space to explore, ethnographically, a more social space: "the web of a web project" (pp. 1938–1939), that is, the network of actors on a new-media project who existed in a "heterarchy" (not a hierarchy) of simultaneous engineering and distributed authority (pp. 1934–1936). Tracing the social network between Web developers, clients, third-party "technology partners," venture capitalists, order fulfillment firms, credit services, and the like, Girard and Stark (p. 1939) concluded that the knowledge necessary to successful delivery of a product in such a business environment is literally "distributed across this web."

Thinking about new media in this way—fragmented in time and space as continual, short-term "project work" for a range of global clients—allows researchers to revisit the history of "old media" labor conditions and industrial landscapes and see how, even though industries such as filmmaking and advertising produced their own professional spaces (Hollywood, Madison Avenue), the existence of organized labor institutions within these places endowed these districts with a different set of meanings. For example, Christopherson (2002, p. 2004) has argued that

> unlike their old-media counterparts, new-media workers (and their employers) did not have the intermediary institutions to set the rules for employment, to define roles in project production, or to facilitate project management. So, when we look at new media, we see idiosyncratic occupational titles (such as technical evangelist), an understanding of work as a commodity rather than a relationship, and a distinctly entrepreneurial approach to career development.

She went on to say that all this "has empowered individual workers but disempowered the workforce as a whole. It has also made collocation a virtual necessity both for employers and for new-media professionals" (p. 2004).

Thinking about both the processes of collocation and the construction of information systems to facilitate this kind of labor brings the geography of new-media production in contact with longstanding LIS research. For example, in her introduction to a recent issue of *Environment and Planning A*, Grabher (2002, p. 1914) explicitly drew on Star and Griesemer's (1989) well-known concept of information artifacts acting as "boundary objects":

> Despite the fuzzy boundaries of professional profiles and roles, the work process in new media does involve a division of labor, no matter how vague and project specific. In the fluid new-media context, reliability of information and validity of expectations across the various domains and across time are achieved through 'boundary objects' which are both plastic enough to adapt to local contexts and constraints of the parties employing them, yet robust enough to maintain a common identity.

Thus, she argued, "new media gravitate towards distinct metropolitan areas, which offer the infrastructural amenities of a central location and yet offer space for sociocultural and physical (re)development"—places, such as Silicon Alley, which contain "a rich pool of specialized labor; a diversified infrastructure of specialized suppliers of intermediate inputs and specialized services; and so-called knowledge spill-overs" (p. 1918). In this way, for a new-media industry marked by short-term projects, fragmented divisions of labor mediated by "boundary objects," and distinct symbolic urban districts of activity, "the knowledge space" of both physical proximity and social networks can help produce what Grabher (p. 1922) called "locally diffused and enduring 'repositories of experience.'"

Other geographers have continued to investigate how these repositories of experience are (re)produced in place. Benner's (2003) work combines traditional "geographies of innovation" research (focused on high-tech regions) with newer "community of practice" studies (focused on informal networks of professionals) to examine how, especially in information technology labor, innovative regional economies are sustained in part by the learning that takes place through organized communities of practice. Using a case study of the "Silicon Valley Webgrrls" (SVW) group to make his point, Benner argued that "significant learning takes place in loosely structured communities of people with similar occupations, skills, and experiences in the regional labor market" and that "these communities of practice emerge not simply through informal social interaction, but are being actively built at least in part through the formal activities of professional associations" (p. 1810). But, crucially, these activities are situated in "geographical space": "Spatial proximity facilitates the exchange of many kinds of information and knowledge, particularly tacit knowledge" (p. 1812). Benner (p. 1825) found that

> When it was fully functional, SVW brought together a community of 1,200 people in the Silicon Valley involved in one way or another with Internet development and Web design. ... In an environment in which social networks have worked to exclude women from positions of influence in the core of the region's high-tech agglomeration, SVW provided the information resources and social networks to help promote their members [sic] careers effectively.

He concluded that "The high levels of trust, openness, and organized incorporation into the community, built through the combination of in-person and online communication, was a critical component of the organization's success" (p. 1826).

Geographical investigations like this can help LIS researchers come to grips with the workings of local labor markets in ICT and ICA industries. But we must also remember that such labor markets are not given, but have to be produced. Many human geographers take the dialectical view that "the spatial division of labour [is] a product of capitalist social relations," a process that must be understood as unfolding historically (Wills, Cumbers, & Berndt, 2000, p. 1524):

Workers did not just "happen" to be in a place of work at a particular time. Rather, they were understood to be there—with a certain package of skills, experiences, and opinions—as a result of previous rounds of economic investment.

This theoretical orientation can be productive when new ICTs and ICAs themselves provide the power to change the rules of the game for labor market production, creating potential employees and employers on a much wider spatial and temporal scale than ever before.

Niles and Hanson (2003) explored this very question, studying the way ICTs and ICAs are providing new methods for job seeking that can potentially (but not always in practice) transcend space. They began by observing that "information—and especially information about opportunities such as education, jobs, and medical care that affect individual livelihoods—circulates through social networks," a process they termed "grounded social relations" (p. 1223). Because, in such social relations, "information available through a social network is partial and constrained by the spatial extent of network members' experiences" (for example, where they've worked and lived in the past), Niles and Hanson (p. 1223) wondered if new ICT tools such as the online job-seeking service Monster.com would change these social relations. Their method involved qualitative, in-depth interviews of nine employers who had advertised openings on Monster.com:

Specifically we wanted to understand whether employers are able to attract qualified candidates from a broader social and geographic spectrum than that represented by their existing workers and whether expanding and diversifying the applicant pool were important reasons for employer use of the Internet as a recruiting tool. (pp. 1230–1231)

What they found was that the ICT of the Web, together with the ICA of Monster.com, was used to conquer time, but not necessarily space:

Using the Internet in this case does not mean dramatically changing the way firms hire people; it means looking for a way to make the existing methods more efficient. It was clear that efficiency is often measured by finding very specifically skilled candidates who already reside within the area inscribed by what the employer deems an appropriate commuting distance. Although hiring specifically like this may be efficient in terms of time and money, it necessarily precludes considering non-traditional, or more distance, applicants. (p. 1241)

Thus a "socially constructed" geography—the perceived space of action on the part of employers when conducting a job search, including the meaning of "appropriate commuting distance"—conflicted with the widened "socially produced" space of recruiting offered by the global ICT of the Web and the transnational corporate ICA of Monster.com.

The Place of Libraries (and LIS) in the "New Geography"

Geography has concentrated heavily on studies of new-media firms— how these new ICAs are produced, reproduced, and understood in relation to new opportunities for action across time and space offered by new ICTs, and how the political economy of pre-existing spaces enables and constrains these processes. Thus, even though geography (so far) has had little to say about nonprofit information agencies such as libraries, one way that LIS might usefully engage with geography is to compare strategies and patterns for taking research on ICTs and ICAs into the realm of political-economic action (as if it were ever really free of this realm). The LIS community, unlike those of many other academic disciplines (but similarly to, say, those of journalism and mass communication), tends to be more comfortable in articulating and defending a core set of social norms defining a public interest, including free and open access to information without regard to ability to pay and without discrimination on the basis of social/cultural affiliation. Libraries—especially public, school, and academic—have long been a part of this public interest. But now, just as the creation of cyberspace threatens to undermine the power of particular urban places, the creation of largely privatized digital libraries of all sorts threatens to undercut public support for physical libraries at all spatial scales. In an environment of both increased private market investment in ICTs (e.g., corporate intranets) and decreased state funding for ICAs (e.g., public libraries), polarized arguments have emerged either (1) touting the inevitable and technologically determined replacement of the material world of printed texts and reference librarians with the virtual world of digital texts and Google queries or (2) declaring the eternal superiority of human versus automated information expertise and the natural comforts of sitting in a plush chair with a thick book versus the obvious difficulty of staring at a glowing screen. On both sides, particular imagined geographies are being invoked—the material versus the virtual, the place-bound versus the placeless, the human society versus the built environment. But on both sides as well, these geographical imaginaries are reductionist and deceptive.

Geographical reductionism is not a bad place to start, but it can reveal only a partial reality. For example, one might start on the "material" side with the enticing fact that "there are 16,180 public library buildings (including branches) in the United States (that's more than McDonald's restaurants)" (Wiegand, 2003, p. 369). One might also gather national-level statistics, such as the 2002 ALA survey, which "found that only 66 percent of respondents had reported using the public library within the past year" (Adkins & Bala, 2004, p. 338). Such efforts at counting the presence and influence of libraries across the landscape have been present in LIS research ever since Wilson's (1938) Depression-era *Geography of Reading*. Today, one might use a GIS-based system such as the Florida GeoLib to identify each one of those library systems, branches, and buildings; with the addition of freely available government census data, one can then compare and correlate libraries and their communities in search of patterns of areal differentiation across the landscape at any particular political scale (national, state, or county) and in hope of finding evidence either praising the library as a co-determinant of successful communities or burying it as a relic too far removed from needy populations (Dorman, 2002; Jue et al., 1999; Koontz, 1997; Ottensman, 1997). Of course, these too were longstanding practices in the pre-GIS years (Chitwood, 1967).

An initial appeal to geography helps us define salient and polarized characteristics of things—pages versus screens, reading rooms versus chat rooms. But these things do not exist in isolation: They exist in relationship to each other in myriad ways that a reductionist view may or may not suggest; moreover, they exist as "moments" in larger social processes that a reductionist view allows us to glimpse only in snapshot. LIS researchers interested in ICAs have long attempted to pin down the "laws" of library siting that would allow LIS professionals not only to win legitimacy from library funding bodies (charitable, corporate, or state) but also to serve effectively both the populations who already demonstrate high demand for library services (elderly adults, young families with children, highly literate communities) and those who remain outside of the library's doors (recent immigrants, those struggling with literacy, or oppressed communities) (Koontz, 1997). They have also tried to quantify the level of library outreach that is "produced" for various sizes and concentrations of metropolitan areas (Adkins & Bala, 2004). But such principles of where and when to build libraries or to pursue outreach must adapt to changing technological contexts. An issue of *The Information Society* on the topic of the digital divide, edited by Strover (2003, p. 275), properly criticized "the mantra equating computer use with economic development and improved social conditions," which drove many early digital divide projects (and which was exploited by large technology vendors such as Microsoft and Dell through value-laden, short-term donations intended to bolster their brand image and increase their long-term market share). One of the problems was that early analyses of the digital divide were often aspatial (focusing on differences between social groups) or crudely reductionist in their spatial terms (rural versus urban, "inner city" versus suburban). In the evaluation of libraries versus cyberspace, more relational and dialectical use of both geographical tools and geographic theory is needed to go beyond utopian or dystopian arguments.

A first step in such a relational research agenda might be geographically focused case studies of ICAs in relation to their communities at particular historical moments. Sarah Anderson's (2003) fascinating

Library Quarterly article on the 135th Street Branch library in New York City's Harlem paid attention to the library within the geographical context of its local community, treating both the organization and the neighborhood as more than just "containers" for social processes and social actors. Anderson (pp. 417–418) argued that

> The story of the 135th Street Branch library is larger than its transformation into a world-renowned repository of knowledge; it serves as a model of the library finding its place in its community. ... It served as a public sphere in which sharply divergent ideas about race, art, literature, and politics could be exchanged. ... Through church pastors, school teachers, artists, poets, playwrights, novelists, political spokesmen, magazine editors, society matrons, and librarians, networks of social contacts were established that filled the library's auditorium and its reading rooms.

Leckie and Hopkins (2002, p. 327) also took a relational and dialectical view of the social processes within which ICAs are embedded in their study of central public libraries in Toronto and Vancouver, arguing that the public library is both a product and producer of "public culture" and, thus, a key institution in supporting the public sphere. Drawing on Zukin's (1995) work, they defined the "public" in the following terms: "Public life is produced and reproduced by social practices that transpire in specific places—public places—and the library is certainly one of those enduring and successful public places" (Leckie & Hopkins, 2002, p. 332). They suggested that such places

> are sites of neutral ground where people are free to come and go at their leisure and all feel welcomed. ... The primary activity is information exchange. ... They operate beyond the regular weekday working hours. ... Ease of access is a priority. ... They attract a regular clientele ... [and] the patrons themselves create a dynamic and animated ambience through their own activities, diversity, and vitality. (Leckie & Hopkins, 2002, p. 332)

Given and Leckie (2003) pursued these patrons and their diverse, vital activities more systematically in a related study that drew on geographic methods of a different sort. Arguing that "the spatial data collection and analysis techniques used by geographers and other social scientists to investigate research questions relating to shopping malls and other social spaces are currently underused in LIS research," they asked "what uses do individuals actually make of the public space of central libraries" (p. 366)? Through careful "seating sweeps" research they explored the interior space-time of their case sites, revealing the daily time-geography of patron numbers (how many?), demographics (what social groups?), locations (where did they go?), transported possessions (what did they carry?), and activities (what did they do?). In a similar way, Sandvig (2003) traced the cyberspace time-space movements of children using library-provided Internet access terminals. His study produced some surprising findings. In the realm of the physical, he found that "children often share the computers at the center ... they are always aware of other users and often watch them. In doing so, they learn about computers from strangers" (p. 179). And in the realm of the virtual, he argued that

> While justifications for Internet access in inner cities often rest on claims of educational benefit, in the EDC [the Electronic Discovery Center in San Francisco, the case study site], content that is explicitly educational was often avoided. In the EDC the Internet appears to be used most often as an active medium of play and leisure. (p. 179)

Such research prods practitioners to "remember to consider users' real, necessary activities, creating policies and areas within libraries that fit their needs and expectations of libraries as places that are socially constructed by the myriad of activities and interactions taking place within them" (Given and Leckie, 2003, p. 384).

In a sense, these studies of user activity in the space-time of the physical library are similar to long-standing LIS studies of the way users interact with online information resources in space and time in nonlibrary contexts, such as the workplace and the home. For example, recent work by Gorman, Lavelle, Delcambre, and Maier (2002, p. 1246) noted that their users of virtual medical records missed the physical cues of browsing—"size, thickness, color, wear and tear of pages"—that they had previously experienced with paper files. And a recent study by Rieh (2004, p. 744) argued that accessing virtual information from household spaces was worthy of scrutiny because "home is considered to be a socially defined setting rather than merely a physical setting in which people play diverse social roles while engaging in various social activities." Her findings, although limited, suggested that "home provides a unique interaction situation in which people conduct searches on the Web in ways different from searching in public settings such as workplaces, schools, and libraries" (p. 752). All of these studies share common ground by investigating the border between the virtual and the physical in practices of information use within different geographical (social, spatial, and temporal) contexts.

This kind of research fits into Wiegand's (2003, p. 372) call for more attention to the process of reading and the "library as place" within LIS. Wiegand (p. 372) wrote:

> To understand values the larger public assigns to the library ... it might be more illuminating to focus on the

library in the life of the user, especially in the areas of "place" and "reading," both of which have already found comfortable homes in American Studies scholarship.

In fact, he pointed not only to American Studies, but also to political communication and community studies (from the classic work of Jürgen Habermas to the recent work of Robert Putnam). Similarly, library professionals and researchers calling for libraries to take their "place at the table" in their local communities (McCook, 2000, p. 1) have often grounded their arguments in claims that libraries foster civic engagement and enact the ideal of the public sphere. But these efforts leave geography out of the mix. This is unfortunate, for, as Wiegand (2003, p. 374) pointed out, libraries can be conceptualized geographically not only as a reductionist "source and site for the act of reading," but also dialectically as a "place" that "influences community honesty and social trust" in the process of reproducing social capital. Similarly, although Leckie and Hopkins (2002, p. 330) recited the customary complaints of critical geographers in an attempt to illustrate the development potential of strong central public libraries—vilifying the automobile, the shopping mall, and gated communities as disasters for urban sustainability and social justice—they exhibited a rather reductionist view of the supposed decentralizing impact of the "information economy" on urban space, writing that

> Due to the rapid transmission of electronic information from one place to any other place, location is becoming irrelevant, and the emergent urban landscape is freed from conventional restrictions imposed by space. Cities are thus increasingly decentralized, fragmented, and seemingly organized by chance.

A corrective to this totalizing view might be found in the LIS literature on community networks and community technology centers, which focuses attention on the way ICTs arranged through certain ICAs can help bolster community social capital rather than fragment it. In their preface to a special issue of *The Information Society* focused on this topic, Huysman and Wulf (2005, p. 82) argue that "by addressing in more detail how people relate to one another, how shared practices emerge, and how communities evolve, we will be able to understand better if, when, how, and why such communities use or do not use technologies." Case studies are the usual methods employed, such as the work of Pettigrew, Durrance, and Unruh (2002) who observed, surveyed, and interviewed users of three community information networks: NorthStarNet in northeastern Illinois, Three Rivers Free-Net in Pittsburgh, and CascadeLink in Portland, Oregon. What they found was that social ties of community were often invoked by individuals who used the network: "Several respondents described how they spoke about their information need or situation with a social tie before searching on-line" or even performed online searches "on behalf of another person (e.g., a relative, friend), and not always at that person's behest" (p. 899). In a similar investigation, Kavanaugh, Reese, Carroll, and Rosson (2005, p. 128) studied community network users in the "wired city" of Blacksburg, Virginia, and found that

> Heavy Internet users with bridging ties [that is, weak social ties to many diverse individuals] have higher social engagement, have greater use of the Internet for social purposes, and have been attending more local meetings and events since going online than non-bridges who use the Internet heavily.

This work illustrates well that reductionist/substitution arguments, according to which time online is automatically either spent away from community or spent building community, are too simplistic.

These and other findings point to the value of relational, dialectical methods in considering the use of ICTs in conjunction with other forms of information seeking in place—the idea that "cyberspace fights against physical space less than it complements it" (Wellman, 2001, p. 247). As Venkatesh (2003, p. 345) argued in *The Information Society*'s special issue on community networks, simply counting and mapping these new spaces is no longer enough: "As befits a maturing field, we need to go beyond Adamic discovery and naming exercises to robust, theoretically informed accounts of community network development as socially embedded and socially constructed artifacts." In doing so, LIS researchers often debunk the notion that such projects, because of their networked nature, can magically thrive without sustained attention from the state. Servon and Nelson (2001, p. 421) described community technology centers in Portland, Austin, and Seattle to argue that these places "have the potential to provide part of a solution to bridging the technology gap, particularly in low-income, urban communities." But, they noted, this technological fix can only do so much on its own: "to think of community-based efforts as the sole bridging solution raises expectations that they will not be able to deliver. Public sector support is necessary to nurture and promote these efforts" (p. 421).

The same caveat holds for the socially embedded and socially constructed artifacts called libraries—long-standing ICAs that, like the newer community technology centers, must now produce and construct new relations between physical and virtual space. Atkinson (2001, p. 7) has noted the peculiar contradiction that in a digital universe of distributed, electronic documents,

> the less important the geographical dispersal and location of objects are for the user, the more important the network of locations becomes for the library. Such a "placeless" culture of

research is only possible if someone behind the scenes is paying a great deal of attention to the geographical places where objects are kept. (p. 8)

In a similar vein, he suggested that in a perfect world of digital information access, physical information spaces might become more, not less, important:

> Precisely because of the increased role of computer-mediated communication, each academic institution, and presumably each civic community, will need an agora of some kind—a central place where people can meet face to face and can work together, using digital and other information objects. (p. 8)

However, Atkinson defined "information" as reductionist "objects" and "knowledge" as "private and personal"—a move resulting in an individualistic, consumption-oriented definition of "information services" as those that "assist individual users in locating and making use of ... information objects" (p. 3). His argument thus fell prey to a third geographical tension, as he both attempted to justify the continued existence of libraries by appealing to their provision of "public or collective benefit" and assumed that they would be maintained by "collectively created support" (p. 3). Yet, if the new geography of information is to be experienced individually, how can information professionals hope to build that geography collectively?

In the following year, D'Elia, Jorgensen, Woelfel, and Rodger (2002) explored that very question by conducting a telephone survey of some 3,000 adults to investigate the relationship between people's use of the Internet and of the library. Their findings revealed a strong connection between the two worlds in the practice of their respondents: "75 percent of Internet users are library users and 60 percent of library users are Internet users" (p. 818). And their respondents voiced particular reasons for using each informational source: "Comments among the focus group participants who used *both* the library and the Internet suggested that the library is maintaining its edge in terms of such aspects as accuracy of information, privacy, and a place to go with children"; however, they also found that for people who use both the library and the Internet, "the library is already beginning to experience competition" in certain uses for which the Internet is chosen exclusively by these users (p. 818). Yet the connections between library space and cyberspace remain tantalizingly vague. D'Elia et al.'s (p. 818) respondents indicated that they appreciated physical libraries in part because of the library's role in "providing for the digital have-nots"; moreover, in areas of competition between the two worlds, the authors admitted that "a critical distinction that cannot be made with this data is whether these preferences for Internet use represent *new demands* for information being satisfied by the *new* provider or demands for information that *were formerly* met by the library." All in all, the study defined libraries and the Internet on the basis of an aspatial "information service provision" model (really a "uses and gratifications" media model), which casts patrons as "consumers," rather than on the basis of a "physical versus virtual space" model, which casts patrons as "citizens."

But the very point of conceptualizing networked ICTs as "cyberspaces"—sites for social action—is that, especially over time, these ICTs are produced, maintained, and used for many purposes other than "information service provision." The same holds true for ICAs like libraries—physical spaces where a variety of social processes take place in a mix that changes over time and space. Graham (1998, p. 180) reminds us that "we need to be extremely wary of the dangers of adopting, even implicitly, deterministic technological models and metaphors of technological change" and that "we need to be equally wary of the dangers of adopting simplistic concepts of *space* and *place*." He warns that "only by maintaining linked, relational conceptions of *both* new information and communication technologies *and* space and place will we ever approach a full understanding of the inter-relationships between them" (p. 181). Two surprising threads of recent research in geography might offer some help through this thicket.

An example of the first strand of research is provided by Adams and Ghose (2003), who explored the virtual and transnational community sustained by many Indian citizens living in the United States. In the course of their study, they pointed to the contradiction that "technologies that appear to collapse space and time can make any community (including an ethnic community) seem more close-knit, and therefore closer to the ideal" (p. 415). Here again, a contradiction was revealed through the time-space reorganizations of ICTs: "Ironically, when 'place-transcending' technologies facilitate the creation of ties through space and reduce the separation between here and there, negating place, this can strengthen a sense of ethnic identity, which implies a tie between self and place" (p. 415). In exploring this contradiction, Adams and Ghose (p. 419) did not use the idea of "cyberspace," but what they termed "bridgespace," in other words, "a collection of interconnected virtual places that support people's movement between two regions or countries and the sustenance of cultural ties at a distance." Bridgespace is made up of both networked ICTs and mass media products such as music CDs and "Bollywood" films, precisely as these networks and products are used to connect real social communities in real geographical sites. Adams and Ghose not only drew on both mass media research and social informatics, but also brought these fields into effective dialogue with geography by observing that "not only are technologies appropriated differently in different places, because of cultural differences, but that people in essence make different kinds of spaces in technologies" (433).

An example of the second strand of research comes from Dodge and Kitchin (2005, p. 162), who have, in a similar vein, moved from analyzing cyberspace to defining what they call "code/space": "Despite the growing use and pervasiveness of [software] code in contemporary society, code and its effects on the production of space have largely been ignored by geographers in favor of studying the technologies and infrastructures that code facilitates." They conceptualize code as "embedded in everyday objects, infrastructures, and processes" (p. 162) and basically follow an actor-network approach to thinking through the place of "code" in society at different scales. Mediated in part by this now ubiquitous code, they argue, "the relationship between human and technology is complex, contingent, relational, and productive" (p. 169). Understanding code/space begins with everyday practice:

> Code enables everyday acts to occur, such as watching television, using the Internet, traveling across a city, buying goods, making transnational phone calls, operating healthcare equipment, and withdrawing money from an ATM. While some of these practices were possible before the invention of code, code is now vital to their operation, and in some cases possible only through the work of code. (p. 170)

The epitome of code/space is thus a social situation in which "coded objects, infrastructures, and processes have entirely replaced older (wholly manual, electromechanical) systems, meaning that they can no longer be undertaken in an alternative way" (p. 173).

Now consider, for a moment, what these two recent examples from the geographical literature might have to offer the study of both physical libraries and the virtual information spaces connected to libraries. In addition to thinking about libraries as sites where the digital divides of information spaces might be leveled out, sites where the agencies of community information networks might be housed, or places where the quality of activities and surroundings affords the growth of social capital, we might think about libraries as sites of "bridgespace" and "code/space." Libraries, serving both as access points to electronic networks and as distribution points for both print and electronic media commodities, provide the ideal location for activities that can bring transnational communication together with transnational media consumption. But this can happen only if these ICAs recognize and orient themselves toward cohesive social groups within their local community service areas that might be able to make use of such bridging tools. Similarly, libraries, currently filled with both public-access computers and staff-only systems, are already profoundly integrated coded spaces, as almost every function of indexing, cataloging, processing and planning has moved into the orbit of electronic algorithms. Yet libraries also remain one of the few sites that defend the process of reading, conversing, meeting, and browsing against the intrusion of that most severe manifestation of code/space, where the only way to acquire information or engage in entertainment is through code-mediated technologies. Putting the physical library in opposition to a virtual cyberspace is both reductionist research and self-defeating policy. Thinking through the many ways that libraries might *uniquely* engage with cyberspace—roles as effective bridgespaces and carefully limited code/spaces are only two possibilities—is, to my mind, the best way that geographic ideas might engage with the LIS agenda.

Fortunately, that agenda is already broad enough to allow such relational work. In their set of wide-ranging essays on the social and contingent nature of classification, *Sorting Things Out*, Bowker and Star (1999) revealed how supposedly scientific and objective systems of classification are actually normative, contradictory, and cultural. Such work, situated at the center of the field of science and technology studies, already provides one disciplinary bridge with LIS (Van House, 2004). But when Bowker and Star suggested that such socially constructed classification schemes might actually become embodied in physical and virtual space, they invoked the geographical imagination as well. We might call such space "classification space," using this term to specify spaces, places, and scales that depend on classification for their use, meaning, and value. Bowker and Star (1999, p. 3) themselves referred to "the material force of categories":

> Try the simple experiment of ignoring your gender classification and use instead whichever toilets are nearest; try to locate a library book shelved under the wrong Library of Congress catalogue number; stand in the immigration queue at a busy foreign airport without the right passport or arrive without the transformer and the adaptor that translates between electrical standards.

Just as code/space is invisibly present in our digitally mediated lives, so is classification space invisibly present in our knowledge-structured lives, making up what Bowker and Star refer to as "infrastructure" (p. 35). And just as bridgespace provides a site for translation between disparate and social worlds, Bowker and Star's classification spaces would necessarily contain what they refer to as "boundary objects," such as information artifacts that are, again, "both plastic enough to adapt to local needs and constraints of the several parties employing them, yet robust enough to maintain a common identity across sites" (p. 297). Expanding on Bowker and Star's metaphors to conceptualize spaces of classification in this way is no mere linguistic exercise: as they themselves point out, "we need a richer vocabulary than that of standardization or formalization with which to characterize the heterogeneity and the processual nature of information ecologies" (p. 293).

For those researchers (and practitioners) who attempt to focus on the social aspects of information production, organization, distribution, and consumption within such "information ecologies," thinking geographically can help to define those ecologies in a way that can bridge the gap between the "L" and the "IS" in LIS. Geographical analysis suggests that libraries are not just *places* in the sense of cultural, social, and communal sites, but also serve as *spaces* of important but fragmented social action, connected to endless digital realms and diverse representational schemes. Interfaces and algorithms are not just more or less efficient ways of storing, accessing, distributing, and evaluating information, but systems that create spatialities of their own, both in abstract representational ways and in concrete experiential ways. And increasingly the social processes that revolve around the production, distribution, and consumption of "information" itself work in, and through, both physical and virtual spaces, through both social networks and technological networks, in such complicated ways that mapping the overlap, the intersection, and the doorways between such spaces is crucial.

LIS researchers are well aware of the difficulties encountered when information artifacts formerly available only in material form—as books and periodicals printed on varying-quality paper, analog audio recordings on magnetic tape, or images on celluloid and microfilm—are suddenly able to be translated into "virtual" form through digital sampling, storage, distribution, and display. The challenge now is to find ways of theorizing, conceptualizing, and studying what happens when human social processes move from material places, spaces, and scales to virtual ones. Not only can human geography help in this pursuit, but it, in turn, can learn much from the long tradition of LIS research. Over 20 years ago, Harvey (1984, p. 11) argued that "geography is too important to be left to geographers. But it is far too important to be left to generals, politicians, and corporate chiefs. ... There is more to geography than the production of knowledge and personnel to be sold as commodities to the highest bidder." Today, geographical knowledge and data (especially mustered through GIS) threatens to be appropriated in the service of reinforcing technologically determinist, normative capitalist myths such as the inevitable networking of society into a global market and media, the decentralizing destruction of physical concentrations of people and texts, and the uncritical acceptance of the necessary secrecy of all sorts of private and government information. Yet, as Sui (2004, p. 67) has observed,

> Geography is a fertile ground for crossing the traditional boundaries of science, social theory, technology, and the humanities, and capacious imaginations will be required to realize the potential of GIS to better understand—and, in some limited cases, even solve—scientific problems, illuminate social injustices, and feed the human spirit.

If researchers, professionals, and activists within the LIS community are to question, manage, and challenge the assumptions that would shake their foundations and undermine their mission, they too must have more than a passing understanding of geography. And I hope that intellectual laborers within geography continue to give them more than a passing glance as well.

References

Abbott, L. T., & Argentati, C. D. (1995). GIS: A new component of public services. *Journal of Academic Librarianship, 21,* 251–256.

Adams, P. C., & Ghose, R. (2003). India.com: The construction of a space between. *Progress in Human Geography, 27,* 414–437.

Adkins, D., & Bala, E. (2004). Public library outreach as a function of staffing and metropolitan location. *Library & Information Science Research, 26,* 338–350.

Adkins, D., & Sturges, D. K. (2004). Library service planning with GIS and census data. *Public Libraries, 43,* 165–170.

Anderson, S. A. (2003). "The place to go": The 135th Street Branch Library and the Harlem Renaissance. *Library Quarterly, 73,* 383–421.

Aoyama, Y. (2003). Sociospatial dimensions of technology adoption: Recent m-commerce and e-commerce developments. *Environment and Planning A, 35,* 1201–1221.

Aoyama, Y., & Sheppard, E. (2003). The dialectics of geographic and virtual space. *Environment and Planning A, 35,* 1151–1156.

Atkinson, R. (2001). Contingency and contradiction: The place(s) of the library at the dawn of the new millennium. *Journal of the American Society for Information Science and Technology, 52,* 3–11.

Benedikt, B. (Ed.). (1991). *Cyberspace: First steps.* Cambridge, MA: MIT Press.

Benner, C. (2003). Learning communities in a learning region: The soft infrastructure of cross-firm learning networks in Silicon Valley. *Environment and Planning A, 35,* 1809–1830.

Benoît, G. (2002). Toward a critical theoretic perspective in information systems. *Library Quarterly, 72,* 441–471.

Benton Foundation. (1997). Buildings, books, and bytes: Libraries and communities in the digital age. *Library Trends, 46,* 178–223.

Bowker, G. C., & Star, S. L. (1999). *Sorting things out: Classification and its consequences.* Cambridge, MA: MIT Press.

Boxall, J. (2003). Geolibraries: Geographers, librarians and spatial collaboration. *The Canadian Geographer, 47,* 18–27.

Boyer, K. (2004). "Miss Remington" goes to work: Gender, space, and technology at the dawn of the information age. *The Professional Geographer, 56,* 201–212.

Brown, B., & O'Hara, K. (2003). Place as a practical concern of mobile workers. *Environment and Planning A, 35,* 1565–1587.

Buschman, J. E. (2003). *Dismantling the public sphere: Situating and sustaining librarianship in the age of the new public philosophy.* Westport, CT: Libraries Unlimited.

Carlin, A. P. (2003). Disciplinary debates and bases of interdisciplinary studies: The place of research ethics in library and information science. *Library & Information Science Research, 25,* 3–18.

Castells, M. (1989). *The informational city: Information technology, economic restructuring, and the urban-regional process*. New York: Blackwell.

Castells, M. (2000). Grassrooting the space of flows. In J. O. Wheeler, Y. Aoyama, & B. Warf (Eds.), *Cities in the telecommunications age: The fracturing of geographies* (pp. 18–27). New York: Routledge.

Chitwood, J. (1967). Library and community: Community analysis, population characteristics, community growth, governmental relationships, library site criteria. In R. J. Shaw (Ed.), *Libraries: Building for the future* (pp. 23–28). Chicago: American Library Association.

Christopherson, S. (2002). Project work in context: Regulatory change and the new geography of media. *Environment and Planning A, 34*, 2003–2015.

Craig, W. J., & Elwood, S. A. (1998). How and why community groups use maps and geographic information. *Cartography and Geographic Information Systems, 25*, 95–104.

Currah, A. (2002). Behind the Web store: The organisational and spatial evolution of multi-channel retailing in Toronto. *Environment and Planning A, 34*, 1411–1441.

D'Elia, G., Jorgensen, C., Woelfel, J., & Rodger, E. J. (2002). The impact of the Internet on public library use: An analysis of the current consumer market for library and Internet services. *Journal of the American Society for Information Science and Technology, 53*, 802–820.

Day, R. E. (2005). Poststructuralism and information studies. *Annual Review of Information Studies and Technology, 39*, 575–609.

Dear, M., & Flusty, S. (2002). Introduction: How to map a radical break. In M. Dear & S. Flusty (Eds.), *The spaces of postmodernity: Readings in human geography* (pp. 1–12). Oxford, UK: Blackwell.

Dodge, M., & Kitchin, R. (2005). Code and the transduction of space. *Annals of the Association of American Geographers, 95*, 162–180.

Dorman, D. C. (2002). GIS provides a new way of seeing service areas. *American Libraries, 33*(2), 62–63.

Dutton, W. H., Blumler, J. G., & Kraemer, K. L. (1987). Continuity and change in conceptions of the wired city. In W. H. Dutton, J. G. Blumler, & K. L. Kraemer (Eds.), *Wired cities: Shaping the future of communications* (pp. 3–26). Boston: G.K. Hall & Co.

Ellis, D., Oldridge, R., & Vasconcelos, A. (2004). Community and virtual community. *Annual Review of Information Science and Technology, 38*, 145–186.

Gandy, M. (2005). Cyborg urbanization: Complexity and monstrosity in the contemporary city. *International Journal of Urban and Regional Research, 29*, 26–49.

Gibbs, J., Kraemer, K. L., & Dedrick, J. (2003). Environment and policy factors shaping global e-commerce diffusion: A cross-country comparison. *The Information Society, 19*(1), 5–18.

Giddens, A. (1990). *The consequences of modernity*. Stanford, CA: Stanford University Press.

Girard, M., & Stark, D. (2002). Distributing intelligence and organizing diversity in new-media projects. *Environment and Planning A, 34*, 1927–1949.

Given, L. M., & Leckie, G. J. (2003). "Sweeping" the library: Mapping the social activity space of the public library. *Library & Information Science Research, 25*, 365–385.

Gluck, M., Danley, E., & Lahmon, J. (1996). Public librarians' views of the public's geospatial information needs. *Library Quarterly, 66*, 408–448.

Gorman, P., Lavelle, M., Delcambre, L., & Maier, D. (2002). Following experts at work in their own information spaces: Using observational methods to develop tools for the digital library. *Journal of the American Society for Information Science and Technology, 53,* 1245–1250.

Goss, J. (1995). "We know who you are and we know where you live": The instrumental rationality of geodemographic systems. *Economic Geography, 71,* 171–198.

Grabher, G. (2002). Fragile sector, robust practice: Project ecologies in new media. *Environment and Planning A, 34,* 1911–1926.

Graham, S. (1998). The end of geography or the explosion of place? Conceptualising space, place and information technology. *Progress in Human Geography, 22,* 165–185.

Graham, S. (2000). Introduction: Cities and infrastructure networks. *International Journal of Urban and Regional Research, 24,* 114–119.

Graham, S. (2001). Information technologies and reconfigurations of urban space. *International Journal of Urban and Regional Research, 25,* 405–410.

Graham, S., & Marvin, S. (1996). *Telecommunications and the city: Electronic spaces, urban places.* London: Routledge.

Grubesic, T. H., & O'Kelly, M. E. (2002). Using points of presence to measure accessibility to the commercial Internet. *The Professional Geographer, 54,* 259–278.

Harley, J. B. (1989). Deconstructing the map. *Cartographica, 26,* 1–20.

Harvey, D. (1973). *Social justice and the city.* Oxford, UK: Basil Blackwell.

Harvey, D. (1982). *The limits to capital.* Oxford, UK: Oxford University Press.

Harvey, D. (1984). On the history and present conditions of geography: An historical materialist manifesto. *The Professional Geographer, 3,* 1–11.

Harvey, D. (1989). *The condition of postmodernity: An enquiry into the origins of cultural change.* Cambridge, MA: Blackwell.

Harvey, D. (1996). *Justice, nature, and the geography of difference.* Cambridge, MA: Blackwell.

Harvey, D. (2004). Retrospect on *The Limits to Capital. Antipode, 36,* 544–549.

Hornbeck, D., Earle, C., & Rodrigue, C. M. (1996). The way we were: Deployments (and redeployments) of time in human geography. In C. Earle, K. Mathewson, & M. S. Kenzer (Eds.), *Concepts in human geography* (pp. 33–61). Lanham, MD: Rowman & Littlefield.

Huysman, M., & Wulf, V. (2005). The role of information technology in building and sustaining the relational base of communities. *The Information Society, 21,* 81–90.

Janelle, D. G. (1991). Global interdependence and its consequences. In S. D. Brunn & T. R. Leinbach (Eds.), *Collapsing space and time: Geographic aspects of communication and information* (pp. 49–81). London: Harper Collins Academic.

Jeong, W., & Gluck, M. (2003). Multimodal geographic information systems: Adding haptic and auditory display. *Journal of the American Society for Information Science and Technology, 54,* 229–242.

Jue, D. K., Koontz, C. M., Magpantay, J. A., Lance, K. C., & Seidl, A. M. (1999). Using public libraries to provide technology access for individuals in poverty: A nationwide analysis of library market areas using a geographic information system. *Library & Information Science Research, 21,* 299–325.

Kavanaugh, A., Reese, D., Carroll, J., & Rosson, M. (2005). Weak ties in networked communities. *The Information Society, 21,* 119–131.

Kitchin, R., & Kneale, J. (2001). Science fiction or future fact? Exploring imaginative geographies of the new millennium. *Progress in Human Geography, 25*, 19–35.

Kitchin, R., & Tate, N. J. (2000). Thinking about research. In R. Kitchin & N. J. Tate, *Conducting research in human geography* (pp. 1–27). New York: Prentice-Hall.

Kling, R. (Ed.). (1996). *Computerization and controversy: Value conflicts and social choices* (2nd ed.). San Diego, CA: Academic Press.

Koontz, C. M. (1997). *Library facility siting and location handbook*. Westport, CT: Greenwood.

Koontz, C. M., Jue, D. K., McClure, C. M., & Bertot, J. C. (2004). The public library geographic database: What can it do for you and your library? *Public Libraries, 43*, 113–118.

Leckie, G. J., & Hopkins, J. (2002). The public place of central libraries: Findings from Toronto and Vancouver. *Library Quarterly, 72*, 326–372.

Leitner, H., & Sheppard, E. (2002). "The city is dead, long live the net": Harnessing European interurban networks for a neoliberal agenda. *Antipode, 34*, 495–518.

Leyshon, A. (2001). Time-space (and digital) compression: Software formats, musical networks, and the reorganisation of the music industry. *Environment and Planning A, 33*, 49–77.

Li, F., Whalley, J., & Williams, H. (2001). Between physical and electronic spaces: The implications for organisations in the networked economy. *Environment and Planning A, 33*, 699–716.

Lievrouw, L. A., & Farb, S. E. (2003). Information and equity. *Annual Review of Information Science and Technology, 37*, 499–540.

Lim, E.-P., Liu, Z., Yin, M., Goh, D. H.-L., Theng, Y. L., & Ng, W. K. (2005). On organizing and accessing geospatial and georeferenced Web resources using the G-Portal system. *Information Processing & Management, 41*, 1277–1297.

Martell, C. (1999). Human geography/cyber geography. *Journal of Academic Librarianship, 25*, 50–51.

McCook, K. (2000). *A place at the table: Participating in community building*. Chicago: American Library Association.

Mihalache, A. (2002). The cyber space–time continuum: Meaning and metaphor. *The Information Society, 18*, 293–301.

Mitchell, W. J. (1995). *City of bits: Space, place, and the infobahn*. Cambridge, MA: MIT Press.

Molz, R. K., & Dain, P. (1999). *Civic space/cyberspace: The American public library in the information age*. Cambridge, MA: MIT Press.

Murphy, A. J. (2003). (Re)solving space and time: Fulfilment issues in online grocery retailing. *Environment and Planning A, 35*, 1173–1200.

Niles, S., & Hanson, S. (2003). The geographies of online job search: Preliminary findings from Worcester, MA. *Environment and Planning A, 35*, 1223–1243.

Ó Riain, S., Parthasarathy, B., & Zook, M. A. (2004). Flows and filters: The politics of ICT regions in a global economy. *International Journal of Urban and Regional Research, 28*, 617–620.

Openshaw, S. (1991). A view on the GIS crisis in geography, or, using GIS to put Humpty Dumpty back together again. *Environment and Planning A, 23*, 621–628.

Orr, J. E. (1996). *Talking about machines: An ethnography of a modern job*. Ithaca, NY: Cornell University Press.

Ottensmann, J. R. (1997). Using geographic information systems to analyze library utilization. *Library Quarterly, 67*, 24–49.

Pettigrew, K. E., Durrance, J. C., & Unruh, K. T. (2002). Facilitating community information seeking using the Internet: Findings from three public library-community network systems. *Journal of the American Society for Information Science and Technology, 53*, 894–902.

Pickles, J. (1999). Social and cultural cartographies and the spatial turn in social theory. *Journal of Historical Geography, 25*, 93–98.

Rieh, S. Y. (2004). On the Web at home: Information seeking and Web searching in the home environment. *Journal of the American Society for Information Science and Technology, 55*, 743–754.

Rorty, R. (Ed.). (1967). *The linguistic turn: Essays in philosophical method.* Chicago: University of Chicago Press.

Sandvig, C. (2003). Public Internet access for young children in the inner city: Evidence to inform access subsidy and content regulation. *The Information Society, 19*, 171–184.

Sawyer, S., & Eschenfelder, K. R. (2002). Social informatics: Perspectives, examples, and trends. *Annual Review of Information Science and Technology, 36*, 427–466.

Schoenberger, E. (1997). *The cultural crisis of the firm.* Cambridge, MA: Blackwell.

Schoenberger, E. (1998). Discourse and practice in human geography. *Progress in Human Geography, 22*, 1–14.

Schoenberger, E. (2001). Interdisciplinarity and social power. *Progress in Human Geography, 25*, 365–382.

Schoenberger, E. (2004). The spatial fix revisited. *Antipode, 36*, 427–433.

Schumpeter, J. A. (1942). *Capitalism, socialism, and democracy.* New York: Harper & Brothers.

Servon, L. J., & Nelson, M. K. (2001). Community technology centers and the urban technology gap. *International Journal of Urban and Regional Research, 25*, 419–426.

Sheppard, E. (1995). GIS and society: Towards a research agenda. *Cartography and Geographic Information Systems, 22*, 5–16.

Sheppard, E. (2001). Quantitative geography: Representations, practices, and possibilities. *Environment and Planning D: Society and Space, 19*, 535–554.

Sheppard, E. (2004). The spatiality of *The Limits to Capital. Antipode, 36*, 470–479.

Smith, L. C., & Gluck, M. (Eds.). (1996). *Geographic information systems and libraries: Patrons, maps, and spatial information.* Urbana: University of Illinois.

Smith, N. (1990). *Uneven development: Nature, capital, and the production of space* (2nd ed.). New York: Blackwell.

Star, S. L., & Griesemer, J. R. (1989). Institutional ecology, "translations" and boundary objects: Amateurs and professionals in Berkeley's Museum of Vertebrate Zoology, 1907–39. *Social Studies of Science, 19*, 387–420.

Stolfi, F., & Sussman, G. (2001). Telecommunications and transnationalism: The polarization of social space. *The Information Society, 17*, 49–62.

Strover, S. (2003). Remapping the digital divide. *The Information Society, 19*, 275–277.

Sui, D. Z. (2004). GIS, cartography, and the "third culture": Geographic imaginations in the computer age. *The Professional Geographer, 56*, 62–72.

Ueno, N., & Kawatoko, Y. (2003). Technologies making space visible. *Environment and Planning A, 35*, 1529–1545.

Van House, N. A. (2004). Science and technology studies and information studies. *Annual Review of Information Science and Technology, 38*, 3–86.

Venkatesh, M. (2003). The community network lifecycle: A framework for research and action. *The Information Society, 19*, 339–347.

Watters, C., & Amoudi, G. (2003). GeoSearcher: Location-based ranking of search engine results. *Journal of the American Society for Information Science and Technology, 54*, 140–151.

Wellman, B. (2001). Physical place and cyberplace: The rise of personalized networking. *International Journal of Urban and Regional Research, 25*, 227–252.

Wiegand, W. A. (1999). Tunnel vision and blind spots: What the past tells us about the present; Reflections on the twentieth-century history of American librarianship. *Library Quarterly, 69*, 1–32.

Wiegand, W. A. (2003). To reposition a research agenda: What American studies can teach the LIS community about the library in the life of the user. *Library Quarterly, 73*, 369–383.

Wills, J., Cumbers, A., & Berndt, C. (2000). The workplace at the millennium: New geographies of employment. *Environment and Planning A, 32*, 1523–1528.

Wilson, L. R. (1938). *The geography of reading: A study of the distribution and status of libraries in the United States*. Chicago: American Library Association and University of Chicago Press.

Wilson, M. (2003). Chips, bits, and the law: An economic geography of Internet gambling. *Environment and Planning A, 35*, 1245–1260.

Winchester, H. P. M. (2000). Qualitative research and its place in human geography. In I. Hay (Ed.), *Qualitative research methods in human geography* (pp. 1–20). Oxford, UK: Oxford University Press.

Winner, L. (1986). *The whale and the reactor: A search for limits in an age of high technology*. Chicago: University of Chicago.

Xia, J. (2004). Using GIS to measure in-library book-use behavior. *Information Technology and Libraries, 23*, 184–191.

Zellner, L. (2004). How homeland security affects spatial information. *Computers in Libraries, 24*, 6–8, 37–40.

Zook, M. A. (2000). The Web of production: The economic geography of commercial Internet content production in the United States. *Environment and Planning A, 32*, 411–426.

Zook, M. A. (2006). The geography of the Internet. *Annual Review of Information Science and Technology, 40*, 53–78.

Zukin, S. (1995). *The cultures of cities*. Cambridge, MA: Blackwell.

Index

5S model of digital library space, 236

A

A Language for Process Specification
  (ALPS), 73
Abbate, J., 30
Abbattista, F., 242, 252
Abbott, A., 27
Abbott, L. T., 691
Abdul-Rauf, M., 518
Abed, E., 516
Abel, J. R., 192, 210–211
Abell, A., 278
Abels, E. G., 336
Abelson, H., 23
Aberg, Y., 582
ABM (agent-based modeling), 574–575,
  581–582
Abrahamsen, K. T., 390
Abrams, D., 454, 471, 475, 478
Abrams, S., 247
Abu El-Khair, I., 515
Abu-Salem, H., 511, 520, 526
academic publishing, see scholarly
  publishing
access to resources, see universal service
Accomazzi, A., 249, 252, 624
Ackerman, M. S., 467
ACLS (American Council of Learned
  Societies), 226–227
ACM (Association for Computing
  Machinery), 7–8, 224, 492, 506
acquisitions for digital libraries, 244
active semantic relations, 404
Acton, S. T., 231
ADA (Americans with Disabilities Act),
  176, 196

Adair, W. C., 108–109
Adam, N. R., 237
Adame, D. D., 331
Adamic, L. A., 553, 583
Adams, A., 229
Adams, A. A., 228
Adams, P. C., 718
Adar, E., 491, 553
Adaval, R., 328
Adessa, C., 649, 658–659
ADI (American Documentation Institute),
  10, 16, 102
Adkins, D., 691, 711–712
Adkinson, B. W., 8
Adler, S., 321
affix removal method of stemming for
  information retrieval, 512–515
agent-based modeling (ABM), 574–575,
  581–582
Agosti, M., 228, 231, 243, 246
Agosto, D. E., 319
Agre, P. E., 251
Ahluwalia, P., 440
AI (artificial intelligence), 70, 407, 425,
  427, 460
AIHT (Archive Ingest and Handling
  Test), 247
Aikman, W. F., 204
Ajeeb English-to-Arabic translation Web
  site, 516, 522
Akoumianakis, D., 179
Alberair, A., 521, 526
Albert, R., 539, 558–561, 572–574, 584
Albrechtsen, H., 32
Aldag, B., 414
Aldrich, H. E., 277
Alexander, J., 340
Alexander, J. E., 340

Further Reading in Information Science & Technology

Theories of Information Behavior

Edited by Karen E. Fisher, Sanda Erdelez, and Lynne (E. F.) McKechnie

This unique book presents authoritative overviews of more than 70 conceptual frameworks for understanding how people seek, manage, share, and use information in different contexts. Covering both established and newly proposed theories of information behavior, the book includes contributions from 85 scholars from 10 countries. Theory descriptions cover origins, propositions, methodological implications, usage, and links to related theories.

456 pp/hardbound/ISBN 1-57387-230-X

ASIST Members $39.60 • Nonmembers $49.50

Covert and Overt

Recollecting and Connecting Intelligence Service and Information Science

Edited by Robert V. Williams and Ben-Ami Lipetz

This book explores the historical relationships between covert intelligence work and information/computer science. It first examines the pivotal strides to utilize technology to gather and disseminate government/military intelligence during WWII. Next, it traces the evolution of the relationship between spymasters, computers, and systems developers through the years of the Cold War.

256 pp/hardbound/ISBN 1-57387-234-2

ASIST Members $39.60 • Nonmembers $49.50

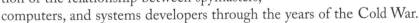

Information Representation and Retrieval in the Digital Age

By Heting Chu

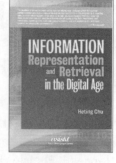

This is the first book to offer a clear, comprehensive view of Information Represetation and Retrieval (IRR). With an emphasis on principles and fundamentals, the author first reviews key concepts and major developmental stages of the field, then systematically examines information representation methods, IRR languages, retrieval techniques and models, and Internet retrieval systems.

264pp/hardbound/ISBN 1-57387-172-9
ASIST members $35.60 • Nonmembers $44.50

The Web Knowledge

A Festschrift in Honor of Eugene Garfield

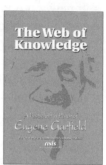

Edited by Blaise Cronin and Helen Barsky Atkins

Dr. Eugene Garfield, the founder of ISI, devoted years to fulfilling his dream of creating a multidisciplinary citation index. The development of the *Science Citation Index* represented a fundamental breakthrough in scientific informatin retrieval.

This ASIST monograph is the first to comprehensively address the history, theory, and practical applications of citation analysis—a field which has grown from Garfield's seed of an idea—and to examine its impact on scholarly research 40 years after its inception. In bringing together the analyses, insights, and reflections of more than 35 leading lights, editors Cronin and Atkins have produced both a comprehensive survey of citation indexing and its applications and a beautifully-realized tribute to Eugene Garfield and his vision.

544 pp/hardbound/ISBN 1-57387-099-4
ASIST members $39.60 • Nonmembers $49.50

Introductory Concepts in Information Science

By Melanie J. Norton

Melanie J. Norton presents a unique introduction to the practical and theoretical concepts of information science while examining the impact of the Information Age on society. Drawing on recent research into the field, as well as from scholarly and trade publications, the monograph provides a brief history of information science and coverage of key topics, including communications and cognition, information retrieval, bibliometrics, modeling, economics, information policies, and the impact of information technology on modern management. This is an essential volume for graduate students, practitioners, and any professional who needs a solid grounding in the field of information science.

127 pp/hardbound/ISBN 1-57387-087-0
ASIST members $31.60 • Nonmembers $39.50

Editorial Peer Review

Its Strengths and Weaknesses

By Ann C. Weller

This important book is the first to provide an in-depth analysis of the peer review process in scholarly publishing. Author Weller (Associate Professor and Deputy Director at the Library of the Health Sciences, University of Illinois at Chicago) offers a carefully researched, systematic review of published studies of editorial peer review in the following broad categories: general studies of rejection rates, studies of editors, studies of authors, and studies of reviewers. The book concludes with an examination of new models of editorial peer review intended to enhance the scientific communication process as it moves from a print to an electronic environment. *Editorial Peer Review* is an essential monograph for editors, reviewers, publishers, professionals from learned societies, writers, scholars, and librarians who purchase and disseminate scholarly material.

360 pp/hardbound/ISBN 1-57387-100-1
ASIST members $35.60 • Nonmembers $44.50

Statistical Methods for the Information Profesional

By Liwen Vaughan

Author and educator Liwen Vaughan clearly explains the statistical methods used in information science research, focusing on basic logic rather than mathematical intricacies. Her emphasis is on the meaning of statistics, when and how to apply them, and how to interpret the results of statistical analysis. Through the use of real-world examples, she shows how statistics can be used to improve services, make better decisions, and conduct more effective research.

240pp/hardbound/ISBN 1-57387-110-9
ASIST members $31.60 • Nonmembers $39.50

Evaluating Networked Information Services

Techniques, Policy, and Issues

Edited by Charles R. McClure and John Carlo Bertot

As information services and resources are made available in the global networked environment, there is a critical need to evaluate their usefulness, impact, cost, and effectiveness. This monograph brings together an introduction and overview of evaluation techniques and methods, informaton policy issues and initiatives, and other critical issues related to the evaluation of networked information services.

300 pp/hardbound/ISBN 1-57387-118-4
ASIST members $35.60 • Nonmembers $44.50

Knowledge Management Lessons Learned
What Works and What Doesn't

Edited by Michael E. D. Koenig and T. Kanti Srikantaiah

A follow-up to Srikantaiah and Koenig's ground-breaking *Knowledge Management for the Information Professional* (2000), this new book surveys recent applications and innovations in KM. More than 30 experts describe KM in practice, revealing what has been learned, what works, and what doesn't. Includes projects undertaken by organizations at the forefront of KM, and coverage of KM strategy and implementation, cost analysis, education and training, content management, communities of practice, competitive intelligence, and much more.

624 pp/hardbound/ISBN 1-57387-181-8
ASIST members $35.60 • Nonmembers $44.50

Knowledge Management for the Information Professional
Edited by T. Kanti Srikantaiah and Michael E. D. Koenig

Written from the perspective of the information community, this book examines the business community's recent enthusiasm for Knowledge Management (KM). With contributions from 26 leading KM practitioners, academicians, and information professionals, editors Srikantaiah and Koenig bridge the gap between two distinct perspectives, equipping information professionals with the tools to make a broader and more effective contribution in developing KM systems and creating a Knowledge Management culture within their organizations.

608 pp/hardbound/ISBN 1-57387-079-X
ASIST members $35.60 • Nonmembers $44.50

ASIST Thesaurus of Information Science, Technology, and Librarianship, Third Edition

Edited by Alice Redmond-Neal
and Marjorie M. K. Hlava

The *ASIST Thesaurus* is the authoritative reference to
the terminology of information science, technology,
and librarianship. This updated third edition is an
essential resource for indexers, researchers, scholars,
students, and practitioners. An optional CD-ROM includes the complete
contents of the print thesaurus along with Data Harmony's Thesaurus Master
software. In addition to powerful search and display features, the CD-ROM
allows users to add, change, and delete terms, and to learn the basics of
thesaurus construction while exploring the vocabulary of library and
information science and technology.

Book with CD-ROM: 272pp/softbound/ISBN 1-57387-244-X
ASIST members $63.95 • Nonmembers $79.95

Book only: 272pp/softbound/ISBN 1-57387-243-1
ASIST members $39.95 • Nonmembers $49.95

Understanding and Communicating Social Informatics

A Framework for Studying and Teaching the Human
Contexts of Information and Communication Technologies

By Rob Kling, Howard Rosenbaum, and Steve Sawyer

Here is a sustained investigation into the human
contexts of information and communication
technologies (ICTs), covering both research and
theory. The authors demonstrate that the design,
adoption, and use of ICTs are deeply connected to people's actions as well
as to the environments in which ICTs are used. They offer a pragmatic
overview of social informatics, articulating its fundamental ideas for
specific audiences and presenting important research findings.

240 pp/hardbound/ISBN 1-57387-228-8/$39.50

To order or for a complete catalog, contact:

Information Today, Inc.

143 Old Marlton Pike, Medford, NJ 08055 • 609/654-6266
email: custserv@infotoday.com • Web site: www.infotoday.com